The Editor

MICHAEL MOON is Professor of English at The Johns Hopkins University. He is the author of *Disseminating Whitman: Revision and Corporeality in "Leaves of Grass"* and *A Small Boy and Others: Imitation and Initiation in American Culture from Henry James to Andy Warhol.* He co-edited, with Cathy N. Davidson, *Subjects and Citizens: Nation, Race, and Gender from "Oroonoko" to Anita Hill.*

A NORTON CRITICAL EDITION

Walt Whitman
LEAVES OF GRASS
AND OTHER WRITINGS

AUTHORITATIVE TEXTS
OTHER POETRY AND PROSE
CRITICISM

Edited by

MICHAEL MOON

THE JOHNS HOPKINS UNIVERSITY

*An expanded and revised edition based on the
Norton Critical Edition of* Leaves of Grass, *edited by*

SCULLEY BRADLEY   *and*   HAROLD W. BLODGETT

LATE OF THE UNIVERSITY   LATE OF UNION COLLEGE
OF PENNSYLVANIA

W • W • NORTON & COMPANY • *New York* • *London*

Reprinted by arrangement with New York University Press.

Printed in the United States of America.
The text of this book is composed in Fairfield Medium
with the display set in Bernhard Modern.
Composition by PennSet, Inc.
Manufacturing by Courier.
Book design by Antonina Krass.

Library of Congress Cataloging-in-Publication Data

Whitman, Walt, 1819–1892.
  [Selections. 2001]
  Leaves of grass and other writings : authoritative texts, prefaces, Whitman on
    his art, criticism / Walt Whitman ; edited by Michael Moon.
      p. cm.— (A Norton critical edition)
  "An expanded and revised edition based on the Norton critical edition of Leaves
    of grass edited by Sculley Bradley and Harold W. Blodgett."
  Includes bibliographical references and index.

          ISBN 0-393-97496-0 (pbk.)

  I. Moon, Michael. II. Bradley, Sculley, 1897– III. Blodgett, Harold William,
    1900– IV. Title.

  PS3204 2001
  811'.3—dc21   2001045248

W. W. Norton & Company, Inc., 500 Fifth Avenue, New York, N.Y. 10110
www.wwnorton.com

W. W. Norton & Company Ltd., Castle House, 75/76 Wells Street,
London W1T 3QT

3 4 5 6 7 8 9 0

Contents

The Text of *Leaves of Grass*, 1891–1892

An Album of Whitman Portraits 493

Other Poetry and Prose

Criticism

Preface

This volume represents a revision of Sculley Bradley and Harold W. Blodgett's venerable 1973 Norton Critical Edition of Walt Whitman's *Leaves of Grass*, which was in turn based on the last (1891–92) issue of the book published in the poet's lifetime. The present editor has made no changes in the body of the poetic text, which remains Bradley and Blodgett's "Reader's Edition," based on their still-definitive *Leaves of Grass* variorum. Owing to changes in printing technology, it has not always been possible to preserve the previous edition's strict adherence to the breaking of the run-on lines precisely as they appeared in the 1891–92 *Leaves of Grass*; interested scholars should consult the *Variorum*. I have, with a sparing hand, updated some of the footnotes, revising and expanding them in view of the massive amount of scholarship on Whitman's book and its contexts that has emerged in the past thirty years.

The debt of much of this scholarship to Bradley and Blodgett's editorial labors is incalculably large. Whitman continued to rewrite and move poems around in *Leaves of Grass* throughout his life, and it was Bradley and Blodgett who first made it possible for the interested reader to compare several different versions of a Whitman poem with ease and convenience. Before the appearance of their Variorum Edition from New York University Press in 1965, only a handful of professional scholars who enjoyed the rare privilege of examining copies of early editions of *Leaves of Grass* had the means of making the kinds of discoveries that have repeatedly arisen as Whitman's genius for revision has become more widely recognized.

I have added the full text of Whitman's first (1855) edition of *Leaves of Grass* to this volume so that students can compare the poet's relatively short first version of his book—one that contained only twelve poems—with the compendious final work that he left at the time of his death thirty-seven years later. For similar comparison, I have also added the text of "Live Oak, with Moss," the initial group of poems out of which Whitman developed the celebrated "Calamus" section of *Leaves of Grass*. I thank Professor Hershel Parker for permission to reprint in this volume the version of this poetic "cluster" (to use Whitman's term) that he edited for *The Norton Anthology of American Literature*. I have also added substantial excerpts from Whitman's two great prose works, *Democratic Vistas* and *Specimen Days*.

The "Criticism" section of the volume has been thoroughly revised. The selections from Whitman's contemporaries have been supplemented with the responses of a number of writers who were either known only to literary and cultural historians at the time Bradley and Blodgett made their selection of criticism but have since come to be recognized as important literary figures, such as Fanny Fern (Sara Willis Parton), or who were well known but whose provocative responses to Whitman's writing were long ignored, such as Thoreau or Henry James. The most extensive revisions in this volume have been made in the selection of more recent criticism; the group of articles provided in the previous edition barely reached 1960. For a further sampling of the many rich developments in Whitman criticism over the past forty years, the reader is referred to the "Selected Bibliography" at the end of the volume.

Scholars have done much in recent decades to increase our understanding of the sources and implications of Whitman's writing, exploring a wide range of questions, from the intimate meaning of the poet's avowed love for other men (including some he merely glimpsed in public places, and others to whom he devoted himself for years) to his experience of life as a young bohemian newspaperman in the burgeoning metropolis of 1850s New York City, as a visiting nurse to the great Civil War hospitals in Washington, D.C., or—later—as a poet gradually achieving an international reputation while living, often in poor health, in a working-class section of Camden, N.J. Whitman, who was often represented by earlier critics as an anomalous figure, a great poet who inexplicably arose from a humble, even vulgar, background, has, thanks to much fine historicist criticism of the past several decades, come to "make sense" as a product as well as a producer of the violently energetic urban culture of the United States of his time. Many critics have also come to accept the notion—fiercely resisted for a long time—that Whitman may have enacted in his life some version of the "fluid," "adhesive" sexuality he celebrates in his poetry.

In their original introduction to the Norton Critical Edition of *Leaves of Grass,* Bradley and Blodgett modestly stated that their intention was "only to show the honored text without interruption, for the satisfaction of the reader." It is my hope that this revised edition will provide a new generation of students with the "satisfactions" of the previous edition, while also serving to introduce them to the critical literature on the poet.

I wish to express my gratitude to three young Americanist scholars who each provided invaluable aid to me during successive phases of this project: John Vincent, Ada Norris, and Christopher Lukasik. Thanks also to Carol Bemis, Kate Lovelady, and Brian Baker at Norton for their patient good humor as well as for the high level of professional dedication they have brought to this project. Closer to home, Jonathan Goldberg provided unfailing support and editorial counsel, for which I thank him.

MICHAEL MOON

Abbreviations

AANC	*After All, Not to Create Only* (1871)
AL	*American Literature*, quarterly, Duke University Press
Allen	Gay Wilson Allen, *The Solitary Singer* (1955)
AS	*American Speech*
ASB	Whitman, *As a Strong Bird on Pinions Free and Other Poems* (1872)
Asselineau	Roger Asselineau, *L'Evolution de Walt Whitman* (1954)
Asselineau (2)	Roger Asselineau, *The Evolution of Walt Whitman*, Eng. tr. 2 vols. (1960, 1962)
Aurora	Jay Rubin and Charles H. Brown, eds., *Walt Whitman of the New York Aurora* (1950)
Barrett	Clifton Waller Barrett Collection, University of Virginia
Barrus	Clara Barrus, *Whitman and Burroughs, Comrades* (1931)
Bayley	William D. Bayley Collection, Ohio Wesleyan University
Berg	Henry W. and Albert A. Berg Collection, New York Public Library
Blodgett	Harold Blodgett, *Walt Whitman in England* (1934)
Blue Copy	LG 1860 with WW's corrections, Lion Collection, New York Public Library
BNYPL	*Bulletin of the New York Public Library*
Bowers	Fredson Bowers, *Whitman's Manuscripts, Leaves of Grass 1860* (1955)
BPL	Boston Public Library
Brown	Brown University Library
Bucke	Richard Maurice Bucke, *Walt Whitman* (1883)
Calamus	*Calamus: A Series of Letters written during the Years 1868–1880 by Whitman to a Young Friend* (Peter Doyle), ed. by R. M. Bucke (1897)
Canby	Henry Seidel Canby, *Walt Whitman: An American* (1943)
Coll W	*Collected Writings of Walt Whitman*, 21 vols. (N.Y.U. Press, 1961–84)
Corr.	*Correspondence of Walt Whitman*, ed. by Edwin H. Miller, 6 vols. (1961–77); in *Coll W*
CPP	*Complete Poems & Prose of Walt Whitman, 1855–1888* (1888)

CPSP	*Complete Poetry and Selected Prose and Letters,* Nonesuch Edition, ed. by Emory Holloway (1938)
CPW	Whitman, *Complete Prose Works* (1892)
CW	*Complete Writings of Walt Whitman,* ed. by R. M. Bucke and others, 10 vols. (1902)
DAB	*Dictionary of American Biography*
DNB	*Dictionary of National Biography* (British)
Doheny	Estelle Doheny Collection, Doheny Memorial Library, St. John's Seminary, Camarillo, California
Donaldson	Thomas Donaldson, *Walt Whitman the Man* (1896)
DT	Whitman, *Drum-Taps* (1865–66)
Duke	Library of Duke University: Trent Collection
DV	Whitman, *Democratic Vistas* (1871)
EA	*Etudes Anglaises*
EJ	*English Journal*
ELH	*Journal of English Literary History*
ESQ	*Emerson Society Quarterly*
Expli	*Explicator*
Faner	Robert D. Faner, *Walt Whitman and Opera* (1951)
FBW	William Sloane Kennedy, *The Fight of a Book for the World* (1926)
FCI	*Faint Clews and Indirections* (Trent MS Collection), ed. by Clarence Gohdes and Rollo G. Silver (1949)
Feinberg	Charles E. Feinberg Collection
Furness	Clifton J. Furness, *Walt Whitman's Workshop* (1928)
GBF	Whitman, *Good-Bye My Fancy* (1891)
GF	*Gathering of the Forces,* ed. by Cleveland Rogers and John Black, 2 vols. (1920)
Gilchrist	Herbert H. Gilchrist, *Anne Gilchrist: Her Life and Writings* (1887)
Glicksberg	Charles I. Glicksberg, *Walt Whitman and the Civil War* (1933)
Handbook	Gay Wilson Allen, *Walt Whitman Handbook* (1946)
Hanley	T. E. Hanley Collection, University of Texas
Harned	*The Letters of Anne Gilchrist and Walt Whitman,* ed. by Thomas B. Harned (1918)
HLQ	*Huntington Library Quarterly*
Holloway	Emory Holloway, *Whitman: An Interpretation in Narrative* (1926)
Houghton	Houghton Library, Harvard University
Huntington	Henry E. Huntington Library, San Marino, California
Imprints	*Leaves of Grass Imprints* (1860)
Inclusive LG	*Leaves of Grass,* Inclusive Edition, ed. by Emory Holloway (1924 *et seq.*)
In Re	*In Re Walt Whitman,* ed. by Horace L. Traubel, R. M. Bucke, T. B. Harned (1893)
ISL	*I Sit and Look Out,* ed. by Emory Holloway and Vernolian Schwartz (1932)

Kennedy	William Sloan Kennedy, *Reminiscences of Walt Whitman* (1896)
LC	Library of Congress
LC *Whitman*	*Walt Whitman: Catalog Based upon the Collections of the Library of Congress* (1955)
LG	*Leaves of Grass* (*LG, LG* 1860, etc.)
Lion	Oscar Lion Collection, New York Public Library
Livezey	Livezey Collection, University of California
Memoranda	Whitman, *Memoranda During the War* (1875)
Miller	James E. Miller, Jr., *A Critical Guide to Leaves of Grass* (1957)
MLN	*Modern Language Notes*
Morgan	Pierpont Morgan Library, New York City
Mott	Frank Luther Mott, *A History of American Magazines,* 4 vols.
MP	*Modern Philology*
N *and* F	*Notes and Fragments,* ed. by R. M. Bucke (1899): republished, *CW,* Vol. IX
NB	Whitman, *November Boughs* (1888)
NED	*New English Dictionary*
NEQ	*New England Quarterly*
NYD	*New York Dissected,* ed. Emory Holloway and Ralph Adimari (1936)
NYPL	New York Public Library; See Berg, See Lion
PBSA	*Publications of the Bibliographical Society of America*
Pennsylvania	University of Pennsylvania Library, Philadelphia
Perry	Bliss Perry, *Walt Whitman* (1906)
PI	Whitman, *Passage to India* (1871)
PMLA	*Publications of the Modern Language Ass'n*
PT	Partial text
SB	*Studies in Bibliography*
SDC	Whitman, *Specimen Days & Collect* (1882)
Texas	Library of the University of Texas: Hanley
Traubel	Horace Traubel, *With Walt Whitman in Camden,* 3 vols. (1906–1914); Vol. IV, ed. by Sculley Bradley (1953): Vol. V, ed. by Gertrude Traubel (1964)
TR	Whitman, *Two Rivulets* (1876)
Trent	Trent Memorial Collection; cf. Duke
TSE	*Tulane Studies in English*
UPP	*The Uncollected Poetry and Prose of Walt Whitman,* 2 vols. ed. by Emory Holloway (1921)
Va.	Library of the University of Virginia, Charlottesville
Visits	*Visits to Walt Whitman in 1890–1891 by two Lancashire Friends,* John Johnston and J. W. Wallace (London, 1917; New York, 1918)
WD	Whitman, *The Wound Dresser,* ed. by R. M. Bucke (1898)
WDC	Whitman, *Walt Whitman's Diary in Canada,* ed. by William Sloane Kennedy (1904)

Wells	Carolyn Wells and Alfred F. Goldsmith, *A Concise Bibliography of the Works of Walt Whitman* (1922)
WW	Walt Whitman
WWM	Gay W. Allen and E. Allen, *Walt Whitman as Man, Poet and Legend* (1960)
WWN	*Walt Whitman Newsletter*, Vol I, 1–4 (New York University Press, 1955)
WWP	*Walt Whitman Poems*, ed. by Gay W. Allen and Charles T. Davis (1955)
WWQR	*Walt Whitman Quarterly Review*
WWR	*Walt Whitman Review* (successor to the *Newsletter*), Wayne State University Press, Vol. II *et seq.* (1956–)
Yale	Yale Collection of American Literature

Introduction

The Growth of "Leaves of Grass"

In the Variorum Edition,[1] which presents for the first time all the poems of *Leaves of Grass* in chronological order, a full analysis is made of the almost incessant revision, reordering, and augmentation that culminated in the final 1881 arrangement. It is pertinent here briefly to characterize and outline this process, which has often been described by mutually exclusive images—a cathedral constructed from a blueprint in the poet's mind, or a tree growing from year to year, its rings marking the successive editions. A better image is one the poet used in a postcard to his friend William Douglas O'Connor, March 5, 1889, upon sending him the 1888 one-volume *Complete Poems & Prose*: "I can hardly tell why, but feel very positively that if anything can justify my revolutionary attempts & utterances, it is such *ensemble*—like a great city to modern civilization & a whole combined clustering paradoxical identity a man, a woman . . ."

Actually the successive nine editions of the poet's lifetime grew out of his vivid sense of endless materials, a creative pressure welling from profound depths, and a boundless acceptance which expressed itself in an urgent inclusiveness rather than in the artful limits of deliberate design. In franker moments the poet recognized this. In a very late note, December 6, 1891, he speaks of "hackling" at *Leaves of Grass* for *thirty-six* years, of its "cumulous" character, even its "jaggedness." And more than once he testified to his intuitive approach. "I do not suppose," he said, "that I shall ever again have the *afflatus* I had in writing the first *Leaves of Grass*," and he spoke of his experiment as a radical utterance out of the abysms of the Soul. In such phrases Whitman was describing the workings of the creative mind, which plans and constructs indeed with the impassioned power of discovery.

The poet was receptive to its promptings. He had to wait upon the event, and in his case, the event was the whole life of his nation. So Whitman was surely justified in insisting upon identifying the growth of his *Leaves* with the growth of his country. He had new things to say, new approaches, shifts of insight and mood as he and his land developed: "as I have lived in fresh lands, inchoate, and in a revolutionary age, future-founding," he wrote in his 1876 Preface, "I have felt to identify the points of that age, these lands, in my recitatives

---

1. Sculley Bradley, Harold W. Blodgett, Arthur Golden, and William White, eds., *Leaves of Grass: A Textual Variorum of the Printed Poems,* 3 vols. (New York: New York University Press, 1965).

. . . Within my time the United States have emerg'd from nebulous vagueness and suspense, to full orbic, (though varied) decision . . . Out of that stretch of time . . . my Poems too have found genesis."

Here, in outline summary, is the record: The twelve poems of *LG* 1855, in which the introductory poem, to be called "Song of Myself," is longer than the other eleven poems taken together, boldly eschew all distinction of title, and indeed the whole design seems to emphasize the singleness of the poet's song—variations upon one utterance. In the second edition, *LG* 1856, Whitman began to count his poems. He added twenty—among them some of his best—and in his exuberant letter to Emerson, really his 1856 Preface, he boasts that he will keep on until he has made a hundred and then several hundred, perhaps a thousand! He also fashioned titles, some absurdly long, some reduced to a syllable—"Clef Poem," or "Bunch Poem." It was an odd and yet arresting table of contents from a writer uncommitted to a pattern.

Within the next four years his now intense creative energy produced no less than 124 poems for his third edition, *LG* 1860, making 156 in all; and yet at the same time he was hopefully pondering, as a kind of "wander-teacher," a program of lectures corresponding with his *Leaves,* to reach his countrymen if his poems should not. *LG* 1860 was the first to display a group arrangement of sorts, emphasized by eccentric typography; and yet an examination of his manuscripts shows (*vide* Bowers) that probably as late as 1859 Whitman had had no decisive intention whatever of dividing his poems into groups. The compelling factor was his sudden focusing upon two special themes, and later a third: the celebration of comradeship in "Calamus," of procreation in "Children of Adam," and of the nation at war in *Drum-Taps.* Such new demands led the poet to observe (in the *Saturday Press,* January 7, 1860) that *Leaves of Grass* had not yet really been published at all—he was slowly trying his hand at the structure he had undertaken. And these three groups did possess a homogeneity so vital that through all succeeding editions they remained essentially undisturbed by the considerable shifting to which the poet subjected them—so considerable, indeed, that only thirty-eight of the seventy-one pieces in the 1865–66 *Drum-Taps* and "Sequel to Drum-Taps" were held in place, thirty-three poems being eventually dispersed into no less than nine other groups. To return to the third edition, its remaining clusters—the remarkable "Chants Democratic," the numbered "Leaves of Grass," and the "Messenger Leaves" demonstrated no survival value *as groups,* and so disappeared. The poet had no certain structural plan, and this uncertainty, deepening under the perturbation of a personal crisis, even led him, in three of the 1860 poems, to question whether he should go on.

But of course he was bound to go on, and plans multiplied. Late in 1860 his Boston publisher announced a separate volume, *Banner at Daybreak,* but it never appeared. In an MS draft of an unpublished preface originally dated May 31, 1861, the poet complained, "the paths to the house are made, but where is the house itself?" But when presently the poems of *Drum-Taps* began to form under the immediate stress of war, the poet grew in confidence. "I *must* be continually bring-ing out poems—now is the hey day," he wrote on November 17, 1863, to his publisher, Eldrige, and much of his creative concentration may be sensed from the annotations that crowd the pages of his third edi-tion toward his next. Fortunately these annotations are extant in the *LG* 1860 "Blue Copy," now in the Lion Collection—the very volume, WW averred (Traubel, III, 474), which James Harlan, secretary of the Interior, had surreptitiously examined before he dismissed the poet from his Washington clerkship. "Transfer to Drum-Taps?" the poet questions at the top of a page, or "Out—out altogether" he scrawls in the margin of others, and some annotations indicate that he was pon-dering still other volumes or groupings under such titles as "Leaves-Droppings" or "Pioneers."

The book *Drum-Taps* (1865), turning upon the pivotal issue of the Civil War, was very important to the poet both as document and as art, and with its "Sequel" (1865–66), he began the practice of devel-oping supplements with their own pagination, to be bound up with the parent volume or issued separately. In August, 1866, he wrote to Abby Price of going to New York to bring out a new and much better edition of *Leaves of Grass*—"that unkillable work." This was to be the fourth edition of 1867, which he designated in the Bucke biography as beginning the order and classification eventually settled upon. Yet this order, more flexible than in *LG* 1860, is notably casual, and not so much an advance in thematic sequence as in variety of content. The supplements—now augmented by "Songs Before Parting"—were so variously combined with the major text that *LG* 1867 exists in four different forms. Of the various groupings, only "Calamus" and "Chil-dren of Adam" were "clusters" in Whitman's sense of that word: only these fifty-six poems, exclusive of the supplements, possessed an un-mistakable consistency of theme. Seventy-six of the other poems were distributed among untitled groups, and the remaining twenty-six were arranged in a series of four "Leaves of Grass" groups and one group of "Thoughts," carried over intact from the "Thoughts" of 1860. No patent unity of theme distinguished the "Leaves of Grass" groups—the title being a mere convenience—and in later editions the poems comprising them were thoroughly scattered.

With all its supplements, *LG* 1867 included 236 poems, only 57 short of the 293 which were to compose the final arrangement of 1881. And very soon—as early as May 1869—Whitman began to hint of his final edition, and of turning to religious themes. These specu-lations occupied his thoughts in both the 1872 and 1876 Prefaces: *Leaves of Grass* he felt to be as complete as he could make it, and its "surplusage" might become a supplementary volume, the voice—as he wrote in 1872—of "a composite, electric, democratic personality," or —as he put it in 1876—"of those convictions which make the unseen Soul govern absolutely at last."

These aims, really explicit from the first, were purposefully stressed in later poems—superbly so in "Passage to India"—but the structural problem was not solved. Indeed it could not be. Instead there was the improvising of an arrangement for a body of work already largely complete. The 1871 *Leaves of Grass,* with only nine new poems, was formed into twenty-two groups, sixteen of them titled—some simply as "Leaves of Grass"—and the other six untitled. The 1871 pamphlet *Passage to India,* with only twenty-two of its seventy-four poems new, was formed into six titled groups and three untitled, the poet at once binding it in as a supplement in *LG* 1872.

Five years after the 1871 edition appeared *LG* 1876, identical except for a few intercalations. Its companion volume, *Two Rivulets,* was a medley of prose, fourteen new poems under the "Two Rivulets" title, four "Centennial Songs," seven poems under the title piece, "As a Strong Bird on Pinions Free," and the 1871 collection, *Passage to India.* Undoubtedly Whitman had made a practical solution of the problem of arranging a two-volume edition to signalize the centennial year, but his perplexity had been pressing. A notebook belonging to the mid-1870s addresses questions to himself: "Qu—whether to make a new Vol of these pieces including *Whispers of Heavenly Death?*—qu—whether to finish up *Leaves of Grass* in one Vol—*Drum-Taps* in another . . .—*Whispers* etc in another."

The questions ended in mid-air, but the poet now resolved to end his problem by a thorough reshuffling of all his poems into the final arrangement of 1881, a process in which several group titles (some very good, for Whitman had a gift for titles) disappear, their contents absorbed into the surviving groups. The cluster "Inscriptions," first faintly suggested in 1867, is an appropriate introduction, although certain announcement poems elsewhere are quite as inscriptive as these. Such groups as "Birds of Passage," "By the Roadside," "Autumn Rivulets," and "From Noon to Starry Night" do possess a casual consonance of theme, but attempts to demonstrate a rule of logical continuity in them are embarrassed by too many exceptions. On the other hand, two of the groups carrying over from *Passage to India*—"Sea-Drift" (formerly "Sea-Shore Memories") and "Whispers of Heavenly Death"—are very closely knit, and so is the final group "Songs of Parting," sounding a farewell with poems that had appeared over a period of more than twenty years. The sense of departure had haunted Whitman's pages ever since "So Long!" had closed the 1860 edition. For the rest, there are the three stalwarts—"Children of Adam," "Calamus," and "Drum-Taps," together with the twenty-five major poems to which the poet gave the importance of standing by themselves. Perhaps it should be noted that in this whole process not only have groups constantly shifted, but also the poems within the groups, so that a given poem may have appeared in three or four different groups from 1860 to 1881. There was to be no more shifting, but there would be addition: the sixty-five poems of "Sands at Seventy," first separately published in *November Boughs* (1888), and the thirty-one poems of "Good-Bye My Fancy," first separately published in 1891. Both "annexes" were to round out the 1891–92 edition, the poet's sole authorized text.

This is the poet's structure—neither the "Leaves" in the order of their growth nor the cathedral of prefigured design. These figures were ideals which gave solace and strength to a task which had often to face a bleak reality of contingency and crisis. Certain comment, arguing from the 1881 arrangement, has attributed to Whitman a prescience which robs him of his true stature. It is just as erroneous to argue, as some critics have, that the poet's constant revisions, shiftings, and insertions betray indecisiveness or uncertainty. There is never any doubt of a purpose kept consciously in view, an aim never deviated from; nor is there doubt that Whitman intended and achieved structure. Still, it was a structure that grew as the poet grew, that was adapted to the necessities he met and molded by the pressures his own life felt—its materials altered, added to, subtracted from, transposed as time and need required. And so it was alive. The construction of *Leaves of Grass* is best to be regarded, not as a hierarchic system of themes, but as resourceful editing by a man who was obliged to be his own publisher for most of his life, who serenely confronted a hostile literary market, who enjoyed little benefit of professional advice, and who nevertheless essentially achieved what he had set out to do. It took resolution—the resolution of the poet who told himself, "Now voyager sail thou forth to seek and find."

The Poems of the Canon

Yet in one's absorption with the tortuous process by which the poet arrived at his final structure—the preferred and authorized text of 1891–92—one should not fail to acknowledge the impressive and, on the whole, triumphal advance of the poet's genius in its hard-won path.

To begin in 1855 with "Song of Myself," untitled and in no signal way distinguished from its accompanying eleven poems, was directly to assert without skirmish or equivocation the basic theme of this poet's creative intent: to improve and transform life (the poet as maker and reformer), to discern and set forth its miraculousness (the poet as celebrator), and to sing the transcendence of human love, envisioned as divine (the poet as lover). The companion poems of the first edition were—as in a sense were also the future poems of *Leaves of Grass*—an extension of the prime purpose, celebration of the individual, of the nation, and of spiritual possibility. So, for example, we have (employing the final titles) "A Song for Occupations," the poem of daily work which in later editions was to undergo severe revision; "To Think of Time," also to be much revised but even now strongly anticipating "Crossing Brooklyn Ferry" in its poignant concern with time and death; "The Sleepers," powerfully original in imaginative grasp—a twentieth century poem in its penetration into subconscious states; "I Sing the Body Electric," an announcement poem, really, for what was to be one of the great groups of the third edition; "Faces," of audacious imagery, limning both the victorious and the broken; "Song of the Answerer," to be fused later with a kindred poem largely derived from the 1855 Preface; and "There was a Child Went Forth," simple and profound in its Lockean grasp of the relation of experience to knowledge.

His ambition undaunted by massive indifference toward his first edition, the poet prefaced his second by the brash exuberance of his "Dear Master" letter to Emerson—a kind of *Democratic Vistas* in embryo, calling for identity, for national character, and individuality. He now had twenty new poems to strengthen his poetic evangelism, and remarkable poems some of them were, including the strange "Poem of the Propositions of Nakedness" (later "Respondez!"), which he was to exclude, retaining two passages as mementos of a passionate deviation into irony. Four of the poems derive much of their being from the poetic storehouse of the 1855 Preface—notably the somewhat confused "Poem of Many in One" ("By Blue Ontario's Shore"), which elaborates the thesis of the American Bard for America, an outburst to be greatly modified in later editions; and "Poem of the Last Explanations of Prudence" ("Song of Prudence"), an Emersonian meditation on value.

Other salient—and successful—compositions are "Poem of Salutation" ("Salut au Monde!"), a vigorously expressive recognition of the peoples of the earth, their cultures and religions; the assuring and intimate "To You"; the buoyant "Poem of the Road" ("Song of the Open Road"), the most famous of the invitation poems; and "Broad-Axe Poem" ("Song of the Broad-Axe"), with its flawless opening lines and its evocation of the shapes of America, among which the poet at first included himself. Two of the bold new poems, "A Woman Waits for Me" and "Spontaneous Me," were to find their fitting place in the "Enfans d'Adam" of the third edition. But the most beautiful poem of the second edition was "Sun-Down Poem" ("Crossing Brooklyn Ferry"), with its descriptions of the "glories strung like beads on my smallest sights and hearings," and its vision, penetrating beyond time and appearance to an eternal and changeless reality.

The thirty-two poems of the first two editions were a prelude to an extraordinary burst of creative energy in the next three years. Indeed by June 1857 (the date is surmised by Dr. Bucke), WW made a cryptic reference to "the three hundred and sixty-five" as the goal he had set himself for the "Great Construction of the New Bible" (*N and F*, 57). Whether the figure refers to poems or days, we do not know, but in a letter of the following July 20 he speaks of wanting to bring out a third edition, for which he already has a hundred poems. We know, too, from manuscript evidence that even before this date he was working on poems that were to appear in *LG* 1860. His failure to publish his third edition in 1857 may be attributed to a number of reasons— perhaps his absorption in the editorship of the *Brooklyn Times,* perhaps the difficulty of finding a publisher in a year of business depression, perhaps his own financial straits. At any rate it seems fortunate, in retrospect, that Thayer and Eldridge were not to make the enthusiastic offer that eventuated in the third edition until February 10, 1860, for early in 1859 the poet experienced another access of poetic energy whose source seems to be a profound need that changed the current of his important opening poem, "Proto-Leaf" ("Starting from Paumanok") and produced two great new clusters—"Calamus" and

"Enfans d'Adam." With the encouragement of publishers who believed in him and with 124 poems added to the existing 32, he was now for the first time to arrange his poems into a structural pattern which should emphasize the basic themes—as he announced them in "Proto-Leaf"—of "the greatness of Love and Democracy—and the greatness of Religion."

"Proto-Leaf" is not only an announcement of themes, but a moving declaration that the poet "will write the evangel-poem of comrades and of love"; and this he does in the forty-five new poems of the "Calamus" cluster which in their sensibility and candor are art of a high order, superior in delicacy to the more literal-seeming "Enfans d'Adam," which WW was to defend in his famous talk with Emerson on Boston Common and also in his prose piece, "A Memorandum at a Venture." This group of fifteen poems, twelve of which were new, was introduced by the brilliant "To the Garden the World," evoking the figure of Adam, who with conscious art appears again in the final poem of the cluster.

The other clusters were less successful, and so did not survive. The twenty-one "Chants Democratic," advertising themselves in subtitle as "Native American," displayed a certain confident strength, derived in part from six poems of the earlier editions, and also one interesting failure, "Apostroph," a curious exercise in ecstatic exclamation. These poems were to be widely dispersed, as were those of the group of twenty-four simply titled "Leaves of Grass," which opened with a remarkable confession later to be called "As I Ebb'd with the Ocean of Life." The poet, addressing the ocean as father and rejecting "all the blab whose echoes recoil upon me," avows in humility the terrible burden of trying to penetrate the meaning of existence. "O I perceive I have not understood anything—not a single object—and that no man ever can." One more cluster, "Messenger Leaves," does have a single theme to hold its fifteen poems together, in the sense that they are indeed all messages, beginning with the moving "To You" of the second edition, but their sequence was not to be maintained—the poet assuming in later editions, perhaps, that the whole of *Leaves of Grass* is a message, properly considered.

In comparative estimates, few would question that the finest single achievement of the third edition is "Out of the Cradle," first published as "A Child's Reminiscence" in the New York *Saturday Press*, December 24, 1859, and in *LG* 1860 as "A Word Out of the Sea." Its variants are worth special study, for the poet worked long on this poem, which has been characterized by D. H. Lawrence as "the perfect utterance of a concentrated, spontaneous soul." Whether or not the poet here sublimated a personal grief over the loss of a lover, it is certain that he revealed his own poetic birth. "My own songs awakened from that hour."

The 1860 edition closed, strangely for a poet scarcely turned forty, with a note of leave-taking: the seemingly casual "So Long!" which announces what shall come after him and ends with an exalted farewell: "Remember my words—I love you—I depart from materials, / I

am as one disembodied, triumphant, dead." Altogether, as Roy Harvey
Pearce has declared in his facsimile edition, *LG 1860* is a great book
—he believes the poet's greatest. But Whitman's greatness was not yet
expended.

He was to experience a great new source of poetic inspiration—the
Civil War—of which the 1865 *Drum-Taps* and its 1865–66 "Sequel"
were the consequence. Despite the circumstance that a number of
these seventy-one poems were probably composed before the actual
conflict, and that many of them were later dispersed into other groups,
they derive their strength and centrality from the poet's total commit-
ment to the tremendous crisis of his beloved democracy. He wrote
them, as he put it, "on the field, in the hospitals, as I worked with the
soldier boys . . . ," and later he averred, "Without those three or four
years and the experiences they gave, *Leaves of Grass* would not now be
existing." We cannot accept this statement in view of such achieve-
ments as "Song of Myself," "Crossing Brooklyn Ferry," and "Out of
the Cradle Endlessly Rocking," but we see what the poet meant when
we consider his equally remarkable statement in a letter on *Drum-
Taps* to William Douglas O'Connor, January 6, 1865: "It is in my opin-
ion superior to Leaves of Grass—certainly more perfect as a work of
art . . ." He goes on to stress such qualities as proportion, control, and
the removal of all verbal superfluity.

Drum-Taps, then, was a highly conscious achievement in craft.
Working with great materials on a task that he said had haunted him—
"the pending action of this *Time & Land we swim in*"—Whitman
found artistic resources in himself which were quite unrecognized in
the poetic practices of the day, and, incidentally, unperceived by two
young reviewers of *Drum-Taps,* William Dean Howells and Henry
James, both of whom complained of the poet's lack of art. These re-
sources manifested themselves in an ability at stark depiction of war
scenes, whose realism in such poems as "A Sight in Camp . . ." or
"The Wound-Dresser" look forward to the specificity of a Crane or a
Hemingway; and in sharply etched vignettes such as "Cavalry Crossing
a Ford" or "An Army Corps on the March," which reveal an artist's
fascination with the sight and show of war. But even more than de-
scriptive power or objective reporting, the poems evince another qual-
ity which informs their aesthetic sensibility—the compassion and love
which, lifted above the desperation of some of the "Calamus" poems,
animates the whole enterprise with a sympathetic imaginativeness
whose richest expression is the great threnody, "When Lilacs Last in
the Dooryard Bloom'd"—"the most sweet and sonorous nocturne,"
exclaimed Swinburne, "ever chanted in the church of the world." Some
critics consider this to be Whitman's greatest poem; some disagree,
feeling a sense of artifice in its deployment of symbols; but certainly
it may stand as the high point of the poet's personal engagement with
war and with the issues of his nation, commemorating not alone the
death of a great hero but the heroic and the truly great in humanity.

But if the Lincoln elegy is the high point, what is to be said of WW's
poetic performance thereafter—the new verses of the six editions of

LG still to come, as well as certain poems in separate publication? It has become almost a cliché of one school of Whitman criticism to stress not only a falling-off of poetic energy (which was to be expected), but a regrettable change of intent, the complaint being that in later years Whitman the visionary was overtaken by Whitman the prophet —that the poet was conquered by the propagandist. There is directness in this charge, and some evidence to support it, but one should heed the poet's own insistence that he wanted a full, not a partial judgment upon his work—that he was not to be known as a piece of something but as a totality (Traubel, I, 272). When we consider Whitman's totality, we are persuaded of its genuineness and of its steady adherence to a crowning purpose, painstakingly detailed in "A Backward Glance . . .": to "formulate a poem whose every thought or fact should directly or indirectly be or connive at an implicit belief in the wisdom, health, mystery, beauty of every process, every concrete object, every human or other existence, not only consider'd from the point of view of all, but of each."

Let us briefly summarize the record from this point. After the *Drum-Taps* poems, and exclusive of the two annexes, "Sands at Seventy" and "Good-bye My Fancy," Whitman was to publish nearly ninety poems. It must be said that, taken together, they give an impression of appetite for life, of unwaning poetic interest, and a high degree of distinctive performance despite the hazards and disabilities of the oncoming years. More than a fourth of them are short lyrics of less than eight or ten lines, some of them designed for the introductory "Inscriptions" cluster; a number, such as "Outlines for a Tomb" or "O Star of France" are poems of occasion; several, of which the greatest is "The Return of the Heroes" (originally "A Carol of Harvest, for 1867"), deal with the still harrowing memory of the war and the crucial problems for democratic society left in its wake. In fact, the problems as well as the potentialities of democracy were to furnish the substance of three major poems that WW composed in response to public invitation, poems that furnished, too, a certain temptation for the poet to act as America's official voice. These were "Song of the Exposition" (American Institute, New York, 1871), "Thou Mother with Thy Equal Brood" (Dartmouth College, 1872), and "Song of the Universal" (Tufts College, 1874). Of these the last is the best, if only that in expressing his theme—the reaffirmation of his idealism—the poet uses a pattern that is direct, terse, almost epigrammatic. In the first, and to a lesser extent in the second of these public poems, the poet is occasionally betrayed into a Polonius-like sententiousness, so earnest a spokesman for America that he sounds at times more like her agent than her lover. Yet even here the bold, original image may be found. Who else could speak of installing the Muse among the kitchenware?

The most distinguished poem of the later period is *Passage to India,* first separately published in 1871, and then incorporated into *LG* 1872 and *TR* 1876. Writing with characteristic exultation in the achievement of three great advances in communication—the opening of the Suez Canal, the completion of the continental railway system in his own country, and the laying of the Atlantic and Pacific cables—the poet moves swiftly to his great dream of international brotherhood, and so to his "passage to more than India," the venturing of the soul into the seas of God. As with his "Proud Music of the Storm," "The Mystic Trumpeter," "Prayer of Columbus," and "Song of the Redwood Tree," the poet in "Passage to India" finds and skillfully employs images of strength, love, and endurance that lift his expression into poetry beautifully free from the encumbrance of rhetoric.

The impressive poems of Whitman's later years illustrate, then, the turn of direction and emphasis that he himself noted in both his 1872 and 1876 Prefaces—the singing of the "unseen Soul" and "Spiritual Law." These poems were destined never to fill the "further, equally needed Volume" the poet had projected, but nevertheless they found their proper place in the parent—and only—*Leaves of Grass*. Included among them were not only the longer poems of major effort but such exquisite brief lyrics as "Darest Thou Now O Soul," "Whispers of Heavenly Death," "On the Beach at Night," and "The Last Invocation."

Finally, let us remind ourselves that this poet never—even toward the end, when he was bedridden and helpless—lost his power over his own idiom. It informs his expression to the last—in, for example, such poems of the annexes as "A Prairie Sunset," "Old Salt Kossabone," "Twilight," and "Fancies at Navesink." "Garrulous to the very last," he cheerfully wrote. Garrulous, yes, but also possessed to the very last with his own gift and self.

Poems and Passages Excluded from "Leaves of Grass"

An important category of Whitman's complete poems in the present edition is represented in two sections: "Poems Excluded from *Leaves of Grass*" and "Passages Excluded from *Leaves of Grass* Poems." (See these headings in Table of Contents for locations.) As in the case of those *Leaves of Grass* poems which Whitman finally retained, these texts have also been established in this edition by a new collation of all *LG* volumes authorized by Whitman from 1855 to 1891–92, including the concurrent "Supplements" and "Clusters" from *Drum-Taps* (1865) to *Good-Bye My Fancy* (1891). This new collation of texts appears in *Leaves of Grass: A Textual Variorum*.

An earlier variorum prepared by Oscar Lovell Triggs appeared as an appendix to *Leaves of Grass* in *Complete Writings of Walt Whitman* (New York, 1902). Emory Holloway, in his familiar *Leaves of Grass, Inclusive Edition* (1924), added four poems to the twenty-five "Rejected Poems" in the Triggs Appendix, and reprinted the same twenty-nine in the appendix to his "Nonesuch Press Edition" of the *Leaves* (ca. 1938). The present editors have preferred to refer to these as "Excluded Poems" and we have been able to add sixteen, bringing the total to forty-five, while making alterations and amplifications in the texts as presented by Triggs. From the close study of these poems one gets the impression that they have been unduly neglected and that they will gain approval and importance by their association, in the present edition, with the groups of poems not before collected or surviving in manuscript unpublished. They deserve comparison with the canon poems of *LG,* from which they were excluded for reasons not always unfavorable to their merits.

The complete collation of *LG* texts and supplements also identified the large number of lines, fragments, and passages of larger scope which Whitman excluded from *LG* poems in the process of revision, not primarily because he disapproved of them as creative work. Triggs also showed many such passages in his variorum, remote from and subordinated to the *Leaves of Grass* poems. The present editors were impressed by the genuine insight and poetic merit, the poem-like unity and independence, of many of the excluded passages; of these we chose, frankly, those that pleased us most, twenty-eight in number, to stand as a separate group in association with the other *Leaves of Grass* texts. The student will find the entire body of excluded lines, passages, and poems in the variorum in this Norton Critical Edition. We have had to supply titles for all these passages, of course, and for eight of the forty-five excluded poems.

We have called these "excluded," instead of continuing the familiar term, "rejected," because we find the latter to be somewhat pejorative, and unjustified in view of the value of many of these pieces as creations, revelations, doctrines, or precepts, or as stages in the growth of the poet or his work. Each of these passages has the merit that it was once judged by the poet worthy to be included in *Leaves of Grass,* where a number remained for a decade or two. They are integral to *Leaves of Grass* considered as a construct of Whitman's mind through a period of years, and they are enormously valuable either to the scholar or to the general reader interested in the growth of Whitman's art, mind, methods of composition, and critical interpretation of life. We have attempted to facilitate this critical approach by subtending to each poem or passage the dates of first and last appearance in an *LG* edition; also, our first footnote gives the provenance and life history of the passage and whatever commentary may seem to be useful.

A number of the excluded poems, particularly those originating in the 1860 *Leaves,* appeared only in one edition, like that attractive image, "In the New Garden," to which reference will be made below. More poems of early origin—such as "Think of the Soul," "Respondez!", and "Thought"—continued to reappear for as long as twenty years without fundamental alterations. Like previous editors, we chose to show each of these in the text of its last appearance, unless special circumstances, explained by a note, required another choice. Since the exclusions range in date from 1860 to 1891, the last texts of these poems are not consistent in formal conventions, because Whitman was experimenting during this period with changes of style involving the use of asterisks, points, dashes, brackets, foreign words, neologisms and classical derivatives, the elision of the "e" before "d" in past-tense constructions, and the like. We have not attempted regularization, preferring these poems to appear in their natural diversity, each representing the characteristics of the edition from which it was extracted.

The same diversity will appear, of course, in the formal style of the passages excluded from poems.

Really complex questions developed in choosing the appropriate text to be honored when a poem, during the course of its life, had been fragmented by the poet's borrowing from it lines used in later poems; or when it had been changed by the exclusion of some secondary theme, or had been divided into two or more poems, of which one or more were later excluded; or when, as happened, two early poems had been combined to form a third, which then might have been excluded but in fact was actually retained in the canon. All of these changes occurred, and others also, which, however defensible on creative grounds, are calculated to dismay the editor who must choose one text, or one stage of the text, for publication. The present editors frequently made a choice at variance with that of Triggs, who generally—but not consistently—favored the latest text that appeared, and who usually excluded from his text of a "rejected" poem all those passages that had appeared in poems in the final 1881 *Leaves*. We have attempted to treat each poem as a separate problem, and since this edition is meant to serve the reader primarily—the scholar will also use the Variorum Edition—we chose in each case the text that gives the completest idea of the original poem, with an accompanying note that in most cases will enable the attentive student to reconstruct the changes that occurred in its text.

The comparison of texts of these excluded poems made clear that, as in the case of the *Leaves of Grass* poems in general, Whitman worked prodigiously at their improvement in manuscript and in various forms of trial run before he included them in the *Leaves*. His "exclusion" of the poem from the *Leaves* did not necessarily indicate its rejection for creative shortcomings. Like other poems similarly revised, some of these were shifted from "cluster" to "cluster," from 1856 to 1881, in the poet's persistent effort to secure unity and order among the topics of his great book. As the footnotes will show, other reasons for excluding poems and passages were certain changes in his own ideas or convictions, or in his attitude toward the propriety or usefulness of emphasizing them; changes in the temper of the times because of the changing conditions of a war-torn country; and changes that occurred about 1871 in the meanings to be emphasized in his book as a whole. In short, the idea that the excluded poems and passages were necessarily of inferior creative value to those retained should not be lightly accepted. Whitman continued to borrow lines from excluded poems, as from early manuscripts that he had frugally hoarded, long after he had set them aside.

As was said, the poet's borrowing of lines from a previous poem produced one of the difficult textual problems. For example, "Debris," a luxuriant poem of sixty lines, appears only in *LG* 1860. By 1872 nearly half its lines had been distributed among seven new poems, of which six survived in the final collection of *Leaves of Grass* (1881). A seventh *LG* poem, "Stronger Lessons," a couplet borrowed from "Debris," appeared in *November Boughs* (1888) and was transferred to the

"First Annex" of the 1891–92 edition. In accord, presumably, with his general practice, Triggs published only what he regarded as the un-distributed remnant of "Debris"—thirty-five lines (by our count it would be only thirty-one). What has come down to readers in Triggs's edition is neither "Debris" nor any poem that Whitman authorized. The present edition gives the complete 1860 text of sixty lines, with a note showing the distribution of lines to other poems. The excluded poem, "States," appeared only in the 1860 edition, but the reader ac-quainted with *Leaves of Grass* will recognize the last three stanzas with particular pleasure. Whitman borrowed these stanzas, adding a refrain to each of the first two in *LG* 1867 and thereby created his most admired "Calamus" poem, "For you, O Democracy." Of the original "States," Triggs published only the first thirty-five lines, omitting the seven-line conclusion that the poet had transposed. But Whitman had borrowed even earlier, in 1865, the nineteen lines from "States" that form the body of the memorable Civil War poem, "Over the Carnage Rose Prophetic a Voice," which also remained in the final *LG* selec-tion. Triggs must have forgotten this—he mentions the transposition in his variorum—but had he remembered it, the application of his editorial principle would have reduced the poem to a disorderly rem-nant of sixteen lines. The present text represents the original forty-two lines of the 1860 text, showing "States" as a poem of independent merits.

Certain poems, which in the earlier versions were a fusion or con-trast of two or more themes, were revised by the cancellation of a secondary theme, thereby emphasizing the principal motif. "Great Are the Myths" (1855), which in 1860 numbered seventy-one lines, was reduced, in *LG* 1867, to forty-nine lines by the cancellation of three sections. This eliminated the secondary theme, which dealt with the accumulation of belief in human values, tested by the duration of his-torical time. In the shortened version this poem, important in concep-tion but weak in its execution, was not excluded until the definitive selection of 1881. The present text is the uncut version of 1860, seventy-one lines, in which the interest of a paradox is contributed by the minor theme. By following the instruction of the footnote, the reader may compare the two versions. Triggs, with consistency, gave the abbreviated version of forty-nine lines, apparently unaware that four of these lines were actually retained in 1881, as the "new" poem, "Youth, Day, Old Age, and Night."

Similarly, "Says" contained two themes each appearing antiphonally in a series of eight stanzas. In his mood of postwar reconciliation the poet cancelled, in *LG* 1867, the four stanzas condemning the system of slavery and its intellectual hypocrisies, leaving only the theme of democratic individualism. Although the poem was now deprived of any of its interesting tension, it was not excluded until the 1881 edition. Since none of the poem appeared in the final selection, Triggs was consistent in publishing the entire 1860 text, in spite of the exclusions of 1867. The present edition of the same text shows, in the note, the verbal changes that occurred in the title and in the abbreviated text.

Unlike "Says," several of the poems ultimately excluded were improved by pruning and fundamental revision. Two noteworthy examples are "Poem of Remembrances for a Girl or a Boy of These States" (1856) and "Apostroph" (1860); each yielded in revision a much better short poem that was excluded in 1881, although each possessed sufficient independence and interest to justify its retention. In 1867 the poet rejected the first twenty-one lines of "Poem of Remembrances . . ." and retained the last twenty-three, with some revision, as "Think of the Soul." In the present edition, the rejected first half of the original poem is shown in its latest text (1860) and "Think of the Soul" follows in its latest text (1867), so that both the poem as a whole and the derivative poem are available to the reader. A somewhat different editorial problem was that of "Apostroph," an unwieldy and declamatory poem of the 1860 edition. Its aforementioned derivative, the impressive "O Sun of Real Peace," was based primarily on the last nineteen lines of the original. The two versions are so different in effect, however, that it seemed better to the present editors, as to their predecessors, to reproduce the entire last text of both the parent and the derived poem, in succession.

Triggs's extreme application of his rule, that lines surviving in poems of the final *LG* 1881 could not be shown in the text of the related excluded poems, caused at least two good poems to disappear completely from the *Leaves of Grass* collections. Their lines were indeed consumed by four poems of the 1881 canon, a fact not surprising, considering that these despoiled ancestors comprised collectively only ten lines to begin with. The two poems are "Thoughts—2" and "Thoughts—4" (see notes to these poems). For the first time in any collection we show them as they originally appeared in the 1860 cluster "Thoughts," which included seven valuable small poems. Numbers "2" and "4" each had an independent vitality, and it seems appropriate to restore them. A similar reward of the new collation was the rediscovery, in *LG* 1867, of the first version of "When I Read the Book" (*q.v.* in "Excluded Poems"). This is, of course, familiar as the title of the ninth of the poems among the initial "Inscriptions" section of the *Leaves*; and Triggs's principle of choice would have barred it from his collection. In the original form, however, the single last line, at once epigrammatic and profound, raises the poem to the top level of Whitman's dramatic intensity. In transferring it to the "Inscriptions" in 1871, he replaced this line with three lines which by comparison are only honest, prosaic exposition.

In retrospect the editors would add a comment, perhaps out of context, in praise of the pioneer textual work that Oscar Lovell Triggs accomplished in analyzing the *Leaves of Grass* editions. With respect to the lacunae in his "rejected poems" collection, it may be presumed that he defined his purpose as the simple collection of all lines and fragments, from any *LG* edition, that were not represented in the final *LG* selection. The present editors have a different purpose: the faithful reproduction of the most complete and satisfactory text, for the general reader, of every poem excluded from *LG* or its supplements.

The previous discussion of textual problems made reference to the literary values that a number of these poems possess. That so many of them are impressive is the more noteworthy when one considers that the present collection is defined as complete, without discrimination on the ground of merit. However, the "Passages excluded from *Leaves of Grass* Poems" include only the best of those that combine a certain independence and formal unity with poetic values. Unlike the excluded poems, the excluded passages did not impose on the editors any necessity for making a complete collection. The Variorum Edition in its completeness will show that many worthy passages still remained in discard. The jewel of them all, perhaps, was left unused in the remnant of "Debris," lines 35–43 (*q.v.*), which may be recalled by its central line, "I will take an egg out of the robin's nest in the orchard." This is the kind of nature lyric—simple, rapt, and luminous—that the young Sandburg learned, perhaps from Whitman, to make out of common things and the common speech of the people.

Numerous trial manuscripts of passages finally dropped from poems of *Leaves of Grass* survived at the poet's death, some of them to be transcribed in Bucke's familiar *Notes and Fragments* before appearing again in Triggs's variorum. Of these, the "Black Lucifer" poem proved at once the most baffling and the most meritorious. In the present edition it appears with the first-line title, "Now Lucifer Was Not Dead," in a text resulting from the collation of the successive editions of "The Sleepers," one of Whitman's major poems, in which the Lucifer canto remained from 1855 until 1876. It is evidently an invective parable against slavery, predicting the Negro's inevitable revenge, and its concluding metaphor (*q.v.*), although terrifying even a century later, is one of Whitman's greatest. Conjecturally, it was canceled from "The Sleepers" because the revisions of that poem had made it an embodiment of human love in which revenge had no place, and because of Whitman's sense of reconciliation after the war, which influenced his revision of several other poems. Another excluded canto of "The Sleepers," "O Hot-Cheek'd and Blushing" (as named by its first line) is also one of Whitman's most creative passages, in which, again, symbol, emotion, and subject are in effective balance. It contains perhaps the most subtle sexual imagery of all Whitman's poems (see note), but by 1876 it also was inappropriate in the context of the parent poem and out of harmony with Whitman's objective treatment of sexual themes in this late period. In the same spirit, much earlier, was one of his most memorable passages, the three-stanza introduction for "You Felons on Trial in Courts," when it first appeared in 1860. In this edition, under its first-line title, "O Bitter Sprig," this indeed seems to be a "confession sprig," as the poet said, and he may have been influenced to exclude it in the next edition because of his hard-won caution suggesting greater objectivity, or less intimacy, in treating sexual themes. In 1859, in the manuscript of "Once I Passed Through a Populous City," he had changed the lover from a man to a woman; and in the 1860 edition, three good poems open to the same sort of criticism were not again published. They appear in the present collection: See

"Who Is Now Reading This," "Long I Thought that Knowledge Alone Would Suffice," and "Hours Continuing Long." One can think of no good reason, however, for Whitman's excluding, after 1860, the excellent little poem, "In the New Garden," which provides a compatible twin for another 1860 poem, "As Adam Early in the Morning," that finally came to rest as the last of the "Children of Adam" cluster. The "new garden" contained the "new Adam," seeking "this moment, . . . the woman of the future," in contrast with the first Adam of the other poem. Among other small poems in this collection which show interesting evidence of Whitman's craftsmanship, "To You" (see note) is particularly recommended because the poet rescued it from mawkishness by inserting a single line; and also "To the Reader at Parting," which Whitman rehabilitated almost by sleight-of-hand, then excluded after all.

The editors have no desire to gild the lilies that the reader might otherwise gather unblemished, but since they have made a value choice among many interesting excluded passages, it is probable that certain values should be identified. A good many of these passages seem to be felicitous expressions of some prevalent theme or quality in *Leaves of Grass*. A number of them illustrate Whitman's practical idealism, or his almost metaphysical concept of reality. One such theme is the function of the poet as bard or prophet; however, in "Facts Showered Over with Light" he includes, with the poet, the "literat," the writer in general, the man of ideas and expressive power. "As he emits himself facts are showered over with light, . . . Each precise object," whether common or refined, "gleams with unmatched beauty." There is a serenely controlled power in this expression of a familiar credo dropped by the wayside. Metaphysical indeed, besides manifesting beauty and power, is Whitman's quite unusually explicit expression of faith in personal survival beyond death (*cf.* "A Thought of the Clef of Eternity"). Metaphysical to the point of being Emersonian is the quatrain (*cf.* "You Dumb, Beautiful Ministers"), which was deleted from "Crossing Brooklyn Ferry," possibly because it too explicitly defined a motif in the poem more subtly expressed in another passage. Still, even in the excluded passage, the identification of spiritual with material realities is by no means superficial.

A significant number of worthy passages were canceled from the poems apparently because the luxuriance of Whitman's perception had defied the scope of the book to contain, even in the form of inventories, all the good things he had found in the abundance of daily life. Hence the tally of "Old Forever New Things," excluded from "A Song for Occupations," reproduces by the free association of carefully selected common things the immediate sense of the physical world of the workman of New York a century ago. "What Do You Hear, Walt Whitman?" excluded from "Salut au Monde," is a diapason of the sounds of gusto and delight with which mankind makes its "salute to the world" of nature and primitive activity. Almost enough musical themes for a symphony are suggested in this passage alone. These are the sounds that man knew—and made—from the beginning of his existence. Also primordial are the questions that this prodigal poet dropped by the wayside in "The Teeming Mother of Mothers" (from "I Sing the Body Electric")—simple questions which suddenly subsume all the individual responsibilities for the continuity of being.

Other passages are small poems in which suddenly we find some aspect of our protean poet himself—superficially comic or deeply moved, as the case may be. Comic certainly, when we realize that "His Shape Arises" (from "Song of the Broad-Axe"), which begins as an impressive description of the heroic shape of the "New Man," gradually takes on the unmistakable aspect of the young poet's picture of himself; he may have suppressed it for that reason. However, in "Readers to Come," our title for the excluded stanzas from "Poets to Come," one suddenly feels the pathos of Whitman's situation—a genuine poet, under the compulsion of a mission and a message, who found apparently none to hear, unless they lay still asleep behind the locked doors of tomorrow. "Give Me the Clue" may suggest a personal dimension involving the poet with the bereaved mockingbird, mourning for the loss of a "beloved" mate in "Out of the Cradle Endlessly Rocking," from which this stanza was excluded—but why?

These and many more values found by the editors in the poems and passages excluded from *Leaves of Grass* resulted in the determination to edit them in depth, and to give them a place closely associated with the canon poems of *Leaves of Grass* in this comprehensive edition of the poems that Whitman created after the beginning of the *Leaves*.

The Uncollected Poems

Among the poet's many jottings for titles were "Leaves Supervened" or "Plus-Leaves,"—i.e., leaves additional or leaves to be added. He wrote with such abundance that he knew selection to be an unceasing problem, as it is indeed that of any artist, but with him a particularly pressing one, for he had a gradually developing schema within which to direct his essential purpose—to celebrate the individual (himself as symbol), the nation, and his intuition of final things. To conform to this purpose, he had worked out through the years, as we have seen, a structure that was essentially complete by 1881. To this he adhered faithfully, but he had much left over—much that was good as well as some that was negligible, and—practically speaking—he could not bring himself to throw anything away even if he could find no place for it. It is a great mistake to think of Whitman as an uncritical genius whose prodigality led him into wastefulness. So it is that we find poems and fragments outside the canon, both in unpublished and in published MSS. Of the sixty-five "Uncollected Poems" presented here, forty-three have been printed—thirty-six in books, seven in periodicals.

A few of these poems—notably "Pictures"—may be regarded as preliminary sketches which in both subject and technique prefigure the accomplishment manifest in *Leaves of Grass*. Others are indeed "additional"—not workings of themes later amplified in *Leaves of Grass*, but subjects or promptings that the poet decided not to include in his canon. Such a poem, for example, is "The Two Vaults," suggested by the scene in Pfaff's underground Broadway restaurant, where the poet, as in more than one "Leaves of Grass" poem, is caught by the doubt of reality. A few of the poems have such distinction that one imagines the poet must have been reluctant to reject them. Consider, for instance, the powerful scorn of "Scantlings," the poignance of the lyric, "Of Your Soul," the exultant dedication of "To an Exclusive." Yet the poet knew that the same ideas, the same fervor, were already present in the *Leaves* of his final choice.

The "Uncollected Poems" range in time from compositions that antedate the first edition to the early 1880s, and their range of interest and topic is roughly that of *Leaves of Grass* itself—from the "celebrations" of 1855–60 to the absorption in the great war, to the themes of union and nationalism thereafter, and near the end to the delicate grace of "Wood Odors." The manuscripts exist in many collections and in many forms, but notably in the poet's invaluable notebooks and the scattered leaves that Dr. Bucke faithfully gathered in *Notes and Fragments*.

Twenty-two of the sixty-five "Uncollected Poems" are here published for the first time, from eight separate manuscript collections, ranging from the banal "A Soul Duet," which in all probability dates from the 1840s, to the appealing "Champagne in Ice," which if not poetry, is a human document of interest penned cheerfully in the extremities of age. Several deal with the war days whose immediacy never failed in the poet's mind; all of them relate to his basic themes that he tried to summarize in one of them, "Last Words." In the poet's judgment they were not momentous enough or artful enough to be honored by inclusion in *Leaves of Grass*, but all—as do the other uncollected poems—testify to a persistent exertion of idiom and interest.

The Uncollected Manuscript Fragments

The poetic fragments encountered by the forager into Whitman manuscripts are of two sorts according to the status given them by the poet. On the one hand are the passages definitely related to the poems of the *LG* canon as alternative or additional readings; on the other are the passages related to compositions that would have become poems in *Leaves of Grass* if the poet's power had fulfilled his intention. The poet's work was incessant, and such lines as these were his daily exercise. The fragments related to the *LG* poems are of course to be collated in the Variorum Edition, and they are also drawn upon in the annotations of this edition as they may serve to illustrate a point or elucidate the text. The other fragments—"outside" the *Leaves*, so to speak—are here selected for the reader's interest; they also will be fully represented in the Variorum Edition.

A few of the fragments can be roughly dated by subject (*vide* the war poems) or by the circumstances of being written on identifiable stationery or letterhead, but with most of them the time of composition is only a matter of guesswork. A good guess would be the period

1847–60, for both in tone and theme they are akin to the earlier poems. If it be asked how one can always be sure that a given passage *is* a fragment rather than a complete poem, the answer is simply that one can't. When the poet leaves a MS passage without title, this may be an indication that it is only a fragment, for he usually titled his poems or numbered them in the original composition, but this rule cannot be relied upon. But the problem does not press: one feels reasonably confident that a particular cluster of lines achieves aesthetic wholeness, or that—as here—the composition is a fragment to await completion. Even so, the lines may elicit delight.

The Manuscript Sources

A notable advantage of this edition is that it is the first fully to take into account and employ the resources of the considerable accumulation of the poet's manuscripts, held in many public and private collections. After Whitman died his surviving unattached literary materials were distributed, as is well known, into the custody of three literary executors, Dr. Richard Maurice Bucke, Thomas B. Harned, and Horace Traubel. Of the three Dr. Bucke was the only one to undertake the responsibility of editing those MSS that had come into his hands. His *Notes and Fragments* (1899) is invaluable; and, considering that he was not a professional scholar, his editing is admirably faithful to its responsibilities. There are errors, to be sure, but they are few.

Since this major distribution of the poet's MSS, they have passed through many hands and are widely scattered. They are of many sorts and their variety is formidable: notes and ideas toward poems, often jotted down with lists of titles; working notes and phrases; trial lines; rough drafts; amended drafts; fair copies for the printer—even, on occasion, longhand copies for souvenir purposes—of poems already printed. They exist in many conditions and forms: in the invaluable notebooks of few or many pages which the poet habitually carried about with him, on tax forms or other "waste paper," economically garnered, on the backs of letters and opened envelopes, on wrapping paper and on scrap paper of all sorts. A single page of MS may be written on as many as six or seven strips of paper pasted together, and the medium may be of four or five kinds—pencil, blue crayon, black ink, lighter ink, red ink—and sometimes the revisions and deletions are so crowded and intricate that the MS is a pastiche of line and color. Also, a MS may exist in an orderly succession of sheets on which the lines are neatly transcribed.

This rich store is, of course, specifically drawn upon for line-by-line collation in the Variorum Edition, but its value to this Norton Critical Edition is salient as well—not only in aiding interpretation of certain passages but also in furnishing, on occasion, variant readings that illuminate beyond the power of the immediate text. For instance, we learn from manuscript that "Starting from Paumanok" was first titled "Premonition," and that the "Calamus" poem "We Two Boys Together

Clinging" originally carried the exotic title "Razzia," an Arabic word meaning "raid" or "foray." We learn, too, that in "Song of Myself" the magnificent phrase "Far-swooping elbow'd earth" was first "Earth of far arms," and that in the same passage "Still nodding night" was originally "Still slumberous night." And had the poet retained his MS revision of the title and first line of "A Woman Waits for Me"—"A Woman America Knows (or Shall Yet Know)"—the poem would not, perhaps, have had the inference of assignation that some critics erroneously found in it.

These are illustrations among many of how our annotations have often profited by MS sources. More important, no less than twenty-two poems are here printed from MS for the first time, as well as a large number of selected fragments, a full presentation of which will be the province of the Variorum Edition. In his 1902 variorum readings, Oscar L. Triggs drew rather fitfully and without identification upon MS sources introduced by the phrase: "Early manuscript readings of lines in this section." He was faithful to his editorial responsibility, but he did not have access to all sources; and both this Norton Critical Edition and the Variorum Edition, concerned to scrutinize all MS resources extant and available, take account of much that he did not note.

William Carlos Williams, whose interesting comments on Whitman were sometimes affected by inadequate knowledge, once said: "Whitman didn't have the training to construct his verses after a conscious mold which would have given him power over them to turn them this way, then that, at will. He only knew how to give them birth and to release them to go their own way." (*Leaves of Grass One Hundred Years After*, ed. by Milton Hindus, p. 23). How wrong he was the MSS show—they show, indeed, that the poet released his verses only after he had recast them again and again to find the form he wanted.

The Prefaces

This edition of *Leaves of Grass* gives more than the usual attention to Whitman's prefaces and to the writings functioning as prefaces in *Leaves of Grass* editions of 1855, 1856, 1872, 1876, and 1891–92. These writings are not all shown in consecutive order; "A Backward Glance . . ." is retained in the position that it occupied in the text which we have honored, the *Leaves of Grass* dated 1891–92, in which Whitman placed "A Backward Glance O'er Travel'd Roads" after the text of the poems and included the note which approved that edition, with this essay, for future publication. It seems to have gone without comment that "A Backward Glance . . ." first appeared in this position—with the same injunction—in the *Leaves* of 1889, but since the poet then supposed, with apparent good reason, that this edition was his last before death, the authorization of the final arrangement is only made more compelling. In the 1889 edition, Whitman also commemorated his seventieth birthday by prefacing the retrospective essay with a "Letter to the Reader," which was so serene in facing imminent mortality, so "garrulous to the very last," and so character-istic of the mood of those last years in which he made the few but important decisions affecting the final construction of his book, that the present editors have included it, as prefatory to "A Backward Glance . . ." in this edition also. The remainder of the prefaces appear consecutively as a group. We have annotated them with the object of emphasizing their values for the general reader of Whitman's poetry. These essays, in chronological order, usefully explicate Whitman's con-cept of the unity existing between the poet, his art, his experience, and his theory of nature; they mark, also, certain stages in his con-struction of what he supposed could become a single poem composed of poems. We wish also to call renewed attention to the values of the earliest preface, which appeared in the first *Leaves of Grass* (1855).

Like Wordsworth's introduction to the second issue of *Lyrical Bal-lads* in 1800, Whitman's preface to the first *Leaves of Grass* edition influenced the changing course of poetry by predicting and defining the functions of the poet and the form and range of poetry in the age to come. Unlike Wordsworth, Whitman did not live to know that he measurably succeeded; his poetry was so advanced in psychological and social insight, and so radically sophisticated in form and symbol-ism, that younger poets did not recognize their indebtedness until after 1915. Whitman's first preface was a radical prose composition, poised on the very brink of lyrical communication. A bit more of tension in the metaphors, a heightening of the rhythmic regulation, and the emo-tional forces were ready to go into independent orbit. And they did so.

They did so, from one angle of vision, because Whitman extracted numerous lines and groups of lines from this preface, to be rewritten, paraphrased, or even transcribed into poems that appeared for the most part in the *Leaves* of 1856 or 1860. None of these derivatives are among Whitman's masterpieces, although "By Blue Ontario's Shore" and "Song of the Answerer," after indispensable revisions, took a po-sition among those poems that support the meaning of *Leaves of Grass* as a whole. Much more important, the Preface of 1855 went into independent orbit as an impassioned prose masterpiece. The ingenu-ous force and fervor that expressed a radical creed, and perhaps a revelation—with but a handful of poems for illustration—is now seen to have been prophetic with respect to Whitman's final accomplish-ment and the acceptance, in the present century, of his psychological basis and his organic structure of poetry. Certainly Whitman in his full accomplishment remained faithful to his creed. Numerous critics have observed Traubel's report that the poet more than thirty years later expressed doubt concerning the continuing importance of his first preface, but his remark is not disparaging in view of Whitman's knowl-edge that every idea in the 1855 Preface had been somewhere trans-lated into his poems. The poems of the 1855 edition likewise give the impression of being a spontaneous first expression of an overwhelming and sudden discovery affecting the poet's theory of man's personality and the nature of existence. The Preface and the poems of 1855 are in remarkable accord; literary history knows very few examples of such consistency between the art and the theory of a creative writer. From all points of view this essay is among the great writings of American literature. Of Whitman's critical pronouncements, only "A Backward Glance O'er Travel'd Roads," his last recapitulation of his poetry, has so much material value, and even that lacks the stylistic felicity of the first preface.

The long neglect of the special values of the 1855 Preface may justify the special emphasis upon it in this edition. In 1882 and in later collections of his prose, Whitman published an abbreviated version, shorter by some 328 equivalent lines, or nearly one-third the original bulk. Most of the cancellations apparently resulted from the poet's desire to omit certain lines of prose that had been translated into the poems. For whatever reason, his revisions diminished the essay's lyric élan and its exciting vigor as a manifesto. The shorter version, as finally published in the poet's *Complete Prose Works* (1892), is included in the present collection in the second volume of *Prose Works 1892*, where it is collated with all earlier texts.

The present version is the entire 1855 text, printed from a facsimile, including the punctuation, which represents Whitman's earlier practice. Our notes identify the lines of the essay that were borrowed for the eight poems most affected, and they also give the lines that Whitman inserted in later editions of this preface. The reader is referred to the first note on the text of this preface for further detail.

The second edition, *Leaves of Grass* (1856), had no preface in the accepted sense, yet we have no doubt that Whitman's open letter to Emerson, which followed the poems in this overstuffed little book, was intended by its author to serve the function of a preface; the well-publicized fact that Emerson had generously praised the first *Leaves* was sufficient to capture the attention of every informed reader. Except for the epistolary opening and closing paragraphs, this letter has the character of an introduction, calling attention to certain ideas already strongly expressed in the poetry of the volume. In part it is a searching, rebellious satire on the failure of American society, in spite of the principles of its famous revolutionary foundation, to develop the concept of individualism at the level of great leadership and new revelations. In consistency with the same idea, the essay calls for the development of an American literature that shall be "inherent"—not simply nationalistic; that shall produce poets able to reveal, in American life, "the indefinable hard something that is Nature." Finally, and in the same vein, this essay is perhaps Whitman's most explicit and fullest prose exposition of his belief that the sexual nature of man is the source of creativeness and individualism and must be made illustrious—this on psychological grounds only lately familiar in twentieth-century American thought. This open letter was Whitman's reply to the familiar letter that Emerson had sent him on July 21, 1855, praising the first edition of *Leaves of Grass* with unequivocal and characteristic understanding of the full meaning of these poems and with knowledge that they would offend readers in general. Having within three months been "persuaded" by editor Charles A. Dana to make Emerson's letter public in the *New York Tribune*, Whitman now replied by this open letter, dated August 1856, and he printed the two letters together in the 1856 *Leaves* in an appendix entitled "Leaves Droppings." Still without asking Emerson's permission, as if bent on social suicide, the Brooklyn poet had the spine of the volume ornamented with a gold-stamped copy of Emerson's words from the letter: "I Greet you at the / Beginning of A / Great Career / R. W. Emerson. Emerson, it is reported, only remarked to Samuel Longfellow that Whitman "has done a strange rude thing," but he remained his staunch friend. The reader will find other specific information in the note on the text, "Letter to Emerson, 1856."

The Preface of 1872, originally the introduction to the small volume of poems entitled *As a Strong Bird on Pinions Free,* and the Preface of 1876, which was prepared for the "Centennial" volume, *Two Rivulets,* are in the present edition brought into close association with each other by the footnotes. Like the "Preface 1855" and "A Backward Glance O'er Travel'd Roads," the prefaces of 1872 and 1876 may be found in numerous collections of Whitman's poems and prose, but none of these have been annotated. As a whole, these prefaces constitute a progressive revelation of Whitman the man and poet, but the prefaces of 1872 and 1876 have an additional interest for the reader and critic. They show that Whitman, during these years, was going through a "mid-channel" crisis of illness and confused aims. He had not yet quite realized that, whether from illness or other causes, his great period of creativity had closed, indeed had begun to close about 1867. In Preface 1872 he declared an intention to write another book, parallel to *Leaves of Grass.* The former work had established, he thought, the theme of democratic individualism; the companion volume was to be dedicated to the theme of the democratic society and in particular to its religious values. "As a Strong Bird on Pinions Free," he thought, might prove to be the beginning of this new cycle. Very likely a few poems of the early 1870s—certainly "Passage to India" and "Prayer of Columbus"—were related to the plan, but as our notes make clear, Whitman was destined never to regain the health and creative imagination that, from 1850 to 1865, had supported an astonishing creativity and originality.

This commentary on the prefaces began with a reference to "A Backward Glance O'er Travel'd Roads," and we should return at least briefly to it, as the last to be completed of all Whitman's major essays in self-criticism. Its first appearance in *November Boughs* (1888) was prepared for by a number of trial runs of its related major themes in a succession of essays over a period of several years, and this complex process of growth is indicated in the textual footnotes of the present edition. The essay is so familiar that, although it is the most generous in its information among the articles functioning as prefaces, it may be treated somewhat less fully than the Preface 1855. Generally speaking, it divides into two related subjects: the personality of the poet in the perspective of the history of his times, of which he believed the Civil War to be the central event; and secondly, his theory of poetry, involving the recognition of that experience that excited his creativity and gave him, for a time, a dedication that seemed to represent the inspiration of some vast power outside him. It was pointed out above that the present edition of "A Backward Glance . . ." is supported, as in the 1889 *Leaves*, by the prefatory "Letter to the Reader." This, and the "Letter to Emerson, 1856," have not previously appeared in an edition of Whitman's prefaces.

The Text and the Notes

The selection of the text to be honored in any edition is of first concern; but in fact the text reproduced here had already been identified by the same editors in their work on *Leaves of Grass: A Textual Variorum*. By definition the Variorum Edition deals strictly and exhaustively with all textual variants and evidence that may be derived from the collation of all extant texts of each poem. The present "Reader's Edition" intends only to show the honored text without interruption, for the satisfaction of the reader. For the satisfaction of the reader-turned-student, footnotes for each poem summarize the history of the text, clarify foreign or archaic expressions, and identify allusions now generally unfamiliar.

The text was printed directly from a photographic facsimile, which was corrected for mechanical defects. As was said above, this edition is one of the two issues of 1891–92, containing the prefatory note recommending that future editions be "a copy and facsimile, indeed of the text of these . . . pages." The contents of the edition are indicated by its bibliographical description: *Leaves of Grass*/Including/ SANDS AT SEVENTY . . . *1st Annex,*/GOOD-BYE MY FANCY . . . *2nd Annex,*/ A BACKWARD GLANCE O'ER TRAVEL'D ROADS,/*and Portrait from Life.*// *Walt Whitman* [facsimile autograph] beneath the poem, "Come, said my Soul,"//PHILADELPHIA/DAVID MCKAY, PUBLISHER/23 SOUTH NINTH STREET/1891–2//

As Whitman bibliographers have noted, this issue appears in two forms, with identical title pages, contents, and pagination but different in binding. One form is bound in heavy paper, the covers plain, the spine showing only a pasted-on label on which is printed the title and the author's name, the covers usually grey in color or dark chocolate brown (called the "brownstone front" by Whitman's familiars). Of the softbound issue, only a small number were hurriedly bound up in advance of the whole edition so that the bedfast author could autograph copies as Christmas gifts for his friends. They were available in November. However, the report that Whitman's increasing weakness prevented him from completing his task is sustained by the survival of copies forwarded on behalf of the poet by Horace Traubel. The early copy at the University of Pennsylvania, inscribed to J. W. Wallace in Whitman's hand but not dated, must have been mailed in mid-November, 1891, since it reached Wallace at his home in Bolton, England, about December 17 (J. Johnston and J. W. Wallace, *Visits to Walt Whitman . . .* , London, 1917, p. 231). The bulk of the 1891–

92 edition was the second form, bound in dark green cloth; the covers are plain, the spine gold-stamped with the title and the names of author and publisher. No copy bearing Whitman's autograph has been seen, although a copy in Gay W. Allen's collection bears the acquisition date of "May/92" and the poet lived until March 26. The term, "deathbed edition" has been applied to both issues, but more appropriately to the softbound form.

Many of these facts have long been known, but it has not previously been reported that the softbound issue does not contain the verbal changes and mechanical variants that first appeared in Whitman's revised *Leaves of Grass* in 1888 and 1889. These revisions did appear, however, in the hardbound issue of 1891–92. The differences between the two issues have been verified by the comparison of a significant number of copies of each form in several collections, and by the thorough examination of the Feinberg MS of the volume as made up for the printer, in which loose signatures of *LG* 1889 constitute the copy for the canon poems and show the corrections of 1888 and 1889 that appear only in the clothbound issue of 1891–92, not in softbound copies. Therefore the present editors have honored, in the text of this volume, that of the green cloth hardbound issue of 1891–92. Important variants between the two issues—those that affect the meaning —are shown in the footnotes.

The preparation of the Variorum Edition, which will report all variants of every kind, also sorted out the successive texts of the "Poems Excluded from *Leaves of Grass*" and "Passages Excluded from Poems of *Leaves of Grass*," two separate sections following the *Leaves of Grass*, 1891–92, in this edition. The new variorum provided information reflected in the report of the textual history in notes to the poems of the *Leaves of Grass* canon.

Whitman's prefaces, like the poems, created the problem of selecting the text to be honored. We chose in all cases the first edition texts that appeared in the volumes of Whitman's poems that they heralded. Read consecutively in this arrangement they represent in their way the poet's apologia, his stirring critical defense of what he knew was then a radical poetry. We hope they will again make available for a new generation the immediate urgency of this poetry in its first appearance, and demonstrate its continuing relationship to the American ideology. Never before have all these pieces appeared together in association with the complete text of the *Leaves of Grass*. Not even Whitman, in *Complete Prose Works*, 1892, included the prefatorial "Letter to Emerson" 1856 or the "Letter to the Reader" of 1889. All the other prefaces appear in the present *Collected Writings, Prose Works*, 1892, but necessarily in their last edition texts. Professor Floyd Stovall has edited them so as to show by footnotes what were their first-edition sources, while we here have edited the first edition texts with reference to their last-edition derivatives—a calculated dualism of *a quo* and *ad quem* in these *Collected Writings of Walt Whitman*.

Among mechanical characteristics that should be noted in this text is the treatment of run-on or spill-over lines in the canon poems of

Leaves of Grass. This body of Whitman's poems retained unchanged the same paginations and type-face established by the plates of the Boston edition of 1881 until the poet's last edition of 1891–92; Whitman's verbal alterations during this period were accommodated to the existing space. We have not indicated the numbering of stanzas, or groups of stanzas, except for the last edition, our present text. However, since our pagination is different from that of the 1891–92 edition, we were able to restore the space between stanzas whenever a stanza break occurring in earlier editions was accidentally obscured in the texts of 1881 and later by the ending of a stanza at the last line of a page. The failure of twentieth-century editions to do this resulted in some severe distortions. For example, the restoration of "To the Man-of-War Bird" in a three-stanza form (instead of two) contributes to the understanding of its dramatic development and its rhythmic pattern. The characteristics treated above do not apply, of course, to the excluded poems or fragments, or to uncollected poems, because they vary with respect to typography, stanza divisions, and spill-overs from one edition, or one MS, to another. Our selections of the best text for poems not in the canon therefore led to inconsistencies in the poetry outside the 1891 *Leaves*.

We call attention also to the dating of the literature of this edition. In all cases the dates, if known, will appear below the concluding line of text, the date at the left margin representing the first appearance in print and the date at the right margin indicating the appearance of the writing in its last approved form as shown. Date of composition, if known, will appear in the first footnote (the headnote or title-note) and more detailed information dating the publications may also appear in the same place. This use of the headnote has been especially necessary in dating the poems excluded from early issues. We commonly abbreviate the title and date of a Whitman edition: *LG* 1860 (*Leaves of Grass*); *DT* 1865 (*Drum-Taps*); *CPW* 1892 (*Complete Prose Works*). In addition, for a clothbound or hardbound volume, or for a paperbound edition, find respectively "hb" and "sb"; but see complete "list of abbreviations."

SCULLEY BRADLEY
HAROLD W. BLODGETT

The Text of
LEAVES OF GRASS
1891–1892

Leaves of Grass

Including

SANDS AT SEVENTY... *1st Annex,*
GOOD-BYE MY FANCY... *2d Annex,*
A BACKWARD GLANCE O'ER TRAVEL'D ROADS,
and Portrait from Life.

COME, said my Soul,[1]
Such verses for my Body let us write, (for we are one,)
That should I after death invisibly return,
Or, long, long hence, in other spheres,
There to some group of mates the chants resuming,
(Tallying Earth's soil, trees, winds, tumultuous waves,)
Ever with pleas'd smile I may keep on,
Ever and ever yet the verses owning—as, first, I here and now,
Signing for Soul and Body, set to them my name,

Walt Whitman

PHILADELPHIA
DAVID McKAY, PUBLISHER
23 SOUTH NINTH STREET
1891-'2

---

1. First printed in the Christmas number of the *New York Daily Graphic,* December 1874, then in the *New York Tribune,* February 19, 1876, this poem, signed by WW, became the title-page epigraph of *LG* 1876, *LG* 1882 (Camden), *CPP* 1888, and finally *LG* 1891–92, where it was restored after having disappeared from the title-pages of *LG* 1881 and 1883–84. Numerous MSS (Barrett, Berg, BPL, Huntington) show elaborate revision. See *CW*, X, 131–34 for earlier versions, originally transcribed by W. S. Kennedy in *The Conservator,* June 1896.

INSCRIPTIONS

One's-Self I Sing[1]

One's-Self[2] I sing, a simple separate person,
Yet utter the word Democratic, the word En-Masse.[3]

Of physiology from top to toe I sing,
Not physiognomy alone nor brain alone is worthy for the
     Muse, I say the Form complete is worthier far,
The Female equally with the Male I sing.   5

Of Life immense in passion, pulse, and power,
Cheerful, for freest action form'd under the laws divine,
The Modern Man I sing.
1867   *1871*

As I Ponder'd in Silence[4]

As I ponder'd in silence,
Returning upon my poems, considering, lingering long,
A Phantom arose before me with distrustful aspect,
Terrible in beauty, age, and power,
The genius of poets of old lands,   5
As to me directing like flame its eyes,
With finger pointing to many immortal songs,
And menacing voice, *What singest thou?* it said,
Know'st thou not there is but one theme for ever-enduring bards?
And that is the theme of War, the fortune of battles,   10
The making of perfect soldiers.

Inscriptions: "Inscriptions" first became a group title for the opening nine poems of *LG* 1871. In *LG* 1881 the group was increased to the present twenty-four poems, of which one was new.

1. This poem is a shorter rendering of the "Inscription" italicized on the frontispiece of *LG* 1867, and reprinted in the "Sands at Seventy" group of *NB* (1888) under the title "Small the Theme of my Chant." The present version was first printed in *LG* 1871. Both versions were derived from drafts in seven small notebooks that WW had fastened into his own copy of the first edition of *LG*, and that were edited by Clifton Joseph Furness in 1929. See Furness, "Introductions intended for American editions of *Leaves of Grass*," 115–37, and "Appendix," 165–74.
2. The expanded self that WW celebrates here and elsewhere in *LG* seems paradoxically to include both the "self" in the ordinary sense ("a simple separate person") and a larger, more inclusive, "Democratic" self.
3. WW was fond of this borrowed word, using it in his first poem, "Song of Myself" (line 478).
4. In this and the next poem WW begins a use of italics whose flexibility and variety students will find interesting to note as they proceed through *LG*. Here the form is question and answer, but in the following poem it is imagined response. In "Song of the Redwood-Tree," as in "Out of the Cradle . . ." and "Out of the Rolling Ocean . . . ," it is direct first person. In the thrush song of "When Lilacs Last . . ." it is a voice overheard, and so on.

3

Be it so, then I answer'd,
*I too haughty Shade also sing war, and a longer and greater one
    than any,*
*Waged in my book with varying fortune, with flight, advance
    and retreat, victory deferr'd and wavering,*
*(Yet methinks certain, or as good as certain, at the last,) the field
    the world,*   15
For life and death, for the Body and for the eternal Soul,
Lo, I too am come, chanting the chant of battles,
I above all promote brave soldiers.
    1871   *1871*

In Cabin'd Ships at Sea[5]

In cabin'd ships at sea,
The boundless blue on every side expanding,
With whistling winds and music of the waves, the large
    imperious waves,
Or some lone bark buoy'd on the dense marine,
Where joyous full of faith, spreading white sails,   5
She cleaves the ether[6] mid the sparkle and the foam of day, or
    under many a star at night,
By sailors young and old haply will I, a reminiscence of the
    land, be read,
In full rapport at last.

Here are our thoughts, voyagers' thoughts,
*Here not the land, firm land, alone appears, may then by them
    be said,*   10
*The sky o'erarches here, we feel the undulating deck beneath our
    feet,*
We feel the long pulsation, ebb and flow of endless motion,
*The tones of unseen mystery, the vague and vast suggestions of
    the briny world, the liquid-flowing syllables,*
*The perfume, the faint creaking of the cordage,[7] the melancholy
    rhythm,*
The boundless vista and the horizon far and dim are all here,   15
And this is ocean's poem.

Then falter not O book, fulfil your destiny,
You not a reminiscence of the land alone,

---

5. First published in the 1871 "Inscriptions" in the positions they now occupy, both this poem
   and the preceding "As I Ponder'd in Silence" are concerned with the destiny of *LG.* W. S.
   Kennedy, WW's friend and commentator, said (*Conservator*, no. 12 [February 1907]: 184)
   that this poem was suggested by a passage in Pindar's fifth ode:

   > Speed thou, my dulcet lay,
   > In every bark and pinnace o'er the deep.

   Note the structural regularity of this poem: three stanzas of eight iambic lines each, begin-
   ning and ending with shorter lines.
6. The element that, according to Aristotle, filled the rarefied upper spaces.
7. The ropes in the rigging of a ship.

You too as a lone bark cleaving the ether, purpos'd I know not
  whither, yet ever full of faith,
Consort to every ship that sails, sail you!   20
Bear forth to them folded my love, (dear mariners, for you I
  fold it here in every leaf;)
Speed on my book! spread your white sails my little bark
  athwart the imperious waves,
Chant on, sail on, bear o'er the boundless blue from me to
  every sea,
This song for mariners and all their ships.
  1871   *1871*

To Foreign Lands[8]

I heard that you ask'd for something to prove this puzzle the
  New World,
And to define America, her athletic Democracy,
Therefore I send you my poems that you behold in them what
  you wanted.
  1860   *1871*

To a Historian[9]

You who celebrate bygones,
Who have explored the outward, the surfaces of the races, the
  life that has exhibited itself,
Who have treated of man as the creature of politics,
  aggregates, rulers and priests,
I, habitan of the Alleghanies,[1] treating of him as he is in
  himself in his own rights,
Pressing the pulse of the life that has seldom exhibited itself,
  (the great pride of man in himself,)   5
Chanter of Personality, outlining what is yet to be,
I project the history of the future.
  1860   *1871*

---

8. First appeared among the "Messenger Leaves" group of *LG* 1860.
9. Compare this poem with its inflated first version, "Chants Democratic" No. 10, *LG* 1860.
1. "Habitan" is apparently the poet's coinage, perhaps derived from "habitant," a native of
  Canada (or Louisiana) of French descent. The Alleghenies are the oldest mountains in the
  United States; thus WW is allegorically identifying himself with the ancient geologic past of
  his land. "Alleghanies" is Whitman's own spelling.

To Thee Old Cause[2]

To thee old cause!
Thou peerless, passionate, good cause,
Thou stern, remorseless, sweet idea,
Deathless throughout the ages, races, lands,
After a strange sad war, great war for thee,   5
(I think all war through time was really fought, and ever will
      be really fought, for thee,)
These chants for thee, the eternal march of thee.

(A war O soldiers not for itself alone,
Far, far more stood silently waiting behind, now to advance in
      this book.)

Thou orb of many orbs!   10
Thou seething principle! thou well-kept, latent germ! thou
      centre!
Around the idea of thee the war revolving,
With all its angry and vehement play of causes,
(With vast results to come for thrice a thousand years,)
These recitatives for thee,—my book and the war are one,   15
Merged in its spirit I and mine, as the contest hinged on thee,
As a wheel on its axis turns, this book unwitting to itself,
Around the idea of thee.
    1871   *1881*

Eidólons[3]

    I met a seer,
Passing the hues and objects of the world,
The fields of art and learning, pleasure, sense,
    To glean eidólons.

---

2. WW frequently refers—in similar phrase—to "the good old cause," and comes closest to
   defining it in the 1860 "To a Certain Cantatrice" as "the progress and freedom of the race."
   In addressing the cause as "Thou orb of many orbs!" the poet employs the word in the older
   sense of "sphere of activity." In "Whitman and the 'Good Old Cause,' " (*AL* 34 [November
   1962]: 400–403), Clarence Gohdes offers evidence to show why the poet could take for
   granted that his contemporaries would understand the phrase. See also WW's MS note on
   the "good old cause" in *N and F,* I, 55.
3. First published in the *New York Tribune,* February 19, 1876, then in *TR* (1876), and trans-
   ferred to "Inscriptions" in 1881. WW entered in his MS "Notebook on Words" (Feinberg):
   "Ei-do-lon (Gr) phantom—the *image* of a Helen at Troy instead of real flesh and blood
   woman." Years later he told Traubel, "It is the custom everywhere to pronounce the word
   eidolons: I always make it *eidolons:* this is right, too. I make considerable use of the word."
   (Traubel, III, 131). WW employs the word as a refrain to express the concept, central in
   LG, that behind all appearance is soul, the ultimate reality, eternal and changeless. W. S.
   Kennedy (*FBW,* 181–82) suggests the influence of Balfour Stewart and P. G. Tait's *The
   Unseen Universe* (1875), whose thesis is "that each organic or inorganic object on the earth
   makes, in the process of its growth, a delicate facsimile register of itself on the living sensitive
   ether that lies immediately around it and bathes and interpenetrates its every atom."

Put in thy chants said he,   5
No more the puzzling hour nor day, nor segments, parts, put in,
Put first before the rest as light for all and entrance-song of all,
    That of eidólons.

Ever the dim beginning,
Ever the growth, the rounding of the circle,   10
Ever the summit and the merge at last, (to surely start again,)
    Eidólons! eidólons!

Ever the mutable,
Ever materials, changing, crumbling, re-cohering,
Ever the ateliers, the factories divine,   15
    Issuing eidólons.

Lo, I or you,
Or woman, man, or state, known or unknown,
We seeming solid wealth, strength, beauty build,
    But really build eidólons.   20

The ostent[4] evanescent,
The substance of an artist's mood or savan's studies long,
Or warrior's, martyr's, hero's toils,
    To fashion his eidólon.

Of every human life,   25
(The units gather'd, posted, not a thought, emotion, deed, left out,)
The whole or large or small summ'd, added up,
    In its eidólon.

The old, old urge,
Based on the ancient pinnacles, lo, newer, higher pinnacles,   30
From science and the modern still impell'd,
    The old, old urge, eidólons.

The present now and here,
America's busy, teeming, intricate whirl,
Of aggregate and segregate for only thence releasing,   35
    To-day's eidólons.

These with the past,
Of vanish'd lands, of all the reigns of kings across the sea,
Old conquerors, old campaigns, old sailors' voyages,
    Joining eidólons.   40

Densities, growth, façades,
Strata of mountains, soils, rocks, giant trees,

---

4. A token or portent.

Far-born, far-dying, living long, to leave,
    Eidólons everlasting.

    Exaltè, rapt, ecstatic,   45
The visible but their womb of birth,
Of orbic tendencies to shape and shape and shape,
    The mighty earth-eidólon.

    All space, all time,
(The stars, the terrible perturbations of the suns,   50
Swelling, collapsing, ending, serving their longer, shorter use,)
    Fill'd with eidólons only.

    The noiseless myriads,
The infinite oceans where the rivers empty,
The separate countless free identities, like eyesight,   55
    The true realities, eidólons.

    Not this the world,
Nor these the universes, they the universes,
Purport and end, ever the permanent life of life,
    Eidólons, eidólons.   60

    Beyond thy lectures learn'd professor,
Beyond thy telescope or spectroscope observer keen, beyond all
    mathematics,
Beyond the doctor's surgery, anatomy, beyond the chemist with
    his chemistry,
    The entities of entities, eidólons.

    Unfix'd yet fix'd,   65
Ever shall be, ever have been and are,
Sweeping the present to the infinite future,
    Eidólons, eidólons, eidólons.

    The prophet and the bard,
Shall yet maintain themselves, in higher stages yet,   70
Shall mediate to the Modern, to Democracy, interpret yet to them,
    God and eidólons.

    And thee my soul,
Joys, ceaseless exercises, exaltations,
Thy yearning amply fed at last, prepared to meet,   75
    Thy mates, eidólons.

    Thy body permanent,
The body lurking there within thy body,
The only purport of the form thou art, the real I myself,
    An image, an eidólon.   80

Thy very songs not in thy songs,
No special strains to sing, none for itself,
But from the whole resulting, rising at last and floating,
    A round full-orb'd eidólon.
1876   1876

For Him I Sing[5]

For him I sing,
I raise the present on the past,
(As some perennial tree out of its roots, the present on the past,)
With time and space I him dilate and fuse the immortal laws,
To make himself by them the law unto himself.   5
1871   1871

When I Read the Book[6]

When I read the book, the biography famous,
And is this then (said I) what the author calls a man's life?
And so will some one when I am dead and gone write my life?
(As if any man really knew aught of my life,
Why even I myself I often think know little or nothing of my
    real life,   5
Only a few hints, a few diffused faint clews and indirections
I seek for my own use to trace out here.)
1867   1871

Beginning My Studies[7]

Beginning my studies the first step pleas'd me so much,
The mere fact consciousness, these forms, the power of motion,
The least insect or animal, the senses, eyesight, love,
The first step I say awed me and pleas'd me so much,
I have hardly gone and hardly wish'd to go any farther,   5
But stop and loiter all the time to sing it in ecstatic songs.
1865   1871

---

5. First appeared in the "Inscriptions" of *LG* 1871.
6. The first (and more powerful) version of this poem in *LG* 1867 was limited to five lines, the first four as they are now, the fifth completing the parenthesis: "As if you, O cunning Soul, did not keep your secret well!" The ms (Lion) shows many variants.
7. First appeared in the 1865 *Drum-Taps,* and was transferred to "Inscriptions" in 1871.

Beginners[8]

How they are provided for upon the earth, (appearing at
    intervals,)
How dear and dreadful they are to the earth,
How they inure to themselves as much as to any—what a
    paradox appears their age,
How people respond to them, yet know them not,
How there is something relentless in their fate all times,   5
How all times mischoose the objects of their adulation and
    reward,
And how the same inexorable price must still be paid for the
    same great purchase.
1860   *1860*

To the States[9]

To the States or any one of them, or any city of the States,
    Resist much, obey little,
Once unquestioning obedience, once fully enslaved,
Once fully enslaved, no nation, state, city of this earth, ever
    afterward resumes its liberty.
1860   *1881*

On Journeys through the States[1]

On journeys through the States we start,
(Ay through the world, urged by these songs,
Sailing henceforth to every land, to every sea,)
We willing learners of all, teachers of all, and lovers of all.

We have watch'd the seasons dispensing themselves and
    passing on,   5
And have said, Why should not a man or woman do as much
    as the seasons, and effuse as much?

We dwell a while in every city and town,
We pass through Kanada,[2] the North-east, the vast valley of
    the Mississippi, and the Southern States,

---

8. This distinguished little poem, which first appeared in *LG* 1860, shows WW's power to withhold and challenge. The word "beginners" is to be taken in no obvious sense: the beginners are the great innovators.
9. First titled "Walt Whitman's Caution," this poem was one of the "Messenger Leaves" of *LG* 1860 and, appropriately, one of the "Songs of Insurrection" of the 1871 and 1876 editions.
1. No. 17 of the "Chants Democratic" of *LG* 1860, this poem was dropped from the 1867 edition, and then restored in the 1871 *Passage to India*, also in the "Passage to India" annexes of *LG* 1872 and the 1876 *Two Rivulets*. The poet's theme is accurately conveyed in an MS title he was not to use—"Wander-Teachers" (Bowers, 164).
2. This spelling of "Canada"—and its adjectival form, "Kanadian"—is consistent in *LG*, and purely idiosyncratic.

We confer on equal terms with each of the States,
We make trial of ourselves and invite men and women to hear,   10
We say to ourselves, Remember, fear not, be candid, promulge
    the body and the soul,
Dwell a while and pass on, be copious, temperate, chaste,
    magnetic,
And what you effuse may then return as the seasons return,
And may be just as much as the seasons.
    1860   *1871*

To a Certain Cantatrice[3]

Here, take this gift,
I was reserving it for some hero, speaker, or general,
One who should serve the good old cause, the great idea, the
    progress and freedom of the race,
Some brave confronter of despots, some daring rebel;
But I see that what I was reserving belongs to you just as
    much as to any.   5
    1860   *1871*

Me Imperturbe[4]

Me imperturbe, standing at ease in Nature,
Master of all or mistress of all, aplomb in the midst of
    irrational things,
Imbued as they, passive, receptive, silent as they,
Finding my occupation, poverty, notoriety, foibles, crimes, less
    important than I thought,
Me toward the Mexican sea, or in the Mannahatta[5] or the
    Tennessee, or far north or inland,   5
A river man, or a man of the woods, or of any farm-life of
    these States or of the coast, or the lakes or Kanada,
Me wherever my life is lived, O to be self-balanced for
    contingencies,
To confront night, storms, hunger, ridicule, accidents, rebuffs,
    as the trees and animals do.
    1860   *1881*

---

3. One of the "Messenger Leaves" of *LG* 1860, this poem was transferred to "Songs of Insurrection" in 1871 and 1876, and to "Inscriptions" in 1881. The tribute is addressed to Madame Marietta Alboni, great coloratura soprano, who in the New York season of 1852–53 appeared in ten operas, every one attended by the poet, as he proudly testified (*CW*, IV, 26).
4. No. 18 of the "Chants Democratic" of *LG* 1860, this poem was transferred to "Inscriptions" in 1881. It is remindful of the counsels to himself that WW often entered in his notebooks, and it is little changed from the original MS.
5. This Indian name for his city so pleased WW that he used it many times in his poetry. Irving had also popularized it in his *Knickerbocker's History of New York* (1809), Book III, chap. I: ". . . the lovely island of Mannahatta." The name is an Algonquian word, meaning "large island" (*Proceedings of the New York State Historical Association*, 1906, pp. 13–14, "Indian Geographical Names").

Savantism[6]

Thither as I look I see each result and glory retracing itself
    and nestling close, always obligated,
Thither hours, months, years—thither trades, compacts,
    establishments, even the most minute,
Thither every-day life, speech, utensils, politics, persons,
    estates;
Thither we also, I with my leaves and songs, trustful, admirant,
As a father to his father going takes his children along with
    him.   5
1860   *1860*

The Ship Starting[7]

Lo, the unbounded sea,
On its breast a ship starting, spreading all sails, carrying even
    her moonsails,
The pennant is flying aloft as she speeds she speeds so stately—
    below emulous waves press forward,
They surround the ship with shining curving motions and
    foam.
1865   *1881*

I Hear America Singing[8]

I hear America singing, the varied carols I hear,
Those of mechanics, each one singing his as it should be
    blithe and strong,
The carpenter singing his as he measures his plank or beam,
The mason singing his as he makes ready for work, or leaves
    off work,
The boatman singing what belongs to him in his boat, the
    deck-hand singing on the steamboat deck,   5
The shoemaker singing as he sits on his bench, the hatter
    singing as he stands,

6. This 1860 poem was transferred to *Passage to India* in 1871, and hence to the "Passage to India" annexes of *LG* 1872 and the 1876 *Two Rivulets,* and to "Inscriptions" in 1881. "Savantism" may be interpreted as the wisdom that perceives the relationship and indebtedness of all appearance to its spiritual source.
7. Originally an 1865 *Drum-Taps* poem, "The Ship Starting" was grouped with ". . . Paumanok" in 1871 and 1876 and was transferred to "Inscriptions" in 1881.
8. This poem was first published in *LG* 1860 as No. 20 of "Chants Democratic"; for the next edition, 1867, WW had achieved the title and the first line we now know, an inspired improvement upon the original "American mouth-songs." The poem was transferred to "Inscriptions" in 1881. Inevitably it has received many musical adaptations—notably as a cantata for mixed voices by Harvey B. Gaul (1925) and by George Kleinsinger (1941). Also it became the title song of a group of WW's poems for mixed voices by Normand Lockwood (1954).

The wood-cutter's song, the ploughboy's on his way in the
    morning, or at noon intermission or at sundown,
The delicious singing of the mother, or of the young wife at
    work, or of the girl sewing or washing,
Each singing what belongs to him or her and to none else,
The day what belongs to the day—at night the party of young
    fellows, robust, friendly,   10
Singing with open mouths their strong melodious songs.
    1860   1867

What Place Is Besieged?[9]

What place is besieged, and vainly tries to raise the siege?
Lo, I send to that place a commander, swift, brave, immortal,
And with him horse and foot, and parks of artillery,
And artillery-men, the deadliest that ever fired gun.
    1860   1867

Still Though the One I Sing[1]

Still though the one I sing,
(One, yet of contradictions made,) I dedicate to Nationality,
I leave in him revolt, (O latent right of insurrection! O
    quenchless, indispensable fire!)
    1871   1871

Shut Not Your Doors[2]

Shut not your doors to me proud libraries,
For that which was lacking on all your well-fill'd shelves, yet
    needed most, I bring,
Forth from the war emerging, a book I have made,
The words of my book nothing, the drift of it every thing,
A book separate, not link'd with the rest nor felt by the
    intellect,   5
But you ye untold latencies will thrill to every page.
    1865   1881

9. Originally this poem constituted the last four lines of an eight-line poem printed as "Cala-
mus" No. 31 in *LG* 1860. In the next edition, 1867, it appeared under its present title, and
the first four lines of the original piece also became a separate piece under the title "Here,
Sailor!" now "What Ship Puzzled at Sea." "What Place is Besieged?" was transferred to
"Inscriptions" in 1881.
1. This was the introductory poem (and the only new one) of a group of six labelled "Songs of
Insurrection" that WW arranged for the 1871 and 1876 editions; it then became one of the
"Inscriptions" in 1881.
2. First a *Drum-Taps* poem, this piece was much improved in revision, achieving its final—and
best—form in the 1881 "Inscriptions." Among the changes was the dropping of four lines
in the 1871 version to become in 1881 part of another poem, "As They Draw to a Close."

Poets to Come[3]

Poets to come! orators, singers, musicians to come!
Not to-day is to justify me and answer what I am for,
But you, a new brood, native, athletic, continental, greater
    than before known,
Arouse! for you must justify me.

I myself but write one or two indicative words for the future,   5
I but advance a moment only to wheel and hurry back in the
    darkness.

I am a man who, sauntering along without fully stopping,
    turns a casual look upon you and then averts his face,
Leaving it to you to prove and define it,
Expecting the main things from you.
    1860   *1867*

To You[4]

Stranger, if you passing meet me and desire to speak to me,
    why should you not speak to me?
And why should I not speak to you?
    1860   *1860*

Thou Reader[5]

Thou reader throbbest life and pride and love the same as I,
Therefore for thee the following chants.
    1881   *1881*

---

3. Originally No. 14 of "Chants Democratic," *LG* 1860, this poem was shortened and improved in 1867, transferred to "The Answerer" group in 1871 and 1876, and finally to "Inscriptions" in 1881.
4. The last of the "Messenger Leaves" of *LG* 1860, this poem was transferred to "Inscriptions" in 1881.
5. This final poem of the "Inscriptions" group was one of the seventeen new poems in *LG* 1881.

Starting from Paumanok[1]

1

Starting from fish-shape Paumanok where I was born,
Well-begotten, and rais'd by a perfect mother,
After roaming many lands, lover of populous pavements,
Dweller in Mannahatta[2] my city, or on southern savannas,
Or a soldier camp'd or carrying my knapsack and gun, or a
    miner in California,   5
Or rude in my home in Dakota's woods, my diet meat, my
    drink from the spring,
Or withdrawn to muse and meditate in some deep recess,
Far from the clank of crowds intervals passing rapt and happy,
Aware of the fresh free giver the flowing Missouri, aware of
    mighty Niagara,
Aware of the buffalo herds grazing the plains, the hirsute and
    strong-breasted bull,   10
Of earth, rocks, Fifth-month flowers experienced, stars, rain,
    snow, my amaze,
Having studied the mocking-bird's tones and the flight of the
    mountain-hawk,
And heard at dawn[3] the unrivall'd one, the hermit thrush from
    the swamp-cedars,
Solitary, singing in the West, I strike up for a New World.

2

Victory, union, faith, identity, time,   15
The indissoluble compacts, riches, mystery,
Eternal progress, the kosmos, and the modern reports.

This then is life,
Here is what has come to the surface after so many throes and
    convulsions.

How curious! how real!   20
Underfoot the divine soil, overhead the sun.
See revolving the globe,

---

1. The introductory poem of the 1860 edition, under the title "Proto-Leaf," this fervent an-
nouncement of the poet's theme and purpose was originally entitled "Premonition," as the
MS (Barrett) shows. See Bowers, 2–36, which also prints (40–56) a WW notebook of 1856
(Feinberg) containing many first-draft lines for this poem, whose composition was begun
immediately after the appearance of the first edition of LG. Its present title first appeared
in the 1867 edition, which contains more revisions than any other. These revisions are of
considerable interest and should be studied. The poem was placed in its present position,
immediately following the "Inscriptions" group, in LG 1871. It is itself an extended "Inscrip-
tion," as the original titles "Premonition" and "Proto-Leaf" also suggest. But it is much more
than an announcement of intent; like "Song of Myself" it is both a mythic and personal
portrait of the poet—the new man of the Western World. For commentary, see Handbook,
38–40; and Miller, 192–96.
2. Cf. "Me Imperturbe," line 5, note.
3. The softbound issue, unlike the hardbound issue of the 1891–92 text, reads "dusk," as in
editions previous to 1888.

The ancestor-continents away group'd together,
The present and future continents north and south, with the
    isthmus between.

See, vast trackless spaces,   25
As in a dream they change, they swiftly fill,
Countless masses debouch upon them,
They are now cover'd with the foremost people, arts,
    institutions, known.

See, projected through time,
For me an audience interminable.   30

With firm and regular step they wend, they never stop,
Successions of men, Americanos, a hundred millions,
One generation playing its part and passing on,
Another generation playing its part and passing on in its turn,
With faces turn'd sideways or backward towards me to listen,   35
With eyes retrospective towards me.

3

Americanos! conquerors! marches humanitarian!
Foremost! century marches! Libertad![4] masses!
For you a programme of chants.

Chants of the prairies,   40
Chants of the long-running Mississippi, and down to the
    Mexican sea,
Chants of Ohio, Indiana, Illinois, Iowa, Wisconsin and
    Minnesota,
Chants going forth from the centre from Kansas, and thence
    equidistant,
Shooting in pulses of fire ceaseless to vivify all.

4

Take my leaves America, take them South and take them
    North,   45
Make welcome for them everywhere, for they are your own
    offspring,
Surround them East and West, for they would surround you,
And you precedents, connect lovingly with them, for they
    connect lovingly with you.

I conn'd old times,
I sat studying at the feet of the great masters,   50
Now if eligible O that the great masters might return and
    study me.

---

4. This Spanish word for "freedom" or "Liberty" is a favorite borrowing, appearing frequently
in *LG*.

In the name of these States shall I scorn the antique?
Why these are the children of the antique to justify it.

5

Dead poets, philosophs,[5] priests,
Martyrs, artists, inventors, governments long since,   55
Language-shapers on other shores,
Nations once powerful, now reduced, withdrawn, or desolate,
I dare not proceed till I respectfully credit what you have left
      wafted hither,
I have perused it, own it is admirable, (moving awhile among it,)
Think nothing can ever be greater, nothing can ever deserve
      more than it deserves,   60
Regarding it all intently a long while, then dismissing it,
I stand in my place with my own day here.

Here lands female and male,
Here the heir-ship and heiress-ship of the world, here the
      flame of materials,
Here spirituality the translatress, the openly-avow'd,   65
The ever-tending, the finalè[6] of visible forms,
The satisfier, after due long-waiting now advancing,
Yes here comes my mistress the soul.

6

The soul,
Forever and forever—longer than soil is brown and solid—
      longer than water ebbs and flows.   70

I will make the poems of materials, for I think they are to be
      the most spiritual poems,
And I will make the poems of my body and of mortality,
For I think I shall then supply myself with the poems of my
      soul and of immortality.

I will make a song for these States that no one State may
      under any circumstances be subjected to another State,
And I will make a song that there shall be comity by day and
      by night between all the States, and between any two of
      them,   75
And I will make a song for the ears of the President, full of
      weapons with menacing points,
And behind the weapons countless dissatisfied faces;
And a song make I of the One form'd out of all,
The fang'd and glittering One whose head is over all,

5. WW was fond of this variant of "philosopher," from the French "philosophe," a term often
      referring to the popular quasi-philosophers of the eighteenth-century French Enlightenment.
6. Properly, finale; the error was introduced in the Rees Welsh edition, 1882.

Resolute warlike One including and over all,   80
(However high the head of any else that head is over all.)[7]

I will acknowledge contemporary lands,
I will trail the whole geography of the globe and salute
      courteously every city large and small,
And employments! I will put in my poems that with you is
      heroism upon land and sea,
And I will report all heroism from an American point of view.   85

I will sing the song of companionship,
I will show what alone must finally compact these,
I believe these are to found their own ideal of manly love,
      indicating it in me,
I will therefore let flame from me the burning fires that were
      threatening to consume me,
I will lift what has too long kept down those smouldering fires,   90
I will give them complete abandonment,
I will write the evangel-poem of comrades and of love,
For who but I should understand love with all its sorrow and joy?
And who but I should be the poet of comrades?

7

I am the credulous man of qualities, ages, races,   95
I advance from the people in their own spirit,
Here is what sings unrestricted faith.

Omnes! omnes![8] let others ignore what they may,
I make the poem of evil also, I commemorate that part also,
I am myself just as much evil as good, and my nation is—and
      I say there is in fact no evil,   100
(Or if there is I say it is just as important to you, to the land
      or to me, as any thing else.)

I too, following many and follow'd by many, inaugurate a
      religion, I descend into the arena,
(It may be I am destin'd to utter the loudest cries there, the
      winner's pealing shouts,
Who knows? they may rise from me yet, and soar above every
      thing.)

Each is not for its own sake,   105
I say the whole earth and all the stars in the sky are for
      religion's sake.

---

7. This four-line passage was added in *LG* 1867. Compare with the eleventh stanza of "Pio-
   neers! O Pioneers!" in which the "fang'd and warlike mistress" is evidently the flag waving
   over the warlike procession.
8. Latin plural: "all"; here the meaning is extended to suggest "the all."

I say no man has ever yet been half devout enough,
None has ever yet adored or worship'd half enough,
None has begun to think how divine he himself is, and how
    certain the future is.

I say that the real and permanent grandeur of these States
    must be their religion,   110
Otherwise there is no real and permanent grandeur;
(Nor character nor life worthy the name without religion,
Nor land nor man or woman without religion.)

8

What are you doing young man?
Are you so earnest, so given up to literature, science, art,
    amours?   115
These ostensible realities, politics, points?
Your ambition or business whatever it may be?

It is well—against such I say not a word, I am their poet also,
But behold! such swiftly subside, burnt up for religion's sake,
For not all matter is fuel to heat, impalpable flame, the
    essential life of the earth,   120
Any more than such are to religion.

9

What do you seek so pensive and silent?
What do you need camerado?[9]
Dear son do you think it is love?

Listen dear son—listen America, daughter or son,   125
It is a painful thing to love a man or woman to excess, and yet
    it satisfies, it is great,
But there is something else very great, it makes the whole
    coincide,
It, magnificent, beyond materials, with continuous hands
    sweeps and provides for all.

10

Know you, solely to drop in the earth the germs of a greater
    religion,
The following chants each for its kind I sing.   130

My comrade!
For you to share with me two greatnesses, and a third one
    rising inclusive and more resplendent,

9. This favorite word of WW for "comrade"—to be used in *LG* seven times, beginning with
"Song of Myself"—is neither the present French *camarade* nor the Spanish *camarada*, but,
as Louise Pound noted in "Walt Whitman and the French Language," *American Speech* 1
(May 1926): 424, "an old English form of the Spanish word which he had from the Waverley
novels."

The greatness of Love and Democracy, and the greatness of
    Religion.[1]

Melange[2] mine own, the unseen and the seen,
Mysterious ocean where the streams empty,   135
Prophetic spirit of materials shifting and flickering around me,
Living beings, identities now doubtless near us in the air that
    we know not of,
Contact daily and hourly that will not release me,
These selecting, these in hints demanded of me.

Not he with a daily kiss onward from childhood kissing me,   140
Has winded and twisted around me that which holds me to him,
Any more than I am held to the heavens and all the spiritual
    world,
After what they have done to me, suggesting themes.

O such themes—equalities! O divine average!
Warblings under the sun, usher'd as now, or at noon, or
    setting,   145
Strains musical flowing through ages, now reaching hither,
I take to your reckless and composite chords, add to them, and
    cheerfully pass them forward.

11

As I have walk'd in Alabama my morning walk,
I have seen where the she-bird the mocking-bird sat on her
    nest in the briers hatching her brood.

I have seen the he-bird also,   150
I have paus'd to hear him near at hand inflating his throat and
    joyfully singing.

And while I paus'd it came to me that what he really sang for
    was not there only,
Nor for his mate nor himself only, nor all sent back by the echoes,
But subtle, clandestine, away beyond,
A charge transmitted and gift occult for those being born.   155

12

Democracy! near at hand to you a throat is now inflating itself
    and joyfully singing.

---

1. With these three "greatnesses" WW summarized, in 1860, the essential themes of *LG*.
2. French: a mixture; here the commingled elements in the following lines.

Ma femme![3] for the brood beyond us and of us,
For those who belong here and those to come,
I exultant to be ready for them will now shake out carols
    stronger and haughtier than have ever yet been heard
    upon earth.

I will make the songs of passion to give them their way,   160
And your songs outlaw'd offenders, for I scan you with kindred
    eyes, and carry you with me the same as any.

I will make the true poem of riches,
To earn for the body and the mind whatever adheres and goes
    forward and is not dropt by death;
I will effuse egotism and show it underlying all, and I will be
    the bard of personality,
And I will show of male and female that either is but the
    equal of the other,   165
And sexual organs and acts! do you concentrate in me, for I
    am determin'd to tell you with courageous clear voice to
    prove you illustrious,[4]
And I will show that there is no imperfection in the present,
    and can be none in the future,
And I will show that whatever happens to anybody it may be
    turn'd to beautiful results,
And I will show that nothing can happen more beautiful than
    death,
And I will thread a thread through my poems that time and
    events are compact,   170
And that all the things of the universe are perfect miracles,
    each as profound as any.

I will not make poems with reference to parts,
But I will make poems, songs, thoughts, with reference to
    ensemble,
And I will not sing with reference to a day, but with reference
    to all days,
And I will not make a poem nor the least part of a poem but
    has reference to the soul,   175
Because having look'd at the objects of the universe, I find
    there is no one nor any particle of one but has reference
    to the soul.

13

Was somebody asking to see the soul?[5]
See, your own shape and countenance, persons, substances,
    beasts, the trees, the running rivers, the rocks and sands.

---

3. WW addresses Democracy as "Ma femme!" in two other poems of 1860—"For You O De-
mocracy" and "France: The 18th Year of these States."
4. This line was transferred to its present position in 1871. Originally it followed line 85.
5. See N and F, I, 27, item 65, for MS variant of this section.

All hold spiritual joys and afterwards loosen them;
How can the real body ever die and be buried? 180

Of your real body and any man's or woman's real body,
Item for item it will elude the hands of the corpse-cleaners
and pass to fitting spheres,
Carrying what has accrued to it from the moment of birth to
the moment of death.

Not the types set up by the printer return their impression, the
meaning, the main concern,
Any more than a man's substance and life or a woman's
substance and life return in the body and the soul, 185
Indifferently before death and after death.

Behold, the body includes and is the meaning, the main
concern, and includes and is the soul;
Whoever you are, how superb and how divine is your body, or
any part of it!

14

Whoever you are, to you endless announcements!

Daughter of the lands did you wait for your poet? 190
Did you wait for one with a flowing mouth and indicative hand?
Toward the male of the States, and toward the female of the
States,
Exulting words, words to Democracy's lands.

Interlink'd, food-yielding lands!
Land of coal and iron! land of gold! land of cotton, sugar, rice! 195
Land of wheat, beef, pork! land of wool and hemp! land of the
apple and the grape!
Land of the pastoral plains, the grass-fields of the world! land
of those sweet-air'd interminable plateaus!
Land of the herd, the garden, the healthy house of adobie![6]
Lands where the north-west Columbia winds, and where the
southwest Colorado winds!
Land of the eastern Chesapeake! land of the Delaware! 200
Land of Ontario, Erie, Huron, Michigan!
Land of the Old Thirteen! Massachusetts land! land of
Vermont and Connecticut!
Land of the ocean shores! land of sierras and peaks!
Land of boatmen and sailors! fishermen's land!
Inextricable lands! the clutch'd together! the passionate ones! 205
The side by side! the elder and younger brothers! the bony-
limb'd!

---

6. WW's spelling in all editions of this poem, here and in line 221. *Cf.* "Song of Myself," line
323, note.

The great women's land! the feminine! the experienced sisters
    and the inexperienced sisters!
Far breath'd land! Arctic braced! Mexican breez'd! the diverse!
    the compact!
The Pennsylvanian! the Virginian! the double Carolinian!
O all and each well-loved by me! my intrepid nations! O I at
    any rate include you all with perfect love!   210
I cannot be discharged from you! not from one any sooner
    than another!
O death! O for all that, I am yet of you unseen this hour with
    irrepressible love,
Walking New England, a friend, a traveler,[7]
Splashing my bare feet in the edge of the summer ripples on
    Paumanok's sands,
Crossing the prairies, dwelling again in Chicago, dwelling in
    every town,   215
Observing shows, births, improvements, structures, arts,
Listening to orators and oratresses in public halls,
Of and through the States as during life, each man and
    woman my neighbor,
The Louisianian, the Georgian, as near to me, and I as near to
    him and her,
The Mississippian and Arkansian yet with me, and I yet with
    any of them,   220
Yet upon the plains west of the spinal river, yet in my house of
    adobie,
Yet returning eastward, yet in the Seaside State or in
    Maryland,
Yet Kanadian cheerily braving the winter, the snow and ice
    welcome to me,
Yet a true son either of Maine or of the Granite State, or the
    Narragansett Bay State, or the Empire State,
Yet sailing to other shores to annex the same, yet welcoming
    every new brother,   225
Hereby applying these leaves to the new ones from the hour
    they unite with the old ones,
Coming among the new ones myself to be their companion
    and equal, coming personally to you now,
Enjoining you to acts, characters, spectacles, with me.

15

With me with firm holding, yet haste, haste on.

For your life adhere to me,   230
(I may have to be persuaded many times before I consent to
    give myself really to you, but what of that?
Must not Nature be persuaded many times?)

---

7. The softbound issue, unlike the hardbound issue of the 1891–92 text, reads "traveller."

No dainty dolce affettuoso[8] I,
Bearded, sun-burnt, gray-neck'd, forbidding, I have arrived,
To be wrestled with as I pass for the solid prizes of the
    universe,   235
For such I afford whoever can persevere to win them.

16

On my way a moment I pause,
Here for you! and here for America!
Still the present I raise aloft, still the future of the States I
    harbinge[9] glad and sublime,
And for the past I pronounce what the air holds of the red
    aborigines.   240

The red aborigines,
Leaving natural breaths, sounds of rain and winds, calls as of
    birds and animals in the woods, syllabled to us for names,
Okonee, Koosa, Ottawa, Monongahela, Sauk, Natchez,
    Chattahoochee, Kaqueta, Oronoco,
Wabash, Miami, Saginaw, Chippewa, Oshkosh, Walla-Walla,
Leaving such to the States they melt, they depart, charging the
    water and the land with names.   245

17

Expanding and swift, henceforth,
Elements, breeds, adjustments, turbulent, quick and audacious,
A world primal again, vistas of glory incessant and branching,
A new race dominating previous ones and grander far, with
    new contests,
New politics, new literatures and religions, new inventions and
    arts.   250

These, my voice announcing—I will sleep no more but arise,
You oceans that have been calm within me! how I feel you,
    fathomless, stirring, preparing unprecedented waves and
    storms.

18

See, steamers steaming through my poems,
See, in my poems immigrants continually coming and landing,
See, in arriere, the wigwam, the trail, the hunter's hut, the
    flat-boat, the maize-leaf, the claim, the rude fence, and
    the backwoods village,   255
See, on the one side the Western Sea and on the other the

8. Two Italian words familiar as directions in music, suggesting sweet, dainty sentiment by
   contrast with the following lines.
9. Foretell.

Eastern Sea, how they advance and retreat upon my
poems as upon their own shores,
See, pastures and forests in my poems—see, animals wild and
tame—see, beyond the Kaw,[1] countless herds of buffalo
feeding on short curly grass,
See, in my poems, cities, solid, vast, inland, with paved streets,
with iron and stone edifices, ceaseless vehicles, and
commerce,
See, the many-cylinder'd steam printing-press—see, the
electric telegraph stretching across the continent,
See, through Atlantica's[2] depths pulses American Europe
reaching, pulses of Europe duly return'd,   260
See, the strong and quick locomotive as it departs, panting,
blowing the steam-whistle,[3]
See, ploughmen ploughing farms—see, miners digging mines
—see, the numberless factories,
See, mechanics busy at their benches with tools—see from
among them superior judges, philosophs, Presidents,
emerge, drest in working dresses,
See, lounging through the shops and fields of the States, me
well-belov'd, close-held by day and night,
Here the loud echoes of my songs there—read the hints come
at last.   265

19

O camerado close! O you and me at last, and us two only.[4]
O a word to clear one's path ahead endlessly!
O something ecstatic and undemonstrable! O music wild!
O now I triumph—and you shall also;
O hand in hand—O wholesome pleasure—O one more desirer
and lover!   270
O to haste firm holding—to haste, haste on with me.
    (1856) 1860   *1881*

1. Originally, a tribe of Siouan Indians after whom the state of Kansas is named. The Kaw is
   also a river in Kansas.
2. Originally Atlantica was one of the names for Atlantis or Atalantis, fabled island in the
   Atlantic Ocean. Here, it is WW's poetic name for the Atlantic.
3. Note the comparative recency of some of the inventions here cited: the rotary printing press,
   1846; the electric telegraph, 1832; the steam locomotive, 1829.
4. The reader should compare this section with its first 1860 version, in which the "Calamus"
   sentiment of "adhesiveness" is expressed in lines that were dropped from all succeeding
   editions. In the first version, the following lines appeared between lines 266 and 267:

   O power, liberty, eternity at last!
   O to be relieved of distinctions! to make as much of vices as virtues!
   O to level occupations and the sexes! O to bring all to common ground! O adhesiveness!
   O the pensive aching to be together—you know not why, and I know not why.

Song of Myself[1]

1

I celebrate myself, and sing myself,
And what I assume you shall assume,
For every atom belonging to me as good belongs to you.

I loafe and invite my soul,
I lean and loafe at my ease observing a spear of summer grass.   5

My tongue, every atom of my blood, form'd from this soil, this air,
Born here of parents born here from parents the same, and
      their parents the same,
I, now thirty-seven years old in perfect health begin,
Hoping to cease not till death.

Creeds and schools in abeyance,   10
Retiring back a while sufficed at what they are, but never
      forgotten,
I harbor for good or bad, I permit to speak at every hazard,
Nature without check with original energy.

2

Houses and rooms are full of perfumes, the shelves are
      crowded with perfumes,
I breathe the fragrance myself and know it and like it,   15
The distillation would intoxicate me also, but I shall not let it.

The atmosphere is not a perfume, it has no taste of the
      distillation, it is odorless,
It is for my mouth forever, I am in love with it,
I will go to the bank by the wood and become undisguised and
      naked,
I am mad for it to be in contact with me.[2]   20

---

1. This poem, untitled and unsectioned in 1855, occupied more than half of the first edition
of *LG*. In 1856 it was titled "Poem of Walt Whitman, an American"; in the 1860 and
succeeding editions it was titled simply "Walt Whitman," until in 1881 it became "Song of
Myself." As the variorum readings indicate, its evolution, beginning in the notebooks of
1847–48 (see *UPP*, II, 69–86) and continuing with many revisions through seven editions,
was not complete until 1881, although the poet never altered the poem fundamentally,
restricting himself to changes in diction and rhythm. "Song of Myself" is essentially the
epitome of the poet's "haughty" song, sure in its intent; and what to early commentators
seemed a kind of chaos of poetic exuberance is now recognized as deliberate structure—
perhaps an early modern example of the method of free association, but artful and controlled
in its reporting of what comes into awareness. The movement of "Song of Myself" is circular
rather than progressive, returning upon itself in evocation of ecstasy and confession, of
identification and recognition, of rapturous union with earth and spirit—truly a celebration
both personal and universal. For a generous survey of critical opinion regarding "Song of
Myself," see Edwin Haviland Miller, ed., *Walt Whitman's "Song of Myself": A Mosaic of
Interpretations* (Iowa City: University of Iowa Press, 1989), xviii–xxviii.
2. The symbolism of this passage, lines 14–20, suggests the opposition between experience
from shelved books and experience from Nature—a Wordsworthian concept. See Alice L.
Cooke, "A Note on Whitman's Symbolism in 'Song of Myself,' " *MLN* 65: 228–32.

The smoke of my own breath,
Echoes, ripples, buzz'd whispers, love-root, silk-thread, crotch
    and vine,
My respiration and inspiration, the beating of my heart, the
    passing of blood and air through my lungs,
The sniff of green leaves and dry leaves, and of the shore and
    dark-color'd sea-rocks, and of hay in the barn,
The sound of the belch'd words of my voice loos'd to the
    eddies of the wind,   25
A few light kisses, a few embraces, a reaching around of arms,
The play of shine and shade on the trees as the supple boughs
    wag,
The delight alone or in the rush of the streets, or along the
    fields and hill-sides,
The feeling of health, the full-noon trill, the song of me rising
    from bed and meeting the sun.

Have you reckon'd a thousand acres much? have you reckon'd
    the earth much?   30
Have you practis'd so long to learn to read?
Have you felt so proud to get at the meaning of poems?

Stop this day and night with me and you shall possess the
    origin of all poems,
You shall possess the good of the earth and sun, (there are
    millions of suns left,)[3]
You shall no longer take things at second or third hand, nor
    look through the eyes of the dead, nor feed on the
    spectres in books,   35
You shall not look through my eyes either, not take things
    from me,
You shall listen to all sides and filter them from your self.

3

I have heard what the talkers were talking, the talk of the
    beginning and the end,
But I do not talk of the beginning or the end.

There was never any more inception than there is now,   40
Nor any more youth or age than there is now,
And will never be any more perfection than there is now,
Nor any more heaven or hell than there is now.

Urge and urge and urge,
Always the procreant urge of the world.   45

---

3. WW was stirred by astronomical immensity, and his grasp of solar data was advanced for
his day. He was probably influenced by the New York lectures of the Cincinnati astronomer
Ormsby MacKnight Mitchel in December 1847. See Joseph Beaver, *Walt Whitman—Poet
of Science* (New York: King's Crown Press, 1951), 44, 63ff.

Out of the dimness opposite equals advance, always substance
and increase, always sex,
Always a knit of identity, always distinction, always a breed of
life.

To elaborate is no avail, learn'd and unlearn'd feel that it is so.

Sure as the most certain sure, plumb in the uprights, well
entretied,[4] braced in the beams,
Stout as a horse, affectionate, haughty, electrical,   50
I and this mystery here we stand.

Clear and sweet is my soul, and clear and sweet is all that is
not my soul.

Lack one lacks both, and the unseen is proved by the seen,
Till that becomes unseen and receives proof in its turn.

Showing the best and dividing it from the worst age vexes age,[5]   55
Knowing the perfect fitness and equanimity of things, while
they discuss I am silent, and go bathe and admire myself.

Welcome is every organ and attribute of me, and of any man
hearty and clean,
Not an inch nor a particle of an inch is vile, and none shall be
less familiar than the rest.

I am satisfied—I see, dance, laugh, sing;
As the hugging and loving bed-fellow sleeps at my side through
the night, and withdraws at the peep of the day with
stealthy tread,[6]
Leaving me baskets cover'd with white towels swelling the   60
house with their plenty,
Shall I postpone my acceptation and realization and scream at
my eyes,
That they turn from gazing after and down the road,
And forthwith cipher and show me to a cent,[7]
Exactly the value of one and exactly the value of two, and
which is ahead?   65

4. A carpenter's term meaning "cross-braced," as between two joists or walls. Here WW is
   drawing upon the vernacular of his experience as a house builder with his father.
5. In the first four editions of LG, a comma was placed between "worst" and "age," narrowing
   the sense.
6. The 1855 version of this line is explicit: "As God comes a loving bed-fellow and sleeps at
   my side all night and close on the peep of the day,"
7. Reads "show to me a cent" from 1881 to 1888; corrected by WW in LG 1889. Appears
   correctly in the hardbound form of LG 1891–92, but not in the softbound issue of this
   edition.

4

Trippers and askers surround me,
People I meet, the effect upon me of my early life or the ward
    and city I live in, or the nation,
The latest dates, discoveries, inventions, societies, authors old
    and new,
My dinner, dress, associates, looks, compliments, dues,
The real or fancied indifference of some man or woman I love,   70
The sickness of one of my folks or of myself, or ill-doing or
    loss or lack of money, or depressions or exaltations,
Battles, the horrors of fratricidal war, the fever of doubtful
    news, the fitful events;
These come to me days and nights and go from me again,
But they are not the Me myself.

Apart from the pulling and hauling stands what I am,   75
Stands amused, complacent, compassionating, idle, unitary,
Looks down, is erect, or bends an arm on an impalpable
    certain rest,
Looking with side-curved head curious what will come next,
Both in and out of the game and watching and wondering at it.

Backward I see in my own days where I sweated through fog
    with linguists and contenders,
I have no mockings or arguments, I witness and wait.   80

5

I believe in you my soul, the other I am must not abase itself
    to you,[8]
And you must not be abased to the other.

Loafe with me on the grass, loose the stop from your throat,
Not words, not music or rhyme I want, not custom or lecture,
    not even the best,   85
Only the lull I like, the hum of your valvèd voice.

I mind how once we lay such a transparent summer morning,
How you settled your head athwart my hips and gently turn'd
    over upon me,
And parted the shirt from my bosom-bone, and plunged your
    tongue to my bare-stript heart,
And reach'd till you felt my beard, and reach'd till you held my
    feet.   90

8. In this section, an invitation to the "soul" to "loafe . . . on the grass" eventuates in an erotic
scene (lines 87–90) between soul and body, an exchange that appears to produce a sense of
profound peace in the self. Compare section 21, line 1, and section 48, lines 1–2, which
insist that the body is in no way inferior to the soul. To get a sense of the wide range of
critical response to this, perhaps the most hotly debated section in *LG*, the reader may
consult Miller, ed., *Walt Whitman's "Song of Myself": A Mosaic of Interpretations*, 59–67.

Swiftly arose and spread around me the peace and knowledge
    that pass all the argument of the earth,
And I know that the hand of God is the promise of my own,
And I know that the spirit of God is the brother of my own,
And that all the men ever born are also my brothers, and the
    women my sisters and lovers,
And that a kelson of the creation is love,   95
And limitless are leaves stiff or drooping in the fields,
And brown ants in the little wells beneath them,
And mossy scabs of the worm fence, heap'd stones, elder,
    mullein and poke-weed.

6

A child said *What is the grass?* fetching it to me with full hands;
How could I answer the child? I do not know what it is any
    more than he.   100

I guess it must be the flag of my disposition, out of hopeful
    green stuff woven.

Or I guess it is the handkerchief of the Lord,
A scented gift and remembrancer designedly dropt,
Bearing the owner's name someway in the corners, that we
    may see and remark, and say *Whose?*

Or I guess the grass is itself a child, the produced babe of the
    vegetation.   105

Or I guess it is a uniform hieroglyphic,
And it means, Sprouting alike in broad zones and narrow zones,
Growing among black folks as among white,
Kanuck, Tuckahoe, Congressman, Cuff,[9] I give them the same,
    I receive them the same.

And now it seems to me the beautiful uncut hair of graves.   110

Tenderly will I use you curling grass,
It may be you transpire from the breasts of young men,
It may be if I had known them I would have loved them,
It may be you are from old people, or from offspring taken
    soon out of their mothers' laps,
And here you are the mothers' laps.   115

---

9. "Kanuck": (now considered pejorative) French Canadian; "Tuckahoe": tidewater Virginian
who eats "tuckahoe," a brown fungus sometimes called "Virginia truffle"; "Cuff": African
day-name for a male born on a Friday; for this last, see under "cuffy" in Frederic G. Cassidy,
ed., *Dictionary of American Regional English* (Cambridge, Mass.: Harvard University Press,
1985), vol. I.

This grass is very dark to be from the white heads of old
    mothers,
Darker than the colorless beards of old men,
Dark to come from under the faint red roofs of mouths.

O I perceive after all so many uttering tongues,
And I perceive they do not come from the roofs of mouths for
    nothing.   120

I wish I could translate the hints about the dead young men
    and women,
And the hints about old men and mothers, and the offspring
    taken soon out of their laps.

What do you think has become of the young and old men?
And what do you think has become of the women and children?

They are alive and well somewhere,   125
The smallest sprout shows there is really no death,
And if ever there was it led forward life, and does not wait at
    the end to arrest it,
And ceas'd the moment life appear'd.

All goes onward and outward, nothing collapses,
And to die is different from what any one supposed, and
    luckier.   130

7

Has any one supposed it lucky to be born?
I hasten to inform him or her it is just as lucky to die, and I
    know it.

I pass death with the dying and birth with the new-wash'd
    babe, and am not contain'd between my hat and boots,
And peruse manifold objects, no two alike and every one good,
The earth good and the stars good, and their adjuncts all good.   135

I am not an earth nor an adjunct of an earth,
I am the mate and companion of people, all just as immortal
    and fathomless as myself,
(They do not know how immortal, but I know.)

Every kind for itself and its own, for me mine male and
    female,
For me those that have been boys and that love women,   140
For me the man that is proud and feels how it stings to be
    slighted,
For me the sweet-heart and the old maid, for me mothers and
    the mothers of mothers,

For me lips that have smiled, eyes that have shed tears,
For me children and the begetters of children.

Undrape! you are not guilty to me, nor stale nor discarded,   145
I see through the broadcloth and gingham whether or no,
And am around, tenacious, acquisitive, tireless, and cannot be
    shaken away.

8

The little one sleeps in its cradle,
I lift the gauze and look a long time, and silently brush away
    flies with my hand.

The youngster and the red-faced girl turn aside up the bushy
    hill,   150
I peeringly view them from the top.

The suicide sprawls on the bloody floor of the bedroom,
I witness the corpse with its dabbled hair, I note where the
    pistol has fallen.

The blab of the pave, tires of carts, sluff of boot-soles, talk of
    the promenaders,
The heavy omnibus, the driver with his interrogating thumb,
    the clank of the shod horses on the granite floor,   155
The snow-sleighs, clinking, shouted jokes, pelts of snow-balls,
The hurrahs for popular favorites, the fury of rous'd mobs,
The flap of the curtain'd litter, a sick man inside borne to the
    hospital,
The meeting of enemies, the sudden oath, the blows and fall,
The excited crowd, the policeman with his star quickly working
    his passage to the centre of the crowd,   160
The impassive stones that receive and return so many echoes,
What groans of over-fed or half-starv'd who fall sunstruck or in
    fits,
What exclamations of women taken suddenly who hurry home
    and give birth to babes,
What living and buried speech is always vibrating here, what
    howls restrain'd by decorum,
Arrests of criminals, slights, adulterous offers made,
    acceptances, rejections with convex lips,   165
I mind them or the show or resonance of them—I come and I
    depart.

9

The big doors of the country barn stand open and ready,
The dried grass of the harvest-time loads the slow-drawn wagon,
The clear light plays on the brown gray and green intertinged,
The armfuls are pack'd to the sagging mow.   170

I am there, I help, I came stretch'd atop of the load,
I felt its soft jolts, one leg reclined on the other,
I jump from the cross-beams and seize the clover and timothy,
And roll head over heels and tangle my hair full of wisps.

10

Alone far in the wilds and mountains I hunt,   175
Wandering amazed at my own lightness and glee,
In the late afternoon choosing a safe spot to pass the night,
Kindling a fire and broiling the fresh-kill'd game,
Falling asleep on the gather'd leaves with my dog and gun by
    my side.

The Yankee clipper is under her sky-sails, she cuts the sparkle
    and scud,   180
My eyes settle the land, I bend at her prow or shout joyously
    from the deck.

The boatmen and clam-diggers arose early and stopt for me,
I tuck'd my trowser-ends in my boots and went and had a good
    time;
You should have been with us that day round the chowder-
    kettle.

I saw the marriage of the trapper in the open air in the far
    west, the bride was a red girl,   185
Her father and his friends sat near cross-legged and dumbly
    smoking, they had moccasins to their feet and large thick
    blankets hanging from their shoulders,
On a bank lounged the trapper, he was drest mostly in skins,
    his luxuriant beard and curls protected his neck, he held
    his bride by the hand,
She had long eyelashes, her head was bare, her coarse straight
    locks descended upon her voluptuous limbs and reach'd to
    her feet.[1]

The runaway slave came to my house and stopt outside,
I heard his motions crackling the twigs of the woodpile,   190
Through the swung half-door of the kitchen I saw him limpsy
    and weak,
And went where he sat on a log and led him in and assured him,

1. The preceding four lines are based on a painting entitled "The Trapper's Bride," by the
Baltimore artist Alfred Jacob Miller (1810–1874). See Edgeley W. Todd, "Indian Pictures
and Two Whitman Poems," *HLQ* 19:1–11. Section 10 is in its entirety a good instance of
WW's customary mingling of his own experience with extrapolated experience like the bard
or ballader of old—the clamming incident from his actual youth, the runaway slave episode
probably experienced or witnessed, the imagined experience of the hunters (from literary or
actual hear-say), and the extrapolation of the Indian bride by the agency of a painting. All
with the ballad "I."

And brought water and fill'd a tub for his sweated body and
    bruis'd feet,
And gave him a room that enter'd from my own, and gave him
    some coarse clean clothes,
And remember perfectly well his revolving eyes and his
    awkwardness,   195
And remember putting plasters on the galls of his neck and
    ankles;
He staid with me a week before he was recuperated and pass'd
    north,
I had him sit next me at table, my fire-lock lean'd in the corner.

11

Twenty-eight young men bathe by the shore,[2]
Twenty-eight young men and all so friendly;   200
Twenty-eight years of womanly life and all so lonesome.

She owns the fine house by the rise of the bank,
She hides handsome and richly drest aft the blinds of the window.

Which of the young men does she like the best?
Ah the homeliest of them is beautiful to her.   205

Where are you off to, lady? for I see you,
You splash in the water there, yet stay stock still in your room.

Dancing and laughing along the beach came the twenty-ninth
    bather,
The rest did not see her, but she saw them and loved them.

The beards of the young men glisten'd with wet, it ran from
    their long hair,   210
Little streams pass'd all over their bodies.

An unseen hand also pass'd over their bodies,
It descended tremblingly from their temples and ribs.

The young men float on their backs, their white bellies bulge
    to the sun, they do not ask who seizes fast to them,
They do not know who puffs and declines with pendant and
    bending arch,   215
They do not think whom they souse with spray.

---

2. This parable—WW's first—is audacious for its time, and extraordinarily delicate in its sen-
   sitive recognition of loneliness and desire. For a sampling of critical response to this section,
   see Miller, ed. *Walt Whitman's "Song of Myself": A Mosaic of Interpretations*, 74–77. See
   also Michael Moon's commentary on this passage, reprinted in this volume, p. 863.

12

The butcher-boy puts off his killing-clothes, or sharpens his
    knife at the stall in the market,
I loiter enjoying his repartee and his shuffle and break-down.[3]

Blacksmiths with grimed and hairy chests environ the anvil,
Each has his main-sledge, they are all out, there is a great heat
    in the fire.   220

From the cinder-strew'd threshold I follow their movements,
The lithe sheer of their waists plays even with their massive arms,
Overhand the hammers swing, overhand so slow, overhand so
    sure,
They do not hasten, each man hits in his place.

13

The negro holds firmly the reins of his four horses, the block
    swags underneath on its tied-over chain,   225
The negro that drives the long dray of the stone-yard, steady
    and tall he stands pois'd on one leg on the string-piece,[4]
His blue shirt exposes his ample neck and breast and loosens
    over his hip-band,
His glance is calm and commanding, he tosses the slouch of
    his hat away from his forehead,
The sun falls on his crispy hair and mustache, falls on the
    black of his polish'd and perfect limbs.

I behold the picturesque giant and love him, and I do not stop
    there,   230
I go with the team also.

In me the caresser of life wherever moving, backward as well
    as forward sluing,
To niches aside and junior bending, not a person or object
    missing,
Absorbing all to myself and for this song.

Oxen that rattle the yoke and chain or halt in the leafy shade,
    what is that you express in your eyes?   235
It seems to me more than all the print I have read in my life.

My tread scares the wood-drake and wood-duck on my distant
    and day-long ramble,
They rise together, they slowly circle around.

3. Shuffle is a slow (or adagio) dance with sliding movements; break-down is a rollicking, noisy
   dance. Both were then familiar in popular entertainment and minstrelsy.
4. Long piece of heavy squared timber used in shoring or construction.

I believe in those wing'd purposes,
And acknowledge red, yellow, white, playing within me,   240
And consider green and violet and the tufted crown
    intentional,
And do not call the tortoise unworthy because she is not
    something else,
And the jay in the woods never studied the gamut, yet trills
    pretty well to me,
And the look of the bay mare shames silliness out of me.

14

The wild gander leads his flock through the cool night,   245
Ya-honk he says, and sounds it down to me like an invitation,
The pert may suppose it meaningless, but I listening close,
Find its purpose and place up there toward the wintry sky.

The sharp-hoof'd moose of the north, the cat on the house-sill,
    the chickadee, the prairie-dog,
The litter of the grunting sow as they tug at her teats,   250
The brood of the turkey-hen and she with her half-spread wings,
I see in them and myself the same old law.

The press of my foot to the earth springs a hundred affections,
They scorn the best I can do to relate them.

I am enamour'd of growing out-doors,   255
Of men that live among cattle or taste of the ocean or woods,
Of the builders and steerers of ships and the wielders of axes
    and mauls, and the drivers of horses,
I can eat and sleep with them week in and week out.

What is commonest, cheapest, nearest, easiest, is Me,
Me going in for my chances, spending for vast returns,   260
Adorning myself to bestow myself on the first that will take me,
Not asking the sky to come down to my good will,
Scattering it freely forever.

15

The pure contralto sings in the organ loft,
The carpenter dresses his plank, the tongue of his foreplane
    whistles its wild ascending lisp,   265
The married and unmarried children ride home to their
    Thanksgiving dinner,
The pilot seizes the king-pin,[5] he heaves down with a strong arm,

---

5. A much extended spoke of the pilot wheel, providing greater leverage in strong currents.

The mate stands braced in the whale-boat, lance and harpoon
    are ready,
The duck-shooter walks by silent and cautious stretches,
The deacons are ordain'd with cross'd hands at the altar,   270
The spinning-girl retreats and advances to the hum of the big
    wheel,
The farmer stops by the bars as he walks on a First-day[6] loafe
    and looks at the oats and rye,
The lunatic is carried at last to the asylum a confirm'd case,
(He will never sleep any more as he did in the cot in his
    mother's bed-room;)
The jour printer[7] with gray head and gaunt jaws works at his
    case,   275
He turns his quid of tobacco while his eyes blurr with the
    manuscript;
The malform'd limbs are tied to the surgeon's table,
What is removed drops horribly in a pail;
The quadroon girl is sold at the auction-stand, the drunkard
    nods by the bar-room stove,
The machinist rolls up his sleeves, the policeman travels his
    beat, the gate-keeper marks who pass,   280
The young fellow drives the express-wagon, (I love him, though
    I do not know him;)
The half-breed straps on his light boots to compete in the race,
The western turkey-shooting draws old and young, some lean
    on their rifles, some sit on logs,
Out from the crowd steps the marksman, takes his position,
    levels his piece;
The groups of newly-come immigrants cover the wharf or
    levee,   285
As the woolly-pates hoe in the sugar-field, the overseer views
    them from his saddle,
The bugle calls in the ball-room, the gentlemen run for their
    partners, the dancers bow to each other,
The youth lies awake in the cedar-roof'd garret and harks to
    the musical rain,
The Wolverine[8] sets traps on the creek that helps fill the Huron,
The squaw wrapt in her yellow-hemm'd cloth is offering
    moccasins and bead-bags for sale,   290
The connoisseur peers along the exhibition-gallery with half-
    shut eyes bent sideways,
As the deck-hands make fast the steamboat the plank is
    thrown for the shore-going passengers,
The young sister holds out the skein while the elder sister
    winds it off in a ball, and stops now and then for the
    knots,

---

6. Quaker designation for Sunday.
7. Journeyman printer.
8. Native of Michigan.

The one-year wife is recovering and happy having a week ago
    borne her first child,
The clean-hair'd Yankee girl works with her sewing-machine or
    in the factory or mill,   295
The paving-man leans on his two-handed rammer, the
    reporter's lead flies swiftly over the note-book, the sign-
    painter is lettering with blue and gold,
The canal boy trots on the tow-path, the book-keeper counts at
    his desk, the shoemaker waxes his thread,
The conductor beats time for the band and all the performers
    follow him,
The child is baptized, the convert is making his first
    professions,
The regatta is spread on the bay, the race is begun, (how the
    white sails sparkle!)   300
The drover watching his drove sings out to them that would stray,
The pedler sweats with his pack on his back, (the purchaser
    higgling about the odd cent;)
The bride unrumples her white dress, the minute-hand of the
    clock moves slowly,
The opium-eater reclines with rigid head and just-open'd lips,
The prostitute draggles her shawl, her bonnet bobs on her
    tipsy and pimpled neck,   305
The crowd laugh at her blackguard oaths, the men jeer and
    wink to each other,
(Miserable! I do not laugh at your oaths nor jeer you;)
The President holding a cabinet council is surrounded by the
    great Secretaries,
On the piazza walk three matrons stately and friendly with
    twined arms,
The crew of the fish-smack pack repeated layers of halibut in
    the hold,   310
The Missourian crosses the plains toting his wares and his cattle,
As the fare-collector goes through the train he gives notice by
    the jingling of loose change,
The floor-men are laying the floor, the tinners are tinning the
    roof, the masons are calling for mortar,
In single file each shouldering his hod pass onward the laborers;
Seasons pursuing each other the indescribable crowd is
    gather'd, it is the fourth of Seventh-month,[9] (what salutes
    of cannon and small arms!)   315
Seasons pursuing each other the plougher ploughs, the mower
    mows, and the winter-grain falls in the ground;
Off on the lakes the pike-fisher watches and waits by the hole
    in the frozen surface,

9. Quaker designation for the Fourth of July.

The stumps stand thick round the clearing, the squatter strikes
    deep with his axe,
Flatboatmen make fast towards dusk near the cotton-wood or
    pecan-trees,
Coon-seekers go through the regions of the Red river or
    through those drain'd by the Tennessee, or through those
    of the Arkansas,   320
Torches shine in the dark that hangs on the Chattahooche or
    Altamahaw,[1]
Patriarchs sit at supper with sons and grandsons and great-
    grandsons around them,
In walls of adobie,[2] in canvas tents, rest hunters and trappers
    after their day's sport,
The city sleeps and the country sleeps,
The living sleep for their time, the dead sleep for their time,   325
The old husband sleeps by his wife and the young husband
    sleeps by his wife;
And these tend inward to me, and I tend outward to them,
And such as it is to be of these more or less I am,
And of these one and all I weave the song of myself.

16

I am of old and young, of the foolish as much as the wise,   330
Regardless of others, ever regardful of others,
Maternal as well as paternal, a child as well as a man,
Stuff'd with the stuff that is coarse and stuff'd with the stuff
    that is fine,
One of the Nation of many nations, the smallest the same and
    the largest the same,
A Southerner soon as a Northerner, a planter nonchalant and
    hospitable down by the Oconee I live,   335
A Yankee bound my own way ready for trade, my joints the
    limberest joints on earth and the sternest joints on earth,
A Kentuckian walking the vale of the Elkhorn in my deer-skin
    leggings, a Louisianian or Georgian,
A boatman over lakes or bays or along coasts, a Hoosier,
    Badger, Buckeye;[3]
At home on Kanadian snow-shoes or up in the bush, or with
    fishermen off Newfoundland,
At home in the fleet of ice-boats, sailing with the rest and
    tacking,   340
At home on the hills of Vermont or in the woods of Maine, or
    the Texan ranch,
Comrade of Californians, comrade of free North-Westerners,
    (loving their big proportions,)

1. Southern rivers. The first (from which Whitman omits a final "e") forms a boundary between
    Georgia and Alabama and Georgia and Florida; the second is in Georgia.
2. In 1855, "abode"; in 1856, "adobe"; from 1860, "adobie." Cf. "Starting from Paumanok,"
    line 198, note.
3. Nicknames for people from Indiana, Wisconsin, and Ohio respectively.

Comrade of raftsmen and coalmen, comrade of all who shake
    hands and welcome to drink and meat,
A learner with the simplest, a teacher of the thoughtfullest,
A novice beginning yet experient of myriads of seasons,   345
Of every hue and caste am I, of every rank and religion,
A farmer, mechanic, artist, gentleman, sailor, quaker,
Prisoner, fancy-man, rowdy, lawyer, physician, priest.

I resist any thing better than my own diversity,
Breathe the air but leave plenty after me,   350
And am not stuck up, and am in my place.

(The moth and the fish-eggs are in their place,
The bright suns I see and the dark suns I cannot see are in
    their place,
The palpable is in its place and the impalpable is in its place.)

17

These are really the thoughts of all men in all ages and lands,
    they are not original with me,   355
If they are not yours as much as mine they are nothing, or
    next to nothing,
If they are not the riddle and the untying of the riddle they are
    nothing,
If they are not just as close as they are distant they are nothing.

This is the grass that grows wherever the land is and the water is,
This the common air that bathes the globe.   360

18

With music strong I come, with my cornets and my drums,
I play not marches for accepted victors only, I play marches
    for conquer'd and slain persons.

Have you heard that it was good to gain the day?
I also say it is good to fall, battles are lost in the same spirit in
    which they are won.

I beat and pound for the dead,   365
I blow through my embouchures[4] my loudest and gayest for them.

Vivas to those who have fail'd!
And to those whose war-vessels sank in the sea!
And to those themselves who sank in the sea!

---

4. Mouthpieces of wind instruments. Also, the shape of the mouth and lips in blowing.

And to all generals that lost engagements, and all overcome
    heroes!   370
And the numberless unknown heroes equal to the greatest
    heroes known!

19

This is the meal equally set, this the meat for natural hunger,
It is for the wicked just the same as the righteous, I make
    appointments with all,
I will not have a single person slighted or left away,
The kept-woman, sponger, thief, are hereby invited,   375
The heavy-lipp'd slave is invited, the venerealee is invited;
There shall be no difference between them and the rest.

This is the press of a bashful hand, this the float and odor of hair,
This the touch of my lips to yours, this the murmur of yearning,
This the far-off depth and height reflecting my own face,   380
This the thoughtful merge of myself, and the outlet again.

Do you guess I have some intricate purpose?
Well I have, for the Fourth-month showers have, and the mica
    on the side of a rock has.

Do you take it I would astonish?
Does the daylight astonish? does the early redstart twittering
    through the woods?   385
Do I astonish more than they?

This hour I tell things in confidence,
I might not tell everybody, but I will tell you.

20

Who goes there? hankering, gross, mystical, nude;
How is it I extract strength from the beef I eat?   390

What is a man anyhow? what am I? what are you?

All I mark as my own you shall offset it with your own,
Else it were time lost listening to me.

I do not snivel that snivel the world over,
That months are vacuums and the ground but wallow and
    filth.   395

Whimpering and truckling fold with powders for invalids,[5]
    conformity goes to the fourth-remov'd,
I wear my hat as I please indoors or out.

Why should I pray? why should I venerate and be ceremonious?

Having pried through the strata, analyzed to a hair, counsel'd
    with doctors and calculated close,
I find no sweeter fat than sticks to my own bones.   400

In all people I see myself, none more and not one a barley-
    corn less,
And the good or bad I say of myself I say of them.

I know I am solid and sound,
To me the converging objects of the universe perpetually flow,
All are written to me, and I must get what the writing means.   405

I know I am deathless,
I know this orbit of mine cannot be swept by a carpenter's
    compass,
I know I shall not pass like a child's carlacue[6] cut with a burnt
    stick at night.

I know I am august,
I do not trouble my spirit to vindicate itself or be understood,   410
I see that the elementary laws never apologize,
(I reckon I behave no prouder than the level I plant my house
    by, after all.)

I exist as I am, that is, enough,
If no other in the world be aware I sit content,
And if each and all be aware I sit content.   415

One world is aware and by far the largest to me, and that is
    myself,
And whether I come to my own to-day or in ten thousand or
    ten million years,
I can cheerfully take it now, or with equal cheerfulness I can wait.

My foothold is tenon'd and mortis'd in granite,
I laugh at what you call dissolution,   420
And I know the amplitude of time.

5. Powdered medicine was then folded in doses in small papers prepared by the physician.
6. A variant of "curlicue," something fancifully curled, as a flourish in writing.

21

I am the poet of the Body and I am the poet of the Soul,
The pleasures of heaven are with me and the pains of hell are
    with me,
The first, I graft and increase upon myself, the latter I
    translate into a new tongue.

I am the poet of the woman the same as the man,   425
And I say it is as great to be a woman as to be a man,
And I say there is nothing greater than the mother of men.

I chant the chant of dilation or pride,
We have had ducking and deprecating about enough,
I show that size is only development.   430

Have you outstript the rest? are you the President?
It is a trifle, they will more than arrive there every one, and
    still pass on.

I am he that walks with the tender and growing night,
I call to the earth and sea half-held by the night.

Press close bare-bosom'd night—press close magnetic
    nourishing night!   435
Night of south winds—night of the large few stars!
Still nodding night—mad naked summer night.

Smile O voluptuous cool-breath'd earth!
Earth of the slumbering and liquid trees!
Earth of departed sunset—earth of the mountains misty-topt!   440
Earth of the vitreous pour of the full moon just tinged with blue!
Earth of shine and dark mottling the tide of the river!
Earth of the limpid gray of clouds brighter and clearer for my sake!
Far-swooping elbow'd earth—rich apple-blossom'd earth!
Smile, for your lover comes.[7]   445

Prodigal, you have given me love—therefore I to you give love!
O unspeakable passionate love.

22

You sea! I resign myself to you also—I guess what you mean,
I behold from the beach your crooked inviting fingers,
I believe you refuse to go back without feeling of me,   450

7. The MS draft (Lion) of this passage shows that its superb phrasing was not immediately
    achieved. Originally "Still nodding night" was "Still slumberous night"; "O voluptuous cool-
    breath'd earth!" was "O voluptuous procreant Earth!"; "vitreous pour of the full moon" was
    "vitreous fall of the full moon"; and "Far-swooping elbow'd earth" was "Earth of far arms."

We must have a turn together, I undress, hurry me out of
    sight of the land,
Cushion me soft, rock me in billowy drowse,
Dash me with amorous wet, I can repay you.

Sea of stretch'd ground-swells,
Sea breathing broad and convulsive breaths,   455
Sea of the brine of life and of unshovell'd yet always-ready
    graves,
Howler and scooper of storms, capricious and dainty sea,
I am integral with you, I too am of one phase and of all phases.

Partaker of influx and efflux I, extoller of hate and conciliation,
Extoller of amies and those that sleep in each others' arms.   460

I am he attesting sympathy,
(Shall I make my list of things in the house and skip the house
    that supports them?)

I am not the poet of goodness only, I do not decline to be the
    poet of wickedness also.

What blurt is this about virtue and about vice?
Evil propels me and reform of evil propels me, I stand
    indifferent,   465
My gait is no fault-finder's or rejecter's gait,
I moisten the roots of all that has grown.

Did you fear some scrofula out of the unflagging pregnancy?
Did you guess the celestial laws are yet to be work'd over and
    rectified?

I find one side a balance and the antipodal side a balance,   470
Soft doctrine as steady help as stable doctrine,
Thoughts and deeds of the present our rouse and early start.

This minute that comes to me over the past decillions,
There is no better than it and now.

What behaved well in the past or behaves well to-day is not
    such a wonder,   475
The wonder is always and always how there can be a mean
    man or an infidel.[8]

---

8. In their reconciliation of apparent opposites, lines 464–76 suggest the influence of Hegel,
   in whose dialectic WW was much interested. For more on the possible significance of the
   German philosopher for WW, see the entry on Hegel in J. R. LeMaster and Donald D.
   Kummings, eds., *Walt Whitman: An Encyclopedia* (New York: Garland, 1998), 271–72.

23

Endless unfolding of words of ages!
And mine a word of the modern, the word En-Masse.

A word of the faith that never balks,
Here or henceforward it is all the same to me, I accept Time
    absolutely.   480

It alone is without flaw, it alone rounds and completes all,
That mystic baffling wonder alone completes all.

I accept Reality and dare not question it,
Materialism first and last imbuing.

Hurrah for positive science! long live exact demonstration!   485
Fetch stonecrop[9] mixt with cedar and branches of lilac,
This is the lexicographer, this the chemist, this made a
    grammar of the old cartouches,[1]
These mariners put the ship through dangerous unknown seas,
This is the geologist, this works with the scalpel, and this is a
    mathematician.

Gentlemen, to you the first honors always!   490
Your facts are useful, and yet they are not my dwelling,
I but enter by them to an area of my dwelling.

Less the reminders of properties told my words,
And more the reminders they of life untold, and of freedom
    and extrication,
And make short account of neuters and geldings, and favor
    men and women fully equipt,   495
And beat the gong of revolt, and stop with fugitives and them
    that plot and conspire.

24

Walt Whitman, a kosmos, of Manhattan the son,[2]
Turbulent, fleshy, sensual, eating, drinking and breeding,

9. A hardy sedum, some varieties long esteemed in folk medicine as a vulnerary or healing for
   wounds; it is here "mixt with cedar," a tree long associated with graveyards and comfort for
   the bereaved—as in WW's threnody to Lincoln (see p. 276) where the lilac functions (as
   here) as a symbol of love and male comradeship.
1. Scroll-shaped carvings especially prevalent on ancient columns and entablatures. The Egyp-
   tian cartouches on memorials to monarchs bore hieroglyphs of importance in establishing
   the language. In the mid-fifties WW was a frequenter and publicist of Dr. Henry Abbott's
   Museum of Egyptian Antiquities on Broadway. See NYD, 27–40. For more on WW's interest
   in and knowledge of ancient Egypt, see the selection by John Irwin reprinted in this volume,
   p. 863.
2. Through the first three editions this line read "Walt Whitman, an American, one of the
   roughs, a kosmos." "Kosmos" was then a word of particular import, hypothesizing the sublime
   order of the universe, and befitting an Emersonian, as WW was. Briefly, in 1867, the word
   was dropped, and the line became "Walt Whitman am I, of mighty Manhattan the son:"
   then restored to read "Walt Whitman am I, a Kosmos, of mighty Manhattan the son." Finally,
   in 1881 the poet, triumphing over rhetoric, achieved the present reading.

No sentimentalist, no stander above men and women or apart
    from them,
No more modest than immodest.   500

Unscrew the locks from the doors!
Unscrew the doors themselves from their jambs!

Whoever degrades another degrades me,
And whatever is done or said returns at last to me.

Through me the afflatus[3] surging and surging, through me the
    current and index.   505

I speak the pass-word primeval, I give the sign of democracy,
By God! I will accept nothing which all cannot have their
    counterpart of on the same terms.

Through me many long dumb voices,
Voices of the interminable generations of prisoners and slaves,
Voices of the diseas'd and despairing and of thieves and
    dwarfs,   510
Voices of cycles of preparation and accretion,
And of the threads that connect the stars, and of wombs and
    of the father-stuff,
And of the rights of them the others are down upon,
Of the deform'd, trivial, flat, foolish, despised,
Fog in the air, beetles rolling balls of dung.   515

Through me forbidden voices,
Voices of sexes and lusts, voices veil'd and I remove the veil,
Voices indecent by me clarified and transfigur'd.

I do not press my fingers across my mouth,
I keep as delicate around the bowels as around the head and
    heart,   520
Copulation is no more rank to me than death is.

I believe in the flesh and the appetites,
Seeing, hearing, feeling, are miracles, and each part and tag of
    me is a miracle.

Divine am I inside and out, and I make holy whatever I touch
    or am touch'd from,
The scent of these arm-pits aroma finer than prayer,   525
This head more than churches, bibles, and all the creeds.

If I worship one thing more than another it shall be the spread
    of my own body, or any part of it,

---

3. Latin *afflare, afflatum,* to breathe or blow on. In this context, a divine impartation of power
  or inspiration.

Translucent mould of me it shall be you!
Shaded ledges and rests it shall be you!
Firm masculine colter[4] it shall be you!   530
Whatever goes to the tilth[5] of me it shall be you!
You my rich blood! your milky stream pale strippings of my life!
Breast that presses against other breasts it shall be you!
My brain it shall be your occult convolutions!
Root of wash'd sweet-flag! timorous pond-snipe! nest of
     guarded duplicate eggs! it shall be you![6]   535
Mix'd tussled hay of head, beard, brawn, it shall be you!
Trickling sap of maple, fibre of manly wheat, it shall be you!
Sun so generous it shall be you!
Vapors lighting and shading my face it shall be you!
You sweaty brooks and dews it shall be you!   540
Winds whose soft-tickling genitals rub against me it shall be you!
Broad muscular fields, branches of live oak, loving lounger in
     my winding paths, it shall be you!
Hands I have taken, face I have kiss'd, mortal I have ever
     touch'd, it shall be you.

I dote on myself, there is that lot of me and all so luscious,
Each moment and whatever happens thrills me with joy,   545
I cannot tell how my ankles bend, nor whence the cause of my
     faintest wish,
Nor the cause of the friendship I emit, nor the cause of the
     friendship I take again.

That I walk up my stoop, I pause to consider if it really be,
A morning-glory at my window satisfies me more than the
     metaphysics of books.

To behold the day-break!   550
The little light fades the immense and diaphanous shadows,
The air tastes good to my palate.

Hefts of the moving world at innocent gambols silently rising,
     freshly exuding,
Scooting obliquely high and low.

Something I cannot see puts upward libidinous prongs,   555
Seas of bright juice suffuse heaven.

The earth by the sky staid with, the daily close of their junction,
The heav'd challenge from the east that moment over my head,
The mocking taunt, See then whether you shall be master![7]

4. In nonsymbolic terms the colter is the prong that directs the plow into the turf.
5. Cultivation or tillage of the soil.
6. The natural objects evoked in this line suggest the shapes of the male genitals.
7. In the preceding passage, the procreative impulse of the individual (lines 528–43) gives way
   to the cosmic energies symbolized in the sunrise (lines 550–59).

25

Dazzling and tremendous how quick the sun-rise would kill
    me,
If I could not now and always send sun-rise out of me.   560

We also ascend dazzling and tremendous as the sun,
We found our own O my soul in the calm and cool of the day-
    break.

My voice goes after what my eyes cannot reach,
With the twirl of my tongue I encompass worlds and volumes
    of worlds.   565

Speech is the twin of my vision, it is unequal to measure itself,
It provokes me forever, it says sarcastically,
Walt you contain enough, why don't you let it out then?

Come now I will not be tantalized, you conceive too much of
    articulation,
Do you not know O speech how the buds beneath you are
    folded?   570
Waiting in gloom, protected by frost,
The dirt receding before my prophetical screams,
I underlying causes to balance them at last,
My knowledge my live parts, it keeping tally with the meaning
    of all things,
Happiness, (which whoever hears me let him or her set out in
    search of this day.)   575

My final merit I refuse you, I refuse putting from me what I
    really am,
Encompass worlds, but never try to encompass me,
I crowd your sleekest and best by simply looking toward you.

Writing and talk do not prove me,
I carry the plenum[8] of proof and every thing else in my face,   580
With the hush of my lips I wholly confound the skeptic.

26

Now I will do nothing but listen,
To accrue what I hear into this song, to let sounds contribute
    toward it.

8. Fullness.

I hear bravuras of birds, bustle of growing wheat, gossip of
    flames, clack of sticks cooking my meals,
I hear the sound I love, the sound of the human voice,   585
I hear all sounds running together, combined, fused or following,
Sounds of the city and sounds out of the city, sounds of the
    day and night,
Talkative young ones to those that like them, the loud laugh of
    work-people at their meals,
The angry base of disjointed friendship, the faint tones of the sick,
The judge with hands tight to the desk, his pallid lips
    pronouncing a death-sentence,   590
The heave'e'yo of stevedores unlading ships by the wharves,
    the refrain of the anchor-lifters,
The ring of alarm-bells, the cry of fire, the whirr of swift-
    streaking engines and hose-carts with premonitory tinkles
    and color'd lights,
The steam-whistle, the solid roll of the train of approaching cars,
The slow march play'd at the head of the association marching
    two and two,
(They go to guard some corpse, the flag-tops are draped with
    black muslin.)   595

I hear the violoncello, ('tis the young man's heart's complaint,)
I hear the key'd cornet, it glides quickly in through my ears,
It shakes mad-sweet pangs through my belly and breast.

I hear the chorus, it is a grand opera,
Ah this indeed is music—this suits me.   600

A tenor large and fresh as the creation fills me,
The orbic flex of his mouth is pouring and filling me full.

I hear the train'd soprano (what work with hers is this?)
The orchestra whirls me wider than Uranus[9] flies,
It wrenches such ardors from me I did not know I possess'd
    them,   605
It sails me, I dab with bare feet, they are lick'd by the indolent
    waves,
I am cut by bitter and angry hail, I lose my breath,
Steep'd amid honey'd morphine, my windpipe throttled in fakes[1]
    of death,
At length let up again to feel the puzzle of puzzles,
And that we call Being.   610

---

9. The seventh planet, long believed the most remote: the Greek personification of Heaven.
1. The turns or coils of a rope.

27

To be in any form, what is that?
(Round and round we go, all of us, and ever come back thither,)
If nothing lay more develop'd the quahaug[2] in its callous shell
        were enough.

Mine is no callous shell,
I have instant conductors all over me whether I pass or stop,   615
They seize every object and lead it harmlessly through me.

I merely stir, press, feel with my fingers, and am happy,
To touch my person to some one else's is about as much as I
        can stand.

28

Is this then a touch? quivering me to a new identity,
Flames and ether making a rush for my veins,   620
Treacherous tip of me reaching and crowding to help them,
My flesh and blood playing out lightning to strike what is
        hardly different from myself,
On all sides prurient provokers stiffening my limbs,
Straining the udder of my heart for its withheld drip,
Behaving licentious toward me, taking no denial,   625
Depriving me of my best as for a purpose,
Unbuttoning my clothes, holding me by the bare waist,
Deluding my confusion with the calm of the sunlight and
        pasture-fields,
Immodestly sliding the fellow-senses away,
They bribed to swap off with touch and go and graze at the
        edges of me,
No consideration, no regard for my draining strength or my   630
        anger,
Fetching the rest of the herd around to enjoy them a while,
Then all uniting to stand on a headland and worry me.

The sentries desert every other part of me,
They have left me helpless to a red marauder,   635
They all come to the headland to witness and assist against me.

I am given up by traitors,
I talk wildly, I have lost my wits, I and nobody else am the
        greatest traitor,
I went myself first to the headland, my own hands carried me
        there.

2. An Atlantic coast clam.

You villain touch! what are you doing? my breath is tight in its
    throat,   640
Unclench your floodgates, you are too much for me.

29

Blind loving wrestling touch, sheath'd hooded sharp-tooth'd touch!
Did it make you ache so, leaving me?

Parting track'd by arriving, perpetual payment of perpetual loan,
Rich showering rain, and recompense richer afterward.   645

Sprouts take and accumulate, stand by the curb prolific and vital,
Landscapes projected masculine, full-sized and golden.

30

All truths wait in all things,
They neither hasten their own delivery nor resist it,
They do not need the obstetric forceps of the surgeon,   650
The insignificant is as big to me as any,
(What is less or more than a touch?)

Logic and sermons never convince,
The damp of the night drives deeper into my soul.

(Only what proves itself to every man and woman is so,   655
Only what nobody denies is so.)

A minute and a drop of me settle my brain,
I believe the soggy clods shall become lovers and lamps,
And a compend of compends is the meat of a man or woman,
And a summit and flower there is the feeling they have for
    each other,   660
And they are to branch boundlessly out of that lesson until it
    becomes omnific,
And until one and all shall delight us, and we them.

31

I believe a leaf of grass is no less than the journey-work of the
    stars,
And the pismire[3] is equally perfect, and a grain of sand, and
    the egg of the wren,
And the tree-toad is a chef-d'œuvre for the highest,   665
And the running blackberry would adorn the parlors of heaven,

3. An ant.

And the narrowest hinge in my hand puts to scorn all
    machinery,
And the cow crunching with depress'd head surpasses any
    statue,
And a mouse is miracle enough to stagger sextillions of infidels.

I find I incorporate gneiss, coal, long-threaded moss, fruits,
    grains, esculent roots,   670
And am stucco'd with quadrupeds and birds all over,[4]
And have distanced what is behind me for good reasons,
But call any thing back again when I desire it.

In vain the speeding or shyness,
In vain the plutonic rocks[5] send their old heat against my
    approach,   675
In vain the mastodon retreats beneath its own powder'd bones,
In vain objects stand leagues off and assume manifold shapes,
In vain the ocean settling in hollows and the great monsters
    lying low,
In vain the buzzard houses herself with the sky,
In vain the snake slides through the creepers and logs,   680
In vain the elk takes to the inner passes of the woods,
In vain the razor-bill'd auk sails far north to Labrador,
I follow quickly, I ascend to the nest in the fissure of the cliff.

32

I think I could turn and live with animals, they are so placid
    and self-contain'd,
I stand and look at them long and long.   685

They do not sweat and whine about their condition,
They do not lie awake in the dark and weep for their sins,
They do not make me sick discussing their duty to God,
Not one is dissatisfied, not one is demented with the mania of
    owning things,
Not one kneels to another, nor to his kind that lived thousands
    of years ago,   690
Not one is respectable or unhappy over the whole earth.

4. *Cf.* lines 670–71 with WW's notebook observation: "The soul or spirit transmits itself into
all matter—into rocks, and can live the life of a rock—into the sea, and can feel itself the
sea—into the oak, or other tree—into an animal, and feel itself a horse, a fish, or bird—
into the earth—into the motions of the suns and stars" (*UPP*, II, 64). Lines 670–83 typify
WW's own understanding of evolutionary theory. Charles Darwin's *The Origin of Species*
first appeared four years after the 1855 *LG*. Several critics have related passages such as
this one to the evolutionary theory of Lamarck. See David C. Leonard, "Lamarckian Evo-
lution in Whitman's 'Song of Myself,' " *WWR* 24, no. 1 (March 1978): 21–28.
5. Solidified from the molten conglomerate deep in the earth, here associated with the earliest
(Archeozoic) earth history.

So they show their relations to me and I accept them,
They bring me tokens of myself, they evince them plainly in
    their possession.

I wonder where they get those tokens,
Did I pass that way huge times ago and negligently drop them?   695

Myself moving forward then and now and forever,
Gathering and showing more always and with velocity,
Infinite and omnigenous,[6] and the like of these among them,
Not too exclusive toward the reachers of my remembrancers,
Picking out here one that I love, and now go with him on
    brotherly terms.   700

A gigantic beauty of a stallion, fresh and responsive to my
    caresses,
Head high in the forehead, wide between the ears,
Limbs glossy and supple, tail dusting the ground,
Eyes full of sparkling wickedness, ears finely cut, flexibly moving.

His nostrils dilate as my heels embrace him,   705
His well-built limbs tremble with pleasure as we race around
    and return.

I but use you a minute, then I resign you, stallion,
Why do I need your paces when I myself out-gallop them?
Even as I stand or sit passing faster than you.

33

Space and Time! now I see it is true, what I guess'd at,[7]   710
What I guess'd when I loaf'd on the grass,
What I guess'd while I lay alone in my bed,
And again as I walk'd the beach under the paling stars of the
    morning.

My ties and ballasts leave me, my elbows rest in sea-gaps,
I skirt sierras, my palms cover continents,   715
I am afoot with my vision.

By the city's quadrangular houses—in log huts, camping with
    lumbermen,[8]

6. Of all kinds.
7. Read "guessed" in the softbound form of this edition. The hardbound issue, which is followed here, reflects WW's elision of this "e" in the two previous editions (1888–89).
8. WW's so-called "cataloguing," brilliantly illustrated in lines 717–97, as in many later passages of *LG*, used to be occasionally cited as evidence of his "barbarism" or naïveté as an artist. Now this aspect of his technique is generally recognized for what it is—the powerful employment of a great imagination that delights to celebrate "God in every object" with loving, exact art. Among articles on this subject, note especially Stanley K. Coffman's " 'Crossing Brooklyn Ferry': A Note on the Catalogue Technique in Whitman's Poetry," *MP* 51: 225–32.

Along the ruts of the turnpike, along the dry gulch and rivulet bed,
Weeding my onion-patch or hoeing rows of carrots and
    parsnips, crossing savannas, trailing in forests,
Prospecting, gold-digging, girdling the trees of a new purchase,   720
Scorch'd ankle-deep by the hot sand, hauling my boat down
    the shallow river,
Where the panther walks to and fro on a limb overhead, where
    the buck turns furiously at the hunter,
Where the rattlesnake suns his flabby length on a rock, where
    the otter is feeding on fish,
Where the alligator in his tough pimples sleeps by the bayou,
Where the black bear is searching for roots or honey, where
    the beaver pats the mud with his paddle-shaped tail;   725
Over the growing sugar, over the yellow-flower'd cotton plant,
    over the rice in its low moist field,
Over the sharp-peak'd farm house, with its scallop'd scum[9] and
    slender shoots from the gutters,
Over the western persimmon, over the long-leav'd corn, over
    the delicate blue-flower flax,
Over the white and brown buckwheat, a hummer and buzzer
    there with the rest,
Over the dusky green of the rye as it ripples and shades in the
    breeze;   730
Scaling mountains, pulling myself cautiously up, holding on by
    low scragged limbs,
Walking the path worn in the grass and beat through the
    leaves of the brush,
Where the quail is whistling betwixt the woods and the wheat-lot,
Where the bat flies in the Seventh-month eve, where the great
    gold-bug drops through the dark,
Where the brook puts out of the roots of the old tree and
    flows to the meadow,   735
Where cattle stand and shake away flies with the tremulous
    shuddering of their hides,
Where the cheese-cloth hangs in the kitchen, where andirons
    straddle the hearth-slab, where cobwebs fall in festoons
    from the rafters;
Where trip-hammers crash, where the press is whirling its
    cylinders,
Wherever the human heart beats with terrible throes under its
    ribs,
Where the pear-shaped balloon is floating aloft, (floating in it
    myself and looking composedly down,)   740
Where the life-car[1] is drawn on the slip-noose, where the heat
    hatches pale-green eggs in the dented sand,

---

9. The rain-washed sediment on the roof of old farm houses. Such houses often sustained
  weeds on their roofs, much in the European tradition.
1. A watertight vehicle traveling along a rope strung from aloft on a ship, for the purpose of
  removing passengers, usually in a disaster.

Where the she-whale swims with her calf and never forsakes it,
Where the steam-ship trails hind-ways its long pennant of
    smoke,
Where the fin of the shark cuts like a black chip out of the
    water,
Where the half-burn'd brig is riding on unknown currents,   745
Where shells grow to her slimy deck, where the dead are
    corrupting below;
Where the dense-starr'd flag is borne at the head of the
    regiments,
Approaching Manhattan up by the long-stretching island,
Under Niagara, the cataract falling like a veil over my
    countenance,
Upon a door-step, upon the horse-block of hard wood outside,   750
Upon the race-course, or enjoying picnics or jigs or a good
    game of base-ball,
At he-festivals, with blackguard gibes, ironical license, bull-
    dances,[2] drinking, laughter,
At the cider-mill tasting the sweets of the brown mash, sucking
    the juice through a straw,
At apple-peelings[3] wanting kisses for all the red fruit I find,
At musters,[4] beach-parties, friendly bees, huskings, house-
    raisings;   755
Where the mocking-bird sounds his delicious gurgles, cackles,
    screams, weeps,
Where the hay-rick stands in the barn-yard, where the dry-stalks
    are scatter'd, where the brood-cow waits in the hovel,
Where the bull advances to do his masculine work, where the
    stud to the mare, where the cock is treading the hen,
Where the heifers browse, where geese nip their food with
    short jerks;
Where sun-down shadows lengthen over the limitless and
    lonesome prairie,   760
Where herds of buffalo make a crawling spread of the square
    miles far and near;
Where the humming-bird shimmers, where the neck of the
    long-lived swan is curving and winding,
Where the laughing-gull scoots by the shore, where she laughs
    her near-human laugh,
Where bee-hives range on a gray bench in the garden half hid
    by the high weeds,
Where band-neck'd partridges roost in a ring on the ground
    with their heads out,   765
Where burial coaches enter the arch'd gates of a cemetery,

2. A slang term for "buffalo-dance," originally danced by some Native American peoples.
3. The use of this term in *LG* is perhaps the earliest in print, although "apple-paring" appeared
    as early as 1819. See William D. Templeman, "On Whitman's Apple-peelings," *PQ* (April
    1956): 200–202.
4. A localism, now rare, for assemblages of people.

Where winter wolves bark amid wastes of snow and icicled trees,
Where the yellow-crown'd heron comes to the edge of the
     marsh at night and feeds upon small crabs,
Where the splash of swimmers and divers cools the warm noon,
Where the katy-did works her chromatic reed on the walnut-
     tree over the well,   770
Through patches of citrons and cucumbers with silver-wired
     leaves,
Through the salt-lick or orange glade, or under conical firs,
Through the gymnasium, through the curtain'd saloon, through
     the office or public hall;
Pleas'd with the native and pleas'd with the foreign, pleas'd
     with the new and old,
Pleas'd with the homely woman as well as the handsome,   775
Pleas'd with the quakeress as she puts off her bonnet and talks
     melodiously,
Pleas'd with the tune of the choir of the whitewash'd church,
Pleas'd with the earnest words of the sweating Methodist
     preacher, impress'd seriously at the camp-meeting;
Looking in at the shop-windows of Broadway the whole
     forenoon, flatting the flesh of my nose on the thick plate
     glass,
Wandering the same afternoon with my face turn'd up to the
     clouds, or down a lane or along the beach,   780
My right and left arms round the sides of two friends, and I in
     the middle;
Coming home with the silent and dark-cheek'd bush-boy,
     (behind me he rides at the drape of the day,[5])
Far from the settlements studying the print of animals' feet, or
     the moccasin print,
By the cot in the hospital reaching lemonade to a feverish patient,
Nigh the coffin'd corpse when all is still, examining with a
     candle;   785
Voyaging to every port to dicker and adventure,
Hurrying with the modern crowd as eager and fickle as any,
Hot toward one I hate, ready in my madness to knife him,
Solitary at midnight in my back yard, my thoughts gone from
     me a long while,
Walking the old hills of Judea with the beautiful gentle God by
     my side,   790
Speeding through space, speeding through heaven and the stars,
Speeding amid the seven satellites and the broad ring, and the
     diameter of eighty thousand miles,
Speeding with tail'd meteors, throwing fire-balls like the rest,
Carrying the crescent child that carries its own full mother in
     its belly,

5. Close of day.

Storming, enjoying, planning, loving, cautioning,   795
Backing and filling, appearing and disappearing,
I tread day and night such roads.

I visit the orchards of spheres and look at the product,
And look at quintillions ripen'd and look at quintillions green.

I fly those flights of a fluid and swallowing soul,   800
My course runs below the soundings of plummets.

I help myself to material and immaterial,
No guard can shut me off, no law prevent me.

I anchor my ship for a little while only,
My messengers continually cruise away or bring their returns
     to me.   805

I go hunting polar furs and the seal, leaping chasms with a
     pike-pointed staff, clinging to topples⁶ of brittle and blue.

I ascend to the Foretruck,
I take my place late at night in the crow's-nest,
We sail the arctic sea, it is plenty light enough,
Through the clear atmosphere I stretch around on the
     wonderful beauty,   810
The enormous masses of ice pass me and I pass them, the
     scenery is plain in all directions,
The white-topt mountains show in the distance, I fling out my
     fancies toward them,
We are approaching some great battle-field in which we are
     soon to be engaged,
We pass the colossal outposts of the encampment, we pass
     with still feet and caution,
Or we are entering by the suburbs some vast and ruin'd city,   815
The blocks and fallen architecture more than all the living
     cities of the globe.

I am a free companion, I bivouac by invading watchfires,
I turn the bridegroom out of bed and stay with the bride myself,
I tighten her all night to my thighs and lips.

My voice is the wife's voice, the screech by the rail of the
     stairs,   820
They fetch my man's body up dripping and drown'd.

---

6. Dictionaries do not list a noun form of this word; the poet is apparently referring to an
   overhanging protrusion of ice that has "toppled" from above.

I understand the large hearts of heroes,
The courage of present times and all times,
How the skipper saw the crowded and rudderless wreck of the
    steam-ship, and Death chasing it up and down the storm,
How he knuckled tight and gave not back an inch, and was
    faithful of days and faithful of nights,   825
And chalk'd in large letters on a board, *Be of good cheer, we
    will not desert you;*
How he follow'd with them and tack'd with them three days
    and would not give it up,
How he saved the drifting company at last,
How the lank loose-gown'd women look'd when boated from
    the side of their prepared graves,
How the silent old-faced infants and the lifted sick, and the
    sharp-lipp'd unshaved men;   830
All this I swallow, it tastes good, I like it well, it becomes mine,
I am the man, I suffer'd, I was there.[7]

The disdain and calmness of martyrs,
The mother of old, condemn'd for a witch, burnt with dry
    wood, her children gazing on,
The hounded slave that flags in the race, leans by the fence,
    blowing, cover'd with sweat,
The twinges that sting like needles his legs and neck, the   835
    murderous buckshot and the bullets,
All these I feel or am.

I am the hounded slave, I wince at the bite of the dogs,
Hell and despair are upon me, crack and again crack the
    marksmen,
I clutch the rails of the fence, my gore dribs,[8] thinn'd with the
    ooze of my skin,   840
I fall on the weeds and stones,
The riders spur their unwilling horses, haul close,
Taunt my dizzy ears and beat me violently over the head with
    whip-stocks.

Agonies are one of my changes of garments,
I do not ask the wounded person how he feels, I myself
    become the wounded person,   845
My hurts turn livid upon me as I lean on a cane and observe.

I am the mash'd fireman with breast-bone broken,
Tumbling walls buried me in their debris,

7. The shipwreck described in lines 824–30 was that of the *San Francisco,* which sailed from
   New York December 22, 1853, bound for South America, and was caught in a gale within
   a few hundred miles of the city. From December 23 until January 5 she was helpless, 150
   people being at one time washed away in a single sea. The disaster was reported in the *New
   York Weekly Tribune* of January 21, 1854, a copy of which was later found among WW's
   effects. See Bucke, "Notes on the Text of 'Leaves of Grass,' " *Conservator* 7 (May 1896): 40.
8. Obsolete form of "dribbles" (*cf.* "drips").

Heat and smoke I inspired, I heard the yelling shouts of my
    comrades,
I heard the distant click of their picks and shovels,   850
They have clear'd the beams away, they tenderly lift me forth.

I lie in the night air in my red shirt, the pervading hush is for
    my sake,
Painless after all I lie exhausted but not so unhappy,
White and beautiful are the faces around me, the heads are
    bared of their fire-caps,
The kneeling crowd fades with the light of the torches.   855

Distant and dead resuscitate,
They show as the dial or move as the hands of me, I am the
    clock myself.

I am an old artillerist, I tell of my fort's bombardment,
I am there again.

Again the long roll of the drummers,   860
Again the attacking cannon, mortars,
Again to my listening ears the cannon responsive.

I take part, I see and hear the whole,
The cries, curses, roar, the plaudits for well-aim'd shots,
The ambulanza[9] slowly passing trailing its red drip,   865
Workmen searching after damages, making indispensable
    repairs,
The fall of grenades through the rent roof, the fan-shaped
    explosion,
The whizz of limbs, heads, stone, wood, iron, high in the air.

Again gurgles the mouth of my dying general, he furiously
    waves with his hand,
He gasps through the clot *Mind not me—mind—the*
    entrenchments.   870

34

Now I tell what I knew in Texas in my early youth,
(I tell not the fall of Alamo,
Not one escaped to tell the fall of Alamo,
The hundred and fifty are dumb yet at Alamo,)
'Tis the tale of the murder in cold blood of four hundred and
    twelve young men.[1]   875

Retreating they had form'd in a hollow square with their
    baggage for breastworks,

9. Apparently Whitman's incorrect Spanish for "ambulance." The proper form is "ambulancia."
1. This is the tale of the massacre by the Mexican enemy of Captain Fannin and his company
   of 371 Texans after their surrender at Goliad, March 27, 1836.

Nine hundred lives out of the surrounding enemy's, nine times
    their number, was the price they took in advance,
Their colonel was wounded and their ammunition gone,
They treated for an honorable capitulation, receiv'd writing and
    seal, gave up their arms and march'd back prisoners of war.

They were the glory of the race of rangers,   880
Matchless with horse, rifle, song, supper, courtship,
Large, turbulent, generous, handsome, proud, and affectionate,
Bearded, sunburnt, drest in the free costume of hunters,
Not a single one over thirty years of age.

The second First-day[2] morning they were brought out in
    squads and massacred, it was beautiful early summer,   885
The work commenced about five o'clock and was over by eight.

None obey'd the command to kneel,
Some made a mad and helpless rush, some stood stark and
    straight,
A few fell at once, shot in the temple or heart, the living and
    dead lay together,
The maim'd and mangled dug in the dirt, the new-comers saw
    them there,   890
Some half-kill'd attempted to crawl away,
These were despatch'd with bayonets or batter'd with the
    blunts of muskets,
A youth not seventeen years old seiz'd his assassin till two
    more came to release him,
The three were all torn and cover'd with the boy's blood.

At eleven o'clock began the burning of the bodies;   895
That is the tale of the murder of the four hundred and twelve
    young men.

35

Would you hear of an old-time sea-fight?
Would you learn who won by the light of the moon and stars?
List to the yarn, as my grandmother's father the sailor told it to me.[3]

---

2. Sunday in the parlance of the Quakers, who strongly influenced WW's youth. Their pacifist
inclination unites with the ideas of Sunday in strong contrast with the massacre here
described.
3. This line first appeared in the 1867 edition; in the three earlier editions the poet had asked,
"Did you read in the seabooks of the oldfashioned frigate-fight?" Actually, his sources were
both the tales told him by his maternal grandmother Naomi Van Velsor, whose father, Capt.
John Williams, had served under John Paul Jones, and the account by Jones himself in a
letter to Benjamin Franklin about the battle on September 23, 1779, between his *BonHomme
Richard* and the British *Serapis* off Flamborough Head. This letter, printed in *Old South
Leaflets* (Boston, n.d.), VII, 36–39, is followed by WW with close parallelism. See David
Goodale, "Some of Walt Whitman's Borrowings," *AL* 10: 202–13.

Our foe was no skulk in his ship I tell you, (said he,)   900
His was the surly English pluck, and there is no tougher or
    truer, and never was, and never will be;
Along the lower'd eve he came horribly raking us.

We closed with him, the yards entangled, the cannon touch'd,
My captain lash'd fast with his own hands.

We had receiv'd some eighteen pound shots under the water,   905
On our lower-gun-deck two large pieces had burst at the first
    fire, killing all around and blowing up overhead.

Fighting at sun-down, fighting at dark,
Ten o'clock at night, the full moon well up, our leaks on the
    gain, and five feet of water reported,
The master-at-arms loosing the prisoners confined in the after-
    hold to give them a chance for themselves.

The transit to and from the magazine is now stopt by the
    sentinels,   910
They see so many strange faces they do not know whom to trust.

Our frigate takes fire,
The other asks if we demand quarter?
If our colors are struck and the fighting done?

Now I laugh content, for I hear the voice of my little captain,   915
We have not struck, he composedly cries, *we have just begun
    our part of the fighting.*

Only three guns are in use,
One is directed by the captain himself against the enemy's
    main-mast,
Two well serv'd with grape and canister silence his musketry
    and clear his decks.

The tops alone second the fire of this little battery, especially
    the main-top,   920
They hold out bravely during the whole of the action.

Not a moment's cease,
The leaks gain fast on the pumps, the fire eats toward the
    powder-magazine.

One of the pumps has been shot away, it is generally thought
    we are sinking.

Serene stands the little captain,   925
He is not hurried, his voice is neither high nor low,
His eyes give more light to us than our battle-lanterns.

Toward twelve there in the beams of the moon they surrender
    to us.

36

Stretch'd and still lies the midnight,
Two great hulls motionless on the breast of the darkness,   930
Our vessel riddled and slowly sinking, preparations to pass to
    the one we have conquer'd,
The captain on the quarter-deck coldly giving his orders
    through a countenance white as a sheet,
Near by the corpse of the child that serv'd in the cabin,
The dead face of an old salt with long white hair and carefully
    curl'd whiskers,
The flames spite of all that can be done flickering aloft and
    below,   935
The husky voices of the two or three officers yet fit for duty,
Formless stacks of bodies and bodies by themselves, dabs of
    flesh upon the masts and spars,
Cut of cordage, dangle of rigging, slight shock of the soothe of
    waves,
Black and impassive guns, litter of powder-parcels, strong scent,
A few large stars overhead, silent and mournful shining,   940
Delicate sniffs of sea-breeze, smells of sedgy grass and fields by
    the shore, death-messages given in charge to survivors,
The hiss of the surgeon's knife, the gnawing teeth of his saw,
Wheeze, cluck, swash of falling blood, short wild scream, and
    long, dull, tapering groan,
These so, these irretrievable.

37

You laggards there on guard! look to your arms!   945
In at the conquer'd doors they crowd! I am possess'd!
Embody all presences outlaw'd or suffering,
See myself in prison shaped like another man,
And feel the dull unintermitted pain.

For me the keepers of convicts shoulder their carbines and
    keep watch,
It is I let out in the morning and barr'd at night.   950

Not a mutineer walks handcuff'd to jail but I am handcuff'd to
    him and walk by his side,
(I am less the jolly one there, and more the silent one with
    sweat on my twitching lips.)

Not a youngster is taken for larceny but I go up too, and am
    tried and sentenced.

Not a cholera patient lies at the last gasp but I also lie at the
    last gasp, 955
My face is ash-color'd, my sinews gnarl, away from me people
    retreat.

Askers embody themselves in me and I am embodied in them,
I project my hat, sit shame-faced, and beg.[4]

38

Enough! enough! enough!
Somehow I have been stunn'd. Stand back! 960
Give me a little time beyond my cuff'd head, slumbers, dreams,
    gaping,
I discover myself on the verge of a usual mistake.

That I could forget the mockers and insults!
That I could forget the trickling tears and the blows of the
    bludgeons and hammers!
That I could look with a separate look on my own crucifixion
    and bloody crowning. 965

I remember now,
I resume the overstaid fraction,
The grave of rock multiplies what has been confided to it, or
    to any graves,
Corpses rise, gashes heal, fastenings roll from me.

I troop forth replenish'd with supreme power, one of an
    average unending procession, 970
Inland and sea-coast we go, and pass all boundary lines,
Our swift ordinances on their way over the whole earth,
The blossoms we wear in our hats the growth of thousands of
    years.

Eleves,[5] I salute you! come forward!
Continue your annotations, continue your questionings. 975

39

The friendly and flowing savage, who is he?
Is he waiting for civilization, or past it and mastering it?

Is he some Southwesterner rais'd out-doors? is he Kanadian?
Is he from the Mississippi country? Iowa, Oregon, California?
The mountains? prairie-life, bush-life? or sailor from the sea? 980

4. The beggar then commonly extended his hat to receive alms.
5. French: pupils or disciples.

Wherever he goes men and women accept and desire him,
They desire he should like them, touch them, speak to them,
    stay with them.

Behavior lawless as snow-flakes, words simple as grass,
    uncomb'd head, laughter, and naivetè,
Slow-stepping feet, common features, common modes and
    emanations,
They descend in new forms from the tips of his fingers,   985
They are waited with the odor of his body or breath, they fly
    out of the glance of his eyes.

40

Flaunt of the sunshine I need not your bask—lie over!
You light surfaces only, I force surfaces and depths also.

Earth! you seem to look for something at my hands,
Say, old top-knot,[6] what do you want?   990

Man or woman, I might tell how I like you, but cannot,
And might tell what it is in me and what it is in you, but cannot,
And might tell that pining I have, that pulse of my nights and days.

Behold, I do not give lectures or a little charity,
When I give I give myself.   995

You there, impotent, loose in the knees,
Open your scarf'd chops[7] till I blow grit within you,
Spread your palms and lift the flaps of your pockets,
I am not to be denied, I compel, I have stores plenty and to
    spare,
And any thing I have I bestow.   1000

I do not ask who you are, that is not important to me,
You can do nothing and be nothing but what I will infold you.

To cotton-field drudge or cleaner of privies I lean,
On his right cheek I put the family kiss,
And in my soul I swear I never will deny him.   1005

On women fit for conception I start bigger and nimbler babes,
(This day I am jetting the stuff of far more arrogant republics.)

6. An epithet common in frontier humor, denoting either the head itself or the tuft of hair
    gathered at the top of the head—a style associated with both Asian and Native American
    men in WW's time. Perhaps we have here a conscious echo from the reference to the
    "friendly and flowing savage" of line 976.
7. Scarf'd: scarified or channeled, hence lined or "worn-down" face.

To any one dying, thither I speed and twist the knob of the door,
Turn the bed-clothes toward the foot of the bed,
Let the physician and the priest go home.   1010

I seize the descending man and raise him with resistless will,
O despairer, here is my neck,
By God, you shall not go down! hang your whole weight upon me.

I dilate you with tremendous breath, I buoy you up,
Every room of the house do I fill with an arm'd force,   1015
Lovers of me, bafflers of graves.

Sleep—I and they keep guard all night,
Not doubt, not decease[8] shall dare to lay finger upon you,
I have embraced you, and henceforth possess you to myself,
And when you rise in the morning you will find what I tell you
    is so.   1020

41

I am he bringing help for the sick as they pant on their backs,
And for strong upright men I bring yet more needed help.

I heard what was said of the universe,
Heard it and heard it of several thousand years;
It is middling well as far as it goes—but is that all?   1025

Magnifying and applying come I,
Outbidding at the start the old cautious hucksters,
Taking myself the exact dimensions of Jehovah,
Lithographing Kronos, Zeus his son, and Hercules his grandson,
Buying drafts of Osiris, Isis, Belus, Brahma, Buddha,   1030
In my portfolio placing Manito loose, Allah on a leaf, the
    crucifix engraved,
With Odin and the hideous-faced Mexitli and every idol and image,[9]
Taking them all for what they are worth and not a cent more,
Admitting they were alive and did the work of their days,
(They bore mites as for unfledg'd birds who have now to rise
    and fly and sing for themselves,)   1035
Accepting the rough deific sketches to fill out better in myself,
    bestowing them freely on each man and woman I see,

8. This word was misprinted as "disease" in the 1902 *CW*, and the error seems to have been
   repeated in most later editions.
9. Lines 1029–32—*Kronos*: the Titan, son of Uranus and Gaea, who dethroned his father and
   was in turn dethroned by his son, Zeus. *Osiris*: Egyptian god of the lower world. *Isis*: Egyptian
   goddess of fertility, sister and wife of Osiris. *Belus*: legendary king of Assyria. *Manito*: nature
   spirit of the Algonquian Indians. *Mexitli*: Aztec god of war. *Brahma*: in Hindu religion, the
   supreme soul of the universe. *Odin*: in Norse mythology, the god of war.

Discovering as much or more in a framer framing a house,
Putting higher claims for him there with his roll'd-up sleeves
    driving the mallet and chisel,
Not objecting to special revelations, considering a curl of
    smoke or a hair on the back of my hand just as curious as
    any revelation,
Lads ahold of fire-engines and hook-and-ladder ropes no less
    to me than the gods of the antique wars,   1040
Minding their voices peal through the crash of destruction,
Their brawny limbs passing safe over charr'd laths, their white
    foreheads whole and unhurt out of the flames;
By the mechanic's wife with her babe at her nipple interceding
    for every person born,
Three scythes at harvest whizzing in a row from three lusty
    angels with shirts bagg'd out at their waists,
The snag-tooth'd hostler with red hair redeeming sins past and
    to come,   1045
Selling all the possesses, traveling on foot to fee lawyers for his
    brother and sit by him while he is tried for forgery;
What was strewn in the amplest strewing the square rod about
    me, and not filling the square rod then,
The bull and the bug never worshipp'd half enough,[1]
Dung and dirt more admirable than was dream'd,
The supernatural of no account, myself waiting my time to be
    one of the supremes,   1050
The day getting ready for me when I shall do as much good as
    the best, and be as prodigious;
By my life-lumps! becoming already a creator,
Putting myself here and now to the ambush'd womb of the shadows.

42

A call in the midst of the crowd,
My own voice, orotund sweeping and final.   1055

Come my children,
Come my boys and girls, my women, household and intimates,
Now the performer launches his nerve, he has pass'd his
    prelude on the reeds within.

Easily written loose-finger'd chords—I feel the thrum of your
    climax and close.

My head slues round on my neck,   1060
Music rolls, but not from the organ,
Folks are around me, but they are no household of mine.

---

1. Probably chosen as common objects; yet the bull was worshipped in Greece as the embod-
iment of Dionysus, and also held sacred by the Egyptians and believed by the Moslems to
support the earth on its back. The scarabaeus, a dung beetle, was the model for icons of the
Egyptian sun god, Khepera.

Ever the hard unsunk ground,
Ever the eaters and drinkers, ever the upward and downward
    sun, ever the air and the ceaseless tides,
Ever myself and my neighbors, refreshing, wicked, real,   1065
Ever the old inexplicable query, ever that thorn'd thumb,[2] that
    breath of itches and thirsts,
Ever the vexer's *hoot! hoot!* till we find where the sly one hides
    and bring him forth,
Ever love, ever the sobbing liquid of life,
Ever the bandage under the chin, ever the trestles of death.[3]

Here and there with dimes on the eyes walking,[4]   1070
To feed the greed of the belly the brains liberally spooning,
Tickets buying, taking, selling, but in to the feast never once
    going,
Many sweating, ploughing, thrashing, and then the chaff for
    payment receiving,
A few idly owning, and they the wheat continually claiming.

This is the city and I am one of the citizens,   1075
Whatever interests the rest interests me, politics, wars,
    markets, newspapers, schools,
The mayor and councils, banks, tariffs, steamships, factories,
    stocks, stores, real estate and personal estate.

The little plentiful manikins skipping around in collars and
    tail'd coats,
I am aware who they are, (they are positively not worms or fleas,)
I acknowledge the duplicates of myself, the weakest and
    shallowest is deathless with me,   1080
What I do and say the same waits for them,
Every thought that flounders in me the same flounders in them.

I know perfectly well my own egotism,
Know my omnivorous lines and must not write any less,
And would fetch you whoever you are flush with myself.   1085

Not words of routine this song of mine,
But abruptly to question, to leap beyond yet nearer bring;
This printed and bound book—but the printer and the
    printing-office boy?
The well-taken photographs—but your wife or friend close and
    solid in your arms?

2. WW's version of the familiar metaphor, "thorn in the flesh," an image of vexation.
3. The supports on which the dead lie; the same image is employed in "Beat! Beat! Drums!"
4. The phrase powerfully combines the previous image of death (dimes keep the eye-lids closed
    until the funeral) and that of greed, following. *Cf.* E. A. Robinson's sonnet on Aaron Stark:

        A miser was he, with a miser's nose,
        And eyes like little dollars in the dark.

The black ship mail'd with iron, her mighty guns in her turrets
   —but the pluck of the captain and engineers?   1090
In the houses the dishes and fare and furniture—but the host
   and hostess, and the look out of their eyes?
The sky up there—yet here or next door, or across the way?
The saints and sages in history—but you yourself?
Sermons, creeds, theology—but the fathomless human brain,
And what is reason? and what is love? and what is life?   1095

43

I do not despise you priests, all time, the world over,
My faith is the greatest of faiths and the least of faiths,
Enclosing worship ancient and modern and all between
   ancient and modern,
Believing I shall come again upon the earth after five thousand
   years,
Waiting responses from oracles, honoring the gods, saluting
   the sun,   1100
Making a fetich of the first rock or stump, powowing with
   sticks in the circle of obis,[5]
Helping the llama[6] or brahmin as he trims the lamps of the idols,
Dancing yet through the streets in a phallic procession, rapt
   and austere in the woods a gymnosophist,[7]
Drinking mead from the skull-cup, to Shastas and Vedas
   admirant,[8] minding the Koran,
Walking the teokallis,[9] spotted with gore from the stone and
   knife, beating the serpent-skin drum,   1105
Accepting the Gospels, accepting him that was crucified,
   knowing assuredly that he is divine,
To the mass kneeling or the puritan's prayer rising, or sitting
   patiently in a pew,
Ranting and frothing in my insane crisis, or waiting dead-like
   till my spirit arouses me,
Looking forth on pavement and land, or outside of pavement
   and land,
Belonging to the winders of the circuit of circuits.   1110

One of that centripetal and centrifugal gang[1] I turn and talk
   like a man leaving charges before a journey.

---

5. Shell fragments used in divination systems that are part of Yoruba-based *vodun* ("voodoo")
   practices of African-diasporic communities in the Caribbean and the United States.
6. Properly, "lama," Tibetan high priest.
7. Member of an ancient Hindu sect of ascetics who wore little or no clothing.
8. Shastas (properly "shastras") and Vedas are collections of the ancient sacred literature of
   Hinduism.
9. Aztec temples, usually built upon a truncated pyramid.
1. In the obsolescent sense of a group of people traveling in the same direction; not then a
   disparaging term.

Down-hearted doubters dull and excluded,
Frivolous, sullen, moping, angry, affected, dishearten'd,
  atheistical,
I know every one of you, I know the sea of torment, doubt,
  despair and unbelief.

How the flukes splash!   1115
How they contort rapid as lightning, with spasms and spouts of
  blood!

Be at peace bloody flukes[2] of doubters and sullen mopers,
I take my place among you as much as among any,
The past is the push of you, me, all, precisely the same,
And what is yet untried and afterward is for you, me, all,
  precisely the same.   1120

I do not know what is untried and afterward,
But I know it will in its turn prove sufficient, and cannot fail.

Each who passes is consider'd, each who stops is consider'd,
  not a single one can it fail.

It cannot fail the young man who died and was buried,
Nor the young woman who died and was put by his side,   1125
Nor the little child that peep'd in at the door, and then drew
  back and was never seen again,
Nor the old man who has lived without purpose, and feels it
  with bitterness worse than gall,
Nor him in the poor house tubercled by rum and the bad
  disorder,
Nor the numberless slaughter'd and wreck'd, nor the brutish
  koboo[3] call'd the ordure of humanity,
Nor the sacs merely floating with open mouths for food to slip
  in,   1130
Nor any thing in the earth, or down in the oldest graves of the
  earth,
Nor any thing in the myriads of spheres, nor the myriads of
  myriads that inhabit them,
Nor the present, nor the least wisp that is known.

44

It is time to explain myself—let us stand up.

What is known I strip away,   1135
I launch all men and women forward with me into the
  Unknown.

2. As the flukes (tail fins) of a stricken whale.
3. A native of Palembang on the east coast of Sumatra. See T. O. Mabbott, *Expli.* 11:34.

The clock indicates the moment—but what does eternity
    indicate?

We have thus far exhausted trillions of winters and summers,
There are trillions ahead, and trillions ahead of them.

Births have brought us richness and variety,   1140
And other births will bring us richness and variety.

I do not call one greater and one smaller,
That which fills its period and place is equal to any.

Were mankind murderous or jealous upon you, my brother, my
    sister?
I am sorry for you, they are not murderous or jealous upon
    me,   1145
All has been gentle with me, I keep no account with
    lamentation,
(What have I to do with lamentation?)

I am an acme of things accomplish'd, and I an encloser of
    things to be.[4]

My feet strike an apex of the apices of the stairs,
On every step bunches of ages, and larger bunches between
    the steps,   1150
All below duly travel'd, and still I mount and mount.

Rise after rise bow the phantoms behind me,
Afar down I see the huge first Nothing, I know I was even
    there,
I waited unseen and always, and slept through the lethargic
    mist,
And took my time, and took no hurt from the fetid carbon.   1155

Long I was hugg'd close—long and long.

Immense have been the preparations for me,
Faithful and friendly the arms that have help'd me.

Cycles ferried my cradle, rowing and rowing like cheerful
    boatmen,
For room to me stars kept aside in their own rings,   1160
They sent influences to look after what was to hold me.

Before I was born out of my mother generations guided me,
My embryo has never been torpid, nothing could overlay it.

4. For lines 1148–69, *cf.* note to line 671.

For it the nebula cohered to an orb,
The long slow strata piled to rest it on,   1165
Vast vegetables gave it sustenance,
Monstrous sauroids transported it in their mouths and
        deposited it with care.[5]

All forces have been steadily employ'd to complete and delight me,
Now on this spot I stand with my robust soul.

45

O span of youth! ever-push'd elasticity!   1170
O manhood, balanced, florid and full.

My lovers suffocate me,
Crowding my lips, thick in the pores of my skin,
Jostling me through streets and public halls, coming naked to
        me at night,
Crying by day *Ahoy!* from the rocks of the river, swinging and
        chirping over my head,   1175
Calling my name from flower-beds, vines, tangled underbrush,
Lighting on every moment of my life,
Bussing my body with soft balsamic busses,
Noiselessly passing handfuls out of their hearts and giving
        them to be mine.

Old age superbly rising! O welcome, ineffable grace of dying
        days!   1180

Every condition promulges not only itself, it promulges what
        grows after and out of itself,
And the dark hush promulges[6] as much as any.

I open my scuttle at night and see the far-sprinkled systems,
And all I see multiplied as high as I can cipher edge but the
        rim of the farther systems.

Wider and wider they spread, expanding, always expanding,   1185
Outward and outward and forever outward.

My sun has his sun and round him obediently wheels,
He joins with his partners a group of superior circuit,
And greater sets follow, making specks of the greatest inside
        them.

There is no stoppage and never can be stoppage,   1190

5. Sauria, prehistoric mammoth reptiles, were thought according to legend to carry their eggs
   in their mouths—a folk superstition that, with respect to snakes, has survived to modern
   times.
6. Archaic form of "promulgate," to make known, to make widespread.

If I, you, and the worlds, and all beneath or upon their
      surfaces, were this moment reduced back to a pallid float,
      it would not avail in the long run,
We should surely bring up again where we now stand,
And surely go as much farther, and then farther and farther.

A few quadrillions of eras, a few octillions of cubic leagues, do
      not hazard the span or make it impatient,
They are but parts, any thing is but a part.   1195

See ever so far, there is limitless space outside of that,
Count ever so much, there is limitless time around that.

My rendezvous is appointed, it is certain,
The Lord will be there and wait till I come on perfect terms,
The great Camerado, the lover true for whom I pine will be
      there.   1200

46

I know I have the best of time and space, and was never
      measured and never will be measured.

I tramp a perpetual journey, (come listen all!)
My signs are a rain-proof coat, good shoes, and a staff cut
      from the woods,
No friend of mine takes his ease in my chair,
I have no chair, no church, no philosophy,   1205
I lead no man to a dinner-table, library, exchange,
But each man and each woman of you I lead upon a knoll,
My left hand hooking you round the waist,
My right hand pointing to landscapes of continents and the
      public road.

Not I, not any one else can travel that road for you,   1210
You must travel it for yourself.

It is not far, it is within reach,
Perhaps you have been on it since you were born and did not
      know,
Perhaps it is everywhere on water and on land.

Shoulder your duds dear son, and I will mine, and let us
      hasten forth,   1215
Wonderful cities and free nations we shall fetch as we go.

If you tire, give me both burdens, and rest the chuff[7] of your
      hand on my hip,

---

7. English dialectical adjective meaning "chubby" or "fat"; here converted into a noun referring
   to the heel of the hand.

And in due time you shall repay the same service to me,
For after we start we never lie by again.

This day before dawn I ascended a hill and look'd at the
    crowded heaven,   1220
And I said to my spirit *When we become the enfolders of those*
    orbs, and the pleasure and knowledge of every thing in
    them, shall we be fill'd and satisfied then?
And my spirit said *No, we but level that lift to pass and*
    continue beyond.

You are also asking me questions and I hear you,
I answer that I cannot answer, you must find out for yourself.

Sit a while dear son,   1225
Here are biscuits to eat and here is milk to drink,
But as soon as you sleep and renew yourself in sweet clothes, I
    kiss you with a good-by kiss and open the gate for your
    egress hence.

Long enough have you dream'd contemptible dreams,
Now I wash the gum from your eyes,
You must habit yourself to the dazzle of the light and of every
    moment of your life.   1230

Long have you timidly waded holding a plank by the shore,
Now I will you to be a bold swimmer,
To jump off in the midst of the sea, rise again, nod to me,
    shout, and laughingly dash with your hair.

47

I am the teacher of athletes,
He that by me spreads a wider breast than my own proves the
    width of my own,   1235
He most honors my style who learns under it to destroy the
    teacher.

The boy I love, the same becomes a man not through derived
    power, but in his own right,
Wicked rather than virtuous out of conformity or fear,
Fond of his sweetheart, relishing well his steak,
Unrequited love or a slight cutting him worse than sharp steel
    cuts,   1240
First-rate to ride, to fight, to hit the bull's eye, to sail a skiff, to
    sing a song or play on the banjo,
Preferring scars and the beard and faces pitted with small-pox
    over all latherers,
And those well-tann'd to those that keep out of the sun.

I teach straying from me, yet who can stray from me?
I follow you whoever you are from the present hour,   1245
My words itch at your ears till you understand them.

I do not say these things for a dollar or to fill up the time
      while I wait for a boat,
(It is you talking just as much as myself, I act as the tongue of
      you,
Tied in your mouth, in mine it begins to be loosen'd.)

I swear I will never again mention love or death inside a
      house,   1250
And I swear I will never translate myself at all, only to him or
      her who privately stays with me in the open air.

If you would understand me go to the heights or water-shore,
The nearest gnat is an explanation, and a drop or motion of
      waves a key,
The maul, the oar, the hand-saw, second my words.

No shutter'd room or school can commune with me,   1255
But roughs and little children better than they.

The young mechanic is closest to me, he knows me well,
The woodman that takes his axe and jug with him shall take
      me with him all day,
The farm-boy ploughing in the field feels good at the sound of
      my voice,
In vessels that sail my words sail, I go with fishermen and
      seamen and love them.   1260

The soldier camp'd or upon the march is mine,
On the night ere the pending battle many seek me, and I do
      not fail them,
On that solemn night (it may be their last) those that know me
      seek me.

My face rubs to the hunter's face when he lies down alone in
      his blanket,
The driver thinking of me does not mind the jolt of his wagon,   1265
The young mother and old mother comprehend me,
The girl and the wife rest the needle a moment and forget
      where they are,
They and all would resume what I have told them.

48

I have said that the soul is not more than the body,
And I have said that the body is not more than the soul,   1270

And nothing, not God, is greater to one than one's self is,
And whoever walks a furlong without sympathy walks to his
    own funeral drest in his shroud,
And I or you pocketless of a dime may purchase the pick of
    the earth,
And to glance with an eye or show a bean in its pod
    confounds the learning of all times,
And there is no trade or employment but the young man
    following it may become a hero,   1275
And there is no object so soft but it makes a hub for the
    wheel'd universe,
And I say to any man or woman, Let your soul stand cool and
    composed before a million universes.

And I say to mankind, Be not curious about God,
For I who am curious about each am not curious about God,
(No array of terms can say how much I am at peace about
    God and about death.)   1280

I hear and behold God in every object, yet understand God not
    in the least,
Nor do I understand who there can be more wonderful than
    myself.

Why should I wish to see God better than this day?
I see something of God each hour of the twenty-four, and
    each moment then,
In the faces of men and women I see God, and in my own
    face in the glass,   1285
I find letters from God dropt in the street, and every one is
    sign'd by God's name,
And I leave them where they are, for I know that wheresoe'er I
    go,
Others will punctually come for ever and ever.

49

And as to you Death, and you bitter hug of mortality, it is idle
    to try to alarm me.

To his work without flinching the accoucheur[8] comes,   1290
I see the elder-hand pressing receiving supporting,
I recline by the sills of the exquisite flexible doors,
And mark the outlet, and mark the relief and escape.

And as to you Corpse I think you are good manure, but that
    does not offend me,
I smell the white roses sweet-scented and growing,   1295

8. Midwife, obstetrician; note also "the elder-hand" below.

I reach to the leafy lips, I reach to the polish'd breasts of melons.

And as to you Life I reckon you are the leavings of many deaths,
(No doubt I have died myself ten thousand times before.)

I hear you whispering there O stars of heaven,
O suns—O grass of graves—O perpetual transfers and
    promotions,   1300
If you do not say any thing how can I say any thing?

Of the turbid pool that lies in the autumn forest,
Of the moon that descends the steeps of the soughing twilight,
Toss, sparkles of day and dusk—toss on the black stems that
    decay in the muck,
Toss to the moaning gibberish of the dry limbs.   1305

I ascend from the moon, I ascend from the night,
I perceive that the ghastly glimmer is noonday sunbeams
    reflected,
And debouch[9] to the steady and central from the offspring
    great or small.

50

There is that in me—I do not know what it is—but I know it
    is in me.

Wrench'd and sweaty—calm and cool then my body becomes,   1310
I sleep—I sleep long.

I do not know it—it is without name—it is a word unsaid,
It is not in any dictionary, utterance, symbol.

Something it swings on more than the earth I swing on,
To it the creation is the friend whose embracing awakes me.   1315

Perhaps I might tell more. Outlines! I plead for my brothers
    and sisters.

Do you see O my brothers and sisters?
It is not chaos or death—it is form, union, plan—it is eternal
    life—it is Happiness.[1]

---

9. Emerge. *Cf.* the French "bouche," a mouth; and note the "flexible doors" (line 1293). "I"
   is apparently the subject of the verb, and if so, "offspring" may be interpreted as "point of
   departure."
1. For a succinct survey of critical commentary on Section 50, see Miller, ed., *Walt Whitman's
   "Song of Myself": A Mosaic of Interpretations*, 134–35.

51

The past and present wilt—I have fill'd them, emptied them,
And proceed to fill my next fold of the future.   1320

Listener up there! what have you to confide to me?
Look in my face while I snuff the sidle of evening,[2]
(Talk honestly, no one else hears you, and I stay only a minute
    longer.)

Do I contradict myself?
Very well then I contradict myself,[3]   1325
(I am large, I contain multitudes.)

I concentrate toward them that are nigh, I wait on the door-slab.

Who has done his day's work? who will soonest be through
    with his supper?
Who wishes to walk with me?

Will you speak before I am gone? will you prove already too
    late?   1330

52

The spotted hawk swoops by and accuses me, he complains of
    my gab and my loitering.

I too am not a bit tamed, I too am untranslatable,
I sound my barbaric yawp over the roofs of the world.

The last scud of day holds back for me,
It flings my likeness after the rest and true as any on the
    shadow'd wilds,   1335
It coaxes me to the vapor and the dusk.

I depart as air, I shake my white locks at the runaway sun,
I effuse my flesh in eddies, and drift it in lacy jags.

I bequeath myself to the dirt to grow from the grass I love,
If you want me again look for me under your boot-soles.   1340

You will hardly know who I am or what I mean,
But I shall be good health to you nevertheless,
And filter and fibre your blood.

---

2. *Cf.* the colloquial phrase to "snuff out" (extinguish) a light—in this case the sidelong glimmer
   of evening.
3. *Cf.* Emerson's "A foolish consistency is the hobgoblin of little minds, adored by little states-
   men and philosophers and divines" ("Self-Reliance," *Essays: First Series,* 1841).

Failing to fetch me at first keep encouraged,
Missing me one place search another, 1345
I stop somewhere waiting for you.[4]
1855 *1881*

CHILDREN OF ADAM

To the Garden the World[1]

To the garden the world anew ascending,
Potent mates, daughters, sons, preluding,
The love, the life of their bodies, meaning and being,
Curious here behold my resurrection after slumber,
The revolving cycles in their wide sweep having brought me
    again, 5
Amorous, mature, all beautiful to me, all wondrous,
My limbs and the quivering fire that ever plays through them,
    for reasons, most wondrous,
Existing I peer and penetrate still,
Content with the present, content with the past,
By my side or back of me Eve following, 10
Or in front, and I following her just the same.
1860 *1867*

---

4. Through a series of bold images—the hawk, the meteorlike scud or loose eddies of evening
mist, the dirt that nourishes the grass—the poet leaves the reader with his legacy of great
natural force, untranslatable but found everywhere—in the sky or underfoot.

  Children of Adam: In two of his notes toward poems WW set forth his ideas for this group.
One reads: "A string of Poems (short, etc.), embodying the amative love of woman—the
same as Live Oak Leaves do the passion of friendship for man." (MS unlocated; *N and F,* I,
169, item 63). The other, evidently written after the "Live Oak Leaves" had been replaced
by "Calamus" as a symbol, is more explicit: "Theory of a Cluster of Poems the same *to the
passion of Woman-Love* as the "Calamus-Leaves" are to adhesiveness, manly love. Full of
animal-fire, tender, burning,—the tremulous ache, delicious, yet such a torment. The swell-
ing elate and vehement, that will not be denied. Adam, as a central figure and type. One
piece presenting a vivid picture (in connection with the spirit) of a fully complete, well-
developed man, eld, bearded, swart, fiery,—as a more than rival of the youthful type-hero
of novels and love poems" (Trent; *N and F,* I, 124, item 142).
  Under the title "Enfans d'Adam" the group first appeared in *LG* 1860 as fifteen poems,
twelve of which were new. In the 1867 edition the title was changed to "Children of Adam,"
and one of the poems, "In the New Garden, in all the Parts," was dropped. In 1871 the
fourteen poems of the preceding edition were retained, together with two transfers from the
Drum-Taps poems, to make a total of sixteen; thereafter the group remained unchanged,
although the present order is slightly different from that of the original. WW was formally
to defend this group in his "A Memorandum at a Venture," *North American Review* 134
(June 1882): 456–60, as a few months earlier he had defended it in talk with Emerson on
the Boston Common. He is reported by Traubel as remarking, " 'Children of Adam' stumps
the worst and the best; I have even tried hard to see if it might not as I grow older or
experience new moods stump me; I have even almost deliberately tried to retreat. But it
would not do. When I tried to take those pieces out of the scheme the whole scheme came
down about my ears" (Traubel, I, 3).
1. Two MS versions of this poem, under the title "Leaves-Droppings," are in the Barrett collec-
tion (see *WWM,* 58), and as WW's second note on the "Children of Adam" group indicates,
"Adam, as a central figure and type," is here made the controlling symbol of the group, the
subject of its first poem and its last. The poet left this fine poem unaltered through the
successive editions.

From Pent-up Aching Rivers[2]

From pent-up aching rivers,
From that of myself without which I were nothing,
From what I am determin'd to make illustrious, even if I stand
    sole among men,
From my own voice resonant, singing the phallus,
Singing the song of procreation,   5
Singing the need of superb children and therein superb grown
    people,
Singing the muscular urge and the blending,
Singing the bedfellow's song, (O resistless yearning!
O for any and each the body correlative attracting!
O for you whoever you are your correlative body! O it, more
    than all else, you delighting!)   10
From the hungry gnaw that eats me night and day,
From native moments, from bashful pains, singing them,
Seeking something yet unfound though I have diligently sought
    it many a long year,
Singing the true song of the soul fitful at random,
Renascent with grossest Nature or among animals,   15
Of that, of them and what goes with them my poems
    informing,
Of the smell of apples and lemons, of the pairing of birds,
Of the wet of woods, of the lapping of waves,
Of the mad pushes of waves upon the land, I them chanting,
The overture lightly sounding, the strain anticipating,   20
The welcome nearness, the sight of the perfect body,
The swimmer swimming naked in the bath, or motionless on
    his back lying and floating,
The female form approaching, I pensive, love-flesh tremulous
    aching,
The divine list for myself or you or for any one making,
The face, the limbs, the index from head to foot, and what it
    arouses,   25
The mystic deliria, the madness amorous, the utter
    abandonment,
(Hark close and still what I now whisper to you,
I love you, O you entirely possess me,
O that you and I escape from the rest and go utterly off, free
    and lawless,

2. Originally "Enfans d'Adam" No. 2 in the 1860 edition, this poem took its present title in the
next edition (1867) from what had been its tenth line, although the poet had tentatively
entered the title "Song of Procreation" in his MS revisions. It is a daring and original cele-
bration of the drive of sex, not only the procreative instinct but the whole appetite for the
context of creation—the smell of apples, the wet of woods. The poem remained compara-
tively unchanged although a few lines were later omitted, including, in 1881, the passage:

    Singing what, to the Soul, entirely redeemed her,
        the faithful one, the prostitute, who detained
        me when I went to the city;
    Singing the song of prostitutes.

Two hawks in the air, two fishes swimming in the sea not
    more lawless than we;)   30
The furious storm through me careering, I passionately
    trembling,
The oath of the inseparableness of two together, of the woman
    that loves me and whom I love more than my life, that
    oath swearing,
(O I willingly stake all for you,
O let me be lost if it must be so!
O you and I! what is it to us what the rest do or think?   35
What is all else to us? only that we enjoy each other and
    exhaust each other if it must be so;)
From the master, the pilot I yield the vessel to,
The general commanding me, commanding all, from him
    permission taking,
From time the programme hastening, (I have loiter'd too long
    as it is,)
From sex, from the warp and from the woof,[3]   40
From privacy, from frequent repinings alone,
From plenty of persons near and yet the right person not near,
From the soft sliding of hands over me and thrusting of fingers
    through my hair and beard,
From the long sustain'd kiss upon the mouth or bosom,
From the close pressure that makes me or any man drunk,
    fainting with excess,   45
From what the divine husband knows, from the work of
    fatherhood,
From exultation, victory and relief, from the bedfellow's
    embrace in the night,
From the act-poems of eyes, hands, hips and bosoms,
From the cling of the trembling arm,
From the bending curve and the clinch,   50
From side by side the pliant coverlet off-throwing,
From the one so unwilling to have me leave, and me just as
    unwilling to leave,
(Yet a moment O tender waiter, and I return,)
From the hour of shining stars and dropping dews,
From the night a moment I emerging flitting out,   55
Celebrate you act divine and you children prepared for,
And you stalwart loins.
    1860   *1881*

---

3. Associated with the word "sex," the interweaving vertical and horizontal strands on a loom
    suggest masculine and feminine opposites.

I Sing the Body Electric[4]

1

I sing the body electric,
The armies of those I love engirth me and I engirth them,
They will not let me off till I go with them, respond to them,
And discorrupt them, and charge them full with the charge of
    the soul.

Was it doubted that those who corrupt their own bodies
    conceal themselves? 5
And if those who defile the living are as bad as they who defile
    the dead?
And if the body does not do fully as much as the soul?
And if the body were not the soul, what is the soul?

2

The love of the body of man or woman balks account, the
    body itself balks account,
That of the male is perfect, and that of the female is perfect. 10

The expression of the face balks account,
But the expression of a well-made man appears not only in his
    face,
It is in his limbs and joints also, it is curiously in the joints of
    his hips and wrists,
It is in his walk, the carriage of his neck, the flex of his waist
    and knees, dress does not hide him,
The strong sweet quality he has strikes through the cotton and
    broadcloth, 15
To see him pass conveys as much as the best poem, perhaps more,
You linger to see his back, and the back of his neck and
    shoulder-side.

The sprawl and fulness of babes, the bosoms and heads of
    women, the folds of their dress, their style as we pass in
    the street, the contour of their shape downwards,
The swimmer naked in the swimming-bath, seen as he swims
    through the transparent green-shine, or lies with his face
    up and rolls silently to and fro in the heave of the water,

---

4. No. 5 of the twelve poems of the 1855 edition, "I Sing the Body Electric," untitled and
unsectioned, became "Poem of the Body" in the 1856 edition, augmented with the remark-
able anatomical inventory that now concludes the poem. The poet's MS notes thereon are
now in the Trent Duke collection (N and F, I, 172, item 84). In 1860 the poem became
"Enfans d'Adam" No. 3 with a few minor revisions; and in 1867 it acquired its present
sectioning and title, which was also its opening line. There were minor changes in 1871 and
1881. What the poet sang—lovingly, boldly to the limit of specificity—was this world's body,
in whose movements he found insatiable delight; but also, as he tells us repeatedly, he is
singing the soul.

The bending forward and backward of rowers in row-boats, the
    horseman in his saddle,   20
Girls, mothers, house-keepers, in all their performances,
The group of laborers seated at noon-time with their open
    dinner-kettles, and their wives waiting,
The female soothing a child, the farmer's daughter in the
    garden or cow-yard,
The young fellow hoeing corn, the sleigh-driver driving his six
    horses through the crowd,
The wrestle of wrestlers, two apprentice-boys, quite grown,
    lusty, good-natured, native-born, out on the vacant lot at
    sun-down after work,   25
The coats and caps thrown down, the embrace of love and
    resistance,
The upper-hold and under-hold, the hair rumpled over and
    blinding the eyes;
The march of firemen in their own costumes, the play of
    masculine muscle through clean-setting trowsers and
    waist-straps,
The slow return from the fire, the pause when the bell strikes
    suddenly again, and the listening on the alert,
The natural, perfect, varied attitudes, the bent head, the curv'd
    neck and the counting;   30
Such-like I love—I loosen myself, pass freely, am at the
    mother's breast with the little child,
Swim with the swimmers, wrestle with wrestlers, march in line
    with the firemen, and pause, listen, count.

3

I knew a man, a common farmer, the father of five sons,
And in them the fathers of sons, and in them the fathers of sons.

This man was of wonderful vigor, calmness, beauty of person,   35
The shape of his head, the pale yellow and white of his hair
    and beard, the immeasurable meaning of his black eyes,
    the richness and breadth of his manners,
These I used to go and visit him to see, he was wise also,
He was six feet tall, he was over eighty years old, his sons were
    massive, clean, bearded, tan-faced, handsome,
They and his daughters loved him, all who saw him loved him,
They did not love him by allowance, they loved him with
    personal love,   40
He drank water only, the blood show'd like scarlet through the
    clear-brown skin of his face,
He was a frequent gunner and fisher, he sail'd his boat
    himself, he had a fine one presented to him by a ship-
    joiner, he had fowling-pieces presented to him by men
    that loved him,
When he went with his five sons and many grand-sons to hunt

or fish, you would pick him out as the most beautiful and
   vigorous of the gang,
You would wish long and long to be with him, you would wish
   to sit by him in the boat that you and he might touch
   each other.

4

I have perceiv'd that to be with those I like is enough,   45
To stop in company with the rest at evening is enough,
To be surrounded by beautiful, curious, breathing, laughing
   flesh is enough,
To pass among them or touch any one, or rest my arm ever so
   lightly round his or her neck for a moment, what is this
   then?
I do not ask any more delight, I swim in it as in a sea.

There is something in staying close to men and women and
   looking on them, and in the contact and odor of them,
   that pleases the soul well,   50
All things please the soul, but these please the soul well.

5

This is the female form,
A divine nimbus exhales from it from head to foot,
It attracts with fierce undeniable attraction,
I am drawn by its breath as if I were no more than a helpless
   vapor, all falls aside but myself and it,   55
Books, art, religion, time, the visible and solid earth, and what
   was expected of heaven or fear'd of hell, are now
   consumed,
Mad filaments, ungovernable shoots play out of it, the
   response likewise ungovernable,
Hair, bosom, hips, bend of legs, negligent falling hands all
   diffused, mine too diffused,
Ebb stung by the flow and flow stung by the ebb, love-flesh
   swelling and deliciously aching,
Limitless limpid jets of love hot and enormous, quivering jelly
   of love, white-blow and delirious juice,   60
Bridegroom night of love working surely and softly into the
   prostrate dawn,
Undulating into the willing and yielding day,
Lost in the cleave of the clasping and sweet-flesh'd day.

This the nucleus—after the child is born of woman, man is
   born of woman,
This the bath of birth, this the merge of small and large, and
   the outlet again.

Be not ashamed women, your privilege encloses the rest, and
    is the exit of the rest,
You are the gates of the body, and you are the gates of the soul.

The female contains all qualities and tempers them,
She is in her place and moves with perfect balance,
She is all things duly veil'd, she is both passive and active,   70
She is to conceive daughters as well as sons, and sons as well
    as daughters.

As I see my soul reflected in Nature,
As I see through a mist, One with inexpressible completeness,
    sanity, beauty,
See the bent head and arms folded over the breast, the Female
    I see.

6

The male is not less the soul nor more, he too is in his place,   75
He too is all qualities, he is action and power,
The flush of the known universe is in him,
Scorn becomes him well, and appetite and defiance become
    him well,
The wildest largest passions, bliss that is utmost, sorrow that is
    utmost become him well, pride is for him,
The full-spread pride of man is calming and excellent to the
    soul,   80
Knowledge becomes him, he likes it always, he brings every
    thing to the test of himself,
Whatever the survey, whatever the sea and the sail he strikes
    soundings at last only here,
(Where else does he strike soundings except here?)

The man's body is sacred and the woman's body is sacred,
No matter who it is, it is sacred—is it the meanest one in the
    laborers' gang?
Is it one of the dull-faced immigrants just landed on the wharf?   85
Each belongs here or anywhere just as much as the well-off,
    just as much as you,
Each has his or her place in the procession.

(All is a procession,
The universe is a procession with measured and perfect
    motion.)   90

Do you know so much yourself that you call the meanest
    ignorant?
Do you suppose you have a right to a good sight, and he or
    she has no right to a sight?
Do you think matter has cohered together from its diffuse

float, and the soil is on the surface, and water runs and
    vegetation sprouts,
For you only, and not for him and her?

7

A man's body at auction,   95
(For before the war I often go to the slave-mart and watch the
    sale,)[5]
I help the auctioneer, the sloven does not half know his business.

Gentlemen look on this wonder,
Whatever the bids of the bidders they cannot be high enough for it,
For it the globe lay preparing quintillions of years without one
    animal or plant,   100
For it the revolving cycles truly and steadily roll'd.

In this head the all-baffling brain,
In it and below it the makings of heroes.

Examine these limbs, red, black, or white, they are cunning in
    tendon and nerve,
They shall be stript that you may see them.   105

Exquisite senses, life-lit eyes, pluck, volition,
Flakes of breast-muscle, pliant backbone and neck, flesh not
    flabby, good-sized arms and legs,
And wonders within there yet.

Within there runs blood,
The same old blood! the same red-running blood!   110
There swells and jets a heart, there all passions, desires,
    reachings, aspirations,
(Do you think they are not there because they are not
    express'd in parlors and lecture-rooms?)

This is not only one man, this the father of those who shall be
    fathers in their turns,
In him the start of populous states and rich republics,
Of him countless immortal lives with countless embodiments
    and enjoyments.   115

How do you know who shall come from the offspring of his
    offspring through the centuries?
(Who might you find you have come from yourself, if you
    could trace back through the centuries?)

5. This line was added in 1881.

8

A woman's body at auction,
She too is not only herself, she is the teeming mother of mothers,
She is the bearer of them that shall grow and be mates to the
    mothers.   120

Have you ever loved the body of a woman?
Have you ever loved the body of a man?
Do you not see that these are exactly the same to all in all
    nations and times all over the earth?

If any thing is sacred the human body is sacred,
And the glory and sweet of a man is the token of manhood
    untainted,   125
And in man or woman a clean, strong, firm-fibred body, is
    more beautiful than the most beautiful face.

Have you seen the fool that corrupted his own live body? or
    the fool that corrupted her own live body?
For they do not conceal themselves, and cannot conceal
    themselves.

9

O my body! I dare not desert the likes of you in other men and
    women, nor the likes of the parts of you,
I believe the likes of you are to stand or fall with the likes of
    the soul, (and that they are the soul,)   130
I believe the likes of you shall stand or fall with my poems,
    and that they are my poems,
Man's, woman's, child's, youth's, wife's, husband's, mother's,
    father's, young man's, young woman's poems,
Head, neck, hair, ears, drop and tympan of the ears,
Eyes, eye-fringes, iris of the eye, eyebrows, and the waking or
    sleeping of the lids,
Mouth, tongue, lips, teeth, roof of the mouth, jaws, and the
    jaw-hinges,   135
Nose, nostrils of the nose, and the partition,
Cheeks, temples, forehead, chin, throat, back of the neck,
    neck-slue,
Strong shoulders, manly beard, scapula, hind-shoulders, and
    the ample side-round of the chest,
Upper-arm, armpit, elbow-socket, lower-arm, arm-sinews, arm-bones,
Wrist and wrist-joints, hand, palm, knuckles, thumb,
    forefinger, finger-joints, finger-nails,   140
Broad breast-front, curling hair of the breast, breast-bone,
    breast-side,
Ribs, belly, backbone, joints of the backbone,

Hips, hip-sockets, hip-strength, inward and outward round,
      man-balls, man-root,
Strong set of thighs, well carrying the trunk above,
Leg-fibres, knee, knee-pan, upper-leg, under-leg,   145
Ankles, instep, foot-ball, toes, toe-joints, the heel;
All attitudes, all the shapeliness, all the belongings of my or
      your body or of any one's body, male or female,
The lung-sponges, the stomach-sac, the bowels sweet and clean,
The brain in its folds inside the skull-frame,
Sympathies, heart-valves, palate-valves, sexuality, maternity,   150
Womanhood, and all that is a woman, and the man that comes
      from woman,
The womb, the teats, nipples, breast-milk, tears, laughter,
      weeping, love-looks, love-perturbations and risings,
The voice, articulation, language, whispering, shouting aloud,
Food, drink, pulse, digestion, sweat, sleep, walking, swimming,
Poise on the hips, leaping, reclining, embracing, arm-curving
      and tightening,   155
The continual changes of the flex of the mouth, and around
      the eyes,
The skin, the sunburnt shade, freckles, hair,
The curious sympathy one feels when feeling with the hand
      the naked meat of the body,
The circling rivers the breath, and breathing it in and out,
The beauty of the waist, and thence of the hips, and thence
      downward toward the knees,   160
The thin red jellies within you or within me, the bones and the
      marrow in the bones,
The exquisite realization of health;
O I say these are not the parts and poems of the body only,
      but of the soul,
O I say now these are the soul!
    1855   *1881*

A Woman Waits for Me[6]

A woman waits for me, she contains all, nothing is lacking,
Yet all were lacking if sex were lacking, or if the moisture of
      the right man were lacking.

Sex contains all, bodies, souls,
Meanings, proofs, purities, delicacies, results, promulgations,

6. Originally an 1856 poem with the title "Poem of Procreation" and becoming "Enfans
d'Adam" No. 4 in 1860, "A Woman Waits for Me" took its present title from its first line in
1867. Had WW honored the title and first line he had tentatively ventured in his 1860 MS
revisions, "A woman America knows (or shall yet know)—she contains all, nothing is lack-
ing," his poem would probably have earned less opprobrium than it did then, with its seeming
suggestion of assignation. Later changes were minor: a few lines were omitted, notably "O
I will fetch bully breeds of children yet!"

Songs, commands, health, pride, the maternal mystery, the
    seminal milk,   5
All hopes, benefactions, bestowals, all the passions, loves,
    beauties, delights of the earth,
All the governments, judges, gods, follow'd persons of the earth,
These are contain'd in sex as parts of itself and justifications of
    itself.

Without shame the man I like knows and avows the
    deliciousness of his sex,
Without shame the woman I like knows and avows hers.   10

Now I will dismiss myself from impassive women,
I will go stay with her who waits for me, and with those
    women that are warm-blooded and sufficient for me,
I see that they understand me and do not deny me,
I see that they are worthy of me, I will be the robust husband
    of those women.

They are not one jot less than I am,   15
They are tann'd in the face by shining suns and blowing winds,
Their flesh has the old divine suppleness and strength,
They know how to swim, row, ride, wrestle, shoot, run, strike,
    retreat, advance, resist, defend themselves,
They are ultimate in their own right—they are calm, clear,
    well-possess'd of themselves.

I draw you close to me, you women,
I cannot let you go, I would do you good,   20
I am for you, and you are for me, not only for our own sake,
    but for others' sakes,
Envelop'd in you sleep greater heroes and bards,
They refuse to awake at the touch of any man but me.

It is I, you women, I make my way,   25
I am stern, acrid, large, undissuadable, but I love you,
I do not hurt you any more than is necessary for you,
I pour the stuff to start sons and daughters fit for these States,
    I press with slow rude muscle,
I brace myself effectually, I listen to no entreaties,
I dare not withdraw till I deposit what has so long
    accumulated within me.   30

Through you I drain the pent-up rivers of myself,
In you I wrap a thousand onward years,
On you I graft the grafts of the best-beloved of me and
    America,
The drops I distil upon you shall grow fierce and athletic girls,
    new artists, musicians, and singers,
The babes I beget upon you are to beget babes in their turn,   35

I shall demand perfect men and women out of my love-
    spendings,
I shall expect them to interpenetrate with others, as I and you
    interpenetrate now,
I shall count on the fruits of the gushing showers of them, as I
    count on the fruits of the gushing showers I give now,
I shall look for loving crops from the birth, life, death,
    immortality, I plant so lovingly now.

1856   1871

Spontaneous Me[7]

Spontaneous me, Nature,
The loving day, the mounting sun, the friend I am happy with,
The arm of my friend hanging idly over my shoulder,
The hillside whiten'd with blossoms of the mountain ash,
The same late in autumn, the hues of red, yellow, drab,
    purple, and light and dark green,   5
The rich coverlet of the grass, animals and birds, the private
    untrimm'd bank, the primitive apples, the pebble-stones,
Beautiful dripping fragments, the negligent list of one after
    another as I happen to call them to me or think of them,
The real poems, (what we call poems being merely pictures,)
The poems of the privacy of the night, and of men like me,
This poem drooping shy and unseen that I always carry, and
    that all men carry,   10
(Know once for all, avow'd on purpose, wherever are men like
    me, are our lusty lurking masculine poems,)
Love-thoughts, love-juice, love-odor, love-yielding, love-
    climbers, and the climbing sap,
Arms and hands of love, lips of love, phallic thumb of love,
    breasts of love, bellies press'd and glued together with
    love,
Earth of chaste love, life that is only life after love,
The body of my love, the body of the woman I love, the body
    of the man, the body of the earth,   15
Soft forenoon airs that blow from the south-west,
The hairy wild-bee that murmurs and hankers up and down,
    that gripes the full-grown lady-flower,[8] curves upon her
    with amorous firm legs, takes his will of her, and holds
    himself tremulous and tight till he is satisfied;
The wet of woods through the early hours,

---

7. Oddly titled "Bunch Poem" (after its final image) when it appeared in the 1856 edition, this poem became No. 5 of the "Enfans d'Adam" group in 1860, and in 1867 it took its present title from the first line, which was added in 1860. Another addition of 1860, the phrase "my Adamic and fresh daughters," relates it to the "Adam" image that informs the whole group. Intense and frank in sexual imagery, it is remarkable for its time. In his "Blue Copy" revisions of the 1860 edition, WW had marked the tenth line for deletion, but he retained it, and indeed he marked the poem "satisfactory—Jan. '65."
8. The generic suggestion of "female" is enriched by popular memory of the "Lady's Slipper," the familiar little orchid of field and garden, formally named *Cypripedium*, "Venus' Foot."

Two sleepers at night lying close together as they sleep, one
    with an arm slanting down across and below the waist of
    the other,
The smell of apples, aromas from crush'd sage-plant, mint,
    birch-bark,   20
The boy's longings, the glow and pressure as he confides to me
    what he was dreaming,
The dead leaf whirling its spiral whirl and falling still and
    content to the ground,
The no-form'd stings that sights, people, objects, sting me with,
The hubb'd[9] sting of myself, stinging me as much as it ever
    can any one,
The sensitive, orbic, underlapp'd brothers, that only privileged
    feelers may be intimate where they are,   25
The curious roamer the hand roaming all over the body, the
    bashful withdrawing of flesh where the fingers soothingly
    pause and edge themselves,
The limpid liquid within the young man,
The vex'd corrosion so pensive and so painful,
The torment, the irritable tide that will not be at rest,
The like of the same I feel, the like of the same in others,   30
The young man that flushes and flushes, and the young
    woman that flushes and flushes,
The young man that wakes deep at night, the hot hand seeking
    to repress what would master him,
The mystic amorous night, the strange half-welcome pangs,
    visions, sweats,
The pulse pounding through palms and trembling encircling
    fingers, the young man all color'd, red, ashamed, angry;
The souse upon me of my lover the sea, as I lie willing and
    naked,   35
The merriment of the twin babes that crawl over the grass in
    the sun, the mother never turning her vigilant eyes from
    them,
The walnut-trunk, the walnut-husks, and the ripening or
    ripen'd long-round walnuts,
The continence of vegetables, birds, animals,
The consequent meanness of me should I skulk or find myself
    indecent, while birds and animals never once skulk or find
    themselves indecent,
The great chastity of paternity, to match the great chastity of
    maternity,   40
The oath of procreation I have sworn, my Adamic and fresh
    daughters,
The greed that eats me day and night with hungry gnaw, till I
    saturate what shall produce boys to fill my place when I
    am through,
The wholesome relief, repose, content,

---

9. Centered, as in a wheel's hub; and *cf.* "no-form'd," just above.

And this bunch pluck'd at random from myself,
It has done its work—I toss it carelessly to fall where it may.   45
   1856   *1867*

One Hour to Madness and Joy[1]

One hour to madness and joy! O furious! O confine me not!
(What is this that frees me so in storms?
What do my shouts amid lightnings and raging winds mean?)

O to drink the mystic deliria deeper than any other man!
O savage and tender achings! (I bequeath them to you my
    children,   5
I tell them to you, for reasons, O bridegroom and bride.)
O to be yielded to you whoever you are, and you to be yielded
    to me in defiance of the world!
O to return to Paradise! O bashful and feminine!
O to draw you to me, to plant on you for the first time the lips
    of a determin'd man.

O the puzzle, the thrice-tied knot, the deep and dark pool, all
    untied and illumin'd!   10
O to speed where there is space enough and air enough at last!
To be absolv'd from previous ties and conventions, I from mine
    and you from yours!
To find a new unthought-of nonchalance with the best of
    Nature!
To have the gag remov'd from one's mouth!
To have the feeling to-day or any day I am sufficient as I am.   15

O something unprov'd! something in a trance!
To escape utterly from others' anchors and holds!
To drive free! to love free! to dash reckless and dangerous!
To court destruction with taunts, with invitations!
To ascend, to leap to the heavens of the love indicated to me!   20
To rise thither with my inebriate soul!
To be lost if it must be so!
To feed the remainder of life with one hour of fulness and
    freedom!
With one brief hour of madness and joy.
   1860   *1881*

---

1. Originally No. 6 of the "Enfans d'Adam" group, this poem took its present title from the first
line, added in 1867. Another significant change for the 1867 edition was the dropping, after
line 7, of the lover's adjuration:

      Know, I am a man, attracting, at any time, her I
         but look upon, or touch with the tips of my fingers,
      Or that touches my face, or leans against me.)

After 1867 the text remained as it is, except for minor changes.

Out of the Rolling Ocean the Crowd[2]

Out of the rolling ocean the crowd came a drop gently to me,
Whispering *I love you, before long I die,*
I have travel'd a long way merely to look on you to touch you,
For I could not die till I once look'd on you,
For I fear'd I might afterward lose you.   5

Now we have met, we have look'd, we are safe,
Return in peace to the ocean my love,
I too am part of that ocean my love, we are not so much
    separated,
Behold the great rondure, the cohesion of all, how perfect!
But as for me, for you, the irresistible sea is to separate us,   10
As for an hour carrying us diverse, yet cannot carry us diverse
    forever;
Be not impatient—a little space—know you I salute the air,
    the ocean and the land,
Every day at sundown for your dear sake my love.
    1865   *1881*

Ages and Ages Returning at Intervals[3]

Ages and ages returning at intervals,
Undestroy'd, wandering immortal,
Lusty, phallic, with the potent original loins, perfectly sweet,
I, chanter of Adamic songs,
Through the new garden the West, the great cities calling,   5
Deliriate, thus prelude what is generated, offering these,
    offering myself,
Bathing myself, bathing my songs in Sex,
Offspring of my loins.
    1860   *1867*

We Two, How Long We Were Fool'd[4]

We two, how long we were fool'd,
Now transmuted, we swiftly escape as Nature escapes,
We are Nature, long have we been absent, but now we return,

---

2. This poem, probably composed in the early 1860s, was originally a *Drum-Taps* poem (1865) and was transferred to the "Children of Adam" group in 1871. Before 1881 the poem's two sections were numbered, the second being enclosed within parentheses. Note the characteristic use of italics for direct address.
3. In 1860, No. 12 of the "Enfans d'Adam" group, this poem remained unchanged through later editions except for the capitalizing of the word "Sex" in 1867, at which time it assumed its present title.
4. In 1860, No. 7 of the "Enfans d'Adam" group, this poem began with the line "You and I— what the earth is, we are," which was dropped in 1867 when the poem took its title from the present first line. Another line was also dropped, and there were further minor changes.

We become plants, trunks, foliage, roots, bark,
We are bedded in the ground, we are rocks,   5
We are oaks, we grow in the openings side by side,
We browse, we are two among the wild herds spontaneous as any,
We are two fishes swimming in the sea together,
We are what locust blossoms are, we drop scent around lanes
    mornings and evenings,
We are also the coarse smut of beasts, vegetables, minerals,   10
We are two predatory hawks, we soar above and look down,
We are two resplendent suns, we it is who balance ourselves
    orbic and stellar, we are as two comets,
We prowl fang'd and four-footed in the woods, we spring on prey,
We are two clouds forenoons and afternoons driving overhead,
We are seas mingling, we are two of those cheerful waves
    rolling over each other and interwetting each other,   15
We are what the atmosphere is, transparent, receptive,
    pervious, impervious,
We are snow, rain, cold, darkness, we are each product and
    influence of the globe,
We have circled and circled till we have arrived home again,
    we two,
We have voided all but freedom and all but our own joy.
    1860   *1881*

O Hymen! O Hymenee![5]

O hymen! O hymenee! why do you tantalize me thus?
O why sting me for a swift moment only?
Why can you not continue? O why do you now cease?
Is it because if you continued beyond the swift moment you
    would soon certainly kill me?
    1860   *1867*

I Am He That Aches with Love[6]

I am he that aches with amorous love;
Does the earth gravitate? does not all matter, aching, attract all
    matter?
So the body of me to all I meet or know.
    1860   *1867*

---

5. This poem was No. 13 of the "Enfans d'Adam" in 1860, taking its present title in 1867.
6. No. 14 of the "Enfans d'Adam" group in 1860, this poem took its present title in 1867 and
    remained unchanged except for the addition of "amorous" in the first line.

Native Moments[7]

Native moments—when you come upon me—ah you are here now,
Give me now libidinous joys only,
Give me the drench of my passions, give me life coarse and rank,
To-day I go consort with Nature's darlings, to-night too,
I am for those who believe in loose delights, I share the
    midnight orgies of young men,   5
I dance with the dancers and drink with the drinkers,
The echoes ring with our indecent calls, I pick out some low
    person for my dearest friend,
He shall be lawless, rude, illiterate, he shall be one condemn'd
    by others for deeds done,
I will play a part no longer, why should I exile myself from my
    companions?
O you shunn'd persons, I at least do not shun you,   10
I come forthwith in your midst, I will be your poet,
I will be more to you than to any of the rest.
    1860   *1881*

Once I Pass'd through a Populous City[8]

Once I pass'd through a populous city imprinting my brain for
    future use with its shows, architecture, customs,
    traditions,
Yet now of all that city I remember only a woman I casually
    met there who detain'd me for love of me,
Day by day and night by night we were together—all else has
    long been forgotten by me,
I remember I say only that woman who passionately clung to me,
Again we wander, we love, we separate again,   5
Again she holds me by the hand, I must not go,
I see her close beside me with silent lips sad and tremulous.
    1860   *1861*

---

7. This poem, No. 8 of the "Enfans d'Adam" group in 1860, took its present title in 1867 and
has remained unchanged except for the dropping in 1881 of the phrase "I take for my love
some prostitute—" after "indecent calls" in the seventh line. The MS (Barrett) reveals other
rejected phrases: "Give me fierce pleasures only! Give me the weedy luxuriance!"
8. This poem, No. 9 of the "Enfans d'Adam" group, has remained unchanged through all the
editions, but its MS (Barrett; printed in *UPP*, II, 102 and Bowers, 64) significantly alters the
whole import of the poem. The second line of the MS reads:

        But now of all that city I remember only the man
            who wandered with me, there, for love of me.

and the fourth line reads, in part:

        —I remember, I say, only one rude and ignorant man

I Heard You Solemn-Sweet Pipes of the Organ[9]

I heard you solemn-sweet pipes of the organ as last Sunday
    morn I pass'd the church,
Winds of autumn, as I walk'd the woods at dusk I heard your
    long-stretch'd sighs up above so mournful,
I heard the perfect Italian tenor singing at the opera, I heard
    the soprano in the midst of the quartet singing;
Heart of my love! you too I heard murmuring low through one
    of the wrists around my head,
Heard the pulse of you when all was still ringing little bells
    last night under my ear.   5
1861   *1867*

Facing West from California's Shores[1]

Facing west from California's shores,
Inquiring, tireless, seeking what is yet unfound,
I, a child, very old, over waves, towards the house of maternity,
    the land of migrations, look afar,
Look off the shores of my Western sea, the circle almost circled;
For starting westward from Hindustan, from the vales of
    Kashmere,   5
From Asia, from the north, from the God, the sage, and the hero,
From the south, from the flowery peninsulas and the spice islands,
Long having wander'd since, round the earth having wander'd,
Now I face home again, very pleas'd and joyous,
(But where is what I started for so long ago?   10
And why is it yet unfound?)
1860   *1867*

---

9. Originally, this poem reflected the sentiments of love and war appropriate to the time of its first appearance, in the *New York Leader,* October 12, 1861, under the title "Little Bells Last Night," and beginning:

    War-suggesting trumpets, I heard you.

The opening three lines and a seventh were omitted when WW again printed it in the "Sequel to Drum-Taps," 1865–66; with no further alterations it was transferred to the "Children of Adam" group in 1871.
1. No. 10 of the 1860 "Enfans d'Adam," this poem acquired its title and first line in 1867. The MS version (Barrett) begins with the present third line, under the title, "Hindustan, from the Western Sea."

As Adam Early in the Morning[2]

As Adam early in the morning,
Walking forth from the bower refresh'd with sleep,
Behold me where I pass, hear my voice, approach,
Touch me, touch the palm of your hand to my body as I pass,
Be not afraid of my body.   5
1861   *1867*

CALAMUS

In Paths Untrodden[1]

In paths untrodden,
In the growth by margins of pond-waters,
Escaped from the life that exhibits itself,
From all the standards hitherto publish'd, from the pleasures,
    profits, conformities,
Which too long I was offering to feed my soul,   5
Clear to me now standards not yet publish'd, clear to me that
    my soul,
That the soul of the man I speak for rejoices in comrades,
Here by myself away from the clank of the world,

2. The final (No. 15) poem of the "Enfans d'Adam" group. The first line, "Early in the morning,"
was altered in 1867 to its present reading so that the controlling symbol, Adam in the
Garden, is the specific image of the entire poem.
1. In all editions this resolute announcement opens the "Calamus" group, taking its present
title in 1867 although in the revisions of his 1860 copy WW had considered the alternate
title, "By the Calamus Pond I Wander." Three different MSS (Trent; Barrett; and *N and F,*
I, 45, item 149) offer variant readings, including the lines:

> And now I care not to walk the earth unless a friend walk by my side,
> And now I dare not sing no other songs only those of lovers,

Calamus: Of all the groups in *LG*, the "Calamus" poems, first appearing in the text in 1860,
possess the closest autonomy, held together by a sentiment of manly attachment ("adhe-
siveness" was WW's term) that some readers find more intimate and compelling than that
of "Children of Adam." This important cluster had its beginnings in a manuscript of twelve
poems that may have been modeled on Shakespeare's sonnets, important precedents for
Whitman and his contemporaries in writing about passion between men. For some critics,
including Hershel Parker, this earlier poetic project represents a more positive, less occluded
version of a male-male love affair than does the much revised, reordered, and expanded
sequence of poems WW eventually published as "Calamus." The earlier sequence of twelve
poems, under the title "Live Oak, with Moss," appear on pp. 752–56 of this volume. Readers
interested in the recent critical controversy over the significance of the "Live Oak" sequence
and its relation to the "Calamus" section may consult Alan Helms, "Whitman's 'Live Oak
with Moss,' " in Robert K. Martin, ed., *The Continuing Presence of Walt Whitman: The Life
after the Life* (Iowa City: University of Iowa Press, 1992), 185–205; and Hershel Parker,
"The Real 'Live Oak, with Moss': Straight Talk about Whitman's 'Gay Manifesto,' "
Nineteenth-Century Literature 51, no. 2 (September 1996): 145–60.
    For the benefit of his English editor, W. M. Rosetti, WW defined his symbol as follows:
"Calamus is a common word here. It is the very large & aromatic grass, or rush, growing
about water-ponds in the valleys—spears about three feet high—often called 'sweet flag'—
grows all over the Northern and Middle States . . . The recherché or ethereal sense of the

Tallying and talk'd to here by tongues aromatic,
No longer abash'd, (for in this secluded spot I can respond as I
    would not dare elsewhere,)   10
Strong upon me the life that does not exhibit itself, yet
    contains all the rest,
Resolv'd to sing no songs to-day but those of manly
    attachment,
Projecting them along that substantial life,
Bequeathing hence types of athletic love,
Afternoon this delicious Ninth-month in my forty-first year,[2]   15
I proceed for all who are or have been young men,
To tell the secret of my nights and days,
To celebrate the need of comrades.
1860   1867

Scented Herbage of My Breast[3]

Scented herbage of my breast,
Leaves from you I glean, I write, to be perused best afterwards,
Tomb-leaves, body-leaves growing up above me above death,

---

term, as used in my book, arises probably from the actual Calamus presenting the biggest &
hardiest kind of spears of grass—and the fresh, acquatic, pungent bouquet" (*Corr.* I, 347).
That the symbol also possessed a specific sexual significance is apparent from its use five
years earlier in "Song of Myself" (see line 535). In response to John Addington Symonds's
implicitly hopeful inquiry about whether the "Calamus" sentiment might be homoerotic, the
aged WW may have protested too much, emphatically denying the possibility, and attempting
to quiet any doubts about his heterosexuality by claiming to have fathered six children (no
trace of whom has ever otherwise manifested itself).

    Both in *Democratic Vistas* and in his 1876 Preface to *LG*, WW was at pains to insist that
the meaning of "Calamus" resides mainly in its political significance,—e.g., "It is to the
development, identification, and general prevalence of that fervid comradeship, (the adhesive
love, at least rivaling the amative love hitherto possessing imaginative literature, if not going
beyond it,) that I look for the counterbalance and offset of our materialistic and vulgar
American democracy, and for the spiritualization thereof."

    Through the remaining six editions of *LG*, this group of poems retained its identity with
surprisingly little change. The forty-five poems of 1860 were reduced in 1867 to forty-two,
with three poems rejected; in 1871 one poem was added and four were transferred to *Passage
to India* to make a total of thirty-nine, which is the number retained for the final arrangement
of 1881.

2. September, 1859.
3. The second of the 1860 "Calamus" group, this poem remained substantially unchanged
   except for the dropping in 1881 of the following line after the present seventh line:

      O burning and throbbing—surely all will one day be accomplished;

The intricate symbolism of the "emblematic and capricious blades" is difficult to follow—
even the poet (line 22) cries that they serve him not, but it is clear that in this poignant
confession love has led him to think of death as a deliverance. D. H. Lawrence, reflecting
upon this poem (see *Studies in Classic American Literature,* 1922) remarks that "Whitman
is a very great poet, of the end of life." The exultant celebrator of life is also the solicitor of
death, which to him is not morbid, but beautiful. Esther Shephard has made the interesting
discovery that in his concept of tomb leaves growing out of his breast, WW was influenced
by poring over illustrations in Ippolito Rosellini's account of the Egyptians (Pisa, 1844),
which show the burial chamber of Osiris, from whose mummy are sprouting leaves of grain.
WW had seen the plates of the book in the Astor Library and wrote of it in *Life Illustrated,*
December 8, 1855. See Shephard, "Possible Sources of Some of Whitman's Ideas and Sym-
bols in *Hermes Mercurius Trismegistus* and Other Works," *MLQ* 14:60–81. See also the
selection by John Irwin in this volume, pp. 863–72.

Perennial roots, tall leaves, O the winter shall not freeze you
    delicate leaves,
Every year shall you bloom again, out from where you retired
    you shall emerge again;
O I do not know whether many passing by will discover you or
    inhale your faint odor, but I believe a few will;
O slender leaves! O blossoms of my blood! I permit you to tell
    in your own way of the heart that is under you,
O I do not know what you mean there underneath yourselves,
    you are not happiness,
You are often more bitter than I can bear, you burn and sting
    me,
Yet you are beautiful to me you faint tinged roots, you make
    me think of death,
Death is beautiful from you, (what indeed is finally beautiful
    except death and love?)
O I think it is not for life I am chanting here my chant of
    lovers, I think it must be for death,
For how calm, how solemn it grows to ascend to the
    atmosphere of lovers,
Death or life I am then indifferent, my soul declines to prefer,
(I am not sure but the high soul of lovers welcomes death
    most,)
Indeed O death, I think now these leaves mean precisely the
    same as you mean,
Grow up taller sweet leaves that I may see! grow up out of my
    breast!
Spring away from the conceal'd heart there!
Do not fold yourself so in your pink-tinged roots timid leaves!
Do not remain down there so ashamed, herbage of my breast!
Come I am determin'd to unbare this broad breast of mine, I
    have long enough stifled and choked;
Emblematic and capricious blades I leave you, now you serve
    me not,
I will say what I have to say by itself,
I will sound myself and comrades only, I will never again utter
    a call only their call,
I will raise with it immortal reverberations through the States,
I will give an example to lovers to take permanent shape and
    will through the States,
Through me shall the words be said to make death
    exhilarating,
Give me your tone therefore O death, that I may accord with it,
Give me yourself, for I see that you belong to me now above
    all, and are folded inseparably together, you love and
    death are,
Nor will I allow you to balk me any more with what I was
    calling life,
For now it is convey'd to me that you are the purports
    essential,

5

10

15

20

25

30

That you hide in these shifting forms of life, for reasons, and
    that they are mainly for you,
That you beyond them come forth to remain, the real reality,
That behind the mask of materials you patiently wait, no
    matter how long,
That you will one day perhaps take control of all,   35
That you will perhaps dissipate this entire show of appearance,
That may-be you are what it is all for, but it does not last so
    very long,
But you will last very long.
1860   1881

Whoever You Are Holding Me Now in Hand[4]

Whoever you are holding me now in hand,
Without one thing all will be useless,
I give you fair warning before you attempt me further,
I am not what you supposed, but far different.

Who is he that would become my follower?   5
Who would sign himself a candidate for my affections?

The way is suspicious, the result uncertain, perhaps destructive,
You would have to give up all else, I alone would expect to be
    your sole and exclusive standard,
Your novitiate would even then be long and exhausting,
The whole past theory of your life and all conformity to the
    lives around you would have to be abandon'd,   10
Therefore release me now before troubling yourself any
    further, let go your hand from my shoulders,
Put me down and depart on your way.

Or else by stealth in some wood for trial,
Or back of a rock in the open air,
(For in any roof'd room of a house I emerge not, nor in
    company,   15
And in libraries I lie as one dumb, a gawk, or unborn, or dead,)
But just possibly with you on a high hill, first watching lest
    any person for miles around approach unawares,
Or possibly with you sailing at sea, or on the beach of the sea
    or some quiet island,

---

4. This poem, the third of the 1860 "Calamus" group, underwent no substantial change after
taking its present title in 1867, although in his 1860 MS revisions the poet had considered
the title "These leaves conning, you con at peril." In the role of prophet or redeemer, the
poet makes his absolute demands upon his followers, offering challenges rather than assur-
ances. For more on this poem, see Allen Grossman, "Whitman's 'Whoever You Are, Holding
Me Now in Hand': Remarks on the Endlessly Repeated Rediscovery of the Incommensura-
bility of the Person," in Betsy Erkkila and Jay Grossman, eds., *Breaking Bounds: Whitman
and American Cultural Studies* (New York: Oxford University Press, 1996), 112–22.

Here to put your lips upon mine I permit you,
With the comrade's long-dwelling kiss or the new husband's
  kiss,   20
For I am the new husband and I am the comrade.

Or if you will, thrusting me beneath your clothing,[5]
Where I may feel the throbs of your heart or rest upon your hip,
Carry me when you go forth over land or sea;
For thus merely touching you is enough, is best,   25
And thus touching you would I silently sleep and be carried
  eternally.

But these leaves conning you con at peril,
For these leaves and me you will not understand,
They will elude you at first and still more afterward, I will
  certainly elude you,
Even while you should think you had unquestionably caught
  me, behold!   30
Already you see I have escaped from you.

For it is not for what I have put into it that I have written this book,
Nor is it by reading it you will acquire it,
Nor do those know me best who admire me and vauntingly
  praise me,
Nor will the candidates for my love (unless at most a very few)
  prove victorious,   35
Nor will my poems do good only, they will do just as much
  evil, perhaps more,
For all is useless without that which you may guess at many
  times and not hit, that which I hinted at;
Therefore release me and depart on your way.
  1860   *1881*

For You O Democracy[6]

Come, I will make the continent indissoluble,
I will make the most splendid race the sun ever shone upon,
I will make divine magnetic lands,
              With the love of comrades,
              With the life-long love of comrades.   5

---

5. The poet identifies himself with his book in the first 26 lines; however, in lines 27–38 he
   becomes the commentator.
6. In 1860 this poem was part of "Calamus" No. 5, a fifteen-stanza poem of forty-two lines. In
   1865 lines from the first twelve stanzas were rearranged, with additions, to make the *Drum-
   Taps* poem "Over the Carnage Rose Prophetic a Voice"; in 1867 the present poem was made
   from the last three stanzas, with the repetend added, and entitled "A Song." Under this title
   it again appeared in 1871 and 1876, and with the present title in 1881. In 1902 the first
   twelve stanzas in their original form were reprinted among the "Rejected Poems" under the
   title, "[States]," *q.v.* below: "Poems Excluded from *Leaves of Grass*."

I will plant companionship thick as trees along all the rivers of
     America, and along the shores of the great lakes, and all
     over the prairies,
I will make inseparable cities with their arms about each
     other's necks,
           By the love of comrades,
            By the manly love of comrades.

For you these from me, O Democracy, to serve you ma femme!   10
For you, for you I am trilling these songs.
1860   *1881*

These I Singing in Spring[7]

These I singing in spring collect for lovers,
(For who but I should understand lovers and all their sorrow
     and joy?
And who but I should be the poet of comrades?)
Collecting I traverse the garden the world, but soon I pass the
     gates,
Now along the pond-side, now wading in a little, fearing not
     the wet,   5
Now by the post-and-rail fences where the old stones thrown
     there, pick'd from the fields, have accumulated,
(Wild-flowers and vines and weeds come up through the
     stones and partly cover them, beyond these I pass,)
Far, far in the forest, or sauntering later in summer, before I
     think where I go,
Solitary, smelling the earthy smell, stopping now and then in
     the silence,
Alone I had thought, yet soon a troop gathers around me,   10
Some walk by my side and some behind, and some embrace
     my arms or neck,
They the spirits of dear friends dead or alive, thicker they
     come, a great crowd, and I in the middle,
Collecting, dispensing, singing, there I wander with them,
Plucking something for tokens, tossing toward whoever is near
     me,
Here, lilac, with a branch of pine,   15
Here, out of my pocket, some moss which I pull'd off a live-
     oak in Florida as it hung trailing down,
Here, some pinks and laurel leaves, and a handful of sage,
And here what I now draw from the water, wading in the
     pond-side,

7. The antecedent of "These" is apparently the "tokens" (line 14) that the poet collects for
lovers, but of them all only the calamus root, drawn from the water by the pond-side, pos-
sesses a special significance for those who "love as I myself am capable of loving." In his
1860 MS emendations, WW considered, but fortunately abandoned, the sentimental title,
"As I walk alone at candlelight." The poem took its present title in 1867 and remained
unchanged thereafter.

(O here I last saw him that tenderly loves me, and returns
    again never to separate from me,
And this, O this shall henceforth be the token of comrades,
    this calamus-root shall,   20
Interchange it youths with each other! let none render it back!)
And twigs of maple and a bunch of wild orange and chestnut,
And stems of currants and plum-blows, and the aromatic cedar,
These I compass'd around by a thick cloud of spirits,
Wandering, point to or touch as I pass, or throw them loosely
    from me,   25
Indicating to each one what he shall have, giving something to
    each;
But what I drew from the water by the pond-side, that I reserve,
I will give of it, but only to them that love as I myself am
    capable of loving.
1860   *1867*

Not Heaving from my Ribb'd Breast Only[8]

Not heaving from my ribb'd breast only,
Not in sighs at night in rage dissatisfied with myself,
Not in those long-drawn, ill-supprest sighs,
Not in many an oath and promise broken,
Not in my wilful and savage soul's volition,   5
Not in the subtle nourishment of the air,
Not in this beating and pounding at my temples and wrists,
Not in the curious systole and diastole within which will one
    day cease,
Not in many a hungry wish told to the skies only,
Not in cries, laughter, defiances, thrown from me when alone
    far in the wilds,   10
Not in husky pantings through clinch'd teeth,
Not in sounded and resounded words, chattering words,
    echoes, dead words,
Not in the murmurs of my dreams while I sleep,
Nor the other murmurs of these incredible dreams of every day,
Nor in the limbs and senses of my body that take you and
    dismiss you continually—not there,   15
Not in any or all of them O adhesiveness![9] O pulse of my life!
Need I that you exist and show yourself any more than in
    these songs.
1860   *1867*

8. No. 6 of the "Calamus" group in 1860, this poem remained unchanged through all editions,
taking its title in 1867.
9. This is a phrenological term, meaning the propensity for friendship between persons of the
same sex; for WW, "adhesiveness" sometimes signifies an intense, even passionate, bond.
See Michael Lynch, " 'Here Is Adhesiveness': From Friendship to Homosexuality," *Victorian
Studies* 29, no. 1 (Autumn 1985): 67–96.

Of the Terrible Doubt of Appearances[1]

Of the terrible doubt of appearances,
Of the uncertainty after all, that we may be deluded,
That may-be reliance and hope are but speculations after all,
That may-be identity beyond the grave is a beautiful fable only,
May-be the things I perceive, the animals, plants, men, hills,
    shining and flowing waters,   5
The skies of day and night, colors, densities, forms, may-be
    these are (as doubtless they are) only apparitions, and the
    real something has yet to be known,
(How often they dart out of themselves as if to confound me
    and mock me!
How often I think neither I know, nor any man knows, aught
    of them,)
May-be seeming to me what they are (as doubtless they indeed
    but seem) as from my present point of view, and might
    prove (as of course they would) nought of what they
    appear, or nought anyhow, from entirely changed points of
    view;
To me these and the like of these are curiously answer'd by my
    lovers, my dear friends,   10
When he whom I love travels with me or sits a long while
    holding me by the hand,
When the subtle air, the impalpable, the sense that words and
    reason hold not, surround us and pervade us,
Then I am charged with untold and untellable wisdom, I am
    silent, I require nothing further,
I cannot answer the question of appearances or that of identity
    beyond the grave,
But I walk or sit indifferent, I am satisfied,   15
He ahold of my hand has completely satisfied me.
1860   *1867*

The Base of All Metaphysics[2]

And now gentlemen,
A word I give to remain in your memories and minds,
As base and finalè[3] too for all metaphysics.

---

1. Compare with lines 32–33 of "Scented Herbage of my Breast" in which the "real reality" is
   contrasted with "these shifting forms of life." Here the same idea—that only love confirms
   reality—is developed into powerful form. This "Calamus" No. 7 was given its present title
   in 1867. It is interesting that in his 1860 revisions WW deleted the syntactically involved
   line 9, and then decided to let it stand.
2. This poem, added to the "Calamus" group in 1871, sublimates the sentiment of "adhesive-
   ness" to lofty universal principle. A MS draft (BPL) has the title, "The Professor's Answer."
3. The incorrect use of an accent was introduced in the Osgood *LG* 1881 and prevails in all
   later editions, including the final *LG* 1892.

(So to the students the old professor,
At the close of his crowded course.)   5

Having studied the new and antique, the Greek and Germanic
    systems,
Kant having studied and stated, Fichte and Schelling and Hegel,
Stated the lore of Plato, and Socrates greater than Plato,
And greater than Socrates sought and stated, Christ divine
    having studied long,
I see reminiscent to-day those Greek and Germanic systems,   10
See the philosophies all, Christian churches and tenets see,
Yet underneath Socrates clearly see, and underneath Christ
    the divine I see,
The dear love of man for his comrade, the attraction of friend
    to friend,
Of the well-married husband and wife, of children and parents,
Of city for city and land for land.   15
1871   *1871*

Recorders Ages Hence[4]

Recorders ages hence,
Come, I will take you down underneath this impassive exterior,
    I will tell you what to say of me,
Publish my name and hang up my picture as that of the
    tenderest lover,
The friend the lover's portrait, of whom his friend his lover
    was fondest,
Who was not proud of his songs, but of the measureless ocean
    of love within him, and freely pour'd it forth,   5
Who often walk'd lonesome walks thinking of his dear friends,
    his lovers,
Who pensive away from one he lov'd often lay sleepless and
    dissatisfied at night,
Who knew too well the sick, sick dread lest the one he lov'd
    might secretly be indifferent to him,
Whose happiest days were far away through fields, in woods,
    on hills, he and another wandering hand in hand, they
    twain apart from other men,
Who oft as he saunter'd the streets curv'd with his arm the
    shoulder of his friend, while the arm of his friend rested
    upon him also.   10
1860   *1867*

---

4. Both the MS (Barrett) and the 1860 text of this poem began with the following two lines,
dropped in 1867 when it tooks its present title and form:

    You bards of ages hence! when you refer to me, mind not so much my poems,
    Nor speak of me that I prophesied of The States, and led them the way of their glories;

When I Heard at the Close of the Day[5]

When I heard at the close of the day how my name had been
    receiv'd with plaudits in the capitol, still it was not a
    happy night for me that follow'd,
And else when I carous'd, or when my plans were
    accomplish'd, still I was not happy,
But the day when I rose at dawn from the bed of perfect
    health, refresh'd, singing, inhaling the ripe breath of
    autumn,
When I saw the full moon in the west grow pale and disappear
    in the morning light,
When I wander'd alone over the beach, and undressing bathed,
    laughing with the cool waters, and saw the sun rise,   5
And when I thought how my dear friend my lover was on his
    way coming, O then I was happy,
O then each breath tasted sweeter, and all that day my food
    nourish'd me more, and the beautiful day pass'd well,
And the next came with equal joy, and with the next at
    evening came my friend,
And that night while all was still I heard the waters roll slowly
    continually up the shores,
I heard the hissing rustle of the liquid and sands as directed to
    me whispering to congratulate me,   10
For the one I love most lay sleeping by me under the same
    cover in the cool night,
In the stillness in the autumn moonbeams his face was
    inclined toward me,
And his arm lay lightly around my breast—and that night I
    was happy.

1860   *1867*

Are You the New Person Drawn toward Me?[6]

Are you the new person drawn toward me?
To begin with take warning, I am surely far different from
    what you suppose;
Do you suppose you will find in me your ideal?
Do you think it so easy to have me become your lover?
Do you think the friendship of me would be unalloy'd
    satisfaction?   5
Do you think I am trusty and faithful?

5. Both this poem ("Calamus" No. 11) and the preceding poem ("Calamus" No. 10) were
originally indicated with Roman numerals III and VII respectively in the series of twelve
poems, apparently so numbered in the MS (Barrett) in order to commemorate a single epi-
sode. This poem remained unchanged after taking its present title in 1867.
6. The MS (Barrett) of this "Calamus" No. 12 has a more intimate title, "To a new personal
admirer." In his 1860 revisions WW had made the marginal notation "Out without fail" for
the whole poem, but instead he dropped the final two-and-one-half lines of the 1860 text
and reprinted it in the next edition under the present title.

Do you see no further than this façade, this smooth and
tolerant manner of me?
Do you suppose yourself advancing on real ground toward a
real heroic man?
Have you no thought O dreamer that it may be all maya,
illusion?
1860   *1867*

Roots and Leaves Themselves Alone[7]

Roots and leaves themselves alone are these,
Scents brought to men and women from the wild woods and
pond-side,
Breast-sorrel and pinks of love, fingers that wind around
tighter than vines,
Gushes from the throats of birds hid in the foliage of trees as
the sun is risen,
Breezes of land and love set from living shores to you on the
living sea, to you O sailors!   5
Frost-mellow'd berries and Third-month twigs offer'd fresh to
young persons wandering out in the fields when the
winter breaks up,
Love-buds put before you and within you whoever you are,
Buds to be unfolded on the old terms,
If you bring the warmth of the sun to them they will open and
bring form, color, perfume, to you,
If you become the aliment and the wet they will become
flowers, fruits, tall branches and trees.   10
1860   *1867*

Not Heat Flames Up and Consumes[8]

Not heat flames up and consumes,
Not sea-waves hurry in and out,
Not the air delicious and dry, the air of ripe summer, bears
lightly along white down-balls of myriads of seeds,
Wafted, sailing gracefully, to drop where they may;
Not these, O none of these more than the flames of me,
consuming, burning for his love whom I love,   5
O none more than I hurrying in and out;

---

7. WW improved the 1867 text of this "Calamus" No. 13 by dropping the first two lines and
the last three from the poem. The opening lines of the 1860 text had read:

Calamus taste,
(For I must change the strain—these are not to be pensive leaves, but leaves of joy,)

and the original MS (Barrett) title was "Buds."
8. This "Calamus" No. 14, unchanged since it took its present title in 1867, was originally, as
the MS (Barrett) shows, numbered I in the Roman numeral series already referred to, and it
carried the title "Calamus-Leaves," altered from a still earlier title, "Live Oak, with Moss."
See the poetic sequence which WW wrote under this title, on pp. 752–57 of this volume.

Does the tide hurry, seeking something, and never give up? O
    I the same,
O nor down-balls nor perfumes, nor the high rain-emitting
    clouds, are borne through the open air,
Any more than my soul is borne through the open air,
Wafted in all directions O love, for friendship, for you.   10
   1860   1867

Trickle Drops[9]

Trickle drops! my blue veins leaving!
O drops of me! trickle, slow drops,
Candid from me falling, drip, bleeding drops,
From wounds made to free you whence you were prison'd,
From my face, from my forehead and lips,   5
From my breast, from within where I was conceal'd, press
    forth red drops, confession drops,
Stain every page, stain every song I sing, every word I say,
    bloody drops,
Let them know your scarlet heat, let them glisten,
Saturate them with yourself all ashamed and wet,
Glow upon all I have written or shall write, bleeding drops,   10
Let it all be seen in your light, blushing drops.
   1860   1867

City of Orgies[1]

City of orgies, walks and joys,
City whom that I have lived and sung in your midst will one
    day make you illustrious,
Not the pageants of you, not your shifting tableaus, your
    spectacles, repay me,
Not the interminable rows of your houses, nor the ships at the
    wharves,
Nor the processions in the streets, nor the bright windows with
    goods in them,   5
Nor to converse with learn'd persons, or bear my share in the
    soiree or feast;
Not those, but as I pass O Manhattan, your frequent and swift
    flash of eyes offering me love,
Offering response to my own—these repay me,
Lovers, continual lovers, only repay me.
   1860   1867

9. The first line of this "Calamus" No. 15 was added in 1867. There were no further changes. The 1860 MS (Barrett) has the title "Confession Drops," which supports the meaning of line 6.
1. Compare this poem with the *Drum-Taps* poem "City of Ships," also celebrating Manhattan, but with a different emphasis. In the MS (Barrett), the name of the city is not given. The poem, originally "Calamus" No. 18, has remained unchanged since it took its title in 1867.

Behold This Swarthy Face[2]

Behold this swarthy face, these gray eyes,
This beard, the white wool unclipt upon my neck,
My brown hands and the silent manner of me without charm;
Yet comes one a Manhattanese and ever at parting kisses me
    lightly on the lips with robust love,
And I on the crossing of the street or on the ship's deck give a
    kiss in return,   5
We observe that salute of American comrades land and sea,
We are those two natural and nonchalant persons.
  1860   *1871*

I Saw in Louisiana a Live-Oak Growing[3]

I saw in Louisiana a live-oak growing,
All alone stood it and the moss hung down from the branches,
Without any companion it grew there uttering joyous leaves of
    dark green,
And its look, rude, unbending, lusty, made me think of myself,
But I wonder'd how it could utter joyous leaves standing alone
    there without its friend near, for I knew I could not,   5
And I broke off a twig with a certain number of leaves upon it,
    and twined around it a little moss,
And brought it away, and I have placed it in sight in my room,
It is not needed to remind me as of my own dear friends,
(For I believe lately I think of little else than of them,)
Yet it remains to me a curious token, it makes me think of
    manly love;   10
For all that, and though the live-oak glistens there in
    Louisiana solitary in a wide flat space,
Uttering joyous leaves all its life without a friend a lover near,
I know very well I could not.
  1860   *1867*

---

2. WW improved the 1860 version of this "Calamus" No. 19 by omitting for the next edition
the opening two-line stanza:

> Mind you the timid models of the rest, the majority?
> Long I minded them, but hence I will not—for I have
>   adopted models for myself, and now offer them to The
>   Lands.

3. Two MSS of this poem (Barrett, Berg) show little revision except for line rearrangement. It
is numbered II in the Roman numeral series and No. 20 of the 1860 "Calamus" group,
receiving its title and final text in 1867.

To a Stranger[4]

Passing stranger! you do not know how longingly I look upon
    you,
You must be he I was seeking, or she I was seeking, (it comes
    to me as of a dream,)
I have somewhere surely lived a life of joy with you,
All is recall'd as we flit by each other, fluid, affectionate,
    chaste, matured,
You grew up with me, were a boy with me or a girl with me,   5
I ate with you and slept with you, your body has become not
    yours only nor left my body mine only,
You give me the pleasure of your eyes, face, flesh, as we pass,
    you take of my beard, breast, hands, in return,
I am not to speak to you, I am to think of you when I sit alone
    or wake at night alone,
I am to wait, I do not doubt I am to meet you again,
I am to see to it that I do not lose you.   10
1860   *1867*

This Moment Yearning and Thoughtful[5]

This moment yearning and thoughtful sitting alone,
It seems to me there are other men in other lands yearning
    and thoughtful,
It seems to me I can look over and behold them in Germany,
    Italy, France, Spain,
Or far, far away, in China, or in Russia or Japan, talking other
    dialects,
And it seems to me if I could know those men I should
    become attached to them as I do to men in my own lands,   5
O I know we should be brethren and lovers,
I know I should be happy with them.
1860   *1881*

---

4. The MS (Barrett) of this poem, "Calamus" No. 22, gives it the present title, printed in 1867
without further changes.
5. This "Calamus" No. 23 was designated in MS (Barrett) as IV in Roman numerals. In 1867
a line following the present fourth line,

    It seems to me they are as wise, beautiful, benevolent, as any in my own lands;—

was dropped, and in 1881 the present lines 3 and 4 were constructed from the former
line 3.

I Hear It Was Charged against Me[6]

I hear it was charged against me that I sought to destroy
    institutions,
But really I am neither for nor against institutions,
(What indeed have I in common with them? or what with the
    destruction of them?)
Only I will establish in the Mannahatta and in every city of
    these States inland and seaboard,
And in the fields and woods, and above every keel little or
    large that dents the water,   5
Without edifices or rules or trustees or any argument,
The institution of the dear love of comrades.
    1860   *1867*

The Prairie-Grass Dividing[7]

The prairie-grass dividing, its special odor breathing,
I demand of it the spiritual corresponding,
Demand the most copious and close companionship of men,
Demand the blades to rise of words, acts, beings,
Those of the open atmosphere, coarse, sunlit, fresh, nutritious,   5
Those that go their own gait, erect, stepping with freedom and
    command, leading not following,
Those with a never-quell'd audacity, those with sweet and lusty
    flesh clear of taint,
Those that look carelessly in the faces of Presidents and
    governors, as to say *Who are you?*
Those of earth-born passion, simple, never constrain'd, never
    obedient,
Those of inland America.   10
    1860   *1867*

When I Peruse the Conquer'd Fame[8]

When I peruse the conquer'd fame of heroes and the victories
    of mighty generals, I do not envy the generals,
Nor the President in his Presidency, nor the rich in his great
    house,

---

6. In 1860 the first line of this "Calamus" No. 24 was in present tense. There were no further changes after the poem took its title in 1867. The poem is to be taken, not as a reaction to a specific charge, but as the spirited rhetorical challenge of a man whose visionary utterance is not to be confined by the institutional.
7. In 1860 the first line of this "Calamus" No. 25 read "own" for "special"; and "choice and chary of its love-power," followed "taint," in line 7. The poem took its present title and form in 1867.
8. WW considered the title "When I perused the fame of heroes" in his 1860 MS revisions of this "Calamus" No. 28, but he gave it the present title in 1867. There were very minor alterations in 1871.

But when I hear of the brotherhood of lovers, how it was with
    them,
How together through life, through dangers, odium,
    unchanging, long and long,
Through youth and through middle and old age, how
    unfaltering, how affectionate and faithful they were,   5
Then I am pensive—I hastily walk away fill'd with the bitterest
    envy.
1860   *1871*

We Two Boys Together Clinging[9]

We two boys together clinging,
One the other never leaving,
Up and down the roads going, North and South excursions
    making,
Power enjoying, elbows stretching, fingers clutching,
Arm'd and fearless, eating, drinking, sleeping, loving,   5
No law less than ourselves owning, sailing, soldiering, thieving,
    threatening,
Misers, menials, priests alarming, air breathing, water drinking,
    on the turf or the sea-beach dancing,
Cities wrenching, ease scorning, statutes mocking, feebleness
    chasing,
Fulfilling our foray.
1860   *1867*

A Promise to California[1]

A promise to California,
Or inland to the great pastoral Plains, and on to Puget sound
    and Oregon;
Sojourning east a while longer, soon I travel toward you, to
    remain, to teach robust American love,
For I know very well that I and robust love belong among you,
    inland, and along the Western sea;
For these States tend inland and toward the Western sea, and
    I will also.   5
1860   *1867*

---

9. The following line, dropped in 1867, appeared after the present seventh line in the 1860
text of this "Calamus" No. 26:

    With birds singing—With fishes swimming—With trees branching and leafing,

In the Barrett MS WW headed the poem with the exotic title "Razzia," a word of Arabic
origin meaning "raid" or "foray." The poem took its present title in 1867.

1. The MS (Barrett) of this "Calamus" No. 30 makes no mention of California, the first line
reading "A promise to Indiana, Nebraska, Kansas, Iowa, Minnesota, and others:" nor is there
any mention in the text of "robust American love." The poem took its present title in 1867.

Here the Frailest Leaves of Me[2]

Here the frailest leaves of me and yet my strongest lasting,
Here I shade and hide my thoughts, I myself do not expose
    them,
And yet they expose me more than all my other poems.
    1860   *1871*

No Labor-Saving Machine[3]

No labor-saving machine,
Nor discovery have I made,
Nor will I be able to leave behind me any wealthy bequest to
    found a hospital or library,
Nor reminiscence of any deed of courage for America,
Nor literary success nor intellect, nor book for the book-shelf,   5
But a few carols vibrating through the air I leave,
For comrades and lovers.
    1860   *1881*

A Glimpse[4]

A glimpse through an interstice caught,
Of a crowd of workmen and drivers in a bar-room around the
    stove late of a winter night, and I unremark'd seated in a
    corner,
Of a youth who loves me and whom I love, silently
    approaching and seating himself near, that he may hold
    me by the hand,
A long while amid the noises of coming and going, of drinking
    and oath and smutty jest,
There we two, content, happy in being together, speaking little,
    perhaps not a word.   5
    1860   *1867*

---

2. The 1860 text of this "Calamus" No. 44 opened with the line (not in the Barrett MS) "Here
   my last words, and the most baffling," subsequently dropped in 1867. The poem took its
   present title in 1867.
3. The opening phrase of the sixth line of this "Calamus" No. 33, reading "Only these carols,"
   was changed in 1867 to read "Only a few carols," and in 1881 to "But a few carols." It took
   its present title in 1867.
4. The first line of this "Calamus" No. 29 was very slightly revised in 1867, and 1860 MS
   revisions indicate that WW had considered the more extended title "A Glimpse Caught
   Through an Interstice."

A Leaf for Hand in Hand[5]

A leaf for hand in hand;
You natural persons old and young!
You on the Mississippi and on all the branches and bayous of
    the Mississippi!
You friendly boatmen and mechanics! you roughs!
You twain! and all processions moving along the streets!   5
I wish to infuse myself among you till I see it common for you
    to walk hand in hand.
  1860   *1867*

Earth, My Likeness[6]

Earth, my likeness,
Though you look so impassive, ample and spheric there,
I now suspect that is not all;
I now suspect there is something fierce in you eligible to burst
    forth,
For an athlete is enamour'd of me, and I of him,   5
But toward him there is something fierce and terrible in me
    eligible to burst forth,
I dare not tell it in words, not even in these songs.
  1860   *1867*

I Dream'd in a Dream[7]

I dream'd in a dream I saw a city invincible to the attacks of
    the whole of the rest of the earth,
I dream'd that was the new city of Friends,
Nothing was greater there than the quality of robust love, it
    led the rest,
It was seen every hour in the actions of the men of that city,
And in all their looks and words.   5
  1860   *1867*

---

5. WW's MS version (Barrett) of this "Calamus" No. 37 (see Bowers, 112) may be preferred to
    its first text (1860), which, incidentally, included in line 2 the phrase "You on the Eastern
    Sea, and you on the Western!" dropped in 1867 when the poem took its present title and
    form.
6. In the Barrett MS this "Calamus" No. 36 is numbered XI, but in another MS (Feinberg) it is
    marked as VI. The poem took its present title in 1867 but otherwise remained unchanged.
7. Compare this "Calamus" No. 34 with the Barrett MS reading (Bowers, 114), whose phrasing
    is simpler and more direct. It is numbered IX in the Roman numeral series. The poem has
    remained unchanged since it took its present title in 1867.

What Think You I Take My Pen in Hand?[8]

What think you I take my pen in hand to record?
The battle-ship, perfect-model'd, majestic, that I saw pass the
    offing to-day under full sail?
The splendors of the past day? or the splendor of the night
    that envelops me?
Or the vaunted glory and growth of the great city spread
    around me?—no;
But merely of two simple men I saw to-day on the pier in the
    midst of the crowd, parting the parting of dear friends,   5
The one to remain hung on the other's neck and passionately
    kiss'd him,
While the one to depart tightly prest the one to remain in his
    arms.
1860   *1881*

To the East and to the West[9]

To the East and to the West,
To the man of the Seaside State and of Pennsylvania,
To the Kanadian of the north, to the Southerner I love,
These with perfect trust to depict you as myself, the germs are
    in all men,
I believe the main purport of these States is to found a superb
    friendship, exaltè, previously unknown,   5
Because I perceive it waits, and has been always waiting, latent
    in all men.
1860   *1867*

Sometimes with One I Love[1]

Sometimes with one I love I fill myself with rage for fear I
    effuse unreturn'd love,
But now I think there is no unreturn'd love, the pay is certain
    one way or another,

---

8. The Barrett MS of this "Calamus" No. 32 shows it to be VI in the Roman numeral series. It
has remained unchanged since it took its present title in 1867, except for the substitution
in 1881 of "But merely" for "But I record" in the beginning of the fifth line.
9. In 1860 the first line of this "Calamus" No. 35 read, "To you of New England"; this was
excluded under the present title in 1867.
1. Both the MS (Barrett) and the 1860 text of this "Calamus" No. 39 conclude with a third
line, as follows:

> Doubtless I could not have perceived the universe,
>   or written one of my poems, if I had not freely
>   given myself to comrades, to love.

The poem took its title and present reading in 1867.

(I loved a certain person ardently and my love was not return'd,
Yet out of that I have written these songs.)
1860   1867

To a Western Boy[2]

Many things to absorb I teach to help you become eleve[3] of
     mine;
Yet if blood like mine circle not in your veins,
If you be not silently selected by lovers and do not silently
     select lovers,
Of what use is it that you seek to become eleve of mine?
1860   1881

Fast Anchor'd Eternal O Love![4]

Fast-anchor'd eternal O love! O woman I love!
O bride! O wife! more resistless than I can tell, the thought of
     you!
Then separate, as disembodied or another born,
Ethereal, the last athletic reality, my consolation,
I ascend, I float in the regions of your love O man,   5
O sharer of my roving life.
1860   1867

Among the Multitude[5]

Among the men and women the multitude,
I perceive one picking me out by secret and divine signs,
Acknowledging none else, not parent, wife, husband, brother,
     child, any nearer than I am,
Some are baffled, but that one is not—that one knows me.

Ah lover and perfect equal,   5
I meant that you should discover me so by faint indirections,
And I when I meet you mean to discover you by the like in
     you.
1860   1881

---

2. The MS (Barrett) of this "Calamus" No. 42 shows it to be XII in the Roman numeral series.
   In 1867 it received its present title and an opening line, "O Boy of the West!" that was
   dropped, with some further minor revision, in 1881.
3. Pupil.
4. Both in the Barrett MS and in the 1860 text, the first line of this "Calamus" No. 38 read,
   "Primeval my love for the woman I love." In all editions, "Fast-anchor'd" lacks the hyphen
   in the title.
5. This "Calamus" No. 41 is but slightly revised from its original in the Barrett MS and 1860
   text. It took its present title in 1867. Note the echo of line 6 in the phrase "faint clews and
   indirections" in the 1867 "Inscription," "When I Read the Book."

O You Whom I Often and Silently Come[6]

O you whom I often and silently come where you are that I
    may be with you,
As I walk by your side or sit near, or remain in the same room
    with you,
Little you know the subtle electric fire that for your sake is
    playing within me.
1860   *1867*

That Shadow My Likeness[7]

That shadow my likeness that goes to and fro seeking a
    livelihood, chattering, chaffering,[8]
How often I find myself standing and looking at it where it flits,
How often I question and doubt whether that is really me;
But among my lovers and caroling these songs,
O I never doubt whether that is really me.   5
1860   *1881*

Full of Life Now[9]

Full of life now, compact, visible,
I, forty years old the eighty-third year of the States,
To one a century hence or any number of centuries hence,
To you yet unborn these, seeking you.

When you read these I that was visible am become invisible,   5
Now it is you, compact, visible, realizing my poems, seeking me,
Fancying how happy you were if I could be with you and
    become your comrade;
Be it as if I were with you. (Be not too certain but I am now
    with you.)
1860   *1871*

---

6. This "Calamus" No. 43, whose MS (Barrett) designates it as X of the Roman numeral series, has remained unchanged through all the editions, taking its present title in 1867.
7. The gist of this poem, "Calamus" No. 40, is contained in three lines jotted down in an 1859 notebook (LC 89) transcribed in *UPP*, II, 91. It took its title in 1867, and its fourth line was slightly revised in 1881.
8. Bantering. This is a meaning, long in use, from "chaffer" (noun, fl. ca. 1850), a banterer or a joker at the expense of others (Partridge, *A Dictionary of Slang and Unconventional English*, 1961).
9. The MS (Barrett) of this "Calamus" No. 45 contains the rejected opening line

      Throwing far, throwing over the head of death, I, full of affection,

and its second line (now the first and second lines) reads "thirty-eight years old the eighty-first year of The States," indicating that WW composed the poem in 1857. It took its present title in 1867; it was slightly revised then, and also in 1871.

Salut au Monde![1]

1

O take my hand Walt Whitman!
Such gliding wonders! such sights and sounds!
Such join'd unended links, each hook'd to the next,
Each answering all, each sharing the earth with all.

What widens within you Walt Whitman?   5
What waves and soils exuding?
What climes? what persons and cities are here?
Who are the infants, some playing, some slumbering?
Who are the girls? who are the married women?
Who are the groups of old men going slowly with their arms
    about each other's necks?   10
What rivers are these? what forests and fruits are these?
What are the mountains call'd that rise so high in the mists?
What myriads of dwellings are they fill'd with dwellers?

2

Within me latitude widens, longitude lengthens,
Asia, Africa, Europe, are to the east—America is provided for
    in the west,   15
Banding the bulge of the earth winds the hot equator,
Curiously north and south turn the axis-ends,
Within me is the longest day, the sun wheels in slanting rings,
    it does not set for months,
Stretch'd in due time within me the midnight sun just rises
    above the horizon and sinks again,
Within me zones, seas, cataracts, forests, volcanoes, groups,   20
Malaysia, Polynesia, and the great West Indian islands.

3

What do you hear Walt Whitman?

I hear the workman singing and the farmer's wife singing,
I hear in the distance the sounds of children and of animals
    early in the day,
I hear emulous shouts of Australians pursuing the wild horse,   25

---

1. The third poem of the second edition of *LG* 1856, under the title "Poem of Salutation," this poem took its present title in 1860. In his 1855 Preface WW had said of the American bard that "to him the other continents arrive as contributions"; and so, early in the development of *LG*, he undertook to express a world vision—"within me latitude widens, longitude lengthens"—that tempered and balanced his nationalism. His revisions were fairly constant but preserved the general proportion. Notably, he added in 1860 the effective salutation of the closing four lines, and for the final 1881 version he removed, with discrimination, quite a number of lines that were descriptive of the United States, so limiting his point of view outward from America to other lands. In composing his poem, WW was much influenced by his reading of Volney's *Ruins*. See Betsy Erkkila, *Whitman Among the French* (Princeton, N.J.: Princeton University Press, 1980), 14–19.

I hear the Spanish dance with castanets in the chestnut shade,
    to the rebeck and guitar,
I hear continual echoes from the Thames,
I hear fierce French liberty songs,
I hear of the Italian boat-sculler the musical recitative of old
    poems,
I hear the locusts in Syria as they strike the grain and grass
    with the showers of their terrible clouds,   30
I hear the Coptic refrain toward sundown, pensively falling on
    the breast of the black venerable vast mother the Nile,
I hear the chirp of the Mexican muleteer, and the bells of the
    mule,
I hear the Arab muezzin calling from the top of the mosque,
I hear the Christian priests at the altars of their churches, I
    hear the responsive base² and soprano,
I hear the cry of the Cossack, and the sailor's voice putting to
    sea at Okotsk,³   35
I hear the wheeze of the slave-coffle⁴ as the slaves march on,
    as the husky gangs pass on by twos and threes, fasten'd
    together with wrist-chains and ankle-chains,
I hear the Hebrew reading his records and psalms,
I hear the rhythmic myths of the Greeks, and the strong
    legends of the Romans,
I hear the tale of the divine life and bloody death of the
    beautiful God the Christ,
I hear the Hindoo teaching his favorite pupil the loves, wars,
    adages, transmitted safely to this day from poets who
    wrote three thousand years ago.   40

4

What do you see Walt Whitman?
Who are they you salute, and that one after another salute you?

I see a great round wonder rolling through space,
I see diminute farms, hamlets, ruins, graveyards, jails,
    factories, palaces, hovels, huts of barbarians, tents of
    nomads upon the surface,
I see the shaded part on one side where the sleepers are
    sleeping, and the sunlit part on the other side,
I see the curious rapid change of the light and shade,   45
I see distant lands, as real and near to the inhabitants of them
    as my land is to me.

I see plenteous waters,
I see mountain peaks, I see the sierras of Andes where they
    range,

---

2. Properly, "bass," in harmonic music the lower range of instrument or voice.
3. Seaport of eastern Siberia.
4. Slave caravan.

I see plainly the Himalayas, Chian Shahs, Altays, Ghauts,[5]   50
I see the giant pinnacles of Elbruz, Kazbek, Bazardjusi,[6]
I see the Styrian Alps, and the Karnac Alps,[7]
I see the Pyrenees, Balks, Carpathians, and to the north the
    Dofrafields, and off at sea mount Hecla,[8]
I see Vesuvius and Etna, the mountains of the Moon,[9] and the
    Red mountains of Madagascar,
I see the Lybian, Arabian, and Asiatic deserts,   55
I see huge dreadful Arctic and Antarctic icebergs,
I see the superior oceans and the inferior ones, the Atlantic
    and Pacific, the sea of Mexico, the Brazilian sea, and the
    sea of Peru,
The waters of Hindustan, the China sea, and the gulf of Guinea,
The Japan waters, the beautiful bay of Nagasaki[1] land-lock'd in
    its mountains,
The spread of the Baltic, Caspian, Bothnia, the British shores,
    and the bay of Biscay,   60
The clear-sunn'd Mediterranean, and from one to another of
    its islands,
The White sea, and the sea around Greenland.

I behold the mariners of the world,
Some are in storms, some in the night with the watch on the
    lookout,
Some drifting helplessly, some with contagious diseases.   65

I behold the sail and steamships of the world, some in clusters
    in port, some on their voyages,
Some double the cape of Storms, some cape Verde, others
    capes Guardafui, Bon, or Bajadore,[2]
Others Dondra head, others pass the straits of Sunda, others
    cape Lopatka, others Behring's straits,[3]
Others cape Horn, others sail the gulf of Mexico or along
    Cuba or Hayti, others Hudson's bay or Baffin's bay,
Others pass the straits of Dover, others enter the Wash, others
    the firth of Solway, others round cape Clear, others the
    Land's End,   70
Others traverse the Zuyder Zee or the Scheld,[4]
Others as comers and goers at Gibraltar or the Dardanelles,

5. Mountain systems in China, Siberia, and British India respectively.
6. Mountain peaks in the Caucasus.
7. Austrian and Italian Alps.
8. Volcano in southwest Iceland.
9. A range placed by Ptolemy in the interior of Africa.
1. Reads "Nagusaki" in the softbound, but not in the hardbound issue of 1891–92. The error
   occurred in 1881, was corrected in *LG* 1889.
2. *Cape of Storms*: the name given by Bartholomeu Dias to the Cape of Good Hope; *cape Verde*:
   westernmost point of Africa; *Guardafui*: northeastern extremity of the Somali country, Africa;
   Bon: northeast Tunis, Africa; *Bajadore*: unidentified.
3. *Dondra head*: southernmost cape of Ceylon; *straits of Sunda*: sea passage separating Sumatra
   and Java; *cape Lopatka*: southern extremity of Kamchatka.
4. River of France, Belgium, and the Netherlands, flowing to the North Sea. Now spelled
   Schelde or Scheldt.

Others sternly push their way through the northern winter-packs,
Others descend or ascend the Obi or the Lena,[5]
Others the Niger or the Congo, others the Indus, the
    Burampooter and Cambodia,[6]   75
Others wait steam'd up ready to start in the ports of Australia,
Wait at Liverpool, Glasgow, Dublin, Marseilles, Lisbon,
    Naples, Hamburg, Bremen, Bordeaux, the Hague,
    Copenhagen,
Wait at Valparaiso, Rio Janeiro, Panama.

5

I see the tracks of the railroads of the earth,
I see them in Great Britain, I see them in Europe,   80
I see them in Asia and in Africa.

I see the electric telegraphs of the earth,
I see the filaments of the news of the wars, deaths, losses,
    gains, passions, of my race.

I see the long river-stripes of the earth,
I see the Amazon and the Paraguay,   85
I see the four great rivers of China, the Amour,[7] the Yellow
    River, the Yiang-tse, and the Pearl,
I see where the Seine flows, and where the Danube, the Loire,
    the Rhone, and the Guadalquiver[8] flow,
I see the windings of the Volga, the Dnieper, the Oder,[9]
I see the Tuscan going down the Arno, and the Venetian along
    the Po,
I see the Greek seaman sailing out of Egina bay.   90

6

I see the site of the old empire of Assyria, and that of Persia,
    and that of India,
I see the falling of the Ganges over the high rim of Saukara.[1]

---

5. *Obi:* inlet of Arctic Ocean, north of Siberia; *Lena:* one of the chief rivers of Siberia.
6. *Niger or the Congo:* African rivers; *Indus, the Burampooter and Cambodia:* Asian rivers.
7. Whitman's spelling for Amur, a river of East Asia.
8. River in southern Spain.
9. One of the chief rivers of Germany.
1. Probably a misspelling for "Sankara" in WW's source, reflected in his MS and in the first
    edition of the poem, 1856. Sankara is a familiar alternative name for Siva, in ancient Hindu
    literature the male divinity associated with both destruction and rebirth, hence fertility. From
    the head of Siva, or Sankara, sprang the Ganges, cascading over "the high rim" of his hair,
    which was piled in rows of curls above the brow. The present line and the next are the
    remnant of four in the MS, which substantiate the idea above:
        The Sanscrit—the ancient poems and laws;
        The idea of Gods incarnated by their avatars in man and woman;
        The falling of the waters of the Ganges over the high rim of Saukara;
        The poems descended safely to this day from poets of three thousand years ago.
    For the identification of Sankara (Shankara) with Siva (Shiva) see p. 22, and for the fall of
    the Ganges see p. 104, in P. Thomas, *Epics, Myths, and Legends of India* (Bombay, 1940,
    3rd ed., n.d.).

I see the place of the idea of the Deity incarnated by avatars
    in human forms,[2]
I see the spots of the successions of priests on the earth,
    oracles, sacrificers, brahmins, sabians, llamas, monks,
    muftis, exhorters,[3]
I see where druids walk'd the groves of Mona, I see the
    mistletoe and vervain,[4]   95
I see the temples of the deaths of the bodies of Gods, I see
    the old signifiers.

I see Christ eating the bread of his last supper in the midst of
    youths and old persons,
I see where the strong divine young man the Hercules toil'd
    faithfully and long and then died,
I see the place of the innocent rich life and hapless fate of the
    beautiful nocturnal son, the full-limb'd Bacchus,
I see Kneph,[5] blooming, drest in blue, with the crown of
    feathers on his head,   100
I see Hermes,[6] unsuspected, dying, well-belov'd, saying to the
    people *Do not weep for me,*
This is not my true country, I have lived banish'd from my true
    country, I now go back there,
I return to the celestial sphere where every one goes in his turn.

7

I see the battle-fields of the earth, grass grows upon them and
    blossoms and corn,
I see the tracks of ancient and modern expeditions.   105

I see the nameless masonries, venerable messages of the
    unknown events, heroes, records of the earth.

I see the places of the sagas,
I see pine-trees and fir-trees torn by northern blasts,
I see granite bowlders and cliffs, I see green meadows and lakes,
I see the burial-cairns of Scandinavian warriors,   110
I see them raised high with stones by the marge of restless
    oceans, that the dead men's spirits when they wearied of
    their quiet graves might rise up through the mounds and

---

2. The incarnation of the deity by an avatar in human form occurs in several religions, including
    the Hindu and Egyptian.
3. *Sabians*: originally a semi-Christian sect of Babylonia, and later a semi-Moslem sect of Mes-
    opotamia; *llamas*: properly, "lamas," Tibetan priests; *muftis*: official expounders of Moham-
    medan law.
4. *Groves of Mona*: Latin name of Anglesea, county of North Wales; *vervain*: a European mal-
    low, like mistletoe a legendary association with Druid worship.
5. In Egyptian mythology, a god with the body of a man and the head of a sheep.
6. In Greek mythology the messenger of the gods. WW took this passage about Kneph and
    Hermes almost literally from Volney's *Ruins*.

gaze on the tossing billows, and be refresh'd by storms,
immensity, liberty, action.[7]

I see the steppes of Asia,
I see the tumuli of Mongolia, I see the tents of Kalmucks and
Baskirs,[8]
I see the nomadic tribes with herds of oxen and cows,
I see the table-lands notch'd with ravines, I see the jungles and
deserts,   115
I see the camel, the wild steed, the bustard, the fat-tail'd
sheep, the antelope, and the burrowing wolf.

I see the highlands of Abyssinia,
I see flocks of goats feeding, and see the fig-tree, tamarind, date,
And see fields of teff-wheat[9] and places of verdure and gold.

I see the Brazilian vaquero,   120
I see the Bolivian ascending mount Sorata,
I see the Wacho[1] crossing the plains, I see the incomparable
rider of horses with his lasso on his arm,
I see over the pampas the pursuit of wild cattle for their hides.

8[2]

I see the regions of snow and ice,
I see the sharp-eyed Samoiede[3] and the Finn,   125
I see the seal-seeker in his boat poising his lance,
I see the Siberian on his slight-built sledge drawn by dogs,
I see the porpoise-hunters, I see the whale-crews of the south
Pacific and the north Atlantic,
I see the cliffs, glaciers, torrents, valleys, of Switzerland—I
mark the long winters and the isolation.

I see the cities of the earth and make myself at random a part
of them,
I am a real Parisian,   130
I am a habitan of Vienna, St. Petersburg, Berlin,
Constantinople,
I am of Adelaide, Sidney, Melbourne,
I am of London, Manchester, Bristol, Edinburgh, Limerick,
I am of Madrid, Cadiz, Barcelona, Oporto, Lyons, Brussels,
Berne, Frankfort, Stuttgart, Turin, Florence,   135
I belong in Moscow, Cracow, Warsaw, or northward in

7. These lines about the Scandinavian warriors were directly developed from a newspaper clip-
ping found in one of WW's notebooks. See Bucke, *N and F*, I, 43*n*.
8. Nomadic tribes of Mongolia.
9. An Abyssinian grain plant.
1. A member of a Caddoan Indian tribe, Texas.
2. In 1881 WW excluded a former section 8, transposing seven of its eight lines to "A Pau-
manok Picture" (see note, p. 391). Former section 9 then became section 8 and the number
9 was cancelled from the sequence.
3. A member of the Samoyedes, a neo-Siberian tribe in the region of the Altai mountains.

Christiania or Stockholm, or in Siberian Irkutsk, or in
    some street in Iceland,
I descend upon all those cities, and rise from them again.

10

I see vapors exhaling from unexplored countries,
I see the savage types, the bow and arrow, the poison'd splint,
    the fetich, and the obi.

I see African and Asiatic towns,   140
I see Algiers, Tripoli, Derne, Mogadore, Timbuctoo, Monrovia,
I see the swarms of Pekin, Canton, Benares, Delhi, Calcutta,
    Tokio,
I see the Kruman[4] in his hut, and the Dahoman and Ashantee-
    man in their huts,
I see the Turk smoking opium in Aleppo,
I see the picturesque crowds at the fairs of Khiva and those of
    Herat,[5]   145
I see Teheran, I see Muscat and Medina and the intervening
    sands,[6] I see the caravans toiling onward,
I see Egypt and the Egyptians, I see the pyramids and obelisks,
I look on chisell'd histories, records of conquering kings,
    dynasties, cut in slabs of sand-stone, or on granite-blocks,
I see at Memphis mummy-pits containing mummies embalm'd,
    swathed in linen cloth, lying there many centuries,
I look on the fall'n Theban, the large-ball'd eyes, the side-
    drooping neck, the hands folded across the breast.   150

I see all the menials of the earth, laboring,
I see all the prisoners in the prisons,
I see the defective human bodies of the earth,
The blind, the deaf and dumb, idiots, hunchbacks, lunatics,
The pirates, thieves, betrayers, murderers, slave-makers of the
    earth,   155
The helpless infants, and the helpless old men and women.

I see male and female everywhere,
I see the serene brotherhood of philosophs,
I see the constructiveness of my race,
I see the results of the perseverance and industry of my race,   160
I see ranks, colors, barbarisms, civilizations, I go among them,
    I mix indiscriminately,
And I salute all the inhabitants of the earth.

4. Tribesman of Liberia, West Africa.
5. *Khiva*: former khanate in western Asia, now in Uzbekistan; *Herat*: city of northwestern
    Afghanistan.
6. *Teheran*: capital of Iran; *Muscat*: capital of Oman, Arabia; *Medina*: city in Hejaz, Saudi
    Arabia.

11

You whoever you are!
You daughter or son of England!
You of the mighty Slavic tribes and empires! you Russ in
    Russia!   165
You dim-descended, black, divine-soul'd African, large, fine-
    headed, nobly-form'd, superbly destin'd, on equal terms
    with me!
You Norwegian! Swede! Dane! Icelander! you Prussian!
You Spaniard of Spain! you Portuguese!
You Frenchwoman and Frenchman of France!
You Belge! you liberty-lover of the Netherlands! (you stock
    whence I myself have descended;)   170
You sturdy Austrian! you Lombard! Hun! Bohemian! farmer of
    Styria!⁷
You neighbor of the Danube!
You working-man of the Rhine, the Elbe, or the Weser!⁸ you
    working-woman too!
You Sardinian! you Bavarian! Swabian! Saxon! Wallachian!⁹
    Bulgarian!
You Roman! Neapolitan! you Greek!   175
You lithe matador in the arena at Seville!
You mountaineer living lawlessly on the Taurus or Caucasus!¹
You Bokh² horse-herd watching your mares and stallions feeding!
You beautiful-bodied Persian at full speed in the saddle
    shooting arrows to the mark!
You Chinaman and Chinawoman of China! you Tartar of
    Tartary!   180
You women of the earth subordinated at your tasks!
You Jew journeying in your old age through every risk to stand
    once on Syrian ground!
You other Jews waiting in all lands for your Messiah!
You thoughtful Armenian pondering by some stream of the
    Euphrates! you peering amid the ruins of Nineveh! you
    ascending mount Ararat!
You foot-worn pilgrim welcoming the far-away sparkle of the
    minarets of Mecca!   185
You sheiks along the stretch from Suez to Bab-el-mandeb³
    ruling your families and tribes!
You olive-grower tending your fruit on fields of Nazareth,
    Damascus, or lake Tiberias!⁴

---

7. A province of southeastern Austria.
8. River in Germany.
9. *Swabian*: native of Swabia, now a district of southwestern Bavaria; *Wallachian*: native of
    Wallachia, now a part of Romania.
1. *Taurus*: a mountain range in southern Asia Minor, in Turkey; *Caucasus*: mountain range
    between the Black Sea and the Caspian.
2. Referring to Bokhara, a khanate in Central Asia.
3. A strait connecting the Red Sea with the Indian Ocean.
4. The Sea of Galilee in Palestine.

You Thibet trader on the wide inland or bargaining in the
    shops of Lassa!
You Japanese man or woman! you liver in Madagascar, Ceylon,
    Sumatra, Borneo!
All you continentals of Asia, Africa, Europe, Australia,
    indifferent of place!   190
All you on the numberless islands of the archipelagoes of the sea!
And you of centuries hence when you listen to me!
And you each and everywhere whom I specify not, but include
    just the same!
Health to you! good will to you all, from me and America sent!

Each of us inevitable,   195
Each of us limitless—each of us with his or her right upon the
    earth,
Each of us allow'd the eternal purports of the earth,
Each of us here as divinely as any is here.

12

You Hottentot[5] with clicking palate! you woolly-hair'd hordes!
You own'd persons dropping sweat-drops or blood-drops!   200
You human forms with the fathomless ever-impressive
    countenances of brutes!
You poor koboo[6] whom the meanest of the rest look down
    upon for all your glimmering language and spirituality!
You dwarf'd Kamtschatkan,[7] Greenlander, Lapp!
You Austral negro, naked, red, sooty, with protrusive lip,
    groveling, seeking your food!
You Caffre, Berber, Soudanese!   205
You haggard, uncouth, untutor'd Bedowee![8]
You plague-swarms in Madras, Nankin, Kaubul, Cairo![9]
You benighted roamer of Amazonia! you Patagonian! you
    Feejee-man!
I do not prefer others so very much before you either,
I do not say one word against you away back there where you
    stand,   210
(You will come forward in due time to my side.)

13

My spirit has pass'd in compassion and determination around
    the whole earth,

---

5. A people of southern Africa who call themselves Khoikhoin; "Hottentot," now considered
   pejorative, was the name given them by Dutch (later Afrikaner) settlers. Khoikhoin languages
   make extensive use of click sounds.
6. Kubu, Malayan forest tribe of south-central Sumatra.
7. Native of Kamchatka, a peninsula in northeastern Siberia.
8. Bedouin, a nomadic Arabian.
9. *Madras*: state and capital of southeastern India; *Nankin*: a city in southeastern. China, former
   capital, usually spelled Nanking; *Kaubul*: Kabul, capital of Afghanistan.

I have look'd for equals and lovers and found them ready for
    me in all lands,
I think some divine rapport has equalized me with them.

You vapors, I think I have risen with you, moved away to
    distant continents, and fallen down there, for reasons,   215
I think I have blown with you you winds;
You waters I have finger'd every shore with you,
I have run through what any river or strait of the globe has
    run through,
I have taken my stand on the bases of peninsulas and on the
    high embedded rocks, to cry thence:

Salut au monde!   220
What cities the light or warmth penetrates I penetrate those
    cities myself,
All islands to which birds wing their way I wing my way myself.

Toward you all, in America's name,
I raise high the perpendicular hand, I make the signal,
To remain after me in sight forever,   225
For all the haunts and homes of men.
   1856   *1881*

Song of the Open Road[1]

1

A foot and light-hearted I take to the open road,
Healthy, free, the world before me,
The long brown path before me leading wherever I choose.

Henceforth I ask not good-fortune, I myself am good-fortune,
Henceforth I whimper no more, postpone no more, need
    nothing,   5
Done with indoor complaints, libraries, querulous criticisms,[2]
Strong and content I travel the open road.

---

1. Entitled "Poem of the Road" in 1856 and 1860, and taking its present title in 1867, this famous second-edition poem underwent only slight revision, one line being added in 1881 and ten others being dropped either in 1871 or in 1881. Of all WW's poems, it perhaps best meets the expectation of the general reader with its elation, its buoyant invitation to adventure, and its confident promise. Yet, as in all the greater poems, its power resides in its symbolic import without diminution of the literal and realistic. W. S. Kennedy has surmised that WW found inspiration for this poem in a passage from George Sand's novel *Consuelo*: "What is there more beautiful than a road? It is the symbol and the image of an active and varied life . . . And then that road is the passage of Humanity, the route of the Universe . . . So far as the sight can read, the road is a land of liberty . . ." (see *Conservator*, February 1907, 184–85).
2. This line was added in 1881. WW's continued illness confirmed his belief that he must now consider *LG* completed. *Cf.* "Prefaces," 1872 and 1876.

The earth, that is sufficient,
I do not want the constellations any nearer,
I know they are very well where they are,   10
I know they suffice for those who belong to them.

(Still here I carry my old delicious burdens,
I carry them, men and women, I carry them with me wherever I go,
I swear it is impossible for me to get rid of them,
I am fill'd with them, and I will fill them in return.)   15

                                   2

You road I enter upon and look around, I believe you are not
     all that is here,
I believe that much unseen is also here.

Here the profound lesson of reception, nor preference nor denial,
The black with his woolly head, the felon, the diseas'd, the
     illiterate person, are not denied;
The birth, the hasting after the physician, the beggar's tramp,
     the drunkard's stagger, the laughing party of mechanics,   20
The escaped youth, the rich person's carriage, the fop, the
     eloping couple,
The early market-man, the hearse, the moving of furniture into
     the town, the return back from the town,
They pass, I also pass, any thing passes, none can be interdicted,
None but are accepted, none but shall be dear to me.

                                   3

You air that serves me with breath to speak!   25
You objects that call from diffusion my meanings and give
     them shape!
You light that wraps me and all things in delicate equable showers!
You paths worn in the irregular hollows by the roadsides!
I believe you are latent with unseen existences, you are so dear
     to me.

You flagg'd walks of the cities! you strong curbs at the edges!   30
You ferries! you planks and posts of wharves! you timber-lined
     sides! you distant ships!
You rows of houses! you window-pierc'd façades! you roofs!
You porches and entrances! you copings and iron guards!
You windows whose transparent shells might expose so much!
You doors and ascending steps! you arches!   35
You gray stones of interminable pavements! you trodden
     crossings!
From all that has touch'd you I believe you have imparted to

yourselves, and now would impart the same secretly to me,
From the living and the dead you have peopled your impassive
surfaces, and the spirits thereof would be evident and
amicable with me.

4

The earth expanding right hand and left hand,
The picture alive, every part in its best light,   40
The music falling in where it is wanted, and stopping where it
is not wanted,
The cheerful voice of the public road, the gay fresh sentiment
of the road.

O highway I travel, do you say to me *Do not leave me?*
Do you say *Venture not—if you leave me you are lost?*
Do you say *I am already prepared, I am well-beaten and
undenied, adhere to me?*   45

O public road, I say back I am not afraid to leave you, yet I
love you,
You express me better than I can express myself,
You shall be more to me than my poem.

I think heroic deeds were all conceiv'd in the open air, and all
free poems also,
I think I could stop here myself and do miracles,   50
I think whatever I shall meet on the road I shall like, and
whoever beholds me shall like me,
I think whoever I see must be happy.

5

From this hour I ordain myself loos'd of limits and imaginary
lines,
Going where I list, my own master total and absolute,
Listening to others, considering well what they say,   55
Pausing, searching, receiving, contemplating,
Gently, but with undeniable will, divesting myself of the holds
that would hold me.

I inhale great draughts of space,
The east and the west are mine, and the north and the south
are mine.

I am larger, better than I thought,   60
I did not know I held so much goodness.

All seems beautiful to me,
I can repeat over to men and women You have done such good
to me I would do the same to you,

I will recruit for myself and you as I go,
I will scatter myself among men and women as I go,   65
I will toss a new gladness and roughness among them,
Whoever denies me it shall not trouble me,
Whoever accepts me he or she shall be blessed and shall bless me.

6

Now if a thousand perfect men were to appear it would not
    amaze me,
Now if a thousand beautiful forms of women appear'd it would
    not astonish me.   70

Now I see the secret of the making of the best persons,
It is to grow in the open air and to eat and sleep with the earth.

Here a great personal deed has room,
(Such a deed seizes upon the hearts of the whole race of men,
Its effusion of strength and will overwhelms law and mocks all
    authority and all argument against it.)   75

Here is the test of wisdom,
Wisdom is not finally tested in schools,
Wisdom cannot be pass'd from one having it to another not
    having it,
Wisdom is of the soul, is not susceptible of proof, is its own proof,
Applies to all stages and objects and qualities and is content,   80
Is the certainty of the reality and immortality of things, and
    the excellence of things;
Something there is in the float of the sight of things that
    provokes it out of the soul.[3]

Now I re-examine philosophies and religions,
They may prove well in lecture-rooms, yet not prove at all
    under the spacious clouds and along the landscape and
    flowing currents.

Here is realization,   85
Here is a man tallied[4]—he realizes here what he has in him,
The past, the future, majesty, love—if they are vacant of you,
    you are vacant of them.

3. The "float of the sight of things" suggests the "flood" or "flowing" of the appearances that
   provoke wisdom (call it forth) out of the soul. *Cf.* line 62, "Crossing Brooklyn Ferry." Par-
   ticularly WW would be aware of the meaning of "float" as the footlights on the stage, i.e.,
   a flood of light.
4. Colloquially, "added up." Sometimes WW used the word in the further sense of "to evaluate
   or estimate."

Only the kernel of every object nourishes;
Where is he who tears off the husks for you and me?
Where is he that undoes stratagems and envelopes for you and
    me?   90

Here is adhesiveness, it is not previously fashion'd, it is apropos;[5]
Do you know what it is as you pass to be loved by strangers?
Do you know the talk of those turning eye-balls?

7

Here is the efflux of the soul,
The efflux of the soul comes from within through embower'd
    gates, ever provoking questions,   95
These yearnings why are they? these thoughts in the darkness
    why are they?
Why are there men and women that while they are nigh me
    the sunlight expands my blood?
Why when they leave me do my pennants of joy sink flat and lank?
Why are there trees I never walk under but large and
    melodious thoughts descend upon me?
(I think they hang there winter and summer on those trees
    and always drop fruit as I pass;)   100
What is it I interchange so suddenly with strangers?
What with some driver as I ride on the seat by his side?
What with some fisherman drawing his seine by the shore as I
    walk by and pause?
What gives me to be free to a woman's and man's good-will?
    what gives them to be free to mine?

8

The efflux of the soul is happiness, here is happiness,   105
I think it pervades the open air, waiting at all times,
Now it flows unto us, we are rightly charged.

Here rises the fluid and attaching character,
The fluid and attaching character is the freshness and
    sweetness of man and woman,
(The herbs of the morning sprout no fresher and sweeter every
    day out of the roots of themselves, than it sprouts fresh
    and sweet continually out of itself.)   110

Toward the fluid and attaching character exudes the sweat of
    the love of young and old,
From it falls distill'd the charm that mocks beauty and
    attainments,
Toward it heaves the shuddering longing ache of contact.

---

5. Meaning here, in the context, "appropriate" or "timely."

9

Allons![6] whoever you are come travel with me!
Traveling with me you find what never tires.   115

The earth never tires,
The earth is rude, silent, incomprehensible at first, Nature is
    rude and incomprehensible at first,
Be not discouraged, keep on, there are divine things well
    envelop'd,
I swear to you there are divine things more beautiful than
    words can tell.

Allons! we must not stop here,   120
However sweet these laid-up stores, however convenient this
    dwelling we cannot remain here,
However shelter'd this port and however calm these waters we
    must not anchor here,
However welcome the hospitality that surrounds us we are
    permitted to receive it but a little while.

10

Allons! the inducements shall be greater,
We will sail pathless and wild seas,   125
We will go where winds blow, waves dash, and the Yankee
    clipper speeds by under full sail.

Allons! with power, liberty, the earth, the elements,
Health, defiance, gayety, self-esteem, curiosity;
Allons! from all formules![7]
From your formules, O bat-eyed and materialistic priests.   130

The stale cadaver blocks up the passage—the burial waits no
    longer.

Allons! yet take warning!
He traveling with me needs the best blood, thews, endurance,
None may come to the trial till he or she bring courage and
    health,
Come not here if you have already spent the best of yourself,   135
Only those may come who come in sweet and determin'd bodies,
No diseas'd person, no rum-drinker or venereal taint is
    permitted here.

(I and mine do not convince by arguments, similes, rhymes,
We convince by our presence.)

6. French: "Let us go!" In the succeeding canto, it becomes martial.
7. French: "formulas." In his "Blue Copy" revisions of the 1860 edition of *LG*, WW deleted
   this and the following two lines, but he retained them in the 1867 edition nevertheless.

11

Listen! I will be honest with you,   140
I do not offer the old smooth prizes, but offer rough new prizes,
These are the days that must happen to you:
You shall not heap up what is call'd riches,
You shall scatter with lavish hand all that you earn or achieve,
You but arrive at the city to which you were destin'd, you
    hardly settle yourself to satisfaction before you are call'd
    by an irresistible call to depart,   145
You shall be treated to the ironical smiles and mockings of
    those who remain behind you,
What beckonings of love you receive you shall only answer
    with passionate kisses of parting,
You shall not allow the hold of those who spread their reach'd
    hands toward you.

12

Allons! after the great Companions, and to belong to them!
They too are on the road—they are the swift and majestic men
    —they are the greatest women,   150
Enjoyers of calms of seas and storms of seas,
Sailors of many a ship, walkers of many a mile of land,
Habituès of many distant countries, habituès of far-distant
    dwellings,
Trusters of men and women, observers of cities, solitary toilers,
Pausers and contemplators of tufts, blossoms, shells of the
    shore,   155
Dancers at wedding-dances, kissers of brides, tender helpers of
    children, bearers of children,
Soldiers of revolts, standers by gaping graves, lowerers-down of
    coffins,
Journeyers over consecutive seasons, over the years, the
    curious years each emerging from that which preceded it,
Journeyers as with companions, namely their own diverse
    phases,
Forth-steppers from the latent unrealized baby-days,   160
Journeyers gayly with their own youth, journeyers with their
    bearded and well-grain'd manhood,
Journeyers with their womanhood, ample, unsurpass'd, content,
Journeyers with their own sublime old age of manhood or
    womanhood,
Old age, calm, expanded, broad with the haughty breadth of
    the universe,
Old age, flowing free with the delicious near-by freedom of
    death.   165

13

Allons! to that which is endless as it was beginningless,
To undergo much, tramps of days, rests of nights,
To merge all in the travel they tend to, and the days and
    nights they tend to,
Again to merge them in the start of superior journeys,
To see nothing anywhere but what you may reach it and pass
    it,   110
To conceive no time, however distant, but what you may reach
    it and pass it,
To look up or down no road but it stretches and waits for you,
    however long but it stretches and waits for you,
To see no being, not God's or any, but you also go thither,
To see no possession but you may possess it, enjoying all
    without labor or purchase, abstracting the feast yet not
    abstracting one particle of it,
To take the best of the farmer's farm and the rich man's
    elegant villa, and the chaste blessings of the well-married
    couple, and the fruits of orchards and flowers of gardens,   175
To take to your use out of the compact cities as you pass
    through,
To carry buildings and streets with you afterward wherever you
    go,
To gather the minds of men out of their brains as you
    encounter them, to gather the love out of their hearts,
To take your lovers on the road with you, for all that you leave
    them behind you,
To know the universe itself as a road, as many roads, as roads
    for traveling souls.   180

All parts away for the progress of souls,
All religion, all solid things, arts, governments—all that was or
    is apparent upon this globe or any globe, falls into niches
    and corners before the procession of souls along the grand
    roads of the universe.

Of the progress of the souls of men and women along the
    grand roads of the universe, all other progress is the
    needed emblem and sustenance.

Forever alive, forever forward,
Stately, solemn, sad, withdrawn, baffled, mad, turbulent,
    feeble, dissatisfied,   185
Desperate, proud, fond, sick, accepted by men, rejected by men,
They go! they go! I know that they go, but I know not where
    they go,
But I know that they go toward the best—toward something great.

Whoever you are, come forth! or man or woman come forth!
You must not stay sleeping and dallying there in the house,
     though you built it, or though it has been built for you.   190

Out of the dark confinement! out from behind the screen!
It is useless to protest, I know all and expose it.

Behold through you as bad as the rest,
Through the laughter, dancing, dining, supping, of people,
Inside of dresses and ornaments, inside of those wash'd and
     trimm'd faces,   195
Behold a secret silent loathing and despair.

No husband, no wife, no friend, trusted to hear the confession,
Another self, a duplicate of every one, skulking and hiding it
     goes,
Formless and wordless through the streets of the cities, polite
     and bland in the parlors,
In the cars of railroads, in steamboats, in the public assembly,   200
Home to the houses of men and women, at the table, in the
     bedroom, everywhere,
Smartly attired, countenance smiling, form upright, death
     under the breast-bones, hell under the skull-bones,
Under the broadcloth and gloves, under the ribbons and
     artificial flowers,
Keeping fair with the customs, speaking not a syllable of itself,
Speaking of any thing else but never of itself.   205

14

Allons! through struggles and wars!
The goal that was named cannot be countermanded.

Have the past struggles succeeded?
What has succeeded? yourself? your nation? Nature?
Now understand me well—it is provided in the essence of
     things that from any fruition of success, no matter what,
     shall come forth something to make a greater struggle
     necessary.   210

My call is the call of battle, I nourish active rebellion,
He going with me must go well arm'd,
He going with me goes often with spare diet, poverty, angry
     enemies, desertions.

15

Allons! the road is before us!
It is safe—I have tried it—my own feet have tried it well—be
     not detain'd!   215

Let the paper remain on the desk unwritten, and the book on
the shelf unopen'd!
Let the tools remain in the workshop! let the money remain
unearn'd!
Let the school stand! mind not the cry of the teacher!
Let the preacher preach in his pulpit! let the lawyer plead in
the court, and the judge expound the law.

Camerado, I give you my hand!   220
I give you my love more precious than money,
I give you myself before preaching or law;
Will you give me yourself? will you come travel with me?
Shall we stick by each other as long as we live?
    1856   *1881*

Crossing Brooklyn Ferry[1]

1

Flood-tide below me! I see you face to face!
Clouds of the west—sun there half an hour high—I see you
also face to face.

Crowds of men and women attired in the usual costumes, how
curious you are to me!
On the ferry-boats the hundreds and hundreds that cross,
returning home, are more curious to me than you
suppose,
And you that shall cross from shore to shore years hence are
more to me, and more in my meditations, than you might
suppose.   5

2

The impalpable sustenance of me from all things at all hours
of the day,

1. This was the "Sun-Down Poem" of the second edition, the most distinguished of the new
poems of 1856, taking its present title in 1860. It is possible that WW began its composition
even before the first edition went to press, for many of its lines are entered into one of his
notebooks of the period. See *An 1855–56 Notebook Toward the Second Edition of Leaves of
Grass*, ed. by Harold W. Blodgett (Carbondale: Southern Illinois University Press, 1959).
The revisions through the various editions—some fourteen lines were dropped and quite a
number of phrases amended—reveal the constant improvement in a composition whose first
version evidenced mastery of artistic power. With exalted and sustained inspiration the poet
presents a transcendent reality unlimited by the tyranny of time or person or space, a poetic
demonstration of the power of appearances—"dumb, beautiful ministers"—to affirm the
soul. Philosophical in theme, the poem is yet profoundly personal—his own daily experience
made illustrious—and its strength lies in its aesthetic vision. For a detailed analysis, see
Stanley K. Coffman's " 'Crossing Brooklyn Ferry': A Note on the Catalogue Technique in
Whitman's Poetry." *MP* 51: 225–32. Also helpful are M. Wynn Thomas, *The Lunar Light
of Whitman's Poetry* (Cambridge, Mass.: Harvard University Press, 1987), 92–123; and James
Dougherty, *Walt Whitman and the Citizen's Eye* (Baton Rouge: Louisiana State University
Press, 1993), 143–54.

The simple, compact, well-join'd scheme, myself disintegrated,
    every one disintegrated yet part of the scheme,
The similitudes of the past and those of the future,
The glories strung like beads on my smallest sights and
    hearings, on the walk in the street and the passage over
    the river,
The current rushing so swiftly and swimming with me far
    away,   10
The others that are to follow me, the ties between me and them,
The certainty of others, the life, love, sight, hearing of others.

Others will enter the gates of the ferry and cross from shore to
    shore,
Others will watch the run of the flood-tide,
Others will see the shipping of Manhattan north and west, and
    the heights of Brooklyn to the south and east,   15
Others will see the islands large and small;
Fifty years hence, others will see them as they cross, the sun
    half an hour high,
A hundred years hence, or ever so many hundred years hence,
    others will see them,
Will enjoy the sunset, the pouring-in of the flood-tide, the
    falling-back to the sea of the ebb-tide.

3

It avails not, time nor place—distance avails not,   20
I am with you, you men and women of a generation, or ever so
    many generations hence,
Just as you feel when you look on the river and sky, so I felt,
Just as any of you is one of a living crowd, I was one of a crowd,
Just as you are refresh'd by the gladness of the river and the
    bright flow, I was refresh'd,
Just as you stand and lean on the rail, yet hurry with the swift
    current, I stood yet was hurried,   25
Just as you look on the numberless masts of ships and the
    thick-stemm'd pipes of steamboats, I look'd.

I too many and many a time cross'd the river of old,
Watched the Twelfth-month sea-gulls,[2] saw them high in the
    air floating with motionless wings, oscillating their bodies,
Saw how the glistening yellow lit up parts of their bodies and
    left the rest in strong shadow,
Saw the slow-wheeling circles and the gradual edging toward
    the south,   30
Saw the reflection of the summer sky in the water,
Had my eyes dazzled by the shimmering track of beams,

2. WW's use of the Quaker designation for the days and months often produced a more musical
    phrase.

Look'd at the fine centrifugal spokes of light round the shape
    of my head in the sunlit water,[3]
Look'd on the haze on the hills southward and south-westward,
Look'd on the vapor as it flew in fleeces tinged with violet,   35
Look'd toward the lower bay to notice the vessels arriving,
Saw their approach, saw aboard those that were near me,
Saw the white sails of schooners and sloops, saw the ships at
    anchor,
The sailors at work in the rigging or out astride the spars,
The round masts, the swinging motion of the hulls, the slender
    serpentine pennants,   40
The large and small steamers in motion, the pilots in their
    pilot-houses,
The white wake left by the passage, the quick tremulous whirl
    of the wheels,
The flags of all nations, the falling of them at sunset,
The scallop-edged waves in the twilight, the ladled cups, the
    frolicsome crests and glistening,
The stretch afar growing dimmer and dimmer, the gray walls
    of the granite storehouses by the docks,   45
On the river the shadowy group, the big steam-tug closely
    flank'd on each side by the barges, the hay-boat, the
    belated lighter,
On the neighboring shore the fires from the foundry chimneys
    burning high and glaringly into the night,
Casting their flicker of black contrasted with wild red and
    yellow light over the tops of houses, and down into the
    clefts of streets.

4

These and all else were to me the same as they are to you,
I loved well those cities, loved well the stately and rapid river,   50
The men and women I saw were all near to me,
Others the same—others who look back on me because I
    look'd forward to them,
(The time will come, though I stop here to-day and to-night.)

5

What is it then between us?
What is the count of the scores or hundreds of years between
    us?   55

Whatever it is, it avails not—distance avails not, and place
    avails not,
I too lived, Brooklyn of ample hills was mine,
I too walk'd the streets of Manhattan island, and bathed in the
    waters around it,
I too felt the curious abrupt questionings stir within me,

---

3. An aureole available to anyone.

In the day among crowds of people sometimes they came upon
    me,   60
In my walks home late at night or as I lay in my bed they
    came upon me,
I too had been struck from the float forever held in solution,
I too had receiv'd identity by my body,
That I was I knew was of my body, and what I should be I
    knew I should be of my body.

6

It is not upon you alone the dark patches fall,   65
The dark threw its patches down upon me also,
The best I had done seem'd to me blank and suspicious,
My great thoughts as I supposed them, were they not in reality
    meagre?
Nor is it you alone who know what it is to be evil,
I am he who knew what it was to be evil,   70
I too knitted the old knot of contrariety,
Blabb'd, blush'd, resented, lied, stole, grudg'd,
Had guile, anger, lust, hot wishes I dared not speak,
Was wayward, vain, greedy, shallow, sly, cowardly, malignant,
The wolf, the snake, the hog, not wanting in me,   75
The cheating look, the frivolous word, the adulterous wish, not
    wanting,
Refusals, hates, postponements, meanness, laziness, none of
    these wanting,
Was one with the rest, the days and haps of the rest,
Was call'd by my nighest name by clear loud voices of young
    men as they saw me approaching or passing,
Felt their arms on my neck as I stood, or the negligent leaning
    of their flesh against me as I sat,   80
Saw many I loved in the street or ferry-boat or public
    assembly, yet never told them a word,
Lived the same life with the rest, the same old laughing,
    gnawing, sleeping,
Play'd the part that still looks back on the actor or actress,
The same old role, the role that is what we make it, as great as
    we like,
Or as small as we like, or both great and small.   85

7

Closer yet I approach you,
What thought you have of me now, I had as much of you—I
    laid in my stores in advance,
I consider'd long and seriously of you before you were born.

Who was to know what should come home to me?
Who knows but I am enjoying this?   90

Who knows, for all the distance, but I am as good as looking
    at you now, for all you cannot see me?[4]

8

Ah, what can ever be more stately and admirable to me than
    mast-hemm'd Manhattan?
River and sunset and scallop-edg'd waves of flood-tide?
The sea-gulls oscillating their bodies, the hay-boat in the
    twilight, and the belated lighter?
What gods can exceed these that clasp me by the hand, and
    with voices I love call me promptly and loudly by my
    nighest name as I approach?   95
What is more subtle than this which ties me to the woman or
    man that looks in my face?
Which fuses me into you now, and pours my meaning into you?

We understand then do we not?
What I promis'd without mentioning it, have you not accepted?
What the study could not teach—what the preaching could
    not accomplish is accomplish'd, is it not?   100

9

Flow on, river! flow with the flood-tide, and ebb with the ebb-tide!
Frolic on, crested and scallop-edg'd waves!
Gorgeous clouds of the sunset! drench with your splendor me,
    or the men and women generations after me!
Cross from shore to shore, countless crowds of passengers!
Stand up, tall masts of Mannahatta! stand up, beautiful hills of
    Brooklyn!   105
Throb, baffled and curious brain! throw out questions and
    answers!
Suspend here and everywhere, eternal float of solution!
Gaze, loving and thirsting eyes, in the house or street or public
    assembly!
Sound out, voices of young men! loudly and musically call me
    by my nighest name!
Live, old life! play the part that looks back on the actor or
    actress!   110
Play the old role, the role that is great or small according as
    one makes it!
Consider, you who peruse me, whether I may not in unknown
    ways be looking upon you;
Be firm, rail over the river, to support those who lean idly, yet
    haste with the hasting current;
Fly on, sea-birds! fly sideways, or wheel in large circles high in
    the air;

---

4. For lines 89–91, *cf.* endings of "Song of Myself" and "So Long."

Receive the summer sky, you water, and faithfully hold it till
    all downcast eyes have time to take it from you!   115
Diverge, fine spokes of light, from the shape of my head, or
    any one's head, in the sunlit water!
Come on, ships from the lower bay! pass up or down, white-
    sail'd schooners, sloops, lighters!
Flaunt away, flags of all nations! be duly lower'd at sunset!
Burn high your fires, foundry chimneys! cast black shadows at
    nightfall! cast red and yellow light over the tops of the
    houses!
Appearances, now or henceforth, indicate what you are,   120
You necessary film, continue to envelop the soul,
About my body for me, and your body for you, be hung our
    divinest aromas,
Thrive, cities—bring your freight, bring your shows, ample and
    sufficient rivers,
Expand, being than which none else is perhaps more spiritual,
Keep your places, objects than which none else is more lasting. 125

You have waited, you always wait, you dumb, beautiful
    ministers,
We receive you with free sense at last, and are insatiate hence-
    forward,
Not you any more shall be able to foil us, or withhold
    yourselves from us,
We use you, and do not cast you aside—we plant you
    permanently within us,
We fathom you not—we love you—there is perfection in you
    also,   130
You furnish your parts toward eternity,
Great or small, you furnish your parts toward the soul.
    1856   *1881*

Song of the Answerer[1]

1

Now list to my morning's romanza,[2] I tell the signs of the
    Answerer,
To the cities and farms I sing as they spread in the sunshine
    before me.

A young man comes to me bearing a message from his brother,
How shall the young man know the whether and when of his
    brother?
Tell him to send me the signs.   5

And I stand before the young man face to face, and take his
    right hand in my left hand and his left hand in my right
    hand,
And I answer for his brother and for men, and I answer for
    him that answers for all, and send these signs.

Him all wait for, him all yield up to, his word is decisive and
    final,
Him they accept, in him lave, in him perceive themselves as
    amid light,
Him they immerse and he immerses them.   10

Beautiful women, the haughtiest nations, laws, the landscape,
    people, animals,
The profound earth and its attributes and the unquiet ocean,
    (so tell I my morning's romanza,)
All enjoyments and properties and money, and whatever money
    will buy,
The best farms, others toiling and planting and he unavoidably
    reaps,
The noblest and costliest cities, others grading and building
    and he domiciles there,   15
Nothing for any one but what is for him, near and far are for
    him, the ships in the offing,
The perpetual shows and marches on land are for him if they
    are for anybody.

1. For the 1881 edition this poem was created from what had been two separate poems, the
first section having originally been one of the twelve untitled poems of the first edition,
becoming "Poem of the Poet" in the second edition, "Leaves of Grass" No. 3 in the third,
and in the fourth "Now List to My Morning Romanza," a title taken from the then added
two-line opening passage, and retained until the second section and present title were added
in 1881. The second section began in 1856 as "Poem of The Singers and of The Words of
Poems" became "Leaves of Grass" No. 6 in the third edition, and "The Indications" in the
fourth, fifth, and sixth editions, until in 1881 it took its present position. The joining of the
two poems is obviously appropriate, for the Poet of the second section is the Answerer of
the first; and in fact the two were consecutive in the editions of 1871 and 1876. As it now
stands, the composition is the result of not a little revision. From the first section the last
four lines were dropped in 1867; and some lines of the second section were adapted from
the 1855 Preface.
2. Italian: ballad or air.

He puts things in their attitudes,
He puts to-day out of himself with plasticity and love,
He places his own times, reminiscences, parents, brothers and
    sisters, associations, employment, politics, so that the rest
    never shame them afterward, nor assume to command
    them.   20

He is the Answerer,
What can be answer'd he answers, and what cannot be
    answer'd he shows how it cannot be answer'd.

A man is a summons and challenge,
(It is vain to skulk—do you hear that mocking and laughter?
    do you hear the ironical echoes?)

Books, friendships, philosophers, priests, action, pleasure,
    pride, beat up and down seeking to give satisfaction,   25
He indicates the satisfaction, and indicates them that beat up
    and down also.

Whichever the sex, whatever the season or place, he may go
    freshly and gently and safely by day or by night,
He has the pass-key of hearts, to him the response of the
    prying of hands on the knobs.

His welcome is universal, the flow of beauty is not more
    welcome or universal than he is,
The person he favors by day or sleeps with at night is blessed.   30

Every existence has its idiom, every thing has an idiom and
    tongue,
He resolves all tongues into his own and bestows it upon men,
    and any man translates, and any man translates himself
    also,
One part does not counteract another part, he is the joiner, he
    sees how they join.

He says indifferently and alike *How are you friend?* to the
    President at his levee,
And he says *Good-day my brother,* to Cudge[3] that hoes in the
    sugar-field,   35
And both understand him and know that his speech is right.

He walks with perfect ease in the capitol,
He walks among the Congress, and one Representative says to
    another, *Here is our equal appearing and new.*

3. From "Cudjoe," African day-name for a male born on a Monday. *Cf.* "Cuff," line 109, "Song
   of Myself."

Then the mechanics take him for a mechanic,
And the soldiers suppose him to be a soldier, and the sailors
    that he has follow'd the sea,   40
And the authors take him for an author, and the artists for an
    artist,
And the laborers perceive he could labor with them and love
    them,
No matter what the work is, that he is the one to follow it or
    has follow'd it,
No matter what the nation, that he might find his brothers
    and sisters there.

The English believe he comes of their English stock,   45
A Jew to the Jew he seems, a Russ to the Russ, usual and
    near, removed from none.

Whoever he looks at in the traveler's coffee-house claims him,
The Italian or Frenchman is sure, the German is sure, the
    Spaniard is sure, and the island Cuban is sure,
The engineer, the deck-hand on the great lakes, or on the
    Mississippi or St. Lawrence or Sacramento, or Hudson or
    Paumanok sound, claims him.

The gentleman of perfect blood acknowledges his perfect
    blood,   50
The insulter, the prostitute, the angry person, the beggar, see
    themselves in the ways of him, he strangely transmutes
    them,
They are not vile any more, they hardly know themselves they
    are so grown.

2

The indications and tally of time,
Perfect sanity shows the master among philosophs,
Time, always without break, indicates itself in parts,   55
What always indicates the poet is the crowd of the pleasant
    company of singers, and their words,
The words of the singers are the hours or minutes of the light
    or dark, but the words of the maker of poems are the
    general light and dark,
The maker of poems settles justice, reality, immortality,
His insight and power encircle things and the human race,
He is the glory and extract thus far of things and of the
    human race.   60

The singers do not beget, only the Poet begets,
The singers are welcom'd, understood, appear often enough,
    but rare has the day been, likewise the spot, of the birth
    of the maker of poems, the Answerer,
(Not every century nor every five centuries has contain'd such
    a day, for all its names.)

The singers of successive hours of centuries may have
   ostensible names, but the name of each of them is one of
   the singers,
The name of each is, eye-singer, ear-singer, head-singer, sweet-
   singer, night-singer, parlor-singer, love-singer, weird-
   singer, or something else.   65

All this time and at all times wait the words of true poems,
The words of true poems do not merely please,
The true poets are not followers of beauty but the august
   masters of beauty;
The greatness of sons is the exuding of the greatness of
   mothers and fathers,
The words of true poems are the tuft[4] and final applause of
   science.   70

Divine instinct, breadth of vision, the law of reason, health,
   rudeness of body, withdrawness,
Gayety, sun-tan, air-sweetness, such are some of the words of
   poems.

The sailor and traveler underlie the maker of poems, the
   Answerer,
The builder, geometer, chemist, anatomist, phrenologist,[5]
   artist, all these underlie the maker of poems, the
   Answerer.

The words of the true poems give you more than poems,   75
They give you to form for yourself poems, religions, politics,
   war, peace, behavior, histories, essays, daily life, and every
   thing else,
They balance ranks, colors, races, creeds, and the sexes,
They do not seek beauty, they are sought,
Forever touching them or close upon them follows beauty,
   longing, fain, love-sick.

They prepare for death, yet are they not the finish, but rather
   the outset,   80
They bring none to his or her terminus or to be content and
   full,
Whom they take they take into space to behold the birth of
   stars, to learn one of the meanings,
To launch off with absolute faith, to sweep through the
   ceaseless rings and never be quiet again.
   1855, 1856   *1881*

---

4. A small flexible cluster, but in WW's figure, suggesting a culminating adornment, familiar
   in the male bird's crest or the Native American's feathered topknot. This line is one of several
   adapted from the 1855 Preface.
5. Phrenology then occupied a place in public imagination later to be taken by the infant
   science of psychology.

Our Old Feuillage[1]

Always our old feuillage!
Always Florida's green peninsula—always the priceless delta of
    Louisiana—always the cotton-fields of Alabama and Texas,
Always California's golden hills and hollows, and the silver
    mountains of New Mexico—always soft-breath'd Cuba,
Always the vast slope drain'd by the Southern sea, inseparable
    with the slopes drain'd by the Eastern and Western seas,
The area the eighty-third year[2] of these States, the three and a
    half millions of square miles,   5
The eighteen thousand miles of sea-coast and bay-coast on the
    main, the thirty thousand miles of river navigation,
The seven millions of distinct families and the same number of
    dwellings—always these, and more, branching forth into
    numberless branches,
Always the free range and diversity—always the continent of
    Democracy;
Always the prairies, pastures, forests, vast cities, travelers,
    Kanada, the snows;
Always these compact lands tied at the hips with the belt
    stringing the huge oval lakes;   10
Always the West with strong native persons, the increasing
    density there, the habitans, friendly, threatening, ironical,
    scorning invaders;
All sights, South, North, East—all deeds, promiscuously done
    at all times,
All characters, movements, growths, a few noticed, myriads
    unnoticed,
Through Mannahatta's streets I walking, these things
    gathering,
On interior rivers by night in the glare of pine knots,
    steamboats wooding up,   15
Sunlight by day on the valley of the Susquehanna, and on the
    valleys of the Potomac and Rappahannock, and the valleys
    of the Roanoke and Delaware,
In their northerly wilds beasts of prey haunting the
    Adirondacks the hills, or lapping the Saginaw waters to
    drink,

1. French for "foliage," here used symbolically as a universal particular, like leaves of grass.
WW himself interpreted this poem in the first paragraph of a letter he wrote offering it to
Harper's Magazine, January 7, 1860: "The theory of 'A Chant of National Feuillage' is to
bring in, (devoting a line, or two or three lines to each,) a comprehensive collection of
touches, locales, incidents, idiomatic scenes, from every section. South, West, North, East,
Kanada, Texas, Maine, Virginia, the Mississippi Valley, etc, etc, etc.—all intensely fused to
the urgency of compact America, 'America always'—all in a vein of graphic, short, clear,
hasting along—as having a huge bouquet to collect, and quickly taking and binding in every
characteristic subject that offers itself—making a compact, the-whole-surrounding, *National
Poem*, after its sort, after my own style." The poem was rejected. Although it appeared in
the 1860 edition as "Chants Democratic" No. 4, the MS (Barrett) shows that it was composed,
at least in part, as early as 1856. The poem has undergone little change. In 1867 it was
titled "American Feuillage," and it first took its present title in 1881.
2. The MS reads "Eightieth year," indicating that the poem was worked upon as early as 1856.

In a lonesome inlet a sheldrake lost from the flock, sitting on
  the water rocking silently,
In farmers' barns oxen in the stable, their harvest labor done,
  they rest standing, they are too tired,
Afar on arctic ice the she-walrus lying drowsily while her cubs
  play around,   20
The hawk sailing where men have not yet sail'd, the farthest
  polar sea, ripply, crystalline, open, beyond the floes,
White drift spooning ahead where the ship in the tempest
  dashes,
On solid land what is done in cities as the bells strike
  midnight together,
In primitive woods the sounds there also sounding, the howl of
  the wolf, the scream of the panther, and the hoarse
  bellow of the elk,
In winter beneath the hard blue ice of Moosehead lake, in
  summer visible through the clear waters, the great trout
  swimming,   25
In lower latitudes in warmer air in the Carolinas the large
  black buzzard floating slowly high beyond the tree tops,
Below, the red cedar festoon'd with tylandria,³ the pines and
  cypresses growing out of the white sand that spreads far
  and flat,
Rude boats descending the big Pedee,⁴ climbing plants,
  parasites with color'd flowers and berries enveloping huge
  trees,
The waving drapery on the live-oak trailing long and low,
  noiselessly waved by the wind,
The camp of Georgia wagoners just after dark, the supper-fires
  and the cooking and eating by whites and negroes,   30
Thirty or forty great wagons, the mules, cattle, horses, feeding
  from troughs,
The shadows, gleams, up under the leaves of the old sycamore-
  trees, the flames with the black smoke from the pitch-pine
  curling and rising;
Southern fishermen fishing, the sounds and inlets of North
  Carolina's coast, the shad-fishery and the herring-fishery,
  the large sweep-seines, the windlasses on shore work'd by
  horses, the clearing, curing, and packing-houses;
Deep in the forest in piney woods turpentine dropping from
  the incisions in the trees, there are the turpentine works,
There are the negroes at work in good health, the ground in all
  directions is cover'd with pine straw;   35
In Tennessee and Kentucky slaves busy in the coalings, at the
  forge, by the furnace-blaze, or at the corn-shucking,
In Virginia, the planter's son returning after a long absence,
  joyfully welcom'd and kiss'd by the aged mulatto nurse,

3. Properly, tillandsia, or Spanish moss.
4. Name given to the Yadkin river after it enters South Carolina.

On rivers boatmen safely moor'd at nightfall in their boats
    under shelter of high banks,
Some of the younger men dance to the sound of the banjo or
    fiddle, others sit on the gunwale smoking and talking;
Late in the afternoon the mocking-bird, the American mimic,
    singing in the Great Dismal Swamp,[5] 40
There are the greenish waters, the resinous odor, the plenteous
    moss, the cypress-tree, and the juniper-tree;
Northward, young men of Mannahatta, the target company
    from an excursion returning home at evening, the musket-
    muzzles all bear bunches of flowers presented by women;
Children at play, or on his father's lap a young boy fallen
    asleep, (how his lips move! how he smiles in his sleep!)
The scout riding on horseback over the plains west of the
    Missisippi, he ascends a knoll and sweeps his eyes around;
California life, the miner, bearded, dress'd in his rude
    costume, the stanch California friendship, the sweet air,
    the graves one in passing meets solitary just aside the
    horse-path; 45
Down in Texas the cotton-field, the negro-cabins, drivers
    driving mules or oxen before rude carts, cotton bales piled
    on banks and wharves;
Encircling all, vast-darting up and wide, the American Soul,
    with equal hemispheres, one Love, one Dilation or Pride;
In arriere[6] the peace-talk with the Iroquois the aborigines, the
    calumet, the pipe of good-will, arbitration, and
    indorsement,
The sachem blowing the smoke first toward the sun and then
    toward the earth,
The drama of the scalp-dance enacted with painted faces and
    guttural exclamations, 50
The setting out of the war-party, the long and stealthy march,
The single file, the swinging hatchets, the surprise and
    slaughter of enemies;
All the acts, scenes, ways, persons, attitudes of these States,
    reminiscences, institutions,
All these States compact, every square mile of these States
    without excepting a particle;
Me pleas'd, rambling in lanes and country fields, Paumanok's
    fields, 55
Observing the spiral flight of two little yellow butterflies
    shuffling between each other, ascending high in the air,
The darting swallow, the destroyer of insects, the fall traveler
    southward but returning northward early in the spring,
The country boy at the close of the day driving the herd of
    cows and shouting to them as they loiter to browse by the
    roadside,

---

5. Marshy region north of Albermarle Sound, North Carolina.
6. French: properly arrière, "behind," "in the rear," but here meaning "in the past."

The city wharf, Boston, Philadelphia, Baltimore, Charleston,
    New Orleans, San Francisco,
The departing ships when the sailors heave the capstan;   60
Evening—me in my room—the setting sun,
The setting summer sun shining in my open window, showing
    the swarm of flies, suspended, balancing in the air in the
    centre of the room, darting athwart, up and down, casting
    swift shadows in specks on the opposite wall where the
    shine is;
The athletic American matron speaking in public to crowds of
    listeners,
Males, females, immigrants, combinations, the copiousness,
    the individuality of the States, each for itself—the money-
    makers,
Factories, machinery, the mechanical forces, the windlass,
    lever, pulley, all certainties,   65
The certainty of space, increase, freedom, futurity,
In space the sporades,[7] the scatter'd islands, the stars—on the
    firm earth, the lands, my lands,
O lands! all so dear to me—what you are, (whatever it is,) I
    putting it at random in these songs, become a part of that,
    whatever it is,
Southward there, I screaming, with wings slow flapping, with
    the myriads of gulls wintering along the coasts of Florida,
Otherways there atwixt the banks of the Arkansaw, the Rio
    Grande, the Nueces, the Brazos, the Tombigbee,[8] the Red
    River, the Saskatchawan or the Osage, I with the spring
    waters laughing and skipping and running,   70
Northward, on the sands, on some shallow bay of Paumanok, I
    with parties of snowy herons wading in the wet to seek
    worms and aquatic plants,
Retreating, triumphantly twittering, the king-bird, from
    piercing the crow with its bill, for amusement—and I
    triumphantly twittering,
The migrating flock of wild geese alighting in autumn to
    refresh themselves, the body of the flock feed, the
    sentinels outside move around with erect heads watching,
    and are from time to time reliev'd by other sentinels—and
    I feeding and taking turns with the rest,[9]
In Kanadian forests the moose, large as an ox, corner'd by
    hunters, rising desperately on his hind-feet, and plunging
    with his fore-feet, the hoofs as sharp as knives—and I,
    plunging at the hunters, corner'd and desperate,

7. Designating both "the scattered islands"—Greek isles in the Aegean, with a capital "S"—
    and the sporadic stars not belonging to any constellation.
8. *Nueces*: river in southwestern Texas; *Brazos*: river in Texas, southwest of Galveston; *Tom-*
    bigbee: river in eastern Mississippi and western Alabama.
9. Such lines as 71–73 on the behavior of birds testify to WW's close observation. In a letter
    of August 24, 1879, John Burroughs, who had been composing an article on "Nature and
    the Poets," confessed: "I cannot catch you in any mistake, as I wish I could, for that is my
    game." (Traubel, III, 260)

In the Mannahatta, streets, piers, shipping, store-houses, and
    the countless workmen working in the shops,   75
And I too of the Mannahatta, singing thereof—and no less in
    myself than the whole of the Mannahatta in itself,
Singing the song of These, my ever-united lands—my body no
    more inevitably united, part to part, and made out of a
    thousand diverse contributions one identity, any more
    than my lands are inevitably united and made ONE
    IDENTITY;
Nativities, climates, the grass of the great pastoral Plains,
Cities, labors, death, animals, products, war, good and evil—
    these me,
These affording, in all their particulars, the old feuillage to me
    and to America, how can I do less than pass the clew of
    the union of them, to afford the like to you?   80
Whoever you are! how can I but offer you divine leaves, that
    you also be eligible as I am?
How can I but as here chanting, invite you for yourself to
    collect bouquets of the incomparable feuillage of these
    States?
1860   *1881*

A Song of Joys[1]

O to make the most jubilant song!
Full of music—full of manhood, womanhood, infancy!
Full of common employments—full of grain and trees.

O for the voices of animals—O for the swiftness and balance
    of fishes!
O for the dropping of raindrops in a song!   5
O for the sunshine and motion of waves in a song!

O the joy of my spirit—it is uncaged—it darts like lightning!
It is not enough to have this globe or a certain time,
I will have thousands of globes and all time.

O the engineer's joys! to go with a locomotive!   10

1. Entitled "Poem of Joys" when it first appeared in 1860, and "Poems of Joy" in 1867, the
poem reverted to its first title in 1871 and 1876 and took its present title in 1881. Based
on personal reminiscences, but designed, like "Song of the Open Road," to celebrate the
American experience generally, the poem underwent considerable alteration by excision, ad-
dition, and transposition. The most notable addition was that in 1871 of a passage (lines
121 through 133) that may indicate a fresh access of confidence after the tribulations of the
Civil War. The MSS show that WW had been working upon this theme since the early 1850s.
For example, he made the following entry in a pre-1855 notebook (LC *Whitman*, No. 85):
"Poem incarnating the mind of an old man, whose life has been magnificently developed—
the wildest and most exuberant joy—the utterance of hope and floods of anticipation—faith
in whatever happens—but all enfolded on Joy Joy Joy which underlies and overtops the
whole effusion."

To hear the hiss of steam, the merry shriek, the steam-whistle,
the laughing locomotive!
To push with resistless way and speed off in the distance.

O the gleesome saunter over fields and hillsides!
The leaves and flowers of the commonest weeds, the moist
fresh stillness of the woods,
The exquisite smell of the earth at daybreak, and all through
the forenoon.   15

O the horseman's and horsewoman's joys!
The saddle, the gallop, the pressure upon the seat, the cool
gurgling by the ears and hair.

O the fireman's joys!
I hear the alarm at dead of night,
I hear bells, shouts! I pass the crowd, I run!   20
The sight of the flames maddens me with pleasure.

O the joy of the strong-brawn'd fighter, towering in the arena
in perfect condition, conscious of power, thirsting to meet
his opponent.

O the joy of that vast elemental sympathy which only the
human soul is capable of generating and emitting in
steady and limitless floods.

O the mother's joys!
The watching, the endurance, the precious love, the anguish,
the patiently yielded life.   25

O the joy of increase, growth, recuperation,
The joy of soothing and pacifying, the joy of concord and
harmony.

O to go back to the place where I was born,
To hear the birds sing once more,
To ramble about the house and barn and over the fields once
more,   30
And through the orchard and along the old lanes once more.

O to have been brought up on bays, lagoons, creeks, or along
the coast,
To continue and be employ'd there all my life,
The briny and damp smell, the shore, the salt weeds exposed
at low water,
The work of fishermen, the work of the eel-fisher and clam-
fisher;[2]   35

2. Lines 28–47 reflect actual memories of the poet's boyhood and the Long Island shore, where
clamming and fishing were then local industries. *Cf.* "Song of Myself," lines 182–84.

I come with my clam-rake and spade, I come with my eel-spear,
Is the tide out? I join the group of clam-diggers on the flats,
I laugh and work with them, I joke at my work like a
      mettlesome young man;
In winter I take my eel-basket and eel-spear and travel out on
      foot on the ice—I have a small axe to cut holes in the ice,
Behold me well-clothed going gayly or returning in the
      afternoon, my brood of tough boys accompanying me,   40
My brood of grown and part-grown boys, who love to be with
      no one else so well as they love to be with me,
By day to work with me, and by night to sleep with me.

Another time in warm weather out in a boat, to lift the lobster-
      pots where they are sunk with heavy stones, (I know the
      buoys,)
O the sweetness of the Fifth-month[3] morning upon the water
      as I row just before sunrise toward the buoys,
I pull the wicker pots up slantingly, the dark green lobsters are
      desperate with their claws as I take them out, I insert
      wooden pegs in the joints of their pincers,   45
I go to all the places one after another, and then row back to
      the shore,
There in a huge kettle of boiling water the lobsters shall be
      boil'd till their color becomes scarlet.

Another time mackerel-taking,
Voracious, mad for the hook, near the surface, they seem to
      fill the water for miles;
Another time fishing for rock-fish in Chesapeake bay, I one of
      the brown-faced crew;   50
Another time trailing for blue-fish off Paumanok, I stand with
      braced body,
My left foot is on the gunwale, my right arm throws far out
      the coils of slender rope,
In sight around me the quick veering and darting of fifty skiffs,
      my companions.

O boating on the rivers,
The voyage down the St. Lawrence, the superb scenery, the
      steamers,   55
The ships sailing, the Thousand Islands, the occasional timber-
      raft and the raftsmen with long-reaching sweep-oars,
The little huts on the rafts, and the steam of smoke when they
      cook supper at evening.

(O something pernicious and dread!
Something far away from a puny and pious life!

3. In Quaker parlance, the month of May.

Something unproved! something in a trance!   60
Something escaped from the anchorage and driving free.)

O to work in mines, or forging iron,
Foundry casting, the foundry itself, the rude high roof, the
    ample and shadow'd space,
The furnace, the hot liquid pour'd out and running.

O to resume the joys of the soldier!   65
To feel the presence of a brave commanding officer—to feel
    his sympathy!
To behold his calmness—to be warm'd in the rays of his smile!
To go to battle—to hear the bugles play and the drums beat!
To hear the crash of artillery—to see the glittering of the
    bayonets and musket-barrels in the sun!
To see men fall and die and not complain!   70
To taste the savage taste of blood—to be so devilish!
To gloat so over the wounds and deaths of the enemy.

O the whaleman's joys! O I cruise my old cruise again!
I feel the ship's motion under me, I feel the Atlantic breezes
    fanning me,
I hear the cry again sent down from the mast-head, *There—
    she blows!*   75
Again I spring up the rigging to look with the rest—we
    descend, wild with excitement,
I leap in the lower'd boat, we row toward our prey where he lies,
We approach stealthy and silent, I see the mountainous mass,
    lethargic, basking,
I see the harpooneer standing up, I see the weapon dart from
    his vigorous arm;
O swift again far out in the ocean the wounded whale,
    settling, running to windward, tows me,   80
Again I see him rise to breathe, we row close again,
I see a lance driven through his side, press'd deep, turn'd in
    the wound,
Again we back off, I see him settle again, the life is leaving
    him fast,
As he rises he spouts blood, I see him swim in circles narrower
    and narrower, swiftly cutting the water—I see him die,
He gives one convulsive leap in the centre of the circle, and
    then falls flat and still in the bloody foam.   85

O the old manhood of me, my noblest joy of all!
My children and grand-children, my white hair and beard,
My largeness, calmness, majesty, out of the long stretch of my
    life.

O ripen'd joy of womanhood! O happiness at last!
I am more than eighty years of age, I am the most venerable
      mother,   90
How clear is my mind—how all people draw nigh to me!
What attractions are these beyond any before? what bloom
      more than the bloom of youth?
What beauty is this that descends upon me and rises out of me?

O the orator's joys!
To inflate the chest, to roll the thunder of the voice out from
      the ribs and throat,   95
To make the people rage, weep, hate, desire, with yourself,
To lead America—to quell America with a great tongue.

O the joy of my soul leaning pois'd on itself, receiving identity
      through materials and loving them, observing characters
      and absorbing them,
My soul vibrated back to me from them, from sight, hearing,
      touch, reason, articulation, comparison, memory, and the
      like,
The real life of my senses and flesh transcending my senses
      and flesh,   100
My body done with materials, my sight done with my material
      eyes,
Proved to me this day beyond cavil that it is not my material
      eyes which finally see,
Nor my material body which finally loves, walks, laughs,
      shouts, embraces, procreates.

O the farmer's joys!
Ohioan's, Illinoisian's, Wisconsinese', Kanadian's, Iowan's,
      Kansian's, Missourian's, Oregonese' joys!   105
To rise at peep of day and pass forth nimbly to work,
To plough land in the fall for winter-sown crops,
To plough land in the spring for maize,
To train orchards, to graft the trees, to gather apples in the fall.

O to bathe in the swimming-bath, or in a good place along
      shore,   110
To splash the water! to walk ankle-deep, or race naked along
      the shore.

O to realize space!
The plenteousness of all, that there are no bounds,
To emerge and be of the sky, of the sun and moon and flying
      clouds, as one with them.

O the joy of a manly self-hood!   115
To be servile to none, to defer to none, not to any tyrant
    known or unknown,
To walk with erect carriage, a step springy and elastic,
To look with calm gaze or with a flashing eye,
To speak with a full and sonorous voice out of a broad chest,
To confront with your personality all the other personalities of
    the earth.   120

Know'st thou the excellent joys of youth?
Joys of the dear companions and of the merry word and
    laughing face?
Joy of the glad light-beaming day, joy of the wide-breath'd
    games?
Joy of sweet music, joy of the lighted ball-room and the
    dancers?
Joy of the plenteous dinner, strong carouse and drinking?   125

Yet O my soul supreme!
Know'st thou the joys of pensive thought?
Joys of the free and lonesome heart, the tender, gloomy heart?
Joys of the solitary walk, the spirit bow'd yet proud, the
    suffering and the struggle?
The agonistic[4] throes, the ecstasies, joys of the solemn musings
    day or night?   130
Joys of the thought of Death, the great spheres Time and Space?
Prophetic joys of better, loftier love's ideals, the divine wife,
    the sweet, eternal, perfect comrade?
Joys all thine own undying one, joys worthy thee O soul.

O while I live to be the ruler of life, not a slave,
To meet life as a powerful conqueror,   135
No fumes, no ennui, no more complaints or scornful
    criticisms,
To these proud laws of the air, the water and the ground,
    proving my interior soul impregnable,
And nothing exterior shall ever take command of me.

For not life's joys alone I sing, repeating—the joy of death!
The beautiful touch of Death, soothing and benumbing a few
    moments, for reasons,   140
Myself discharging my excrementitious body to be burn'd, or
    render'd to powder, or buried,
My real body doubtless left to me for other spheres,
My voided body nothing more to me, returning to the
    purifications, further offices, eternal uses of the earth.

4. In its primary Greek meaning, relating to the contest in athletics or the arts.

O to attract by more than attraction!
How it is I know not—yet behold! the something which obeys
    none of the rest,   145
It is offensive, never defensive—yet how magnetic it draws.

O to struggle against great odds, to meet enemies undaunted!
To be entirely alone with them, to find how much one can stand!
To look strife, torture, prison, popular odium, face to face!
To mount the scaffold, to advance to the muzzles of guns with
    perfect nonchalance!   150
To be indeed a God!

O to sail to sea in a ship!
To leave this steady unendurable land,
To leave the tiresome sameness of the streets, the sidewalks
    and the houses,
To leave you O you solid motionless land, and entering a ship,   155
To sail and sail and sail!

O to have life henceforth a poem of new joys!
To dance, clap hands, exult, shout, skip, leap, roll on, float on!
To be a sailor of the world bound for all ports,
A ship itself, (see indeed these sails I spread to the sun and
    air,)   160
A swift and swelling ship full of rich words, full of joys.
1860   *1881*

Song of the Broad-Axe[1]

1

Weapon shapely, naked, wan,
Head from the mother's bowels drawn,
Wooded flesh and metal bone, limb only one and lip only one,
Gray-blue leaf by red-heat grown, helve produced from a little
    seed sown,
Resting the grass amid and upon,   5
To be lean'd and to lean on.

Strong shapes and attributes of strong shapes, masculine
    trades, sights and sounds,

1. Entitled "Broad-Axe Poem" in 1856 and "Chants Democratic" No. 2 in 1860, this poem
took its present title in 1867. From the 390 lines of the first version to the 254 of its final
form, it has been much revised, although the superb first six lines and indeed the whole
poem's essential quality was achieved in the 1856 text. The most considerable change is the
disappearance after 1860 of eighteen lines, just before its final section, that exuberantly
described the idealized "shape" of the poet himself, "arrogant, masculine, naive, rowdy-
ish . . ." For discussions of this poem, see Dorothy M.-T. Gregory, "The Celebration of
Nativity: 'Broad-Axe Poem,' " *WWQR* 2, no. 1 (Summer 1984): 1–11; and David Cavitch,
"The Lament in 'Song of the Broad-Axe',", in Joann P. Krieg, ed., *Walt Whitman: Here and
Now* (Westport, Conn.: Greenwood, 1985), 125–35.

Long varied train of an emblem, dabs of music,
Fingers of the organist skipping staccato over the keys of the
 great organ.

2

Welcome are all earth's lands, each for its kind,   10
Welcome are lands of pine and oak,
Welcome are lands of the lemon and fig,
Welcome are lands of gold,
Welcome are lands of wheat and maize, welcome those of the
 grape,
Welcome are lands of sugar and rice,   15
Welcome the cotton-lands, welcome those of the white potato
 and sweet potato,
Welcome are mountains, flats, sands, forests, prairies,
Welcome the rich borders of rivers, table-lands, openings,
Welcome the measureless grazing-lands, welcome the teeming
 soil of orchards, flax, honey, hemp;
Welcome just as much the other more hard-faced lands,   20
Lands rich as lands of gold or wheat and fruit lands,
Lands of mines, lands of the manly and rugged ores,
Lands of coal, copper, lead, tin, zinc,
Lands of iron—lands of the make of the axe.

3

The log at the wood-pile, the axe supported by it,   25
The sylvan hut, the vine over the doorway, the space clear'd
 for a garden,
The irregular tapping of rain down on the leaves after the
 storm is lull'd,
The wailing and moaning at intervals, the thought of the sea,
The thought of ships struck in the storm and put on their
 beam ends, and the cutting away of masts,
The sentiment of the huge timbers of old-fashion'd houses and
 barns,   30
The remember'd print or narrative, the voyage at a venture of
 men, families, goods,
The disembarkation, the founding of a new city,
The voyage of those who sought a New England and found it,
 the outset anywhere,
The settlements of the Arkansas, Colorado, Ottawa,
 Willamette,[2]
The slow progress, the scant fare, the axe, rifle, saddle-bags;   35
The beauty of all adventurous and daring persons,
The beauty of wood-boys and wood-men with their clear
 untrimm'd faces,

---

2. *Ottawa*: river in Canada between Ontario and Quebec; *Willamette*: river in western Oregon,
flowing into the Columbia river.

The beauty of independence, departure, actions that rely on
    themselves,
The American contempt for statutes and ceremonies, the
    boundless impatience of restraint,
The loose drift of character, the inkling through random types,
    the solidification;   40
The butcher in the slaughter-house, the hands aboard
    schooners and sloops, the raftsman, the pioneer,
Lumbermen in their winter camp, daybreak in the woods,
    stripes of snow on the limbs of trees, the occasional
    snapping,
The glad clear sound of one's own voice, the merry song, the
    natural life of the woods, the strong day's work,
The blazing fire at night, the sweet taste of supper, the talk,
    the bed of hemlock-boughs and the bear-skin;
The house-builder at work in cities or anywhere,[3]   45
The preparatory jointing, squaring, sawing, mortising,
The hoist-up of beams, the push of them in their places, laying
    them regular,
Setting the studs by their tenons in the mortises according as
    they were prepared,
The blows of mallets and hammers, the attitudes of the men,
    their curv'd limbs,
Bending, standing, astride the beams, driving in pins, holding
    on by posts and braces,   50
The hook'd arm over the plate, the other arm wielding the axe,
The floor-men forcing the planks close to be nail'd,
Their postures bringing their weapons downward on the bearers,
The echoes resounding through the vacant building;
The huge storehouse carried up in the city well under way,   55
The six framing-men, two in the middle and two at each end,
    carefully bearing on their shoulders a heavy stick for a
    cross-beam,
The crowded line of masons with trowels in their right hands
    rapidly laying the long side-wall, two hundred feet from
    front to rear,
The flexible rise and fall of backs, the continual click of the
    trowels striking the bricks,
The bricks one after another each laid so workmanlike in its
    place, and set with a knock of the trowel-handle,
The piles of materials, the mortar on the mortar-boards, and
    the steady replenishing by the hod-men;   60
Spar-makers in the spar-yard, the swarming row of well-grown
    apprentices,
The swing of their axes on the square-hew'd log shaping it
    toward the shape of a mast,

---

3. Lines 45–72 reflect the poet's youthful experience as a carpenter, his love of the trustworthy
   tools, the well-joined wood, the familiar excitement of the fire in that fire-prone age.

The brisk short crackle of the steel driven slantingly into the pine,
The butter-color'd chips flying off in great flakes and slivers,
The limber motion of brawny young arms and hips in easy
    costumes,   65
The constructor of wharves, bridges, piers, bulk-heads, floats,
    stays against the sea;
The city fireman, the fire that suddenly bursts forth in the
    close-pack'd square,
The arriving engines, the hoarse shouts, the nimble stepping
    and daring,
The strong command through the fire-trumpets, the falling in
    line, the rise and fall of the arms forcing the water,
The slender, spasmic, blue-white jets, the bringing to bear of
    the hooks and ladders and their execution,   70
The crash and cut away of connecting wood-work, or through
    floors if the fire smoulders under them,
The crowd with their lit faces watching, the glare and dense
    shadows;
The forger at his forge-furnace and the user of iron after him,
The maker of the axe large and small, and the welder and
    temperer,
The chooser breathing his breath on the cold steel and trying
    the edge with his thumb,   75
The one who clean-shapes the handle and sets it firmly in the
    socket;
The shadowy processions of the portraits of the past users also,
The primal patient mechanics, the architects and engineers,
The far-off Assyrian edifice and Mizra[4] edifice,
The Roman lictors[5] preceding the consuls,   80
The antique European warrior with his axe in combat,
The uplifted arm, the clatter of blows on the helmeted head,
The death-howl, the limpsy tumbling body, the rush of friend
    and foe thither,
The siege of revolted lieges determin'd for liberty,
The summons to surrender, the battering at castle gates, the
    truce and parley,   85
The sack of an old city in its time,
The bursting in of mercenaries and bigots tumultuously and
    disorderly,
Roar, flames, blood, drunkenness, madness,
Goods freely rifled from houses and temples, screams of
    women in the gripe of brigands,
Craft and thievery of camp-followers, men running, old
    persons despairing,   90
The hell of war, the cruelties of creeds,
The list of all executive deeds and words just or unjust,
The power of personality just or unjust.

4. Egyptian, after "Mizraim," biblical name for Egypt.
5. Minor Roman officials who carried the fasces (rods and axe), symbol of authority, in
    procession.

4

Muscle and pluck forever!
What invigorates life invigorates death, 95
And the dead advance as much as the living advance,
And the future is no more uncertain than the present,
For the roughness of the earth and of man encloses as much
      as the delicatesse[6] of the earth and of man,
And nothing endures but personal qualities.

What do you think endures? 100
Do you think a great city endures?
Or a teeming manufacturing state? or a prepared constitution?
      or the best built steamships?
Or hotels of granite and iron? or any chef-d'œuvres of
      engineering, forts, armaments?
Away! these are not to be cherish'd for themselves,
They fill their hour, the dancers dance, the musicians play for
      them, 105
The show passes, all does well enough of course,
All does very well till one flash of defiance.

A great city is that which has the greatest men and women,
If it be a few ragged huts it is still the greatest city in the
      whole world.

5

The place where a great city stands is not the place of
      stretch'd wharves, docks, manufactures, deposits of
      produce merely, 110
Nor the place of ceaseless salutes of new-comers or the
      anchor-lifters of the departing,
Nor the place of the tallest and costliest buildings or shops
      selling goods from the rest of the earth,
Nor the place of the best libraries and schools, nor the place
      where money is plentiest,
Nor the place of the most numerous population.

Where the city stands with the brawniest breed of orators and
      bards, 115
Where the city stands that is belov'd by these, and loves them
      in return and understands them,
Where no monuments exist to heroes but in the common
      words and deeds,
Where thrift is in its place, and prudence is in its place,[7]
Where the men and women think lightly of the laws,
Where the slave ceases, and the master of slaves ceases, 120

---

6. French: properly "délicatesse," "delicacy."
7. Cf. "Song of Prudence" and note thereon. To WW prudence was not merely a pragmatic
   virtue, but intrinsic and inseparable in every virtuous thought or deed, recalling its original
   association with "providence."

Where the populace rise at once against the never-ending
　　audacity of elected persons,
Where fierce men and women pour forth as the sea to the
　　whistle of death pours its sweeping and unript waves,
Where outside authority enters always after the precedence of
　　inside authority,
Where the citizen is always the head and ideal, and President,
　　Mayor, Governor and what not, are agents for pay,
Where children are taught to be laws to themselves, and to
　　depend on themselves,　　　　　　　　　　　　　　　　125
Where equanimity is illustrated in affairs,
Where speculations on the soul are encouraged,
Where women walk in public processions in the streets the
　　same as the men,
Where they enter the public assembly and take places the
　　same as the men;
Where the city of the faithfulest friends stands,　　　　　130
Where the city of the cleanliness of the sexes stands,
Where the city of the healthiest fathers stands,
Where the city of the best-bodied mothers stands,
There the great city stands.

6

How beggarly appear arguments before a defiant deed!　　135
How the floridness of the materials of cities shrivels before a
　　man's or woman's look!

All waits or goes by default till a strong being appears;
A strong being is the proof of the race and of the ability of the
　　universe,
When he or she appears materials are overaw'd,
The dispute on the soul stops,　　　　　　　　　　　　　140
The old customs and phrases are confronted, turn'd back, or
　　laid away.

What is your money-making now? what can it do now?
What is your respectability now?
What are your theology, tuition, society, traditions, statute-
　　books, now?
Where are your jibes of being now?　　　　　　　　　　145
Where are your cavils about the soul now?

7

A sterile landscape covers the ore, there is as good as the best
　　for all the forbidding appearance.

There is the mine, there are the miners,
The forge-furnace is there, the melt is accomplish'd, the
　　hammers-men are at hand with their tongs and hammers,
What always served and always serves is at hand.　　　　150

Than this nothing has better served, it has served all,
Served the fluent-tongued and subtle-sensed Greek, and long
 ere the Greek,
Served in building the buildings that last longer than any,
Served the Hebrew, the Persian, the most ancient Hindustanee,
Served the mound-raiser on the Mississippi, served those
 whose relics remain in Central America,   155
Served Albic[8] temples in woods or on plains, with unhewn
 pillars and the druids,
Served the artificial clefts, vast, high, silent, on the snow-
 cover'd hills of Scandinavia,
Served those who time out of mind made on the granite walls
 rough sketches of the sun, moon, stars, ships, ocean
 waves,
Served the paths of the irruptions of the Goths, served the
 pastoral tribes and nomads,
Served the long distant Kelt, served the hardy pirates of the
 Baltic,   160
Served before any of those the venerable and harmless men of
 Ethiopia,
Served the making of helms for the galleys of pleasure and the
 making of those for war,
Served all great works on land and all great works on the sea,
For the mediæval ages and before the mediæval ages,
Served not the living only then as now, but served the dead.   165

8

I see the European headsman,
He stands mask'd, clothed in red, with huge legs and strong
 naked arms,
And leans on a ponderous axe.

(Whom have you slaughter'd lately European headsman?
Whose is that blood upon you so wet and sticky?)   170

I see the clear sunset of the martyrs,
I see from the scaffolds the descending ghosts,
Ghosts of dead lords, uncrown'd ladies, impeach'd ministers,
 rejected kings,
Rivals, traitors, poisoners, disgraced chieftains and the rest.

I see those who in any land have died for the good cause,   175
The seed is spare, nevertheless the crop shall never run out,
(Mind you O foreign kings, O priests, the crop shall never run out.)

8. English, from "Albion," ancient name for England.

I see the blood wash'd entirely away from the axe,
Both blade and helve are clean,
They spirt no more the blood of European nobles, they clasp
    no more the necks of queens.   180

I see the headsman withdraw and become useless,
I see the scaffold untrodden and mouldy, I see no longer any
    axe upon it,
I see the mighty and friendly emblem of the power of my own
    race, the newest, largest race.

9

(America! I do not vaunt my love for you,
I have what I have.)   185

The axe leaps!
The solid forest gives fluid utterances,
They tumble forth, they rise and form,
Hut, tent, landing, survey,
Flail, plough, pick, crowbar, spade,   190
Shingle, rail, prop, wainscot, jamb, lath, panel, gable,
Citadel, ceiling, saloon, academy, organ, exhibition-house, library,
Cornice, trellis, pilaster, balcony, window, turret, porch,
Hoe, rake, pitchfork, pencil, wagon, staff, saw, jack-plane,
    mallet, wedge, rounce,[9]
Chair, tub, hoop, table, wicket, vane, sash, floor,   195
Work-box, chest, string'd instrument, boat, frame, and what not,
Capitols of States, and capitol of the nation of States,
Long stately rows in avenues, hospitals for orphans or for the
    poor or sick,
Manhattan steamboats and clippers taking the measure of all seas.

The shapes arise!   200
Shapes of the using of axes anyhow, and the users and all that
    neighbors them,
Cutters down of wood and haulers of it to the Penobscot or
    Kennebec,
Dwellers in cabins among the Californian mountains or by the
    little lakes, or on the Columbia,
Dwellers south on the banks of the Gila or Rio Grande,
    friendly gatherings, the characters and fun,
Dwellers along the St. Lawrence, or north in Kanada, or down
    by the Yellowstone, dwellers on coasts and off coasts,   205
Seal-fishers, whalers, arctic seamen breaking passages through
    the ice.

9. Handle of a hand press.

The shapes arise!
Shapes of factories, arsenals, foundries, markets,
Shapes of the two-threaded tracks of railroads,
Shapes of the sleepers of bridges, vast frameworks, girders,
    arches,   210
Shapes of the fleets of barges, tows, lake and canal craft, river
    craft,
Ship-yards and dry-docks along the Eastern and Western seas,
    and in many a bay and by-place,
The live-oak kelsons, the pine planks, the spars, the
    hackmatack-roots for knees,[1]
The ships themselves on their ways, the tiers of scaffolds, the
    workmen busy outside and inside,
The tools lying around, the great auger and little auger, the
    adze, bolt, line, square, gouge, and bead-plane.   215

10

The shapes arise!
The shape measur'd, saw'd, jack'd, join'd, stain'd,
The coffin-shape for the dead to lie within in his shroud,
The shape got out in posts, in the bedstead posts, in the posts
    of the bride's bed,
The shape of the little trough, the shape of the rockers
    beneath, the shape of the babe's cradle,   220
The shape of the floor-planks, the floor-planks for dancers' feet,
The shape of the planks of the family home, the home of the
    friendly parents and children,
The shape of the roof of the home of the happy young man
    and woman, the roof over the well-married young man
    and woman,
The roof over the supper joyously cook'd by the chaste wife,
    and joyously eaten by the chaste husband, content after
    his day's work.

The shapes arise!   225
The shape of the prisoner's place in the court-room, and of
    him or her seated in the place,
The shape of the liquor-bar lean'd against by the young rum-
    drinker and the old rum-drinker,
The shape of the shamed and angry stairs trod by sneaking
    footsteps,
The shape of the sly settee, and the adulterous unwholesome
    couple,
The shape of the gambling-board with its devilish winnings
    and losings,   230
The shape of the step-ladder for the convicted and sentenced

---

1. Larch or juniper roots; the "knees" are structural members of bent wood that bear strains.

murderer, the murderer with haggard face and pinion'd arms,
The sheriff at hand with his deputies, the silent and white-
    lipp'd crowd, the dangling of the rope.

The shapes arise!
Shapes of doors giving many exits and entrances,
The door passing the dissever'd friend flush'd and in haste,   235
The door that admits good news and bad news,
The door whence the son left home confident and puff'd up,
The door he enter'd again from a long and scandalous absence,
    diseas'd, broken down, without innocence, without means.

11

Her shape arises,
She less guarded than ever, yet more guarded than ever,   240
The gross and soil'd she moves among do not make her gross
    and soil'd,
She knows the thoughts as she passes, nothing is conceal'd
    from her,
She is none the less considerate or friendly therefor,
She is the best belov'd, it is without exception, she has no
    reason to fear and she does not fear,
Oaths, quarrels, hiccup'd songs, smutty expressions, are idle to
    her as she passes,   245
She is silent, she is possess'd of herself, they do not offend her,
She receives them as the laws of Nature receive them, she is
    strong,
She too is a law of Nature—there is no law stronger than she is.

12

The main shapes arise!
Shapes of Democracy total, result of centuries,   250
Shapes ever projecting other shapes,
Shapes of turbulent manly cities,
Shapes of the friends and home-givers of the whole earth,
Shapes bracing the earth and braced with the whole earth.
   1856   *1881*

Song of the Exposition[1]

1

(Ah little recks the laborer,
How near his work is holding him to God,
The loving Laborer through space and time.)

After all not to create only, or found only,
But to bring perhaps from afar what is already founded,   5
To give it our own identity, average, limitless, free,
To fill the gross the torpid bulk with vital religious fire,
Not to repel or destroy so much as accept, fuse, rehabilitate,
To obey as well as command, to follow more than to lead,
These also are the lessons of our New World;   10
While how little the New after all, how much the Old, Old
    World!

Long and long has the grass been growing,
Long and long has the rain been falling,
Long has the globe been rolling round.

2

Come Muse migrate from Greece and Ionia,   15
Cross out please those immensely overpaid accounts,
That matter of Troy and Achilles' wrath, and Æneas',
    Odysseus' wanderings,[2]
Placard "Removed" and "To Let" on the rocks of your snowy
    Parnassus,[3]
Repeat at Jerusalem, place the notice high on Jaffa's gate and
    on Mount Moriah,[4]
The same on the walls of your German, French and Spanish
    castles, and Italian collections,   20
For know a better, fresher, busier sphere, a wide, untried
    domain awaits, demands you.

1. Composed in response to the invitation of the American Institute to read a poem at the opening of its fortieth Annual Exhibition in New York City, September 7, 1871, this piece was published in the same year as a booklet under the title *After All, Not to Create Only* following its appearance in a dozen newspapers, including the *Washington Daily Morning Chronicle,* the *New York Evening Post,* and the *Springfield Republican,* on the occasion of its presentation at the Exhibition. In fact, WW did his best to publicize the event, furnishing copy himself, and later defending the poem anonymously against a prevailingly hostile press. One editorial (*New York Globe,* September 7, 1871) boasted of the poet's foreign reputation with details that WW himself must have supplied, if indeed he were not the actual author. See Allen, 432–35 and Traubel, I, 324–29. The poem appeared under its first title at the end of the 1872 *Leaves of Grass,* and in the *Two Rivulets* of 1876 under its present title, "Song of the Exposition," prefaced by an editorial. For the final 1881 text, the poem was improved by the addition of the opening three lines and the deletion of some twenty lines.
2. These are, of course, references to the Homeric epics and to Virgil's *Aeneid.*
3. A peak in southern Greece, sacred to the Muses and hence a symbol of the realm of poetry.
4. Jaffa is a seaport in Israel; *Mount Moriah*: hill of Jerusalem on which Solomon's temple was built.

3

Responsive to our summons,
Or rather to her long-nurs'd inclination,
Join'd with an irresistible, natural gravitation,
She comes! I hear the rustling of her gown,   25
I scent the odor of her breath's delicious fragrance,
I mark her step divine, her curious eyes a-turning, rolling,
Upon this very scene.

The dame of dames! can I believe then,
Those ancient temples, sculptures classic, could none of them
    retain[5] her?   30
Nor shades of Virgil and Dante, nor myriad memories, poems,
    old associations, magnetize and hold on to her?
But that she's left them all—and here?

Yes, if you will allow me to say so,
I, my friends, if you do not, can plainly see her,
The same undying soul of earth's, activity's, beauty's, heroism's
    expression,   35
Out from her evolutions hither come, ended the strata of her
    former themes,
Hidden and cover'd by to-day's, foundation of to-day's,
Ended, deceas'd through time, her voice by Castaly's fountain,[6]
Silent the broken-lipp'd Sphynx in Egypt, silent all those
    century-baffling tombs,
Ended for aye the epics of Asia's, Europe's helmeted warriors,
    ended the primitive call of the muses,   40
Calliope's call forever closed, Clio, Melpomene, Thalia dead,[7]
Ended the stately rhythmus of Una and Oriana, ended the
    quest of the holy Graal,[8]
Jerusalem a handful of ashes blown by the wind, extinct,
The Crusaders' streams of shadowy midnight troops sped with
    the sunrise,
Amadis, Tancred, utterly gone, Charlemagne, Roland, Oliver
    gone,[9]   45
Palmerin, ogre, departed, vanish'd the turrets that Usk from its
    waters reflected,[1]

---

5. This word is "restrain" both in MS and in the 1871 edition.
6. A spring on Mount Parnassus whose waters were thought to be a source of poetic inspiration.
7. Respectively, the muses of epic poetry, history, tragedy, and comedy.
8. *Una*: the character who symbolizes true religion in Book I of Spenser's *Faerie Queene*. *Oriana*: a character in the romance *Amadis of Gaul*, also the name given by Elizabethan poets to Queen Elizabeth; *holy Graal*: more commonly spelled "Grail," the legendary cup used by Jesus at the Last Supper.
9. *Amadis*: hero of medieval romances; *Tancred*: Norman leader of the first Crusade; *Charlemagne*: king of the Franks, 800–814; *Roland*: legendary hero of the Charlemagne exploits; *Oliver*: a friend of Roland and one of Charlemagne's twelve peers.
1. *Palmerin*: hero of the Portuguese romance, *Palmerin of England*; *Usk*: river of Wales and England, associated with Arthurian legend.

Arthur vanish'd with all his knights, Merlin and Lancelot and
    Galahad,[2] all gone, dissolv'd utterly like an exhalation;
Pass'd! pass'd! for us, forever pass'd, that once so mighty
    world, now void, inanimate, phantom world,
Embroider'd, dazzling, foreign world, with all its gorgeous
    legends, myths,
Its kings and castles proud, its priests and warlike lords and
    courtly dames,   50
Pass'd to its charnel vault, coffin'd with crown and armor on,
Blazon'd with Shakspere's purple page,
And dirged by Tennyson's sweet sad rhyme.[3]

I say I see, my friends, if you do not, the illustrious emigré,
    (having it is true in her day, although the same, changed,
    journey'd considerable,)
Making directly for this rendezvous, vigorously clearing a path
    for herself, striding through the confusion,   55
By thud of machinery and shrill steam-whistle undismay'd,
Bluff'd not a bit by drain-pipe, gasometers, artificial fertilizers,
Smiling and pleas'd with palpable intent to stay,
She's here, install'd amid the kitchen ware!

4

But hold—don't I forget my manners?   60
To introduce the stranger, (what else indeed do I live to chant
    for?) to thee Columbia;
In liberty's name welcome immortal! clasp hands,
And ever henceforth sisters dear be both.

Fear not O Muse! truly new ways and days receive, surround you,
I candidly confess a queer, queer race, of novel fashion,   65
And yet the same old human race, the same within, without,
Faces and hearts the same, feelings the same, yearnings the same,
The same old love, beauty and use the same.

5

We do not blame thee elder World, nor really separate
    ourselves from thee,
(Would the son separate himself from the father?)   70

---

2. *Arthur*: legendary king of Britain, sixth century, founder of the Round Table; *Merlin*: ma-
gician and seer, helper of King Arthur; *Lancelot*: bravest among King Arthur's knights, lover
of Queen Guinevere; *Galahad*: noblest of the knights of the Round Table, son of Lancelot
and Elaine.
3. Tennyson's romances, *Idylls of the King*, 1859–85, were then—it should be remembered
—strictly contemporary.

Looking back on thee, seeing thee to thy duties, grandeurs,
  through past ages bending, building,
We build to ours to-day.

Mightier than Egypt's tombs,
Fairer than Grecia's, Roma's temples,
Prouder than Milan's statued, spired cathedral,   75
More picturesque than Rhenish castle-keeps,
We plan even now to raise, beyond them all,
Thy great cathedral sacred industry, no tomb,
A keep for life for practical invention.

As in a waking vision,   80
E'en while I chant I see it rise, I scan and prophesy outside
  and in,
Its manifold ensemble.

Around a palace, loftier, fairer, ampler than any yet,[4]
Earth's modern wonder, history's seven outstripping,
High rising tier on tier with glass and iron façades,   85
Gladdening the sun and sky, enhued in cheerfulest hues,
Bronze, lilac, robin's-egg, marine and crimson,
Over whose golden roof shall flaunt, beneath thy banner
  Freedom,
The banners of the States and flags of every land,
A brood of lofty, fair, but lesser palaces shall cluster.   90

Somewhere within their walls shall all that forwards perfect
  human life be started,
Tried, taught, advanced, visibly exhibited.

Not only all the world of works, trade, products,
But all the workmen of the world here to be represented.

Here shall you trace in flowing operation,   95
In every state of practical, busy movement, the rills of
  civilization,
Materials here under your eye shall change their shape as if by
  magic,
The cotton shall be pick'd almost in the very field,
Shall be dried, clean'd, ginn'd, baled, spun into thread and
  cloth before you,
You shall see hands at work at all the old processes and all the
  new ones,   100
You shall see the various grains and how flour is made and
  then bread baked by the bakers,

4. Lines 83–90, are descriptive of the famous exhibition structures of the time—the great
Crystal Palace of London, built to house the International Exhibition of 1851, and the
American Crystal Palace opened in 1853 to house a World's Fair at what is now Bryant
Park, New York City.

You shall see the crude ores of California and Nevada passing
    on and on till they become bullion,
You shall watch how the printer sets type, and learn what a
    composing-stick is,
You shall mark in amazement the Hoe press[5] whirling its
    cylinders, shedding the printed leaves steady and fast,
The photograph, model, watch, pin, nail, shall be created
    before you.   105

In large calm halls, a stately museum shall teach you the
    infinite lessons of minerals,
In another, woods, plants, vegetation shall be illustrated—in
    another animals, animal life and development.

One stately house shall be the music house,
Others for other arts—learning, the sciences, shall all be here,
None shall be slighted, none but shall here be honor'd, help'd,
    exampled.   110

6

(This, this and these, America, shall be *your* pyramids and obelisks,
Your Alexandrian Pharos,[6] gardens of Babylon,
Your temple at Olympia.[7])

The male and female many laboring not,
Shall ever here confront the laboring many,   115
With precious benefits to both, glory to all,
To thee America, and thee eternal Muse.

And here shall ye inhabit powerful Matrons!
In your vast state vaster than all the old,
Echoed through long, long centuries to come,   120
To sound of different, prouder songs, with stronger themes,
Practical, peaceful life, the people's life, the People themselves,
Lifted, illumin'd, bathed in peace—elate, secure in peace.

7

Away with themes of war![8] away with war itself!
Hence from my shuddering sight to never more return that
    show of blacken'd, mutilated corpses!   125
That hell unpent and raid of blood, fit for wild tigers or for
    lop-tongued wolves, not reasoning men,

---

5. Rotary press invented in 1846 by Richard March Hoe, and on display at the Exposition.
6. Lighthouse near Alexandria, Egypt, one of the seven wonders of the ancient world, as were also the Gardens of Babylon.
7. In ancient Elis, Greece, famous for colossal statue of Zeus by Phidias.
8. *Cf.* "As I Ponder'd in Silence," where the war of bloodshed is supplanted by the war of ideas. Here the poet suggests that technology will conquer war.

And in its stead speed industry's campaigns,
With thy undaunted armies, engineering,
Thy pennants labor, loosen'd to the breeze,
Thy bugles sounding loud and clear.   130

Away with old romance![9]
Away with novels, plots and plays of foreign courts,
Away with love-verses sugar'd in rhyme, the intrigues, amours
    of idlers,
Fitted for only banquets of the night where dancers to late
    music slide,
The unhealthy pleasures, extravagant dissipations of the few,   135
With perfumes, heat and wine, beneath the dazzling chandeliers.

To you ye reverent sane sisters,[1]
I raise a voice for far superber themes for poets and for art,
To exalt the present and the real,
To teach the average man the glory of his daily walk and trade,   140
To sing in songs how exercise and chemical life are never to be
    baffled,
To manual work for each and all, to plough, hoe, dig,
To plant and tend the tree, the berry, vegetables, flowers,
For every man to see to it that he really do something, for
    every woman too;
To use the hammer and the saw, (rip, or cross-cut,)   145
To cultivate a turn for carpentering, plastering, painting,
To work as tailor, tailoress, nurse, hostler, porter,
To invent a little, something ingenious, to aid the washing,
    cooking, cleaning,
And hold it no disgrace to take a hand at them themselves.

I say I bring thee Muse to-day and here,   150
All occupations, duties broad and close,
Toil, healthy toil and sweat, endless, without cessation,
The old, old practical burdens, interests, joys,
The family, parentage, childhood, husband and wife,
The house-comforts, the house itself and all its belongings,   155
Food and its preservation, chemistry applied to it,
Whatever forms the average, strong, complete, sweet-blooded
    man or woman, the perfect longeve[2] personality,
And helps its present life to health and happiness, and shapes
    its soul,
For the eternal real life to come.

With latest connections, works, the inter-transportation of the
    world,   160

9. Persistently anti-romantic both in poetry and prose criticism, WW associated his idea of
    romanticism with intrigues, amours, and the extravagant dissipation of an effete civilization.
1. The nine Muses.
2. Long-lasting.

Steam-power, the great express lines, gas, petroleum,
These triumphs of our time, the Atlantic's delicate cable,
The Pacific railroad, the Suez canal, the Mont Cenis and
    Gothard and Hoosac tunnels,[3] the Brooklyn bridge,
This earth all spann'd with iron rails, with lines of steamships
    threading every sea,
Our own rondure, the current globe I bring.   165

8

And thou America,
Thy offspring towering e'er so high, yet higher Thee above all
    towering,
With Victory on thy left, and at thy right hand Law;
Thou Union holding all, fusing, absorbing, tolerating all,
Thee, ever thee, I sing.   170

Thou, also thou, a World,
With all thy wide geographies, manifold, different, distant,
Rounded by thee in one—one common orbic language,
One common indivisible destiny for All.

And by the spells which ye vouchsafe to those your ministers
    in earnest,   175
I here personify and call my themes, to make them pass before ye.

Behold, America! (and thou, ineffable guest and sister!)
For thee come trooping up thy waters and thy lands;
Behold! thy fields and farms, thy far-off woods and mountains,
As in procession coming.   180

Behold, the sea itself,
And on its limitless, heaving breast, the ships;
See, where their white sails, bellying in the wind, speckle the
    green and blue,
See, the steamers coming and going, steaming in or out of port,
See, dusky and undulating, the long pennants of smoke.   185

Behold, in Oregon, far in the north and west,
Or in Maine, far in the north and east, thy cheerful axemen,
Wielding all day their axes.

Behold, on the lakes, thy pilots at their wheels, thy oarsmen,
How the ash writhes under those muscular arms!   190

---

3. Respectively, an 8-mile tunnel joining France and Italy through Alpine Mount Cenis; a
9¼-mile tunnel beneath St. Gotthard pass between Switzerland and Italy; a 4½-mile tunnel
in Massachusetts on the Fitchburg railroad.

There by the furnace, and there by the anvil,
Behold thy sturdy blacksmiths swinging their sledges,
Overhand so steady, overhand they turn and fall with joyous clank,
Like a tumult of laughter.

Mark the spirit of invention everywhere, thy rapid patents,   195
Thy continual workshops, foundries, risen or rising,
See, from their chimneys how the tall flame-fires stream.

Mark, thy interminable farms, North, South,
Thy wealthy daughter-states, Eastern and Western,
The varied products of Ohio, Pennsylvania, Missouri, Georgia,
    Texas, and the rest,   200
Thy limitless crops, grass, wheat, sugar, oil, corn, rice, hemp,
    hops,
Thy barns all fill'd, the endless freight-train and the bulging
    storehouse,
The grapes that ripen on thy vines, the apples in thy orchards,
Thy incalculable lumber, beef, pork, potatoes, thy coal, thy
    gold and silver,
The inexhaustible iron in thy mines.   205

All thine O sacred Union!
Ships, farms, shops, barns, factories, mines,
City and State, North, South, item and aggregate,
We dedicate, dread Mother, all to thee!

Protectress absolute, thou! bulwark of all!   210
For well we know that while thou givest each and all,
    (generous as God,)
Without thee neither all nor each, nor land, home,
Nor ship, nor mine, nor any here this day secure,
Nor aught, nor any day secure.

9

And thou, the Emblem waving over all!   215
Delicate beauty, a word to thee, (it may be salutary,)
Remember thou hast not always been as here to-day so
    comfortably ensovereign'd,
In other scenes than these have I observ'd thee flag,
Not quite so trim and whole and freshly blooming in folds of
    stainless silk,
But I have seen thee bunting, to tatters torn upon thy
    splinter'd staff,   220
Or clutch'd to some young color-bearer's breast with desperate
    hands,
Savagely struggled for, for life or death, fought over long,
'Mid cannons' thunder-crash and many a curse and groan and
    yell, and rifle-volleys cracking sharp,

And moving masses as wild demons surging, and lives as
 nothing risk'd,
For thy mere remnant grimed with dirt and smoke and sopp'd
 in blood,   225
For sake of that, my beauty, and that thou might'st dally as
 now secure up there,
Many a good man have I seen go under.

Now here and these and hence in peace, all thine O Flag!
And here and hence for thee, O universal Muse! and thou for them!
And here and hence O Union, all the work and workmen
 thine!   230
None separate from thee—henceforth One only, we and thou,
(For the blood of the children, what is it, only the blood maternal?
And lives and works, what are they all at last, except the roads
 to faith and death?)

While we rehearse our measureless wealth, it is for thee, dear
 Mother,
We own it all and several to-day indissoluble in thee;   235
Think not our chant, our show, merely for products gross or
 lucre—it is for thee, the soul in thee, electric, spiritual!
Our farms, inventions, crops, we own in thee! cities and States
 in thee!
Our freedom all in thee! our very lives in thee!
1871   *1881*

Song of the Redwood-Tree[1]

1

A California song,
A prophecy and indirection, a thought impalpable to breathe as
 air,
A chorus of dryads, fading, departing, or hamadryads
 departing,
A murmuring, fateful, giant voice, out of the earth and sky,
Voice of a mighty dying tree in the redwood forest dense.   5

1. WW composed this poem in the fall of 1873, asking and receiving $100 for it from *Harper's
Magazine*, which printed it in its issue of February 1874. It next appeared among the "Cen-
tennial Songs" of the 1876 *Two Rivulets*, and then in *LG* 1881, remaining unchanged in
title and—except for one or two words—in text. Among the MS drafts (Barrett and Trent)
is WW's own note to himself on its theme: "The spinal idea of the poem I (the tree) have
fill'd my time and fill'd it grandly All is prepared for you—my termination comes prophecy
[sic] a great race—great as the mountains and the trees Intersperse with *italic* (first person
speaking) the same as in 'Out of the Cradle endlessly rocking.'" To Rudolf Schmidt WW
wrote, March 4, 1874, that he had written the poem "to idealize our great Pacific half of
America, (the future *better half*)—" (*Corr.*, II, 282). A diplomatic reprint of two MSS (Barrett-
Va.) of the poem, one rough and the other comparatively finished, is presented by Fredson
Bowers in *PBSA* 50 (1st quarter, 1956): 53–85.

Farewell my brethren,
Farewell O earth and sky, farewell ye neighboring waters,
My time has ended, my term has come,

Along the northern coast,
Just back from the rock-bound shore and the caves,   10
In the saline air from the sea in the Mendocino country,[2]
With the surge for base and accompaniment low and hoarse,
With crackling blows of axes sounding musically driven by
    strong arms,
Riven deep by the sharp tongues of the axes, there in the
    redwood forest dense,
I heard the mighty tree its death-chant chanting.   15

The choppers heard not, the camp shanties[3] echoed not,
The quick-ear'd teamsters and chain and jack-screw men heard
    not,
As the wood-spirits came from their haunts of a thousand
    years to join the refrain,
But in my soul I plainly heard.

Murmuring out of its myriad leaves,   20
Down from its lofty top rising two hundred feet high,
Out of its stalwart trunk and limbs, out of its foot-thick bark,
That chant of the seasons and time, chant not of the past only
    but the future.

You untold life of me,
And all you venerable and innocent joys,   25
Perennial hardy life of me with joys 'mid rain and many a
    summer sun,
And the white snows and night and the wild winds;
O the great patient rugged joys, my soul's strong joys unreck'd by
    man,
(For know I bear the soul befitting me, I too have consciousness,
    identity,
And all the rocks and mountains have, and all the earth,)   30
Joys of the life befitting me and brothers mine,
Our time, our term has come.

Nor yield we mournfully majestic brothers,
We who have grandly fill'd our time;
With Nature's calm content, with tacit huge delight,   35
We welcome what we wrought for through the past,
And leave the field for them.

For them predicted long,
For a superber race, they too to grandly fill their time,

2. California coastal county north of San Francisco.
3. Suggesting both huts and work-songs.

For them we abdicate, in them ourselves ye forest kings!   40
In them these skies and airs, these mountain peaks, Shasta,
    Nevadas,[4]
These huge precipitous cliffs, this amplitude, these valleys, far
    Yosemite,
To be in them absorb'd, assimilated.

Then to a loftier strain,
Still prouder, more ecstatic rose the chant,   45
As if the heirs, the deities of the West,
Joining with master-tongue bore part.

Not wan from Asia's fetiches,
Nor red from Europe's old dynastic slaughter-house,
(Area of murder-plots of thrones, with scent left yet of wars and
    scaffolds everywhere,)   50
But come from Nature's long and harmless throes, peacefully
    builded thence,
These virgin lands, lands of the Western shore,
To the new culminating man, to you, the empire new,
You promis'd long, we pledge, we dedicate.

You occult deep volitions,   55
You average spiritual manhood, purpose of all, pois'd on yourself,
    giving not taking law,
You womanhood divine, mistress and source of all, whence life
    and love and aught that comes from life and love,
You unseen moral essence of all the vast materials of America,
    (age upon age working in death the same as life,)
You that, sometimes known, oftener unknown, really shape and
    mould the New World, adjusting it to Time and Space,
You hidden national will lying in your abysms, conceal'd but
    ever alert,   60
You past and present purposes tenaciously pursued, may-be
    unconscious of yourselves,
Unswerv'd by all the passing errors, perturbations of the surface;
You vital, universal, deathless germs, beneath all creeds, arts,
    statutes, literatures,
Here build your homes for good, establish here, these areas
    entire, lands of the Western shore,
We pledge, we dedicate to you.[5]   65

For man of you, your characteristic race,
Here may he hardly, sweet, gigantic grow, here tower
    proportionate to Nature,
Here climb the vast pure spaces unconfined, uncheck'd by wall
    or roof,
Here laugh with storm or sun, here joy, here patiently inure,

4. *Shasta*: mountain peak in Siskiyou County, California; *Nevadas*: Sierra Nevada, mountain
    range in eastern California.
5. An early working draft (Trent-Duke) of lines 55–65 is printed in *FCI*, 8–9.

Here heed himself, unfold himself, (not others' formulas heed,)
    here fill his time,   70
To duly fall, to aid, unreck'd at last,
To disappear, to serve.

Thus on the northern coast,
In the echo of teamsters' calls and the clinking chains, and the
    music of choppers' axes,
The falling trunk and limbs, the crash, the muffled shriek, the
    groan,   75
Such words combined from the redwood-tree, as of voices
    ecstatic, ancient and rustling,
The century-lasting, unseen dryads, singing, withdrawing,
All their recesses of forests and mountains leaving,
From the Cascade range to the Wahsatch,[6] or Idaho far, or Utah,
To the deities of the modern henceforth yielding,   80
The chorus and indications, the vistas of coming humanity, the
    settlements, features all,
In the Mendocino woods I caught.

2

The flashing and golden pageant of California,
The sudden and gorgeous drama, the sunny and ample lands,
The long and varied stretch from Puget sound to Colorado
    south,   85
Lands bathed in sweeter, rarer, healthier air, valleys and
    mountain cliffs,
The fields of Nature long prepared and fallow, the silent, cyclic
    chemistry,
The slow and steady ages plodding, the unoccupied surface
    ripening, the rich ores forming beneath;
At last the New arriving, assuming, taking possession,
A swarming and busy race settling and organizing everywhere,   90
Ships coming in from the whole round world, and going out to
    the whole world,
To India and China and Australia and the thousand island
    paradises of the Pacific,
Populous cities, the latest inventions, the steamers on the
    rivers, the railroads, with many a thrifty farm, with
    machinery,
And wool and wheat and the grape, and diggings of yellow gold.

3

But more in you than these, lands of the Western shore,   95
(These but the means, the implements, the standing-ground,)

6. *Cascade*: range of mountains in Oregon, Washington, and British Columbia; *Wahsatch*: more
    commonly Wasatch, a range in northern Utah and southeastern Idaho.

I see in you, certain to come, the promise of thousands of
    years, till now deferr'd,
Promis'd to be fulfill'd, our common kind, the race.

The new society at last, proportionate to Nature,
In man of you, more than your mountain peaks or stalwart
    trees imperial,   100
In woman more, far more, than all your gold or vines, or even
    vital air.

Fresh come, to a new world indeed, yet long prepared,
I see the genius of the modern, child of the real and ideal,
Clearing the ground for broad humanity, the true America,
    heir of the past so grand,
To build a grander future.   105
    1874   *1881*

A Song for Occupations[1]

1

A song for occupations!
In the labor of engines and trades and the labor of fields I find
    the developments,
And find the eternal meanings.

Workmen and Workwomen!
Were all educations practical and ornamental well display'd out
    of me, what would it amount to?   5
Were I as the head teacher, charitable proprietor, wise
    statesman, what would it amount to?
Were I to you as the boss employing and paying you, would
    that satisfy you?

---

1. The second of the twelve untitled poems of the first edition. It was subsequently "Poem of The Daily Work of The Workmen and Workwomen of These States" (1856), No. 3 of the "Chants Democratic" (1860), "To Workingmen" (1867), and "Carol of Occupations" (1871 and 1876); in 1881 it received its present title. WW worked at it persistently, regarding it as a major pronouncement. In the MS revisions of his 1860 text he suggested such titles as "Song of Trades and Implements" or "Chant of Mechanics," and although he wrote on the title page, "This is satisfactory as it now is, Dec. 7, 1864," he marked for deletion much of what is now the fifth section and labeled the final section "out without fail!" Section 5 contained 65 lines in 1855, was expanded to 80 lines in 1860, and finally reduced to its present 38. The 178 lines of the original poem became 196 in 1856, 205 in 1860, 158 in 1871 and 1876, and finally 151. The general effect was to shorten the catalogues and diminish the sense of intimacy. For example, the opening passage (dropped in 1881) began:

> Come closer to me,
> Push close my lovers and take the best I possess,
> Yield closer and closer and give me the best you possess.

Compare lines 1309–13, "Song of Myself," with lines 44–48 of this "Song" for examples of the consistency in spirit of the first *Leaves*.

    On the question of the relation of this and other poems of WW's to the history of labor, see Alan Trachtenberg, "The Politics of Labor and the Poet's Work," and M. Wynn Thomas, "Whitman and the Dreams of Labor," both in Ed Folsom, ed., *Walt Whitman: The Centennial Essays* (Iowa City: University of Iowa Press, 1994), 120–32 and 133–52, respectively.

The learn'd, virtuous, benevolent, and the usual terms,
A man like me and never the usual terms.

Neither a servant nor a master I,   10
I take no sooner a large price than a small price, I will have
    my own whoever enjoys me,
I will be even with you and you shall be even with me.

If you stand at work in a shop I stand as nigh as the nighest in
    the same shop,
If you bestow gifts on your brother or dearest friend I demand
    as good as your brother or dearest friend,
If your lover, husband, wife, is welcome by day or night, I
    must be personally as welcome,   15
If you become degraded, criminal, ill, then I become so for
    your sake,
If you remember your foolish and outlaw'd deeds, do you think
    I cannot remember my own foolish and outlaw'd deeds?
If you carouse at the table I carouse at the opposite side of the
    table,
If you meet some stranger in the streets and love him or her,
    why I often meet strangers in the street and love them.

Why what have you thought of yourself?   20
Is it you then that thought yourself less?
Is it you that thought the President greater than you?
Or the rich better off than you? or the educated wiser than you?

(Because you are greasy or pimpled, or were once drunk, or a thief,
Or that you are diseas'd, or rheumatic, or a prostitute,   25
Or from frivolity or impotence, or that you are no scholar and
    never saw your name in print,
Do you give in that you are any less immortal?)

2

Souls of men and women! it is not you I call unseen, unheard,
    untouchable and untouching,
It is not you I go argue pro and con about, and to settle
    whether you are alive or no,
I own publicly who you are, if nobody else owns.   30

Grown, half-grown and babe, of this country and every
    country, indoors and out-doors, one just as much as the
    other, I see,
And all else behind or through them.

The wife, and she is not one jot less than the husband,
The daughter, and she is just as good as the son,
The mother, and she is every bit as much as the father.   35

Offspring of ignorant and poor, boys apprenticed to trades,
Young fellows working on farms and old fellows working on farms,
Sailor-men, merchant-men, coasters, immigrants,
All these I see, but nigher and farther the same I see,
None shall escape me and none shall wish to escape me.   40

I bring what you much need yet always have,
Not money, amours, dress, eating, erudition, but as good,
I send no agent or medium, offer no representative of value,
    but offer the value itself.

There is something that comes to one now and perpetually,
It is not what is printed, preach'd, discussed, it eludes
    discussion and print,   45
It is not to be put in a book, it is not in this book,
It is for you whoever you are, it is no farther from you than
    your hearing and sight are from you,
It is hinted by nearest, commonest, readiest, it is ever
    provoked by them.

You may read in many languages, yet read nothing about it,
You may read the President's message and read nothing about
    it there,   50
Nothing in the reports from the State department or Treasury
    department, or in the daily papers or weekly papers,
Or in the census or revenue returns, prices current, or any
    accounts of stock.

3

The sun and stars that float in the open air,
The apple-shaped earth and we upon it, surely the drift of
    them is something grand,
I do not know what it is except that it is grand, and that it is
    happiness,   55
And that the enclosing purport of us here is not a speculation
    or bon-mot or reconnoissance,
And that it is not something which by luck may turn out well
    for us, and without luck must be a failure for us,
And not something which may yet be retracted in a certain
    contingency.

The light and shade, the curious sense of body and identity,
    the greed that with perfect complaisance devours all
    things,
The endless pride and outstretching of man, unspeakable joys
    and sorrows,   60
The wonder every one sees in every one else he sees, and the
    wonders that fill each minute of time forever,
What have you reckon'd them for, camerado?

Have you reckon'd them for your trade or farm-work? or for
    the profits of your store?
Or to achieve yourself a position? or to fill a gentleman's
    leisure, or a lady's leisure?

Have you reckon'd that the landscape took substance and form
    that it might be painted in a picture?   65
Or men and women that they might be written of, and songs
    sung?
Or the attraction of gravity, and the great laws and harmonious
    combinations and the fluids of the air, as subjects for the
    savans?[2]
Or the brown land and the blue sea for maps and charts?
Or the stars to be put in constellations and named fancy names?
Or that the growth of seeds is for agricultural tables, or
    agriculture itself?   70

Old institutions, these arts, libraries, legends, collections, and
    the practice handed along in manufactures, will we rate
    them so high?
Will we rate our cash and business high? I have no objection,
I rate them as high as the highest—then a child born of a
    woman and man I rate beyond all rate.

We thought our Union grand, and our Constitution grand,
I do not say they are not grand and good, for they are,   75
I am this day just as much in love with them as you,
Then I am in love with You, and with all my fellows upon the earth.

We consider bibles[3] and religions divine—I do not say they are
    not divine,
I say they have all grown out of you, and may grow out of you still,
It is not they who give the life, it is you who give the life,   80
Leaves are not more shed from the trees, or trees from the
    earth, than they are shed out of you.

4

The sum of all known reverence I add up in you whoever you are,
The President is there in the White House for you, it is not
    you who are here for him,
The Secretaries act in their bureaus for you, not you here for them,
The Congress convenes every Twelfth-month for you,   85
Laws, courts, the forming of States, the charters of cities, the
    going and coming of commerce and mails, are all for you.

2. WW's spelling for "savants," learned men. *Cf.* "philosophs."
3. Not capitalized: any book regarded as authoritative.

List close my scholars dear,
Doctrines, politics and civilization exurge[4] from you,
Sculpture and monuments and any thing inscribed anywhere
    are tallied in you,
The gist of histories and statistics as far back as the records
    reach is in you this hour, and myths and tales the same,   90
If you were not breathing and walking here, where would they
    all be?
The most renown'd poems would be ashes, orations and plays
    would be vacuums.

All architecture is what you do to it when you look upon it,
(Did you think it was in the white or gray stone? or the lines
    of the arches and cornices?)

All music is what awakes from you when you are reminded by
    the instruments,   95
It is not the violins and the cornets, it is not the oboe nor the
    beating drums, nor the score of the baritone singer singing
    his sweet romanza, nor that of the men's chorus, nor that
    of the women's chorus,
It is nearer and farther than they.[5]

5

Will the whole come back then?
Can each see signs of the best by a look in the looking-glass?
    is there nothing greater or more?
Does all sit there with you, with the mystic unseen soul?   100

Strange and hard that paradox true I give,
Objects gross and the unseen soul are one.

House-building, measuring, sawing the boards,
Blacksmithing, glass-blowing, nail-making, coopering, tin-
    roofing, shingle-dressing,
Ship-joining, dock-building, fish-curing, flagging of sidewalks
    by flaggers,   105
The pump, the pile-driver, the great derrick, the coal-kiln and
    brick-kiln,
Coal-mines and all that is down there, the lamps in the
    darkness, echoes, songs, what meditations, what vast
    native thoughts looking through smutch'd faces,
Iron-works, forge-fires in the mountains or by river-banks, men
    around feeling the melt with huge crowbars, lumps of ore,
    the due combining of ore, limestone, coal,

---

4. To rise or come into view. Usually "exsurge." WW's form is cited in *NED*.
5. For lines 88–97, *cf.* lines 82–88 of "A Song of the Rolling Earth."

The blast-furnace and the puddling-furnace, the loup-lump at
    the bottom of the melt at last,[6] the rolling-mill, the
    stumpy bars of pig-iron, the strong clean-shaped T-rail for
    railroads,
Oil-works, silk-works, white-lead-works, the sugar-house,
    steam-saws, the great mills and factories,   110
Stone-cutting, shapely trimmings for facades or window or
    door-lintels, the mallet, the tooth-chisel, the jib to protect
    the thumb,[7]
The calking-iron, the kettle of boiling vault-cement, and the
    fire under the kettle,
The cotton-bale, the stevedore's hook, the saw and buck of the
    sawyer, the mould of the moulder, the working-knife of
    the butcher, the ice-saw, and all the work with ice,
The work and tools of the rigger, grappler, sail-maker, block-
    maker,
Goods of gutta-percha, papier-maché, colors, brushes, brush-
    making, glazier's implements,   115
The veneer and glue-pot, the confectioner's ornaments, the
    decanter and glasses, the shears and flat-iron,
The awl and knee-strap, the pint measure and quart measure,
    the counter and stool, the writing-pen of quill or metal,
    the making of all sorts of edged tools,
The brewery, brewing, the malt, the vats, every thing that is
    done by brewers, wine-makers, vinegar-makers,
Leather-dressing, coach-making, boiler-making, rope-twisting,
    distilling, sign-painting, lime-burning, cotton-picking,
    electroplating, electrotyping, stereotyping,
Stave-machines, planning-machines, reaping-machines,
    ploughing-machines, thrashing-machines, steam wagons,   120
The cart of the carman, the omnibus, the ponderous dray,
Pyrotechny, letting off color'd fireworks at night, fancy figures
    and jets;
Beef on the butcher's stall, the slaughter-house of the butcher,
    the butcher in his killing-clothes,
The pens of live pork, the killing-hammer, the hog-hook, the
    scalder's tub, gutting, the cutter's cleaver, the packer's
    maul, and the plenteous winterwork of pork-packing,
Flour-works, grinding of wheat, rye, maize, rice, the barrels
    and the half and quarter barrels, the loaded barges, the
    high piles on wharves and levees,   125
The men and the work of the men on ferries, railroads,
    coasters, fish-boats, canals;
The hourly routine of your own or any man's life, the shop,
    yard, store, or factory,
These shows all near you by day and night—workman!
    whoever you are, your daily life!

6. The pasty mass of iron at the bottom of the melt—the product sought in the smelting
process.
7. Projecting shield.

In that and them the heft of the heaviest—in that and them
    far more than you estimated, (and far less also,)
In them realities for you and me, in them poems for you and
    me,   130
In them, not yourself—you and your soul enclose all things,
    regardless of estimation,
In them the development good—in them all themes, hints,
    possibilities.

I do not affirm that what you see beyond is futile, I do not
    advise you to stop,
I do not say leadings you thought great are not great,
But I say that none lead to greater than these lead to.   135

6

Will you seek afar off? you surely come back at last,
In things best known to you finding the best, or as good as the
    best,
In folks nearest to you finding the sweetest, strongest,
    lovingest,
Happiness, knowledge, not in another place but this place, not
    for another hour but this hour,
Man in the first you see or touch, always in friend, brother,
    nighest neighbor—woman in mother, sister, wife,   140
The popular tastes and employments taking precedence in
    poems or anywhere,
You workwomen and workmen of these States having your own
    divine and strong life,
And all else giving place to men and women like you.

When the psalm sings instead of the singer,
When the script preaches instead of the preacher,   145
When the pulpit descends and goes instead of the carver that
    carved the supporting desk,
When I can touch the body of books by night or by day, and
    when they touch my body back again,
When a university course convinces like a slumbering woman
    and child convince,
When the minted gold in the vault smiles like the night-
    watchman's daughter,
When warrantee deeds loafe in chairs opposite and are my
    friendly companions,   150
I intend to reach them my hand, and make as much of them
    as I do of men and women like you.

1855   *1881*

A Song of the Rolling Earth[1]

1

A song of the rolling earth, and of words according,
Were you thinking that those were the words, those upright
    lines? those curves, angles, dots?
No, those are not the words, the substantial words are in the
    ground and sea,
They are in the air, they are in you.

Were you thinking that those were the words, those delicious
    sounds out of your friends' mouths?   5
No, the real words are more delicious than they.

Human bodies are words, myriads of words,
(In the best poems re-appears the body, man's or woman's,
    well-shaped, natural, gay,
Every part able, active, receptive, without shame or the need of
    shame.)

Air, soil, water, fire—those are words,   10
I myself am a word with them—my qualities interpenetrate
    with theirs—my name is nothing to them,
Though it were told in the three thousand languages, what
    would air, soil, water, fire, know of my name?

A healthy presence, a friendly or commanding gesture, are
    words, sayings, meanings,
The charms that go with the mere looks of some men and
    women, are sayings and meanings also.

The workmanship of souls is by those inaudible words of the
    earth,   15
The masters know the earth's words and use them more than
    audible words.

1. This 1856 poem underwent comparatively slight revision except for its title and beginning.
The changes in title themselves indicate successive emphasis upon the sayers, the words,
and the earth: "Poem of The Sayers of The Words of The Earth" (1856); "To the Sayers of
Words" (1860, 1867); "Carol of Words" (1871, 1876); "A Song of the Rolling Earth" (1881).
The opening two lines, dropped in 1881, provided an explicit clue for the reader:

    Earth, round, rolling, compact—suns, moons, animals—all these are words,
    Watery, vegetable, sauroid advances—beings, premonitions, lispings of the future—
        these are vast words.

In his MS emendations of the 1860 "Blue Copy" text, WW proposed changing the opening
to "This rolling earth is the word to be said," but he withdrew the alteration, and the lines
were retained through 1876. Some of his greatest lines are in this poem, a poetic demon-
stration of the transcendentalist doctrine expounded by Emerson in *Nature*, Part IV, "Lan-
guage" (1836): "Language is a . . . use which Nature subserves to man. Nature is the vehicle
of thought . . . Words are signs of natural facts."

Amelioration is one of the earth's words,
The earth neither lags nor hastens,
It has all attributes, growths, effects, latent in itself from the jump,[2]
It is not half beautiful only, defects and excrescences show just
     as much as perfections show.   20

The earth does not withhold; it is generous enough,
The truths of the earth continually wait, they are not so
     conceal'd either,
They are calm, subtle, untransmissible by print,
They are imbued through all things conveying themselves
     willingly,
Conveying a sentiment and invitation, I utter and utter,   25
I speak not, yet if you hear me not of what avail am I to you?
To bear, to better, lacking these of what avail am I?

(Accouche! accouchez![3]
Will you rot your own fruit in yourself there?
Will you squat and stifle there?)   30

The earth does not argue,
Is not pathetic, has no arrangements,
Does not scream, haste, persuade, threaten, promise,
Makes no discriminations, has no conceivable failures,
Closes nothing, refuses nothing, shuts none out,   35
Of all the powers, objects, states, it notifies, shuts none out.

The earth does not exhibit itself nor refuse to exhibit itself,
     possesses still underneath,
Underneath the ostensible sounds, the august chorus of
     heroes, the wail of slaves,
Persuasions of lovers, curses, gasps of the dying, laughter of
     young people, accents of bargainers,
Underneath these possessing words that never fail.   40

To her children the words of the eloquent dumb great mother
     never fail,
The true words do not fail, for motion does not fail and
     reflection does not fail,
Also the day and night do not fail, and the voyage we pursue
     does not fail.

---

2. For biblical analogy of the primordial word, consider John 1.1: "In the beginning was the Word . . . and the Word was God."
3. French: properly "Accouchée! accouchez!"—i.e., "You pregnant one! be delivered!"

Of the interminable sisters,[4]
Of the ceaseless cotillons[5] of sisters,   45
Of the centripetal and centrifugal sisters, the elder and
    younger sisters,
The beautiful sister we know dances on with the rest.

With her ample back towards every beholder,
With the fascinations of youth and the equal fascinations of age,
Sits she whom I too love like the rest, sits undisturb'd,   50
Holding up in her hand what has the character of a mirror,
    while her eyes glance back from it,
Glance as she sits, inviting none, denying none,
Holding a mirror day and night tirelessly before her own face.

Seen at hand or seen at a distance,
Duly the twenty-four appear in public every day,   55
Duly approach and pass with their companions or a
    companion,
Looking from no countenances of their own, but from the
    countenances of those who are with them,
From the countenances of children or women or the manly
    countenance,
From the open countenances of animals or from inanimate
    things,
From the landscape or waters or from the exquisite apparition
    of the sky,   60
From our countenances, mine and yours, faithfully returning
    them,
Every day in public appearing without fail, but never twice
    with the same companions.

Embracing man, embracing all, proceed the three hundred and
    sixty-five resistlessly round the sun;
Embracing all, soothing, supporting, follow close three
    hundred and sixty-five offsets of the first, sure and
    necessary as they.

Tumbling on steadily, nothing dreading,   65
Sunshine, storm, cold, heat, forever withstanding, passing,
    carrying,
The soul's realization and determination still inheriting,
The fluid vacuum around and ahead still entering and dividing,

4. The sisters, the "ceaseless cotillions," are the stars and planets, among whom is the earth, the "beautiful sister we know," the whole passage, lines 44–72, being governed by the figure of time, the consequence of celestial motion. Cf. the poem "Days" by Emerson, whose "daughters of time" regard man with "scorn" for his paltry use of their gifts. By contrast, WW's unending cotillions of "sisters" dance by—the one (line 50), the "twenty-four" (line 55), the "three hundred and sixty-five" (line 63), making luminous the faces of men and things, "embracing man" and "all" on "the divine ship."
5. This is the French form for a brisk ballroom dance of the nineteenth century, also used in LG 1881 and in the 1902 CW, but in the LG editions of 1856, 1860, 1867, 1871, 1872, and 1876 the English "cotillions" appears.

No balk retarding, no anchor anchoring, on no rock striking,
Swift, glad, content, unbereav'd, nothing losing, 70
Of all able and ready at any time to give strict account,
The divine ship sails the divine sea.

2

Whoever you are! motion and reflection are especially for you,
The divine ship sails the divine sea for you.

Whoever you are! you are he or she for whom the earth is
    solid and liquid, 75
You are he or she for whom the sun and moon hang in the sky,
For none more than you are the present and the past,
For none more than you is immortality.

Each man to himself and each woman to herself, is the word
    of the past and present, and the true word of immortality;
No one can acquire for another—not one, 80
Not one can grow for another—not one.

The song is to the singer, and comes back most to him,
The teaching is to the teacher, and comes back most to him,
The murder is to the murderer, and comes back most to him,
The theft is to the thief, and comes back most to him, 85
The love is to the lover, and comes back most to him,
The gift is to the giver, and comes back most to him—it
    cannot fail,
The oration is to the orator, the acting is to the actor and
    actress not to the audience,
And no man understands any greatness or goodness but his
    own, or the indication of his own.

3

I swear the earth shall surely be complete to him or her who
    shall be complete, 90
The earth remains jagged and broken only to him or her who
    remains jagged and broken.

I swear there is no greatness or power that does not emulate
    those of the earth,
There can be no theory of any account unless it corroborate
    the theory of the earth,
No politics, song, religion, behavior, or what not, is of account,
    unless it compare with the amplitude of the earth,
Unless it face the exactness, vitality, impartiality, rectitude of
    the earth. 95

I swear I begin to see love with sweeter spasms than that
    which responds love,[6]
It is that which contains itself, which never invites and never
    refuses.

I swear I begin to see little or nothing in audible words,
All merges toward the presentation of the unspoken meanings
    of the earth,
Toward him who sings the songs of the body and of the truths
    of the earth,   100
Toward him who makes the dictionaries of words that print
    cannot touch.

I swear I see what is better than to tell the best,
It is always to leave the best untold.

When I undertake to tell the best I find I cannot,
My tongue is ineffectual on its pivots,   105
My breath will not be obedient to its organs,
I become a dumb man.

The best of the earth cannot be told anyhow, all or any is best,
It is not what you anticipated, it is cheaper, easier, nearer,
Things are not dismiss'd from the places they held before,   110
The earth is just as positive and direct as it was before,
Facts, religions, improvements, politics, trades, are as real as
    before,
But the soul is also real, it too is positive and direct,
No reasoning, no proof has establish'd it,
Undeniable growth has establish'd it.   115

4

These to echo the tones of souls and the phrases of souls,
(If they did not echo the phrases of souls what were they then?
If they had not reference to you in especial what were they
    then?)

I swear I will never henceforth have to do with the faith that
    tells the best,
I will have to do only with that faith that leaves the best
    untold.   120

Say on, sayers! sing on, singers!
Delve! mould! pile the words of the earth!
Work on, age after age, nothing is to be lost,
It may have to wait long, but it will certainly come in use,
When the materials are all prepared and ready, the architects
    shall appear.   125

6. WW sometimes coined an intransitive verb into a transitive form; actually the translation of
the Latin roots is transitive, i.e., to "promise back" love.

I swear to you the architects shall appear without fail,
I swear to you they will understand you and justify you,
The greatest among them shall be he who best knows you, and
  encloses all and is faithful to all,
He and the rest shall not forget you, they shall perceive that
  you are not an iota less than they,
You shall be fully glorified in them.   ¹³⁰
 1856   *1881*

Youth, Day, Old Age and Night[1]

Youth, large, lusty, loving—youth full of grace, force,
  fascination,
Do you know that Old Age may come after you with equal
  grace, force, fascination?

Day full-blown and splendid—day of the immense sun, action,
  ambition, laughter,
The Night follows close with millions of suns, and sleep and
  restoring darkness.
 1855   *1881*

BIRDS OF PASSAGE

Song of the Universal[1]

1

Come said the Muse,
Sing me a song no poet yet has chanted,
Sing me the universal.

1. This poem is composed of four lines retained from the 1855 poem "Great Are the Myths" when it was excluded from *LG* 1881. They had been lines 19 through 22 of the original piece, which was the final poem of the first edition.

 Birds of Passage: This group, new to WW's final 1881 arrangement, appears under a title that admirably suggests an abiding element in his poetry—the sense of flight and change. Although the seven component poems each appeared in a different group in various earlier editions of *LG*, they now acquire a casual unity of tone because each deals with movement—whether of the evolution of cultural perfection, or westward expansion, or the search for one's own identity, or the vicissitudes of history.

1. Written in response to the invitation (March 20, 1874) of a group of young men at Tufts College to deliver a poem at commencement, this piece was recited June 17 in absentia because WW's illness prevented his personal appearance. The poem received nearly simultaneous publication in several newspapers—the *New York Daily Graphic* and *Evening Post* on June 17, the *Springfield Republican* on June 18, the *New York World* on June 19, and the *Camden New Republic* on June 20. Its first book appearance was among the "Centennial Songs" of the 1876 *Two Rivulets*, companion volume to *LG*. Composed in the wake of personal trials, notably WW's paralytic stroke January 23, 1873, and the death of his mother the following May 23, it is a strong reaffirmation of faith, its ideal of perfection's culmination being strongly affected by the poet's reading of Hegel. See Allen, 460. The MS drafts (Yale and Berg) show much working over.

In this broad earth of ours,
Amid the measureless grossness and the slag,   5
Enclosed and safe within its central heart,
Nestles the seed perfection.

By every life a share or more or less,
None born but it is born, conceal'd or unconceal'd the seed is
      waiting.

2

Lo! keen-eyed towering science,   10
As from tall peaks the modern overlooking,
Successive absolute fiats issuing.

Yet again, lo! the soul, above all science,
For it has history gather'd like husks around the globe,
For it the entire star-myriads roll through the sky.   15

In spiral routes by long detours,
(As a much-tacking ship upon the sea,)
For it the partial to the permanent flowing,
For it the real to the ideal² tends.

For it the mystic evolution,   20
Not the right only justified, what we call evil also justified.

Forth from their masks, no matter what,
From the huge festering trunk, from craft and guile and tears,
Health to emerge and joy, joy universal.

Out of the bulk, the morbid and the shallow,   25
Out of the bad majority, the varied countless frauds of men
      and states,
Electric, antiseptic yet, cleaving, suffusing all,
Only the good is universal.

3

Over the mountain-growths disease and sorrow,
An uncaught bird is ever hovering, hovering,   30
High in the purer, happier air.

From imperfection's murkiest cloud,
Darts always forth one ray of perfect light,
One flash of heaven's glory.

To fashion's, custom's discord,   35
To the mad Babel-din, the deafening orgies,

2. In the sense of substance and idea.

Soothing each lull a strain is heard, just heard,
From some far shore the final chorus sounding.

O the blest eyes, the happy hearts,
That see, that know the guiding thread so fine,   40
Along the mighty labyrinth.

4

And thou America,
For the scheme's culmination, its thought and its reality,
For these (not for thyself) thou hast arrived.

Thou too surroundest all,   45
Embracing carrying welcoming all, thou too by pathways broad
     and new,
To the ideal tendest.

The measur'd faiths of other lands, the grandeurs of the past,
Are not for thee, but grandeurs of thine own,
Deific faiths and amplitudes, absorbing, comprehending all,   50
All eligible to all.

All, all for immortality,
Love like the light silently wrapping all,
Nature's amelioration blessing all,
The blossoms, fruits of ages, orchards divine and certain,   55
Forms, objects, growths, humanities, to spiritual images ripening.

Give me O God to sing that thought,
Give me, give him or her I love this quenchless faith,
In Thy ensemble,[3] whatever else withheld withhold not from us,
Belief in plan of Thee enclosed in Time and Space,   60
Health, peace, salvation universal.

Is it a dream?
Nay but the lack of it the dream,
And failing it life's lore and wealth a dream,
And all the world a dream.   65
     1874   *1881*

---

3. A transcendental concept, rife in WW's youth, was the integrated ensemble of all microcosms
   in the grand single macrocosm of Being.

Pioneers! O Pioneers![4]

Come my tan-faced children,
Follow well in order, get your weapons ready,
Have you your pistols? have you your sharp-edged axes?
    Pioneers! O pioneers!

For we cannot tarry here,   5
We must march my darlings, we must bear the brunt of danger,
We the youthful sinewy races, all the rest on us depend,
    Pioneers! O pioneers!

O you youths, Western youths,
So impatient, full of action, full of manly pride and friendship,   10
Plain I see you Western youths, see you tramping with the
        foremost;
    Pioneers! O pioneers!

Have the elder races halted?
Do they droop and end their lesson, wearied over there beyond
        the seas?
We take up the task eternal, and the burden and the lesson,   15
    Pioneers! O pioneers!

All the past we leave behind,
We debouch[5] upon a newer mightier world, varied world,
Fresh and strong the world we seize, world of labor and the march,
    Pioneers! O pioneers!   20

We detachments steady throwing,
Down the edges, through the passes, up the mountains steep,
Conquering, holding, daring, venturing as we go the unknown ways,
    Pioneers! O pioneers!

We primeval forests felling,   25
We the rivers stemming, vexing we and piercing deep the
        mines within,
We the surface broad surveying, we the virgin soil upheaving,
    Pioneers! O pioneers!

4. First published in numbered stanzas in the 1865 *Drum-Taps*, again in the 1867 "Drum-
Taps" annex, and in 1871 and 1876 among a *Leaves of Grass* group entitled "Marches Now
the War Is Over," this poem, with its strong trochaic beat, is obviously designed to be a
marching song. Recalling "Eidólons" in its stanza structure, it is one of the more than a
dozen *LG* poems that, in the regularity of their meter, are atypical of WW. Charles B. Willard
has called attention to the influence of Tennyson's "Ulysses" upon this poem (*WWN*, 9–10).
5. To emerge from a narrow pass into open country. *Cf.* WW's use of this word in "Song of
Myself," section 49, the last line.

Colorado men are we,
From the peaks gigantic, from the great sierras and the high
plateaus,
From the mine and from the gully, from the hunting trail we come,
Pioneers! O pioneers!

From Nebraska, from Arkansas,
Central inland race are we, from Missouri, with the continental
blood intervein'd,
All the hands of comrades clasping, all the Southern, all the
Northern,
Pioneers! O pioneers!

O resistless restless race!
O beloved race in all! O my breast aches with tender love for all!
O I mourn and yet exult, I am rapt with love for all,
Pioneers! O pioneers!

Raise the mighty mother mistress,
Waving high the delicate mistress, over all the starry mistress,
(bend your heads all,)
Raise the fang'd and warlike mistress, stern, impassive,
weapon'd mistress,
Pioneers! O pioneers!

See my children, resolute children,
By those swarms upon our rear we must never yield or falter,
Ages back in ghostly millions frowning there behind us urging,
Pioneers! O pioneers!

On and on the compact ranks,
With accessions ever waiting, with the places of the dead
quickly fill'd,
Through the battle, through defeat, moving yet and never stopping,
Pioneers! O pioneers!

O to die advancing on!
Are there some of us to droop and die? has the hour come?
Then upon the march we fittest die, soon and sure the gap is
fill'd,
Pioneers! O pioneers!

All the pulses of the world,
Falling in they beat for us, with the Western movement beat,
Holding single or together, steady moving to the front, all for us,
Pioneers! O pioneers!

Life's involv'd and varied pageants,
All the forms and shows, all the workmen at their work,
All the seamen and the landsmen, all the masters with their slaves,
    Pioneers! O pioneers!

All the hapless silent lovers,   65
All the prisoners in the prisons, all the righteous and the wicked,
All the joyous, all the sorrowing, all the living, all the dying,
    Pioneers! O pioneers!

I too with my soul and body,
We, a curious trio, picking, wandering on our way,   70
Through these shores amid the shadows, with the apparitions
        pressing,
    Pioneers! O pioneers!

Lo, the darting bowling orb!
Lo, the brother orbs around, all the clustering suns and planets,[6]
All the dazzling days, all the mystic nights with dreams,   75
    Pioneers! O pioneers!

These are of us, they are with us,
All for primal needed work, while the followers there in
        embryo wait behind,
We to-day's procession heading, we the route for travel clearing,
    Pioneers! O pioneers!   80

O you daughters of the West!
O you young and elder daughters! O you mothers and you wives!
Never must you be divided, in our ranks you move united,
    Pioneers! O pioneers!

Minstrels latent on the prairies!   85
(Shrouded bards of other lands, you may rest, you have done
        your work,)
Soon I hear you coming warbling, soon you rise and tramp amid us,
    Pioneers! O pioneers!

Not for delectations sweet,
Not the cushion and the slipper, not the peaceful and the
        studious,   90

---

6. Erroneously printed as "sons" in the 1881 revision and thereafter until *LG* 1889. The 1891–92 hardbound issue reads "suns," but the softbound issue of that date retained the error.

Not the riches safe and palling, not for us the tame enjoyment,
    Pioneers! O pioneers!

    Do the feasters gluttonous feast?
Do the corpulent sleepers sleep? have they lock'd and bolted doors?
Still be ours the diet hard, and the blanket on the ground,   95
    Pioneers! O pioneers!

    Has the night descended?
Was the road of late so toilsome? did we stop discouraged
    nodding on our way?
Yet a passing hour I yield you in your tracks to pause oblivious,
    Pioneers! O pioneers!   100

    Till with sound of trumpet,
Far, far off the daybreak call—hark! how loud and clear I hear
    it wind,
Swift! to the head of the army!—swift! spring to your places,
    Pioneers! O pioneers!
1865   1881

To You[7]

Whoever you are, I fear you are walking the walks of dreams,
I fear these supposed realities are to melt from under your feet
    and hands,
Even now your features, joys, speech, house, trade, manners,
    troubles, follies, costume, crimes, dissipate away from you,
Your true soul and body appear before me,
They stand forth out of affairs, out of commerce, shops, work,
    farms, clothes, the house, buying, selling, eating, drinking,
    suffering, dying.   5

Whoever you are, now I place my hand upon you, that you be
    my poem,
I whisper with my lips close to your ear,
I have loved many women and men, but I love none better
    than you.

O I have been dilatory and dumb,
I should have made my way straight to you long ago,   10

7. In 1856 this poem appeared under the title "Poem of You, Whoever You Are," and in 1860
as "To You, Whoever You Are." In 1867 it was simply "Leaves of Grass" No. 4, and from
1871 it has carried its present title. Although three lines have been dropped from the first
text, it has undergone but slight revision, and it remains a striking instance of WW's intimate
address directly to the reader, somewhat in the manner of teacher to disciple. Here the
teacher encourages one of the "divine average" to discover and respect his own personal
identity.

I should have blabb'd nothing but you, I should have chanted
    nothing but you.

I will leave all and come and make the hymns of you,
None has understood you, but I understand you,
None has done justice to you, you have not done justice to
    yourself,
None but has found you imperfect, I only find no imperfection
    in you,
None but would subordinate you, I only am he who will never
    consent to subordinate you,
I only am he who places over you no master, owner, better,
    God, beyond what waits intrinsically in yourself.

Painters have painted their swarming groups and the centre-
    figure of all,
From the head of the centre-figure spreading a nimbus of gold-
    color'd light,
But I paint myriads of heads, but paint no head without its
    nimbus of gold-color'd light,[8]
From my hand from the brain of every man and woman it
    streams, effulgently flowing forever.

O I could sing such grandeurs and glories about you!
You have not known what you are, you have slumber'd upon
    yourself all your life,
Your eyelids have been the same as closed most of the time,
What you have done returns already in mockeries,
(Your thrift, knowledge, prayers, if they do not return in
    mockeries, what is their return?)

The mockeries are not you,
Underneath them and within them I see you lurk,
I pursue you where none else has pursued you,
Silence, the desk, the flippant expression, the night, the
    accustom'd routine, if these conceal you from others or
    from yourself, they do not conceal you from me,
The shaved face, the unsteady eye, the impure complexion, if
    these balk others they do not balk me,
The pert apparel, the deform'd attitude, drunkenness, greed,
    premature death, all these I part aside.

There is no endowment in man or woman that is not tallied in
    you,
There is no virtue, no beauty in man or woman, but as good is
    in you,
No pluck, no endurance in others, but as good is in you,

8. Note that WW endowed the head of the "average" person with its nimbus also in "Crossing
    Brooklyn Ferry," line 116.

No pleasure waiting for others, but an equal pleasure waits for
you.

As for me, I give nothing to any one except I give the like
carefully to you,
I sing the songs of the glory of none, not God, sooner than I
sing the songs of the glory of you.

Whoever you are! claim your own at any hazard!
These shows of the East and West are tame compared to you,   40
These immense meadows, these interminable rivers, you are
immense and interminable as they,
These furies, elements, storms, motions of Nature, throes of
apparent dissolution, you are he or she who is master or
mistress over them,
Master or mistress in your own right over Nature, elements,
pain, passion, dissolution.

The hopples[9] fall from your ankles, you find an unfailing
sufficiency,
Old or young, male or female, rude, low, rejected by the rest,
whatever you are promulges[1] itself,   45
Through birth, life, death, burial, the means are provided,
nothing is scanted,
Through angers, losses, ambition, ignorance, ennui, what you
are picks its way.
1856   *1881*

France[2]

The 18th Year of these States

A great year and place,
A harsh discordant natal scream out-sounding, to touch the
mother's heart closer than any yet.

I walk'd the shores of my Eastern sea,
Heard over the waves the little voice,
Saw the divine infant where she woke mournfully wailing,
amid the roar of cannon, curses, shouts, crash of falling
buildings,   5
Was not so sick from the blood in the gutters running, nor

9. Hobbles or fetters.
1. Publishes, sets forth. *Cf.* "promulgates," a more formal word, which has recently been
preferred.
2. Unchanged in title since its first appearance in the 1860 edition, this poem was appropriately
included in a small group entitled "Songs of Insurrection" in the editions of 1871 and 1876.
WW is, of course, commemorating the year 1794 of the French Revolution, the climactic
year of the Revolutionary Tribunal. The text has undergone but slight revision from its first
MS reading (Barrett).

from the single corpses, nor those in heaps, nor those
    borne away in the tumbrils,
Was not so desperate at the battues[3] of death—was not so
    shock'd at the repeated fusillades of the guns.

Pale, silent, stern, what could I say to that long-accrued
    retribution?
Could I wish humanity different?
Could I wish the people made of wood and stone?   10
Or that there be no justice in destiny or time?

O Liberty! O mate for me!
Here too the blaze, the grape-shot and the axe, in reserve, to
    fetch them out in case of need,
Here too, though long represt, can never be destroy'd,
Here too could rise at last murdering and ecstatic,   15
Here too demanding full arrears of vengeance.

Hence I sign this salute over the sea,
And I do not deny that terrible red birth and baptism,
But remember the little voice that I heard wailing, and wait
    with perfect trust, no matter how long,
And from to-day sad and cogent I maintain the bequeath'd
    cause, as for all lands,   20
And I send these words to Paris with my love,
And I guess some chansonniers[4] there will understand them,
For I guess there is latent music yet in France, floods of it,
O I hear already the bustle of instruments, they will soon be
    drowning all that would interrupt them,
O I think the east wind brings a triumphal and free march,   25
It reaches hither, it swells me to joyful madness,
I will run transpose it in words, to justify it,
I will yet sing a song for you ma femme.[5]
    1860   *1871*

Myself and Mine[6]

Myself and mine gymnastic ever,
To stand the cold or heat, to take good aim with a gun, to sail
    a boat, to manage horses, to beget superb children,

3. The beaten, the wantonly slaughtered, as of helpless crowds.
4. Song writers.
5. Literally, my woman; here, Democracy, personified.
6. In 1860 this poem was No. 10 of the "Leaves of Grass" group, and in 1867 it was No. 2 of
    another group so named. With the 1871, 1872, and 1876 editions it was included in the
    "Passage to India" supplement with its present title. WW dropped the two original opening
    lines in 1867 for the present opening line and at the same time deleted—just before the
    present line 26—two lines confessing "the evil I really am." In its announcement of personal
    intent it could well be one of the "Inscriptions" poems.

To speak readily and clearly, to feel at home among common
    people,
And to hold our own in terrible positions on land and sea.

Not for an embroiderer,   5
(There will always be plenty of embroiderers, I welcome them
    also,)
But for the fibre of things and for inherent men and women.

Not to chisel ornaments,
But to chisel with free stroke the heads and limbs of plenteous
    supreme Gods, that the States may realize them walking
    and talking.

Let me have my own way,   10
Let others promulge[7] the laws, I will make no account of the laws,
Let others praise eminent men and hold up peace, I hold up
    agitation and conflict,
I praise no eminent man, I rebuke to his face the one that was
    thought most worthy.

(Who are you? and what are you secretly guilty of all your life?
Will you turn aside all your life? will you grub and chatter all
    your life?   15
And who are you, blabbing by rote, years, pages, languages,
    reminiscences,
Unwitting to-day that you do not know how to speak properly
    a single word?)

Let others finish specimens, I never finish specimens,
I start them by exhaustless laws as Nature does, fresh and
    modern continually.

I give nothing as duties,   20
What others give as duties I give as living impulses,
(Shall I give the heart's action as a duty?)

Let others dispose of questions, I dispose of nothing, I arouse
    unanswerable questions,
Who are they I see and touch, and what about them?
What about these likes of myself that draw me so close by
    tender directions and indirections?   25

I call to the world to distrust the accounts of my friends, but
    listen to my enemies, as I myself do,
I charge you forever reject those who would expound me, for I
    cannot expound myself,

7. Promulgate. *Cf.* "To You," line 45, note.

I charge that there be no theory or school founded out of me,
I charge you to leave all free, as I have left all free.

After me, vista! 30
O I see life is not short, but immeasurably long,
I henceforth tread the world chaste, temperate, an early riser,
    a steady grower,
Every hour the semen of centuries, and still of centuries.

I must follow up these continual lessons of the air, water, earth,
I perceive I have no time to lose. 35
  1860   *1881*

Year of Meteors[8]

(1859–60)

Year of meteors! brooding year!
I would bind in words retrospective some of your deeds and signs,
I would sing your contest for the 19th Presidentiad,[9]
I would sing how an old man, tall, with white hair, mounted
    the scaffold in Virginia,[1]
(I was at hand, silent I stood with teeth shut close, I watch'd, 5
I stood very near you old man when cool and indifferent, but
    trembling with age and your unheal'd wounds you
    mounted the scaffold;)
I would sing in my copious song your census returns of the States,
The tables of population and products, I would sing of your
    ships and their cargoes,
The proud black ships of Manhattan arriving, some fill'd with
    immigrants, some from the isthmus with cargoes of gold,
Songs thereof would I sing, to all that hitherward comes would
    I welcome give, 10
And you would I sing, fair stripling! welcome to you from me,
    young prince of England![2]
(Remember you surging Manhattan's crowds as you pass'd with
    your cortege of nobles?
There in the crowds stood I, and singled you out with attachment;)

8. In 1865 and 1867 this poem was in *Drum-Taps*; in 1871, 1872, and 1876, in a "Leaves of Grass" group, from which it was transferred to the present group in 1881. Printed in *N and F*, I, 51–52, item 184, are two MS fragments (Berg and Feinberg) in which WW describes two meteor showers: one, November 13, 1833, in a prose paragraph, and the other, November 12–13, 1858, in five trial lines that may have been intended for his "Pictures" poem.
9. The 1860 Lincoln-Douglas electoral contest.
1. John Brown the abolitionist, hanged for treason, December 2, 1859 at Charles Town, Va.
2. Edward, Prince of Wales, who visited New York City on October 11, 1860. WW made a notebook entry on his visit (LC *Whitman*, No. 92). See "Prince of Wales" in *Fragments*.

Nor forget I to sing of the wonder, the ship as she swam up
    my bay,
Well-shaped and stately the Great Eastern[3] swam up my bay,
    she was 600 feet long,   15
Her moving swiftly surrounded by myriads of small craft I
    forget not to sing;
Nor the comet that came unannounced out of the north
    flaring in heaven,
Nor the strange huge meteor-procession dazzling and clear
    shooting over our heads,
(A moment, a moment long it sail'd its balls of unearthly light
    over our heads,
Then departed, dropt in the night, and was gone;)   20
Of such, and fitful as they, I sing—with gleams from them
    would I gleam and patch these chants,
Your chants, O year all mottled with evil and good—year of
    forebodings!
Year of comets and meteors transient and strange—lo! even
    here one equally transient and strange!
As I flit through you hastily, soon to fall and be gone, what is
    this chant,
What am I myself but one of your meteors?   25
  1865   *1881*

With Antecedents[4]

1

With antecedents,
With my fathers and mothers and the accumulations of past ages,
With all which, had it not been, I would not now be here, as I am,
With Egypt, India, Phenicia, Greece and Rome,
With the Kelt, the Scandinavian, the Alb[5] and the Saxon,   5
With antique maritime ventures, laws, artisanship, wars and
    journeys,
With the poet, the skald, the saga, the myth, and the oracle,
With the sale of slaves, with enthusiasts, with the troubadour,
    the crusader, and the monk,
With those old continents whence we have come to this new
    continent,
With the fading kingdoms and kings over there,   10

---

3. Famous British iron steamship, of later tragic history, which reached New York City June
    28, 1860, on her maiden Atlantic crossing.
4. The first publication of this poem was in the *New York Saturday Press*, January 14, 1860,
    under the title, "You and Me and To-day." In the 1860 *LG* it is No. 7 of the "Chants
    Democratic," taking its present title from 1867 on. The MS (Barrett-Va.) proposes two other
    titles: "Poemet," deleted for "Evolutions." The parenthetical phrase of line 23, "(torn, stormy,
    even as I, amid these vehement days,)," was added in 1867.
5. Man of Albion, i.e., England.

With the fading religions and priests,
With the small shores we look back to from our own large and
    present shores,
With countless years drawing themselves onward and arrived at
    these years,
You and me arrived—America arrived and making this year,
This year! sending itself ahead countless years to come.   15

2

O but it is not the years—it is I, it is You,
We touch all laws and tally all antecedents,
We are the skald, the oracle, the monk and the knight, we
    easily include them and more,
We stand amid time beginningless and endless, we stand amid
    evil and good,
All swings around us, there is as much darkness as light,   20
The very sun swings itself and its system of planets around us,
Its sun, and its again, all swing around us.

As for me, (torn, stormy, amid these vehement days,)
I have the idea of all, and am all and believe in all,
I believe materialism is true and spiritualism is true, I reject no
    part.   25

(Have I forgotten any part? any thing in the past?
Come to me whoever and whatever, till I give you recognition.)

I respect Assyria, China, Teutonia, and the Hebrews,
I adopt each theory, myth, god, and demi-god,
I see that the old accounts, bibles, genealogies, are true,
    without exception,   30
I assert that all past days were what they must have been,
And that they could no-how have been better than they were,
And that to-day is what it must be, and that America is,
And that to-day and America could no-how be better than they are.

3

In the name of these States and in your and my name, the Past, 35
And in the name of these States and in your and my name,
    the Present time.

I know that the past was great and the future will be great,
And I know that both curiously conjoint in the present time,
(For the sake of him I typify, for the common average man's
    sake, your sake if you are he,)
And that where I am or you are this present day, there is the
    centre of all days, all races,   40

And there is the meaning to us of all that has ever come of
     races and days, or ever will come.
1860   *1881*

_____

A Broadway Pageant[1]

1

Over the Western sea hither from Niphon[2] come,
Courteous, the swart-cheek'd two-sworded envoys,
Leaning back in their open barouches, bare-headed, impassive,
Ride to-day through Manhattan.

Libertad![3] I do not know whether others behold what I behold,   5
In the procession along with the nobles of Niphon, the errand-
     bearers,
Bringing up the rear, hovering above, around, or in the ranks
     marching,
But I will sing you a song of what I behold Libertad.

When million-footed Manhattan unpent descends to her
     pavements,
When the thunder-cracking guns arouse me with the proud
     roar I love,   10
When the round-mouth'd guns out of the smoke and smell I
     love spit their salutes,
When the fire-flashing guns have fully alerted me, and heaven-
     clouds canopy my city with a delicate thin haze,
When gorgeous the countless straight stems, the forests at the
     wharves, thicken with colors,
When every ship richly drest carries her flag at the peak,
When pennants trail and street-festoons hang from the
     windows,   15
When Broadway is entirely given up to foot-passengers and
     foot-standers, when the mass is densest,
When the façades of the houses are alive with people, when
     eyes gaze riveted tens of thousands at a time,
When the guests from the islands advance, when the pageant
     moves forward visible,

1. This poem was first printed in the *New York Times,* June 27, 1860, under the title "The
   Errand-Bearers," in commemoration of the parade down Broadway eleven days before of the
   Japanese embassy, which had come to America to work on treaty arrangements between
   America and Japan. The title, and the Quaker phrase in the subtitle—"16th 6th Month,
   Year 84 of The States"—were changed when the poem appeared in the 1865 *Drum-Taps* as
   "A Broadway Pageant (Reception Japanese Embassy, June 16, 1860)." The *Drum-Taps* text
   was but slightly changed from the newspaper text, but a significant revision of the opening
   lines was made for the 1871 and succeeding texts. Omitted was the fourth-line phrase "Les-
   son-giving princes," and in general the emphasis was shifted from deference to the Orient
   to the role of America as the mistress of a new world-democracy. In this sense "A Broadway
   Pageant" is a precursor of "Passage to India."
2. Commonly Nippon, Japanese name for Japan.
3. Spanish: "liberty." In WW's usage it is also the personification of freedom.

When the summons is made, when the answer that waited
    thousands of years answers,
I too arising, answering, descend to the pavements, merge with
    the crowd, and gaze with them.   20

2

Superb-faced Manhattan!
Comrade Americanos! to us, then at last the Orient comes.

To us, my city,
Where our tall-topt marble and iron beauties range on opposite
    sides, to walk in the space between,
To-day our Antipodes comes.   25

The Originatress comes,
The nest of languages, the bequeather of poems, the race of eld,[4]
Florid with blood, pensive, rapt with musings, hot with passion,
Sultry with perfume, with ample and flowing garments,
With sunburnt visage, with intense soul and glittering eyes,   30
The race of Brahma comes.

See my cantabile![5] these and more are flashing to us from the
    procession,
As it moves changing, a kaleidoscope divine it moves changing
    before us.

For not the envoys nor the tann'd Japanee from his island only,
Lithe and silent the Hindoo appears, the Asiatic continent
    itself appears, the past, the dead,   35
The murky night-morning of wonder and fable inscrutable,
The envelop'd mysteries, the old and unknown hive-bees,
The north, the sweltering south, eastern Assyria, the Hebrews,
    the ancient of ancients,
Vast desolated cities, the gliding present, all of these and more
    are in the pageant-procession.

Geography, the world, is in it,   40
The Great Sea, the brood of islands, Polynesia, the coast
    beyond,
The coast you henceforth are facing—you Libertad! from your
    Western golden shores,
The countries there with their populations, the millions en-
    masse are curiously here,

---

4. People of olden time.
5. Properly, an adjective meaning "flowing" or "songlike," but WW uses it as a noun, meaning
    "melodious song."

The swarming market-places, the temples with idols ranged
    along the sides or at the end; bonze, brahmin, and llama,[6]
Mandarin, farmer, merchant, mechanic, and fisherman,   45
The singing-girl and the dancing-girl, the ecstatic persons, the
    secluded emperors,
Confucius himself, the great poets and heroes, the warriors,
    the castes, all,
Trooping up, crowding from all directions, from the Altay
    mountains,
From Thibet, from the four winding and far-flowing rivers of China,
From the southern peninsulas and the demi-continental
    islands, from Malaysia,   50
These and whatever belongs to them palpable show forth to
    me, and are seiz'd by me,
And I am seiz'd by them, and friendlily held by them,
Till as here them all I chant, Libertad! for themselves and for you.

For I too raising my voice join the ranks of this pageant,
I am the chanter, I chant aloud over the pageant,   55
I chant the world on my Western sea,
I chant copious the islands beyond, thick as stars in the sky,
I chant the new empire grander than any before, as in a vision
    it comes to me,
I chant America the mistress, I chant a greater supremacy,
I chant projected a thousand blooming cities yet in time on
    those groups of sea-islands,   60
My sail-ships and steam-ships threading the archipelagoes,
My stars and stripes fluttering in the wind,
Commerce opening, the sleep of ages having done its work,
    races reborn, refresh'd,
Lives, work resumed—the object I know not—but the old, the
    Asiatic renew'd as it must be,
Commencing from this day surrounded by the world.   65

3

And you Libertad of the world!
You shall sit in the middle well-pois'd thousands of thousands
    of years,
As to-day from one side the nobles of Asia come to you,
As to-morrow from the other side the queen of England sends
    her eldest son to you.[7]

The sign is reversing, the orb is enclosed,   70
The ring is circled, the journey is done,

6. Respectively, Buddhist monk of Japan, member of the priestly Hindu caste, and Tibetan
    priest (properly spelled "lama").
7. Edward, Prince of Wales, later Edward VII, whose 1860 visit to America is referred to in
    "Year of Meteors."

The box-lid is but perceptibly open'd, nevertheless the perfume
    pours copiously out of the whole box.

Young Libertad! with the venerable Asia, the all-mother,
Be considerate with her now and ever hot Libertad, for you are all,
Bend your proud neck to the long-off mother now sending
    messages over the archipelagoes to you,   75
Bend your proud neck low for once, young Libertad.

Were the children straying westward so long? so wide the
    tramping?
Were the precedent dim ages debouching westward from
    Paradise so long?
Were the centuries steadily footing it that way, all the while
    unknown, for you, for reasons?

They are justified, they are accomplish'd, they shall now be
    turn'd the other way also, to travel toward you thence,   80
They shall now also march obediently eastward for your sake
    Libertad.
1860   *1881*

SEA-DRIFT

Out of the Cradle Endlessly Rocking[1]

Out of the cradle endlessly rocking,
Out of the mocking-bird's throat, the musical shuttle,

> **Sea-Drift**: This group of eleven poems, compiled in *LG* 1881, included the seven poems of
> the "Sea-Shore Memories" cluster in the 1871 *Passage to India*, two new poems, and two
> poems transferred from the 1876 *Two Rivulets*. The new group is one of the poet's most
> consonant arrangements, held together by the impression, deep in childhood memory, of the
> sea and the beach, an influence that is at the heart of his acceptance of the tragic in life.
> 1. First published (MS Berg) under the title "A Child's Reminiscence" in the Christmas issue
> (December 24, 1859) of the *New York Saturday Press,* whose editor, Henry Clapp, was WW's
> friend and companion in the Pfaff Restaurant coterie. The long proem, called "Pre-Verse,"
> syntactically a single sentence, was followed by "Reminiscence," in thirty-five numbered
> stanzas. With concurrent revisions the poem appeared prominently in all *LG* or *Passage to
> India* editions; the present authorized text appeared in *LG* 1881. The revisions of 1860 merit
> close study, while those of 1867 greatly improved the phrasing. In *LG* 1860 and 1867 the
> title was "A Word Out of the Sea." Under its present title it headed the "Sea-Shore Mem-
> ories" group in *Passage to India* in 1871 and until that supplement was consolidated with
> *LG* in 1881.
>   WW himself probably wrote the editorial notice of the poem in the same issue of the
> *Saturday Press*: "Our readers may, if they choose, consider as our Christmas or New Year's
> present to them, the curious warble, by Walt Whitman, of 'A Child's Reminiscence,' on our
> First Page. Like the 'Leaves of Grass,' the purport of this wild and plaintive song, well-
> enveloped, and eluding definition, is positive and unquestionable, like the effect of music.
>   "The piece will bear reading many times—perhaps, indeed only comes forth, as from re-
> cesses, by many repetitions."
>   In "All About a Mocking Bird" (*Saturday Press,* January 7, 1860), WW defended the poem
> against a charge in the *Cincinnati Daily Commercial* (December 28, 1859) that the poem

Out of the Ninth-month midnight,[2]
Over the sterile sands and the fields beyond, where the child
    leaving his bed wander'd alone, bareheaded, barefoot,
Down from the shower'd halo,   5
Up from the mystic play of shadows twining and twisting as if
    they were alive,
Out from the patches of briers and blackberries,
From the memories of the bird that chanted to me,
From your memories sad brother, from the fitful risings and
    fallings I heard,
From under that yellow half-moon late-risen and swollen as if
    with tears,   10
From those beginning notes of yearning and love there in the mist,
From the thousand responses of my heart never to cease,
From the myriad thence-arous'd words,
From the word stronger and more delicious than any,
From such as now they start the scene revisiting,   15
As a flock, twittering, rising, or overhead passing,
Borne hither, ere all eludes me, hurriedly,
A man, yet by these tears a little boy again,
Throwing myself on the sand, confronting the waves,
I, chanter of pains and joys, uniter of here and hereafter,   20
Taking all hints to use them, but swiftly leaping beyond them,
A reminiscence sing.

Once Paumanok,[3]
When the lilac-scent was in the air and Fifth-month grass was
    growing,
Up this seashore in some briers,   25
Two feather'd guests from Alabama, two together,
And their nest, and four light-green eggs spotted with brown,
And every day the he-bird to and fro near at hand,
And every day the she-bird crouch'd on her nest, silent, with
    bright eyes,
And every day I, a curious boy, never too close, never
    disturbing them,   30
Cautiously peering, absorbing, translating.

---

is meaningless. The poem is profoundly autobiographical in that its theme goes to the very center of the poet's experience—how he became a poet and how his songs awoke. Whether or not it is based on a personal loss is not known, but surely its interpretation of love and death relates it to the "Calamus" themes. Helen Price recalled that WW had read it to her family as early as 1858. (See Bucke, 29.) Swinburne called it ". . . the most lovely and wonderful thing I have read for years and years . . . there is such beautiful skill and subtle power in every word of it." An excellent article is Leo Spitzer's " 'Explication de Texte' Applied to Walt Whitman's 'Out of the Cradle Endlessly Rocking,' " *ELH* 16: 229–49.

2. The Quaker designation for September may here suggest the human cycle of fertility and birth, in contrast with "sterile sands" in the next line.

3. WW was especially fond of this Indian name for Long Island as closely associated with his childhood memories.

Shine! shine! shine![4]
Pour down your warmth, great sun!
While we bask, we two together.

Two together!   35
Winds blow south, or winds blow north,
Day come white, or night come black,
Home, or rivers and mountains from home,
Singing all time, minding no time,
While we two keep together.   40

Till of a sudden,
May-be kill'd, unknown to her mate,
One forenoon the she-bird crouch'd not on the nest,
Nor return'd that afternoon, nor the next,
Nor ever appear'd again.   45

And thenceforward all summer in the sound of the sea,
And at night under the full of the moon in calmer weather,
Over the hoarse surging of the sea,
Or flitting from brier to brier by day,
I saw, I heard at intervals the remaining one, the he-bird,   50
The solitary guest from Alabama.

Blow! blow! blow!
Blow up sea-winds along Paumanok's shore;
I wait and I wait till you blow my mate to me.

Yes, when the stars glisten'd,   55
All night long on the prong of a moss-scallop'd stake,
Down almost amid the slapping waves,
Sat the lone singer wonderful causing tears.

He call'd on his mate,
He pour'd forth the meanings which I of all men know.   60

Yes my brother I know,
The rest might not, but I have treasur'd every note,
For more than once dimly down to the beach gliding,
Silent, avoiding the moonbeams, blending myself with the shadows,
Recalling now the obscure shapes, the echoes, the sounds and
    sights after their sorts,   65
The white arms out in the breakers tirelessly tossing,
I, with bare feet, a child, the wind wafting my hair,
Listen'd long and long.

---

4. Comparison with earlier versions shows WW's success in improving the lyrics (printed in
   italics) that resemble birdsong; especially the characteristic reiteration of phrase, the varied
   vocalic modulation of the cadences, and the staccato "twittering" accentuation (lines 80,
   91–92, 110, for example).

Listen'd to keep, to sing, now translating the notes,
Following you my brother.   70

Soothe! soothe! soothe!
Close on its wave soothes the wave behind,
And again another behind embracing and lapping, every one close,
But my love soothes not me, not me.

Low hangs the moon, it rose late,   75
It is lagging—O I think it is heavy with love, with love.

O madly the sea pushes upon the land,
With love, with love.

O night! do I not see my love fluttering out among the breakers?
What is that little black thing I see there in the white?   80

Loud! loud! loud!
Loud I call to you, my love!
High and clear I shoot my voice over the waves,
Surely you must know who is here, is here,
You must know who I am, my love.   85

Low-hanging moon!
What is that dusky spot in your brown yellow?
O it is the shape, the shape of my mate!
O moon do not keep her from me any longer.

Land! land! O land!   90
Whichever way I turn, O I think you could give me my mate
      back again if you only would,
For I am almost sure I see her dimly whichever way I look.

O rising stars!
Perhaps the one I want so much will rise, will rise with some of you.

O throat! O trembling throat!   95
Sound clearer through the atmosphere!
Pierce the woods, the earth,
Somewhere listening to catch you must be the one I want.

Shake out carols!
Solitary here, the night's carols!   100
Carols of lonesome love! death's carols!
Carols under that lagging, yellow, waning moon!
O under that moon where she droops almost down into the sea!
O reckless despairing carols.

But soft! sink low! 105
Soft! let me just murmur,
And do you wait a moment you husky-nois'd sea,
For somewhere I believe I heard my mate responding to me,
So faint, I must be still, be still to listen,
But not altogether still, for then she might not come immediately
    to me. 110

Hither my love!
Here I am! here!
With this just-sustain'd note I announce myself to you,
This gentle call is for you my love, for you.

Do not be decoy'd elsewhere, 115
That is the whistle of the wind, it is not my voice,
That is the fluttering, the fluttering of the spray,
Those are the shadows of leaves.

O darkness! O in vain!
O I am very sick and sorrowful. 120

O brown halo in the sky near the moon, drooping upon the sea!
O troubled reflection in the sea!
O throat! O throbbing heart!
And I singing uselessly, uselessly all the night.

O past! O happy life! O songs of joy! 125
In the air, in the woods, over fields,
Loved! loved! loved! loved! loved!
But my mate no more, no more with me!
We two together no more.

The aria[5] sinking, 130
All else continuing, the stars shining,
The winds blowing, the notes of the bird continuous echoing,
With angry moans the fierce old mother incessantly moaning,
On the sands of Paumanok's shore gray and rustling,
The yellow half-moon enlarged, sagging down, drooping, the
    face of the sea almost touching, 135
The boy ecstatic, with his bare feet the waves, with his hair
    the atmosphere dallying,
The love in the heart long pent, now loose, now at last
    tumultuously bursting,
The aria's meaning, the ears, the soul, swiftly depositing,
The strange tears down the cheeks coursing,
The colloquy there, the trio, each uttering, 140
The undertone, the savage old mother incessantly crying,

---

5. See Robert D. Faner's *Walt Whitman and Opera* (Philadelphia: University of Pennsylvania Press, 1951), especially 173–77, for an analysis of WW's use of this opera form.

To the boy's soul's questions sullenly timing, some drown'd
    secret hissing,
To the outsetting bard.

Demon or bird! (said the boy's soul,)
Is it indeed toward your mate you sing? or is it really to me?   145
For I, that was a child, my tongue's use sleeping, now I have
    heard you,
Now in a moment I know what I am for, I awake,
And already a thousand singers, a thousand songs, clearer,
    louder and more sorrowful than yours,
A thousand warbling echoes have started to life within me,
    never to die.

O you singer solitary, singing by yourself, projecting me,   150
O solitary me listening, never more shall I cease perpetuating you,
Never more shall I escape, never more the reverberations,
Never more the cries of unsatisfied love be absent from me,
Never again leave me to be the peaceful child I was before
    what there in the night,
By the sea under the yellow and sagging moon,   155
The messenger there arous'd, the fire, the sweet hell within,
The unknown want, the destiny of me.

O give me the clew! (it lurks in the night here somewhere,)
O if I am to have so much, let me have more!

A word then, (for I will conquer it,)   160
The word final, superior to all,
Subtle, sent up—what is it?—I listen;
Are you whispering it, and have been all the time, you sea-waves?
Is that it from your liquid rims and wet sands?

Whereto answering, the sea,   165
Delaying not, hurrying not,
Whisper'd me through the night, and very plainly before day-break,
Lisp'd to me the low and delicious word death,
And again death, death, death, death,
Hissing melodious, neither like the bird nor like my arous'd
    child's heart,   170
But edging near as privately for me rustling at my feet,
Creeping thence steadily up to my ears and laving me softly all over,
Death, death, death, death, death.

Which I do not forget,
But fuse the song of my dusky demon and brother,   175

That he sang to me in the moonlight on Paumanok's gray beach,
With the thousand responsive songs at random,
My own songs awaked from that hour,
And with them the key, the word up from the waves,
The word of the sweetest song and all songs,   180
That strong and delicious word which, creeping to my feet,
(Or like some old crone rocking the cradle, swathed in sweet
    garments, bending aside,)
The sea whisper'd me.
    1859   *1881*

As I Ebb'd with the Ocean of Life[6]

1

As I ebb'd with the ocean of life,
As I wended the shores I know,
As I walk'd where the ripples continually wash you Paumanok,
Where they rustle up hoarse and sibilant;
Where the fierce old mother endlessly cries for her castaways,   5
I musing late in the autumn day, gazing off southward,
Held by this electric self out of the pride of which I utter poems,
Was seiz'd by the spirit that trails in the lines underfoot,
The rim, the sediment that stands for all the water and all the
    land of the globe.

Fascinated, my eyes reverting from the south, dropt, to follow
    those slender windrows,   10
Chaff, straw, splinters of wood, weeds, and the sea-gluten,
Scum, scales from shining rocks, leaves of salt-lettuce, left by
    the tide,
Miles walking, the sound of breaking waves the other side of me,

6. Probably composed in 1859; first published as "Bardic Symbols" in the *Atlantic Monthly*, April 1860; in *LG* 1860 it appeared as No. 1 of the "Leaves of Grass" with the restoration of lines 59–60, whose realism had caused editor James Russell Lowell to request their omission from the magazine, in which WW was so eager to appear that he uncharacteristically acceded. (See *Corr.*, I, 47–48.) In *LG* 1867, the title restated the first line, "Elemental Drifts," later dropped. It was so called in the cluster "Sea-Shore Memories" of *Passage to India*, 1871 to 1876, and was given its present title and position in 1881. The MSS (Houghton and Barrett) and printed variants show persistent, though minor, revision.
    The poem is remarkable in its poignant admission of self-doubt and frustration; in the period of its composition WW, having left his editorial post on the *Brooklyn Times*, was unemployed and insecure. Yet the mood of this poem is not that of personal discontent so much as recognition of the "tears of things" in the human condition. It is not the poet alone who identifies himself with the sands and drift, who seeks the consolation of the father, and who at the end is thrown helpless on the shore like a drowned corpse; it is humankind. Other poems—for example, "On the Beach at Night"—make their answer.
    For a helpful reading of "As I Ebb'd with the Ocean of Life," see Tenney Nathanson, *Whitman's Presence: Body, Voice, and Writing in "Leaves of Grass"* (New York: New York University Press, 1992), 444–68.

Paumanok there and then as I thought the old thought of
    likenesses,[7]
These you presented to me you fish-shaped island,   15
As I wended the shores I know,
As I walk'd with that electric self seeking types.

2

As I wend to the shores I know not,
As I list to the dirge, the voices of men and women wreck'd,
As I inhale the impalpable breezes that set in upon me,   20
As the ocean so mysterious rolls toward me closer and closer,
I too but signify at the utmost a little wash'd-up drift,
A few sands and dead leaves to gather,
Gather, and merge myself as part of the sands and drift.

O baffled, balk'd, bent to the very earth,   25
Oppress'd with myself that I have dared to open my mouth,
Aware now that amid all that blab[8] whose echoes recoil upon
    me I have not once had the least idea who or what I am,
But that before all my arrogant poems the real Me stands yet
    untouch'd, untold, altogether unreach'd,
Withdrawn far, mocking me with mock-congratulatory signs
    and bows,
With peals of distant ironical laughter at every word I have
    written,   30
Pointing in silence to these songs, and then to the sand beneath.

I perceive I have not really understood any thing, not a single
    object, and that no man ever can,
Nature here in sight of the sea taking advantage of me to dart
    upon me and sting me,
Because I have dared to open my mouth to sing at all.

3

You oceans both, I close with you,   35
We murmur alike reproachfully rolling sands and drift,
    knowing not why,
These little shreds indeed standing for you and me and all.

You friable shore with trials of debris,
You fish-shaped island, I take what is underfoot,
What is yours is mine my father.[9]   40

7. The correspondence, in transcendental terms, between the "wash'd-up drift" and the poet
   himself.
8. Cf. the "barbaric yawp" of line 1333 of "Song of Myself."
9. Paumanok, the island, his natal land, is here the father symbol as the ocean is the "fierce
   old mother."

I too Paumanok,
I too have bubbled up, floated the measureless float, and been
    wash'd on your shores,
I too am but a trail of drift and debris,
I too leave little wrecks upon you, you fish-shaped island.

I throw myself upon your breast my father,   45
I cling to you so that you cannot unloose me,
I hold you so firm till you answer me something.

Kiss me my father,
Touch me with your lips as I touch those I love,
Breathe to me while I hold you close the secret of the
    murmuring I envy.   50

4

Ebb, ocean of life, (the flow will return,)
Cease not your moaning you fierce old mother,
Endlessly cry for your castaways, but fear not, deny not me,
Rustle not up so hoarse and angry against my feet as I touch
    you or gather from you.

I mean tenderly by you and all,   55
I gather for myself and for this phantom looking down where
    we lead, and following me and mine.

Me and mine, loose windrows, little corpses,
Froth, snowy white, and bubbles,
(See, from my dead lips the ooze exuding at last,
See, the prismatic colors glistening and rolling,)[1]   60
Tufts of straw, sands, fragments,
Buoy'd hither from many moods, one contradicting another,
From the storm, the long calm, the darkness, the swell,
Musing, pondering, a breath, a briny tear, a dab of liquid or soil,
Up just as much out of fathomless workings fermented and
    thrown,   65
A limp blossom or two, torn, just as much over waves floating,
    drifted at random,
Just as much for us that sobbing dirge of Nature,
Just as much whence we come that blare of the cloud-trumpets,
We, capricious, brought hither we know not whence, spread
    out before you,
You up there walking or sitting,   70
Whoever you are, we too lie in drifts at your feet.
1860   *1881*

---

1. Lines 59–60 were excised from the *Atlantic Monthly* copy.

Tears[2]

Tears! tears! tears!
In the night, in solitude, tears,
On the white shore dripping, dripping, suck'd in by the sand,
Tears, not a star shining, all dark and desolate,
Moist tears from the eyes of a muffled head;   5
O who is that ghost? that form in the dark, with tears?
What shapeless lump is that, bent, crouch'd there on the sand?
Streaming tears, sobbing tears, throes, choked with wild cries;
O storm, embodied, rising, careering with swift steps along the
    beach!
O wild and dismal night storm, with wind—O belching and
    desperate!   10
O shade so sedate and decorous by day, with calm
    countenance and regulated pace,
But away at night as you fly, none looking—O then the
    unloosen'd ocean,
Of tears! tears! tears!
1867   *1871*

To the Man-of-War-Bird[3]

Thou who hast slept all night upon the storm,
Waking renew'd on thy prodigious pinions,
(Burst the wild storm? above it thou ascended'st,
And rested on the sky, thy slave that cradled thee,)
Now a blue point, far, far in heaven floating,   5
As to the light emerging here on deck I watch thee,
(Myself a speck, a point on the world's floating vast.)

Far, far at sea,
After the night's fierce drifts have strewn the shore with wrecks,
With re-appearing day as now so happy and serene,   10
The rosy and elastic dawn, the flashing sun,

---

2. This was one of seven new poems added to *LG* 1867, in which it appeared as No. 2 of a
"Leaves of Grass" cluster. In 1871 and 1876 it was transferred to the new "Sea-Shore Mem-
ories" group of *Passage to India*. In "The Fundamental Metrical Principle in Whitman's
Poetry," *AL* 10: 437–59, Sculley Bradley has analyzed the remarkable accentual symmetry
of this poem.
3. This poem first appeared in the *London Athenaeum*, April 1, 1876; it was an intercalation
in some copies of *LG* 1876, again appeared in the *Philadelphia Progress* of November 16,
1878, with a headnote passage from Jules Michelet's *The Bird* (English translation, 1869),
and was finally placed among the "Sea-Drift" group in 1881. The poem is practically a
paraphrase of the English translation of the French original, although WW acknowledges
indebtedness only in the *Progress* publication. Adeline Knapp was the first to note the parallel
in the *Critic* 44: 467–68. WW had read Michelet in English as early as April 1847 and was
much influenced by his work, particularly *The People* (English translation, 1845). The whole
relationship is reviewed by Gay W. Allen in "Walt Whitman and Jules Michelet," *EA* 1: 230–
37.

The limpid spread of air cerulean,
Thou also re-appearest.

Thou born to match the gale, (thou art all wings,)
To cope with heaven and earth and sea and hurricane,   15
Thou ship of air that never furl'st thy sails,
Days, even weeks untired and onward, through spaces, realms
    gyrating,
At dusk that look'st on Senegal,[4] at morn America,
That sport'st amid the lightning-flash and thunder-cloud,
In them, in thy experiences, had'st thou my soul,   20
What joys! what joys were thine![5]
    1876   1881

Aboard at a Ship's Helm[6]

Aboard at a ship's helm,
A young steersman steering with care.

Through fog on a sea-coast dolefully ringing,
An ocean bell—O a warning bell, rock'd by the waves.

O you give good notice indeed, you bell by the sea-reefs
    ringing,   5
Ringing, ringing, to warn the ship from its wreck-place.

For as on the alert O steersman, you mind the loud admonition,
The bows turn, the freighted ship tacking speeds away under
    her gray sails,
The beautiful and noble ship with all her precious wealth
    speeds away gayly and safe.

But O the ship, the immortal ship! O ship aboard the ship!   10
Ship of the body, ship of the soul, voyaging, voyaging,
    voyaging.
    1867   1881

---

4. Territory in French West Africa. Now a republic.
5. Cf. final stanza of Shelley's "To a Skylark" for reversal of the sentiment of lines 20–21.
6. No. 3 of a "Leaves of Grass" group in the 1867 edition, this poem took its present title in
   the "Sea-Shore Memories" group of Passage to India (1871). In 1881 it was finally consoli-
   dated with LG in the "Sea-Drift" cluster.

On the Beach at Night[7]

On the beach at night,
Stands a child with her father,
Watching the east, the autumn sky.

Up through the darkness,
While ravening clouds, the burial clouds, in black masses
    spreading,   5
Lower sullen and fast athwart and down the sky,
Amid a transparent clear belt of ether yet left in the east,
Ascends large and calm the lord-star Jupiter,
And nigh at hand, only a very little above,
Swim the delicate sisters the Pleiades.[8]   10

From the beach the child holding the hand of her father,
Those burial-clouds that lower victorious soon to devour all,
Watching, silently weeps.

Weep not, child,
Weep not, my darling,   15
With these kisses let me remove your tears,
The ravening clouds shall not long be victorious,
They shall not long possess the sky, they devour the stars only
    in apparition,
Jupiter shall emerge, be patient, watch again another night,
    the Pleiades shall emerge,
They are immortal, all those stars both silvery and golden shall
    shine out again,   20
The great stars and the little ones shall shine out again, they
    endure,
The vast immortal suns and the long-enduring pensive moons
    shall again shine.

Then dearest child mournest thou only for Jupiter?
Considerest thou alone the burial of the stars?

Something there is,   25
(With my lips soothing thee, adding I whisper,
I give thee the first suggestion, the problem and indirection,)
Something there is more immortal even than the stars,
(Many the burials, many the days and nights, passing away,)

---

7. This poem, under its present title, first appeared in the "Sea-Shore Memories" of *Passage to India* (1871) and was transferred to the "Sea-Drift" group in 1881. *Cf.* Wordsworth's 1807 sonnet "It is a beauteous evening, calm and free" for an interesting analogy in sensibility.
8. "Sisters" read "brothers" in 1871 and 1876, being corrected in 1881 to conform with the Grecian myth about the Pleiades, the seven daughters of Atlas who were placed by Zeus among the stars; hence the name given to a group of stars in the constellation Taurus.

Something that shall endure longer even than lustrous Jupiter,   30
Longer than sun or any revolving satellite,
Or the radiant sisters the Pleiades.[9]
1871   *1881*

The World Below the Brine[1]

The world below the brine,
Forests at the bottom of the sea, the branches and leaves,
Sea-lettuce, vast lichens, strange flowers and seeds, the thick
    tangle, openings, and pink turf,
Different colors, pale gray and green, purple, white, and gold,
    the play of light through the water,
Dumb swimmers there among the rocks, coral, gluten, grass,
    rushes, and the aliment of the swimmers,   5
Sluggish existences grazing there suspended, or slowly crawling
    close to the bottom,
The sperm-whale at the surface blowing air and spray, or
    disporting with his flukes,
The leaden-eyed shark, the walrus, the turtle, the hairy sea-
    leopard, and the sting-ray,
Passions there, wars, pursuits, tribes, sight in those ocean-
    depths, breathing that thick-breathing air, as so many do,
The change thence to the sight here, and to the subtle air
    breathed by beings like us who walk this sphere,   10
The change onward from ours to that of beings who walk
    other spheres.
1860   *1871*

On the Beach at Night Alone[2]

On the beach at night alone,
As the old mother sways her to and fro singing her husky song,
As I watch the bright stars shining, I think a thought of the
    clef of the universes and of the future.

9. Read "brothers" in 1871 and 1876. See note above.
1. No. 16 of the "Leaves of Grass" group of the 1860 edition, and No. 4 of a group of
   the same name in 1867, this poem received its present title in 1871 when it was placed
   in the "Sea-Shore Memories" group of *Passage to India*. Its MS (Barrett) is simply headed
   "Leaf.—" In 1881 it was transferred to the present position.
2. As the "Clef Poem" ("clef" here used in the sense of "clue" or "key") of *LG* 1856, and
   No. 12 of the "Leaves of Grass" group of *LG* 1860, this poem was more than twice the
   length of its present version, and the "thought of the clef of the universes" was presented
   as an extended, candidly personal reflection. In 1867, as No. 1 of a "Leaves of Grass" cluster,
   the poem was radically revised to its present form, and in 1871 it took its present title as
   one of the "Sea-Shore Memories" of *Passage to India*. In *LG* 1881 it was transferred to the
   "Sea-Drift" group.

A vast similitude interlocks all,[3]
All spheres, grown, ungrown, small, large, suns, moons,
    planets,   5
All distances of place however wide,
All distances of time, all inanimate forms,
All souls, all living bodies though they be ever so different, or
    in different worlds,
All gaseous, watery, vegetable, mineral processes, the fishes,
    the brutes,
All nations, colors, barbarisms, civilizations, languages,   10
All identities that have existed or may exist on this globe, or
    any globe,
All lives and deaths, all of the past, present, future,
This vast similitude spans them, and always has spann'd,
And shall forever span them and compactly hold and enclose
    them.
1856   1881

Song for All Seas, All Ships[4]

1

To-day a rude brief recitative,
Of ships sailing the seas, each with its special flag or ship-signal,
Of unnamed heroes in the ships—of waves spreading and
    spreading far as the eye can reach,
Of dashing spray, and the winds piping and blowing,
And out of these a chant for the sailors of all nations,   5
Fitful, like a surge.

Of sea-captains young or old, and the mates, and of all
    intrepid sailors,
Of the few, very choice, taciturn, whom fate can never surprise
    nor death dismay,
Pick'd sparingly without noise by thee old ocean, chosen by thee,
Thou sea that pickest and cullest the race in time, and unitest
    nations,   10
Suckled by thee, old husky nurse, embodying thee,
Indomitable, untamed as thee.

3. This concept is Hegelian, similar to Emerson's transcendental view that the great macrocosm contains all microcosms—perhaps is the sum of them. See note, lines 464–76, "Song of Myself," for Hegelian influence on WW.
4. This poem, first printed in the *New York Daily Graphic*, April 4, 1873, under the title "Sea Captains, Young or Old," was written in commemoration of two recent marine disasters: the British steamer *Northfleet* was sunk January 22, 1873, in a collision off Dungeness with a loss of 300; and the White Star steamer *Atlantic* was wrecked off Nova Scotia, April 1, 1873, with a loss of 547. Under its present title the poem appeared as one of the four "Centennial Songs" of the 1876 *Two Rivulets,* and finally in the "Sea-Drift" group of *LG* 1881.

(Ever the heroes on water or on land, by ones or twos
    appearing,
Ever the stock preserv'd and never lost, though rare, enough
    for seed preserv'd.)

2

Flaunt out O sea your separate flags of nations! 15
Flaunt out visible as ever the various ship-signals!
But do you reserve especially for yourself and for the soul of
    man one flag above all the rest,
A spiritual woven signal for all nations, emblem of man elate
    above death,
Token of all brave captains and all intrepid sailors and mates,
And all that went down doing their duty, 20
Reminiscent of them, twined from all intrepid captains young
    or old,
A pennant universal, subtly waving all time, o'er all brave sailors,
All seas, all ships.
      1873   1881

Patroling Barnegat[5]

Wild, wild the storm, and the sea high running,
Steady the roar of the gale, with incessant undertone muttering,
Shouts of demoniac laughter fitfully piercing and pealing,
Waves, air, midnight, their savagest trinity lashing,
Out in the shadows there milk-white combs careering, 5
On beachy slush and sand spirts of snow fierce slanting,
Where through the murk the easterly death-wind breasting,
Through cutting swirl and spray watchful and firm advancing,
(That in the distance! is that a wreck? is the red signal flaring?)
Slush and sand of the beach tireless till daylight wending, 10
Steadily, slowly, through hoarse roar never remitting,
Along the midnight edge by those milk-white combs careering,
A group of dim, weird forms, struggling, the night confronting,
That savage trinity warily watching.
      1880   1881

5. This poem was first printed in *The American,* June 1880, reprinted in *Harper's Monthly,* April
   1881, and finally reached its present position in *LG* 1881. The MS drafts (Feinberg) indicate
   much reworking. Barnegat Bay, a large salt inlet about thirty miles long, is off the coast of
   Ocean County, N.J., where WW sometimes visited during his Camden days.

After the Sea-Ship[6]

After the sea-ship, after the whistling winds,
After the white-gray sails taut to their spars and ropes,
Below, a myriad myriad waves hastening, lifting up their necks,
Tending in ceaseless flow toward the track of the ship,
Waves of the ocean bubbling and gurgling, blithely prying,   5
Waves, undulating waves, liquid, uneven, emulous waves,
Toward that whirling current, laughing and buoyant, with curves,
Where the great vessel sailing and tacking displaced the surface,
Larger and smaller waves in the spread of the ocean yearnfully
    flowing,
The wake of the sea-ship after she passes, flashing and
    frolicsome under the sun,   10
A motley procession with many a fleck of foam and many
    fragments,
Following the stately and rapid ship, in the wake following.
1874   *1881*

By the Roadside

A Boston Ballad[1]

(1854)

To get betimes in Boston town I rose this morning early,
Here's a good place at the corner, I must stand and see the show.

---

6. This poem was first published in the Christmas issue of the *New York Daily Graphic*, December 1874, under the title "In the Wake Following." The MS (Mills College) indicates many variants and has still another title, "Waves in the Vessel's Wake." The poem took its present title in the 1876 *Two Rivulets* and in *LG* 1881 became one of the "Sea-Drift" group. *By the Roadside*: The two opening poems of this group are from the first edition of 1855, and three were newly written for the final 1881 arrangement. Sixteen are poems from *LG* 1860, five from the 1865 *Drum-Taps*, one from *LG* 1867, and two from the 1871 *Passage to India*. The title "By the Roadside" suggests no especial assignment of theme, unless the poet meant to evoke the notion of "wayside" topics as they strike the mind during one's passage through life. What we have here seems at first to be simply poetic miscellany: poems of rebellion, of stern admonition, of the questioning of life's meaning, of idealistic vision, of announcement, of descriptive intent. The group is truly a melange held together by the common bond of the poet's experience as roadside observer—passive, but alert and continually recording.

1. Untitled as one of the twelve poems of the first edition, this piece was called in 1856 "Poem of Apparitions in Boston, the 78th Year of These States"; in 1860, "A Boston Ballad, the 78th Year of These States"; in 1867, "To Get Betimes in Boston Town"; and in 1871 received its present title. It belonged to no group before 1881. One of the earliest of the 1855 poems, it was probably composed in June 1854, during the indignant public excitement at the arrest and trial in Boston of the fugitive slave Anthony Burns, shortly after the passage of the Kansas-Nebraska bill. It is melodramatic and bold, but its harsh satire is not native to Whitman's verse, and its rhythms are gawky, although curiously appropriate. See Stephen D. Malin, " 'A Boston Ballad' and the Boston Riot," *WWR*, no. 9 (September 1963): 51–57.

Clear the way there Jonathan![2]
Way for the President's marshal—way for the government
    cannon!
Way for the Federal foot and dragoons, (and the apparitions
    copiously tumbling.)   5

I love to look on the Stars and Stripes, I hope the fifes will
    play Yankee Doodle.
How bright shine the cutlasses of the foremost troops!
Every man holds his revolver, marching stiff through Boston town.

A fog follows, antiques of the same come limping,
Some appear wooden-legged, and some appear bandaged and
    bloodless.   10

Why this is indeed a show—it has called the dead out of the earth!
The old graveyards of the hills have hurried to see!
Phantoms! phantoms countless by flank and rear!
Cock'd hats of mothy mould—crutches made of mist!
Arms in slings—old men leaning on young men's shoulders.   15

What troubles you Yankee phantoms? what is all this
    chattering of bare gums?
Does the ague convulse your limbs? do you mistake your
    crutches for firelocks and level them?

If you blind your eyes with tears you will not see the
    President's marshal,
If you groan such groans you might balk the government cannon.

For shame old maniacs—bring down those toss'd arms, and let
    your white hair be,   20
Here gape your great grandsons, their wives gaze at them from
    the windows,
See how well dress'd, see how orderly they conduct themselves.

Worse and worse—can't you stand it? are you retreating?
Is this hour with the living too dead for you?

Retreat then—pell-mell!   25
To your graves—back—back to the hills old limpers!
I do not think you belong here anyhow.

2. Common name for the New England rustic or Yankee, first popularized by Royall Tyler's
   comedy, *The Contrast* (1787).

But there is one thing that belongs here—shall I tell you what
    it is, gentlemen of Boston?

I will whisper it to the Mayor, he shall send a committee to
    England,
They shall get a grant from the Parliament, go with a cart to
    the royal vault,   30
Dig out King George's coffin, unwrap him quick from the
    grave-clothes, box up his bones for a journey,
Find a swift Yankee clipper—here is freight for you, black-
    bellied clipper,
Up with your anchor—shake out your sails—steer straight
    toward Boston bay.

Now call for the President's marshal again, bring out the
    government cannon,
Fetch home the roarers from Congress, make another
    procession, guard it with foot and dragoons.   35

This centre-piece for them;
Look, all orderly citizens—look from the windows, women!

The committee open the box, set up the regal ribs, glue those
    that will not stay,
Clap the skull on top of the ribs, and clap a crown on top of
    the skull.

You have got your revenge, old buster—the crown is come to
    its own, and more than its own.   40

Stick your hands in your pockets, Jonathan—you are a made
    man from this day,
You are mighty cute—and here is one of your bargains.
1854   *1871*

Europe,[3]

The 72d and 73d Years of These States

Suddenly out of its stale and drowsy lair, the lair of slaves,
Like lightning it le'pt forth half startled at itself,

3. This poem is the earliest of the twelve of 1855, being first published in the *New York Daily Tribune* of June 21, 1850, under the title "Resurgemus," with different line arrangement and occasionally different phrasing. In *LG* 1855 it was, of course, untitled; in 1856 it was "Poem of The Dead Young Men of Europe, the 72nd and 73rd Years of These States"; and in 1860 it took its present title. It belonged to no group until it was placed among the "Songs of Insurrection" in 1871 and 1876, and it was transferred to the present group in 1881. It was inspired, of course, by the year of revolution, 1848, when Louis Philippe was dethroned in France and a second Republic set up February 26; when Ferdinand I of Austria abdicated in favor of his nephew Franz Josef; when freedom was proclaimed in Hungary under Kossuth; and when there were also revolts in Ireland, Lombardy, Venice, Denmark, and Schleswig-Holstein.

Its feet upon the ashes and the rags, its hands tight to the
    throats of kings.

O hope and faith!
O aching close of exiled patriots' lives!
O many a sicken'd heart!
Turn back unto this day and make yourselves afresh.

And you, paid to defile the People—you liars, mark!
Not for numberless agonies, murders, lusts,
For court thieving in its manifold mean forms, worming from
    his simplicity the poor man's wages,
For many a promise sworn by royal lips and broken and
    laugh'd at in the breaking,

Then in their power not for all these did the blows strike
    revenge, or the heads of the nobles fall;
The People scorn'd the ferocity of kings.

But the sweetness of mercy brew'd bitter destruction, and the
    frighten'd monarchs come back,
Each comes in state with his train, hangman, priest, tax-
    gatherer,
Soldier, lawyer, lord, jailer, and sycophant.

Yet behind all lowering stealing, lo, a shape,
Vague as the night, draped interminably, head, front and form,
    in scarlet folds,
Whose face and eyes none may see,
Out of its robes only this, the red robes lifted by the arm,
One finger crook'd pointed high over the top, like the head of
    a snake appears.

Meanwhile corpses lie in new-made graves, bloody corpses of
    young men,
The rope of the gibbet hangs heavily, the bullets of princes are
    flying, the creatures of power laugh aloud,
And all these things bear fruits, and they are good.

Those corpses of young men,
Those martyrs that hang from the gibbets, those hearts pierc'd
    by the gray lead,
Cold and motionless as they seem live elsewhere with
    unslaughter'd vitality.

They live in other young men O kings!
They live in brothers again ready to defy you,
They were purified by death, they were taught and exalted.

Not a grave of the murder'd for freedom but grows seed for
    freedom, in its turn to bear seed,

Which the winds carry afar and re-sow, and the rains and the
    snows nourish.

Not a disembodied spirit can the weapons of tyrants let loose,
But it stalks invisibly over the earth, whispering, counseling,
    cautioning.

Liberty, let others despair of you—I never despair of you.   35

Is the house shut? is the master away?
Nevertheless, be ready, be not weary of watching,
He will soon return, his messengers come anon.
    1850   *1871*

A Hand-Mirror[4]

Hold it up sternly—see this it sends back, (who is it? is it you?)
Outside fair costume, within ashes and filth,
No more a flashing eye, no more a sonorous voice or springy step,
Now some slave's eye, voice, hands, step,
A drunkard's breath, unwholesome eater's face, venerealee's
    flesh,   5
Lungs rotting away piecemeal, stomach sour and cankerous,
Joints rheumatic, bowels clogged with abomination,
Blood circulating dark and poisonous streams,
Words babble, hearing and touch callous,
No brain, no heart left, no magnetism of sex;   10
Such from one look in this looking-glass ere you go hence,
Such a result so soon—and from such a beginning!
    1860   *1860*

Gods[5]

Lover divine and perfect Comrade,
Waiting content, invisible yet, but certain,
Be thou my God.

Thou, thou, the Ideal Man,
Fair, able, beautiful, content, and loving,   5

4. This poem has remained unchanged and with the same title since its first appearance in the
   1860 edition. The MS (Barrett) shows that its original title, deleted, was "Looking-Glass."
5. When this poem was first published in *Passage to India*, 1871, and again in 1876, it opened
   with two lines, dropped in the present 1881 version:

> Thought of the Infinite—the All—
> Be thou my God.

Also dropped was an invocation to "thee, Old Cause" in the fifth stanza.

Complete in body and dilate in spirit,
Be thou my God.

O Death, (for Life has served its turn,)
Opener and usher to the heavenly mansion,
Be thou my God.   10

Aught, aught of mightiest, best I see, conceive, or know,
(To break the stagnant tie—thee, thee to free, O soul,)
Be thou my God.

All great ideas, the races' aspirations,
All heroisms, deeds of rapt enthusiasts,   15
Be ye my Gods.

Or Time and Space,
Or shape of Earth divine and wondrous,
Or some fair shape I viewing, worship,
Or lustrous orb of sun or star by night,   20
Be ye my Gods.
    1871   *1881*

Germs[6]

Forms, qualities, lives, humanity, language, thoughts,
The ones known, and the ones unknown, the ones on the stars,
The stars themselves, some shaped, others unshaped,
Wonders as of those countries, the soil, trees, cities,
        inhabitants, whatever they may be,
Splendid suns, the moons and rings, the countless
        combinations and effects,   5
Such-like, and as good as such-like, visible here or anywhere,
        stand provided for in a handful of space, which I extend
        my arm and half enclose with my hand,
That containing the start of each and all, the virtue, the germs
        of all.
    1860   *1871*

---

6. In *LG* 1860 this poem was "Leaves of Grass" No. 19, and in 1867 it was No. 2 of the
   "Leaves of Grass" in the annex, "Songs Before Parting." It was entitled "Germs" in 1871 and
   finally placed in the cluster "By the Roadside" in 1881. The MS (Barrett) has the title "As
   of Origins." The "germs" are a strikingly concentrated figure of the transcendental "each and
   all." *Cf.* Emerson's poem, "Each and All."

Thoughts[7]

Of ownership—as if one fit to own things could not at
    pleasure enter upon all, and incorporate them into himself
    or herself;
Of vista—suppose some sight in arriere through the formative
    chaos, presuming the growth, fulness, life, now attain'd on
    the journey,
(But I see the road continued, and the journey ever continued;)
Of what was once lacking on earth, and in due time has
    become supplied—and of what will yet be supplied,
Because all I see and know I believe to have its main purport
    in what will yet be supplied.   5
1860   *1881*

When I Heard the Learn'd Astronomer[8]

When I heard the learn'd astronomer,
When the proofs, the figures, were ranged in columns before me,
When I was shown the charts and diagrams, to add, divide,
    and measure them,
When I sitting heard the astronomer where he lectured with
    much applause in the lecture-room,
How soon unaccountable I became tired and sick,   5
Till rising and gliding out I wander'd off by myself,
In the mystical moist night-air, and from time to time,
Look'd up in perfect silence at the stars.
1865   *1865*

Perfections[9]

Only themselves understand themselves and the like of themselves,
As souls only understand souls.
1860   *1860*

---

7. In *LG* 1860 and 1887, a six-line poem identified only as No. 2 of the cluster, "Thoughts."
This consisted of the present lines 2 to 5, preceded by the couplet:

> Of waters, forests, hills;
> Of the earth at large, whispering through medium of me;

In *LG* 1871 the poem became seven lines, WW having superimposed the present first line
(previously the initial line of "Thoughts" No. 4); in *LG* 1881 WW dropped the couplet (the
initial lines of 1860, seen above), reducing the poem finally to the present five lines. The
original poems, "Thoughts" No. 2 and No. 4, will be found in this volume under the heading
"Poems Excluded from *LG*."
8. A *Drum-Taps* poem in 1865 and 1867, this much-authologized piece was in the "Songs of
Parting" group of *LG* in 1871 and 1876 and was included in the present group in 1881.
9. This poem first appeared in the 1860 edition and was reprinted without change in all suc-
ceeding editions.

O Me! O Life![1]

O me! O life! of the questions of these recurring,
Of the endless trains of the faithless, of cities fill'd with the
　　foolish,
Of myself forever reproaching myself, (for who more foolish
　　than I, and who more faithless?)
Of eyes that vainly crave the light, of the objects mean, of the
　　struggle ever renew'd,
Of the poor results of all, of the plodding and sordid crowds I
　　see around me,　　　　　　　　　　　　　　　　　　　　5
Of the empty and useless years of the rest, with the rest me
　　intertwined,
The question, O me! so sad, recurring—What good amid
　　these, O me, O life?

Answer—

That you are here—that life exists and identity,
That the powerful play goes on, and you may contribute a
　　verse.
1865–66　　　　　　　　　　　　　　　　　　　　　　　　1881

To a President[2]

All you are doing and saying is to America dangled mirages,
You have not learn'd of Nature—of the politics of Nature you
　　have not learn'd the great amplitude, rectitude,
　　impartiality,
You have not seen that only such as they are for these States,
And that what is less than they must sooner or later lift off
　　from these States.
1860　　　　　　　　　　　　　　　　　　　　　　　　　1860

I Sit and Look Out[3]

I sit and look out upon all the sorrows of the world, and upon
　　all oppression and shame,
I hear secret convulsive sobs from young men at anguish with
　　themselves, remorseful after deeds done,

---

1. This poem first appeared in the 1865–66 *Sequel to Drum-Taps* and remained unchanged until in *LG* 1881 the word "will" in the last line was changed to "may."
2. This poem began as one of the "Messenger Leaves" of *LG* 1860 and remained unchanged. The president addressed is no doubt James Buchanan, who at this time represented to the poet a democratic failure, soon to be redeemed by Abraham Lincoln.
3. "Leaves of Grass" No. 17 in *LG* 1860; No. 5 in another group so named in *LG* 1867. The poem's present title appeared in 1871, when it was also in a "Leaves of Grass" group; it was transferred in 1881 to "By the Roadside." The MS (Barrett) has the title "Leaf.—"

I see in low life the mother misused by her children, dying,
    neglected, gaunt, desperate,
I see the wife misused by her husband, I see the treacherous
    seducer of young women,
I mark the ranklings of jealousy and unrequited love attempted
    to be hid, I see these sights on the earth,   5
I see the workings of battle, pestilence, tyranny, I see martyrs
    and prisoners,
I observe a famine at sea, I observe the sailors casting lots who
    shall be kill'd to preserve the lives of the rest,
I observe the slights and degradations cast by arrogant persons
    upon laborers, the poor, and upon negroes, and the like;
All these—all the meanness and agony without end I sitting
    look out upon,
See, hear, and am silent.   10
    1860   *1871*

To Rich Givers[4]

What you give me I cheerfully accept,
A little sustenance, a hut and garden, a little money, as I
    rendezvous with my poems,
A traveler's lodging and breakfast as I journey through the
    States,—why should I be ashamed to own such gifts? why
    to advertise for them?
For I myself am not one who bestows nothing upon man and
    woman,
For I bestow upon any man or woman the entrance to all the
    gifts of the universe.   5
    1860   *1881*

The Dalliance of the Eagles[5]

Skirting the river road, (my forenoon walk, my rest,)
Skyward in air a sudden muffled sound, the dalliance of the eagles,
The rushing amorous contact high in space together,
The clinching interlocking claws, a living, fierce, gyrating wheel,
Four beating wings, two beaks, a swirling mass tight grappling,   5
In tumbling turning clustering loops, straight downward falling,
Till o'er the river pois'd, the twain yet one, a moment's lull,

---

4. Under this title, one of the "Messenger Leaves" of *LG* 1860. The poem was ungrouped in
   LG 1867, placed among the "Songs of Parting" in 1871 and 1876, and in the present group
   in 1881.
5. This poem was first printed in *Cope's Tobacco Plant* for November 1880 and was one of the
   new poems of *LG* 1881. The MSS (Barrett, LC *Whitman*, Feinberg) show much reworking.
   According to Clara Barrus, WW, who had never witnessed the mating of eagles, wrote the
   poem from a description given him by John Burroughs, who observed the occurrence in the
   early 1860s at Marlboro on the Hudson River (Barrus, 24: 169–70).

A motionless still balance in the air, then parting, talons loosing,
Upward again on slow-firm pinions slanting, their separate
    diverse flight,
She hers, he his, pursuing.   10
1880   *1881*

Roaming in Thought[6]

(*After reading* HEGEL)

Roaming in thought over the Universe, I saw the little that is
    Good steadily hastening towards immortality,
And the vast all that is call'd Evil I saw hastening to merge
    itself and become lost and dead.
1881   *1881*

A Farm Picture[7]

Through the ample open door of the peaceful country barn,
A sunlit pasture field with cattle and horses feeding,
And haze and vista, and the far horizon fading away.
1865   *1871*

A Child's Amaze[8]

Silent and amazed even when a little boy,
I remember I heard the preacher every Sunday put God in his
    statements,
As contending against some being or influence.
1865   *1867*

The Runner[9]

On a flat road runs the well-train'd runner,
He is lean and sinewy with muscular legs,

6. Like the preceding poem, this two-line piece was new to this group and the 1881 edition.
WW felt that his own idealism was affirmed by Hegel's, whose dialectic—thesis, antithesis,
and synthesis—is essentially illustrated by these lines. The poet's own notes on Hegel were
based mainly on two secondary sources: F. H. Hedge's *The Prose Writers of Germany* (1849)
and Joseph Gostwick's *German Literature* (1854). On WW and Hegel, see note to "Song of
Myself," lines 464–76.
7. Only the first two lines comprised this poem when it appeared in 1865 and in the *LG* 1867
annex as one of the "*Drum-Taps.*" In *LG* 1871 and 1876 it was ungrouped; in *LG* 1881 it
was given its present position.
8. A *Drum-Taps* poem of 1865 and *LG* 1867 annex; ungrouped in *LG* 1871 and 1876; added
to the present group in 1881.
9. First appeared in *LG* 1867; ungrouped in all editions until included in the present group in
1881.

He is thinly clothed, he leans forward as he runs,
With lightly closed fists and arms partially rais'd.
1867   *1867*

Beautiful Women[1]

Women sit or move to and fro, some old, some young,
The young are beautiful—but the old are more beautiful than
    the young.
1860   *1871*

Mother and Babe[2]

I see the sleeping babe nestling the breast of its mother,
The sleeping mother and babe—hush'd, I study them long and
    long.
1865   *1867*

Thought[3]

Of obedience, faith, adhesiveness;
As I stand aloof and look there is to me something profoundly
    affecting in large masses of men following the lead of
    those who do not believe in men.
1860   *1860*

Visor'd[4]

A mask, a perpetual natural disguiser of herself,
Concealing her face, concealing her form,
Changes and transformations every hour, every moment,
Falling upon her even when she sleeps.
1860   *1867*

---

1. These two lines formed a stanza of the poem "Debris" in *LG* 1860, were reprinted under the title "Picture" in *LG* 1867, took the present title in *LG* 1871, and were incorporated into "By the Roadside" in *LG* 1881.
2. This poem first appeared in the 1865 *Drum-Taps,* then in the *LG* 1867 annex; ungrouped in *LG* 1871 and 1876, it was added to the present group in 1881.
3. This was No. 7 of the "Thoughts" in *LG* 1860; was reprinted in 1867 in the same position; took the title "Thought" in *LG* 1871 and 1876, ungrouped; and was placed in "By the Roadside" in *LG* 1881. Its MS (Huntington) numbers the "Thought" as 59.
4. These four lines formed a stanza of the poem "Debris" in *LG* 1860; constituted a poem with the present title, and ungrouped, in *LG* 1867, 1871, and 1876; and were placed in "By the Roadside" in *LG* 1881.

Thought[5]

Of Justice—as if Justice could be any thing but the same
    ample law, expounded by natural judges and saviors,
As if it might be this thing or that thing, according to
    decisions.
  1860   *1860*

Gliding o'er All[6]

Gliding o'er all, through all,
Through Nature, Time, and Space,
As a ship on the waters advancing,
The voyage of the soul—not life alone,
Death, many deaths I'll sing.   5
  1871   *1871*

Hast Never Come to Thee an Hour[7]

Hast never come to thee an hour,
A sudden gleam divine, precipitating, bursting all these
    bubbles, fashions, wealth?
These eager business aims—books, politics, art, amours,
To utter nothingness?
  1881   *1881*

Thought[8]

Of Equality—as if it harm'd me, giving others the same
    chances and rights as myself—as if it were not
    indispensable to my own rights that others possess the
    same.
  1860   *1871*

---

5. These two lines were originally the third and fourth lines of a four-line poem, No. 4 of the "Thoughts" in *LG* 1860 and 1867. In 1871, 1872, and 1876 the poem appeared in *Passage to India*, and in 1881 it was transferred to "By the Roadside."
6. This poem first appeared as the epigraph on the title page of *Passage to India* in 1871, 1872, and 1876 and was transferred to the present group in 1881.
7. A new poem of the 1881 edition. The MS (Barrett) shows two separate drafts on a single leaf, with much revision.
8. This poem was the second line of "Thoughts" No. 4 in the 1860 and 1867 editions; in 1871, 1872, and 1876 it was printed in *Passage to India* as a separate poem under the present title; it was transferred to "By the Roadside" in 1881.

To Old Age[9]

I see in you the estuary that enlarges and spreads itself grandly
  as it pours in the great sea.
1860   *1860*

Locations and Times[1]

Locations and times—what is it in me that meets them all,
  whenever and wherever, and makes me at home?
Forms, colors, densities, odors—what is it in me that
  corresponds with them?
1860   *1871*

Offerings[2]

A thousand perfect men and women appear,
Around each gathers a cluster of friends, and gay children and
  youths, with offerings.
1860   *1871*

To the States[3]

To Identify the 16th, 17th, or 18th Presidentiad

Why reclining, interrogating? why myself and all drowsing?
What deepening twilight—scum floating atop of the waters,
Who are they as bats and night-dogs askant in the capitol?
What a filthy Presidentiad! (O South, your torrid suns! O
  North, your arctic freezings!)

9. In 1860 this poem was one of the "Messenger Leaves"; in 1867 it appeared ungrouped; in 1871, 1872, and 1876 it was transferred to *Passage to India,* and in 1881 to the present group.
1. This poem, first printed as No. 22 of the 1860 "Leaves of Grass" group, is actually a revision of four lines, 133–36, dropped after 1856 from the 1856 "Sun-Down Poem," now "Crossing Brooklyn Ferry." In 1867 it appeared in the annex, "Songs Before Parting"; in 1871, 1872, and 1876 it was transferred under the present title to *Passage to India,* and in 1881 to "By the Roadside."
2. In the 1860 edition this poem was the seventh stanza of "Debris"; in 1867 it was a separate poem entitled "Picture"; in 1871 and 1876 it acquired its present title as a *Passage to India* poem, and it was transferred to "By the Roadside" in 1881.
3. One of the "Messenger Leaves" of the 1860 edition, this poem was reprinted without change in all following editions. WW himself indicates in the MS notes of his "Blue Copy" edition that he composed it in the three years "1857–8–9." The "16th, 17th, or 18th Presidentiad" refers to the administrations of Fillmore, Pierce, and Buchanan, toward which the passionate scorn of the poet found expression not alone in these verses, but also in his political pamphlet, "The Eighteenth Presidency!" unpublished during his lifetime. See Edward F. Grier, *Walt Whitman: The Eighteenth Presidency: A Critical Text* (Lawrence: University of Kansas Press, 1956).

Are those really Congressmen? are those the great Judges? is
    that the President?   5
Then I will sleep awhile yet, for I see that these States sleep,
    for reasons;
(With gathering murk, with muttering thunder and lambent
    shoots we all duly awake,
South, North, East, West, inland and seaboard, we will surely
    awake.)
1860   *1860*

Drum-Taps

First O Songs for a Prelude[1]

First O songs for a prelude,
Lightly strike on the stretch'd tympanum pride and joy in my city,
How she led the rest to arms, how she gave the cue,
How at once with lithe limbs unwaiting a moment she sprang,

Drum-Taps: WW's earliest reference to *Drum-Taps* is in a letter of March 31, 1863, in which he asks his mother to look after the MS, but he was at work on some of the poems by 1860 or earlier, when he was considering the printing of a collection, *Banner at Day-Break,* some of whose titles were later identified as *Drum-Taps* poems (see Allen, 267). WW said *Drum-Taps* was "put together by fits and starts, on the field, in the hospitals, as I worked with the soldier boys . . ." (Traubel, II, 137); and after much persistence against odds, he sent the book to press in May 1865. The first issue was a thin book of 72 pages containing 53 poems, one of which was the short 12-line "Hush'd Be the Camps To-day" about the burial of Lincoln. The great Lincoln elegy, "When Lilacs Last in the Dooryard Bloom'd," was the first of 18 more poems published as "Sequel to Drum-Taps (since the Preceding Came from the Press)," and bound into the second issue of *Drum-Taps.* Five hundred copies were printed, and the reviews were comparatively few and unenthusiastic, notably those by two bright young men of the future, William Dean Howells and Henry James, just turned twenty-eight and twenty-two years, respectively. Such a response saddened the poet, who—as he told O'Connor—felt that *Drum-Taps* was superior as a work of art to *LG.* Despite the distinction, WW was profoundly aware that *Drum-Taps* was a part of *LG,* that indeed the experience of the war had given identity and homogeneity to the whole. He was to say as much years later in "A Backward Glance . . . ." For the publishing history of *Drum-Taps,* see the introduction to F. De Wolfe Miller's facsimile edition of *Drum-Taps* (Gainesville, Fla: Scholars' Facsimiles and Reprints, 1959).

    Because of its subject matter *Drum-Taps* preserved more autonomy through the successive editions of *LG* than most of the groups, despite many changes, as the notes indicate. From the first the group was not limited to war poems, at least 20 of the 71 poems in *Drum-Taps* and in the "Sequel" having nothing to do with the theme suggested by the title; and these —notably "Out of the Rolling Ocean the Crowd" and "Chanting the Square Deific"—were, after 1865–66, placed elsewhere. Of the 53 *Drum-Taps* poems of 1865, only 29 are retained in the final 1881 grouping; and of the 18 poems of the "Sequel," only 9 are retained. The others were shifted, often more than once, to other groups. To put the situation in another way, of the 43 poems now in "Drum-Taps," 38 were either in the original *Drum-Taps* or in the "Sequel," and only 5 originated elsewhere. In his final arrangement, the poet attained a concentration not before achieved.

1. In 1865 and 1867 this introductory poem was simply entitled "Drum-Taps"; in 1871 and 1876, it was preceded by four lines in italics that served as an epigraph for the whole group:

        Aroused and angry,
        I thought to beat the alarum, and urge relentless war;
        But soon my fingers fail'd me, my face droop'd, and I resign'd myself.
        To sit by the wounded and soothe them, or silently watch the dead.

In 1881, the poem took its first line for its title, and the epigraph became the fourth, fifth, and sixth lines of "The Wound-Dresser."

(O superb! O Manhattan, my own, my peerless!   5
O strongest you in the hour of danger, in crisis! O truer than
    steel!)
How you sprang—how you threw off the costumes of peace
    with indifferent hand,
How your soft opera-music changed, and the drum and fife
    were heard in their stead,
How you led to the war, (that shall serve for our prelude,
    songs of soldiers,)
How Manhattan drum-taps led.   10

Forty years had I in my city seen soldiers parading,
Forty years as a pageant, till unawares the lady of this teeming
    and turbulent city,
Sleepless amid her ships, her houses, her incalculable wealth,
With her million children around her, suddenly,
At dead of night, at news from the south,   15
Incens'd struck with clinch'd hand the pavement.

A shock electric, the night sustain'd it,
Till with ominous hum our hive at daybreak pour'd out its
    myriads.

From the houses then and the workshops, and through all the
    doorways,
Leapt they tumultuous, and lo! Manhattan arming.   20

To the drum-taps prompt,
The young men falling in and arming,
The mechanics arming, (the trowel, the jack-plane, the black-
    smith's hammer, tost aside with precipitation,)
The lawyer leaving his office and arming, the judge leaving the
    court,
The driver deserting his wagon in the street, jumping down,
    throwing the reins abruptly down on the horses' backs,   25
The salesman leaving the store, the boss, book-keeper, porter,
    all leaving;
Squads gather everywhere by common consent and arm,
The new recruits, even boys, the old men show them how to
    wear their accoutrements, they buckle the straps carefully,
Outdoors arming, indoors arming, the flash of the musket-
    barrels,
The white tents cluster in camps, the arm'd sentries around,
    the sunrise cannon and again at sunset,   30
Arm'd regiments arrive every day, pass through the city, and
    embark from the wharves,
(How good they look as they tramp down to the river, sweaty,
    with their guns on their shoulders!
How I love them! how I could hug them, with their brown
    faces and their clothes and knapsacks cover'd with dust!)
The blood of the city up—arm'd! arm'd! the cry everywhere,

The flags flung out from the steeples of churches and from all
the public buildings and stores,   35
The tearful parting, the mother kisses her son, the son kisses
his mother,
(Loth is the mother to part, yet not a word does she speak to
detain him,)
The tumultuous escort, the ranks of policemen preceding,
clearing the way,
The unpent enthusiasm, the wild cheers of the crowd for their
favorites,
The artillery, the silent cannons bright as gold, drawn along,
rumble lightly over the stones,   40
(Silent cannons, soon to cease your silence,
Soon unlimber'd to begin the red business;)
All the mutter of preparation, all the determin'd arming,
The hospital service, the lint, bandages and medicines,
The women volunteering for nurses, the work begun for in
earnest, no mere parade now;   45
War! an arm'd race is advancing! the welcome for battle, no
turning away;
War! be it weeks, months, or years, an arm'd race is advancing
to welcome it.

Mannahatta a-march—and it's O to sing it well!
It's O for a manly life in the camp.

And the sturdy artillery,   50
The guns bright as gold, the work for giants, to serve well the
guns,
Unlimber them! (no more as the past forty years for salutes for
courtesies merely,
Put in something now besides powder and wadding.)

And you lady of ships, you Mannahatta,
Old matron of this proud, friendly, turbulent city,   55
Often in peace and wealth you were pensive or covertly
frown'd amid all your children,
But now you smile with joy exulting old Mannahatta.
　1865
                                                                1881

Eighteen Sixty-One[2]

Arm'd year—year of the struggle,
No dainty rhymes or sentimental love verses for you terrible
year,

2. In all editions before 1881, the title of this poem was in figures, "1861." WW attempted to
sell it, October 1, 1861, to the *Atlantic* for $20, but James Russell Lowell, the editor, turned
it down with the odd excuse that before he could use it, its interest, "which is of the
present,—would have passed." See *Corr.*, I, 57, and Traubel, II, 213.

Not you as some pale poetling seated at a desk lisping
    cadenzas piano,
But as a strong man erect, clothed in blue clothes, advancing,
    carrying a rifle on your shoulder,
With well-gristled body and sunburnt face and hands, with a
    knife in the belt at your side,   5
As I heard you shouting loud, your sonorous voice ringing
    across the continent,
Your masculine voice O year, as rising amid the great cities,
Amid the men of Manhattan I saw you as one of the workmen,
    the dwellers in Manhattan,
Or with large steps crossing the prairies out of Illinois and
    Indiana,
Rapidly crossing the West with springy gait and descending the
    Alleghanies,   10
Or down from the great lakes or in Pennsylvania, or on deck
    along the Ohio river,
Or southward along the Tennessee or Cumberland rivers, or at
    Chattanooga on the mountain top,
Saw I your gait and saw I your sinewy limbs clothed in blue,
    bearing weapons, robust year,
Heard your determin'd voice launch'd forth again and again,
Year that suddenly sang by the mouths of the round-lipp'd
    cannon,   15
I repeat you, hurrying, crashing, sad, distracted year.
1865   *1881*

Beat! Beat! Drums![3]

Beat! beat! drums!—blow! bugles! blow!
Through the windows—through doors—burst like a ruthless force,
Into the solemn church, and scatter the congregation,
Into the school where the scholar is studying;
Leave not the bridegroom quiet—no happiness must he have
    now with his bride,   5
Nor the peaceful farmer any peace, ploughing his field or
    gathering his grain,
So fierce you whirr and pound you drums—so shrill you
    bugles blow.

Beat! beat! drums!—blow! bugles! blow!
Over the traffic of cities—over the rumble of wheels in the streets;
Are beds prepared for sleepers at night in the houses? no
    sleepers must sleep in those beds,   10

---

3. This stirring call to arms was first published simultaneously, September 28, 1861, in both
Harper's Weekly and the *New York Leader*. Note the skill with which WW, by spondaic and
anapaestic emphasis, imposes his martial rhythm.

No bargainers' bargains by day—no brokers or speculators—
    would they continue?
Would the talkers be talking? would the singer attempt to sing?
Would the lawyer rise in the court to state his case before the
    judge?
Then rattle quicker, heavier drums—you bugles wilder blow.

Beat! beat! drums!—blow! bugles! blow!   15
Make no parley—stop for no expostulation,
Mind not the timid—mind not the weeper or prayer,
Mind not the old man beseeching the young man,
Let not the child's voice be heard, nor the mother's entreaties,
Make even the trestles to shake the dead where they lie
    awaiting the hearses,   20
So strong you thump O terrible drums—so loud you bugles
    blow.
1861   *1867*

From Paumanok Starting I Fly Like a Bird[4]

From Paumanok starting I fly like a bird,
Around and around to soar to sing the idea of all,
To the north betaking myself to sing there arctic songs,
To Kanada till I absorb Kanada in myself, to Michigan then,
To Wisconsin, Iowa, Minnesota, to sing their songs, (they are
    inimitable;)   5
Then to Ohio and Indiana to sing theirs, to Missouri and
    Kansas and Arkansas to sing theirs,
To Tennessee and Kentucky, to the Carolinas and Georgia to
    sing theirs,
To Texas and so along up toward California, to roam accepted
    everywhere;
To sing first, (to the tap of the war-drum if need be,)
The idea of all, of the Western world one and inseparable,   10
And then the song of each member of these States.
1865   *1867*

---

4. This poem appeared in *Drum-Taps* under this title in all editions.

Song of the Banner at Daybreak[5]

Poet

O a new song, a free song,
Flapping, flapping, flapping, flapping, by sounds, by voices
    clearer, By the wind's voice and that of the drum,
By the banner's voice and child's voice and sea's voice and
    father's voice,
Low on the ground and high in the air,   5
On the ground where father and child stand,
In the upward air where their eyes turn,
Where the banner at daybreak is flapping.

Words! book-words! what are you?
Words no more, for hearken and see,   10
My song is there in the open air, and I must sing,
With the banner and pennant a-flapping.

I'll weave the chord and twine in,
Man's desire and babe's desire, I'll twine them in, I'll put in life,
I'll put the bayonet's flashing point, I'll let bullets and slugs
    whizz,   15
(As one carrying a symbol and menace far into the future,
Crying with trumpet voice, *Arouse and beware! Beware and*
    arouse!)
I'll pour the verse with streams of blood, full of volition, full of
    joy,
Then loosen, launch forth, to go and compete,
With the banner and pennant a-flapping.   20

Pennant

Come up here, bard, bard,
Come up here, soul, soul,
Come up here, dear little child,
To fly in the clouds and winds with me, and play with the
    measureless light.

Child

Father what is that in the sky beckoning to me with long
    finger?   25
And what does it say to me all the while?

---

5. Since in 1861 "Banner at Day-Break" was advertised by WW's publishers, Thayer and Eld-
ridge, as the title poem of a book he had in preparation, it is clear that the poet worked on
this poem at least four years before *Drum-Taps* was published (see Allen, 267). In 1871 and
1876 it was transferred to another group, "Bathed in War's Perfume," which was abandoned
in 1881.

Father

Nothing my babe you see in the sky,
And nothing at all to you it says—but look you my babe,
Look at these dazzling things in the houses, and see you the
    money-shops opening,
And see you the vehicles preparing to crawl along the streets
    with goods;   30
These, ah these, how valued and toil'd for these!
How envied by all the earth.

Poet

Fresh and rosy red the sun is mounting high,
On floats the sea in distant blue careering through its channels,
On floats the wind over the breast of the sea setting in toward
    land,   35
The great steady wind from west or west-by-south,
Floating so buoyant with milk-white foam on the waters.

But I am not the sea nor the red sun,
I am not the wind with girlish laughter,
Not the immense wind which strengthens, not the wind which
    lashes,   40
Not the spirit that ever lashes its own body to terror and death,
But I am that which unseen comes and sings, sings, sings,
Which babbles in brooks and scoots in showers on the land,
Which the birds know in the woods mornings and evenings,
And the shore-sands know and the hissing wave, and that
    banner and pennant,   45
Aloft there flapping and flapping.

Child

O father it is alive—it is full of people—it has children,
O now it seems to me it is talking to its children,
I hear it—it talks to me—O it is wonderful!
O it stretches—it spreads and runs so fast—O my father,   50
It is so broad it covers the whole sky.

Father

Cease, cease, my foolish babe,
What you are saying is sorrowful to me, much it displeases me;
Behold with the rest again I say, behold not banners and
    pennants aloft,
But the well-prepared pavements behold, and mark the solid-
    wall'd houses.   55

Banner and Pennant

Speak to the child O bard out of Manhattan,
To our children all, or north or south of Manhattan,
Point this day, leaving all the rest, to us over all—and yet we
    know not why,
For what are we, mere strips of cloth profiting nothing,
Only flapping in the wind?   60

Poet

I hear and see not strips of cloth alone,
I hear the tramp of armies, I hear the challenging sentry,
I hear the jubilant shouts of millions of men, I hear Liberty!
I hear the drums beat and the trumpets blowing,
I myself move abroad swift-rising flying then,   65
I use the wings of the land-bird and use the wings of the sea-
    bird, and look down as from a height,
I do not deny the precious results of peace, I see populous
    cities with wealth incalculable,
I see numberless farms, I see the farmers working in their
    fields or barns,
I see mechanics working, I see buildings everywhere founded,
    going up, or finish'd,
I see trains of cars swiftly speeding along railroad tracks drawn
    by the locomotives,   70
I see the stores, depots, of Boston, Baltimore, Charleston, New
    Orleans,
I see far in the West the immense area of grain, I dwell awhile
    hovering,
I pass to the lumber forests of the North, and again to the
    Southern plantation, and again to California;
Sweeping the whole I see the countless profit, the busy
    gatherings, earn'd wages,
See the Identity formed out of thirty-eight spacious and
    haughty States, (and many more to come,)   75
See forts on the shores of harbors, see ships sailing in and out;
Then over all, (aye! aye!) my little and lengthen'd pennant
    shaped like a sword,
Runs swiftly up indicating war and defiance—and now the
    halyards have rais'd it,
Side of my banner broad and blue, side of my starry banner,
Discarding peace over all the sea and land.   80

Banner and Pennant

Yet louder, higher, stronger, bard! yet farther, wider cleave!
No longer let our children deem us riches and peace alone,
We may be terror and carnage, and are so now,

Not now are we any one of these spacious and haughty States,
    (nor any five, nor ten,)
Nor market nor depot we, nor money-bank in the city,   85
But these and all, and the brown and spreading land, and the
    mines below, are ours,
And the shores of the sea are ours, and the rivers great and
    small,
And the fields they moisten, and the crops and the fruits are
    ours,
Bays and channels and ships sailing in and out are ours—
    while we over all,
Over the area spread below, the three or four millions of
    square miles, the capitals,   90
The forty millions of people,—O bard! in life and death
    supreme,
We, even we, henceforth flaunt out masterful, high up above,
Not for the present alone, for a thousand years chanting
    through you,
This song to the soul of one poor little child.

Child

O my father I like not the houses,   95
They will never to me be any thing, nor do I like money,
But to mount up there I would like, O father dear, that banner
    I like,
That pennant I would be and must be.

Father

Child of mine you fill me with anguish,
To be that pennant would be too fearful,   100
Little you know what it is this day, and after this day, forever,
It is to gain nothing, but risk and defy every thing,
Forward to stand in front of wars—and O, such wars!—what
    have you to do with them?
With passions of demons, slaughter, premature death?

Banner

Demons and death then I sing,   105
Put in all, aye all will I, sword-shaped pennant for war,
And a pleasure new and ecstatic, and the prattled yearning of
    children,
Blent with the sounds of the peaceful land and the liquid wash
    of the sea,
And the black ships fighting on the sea envelop'd in smoke,
And the icy cool of the far, far north, with rustling cedars and
    pines,   110

And the whirr of drums and the sound of soldiers marching,
    and the hot sun shining south,
And the beach-waves combing over the beach on my Eastern
    shore, and my Western shore the same,
And all between those shores, and my ever running Mississippi
    with bends and chutes,
And my Illinois fields, and my Kansas fields, and my fields of
    Missouri,
The Continent, devoting the whole identity without reserving
    an atom,   115
Pour in! whelm that which asks, which sings, with all and the
    yield of all,
Fusing and holding, claiming, devouring the whole,
No more with tender lip, nor musical labial sound,
But out of the night emerging for good, our voice persuasive
    no more,
Croaking like crows here in the wind.   120

Poet

My limbs, my veins dilate, my theme is clear at last,
Banner so broad advancing out of the night, I sing you
    haughty and resolute,
I burst through where I waited long, too long, deafen'd and
    blinded,
My hearing and tongue are come to me, (a little child taught me,)
I hear from above O pennant of war your ironical call and
    demand,   125
Insensate! insensate! (yet I at any rate chant you,) O banner!
Not houses of peace indeed are you, nor any nor all their
    prosperity, (if need be, you shall again have every one of
    those houses to destroy them,
You thought not to destroy those valuable houses, standing
    fast, full of comfort, built with money,
May they stand fast, then? not an hour except you above them
    and all stand fast;)
O banner, not money so precious are you, not farm produce
    you, nor the material good nutriment,   130
Nor excellent stores, nor landed on wharves from the ships,
Not the superb ships with sail-power or steam-power, fetching
    and carrying cargoes,
Nor machinery, vehicles, trade, nor revenues—but you as
    henceforth I see you
Running up out of the night, bringing your cluster of stars,
    (ever-enlarging stars,)
Divider of daybreak you, cutting the air, touch'd by the sun,
    measuring the sky,   135
(Passionately seen and yearn'd for by one poor little child,
While others remain busy or smartly talking, forever teaching
    thrift, thrift;)

O you up there! O pennant! where you undulate like a snake
    hissing so curious,
Out of reach, an idea only, yet furiously fought for, risking
    bloody death, loved by me,
So loved—O you banner leading the day with stars brought
    from the night!   140
Valueless, object of eyes, over all and demanding all—
    (absolute owner of all)—O banner and pennant!
I too leave the rest—great as it is, it is nothing—houses,
    machines are nothing—I see them not,
I see but you, O warlike pennant! O banner so broad, with
    stripes, I sing you only,
Flapping up there in the wind.
    1865   *1881*

Rise O Days from Your Fathomless Deeps[6]

1

Rise O days from your fathomless deeps, till you loftier, fiercer
    sweep,
Long for my soul hungering gymnastic I devour'd what the
    earth gave me,
Long I roam'd the woods of the north, long I watch'd Niagara
    pouring,
I travel'd the prairies over and slept on their breast, I cross'd
    the Nevadas, I cross'd the plateaus,
I ascended the towering rocks along the Pacific, I sail'd out to
    sea,   5
I sail'd through the storm, I was refresh'd by the storm,
I watch'd with joy the threatening maws of the waves,
I mark'd the white combs where they career'd so high, curling
    over,
I heard the wind piping, I saw the black clouds,
Saw from below what arose and mounted, (O superb! O wild
    as my heart, and powerful!)   10
Heard the continuous thunder as it bellow'd after the
    lightning,
Noted the slender and jagged threads of lightning as sudden
    and fast amid the din they chased each other across the
    sky;
These, and such as these, I, elate, saw—saw with wonder, yet
    pensive and masterful,
All the menacing might of the globe uprisen around me,
Yet there with my soul I fed, I fed content, supercilious.   15

6. This poem has always remained in "Drum-Taps" under this title, and with no revision. Ve-
hement and stirring, it was probably composed in the early days of recruiting, and its sen-
timent, turning from nature's dauntlessness to man's, is echoed in the later "Give Me the
Splendid Silent Sun." Note too, in stanza 3, the poet's exultant relief from the "doubt nau-
seous" that had plagued him when his beloved cities had been the scene of futile political
bickering.

2

'Twas well, O soul—'twas a good preparation you gave me,
Now we advance our latent and ampler hunger to fill,
Now we go forth to receive what the earth and the sea never
  gave us,
Not through the mighty woods we go, but through the
  mightier cities,
Something for us is pouring now more than Niagara pouring,   20
Torrents of men, (sources and rills of the Northwest are you
  indeed inexhaustible?)
What, to pavements and homesteads here, what were those
  storms of the mountains and sea?
What, to passions I witness around me to-day? was the sea risen?
Was the wind piping the pipe of death under the black clouds?
Lo! from deeps more unfathomable, something more deadly
  and savage,   25
Manhattan rising, advancing with menacing front—Cincinnati,
  Chicago, unchain'd;
What was that swell I saw on the ocean? behold what comes here,
How it climbs with daring feet and hands—how it dashes!
How the true thunder bellows after the lightning—how bright
  the flashes of lightning!
How Democracy with desperate vengeful port strides on,
  shown through the dark by those flashes of lightning!   30
(Yet a mournful wail and low sob I fancied I heard through the
  dark,
In a lull of the deafening confusion.)

3

Thunder on! stride on, Democracy! strike with vengeful stroke![7]
And do you rise higher than ever yet O days, O cities!
Crash heavier, heavier yet O storms! you have done me good,   35
My soul prepared in the mountains absorbs your immortal
  strong nutriment,
Long had I walk'd my cities, my country roads through farms,
  only half satisfied,
One doubt nauseous undulating like a snake, crawl'd on the
  ground before me,
Continually preceding my steps, turning upon me oft,
  ironically hissing low;

7. This poem, like "Beat! Beat! Drums!" and perhaps others of the war poems, suggests to some
readers a fundamental inconsistency in the poet of "Reconciliation," who also asserted that
"a kelson of the creation is love." The argument on this poem might consider certain contrary
evidence. Lines 31–32 are poignantly aware of the "mournful wail and low sob" amid the
strong, passionate thunder. Also, many believed that the issue was in fact the survival of
democracy itself. Finally, the naturalistic view that good and evil are compounded in all
reality, one of WW's recurrent themes, is established here by references to the violence
inherent in nature (cf. stanza 1 and the concluding lines, 40–48). Is the poet in fact an
approving participant or a recording observer?

The cities I loved so well I abandon'd and left, I sped to the
  certainties suitable to me,   40
Hungering, hungering, hungering, for primal energies and
  Nature's dauntlessness,
I refresh'd myself with it only, I could relish it only,
I waited the bursting forth of the pent fire—on the water and
  air I waited long;
But now I no longer wait, I am fully satisfied, I am glutted,
I have witness'd the true lightning, I have witness'd my cities
  electric,   45
I have lived to behold man burst forth and warlike America rise,
Hence I will seek no more the food of the northern solitary wilds,
No more the mountains roam or sail the stormy sea.
  1865   1867

Virginia—The West[8]

The noble sire fallen on evil days,
I saw with hand uplifted, menacing, brandishing,
(Memories of old in abeyance, love and faith in abeyance,)
The insane knife toward the Mother of All.

The noble son on sinewy feet advancing,   5
I saw, out of the land of prairies, land of Ohio's waters and of
  Indiana,
To the rescue the stalwart giant hurry his plenteous offspring,
Drest in blue, bearing their trusty rifles on their shoulders.

Then the Mother of All with calm voice speaking,
As to you Rebellious, (I seemed to hear her say,) why strive
  against me, and why seek my life?   10
When you yourself forever provide to defend me?
For you provided me Washington—and now these also.
  1872   1881

City of Ships[9]

City of ships!
(O the black ships! O the fierce ships!

<hr>

8. This satire on Virginia's secession from the democracy that she helped to create, as compared to the loyalty of the Americans from the new West, was not one of the Civil War poems of *Drum-Taps* in 1865, and it was not added to that section until 1881. It is perhaps more closely related to the title poem of the volume in which it first appeared in 1872—"As a Strong Bird on Pinions Free," later called "Thou Mother with thy Equal Brood" in *LG* 1881. This poem (*q.v.*) celebrated a varied chain of different states, yet one identity only. "Virginia—The West" was first printed in the March 1872 issue of *The Kansas Magazine*.
9. Always in *Drum-Taps* under this title, and without revision.

O the beautiful sharp-bow'd steam-ships and sail-ships!)
City of the world! (for all races are here,
All the lands of the earth make contributions here;)   5
City of the sea! city of hurried and glittering tides!
City whose gleeful tides continually rush or recede, whirling in
    and out with eddies and foam!
City of wharves and stores—city of tall façades of marble and
    iron!
Proud and passionate city—mettlesome, mad, extravagant city!
Spring up O city—not for peace alone, but be indeed yourself,
    warlike!   10
Fear not—submit to no models but your own O city!
Behold me—incarnate me as I have incarnated you!
I have rejected nothing you offer'd me—whom you adopted I
    have adopted,
Good or bad I never question you—I love all—I do not
    condemn any thing,
I chant and celebrate all that is yours—yet peace no more,   15
In peace I chanted peace, but now the drum of war is mine,
War, red war is my song through your streets, O city!
    1865   *1867*

The Centenarian's Story[1]

*Volunteer of 1861–2, (at Washington Park, Brooklyn, assisting the
Centenarian)*

Give me your hand old Revolutionary,
The hill-top is nigh, but a few steps, (make room gentlemen,)
Up the path you have follow'd me well, spite of your hundred
    and extra years,
You can walk old man, though your eyes are almost done,
Your faculties serve you, and presently I must have them serve
    me.   5

Rest, while I tell what the crowd around us means,
On the plain below recruits are drilling and exercising,
There is the camp, one regiment departs to-morrow,
Do you hear the officers giving their orders?
Do you hear the clank of the muskets?   10

1. With very minor revision, and under the same title, this poem has remained in the "Drum-Taps" group in all editions. Its story commemorates the Battle of Long Island, August 27, 1776, which took place in the region of Washington Park (Fort Greene), when fortifications raised by rebel troops delayed enemy progress until Washington could make his retreat safely across the East River. WW describes this episode briefly in No. 11 of the "Brooklyniana" articles that he ran at intervals in the *Brooklyn Standard*, 1861–62 (see *UPP*, II, 267–68). According to family tradition, one of the sons of Nehemiah Whitman, WW's great-grandfather, lost his life fighting as a rebel lieutenant in this action. It is evident that this is one of the early composed poems of the group, for it is listed under the title "Washington's First Battle" in the 1860 announcement for WW's never-published volume *Banner at Day-Break*. See note on "Drum-Taps."

Why what comes over you now old man?
Why do you tremble and clutch my hand so convulsively?
The troops are but drilling, they are yet surrounded with smiles,
Around them at hand the well-drest friends and the women,
While splendid and warm the afternoon sun shines down,   15
Green the midsummer verdure and fresh blows the dallying breeze,
O'er proud and peaceful cities and arm of the sea between.

But drill and parade are over, they march back to quarters,
Only hear that approval of hands! hear what a clapping!

As wending the crowds now part and disperse—but we old
    man,   20
Not for nothing have I brought you hither—we must remain,
You to speak in your turn, and I to listen and tell.

The Centenarian

When I clutch'd your hand it was not with terror,
But suddenly pouring about me here on every side,
And below there where the boys were drilling, and up the
    slopes they ran,   25
And where tents are pitch'd, and wherever you see south and
    south-east and south-west,
Over hills, across lowlands, and in the skirts of woods,
And along the shores, in mire (now fill'd over) came again and
    suddenly raged,
As eighty-five years a-gone no mere parade receiv'd with
    applause of friends,
But a battle which I took part in myself—aye, long ago as it is,
    I took part in it,   30
Walking then this hilltop, this same ground.

Aye, this is the ground,
My blind eyes even as I speak behold it re-peopled from graves,
The years recede, pavements and stately houses disappear,
Rude forts appear again, the old hoop'd guns are mounted,   35
I see the lines of rais'd earth stretching from river to bay,
I mark the vista of waters, I mark the uplands and slopes;
Here we lay encamp'd, it was this time in summer also.

As I talk I remember all, I remember the Declaration,[2]
It was read here, the whole army paraded, it was read to us
    here,   40

---

2. The Declaration of Independence, adopted the preceding July 4, was signed by members of
   Congress on August 2, only about three weeks before the battle.

By his staff surrounded the General[3] stood in the middle, he
    held up his unsheath'd sword,
It glitter'd in the sun in full sight of the army.

'Twas a bold act then—the English war-ships had just arrived,
We could watch down the lower bay where they lay at anchor,
And the transports swarming with soldiers.[4]   45

A few days more and they landed, and then the battle.

Twenty thousand were brought against us,
A veteran force furnish'd with good artillery.

I tell not now the whole of the battle,
But one brigade early in the forenoon order'd forward to
    engage the red-coats,   50
Of that brigade I tell, and how steadily it march'd,
And how long and well it stood confronting death.

Who do you think that was marching steadily sternly
    confronting death?
It was the brigade of the youngest men, two thousand strong,
Rais'd in Virginia and Maryland, and most of them known
    personally to the General.   55

Jauntily forward they went with quick step toward Gowanus'
    waters,[5]
Till of a sudden unlook'd for by defiles through the woods,
    gain'd at night,
The British advancing, rounding in from the east, fiercely
    playing their guns,
That brigade of the youngest was cut off and at the enemy's mercy.

The General watch'd them from this hill,   60
They made repeated desperate attempts to burst their environment,
Then drew close together, very compact, their flag flying in the
    middle,
But O from the hills how the cannon were thinning and
    thinning them!

It sickens me yet, that slaughter!
I saw the moisture gather in drops on the face of the General.   65
I saw how he wrung his hands in anguish.

---

3. General George Washington no doubt read the Declaration to the troops some time after
  August 2 (see note above). But he was quartered in New York, General Headquarters of his
  army; General Putnam remained in immediate command at the battle scene on Brooklyn
  Heights.
4. These activities occurred at nearby Staten Island, completely occupied by the British com-
  mander, General Howe, who had been steadily reinforced by the fleet for several weeks.
5. Gowanus Bay is immediately to the southwest of the battleground.

Meanwhile the British manœuvr'd to draw us out for a pitch'd
    battle,
But we dared not trust the chances of a pitch'd battle.

We fought the fight in detachments,
Sallying forth we fought at several points, but in each the luck
    was against us,   70
Our foe advancing, steadily getting the best of it, push'd us
    back to the works on this hill,
Till we turn'd menacing here, and then he left us.

That was the going out of the brigade of the youngest men,
    two thousand strong,
Few return'd, nearly all remain in Brooklyn.

That and here my General's first battle,   75
No women looking on nor sunshine to bask in, it did not
    conclude with applause,
Nobody clapp'd hands here then.

But in darkness in mist on the ground under a chill rain,
Wearied that night we lay foil'd and sullen,
While scornfully laugh'd many an arrogant lord off against us
    encamp'd,   80
Quite within hearing, feasting, clinking wineglasses together
    over their victory.

So dull and damp and another day,
But the night of that, mist lifting, rain ceasing,
Silent as a ghost while they thought they were sure of him, my
    General retreated.[6]

I saw him at the river-side,   85
Down by the ferry lit by torches, hastening the embarcation;
My General waited till the soldiers and wounded were all
    pass'd over,
And then, (it was just ere sunrise,) these eyes rested on him
    for the last time.

Every one else seem'd fill'd with gloom,
Many no doubt thought of capitulation.   90

But when my General pass'd me,
As he stood in his boat and look'd toward the coming sun,
I saw something different from capitulation.

6. Washington's "strategic" retreats set a new pattern of battle logistics, but this first time he
    had the assistance of his enemy, General Howe. Howe's astonishing apathy was to become
    legendary. In this first instance he had only to send a warship or two into the East River
    and prevent the Americans' retreat to New York.

Terminus

Enough, the Centenarian's story ends,
The two, the past and present, have interchanged,   95
I myself as connecter, as chansonnier of a great future, am
    now speaking.

And is this the ground Washington trod?
And these waters I listlessly daily cross, are these the waters he
    cross'd,
As resolute in defeat as other generals in their proudest triumphs?

I must copy the story, and send it eastward and westward,   100
I must preserve that look as it beam'd on you rivers of Brooklyn.

See—as the annual round returns the phantoms return,
It is the 27th of August and the British have landed,
The battle begins and goes against us, behold through the
    smoke Washington's face,[7]
The brigade of Virginia and Maryland have march'd forth to
    intercept the enemy,   105
They are cut off, murderous artillery from the hills plays upon them,
Rank after rank falls, while over them silently droops the flag,
Baptized that day in many a young man's bloody wounds,
In death, defeat, and sisters', mothers' tears.

Ah, hills and slopes of Brooklyn! I perceive you are more
    valuable than your owners supposed;   110
In the midst of you stands an encampment very old,
Stands forever the camp of that dead brigade.
1865   *1881*

Cavalry Crossing a Ford[8]

A line in long array where they wind betwixt green islands,
They take a serpentine course, their arms flash in the sun—
    hark to the musical clank,

7. Following an earlier punctuation, the softbound issue of 1891–92 reads: "The battle begins, and goes against us behold . . ."
8. This poem remained unchanged through all the editions except for the adding of line 6 in 1871. F. O. Matthiessen in *American Renaissance* (1941) noted that many of WW's poems were like the genre painting of certain Dutch and Flemish painters, rendered in words: the subject homely and quiet, the selection of details suggesting the movement of life arrested for a moment, and perhaps intimating but not depicting a story. A representative group of these were assembled by the poet at this point; see the present poem and these following: "Bivouac on a Mountain Side," "An Army Corps on the March," "By the Bivouac's Fitful Flame," "A Sight in Camp in the Daybreak Gray and Dim," "As Toilsome I Wandered Virginia's Woods," "I Saw Old General at Bay," and "Look Down Fair Moon."

Behold the silvery river, in it the splashing horses loitering stop
  to drink,
Behold the brown-faced men, each group, each person a
  picture, the negligent rest on the saddles,[9]
Some emerge on the opposite bank, others are just entering
  the ford—while,
Scarlet and blue and snowy white,   5
The guidon flags flutter gayly in the wind.
  1865   *1871*

Bivouac on a Mountain Side[1]

I see before me now a traveling army halting,
Below a fertile valley spread, with barns and the orchards of
  summer,
Behind, the terraced sides of a mountain, abrupt, in places
  rising high,
Broken, with rocks, with clinging cedars, with tall shapes
  dingily seen,
The numerous camp-fires scatter'd near and far, some away up
  on the mountain,   5
The shadowy forms of men and horses, looming, large-sized,
  flickering,
And over all the sky—the sky! far, far out of reach, studded,
  breaking out, the eternal stars.
  1865   *1871*

An Army Corps on the March[2]

With its cloud of skirmishers in advance,
With now the sound of a single shot snapping like a whip, and
  now an irregular volley,
The swarming ranks press on and on, the dense brigades press on,
Glittering dimly, toiling under the sun—the dust-cover'd men,
In columns rise and fall to the undulations of the ground,   5
With artillery interspers'd—the wheels rumble, the horses sweat,
As the army corps advances.
  1865–66   *1871*

9. Following an earlier punctuation subtly different in meaning, the softbound issue of 1891–
  92 reads: "each group, each person, a picture, . . ."
1. This poem remained unchanged through all the editions except that in 1871 the phrase in
  line 7 "studded with the eternal stars" was revised to the present reading. See note, "Cavalry
  Crossing a Ford," above.
2. First printed in "Sequel to Drum-Taps," 1865–66, and in the 1867 "Drum-Taps" annex
  under the title "An Army on the March," this poem took its present title in 1871 when the
  final line "As the army resistless advances" was revised to the present reading. See note,
  "Cavalry Crossing a Ford," above.

By the Bivouac's Fitful Flame[3]

By the bivouac's fitful flame,
A procession winding around me, solemn and sweet and slow
   —but first I note,
The tents of the sleeping army, the field's and wood's dim
   outline,
The darkness lit by spots of kindled fire, the silence,
Like a phantom far or near an occasional figure moving,   5
The shrubs and trees, (as I lift my eyes they seem to be
   stealthily watching me,)
While wind in procession thoughts, O tender and wondrous
   thoughts,
Of life and death, of home and the past and loved, and of
   those that are far away;
A solemn and slow procession there as I sit on the ground,
By the bivouac's fitful flame.   10
1865   *1867*

Come Up from the Fields Father[4]

Come up from the fields father, here's a letter from our Pete,
And come to the front door mother, here's a letter from thy
   dear son.

Lo, 'tis autumn,
Lo, where the trees, deeper green, yellower and redder,
Cool and sweeten Ohio's villages with leaves fluttering in the
   moderate wind,   5
Where apples ripe in the orchards hang and grapes on the
   trellis'd vines,[5]
(Smell you the smell of the grapes on the vines?
Smell you the buckwheat where the bees were lately buzzing?)

Above all, lo, the sky so calm, so transparent after the rain,
   and with wondrous clouds,
Below too, all calm, all vital and beautiful, and the farm
   prospers well.   10

3. This poem has remained unchanged through all the editions. See note, "Cavalry Crossing a Ford," above.
4. This poem, which—like the following, "Vigil Strange . . ."—has long been a favorite of this group and often anthologized, illustrates WW's power of vivid realization of a scene even though single lines or phrases may seem deficient in poetic quality. The poem remained in "Drum-Taps" unchanged through all editions.
5. This line echoes an observation WW made to his mother in a letter of June 30, 1863, describing a passing cavalry regiment: "Alas, how many of these healthy handsome rollicking young men will lie cold in death, before the apples ripe in the orchards!" (*Corr.*, I, 114).

Down in the fields all prospers well,
But now from the fields come father, come at the daughter's call,
And come to the entry mother, to the front door come right away.

Fast as she can she hurries, something ominous, her steps
    trembling,
She does not tarry to smooth her hair nor adjust her cap. 15

Open the envelope quickly,
O this is not our son's writing, yet his name is sign'd,
O a strange hand writes for our dear son, O stricken mother's
    soul!
All swims before her eyes, flashes with black, she catches the
    main words only,
Sentences broken, *gunshot wound in the breast, cavalry
    skirmish, taken to hospital,* 20
At present low, but will soon be better.

Ah now the single figure to me,
Amid all teeming and wealthy Ohio with all its cities and farms,
Sickly white in the face and dull in the head, very faint,
By the jamb of a door leans. 25

Grieve not so, dear mother, (the just-grown daughter speaks
    through her sobs,
The little sisters huddle around speechless and dismay'd,)
See, dearest mother, the letter says Pete will soon be better.

Alas poor boy, he will never be better, (nor may-be needs to be
    better, that brave and simple soul,)
While they stand at home at the door he is dead already, 30
The only son is dead.

But the mother needs to be better,
She with thin form presently drest in black,
By day her meals untouch'd, then at night fitfully sleeping,
    often waking,
In the midnight waking, weeping, longing with one deep
    longing, 35
O that she might withdraw unnoticed, silent from life escape
    and withdraw,
To follow, to seek, to be with her dear dead son.
   1865   *1867*

Vigil Strange I Kept on the Field One Night[6]

Vigil strange I kept on the field one night;
When you my son and my comrade dropt at my side that day,
One look I but gave which your dear eyes return'd with a look
    I shall never forget,
One touch of your hand to mine O boy, reach'd up as you lay
    on the ground,
Then onward I sped in the battle, the even-contested battle,   5
Till late in the night reliev'd to the place at last again I made
    my way,
Found you in death so cold dear comrade, found your body
    son of responding kisses, (never again on earth
    responding,)
Bared your face in the starlight, curious the scene, cool blew
    the moderate night-wind,
Long there and then in vigil I stood, dimly around me the
    battlefield spreading,
Vigil wondrous and vigil sweet there in the fragrant silent
    night,   10
But not a tear fell, not even a long-drawn sigh, long, long I
    gazed,
Then on the earth partially reclining sat by your side leaning
    my chin in my hands,
Passing sweet hours, immortal and mystic hours with you
    dearest comrade—not a tear, not a word,
Vigil of silence, love and death, vigil for you my son and my
    soldier,
As onward silently stars aloft, eastward new ones upward stole,   15
Vigil final for you brave boy, (I could not save you, swift was
    your death,
I faithfully loved you and cared for you living, I think we shall
    surely meet again,)
Till at latest lingering of the night, indeed just as the dawn
    appear'd,
My comrade I wrapt in his blanket, envelop'd well his form,
Folded the blanket well, tucking it carefully over head and
    carefully under feet,   20
And there and then and bathed by the rising sun, my son in
    his grave, in his rude-dug grave I deposited,
Ending my vigil strange with that, vigil of night and battle-field
    dim,
Vigil for boy of responding kisses, (never again on earth
    responding,)

6. Superior in poetic skill to the preceding poem, with which it is closely allied, this poem, a monologue both lyrical and dramatic, is artfully controlled and profoundly felt. An excellent analysis may be found in Miller, 157–60. It is to be recalled that many young boys were present in the ranks both North and South, some of them underage. The poem remained in "Drum-Taps" practically unchanged through all editions.

Vigil for comrade swiftly slain, vigil I never forget, how as day
    brighten'd,
I rose from the chill ground and folded my soldier well in his
    blanket,
And buried him where he fell.   25
1865   *1867*

A March in the Ranks Hard-Prest, and the Road Unknown[7]

A march in the ranks hard-prest, and the road unknown,
A route through a heavy wood with muffled steps in the
    darkness,
Our army foil'd with loss severe, and the sullen remnant
    retreating,
Till after midnight glimmer upon us the lights of a dim-lighted
    building,
We come to an open space in the woods, and halt by the
    dimlighted building,   5
'Tis a large old church at the crossing roads, now an
    impromptu hospital,
Entering but for a minute I see a sight beyond all the pictures
    and poems ever made,
Shadows of deepest, deepest black, just lit by moving candles
    and lamps,
And by one great pitchy torch stationary with wild red flame
    and clouds of smoke,
By these, crowds, groups of forms vaguely I see on the floor,
    some in the pews laid down,   10
At my feet more distinctly a soldier, a mere lad, in danger of
    bleeding to death, (he is shot in the abdomen,)
I stanch the blood temporarily, (the youngster's face is white
    as a lily,)
Then before I depart I sweep my eyes o'er the scene fain to
    absorb it all,
Faces, varieties, postures beyond description, most in
    obscurity, some of them dead,
Surgeons operating, attendants holding lights, the smell of
    ether, the odor of blood,   15
The crowd, O the crowd of the bloody forms, the yard outside
    also fill'd,
Some on the bare ground, some on planks or stretchers, some
    in the death-spasm sweating,

7. This poem and the following, "A Sight in Camp . . . ," among others, report the scenes of
war with an authenticity that in the 1860s anticipated the realism of Stephen Crane and—
much later—Ernest Hemingway. Their modernity, unappreciated at the time, was achieved
by on-the-spot notation—in this instance in a Washington hospital notebook of 1863–64
(LC *Whitman*, No. 101). Glicksberg (123–25) has transcribed the notebook pages, with their
trial lines, upon which WW drew for the particular scene evoked in the poem. It has re-
mained unchanged in the "Drum-Taps" group through all editions.

An occasional scream or cry, the doctor's shouted orders or calls,
The glisten of the little steel instruments catching the glint of
    the torches,
These I resume as I chant, I see again the forms, I smell the
    odor,   20
Then hear outside the orders given, *Fall in, my men, fall in;*
But first I bend to the dying lad, his eyes open, a half-smile
    gives he me,
Then the eyes close, calmly close, and I speed forth to the
    darkness,
Resuming, marching, ever in darkness marching, on in the ranks,
The unknown road still marching.   25
  1865   *1867*

A Sight in Camp in the Daybreak Gray and Dim[8]

A sight in camp in the daybreak gray and dim,
As from my tent I emerge so early sleepless,
As slow I walk in the cool fresh air the path near by the
    hospital tent,
Three forms I see on stretchers lying, brought out there
    untended lying,
Over each the blanket spread, ample brownish woolen blanket,   5
Gray and heavy blanket, folding, covering all.

Curious I halt and silent stand,
Then with light fingers I from the face of the nearest the first
    just lift the blanket;
Who are you elderly man so gaunt and grim, with well-gray'd
    hair, and flesh all sunken about the eyes?
Who are you my dear comrade?   10

Then to the second I step—and who are you my child and
    darling?
Who are you sweet boy with cheeks yet blooming?

Then to the third—a face nor child nor old, very calm, as of
    beautiful yellow-white ivory;
Young man I think I know you—I think this face is the face of
    the Christ himself,
Dead and divine and brother of all, and here again he lies.   15
  1865   *1867*

---

8. In a notebook of 1862–63 (LC *Whitman*, No. 94) the poet entered the idea for this poem
together with its penultimate line: "Sight at daybreak in camp in front of the hospital tent.
Three dead men lying, each with a blanket spread over him—I lift up one and look at the
young man's face, calm and yellow. 'Tis strange!
    "(Young man: I think this face of yours the face of my dead Christ.)" *UPP*, II, 93. The
poem has remained in the "Drum-Taps" group practically unchanged.

As Toilsome I Wander'd Virginia's Woods[9]

As toilsome I wander'd Virginia's woods,
To the music of rustling leaves kick'd by my feet, (for 'twas
    autumn,)
I mark'd at the foot of a tree the grave of a soldier;
Mortally wounded he and buried on the retreat, (easily all
    could I understand,)
The halt of a mid-day hour, when up! no time to lose—yet this
    sign left,   5
On a tablet scrawl'd and nail'd on the tree by the grave,
Bold, cautious, true, and my loving comrade.

Long, long I muse, then on my way go wandering,
Many a changeful season to follow, and many a scene of life,
Yet at times through changeful season and scene, abrupt,
    alone, or in the crowded street,   10
Comes before me the unknown soldier's grave, comes the
    inscription rude in Virginia's woods,
Bold, cautious, true, and my loving comrade.
  1865   *1867*

Not the Pilot[1]

Not the pilot has charged himself to bring his ship into port,
    though beaten back and many times baffled;
Not the pathfinder penetrating inland weary and long,
By deserts parch'd, snows chill'd, rivers wet, perseveres till he
    reaches his destination,
More than I have charged myself, heeded or unheeded, to
    compose a march for these States,
For a battle-call, rousing to arms if need be, years, centuries
    hence.   5
  1860   *1881*

---

9. This poem has remained unchanged in "Drum-Taps" through all editions. Characteristically,
  as in many other poems of this group, the sense of direct experience is strongly evoked.
1. This poem first appeared untitled in the 1860 group "Debris" and was given its present title
  in 1867. In *LG* 1871 it was transferred to "Drum-Taps" with a revision of the final line,
  which was again improved for the final version of *LG* 1881. The announcement of purpose
  in the fourth line may refer to the forthcoming *Drum-Taps*, but more likely to the whole
  LG—battle call for centuries hence.

Year That Trembled and Reel'd Beneath Me[2]

Year that trembled and reel'd beneath me!
Your summer wind was warm enough, yet the air I breathed
    froze me,
A thick gloom fell through the sunshine and darken'd me,
Must I change my triumphant songs? said I to myself,
Must I indeed learn to chant the cold dirges of the baffled?   5
And sullen hymns of defeat?
    1865   1867

The Wound-Dresser[3]

1

An old man bending I come among new faces,
Years looking backward resuming in answer to children,
Come tell us old man, as from young men and maidens that
    love me,
(Arous'd and angry, I'd thought to beat the alarum, and urge
    relentless war,
But soon my fingers fail'd me, my face droop'd and I resign'd
    myself,   5
To sit by the wounded and soothe them, or silently watch the
    dead;)
Years hence of these scenes, of these furious passions, these
    chances,
Of unsurpass'd heroes, (was one side so brave? the other was
    equally brave;)
Now be witness again, paint the mightiest armies of earth,
Of those armies so rapid so wondrous what saw you to tell us?   10
What stays with you latest and deepest? of curious panics,
Of hard-fought engagements or sieges tremendous what
    deepest remains?

2

O maidens and young men I love and that love me,
What you ask of my days those the strangest and sudden your
    talking recalls,

---

2. This poem has remained unchanged in "Drum-Taps" through all editions. The "Year" may
   be 1863–64, which saw many critical actions. See, for example, WW's piece in SDC, "The
   Wounded from Chancellorsville," dated May 1863.
3. In its first three editions, 1865, 1867, and 1871, this poem was entitled "The Dresser,"
   receiving its present title in 1876. It has always remained in the "Drum-Taps" group, and
   its content is a faithful description of WW's ministrations to the war-wounded in Washington
   hospitals. In fact lines 4, 5, and 6, which first appeared in 1871 and 1876 as a prefatory
   epigraph for the whole "Drum-Taps" group, are WW's recognition of his true role as the
   compassionate comforter of all soldiers, North and South, the poet of "Reconciliation"
   (1865), who knew that "war and all its deeds of carnage must in time be utterly lost." In
   1898 his executor, Richard Maurice Bucke, used this title for his edition of WW's letters to
   soldiers during the war.

Soldier alert I arrive after a long march cover'd with sweat and
    dust,   15
In the nick of time I come, plunge in the fight, loudly shout in
    the rush of successful charge,
Enter the captur'd works—yet lo, like a swift-running river
    they fade,
Pass and are gone they fade—I dwell not on soldiers' perils or
    soldiers' joys,
(Both I remember well—many the hardships, few the joys, yet
    I was content.)

But in silence, in dreams' projections,   20
While the world of gain and appearance and mirth goes on,
So soon what is over forgotten, and waves wash the imprints
    off the sand,
With hinged knees returning I enter the doors, (while for you
    up there,
Whoever you are, follow without noise and be of strong heart.)

Bearing the bandages, water and sponge,   25
Straight and swift to my wounded I go,
Where they lie on the ground after the battle brought in,
Where their priceless blood reddens the grass the ground,
Or to the rows of the hospital tent, or under the roof'd
    hospital,
To the long rows of cots up and down each side I return,   30
To each and all one after another I draw near, not one do I
    miss,
An attendant follows holding a tray, he carries a refuse pail,
Soon to be fill'd with clotted rags and blood, emptied, and fill'd
    again.

I onward go, I stop,
With hinged knees and steady hand to dress wounds,   35
I am firm with each, the pangs are sharp yet unavoidable,
One turns to me his appealing eyes—poor boy! I never knew you,
Yet I think I could not refuse this moment to die for you, if
    that would save you.

3

On, on I go, (open doors of time! open hospital doors!)
The crush'd head I dress, (poor crazed hand tear not the
    bandage away,)   40
The neck of the cavalry-man with the bullet through and
    through I examine,
Hard the breathing rattles, quite glazed already the eye, yet life
    struggles hard,
(Come sweet death! be persuaded O beautiful death!
In mercy come quickly.)

From the stump of the arm, the amputated hand, 45
I undo the clotted lint, remove the slough, wash off the matter
    and blood,
Back on his pillow the soldier bends with curv'd neck and side-
    falling head,
His eyes are closed, his face is pale, he dares not look on the
    bloody stump,
And has not yet look'd on it.

I dress a wound in the side, deep, deep, 50
But a day or two more, for see the frame all wasted and sinking,
And the yellow-blue countenance see.

I dress the perforated shoulder, the foot with the bullet-wound,
Cleanse the one with a gnawing and putrid gangrene, so
    sickening, so offensive,
While the attendant stands behind aside me holding the tray
    and pail. 55

I am faithful, I do not give out,
The fractur'd thigh, the knee, the wound in the abdomen,
These and more I dress with impassive hand, (yet deep in my
    breast a fire, a burning flame.)

4

Thus in silence in dreams' projections,
Returning, resuming, I thread my way through the hospitals, 60
The hurt and wounded I pacify with soothing hand,
I sit by the restless all the dark night, some are so young,
Some suffer so much, I recall the experience sweet and sad,
(Many a soldier's loving arms about this neck have cross'd and
    rested,
Many a soldier's kiss dwells on these bearded lips.) 65
1865   *1881*

Long, Too Long America[4]

Long, too long America,
Traveling roads all even and peaceful you learn'd from joys and
    prosperity only,
But now, ah now, to learn from crises of anguish, advancing,
    grappling with direst fate and recoiling not,
And now to conceive and show to the world what your
    children en-masse really are,

---

4. Until 1881 the title of this poem, taken from its first line, was "Long, Too Long, O Land."
   Both title and first line were then revised to the present reading.

(For who except myself has yet conceiv'd what your children
    en-masse really are?)   5
1865   1881

Give Me the Splendid Silent Sun[5]

1

Give me the splendid silent sun with all his beams full-
    dazzling,
Give me juicy autumnal fruit ripe and red from the orchard,
Give me a field where the unmow'd grass grows,
Give me an arbor, give me the trellis'd grape,
Give me fresh corn and wheat, give me serene-moving animals
    teaching content,   5
Give me nights perfectly quiet as on high plateaus west of the
    Mississippi, and I looking up at the stars,
Give me odorous at sunrise a garden of beautiful flowers
    where I can walk undisturb'd,
Give me for marriage a sweet-breath'd woman of whom I
    should never tire,
Give me a perfect child, give me away aside from the noise of
    the world a rural domestic life,
Give me to warble spontaneous songs recluse by myself, for my
    own ears only,   10
Give me solitude, give me Nature, give me again O Nature
    your primal sanities!

These demanding to have them, (tired with ceaseless
    excitement, and rack'd by the war-strife,)
These to procure incessantly asking, rising in cries from my heart,
While yet incessantly asking still I adhere to my city,
Day upon day and year upon year O city, walking your streets,   15
Where you hold me enchain'd a certain time refusing to give me up,
Yet giving to make me glutted, enrich'd of soul, you give me
    forever faces;
(O I see what I sought to escape, confronting, reversing my cries,
I see my own soul trampling down what it ask'd for.)

---

5. This poem was steadily reprinted without change until *LG* 1881, when the penultimate line was relieved of its final phrase, "with varied chorus and light of the sparkling eyes." The poem is artful in its initial reiteration, the rhythmic balance and tonality of its lines, the antiphonal contrast of its two stanzas, the graphic precision of each visual image, and the effect of free association among them, inducing as a whole the recognition of contrast between the serene delights of nature and the turbulence of war-excited city streets. A MS fragment (Trent)—"Give me something savage and luxuriant . . . Give me large, full-voiced men"—suggests the theme.

2

Keep your splendid silent sun,   20
Keep your woods O Nature, and the quiet places by the woods,
Keep your fields of clover and timothy, and your corn-fields
    and orchards,
Keep the blossoming buckwheat fields where the Ninth-month
    bees hum;
Give me faces and streets—give me these phantoms incessant
    and endless along the trottoirs![6]
Give me interminable eyes—give me women—give me
    comrades and lovers by the thousand!   25
Let me see new ones every day—let me hold new ones by the
    hand every day!
Give me such shows—give me the streets of Manhattan!
Give me Broadway, with the soldiers marching—give me the
    sound of the trumpets and drums!
(The soldiers in companies or regiments—some starting away,
    flush'd and reckless,
Some, their time up, returning with thinn'd ranks, young, yet
    very old, worn, marching, noticing nothing;)   30
Give me the shores and wharves heavy-fringed with black ships!
O such for me! O an intense life, full to repletion and varied!
The life of the theatre, bar-room, huge hotel, for me!
The saloon of the steamer! the crowded excursion for me! the
    torchlight procession!
The dense brigade bound for the war, with high piled military
    wagons following;   35
People, endless, streaming, with strong voices, passions, pageants,
Manhattan streets with their powerful throbs, with beating
    drums as now,
The endless and noisy chorus, the rustle and clank of muskets,
    (even the sight of the wounded,)
Manhattan crowds, with their turbulent musical chorus!
Manhattan faces and eyes forever for me.   40
    1865   *1881*

6. French: "sidewalks."

Dirge for Two Veterans[7]

The last sunbeam
Lightly falls from the finish'd Sabbath,
On the pavement here, and there beyond it is looking,
    Down a new-made double grave.

Lo, the moon ascending,   5
Up from the east the silvery round moon,
Beautiful over the house-tops, ghastly, phantom moon,
    Immense and silent moon.

I see a sad procession,
And I hear the sound of coming full-key'd bugles,   10
All the channels of the city streets they're flooding,
    As with voices and with tears.

I hear the great drums pounding,
And the small drums steady whirring,
And every blow of the great convulsive drums,   15
    Strikes me through and through.

For the son is brought with the father,
(In the foremost ranks of the fierce assault they fell,
Two veterans son and father dropt together,
    And the double grave awaits them.)   20

Now nearer blow the bugles,
And the drums strike more convulsive,
And the daylight o'er the pavement quite has faded,
    And the strong dead-march enwraps me.

In the eastern sky up-buoying,   25
The sorrowful vast phantom moves illumin'd,
('Tis some mother's large transparent face,
    In heaven brighter growing.)

O strong dead-march you please me!
O moon immense with your silvery face you soothe me!   30
O my soldiers twain! O my veterans passing to burial!
    What I have I also give you.

---

7. First appearing in the "Sequel to Drum-Taps," 1865–66, this elegy has remained unchanged in all editions. One of the few poems of *LG* that employ regular stanzaic form, its artistry has been highly praised—among others, by John Bailey, WW's English biographer, who characterizes it as "incomparably fine." In it the solemnity of loss corresponds with the drum beat of a dead-march, and with the plaintive tonality of lines unrhymed or dissonant. Note, for example, the initial consonantal rhyme of sunbeam > Sabbath; the assonantal associations of they're flooding > tears, of pounding > whirring > drums > through, of father > fell > together; and the remarkable four-line reiteration (stanza 2) of "moon," modified by two adjectives in analyzed rhyme—"ascending" and "silent."

The moon gives you light,
And the bugles and the drums give you music,
And my heart, O my soldiers, my veterans,   35
    My heart gives you love.
1865–66   *1867*

Over the Carnage Rose Prophetic a Voice[8]

Over the carnage rose prophetic a voice,
Be not dishearten'd, affection shall solve the problems of
    freedom yet,
Those who love each other shall become invincible,
They shall yet make Columbia victorious.

Sons of the Mother of All, you shall yet be victorious,   5
You shall yet laugh to scorn the attacks of all the remainder of
    the earth.

No danger shall balk Columbia's lovers,
If need be a thousand shall sternly immolate themselves for one.

One from Massachusetts shall be a Missourian's comrade,
From Maine and from hot Carolina, and another an
    Oregonese, shall be friends triune,   10
More precious to each other than all the riches of the earth.

To Michigan, Florida perfumes shall tenderly come,
Not the perfumes of flowers, but sweeter, and wafted beyond death.

It shall be customary in the houses and streets to see manly
    affection,
The most dauntless and rude shall touch face to face lightly,   15
The dependence of Liberty shall be lovers,
The continuance of Equality shall be comrades.

These shall tie you and band you stronger than hoops of iron,
I, ecstatic, O partners! O lands! with the love of lovers tie you.

(Were you looking to be held together by lawyers?   20
Or by an agreement on a paper? or by arms?
Nay, nor the world, nor any living thing, will so cohere.)
1860   *1867*

---

8. All but the first and last lines of this poem were originally part of the 1860 "Calamus"
No. 5, here rearranged. Its present form has remained unchanged since its inclusion in the
1865 *Drum-Taps*. Plainly WW hoped that the sentiment of "manly affection" would be the
cohering principle of the nation in time of peril.

I Saw Old General at Bay[9]

I saw old General at bay,
(Old as he was, his gray eyes yet shone out in battle like stars,)
His small force was now completely hemm'd in, in his works,
He call'd for volunteers to run the enemy's lines, a desperate
    emergency,
I saw a hundred and more step forth from the ranks,[1] but two
    or three were selected,   5
I saw them receive their orders aside, they listen'd with care,
    the adjutant was very grave,
I saw them depart with cheerfulness, freely risking their lives.
1865   1867

The Artilleryman's Vision[2]

While my wife at my side lies slumbering, and the wars are
    over long,
And my head on the pillow rests at home, and the vacant
    midnight passes,
And through the stillness, through the dark, I hear, just hear,
    the breath of my infant,
There in the room as I wake from sleep this vision presses
    upon me;
The engagement opens there and then in fantasy unreal,   5
The skirmishers begin, they crawl cautiously ahead, I hear the
    irregular snap! snap!
I hear the sounds of the different missiles, the short *t-h-t!*
    t-h-t! of the rifle-balls,
I see the shells exploding leaving small white clouds, I hear the
    great shells shrieking as they pass,
The grape like the hum and whirr of wind through the trees,
    (tumultuous now the contest rages,)
All the scenes at the batteries rise in detail before me again,   10
The crashing and smoking, the pride of the men in their pieces,
The chief-gunner ranges and sights his piece and selects a fuse
    of the right time,
After firing I see him lean aside and look eagerly off to note
    the effect;
Elsewhere I hear the cry of a regiment charging, (the young
    colonel leads himself this time with brandish'd sword,)

---

9. Unchanged in "Drum-Taps" through all editions, this poem celebrates the heroic tradition
of war. "Old General" is a prototype, not to be identified.
1. This comma, broken by repeated printings, shows as a period in *LG* 1888 and later issues.
2. Originally "The Veteran's Vision," this poem took its present title, with other very minor
changes, in 1871. It is essentially based on some thirty MS lines set down by WW in a
Washington notebook of 1862–63 (LC *Whitman*, No. 94). They are transcribed in Glicks-
berg, 121–23.

I see the gaps cut by the enemy's volleys, (quickly fill'd up, no
    delay,)   15
I breathe the suffocating smoke, then the flat clouds hover low
    concealing all;
Now a strange lull for a few seconds, not a shot fired on either
    side,
Then resumed the chaos louder than ever, with eager calls and
    orders of officers,
While from some distant part of the field the wind wafts to my
    ears a shout of applause, (some special success,)
And ever the sound of the cannon far or near, (rousing even in
    dreams a devilish exultation and all the old mad joy in the
    depths of my soul,)   20
And ever the hastening of infantry shifting positions, batteries,
    cavalry, moving hither and thither,
(The falling, dying, I heed not, the wounded dripping and red I
    heed not, some to the rear are hobbling,)
Grime, heat, rush, aide-de-camps galloping by or on a full run,
With the patter of small arms, the warning s-s-t of the rifles,
    (these in my vision I hear or see,)
And bombs bursting in air, and at night the vari-color'd
    rockets.   25
1865   *1881*

Ethiopia Saluting the Colors[3]

Who are you dusky woman, so ancient hardly human,
With your woolly-white and turban'd head, and bare bony feet?
Why rising by the roadside here, do you the colors greet?

('Tis while our army lines Carolina's sands and pines,
Forth from thy hovel door thou Ethiopia com'st to me,   5
As under doughty Sherman I march toward the sea.)

Me master years a hundred since from my parents sunder'd,
A little child, they caught me as the savage beast is caught,
Then hither me across the sea the cruel slaver brought.

No further does she say, but lingering all the day,   10
Her high-borne turban'd head she wags, and rolls her darkling eye,
And courtesies to the regiments, the guidons moving by.

---

3. WW composed this poem in 1867 with the title "Ethiopia Commenting" and submitted it
September 7 to the *Galaxy* magazine for $25. Although he thought it was accepted, it was
never printed, and he withdrew it on November 2, 1868. See *Corr.*, I, 337, 341, 354; II, 21,
69. It first appeared in *LG* in 1871 and again in 1876 under its present title, accompanied
by the subtitle "(A Reminiscence of 1864)," and within the group, later dropped, entitled
"Bathed in War's Perfume." It was transferred to "Drum-Taps" in 1881. Note that the poem
not only employs regular stanzaic structure but also both internal and terminal rhyme.

What is it fateful woman, so blear, hardly human?
Why wag your head with turban bound, yellow, red and green?
Are the things so strange and marvelous you see or have seen?   15
1871   *1881*

Not Youth Pertains to Me[4]

Not youth pertains to me,
Nor delicatesse, I cannot beguile the time with talk,
Awkward in the parlor, neither a dancer nor elegant,
In the learn'd coterie sitting constrain'd and still, for learning
    inures not to me,
Beauty, knowledge, inure not to me—yet there are two or
    three things inure to me,   5
I have nourish'd the wounded and sooth'd many a dying soldier,
And at intervals waiting or in the midst of camp,
Composed these songs.
1865   *1871*

Race of Veterans[5]

Race of veterans—race of victors!
Race of the soil, ready for conflict—race of the conquering march!
(No more credulity's race, abiding-temper'd race,)
Race henceforth owning no law but the law of itself,
Race of passion and the storm.   5
1865–66   *1871*

---

4. Compare the last two lines of this poem, revised in 1871, with the original 1865 *Drum-Taps* version:

> And at intervals I have strung together a few songs,
> Fit for war, and the life of the camp.

5. A "Sequel" poem of the 1865–66 *Drum-Taps*, this piece was placed in the group "Marches Now the War is Over" in 1871 and 1876, with its first line "Race of veterans!" expanded by the phrase "race of victors!" The poem was returned to "Drum-Taps" in 1881.

World Take Good Notice[6]

World take good notice, silver stars fading,
Milky hue ript, weft of white detaching,
Coals thirty-eight,[7] baleful and burning,
Scarlet, significant, hands off warning,
Now and henceforth flaunt from these shores.   5
1865   *1881*

O Tan-Faced Prairie-Boy[8]

O tan-faced prairie-boy,
Before you came to camp came many a welcome gift,
Praises and presents came and nourishing food, till at last
    among the recruits,
You came, taciturn, with nothing to give—we but look'd on
    each other,
When lo! more than all the gifts of the world you gave me.   5
1865   *1867*

Look Down Fair Moon[9]

Look down fair moon and bathe this scene,
Pour softly down night's nimbus floods on faces ghastly,
    swollen, purple,
On the dead on their backs with arms toss'd wide,
Pour down your unstinted nimbus sacred moon.
1865   *1881*

---

6. This poem has remained unchanged since its appearance in the 1865 *Drum-Taps*, although
   in 1871 and 1876 it was transferred to the group "Bathed in War's Perfume," then returned
   to "Drum-Taps" in 1881. An earlier MS (Yale) version was published in facsimile by J. H.
   Johnston in the *Century Magazine* 59 (February 1911): 532:

   > *Rise, lurid stars.*
   >
   > Rise, lurid stars, woolly white no more;
   > Change, angry cloth—weft of the silver stars no more;
   > Orbs blushing scarlet—thirty-four stars, red as flame,
   >   On the blue bunting this day we sew.
   >
   > World take good notice, silver stars have vanished;
   > Orbs now of scarlet—mortal coals, all aglow,
   > Dots of molten iron, wakeful and ominous,
   >   On the blue bunting henceforth appear.

   See "Excluded Poems" for another MS (Feinberg) reading, so different as to constitute still
   a third version.
7. The MS version lists "thirty four stars," which would place its composition between January
   29, 1861, the date of admission of Kansas, the thirty-fourth state, and June 19, 1863, the
   date of admission of West Virginia, the thirty-fifth state. The 1865 text reads "coals thirty-
   six," since Nevada, the thirty-sixth state, was admitted October 31, 1864. The thirty-eighth
   state, Colorado, was admitted August 1, 1876.
8. This poem has remained in "Drum-Taps" unchanged through all editions.
9. This poem has remained in "Drum-Taps" unchanged through all editions to 1881, when
   "their" was excluded before "arms" in the third line.

Reconciliation[1]

Word over all, beautiful as the sky,
Beautiful that war and all its deeds of carnage must in time be
    utterly lost,
That the hands of the sisters Death and Night incessantly
    softly wash again, and ever again, this soil'd world;
For my enemy is dead, a man divine as myself is dead,
I look where he lies white-faced and still in the coffin—I draw
    near,   5
Bend down and touch lightly with my lips the white face in
    the coffin.
    1865–66   1881

How Solemn as One by One[2]

(Washington City, 1865)

How solemn as one by one,
As the ranks returning worn and sweaty, as the men file by
    where I stand,
As the faces the masks appear, as I glance at the faces
    studying the masks,
(As I glance upward out of this page studying you, dear friend,
    whoever you are,)
How solemn the thought of my whispering soul to each in the
    ranks, and to you,   5
I see behind each mask that wonder a kindred soul,
O the bullet could never kill what you really are, dear friend,
Nor the bayonet stab what you really are;
The soul! yourself I see, great as any, good as the best,
Waiting secure and content, which the bullet could never kill,   10
Nor the bayonet stab O friend.
    1865–66   1871

---

1. This justly famous poem was first printed in the "Sequel to Drum-Taps, 1865–1866" and
   remained unchanged except for the exclusion, in 1881, of the pronoun "I" opening the last
   line.
2. This poem was one of the "Sequel" pieces of 1865–66 and has remained in "Drum-Taps"
   in all editions. The title note "(Washington City, 1865)" was added in 1871.

As I Lay with My Head in Your Lap Camerado[3]

As I lay with my head in your lap camerado,
The confession I made I resume, what I said to you and the
open air I resume,
I know I am restless and make others so,
I know my words are weapons full of danger, full of death,
For I confront peace, security, and all the settled laws, to
unsettle them,   5
I am more resolute because all have denied me than I could
ever have been had all accepted me,
I heed not and have never heeded either experience, cautions,
majorities, nor ridicule,
And the threat of what is call'd hell is little or nothing to me,
And the lure of what is call'd heaven is little or nothing to me;
Dear camerado! I confess I have urged you onward with me,
and still urge you, without the least idea what is our
destination,   10
Or whether we shall be victorious, or utterly quell'd and
defeated.
1865–66   1881

Delicate Cluster[4]

Delicate cluster! flag of teeming life!
Covering all my lands—all my seashores lining!
Flag of death! (how I watch'd you through the smoke of battle
pressing!
How I heard you flap and rustle, cloth defiant!)
Flag cerulean—sunny flag, with the orbs of night dappled!   5
Ah my silvery beauty—ah my woolly white and crimson!
Ah to sing the song of you, my matron mighty!
My sacred one, my mother.
1871   1871

---

3. Another "Sequel" poem of 1865–66, this piece was transferred in 1871 and 1876 to a
"Leaves of Grass" group, and returned to "Drum-Taps" in 1881, improved by the exclusion
of a parenthetical passage that had followed line 4:

> (Indeed I am myself the real soldier;
> It is not he, there, with his bayonet, and not the
> red-striped artilleryman;).

4. This poem was first published in the group "Bathed in War's Perfume" of the 1871 edition
of *LG*, and transferred to "Drum-Taps" in 1881.

To a Certain Civilian[5]

Did you ask dulcet rhymes from me?
Did you seek the civilian's peaceful and languishing rhymes?
Did you find what I sang erewhile so hard to follow?
Why I was not singing erewhile for you to follow, to
    understand—nor am I now;
(I have been born of the same as the war was born,   5
The drum-corps' rattle is ever to me sweet music, I love well
    the martial dirge,
With slow wail and convulsive throb leading the officer's funeral;)
What to such as you anyhow such a poet as I? therefore leave
    my works,
And go lull yourself with what you can understand, and with
    piano-tunes,
For I lull nobody, and you will never understand me.   10
    1865   *1871*

Lo, Victress on the Peaks[6]

Lo, Victress on the peaks,
Where thou with mighty brow regarding the world,
(The world O Libertad, that vainly conspired against thee,)
Out of its countless beleaguering toils, after thwarting them all,
Dominant, with the dazzling sun around thee,   5
Flauntest now unharm'd in immortal soundness and bloom—
    lo, in these hours supreme,
No poem proud, I chanting bring to thee, nor mastery's
    rapturous verse,
But a cluster containing night's darkness and blood-dripping
    wounds,
And psalms of the dead.
    1865–66   *1881*

5. In the 1865 *Drum-Taps* this defiant poem was composed of six lines only, from the first of which it took its title. In 1871 and 1876 it was included in the supplement, "Passage to India," and in the group "Ashes of Soldiers," with its present title and the addition of lines 2, 5, 6, and 7, as well as the phrase "with piano-tunes" in line 9. In 1881 the poem was returned to "Drum-Taps." At least one biographer has speculated that the poet was here confronting a particular person, but there is no evidence to this effect.
6. This poem, one of the "Sequel" poems of 1865–66, was placed with minor revisions in the group "Bathed in War's Perfume" in 1871 and 1876, and returned to "Drum-Taps" in 1881. "Victress" or "Libertad" is of course the poet's personification of freedom. This is one of the poems in which WW seems to have developed a pattern of line-lengths that corresponds to the undulations of the thought.

Spirit Whose Work Is Done[7]

(Washington City, 1865)

Spirit whose work is done—spirit of dreadful hours!
Ere departing fade from my eyes your forests of bayonets;
Spirit of gloomiest fears and doubts, (yet onward ever
    unfaltering pressing,)
Spirit of many a solemn day and many a savage scene—
    electric spirit,
That with muttering voice through the war now closed, like a
    tireless phantom flitted,   5
Rousing the land with breath of flame, while you beat and
    beat the drum,
Now as the sound of the drum, hollow and harsh to the last,
    reverberates round me,
As your ranks, your immortal ranks, return, return from the
    battles,
As the muskets of the young men yet lean over their shoulders,
As I look on the bayonets bristling over their shoulders,   10
As those slanted bayonets, whole forests of them appearing in
    the distance, approach and pass on, returning homeward,
Moving with steady motion, swaying to and fro to the right and
    left,
Evenly lightly rising and falling while the steps keep time;
Spirit of hours I knew, all hectic red one day, but pale as
    death next day,
Touch my mouth ere you depart, press my lips close,   15
Leave me your pulses of rage—bequeath them to me—fill me
    with currents convulsive,
Let them scorch and blister out of my chants when you are gone,
Let them identify you to the future in these songs.
    1865–66   *1881*

Adieu to a Soldier[8]

Adieu O soldier,
You of the rude campaigning, (which we shared,)
The rapid march, the life of the camp,
The hot contention of opposing fronts, the long manœuvre,
Red battles with their slaughter, the stimulus, the strong
    terrific game,   5

---

7. This poem first appeared in the "Sequel" of 1865–66 and with minor revision has remained
   in "Drum-Taps" through all editions. The title note "(*Washington City*, 1865)" was added in
   1871.
8. This poem was first published in 1871 in the group "Marches Now the War is Over" and
   was transferred to "Drum-Taps" in 1881. Of particular interest is WW's identification of his
   own mission with the hazards of war.

Spell of all brave and manly hearts, the trains of time through
     you and like of you all fill'd,
With war and war's expression.

Adieu dear comrade,
Your mission is fulfill'd—but I, more warlike,
Myself and this contentious soul of mine,   10
Still on our own campaigning bound,
Through untried roads with ambushes opponents lined,
Through many a sharp defeat and many a crisis, often baffled,
Here marching, ever marching on, a war fight out—aye here,
To fiercer, weightier battles give expression.   15
     1871   *1871*

Turn O Libertad[9]

Turn O Libertad, for the war is over,
From it and all henceforth expanding, doubting no more,
     resolute, sweeping the world,
Turn from lands retrospective recording proofs of the past,
From the singers that sing the trailing glories of the past,
From the chants of the feudal world, the triumphs of kings,
     slavery, caste,   5
Turn to the world, the triumphs reserv'd and to come—give up
     that backward world,
Leave to the singers of hitherto, give them the trailing past,
But what remains remains for singers for you—wars to come
     are for you,
(Lo, how the wars of the past have duly inured to you, and the
     wars of the present also inure;)
Then turn, and be not alarm'd O Libertad—turn your undying
     face,   10
To where the future, greater than all the past,
Is swiftly, surely preparing for you.
     1865   *1871*

9. In the *Drum-Taps* of 1865 and 1867 the first line of this poem read, "Turn, O Libertad, no
   more doubting." Then in 1871 and 1876, when it was transferred to the group "Marches
   Now the War is Over," the first line was revised to its present reading and the second line
   added. These changes emphasize WW's persistent conviction that the American historical
   experience marked an epochal change in the entire course of world history. Liberty (Libertad)
   of the individual was won by the Revolution; it was confirmed at last for all the people,
   however obscure, by the Civil War. Before, the poet notes, history was feudalism, kings,
   slavery, caste, but "wars to come are for you, . . . O Libertad."

To the Leaven'd Soil They Trod[1]

To the leaven'd soil they trod calling I sing for the last,
(Forth from my tent emerging for good, loosing, untying the
    tent-ropes,)
In the freshness the forenoon air, in the far-stretching circuits
    and vistas again to peace restored,
In the fiery fields emanative and the endless vistas beyond, to
    the South and the North,
To the leaven'd soil of the general Western world to attest my
    songs,   5
To the Alleghanian hills and the tireless Mississippi,
To the rocks I calling sing, and all the trees in the woods,
To the plains of the poems of heroes, to the prairies spreading wide,
To the far-off sea and the unseen winds, and the sane
    impalpable air;
And responding they answer all, (but not in words,)   10
The average earth, the witness of war and peace, acknowledges
    mutely,
The prairie draws me close, as the father to bosom broad the son,
The Northern ice and rain that began me nourish me to the end,
But the hot sun of the South is to fully ripen my songs.

1865–66   *1881*

---

1. From its first publication in the "Sequel" of 1865–66, this poem has remained the terminal piece of the "Drum-Taps" series, with its purpose to call the "leaven'd sod" to attest the poet's songs. For the final 1881 text the second line, "Not cities, nor man alone, nor war, nor the dead," was dropped; and the seventh line was revised, not for the better, to become the present eleventh line. However, the revision does retain the beautiful phrase "the average earth," on which the emotional force of the poem greatly depends. For in a sense the diverse culture of this continent was first "averaged" by the Civil War.

Memories of President Lincoln

When Lilacs Last in the Dooryard Bloom'd[1]

1

When lilacs last in the dooryard bloom'd,[2]
And the great star[3] early droop'd in the western sky in the night,
I mourn'd, and yet shall mourn with ever-returning spring.

Ever-returning spring, trinity sure to me you bring,
Lilac blooming perennial and drooping star in the west,   5
And thought of him I love.

Memories of President Lincoln: The four poems comprising this group were first brought together in the 1871 and 1876 "Passage to India" annex under the title "President Lincoln's Burial Hymn." They were finally grouped under the present title in 1881.

1. This great threnody, called by Swinburne "the most sweet and sonorous nocturne ever chanted in the church of the world," was composed in the weeks immediately following Lincoln's assassination, April 14, 1865, to become the title poem of the "Sequel" of eighteen poems comprising twenty-four pages, which was printed in the fall to be bound in with *Drum-Taps*. In 1871 and 1876 it headed the group entitled "President Lincoln's Burial Hymn," which was given its present title in the final grouping of 1881. A few minor revisions were made in both 1871 and 1881. For example in 1871 the refrain—the carol of the bird—was italicized for the first time, and the felicitous phrase "retrievements out of the night" was added to line 198. In the Feinberg Collection are two MS pages containing a list of about ninety words expressive of sorrow, evidently compiled by the poet in working on his elegy, and also there are six small notebook pages of MS jottings on the hermit thrush. "He is deeply interested in what I tell him of the Hermit Thrush," wrote John Burroughs to Myron B. Benton in September 1865, "and says he has used largely the information I have given him in one of his principal poems" (Barrus, 24).

    WW's observation of Lincoln as the representative democratic man, the living symbol in many respects of his own message to America, was unremitting. See the several notations on Lincoln in *Specimen Days*, and his memorial lectures, "Death of Abraham Lincoln," *SDC* (1882), and "Abraham Lincoln," *NB* (1888). Lincoln died on the morning of April 15, 1865, and after remaining in Washington until April 21, his body was carried in the long procession through American cities, including Baltimore, Harrisburg, Philadelphia, New York, Albany, Buffalo, Cleveland, Columbus, Indianapolis, and Chicago. Interment took place at Springfield, Ill., on May 4.

2. The lilac's almost universal adaptability, combined with its beauty, made it the most familiar American dooryard shrub. In ancient design, especially in Persian art and literature, the lilac flower, with its heart-shaped leaves and its lobed, paniculated spire of blossoms, acquired erotic significance as a masculine principle. In WW's plant symbolism of male comradeship—calamus, sweet flag, maple, bearded moss, etc.—the lilac occasionally appears, but here it achieves the loftiest transcendence in its dedication to the national martyr.

    Speaking in his Lincoln lecture of the fateful day, April 14, WW said: "I remember where I was stopping at the time, the season being advanced, there were many lilacs in full bloom. By one of those caprices that enter and give tinge to events without being at all a part of them, I find myself always reminded of the great tragedy of that day by the sight and odor of these blossoms." *CW*, V, 246.

    Confirming this association, without reference to WW, Julia Taft, friend from childhood of Lincoln's children, reports of her brother, the surgeon Colonel Charles S. Taft, who tended the dying President through the night, "The yard of the house . . . was full of blossoming lilacs, and as long as Charlie Taft lived the scent of lilacs . . . brought back the black horror of that dreadful night." Julia Taft Bayne, *Tad Lincoln's Father* (1931), 202–4.

3. Venus, low in the western sky at this time. See WW's comment in *SPC* (*Coll. W, Prose Works*, I, 187–88).

2

O powerful western fallen star!
O shades of night—O moody, tearful night!
O great star disappear'd—O the black murk that hides the star!
O cruel hands that hold me powerless—O helpless soul of me!   10
O harsh surrounding cloud that will not free my soul.

3

In the dooryard fronting an old farm-house near the white-
    wash'd palings,
Stands the lilac-bush tall-growing with heart-shaped leaves of
    rich green,
With many a pointed blossom rising delicate, with the perfume
    strong I love,
With every leaf a miracle—and from this bush in the dooryard,   15
With delicate-color'd blossoms and heart-shaped leaves of rich
    green,
A sprig with its flower I break.

4

In the swamp in secluded recesses,
A shy and hidden bird is warbling a song.

Solitary the thrush,   20
The hermit withdrawn to himself, avoiding the settlements,
Sings by himself a song.

Song of the bleeding throat,
Death's outlet song of life, (for well dear brother I know,
If thou wast not granted to sing thou would'st surely die.)   25

5

Over the breast of the spring, the land, amid cities,
Amid lanes and through old woods, where lately the violets
    peep'd from the ground, spotting the gray debris,
Amid the grass in the fields each side of the lanes, passing the
    endless grass,
Passing the yellow-spear'd wheat, every grain from its shroud
    in the dark-brown fields uprisen,
Passing the apple-tree blows of white and pink in the orchards,   30
Carrying a corpse to where it shall rest in the grave,
Night and day journeys a coffin.

6

Coffin that passes through lanes and streets,
Through day and night with the great cloud darkening the
    land,
With the pomp of the inloop'd flags with the cities draped in
    black,   35
With the show of the States themselves as of crape-veil'd
    women standing,
With processions long and winding and the flambeaus of the
    night,
With the countless torches lit, with the silent sea of faces and
    the unbared heads,
With the waiting depot, the arriving coffin, and the sombre
    faces,
With dirges through the night, with the thousand voices rising
    strong and solemn,   40
With all the mournful voices of the dirges pour'd around the
    coffin,
The dim-lit churches and the shuddering organs—where amid
    these you journey,
With the tolling tolling bells' perpetual clang,
Here, coffin that slowly passes,
I give you my sprig of lilac.   45

7

(Nor for you, for one alone,
Blossoms and branches green to coffins all I bring,
For fresh as the morning, thus would I chant a song for you O
    sane and sacred death.

All over bouquets of roses,
O death, I cover you over with roses and early lilies,   50
But mostly and now the lilac that blooms the first,
Copious I break, I break the sprigs from the bushes,
With loaded arms I come, pouring for you,
For you and the coffins all of you O death.)

8

O western orb sailing the heaven,   55
Now I know what you must have meant as a month since I
    walk'd,
As I walk'd in silence the transparent shadowy night,
As I saw you had something to tell as you bent to me night
    after night,
As you droop'd from the sky low down as if to my side, (while
    the other stars all look'd on,)
As we wander'd together the solemn night, (for something I
    know not what kept me from sleep,)   60

As the night advanced, and I saw on the rim of the west how
    full you were of woe,
As I stood on the rising ground in the breeze in the cool
    transparent night,
As I watch'd where you pass'd and was lost in the netherward
    black of the night,
As my soul in its trouble dissatisfied sank, as where you sad orb,
Concluded, dropt in the night, and was gone.   65

9

Sing on there in the swamp,
O singer bashful and tender, I hear your notes, I hear your call,
I hear, I come presently, I understand you,
But a moment I linger, for the lustrous star has detain'd me,
The star my departing comrade holds and detains me.   70

10

O how shall I warble myself for the dead one there I loved?
And how shall I deck my song for the large sweet soul that has gone?
And what shall my perfume be for the grave of him I love?

Sea-winds blown from east and west,
Blown from the Eastern sea and blown from the Western sea,
    till there on the prairies meeting,   75
These and with these and the breath of my chant,
I'll perfume the grave of him I love.

11

O what shall I hang on the chamber walls?
And what shall the pictures be that I hang on the walls,
To adorn the burial-house of him I love?   80

Pictures of growing spring and farms and homes,
With the Fourth-month eve at sundown, and the gray smoke
    lucid and bright,
With floods of the yellow gold of the gorgeous, indolent,
    sinking sun, burning, expanding the air,
With the fresh sweet herbage under foot, and the pale green
    leaves of the trees prolific,
In the distance the flowing glaze, the breast of the river, with a
    wind-dapple here and there,   85
With ranging hills on the banks, with many a line against the
    sky, and shadows,
And the city at hand with dwellings so dense, and stacks of
    chimneys,

And all the scenes of life and the workshops, and the workmen
    homeward returning.

12

Lo, body and soul—this land,
My own Manhattan with spires, and the sparkling and
    hurrying tides, and the ships,   90
The varied and ample land, the South and the North in the
    light, Ohio's shores and flashing Missouri,
And ever the far-spreading prairies cover'd with grass and corn.

Lo, the most excellent sun so calm and haughty,
The violet and purple morn with just-felt breezes,
The gentle soft-born measureless light,   95
The miracle spreading bathing all, the fulfill'd noon,
The coming eve delicious, the welcome night and the stars,
Over my cities shining all, enveloping man and land.

13

Sing on, sing on you gray-brown bird,
Sing from the swamps, the recesses, pour your chant from the
    bushes,   100
Limitless out of the dusk, out of the cedars and pines.

Sing on dearest brother, warble your reedy song,
Loud human song, with voice of uttermost woe.

O liquid and free and tender!
O wild and loose to my soul—O wondrous singer!   105
You only I hear—yet the star holds me, (but will soon depart,)
Yet the lilac with mastering odor holds me.

14

Now while I sat in the day and look'd forth,
In the close of the day with its light and the fields of spring,
    and the farmers preparing their crops,
In the large unconscious scenery of my land with its lakes and
    forests,   110
In the heavenly aerial beauty, (after the perturb'd winds and
    the storms,)
Under the arching heavens of the afternoon swift passing, and
    the voices of children and women,
The many-moving sea-tides, and I saw the ships how they sail'd,
And the summer approaching with richness, and the fields all
    busy with labor,
And the infinite separate houses, how they all went on, each
    with its meals and minutia of daily usages,   115

And the streets how their throbbings throbb'd, and the cities
    pent—lo, then and there,
Falling upon them all and among them all, enveloping me with
    the rest,
Appear'd the cloud, appear'd the long black trail,
And I knew death, its thought, and the sacred knowledge of death.

Then with the knowledge of death as walking one side of me,   120
And the thought of death close-walking the other side of me,
And I in the middle as with companions, and as holding the
    hands of companions,
I fled forth to the hiding receiving night that talks not,
Down to the shores of the water, the path by the swamp in the
    dimness,
To the solemn shadowy cedars and ghostly pines so still.   125

And the singer so shy to the rest receiv'd me,
The gray-brown bird I know receiv'd us comrades three,
And he sang the carol of death, and a verse for him I love.

From deep secluded recesses,
From the fragrant cedars and the ghostly pines so still,   130
Came the carol of the bird.

And the charm of the carol rapt me,
As I held as if by their hands my comrades in the night,
And the voice of my spirit tallied the song of the bird.

Come lovely and soothing death,[4]   135
Undulate round the world, serenely arriving, arriving,
In the day, in the night, to all, to each,
Sooner or later delicate death.

Prais'd be the fathomless universe,
For life and joy, and for objects and knowledge curious,   140
And for love, sweet love—but praise! praise! praise!
For the sure-enwinding arms of cool-enfolding death.

Dark mother always gliding near with soft feet,
Have none chanted for thee a chant of fullest welcome?
Then I chant it for thee, I glorify thee above all,   145
I bring thee a song that when thou must indeed come, come
    unfalteringly.

---

4. In the first 1865–66 version, the song of the bird was not distinguished by italics. In 1871 the italics were used, and the song had its own subtitle, "*Death Carol*," which was dropped in 1881. Compare this lyrical refrain with the songs of the bird in "Out of the Cradle Endlessly Rocking" and the tree in "Song of the Redwood Tree."

Approach strong deliveress,
When it is so, when thou hast taken them I joyously sing the dead,
Lost in the loving floating ocean of thee,
Laved in the flood of thy bliss O death. 150

From me to thee glad serenades,
Dances for thee I propose saluting thee, adornments and
    feastings for thee,
And the sights of the open landscape and the high-spread sky are
    fitting,
And life and the fields, and the huge and thoughtful night.

The night in silence under many a star, 155
The ocean shore and the husky whispering wave whose voice I know,
And the soul turning to thee O vast and well-veil'd death,
And the body gratefully nestling close to thee.

Over the tree-tops I float thee a song,
Over the rising and sinking waves, over the myriad fields and the
    prairies wide, 160
Over the dense-pack'd cities all and the teeming wharves and ways,
I float this carol with joy, with joy to thee O death.

15

To the tally of my soul,
Loud and strong kept up the gray-brown bird,
With pure deliberate notes spreading filling the night. 165

Loud in the pines and cedars dim,
Clear in the freshness moist and the swamp-perfume,
And I with my comrades there in the night.

While my sight that was bound in my eyes unclosed,
As to long panoramas of visions. 170

And I saw askant[5] the armies,
I saw as in noiseless dreams hundreds of battle-flags,
Borne through the smoke of the battles and pierc'd with
    missiles I saw them,
And carried hither and yon through the smoke, and torn and
    bloody,
And at last but a few shreds left on the staffs, (and all in
    silence,) 175
And the staffs all splinter'd and broken.

5. Cf. "askance," obliquely.

I saw battle-corpses, myriads of them,
And the white skeletons of young men, I saw them,
I saw the debris and debris of all the slain soldiers of the war,
But I saw they were not as was thought,   180
They themselves were fully at rest, they suffer'd not,
The living remain'd and suffer'd, the mother suffer'd,
And the wife and the child and the musing comrade suffer'd,
And the armies that remain'd suffer'd.

16

Passing the visions, passing the night,   185
Passing, unloosing the hold of my comrades' hands,
Passing the song of the hermit bird and the tallying song of my soul,
Victorious song, death's outlet song, yet varying ever-altering song,
As low and wailing, yet clear the notes, rising and falling,
      flooding the night,
Sadly sinking and fainting, as warning and warning, and yet
      again bursting with joy,   190
Covering the earth and filling the spread of the heaven,
As that powerful psalm in the night I heard from recesses,
Passing, I leave thee lilac with heart-shaped leaves,
I leave thee there in the door-yard, blooming, returning with spring.

I cease from my song for thee,   195
From my gaze on thee in the west, fronting the west,
      communing with thee,
O comrade lustrous with silver face in the night.

Yet each to keep and all, retrievements out of the night,
The song, the wondrous chant of the gray-brown bird,
And the tallying chant, the echo arous'd in my soul,   200
With the lustrous and drooping star with the countenance full
      of woe,
With the holders holding my hand nearing the call of the bird,
Comrades mine and I in the midst, and their memory ever to
      keep, for the dead I loved so well,
For the sweetest, wisest soul of all my days and lands—and
      this for his dear sake,
Lilac and star and bird twined with the chant of my soul,   205
There in the fragrant pines and the cedars dusk and dim.
    1865–66   *1881*

O Captain! My Captain![6]

O Captain! my Captain! our fearful trip is done,
The ship has weather'd every rack, the prize we sought is won,
The port is near, the bells I hear, the people all exulting,
While follow eyes the steady keel, the vessel grim and daring;
     But O heart! heart! heart! 5
        O the bleeding drops of red,
           Where on the deck my Captain lies,
           Fallen cold and dead.

O Captain! my Captain! rise up and hear the bells;
Rise up—for you the flag is flung—for you the bugle trills, 10
For you bouquets and ribbon'd wreaths—for you the shores
    a-crowding,
For you they call, the swaying mass, their eager faces turning;
     Here Captain! dear father!
        This arm beneath your head!
           It is some dream that on the deck, 15
           You've fallen cold and dead.

My Captain does not answer, his lips are pale and still,
My father does not feel my arm, he has no pulse nor will,
The ship is anchor'd safe and sound, its voyage closed and done,
From fearful trip the victor ship comes in with object won; 20
     Exult O shores, and ring O bells!
        But I with mournful tread,
           Walk the deck my Captain lies,
           Fallen cold and dead.

1865–66   *1871*

6. This is the most widely known and least characteristic poem that WW ever published. It appeared first in the *New York Saturday Press*, November 4, 1865, next in the *Drum-Taps* "Sequel," and then, with several revisions, in the *Passage to India* of 1871 and 1876. It was returned to "Drum-Taps" with no further changes in 1881. The MS readings (Feinberg) show much reworking, and to Traubel the poet confessed that he did not feel at ease with its regularity of form in stanza, meter, and rhyme. He also expressed humorous irritation that the poem had succeeded with the public as his other poems had not. "I'm almost sorry I ever wrote the poem." See Traubel, II, 304, 332–34.

Hush'd Be the Camps To-day[7]

(May 4, 1865)

Hush'd be the camps to-day,
And soldiers let us drape our war-worn weapons,
And each with musing soul retire to celebrate,
Our dear commander's death.
No more for him life's stormy conflicts,   5
Nor victory, nor defeat—no more time's dark events,
Charging like ceaseless clouds across the sky.

But sing poet in our name,
Sing of the love we bore him—because you, dweller in camps,
    know it truly.

As they invault the coffin there,   10
Sing—as they close the doors of earth upon him—one verse,
For the heavy hearts of soldiers.
  1865   *1871*

This Dust Was Once the Man[8]

This dust was once the man,
Gentle, plain, just and resolute, under whose cautious hand,
Against the foulest crime in history known in any land or age,
Was saved the Union of these States.
  1871   *1871*

---

7. WW was able to include this poem in his 1865 *Drum-Taps* before the addition of the "Sequel," but his title note read, "A. L. Buried April 19, 1865," evidently under the misapprehension that interment, as well as the funeral, was to take place in Washington. In the 1871 and 1876 editions he corrected the note to the present reading and also made a number of changes in the final stanza.
8. This poem was first published in 1871 in the "President Lincoln's Burial Hymn" group of *Passage to India*, and again in 1876 in the *Two Rivulets* supplement of the same title. It remained unchanged when it was transferred to "Drum-Taps" in 1881.

By Blue Ontario's Shore[1]

1

By blue Ontario's shore,[2]
As I mused of these warlike days and of peace return'd, and
    the dead that return no more,
A Phantom gigantic superb, with stern visage accosted me,
Chant me the poem, it said, *that comes from the soul of
    America, chant me the carol of victory,*
*And strike up the marches of Libertad, marches more powerful
    yet,*
And sing me before you go the song of the throes of Democracy.   5

(Democracy, the destin'd conqueror, yet treacherous lip-smiles
    everywhere,
And death and infidelity at every step.)

2

A Nation announcing itself,
I myself make the only growth by which I can be appreciated,   10
I reject none, accept all, then reproduce all in my own forms.

A breed whose proof is in time and deeds,
What we are we are, nativity is answer enough to objections,
We wield ourselves as a weapon is wielded,
We are powerful and tremendous in ourselves,   15

1. In theme and intent this poem is essentially the poetical equivalent of the 1855 Preface,
from which, in its present form, it draws more than sixty of its lines—and many more in
the earlier editions. In it WW identifies the purpose of his poetry with the aspiration and
potentiality of his country; in it he presents himself as the bard of his people with a mandate
from the Muse—the Phantom of the opening lines.
    Of all his poems, this poem has undergone the most extensive and ceaseless revision. It
originated as one of the 20 new poems of the second edition under the title "Poem of Many
in One," about one-fourth of its then 280 lines being transfers from the 1855 Preface. In
1860 it was the opening "No. 1" of the "Chants Democratic," 20 lines being dropped and
some 8 added. In *LG* 1867, the fourth edition, the title became "As I Sat Alone by Blue
Ontario's Shore," and notable sections were added—the opening one and several others—
that reflect the poet's experiences and reflections upon the Civil War and expand the text
to 337 lines. In the 1871 and 1876 text the alterations were far fewer, although the additions
brought the poem to 345 lines. Finally, in 1881, the poem took its present title, and some
10 lines were dropped, including the interesting observation, which had first appeared in the
preceding edition, that "As a wheel turns on its axle, so I find my chants turning finally on
the war." The student is advised to make a study of the many variants. Notes on the "Preface
1855" in this volume indicate the lines in that essay that were transposed in some form into
this poem.
    A prose paragraph turned up by Traubel (vol. II, 57) seems to express, as WW agreed, the
idea from which the poem originally advanced:
    "A song America demands that breathes her native air—an utterance to invigorate Democ-
racy. Democracy, the destined conqueror—(yet treacherous lip-smiles everywhere, and death
and infidelity at every step.) Of such a song let me, (for I have had that dream,) initiate here
the NOVICE'S ATTEMPT,—and bravos to the bards, who coming after me, do better far."
2. In this first section, first added in the 1867 edition, compare the address of the Phantom
with its original text:

    Chant me a poem, it said, *of the range of the high Soul of Poets.*
    And chant of the welcome bards that breathe but my native air—Invoke those bards;
    And chant me, before you go, the Song of the throes of Democracy.

We are executive in ourselves, we are sufficient in the variety
    of ourselves,
We are the most beautiful to ourselves and in ourselves,
We stand self-pois'd in the middle, branching thence over the world,
From Missouri, Nebraska, or Kansas, laughing attacks to scorn.

Nothing is sinful to us outside of ourselves,   20
Whatever appears, whatever does not appear, we are beautiful
    or sinful in ourselves only.

(O Mother—O Sisters dear![3]
If we are lost, no victor else has destroy'd us,
It is by ourselves we go down to eternal night.)

3

Have you thought there could be but a single supreme?   25
There can be any number of supremes—one does not
    countervail another any more than one eyesight
    countervails another, or one life countervails another.

All is eligible to all,
All is for individuals, all is for you,
No condition is prohibited, not God's or any.

All comes by the body, only health puts you rapport with the
    universe.   30

Produce great Persons, the rest follows.[4]

4

Piety and conformity to them that like,
Peace, obesity, allegiance, to them that like,
I am he who tauntingly compels men, women, nations,
Crying, Leap from your seats and contend for your lives!   35

I am he who walks the States with a barb'd tongue,
    questioning every one I meet,
Who are you that wanted only to be told what you knew
    before?

---

3. *Mother*: here, as in later references, the Nation personified, representing also Democracy;
Sisters: the States, as elsewhere in *LG*.
4. In the 1867 edition, the following scornful passage, later dropped, was here inserted:

    America isolated I sing;
    I say that works made here in the spirit of other lands, are so much poison to
    These States.

    How dare these insects assume to write poems for America?
    For our armies, and the offspring following the armies.

Who are you that wanted only a book to join you in your
    nonsense?

(With pangs and cries as thine own O bearer of many children,
These clamors wild to a race of pride I give.)   40

O lands, would you be freer than all that has ever been before?
If you would be freer than all that has been before, come
    listen to me.

Fear grace, elegance, civilization, delicatesse,
Fear the mellow sweet, the sucking of honey-juice,
Beware the advancing mortal ripening of Nature,   45
Beware what precedes the decay of the ruggedness of states
    and men.

5

Ages, precedents, have long been accumulating undirected
    materials,
America brings builders, and brings its own styles.

The immortal poets of Asia and Europe have done their work
    and pass'd to other spheres,
A work remains, the work of surpassing all they have done.   50

America, curious toward foreign characters, stands by its own
    at all hazards,
Stands removed, spacious, composite, sound, initiates the true
    use of precedents,[5]
Does not repel them or the past or what they have produced
    under their forms,
Takes the lesson with calmness, perceives the corpse slowly
    borne from the house,
Perceives that it waits a little while in the door, that it was
    fittest for its days,   55
That its life has descended to the stalwart and well-shaped heir
    who approaches,
And that he shall be fittest for his days.

Any period one nation must lead,
One land must be the promise and reliance of the future.

These States are the amplest poem,   60
Here is not merely a nation but a teeming Nation of nations,
Here the doings of men correspond with the broadcast doings
    of the day and night,

---

5. The remainder of this section and most of the following section 6 is composed from the
    1855 Preface.

Here is what moves in magnificent masses careless of particulars,
Here are the roughs, beards, friendliness, combativeness, the
    soul loves,
Here the flowing trains, here the crowds, equality, diversity,
    the soul loves.   65

6

Land of lands and bards to corroborate!
Of them standing among them, one lifts to the light a west-
    bred face,   65
To him the hereditary countenance bequeath'd both mother's
    and father's,
His first parts substances, earth, water, animals, trees,
Built of the common stock, having room for far and near,   70
Used to dispense with other lands, incarnating this land,
Attracting it body and soul to himself, hanging on its neck
    with incomparable love,
Plunging his seminal[6] muscle into its merits and demerits,
Making its cities, beginnings, events, diversities, wars, vocal in
    him,
Making its rivers, lakes, bays, embouchure[7] in him,   75
Mississippi with yearly freshets and changing chutes,
    Columbia, Niagara, Hudson, spending themselves lovingly
    in him,
If the Atlantic coast stretch or the Pacific coast stretch, he
    stretching with them North or South,
Spanning between them East and West, and touching
    whatever is between them,
Growths growing from him to offset the growths of pine,
    cedar, hemlock, live-oak, locust, chestnut, hickory,
    cottonwood, orange, magnolia,
Tangles as tangled in him as any canebrake or swamp,   80
He likening sides and peaks of mountains, forests coated with
    northern transparent ice,
Off him pasturage sweet and natural as savanna, upland, prairie,
Through him flights, whirls, screams, answering those of the
    fish-hawk, mocking-bird, night-heron, and eagle,
His spirit surrounding his country's spirit, unclosed to good
    and evil,
Surrounding the essences of real things, old times and present
    times,   85
Surrounding just found shores, islands, tribes of red aborigines,
Weather-beaten vessels, landings, settlements, embryo stature
    and muscle,

---

6. In the 1856, 1860, and 1867 editions, this adjective was, erroneously, "semitic." So also in
"Preface 1855."
7. The mouth of a river, here used as a verb.

The haughty defiance of the Year One,[8] war, peace, the
  formation of the Constitution,
The separate States, the simple elastic scheme, the immigrants,
The Union always swarming with blatherers and always sure
  and impregnable,   90
The unsurvey'd interior, log-houses, clearings, wild animals,
  hunters, trappers,
Surrounding the multiform agriculture, mines, temperature,
  the gestation of new States,
Congress convening every Twelfth-month, the members duly
  coming up from the uttermost parts,
Surrounding the noble character of mechanics and farmers,
  especially the young men,
Responding their manners, speech, dress, friendships, the gait
  they have of persons who never knew how it felt to stand
  in the presence of superiors,   95
The freshness and candor of their physiognomy, the
  copiousness and decision of their phrenology,
The picturesque looseness of their carriage, their fierceness
  when wrong'd,
The fluency of their speech, their delight in music, their
  curiosity, good temper and open-handedness, the whole
  composite make,
The prevailing ardor and enterprise, the large amativeness,[9]
The perfect equality of the female with the male, the fluid
  movement of the population,   100
The superior marine, free commerce, fisheries, whaling, gold-
  digging,
Wharf-hemm'd cities, railroad and steamboat lines intersecting
  all points,
Factories, mercantile life, labor-saving machinery, the
  Northeast, Northwest, Southwest,
Manhattan firemen, the Yankee swap, southern plantation life,
Slavery—the murderous, treacherous conspiracy to raise it
  upon the ruins of all the rest,   105
On and on to the grapple with it—Assassin! then your life or
  ours be the stake, and respite no more.

                                    7

(Lo, high toward heaven, this day,[1]
Libertad, from the conqueress' field return'd,
I mark the new aureola around your head,
No more of soft astral, but dazzling and fierce,   110
With war's flames and the lambent lightnings playing,

8. The first year of American Independence.
9. Phrenological term for "sexual love."
1. Section 7, beginning with this line, was added in 1867, its MS being pasted by the poet in
  his "Blue Copy" 1860 edition.

And your port immovable where you stand,
With still the inextinguishable glance and the clinch'd and
    lifted fist,
And your foot on the neck of the menacing one, the scorner
    utterly crush'd beneath you,
The menacing arrogant one that strode and advanced with his
    senseless scorn, bearing the murderous knife,   115
The wide-swelling one, the braggart that would yesterday do so
    much,
To-day a carrion dead and damn'd, the despised of all the earth,
An offal rank, to the dunghill maggots spurn'd.)

8

Others take finish, but the Republic is ever constructive and
    ever keeps vista,
Others adorn the past, but you O days of the present, I adorn
    you,   120
O days of the future I believe in you—I isolate myself for your
    sake,
O America because you build for mankind I build for you,
O well-beloved stone-cutters, I lead them who plan with
    decision and science,[2]
Lead the present with friendly hand toward the future.

(Bravas to all impulses sending sane children to the next age!   125
But damn that which spends itself with no thought of the
    stain, pains, dismay, feebleness, it is bequeathing.)

9

I listened to the Phantom by Ontario's shore,
I heard the voice arising demanding bards,
By them all native and grand, by them alone can these States
    be fused into the compact organism of a Nation.

To hold men together by paper and seal or by compulsion is
    no account,   130
That only holds men together which aggregates all in a living
    principle, as the hold of the limbs of the body or the
    fibres of plants.

Of all races and eras these States with veins full of poetical
    stuff most need poets, and are to have the greatest, and
    use them the greatest,
Their Presidents shall not be their common referee so much as
    their poets shall.

2. This line and about twenty lines following in sections 9 and 10 originated in the 1855
Preface.

(Soul of love and tongue of fire!
Eye to pierce the deepest deeps and sweep the world!   135
Ah Mother, prolific and full in all besides, yet how long
     barren, barren?)

                                    10

Of these States the poet is the equable man,[3]
Not in him but off from him things are grotesque, eccentric,
     fail of their full returns,
Nothing out of its place is good, nothing in its place is bad,
He bestows on every object or quality its fit proportion, neither
     more nor less,   140
He is the arbiter of the diverse, he is the key,
He is the equalizer of his age and land,
He supplies what wants supplying, he checks what wants checking,
In peace out of him speaks the spirit of peace, large, rich,
          thrifty, building populous towns, encouraging agriculture,
          arts, commerce, lighting the study of man, the soul,
          health, immortality, government,
In war he is the best backer of the war, he fetches artillery as
     good as the engineer's, he can make every word he speaks
     draw blood,   145
The years straying toward infidelity he witholds by his steady
     faith,
He is no arguer, he is judgment, (Nature accepts him absolutely,)
He judges not as the judge judges but as the sun falling round
     a helpless thing,
As he sees the farthest he has the most faith,
His thoughts are the hymns of the praise of things,   150
In the dispute on God and eternity he is silent,
He sees eternity less like a play with a prologue and denouement,
He sees eternity in men and women, he does not see men and
     women as dreams or dots.

For the great Idea, the idea of perfect and free individuals,
For that, the bard walks in advance, leader of leaders,   155
The attitude of him cheers up slaves and horrifies foreign
     despots.

Without extinction is Liberty, without retrograde is Equality,
They live in the feelings of young men and the best women,
(Not for nothing have the indomitable heads of the earth been
     always ready to fall for Liberty.)

---

3. The portrait of the poet sketched in this section may be found in the sixth paragraph of the
   1855 Preface.

11

For the great Idea,[4]   160
That, O my brethren, that is the mission of poets.

Songs of stern defiance ever ready,
Songs of the rapid arming and the march,
The flag of peace quick-folded, and instead the flag we know,
Warlike flag of the great Idea.   165

(Angry cloth I saw there leaping!
I stand again in leaden rain your flapping folds saluting,
I sing you over all, flying beckoning through the fight—O the
    hard-contested fight!
The cannons ope their rosy-flashing muzzles—the hurtled balls
    scream,
The battle-front forms amid the smoke—the volleys pour
    incessant from the line,   170
Hark, the ringing word *Charge!*—now the tussle and the
    furious maddening yells,
Now the corpses tumble curl'd upon the ground,
Cold, cold in death, for precious life of you,
Angry cloth I saw there leaping.)

12

Are you he who would assume a place to teach or be a poet
    here in the States?   175
The place is august, the terms obdurate.

Who would assume to teach here may well prepare himself
    body and mind,
He may well survey, ponder, arm, fortify, harden, make lithe
    himself,
He shall surely be question'd beforehand by me with many and
    stern questions.

Who are you indeed who would talk or sing to America?   180
Have you studied out the land, its idioms and men?
Have you learn'd the physiology, phrenology, politics,
    geography, pride, freedom, friendship of the land? its
    substratums and objects?
Have you consider'd the organic compact of the first day of the
    first year of Independence, sign'd by the Commissioners,
    ratified by the States, and read by Washington at the head
    of the army?
Have you possess'd yourself of the Federal Constitution?
Do you see who have left all feudal processes and poems

4. This section was added in 1867.

behind them, and assumed the poems and processes of
    Democracy?   185
Are you faithful to things? do you teach what the land and sea,
    the bodies of men, womanhood, amativeness, heroic
    angers, teach?
Have you sped through fleeting customs, popularities?
Can you hold your hand against all seductions, follies, whirls,
    fierce contentions? are you very strong? are you really of
    the whole People?
Are you not of some coterie? some school or mere religion?
Are you done with reviews and criticisms of life? animating
    now to life itself?   190
Have you vivified yourself from the maternity of these States?
Have you too the old ever-fresh forbearance and impartiality?
Do you hold the like love for those hardening to maturity? for
    the last-born? little and big? and for the errant?

What is this you bring my America?   195
Is it uniform with my country?
Is it not something that has been better told or done before?
Have you not imported this or the spirit of it in some ship?
Is it not a mere tale? a rhyme? a prettiness?—is the good old
    cause in it?
Has it not dangled long at the heels of the poets, politicians,
    literats, of enemies' lands?
Does it not assume that what is notoriously gone is still here?   200
Does it answer universal needs? will it improve manners?
Does it sound with trumpet-voice the proud victory of the
    Union in that secession war?
Can your performance face the open fields and the seaside?
Will it absorb into me as I absorb food, air, to appear again in
    my strength, gait, face?
Have real employments contributed to it? original makers, not
    mere amanuenses?   205
Does it meet modern discoveries, calibres, facts, face to face?
What does it mean to American persons, progresses, cities?
    Chicago, Kanada, Arkansas?
Does it see behind the apparent custodians the real custodians
    standing, menacing, silent, the mechanics, Manhattanese,
    Western men, Southerners, significant alike in their
    apathy, and in the promptness of their love?
Does it see what finally befalls, and has always finally befallen,
    each temporizer, patcher, outsider, partialist, alarmist,
    infidel, who has ever ask'd any thing of America?
What mocking and scornful negligence?   210
The track strew'd with the dust of skeletons,
By the roadside others disdainfully toss'd.

13

Rhymes and rhymers pass away, poems distill'd from poems
    pass away,[5]
The swarms of reflectors and the polite pass, and leave ashes,
Admirers, importers, obedient persons, make but the soil of
    literature,   215
America justifies itself, give it time, no disguise can deceive it
    or conceal from it, it is impassive enough,
Only toward the likes of itself will it advance to meet them,
If its poets appear it will in due time advance to meet them,
    there is no fear of mistake,
(The proof of a poet shall be sternly deferr'd till his country
    absorbs him as affectionately as he has absorb'd it.)

He masters whose spirit masters, he tastes sweetest who
    results sweetest in the long run,   220
The blood of the brawn beloved of time is unconstraint;
In the need of songs, philosophy, an appropriate native grand-
    opera, shipcraft, any craft,
He or she is greatest who contributes the greatest original
    practical example.

Already a nonchalant breed, silently emerging, appears on the
    streets,
People's lips salute only doers, lovers, satisfiers, positive
    knowers,   225
There will shortly be no more priests, I say their work is done,
Death is without emergencies here, but life is perpetual
    emergencies here,
Are your body, days, manners, superb? after death you shall be
    superb,
Justice, health, self-esteem, clear the way with irresistible
    power;
How dare you place any thing before a man?   230

14

Fall behind me States![6]
A man before all—myself, typical, before all.

Give me the pay I have served for,
Give me to sing the songs of the great Idea, take all the rest,
I have loved the earth, sun, animals, I have despised riches,   235
I have given alms to every one that ask'd, stood up for the
    stupid and crazy, devoted my income and labor to others,
Hated tyrants, argued not concerning God, had patience and
    indulgence toward the people, taken off my hat to nothing
    known or unknown,

5. This line and several others in section 13 originated in the 1855 Preface.
6. Many of the lines in section 14 originated in the 1855 Preface.

Gone freely with powerful uneducated persons and with the
    young, and with the mothers of families,
Read these leaves to myself in the open air, tried them by
    trees, stars, rivers,
Dismiss'd whatever insulted my own soul or defiled my body,   240
Claim'd nothing to myself which I have not carefully claim'd
    for others on the same terms,
Sped to the camps, and comrades found and accepted from
    every State,
(Upon this breast has many a dying soldier lean'd to breathe
    his last,
This arm, this hand, this voice, have nourish'd, rais'd, restored,
To life recalling many a prostate form;)   245
I am willing to wait to be understood by the growth of the
    taste of myself,
Rejecting none, permitting all.

(Say O Mother, have I not to your thought been faithful?
Have I not through life kept you and yours before me?)

15

I swear I begin to see the meaning of these things,   250
It is not the earth, it is not America who is so great,
It is I who am great or to be great, it is You up there, or any one,
It is to walk rapidly through civilizations, governments, theories,
Through poems, pageants, shows, to form individuals.

Underneath all, individuals,   255
I swear nothing is good to me now that ignores individuals,
The American compact is altogether with individuals,
The only government is that which makes minute of individuals,
The whole theory of the universe is directed unerringly to one
    single individual—namely to You.

(Mother! with subtle sense severe, with the naked sword in
    your hand,
I saw you at last refuse to treat but directly with individuals.)   260

16

Underneath all, Nativity,
I swear I will stand by my own nativity, pious or impious so be it;
I swear I am charm'd with nothing except nativity,
Men, women, cities, nations, are only beautiful from nativity.   265

Underneath all is the Expression of love for men and women,
(I swear I have seen enough of mean and impotent modes of
    expressing love for men and women,

After this day I take my own modes of expressing love for men
  and women.)

I swear I will have each quality of my race in myself,
(Talk as you like, he only suits these States whose manners
  favor the audacity and sublime turbulence of the States.)   270

Underneath the lessons of things, spirits, Nature, governments,
  ownerships, I swear I perceive other lessons,
Underneath all to me is myself, to you yourself, (the same
  monotonous old song.)

17

O I see flashing that this America is only you and me,[7]
Its power, weapons, testimony, are you and me,
Its crimes, lies, thefts, defections, are you and me,   275
Its Congress is you and me, the officers, capitols, armies,
  ships, are you and me,
Its endless gestations of new States are you and me,
The war, (that war so bloody and grim, the war I will
  henceforth forget), was you and me,
Natural and artificial are you and me,
Freedom, language, poems, employments, are you and me,   280
Past, present, future, are you and me.

I dare not shirk any part of myself,
Not any part of America good or bad,
Not to build for that which builds for mankind,
Not to balance ranks, complexions, creeds, and the sexes,   285
Not to justify science nor the march of equality,
Nor to feed the arrogant blood of the brawn belov'd of time.

I am for those that have never been master'd,
For men and women whose tempers have never been master'd,
For those whom laws, theories, conventions, can never master.   290

I am for those who walk abreast with the whole earth,
Who inaugurate one to inaugurate all.

I will not be outfaced by irrational things,
I will penetrate what it is in them that is sarcastic upon me,
I will make cities and civilizations defer to me,   295
This is what I have learnt from America—it is the amount,
  and it I teach again.

7. Compare MS reading of lines 273–92 (*N and F*, I, 14–15, item 27) with section 17.

(Democracy, while weapons were everywhere aim'd at your breast,
I saw you serenely give birth to immortal children, saw in
    dreams your dilating form,
Saw you with spreading mantle covering the world.)

18

I will confront these shows of the day and night,   300
I will know if I am to be less than they,
I will see if I am not as majestic as they,
I will see if I am not as subtle and real as they,
I will see if I am to be less generous than they,
I will see if I have no meaning, while the houses and ships
    have meaning,   305
I will see if the fishes and birds are to be enough for
    themselves, and I am not to be enough for myself.

I match my spirit against yours you orbs, growths, mountains,
    brutes,
Copious as you are I absorb you all in myself, and become the
    master myself,
America isolated yet embodying all, what is it finally except
    myself?
These States, what are they except myself?   310

I know now why the earth is gross, tantalizing, wicked, it is for
    my sake,
I take you specially to be mine, you terrible, rude forms.

(Mother, bend down, bend close to me your face,
I know not what these plots and wars and deferments are for,
I know not fruition's success, but I know that through war and
    crime your work goes on, and must yet go on.)   315

19

Thus by blue Ontario's shore,[8]
While the winds fann'd me and the waves came trooping
    toward me,
I thrill'd with the power's pulsations, and the charm of my
    theme was upon me,
Till the tissues that held me parted their ties upon me.

And I saw the free souls of poets,   320
The loftiest bards of past ages strode before me,
Strange large men, long unwaked, undisclosed, were disclosed
    to me.

---

8. This section was added in 1867.

20

O my rapt verse, my call, mock me not![9]
Not for the bards of the past, not to invoke them have I
    launch'd you forth,
Not to call even those lofty bards here by Ontario's shores,   325
Have I sung so capricious and loud my savage song.

Bards for my own land only I invoke,
(For the war the war is over, the field is clear'd,)
Till they strike up marches henceforth triumphant and onward,
To cheer O Mother your boundless expectant soul.   330

Bards of the great Idea! bards of the peaceful inventions! (for
    the war, the war is over!)
Yet bards of latent armies, a million soldiers waiting ever-ready,
Bards with songs as from burning coals or the lightning's
    fork'd stripes!
Ample Ohio's, Kanada's bards—bards of California! inland
    bards—bards of the war!
You by my charm I invoke.   335
1856   *1881*

Reversals[1]

Let that which stood in front go behind,
Let that which was behind advance to the front,
Let bigots, fools, unclean persons, offer new propositions,
Let the old propositions be postponed,
Let a man seek pleasure everywhere except in himself,   5
Let a woman seek happiness everywhere except in herself.
1856   *1881*

9. This section was added in 1867.
1. The six lines composing this poem were originally part of a 57-line poem of 1856, "Poem of
    the Propositions of Nakedness," in which WW, expressing a mood—rare for him—of ironic
    sarcasm, proposed the reversal of his own affirmations. This 1856 poem became No. 5 of
    the "Chants Democratic" of 1860; was again retitled "Respondez" in 1867, 1871, and 1876;
    and then was rejected in 1881 except for "Reversals" and another three lines to be called
    "Transpositions." See "Respondez" in the section of "Excluded Poems."

AUTUMN RIVULETS

As Consequent, *Etc.*[1]

As consequent from store of summer rains,
Or wayward rivulets in autumn flowing,
Or many a herb-lined brook's reticulations,
Or subterranean sea-rills making for the sea,
Songs of continued years I sing.   5

Life's ever-modern rapids first, (soon, soon to blend,
With the old streams of death.)

Some threading Ohio's farm-fields or the woods,
Some down Colorado's cañons from sources of perpetual snow,
Some half-hid in Oregon, or away southward in Texas,   10
Some in the north finding their way to Erie, Niagara, Ottawa,
Some to Atlantica's bays, and so to the great salt brine.

In you whoe'er you are my book perusing,[2]
In I myself, in all the world, these currents flowing,
All, all toward the mystic ocean tending.   15

Currents for starting a continent new,[3]
Overtures sent to the solid out of the liquid,
Fusion of ocean and land, tender and pensive waves,
(Not safe and peaceful only, waves rous'd and ominous too,

Autumn Rivulets: The thirty-eight poems of this group, new to the final 1881 arrangement, draw upon no less than nine separate editions, from the two 1855 poems to the four here published for the first time. In between are five of 1856, twelve of 1860, three of 1865, one of 1867, five of the 1871 *Passage to India,* one of the 1872 *As a Strong Bird on Pinions Free and Other Poems,* and four of the 1876 *Two Rivulets.* As a group these poems are devoted to no common theme or progression of idea, and they are also disparate in quality. They have perhaps the prevailing mood of retrospective recall, of mature evaluation, and the autumnal wisdom of experience. In short, "Autumn Rivulets" constitute a range, not a focus of the poet's interest.

1. This introductory poem, new to *LG* in 1881, carries forward the metaphor of the group title, the only one of the thirty-eight overtly to do so. However, other poems in the cluster also project the mood of the title, such as "The City Dead-House," "This Compost," "Unnamed Lands," "Outlines for a Tomb," "Laws for Creations," "To a Common Prostitute," "Kosmos," and "Who Learns My Lesson Complete." Although "As Consequent, etc." is new to the 1881 edition, two of its passages are transferred, as the footnotes indicate, from two poems of the 1876 *TR,* now rejected for use here. The imagery of the poem is intricate. The "wayward rivulets" are both WW's own poems and the fructifying currents of the continent; the "little shells," cast up from the sea of Time, are also the tidings of his poems, made out of his life and years; and the "windrow-drift of weeds and shells" are a double metaphor: the poet's discoveries—weeds and shells—being distributed like a windrow on the sea and then drifting ashore to form another line, a "windrow-drift."
2. Lines 13–15 were originally lines 10–12 of "Two Rivulets" in the 1876 *TR.*
3. Lines 16–21 were originally lines 13–18 of the 1876 "Or from That Sea of Time."

Out of the depths the storm's abysmic waves, who knows
    whence? 20
Raging over the vast, with many a broken spar and tatter'd sail.)

Or from the sea of Time, collecting vasting[4] all, I bring,[5]
A windrow-drift of weeds and shells.

O little shells, so curious-convolute, so limpid-cold and voiceless,
Will you not little shells to the tympans of temples held, 25
Murmurs and echoes still call up, eternity's music faint and far,
Wafted inland, sent from Atlantica's rim, strains for the soul of
    the prairies,
Whisper'd reverberations, chords for the ear of the West
    joyously sounding,
Your tidings old, yet ever new and untranslatable,
Infinitesimals out of my life, and many a life, 30
(For not my life and years alone I give—all, all I give,)
These waifs from the deep, cast high and dry,
Wash'd on America's shores?
    1876, 1881   *1881*

The Return of the Heroes[6]

1

For the lands and for these passionate days and for myself,
Now I awhile retire to thee O soil of autumn fields,
Reclining on thy breast, giving myself to thee,

4. "To vast"—short for "avast"—meant "to stop" or "to give up." Perhaps the meaning is "bring-
ing everything to the end of its voyage."
5. Lines 22–33 were originally lines 1–12 of the 1876 "Or from That Sea of Time."
6. This poem was first published in *The Galaxy*, September 1867, under the title "A Carol of
Harvest for 1867," and reprinted in *Tinsley's Magazine* (London) the following month. Then,
with a number of revisions, it was published in the 1871 *Passage to India*. The same text
appeared in the "Passage to India" supplement of the 1876 *TR* with an added headnote: "In
all History, antique or modern, the grandest achievement yet for political Humanity—
grander even than the triumph of THIS UNION over Secession—was the return, disbanding,
and peaceful disintegration from compact military organization, back into agricultural and
civil employments, of the vast Armies, the two millions of embattled men of America—a
problem reserved for Democracy, our day and land, to promptly solve." After some further
revision the poem appeared in *LG* 1881 with present title and text, which has dropped the
original opening passage:

> A song of the grass and fields!
> A song of the soil, and the good green grass!
> A song no more of the city streets;
> A song of the soil of fields.

> A song with the smell of sun-dried hay, where the nimble pitchers
>   handle the pitch-fork;
> A song tasting of new wheat, and of fresh-husk'd maize.

    Examination of the Barrett MS suggests that themes for two separate poems—the abundant
harvest of 1867 and the return of the soldiers—had been skillfully united in a single poem
that sensitively associated the tilled fields of the fecund land with the red fields of war. See
Fredson Bowers' analysis of the MS in *MP* 52, no. 1 (August 1954): 29–51.

Answering the pulses of thy sane and equable heart,
Tuning a verse for thee.   5

O earth that hast no voice, confide to me a voice,
O harvest of my lands—O boundless summer growths,
O lavish brown parturient earth—O infinite teeming womb,
A song to narrate thee.

2

Ever upon this stage,   10
Is acted God's calm annual drama,
Gorgeous processions, songs of birds,
Sunrise that fullest feeds and freshens most the soul,
The heaving sea, the waves upon the shore, the musical,
     strong waves,
The woods, the stalwart trees, the slender, tapering trees,   15
The liliput countless armies of the grass,
The heat, the showers, the measureless pasturages,
The scenery of the snows, the winds' free orchestra,
The stretching light-hung roof of clouds, the clear cerulean
     and the silvery fringes,
The high dilating stars, the placid beckoning stars,   20
The moving flocks and herds, the plains and emerald meadows,
The shows of all the varied lands and all the growths and products.

3

Fecund America—to-day,
Thou art all over set in births and joys!
Thou groan'st with riches, thy wealth clothes thee as a
     swathing-garment,   25
Thou laughest loud with ache of great possessions,
A myriad-twining life like interlacing vines binds all thy vast
     demesne,
As some huge ship freighted to water's edge thou ridest into port,
As rain falls from the heaven and vapors rise from earth, so
     have the precious values fallen upon thee and risen out of
     thee;
Thou envy of the globe! thou miracle!   30
Thou, bathed, choked, swimming in plenty,
Thou lucky Mistress of the tranquil barns,
Thou Prairie Dame that sittest in the middle and lookest out
     upon thy world, and lookest East and lookest West,
Dispensatress, that by a word givest a thousand miles, a
     million farms, and missest nothing,
Thou all-acceptress—thou hospitable, (thou only art hospitable
     as God is hospitable.)   35

4

When late I sang sad was my voice,
Sad were the shows around me with deafening noises of
    hatred and smoke of war;
In the midst of the conflict, the heroes, I stood,
Or pass'd with slow step through the wounded and dying.

But now I sing not war,   40
Nor the measur'd march of soldiers, nor the tents of camps,
Nor the regiments hastily coming up deploying in line of battle;
No more the sad, unnatural shows of war.

Ask'd room those flush'd immortal ranks, the first forth-
    stepping armies?
Ask room alas the ghastly ranks, the armies dread that
    follow'd.   45

(Pass, pass, ye proud brigades, with your tramping sinewy legs,
With your shoulders young and strong, with your knapsacks
    and your muskets;
How elate I stood and watch'd you, where starting off you march'd.

Pass—then rattle drums again,
For an army heaves in sight, O another gathering army,   50
Swarming, trailing on the rear, O you dread accruing army,
O you regiments so piteous, with your mortal diarrhœa, with
    your fever,
O my land's maim'd darlings, with the plenteous bloody
    bandage and the crutch,
Lo, your pallid army follows.)

5

But on these days of brightness,   55
On the far-stretching beauteous landscape, the roads and
    lanes,[7] the high-piled farm-wagons, and the fruits and barns,
Should the dead intrude?

Ah the dead to me mar not, they fit well in Nature,
They fit very well in the landscape under the trees and grass,
And along the edge of the sky in the horizon's far margin.   60

Nor do I forget you Departed,
Nor in winter or summer my lost ones,

7. This edition restores the comma, which was destroyed in an earlier printing.

But most in the open air as now when my soul is rapt and at
    peace, like pleasing phantoms,
Your memories rising glide silently by me.

6

I saw the day the return of the heroes,[8]   65
(Yet the heroes never surpass'd shall never return,
Them that day I saw not.)

I saw the interminable corps, I saw the processions of armies,
I saw them approaching, defiling by with divisions,
Streaming northward, their work done, camping awhile in
    clusters of mighty camps.   70

No holiday soldiers—youthful, yet veterans,
Worn, swart, handsome, strong, of the stock of homestead and
    workshop,
Harden'd of many a long campaign and sweaty march,
Inured on many a hard-fought bloody field.

A pause—the armies wait,   75
A million flush'd embattled conquerors wait,
The world too waits, then soft as breaking night and sure as dawn,
They melt, they disappear.

Exult O lands! victorious lands!
Not there your victory on those red shuddering fields,   80
But here and hence your victory.

Melt, melt away ye armies—disperse ye blue-clad soldiers,
Resolve ye back again, give up for good your deadly arms,
Other the arms the fields henceforth for you, or South or North,
With saner wars, sweet wars, life-giving wars.   85

7

Loud O my throat, and clear O soul!
The season of thanks and the voice of full-yielding,
The chant of joy and power for boundless fertility.

All till'd and untill'd fields expand before me,
I see the true arenas of my race, or first or last,   90
Man's innocent and strong arenas.

I see the heroes at other toils,
I see well-wielded in their hands the better weapons.

8. WW gives an eyewitness account of the soldiers' return to Washington in two of his *Specimen Days* entries: "The Armies Returning" of May 7, 1865, and "The Grand Review" of May 23.

I see where the Mother of All,
With full-spanning eye gazes forth, dwells long,   95
And counts the varied gathering of the products.

Busy the far, the sunlit panorama,
Prairie, orchard, and yellow grain of the North,
Cotton and rice of the South and Louisianian cane,
Open unseeded fallows, rich fields of clover and timothy,   100
Kine and horses feeding, and droves of sheep and swine,
And many a stately river flowing and many a jocund brook,
And healthy uplands with herby-perfumed breezes,
And the good green grass, that delicate miracle the ever-
    recurring grass.

8

Toil on heroes! harvest the products!   105
Not alone on those warlike fields the Mother of All,
With dilated form and lambent eyes watch'd you.

Toil on heroes! toil well! handle the weapons well!
The Mother of All, yet here as ever she watches you.

Well-pleased America thou beholdest,   110
Over the fields of the West those crawling monsters,
The human-divine inventions, the labor-saving implements;
Beholdest moving in every direction imbued as with life the
    revolving hay-rakes,
The steam-power reaping-machines and the horse-power machines,[9]
The engines, thrashers of grain and cleaners of grain, well
    separating the straw, the nimble work of the patent
    pitchfork,   115
Beholdest the newer saw-mill, the southern cotton-gin, and the
    rice-cleanser.

Beneath thy look O Maternal,
With these and else and with their own strong hands the
    heroes harvest.

All gather and all harvest,
Yet but for thee O Powerful, not a scythe might swing as now
    in security,   120
Not a maize-stalk dangle as now its silken tassels in peace.

Under thee only they harvest, even but a wisp of hay under thy
    great face only,

9. This edition restores the comma, which was not present in *LG* 1889 and the 1891–92
   hardbound issue honored here. It appears in the softbound issue and in texts from 1881 to
   1888.

Harvest the wheat of Ohio, Illinois, Wisconsin, every barbed
    spear under thee,
Harvest the maize of Missouri, Kentucky, Tennessee, each ear
    in its light-green sheath,
Gather the hay to its myriad mows in the odorous tranquil
    barns,   125
Oats to their bins, the white potato, the buckwheat of
    Michigan, to theirs;
Gather the cotton in Mississippi or Alabama, dig and hoard
    the golden the sweet potato of Georgia and the Carolinas,
Clip the wool of California or Pennsylvania,
Cut the flax in the Middle States, or hemp or tobacco in the
    Borders,
Pick the pea and the bean, or pull apples from the trees or
    bunches of grapes from the vines,   130
Or aught that ripens in all these States or North or South,
Under the beaming sun and under thee.
    1867   *1881*

There Was a Child Went Forth[1]

There was a child went forth every day,
And the first object he look'd upon, that object he became,
And that object became part of him for the day or a certain
    part of the day,
Or for many years or stretching cycles of years.

The early lilacs became part of this child,   5
And grass and white and red morning-glories, and white and
    red clover, and the song of the phœbe-bird,
And the Third-month lambs and the sow's pink-faint litter, and
    the mare's foal and the cow's calf,
And the noisy brood of the barnyard or by the mire of the pond-side,
And the fish suspending themselves so curiously below there,
    and the beautiful curious liquid,
And the water-plants with their graceful flat heads, all became
    part of him.   10

The field-sprouts of Fourth-month and Fifth-month became
    part of him,
Winter-grain sprouts and those of the light-yellow corn, and
    the esculent roots of the garden,

---

1. The tenth poem of the first edition, this much-anthologized lyric underwent moderate but
constant revision in later texts. In 1856 it was entitled "Poem of the Child That Went Forth,
and Always Goes Forth, Forever and Forever"; in 1860, "Leaves of Grass" No. 9; in 1867,
"No. 1" of another *LG* group; and since 1871 it has had its present title.
    The poem irresistibly suggests autobiography in its vivid identification of the growing child
with WW's own experience. Yet the poet universalized his testimony; a final line, dropped
in 1867, read: "And these become of him or her that peruses them now." Tennyson's line
in "Ulysses"—"I am a part of all that I have met"—makes the same point.

And the apple-trees cover'd with blossoms and the fruit
    afterward, and wood-berries, and the commonest weeds by
    the road,
And the old drunkard staggering home from the outhouse of
    the tavern whence he had lately risen,
And the schoolmistress that pass'd on her way to the school,   15
And the friendly boys that pass'd, and the quarrelsome boys,
And the tidy and fresh-cheek'd girls, and the barefoot negro
    boy and girl,
And all the changes of city and country wherever he went.

His own parents, he that had father'd him and she that had
    conceiv'd him in her womb and birth'd him,
They gave this child more of themselves than that,   20
They gave him afterward every day, they became part of him.

The mother at home quietly placing the dishes on the supper-
    table,
The mother with mild words, clean her cap and gown, a
    wholesome odor falling off her person and clothes as she
    walks by,
The father, strong, self-sufficient, manly, mean, anger'd, unjust,
The blow, the quick loud word, the tight bargain, the crafty
    lure,   25
The family usages, the language, the company, the furniture,
    the yearning and swelling heart,
Affection that will not be gainsay'd, the sense of what is real,
    the thought if after all it should prove unreal,[2]
The doubts of day-time and the doubts of night-time, the
    curious whether and how,
Whether that which appears so is so, or is it all flashes and specks?
Men and women crowding fast in the streets, if they are not
    flashes and specks what are they?   30
The streets themselves and the façades of houses, and goods in
    the windows,
Vehicles, teams, the heavy-plank'd wharves, the huge crossing
    at the ferries,
The village on the highland seen from afar at sunset, the river
    between,
Shadows, aureola and mist, the light falling on roofs and
    gables of white or brown two miles off,
The schooner near by sleepily dropping down the tide, the
    little boat slack-tow'd astern,   35
The hurrying tumbling waves, quick-broken crests, slapping,
The strata of color'd clouds, the long bar of maroon-tint away
    solitary by itself, the spread of purity it lies motionless in,

---

2. Compare the thought of this and the following three lines with that of the 1860 poem "Of
the Terrible Doubt of Appearances."

The horizon's edge, the flying sea-crow, the fragrance of salt
    marsh and shore mud,
These became part of that child who went forth every day, and
    who now goes, and will always go forth every day.
1855   *1871*

Old Ireland[3]

Far hence amid an isle of wondrous beauty,
Crouching over a grave an ancient sorrowful mother,
Once a queen, now lean and tatter'd seated on the ground,
Her old white hair drooping dishevel'd round her shoulders,
At her feet fallen an unused royal harp,   5
Long silent, she too long silent, mourning her shrouded hope
    and heir,
Of all the earth her heart most full of sorrow because most
    full of love.

Yet a word ancient mother,
You need crouch there no longer on the cold ground with
    forehead between your knees,
O you need not sit there veil'd in your old white hair so
    dishevel'd,   10
For know you the one you mourn is not in that grave,
It was an illusion, the son you love was not really dead,
The Lord is not dead, he is risen again young and strong in
    another country,
Even while you wept there by your fallen harp by the grave,
What you wept for was translated, pass'd from the grave,   15
The winds favor'd and the sea sail'd it,
And now with rosy and new blood,
Moves to-day in a new country.
1861   *1867*

The City Dead-House[4]

By the city dead-house by the gate,
As idly sauntering wending my way from the clangor,

---

3. First appeared in the *New York Leader*, November 2, 1861, collected in *Drum-Taps* 1865, and remained unchanged in all *LG* editions. Some variants occur in the magazine text—for example, the phrase "an armed man" after "to-day" in the final line. The Fenian Brotherhood, an Irish-American revolutionary society, was founded in the United States in 1858; in the decade 1851–60, one and a half million Irish, faced with famine and poverty, emigrated to America, while the total remaining population of Ireland was less than six million.
4. This poem was first published in the 1867 *LG*, and it has remained substantially unchanged in text and title. Still very popular was a poem by Thomas Hood, "The Bridge of Sighs" (1844), that depicts and ponders in an insistent dactylic rhythm the suicide of a prostitute, while the author properly maintains aesthetic distance from the subject. Compare WW's poem, which is obviously different.

I curious pause, for lo, an outcast form, a poor dead prostitute
    brought,
Her corpse they deposit unclaim'd, it lies on the damp brick
    pavement,
The divine woman, her body, I see the body, I look on it alone,   5
That house once full of passion and beauty, all else I notice not,
Nor stillness so cold, nor running water from faucet, nor odors
    morbific impress me,
But the house alone—that wondrous house—that delicate fair
    house—that ruin!
That immortal house more than all the rows of dwellings ever
    built!
Or white-domed capitol with majestic figure surmounted, or all
    the old high-spired cathedrals,   10
That little house alone more than them all—poor, desperate
    house!
Fair, fearful wreck—tenement of a soul—itself a soul,
Unclaim'd, avoided house—take one breath from my
    tremulous lips,
Take one tear dropt aside as I go for thought of you,
Dead house of love—house of madness and sin, crumbled,
    crush'd,   15
House of life, erewhile talking and laughing—but ah, poor
    house, dead even then,
Months, years, an echoing, garnish'd house—but dead, dead,
    dead.
1867   1881

This Compost[5]

1

Something startles me where I thought I was safest,
I withdraw from the still woods I loved,
I will not go now on the pastures to walk,
I will not strip the clothes from my body to meet my lover the sea,
I will not touch my flesh to the earth as to other flesh to
    renew me.   5

---

5. First published in *LG* 1856 under the arresting title "Poem of Wonder at The Resurrection of The Wheat"; appeared with revisions in *LG* 1860 as "Leaves of Grass" No. 4; present title in 1867, and completed text, 1881. The poem has undergone much revision, and a sizable MS fragment (Trent), printed in *FCI*, 9–11, shows early stages. A sentence in the chapter "Spring" of Thoreau's *Walden*, published just two years before, expresses a thought of striking similarity: "There was a dead horse in the hollow by the path to my home which compelled me sometimes to go out of my way, especially in the night when the air was heavy, but the assurance it gave me of the strong appetite and inviolable health of Nature was my compensation for this." Both in form and subject this poem is essential Whitman, one of his best. *Cf.* also "Song of Myself," section 49, lines 1294–98.

O how can it be that the ground itself does not sicken?
How can you be alive you growths of spring?
How can you furnish health you blood of herbs, roots,
    orchards, grain?
Are they not continually putting distemper'd corpses within you?
Is not every continent work'd over and over with sour dead?   10

Where have you disposed of their carcasses?
Those drunkards and gluttons of so many generations?
Where have you drawn off all the foul liquid and meat?
I do not see any of it upon you to-day, or perhaps I am deceiv'd,
I will run a furrow with my plough, I will press my spade
    through the sod and turn it up underneath,   15
I am sure I shall expose some of the foul meat.

                         2

Behold this compost! behold it well!
Perhaps every mite has once form'd part of a sick person—yet
    behold!
The grass of spring covers the prairies,
The bean bursts noiselessly through the mould in the garden,   20
The delicate spear of the onion pierces upward,
The apple-buds cluster together on the apple-branches,
The resurrection of the wheat appears with pale visage out of
    its graves,
The tinge awakes over the willow-tree and the mulberry-tree,
The he-birds carol mornings and evenings while the she-birds
    sit on their nests,   25
The young of poultry break through the hatch'd eggs,
The new-born of animals appear, the calf is dropt from the
    cow, the colt from the mare,
Out of its little hill faithfully rise the potato's dark green leaves,
Out of its hill rises the yellow maize-stalk, the lilacs bloom in
    the dooryards,
The summer growth is innocent and disdainful above all those
    strata of sour dead.   30

What chemistry!
That the winds are really not infectious,
That this is no cheat, this transparent green-wash of the sea
    which is so amorous after me,
That it is safe to allow it to lick my naked body all over with
    its tongues,
That it will not endanger me with the fevers that have
    deposited themselves in it,   35
That all is clean forever and forever,
That the cool drink from the well tastes so good,

That blackberries are so flavorous and juicy,
That the fruits of the apple-orchard and the orange-orchard,
 that melons, grapes, peaches, plums, will none of them
 poison me,
That when I recline on the grass I do not catch any disease,   40
Though probably every spear of grass rises out of what was
 once a catching disease.

Now I am terrified at the Earth, it is that calm and patient,
It grows such sweet things out of such corruptions,
It turns harmless and stainless on its axis, with such endless
 successions of diseas'd corpses,
It distills such exquisite winds out of such infused fetor,   45
It renews with such unwitting looks its prodigal, annual,
 sumptuous crops,
It gives such divine materials to men, and accepts such
 leavings from them at last.
1856   *1881*

To a Foil'd European Revolutionaire[6]

Courage yet, my brother or my sister!
Keep on—Liberty is to be subserv'd whatever occurs;
That is nothing that is quell'd by one or two failures, or any
 number of failures,
Or by the indifference or ingratitude of the people, or by any
 unfaithfulness,
Or the show of the tushes[7] of power, soldiers, cannon, penal
 statutes.   5

What we believe in waits latent forever through all the
 continents,
Invites no one, promises nothing, sits in calmness and light, is
 positive and composed, knows no discouragement,
Waiting patiently, waiting its time.

(Not songs of loyalty alone are these,
But songs of insurrection also,   10
For I am the sworn poet of every dauntless rebel the world over,
And he going with me leaves peace and routine behind him,
And stakes his life to be lost at any moment.)

---

6. When first published in *LG* 1856 with several of its lines transferred from the 1855 Preface,
 this poem had the flamboyant title "Liberty Poem for Asia, Africa, Europe, America, Austra-
 lia, Cuba, and The Archipelagoes of the Sea." In 1860 and 1867 it became "To a Foiled
 Revolter or Revoltress," and in 1871 it took its present title. It is evident that the poet meant,
 as he added in 1871, to be the voice "of every dauntless rebel the world over." The text was
 much revised in *LG* editions from 1860 to 1871.
  In the fifth and sixth editions of 1871 and 1876 this poem was one of six placed in a special
 group called "Songs of Insurrection," a division not retained in later editions.
7. Variant of "tusks" or "teeth."

The battle rages with many a loud alarm and frequent advance
    and retreat,
The infidel triumphs, or supposes he triumphs, 15
The prison, scaffold, garroté,[8] handcuffs, iron necklace and
    lead-balls do their work,
The named and unnamed heroes pass to other spheres,
The great speakers and writers are exiled, they lie sick in
    distant lands,
The cause is asleep, the strongest throats are choked with their
    own blood,
The young men droop their eyelashes toward the ground when
    they meet; 20
But for all this Liberty has not gone out of the place, nor the
    infidel enter'd into full possession.

When liberty goes out of a place it is not the first to go, nor
    the second or third to go,
It waits for all the rest to go, it is the last.

When there are no more memories of heroes and martyrs,
And when all life and all the souls of men and women are
    discharged from any part of the earth, 25
Then only shall liberty or the idea of liberty be discharged
    from that part of the earth,
And the infidel come into full possession.

Then courage European revolter, revoltress!
For till all ceases neither must you cease.

I do not know what you are for, (I do not know what I am for
    myself, nor what any thing is for,) 30
But I will search carefully for it even in being foil'd,
In defeat, poverty, misconception, imprisonment—for they too
    are great.

Did we think victory great?
So it is—but now it seems to me, when it cannot be help'd,
    that defeat is great,
And that death and dismay are great. 35
  1856   *1881*

---

8. Erroneous accent added in *CPP* 1888; repeated in hardbound text of *LG* 1891–92, but not
  in the softbound issue.

Unnamed Lands[9]

Nations ten thousand years before these States, and many
    times ten thousand years before these States,
Garner'd clusters of ages that men and women like us grew up
    and travel'd their course and pass'd on,
What vast-built cities, what orderly republics, what pastoral
    tribes and nomads,
What histories, rulers, heroes, perhaps transcending all others,
What laws, customs, wealth, arts, traditions,   5
What sort of marriage, what costumes, what physiology and
    phrenology,
What of liberty and slavery among them, what they thought of
    death and the soul,
Who were witty and wise, who beautiful and poetic, who
    brutish and undevelop'd,
Not a mark, not a record remains—and yet all remains.

O I know that those men and women were not for nothing,
    any more than we are for nothing,   10
I know that they belong to the scheme of the world every bit
    as much as we now belong to it.

Afar they stand, yet near to me they stand,
Some with oval countenances learn'd and calm,
Some naked and savage, some like huge collections of insects,
Some in tents, herdsmen, patriarchs, tribes, horsemen,   15
Some prowling through woods, some living peaceably on farms,
    laboring, reaping, filling barns,
Some traversing paved avenues, amid temples, palaces,
    factories, libraries, shows, courts, theatres, wonderful
    monuments.

Are those billions of men really gone?
Are those women of the old experience of the earth gone?
Do their lives, cities, arts, rest only with us?   20
Did they achieve nothing for good for themselves?

I believe of all those men and women that fill'd the unnamed
    lands, every one exists this hour here or elsewhere,
    invisible to us,
In exact proportion to what he or she grew from in life, and
    out of what he did or she did, felt, became, loved, sinn'd,
    in life.

9. This poem was first published in *LG* 1860 under its present title. The Barrett MS (Bowers,
220–24) and the sucessive texts indicate moderate revision. An early prose MS draft of factual
backgrounds (Trent: "The most immense part of ancient history is altogether unknown,"
etc.) contains several lines later used in the poem (see *N and F*, I, 76–77).

I believe that was not the end of those nations or any person
    of them, any more than this shall be the end of my
    nation, or of me;
Of their languages, governments, marriage, literature, products,
    games, wars, manners, crimes, prisons, slaves, heroes,
    poets,   25
I suspect their results curiously await in the yet unseen world,
    counterparts of what accrued to them in the seen world,
I suspect I shall meet them there,
I suspect I shall there find each old particular of those
    unnamed lands.

1860   *1881*

Song of Prudence[1]

Manhattan's streets I saunter'd pondering,
On Time, Space, Reality—on such as these, and abreast with
    them Prudence.

The last explanation always remains to be made about prudence,
Little and large alike drop quietly aside from the prudence that
    suits immortality.[2]

The soul is of itself,   5
All verges to it, all has reference to what ensues,
All that a person does, says, thinks, is of consequence,
Not a move can a man or woman make, that affects him or
    her in a day, month, any part of the direct lifetime, or the
    hour of death,
But the same affects him or her onward afterward through the
    indirect lifetime.

The indirect is just as much as the direct,   10
The spirit receives from the body just as much as it gives to
    the body, if not more.

Not one word or deed, not venereal sore, discoloration, privacy
    of the onanist,

1. Except for the two opening lines, this 1856 poem is taken, practically in its entirety, from the 1855 Preface and has undergone but minor changes since. In *LG* 1856 it was called "Poem of the Last Explanation of Prudence," in *LG* 1860 "Leaves of Grass" No. 5, and in the following three editions the title was the poem's first line (*q.v.*). In 1881 it took its present title and position.
    One of the most Emersonian of WW's poems, it may have been influenced by Emerson's lecture on "Prudence" (*Essays: First Series,* 1841). Emerson's observation that Prudence is "the outmost action of the inward life" and that "everything in nature, even motes and feathers, go by law and not by luck" strongly supports the poem. A scrap of prose MS (Feinberg) complains that "spiritual prudence" is "nearly altogether omitted in modern formulas, & in the atmosphere of poems & all the literary products."
2. Although "prudence" now familiarly refers to pragmatic caution in worldly affairs, its basic meaning, as here, is "wisdom conducing to moral virtue and discipline."

Putridity of gluttons or rum-drinkers, peculation, cunning,
    betrayal, murder, seduction, prostitution,
But has results beyond death as really as before death.

Charity and personal force are the only investments worth any
    thing.   15

No specification is necessary, all that a male or female does,
    that is vigorous, benevolent, clean, is so much profit to
    him or her,
In the unshakable order of the universe and through the whole
    scope of it forever.

Who has been wise receives interest,
Savage, felon, President, judge,[3] farmer, sailor, mechanic,
    literat, young, old, it is the same,
The interest will come round—all will come round.   20

Singly, wholly, to affect now, affected their time, will forever
    affect, all of the past and all of the present and all of the
    future,
All the brave actions of war and peace,
All help given to relatives, strangers, the poor, old, sorrowful,
    young children, widows, the sick, and to shunn'd persons,
All self-denial that stood steady and aloof on wrecks, and saw
    others fill the seats of the boats,
All offering of substance or life for the good old cause, or for a
    friend's sake, or opinion's sake,   25
All pains of enthusiasts scoff'd at by their neighbors,
All the limitless sweet love and precious suffering of mothers,
All honest men baffled in strifes recorded or unrecorded,
All the grandeur and good of ancient nations whose fragments
    we inherit,
All the good of the dozens of ancient nations unknown to us
    by name, date, location,   30
All that was ever manfully begun, whether it succeeded or no,
All suggestions of the divine mind of man or the divinity of his
    mouth, or the shaping of his great hands,
All that is well thought or said this day on any part of the
    globe, or on any of the wandering stars, or on any of the
    fix'd stars, by those there as we are here,
All that is henceforth to be thought or done by you whoever
    you are, or by any one,
These inure, have inured, shall inure, to the identities from
    which they sprang, or shall spring.   35

Did you guess any thing lived only its moment?
The world does not so exist, no parts palpable or impalpable so
    exist,

3. The word "prostitute" appeared between "judge" and "farmer" in 1856 only.

No consummation exists without being from some long
    previous consummation, and that from some other,
Without the farthest conceivable one coming a bit nearer the
    beginning than any.

Whatever satisfies souls is true;   40
Prudence entirely satisfies the craving and glut of souls,
Itself only finally satisfies the soul,
The soul has that measureless pride which revolts from every
    lesson but its own.

Now I breathe the word of the prudence that walks abreast
    with time, space, reality,
That answers the pride which refuses every lesson but its own.   45

What is prudence is indivisible,
Declines to separate one part of life from every part,
Divides not the righteous from the unrighteous or the living
    from the dead,
Matches every thought or act by its correlative,
Knows no possible forgiveness or deputed atonement,   50
Knows that the young man who composedly peril'd his life and
    lost it has done exceedingly well for himself without doubt,
That he who never peril'd his life, but retains it to old age in
    riches and ease, has probably achiev'd nothing for himself
    worth mentioning,
Knows that only that person has really learn'd who has learn'd
    to prefer results,
Who favors body and soul the same,
Who perceives the indirect assuredly following the direct,   55
Who in his spirit in any emergency whatever neither hurries
    nor avoids death.

1856   *1881*

The Singer in the Prison[4]

1

O sight of pity, shame and dole!
O fearful thought—a convict soul.

4. This poem was first published in the *Saturday Evening Visitor* (Washington), December 25,
1869, before inclusion in the 1871 *Passage to India* and succeeding editions of *LG*. In the
present text (1881) WW excluded the two-line refrain after the first canto and each quatrain
of the hymn.
    The poem celebrates the 1869 concert of the famous singer Parepa-Rosa in Sing Sing
Prison, a performance said to have been attended by the poet himself. (See *In Re*, 370.) It
is one of the few poems in *LG* inspired by an occasion or making any use of conventional
versification. Frankly sentimental, it is burdened with clichés. MS in Huntington.

Rang the refrain along the hall, the prison,
Rose to the roof, the vaults of heaven above,
Pouring in floods of melody in tones so pensive sweet and
    strong the like whereof was never heard,   5
Reaching the far-off sentry and the armed guards, who ceas'd
    their pacing,
Making the hearer's pulses stop for ecstasy and awe.

2

The sun was low in the west one winter day,
When down a narrow aisle amid the thieves and outlaws of the
    land,
(There by the hundreds seated, sear-faced murderers, wily
    counterfeiters,   10
Gather'd to Sunday church in prison walls, the keepers round,
Plenteous, well-armed, watching with vigilant eyes,)
Calmly a lady walk'd holding a little innocent child by either
    hand,
Whom seating on their stools beside her on the platform,
She, first preluding with the instrument a low and musical
    prelude,   15
In voice surpassing all, sang forth a quaint old hymn.

    A soul confined by bars and bands,
    Cries, help! O help! and wrings her hands,
    Blinded her eyes, bleeding her breast,
    Nor pardon finds, nor balm of rest.   20

    Ceaseless she paces to and fro,
    O heart-sick days! O nights of woe!
    Nor hand of friend, nor loving face,
    Nor favor comes, nor word of grace.

    It was not I that sinn'd the sin,   25
    The ruthless body dragg'd me in;
    Though long I strove courageously,
    The body was too much for me.

    Dear prison'd soul bear up a space,
    For soon or late the certain grace;   30
    To set thee free and bear thee home,
    The heavenly pardoner death shall come.

        Convict no more, nor shame, nor dole!
        Depart—a God-enfranchis'd soul!

3

The singer ceas'd,   35
One glance swept from her clear calm eyes o'er all those
    upturn'd faces,

Strange sea of prison faces, a thousand varied, crafty, brutal,
    seam'd and beauteous faces,
Then rising, passing back along the narrow aisle between them,
While her gown touch'd them rustling in the silence,
She vanish'd with her children in the dusk.   40

While upon all, convicts and armed keepers ere they stirr'd,
(Convict forgetting prison, keeper his loaded pistol,)
A hush and pause fell down a wondrous minute,
With deep, half-stiffled sobs and sound of bad men bow'd and
    moved to weeping,
And youth's convulsive breathings, memories of home,   45
The mother's voice in lullaby, the sister's care, the happy
    childhood,
The long-pent spirit rous'd to reminiscence;
A wondrous minute then—but after in the solitary night, to
    many, many there,
Years after, even in the hour of death, the sad refrain, the
    tune, the voice, the words,
Resumed, the large calm lady walks the narrow aisle,   50
The wailing melody again, the singer in the prison sings,

        O sight of pity, shame and dole!
        O fearful thought—a convict soul.
    1869   *1881*

Warble for Lilac-Time[5]

Warble me now for joy of lilac-time, (returning in
    reminiscence,)
Sort me O tongue and lips for Nature's sake, souvenirs of
    earliest summer,
Gather the welcome signs, (as children with pebbles or
    stringing shells,)
Put in April and May, the hylas croaking in the ponds, the
    elastic air,
Bees, butterflies, the sparrow with its simple notes,   5
Blue-bird and darting swallow, nor forget the high-hole
    flashing his golden wings,
The tranquil sunny haze, the clinging smoke, the vapor,
Shimmer of waters with fish in them, the cerulean above,
All that is jocund and sparkling, the brooks running,

---

5. First published in *The Galaxy,* May 1870 (MS in Berg). Reprinted with concurrent slight
revisions in *Passage to India,* 1871; in the *Daily Graphic,* May 12, 1873; in the "Passage to
India" group of *LG* 1872 and *TR* 1876; and with eight lines cancelled, in its present form
in *LG* 1881. One of WW's most successful lyrics, this "jocund and sparkling" spring song
also suggests the emotional range of the lilac symbol (*cf.* note, "When Lilacs Last in the
Dooryard Bloom'd").

The maple woods, the crisp February days and the sugar-
    making,   10
The robin where he hops, bright-eyed, brown-breasted,
With musical clear call at sunrise, and again at sunset,
Or flitting among the trees of the apple-orchard, building the
    nest of his mate,
The melted snow of March, the willow sending forth its
    yellow-green sprouts,
For spring-time is here! the summer is here! and what is this
    in it and from it?   15
Thou, soul, unloosen'd—the restlessness after I know not
    what;
Come, let us lag here no longer, let us be up and away!
O if one could but fly like a bird!
O to escape, to sail forth as in a ship!
To glide with thee O soul, o'er all, in all, as a ship o'er the
    waters;   20
Gathering these hints, the preludes, the blue sky, the grass,
    the morning drops of dew,
The lilac-scent, the bushes with dark green heart-shaped
    leaves,
Wood-violets, the little delicate pale blossoms called
    innocence,
Samples and sorts not for themselves alone, but for their
    atmosphere,
To grace the bush I love—to sing with the birds,   25
A warble for joy of lilac-time, returning in reminiscence.
  1870   *1881*

Outlines for a Tomb[6]

(G. P., Buried 1870)

1

What may we chant, O thou within this tomb?
What tablets, outlines, hang for thee, O millionnaire?[7]
The life thou lived'st we know not,
But that thou walk'dst thy years in barter, 'mid the haunts of
    brokers,
Nor heroism thine, nor war, nor glory.   5

6. First published in *The Galaxy*, January 1870, under the title "Brother of All, with Generous
Hand." Reprinted in *Passage to India*, 1871; in the "Passage to India" group of *LG* 1872 and
TR 1876; and in 1881 under its present title with thirty of its seventy-nine lines cancelled.
An early MS (Trent), printed in *N and F*, I, 44–45, item 147, shows some resemblance to
the poem in its presentation of "tableaus," a favorite device with WW.
7. George Peabody (1795–1869), philanthropist, who died in London, November 4, 1869, his
body being returned by British warship to his native Danvers, Mass., in January 1870. He
founded the Peabody museums at Yale and Harvard.

2

Silent, my soul,
With drooping lids, as waiting, ponder'd,
Turning from all the samples, monuments of heroes.

While through the interior vistas,
Noiseless uprose, phantasmic, (as by night Auroras of the
    north,)
Lambent tableaus, prophetic, bodiless scenes,
Spiritual projections.

In one, among the city streets a laborer's home appear'd,
After his day's work done, cleanly, sweet-air'd, the gaslight
    burning,
The carpet swept and a fire in the cheerful stove.

In one, the sacred parturition scene,
A happy painless mother birth'd a perfect child.

In one, at a bounteous morning meal,
Sat peaceful parents with contented sons.

In one, by twos and threes, young people,
Hundreds concentring, walk'd the paths and streets and roads,
Toward a tall-domed school.

In one a trio beautiful,
Grandmother, loving daughter, loving daughter's daughter, sat,
Chatting and sewing.

In one, along a suite of noble rooms,
'Mid plenteous books and journals, paintings on the walls, fine
    statuettes,
Were groups of friendly journeymen, mechanics young and old,
Reading, conversing.

All, all the shows of laboring life,
City and country, women's, men's and children's,
Their wants provided for, hued in the sun and tinged for once
    with joy,
Marriage, the street, the factory, farm, the house-room,
    lodging-room,
Labor and toil, the bath, gymnasium, playground, library, college,
The student, boy or girl, led forward to be taught,
The sick cared for, the shoeless shod, the orphan father'd and
    mother'd,
The hungry fed, the houseless housed;

(The intentions perfect and divine,
The workings, details, haply human.)

3

O thou within this tomb,   40
From thee such scenes, thou stintless, lavish giver,
Tallying the gifts of earth, large as the earth,
Thy name an earth, with mountains, fields and tides.

Nor by your streams alone, you rivers,
By you, your banks Connecticut,   45
By you and all your teeming life old Thames,
By you Potomac laving the ground Washington trod, by you
    Patapsco,
You Hudson, you endless Mississippi—nor you alone,
But to the high seas launch, my thought, his memory.
1870   *1881*

Out from behind This Mask[8]

(*To Confront a Portrait*)

1

Out from behind this bending rough-cut mask,
These lights and shades, this drama of the whole,
This common curtain of the face contain'd in me for me, in
    you for you, in each for each,
(Tragedies, sorrows, laughter, tears—O heaven!
The passionate teeming plays this curtain hid!)   5
This glaze of God's serenest purest sky,
This film of Satan's seething pit,
This heart's geography's map, this limitless small continent,
    this soundless sea;
Out from the convolutions of this globe,
This subtler astronomic orb than sun or moon, than Jupiter,
    Venus, Mars,   10
This condensation of the universe, (nay here the only universe,

---

8. First published in the *New York Tribune*, February 19, 1876, then in *Two Rivulets* (1876),
a companion volume to *LG*, and in WW's "Centennial Edition" of *LG* in that year. The
poem was WW's description of a portrait in *LG* 1876, facing "The Wound-Dresser," (*q.v.*,
above, among the "Drum-Taps" poems). This portrait, not present in the 1892 edition here
reproduced, was printed from a handsome engraving on wood, by W. J. Linton, of a pho-
tograph of the poet made by G. C. Potter in Washington in 1871. It was to his poetic self-
portrait that WW referred, not to the artist's engraving, in a preview to *TR* that he wrote
appearing in the *New York Daily Tribune*, February 19, 1876: "Whitman gives his own
portrait from life in the book—a large, bending, gray-haired man, 'looking at you.'" See
Blodgett, "Whitman and the Linton Portrait," *WWN*, no. 4 (September 1958): 90–91. No
ambiguity was present in the subtitle to the poem as published in 1876, which read: "To
confront My Portrait, illustrating 'the *Wound-Dresser*,' in LEAVES OF GRASS." In 1881, the
present subtitle was substituted and minor verbal alterations were made to produce the
present, final text.

Here the idea, all in this mystic handful wrapt;)
These burin'd eyes,[9] flashing to you to pass to future time,
To launch and spin through space revolving sideling, from
    these to emanate,
To you whoe'er you are—a look.   15

2

A traveler of thoughts and years, of peace and war,
Of youth long sped and middle age declining,
(As the first volume of a tale perused and laid away, and this
    the second,
Songs, ventures, speculations, presently to close,)
Lingering a moment here and now, to you I opposite turn,   20
As on the road or at some crevice door by chance, or open'd
    window,
Pausing, inclining, baring my head, you specially I greet,
To draw and clinch your soul for once inseparably with mine,
Then travel travel on.
    1876   *1881*

Vocalism[1]

1

Vocalism, measure, concentration, determination, and the
    divine power to speak words;
Are you full-lung'd and limber-lipp'd from long trial? from
    vigorous practice? from physique?
Do you move in these broad lands as broad as they?
Come duly to the divine power to speak words?
For only at last after many years, after chastity, friendship,
    procreation, prudence, and nakedness,   5
After treading ground and breasting river and lake,
After a loosen'd throat, after absorbing eras, temperaments,
    races, after knowledge, freedom, crimes,
After complete faith, after clarifyings, elevations, and removing
    obstructions,
After these and more, it is just possible there comes to a man,
    a woman, the divine power to speak words;
Then toward that man or that woman swiftly hasten all—none
    refuse, all attend,   10

9. "Burin'd" is a technical term meaning "cut by the burin," an engraver's tool.
1. A fusion of two poems in 1881, each of which had developed independently in all editions since *LG* 1860. There they both first appeared—the first stanza of the present poem as No. 12 in the "Chants Democratic" cluster, the second stanza as No. 21 in a "Leaves of Grass" cluster. With intervening changes in phrasing and titles, the poem of stanza 1 above became "To Oratists" in *LG* 1872 to 1876, in which the second stanza also appeared as a separate poem, "Voices." In the conflation of 1881, the first stanza lost thirteen lines while the second stanza dropped two. The fusion was then successful, for both parts celebrate the same theme—the power of the voice, which had so attracted the poet in his earlier days that he had seriously considered the possibility of becoming an orator. See Asselineau, 94–96. The MSS of both stanzas (Barrett) are printed in Bowers, 154–58, 182.

Armies, ships, antiquities, libraries, paintings, machines, cities,
    hate, despair, amity, pain, theft, murder, aspiration, form
    in close ranks,
They debouch as they are wanted to march obediently through
    the mouth of that man or that woman.

2

O what is it in me that makes me tremble so at voices?
Surely whoever speaks to me in the right voice, him or her I
    shall follow,
As the water follows the moon, silently, with fluid steps,
    anywhere around the globe.[2]   15

All waits for the right voices;
Where is the practis'd and perfect organ? where is the
    develop'd soul?
For I see every word utter'd thence has deeper, sweeter, new
    sounds, impossible on less terms.

I see brains and lips closed, tympans and temples unstruck,
Until that comes which has the quality to strike and to
    unclose,   20
Until that comes which has the quality to bring forth what lies
    slumbering forever ready in all words.
1860   *1881*

To Him That Was Crucified[3]

My spirit to yours dear brother,
Do not mind because many sounding your name do not
    understand you,
I do not sound your name, but I understand you,
I specify you with joy O my comrade to salute you, and to
    salute those who are with you, before and since, and
    those to come also,
That we all labor together transmitting the same charge and
    succession,   5
We few equals indifferent of lands, indifferent of times,
We, enclosers of all continents, all castes, allowers of all
    theologies,
Compassionaters, perceivers, rapport of men,
We walk silent among disputes and assertions, but reject not
    the disputers nor any thing that is asserted,

---

2. Lines 14–15 were used by George Eliot as an epigraph for chapter 29, book 4 of her novel
   Daniel Deronda (1876). For her interest in WW, see Blodgett, 169–71.
3. This poem was first published, under this title, in the "Messenger Leaves" group of the 1860
   LG and has remained unchanged except for the dropping in 1881 of the parenthetical phrase
   "(there are others also)" at the end of the third line. The opening lines are plainly a reference
   to Jesus, the poem quickly broadening its meaning to include all crucified ones, of whom
   the poet is the comrade and brother.

We hear the bawling and din, we are reach'd at by divisions,
    jealousies, recrimination on every side,   10
They close peremptorily upon us to surround us, my comrade,
Yet we walk unheld, free, the whole earth over, journeying up
    and down till we make our ineffaceable mark upon time
    and the diverse eras,
Till we saturate time and eras, that the men and women of
    races, ages to come, may prove brethren and lovers as we
    are.
    1860   *1881*

You Felons on Trial in Courts[4]

You felons on trial in courts,
You convicts in prison-cells, you sentenced assassins chain'd
    and handcuff'd with iron,
Who am I too that I am not on trial or in prison?
Me ruthless and devilish as any, that my wrists are not chain'd
    with iron, or my ankles with iron?

You prostitutes flaunting over the trottoirs or obscene in your
    rooms,   5
Who am I that I should call you more obscene than myself?

O culpable! I acknowledge—I exposé!
(O admirers, praise not me—compliment not me—you make
    me wince,
I see what you do not—I know what you do not.)

Inside these breast-bones I lie smutch'd and choked,   10
Beneath this face that appears so impassive hell's tides
    continually run,
Lusts and wickedness are acceptable to me,
I walk with delinquents with passionate love,
I feel I am of them—I belong to those convicts and prostitutes
    myself,

4. First published as "Leaves of Grass" No. 13 in *LG* 1860, beginning with eight lines removed
from all succeeding editions (see below; also in appended section of "Excluded Poems and
Passages"):

> O bitter sprig! Confession sprig!
> In the bouquet I give you place also—I bind you in,
> Proceeding no further till, humbled publicly,
> I give fair warning, once for all.
>
> I own that I have been sly, thievish, mean, a prevaricator, greedy, derelict,
> And I own that I remain so yet.
> What fool thought but I think it—or have in me the stuff out of which
>   it is thought?
> What in darkness in bed at night, alone or with a companion?

There were no other significant changes after 1860, although the confession note was also
struck by a revision of title that WW made in his 1860 "Blue Copy" but never honored:
"Sprig of Confession."

And henceforth I will not deny them—for how can I deny
    myself?   15
1860   1867

Laws for Creations[5]

Laws for creations,
For strong artists and leaders, for fresh broods of teachers and
    perfect literats for America,
For noble savans and coming musicians.

All must have reference to the ensemble of the world, and the
    compact truth of the world,
There shall be no subject too pronounced—all works shall
    illustrate the divine law of indirections.   5

What do you suppose creation is?
What do you suppose will satisfy the soul, except to walk free
    and own no superior?
What do you suppose I would intimate to you in a hundred
    ways, but that man or woman is as good as God?
And that there is no God any more divine than Yourself?
And that that is what the oldest and newest myths finally
    mean?   10
And that you or any one must approach creations through
    such laws?
1860   1872

To a Common Prostitute[6]

Be composed—be at ease with me—I am Walt Whitman,
    liberal and lusty as Nature,
Not till the sun excludes you do I exclude you,
Not till the waters refuse to glisten for you and the leaves to rustle
    for you, do my words refuse to glisten and rustle for you.

My girl I appoint with you an appointment, and I charge you
    that you make preparation to be worthy to meet me,
And I charge you that you be patient and perfect till I come.   5

5. First appeared in *LG* 1860 as No. 13 in the cluster "Chants Democratic." In *LG* 1867, the poem was reduced from eighteen to eleven lines, resulting in the present text, much improved in concentration and effectiveness. Preserved in the Barrett collection are extensive MS notes and drafts for this poem, which are printed in *N and F*, I, 22–23, item 48; also an early MS draft of the whole, printed in Bowers, 158–60, with the rejected title "American Laws."
6. One of the "Messenger Leaves" of the 1860 *LG*, and unchanged in all succeeding editions, this poem has acquired a certain notoriety in having in an earlier period been frequently cited for censorship. In his MS (Huntington) WW had originally written "My love" for "My girl" in the fourth line, and "kiss on your lips" for "significant look" in the sixth. The poet may have thought of this poem as a variation upon the biblical account of the woman taken in adultery (John 8.8–11).

Till then I salute you with a significant look that you do not
    forget me.
1860   *1860*

I Was Looking a Long While[7]

I was looking a long while for Intentions,
For a clew to the history of the past for myself, and for these
    chants—and now I have found it,
It is not in those paged fables in the libraries, (them I neither
    accept nor reject,)
It is no more in the legends than in all else,
It is in the present—it is this earth to-day,   5
It is in Democracy—(the purport and aim of all the past,)
It is the life of one man or one woman to-day—the average
    man of to-day,
It is in languages, social customs, literatures, arts,
It is in the broad show of artificial things, ships, machinery,
    politics, creeds, modern improvements, and the
    interchange of nations,
All for the modern—all for the average man of to-day.   10
1860   *1881*

Thought[8]

Of persons arrived at high positions, ceremonies, wealth,
    scholarships, and the like;
(To me all that those persons have arrived at sinks away from
    them, except as it results to their bodies and souls,
So that often to me they appear gaunt and naked,
And often to me each one mocks the others, and mocks
    himself or herself,
And of each one the core of life, namely happiness, is full of
    the rotten excrement of maggots,   5
And often to me those men and women pass unwittingly the
    true realities of life, and go toward false realities,
And often to me they are alive after what custom has served
    them, but nothing more,
And often to me they are sad, hasty, unwaked sonnambules[9]
    walking the dusk.)
1860   *1871*

---

7. This poem was first published as "Chants Democratic" No. 19 in *LG* 1860 and took its
   present title in 1867. Only minor revisions appear in the comparison of printed texts and
   the MS (Barrett), printed by Bowers, 168. At least three years before publication, trial drafts
   of four of its lines were entered in an 1856–57 notebook (Feinberg). As an announcement
   of purpose, it could well have been an "Inscriptions" poem.
8. This poem was first published as No. 3 of the "Thoughts" group of *LG* 1860 and has re-
   mained unchanged under this title in all succeeding editions. MS in Huntington.
9. French: "sleepwalkers."

Miracles[1]

Why, who makes much of a miracle?
As to me I know of nothing else but miracles,
Whether I walk the streets of Manhattan,
Or dart my sight over the roofs of houses toward the sky,
Or wade with naked feet along the beach just in the edge of
    the water,   5
Or stand under trees in the woods,
Or talk by day with any one I love, or sleep in the bed at night
    with any one I love,
Or sit at table at dinner with the rest,
Or look at strangers opposite me riding in the car,
Or watch honey-bees busy around the hive of a summer
    forenoon,   10
Or animals feeding in the fields,
Or birds, or the wonderfulness of insects in the air,
Or the wonderfulness of the sundown, or of stars shining so
    quiet and bright,
Or the exquisite delicate thin curve of the new moon in spring;
These with the rest, one and all, are to me miracles,   15
The whole referring, yet each distinct and in its place.

To me every hour of the light and dark is a miracle,
Every cubic inch of space is a miracle,
Every square yard of the surface of the earth is spread with the
    same,
Every foot of the interior swarms with the same.   20

To me the sea is a continual miracle,
The fishes that swim—the rocks—the motion of the waves—
    the ships with men in them,
What stranger miracles are there?
1856   *1881*

---

1. Appeared as "Poem of Perfect Miracles" in *LG* 1856 and as "Leaves of Grass" No. 8 in *LG* 1860; present title in 1867. Persistent revision to 1881 shortened it by eleven lines. The theme of the poem had long been on the poet's mind: in a pre-1855 notebook (LC *Whitman*, No. 85) he had written, "We hear of miracles.—But what is there that is not a miracle?" Surpassing this poem in fervor are several revelations in early sections of "Song of Myself," culminating with the miracle of a mouse in section 31, *q.v.*

Sparkles from the Wheel[2]

Where the city's ceaseless crowd moves on the livelong day,
Withdrawn I join a group of children watching, I pause aside
    with them.

By the curb toward the edge of the flagging,
A knife-grinder works at his wheel sharpening a great knife,
Bending over he carefully holds it to the stone, by foot and
    knee,   5
With measur'd tread he turns rapidly, as he presses with light
    but firm hand,
Forth issue then in copious golden jets,
Sparkles from the wheel.

The scene and all its belongings, how they seize and affect me,
The sad sharp-chinn'd old man with worn clothes and broad
    shoulder-band of leather,   10
Myself effusing and fluid, a phantom curiously floating, now
    here absorb'd and arrested,
The group, (an unminded point set in a vast surrounding,)
The attentive, quiet children, the loud, proud, restive base of
    the streets,
The low hoarse purr of the whirling stone, the light-press'd
    blade,
Diffusing, dropping, sideways-darting, in tiny showers of gold,   15
Sparkles from the wheel.
    1871   *1871*

To a Pupil[3]

Is reform needed? is it through you?
The greater the reform needed, the greater the Personality you
    need to accomplish it.

You! do you not see how it would serve to have eyes, blood,
    complexion, clean and sweet?
Do you not see how it would serve to have such a body and
    soul that when you enter the crowd an atmosphere of

---

2. First appeared, with the present title and text, in a "Leaves of Grass" group of the 1871 *Passage to India*. MS scraps (Feinberg) contain trial lines, and the MS of the complete poem (Barrett) is printed by Bowers, 254–56. Older readers will remember the fascination of city children by the itinerant knife-grinder and his treadle wheel; the poem illustrates WW's brilliant power to create a vignette of such scenes, in which, however, the point of view is not entirely objective—the poet, an "arrested phantom," bringing in himself as observer, conscious perhaps of himself as being also a maker of sparkles from the wheel. Compare some of these qualities in Robert Frost's "The Grindstone."
3. One of the "Messenger Leaves" of LG 1860, this poem has remained virtually unchanged through all the editions, and the MS (Barrett), printed in Bowers, 188, shows practically no variations.

desire and command enters with you, and every one is
   impress'd with your Personality?

O the magnet! the flesh over and over!   5
Go, dear friend, if need be give up all else, and commence to-
   day to inure yourself to pluck, reality, self-esteem,
   definiteness, elevatedness,
Rest not till you rivet and publish yourself of your own
   Personality.
1860   *1867*

Unfolded Out of the Folds[4]

Unfolded out of the folds of the woman man comes unfolded,
   and is always to come unfolded,
Unfolded only out of the superbest woman of the earth is to
   come the superbest man of the earth,
Unfolded out of the friendliest woman is to come the
   friendliest man,
Unfolded only out of the perfect body of a woman can a man
   be form'd of perfect body,
Unfolded only out of the inimitable poems of woman can
   come the poems of man, (only thence have my poems
   come;)   5
Unfolded out of the strong and arrogant woman I love, only
   thence can appear the strong and arrogant man I love,
Unfolded by brawny embraces from the well-muscled woman I
   love, only thence come the brawny embraces of the man,
Unfolded out of the folds of the woman's brain come all the
   folds of the man's brain, duly obedient,
Unfolded out of the justice of the woman all justice is
   unfolded,
Unfolded out of the sympathy of the woman is all sympathy;   10
A man is a great thing upon the earth and through eternity,
   but every jot of the greatness of man is unfolded out of
   woman;
First the man is shaped in the woman, he can then be shaped
   in himself.
1856   *1881*

---

4. First appeared in *LG* 1856 as "Poem of Women"; in 1860 and 1867 identified only by its
   number in a "Leaves of Grass" cluster; present title in *LG* 1871 and thereafter, with only
   slight revision. Its emphasis on the eugenic role of women is characteristic.

What Am I After All[5]

What am I after all but a child, pleas'd with the sound of my
    own name? repeating it over and over;
I stand apart to hear—it never tires me.

To you your name also;
Did you think there was nothing but two or three
    pronunciations in the sound of your name?
1860   *1867*

Kosmos[6]

Who includes diversity and is Nature,
Who is the amplitude of the earth, and the coarseness and
    sexuality of the earth, and the great charity of the earth,
    and the equilibrium also,
Who has not look'd forth from the windows the eyes for
    nothing, or whose brain held audience with messengers
    for nothing,
Who contains believers and disbelievers, who is the most
    majestic lover,
Who holds duly his or her triune proportion of realism,
    spiritualism, and of the æsthetic or intellectual,   5
Who having consider'd the body finds all its organs and parts
    good,
Who, out of the theory of the earth and of his or her body
    understands by subtle analogies all other theories,
The theory of a city, a poem, and of the large politics of these
    States;
Who believes not only in our globe with its sun and moon, but
    in other globes with their suns and moons,
Who, constructing the house of himself or herself, not for a
    day but for all time, sees races, eras, dates, generations,   10
The past, the future, dwelling there, like space, inseparable
    together.
1860   *1867*

5. In *LG* 1860 this poem was "Leaves of Grass" No. 22, and in *LG* 1867, No. 4 in the "Songs
Before Parting" supplement; with present title in 1871 as a *Passage to India* poem. In both
the Barrett MS (Bowers, 184) and the 1860 text is a second line, dropped in 1867:

> I cannot tell why it affects me so much, when
>   I hear it from women's voices, and from men's
>   voices, or from my own voice.

6. Usually meaning "an ordered universe," Kosmos is here applied to an individual possessing
a systematic, inclusive harmony—as also in "Song of Myself," section 24, line 1. Identical
in title and text in the Barrett MS (Bowers, 224–26), in *LG* 1860, and all later editions,
except that the terminal phrase of line 7, all other theories," was added in 1867.

Others May Praise What They Like[7]

Others may praise what they like;
But I, from the banks of the running Missouri, praise nothing
    in art or aught else,
Till it has well inhaled the atmosphere of this river, also the
    western prairie-scent,
And exudes it all again.
1865   *1881*

Who Learns My Lesson Complete?[8]

Who learns my lesson complete?
Boss, journeyman, apprentice, churchman and atheist,
The stupid and the wise thinker, parents and offspring,
    merchant, clerk, porter and customer,
Editor, author, artist, and schoolboy—draw nigh and
    commence;
It is no lesson—it lets down the bars to a good lesson,   5
And that to another, and every one to another still.

The great laws take and effuse without argument,
I am of the same style, for I am their friend,
I love them quits and quits, I do not halt and make salaams.

I lie abstracted and hear beautiful tales of things and the
    reasons of things,   10
They are so beautiful I nudge myself to listen.

I cannot say to any person what I hear—I cannot say it to
    myself—it is very wonderful.

It is no small matter, this round and delicious globe moving so
    exactly in its orbit for ever and ever, without one jolt or
    the untruth of a single second,

7. WW first saw the Missouri when he returned from his residence in New Orleans, June 1848,
   and again on his western trip in 1879. Printed in *Drum-Taps* (1865), and with minor revi-
   sions in "Drum-Taps" 1867, *Passage to India* (1871), and the "Passage to India" supplement,
   1872 and 1876, before inclusion in *LG* 1881.
8. The eleventh of the twelve untitled poems of *LG* 1855. In 1856 titled "Lesson Poem," it
   was in *LG* 1860 and 1867 "Leaves of Grass" No. 11 and No. 3, respectively, in *Passage to
   India* (1871) under the present title, and so in *LG* 1881. Considerably revised, the poem
   was most interestingly altered in line 21, which in the first three editions had read:

   And how I was not palpable once, but am now—and was born on the last day
       of May in the Year 43 of America—and passed from a babe, in
       the creeping trance of three summers and three winters, to articulate
       and walk—all this is equally wonderful,
   And that I grew six feet high, and that I have become a man thirty-six years
       old in the Year 79 of America, and that I am here anyhow, are all
       equally wonderful,

I do not think it was made in six days, nor in ten thousand
    years, nor ten billions of years,
Nor plann'd and built one thing after another as an architect
    plans and builds a house.   15

I do not think seventy years is the time of a man or woman,
Nor that seventy millions of years is the time of a man or woman,
Nor that years will ever stop the existence of me, or any one else.

Is it wonderful that I should be immortal? as every one is
    immortal;
I know it is wonderful, but my eyesight is equally wonderful,
    and how I was conceived in my mother's womb is equally
    wonderful,   20
And pass'd from a babe in the creeping trance of a couple of
    summers and winters to articulate and walk—all this is
    equally wonderful.

And that my soul embraces you this hour, and we affect each
    other without ever seeing each other, and never perhaps
    to see each other, is every bit as wonderful.

And that I can think such thoughts as these is just as wonderful,
And that I can remind you, and you think them and know
    them to be true, is just as wonderful.

And that the moon spins round the earth and on with the
    earth, is equally wonderful,   25
And that they balance themselves with the sun and stars is
    equally wonderful.
1855   *1867*

Tests[9]

All submit to them where they sit, inner, secure,
    unapproachable to analysis in the soul,
Not traditions, not the outer authorities are the judges,
They are the judges of outer authorities and of all traditions,
They corroborate as they go only whatever corroborates
    themselves, and touches themselves;
For all that, they have it forever in themselves to corroborate
    far and near without one exception.   5
1860   *1860*

---

9. First printed with the present title in *LG* 1860, and in all succeeding editions without change.
The "tests" in this pronouncement seem to be the intuitive judgments of the soul. MS in
Huntington.

The Torch[1]

On my Northwest coast in the midst of the night a fishermen's
    group stands watching,
Out on the lake that expands before them, others are spearing
    salmon,
The canoe, a dim shadowy thing, moves across the black water,
Bearing a torch ablaze at the prow.

1865   *1871*

O Star of France[2]

1870–71.

O star of France,
The brightness of thy hope and strength and fame,
Like some proud ship that led the fleet so long,
Beseems to-day a wreck driven by the gale, a mastless hulk,
And 'mid its teeming madden'd half-drown'd crowds,   5
Nor helm nor helmsman.

Dim smitten star,
Orb not of France alone, pale symbol of my soul, its dearest
    hopes,
The struggle and the daring, rage divine for liberty,
Of aspirations toward the far ideal, enthusiast's dreams of
    brotherhood,   10
Of terror to the tyrant and the priest.

Star crucified—by traitors sold,
Star panting o'er a land of death, heroic land,
Strange, passionate, mocking, frivolous land.

Miserable! yet for thy errors, vanities, sins, I will not now
    rebuke thee,   15
Thy unexampled woes and pangs have quell'd them all,
And left thee sacred.

---

1. First published in *Drum-Taps* 1865, this memorable vignette remained unchanged after
slight revision in the text of 1871.
2. In the Franco-Prussian War, 1870–71, the defeat of France was acknowledged by the Treaty
of Frankfort, May 10, 1871; ratification by the new French reactionary government provoked
a bloody insurrection of the Commune of Paris, May 21–28. This poem was first published
June 1871 in *The Galaxy*, which paid WW $25 (*Corr.*, II, 121). It was collected in *As a
Strong Bird on Pinions Free and Other Poems* (1872), reprinted in *Two Rivulets* (1876), and
revised in *LG* 1881. The MS in the British Museum agrees with that in the Franco-American
Museum at Blerancourt, as does the magazine text, in giving the final line as "Shall rise
immortal." All texts of the poem preceding that of *LG* 1881 are divided into four stanzas.

In that amid thy many faults thou ever aimedst highly,
In that thou wouldst not really sell thyself however great the
    price,
In that thou surely wakedst weeping from thy drugg'd sleep,   20
In that alone among thy sisters thou, giantess, didst rend the
    ones that shamed thee,
In that thou couldst not, wouldst not, wear the usual chains,
This cross, thy livid face, thy pierced hands and feet,
The spear thrust in thy side.

O star! O ship of France, beat back and baffled long!   25
Bear up O smitten orb! O ship continue on!

Sure as the ship of all, the Earth itself,
Product of deathly fire and turbulent chaos,
Forth from its spasms of fury and its poisons,
Issuing at last in perfect power and beauty,   30
Onward beneath the sun following its course,
So thee O ship of France!

Finish'd the days, the clouds dispel'd,
The travail o'er, the long-sought extrication,
When lo! reborn, high o'er the European world,   35
(In gladness answering thence, as face afar to face, reflecting
    ours Columbia,)
Again thy star O France, fair lustrous star,
In heavenly peace, clearer, more bright than ever,
Shall beam immortal.
    1871   *1880*

The Ox-Tamer[3]

In a far-away northern county in the placid pastoral region,
Lives my farmer friend, the theme of my recitative, a famous
    tamer of oxen,
There they bring him the three-year-olds and the four-year-olds
    to break them,
He will take the wildest steer in the world and break him and
    tame him,
He will go fearless without any whip where the young bullock
    chafes up and down the yard,   5
The bullock's head tosses restless high in the air with raging
    eyes,
Yet see you! how soon his rage subsides—how soon this tamer
    tames him;

3. First published in the *New York Daily Graphic,* December 1874, in a miscellany of prose
and verse called "A Christmas Garland," but apparently composed as early as 1860, for it is
one of ten poems listed by Thayer and Eldridge in an advertisement of that year for the
never-published *Banner at Daybreak.* (See Allen, 267.) The poem appeared in *Two Rivulets*
(1876) and in *LG* 1881.

See you! on the farms hereabout a hundred oxen young and
    old, and he is the man who has tamed them,
They all know him, all are affectionate to him;
See you! some are such beautiful animals, so lofty looking;   10
Some are buff-color'd, some mottled, one has a white line
    running along his back, some are brindled,
Some have wide flaring horns (a good sign)—see you the
    bright hides,
See, the two with stars on their foreheads—see, the round
    bodies and broad backs,
How straight and square they stand on their legs—what fine
    sagacious eyes!
How they watch their tamer—they wish him near them—how
    they turn to look after him!   15
What yearning expression! how uneasy they are when he
    moves away from them;
Now I marvel what it can be he appears to them, (books,
    politics, poems, depart—all else departs,)
I confess I envy only his fascination—my silent, illiterate
    friend,
Whom a hundred oxen love there in his life on farms,
In the northern county far, in the placid pastoral region.   20
  1874   *1881*

An Old Man's Thought of School[4]

For the Inauguration of a Public School, Camden, New Jersey, 1874

An old man's thought of school,
An old man gathering youthful memories and blooms that
    youth itself cannot.

Now only do I know you,
O fair auroral skies—O morning dew upon the grass!

And these I see, these sparkling eyes,   5
These stores of mystic meaning, these young lives,
Building, equipping like a fleet of ships, immortal ships,
Soon to sail out over the measureless seas,
On the soul's voyage.

Only a lot of boys and girls?   10
Only the tiresome spelling, writing, ciphering classes?
Only a public school?

4. First published in the *New York Daily Graphic*, November 3, 1874, with the headnote: "The
following poem was recited personally by the author Saturday afternoon, October 31, at the
inauguration of the fine new Cooper Public School, Camden, New Jersey." It was collected
in *Two Rivulets* (1876), somewhat improved by the omission of three rather prosy lines in
the final stanza, and included in *LG* 1881.

Ah more, infinitely more;
(As George Fox[5] rais'd his warning cry, "Is it this pile of brick
    and mortar, these dead floors, windows, rails, you call the
    church?
Why this is not the church at all—the church is living, ever
    living souls.")   15

And you America,
Cast you the real reckoning for your present?
The lights and shadows of your future, good or evil?
To girlhood, boyhood look, the teacher and the school.
1874   *1881*

Wandering at Morn[6]

Wandering at morn,
Emerging from the night from gloomy thoughts, thee in my
    thoughts,
Yearning for thee harmonious Union! thee, singing bird divine!
Thee coil'd in evil times my country,[7] with craft and black
    dismay, with every meanness, treason thrust upon thee,
This common marvel I beheld—the parent thrush I watch'd
    feeding its young,   5
The singing thrush whose tones of joy and faith ecstatic,
Fail not to certify and cheer my soul.

There ponder'd, felt I,
If worms, snakes, loathsome grubs, may to sweet spiritual
    songs be turn'd,
If vermin so transposed, so used and bless'd may be,   10
Then may I trust in you, your fortunes, days, my country;
Who knows but these may be the lessons fit for you?
From these your future song may rise with joyous trills,
Destin'd to fill the world.
1873   *1881*

5. George Fox (1624–1691), British reformer and founder of the Society of Friends.
6. First published in the *New York Daily Graphic*, March 15, 1873, entitled "The Singing
    Thrush," and dated Washington, March 10. The MS (Feinberg), signed and dated Washing-
    ton, February 28, 1873, shows two discarded titles—"The Future Song" and "The Singing
    Bird"—and also two lines printed in the magazine text, but not in the 1876 *Two Rivulets* or
    in *LG* 1881, in which the poem appeared under its present title.
7. This was a year of financial panic and depression, precipitated by the failure of the banking
    house of Jay Cooke.

Italian Music in Dakota[8]

["The Seventeenth—the finest Regimental Band I ever heard."]

Through the soft evening air enwinding all,
Rocks, woods, fort, cannon, pacing sentries, endless wilds,
In dulcet streams, in flutes' and cornets' notes,
Electric, pensive, turbulent, artificial,
(Yet strangely fitting even here, meanings unknown before,   5
Subtler than ever, more harmony, as if born here, related here,
Not to the city's fresco'd rooms, not to the audience of the
    opera house,
Sounds, echoes, wandering strains, as really here at home,
Sonnambula's innocent love, trios with Norma's anguish,[9]
And thy ecstatic chorus Poliuto;[1])   10
Ray'd in the limpid yellow slanting sundown,
Music, Italian music in Dakota.

While Nature, sovereign of this gnarl'd realm,
Lurking in hidden barbaric grim recesses,
Acknowledging rapport however far remov'd,   15
(As some old root or soil of earth its last-born flower or fruit,)
Listens well pleas'd.
1881   *1881*

With All Thy Gifts[2]

With all thy gifts America,
Standing secure, rapidly tending, overlooking the world,
Power, wealth, extent, vouchsafed to thee—with these and like
    of these vouchsafed to thee,
What if one gift thou lackest? (the ultimate human problem
    never solving,)
The gift of perfect women fit for thee—what if that gift of
    gifts thou lackest?   5

8. This poem, new to LG 1881, is a memorial of WW's western trip of 1879. Never actually in the Dakotas, the poet may have heard the "Seventeenth Regimental Band" while it was on tour in the region he traveled. MS in Yale.
9. Sonnambula's innocent love: in Vincenzo Bellini's opera La Sonnambula (The Sleepwalker, 1831), the innocent heroine, Amina, is falsely accused of unfaithfulness when she walks asleep into the room of a strange man. Her affronted fiancé ultimately realizes the truth of the situation, and the lovers are happily united.
    Norma's anguish: in Bellini's opera Norma (1831), the heroine, a high priestess of a Druid temple, breaks her vows by falling in love with Pollione, a Roman proconsul. When he is unfaithful to her, she incites her people against him, but love makes her powerless to implement her revenge. Pollione, moved by her love, renounces his own perfidy. Together they immolate themselves in a funeral pyre.
1. Opera by Gaetano Donizetti (1797–1848).
2. First published in the New York Daily Graphic, March 6, 1873, then in TR (1876) and LG 1881. The MS (Feinberg) shows no verbal difference.

The towering feminine of thee? the beauty, health, completion,
    fit for thee?
The mothers fit for thee?
1873   *1881*

My Picture-Gallery³

In a little house keep I pictures suspended, it is not a fix'd
    house,
It is round, it is only a few inches from one side to the other;
Yet behold, it has room for all the shows of the world, all
    memories!
Here the tableaus of life, and here the groupings of death;
Here, do you know this? this is cicerone himself,   5
With finger rais'd he points to the prodigal pictures.
1880   *1881*

The Prairie States⁴

A newer garden of creation, no primal solitude,
Dense, joyous, modern, populous millions, cities and farms,
With iron interlaced, composite, tied, many in one,
By all the world contributed—freedom's and law's and thrift's
    society,
The crown and teeming paradise, so far, of time's
    accumulations,   5
To justify the past.
1880   *1881*

---

3. The poet's round house is, of course, the dwelling of his mind, within which the "cicerone"
   guides us among the pictures of memory. The symbolism may remind us of the considerably
   different employment in Poe's "The Haunted Palace" (1839), in which disorder has con-
   quered the guide. First published in *The American*, October 30, 1880, and then in *LG* 1881,
   this poem originated as a small part of a pre-1855 twenty-nine-page notebook, entitled "Pic-
   tures," with the injunction "break all this into Pictures." Passages are reflected in several
   LG poems and fragments. See Holloway, *Pictures* (1927) and "Uncollected Poems" below;
   MS Notebook (Yale); MS of this poem (Barrett).
4. The MS of this poem, dated from Camden, March 15, 1880, was published in facsimile in
   The Art Autograph, May 1880, having been sent there, according to WW's MS note on an
   earlier MS copy (Hanley), "for the Irish famine." The poem was first collected in *LG* 1881.

Proud Music of the Storm[1]

1

Proud music of the storm,
Blast that careers so free, whistling across the prairies,
Strong hum of forest tree-tops—wind of the mountains,
Personified dim shapes—you hidden orchestras,
You serenades of phantoms with instruments alert,   5
Blending with Nature's rhythmus all the tongues of nations;
You chords left as by vast composers—you choruses,
You formless, free, religious dances—you from the Orient,
You undertone of rivers, roar of pouring cataracts,
You sounds from distant guns with galloping cavalry,   10
Echoes of camps with all the different bugle-calls,
Trooping tumultuous, filling the midnight late, bending me
    powerless,
Entering my lonesome slumber-chamber, why have you seiz'd me?

2

Come forward O my soul, and let the rest retire,
Listen, lose not, it is toward thee they tend,   15
Parting the midnight, entering my slumber-chamber,
For thee they sing and dance O soul.

1. Published as "Proud Music of the Sea-Storm" in *The Atlantic Monthly*, February 1869. WW had asked Emerson to offer it to the editor, James T. Fields, and he was paid $100 (*Corr.*, II, 71–73). It was the second, and last, Whitman poem to appear in the *Atlantic*. Asked why he had appealed to Emerson, WW replied: "For several reasons, I may say. But the best reason I had was in his own suggestion that I should permit him to do such things for me when the moment seemed ripe for it." (Traubel, II, 22). WW referred to his achievement in one of his anonymous pieces for the *Washington Star*, January 18, 1869: "The Atlantic for February contains a long poem from his sturdy pen, and one of the very best, to our notion, that he has yet written." With present title and one significant revision—the insertion of the phrase "bridging the way from Life to Death" in the penultimate line—the poem appeared in the 1871 *Passage to India*, the 1876 *Two Rivulets*, and *LG* 1881.
   Critics have praised the musical pattern of this poem—its symphonic structure (*Handbook*, 199–200) and its similarity to an operatic overture (Faner, 153–54)—and such comparisons are provocative; yet it is clear that its essential being resides in its dramatic dedication, brought brilliantly to a climax in the final passage:

> Poems bridging the way from Life to Death, vaguely wafted in
>   night air, uncaught, unwritten,
> Which let us go forth in the bold day and write.

In the beginning, the poet is seized by the music, not alone of physical Nature, but of the "hidden orchestras" of human actions, past and present, which in the varied forms of festival, war, balladry, and all the passionate chants of life are celebrated in the second section of the poem. Then in the third section the poet dwells delightedly on his own musical experience, an experience presently extended to the music of the wide world, heard or imagined, until he cries, "Give me to hold all sounds . . . Fill me with all the voices of the universe. . . ." Then, awakened from his trance, he knows that he has found his "clew" to go forth to "tally" life, refreshed and cheered. One great surmise remains—now in mid-career he feels a new "rhythmus" to fit the poems he has yet to write. Thus "Proud Music of the Storm" announces a new phase in which, as noted in both the 1872 and 1876 prefaces, WW turns to the sphere of "Spiritual Law." The poem is a fitting prelude for "Passage to India." For an extensive analysis see Sydney J. Krause, "Whitman, Music, and *Proud Music of the Storm*," *PMLA* 72 (September 1957): 705–21.

A festival song,
The duet of the bridegroom and the bride, a marriage-march,
With lips of love, and hearts of lovers fill'd to the brim with
    love,   20
The red-flush'd cheeks and perfumes, the cortege swarming
    full of friendly faces young and old,
To flutes' clear notes and sounding harps' cantabile.[2]

Now loud approaching drums,
Victoria![3] see'st thou in powder-smoke the banners torn but
    flying? the rout of the baffled?
Hearest those shouts of a conquering army?   25

(Ah soul, the sobs of women, the wounded greaning in agony,
The hiss and crackle of flames, the blacken'd ruins, the embers
    of cities,
The dirge and desolation of mankind.)

Now airs antique and mediæval fill me,
I see and hear old harpers with their harps at Welsh festivals,   30
I hear the minnesingers singing their lays of love,
I hear the minstrels, gleemen, troubadours, of the middle ages.

Now the great organ sounds,
Tremulous, while underneath, (as the hid footholds of the earth,
On which arising rest, and leaping forth depend,   35
All shapes of beauty, grace and strength, all hues we know,
Green blades of grass and warbling birds, children that gambol
    and play, the clouds of heaven above,)[4]
The strong base stands, and its pulsations intermits not,
Bathing, supporting, merging all the rest, maternity of all the rest,
And with it every instrument in multitudes,   40
The players playing, all the world's musicians,
The solemn hymns and masses rousing adoration,
All passionate heart-chants, sorrowful appeals,
The measureless sweet vocalists of ages,
And for their solvent setting earth's own diapason,   45
Of winds and woods and mighty ocean waves,
A new composite orchestra, binder of years and climes, ten-
    fold renewer,
As of the far-back days the poets tell, the Paradiso,[5]

2. Music in songlike style, appropriate to the wedding procession.
3. England's queen. Perhaps a reference to the Crimean War and the charge of the Light
    Brigade at Balaklava, October 25, 1854; perhaps a taunting reference to the triumphant
    Northern armies (1865) in the light of British "neutrality."
4. The symbolism in lines 34–39 is interesting: that the base (bass) notes of a musical phrase
    represent the maternal basic strength of the whole harmony of creation.
5. The third part of Dante's Divina Commedia, in which the great Italian poet and his Beatrice
    together ascend to their sphere in Heaven, the "wandering done" (line 49).

The straying thence, the separation long, but now the
    wandering done,
The journey done, the journeyman come home,   50
And man and art with Nature fused again.

Tutti![6] for earth and heaven;
(The Almighty leader now for once has signal'd with his wand.)

The manly strophe[7] of the husbands of the world,
And all the wives responding.   55

The tongues of violins,
(I think O tongues ye tell this heart, that cannot tell itself,
This brooding yearning heart, that cannot tell itself.)

3

Ah from a little child,
Thou knowest soul how to me all sounds became music,   60
My mother's voice in lullaby or hymn,
(The voice, O tender voices, memory's loving voices,
Last miracle of all, O dearest mother's, sister's, voices;)
The rain, the growing corn, the breeze among the long-leav'd
    corn,
The measur'd sea-surf beating on the sand,   65
The twittering bird, the hawk's sharp scream,
The wild-fowl's notes at night as flying low migrating north or
    south,
The psalm in the country church or mid the clustering trees,
    the open air camp-meeting,
The fiddler in the tavern, the glee, the long-strung sailor-song,
The lowing cattle, bleating sheep, the crowing cock at dawn.   70

All songs of current lands come sounding round me,
The German airs of friendship, wine and love,
Irish ballads, merry jigs and dances, English warbles,
Chansons of France, Scotch tunes, and o'er the rest,
Italia's peerless compositions.[8]   75

Across the stage with pallor on her face, yet lurid passion,
Stalks Norma[9] brandishing the dagger in her hand.

---

6. Literally, "all, entire!"—a command to the instruments, "all together!" as signaled by the
   orchestra leader of line 53, after the straying from "Paradiso" and the journey home again.
7. Now usually "stanza," but here, as in the Greek choral dance, one in a succession of cor-
   responding movements.
8. The opera, in which WW's interest was inexhaustible.
9. The heroine of Vincenzo Bellini's opera of the same name. *Cf.* note, line 9, "Italian Music
   in Dakota." Norma, brandishing her dagger against her lover, is enacting the climactic scene
   of the opera.

I see poor crazed Lucia's[1] eyes' unnatural gleam,
Her hair down her back falls loose and dishevel'd.

I see where Ernani[2] walking the bridal garden, 80
Amid the scent of night-roses, radiant, holding his bride by the
    hand,
Hears the infernal call, the death-pledge of the horn.

To crossing swords and gray hairs bared to heaven,
The clear electric base and baritone of the world,
The trombone duo, Libertad forever![3] 85

From Spanish chestnut trees' dense shade,
By old and heavy convent walls a wailing song,
Song of lost love, the torch of youth and life quench'd in despair,
Song of the dying swan, Fernando's[4] heart is breaking.

Awaking from her woes at last retriev'd Amina[5] sings, 90
Copious as stars and glad as morning light the torrents of her joy.

(The teeming lady comes,
The lustrious[6] orb, Venus contralto, the blooming mother,
Sister of loftiest gods, Alboni's self I hear.[7])

4

I hear those odes, symphonies, operas, 95
I hear in the *William Tell*[8] the music of an arous'd and angry
    people,
I hear Meyerbeer's *Huguenots*, the *Prophet*, or *Robert*,[9]
Gounod's *Faust*, or Mozart's *Don Juan*.[1]

---

1. The heroine of Gaetano Donizetti's opera *Lucia di Lammermoor*. Tricked into marriage with a man she does not love, Lucia murders him and collapses into madness.
2. The hero of Giuseppe Verdi's opera of the same name. Ernani's secret adoration of a court lady betrothed to a Spanish grandee leads him into a typically complex love intrigue ending in his tragic suicide.
3. Lines 83–85 are a reference to the great trombone duet from Bellini's opera *I Puritani*.
4. The hero of Donizetti's opera *La Favorita*. Lines 86–89 describe one of the poet's most loved scenes, in which Fernando is in despair, believing his beloved Leonora has deceived him by becoming the king's mistress.
5. Soprano role in Bellini's *La Sonnambula*. See note, line 9, "Italian Music in Dakota."
6. In its first appearance (*Atlantic Monthly*, February 1869), read "lustrous." If "lustrious" is in fact a typographical error, it persisted through nine *LG* issues during WW's lifetime, to become "lustrous" once, in 76.2 *TR* (not in the "Centennial") and afterward only posthumously, in *LG* 1897 and later. Conjecturally (*cf.* lustrous > illustrious) to WW the word-worker, Alboni was both the incomparably lustrous Venus and the illustrious songstress. See following note.
7. Marietta Alboni, great operatic prima-donna, introduced to New York during the summer of 1852. WW attended all of her performances and regarded her singing as the most moving of his musical experiences.
8. Rossini's famous opera about the Swiss hero was first produced in 1829.
9. Giacomo Meyerbeer (1791–1863) produced his romantic operas *Robert le Diable*, *Les Huguenots*, and *Le Prophète* in Paris in 1831, 1836, and 1849, respectively.
1. Gounod's *Faust*, an opera based upon Goethe's great poem, was produced in Paris in 1859; Mozart's *Don Juan* (properly, *Don Giovanni*) was produced in Prague October 29, 1787.

I hear the dance-music of all nations,
The waltz, some delicious measure, lapsing, bathing me in
    bliss,   100
The bolero to tinkling guitars and clattering castanets.

I see religious dances old and new,
I hear the sound of the Hebrew lyre,
I see the crusaders marching bearing the cross on high, to the
    martial clang of cymbals,
I hear dervishes monotonously chanting, interspers'd with
    frantic shouts, as they spin around turning always towards
    Mecca,   105
I see the rapt religious dances of the Persians and the Arabs,
Again, at Eleusis, home of Ceres, I see the modern Greeks
    dancing,[2]
I hear them clapping their hands as they bend their bodies,
I hear the metrical shuffling of their feet.

I see again the wild old Corybantian dance, the performers
    wounding each other,[3]   110
I see the Roman youth to the shrill sound of flageolets
    throwing and catching their weapons,
As they fall on their knees and rise again.

I hear from the Mussulman mosque the muezzin calling,
I see the worshippers within, nor form nor sermon, argument
    nor word,
But silent, strange, devout, rais'd, glowing heads, ecstatic faces.   115

I hear the Egyptian harp of many strings,
The primitive chants of the Nile boatmen,
The sacred imperial hymns of China,
To the delicate sounds of the king,[4] (the stricken wood and
    stone,)
Or to Hindu flutes and the fretting twang of the vina,[5]   120
A band of bayaderes.[6]

5

Now Asia, Africa leave me, Europe seizing inflates me,
To organs huge and bands I hear as from vast concourses of
    voices,
Luther's strong hymn *Eine feste Burg ist unser Gott*,[7]

---

2. *Eleusis*: ancient Grecian city, northwest of Athens; *Ceres*: in Roman mythology, goddess of
   the harvest.
3. The Corybants were revelling attendants of the Phrygian goddess, Cybele, whom the Greeks
   adopted from the ancients and associated with Aphrodite and Dionysus in rites celebrating
   the wild delights of nature.
4. Ancient Chinese musical instrument made of resonant stones hung in a wooden frame and
   struck with a hammer.
5. Hindu musical instrument of the zither family.
6. Indian dancing girls.
7. "A strong refuge is our God."

Rossini's *Stabat Mater dolorosa*,[8]   125
Or floating in some high cathedral dim with gorgeous color'd
    windows,
The passionate *Agnus Dei* or *Gloria in Excelsis*.[9]

Composers! mighty maestros!
And you, sweet singers of old lands, soprani, tenori, bassi!
To you a new bard caroling in the West,   130
Obeisant sends his love.

(Such led to thee O soul,
All senses, shows and objects, lead to thee,
But now it seems to me sound leads o'er all the rest.)

I hear the annual singing of the children in St. Paul's
    cathedral,   135
Or, under the high roof of some colossal hall, the symphonies,
    oratorios of Beethoven, Handel, or Haydn,
The *Creation* in billows of godhood laves me.[1]

Give me to hold all sounds, (I madly struggling cry,)
Fill me with all the voices of the universe,
Endow me with their throbbings,[2] Nature's also,   140
The tempests, waters, winds, operas and chants, marches and
    dances,
Utter, pour in, for I would take them all![3]

6

Then I woke softly,
And pausing, questioning awhile the music of my dream,
And questioning all those reminiscences, the tempest in its
    fury,   145
And all the songs of sopranos and tenors,
And those rapt oriental dances of religious fervor,
And the sweet varied instruments, and the diapason of organs,
And all the artless plaints of love and grief and death,
I said to my silent curious soul out of the bed of the slumber-
    chamber,   150
Come, for I have found the clew I sought so long,
Let us go forth refresh'd amid the day,

---

8. Medieval Latin liturgical text, a series of brief meditations on the Virgin Mary standing at
   the foot of the Cross. The text was set by numerous Renaissance and Baroque composers.
   Rossini's early-nineteenth-century setting was a favorite of WW's.
9. Titles of sections of the Mass. Literally, "Lamb of God," "Glory in the Highest."
1. *The Creation* is a famous oratorio by Franz Joseph Haydn.
2. The typographical error "thobbings" occurred in the *LG* 1881 plates. Correction was made
   in *CPP* 1888 and in *LG* 1889 and the hardbound issue of 1891–92 (the present text) but
   not in the softbound issue of that date.
3. In WW's graphic description (lines 102–42) of various consummations of religious experi-
   ence, there is an advance from the frenzied ecstasy of ancient rites to the "billows of god-
   hood," the high spirituality of the greatest composers.

Cheerfully tallying life, walking the world, the real,
Nourish'd henceforth by our celestial dream.

And I said, moreover,   155
Haply what thou hast heard O soul was not the sound of winds,
Nor dream of raging storm, nor sea-hawk's flapping wings nor
    harsh scream,
Nor vocalism of sun-bright Italy,
Nor German organ majestic, nor vast concourse of voices, nor
    layers of harmonies,
Nor strophes of husbands and wives, nor sound of marching
    soldiers,   160
Nor flutes, nor harps, nor the bugle-calls of camps,
But to a new rhythmus fitted for thee,
Poems bridging the way from Life to Death, vaguely wafted in
    night air, uncaught, unwritten,
Which let us go forth in the bold day and write.
1869   *1881*

Passage to India[1]

1

Singing my days,
Singing the great achievements of the present,

---

1. This poem was published in 1871 as the title piece of a paperbound volume of 120 pages, including 75 poems, 23 of which were new. It appeared also in clothbound publication and as a supplement bound into *LG* 1871 without new pagination; so also in *LG* 1872 and *Two Rivulets*, 1876. Then, with very slight revision, these poems were incorporated among the poems of *LG* 1881. This culminating achievement of his later years was apparently the poet's launching song for his unfulfilled project, a "further Volume" which should sing "the unseen Soul" as *LG* sang "the Body and Existence" (1876 Preface). WW continued: "*Passage to India*, and its cluster, are but freer vent and fuller expression to what, from the first, and so throughout, more or less lurks in my writings, underneath every page, every line, everywhere."
    The poem emerged from a long foreground and from a number of separate compositions. In a small notebook (Lion) of fourteen leaves, WW jotted down ideas for the poem, emphasizing Columbus as his heroic symbol. (Diplomatic transcript by Fredson Bowers, *BNYPL* (July 1957): 348–52; also transcribed in Traubel, IV, 399–400.) One leaf (Va.), entitled "Fables," which began as an independent poem, was later incorporated into the second section of this poem. A version of section 5, entitled "Thou Vast Rondure Swimming in Space" (see lines 81–115 and *cf.* MS facsimile, *GF* I, 260), was submitted in 1868–69 to both *The Fortnightly Review* and *The Atlantic Monthly*, but never printed. (*Corr.*, II, 77). A MS (Lion) of twenty-three leaves, incorporating pasted-on proof slips from both "Fables" and "Thou Vast Rondure . . . ," gives evidence that lines 182–223 were first conceived as an independent poem under the title "O Soul, Thou Pleaseth Me." (See Fredson Bowers, *BNYPL* 61: 319–48, for diplomatic text.) A Harvard MS of twenty-one leaves is evidently a fair copy of the Lion MS. (For diplomatic text, see Bowers, *MP* (November 1953): 102–17).
    At the beginning of his poem, the poet evokes the public interest in recent great achievements of communication—the opening of the Suez Canal, the junction of the Union and Central Pacific transcontinental railroads, and the laying of the Atlantic and Pacific cables. But this was not another "poem of materials"; the poet passes swiftly to his noble dream of international brotherhood, and to the great climax of his poem, the passage to more than India, the fearless venturing of the soul to the seas of God. To Traubel, WW said, referring to "Passage to India," "There's more of me, the essential ultimate me, in that than in any of the poems. There is no philosophy, consistent or inconsistent, in that poem . . . but the burden of it is evolution—the one thing escaping the other—the unfolding of cosmic purposes" (Traubel, I, 156–57).

Singing the strong light works of engineers,
Our modern wonders, (the antique ponderous Seven outvied,)[2]
In the Old World the east the Suez canal,[3]   5
The New by its mighty railroad spann'd,[4]
The seas inlaid with eloquent gentle wires;[5]
Yet first to sound, and ever sound, the cry with thee O soul,
The Past! the Past! the Past!

The Past—the dark unfathom'd retrospect!   10
The teeming gulf—the sleepers and the shadows!
The past—the infinite greatness of the past!
For what is the present after all but a growth out of the past?
(As a projectile form'd, impell'd, passing a certain line, still
    keeps on,
So the present, utterly form'd, impell'd by the past.)   15

                                    2

Passage O soul to India!
Eclaircise[6] the myths Asiatic, the primitive fables.

Not you alone proud truths of the world,[7]
Nor you alone ye facts of modern science,
But myths and fables of eld, Asia's, Africa's fables,   20
The far-darting beams of the spirit, the unloos'd dreams,
The deep diving bibles and legends,
The daring plots of the poets, the elder religions;
O you temples fairer than lilies pour'd over by the rising sun!
O you fables spurning the known, eluding the hold of the
    known, mounting to heaven!   25
You lofty and dazzling towers, pinnacled, red as roses,
    burnish'd with gold!
Towers of fables immortal fashion'd from mortal dreams!
You too I welcome and fully the same as the rest!
You too with joy I sing.

Passage to India!   30
Lo, soul, seest thou not God's purpose from the first?
The earth to be spann'd, connected by network,
The races, neighbors, to marry and be given in marriage,
The oceans to be cross'd, the distant brought near,
The lands to be welded together.   35

2. The Seven Wonders of the World of ancient times were the Egyptian pyramids, the Mau-
   soleum at Halicarnassus, the Temple of Artemis at Ephesus, the Hanging Gardens of Bab-
   ylon, the Colossus of Rhodes, the statue of Zeus at Olympia, and the lighthouse at
   Alexandria.
3. The Suez Canal, joining the Mediterranean and Red Seas, was begun April 1859 and opened
   November 17, 1869.
4. The Union Pacific and the Central Pacific railroads were joined at Promontory, Utah, May
   10, 1869.
5. The laying of the Atlantic cable was successfully completed in 1866.
6. French: "clarify."
7. Lines 18–29 were once intended, as the headnote indicates, to be a separate poem under
   the title "Fables."

A worship new I sing,
You captains, voyagers, explorers, yours,
You engineers, you architects, machinists, yours,
You, not for trade or transportation only,
But in God's name, and for thy sake O soul.   40

3

Passage to India!
Lo soul for thee of tableaus twain,
I see in one the Suez canal initiated, open'd,
I see the procession of steamships, the Empress Eugenie's
    leading the van,[8]
I mark from on deck the strange landscape, the pure sky, the
    level sand in the distance,   45
I pass swiftly the picturesque groups, the workmen gather'd,
The gigantic dredging machines.

In one again, different, (yet thine, all thine, O soul, the same,)
I see over my own continent the Pacific railroad surmounting
    every barrier,[9]
I see continual trains of cars winding along the Platte carrying
    freight and passengers,   50
I hear the locomotives rushing and roaring, and the shrill
    steam-whistle,
I hear the echoes reverberate through the grandest scenery in
    the world,
I cross the Laramie plains, I note the rocks in grotesque
    shapes, the buttes,
I see the plentiful larkspur and wild onions, the barren,
    colorless, sage-deserts,
I see in glimpses afar or towering immediately above me the
    great mountains, I see the Wind river and the Wahsatch
    mountains,   55
I see the Monument mountain and the Eagle's Nest, I pass the
    Promontory, I ascend the Nevadas,
I scan the noble Elk mountain and wind around its base,
I see the Humboldt range, I thread the valley and cross the river,
I see the clear waters of lake Tahoe, I see forests of majestic
    pines,
Or crossing the great desert, the alkaline plains, I behold
    enchanting mirages of waters and meadows,   60
Marking through these and after all, in duplicate slender lines,
Bridging the three or four thousand miles of land travel,
Tying the Eastern to the Western sea,
The road between Europe and Asia.

8. The Empress Eugénie, wife of Napoleon III, was on *L'Aigle*, the ship leading the procession
   in the ceremonies opening the Suez canal.
9. Lines 49–63 are descriptive of the railroad route from Omaha to San Francisco.

(Ah Genoese[1] thy dream! thy dream!   65
Centuries after thou art laid in thy grave,
The shore thou foundest verifies thy dream.)

4

Passage to India!
Struggles of many a captain, tales of many a sailor dead,
Over my mood stealing and spreading they come,   70
Like clouds and cloudlets in the unreach'd sky.

Along all history, down the slopes,
As a rivulet running, sinking now, and now again to the
    surface rising,
A ceaseless thought, a varied train—lo, soul, to thee, thy sight,
    they rise,
The plans, the voyages again, the expeditions;   75
Again Vasco de Gama[2] sails forth,
Again the knowledge gain'd, the mariner's compass,
Lands found and nations born, thou born America,
For purpose vast, man's long probation fill'd,
Thou rondure of the world at last accomplish'd.   80

5

O vast Rondure, swimming in space,[3]
Cover'd all over with visible power and beauty,
Alternate light and day and the teeming spiritual darkness,
Unspeakable high processions of sun and moon and countless
    stars above,
Below, the manifold grass and waters, animals, mountains,
    trees,   85
With inscrutable purpose, some hidden prophetic intention,
Now first it seems my thought begins to span thee.

Down from the gardens of Asia descending radiating,
Adam and Eve appear, then their myriad progeny after them,
Wandering, yearning, curious, with restless explorations,   90
With questionings, baffled, formless, feverish, with never-
    happy hearts,
With that sad incessant refrain, *Wherefore unsatisfied soul?* and
    Whither O mocking life?

Ah who shall soothe these feverish children?
Who justify these restless explorations?
Who speak the secret of impassive earth?   95

1. Christopher Columbus. *Cf.* "Prayer of Columbus," the following poem.
2. Correctly, da Gama: Portuguese navigator, first European to sail around Africa to India
   (1497–98).
3. In view of the unity of lines 81–115, it is not surprising that WW offered this passage to
   the magazines for independent prepublication.

Who bind it to us? what is this separate Nature so unnatural?
What is this earth to our affections? (unloving earth, without a
     throb to answer ours,
Cold earth, the place of graves.)

Yet soul be sure the first intent remains, and shall be carried out,
Perhaps even now the time has arrived.   100

After the seas are all cross'd, (as they seem already cross'd,)
After the great captains and engineers have accomplish'd their
     work,
After the noble inventors, after the scientists, the chemist, the
     geologist, ethnologist,
Finally shall come the poet worthy that name,
The true son of God shall come singing his songs.   105

Then not your deeds only O voyagers, O scientists and
     inventors, shall be justified,
All these hearts as of fretted children shall be sooth'd,
All affection shall be fully responded to, the secret shall be told,
All these separations and gaps shall be taken up and hook'd
     and link'd together,
The whole earth, this cold, impassive, voiceless earth, shall be
     completely justified,   110
Trinitas divine shall be gloriously accomplish'd and compacted
     by the true son of God, the poet,
(He shall indeed pass the straits and conquer the mountains,
He shall double the cape of Good Hope to some purpose,)
Nature and Man shall be disjoin'd and diffused no more,
The true son of God shall absolutely fuse them.   115

                              6

Year at whose wide-flung door I sing!
Year of the purpose accomplish'd!
Year of the marriage of continents, climates and oceans!
(No mere doge of Venice now wedding the Adriatic,)[4]
I see O year in you the vast terraqueous globe given and giving
     all,   120
Europe to Asia, Africa join'd, and they to the New World,
The lands, geographies, dancing before you, holding a festival
     garland,
As brides and bridegrooms hand in hand.

4. At the pinnacle of the power of Venice, the doge annually performed a ceremonial wedding
   of the city to the sea by throwing a ring into the Adriatic.

Passage to India!
Cooling airs from Caucasus far, soothing cradle of man,   125
The river Euphrates flowing, the past lit up again.[5]

Lo soul, the retrospect brought forward,
The old, most populous, wealthiest of earth's lands,
The streams of the Indus and the Ganges and their many
     affluents,
(I my shores of America walking to-day behold, resuming all,)   130
The tale of Alexander on his warlike marches suddenly dying,[6]
On one side China and on the other side Persia and Arabia,
To the south the great seas and the bay of Bengal,
The flowing literatures, tremendous epics, religions, castes,
Old occult Brahma interminably far back, the tender and
     junior Buddha,   135
Central and southern empires and all their belongings,
     possessors,
The wars of Tamerlane, the reign of Aurungzebe,[7]
The traders, rulers, explorers, Moslems, Venetians, Byzantium,
     the Arabs, Portuguese,
The first travelers famous yet, Marco Polo, Batouta the Moor,[8]
Doubts to be solv'd, the map incognita, blanks to be fill'd,   140
The foot of man unstay'd, the hands never at rest,
Thyself O soul that will not brook a challenge.

The mediæval navigators rise before me,
The world of 1492, with its awaken'd enterprise,
Something swelling in humanity now like the sap of the earth
     in spring,
                                                                         145
The sunset splendor of chivalry declining.

And who art thou sad shade?
Gigantic, visionary, thyself a visionary,
With majestic limbs and pious beaming eyes,
Spreading around with every look of thine a golden world,   150
Enhuing it with gorgeous hues.

As the chief histrion,
Down to the footlights walks in some great scena,
Dominating the rest I see the Admiral himself,[9]
(History's type of courage, action, faith,)   155

5. The valley of the Euphrates is, traditionally, the cradle of western civilization, and hypo-
   thetically associated with Noah's flood.
6. Alexander the Great died on his return journey from an invasion of India (323 b.c.e.).
7. Three hundred years apart in time, Tamerlane (1336?–1405), "Prince of Destruction," led
   wars of conquest in Turkey, Persia, India, and Russia; Aurungzebe (1618–1707), emperor
   of Hindustan and self-styled "Conqueror of the World," to some extent made good this boast
   in neighboring Mohammedan and Indian principalities.
8. Both Marco Polo (1254–1324), Venetian traveler who penetrated into far Cathay, and Ba-
   touta (1303–1377), a traveler in Africa and Asia, were agents of mercantile expansion.
9. Columbus, "Admiral of the Ocean Sea." Cf., above, "the chief histrion" (actor) and "the
   world of 1492." See also line 65, note.

Behold him sail from Palos[1] leading his little fleet,
His voyage behold, his return, his great fame,
His misfortunes, calumniators, behold him a prisoner, chain'd,
Behold his dejection, poverty, death.

(Curious in time I stand, noting the efforts of heroes,   160
Is the deferment long? bitter the slander, poverty, death?
Lies the seed unreck'd for centuries in the ground? lo, to
      God's due occasion,
Uprising in the night, it sprouts, blooms,
And fills the earth with use and beauty.)

                              7

Passage indeed O soul to primal thought,   165
Not lands and seas alone, thy own clear freshness,
The young maturity of brood and bloom,
To realms of budding bibles.

O soul, repressless, I with thee and thou with me,
Thy circumnavigation of the world begin,   170
Of man, the voyage of his mind's return,
To reason's early paradise,
Back, back to wisdom's birth, to innocent intuitions,
Again with fair creation.

                              8

O we can wait no longer,   175
We too take ship O soul,
Joyous we too launch out on trackless seas,
Fearless for unknown shores on waves of ecstasy to sail,
Amid the wafting winds, (thou pressing me to thee, I thee to
      me, O soul,)
Caroling free, singing our song of God,   180
Chanting our chant of pleasant exploration.

With laugh and many a kiss,[2]
(Let others deprecate, let others weep for sin; remorse, humiliation,)
O soul thou pleasest me, I thee.

Ah more than any priest O soul we too believe in God,   185
But with the mystery of God we dare not dally.

---

1. Spanish seaport from which Columbus sailed on August 3, 1492. Regarding the misfortunes
   of his last years (cf. lines 158–64), see WW's "Prayer of Columbus" (following), in which
   one may perceive an autobiographical overtone.
2. Lines 182–223 made up one of several ultimate components of "Passage to India" that
   originated as independent poems (see headnote). It was entitled "O Soul, Thou Pleaseth
   Me."

O soul thou pleasest me, I thee,
Sailing these seas or on the hills, or waking in the night,
Thoughts, silent thoughts, of Time and Space and Death, like
    waters flowing,
Bear me indeed as through the regions infinite,   190
Whose air I breathe, whose ripples hear, lave me all over,
Bathe me O God in thee, mounting to thee,
I and my soul to range in range of thee.

O Thou transcendent,
Nameless, the fibre and the breath,   195
Light of the light, shedding forth universes, thou centre of them,
Thou mightier centre of the true, the good, the loving,
Thou moral, spiritual fountain—affection's source—thou
    reservoir,
(O pensive soul of me—O thirst unsatisfied—waitest not
    there?
Waitest not haply for us somewhere there the Comrade
    perfect?)   200
Thou pulse—thou motive of the stars, suns, systems,
That, circling, move in order, safe, harmonious,
Athwart the shapeless vastnesses of space,
How should I think, how breathe a single breath, how speak,
    if, out of myself,
I could not launch, to those, superior universe?   205

Swiftly I shrivel at the thought of God,
At Nature and its wonders, Time and Space and Death,
But that I, turning, call to thee O soul, thou actual Me,
And lo, thou gently masterest the orbs,
Thou matest Time, smilest content at Death,   210
And fillest, swellest full the vastnesses of Space.

Greater than stars or suns,
Bounding O soul thou journeyest forth;
What love than thine and ours could wider amplify?
What aspirations, wishes, outvie thine and ours O soul?   215
What dreams of the ideal? what plans of purity, perfection,
    strength?
What cheerful willingness for others' sake to give up all?
For others' sake to suffer all?

Reckoning ahead O soul, when thou, the time achiev'd,
The seas all cross'd, weather'd the capes, the voyage done,   220
Surrounded, copest, frontest God, yieldest, the aim attain'd,
As fill'd with friendship, love complete, the Elder Brother
    found,
The Younger melts in fondness in his arms.

9

Passage to more than India!
Are thy wings plumed indeed for such far flights?   225
O soul, voyagest thou indeed on voyages like those?
Disportest thou on waters such as those?
Soundest below the Sanscrit and the Vedas?[3]
Then have thy bent unleash'd.

Passage to you, your shores, ye aged fierce enigmas!   230
Passage to you, to mastership of you, ye strangling problems!
You, strew'd with the wrecks of skeletons, that, living, never
    reach'd you.

Passage to more than India!
O secret of the earth and sky!
Of you O waters of the sea! O winding creeks and rivers!   235
Of you O woods and fields! of you strong mountains of my land!
Of you O prairies! of you gray rocks!
O morning red! O clouds! O rain and snows!
O day and night, passage to you!

O sun and moon and all you stars! Sirius and Jupiter!   240
Passage to you!

Passage, immediate passage! the blood burns in my veins!
Away O soul! hoist instantly the anchor!
Cut the hawsers—haul out—shake out every sail!
Have we not stood here like trees in the ground long enough?   245
Have we not grovel'd here long enough, eating and drinking
    like mere brutes?
Have we not darken'd and dazed ourselves with books long enough?

Sail forth—steer for the deep waters only,
Reckless O soul, exploring, I with thee, and thou with me,
For we are bound where mariner has not yet dared to go,   250
And we will risk the ship, ourselves and all.

O my brave soul!
O farther farther sail!
O daring joy, but safe! are they not all the seas of God?
O farther, farther, farther sail!   255
1871   *1881*

---

3. The ancient Hindu holy books, the Vedas, written in Sanskrit, became, in translation, influ-
ential in the age of Emerson, Thoreau, and Whitman.

Prayer of Columbus[1]

A batter'd, wreck'd old man,
Thrown on this savage shore, far, far from home,
Pent by the sea and dark rebellious brows, twelve dreary months,
Sore, stiff with many toils, sicken'd and nigh to death,
I take my way along the island's edge,
Venting a heavy heart.   5

I am too full of woe!
Haply I may not live another day;
I cannot rest O God, I cannot eat or drink or sleep,
Till I put forth myself, my prayer, once more to Thee,   10
Breathe, bathe myself once more in Thee, commune with Thee,
Report myself once more to Thee.

Thou knowest my years entire, my life,
My long and crowded life of active work, not adoration merely;
Thou knowest the prayers and vigils of my youth,   15
Thou knowest my manhood's solemn and visionary meditations,
Thou knowest how before I commenced I devoted all to come
    to Thee,
Thou knowest I have in age ratified all those vows and strictly
    kept them,
Thou knowest I have not once lost nor faith nor ecstasy in Thee,
In shackles, prison'd, in disgrace, repining not,[2]   20
Accepting all from Thee, as duly come from Thee.

1. This poem was first published in *Harper's Magazine,* March 1874, WW asking and receiving
$60 (*Corr.*, II, 259). It appeared in *Two Rivulets* (1876) and finally, improved by omission
of two mediocre lines and a phrase from another line, in *LG* 1881. A MS (Feinberg) of some
twenty scraps of paper of varying sizes shows considerable reworking of trial lines. WW wrote
to Ellen O'Connor, "as I see it now I shouldn't wonder if I have unconsciously put a sort of
autobiographical dash in it" (*Corr.*, II, 272). This was conscious understatement, and another
woman admirer, Mrs. Anne Gilchrist, made the identification explicit: "You too have sailed
over stormy seas to your goal—surrounded with mocking disbelievers—you too have paid
the great price of health—our Columbus" (Harned, 108). On January 23 of the preceding
year, WW had suffered a paralytic stroke; just four months later, May 23, he had lost his
mother; and during the 1870s, despite occasional placement of poems in the magazines, he
was feeling the public neglect. He, too, was battered, wrecked, and sore. But the deep
purport linking this poem with "Passage to India" (*cf.* lines 143–64) is the poet's profoundly
felt need of divine sanction for his work, his body of poetry that had come from the "potent,
felt, interior command," for which he, as Columbus, prays. See WW's prefatory note to the
1876 *Two Rivulets* text.
2. Columbus's dark years—his imprisonment after the third voyage, the death of Isabella, the
neglect by Ferdinand, the poverty and physical afflictions—were known to WW through the
pages of Washington Irving's *Life and Voyages of Christopher Columbus* (1828), available in
the 1861 Putnam edition of the *Works* and elsewhere. In fact, in the MS prose jottings
(Feinberg) for this poem, he transcribes several phrases verbatim from Irving's terminal essay,
"Observations on the Character of Columbus."

All my emprises have been fill'd with Thee,
My speculations, plans, begun and carried on in thoughts of Thee,[3]
Sailing the deep or journeying the land for Thee;
Intentions, purports, aspirations mine, leaving results to Thee.   25

O I am sure they really came from Thee,
The urge, the ardor, the unconquerable will,
The potent, felt, interior command, stronger than words,
A message from the Heavens whispering to me even in sleep,
These sped me on.   30

By me and these the work so far accomplish'd,
By me earth's elder cloy'd and stifled lands uncloy'd unloos'd,
By me the hemispheres rounded and tied, the unknown to the
     known.

The end I know not, it is all in Thee,
Or small or great I know not—haply what broad fields, what
     lands,   35
Haply the brutish measureless human undergrowth I know,
Transplanted there may rise to stature, knowledge worthy Thee,
Haply the swords I know may there indeed be turn'd to
     reaping-tools,
Haply the lifeless cross I know, Europe's dead cross, may bud
     and blossom there.

One effort more, my altar this bleak sand;   40
That Thou O God my life hast lighted,
With ray of light, steady, ineffable, vouchsafed of Thee,
Light rare untellable, lighting the very light,
Beyond all signs, descriptions, languages;
For that O God, be it my latest word, here on my knees,   45
Old, poor, and paralyzed, I thank Thee.

My terminus near,
The clouds already closing in upon me,
The voyage balk'd, the course disputed, lost,
I yield my ships to Thee.   50

My hands, my limbs grow nerveless,
My brain feels rack'd, bewilder'd,
Let the old timbers part, I will not part,
I will cling fast to Thee, O God, though the waves buffet me,
Thee, Thee at least I know.   55

Is it the prophet's thought I speak, or am I raving?
What do I know of life? what of myself?

---

3. The eroded comma was restored in the present edition.

I know not even my own work past or present,
Dim ever-shifting guesses of it spread before me,
Of newer better worlds, their mighty parturition,   60
Mocking, perplexing me.

And these things I see suddenly, what mean they?
As if some miracle, some hand divine unseal'd my eyes,
Shadowy vast shapes smile through the air and sky,
And on the distant waves sail countless ships,   65
And anthems in new tongues I hear saluting me.
1874   *1881*

The Sleepers[1]

1

I wander all night in my vision,
Stepping with light feet, swiftly and noiselessly stepping and
     stopping,
Bending with open eyes over the shut eyes of sleepers,
Wandering and confused, lost to myself, ill-assorted,
     contradictory,
Pausing, gazing, bending, and stopping.   5

How solemn they look there, stretch'd and still,
How quiet they breathe, the little children in their cradles.

The wretched features of ennuyés, the white features of
     corpses, the livid faces of drunkards, the sick-gray faces of
     onanists,

1. The fourth of the untitled twelve of the first edition, this poem was called "Night Poem" in
   1856, "Sleep-Chasings" in 1860 and 1867, and "The Sleepers" since 1871. It has undergone
   much revision, particularly in the withdrawal of difficult but interesting passages, not so
   much for aesthetic as for discretionary reasons; and of all WW's poems it may be said that
   this one most repays study of the first 1855 text. It is a powerful and original composition,
   one of the poet's most imaginative, and also one of the most esoteric. It is perhaps the only
   surrealist American poem of the nineteenth century, remarkable in its anticipation of later
   experiment. Bucke, WW's first official biographer and a professional student of the mind,
   was able in 1883 to characterize "The Sleepers" accurately as "a representation of the mind
   during sleep—of connected, half-connected, and disconnected thoughts and feelings as they
   occur in dreams, some commonplace, some weird, some voluptuous, and all given with the
   true and strange emotional accompaniments that belong to them. Sometimes (and these are
   the most astonishing parts of the poem) the vague emotions, without thought, that occa-
   sionally arise in sleep, are given as they actually occur, apart from any idea—the words
   having in the intellectual sense no meaning, but arousing, as music does, the state of feeling
   intended" (Bucke, 171–72). John Burroughs, on the other hand, confessed that he could
   not understand the poem, and he spoke for many (*Whitman: A Study*, 5). Perhaps the poet
   himself could not have explicated certain aspects of his vision, but the main theme is un-
   mistakable and moving. In the world of night the poet is both the dreamer and participant
   in the dreams of others; he identifies his consciousness with theirs—the whole experience
   becoming essentially one in which the darkness, symbolic of spiritual fulfillment, is an agent
   of invigoration and renewal. The penetration, the audacity of metaphor, the psychological
   insight of this poem, with its engagement of sexual fantasy, was unmatched in its time and
   challenges the best achievements—in this kind—of ours. For George B. Hutchinson, the
   poem provides "an ecstatic performance" of "the functions of a healer and prophet"; see his
   The Ecstatic Whitman: Literary Shamanism and the Crisis of the Union (Columbus: Ohio
   State University Press, 1986), 59–67.

The gash'd bodies on battle-fields, the insane in their strong-
    door'd rooms, the sacred idiots, the new-born emerging
    from gates, and the dying emerging from gates,
The night pervades them and infolds them.   10

The married couple sleep calmly in their bed, he with his palm
    on the hip of the wife, and she with her palm on the hip
    of the husband,
The sisters sleep lovingly side by side in their bed,
The men sleep lovingly side by side in theirs,
And the mother sleeps with her little child carefully wrapt.

The blind sleep, and the deaf and dumb sleep,   15
The prisoner sleeps well in the prison, the runaway son sleeps,
The murderer that is to be hung next day, how does he sleep?
And the murder'd person, how does he sleep?

The female that loves unrequited sleeps,
And the male that loves unrequited sleeps,   20
The head of the money-maker that plotted all day sleeps,
And the enraged and treacherous dispositions, all, all sleep.

I stand in the dark with drooping eyes by the worst-suffering
    and the most restless,
I pass my hands soothingly to and fro a few inches from them,
The restless sink in their beds, they fitfully sleep.   25

Now I pierce the darkness, new beings appear,[2]
The earth recedes from me into the night,
I saw that it was beautiful, and I see that what is not the earth
    is beautiful.

I go from bedside to bedside, I sleep close with the other
    sleepers each in turn,
I dream in my dream all the dreams of the other dreamers,   30
And I become the other dreamers.

I am a dance—play up there! the fit is whirling me fast!

I am the ever-laughing—it is new moon and twilight,
I see the hiding of douceurs,[3] I see nimble ghosts whichever
    way I look,
Cache[4] and cache again deep in the ground and sea, and
    where it is neither ground nor sea.   35

2. With this line the poet's vision deepens; he not only dreams but also experiences "the dreams
   of the other dreamers" with whom he identifies.
3. French: plural form of "delight" or "sweetness," but here, delight. From this line to the end
   of the passage (line 41) the poet subtly suggests the pleasures of erotic participation.
4. French: "a hiding place."

Well do they do their jobs those journeymen divine,
Only from me can they hide nothing, and would not if they could,
I reckon I am their boss and they make me a pet besides,
And surround me and lead me and run ahead when I walk,
To lift their cunning⁵ covers to signify me with stretch'd arms,
    and resume the way;   40
Onward we move, a gay gang of blackguards! with mirth-
    shouting music and wild-flapping pennants of joy!

I am the actor, the actress, the voter, the politician,
The emigrant and the exile, the criminal that stood in the box,
He who has been famous and he who shall be famous after to-day,
The stammerer, the well-form'd person, the wasted or feeble
    person.   45

I am she who adorn'd herself and folded her hair expectantly,⁶
My truant lover has come, and it is dark.

Double yourself and receive me darkness,
Receive me and my lover too, he will not let me go without him.

I roll myself upon you as upon a bed, I resign myself to the dusk. 50

He whom I call answers me and takes the place of my lover,
He rises with me silently from the bed.

Darkness, you are gentler than my lover, his flesh was sweaty
    and panting,
I feel the hot moisture yet that he left me.

My hands are spread forth, I pass them in all directions, 55
I would sound up the shadowy shore to which you are journeying.

Be careful darkness! already what was it touch'd me?
I thought my lover had gone, else darkness and he are one,
I hear the heart-beat, I follow, I fade away.

---

5. Used here in the sense of the Germanic root: "knowing," or "possessed of ability"; note that
the covered ones "signify"—make signs to—the speaker.
6. In this episode there seem to be three identities: "she," the lover, and the darkness, a pro-
found generative force of which "she" is aware, before and after the "lover" is received.

2

I descend my western course, my sinews are flaccid,[7]   60
Perfume and youth course through me and I am their wake.

It is my face yellow and wrinkled instead of the old woman's,
I sit low in a straw-bottom chair and carefully darn my
   grandson's stockings.

It is I too, the sleepless widow looking out on the winter mid-night,
I see the sparkles of starshine on the icy and pallid earth.   65

A shroud I see and I am the shroud, I wrap a body and lie in
   the coffin,
It is dark here under ground, it is not evil or pain here, it is
   blank here, for reasons.

(It seems to me that every thing in the light and air ought to
   be happy,
Whoever is not in his coffin and the dark grave let him know
   he has enough.)

3

I see a beautiful gigantic swimmer swimming naked through
   the eddies of the sea,   70
His brown hair lies close and even to his head, he strikes out
   with courageous arms, he urges himself with his legs,
I see his white body, I see his undaunted eyes,
I hate the swift-running eddies that would dash him head-
   foremost on the rocks.

What are you doing you ruffianly red-trickled waves?
Will you kill the courageous giant? will you kill him in the
   prime of his middle age?   75

Steady and long he struggles,
He is baffled, bang'd, bruis'd, he holds out while his strength
   holds out,
The slapping eddies are spotted with his blood, they bear him
   away, they roll him, swing him, turn him,
His beautiful body is borne in the circling eddies, it is
   continually bruis'd on rocks,
Swiftly and out of sight is borne the brave corpse.   80

7. With this line the poet begins to identify himself with a series of dream episodes in which
   death and loss are projected by the struggle of the brave swimmer, the wrecked ship, and—
   in three scenes from actuality—the Battle at Brooklyn Heights, the farewell of Washington
   to his troops, and the visit of the red squaw to the old homestead. *Western course*: the concept
   of the movement of race and culture from east to west was generally reflected in *LG*. *Cf.*
   "Facing West from California's Shores."

4

I turn but do not extricate myself,
Confused, a past-reading, another, but with darkness yet.

The beach is cut by the razory ice-wind, the wreck-guns sound,
The tempest lulls, the moon comes floundering through the drifts.

I look where the ship helplessly heads end on, I hear the burst
    as she strikes, I hear the howls of dismay, they grow
    fainter and fainter.   85

I cannot aid with my wringing fingers,
I can but rush to the surf and let it drench me and freeze
    upon me.

I search with the crowd, not one of the company is wash'd to
    us alive,
In the morning I help pick up the dead and lay them in rows
    in a barn.

5

Now of the older war-days, the defeat at Brooklyn,[8]   90
Washington stands inside the lines, he stands on the
    intrench'd hills amid a crowd of officers,
His face is cold and damp, he cannot repress the weeping drops,
He lifts the glass perpetually to his eyes, the color is blanch'd
    from his cheeks,
He sees the slaughter of the southern braves confided to him
    by their parents.

The same at last and at last when peace is declared,   95
He stands in the room of the old tavern, the well-belov'd
    soldiers all pass through,
The officers speechless and slow draw near in their turns,
The chief encircles their necks with his arm and kisses them
    on the cheek,
He kisses lightly the wet cheeks one after another, he shakes
    hands and bids good-by to the army.

6

Now what my mother told me one day as we sat at dinner
    together,   100

8. After the Battle of Brooklyn Heights, August 27, 1776, in which the Americans were deci-
sively worsted, Washington skillfully managed to ferry his troops across to New York to
prevent total disaster. WW wrote of the episode in his "Brooklyniana" sketches. (See UPP,
II, 267ff.)

Of when she was a nearly grown girl living home with her
    parents on the old homestead.

A red squaw came one breakfast-time to the old homestead,
On her back she carried a bundle of rushes for rush-bottoming
    chairs,
Her hair, straight, shiny, coarse, black, profuse, half-envelop'd
    her face,
Her step was free and elastic, and her voice sounded
    exquisitely as she spoke.   105

My mother look'd in delight and amazement at the stranger,
She look'd at the freshness of her tall-borne face and full and
    pliant limbs,
The more she look'd upon her she loved her,
Never before had she seen such wonderful beauty and purity,
She made her sit on a bench by the jamb of the fireplace, she
    cook'd food for her,   110
She had no work to give her, but she gave her remembrance
    and fondness.

The red squaw staid all the forenoon, and toward the middle
    of the afternoon she went away,
O my mother was loth to have her go away,
All the week she thought of her, she watch'd for her many a month,
She remember'd her many a winter and many a summer,   115
But the red squaw never came nor was heard of there again.

7

A show of the summer softness—a contact of something
    unseen[9]—an amour of the light and air,
I am jealous and overwhelm'd with friendliness,
And will go gallivant with the light and air myself.

O love and summer, you are in the dreams and in me,   120
Autumn and winter are in the dreams, the farmer goes with
    his thrift,
The droves and crops increase, the barns are well-fill'd.

Elements merge in the night, ships make tacks in the dreams,
The sailor sails, the exile returns home,
The fugitive returns unharm'd, the immigrant is back beyond
    months and years,   125
The poor Irishman lives in the simple house of his childhood
    with the well-known neighbors and faces,

---

9. The two final sections, 7 and 8, illustrate the great theme of return and retrievement under
the ministration of the night, the "mother," in whom the poet lay so long, and whom he
loves as much as he does the "rich running day." Compare the last lines, 177–84, with the
earlier passage on darkness, 46–54, and see note to line 46.

They warmly welcome him, he is barefoot again, he forgets he
    is well off,
The Dutchman voyages home, and the Scotchman and
    Welshman voyage home, and the native of the
    Mediterranean voyages home,
To every port of England, France, Spain, enter well-fill'd ships,
The Swiss foots it toward his hills, the Prussian goes his way,
    the Hungarian his way, and the Pole his way,   130
The Swede returns, and the Dane and Norwegian return.

The homeward bound and the outward bound,
The beautiful lost swimmer, the ennuyé, the onanist, the
    female that loves unrequited, the money-maker,
The actor and actress, those through with their parts and those
    waiting to commence,
The affectionate boy, the husband and wife, the voter, the
    nominee that is chosen and the nominee that has fail'd,   135
The great already known and the great any time after to-day,
The stammerer, the sick, the perfect-form'd, the homely,
The criminal that stood in the box, the judge that sat and
    sentenced him, the fluent lawyers, the jury, the audience,
The laugher and weeper, the dancer, the midnight widow, the
    red squaw,
The consumptive, the erysipalite, the idiot, he that is wrong'd,   140
The antipodes, and every one between this and them in the dark,
I swear they are averaged now—one is no better than the other,
The night and sleep have liken'd them and restored them.

I swear they are all beautiful,
Every one that sleeps is beautiful, every thing in the dim light
    is beautiful,   145
The wildest and bloodiest is over, and all is peace.

Peace is always beautiful,
The myth of heaven indicates peace and night.

The myth of heaven indicates the soul,
The soul is always beautiful, it appears more or it appears less,
    it comes or it lags behind,   150
It comes from its embower'd garden and looks pleasantly on
    itself and encloses the world,
Perfect and clean the genitals previously jetting, and perfect
    and clean the womb cohering,
The head well-grown proportion'd and plumb, and the bowels
    and joints proportion'd and plumb.

The soul is always beautiful,
The universe is duly in order, every thing is in its place,   155

What has arrived is in its place and what waits shall be in its
    place,
The twisted skull waits, the watery or rotten blood waits,
The child of the glutton or venerealee waits long, and the child
    of the drunkard waits long, and the drunkard himself
    waits long,
The sleepers that lived and died wait, the far advanced are to
    go on in their turns, and the far behind are to come on in
    their turns,
The diverse shall be no less diverse, but they shall flow and
    unite—they unite now.   160

8

The sleepers are very beautiful as they lie unclothed,
They flow hand in hand over the whole earth from east to west
    as they lie unclothed,
The Asiatic and African are hand in hand, the European and
    American are hand in hand,
Learn'd and unlearn'd are hand in hand, and male and female
    are hand in hand,
The bare arm of the girl crosses the bare breast of her lover,
    they press close without lust, his lips press her neck,   165
The father holds his grown or ungrown son in his arms with
    measureless love, and the son holds the father in his arms
    with measureless love,
The white hair of the mother shines on the white wrist of the
    daughter,
The breath of the boy goes with the breath of the man, friend
    is inarm'd by friend,
The scholar kisses the teacher and the teacher kisses the
    scholar, the wrong'd is made right,
The call of the slave is one with the master's call, and the
    master salutes the slave,   170
The felon steps forth from the prison, the insane becomes
    sane, the suffering of sick persons is reliev'd,
The sweatings and fevers stop, the throat that was unsound is
    sound, the lungs of the consumptive are resumed, the
    poor distress'd head is free,
The joints of the rheumatic move as smoothly as ever, and
    smoother than ever,
Stiflings and passages open, the paralyzed become supple,
The swell'd and convuls'd and congested awake to themselves
    in condition,   175
They pass the invigoration of the night and the chemistry of
    the night, and awake.

I too pass from the night,
I stay a while away O night, but I return to you again and love
    you.

Why should I be afraid to trust myself to you?
I am not afraid, I have been well brought forward by you,   180
I love the rich running day, but I do not desert her in whom I
    lay so long,
I know not how I came of you and I know not where I go with
    you, but I know I came well and shall go well.

I will stop only a time with the night, and rise betimes,
I will duly pass the day O my mother, and duly return to you.
   1855   *1881*

Transpositions[1]

Let the reformers descend from the stands where they are
    forever bawling—let an idiot or insane person appear on
    each of the stands;
Let judges and criminals be transposed—let the prison-keepers
    be put in prison—let those that were prisoners take the
    keys;
Let them that distrust birth and death lead the rest.
   1856   *1881*

To Think of Time[1]

1

To think of time—of all that retrospection,
To think of to-day, and the ages continued henceforward.

Have you guess'd you yourself would not continue?
Have you dreaded these earth-beetles?
Have you fear'd the future would be nothing to you?   5

Is to-day nothing? is the beginningless past nothing?
If the future is nothing they are just as surely nothing.

To think that the sun rose in the east—that men and women
    were flexible, real, alive—that every thing was alive,

---

1. This poem was reconstructed in 1881 from three lines—46, 44, and 22 (in that order)—of
the poem "Respondez," dropped in 1881, and originally titled (1856) "Poem of the Propo-
sitions of Nakedness." See notes on "Respondez" in the section of "Excluded Poems."
1. The third of the untitled twelve of the first edition, this poem was named "Burial Poem" in
1856, "Burial" in 1860 and 1867, and "To Think of Time" since 1871. Like "The Sleepers"
it has been considerably revised, although unchanged in essentials, and a comparison of the
various editions is interesting. As the earlier titles suggest, this poem poses the question of
death, which absorbed such nineteenth-century poets as Poe, Tennyson, Bryant, Words-
worth, and Dickinson. WW's poem, less complex than his other great poem dealing with
time and death, "Crossing Brooklyn Ferry," is nonetheless powerful in its blunt immediacy.
Its unevasive confrontation of the reader with the temporality of possessions and materials,
and with the ironic fact of transience within seeming permanence, is remindful of Emerson's
"Hamatreya."

To think that you and I did not see, feel, think, nor bear our part,
To think that we are now here and bear our part.   10

2

Not a day passes, not a minute or second without an
    accouchement,
Not a day passes, not a minute or second without a corpse.

The dull nights go over and the dull days also,
The soreness of lying so much in bed goes over,
The physician after long putting off gives the silent and
    terrible look for an answer,   15
The children come hurried and weeping, and the brothers and
    sisters are sent for,
Medicines stand unused on the shelf, (the camphor-smell has
    long pervaded the rooms,)
The faithful hand of the living does not desert the hand of the
    dying,
The twitching lips press lightly on the forehead of the dying,
The breath ceases and the pulse of the heart ceases,   20
The corpse stretches on the bed and the living look upon it,
It is palpable as the living are palpable.

The living look upon the corpse with their eyesight,
But without eyesight lingers a different living and looks
    curiously on the corpse.

3

To think the thought of death merged in the thought of
    materials,   25
To think of all these wonders of city and country, and others
    taking great interest in them, and we taking no interest in
    them.

To think how eager we are in building our houses,
To think others shall be just as eager, and we quite indifferent.

(I see one building the house that serves him a few years, or
    seventy or eighty years at most,
I see one building the house that serves him longer than that.)   30

Slow-moving and black lines creep over the whole earth—they
    never cease—they are the burial lines,
He that was President was buried, and he that is now
    President shall surely be buried.

4

A reminiscence of the vulgar fate,
A frequent sample of the life and death of workmen,
Each after his kind.   35

Cold dash of waves at the ferry-wharf, posh[2] and ice in the
    river, half-frozen mud in the streets,
A gray discouraged sky overhead, the short last daylight of
    December,
A hearse and stages, the funeral of an old Broadway stage-
    driver,[3] the cortege mostly drivers.

Steady the trot to the cemetery, duly rattles the death-bell,
The gate is pass'd, the new-dug grave is halted at, the living
    alight, the hearse uncloses,   40
The coffin is pass'd out, lower'd and settled, the whip is laid
    on the coffin,[4] the earth is swiftly shovel'd in,
The mound above is flatted with the spades—silence,
A minute—no one moves or speaks—it is done,
He is decently put away—is there any thing more?

He was a good fellow, free-mouth'd, quick-temper'd, not bad-
    looking,   45
Ready with life or death for a friend, fond of women, gambled,
    ate hearty, drank hearty,
Had known what it was to be flush, grew low-spirited toward
    the last, sicken'd, was help'd by a contribution,
Died, aged forty-one years—and that was his funeral.

Thumb extended, finger uplifted, apron, cape, gloves, strap,
    wet-weather clothes, whip carefully chosen,[5]
Boss, spotter, starter, hostler, somebody loafing on you, you
    loafing on somebody, headway, man before and man
    behind,   50
Good day's work, bad day's work, pet stock, mean stock, first
    out, last out, turning-in at night,
To think that these are so much and so nigh to other drivers,
    and he there takes no interest in them.

5

The markets, the government, the working-man's wages, to
    think what account they are through our nights and days,
To think that other working-men will make just as great
    account of them, yet we make little or no account.

2. Imitative of sound made by walking through slush. WW's use of this word in this line is
   cited in *Webster's Unabridged Dictionary.*
3. Probably WW, who made friends of stage drivers, had attended the funeral of one. See
   "Omnibus Jaunts and Drivers" in *Specimen Days* (*Coll W, Prose Works,* I, 18–19).
4. The driver's whip, according to custom, was buried with him.
5. Lines 49–51 are interesting in their employment of terms of the driver's trade that now
   belong to the past.

The vulgar and the refined, what you call sin and what you
    call goodness, to think how wide a difference,   55
To think the difference will still continue to others, yet we lie
    beyond the difference.

To think how much pleasure there is,
Do you enjoy yourself in the city? or engaged in business? or
    planning a nomination and election? or with your wife and
    family?
Or with your mother and sisters? or in womanly housework? or
    the beautiful maternal cares?
These also flow onward to others, you and I flow onward,   60
But in due time you and I shall take less interest in them.

Your farm, profits, crops—to think how engross'd you are,
To think there will still be farms, profits, crops, yet for you of
    what avail?

6

What will be will be well, for what is is well,
To take interest is well, and not to take interest shall be well.   65

The domestic joys, the daily housework or business, the
    building of houses, are not phantasms, they have weight,
    form, location,
Farms, profits, crops, markets, wages, government, are none of
    them phantasms,
The difference between sin and goodness is no delusion,
The earth is not an echo, man and his life and all the things
    of his life are well-consider'd.

You are not thrown to the winds, you gather certainly and
    safely around yourself,   70
Yourself! yourself! yourself, for ever and ever!

7

It is not to diffuse you that you were born of your mother and
    father, it is to identify you,
It is not that you should be undecided, but that you should be
    decided,
Something long preparing and formless is arrived and form'd in
    you,
You are henceforth secure, whatever comes or goes.   75

The threads that were spun are gather'd, the weft crosses the
    warp, the pattern is systematic.

The preparations have every one been justified,
The orchestra have sufficiently tuned their instruments, the
    baton has given the signal.

The guest that was coming, he waited long, he is now housed,
He is one of those who are beautiful and happy, he is one of
    those that to look upon and be with is enough.   80

The law of the past cannot be eluded,
The law of the present and future cannot be eluded,
The law of the living cannot be eluded, it is eternal,
The law of promotion and transformation cannot be eluded,
The law of heroes and good-doers cannot be eluded,   85
The law of drunkards, informers, mean persons, not one iota
    thereof can be eluded.

8

Slow moving and black lines go ceaselessly over the earth,
Northerner goes carried and Southerner goes carried, and they
    on the Atlantic side and they on the Pacific,
And they between, and all through the Mississippi country,
    and all over the earth.

The great masters and kosmos are well as they go, the heroes
    and good-doers are well,   90
The known leaders and inventors and the rich owners and
    pious and distinguish'd may be well,
But there is more account than that, there is strict account of all.

The interminable hordes of the ignorant and wicked are not
    nothing,
The barbarians of Africa and Asia are not nothing,
The perpetual successions of shallow people are not nothing as
    they go.   95

Of and in all these things,
I have dream'd that we are not to be changed so much, nor
    the law of us changed,
I have dream'd that heroes and good-doers shall be under the
    present and past law,
And that murderers, drunkards, liars, shall be under the
    present and past law,
For I have dream'd that the law they are under now is enough.   100

And I have dream'd that the purpose and essence of the
    known life, the transient,
Is to form and decide identity for the unknown life, the
    permanent.

If all came but to ashes of dung,
If maggots and rats ended us, then Alarum! for we are betray'd,
Then indeed suspicion of death.   105

Do you suspect death? If I were to suspect death I should die now,
Do you think I could walk pleasantly and well-suited toward
    annihilation?

Pleasantly and well-suited I walk,
Whither I walk I cannot define, but I know it is good,
The whole universe indicates that it is good,   110
The past and the present indicate that it is good.

How beautiful and perfect are the animals!
How perfect the earth, and the minutest thing upon it!
What is called good is perfect, and what is called bad is just as
    perfect,
The vegetables and minerals are all perfect, and the
    imponderable fluids perfect;   115
Slowly and surely they have pass'd on to this, and slowly and
    surely they yet pass on.

                            9

I swear I think now that every thing without exception has an
    eternal soul!
The trees have, rooted in the ground! the weeds of the sea
    have! the animals!

I swear I think there is nothing but immortality!
That the exquisite scheme is for it, and the nebulous float is
    for it, and the cohering is for it!
And all preparation is for it—and identity is for it—and life   120
    and materials are altogether for it!
1855   *1881*

WHISPERS OF HEAVENLY DEATH

Darest Thou Now O Soul[1]

Darest thou now O soul,
Walk out with me toward the unknown region,
Where neither ground is for the feet nor any path to follow?

No map there, nor guide,
Nor voice sounding, nor touch of human hand,   5
Nor face with blooming flesh, nor lips, nor eyes, are in that land.

I know it not O soul,
Nor dost thou, all is a blank before us,
All waits undream'd of in that region, that inaccessible land.

Till when the ties loosen,   10
All but the ties eternal, Time and Space,
Nor darkness, gravitation, sense, nor any bounds bounding us.

Then we burst forth, we float,
In Time and Space O soul, prepared for them,
Equal, equipt at last, (O joy! O fruit of all!) them to fulfil O
   soul.   15
1868   *1881*

Whispers of Heavenly Death: This group first appeared in *Passage to India* (1871) as a cluster of thirteen poems. In 1881 the poet added five poems, also from *Passage to India,* to make up the present eighteen. In this final grouping, the consonance of theme is maintained— the exploration of the "unknown region" of spiritual law and the acceptance of death as a fulfillment and a new beginning. One of these poems originated in *LG* 1856, nine in *LG* 1860, two in the 1865 *Drum-Taps,* and six in *LG* 1871. As early as November 22, 1867, the poet had written to his English admirer, William M. Rossetti, "It is quite certain that I shall add to my next edition (carrying out my plan from the first,) a brief cluster of pieces, born of thoughts on the deep themes of Death & Immortality" (*Corr.,* II, 350). Five of the poems had their first appearance in the English *Broadway Magazine* for October 1868: "Whispers of Heavenly Death," "Darest Thou Now O Soul," "A Noiseless Patient Spider," "The Last Invocation," and "Pensive and Faltering"; and by 1870, according to ms evidence (a booklet in the Feinberg Collection), he was considering these pieces, with eight more, either for a separate book or for a supplement that might be bound into a later edition of *LG.* See Harold W. Blodgett, "Whitman's *Whisperings,*" *WWR,* no. 7 (March 1962).
1. Appeared in *Broadway Magazine* (London), October 1868, the second of five numbered poems under the single title "Whispers of Heavenly Death." *Cf.* note above. They had been submitted in response to solicitation from G. Routledge and Sons, December 28, 1867 (Trau-bel, I, 263), to whom WW replied December 30, 1867, and again January 17 and February 19, 1868, accepting $50 in gold for the poems after an asking price of $120. (*Corr.,* I, 355; II, 13, 17–18). The poem was printed in *Passage to India* (1871), in the "Passage to India" supplement of *LG* 1871 and of *Two Rivulets* (1876), and in the present text (1881) with the word "bounding" in the twelfth line as a revision for "bound." The division into three-line stanzas gives an impressive sense of regularity.

Whispers of Heavenly Death[2]

Whispers of heavenly death murmur'd I hear,
Labial gossip of night, sibilant chorals,
Footsteps gently ascending, mystical breezes wafted soft and low,
Ripples of unseen rivers, tides of a current flowing, forever
    flowing,
(Or is it the plashing of tears? the measureless waters of
    human tears?)   5

I see, just see skyward, great cloud-masses,
Mournfully slowly they roll, silently swelling and mixing,
With at times a half-dimm'd sadden'd far-off star,
Appearing and disappearing.

(Some parturition rather, some solemn immortal birth;   10
On the frontiers to eyes impenetrable,
Some soul is passing over.)
1868   *1871*

Chanting the Square Deific[3]

1

Chanting the square deific, out of the One advancing, out of
    the sides,
Out of the old and new, out of the square entirely divine,

---

2. This poem was the first of the *Broadway* poems of October 1868. See above. It remained
unchanged in the 1871 and 1876 "Passage to India" supplement, and in 1881.
3. First printed in "Sequel to Drum-Taps" (1865–66), but WW wrote trial passages on the
theme earlier than *LG* 1855, e.g., see "Pictures" ("Uncollected Poems," below). Another trial
passage begins: "Two antique records . . ." (notebook, 1860–61, LC *Whitman*, No. 91,
published in *UPP*, II, 91–92, and in "Uncollected Poems"; trial titles were "Quadrel," 1860,
for the never-published *Banner at Daybreak*, and "Quadriune" or "Deus Quadriune," written
on the contents page of an *LG* 1860 ("Blue Copy," Lion). The long-mediated poem of 1865–
66 remained unaltered until the final edition except for two slight changes in *LG* 1881—
the substitution, in line 5, of "Time, old" for "Time" and the exclusion, after the present line
21, of the following line:

> (Conqueror yet—for before me all the armies and soldiers of the earth
>   shall yet bow—and all the weapons of war become impotent.)

    Of this poem WW remarked, "It would be hard to give the idea mathematical expression:
the idea of spiritual equity—the north, south, east, west of the constituted universe (even
the soul universe)—the four sides as sustaining the universe (the supernatural something):
this is not the poem but the idea back of the poem or below the poem. I am lame enough
trying to explain it in other words—the idea seems to fit its own words better than mine.
You see, at the time the poem wrote itself: now I am trying to write it" (Traubel, I, 156).
    WW here ignores theological creed or doctrine. Like Emerson's gnomic "Brahma," this
poem deals with the principles, moral and myth-making, that have been constant and com-
pounded in mankind's universal experience of spiritual or moral reality. Four principles ap-
pear, each in a separate canto: first, the elder God, uncreated creator, whose being is soul,
law, authority and time, as symbolized by Jehovah, Brahma, Saturnius, Kronos; second, the
principle of love—herald, messenger, and intercessor, the master of miracle and sacrifice,
typified by Jesus, Hermes, and Hercules. Emblem of revolt, pride, and guilt, Satan (Hebrew,
"enemy") is abundantly represented in the fallen gods and angels, demons and devils in the

Solid, four-sided, (all the sides needed,) from this side Jehovah[4]
    am I,
Old Brahm I, and I Saturnius am;[5]
Not Time affects me—I am Time, old, modern as any,   5
Unpersuadable, relentless, executing righteous judgments,
As the Earth, the Father, the brown old Kronos,[6] with laws,
Aged beyond computation, yet ever new, ever with those
    mighty laws rolling,
Relentless I forgive no man—whoever sins dies—I will have
    that man's life;
Therefore let none expect mercy—have the seasons,
    gravitation, the appointed days, mercy? no more have I,   10
But as the seasons and gravitation, and as all the appointed
    days that forgive not,
I dispense from this side judgments inexorable without the
    least remorse.

2

Consolator most mild, the promis'd one advancing,
With gentle hand extended, the mightier God am I,
Foretold by prophets and poets in their most rapt prophecies
    and poems,   15
From this side, lo! the Lord Christ gazes—lo! Hermes I—lo!
    mine is Hercules' face,
All sorrow, labor, suffering, I, tallying it, absorb in myself,
Many times have I been rejected, taunted, put in prison, and
    crucified, and many times shall be again,
All the world have I given up for my dear brothers' and sisters'
    sake, for the soul's sake,
Wending my way through the homes of men, rich or poor,
    with the kiss of affection,   20
For I am affection, I am the cheer-bringing God, with hope
    and all-enclosing charity,
With indulgent words as to children, with fresh and sane
    words, mine only,
Young and strong I pass knowing well I am destin'd myself to
    an early death;
But my charity has no death—my wisdom dies not, neither
    early nor late,
And my sweet love bequeath'd here and elsewhere never dies.   25

---

myths of man's spiritual adventure. Finally, the reconciling principle of the universal spirit,
"Santa Spirita," pervades all—God, Savior, and Satan.
4. In this context, one notes in Hebrew scriptures the persistence of these attributions: the
divinity of the Godhead; the Word or the One; the lawgiver; and the "consolator."
5. *Brahm*: Brahma—in Hindu theology the supreme spirit of the universe, the timeless and
uncreated creator, hence incomparable. *Saturnius*: Saturn—in Roman mythology the Titan
who preceded Jupiter as head of the Olympian hierarchy. Son of the primordial Uranus, he
was the first of the gods concerned for humanity; as god of seedtime and harvest and as
lawgiver, he produced the first "golden age" for mankind.
6. *Cronus*: in Greek mythology one of the most ancient gods, whom the Romans confused with
Saturn (see above). Born of the father-god, Uranus, whom he overthrew to rule in his place,
he was identified with time and the ancients' discovery of it.

3

Aloof, dissatisfied, plotting revolt,
Comrade of criminals, brother of slaves,
Crafty, despised, a drudge, ignorant,
With sudra face and worn brow, black, but in the depths of
    my heart, proud as any,[7]
Lifted now and always against whoever scorning assumes to
    rule me,   30
Morose, full of guile, full of reminiscences, brooding, with
    many wiles,
(Though it was thought I was baffled and dispel'd, and my
    wiles done, but that will never be,)
Defiant, I, Satan, still live, still utter words, in new lands duly
    appearing, (and old ones also,)
Permanent here from my side, warlike, equal with any, real as any,
Nor time nor change shall ever change me or my words.   35

4

Santa Spirita,[8] breather, life,
Beyond the light, lighter than light,
Beyond the flames of hell, joyous, leaping easily above hell,
Beyond Paradise, perfumed solely with mine own perfume,
Including all life on earth, touching, including God, including
    Saviour and Satan,   40
Ethereal, pervading all, (for without me what were all? what
    were God?)
Essence of forms, life of the real identities, permanent,
    positive, (namely the unseen,)
Life of the great round world, the sun and stars, and of man,
    I, the general soul,
Here the square finishing, the solid, I the most solid,
Breathe my breath also through these songs.   45
    1865–66   *1881*

Of Him I Love Day and Night[9]

Of him I love day and night I dream'd I heard he was dead,
And I dream'd I went where they had buried him I love, but
    he was not in that place,

7. The Sudra is the lowest Hindu caste.
8. The Holy Spirit. The familiar Christian phrases—"Spirito Santo" (Italian) and "Spiritus
    Sanctus" (Latin)—differ from WW's in being masculine and in the usual Latinic word order.
    If not an example of linguistic ignorance, as some suggest, WW's phrase is an inspired
    homonymous invention, affirming at once the secular spirit and the lofty meaning of this
    fourth canto.
9. Originally No. 17 of "Calamus" (*LG* 1860, Barrett MS "Poemet"), the poem acquired its
    present title in *LG* 1867. It was transferred in 1871 from *LG* "Calamus" to the new supple-
    ment, "Passage to India," appropriately, since it is more concerned with "whispers of heav-
    enly death" than with manly love.

And I dream'd I wander'd searching among burial-places to
    find him,
And I found that every place was a burial-place;
The houses full of life were equally full of death, (this house is
    now,)   5
The streets, the shipping, the places of amusement, the
    Chicago, Boston, Philadelphia, the Mannahatta, were as
    full of the dead as of the living,
And fuller, O vastly fuller of the dead than of the living;
And what I dream'd I will henceforth tell to every person and age,
And I stand henceforth bound to what I dream'd,
And now I am willing to disregard burial-places and dispense
    with them,   10
And if the memorials of the dead were put up indifferently
    everywhere, even in the room where I eat or sleep, I
    should be satisfied,
And if the corpse of any one I love, or if my own corpse, be
    duly render'd to powder and pour'd in the sea, I shall be
    satisfied,
Or if it be distributed to the winds I shall be satisfied.
1860   *1867*

Yet, Yet, Ye Downcast Hours[1]

Yet, yet, ye downcast hours, I know ye also,
Weights of lead, how ye clog and cling at my ankles,
Earth to a chamber of mourning turns—I hear the
    o'erweening, mocking voice,
Matter is conqueror—matter, triumphant only, continues onward.

Despairing cries float ceaselessly toward me,   5
The call of my nearest lover, putting forth, alarm'd, uncertain,
The sea I am quickly to sail, come tell me,
Come tell me where I am speeding, tell me my destination.

I understand your anguish, but I cannot help you,
I approach, hear, behold, the sad mouth, the look out of the
    eyes, your mute inquiry,   10
Whither I go from the bed I recline on, come tell me;
Old age, alarm'd, uncertain—a young woman's voice, appealing
    to me for comfort;
A young man's voice, *Shall I not escape?*
1860   *1871*

---

1. The second and third stanzas first appeared in *LG* 1860 as sections 5 and 6 of "Debris";
    they reappeared in *LG* 1867 as the poem "Despairing Cries." In 1871 the first stanza and
    present title were added when the poem appeared among the "Whispers of Heavenly Death"
    in *Passage to India* (1871). In his revised *LG* "Blue Copy," WW noted marginally: "tr[transfer]
    to Religious Leaves."

As If a Phantom Caress'd Me[2]

As if a phantom caress'd me,
I thought I was not alone walking here by the shore;
But the one I thought was with me as now I walk by the
    shore, the one I loved that caress'd me,
As I lean and look through the glimmering light, that one has
    utterly disappear'd,
And those appear that are hateful to me and mock me.   5
    1860   *1867*

Assurances[3]

I need no assurances, I am a man who is pre-occupied of his
    own soul;
I do not doubt that from under the feet and beside the hands
    and face I am cognizant of, are now looking faces I am
    not cognizant of, calm and actual faces,
I do not doubt but the majesty and beauty of the world are
    latent in any iota of the world,
I do not doubt I am limitless, and that the universes are
    limitless, in vain I try to think how limitless,
I do not doubt that the orbs and the systems of orbs play their
    swift sports through the air on purpose, and that I shall
    one day be eligible to do as much as they, and more than
    they,   5
I do not doubt that temporary affairs keep on and on millions
    of years,
I do not doubt interiors have their interiors, and exteriors have
    their exteriors, and that the eyesight has another eyesight,
    and the hearing another hearing, and the voice another
    voice,
I do not doubt that the passionately-wept deaths of young men
    are provided for, and that the deaths of young women and
    the deaths of little children are provided for,
(Did you think Life was so well provided for, and Death, the
    purport of all Life, is not well provided for?)

2. Appeared in *LG* 1860 as the final section of "Debris." In *LG* 1867 were added the first line and the title, and the final clauses of the third and fifth lines, all conforming with the poet's revisions in his "Blue Copy" of *LG* 1860.
3. First appeared in *LG* 1856 as sixteen lines, entitled "Faith Poem," and again without textual change in *LG* 1860, there entitled No. 7 among a "Leaves of Grass" cluster. In *LG* 1867, pruned to twelve lines by exclusion of four declarations, it appeared with the present title in the new cluster, "Songs before Parting." It was transferred in 1871 to the "Whispers of Heavenly Death" cluster in *Passage to India*, in which the present twelve-line text resulted from the exclusion of two lines in favor of two then added. The essential purport of the poem remained unchanged.

I do not doubt that wrecks at sea, no matter what the horrors
 of them, no matter whose wife, child, husband, father,
 lover, has gone down, are provided for, to the minutest
 points,   10
I do not doubt that whatever can possibly happen anywhere at
 any time, is provided for in the inherences of things,
I do not think Life provides for all and for Time and Space,
 but I believe Heavenly Death provides for all.
1856   *1871*

Quicksand Years[4]

Quicksand years that whirl me I know not whither,
Your schemes, politics, fail, lines give way, substances mock
 and elude me,
Only the theme I sing, the great and strong-possess'd soul,
 eludes not,
One's-self must never give way—that is the final substance[5]—
 that out of all is sure,
Out of politics, triumphs, battles, life, what at last finally
 remains?   5
When shows break up what but One's-Self is sure?
1865   *1871*

That Music Always Round Me[6]

That music always round me, unceasing, unbeginning, yet long
 untaught I did not hear,
But now the chorus I hear and am elated,
A tenor, strong, ascending with power and health, with glad
 notes of daybreak I hear,
A soprano at intervals sailing buoyantly over the tops of
 immense waves,
A transparent base shuddering lusciously under and through
 the universe,   5
The triumphant tutti,[7] the funeral wailings with sweet flutes
 and violins, all these I fill myself with,
I hear not the volumes of sound merely, I am moved by the
 exquisite meanings,

---

4. The long first line doubled as title in the first appearance, *Drum-Taps* 1865, and in the
 "Drum-Taps" supplement to *LG* 1867. It was transferred with present title to the "Whispers
 of Heavenly Death" cluster, *Passage to India* (1871). For two earlier MS drafts from an 1862–
 63 notebook (LG *Whitman*, No. 94), see Glicksberg, 125–26.
5. The concept of a "final substance" was reflected in ancient magic, alchemy, and science and
 may be said to survive in modern nuclear research.
6. Originally No. 21 of "Calamus," in *LG* 1860. Present title in 1867; transferred to the present
 group in *Passage to India* (1871). Original text unrevised except by insertion of "That" before
 the first line, a revision by WW in the "Blue Copy," *LG* 1860. The poem is WW's direct
 recognition of the power of music in his inspiration.
7. Italian: musical notation for full tonality of all instruments played simultaneously. See also
 note to line 52, "Proud Music of the Storm."

I listen to the different voices winding in and out, striving,
    contending with fiery vehemence to excel each other in
    emotion;
I do not think the performers know themselves—but now I
    think I begin to know them.
1860   *1867*

What Ship Puzzled at Sea[8]

What ship puzzled at sea, cons for the true reckoning?
Or coming in, to avoid the bars and follow the channel a
    perfect pilot needs?
Here, sailor! here, ship! take aboard the most perfect pilot,
Whom, in a little boat, putting off and rowing, I hailing you
    offer.
1860   *1881*

A Noiseless Patient Spider[9]

A noiseless patient spider,
I mark'd where on a little promontory it stood isolated,
Mark'd how to explore the vacant vast surrounding,
It launch'd forth filament, filament, filament, out of itself,
Ever unreeling them, ever tirelessly speeding them.   5

And you O my soul where you stand,
Surrounded, detached, in measureless oceans of space,
Ceaselessly musing, venturing, throwing, seeking the spheres
    to connect them,
Till the bridge you will need be form'd, till the ductile anchor hold,
Till the gossamer thread you fling catch somewhere, O my
    soul.   10
1868   *1881*

8. In *LG* 1860, the first four lines of "Calamus" No. 31, but in *LG* 1867 a separate poem
   entitled "Here, Sailor!" and so also in the present cluster in the "Passage to India" supple-
   ments in *LG* 1871 and *Two Rivulets* (1876). The present title appeared in *LG* 1881.
9. First appeared in *Broadway Magazine* (London), October 1868, the third of five numbered
   poems printed under the single title "Whispers of Heavenly Death," which survived as the
   title of the cluster in which this poem appeared in the "Passage to India" supplements of
   1871 and 1876. In *LG* 1881 the final revision is the substitution of "detached" for a second
   "surrounded" in line 7. An untitled MS version in a Washington notebook of 1862–63 (LC
   Whitman, No. 94) is significantly different (see *UPP*, II, 93). There the spider's symbolic
   outreaching filaments express the "Calamus" sentiment; here, as elsewhere in this section
   of *LG* (see, e.g., "Of Him I Love Day and Night"), WW's removal of a poem from "Calamus"
   to this section makes especially apparent the consonance between erotic desire and inti-
   mations of mortality in his writing.

O Living Always, Always Dying[1]

O living always, always dying!
O the burials of me past and present,
O me while I stride ahead, material, visible, imperious as ever;
O me, what I was for years, now dead, (I lament not, I am
    content;)
O to disengage myself from those corpses of me, which I turn
    and look at where I cast them,   5
To pass on, (O living! always living!) and leave the corpses
    behind.

1860   *1867*

To One Shortly to Die[2]

From all the rest I single out you, having a message for you,
You are to die—let others tell you what they please, I cannot
    prevaricate,
I am exact and merciless, but I love you—there is no escape
    for you.

Softly I lay my right hand upon you, you just feel it,
I do not argue, I bend my head close and half envelop it,
I sit quietly by, I remain faithful,   5
I am more than nurse, more than parent or neighbor,
I absolve you from all except yourself spiritual bodily, that is
    eternal, you yourself will surely escape,
The corpse you will leave will be but excrementitious.

The sun bursts through in unlooked-for directions,   10
Strong thoughts fill you and confidence, you smile,
You forget you are sick, as I forget you are sick,
You do not see the medicines, you do not mind the weeping
    friends, I am with you,

---

1. No. 27 of the "Calamus" group in *LG* 1860, this poem took its present title in 1867 and
was placed in the "Passage to India" supplement in 1871 and 1876, and in the "Whispers"
cluster in *LG* 1881. The 1860 text began:

        O Love!
        O dying—always dying!

    Present reading of the first line in *LG* 1867. The MS (Barrett) has the title "Leaf."
2. Originally one of the "Messenger Leaves" of *LG* 1860, this poem remained unchanged except
for line 8, to which the clause "you yourself will surely escape" was added in 1871 with the
poem's transfer to the "Passage to India" supplement. It was finally merged with the "Whis-
pers" in *LG* 1881. Of the two MSS (Barrett) one is the present text, but the other, a MS
fragment, gives the following variant:

    I must not deceive you—you are to die,
    I am melancholy and stern, but I love you—there is no escape for you.—
    I do not know your destination, but I know it is real and perfect.

I exclude others from you, there is nothing to be commiserated,
I do not commiserate, I congratulate you.   15
 1860   *1871*

Night on the Prairies[3]

Night on the prairies,
The supper is over, the fire on the ground burns low,
The wearied emigrants sleep, wrapt in their blankets;
I walk by myself—I stand and look at the stars, which I think
    now I never realized before.

Now I absorb immortality and peace,   5
I admire death and test propositions.

How plenteous! how spiritual! how resumé![4]
The same old man and soul—the same old aspirations, and
    the same content.

I was thinking the day most splendid till I saw what the not-
    day[5] exhibited,
I was thinking this globe enough till there sprang out so
    noiseless around me myriads of other globes.   10

Now while the great thoughts of space and eternity fill me I
    will measure myself by them,
And now touch'd with the lives of other globes arrived as far
    along as those of the earth,
Or waiting to arrive, or pass'd on farther than those of the earth,
I henceforth no more ignore them than I ignore my own life,
Or the lives of the earth arrived as far as mine, or waiting to
    arrive.   15

O I see now that life cannot exhibit all to me, as the day cannot,
I see that I am to wait for what will be exhibited by death.
 1860   *1871*

3. First appeared as No. 15 of the cluster "Leaves of Grass" in *LG* 1860; reprinted with WW's
   revisions ("Blue Copy," *LG* 1860) as No. 3 of a "Leaves of Grass" group in *LG* 1867, and
   with present title in the supplement, "Passage to India," 1871 and 1876, and in *LG* 1881
   as one of the "Whispers" cluster. The poet had not yet visited the prairie country when he
   composed his poem, nor when he added the emigrant camp passage (lines 2 and 3) in 1867.
   An interesting literary influence upon the thought of this poem was Joseph Blanco White's
   sonnet "Night," of which Dr. Bucke found WW's clipping. White (1775–1841) was an En-
   glish Unitarian clergyman, admired by Coleridge.
4. French: correctly, *résumé*, "summed up." WW's linguistic borrowings are sometimes effective
   (see note on "Santa Spirita" in "Chanting the Square Deific," above). Others, as in the
   present instance, leave something to be desired—perhaps an English equivalent.
5. *Cf.* in philosophy the classic distinction between the "me" and the "not-me" as two entities
   within the whole of reality. WW's magnificent dichotomy mounts in stages of contrast: of
   earth-light with what is beyond earth's darkness; of measurable space with eternal time; of
   earth-life with life on other globes; and finally, of knowledge of life with knowledge of death.

Thought[6]

As I sit with others at a great feast, suddenly while the music
    is playing,
To my mind, (whence it comes I know not,) spectral[7] in mist
    of a wreck at sea,
Of certain ships, how they sail from port with flying streamers
    and wafted kisses, and that is the last of them,
Of the solemn and murky mystery about the fate of the
    President,[8]
Of the flower of the marine science of fifty generations
    founder'd off the Northeast coast and going down—of the
    steamship Arctic going down,[9]   5
Of the veil'd tableau—women gather'd together on deck, pale,
    heroic, waiting the moment that draws so close—O the
    moment!
A huge sob—a few bubbles—the white foam spirting up—and
    then the women gone,
Sinking there while the passionless wet flows on—and I now
    pondering, Are those women indeed gone?
Are souls drown'd and destroy'd so?
Is only matter triumphant?   10
1860   *1871*

The Last Invocation[1]

At the last, tenderly,
From the walls of the powerful fortress'd house,
From the clasp of the knitted locks, from the keep[2] of the
    well-closed doors,
Let me be wafted.

6. Appeared in *LG* 1860 and 1867 as No. 5 of a cluster of poems entitled "Thoughts." With
the addition of the present lines 3 and 4, it appeared as a separate poem in the supplement,
"Passage to India" in 1871, 1872, and 1876. With no further change, it appeared in the
present cluster of the final 1881 *LG* text.
7. In its context WW's word has double meaning: the following pictures are like a spectre, but
they also have the quality of an image cast by the broken spectrum falling upon the mist.
8. The steamer *President* sailed from New York to Liverpool, March 11, 1841, with 136 persons
on board, and was never heard from again.
9. The steamer *Arctic*, sailing from Liverpool to New York, collided with the French steamer
Vesta on September 27, 1854, in a fog forty miles off Cape Race, Newfoundland; 350 were
lost, including many women and children.
1. The fourth of the five numbered poems first printed in the London *Broadway Magazine*,
October 1868. (See note on "Whispers of Heavenly Death.") Next it appeared in the present
group in the 1871 *Passage to India*; it was reprinted in *LG* 1872, in *Two Rivulets* (1876),
and finally, unaltered, in 1881. Of superb lyrical skill, it has often been set to music by
modern composers—among them, Frank Bridge (1919), Percival Garratt (1920), and James
H. Rogers (1919). In the words of John Livingston Lowes (*Convention and Revolt in Poetry*,
1919), the reader who will "let the words beat their own time" may find the clue to WW's
practice of constructing stanzas on the basis of repetitive accentual patterns of rhythm.
2. This archaic noun refers to the deep underground vaults of a dungeon or castle.

Let me glide noiselessly forth;   5
With the key of softness unlock the locks—with a whisper,
Set ope the doors O soul.

Tenderly—be not impatient,
(Strong is your hold O mortal flesh,
Strong is your hold O love.)   10
    1868   *1871*

As I Watch'd the Ploughman Ploughing[3]

As I watch'd the ploughman ploughing,
Or the sower sowing in the fields, or the harvester harvesting,
I saw there too, O life and death, your analogies;
(Life, life is the tillage, and Death is the harvest according.)
    1871   *1871*

Pensive and Faltering[4]

Pensive and faltering,
The words *the Dead* I write,
For living are the Dead,
(Haply the only living, only real,
And I the apparition, I the spectre.)   5
    1868   *1871*

Thou Mother with Thy Equal Brood[1]

1

Thou Mother with thy equal brood,
Thou varied chain of different States, yet one identity only,

3. This poem was first published in the 1871 *Passage to India,* again in that supplement in *LG* 1872 and *Two Rivulets,* 1876, and finally in *LG* 1881—each time in the cluster "Whispers of Heavenly Death." Remaining unchanged, it is one of the most successfully sustained of WW's little gnomic poems, the entire structure being a harmonious, functional vehicle for the fundamental aphorism (line 4).

4. The last of the five numbered poems first printed in the London *Broadway Magazine,* October 1868, this remained unchanged in the present group in the 1871 *Passage to India,* in *LG* 1872, in *Two Rivulets* (1876), and in the final *LG* 1881. Pertinent here again is the concluding comment in the note to "Ploughing," above.

1. In response to the invitation—not entirely guileless—of a group of Dartmouth seniors to deliver their commencement poem, June 26, 1872, WW composed "As a Strong Bird on Pinions Free," presented it in Hanover with only fair success, then published it that year as the title poem of a small volume containing seven other poems. This volume, without new pagination, became a supplement, bound in with *Two Rivulets* (1876). WW incorporated this poem in *LG* 1881 with minor revisions, adding the present first canto of four stanzas, which in *ASB* 1872 had appeared as "One Song, America, Before I Go." Its first stanza, increased to four lines, reiterated the new title here, and intensified its purport.

A special song before I go I'd sing o'er all the rest,
For thee, the future.
I'd sow a seed for thee of endless Nationality, 5
I'd fashion thy ensemble including body and soul,
I'd show away ahead thy real Union, and how it may be
    accomplish'd.

The paths to the house I seek to make,
But leave to those to come the house itself.

Belief I sing, and preparation; 10
As Life and Nature are not great with reference to the present
    only,
But greater still from what is yet to come,
Out of that formula for thee I sing.

                                2

As a strong bird on pinions free,
Joyous, the amplest spaces heavenward cleaving, 15
Such be the thought I'd think of thee America,
Such be the recitative I'd bring for thee.

The conceits of the poets of other lands I'd bring thee not,
Nor the compliments that have served their turn so long,
Nor rhyme, nor the classics, nor perfume of foreign court or
    indoor library; 20
But an odor I'd bring as from forests of pine in Maine, or
    breath of an Illinois prairie,
With open airs of Virginia or Georgia or Tennessee, or from
    Texas uplands, or Florida's glades,
Or the Saguenay's black stream, or the wide blue spread of Huron,
With presentment of Yellowstone's scenes, or Yosemite,
And murmuring under, pervading all, I'd bring the rustling sea-
    sound, 25
That endlessly sounds from the two Great Seas of the world.

And for thy subtler sense subtler refrains dread Mother,
Preludes of intellect tallying these and thee, mind-formulas
    fitted for thee, real and sane and large as these and thee,

Although the Dartmouth occasion had been arranged with evident intent to annoy the
faculty, WW took it in good faith as justifying his claim to national attention; indeed he
wrote a flamboyant press release for the Washington papers, which refused to run it (see
Perry, 205–10). For the volume of 1872, WW wrote an important preface reviewing his past
hopes and present plans with eloquent candor. This poem has deserved attention as a central
statement of WW's convictions about the role of the "equal brood" of the states in American
democracy, and the future of that democracy in the world order. The power of the idealism
has overcome the rhetoric. For an account of WW's Dartmouth reception, see Perry, 203–
10, and Harold W. Blodgett, "Walt Whitman's Dartmouth Visit," *Dartmouth Alumni Mag-
azine* 25 (February 1933): 13–15: MSS include a notebook with five pages of jottings on the
theme (Yale), some fragments of the poem (LG and Barrett), and the complete MS of the
printer's copy of 1872 (Berg).

Thou! mounting higher, diving deeper than we knew, thou
    transcendental Union!
By thee fact to be justified, blended with thought,   30
Thought of man justified, blended with God,
Through thy idea, lo, the immortal reality!
Through thy reality, lo, the immortal idea!

3

Brain of the New World, what a task is thine,
To formulate the Modern—out of the peerless grandeur of the
    modern,   35
Out of thyself, comprising science, to recast poems, churches, art,
(Recast, may-be discard them, end them—may-be their work is
    done, who knows?)
By vision, hand, conception, on the background of the mighty
    past, the dead,
To limn with absolute faith the mighty living present.

And yet thou living present brain, heir of the dead, the Old
    World brain,   40
Thou that lay folded like an unborn babe within its folds so long,
Thou carefully prepared by it so long—haply thou but
    unfoldest it, only maturest it,
It to eventuate in thee—the essence of the by-gone time
    contain'd in thee,
Its poems, churches, arts, unwitting to themselves, destined
    with reference to thee;
Thou but the apples, long, long, long a-growing,   45
The fruit of all the Old ripening to-day in thee.

4

Sail, sail thy best, ship of Democracy,[2]
Of value is thy freight, 'tis not the Present only,
The Past is also stored in thee,
Thou holdest not the venture of thyself alone, not of the
    Western continent alone,   50
Earth's *résumé* entire floats on thy keel O ship, is steadied by
    thy spars,
With thee Time voyages in trust, the antecedent nations sink
    or swim with thee,
With all their ancient struggles, martyrs, heroes, epics, wars,
    thou bear'st the other continents,
Theirs, theirs as much as thine, the destination-port triumphant;

---

2. Compare WW's use of this image with Longfellow's in the 1850 poem "The Building of the
   Ship," whose most famous passage begins: "Thou, too, sail on, O Ship of State!" WW's stanza
   was given separate publication in the *New York Tribune*, February 19, 1876, under the title
   "Ship of Democracy."

Steer then with good strong hand and wary eye O helmsman,
    thou carriest great companions,   55
Venerable priestly Asia sails this day with thee,
And royal feudal Europe sails with thee,

5

Beautiful world of new superber birth that rises to my eyes,
Like a limitless golden cloud filling the western sky,
Emblem of general maternity lifted above all,   60
Sacred shape of the bearer of daughters and sons,
Out of thy teeming womb thy giant babes in ceaseless
    procession issuing,[3]
Acceding from such gestation, taking and giving continual
    strength and life,
World of the real—world of the twain in one,
World of the soul, born by the world of the real alone, led to
    identity, body, by it alone,   65
Yet in beginning only, incalculable masses of composite
    precious materials,
By history's cycles forwarded, by every nation, language, hither
    sent,
Ready, collected here, a freer, vast, electric world, to be
    constructed here,
(The true New World, the world of orbic science, morals,
    literatures to come,)
Thou wonder world yet undefined, unform'd, neither do I
    define thee,   70
How can I pierce the impenetrable blank of the future?
I feel thy ominous greatness evil as well as good,
I watch thee advancing, absorbing the present, transcending
    the past,
I see thy light lighting, and thy shadow shadowing, as if the
    entire globe,
But I do not undertake to define thee, hardly to comprehend
    thee,   75
I but thee name, thee prophesy, as now,
I merely thee ejaculate!

Thee in thy future,
Thee in thy only permanent life, career, thy own unloosen'd
    mind, thy soaring spirit,
Thee as another equally needed sun, radiant, ablaze, swift-
    moving, fructifying all,   80
Thee risen in potent cheerfulness and joy, in endless great
    hilarity,
Scattering for good the cloud that hung so long, that weigh'd
    so long upon the mind of man,

---

3. Oscar Cargill (*Intellectual America*, New York, 1941) believes that this is the "one poem that
ties him [WW] most completely to his times" as "the natural voice of breeding and prolific
America, the Priapus of the new continent."

The doubt, suspicion, dread, of gradual, certain decadence of man;
Thee in thy larger, saner brood of female, male—thee in thy
    athletes, moral, spiritual, South, North, West, East,
(To thy immortal breasts, Mother of All, thy every daughter,
    son, endear'd alike, forever equal,)
Thee in thy own musicians, singers, artists, unborn yet, but
    certain,
Thee in thy moral wealth and civilization, (until which thy
    proudest material civilization must remain in vain,)
Thee in thy all-supplying, all-enclosing worship—thee in no
    single bible, saviour, merely,
Thy saviours countless, latent within thyself, thy bibles
    incessant within thyself, equal to any, divine as any,
(Thy soaring course thee formulating, not in thy two great
    wars, nor in thy century's visible growth,
But far more in these leaves and chants, thy chants, great
    Mother!)
Thee in an education grown of thee, in teachers, studies,
    students, born of thee,
Thee in thy democratic fêtes en-masse, thy high original
    festivals, operas, lecturers, preachers,
Thee in thy ultimata, (the preparations only now completed,
    the edifice on sure foundations tied,)
Thee in thy pinnacles, intellect, thought, thy topmost rational
    joys, thy love and godlike aspiration,
In thy resplendent coming literati, thy full-lung'd orators, thy
    sacerdotal bards, kosmic savans,
These! these in thee, (certain to come,) to-day I prophesy.

6

Land tolerating all, accepting all, not for the good alone, all
    good for thee,
Land in the realms of God to be a realm unto thyself,
Under the rule of God to be a rule unto thyself.

(Lo, where arise three peerless stars,
To be thy natal stars my country, Ensemble, Evolution, Freedom,
Set in the sky of Law.)

Land of unprecedented faith, God's faith,
Thy soil, thy very subsoil, all upheav'd,
The general inner earth so long so sedulously draped over, now
    hence for what it is boldly laid bare,
Open'd by thee to heaven's light for benefit or bale.

Not for success alone,
Not to fair-sail unintermitted always,

The storm shall dash thy face, the murk of war and worse than
    war shall cover thee all over,   110
(Wert capable of war, its tug and trials? be capable of peace,
    its trials,
For the tug and mortal strain of nations come at last in
    prosperous peace, not war;)
In many a smiling mask death shall approach beguiling thee,
    thou in disease shalt swelter,
The livid cancer spread its hideous claws, clinging upon thy
    breasts, seeking to strike thee deep within,
Consumption of the worst, moral consumption, shall rouge thy
    face with hectic,   115
But thou shalt face thy fortunes, thy diseases, and surmount
    them all,
Whatever they are to-day and whatever through time they may be,
They each and all shall lift and pass away and cease from thee,
While thou, Time's spirals rounding, out of thyself, thyself still
    extricating, fusing,
Equable, natural, mystical Union thou, (the mortal with
    immortal blent,)   120
Shalt soar toward the fulfilment of the future, the spirit of the
    body and the mind,
The soul, its destinies.

The soul, its destinies, the real real,
(Purport of all these apparitions of the real;)
In thee America, the soul, its destinies,   125
Thou globe of globes! thou wonder nebulous!
By many a throe of heat and cold convuls'd, (by these thyself
    solidifying,)
Thou mental, moral orb—thou New, indeed new, Spiritual
    World!
The Present holds thee not—for such vast growth as thine,
For such unparallel'd flight as thine, such brood as thine,   130
The Future only holds thee and can hold thee.
    1872   *1881*

A Paumanok Picture[1]

Two boats with nets lying off the sea-beach, quite still,
Ten fishermen waiting—they discover a thick school of

---

1. From *LG* 1856 through *LG* 1876, these seven lines constituted canto 8 of "Salut au Monde!"
together with an opening line now dropped. Then, with a sure aesthetic instinct, the poet
transferred them, almost without revision, to his 1881 edition as a single poem. In his 1902
"Variorum Readings," Oscar Lovell Triggs had noted the dropping of the lines without rec-
ognizing their happy reappearance. From the beginning, WW was able to transmit without
discussion the meaning of such quiet scenes, which have been compared with genre painting.
Such scenes are displayed with virtuosity in *Drum-Taps* (1865).

    mossbonkers[2]—they drop the join'd seine-ends in the water,
The boats separate and row off, each on its rounding course to
    the beach,[3] enclosing the mossbonkers,
The net is drawn in by a windlass by those who stop ashore,
Some of the fishermen lounge in their boats, others stand
    ankle-deep in the water, pois'd on strong legs,   5
The boats partly drawn up, the water slapping against them,
Strew'd on the sand in heaps and windrows, well out from the
    water, the green-back'd spotted mossbonkers.
1881   *1881*

FROM NOON TO STARRY NIGHT

Thou Orb Aloft Full-Dazzling[1]

Thou orb aloft full-dazzling! thou hot October noon!
Flooding with sheeny light the gray beach sand,
The sibilant near sea with vistas far and foam,
And tawny streaks and shades and spreading blue;
O sun of noon refulgent! my special word to thee.   5

Hear me illustrious!
Thy lover me, for always I have loved thee,
Even as basking babe, then happy boy alone by some wood
    edge, thy touching-distant beams enough,

2. Also "mossbunkers." The menhaden, a fish used for bait, or converted into oil and fertilizer.
3. Having joined the ends of two seine nets offshore, the boats return to the shore with the free ends, in opposite directions around a semicircle, trapping the fish in the looped nets.

From Noon to Starry Night: It is difficult to find an unmistakable unifying principle in this cluster, which is new to the final 1881 arrangement of *LG*, and one may sensibly conclude that the poet had none in mind. It is a miscellany both in source and theme, its twenty-two poems being brought together from seven different editions, 1855 to 1881. Here is the 1855 "Faces," a poem so salient that one wonders why WW did not give it a place to itself in the final arrangement, as he did to twenty-five other poems. Here also is the 1856 "Excelsior," a sort of confident catechism whose position has often shifted in the editions. Here are six brief poems of "inscriptive" intent from the third edition, and four from the *Drum-Taps* group. Nearly half of the poems are late arrivals—five, in fact, are new to the 1881 edition. However lacking in unity of theme or period of creation, the group as a whole is prevailingly reflective or retrospective, and characterized by lyric power and truth. At times the lyric satisfaction is only sporadic in a poem, as at the beginning of "Thou Orb Aloft . . ." or the end of "All is Truth." In the most noteworthy examples, chiefly shorter poems, the lyric propriety is nobly sustained—as in "To a Locomotive in Winter," "Mannahatta," "Spirit That Form'd This Scene," and "By Broad Potomac's Shore." Fittingly, the poet closes with "A Clear Midnight," excellent little coda of four lines, a strain appropriate to his concluding group, "Songs of Parting," which follows.
1. Published in *The American*, June 4, 1881, under the title "A Summer Invocation"; included under its present title in *LG* 1881. In a diary note of May 1881 (*Walt Whitman's Diary in Canada*, ed. by W. S. Kennedy, pp. 58–59), WW records: "Received back to-day the MS of the little piece of "A Summer's Invocation," which I had sent to H's [Harper's] magazine. The editor said he returned it because his readers wouldn't understand any meaning to it." Yet the poem is clearly a hymn to the sun, invoking its creative "fructifying light" to "strike through these chants" into the twilight and "starry nights" of his descending life. It is one of the better poems of the autumnal years. In the MS (LC *Whitman*, No. 29) the poet suggests several other titles, including "Sun-up" and "A Seashore Invocation."

Or man matured, or young or old, as now to thee I launch my
    invocation.

(Thou canst not with thy dumbness me deceive,   10
I know before the fitting man all Nature yields,
Though answering not in words, the skies, trees, hear his voice
    —and thou O sun,
As for thy throes, thy perturbations, sudden breaks and shafts
    of flame gigantic,
I understand them, I know those flames, those perturbations well.)

Thou that with fructifying heat and light,   15
O'er myriad farms, o'er lands and waters North and South,
O'er Mississippi's endless course, o'er Texas' grassy plains,
    Kanada's woods,
O'er all the globe that turns its face to thee shining in space,
Thou that impartially infoldest all, not only continents, seas,
Thou that to grapes and weeds and little wild flowers givest so
    liberally,   20
Shed, shed thyself on mine and me, with but a fleeting ray out
    of thy million millions,
Strike through these chants.

Nor only launch thy subtle dazzle and thy strength for these,
Prepare the later afternoon of me myself—prepare my
    lengthening shadows,
Prepare my starry nights.   25
1881   *1881*

Faces[2]

1

Sauntering the pavement or riding the country by-road, lo,
    such faces!
Faces of friendship, precision, caution, suavity, ideality,
The spiritual-prescient face, the always welcome common
    benevolent face,
The face of the singing of music, the grand faces of natural
    lawyers and judges broad at the back-top,
The faces of hunters and fishers bulged at the brows, the
    shaved blanch'd faces of orthodox citizens,   5
The pure, extravagant, yearning, questioning artist's face,

2. The sixth of the untitled twelve of the first edition, this poem was "Poem of Faces" in 1856,
"Leaf of Faces" in 1860, "A Leaf of Faces" in 1867, and "Faces" since 1871. Both the
surviving MS fragments (Barrett, Trent) and the revisions through the seven editions to 1881
show constant, but minor, reworking. The poet, always intent on the balance of real with
ideal, with brilliant imagery limns the faces of actuality, but his insistence is on fulfillment,
and his final images are those of victory and fruition.

The ugly face of some beautiful soul, the handsome detested
    or despised face,
The sacred faces of infants, the illuminated face of the mother
    of many children,
The face of an armour, the face of veneration,
The face as of a dream, the face of an immobile rock,   10
The face withdrawn of its good and bad, a castrated face,
A wild hawk, his wings clipp'd by the clipper,
A stallion that yielded at last to the thongs and knife of the
    gelder.

Sauntering the pavement thus, or crossing the ceaseless ferry,
    faces and faces and faces,
I see them and complain not, and am content with all.   15

2

Do you suppose I could be content with all if I thought them
    their own finalè?

This now is too lamentable a face for a man,
Some abject louse asking leave to be, cringing for it,
Some milk-nosed maggot blessing what lets it wrig[3] to its hole.

This face is a dog's snout sniffing[4] for garbage,   20
Snakes nest in that mouth, I hear the sibilant threat.

This face is a haze more chill than the arctic sea,
Its sleepy and wabbling[5] icebergs crunch as they go.

This is a face of bitter herbs, this an emetic, they need no label,
And more of the drug-shelf, laudanum, caoutchouc,[6] or hog's-
    lard.   25

This face is an epilepsy, its wordless tongue gives out the
    unearthly cry,
Its veins down the neck distend, its eyes roll till they show
    nothing but their whites,
Its teeth grit, the palms of the hands are cut by the turn'd-in
    nails,
The man falls struggling and foaming to the ground, while he
    speculates[7] well.

This face is bitten by vermin and worms,   30
And this is some murderer's knife with a half-pull'd scabbard.

---

3. A shortened form, now obsolete, of "wriggle."
4. Appeared as "sniffling" in *LG* 1860 only; corrected by WW in his "Blue Copy" revisions.
5. Spelled "wobbling" until *LG* 1881; colloquial, meaning "uncertainly toppling back and forth."
6. Crude rubber.
7. With the meaning, now rare, "to see, or contemplate."

This face owes to the sexton his dismalest fee,
An unceasing death-bell tolls there.

3

Features of my equals would you trick me with your creas'd
    and cadaverous march?
Well, you cannot trick me.   35

I see your rounded never-erased flow,
I see 'neath the rims of your haggard and mean disguises.

Splay and twist as you like, poke with the tangling fores of
    fishes or rats,[8]
You'll be unmuzzled, you certainly will.

I saw the face of the most smear'd and slobbering idiot they
    had at the asylum,   40
And I knew for my consolation what they knew not,
I knew of the agents that emptied and broke my brother,[9]
The same wait to clear the rubbish from the fallen tenement,
And I shall look again in a score or two of ages,
And I shall meet the real landlord perfect and unharm'd, every
    inch as good as myself.   45

4

The Lord advances, and yet advances,
Always the shadow in front, always the reach'd hand bringing
    up the laggards.

Out of this face emerge banners and horses—O superb! I see
    what is coming,
I see the high pioneer-caps, see staves of runners clearing the way,[1]
I hear victorious drums.   50

This face is a life-boat,
This is the face commanding and bearded, it asks no odds of
    the rest,
This face is flavor'd fruit ready for eating,
This face of a healthy honest boy is the programme of all good.

8. *Splay*: as verb: "spread open" or "cut open." *Fores*: When Dr. Bucke asked WW what he
    meant by this word, the poet answered, " 'fores': the front, the snout, whatever" (Traubel,
    IV, 243). In nautical language, the word in WW's time meant the "forward" part of anything;
    as for the "snout," those of fish and rat are similar in outline.
9. WW's brother, Eddie, born in 1835, was considered feebleminded and was cared for by the
    poet, whom he was to outlive by eight months.
1. The staff of authority, from ancient times, was carried before rulers or judges to clear the
    way.

These faces bear testimony slumbering or awake,   55
They show their descent from the Master himself.

Off the word I have spoken I except not one—red, white,
    black, are all deific,
In each house is the ovum, it comes forth after a thousand years.

Spots or cracks at the windows do not disturb me,
Tall and sufficient stand behind and make signs to me,   60
I read the promise and patiently wait.

This is a full-grown lily's face,
She speaks to the limber-hipp'd man near the garden pickets,
Come here she blushingly cries, *Come nigh to me limber-hipp'd*
    man,
Stand at my side till I lean as high as I can upon you,   65
Fill me with albescent honey, bend down to me,
Rub to me with your chafing beard, rub to my breast and
    shoulders.

5

The old face of the mother of many children,
Whist! I am fully content.

Lull'd and late is the smoke of the First-day morning,   70
It hangs low over the rows of trees by the fences,
It hangs thin by the sassafras and wild-cherry and cat-brier
    under them.

I saw the rich ladies in full dress at the soiree,
I heard what the singers were singing so long,
Heard who sprang in crimson youth from the white froth and
    the water-blue.   75

Behold a woman![2]
She looks out from her quaker cap, her face is clearer and
    more beautiful than the sky.

She sits in an armchair under the shaded porch of the farmhouse,
The sun just shines on her old white head.

Her ample gown is of cream-hued linen,   80
Her grandsons raised the flax, and her grand-daughters spun it
    with the distaff and the wheel.

---

2. The poet may here be portraying his maternal grandmother, Naomi Williams Van Velsor.
   See *FCI*, 44–45.

The melodious character of the earth,
The finish beyond which philosophy cannot go and does not
    wish to go,
The justified mother of men.
1855   1881

The Mystic Trumpeter[3]

1

Hark, some wild trumpeter, some strange musician,
Hovering unseen in air, vibrates capricious tunes to-night.

I hear thee trumpeter, listening alert I catch thy notes,
Now pouring, whirling like a tempest round me,
Now low, subdued, now in the distance lost.   5

2

Come nearer bodiless one, haply in thee resounds
Some dead composer, haply thy pensive life
Was fill'd with aspirations high, unform'd ideals,
Waves, oceans musical, chaotically surging,
That now ecstatic ghost, close to me bending, thy cornet
    echoing, pealing,   10
Gives out to no one's ears but mine, but freely gives to mine,
That I may thee translate.

3

Blow trumpeter free and clear, I follow thee,
While at thy liquid prelude, glad, serene,
The fretting world, the streets, the noisy hours of day
    withdraw,   15
A holy calm descends like dew upon me,
I walk in cool refreshing night the walks of Paradise,
I scent the grass, the moist air and the roses;
Thy song expands my numb'd imbonded[4] spirit, thou freest,
    launchest me,
Floating and basking upon heaven's lake.   20

---

3. First published in *The Kansas Magazine* for February 1872, which WW characterized in a letter to his brother Jeff of January 26, 1872, as "a new magazine, same style as the Atlantic— intended *for Western thought* & reminiscences etc—" (*Corr.*, II, 157). Successively reprinted in the 1872 volume *As a Strong Bird on Pinions Free*, in the 1876 *Two Rivulets*, and finally in its present position in *LG* 1881, in which the sole change was the removal of the adjective "wild" before "alarums" in line 43. Surviving MSS (Feinberg, Barrett, Trent, Hanley) show a great profusion of trial phrases and reworking from the first note to its final form. (See *FCI*, 13–14).
    For a suggestive reading of this poem, see Monica R. Weis, " 'Translating the Untrans-latable': A Note on 'The Mystic Trumpeter,' " *WWQR* 1, no. 4 (March 1984): 27–31.
4. Apparently a neologism, meaning "confined" or "fettered."

4

Blow again trumpeter! and for my sensuous eyes,
Bring the old pageants, show the feudal world.

What charm thy music works! thou makest pass before me,
Ladies and cavaliers long dead, barons are in their castle halls,
   the troubadours are singing,
Arm'd knights go forth to redress wrongs, some in quest of the
   holy Graal;   25
I see the tournament, I see the contestants incased in heavy
   armor seated on stately champing horses,
I hear the shouts, the sounds of blows and smiting steel;
I see the Crusaders' tumultuous armies—hark, how the
   cymbals clang,
Lo, where the monks walk in advance, bearing the cross on high.

5

Blow again trumpeter! and for thy theme,   30
Take now the enclosing theme of all, the solvent and the setting,
Love, that is pulse of all, the sustenance and the pang,
The heart of man and woman all for love,
No other theme but love—knitting, enclosing, all-diffusing love.

O how the immortal phantoms crowd around me!   35
I see the vast alembic ever working, I see and know the flames
   that heat the world,
The glow, the blush, the beating hearts of lovers,
So blissful happy some, and some so silent, dark, and nigh to
   death;
Love, that is all the earth to lovers—love, that mocks time and
   space,
Love, that is day and night—love, that is sun and moon and
   stars,   40
Love, that is crimson, sumptuous, sick with perfume,
No other words but words of love, no other thought but love.

6

Blow again trumpeter—conjure war's alarums.

Swift to thy spell a shuddering hum like distant thunder rolls,
Lo, where the arm'd men hasten—lo, mid the clouds of dust
   the glint of bayonets,   45
I see the grime-faced cannoneers, I mark the rosy flash amid
   the smoke, I hear the cracking of the guns;

Nor war alone—thy fearful music-song, wild player,[5] brings
    every sight of fear,
The deeds of ruthless brigands, rapine, murder—I hear the
    cries for help!
I see ships foundering at sea, I behold on deck and below deck
    the terrible tableaus.

7

O trumpeter, methinks I am myself the instrument thou
    playest,   50
Thou melt'st my heart, my brain—thou movest, drawest,
    changest them at will;
And now thy sullen notes send darkness through me,
Thou takest away all cheering light, all hope,
I see the enslaved, the overthrown, the hurt, the opprest of the
    whole earth,
I feel the measureless shame and humiliation of my race, it
    becomes all mine,   55
Mine too the revenges of humanity, the wrongs of ages, baffled
    feuds and hatreds,
Utter defeat upon me weighs—all lost—the foe victorious,
(Yet 'mid the ruins Pride colossal stands unshaken to the last,
Endurance, resolution to the last.)

8

Now trumpeter for thy close,   60
Vouchsafe a higher strain than any yet,
Sing to my soul, renew its languishing faith and hope,
Rouse up my slow belief, give me some vision of the future,
Give me for once its prophecy and joy.

O glad, exulting, culminating song!   65
A vigor more than earth's is in thy notes,
Marches of victory—man disenthral'd—the conqueror at last,
Hymns to the universal God from universal man—all joy!
A reborn race appears—a perfect world; all joy!
Women and men in wisdom innocence and health—all joy!   70
Riotous laughing bacchanals fill'd with joy!
War, sorrow, suffering gone—the rank earth purged—nothing
    but joy left!
The ocean fill'd with joy—the atmosphere all joy!
Joy! joy! in freedom, worship, love! joy in the ecstasy of life!
Enough to merely be! enough to breathe!   75
Joy! joy! all over joy!
    1872   *1881*

---

5. Erroneously printed as "prayer" in the *LG* 1924 "Inclusive Edition" and in several subsequent
    editions.

To a Locomotive in Winter[6]

Thee for my recitative,
Thee in the driving storm even as now, the snow, the winter-
    day declining,
Thee in thy panoply, thy measur'd dual throbbing and thy beat
    convulsive,
Thy black cylindric body, golden brass and silvery steel,
Thy ponderous side-bars, parallel and connecting rods,
    gyrating, shuttling at thy sides,   5
Thy metrical, now swelling pant and roar, now tapering in the
    distance,
Thy great protruding head-light fix'd in front,
Thy long, pale, floating vapor-pennants, tinged with delicate
    purple,
The dense and murky clouds out-belching from thy smoke-stack,
Thy knitted frame, thy springs and valves, the tremulous
    twinkle of thy wheels,   10
Thy train of cars behind, obedient, merrily following,
Through gale or calm, now swift, now slack, yet steadily
    careering;
Type of the modern—emblem of motion and power—pulse of
    the continent,
For once come serve the Muse and merge in verse, even as
    here I see thee,
With storm and buffeting gusts of wind and falling snow,   15
By day thy warning ringing bell to sound its notes,
By night thy silent signal lamps to swing.

Fierce-throated beauty!
Roll through my chant with all thy lawless music, thy swinging
    lamps at night,
Thy madly-whistled laughter, echoing, rumbling like an
    earthquake, rousing all,   20
Law of thyself complete, thine own track firmly holding,
(No sweetness debonair of tearful harp or glib piano thine,)
Thy trills of shrieks by rocks and hills return'd,
Launch'd o'er the prairies wide, across the lakes,
To the free skies unpent and glad and strong.   25
1876   *1881*

---

6. First published in a preview of *Two Rivulets* in the *New York Daily Tribune*, February 19,
1876, before the volume appeared; included without change in its present position in *LG*
1881. Fourteen pages of MS working notes, trial lines, and rough draft (Feinberg) show
the poet's effort to embody his conception. Notes on the intention of the poem include the
following: "The two ideas of Power & Motion (twins, dear to the modern) / Address the
locomotive as personally inviting it / Ring the bell all through & blow the whistle." The final
MS draft is in the Boston Public Library.
    Although very different as poets, both WW and Emily Dickinson, refusing the romantic
posture that science and industry are inimical to the Muse, were inspired by the locomotive.
Cf. Dickinson's "I like to see it lap the miles—."

O Magnet-South[7]

O magnet-South! O glistening perfumed South! my South!
O quick mettle, rich blood, impulse and love! good and evil!
    O all dear to me!
O dear to me my birth-things—all moving things and the trees
    where I was born—the grains, plants, rivers,
Dear to me my own slow sluggish rivers where they flow,
    distant, over flats of silvery sands or through swamps,
Dear to me the Roanoke, the Savannah, the Altamahaw, the
    Pedee, the Tombigbee, the Santee, the Coosa and the
    Sabine,[8]   5
O pensive, far away wandering, I return with my soul to haunt
    their banks again,
Again in Florida I float on transparent lakes, I float on the
    Okeechobee,[9] I cross the hummock-land or through
    pleasant openings or dense forests,
I see the parrots in the woods, I see the papaw-tree and the
    blossoming titi;
Again, sailing in my coaster on deck, I coast off Georgia, I
    coast up the Carolinas,
I see where the live-oak is growing, I see where the yellow-
    pine, the scented bay-tree, the lemon and orange, the
    cypress, the graceful palmetto,   10
I pass rude sea-headlands and enter Pamlico sound[1] through
    an inlet, and dart my vision inland;
O the cotton plant! the growing fields of rice, sugar, hemp!
The cactus guarded with thorns, the laurel-tree with large
    white flowers,
The range afar, the richness and barrenness, the old woods
    charged with mistletoe and trailing moss,
The piney odor and the gloom, the awful natural stillness,
    (here in these dense swamps the freebooter carries his
    gun, and the fugitive has his conceal'd hut;)   15
O the strange fascination of these half-known half-impassable
    swamps, infested by reptiles, resounding with the bellow
    of the alligator, the sad noises of the night-owl and the
    wild-cat, and the whirr of the rattlesnake,
The mocking-bird, the American mimic, singing all the
    forenoon, singing through the moon-lit night,
The humming-bird, the wild turkey, the raccoon, the opossum;

7. First printed in *LG* 1860 and in the July 15, 1860, issue of *The Southern Literary Messenger*
as "Longings for Home," the poem was reprinted unchanged in text and title through the
editions of 1867, 1871, and 1876. In 1881 it received its present title and position, with
two changes: "Tennessee" was dropped for "Kentucky" in line 19, and the following line
after the present line 19 was also dropped: "An Arkansas prairie—a sleeping lake, or still
bayou." WW's liking for the South, recalling his New Orleans days, is of course genuine
enough; yet the passion expressed here, with its luxuriant phrasing, may seem faintly facti-
tious, as if for the occasion.
8. Rivers of the Deep South.
9. Lake in south-central Florida.
1. Channel between the coast and islands off North Carolina.

A Kentucky corn-field, the tall, graceful, long-leav'd corn,
    slender, flapping, bright green, with tassels, with beautiful
    ears each well-sheath'd in its husk;
O my heart! O tender and fierce pangs, I can stand them not,
    I will depart;   20
O to be a Virginian where I grew up! O to be a Carolinian!
O longings irrepressible! O I will go back to old Tennessee and
    never wander more.

1860   *1881*

Mannahatta[2]

I was asking for something specific and perfect for my city,
Whereupon lo! upsprang the aboriginal name.[3]

Now I see what there is in a name, a word, liquid, sane,
    unruly, musical, self-sufficient,
I see that the word of my city is that word from of old,
Because I see that word nested in nests of water-bays, superb,   5
Rich, hemm'd thick all around with sailships and steamships,
    an island sixteen miles long, solid-founded,
Numberless crowded streets, high growths of iron, slender,
    strong, light, splendidly uprising toward clear skies,
Tides swift and ample, well-loved by me, toward sundown,
The flowing sea-currents, the little islands, larger adjoining
    islands, the heights, the villas,
The countless masts, the white shore-steamers, the lighters,
    the ferry-boats, the black sea-steamers well-model'd,   10
The down-town streets, the jobbers' houses of business, the
    houses of business of the ship-merchants and money-
    brokers, the river-streets,
Immigrants arriving, fifteen or twenty thousand in a week,
The carts hauling goods, the manly race of drivers of horses,
    the brown-faced sailors,

2. First appeared, with the present title, in *LG* 1860; reprinted in *LG* 1867; incorporated in a
    "Leaves of Grass" group in *LG* 1871 and in the present cluster in *LG* 1881 with three
    concluding lines—after line 17—that are substituted for an excluded seven-line conclusion
    that is worth the attention of the student:

        The parades, processions, bugles playing, flags flying, drums beating;
        A million people—manners free and superb—open voices—hospitality—
            the most courageous and friendly young men;
        The free city! no slaves! no owners of slaves!
        The beautiful city, the city of hurried and sparkling waters! the city of
            spires and masts!
        The city nested in bays! my city!
        The city of such women, I am mad to be with them! I will return after
            death to be with them!
        The city of such young men, I swear I cannot live happy without I often
            go talk, walk, eat, drink, sleep, with them!

    "Mannahatta" is unquestionably WW's city, and he is its bard. The MS (Barrett) shows little
    variation from the text.
3. *Cf.* note, line 5, "Me Imperturbe."

The summer air, the bright sun shining, and the sailing clouds
    aloft,
The winter snows, the sleigh-bells, the broken ice in the river,
    passing along up or down with the flood-tide or ebb-tide,   15
The mechanics of the city, the masters, well-form'd, beautiful-
    faced, looking you straight in the eyes,
Trottoirs throng'd, vehicles, Broadway, the women, the shops
    and shows,
A million people—manners free and superb—open voices—
    hospitality—the most courageous and friendly young men,
City of hurried and sparkling waters! city of spires and masts!
City nested in bays! my city!   20
    1860   *1881*

All is Truth[4]

O me, man of slack faith so long,
Standing aloof, denying portions so long,
Only aware to-day of compact all-diffused truth,
Discovering to-day there is no lie or form of lie, and can be
    none, but grows as inevitably upon itself as the truth does
    upon itself,
Or as any law of the earth or any natural production of the
    earth does.   5

(This is curious and may not be realized immediately, but it
    must be realized,
I feel in myself that I represent falsehoods equally with the rest,
And that the universe does.)

Where has fail'd a perfect return indifferent of lies or the truth?
Is it upon the ground, or in water or fire? or in the spirit of
    man? or in the meat and blood?   10

Meditating among liars and retreating sternly into myself, I see
    that there are really no liars or lies after all,

---

4. Appeared as "Leaves of Grass" No. 18 in *LG* 1860; as "Leaves of Grass" No. 1 in the
supplementary "Songs Before Parting" of *LG* 1867; again as part of another "Leaves of Grass"
group in *LG* 1871 but with its present title; and finally in the present cluster in *LG* 1881.
MS title, "As of the Truth" (Barrett). The text remained unchanged except that, after *LG*
1860, WW dropped the interesting third line: "Me with mole's eyes, unrisen to buoyancy
and vision—unfree."
    WW's answer to Pilate's eternal question, "What is truth," was influenced by Hegelian
idealism, reflected through Emerson, Coleridge, and other authors familiar to his youth. The
relation of truth > falsehood, like that of good > evil, presented to the poet a genuine
philosophic dichotomy, the two seemingly integral halves of the whole being, like positive
and negative, attracted by and dependent upon each other. In the long run, WW says, in
the "perfect return," each of these temporal microcosms is comprised in the eternal mac-
rocosm. The poem may express WW's personal solution of this perplexing paradox, leaving
him free to "sing and laugh and deny nothing." See Emerson's poem, "Each and All."

And that nothing fails its perfect return, and that what are
    called lies are perfect returns,
And that each thing exactly represents itself and what has
    preceded it,
And that the truth includes all, and is compact just as much
    as space is compact,
And that there is no flaw or vacuum in the amount of the
    truth—but that all is truth without exception;   15
And henceforth I will go celebrate any thing I see or am,
And sing and laugh and deny nothing.
1860   *1871*

A Riddle Song[5]

That which eludes this verse and any verse,
Unheard by sharpest ear, unform'd in clearest eye or
    cunningest mind,
Nor lore nor fame, nor happiness nor wealth,
And yet the pulse of every heart and life throughout the world
    incessantly,
Which you and I and all pursuing ever ever miss,   5
Open but still a secret, the real of the real, an illusion,
Costless, vouchsafed to each, yet never man the owner,
Which poets vainly seek to put in rhyme, historians in prose,
Which sculptor never chisel'd yet, nor painter painted,
Which vocalist never sung, nor orator nor actor ever utter'd,   10
Invoking here and now I challenge for my song.

Indifferently, 'mid public, private haunts, in solitude,
Behind the mountain and the wood,
Companion of the city's busiest streets, through the assemblage,
It and its radiations constantly glide.   15

In looks of fair unconscious babes,
Or strangely in the coffin'd dead,
Or show of breaking dawn or stars by night,
As some dissolving delicate film of dreams,
Hiding yet lingering.   20

Two little breaths of words comprising it,
Two words, yet all from first to last comprised in it.

---

5. One of the new poems of the 1881 *LG*, "A Riddle Song" was first published in *Forney's Progress*, Philadelphia, April 17, 1880, with acknowledgement to the "Sunnyside Press" (WW's letter, May 9, 1880, to John Burroughs; Barrus, 191). Dr. R. M. Bucke wrote to WW August 29, 1888, that he had been thinking over the "Riddle Song" and had made up his mind that the answer was "good cause" or "old cause." Traubel reports that the poet would not verify. "Horace, I made the puzzle: it's not my business to solve" (Traubel, II, 228). In his *The Fight of a Book for the World*, page 188, W. S. Kennedy ventures another guess,—that the "two words" are "The Ideal."

How ardently for it!
How many ships have sail'd and sunk for it!
How many travelers started from their homes and ne'er return'd!   25
How much of genius boldly staked and lost for it!
What countless stores of beauty, love, ventur'd for it!
How all superbest deeds since Time began are traceable to it—
      and shall be to the end!
How all heroic martyrdoms to it!
How, justified by it, the horrors, evils, battles of the earth!   30
How the bright fascinating lambent flames of it, in every age
      and land, have drawn men's eyes,
Rich as a sunset on the Norway coast, the sky, the islands, and
      the cliffs,
Or midnight's silent glowing northern lights unreachable.

Haply God's riddle it, so vague and yet so certain,
The soul for it, and all the visible universe for it,   35
And heaven at last for it.
      1880   *1881*

Excelsior[6]

Who has gone farthest? for I would go farther,
And who has been just? for I would be the most just person of
      the earth,
And who most cautious? for I would be more cautious,
And who has been happiest? O I think it is I—I think no one
      was ever happier than I,
And who has lavish'd all? for I lavish constantly the best I
      have,   5
And who proudest? for I think I have reason to be the
      proudest son alive—for I am the son of the brawny and
      tall-topt city,
And who has been bold and true? for I would be the boldest
      and truest being of the universe,

---

6. Appeared in *LG* 1856 with the title "Poem of The Heart of The Son of Manhattan Island,"
   affirming its character as personal credo; entitled "Chants Democratic" No. 15 in *LG* 1860;
   gained present title in 1867. Appeared in 1871 in the "Passage to India" supplement, and
   in *LG* 1881 in the present group. The shaping process was interesting. Two lines suggested
   in *LG* 1860 "Blue Copy" revisions were not added:
   > And who has adopted the loftiest motto?
   > O I will put my motto over it, as it is over the top of this Song!

   The following line, the tenth of the 1856 text, was dropped, after the 1871 revision, in 1881:
   > And who has projected beautiful words through the longest time? By God!
   > I will outvie him! I will say such words, they shall stretch through
   > longer time!

   Still another line, the twelfth of the 1856 text, was dropped in 1871:
   > And to whom has been given the sweetest from women, and paid them in
   > kind? For I will take the like sweets, and pay them in kind.

And who benevolent? for I would show more benevolence than
 all the rest,
And who has receiv'd the love of the most friends? for I know
 what it is to receive the passionate love of many friends,
And who possesses a perfect and enamour'd body? for I do not
 believe any one possesses a more perfect or enamour'd
 body than mine,   10
And who thinks the amplest thoughts? for I would surround
 those thoughts,
And who has made hymns fit for the earth? for I am mad with
 devouring ecstasy to make joyous hymns for the whole
 earth.
1856   *1881*

Ah Poverties, Wincings, and Sulky Retreats[7]

Ah poverties, wincings, and sulky retreats,
Ah you foes that in conflict have overcome me,
(For what is my life or any man's life but a conflict with foes,
 the old, the incessant war?)
You degradations, you tussle with passions and appetites,
You smarts from dissatisfied friendships, (ah wounds the
 sharpest of all!)   5
You toil of painful and choked articulations, you meannesses,
You shallow tongue-talks at tables, (my tongue the shallowest
 of any;)
You broken resolutions, you racking angers, you smother'd ennuis!
Ah think not you finally triumph, my real self has yet to come
 forth,
It shall yet march forth o'ermastering, till all lies beneath me, 10
It shall yet stand up the soldier of ultimate victory.
1865–66   *1881*

Thoughts[8]

Of public opinion,
Of a calm and cool fiat sooner or later, (how impassive! how
 certain and final!)

---

7. Appeared in "Sequel to Drum-Taps" (1865–66), and reprinted in all later editions without change of title or text, except for the substitution, in *LG* 1881, of "ultimate" for "unquestioned." During the crisis years of the early 1860s, the poet, deeply perturbed but invincibly hopeful, entered into his notebooks just such adjuration to himself as the sentiments here express.
8. Entitled "Thought" in *LG* 1860 and 1867, and "Thoughts" thereafter. In the 1860 *LG* "Blue Copy" revisions WW cancelled this poem, but he retained it in all editions, with the minor revision of two words in 1881. The theme is a common one with the poet—the celebration of democracy sustained by the intuitive wisdom of the people as against the impotence of institutionalism.

Of the President with pale face asking secretly to himself,
What will the people say at last?
Of the frivolous Judge—of the corrupt Congressman,
Governor, Mayor—of such as these standing helpless and
exposed,
Of the mumbling and screaming priest, (received, soon deserted,)   5
Of the lessening year by year of venerableness, and of the
dicta of officers, statutes, pulpits, schools,
Of the rising forever taller and stronger and broader of the
intuitions of men and women, and of Self-esteem and
Personality;
Of the true New World—of the Democracies resplendent en-masse,
Of the conformity of politics, armies, navies, to them,
Of the shining sun by them—of the inherent light, greater
than the rest,   10
Of the envelopment of all by them, and the effusion of all
from them.
1860   1881

Mediums[9]

They shall arise in the States,
They shall report Nature, laws, physiology, and happiness,
They shall illustrate Democracy and the kosmos,
They shall be alimentive, amative, perceptive,
They shall be complete women and men, their pose brawny
and supple, their drink water, their blood clean and clear,   5
They shall fully enjoy materialism and the sight of products,
they shall enjoy the sight of the beef, lumber, bread-stuffs,
of Chicago the great city,
They shall train themselves to go in public to become orators
and oratresses,
Strong and sweet shall their tongues be, poems and materials
of poems shall come from their lives, they shall be makers
and finders,
Of them and of their works shall emerge divine conveyers, to
convey gospels,[1]
Characters, events, retrospections, shall be convey'd in gospels,
trees, animals, waters, shall be convey'd.   10
Death, the future, the invisible faith, shall all be convey'd.
1860   1871

9. Originally "Chants Democratic" No. 16 in *LG* 1860; received present title in 1867; trans-
ferred in 1871 to *Passage to India* and in *LG* 1881 to the present cluster. The one significant
variant shows only in the MS (Barrett)—"America" instead of "Democracy" in the third line;
the few revisions in the printed text were minor. The poem was probably composed in the
mid-1850s, being clearly related to the prophetic tenor of the first poems.
1. In its original meaning, "good tidings."

Weave in, My Hardy Life[2]

Weave in, weave in, my hardy life,
Weave yet a soldier strong and full for great campaigns to come,
Weave in red blood, weave sinews in like ropes, the senses,
    sight weave in,
Weave lasting sure, weave day and night the weft, the warp,
    incessant weave, tire not,
(We know not what the use O life, nor know the aim, the end,
    nor really aught we know,   5
But know the work, the need goes on and shall go on, the
    death-envelop'd march of peace as well as war goes on,)
For great campaigns of peace the same the wiry threads to
    weave,
We know not why or what, yet weave, forever weave.
  1865   *1881*

Spain, 1873–74[3]

Out of the murk of heaviest clouds,
Out of the feudal wrecks and heap'd-up skeletons of kings,
Out of that old entire European debris, the shatter'd
    mummeries,
Ruin'd cathedrals, crumble of palaces, tombs of priests,
Lo, Freedom's features fresh undimm'd look forth—the same
    immortal face looks forth;   5
(A glimpse as of thy Mother's face Columbia,
A flash significant as of a sword,
Beaming towards thee.)

Nor think we forget thee maternal;
Lag'd'st thou so long? shall the clouds close again upon thee?   10
Ah, but thou hast thyself now appear'd to us—we know thee,
Thou hast given us a sure proof, the glimpse of thyself,
Thou waitest there as everywhere thy time.
  1873   *1881*

2. A *Drum-Taps* poem of 1865 and 1867; transferred in 1871 to the group "Marches Now the War is Over" and to the present cluster in 1881. There were minor verbal changes in *LG* 1871 and *LG* 1881 only.
3. First printed in the *New York Daily Graphic*, March 24, 1873, then in the 1876 *Two Rivulets*, and in *LG* 1881 in its present position. The attempt to establish a constitutional republic in Spain produced a virtual condition of anarchy from February 1873 until January 1874 but failed to prevent the restoration of the Bourbons with the proclamation of Don Alfonso as king, December 29, 1874. Sympathetic with the democratic revolution, WW reminds America of her own birth from Freedom and in the second stanza predicts the final victory of Democracy everywhere.

By Broad Potomac's Shore[4]

By broad Potomac's shore, again old tongue,
(Still uttering, still ejaculating, canst never cease this babble?)
Again old heart so gay, again to you, your sense, the full flush
    spring returning,
Again the freshness and the odors, again Virginia's summer
    sky, pellucid blue and silver,
Again the forenoon purple of the hills,   5
Again the deathless grass, so noiseless soft and green,
Again the blood-red roses blooming.

Perfume this book of mine O blood-red roses!
Lave subtly with your waters every line Potomac!
Give me of you O spring, before I close, to put between its
    pages!   10
O forenoon purple of the hills, before I close, of you!
O deathless grass, of you!
  1872

                                  1881

From Far Dakota's Cañons[5]

June 25, 1876

From far Dakota's cañons,
Lands of the wild ravine, the dusky Sioux, the lonesome
    stretch, the silence,
Haply to-day a mournful wail, haply a trumpet-note for heroes.

The battle-bulletin,
The Indian ambuscade, the craft, the fatal environment,   5
The cavalry companies fighting to the last in sternest heroism,
In the midst of their little circle, with their slaughter'd horses
    for breastworks,
The fall of Custer and all his officers and men.

4. This poem was first published as the last of the group of seven poems composing the 1872 supplementary volume, *As a Strong Bird on Pinions Free.* It was then reprinted in the 1872 *Two Rivulets,* and finally in its present position in *LG* 1881. Its lyric power, delicate beyond the clichés of sentiment, is sustained by memory and experience in a troubled year (1872). The ravages of war were still fresh, the Washington clerkship was interrupted by necessary trips away, and illness threatened both the poet and his mother. No wonder his imagination was moved by symbol—the "blood-red roses" for friendship and the "perfume" for memory.
5. First named "A Death Sonnet for Custer" and published in the *New York Tribune,* June 10, 1876. WW was paid $10 (see letter of July 18, 1876, *Corr.,* III, 54). The poem appeared as an intercalation in some copies of *LG* 1876, and in its present title and position in *LG* 1881. Five MS notebooks (Feinberg), working notes and trial phrases show Custer's death in the Sioux massacre on the banks of the Little Big Horn as inspiring heroism in a slack time— an idea the poet phrases in his fourth stanza. There is a MS draft (Feinberg) of the complete poem, and a MS draft (Berg) for the *New York Tribune* version.

Continues yet the old, old legend of our race,
The loftiest of life upheld by death,   10
The ancient banner perfectly maintain'd,
O lesson opportune, O how I welcome thee!

As sitting in dark days,
Lone, sulky, through the time's thick murk looking in vain for
      light, for hope,
From unsuspected parts a fierce and momentary proof,   15
(The sun there at the centre though conceal'd,
Electric life forever at the centre,)
Breaks forth a lightning flash.

Thou of the tawny flowing hair in battle,
I erewhile saw, with erect head, pressing ever in front, bearing
      a bright sword in thy hand,   20
Now ending well in death the splendid fever of thy deeds,
(I bring no dirge for it or thee, I bring a glad triumphal sonnet,)
Desperate and glorious, aye in defeat most desperate, most
      glorious,
After thy many battles in which never yielding up a gun or a
      color,
Leaving behind thee a memory sweet to soldiers,   25
Thou yieldest up thyself.
      1876   *1881*

Old War-Dreams[6]

In midnight sleep of many a face of anguish,
Of the look at first of the mortally wounded, (of that
      indescribable look,)
Of the dead on their backs with arms extended wide,
      I dream, I dream, I dream.

Of scenes of Nature, fields and mountains,   5
Of skies so beauteous after a storm, and at night the moon so
      unearthly bright,
Shining sweetly, shining down, where we dig the trenches and
      gather the heaps,
      I dream, I dream, I dream.

6. This poem appeared in the "Sequel to Drum-Taps," 1865–66, and in the 1867 "Drum-Taps"
   annex under the title "In Clouds Descending, in Midnight Sleep," the opening phrase of the
   first line, which was revised to its present form in 1871. The 1871 text, transferred to the
   "Ashes of Soldiers" group of *Passage to India,* has the title "In Midnight Sleep" together with
   other minor revisions. Present title and position came in the 1881 LG. Note the regularity
   of stanza form and the use of refrain.

Long have they pass'd, faces and trenches and fields,
Where through the carnage I moved with a callous composure,
     or away from the fallen,   10
Onward I sped at the time—but now of their forms at night,
     I dream, I dream, I dream.
1865–66   *1881*

Thick-Sprinkled Bunting[7]

Thick-sprinkled bunting! flag of stars!
Long yet your road, fateful flag—long yet your road, and lined
     with bloody death,
For the prize I see at issue at last is the world,
All its ships and shores I see interwoven with your threads
     greedy banner;
Dream'd again the flags of kings, highest borne, to flaunt
     unrival'd?   5
O hasten flag of man—O with sure and steady step, passing
     highest flags of kings,
Walk supreme to the heavens mighty symbol—run up above
     them all,
Flag of stars! thick-sprinkled bunting!
1865   *1881*

What Best I See in Thee[8]

To U.S.G. return'd from his World's Tour

What best I see in thee,
Is not that where thou mov'st down history's great highways,
Ever undimm'd by time shoots warlike victory's dazzle,
Or that thou sat'st where Washington sat, ruling the land in
     peace,
Or thou the man whom feudal Europe feted, venerable Asia
     swarm'd upon,   5
Who walk'd with kings with even pace the round world's
     promenade;
But that in foreign lands, in all thy walks with kings,
Those prairie sovereigns of the West, Kansas, Missouri,
     Illinois,

---

7. Appeared in the 1865 *Drum-Taps* and the "Drum-Taps" supplement to *LG* 1867, under the title "Flag of stars, thick-sprinkled bunting," which was its first line; in *LG* 1871 with the present title and first line, included in the "Bathed in War's Perfume" cluster; and in *LG* 1881 in the present cluster. *N and F*, I, 46, item 153, is a printing of the MS with variant readings.
8. First appeared in *LG* 1881. General Grant began his world tour in the spring of 1877 upon completing his eight years as president; he returned in September 1879, having been received in England, Europe, and the Far East with distinguished honors. WW's comment, "The Silent General" in *Specimen Days*, parallels the sentiment of the poem (*Coll W, Prose*, I, 226).

Ohio's, Indiana's millions, comrades, farmers, soldiers, all to
   the front,
Invisibly with thee walking with kings with even pace the
   round world's promenade,   10
Were all so justified.
1881   *1881*

Spirit That Form'd This Scene[9]

Written in Platte Cañon, Colorado

Spirit that form'd this scene,
These tumbled rock-piles grim and red,
These reckless heaven-ambitious peaks,
These gorges, turbulent-clear streams, this naked freshness,
These formless wild arrays, for reasons of their own,   5
I know thee, savage spirit—we have communed together,
Mine too such wild arrays,[1] for reasons of their own;
Was't charged against my chants they had forgotten art?
To fuse within themselves its rules precise and delicatesse?
The lyrist's measur'd beat, the wrought-out temple's grace—
   column and polish'd arch forgot?   10
But thou that revelest here—spirit that form'd this scene,
They have remember'd thee.
1881   *1881*

As I Walk These Broad Majestic Days[2]

As I walk these broad majestic days of peace,
(For the war, the struggle of blood finish'd, wherein, O terrific
   Ideal,
Against vast odds erewhile having gloriously won,
Now thou stridest on, yet perhaps in time toward denser wars,
Perhaps to engage in time in still more dreadful contest,
   dangers,   5
Longer campaigns and crises, labors beyond all others,)
Around me I hear that eclat of the world, politics, produce,

9. First appeared in *LG* 1881, and in the *Critic*, September 10 of the same year. A memory of WW's western trip in 1879, it may be compared with its prose counterpart, "An Egotistical Find," in *Specimen Days* (*Coll W, Prose*, I, 210–11). MS in Feinberg Collection.
1. It is notable that in the lyric mastery of these lines, WW not only meets the charge of his critics but demonstrates its falsity.
2. Originally No. 21 of "Chants Democratic" in *LG* 1860; transferred to the "Songs Before Parting" supplement to *LG* 1867 under the title "As I Walk Solitary, Unattended," then to the cluster "Marches Now the War is Over" in *LG* 1871 under its present title. Achieved present position in 1881. It has undergone considerable change, notably in the addition in 1871 of the opening six lines prompted by the Civil War, and the exclusion in 1881 of a final passage of five lines probably not essential to the theme. A fundamental tenet is WW's subject here—that he regards the nonmaterial realities of idea and ideals as more real, more permanent, than the material realities, however much he celebrates their immediate utility.

The announcements of recognized things, science,
The approved growth of cities and the spread of inventions.

I see the ships, (they will last a few years,)   10
The vast factories with their foremen and workmen,
And hear the indorsement of all, and do not object to it.

But I too announce solid things,
Science, ships, politics, cities, factories, are not nothing,
Like a grand procession to music of distant bugles pouring,
    triumphantly moving, and grander heaving in sight,   15
They stand for realities—all is as it should be.

Then my realities;
What else is so real as mine?
Libertad and the divine average, freedom to every slave on the
    face of the earth,
The rapt promises and lumine[3] of seers, the spiritual world,
    these centuries-lasting songs,   20
And our visions, the visions of poets, the most solid
    announcements of any.
    1860   *1881*

A Clear Midnight[4]

This is thy hour O Soul, thy free flight into the wordless,
Away from books, away from art, the day erased, the lesson
    done,
Thee fully forth emerging, silent, gazing, pondering the themes
    thou lovest best,
Night, sleep, death and the stars.
    1881   *1881*

3. In context the meaning of this invented word is clear, but its derivation, whether from lumen,
   "light," or luminary, "a light-giving body," has not been elucidated.
4. First appeared in *LG* 1881. Its MS (LC *Whitman*, No. 28), reproduced in Furness, 174,
   carries the MS note: "for end of poem." The last, revised MS draft (Feinberg) is written on
   the back of a letter dated December 2, 1880.

SONGS OF PARTING

As the Time Draws Nigh[1]

As the time draws nigh glooming a cloud,
A dread beyond of I know not what darkens me.

I shall go forth,
I shall traverse the States awhile, but I cannot tell whither or
    how long,
Perhaps soon some day or night while I am singing my voice
    will suddenly cease.   5

O book, O chants! must all then amount to but this?
Must we barely arrive at this beginning of us?—and yet it is
    enough, O soul;
O soul, we have positively appear'd—that is enough.
1860   *1871*

Songs of Parting: Of the seventeen poems in this final cluster, four are from *LG* 1860, four from the 1865 *Drum-Taps,* six from the 1871 *Passage to India,* one from the 1872 *As a Strong Bird on Pinions Free,* and two are new to the 1881 edition. It is not incongruous that they should have appeared over a period of more than twenty years and in five different editions. The imminence of departure had entered the poet's pages as early as 1860, when, moved by a sense of dread lest his songs should cease, he recalled in "As the Time Draws Nigh" the joys he had taken in life. Now in 1881 this poem opens the final section with equal propriety, the personal note muted by time. The three other 1860 poems still apply, most notably "So Long!" Equally suitable here are the poems not yet distributed into other groups—poems from the "Songs Before Parting" of *LG* 1867, the "Songs of Parting" of *LG* 1871, the "Now Finalè to the Shore" of *Passage to India,* and four poems from the 1886 *Drum-Taps.* Two of this cluster of 1881 were new poems. Perhaps the most genuine of the group—if we except the ceremonious "So Long!"—is "Song at Sunset," a carol of adoration. In these lyrics, reflecting a life passed a century ago, today's reader may find familiar the same terrifying pace of change, the same vast gulfs of ignorance, the same world hopes and fears, the same knowledge that at the end one has little to bequeath save only what is in memory, and that, from the discovery of "endless Finalés," one knows that "in my end is my beginning." The poet wrought well with his group, for only one who possesses greatly can relinquish greatly, and what we feel at last is not the sense of the end, but of continued life.

1. The original poem of nineteen lines in *LG* 1860, entitled "To My Soul," was more than twice the present length, and far more intimate, taking note as in farewell of "the unspeakable love I interchanged with women," "the curious attachment of young men to me," and "the tracks which I leave, upon the side-walks and fields. . . ." The poet outlived the immediate crisis implicit in poems of 1860 and retained the more important, general human condition in his revisions. A MS (Barrett) of the early version associates the phrase "suddenly at the height and close of my career" with the cloud that darkens, but otherwise it varies little from the 1860 text. The poem next appeared in the *LG* 1867 supplement, "Songs Before Parting," cut practically to its present text, under the title "As Nearing Departure." With little further revision in the 1871–76 text, it was placed in the "Songs of Parting" group with the present title.

Years of the Modern[2]

Years of the modern! years of the unperform'd!
Your horizon rises, I see it parting away for more august dramas,
I see not America only, not only Liberty's nation but other
    nations preparing,
I see tremendous entrances and exits, new combinations, the
    solidarity of races,
I see that force advancing with irresistible power on the
    world's stage,   5
(Have the old forces, the old wars, played their parts? are the
    acts suitable to them closed?)
I see Freedom, completely arm'd and victorious and very
    haughty, with Law on one side and Peace on the other,
A stupendous trio all issuing forth against the idea of caste;
What historic denouements are these we so rapidly approach?
I see men marching and countermarching by swift millions,   10
I see the frontiers and boundaries of the old aristocracies
    broken,[3]
I see the landmarks of European kings removed,
I see this day the People beginning their landmarks, (all others
    give way;)
Never were such sharp questions ask'd as this day,
Never was average man, his soul, more energetic, more like a
    God,   15
Lo, how he urges and urges, leaving the masses no rest!
His daring foot is on land and sea everywhere, he colonizes the
    Pacific, the archipelagoes,
With the steamship, the electric telegraph, the newspaper, the
    wholesale engines of war,
With these and the world-spreading factories he interlinks all
    geography, all lands;
What whispers are these O lands, running ahead of you,
    passing under the seas?   20
Are all nations communing? is there going to be but one heart
    to the globe?
Is humanity forming en-masse? for lo, tyrants tremble, crowns
    grow dim,
The earth, restive, confronts a new era, perhaps a general
    divine war,
No one knows what will happen next, such portents fill the
    days and nights;

---

2. First appeared in the 1865 *Drum-Taps* with the title "Years of the Unperformed"; transferred
   with present title and minor textual alterations to the "Songs of Parting" group of *LG* 1872
   and *LG* 1881. Holloway (*CPSP*) was the first to note that in fact about half of the poem's
   lines are taken directly from the final section, "The World's Portents, Issues, the 80th Year
   of These States," of WW's unpublished 1856 political tract, *The Eighteenth Presidency!*, ed.
   Edward F. Grier (Lawrence, Kans., 1956), 42–45.
3. From line 11 through line 24 the phrasing is taken from the final section of *The Eighteenth
   Presidency!*

Years prophetical! the space ahead as I walk, as I vainly try to
    pierce it, is full of phantoms,   25
Unborn deeds, things soon to be, project their shapes around me,
This incredible rush and heat, this strange ecstatic fever of
    dreams O years!
Your dreams O years, how they penetrate through me! (I know
    not whether I sleep or wake;)
The perform'd America and Europe grow dim, retiring in
    shadow behind me,
The unperform'd, more gigantic than ever, advance, advance
    upon me.   30
1865   *1881*

Ashes of Soldiers[4]

Ashes of soldiers South or North,
As I muse retrospective murmuring a chant in thought,
The war resumes, again to my sense your shapes,
And again the advance of the armies.

Noiseless as mists and vapors,   5
From their graves in the trenches ascending,
From cemeteries all through Virginia and Tennessee,
From every point of the compass out of the countless graves,
In wafted clouds, in myriads large, or squads of twos or threes
    or single ones they come,
And silently gather round me.   10

Now sound no note O trumpeters,
Not at the head of my cavalry parading on spirited horses,
With sabres drawn and glistening, and carbines by their thighs,
    (ah my brave horsemen!
My handsome tan-faced horsemen! what life, what joy and pride,
With all the perils were yours.)   15

---

4. First published in the 1865 *Drum-Taps*, an elegy entitled "Hymn of Dead Soldiers," shorter
by ten lines than it is now. Transferred to the supplement "Passage to India" 1871, the poem
was essentially altered by the addition of the present first two stanzas and, as "Ashes of
Soldiers," became the title poem for a cluster of the same name, with the following epigraph:

> Again a verse for sake of you,
> You soldiers in the ranks—you Volunteers,
> Who bravely fighting, silent fell,
> To fill unmention'd graves.

Without significant textual change, the poem retained its place in this supplement to *LG*
1872 and *Two Rivulets* (1876). It achieved its final text and present position in *LG* 1881,
without the epigraph. A MS fragment (Feinberg) of seven lines, not used in the poem's
revision, also develops the "ashes" metaphor that now informs both the opening and closing
passages of this compassionate poem.

Nor you drummers, neither at reveillé at dawn,
Nor the long roll alarming the camp, nor even the muffled
　　beat for a burial,
Nothing from you this time O drummers bearing my warlike drums.

But aside from these and the marts of wealth and the crowded
　　promenade,
Admitting around me comrades close unseen by the rest and
　　voiceless,　　　　　　　　　　　　　　　　　　　　　　　20
The slain elate and alive again, the dust and debris alive,
I chant this chant of my silent soul in the name of all dead
　　soldiers.

Faces so pale with wondrous eyes, very dear, gather closer yet,
Draw close, but speak not.

Phantoms of countless lost,　　　　　　　　　　　　　　　25
Invisible to the rest henceforth become my companions,
Follow me ever—desert me not while I live.

Sweet are the blooming cheeks of the living—sweet are the
　　musical voices sounding,
But sweet, ah sweet, are the dead with their silent eyes.

Dearest comrades, all is over and long gone,　　　　　　　30
But love is not over—and what love, O comrades!
Perfume from battle-fields rising, up from the fœtor arising.

Perfume therefore my chant, O love, immortal love,
Give me to bathe the memories of all dead soldiers,
Shroud them, embalm them, cover them all over with tender
　　pride.　　　　　　　　　　　　　　　　　　　　　　　35

Perfume all—make all wholesome,
Make these ashes to nourish and blossom,
O love, solve all, fructify all with the last chemistry.

Give me exhaustless, make me a fountain,
That I exhale love from me wherever I go like a moist
　　perennial dew,　　　　　　　　　　　　　　　　　　　40
For the ashes of all dead soldiers South or North.
1865　　　　　　　　　　　　　　　　　　　　　*1881*

Thoughts[5]

1

Of these years I sing,
How they pass and have pass'd through convuls'd pains, as
through parturitions,
How America illustrates birth, muscular youth, the promise,
the sure fulfilment, the absolute success, despite of people
—illustrates evil as well as good,
The vehement struggle so fierce for unity in one's-self;
How many hold despairingly yet to the models departed, caste,
myths, obedience, compulsion, and to infidelity,   5
How few see the arrived models, the athletes, the Western
States, or see freedom or spirituality, or hold any faith in
results,
(But I see the athletes, and I see the results of the war
glorious and inevitable, and they again leading to other
results.)

How the great cities appear—how the Democratic masses,
turbulent, wilful, as I love them,
How the whirl, the contest, the wrestle of evil with good, the
sounding and resounding, keep on and on,
How society waits unform'd, and is for a while between things
ended and things begun,   10
How America is the continent of glories, and of the triumph of
freedom and of the Democracies, and of the fruits of
society, and of all that is begun,
And how the States are complete in themselves—and how all
triumphs and glories are complete in themselves, to lead
onward,
And how these of mine and of the States will in their turn be
convuls'd, and serve other parturitions and transitions,
And how all people, sights, combinations, the democratic
masses too, serve—and how every fact, and war itself,
with all its horrors, serves,
And how now or at any time each serves the exquisite
transition of death.   15

5. Originally two separate poems—"Chants Democratic" No. 9 and No. 11 in *LG* 1860; com-
bined in *LG* 1867 as sections 1 and 2 of "Thoughts" in the supplement, "Songs Before
Parting." With little further revision "Thoughts" appeared in *LG* 1871 in the "Songs of
Parting" cluster and achieved present position in *LG* 1881. The mss (Barrett) of the two
1860 poems are closely followed in the texts. In the *LG* 1860 "Blue Copy" revisions, WW
gave the title "Thought" to each and indicated their transfer (unfulfilled) to *Drum-Taps*. As
stanzas of a single poem, they compose a unified vision of "immense spiritual results" for
western democracy.

2

Of seeds dropping into the ground, of births,
Of the steady concentration of America, inland, upward, to
    impregnable and swarming places,
Of what Indiana, Kentucky, Arkansas, and the rest, are to be,
Of what a few years will show there in Nebraska, Colorado,
    Nevada, and the rest,
(Or afar, mounting the Northern Pacific to Sitka or Aliaska,)[6]   20
Of what the feuillage of America is the preparation for—and
    of what all sights, North, South, East and West, are,
Of this Union welded in blood, of the solemn price paid, of
    the unnamed lost ever present in my mind;
Of the temporary use of materials for identity's sake,
Of the present, passing, departing—of the growth of completer
    men than any yet,
Of all sloping down there where the fresh free giver the
    mother, the Mississippi flows,   25
Of mighty inland cities yet unsurvey'd and unsuspected,
Of the new and good names, of the modern developments, of
    inalienable homesteads,
Of a free and original life there, of simple diet and clean and
    sweet blood,
Of litheness, majestic faces, clear eyes, and perfect physique
    there,
Of immense spiritual results future years far West, each side
    of the Anahuacs,[7]   30
Of these songs, well understood there, (being made for that area,)
Of the native scorn of grossness and gain there,
(O it lurks in me night and day—what is gain after all to
    savageness and freedom?)
1860   *1881*

Song at Sunset[8]

Splendor of ended day floating and filling me,
Hour prophetic, hour resuming the past,
Inflating my throat, you divine average,
You earth and life till the last ray gleams I sing.

---

6. Sitka is a town in southeastern Alaska on Baranof Island; "Aliaska" is an early spelling of
   "Alaska."
7. An Aztec name signifying the plateau valley in which the city of Mexico is located. Crossing
   its highest part is a series of ranges, part of which is called "Condillera de Anahuac."
   The sense of the line and the plural form indicates that WW is referring to the mountain
   ranges.
8. This brilliant paean, first printed in *LG* 1860 as "Chants Democratic" No. 8, received its
   present title in *LG* 1867 in the supplement, "Songs Before Parting," p. 29, and was trans-
   ferred to the "Songs of Parting" cluster in *LG* 1871. In MS (Barrett) the title reads, "A Sunset
   Carol"; in WW's 1860. "Blue Copy" revisions is the same title with two words in the margin
   opposite—"finale" and "religious." The poem received but little revision.

Open mouth of my soul uttering gladness,   5
Eyes of my soul seeing perfection,
Natural life of me faithfully praising things,
Corroborating forever the triumph of things.

Illustrious every one!
Illustrious what we name space, sphere of unnumber'd spirits,   10
Illustrious the mystery of motion in all beings, even the tiniest
        insect,
Illustrious the attribute of speech, the senses, the body,
Illustrious the passing light—illustrious the pale reflection on
        the new moon in the western sky,
Illustrious whatever I see or hear or touch, to the last.

Good in all,   15
In the satisfaction and aplomb of animals,
In the annual return of the seasons,
In the hilarity of youth,
In the strength and flush of manhood,
In the grandeur and exquisiteness of old age,   20
In the superb vistas of death.

Wonderful to depart!
Wonderful to be here!
The heart, to jet the all-alike and innocent blood!
To breathe the air, how delicious!   25
To speak—to walk—to seize something by the hand!
To prepare for sleep, for bed, to look on my rose-color'd flesh!
To be conscious of my body, so satisfied, so large!
To be this incredible God I am!
To have gone forth among other Gods, these men and women
        I love.   30

Wonderful how I celebrate you and myself!
How my thoughts play subtly at the spectacles around!
How the clouds pass silently overhead!
How the earth darts on and on! and how the sun, moon, stars,
        dart on and on!
How the water sports and sings! (surely it is alive!)   35
How the trees rise and stand up, with strong trunks, with
        branches and leaves!
(Surely there is something more in each of the trees, some
        living soul.)

O amazement of things—even the least particle!
O spirituality of things!
O strain musical flowing through ages and continents, now
        reaching me and America!   40
I take your strong chords, intersperse them, and cheerfully
        pass them forward.

I too carol the sun, usher'd or at noon, or as now, setting,
I too throb to the brain and beauty of the earth and of all the
  growths of the earth,
I too have felt the resistless call of myself.

As I steam'd down the Mississippi,   45
As I wander'd over the prairies,
As I have lived, as I have look'd through my windows my eyes,
As I went forth in the morning, as I beheld the light breaking
  in the east,
As I bathed on the beach of the Eastern Sea, and again on the
  beach of the Western Sea,⁹
As I roam'd the streets of inland Chicago, whatever streets I
  have roam'd,   50
Or cities or silent woods, or even amid the sights of war,
Wherever I have been I have charged myself with contentment
  and triumph.

I sing to the last the equalities modern or old,
I sing the endless finalés of things,
I say Nature continues, glory continues,   55
I praise with electric voice,
For I do not see one imperfection in the universe,
And I do not see one cause or result lamentable at last in the
  universe.

O setting sun! though the time has come,
I still warble under you, if none else does, unmitigated
  adoration.   60
1860   *1881*

As at Thy Portals Also Death¹

As at thy portals also death,
Entering thy sovereign, dim, illimitable grounds,
To memories of my mother, to the divine blending, maternity,
To her, buried and gone, yet buried not, gone not from me,
(I see again the calm benignant face fresh and beautiful still,   5
I sit by the form in the coffin,
I kiss and kiss convulsively again the sweet old lips, the
  cheeks, the closed eyes in the coffin;)
To her, the ideal woman, practical, spiritual, of all of earth,
  life, love, to me the best,

9. WW never reached the Pacific in his travels, but from the times of the Greek navigators the
  "western sea" has been in the common stock of poetry as a symbol for the far-off or unat-
  tainable. *Cf.* Tennyson's "Stars of the western sea" in a song of *The Princess* (1847), familiar
  to WW.
1. An elegy to the poet's mother, Louisa Van Velsor Whitman, who died May 23, 1873, in her
  seventy-eighth year, a period when WW himself—as the first line intimates—felt pertur-
  bations of death. The poem is one of the seventeen new to *LG* 1881.

I grave a monumental line, before I go, amid these songs,
And set a tombstone here.   10
   1881   *1881*

My Legacy[2]

The business man the acquirer vast,
After assiduous years surveying results, preparing for
     departure,
Devises houses and lands to his children, bequeaths stocks,
     goods, funds for a school or hospital,
Leaves money to certain companions to buy tokens, souvenirs
     of gems and gold.

But I, my life surveying, closing,   5
With nothing to show to devise from its idle years,
Nor houses nor lands, nor tokens of gems or gold for my friends,[3]
Yet certain remembrances of the war for you, and after you,
And little souvenirs of camps and soldiers, with my love,
I bind together and bequeath in this bundle of songs.   10
   1872   *1881*

Pensive on Her Dead Gazing[4]

Pensive on her dead gazing I heard the Mother of All,
Desperate on the torn bodies, on the forms covering the battle-
     fields gazing,
(As the last gun ceased, but the scent of the powder-smoke
     linger'd,)
As she call'd to her earth with mournful voice while she stalk'd,

---

2. Originated as an epigraph entitled "Souvenirs of Democracy," introducing *As a Strong Bird on Pinions Free* (1872), which became a supplement incorporated with others in *Two Rivulets* (1876). With the present title in *LG* 1881, the poem shows considerable revision in the second stanza not shown in Triggs' "Variorum Readings" of 1902.
3. Following this line in the first 1871–76 version, the poem continues:

> Only these Souvenirs of Democracy—In them—in
>   all my songs—behind me leaving,
> To You, whoever you are, (bathing, leavening this
>   leaf especially with my breath—pressing on it
>   a moment with my own hands;
> —Here! feel how the pulse beats in my wrists!—how
>   my heart's blood is swelling, contracting!)
> I will You, in all, Myself, with promise to never
>   desert you,
> To which I sign my name,
>   Walt Whitman

4. Appeared in *Drum-Taps* (1865) and in the same supplement to *LG* 1867; transferred to the "Ashes of Soldiers" group in *Passage to India* (1871) with the insertion of present line 3; printed finally, with minor textual revisions, in *LG* 1881 with present shortened title instead of the whole first line.

Absorb them well O my earth, she cried, I charge you lose not
    my sons, lose not an atom,   5
And you streams absorb them well, taking their dear blood,
And you local spots, and you airs that swim above lightly
    impalpable,
And all you essences of soil and growth, and you my rivers' depths,
And you mountain sides, and the woods where my dear
    children's blood trickling redden'd,
And you trees down in your roots to bequeath to all future
    trees,   10
My dead absorb or South or North—my young men's bodies
    absorb, and their precious precious blood,
Which holding in trust for me faithfully back again give me
    many a year hence,
In unseen essence and odor of surface and grass, centuries hence,
In blowing airs from the fields back again give me my darlings,
    give my immortal heroes,
Exhale me them centuries hence, breathe me their breath, let
    not an atom be lost,   15
O years and graves! O air and soil! O my dead, an aroma sweet!
Exhale them perennial sweet death, years, centuries hence.
1865   *1881*

Camps of Green[5]

Not alone those camps of white, old comrades of the wars,
When as order'd forward, after a long march,
Footsore and weary, soon as the light lessens we halt for the
    night,
Some of us so fatigued carrying the gun and knapsack,
    dropping asleep in our tracks,
Others pitching the little tents, and the fires lit up begin to
    sparkle,   5
Outposts of pickets posted surrounding alert through the dark,
And a word provided for countersign, careful for safety,
Till to the call of the drummers at daybreak loudly beating the
    drums,
We rise up refresh'd, the night and sleep pass'd over, and
    resume our journey,
Or proceed to battle.   10

Lo, the camps of the tents of green,
Which the days of peace keep filling, and the days of war keep
    filling,

---

5. Appeared with the present title in *Drum-Taps* (1865) and in the same supplement to *LG* 1867; transferred to the "Ashes of Soldiers" group in *Passage to India* (1871), with minor revisions then and in its present relocation in *LG* 1881.

With a mystic army, (is it too order'd forward? is it too only
    halting awhile,
Till night and sleep pass over?)

Now in those camps of green, in their tents dotting the world,   15
In the parents, children, husbands, wives, in them, in the old
    and young,
Sleeping under the sunlight, sleeping under the moonlight,
    content and silent there at last,
Behold the mighty bivouac-field and waiting-camp of all,
Of the corps and generals all, and the President over the corps
    and generals all,
And of each of us O soldiers, and of each and all in the ranks
    we fought,   20
(There without hatred we all, all meet.)

For presently O soldiers, we too camp in our place in the
    bivouac-camps of green,
But we need not provide for outposts, nor word for the
    countersign,
Nor drummer to beat the morning drum.
1865   *1881*

The Sobbing of the Bells[6]

(*Midnight, Sept. 19–20, 1881*)

The sobbing of the bells, the sudden death-news everywhere,
The slumberers rouse, the rapport of the People,
(Full well they know that message in the darkness,
Full well return, respond within their breasts, their brains, the
    sad reverberations,)
The passionate toll and clang—city to city, joining, sounding,
    passing,

Those heart-beats of a Nation in the night.
1881   *1881*

6. The poet was in Boston, supervising the printing of his 1881 edition of *LG*, when the news came of President Garfield's death, near midnight, September 19, 1881, from an assassin's attack of the previous July 2. He first published the poem in the *Boston Daily Globe*, September 27, 1881, and then inserted it in the 1881 *LG* edition just before the last pages were stereotyped. The two MSS (Feinberg and Berg) were both published in facsimile (cf. Traubel, II, 137, and Bucke, 55). The poem was reprinted in *The Poets' Tribute to Garfield* (Cambridge, 1881). On WW's friendship with Garfield, whom he had known in Washington when the latter was a young congressman from Ohio, see Allen, 495.

As They Draw to a Close[7]

As they draw to a close,
Of what underlies the precedent songs—of my aims in them,
Of the seed I have sought to plant in them,
Of joy, sweet joy, through many a year, in them,
(For them, for them have I lived, in them my work is done,)   5
Of many an aspiration fond, of many a dream and plan;
Through Space and Time fused in a chant, and the flowing
    eternal identity,
To Nature encompassing these, encompassing God—to the
    joyous, electric all,
To the sense of Death, and accepting exulting in Death in its
    turn the same as life,
The entrance of man to sing;   10
To compact you, ye parted, diverse lives,
To put rapport the mountains and rocks and streams,
And the winds of the north, and the forests of oak and pine,
With you O soul.
1871   *1881*

Joy, Shipmate, Joy![8]

Joy, shipmate, joy![9]
(Pleas'd to my soul at death I cry,)
Our life is closed, our life begins,
The long, long anchorage we leave,
The ship is clear at last, she leaps!   5
She swiftly courses from the shore,
Joy, shipmate, joy.
1871   *1871*

The Untold Want

The untold want by life and land ne'er granted,
Now voyager sail thou forth to seek and find.
1871   *1871*

---

7. First published in the 1871 *Passage to India*, entitled "Thought" in the cluster "Now Finalè to the Shore," but without the present lines 7–10; these were present in the preceding poem of the same group as the last four lines of "Shut Not Your Doors." The seventh line of the original poem was dropped in *LG* 1881:

> O you, O mystery great!—to place on record faith in you, O death!

8. The following four poems were first published in the 1871 *Passage to India* (though not in this order), in the group "Now Finalè to the Shore," with present titles and texts.
9. The reader may observe that this poem and the following three concluding this cluster emphasize a persistent motivation of the "Songs of Parting" (see headnote to that title above), a theme dominant in the beginning of the cluster in "As the Time Draws Nigh," "Ashes of Soldiers," and "Song at Sunset."

Portals

What are those of the known but to ascend and enter the
    Unknown?
And what are those of life but for Death?
1871   *1871*

These Carols

These carols sung to cheer my passage through the world I see,
For completion I dedicate to the Invisible World.
1871   *1871*

Now Finalè to the Shore[1]

Now finalè to the shore,[2]
Now, land and life finalè and farewell,
Now Voyager depart, (much, much for thee is yet in store,)
Often enough hast thou adventur'd o'er the seas,
Cautiously cruising, studying the charts,   5
Duly again to port and hawser's tie returning;
But now obey thy cherish'd secret wish,
Embrace thy friends, leave all in order,
To port and hawser's tie no more returning,
Depart upon thy endless cruise old Sailor.   10
1871   *1871*

1. First published in the 1871 *Passage to India* in a group of the same title, the poem appeared in 1881 with present title and text. Twenty years after "Now Finalè . . ." was written, WW included it in *Good-bye My Fancy* (1891), except for the first line. It terminates the small essay "A Death-Bouquet," and he introduces the poem with the following words: "Like an invisible breeze after a long and sultry day, death sometimes sets in at last, soothingly and refreshingly, almost vitally . . . It is a curious suggestion of immortality that the mental and emotional powers remain to their clearest through all, while the senses of pain and flesh-volitions are blunted or even gone."
2. A peculiarity of the 1892 text is the use of the grave accent for "finale" in the title and in lines 1 and 2. The accent was, however, correctly omitted in this edition from the same word in "Song at Sunset," line 54 (*q.v.*). *Cf.* "Starting from Paumanok," line 66, note.

So Long![3]

To conclude, I announce what comes after me.

I remember I said before my leaves sprang at all,
I would raise my voice jocund and strong with reference to
     consummations.

When America does what was promis'd,
When through these States walk a hundred millions of superb
     persons,   5
When the rest part away for superb persons and contribute to
     them,
When breeds of the most perfect mothers denote America,
Then to me and mine our due fruition.

I have press'd through in my own right,
I have sung the body and the soul, war and peace have I sung,
     and the songs of life and death,   10
And the songs of birth, and shown that there are many births.

I have offer'd my style to every one, I have journey'd with
     confident step;
While my pleasure is yet at the full I whisper *So long!*
And take the young woman's hand and the young man's hand
     for the last time.

I announce natural persons to arise,   15
I announce justice triumphant,
I announce uncompromising liberty and equality,
I announce the justification of candor and the justification of
     pride.

I announce that the identity of these States is a single identity
     only,
I announce the Union more and more compact, indissoluble,   20
I announce splendors and majesties to make all the previous
     politics of the earth insignificant.

3. This farewell poem—"My songs cease, I abandon them"—has terminated *LG* ever since the
third edition (1860), although considerably revised in text, if not in essential meaning. For
the 1867 edition twenty-one lines were cancelled, in accordance with WW's revised *LG* 1860
"Blue Copy," and three lines were added in the 1871 edition. WW excluded earlier passages
that struck a brasher note, producing in the final revision a certain humility and quiet con-
fidence in ultimate recognition: "When America does what was promis'd . . . Then to me
and mine our due fruition." Lines 53–54 and 64–65 are paraphrased from "Leaves of Grass"
No. 24 in *LG* 1860, which then became "Now Lift Me Close" in 1867, reappeared as "To
the Reader at Parting" in *Passage to India* (1871) and in successive combinations of that
supplement with *LG* 1872 and *TR* (1876), and then dropped altogether. William Sloane
Kennedy (FBW, 110) notes that WW was early in using the expression "So Long!" and that
when he asked the poet to define it, he replied: "A salutation of departure, greatly used
among sailors, sports, and prostitutes. The sense of it is 'Till we meet again,'—conveying an
inference that somehow they will doubtless so meet, sooner or later."

I announce adhesiveness,[4] I say it shall be limitless, unloosen'd,
I say you shall yet find the friend you were looking for.

I announce a man or woman coming, perhaps you are the one,
    (*So long!*)
I announce the great individual, fluid as Nature, chaste,
    affectionate, compassionate, fully arm'd.   25

I announce a life that shall be copious, vehement, spiritual, bold,
I announce an end that shall lightly and joyfully meet its
    translation.

I announce myriads of youths, beautiful, gigantic, sweet-blooded,
I announce a race of splendid and savage old men.

O thicker and faster—(*So long!*)   30
O crowding too close upon me,
I foresee too much, it means more than I thought,
It appears to me I am dying.

Hasten throat and sound your last,
Salute me—salute the days once more. Peal the old cry once
    more.   35

Screaming electric, the atmosphere using,
At random glancing, each as I notice absorbing,
Swiftly on, but a little while alighting,
Curious envelop'd messages delivering,
Sparkles hot, seed ethereal down in the dirt dropping,   40
Myself unknowing, my commission obeying, to question it
    never daring,
To ages and ages yet the growth of the seed leaving,
To troops out of the war arising, they the tasks I have set
    promulging,
To women certain whispers of myself bequeathing, their
    affection me more clearly explaining,
To young men my problems offering—no dallier I—I the
    muscle of their brains trying,   45
So I pass, a little time vocal, visible, contrary,
Afterward a melodious echo, passionately bent for, (death
    making me really undying,)
The best of me then when no longer visible, for toward that I
    have been incessantly preparing.

4. A phrenological term designating the faculty of friendship, used by WW in his earlier poems
to designate manly love. There is much in his writings and attitude to suggest that later he
broadened his reference to include friendship between man and woman, and woman and
woman as well. For more on "adhesiveness," see note to "Not Heaving from my Ribb'd Breast
Only."

What is there more, that I lag and pause and crouch extended
    with unshut mouth?
Is there a single final farewell?   50

My songs cease, I abandon them,
From behind the screen where I hid I advance personally
    solely to you.

Camerado, this is no book,
Who touches this touches a man,
(Is it night? are we here together alone?)   55
It is I you hold and who holds you,
I spring from the pages into your arms—decease calls me forth.

O how your fingers drowse me,
Your breath falls around me like dew, your pulse lulls the
    tympans of my ears,
I feel immerged from head to foot,   60
Delicious, enough.

Enough O deed impromptu and secret,
Enough O gliding present—enough O summ'd-up past.

Dear friend whoever you are take this kiss,
I give it especially to you, do not forget me,   65
I feel like one who has done work for the day to retire awhile,
I receive now again of my many translations, from my avataras[5]
    ascending, while others doubtless await me,
An unknown sphere more real than I dream'd, more direct,
    darts awakening rays about me, *So long!*
Remember my words, I may again return,
I love you, I depart from materials,   70
I am as one disembodied, triumphant, dead.
    1860   *1881*

5. A Sanskrit word (*cf.* English "avatar") meaning "incarnation" or "embodiment"—in Hinduism associated with the appearances of the deity, Vishnu, as Krishna.

FIRST ANNEX
SANDS AT SEVENTY

Mannahatta[1]

My city's fit and noble name resumed,
Choice aboriginal name, with marvellous beauty, meaning,
A *rocky founded island—shores where ever. gayly dash the*
    coming, going, hurring sea waves.
1888   *1888–89*

Paumanok[2]

Sea-beauty! stretch'd and basking!
One side thy inland ocean laving, broad, with copious
    commerce, steamers, sails,
And one the Atlantic's wind caressing, fierce or gentle—mighty
    hulls dark-gliding in the distance.
Isle of sweet brooks of drinking-water—healthy air and soil!
Isle of the salty shore and breeze and brine!   5
1888   *1888–89*

Sands at Seventy: In the editions of *LG* from 1860 to 1881, and in the supplementary vol-
umes, beginning with *Drum-Taps* (1865), the poet attempted—by the continuous revision
of the poems, by exluding some and adding some newly created, by arranging and rearranging
clusters of related poems under group titles frequently altered or recombined—to achieve a
topical organization referring to chronology only as the typical sequence of experience in the
life of the so-called average man, spanning the nineteenth century as his own life almost
did. He had come to think of *LG* as a "single poem"; he had hoped to continue with another
such, designed to represent the spiritual anabasis of modern man. By 1881 his mounting
infirmities brought him to a halt with only "this bundle of songs" bequeathed "to the Invisible
World." By 1888 he had completed a number of new pieces, many of them for newspaper
or periodical publication, and a major prose essay, "A Backward Glance O'er Travel'd Roads"
(see below). These, with other prose pieces, appeared as a book, *November Boughs* (1888),
in which the poems were headed "Sands at Seventy." This title did not come easily; several
MS collections (Berg, Trent, Yale) possess scribblings of other possibilities—"Halcyon Days,"
"Sands on the Shores," "Carols at Candlelight," "Carols Closing Sixty-nine," etc. The poems
of *November Boughs* appeared as an annex, "Sands at Seventy," in reprints of *LG* 1884, some
with a new title page dated 1888, and again in *LG* 1889, all with the new penultimate poem,
"Old Age's Lambent Peaks," as in the present text. In the 1891–92 *LG*, the following group
was introduced by a title page, backed by a table of "Contents." The title page read: "ANNEX
/ TO PRECEDING PAGES. / SANDS AT SEVENTY. / Copyright, 1888, by Walt Whitman. / (SEE
'NOVEMBER BOUGHS')." The pagination of this group followed in sequence that of the pre-
ceding text.
1. First published in the *New York Herald*, February 27, 1888, with the third line unitalicized.
2. First published in the *New York Herald*, February 29, 1888. *Cf.* WW's lengthy autobiograph-
   ical poem "Starting from Paumanok" (i.e., Long Island).

From Montauk Point[3]

I stand as on some mighty eagle's beak,
Eastward the sea absorbing, viewing, (nothing but sea and sky,)
The tossing waves, the foam, the ships in the distance,
The wild unrest, the snowy, curling caps—that inbound urge
    and urge of waves,
Seeking the shores forever.   5
  1888   *1888–89*

To Those Who've Fail'd[4]

To those who've fail'd, in aspiration vast,
To unnam'd soldiers fallen in front on the lead,
To calm, devoted engineers—to over-ardent travelers—to pilots
    on their ships,
To many a lofty song and picture without recognition—I'd rear
    a laurel-cover'd monument,
High, high above the rest—To all cut off before their time,   5
Possess'd by some strange spirit of fire,
Quench'd by an early death.
  1888   *1888–89*

A Carol Closing Sixty-nine[5]

A carol closing sixty-nine—a *résumé*—a repetition,
My lines in joy and hope continuing on the same,
Of ye, O God, Life, Nature, Freedom, Poetry;
Of you, my Land—your rivers, prairies, States—you, mottled
    Flag I love,
Your aggregate retain'd entire—Of north, south, east and west,
    your items all;   5
Of me myself—the jocund heart yet beating in my breast,
The body wreck'd, old, poor and paralyzed—the strange inertia
    falling pall-like round me,
The burning fires down in my sluggish blood not yet extinct,
The undiminish'd faith—the groups of loving friends.
  1888   *1888–89*

3. First published in the *New York Herald*, March 1, 1888. The place is a headland at the eastern end of Long Island, familiar in WW's earliest youth.
4. First published in the *New York Herald*, January 27, 1888, with "aspiration" in the plural. The MS (Berg) shows the title "A laurel wreath to those who've fail'd."
5. First published in the *New York Herald*, May 21, 1888. WW's MS (Barrett) shows the note, "sent to Lippincott's," and the cancellation of two other titles: "Carols at nearing Seventy" and "A Carol-Cluster at 69."

The Bravest Soldiers[6]

Brave, brave were the soldiers (high named to-day) who lived
    through the fight;
But the bravest press'd to the front and fell, unnamed,
    unknown.
1888   *1888–89*

A Font of Type[7]

This latent mine—these unlaunch'd voices—passionate powers,
Wrath, argument, or praise, or comic leer, or prayer devout,
(Not nonpareil, brevier, bourgeois, long primer[8] merely,)
These ocean waves arousable to fury and to death,
Or sooth'd to ease and sheeny sun and sleep,   5
Within the pallid slivers slumbering.
1888   *1888–89*

As I Sit Writing Here[9]

As I sit writing here, sick and grown old,
Not my least burden is that dulness of the years, querilities,
Ungracious glooms, aches, lethargy, constipation, whimpering
    ennui,
May filter in my daily songs.
1888   *1888–89*

My Canary Bird[1]

Did we count great, O soul, to penetrate the themes of mighty
    books,
Absorbing deep and full from thoughts, plays, speculations?
But now from thee to me, caged bird, to feel thy joyous warble,
Filling the air, the lonesome room, the long forenoon,
Is it not just as great, O soul?   5
1888   *1888–89*

6. First published in the *New York Herald,* March 18, 1888.
7. John Russell Young's *Men and Memories* (New York, 1901, p. 107) contains a slightly different version of this poem, which, says the editor, was sent to Mr. Young marked "personal—don't print." First published in this group, in *November Boughs* (1888).
8. The preceding are the names of types in the sizes from six to ten points, then most in use.
9. First published in the *New York Herald,* May 14, 1888. The word "querilities," so spelled by WW in the second line, should be "querulities." The error appeared both in the *Herald* and in *November Boughs.*
1. First published in the *New York Herald,* March 2, 1888.

Queries to My Seventieth Year[2]

Approaching, nearing, curious,
Thou dim, uncertain spectre—bringest thou life or death?
Strength, weakness, blindness, more paralysis and heavier?
Or placid skies and sun? Wilt stir the waters yet?
Or haply cut me short for good? Or leave me here as now,   5
Dull, parrot-like and old, with crack'd voice harping,[3]
      screeching?
1888   *1888–89*

The Wallabout Martyrs[4]

[In Brooklyn, in an old vault, mark'd by no special recognition, lie huddled at this moment the
undoubtedly authentic remains of the stanchest and earliest revolutionary patriots from the
British prison ships and prisons of the times of 1776–83, in and around New York, and from
all over Long Island; originally buried—many thousands of them—in trenches in the Wallabout
sands.]

Greater than memory of Achilles or Ulysses,
More, more by far to thee than tomb of Alexander,
Those cart loads of old charnel ashes, scales and splints of
      mouldy bones,
Once living men—once resolute courage, aspiration, strength,
The stepping stones to thee to-day and here, America.   5
1888   *1888–89*

The First Dandelion[5]

Simple and fresh and fair from winter's close emerging,
As if no artifice of fashion, business, politics, had ever been,
Forth from its sunny nook of shelter'd grass—innocent,
      golden, calm as the dawn,
The spring's first dandelion shows its trustful face.
1888   *1888–89*

2. First published in the *New York Herald,* May 2, 1888. MSS, Huntington and Feinberg. The
   Feinberg version includes three lines not printed:
       Steep me in immobility
       As we grow old we narrow on ourselves concentrating
       Something to us unspeakably pensive in our own age—our sorrows—
3. In the more colloquial sense of tedious repetition.
4. First published in the *New York Herald,* March 16, 1888. MS in Barrett. Wallabout Bay is
   at the bend of the East River, present site of the Brooklyn Navy Yard.
5. First published in the *New York Herald,* March 12, 1888, a salute to spring that appeared
   the day after the beginning of the great blizzard of 1888. MS in Barrett.

America[6]

Centre of equal daughters, equal sons,
All, all alike endear'd, grown, ungrown, young or old,
Strong, ample, fair, enduring, capable, rich,
Perennial with the Earth, with Freedom, Law and Love,
A grand, sane, towering, seated Mother,   5
Chair'd in the adamant of Time.
1888   *1888–89*

Memories[7]

How sweet the silent backward tracings!
The wanderings as in dreams—the meditation of old times
    resumed—their loves, joys, persons, voyages.
1888   *1888–89*

To-day and Thee[8]

The appointed winners in a long-stretch'd game;
The course of Time and nations—Egypt, India, Greece and
    Rome;
The past entire, with all its heroes, histories, arts, experiments,
Its store of songs, inventions, voyages, teachers, books,
Garner'd for now and thee—To think of it!   5
The heirdom all converged in thee!
1888   *1888–89*

After the Dazzle of Day[9]

After the dazzle of day is gone,
Only the dark, dark night shows to my eyes the stars;
After the clangor of organ majestic, or chorus, or perfect band,
Silent, athwart my soul, moves the symphony true.
1888   *1888–89*

6. First published in the *New York Herald,* February 11, 1888. *Cf.* "Thou Mother with Thy Equal Brood"; also "To-day and Thee," below.
7. First published in this group in *November Boughs* (1888). MS in Feinberg.
8. First published in the *New York Herald,* April 23, 1888. MS in Barrett.
9. First published in the *New York Herald,* February 3, 1888. MS in Feinberg.

Abraham Lincoln, Born Feb. 12, 1809[1]

To-day, from each and all, a breath of prayer—a pulse of
    thought,
To memory of Him—to birth of Him.
    Publish'd Feb. 12, 1888.
1888   *1888–89*

Out of May's Shows Selected[2]

Apple orchards, the trees all cover'd with blossoms;
Wheat fields carpeted far and near in vital emerald green;
The eternal, exhaustless freshness of each early morning;
The yellow, golden, transparent haze of the warm afternoon sun;
The aspiring lilac bushes with profuse purple or white flowers.   5
1888   *1888–89*

Halcyon Days[3]

Not from successful love alone,
Nor wealth, nor honor'd middle age, nor victories of politics or
    war;
But as life wanes, and all the turbulent passions calm,
As gorgeous, vapory, silent hues cover the evening sky,
As softness, fulness, rest, suffuse the frame, like fresher,
    balmier air,   5
As the days take on a mellower light, and the apple at last
    hangs really finish'd and indolent-ripe on the tree,
Then for the teeming quietest, happiest days of all!
The brooding and blissful halcyon days![4]
1888   *1888–89*

---

1. First published in the *New York Herald,* February 12, 1888. WW gave his first public lecture
on Lincoln on April 14, 1879, and gave others at intervals until 1890, including one in
Philadelphia in 1886 and one in New York in 1887.
2. First published in the *New York Herald,* May 10, 1888.
3. First published in the *New York Herald,* January 29, 1888. MS in Hanley.
4. WW, bird watcher and naturalist, probably knew the Greek fable that the *halkyon*, a mythical
kingfisher, nested at sea and calmed the waves of the winter solstice.

Fancies at Navesink[5]

The Pilot in the Mist

Steaming the northern rapids—(an old St. Lawrence
    reminiscence,
A sudden memory-flash comes back, I know not why,
Here waiting for the sunrise, gazing from this hill;)[6]
Again 'tis just at morning—a heavy haze contends with day-break,
Again the trembling, laboring vessel veers me—I press through
    foam-dash'd rocks that almost touch me,   5
Again I mark where aft the small thin Indian helmsman
Looms in the mist, with brow elate and governing hand.
   1885   *1888–89*

Had I the Choice

Had I the choice to tally greatest bards,
To limn their portraits, stately, beautiful, and emulate at will,
Homer with all his wars and warriors—Hector, Achilles, Ajax,
Or Shakspere's woe-entangled Hamlet, Lear, Othello—
    Tennyson's fair ladies,
Metre or wit the best, or choice conceit to wield in perfect
    rhyme, delight of singers;   5
These, these, O sea, all these I'd gladly barter,
Would you the undulation of one wave, its trick to me transfer,
Or breathe one breath of yours upon my verse,
And leave its odor there.
   1885   *1888–89*

You Tides with Ceaseless Swell

You tides with ceaseless swell! you power that does this work!
You unseen force, centripetal, centrifugal, through space's spread,

---

5. This group of eight poems, after rejection by W. H. Alden, editor of *Harper's* (Traubel, I, 61), was first published in *Nineteenth Century,* August 1885. It takes its place with the "Sea-Drift" cluster, which it indeed surpasses with respect to sustained unity of theme and mood, as evidence of the fascination of the sea upon the poet's mind and art, and his sense of kinship with its rhythms. Abundant MS material—fifty-four scraps and fragments at LC, eighteen pages at Yale, other pages in Barrett, Berg, Hanley, Huntington—show how thoroughly WW worked upon this series, composing, amending, and rejecting. There is manuscript evidence that he had considered a grouping somewhat different from the one printed, including some poems later separately placed. Navesink is a seaside elevation on the New Jersey coast, at the lower entrance of New York Bay.
6. "Navesink—a sea-side mountain, lower entrance of New York Bay" [WW's note].

Rapport of sun, moon, earth, and all the constellations,
What are the messages by you from distant stars to us? what
    Sirius'? what Capella's?
What central heart—and you the pulse—vivifies all? what
    boundless aggregate of all?   5
What subtle indirection and significance in you? what clue to
    all in you? what fluid, vast identity,
Holding the universe with all its parts as one—as sailing in a
    ship?
1885   *1888–89*

Last of Ebb, and Daylight Waning

Last of ebb, and daylight waning,
Scented sea-cool landward making, smells of sedge and salt
    incoming,
With many a half-caught voice sent up from the eddies,
Many a muffled confession—many a sob and whisper'd word,
As of speakers far or hid.   5

How they sweep down and out! how they mutter!
Poets unnamed—artists greatest of any, with cherish'd lost
    designs,
Love's unresponse—a chorus of age's complaints—hope's last
    words,
Some suicide's despairing cry, *Away to the boundless waste, and
    never again return.*

On to oblivion then!   10
On, on, and do your part, ye burying, ebbing tide!
On for your time, ye furious debouché!
1885   *1888–89*

And Yet Not You Alone

And yet not you alone, twilight and burying ebb,
Nor you, ye lost designs alone—nor failures, aspirations;
I know, divine deceitful ones, your glamour's seeming;
Duly by you, from you, the tide and light again—duly the
    hinges turning,
Duly the needed discord-parts offsetting, blending,   5
Weaving from you, from Sleep, Night, Death itself,
The rhythmus of Birth eternal.
1885   *1888–89*

Proudly the Flood Comes In

Proudly the flood comes in, shouting, foaming, advancing,
Long it holds at the high, with bosom broad outswelling,
All throbs, dilates—the farms, woods, streets of cities—
    workmen at work,
Mainsails, topsails, jibs, appear in the offing—steamers'
    pennants of smoke—and under the forenoon sun,
Freighted with human lives, gaily the outward bound, gaily the
    inward bound,   5
Flaunting from many a spar the flag I love.
    1885   *1888–89*

By That Long Scan of Waves

By that long scan of waves, myself call'd back, resumed upon
    myself,
In every crest some undulating light or shade—some
    retrospect,
Joys, travels, studies, silent panoramas—scenes ephemeral,
The long past war, the battles, hospital sights, the wounded
    and the dead,
Myself through every by-gone phase—my idle youth—old age
    at hand,   5
My three-score years of life summ'd up, and more, and past,
By any grand ideal tried, intentionless, the whole a nothing,
And haply yet some drop within God's scheme's ensemble—
    some wave, or part of wave,
Like one of yours, ye multitudinous ocean.
    1885   *1888–89*

Then Last of All[7]

Then last of all, caught from these shores, this hill,
Of you O tides, the mystic human meaning:
Only by law of you, your swell and ebb, enclosing me the same,
The brain that shapes, the voice that chants this song.
    1885   *1888–89*

---

7. The "Fancies at Navesink" end with this poem.

Election Day, November, 1884[8]

If I should need to name, O Western World, your powerfulest
  scene and show,
'Twould not be you, Niagara—nor you, ye limitless prairies—
  nor your huge rifts of canyons, Colorado,
Nor you, Yosemite—nor Yellowstone, with all its spasmic
  geyser-loops ascending to the skies, appearing and
  disappearing,
Nor Oregon's white cones—nor Huron's belt of mighty lakes—
  nor Mississippi's stream:
—This seething hemisphere's humanity, as now, I'd name—
  the still small voice vibrating—America's choosing day,   5
(The heart of it not in the chosen—the act itself the main, the
  quadriennial choosing,)
The stretch of North and South arous'd—sea-board and inland
  —Texas to Maine—the Prairie States—Vermont, Virginia,
  California,
The final ballot-shower from East to West—the paradox and
  conflict,
The countless snow-flakes falling—(a swordless conflict,
Yet more than all Rome's wars of old, or modern Napoleon's:)
  the peaceful choice of all,   10
Or good or ill humanity—welcoming the darker odds, the dross:
—Foams and ferments the wine? it serves to purify—while the
  heart pants, life glows:
These stormy gusts and winds waft precious ships,
Swell'd Washington's, Jefferson's, Lincoln's sails.
  1884

1888–89

8. Under the title "If I Should Need to Name, O Western World," this poem was first published in the *Philadelphia Press,* October 26, 1884. The opposing candidates in 1884 were James G. Blaine and Cleveland, Blaine suffering defeat after the defection of Roscoe Conkling. "There is no question at issue of any importance," WW wrote (the issues happened to be the tariff and Chinese exclusion), "But," he went on, "I like well the *fact* of all these national elections—have written a little poem about it" (*Walt Whitman's Diary in Canada,* 1904, p. 73).

With Husky-Haughty Lips, O Sea![9]

With husky-haughty lips, O sea!
Where day and night I wend thy surf-beat shore,
Imaging to my sense thy varied strange suggestions,
(I see and plainly list thy talk and conference here,)[1]
Thy troops of white-maned racers racing to the goal,   5
Thy ample, smiling face, dash'd with the sparkling dimples of
    the sun,
Thy brooding scowl and murk—thy unloos'd hurricanes,
Thy unsubduedness, caprices, wilfulness;
Great as thou art above the rest, thy many tears—a lack from
    all eternity in thy content,
(Naught but the greatest struggles, wrongs, defeats, could
    make thee greatest—no less could make thee,)   10
Thy lonely state—something thou ever seek'st and seek'st, yet
    never gain'st,
Surely some right withheld—some voice, in huge monotonous
    rage, of freedom-lover pent,
Some vast heart, like a planet's, chain'd and chafing in those
    breakers,
By lengthen'd swell, and spasm, and panting breath,
And rhythmic rasping of thy sands and waves,   15
And serpent hiss, and savage peals of laughter,
And understones of distant lion roar,
(Sounding, appealing to the sky's deaf ear—but now, rapport
    for once,
A phantom in the night thy confidant for once,)
The first and last confession of the globe,   20
Outsurging, muttering from thy soul's abysms,
The tale of cosmic elemental passion,
Thou tellest to a kindred soul.
    1884

                                              1888–89

---

9. First published in *Harper's Monthly*, March 1884, which paid WW $50. The poem is a record of WW's visit to Ocean Grove, New Jersey, for a week with John Burroughs in September and October 1883, when he jotted down some of its phrases in a thirteen-page notebook (Lion). Several trial lines were also penciled on a page with letterhead reading Sheldon House, Ocean Grove (Feinberg). Four more MS pages (Yale) record variants and final draft. One discarded title is "By thine own lips, O Sea." WW's remarkable sequence of "Fancies at Navesink," above, may also have been influenced in part by this holiday. Burroughs (diary, September 29), referring to a walk on the beach, noted,

> there is something grainy and saline in him, as in the voice of the sea . . . sometimes his talk is . . . eliptical and unfinished; again there comes a long, splendid roll of thought that . . . swings you quite free from your moorings.

1. This line was added, after magazine publication, for the 1888–89 text, followed here.

Death of General Grant[2]

As one by one withdraw the lofty actors,
From that great play on history's stage eterne,
That lurid, partial act of war and peace—of old and new
    contending,
Fought out through wrath, fears, dark dismays, and many a
    long suspense;
All past—and since, in countless graves receding, mellowing,   5
Victor's and vanquish'd—Lincoln's and Lee's—now thou with
    them,
Man of the mighty days—and equal to the days!
Thou from the prairies!—tangled and many-vein'd and hard
    has been thy part,
To admiration has it been enacted!
1885   *1888–89*

Red Jacket (from Aloft)[3]

[Impromptu on Buffalo City's monument to, and re-burial of the old Iroquois orator,
October 9, 1884]

Upon this scene, this show,
Yielded to-day by fashion, learning, wealth,
(Nor in caprice alone—some grains of deepest meaning,)
Haply, aloft, (who knows?) from distant sky-clouds' blended
    shapes,
As some old tree, or rock or cliff, thrill'd with its soul,   5
Product of Nature's sun, stars, earth direct—a towering
    human form,
In hunting-shirt of film, arm'd with the rifle, a half-ironical
    smile curving its phantom lips,
Like one of Ossian's ghosts looks down.[4]
1884   *1888–89*

---

2. When this poem was first published in *Harper's Weekly*, May 16, 1885, General Grant was
   still living. The title was the poem's first line, and a second stanza read:

   > And still shall be:—resume thou hero heart!
   > Strengthen to firmest day, O rosy dawn of hope!
   > Tho dirge I started first, to joyful shout reverse—and thou O grave,
   > Wait long and long!

   Although Grant died July 23, 1885, the first version was reprinted in the *Critic*, August 15,
   1885. Present version, *November Boughs* (1888). A MS is in the library of St. John's Seminary,
   Camarillo, Calif.
3. First published in the *Philadelphia Press*, October 10, 1884, and also in the *Transactions of
   the Buffalo Historical Society* (1885). Red Jacket (1750–1830), grand sachem of the Iroquois,
   is credited with turning Iroquois support to the American side in the War of 1812. WW did
   not attend the ceremony here celebrated.
4. Ossian was the legendary third-century Gaelic bard whose poems James Macpherson (1736–
   1796) professed to translate in a rhythmic prose influential in the romanticism of the eight-
   eenth century.

Washington's Monument, February, 1885[5]

Ah, not this marble, dead and cold:
Far from its base and shaft expanding—the round zones
    circling, comprehending,
Thou, Washington, art all the world's, the continents' entire—
    not yours alone, America,
Europe's as well, in every part, castle of lord or laborer's cot,
Or frozen North, or sultry South—the African's—the Arab's in
    his tent,   5
Old Asia's there with venerable smile, seated amid her ruins;
(Greets the antique the hero new? 'tis but the same—the heir
    legitimate, continued ever,
The indomitable heart and arm—proofs of the never-broken
    line,
Courage, alertness, patience, faith, the same—e'en in defeat
    defeated not, the same:)
Wherever sails a ship, or house is built on land, or day or night,   10
Through teeming cities' streets, indoors or out, factories or farms,
Now, or to come, or past—where patriot wills existed or exist,
Wherever Freedom, pois'd by Toleration, sway'd by Law,
Stands or is rising thy true monument.
    1885   1888–89

Of That Blithe Throat of Thine[6]

[More than eighty-three degrees north—about a good day's steaming distance to the Pole by one of our fast oceaners in clear water—Greely the explorer heard the song of a single snowbird merrily sounding over the desolation.]

Of that blithe throat of thine from arctic bleak and blank,
I'll mind the lesson, solitary bird—let me too welcome chilling
    drifts,
E'en the profoundest chill, as now—a torpid pulse, a brain
    unnerv'd,
Old age land-lock'd within its winter bay—(cold, cold, O cold!)
These snowy hairs, my feeble arm, my frozen feet,   5
For them thy faith, thy rule I take, and grave it to the last;
Not summer's zones alone—not chants of youth, or south's
    warm tides alone,
But held by sluggish floes, pack'd in the northern ice, the
    cumulus of years,
These with gay heart I also sing.
    1885   1888–89

---

5. First published in the *Philadelphia Press*, February 22, 1885, under the title "Ah, Not This Granite Dead and Cold." Of four MS pages (Morgan), three are work sheets; another MS, privately owned (De Gruson), is printer's copy for the 1888 *November Boughs*.
6. First published in *Harper's Monthly*, January 1885, which paid WW $30. MSS in LC and Feinberg.

Broadway[7]

What hurrying human tides, or day or night!
What passions, winnings, losses, ardors, swim thy waters!
What whirls of evil, bliss and sorrow, stem thee!
What curious questioning glances—glints of love!
Leer, envy, scorn, contempt, hope, aspiration!   5
Thou portal—thou arena—thou of the myriad long-drawn
    lines and groups!
(Could but thy flagstones, curbs, façades, tell their inimitable
    tales;
Thy windows rich, and huge hotels—thy side-walks wide;)
Thou of the endless sliding, mincing, shuffling feet!
Thou, like the parti-colored world itself—like infinite, teeming,
    mocking life!   10
Thou visor'd, vast, unspeakable show and lesson!
    1888   *1888–89*

To Get the Final Lilt of Songs[8]

To get the final lilt of songs,
To penetrate the inmost lore of poets—to know the mighty ones,
Job, Homer, Eschylus, Dante, Shakspere, Tennyson, Emerson;
To diagnose the shifting-delicate tints of love and pride and
    doubt—to truly understand,
To encompass these, the last keen faculty and entrance-price,   5
Old age, and what it brings from all its past experiences.
    1888   *1888–89*

Old Salt Kossabone[9]

Far back, related on my mother's side,
Old Salt Kossabone, I'll tell you how he died:
(Had been a sailor all his life—was nearly 90—lived with his
    married grandchild, Jenny;
House on a hill, with view of bay at hand, and distant cape,
    and stretch to open sea;)
The last of afternoons, the evening hours, for many a year his
    regular custom,   5

---

7. First published in the *New York Herald,* April 10, 1888. MS in Barrett.
8. First published in the *New York Herald,* April 16, 1888, under the title "The Final Lilt of
   Songs."
9. First published in the *New York Herald,* February 25, 1888. The MS (Feinberg), endorsed
   by the actress Ellen Terry, was presented to her by the poet. "Dutch Kossabone" was the
   father of Mary Kossabone (ca. 1745–ca. 1792), who married Garrett Van Velsor (1742–
   1812). Their son, Major Cornelius Van Velsor (1768–1837), married Naomi Williams (d.
   1826). The poet's mother, Louisa Van Velsor (1795–1873), was the daughter of this
   marriage.

In his great arm chair by the window seated,
(Sometimes, indeed, through half the day,)
Watching the coming, going of the vessels, he mutters to
    himself—And now the close of all:
One struggling outbound brig, one day, baffled for long—
    cross-tides and much wrong going,
At last at nightfall strikes the breeze aright, her whole luck
    veering,   10
And swiftly bending round the cape, the darkness proudly
    entering, cleaving, as he watches,
"She's free—she's on her destination"—these the last words—
    when Jenny came, he sat there dead,
Dutch Kossabone, Old Salt, related on my mother's side, far
    back.
    1888   *1888–89*

The Dead Tenor[1]

As down the stage again,
With Spanish hat and plumes, and gait inimitable,
Back from the fading lessons of the past, I'd call, I'd tell and
    own,
How much from thee! the revelation of the singing voice from
    thee!
(So firm—so liquid-soft—again that tremulous, manly timbre!   5
The perfect singing voice—deepest of all to me the lesson—
    trial and test of all:)
How through those strains distill'd—how the rapt ears, the
    soul of me, absorbing
Fernando's heart, *Manrico's* passionate call, *Ernani's*, sweet
    Gennaro's,[2]
I fold thenceforth, or seek to fold, within my chants
    transmuting,
Freedom's and Love's and Faith's unloos'd cantabile,   10
(As perfume's, color's, sunlight's correlation:)
From these, for these, with these, a hurried line, dead tenor,
A wafted autumn leaf, dropt in the closing grave, the shovel'd
    earth,
To memory of thee.
    1884   *1888–89*

1. First published in the *Critic*, November 8, 1884. The poem is a tribute to Signor Pasquale Brignole, whose funeral in New York City, November 3, 1884, is recorded in a newspaper clipping attached to the MS (Hanley). WW himself identified the singer on an envelope in which he mailed the poem to his friend William Douglas O'Connor.
2. Characters in, respectively, Donizetti's opera *La Favorita*, Verdi's *Il Trovatore*, Verdi's *Ernani*, and Donizetti's *Lucrezia Borgia*.

Continuities[3]

[From a talk I had lately with a German spiritualist]

Nothing is ever really lost, or can be lost,
No birth, identity, form—no object of the world.
Nor life, nor force, nor any visible thing;
Appearance must not foil, nor shifted sphere confuse thy brain.
Ample are time and space—ample the fields of Nature.   5

The body, sluggish, aged, cold—the embers left from earlier fires,
The light in the eye grown dim, shall duly flame again;
The sun now low in the west rises for mornings and for noons
      continual;
To frozen clods ever the spring's invisible law returns,
With grass and flowers and summer fruits and corn.   10
   1888   *1888–89*

Yonnondio[4]

[The sense of the word is *lament for the aborigines.* It is an Iroquois term; and has been used for a personal name.]

A song, a poem of itself—the word itself a dirge,
Amid the wilds, the rocks, the storm and wintry night,
To me such misty, strange tableaux the syllables calling up;
Yonnondio—I see, far in the west or north, a limitless ravine,
      with plains and mountains dark,
I see swarms of stalwart chieftains, medicine-men, and
      warriors,   5
As flitting by like clouds of ghosts, they pass and are gone in
      the twilight,
(Race of the woods, the landscapes free, and the falls!
No picture, poem, statement, passing them to the future:)
Yonnondio! Yonnondio!—unlimn'd they disappear;
To-day gives place, and fades—the cities, farms, factories fade;   10
A muffled sonorous sound, a wailing word is borne through
      the air for a moment,
Then blank and gone and still, and utterly lost.
   1887   *1888–89*

---

3. First published in the *New York Herald*, March 20, 1888. MSS include a work sheet of trial lines (Feinberg) and a complete draft (Barrett).
4. First published in the *Critic*, November 26, 1887. The poem is one of the many memorials of WW's interest in American names.

Life[5]

Ever the undiscouraged, resolute, struggling soul of man;
(Have former armies fail'd? then we send fresh armies—and
  fresh again;)
Ever the grappled mystery of all earth's ages old or new;
Ever the eager eyes, hurrahs, the welcome-clapping hands, the
  loud applause;
Ever the soul dissatisfied, curious, unconvinced at last;   5
Struggling to-day the same—battling the same.
  1888   *1888–89*

"Going Somewhere"[6]

My science-friend, my noblest woman-friend,
(Now buried in an English grave—and this a memory-leaf for
  her dear sake,)
Ended our talk—"The sum, concluding all we know of old or
  modern learning, intuitions deep,
"Of all Geologies—Histories—of all Astronomy—of Evolution,
  Metaphysics all,
"Is, that we all are onward, onward, speeding slowly, surely
  bettering,   5
"Life, life an endless march, an endless army, (no halt, but it
  is duly over,)
"The world, the race, the soul—in space and time the
  universes,
"All bound as is befitting each—all surely going somewhere."
  1887   *1888–89*

Small the Theme of My Chant[7]

Small the theme of my Chant, yet the greatest—namely,
  One's-Self—a simple, separate person. That, for the use
  of the New World, I sing.
Man's physiology complete, from top to toe, I sing. Not
  physiognomy alone, nor brain alone, is worthy for the

5. First published in the *New York Herald,* April 15, 1888. A sheet of rough draft lines (Feinberg) for this poem was used by the poet in a letter of May 7, 1888, to Robert Pearsall Smith, containing the postscript: "I see I have taken a sheet of paper with a rambling first draft of one of my *Herald* yaps—but n'importe."
6. First published in *Lippincott's Magazine,* November 1887. A facsimile of the MS printer's copy is reproduced opposite page 75 of Thomas C. Donaldson's *Walt Whitman, the Man* (1896). The "science-friend" is Anne Gilchrist, who died November 29, 1885. For the story of her friendship with WW, see Marion Walker Alcaro, *Walt Whitman's Mrs. G: A Biography of Anne Gilchrist* (Madison, N.J.: Fairleigh Dickinson University Press, 1991).
7. With minor variants this poem first appeared on the flyleaf before the poems of *LG* 1867, a shorter version later opening the "Inscriptions" group of *LG* 1871. See note to "One's-Self I Sing." MSS are in the Barrett, Dartmouth, LC, and Yale collections.

Muse;—I say the Form complete is worthier far. The
Female equally with the Male, I sing.

Nor cease at the theme of One's-Self. I speak the word of the
modern, the word En-Masse.
My Days I sing, and the Lands—with interstice I knew of
hapless War.
(O friend, whoe'er you are, at last arriving hither to
commence, I feel through every leaf the pressure of your
hand, which I return.   5
And thus upon our journey, footing the road, and more than
once, and link'd together let us go.)
1867   *1888–89*

True Conquerors[8]

Old farmers, travelers, workmen (no matter how crippled or
bent,)
Old sailors, out of many a perilous voyage, storm and wreck,
Old soldiers from campaigns, with all their wounds, defeats
and scars;
Enough that they've survived at all—long life's unflinching ones!
Forth from their struggles, trials, fights, to have emerged at all
—in that alone,   5
True conquerors o'er all the rest.
1888   *1888–89*

The United States to Old World Critics[9]

Here first the duties of to-day, the lessons of the concrete,
Wealth, order, travel, shelter, products, plenty;
As of the building of some varied, vast, perpetual edifice,
Whence to arise inevitable in time, the towering roofs, the lamps,
The solid-planted spires tall shooting to the stars.   5
1888   *1888–89*

The Calming Thought of All[1]

That coursing on, whate'er men's speculations,
Amid the changing schools, theologies, philosophies,

---

8. First published in the *New York Herald*, February 15, 1888.
9. First published in the *New York Herald*, May 8, 1888. Among the "old world critics" who
   especially interested WW in the 1880s were Matthew Arnold, Robert Buchanan, Thomas
   Carlyle, and Oscar Wilde. See Blodgett, *passim.*
1. First published in the *New York Herald*, May 27, 1888.

Amid the bawling presentations new and old,
The round earth's silent vital laws, facts, modes continue.
1888   *1888–89*

Thanks in Old Age[2]

Thanks in old age—thanks ere I go,
For health, the midday sun, the impalpable air—for life, mere
    life,
For precious ever-lingering memories, (of you my mother dear
    —you, father—you, brothers, sisters, friends,)
For all my days—not those of peace alone—the days of war
    the same,
For gentle words, caresses, gifts from foreign lands,   5
For shelter, wine and meat—for sweet appreciation,
(You distant, dim unknown—or young or old—countless,
    unspecified, readers belov'd,
We never met, and ne'er shall meet—and yet our souls
    embrace, long, close and long;)
For beings, group, love, deeds, words, books—for colors, forms,
For all the brave strong men—devoted, hardy men—who've
    forward sprung in freedom's help, all years, all lands,   10
For braver, stronger, more devoted men—(a special laurel ere I
    go, to life's war's chosen ones,
The cannoneers of song and thought—the great artillerists—
    the foremost leaders, captains of the soul:)
As soldier from an ended war return'd—As traveler out of
    myriads, to the long procession retrospective,
Thanks—joyful thanks!—a soldier's, traveler's thanks.
1888   *1888–89*

Life and Death[3]

The two old, simple problems ever intertwined,
Close home, elusive, present, baffled, grappled.
By each successive age insoluble, pass'd on,
To ours to-day—and we pass on the same.
1888   *1888–89*

---

2. One MS scrap (Hanley) is a rough draft of the first eight lines; another (Huntington) of the
last five. Although the Hanley MS bears WW's notation "published Nov. 25, '87," it was
actually published November 24, in the *Philadelphia Press.* It was reprinted in the *New York
World,* November 23, 1890, there entitled "Walt Whitman's Thanksgiving."
3. First published in the *New York Herald,* May 23, 1888.

The Voice of the Rain[4]

And who art thou? said I to the soft-falling shower,
Which, strange to tell, gave me an answer, as here translated:
I am the Poem of Earth, said the voice of the rain,
Eternal I rise impalpable out of the land and the bottomless sea,
Upward to heaven, whence, vaguely form'd, altogether
    changed, and yet the same,   5
I descend to lave the drouths, atomies, dust-layers of the globe,
And all that in them without me were seeds only, latent, unborn;
And forever, by day and night, I give back life to my own
    origin, and make pure and beautify it:
(For song, issuing from its birth-place, after fulfilment,
    wandering,
Reck'd or unreck'd, duly with love returns.)   10
  1885   *1888–89*

Soon Shall the Winter's Foil Be Here[5]

Soon shall the winter's foil be here;
Soon shall these icy ligatures unbind and melt—A little while,
And air, soil, wave, suffused shall be in softness, bloom and
    growth—a thousand forms shall rise
From these dead clods and chills as from low burial graves.

Thine eyes, ears—all thy best attributes—all that takes
    cognizance of natural beauty,   5
Shall wake and fill. Thou shalt perceive the simple shows, the
    delicate miracles of earth,
Dandelions, clover, the emerald grass, the early scents and
    flowers,
The arbutus under foot, the willow's yellow-green, the
    blossoming plum and cherry;
With these the robin, lark and thrush, singing their songs—the
    flitting bluebird;
For such the scenes the annual play brings on.   10
  1888   *1888–89*

4. First published in *Outing*, August 1885. In a proof sheet (Feinberg) of this poem, the title "A Rain Enigma" is rejected.
5. First published in the *New York Herald*, February 21, 1888. MS in Huntington.

While Not the Past Forgetting[6]

While not the past forgetting,
To-day, at least, contention sunk entire—peace, brotherhood
    uprisen;
For sign reciprocal our Northern, Southern hands,
Lay on the graves of all dead soldiers, North or South,
(Nor for the past alone—for meanings to the future,)   5
Wreaths of roses and branches of palm.

                          1888–89

The Dying Veteran[7]

[A Long Island incident—early part of the present century]

Amid these days of order, ease, prosperity,
Amid the current songs of beauty, peace, decorum,
I cast a reminiscence—(likely 'twill offend you,
I heard it in my boyhood;)—More than a generation since,
A queer old savage man, a fighter under Washington himself,   5
(Large, brave, cleanly, hot-blooded, no talker, rather spiritualistic,
Had fought in the ranks—fought well—had been all through
    the Revolutionary war,)
Lay dying—sons, daughters, church-deacons, lovingly tending
    him,
Sharping their sense, their ears, towards his murmuring, half-
    caught words:
"Let me return again to my war-days,   10
To the sights and scenes—to forming the line of battle,
To the scouts ahead reconnoitering,
To the cannons, the grim artillery,
To the galloping aids, carrying orders,
To the wounded, the fallen, the heat, the suspense,   15
The perfume strong, the smoke, the deafening noise;
Away with your life of peace!—your joys of peace!
Give me my old wild battle-life again!"
  1887   1888–89

---

6. WW's note on publication of this Decoration Day poem ("Publish'd May 30, 1888") has not been substantiated, its first appearance evidently being in *November Boughs* (1888). The MS (Feinberg) is a worksheet of trial lines.
7. First published in *McClure's Magazine*, June 1887. WW told William Sloane Kennedy (*Reminiscences of Walt Whitman*, 55) that he received $25 for it—"far more than it is worth." MS in Feinberg Collection.

Stronger Lessons[8]

Have you learn'd lessons only of those who admired you, and
    were tender with you, and stood aside for you?
Have you not learn'd great lessons from those who reject you,
    and brace themselves against you? or who treat you with
    contempt, or dispute the passage with you?
    1860   1888–89

A Prairie Sunset[9]

Shot gold, maroon and violet, dazzling silver, emerald, fawn,
The earth's whole amplitude and Nature's multiform power
    consign'd for once to colors;
The light, the general air possess'd by them—colors till now
    unknown,
No limit, confine—not the Western sky alone—the high
    meridian—North, South, all,
Pure luminous color fighting the silent shadows to the last.   5
    1888   1888–89

Twenty Years[1]

Down on the ancient wharf, the sand, I sit, with a new-comer
    chatting:
He shipp'd as green-hand boy, and sail'd away, (took some
    sudden, vehement notion;)
Since, twenty years and more have circled round and round,
While he the globe was circling round and round,—and now
    returns:
How changed the place—all the old land-marks gone—the
    parents dead;   5
(Yes, he comes back to lay in port for good—to settle—has a
    well-fill'd purse—no spot will do but this;)
The little boat that scull'd him from the sloop, now held in
    leash I see,
I hear the slapping waves, the restless keel, the rocking in the
    sand,
I see the sailor kit, the canvas bag, the great box bound with
    brass,
I scan the face all berry-brown and bearded—the stout-strong
    frame,   10

8. These two lines were first published as part of "Debris" in LG 1860, then separately with
the present title in LG 1867, but not in succeeding editions before November Boughs annex,
1888.
9. First published in the New York Herald, March 9, 1888.
1. First published in The Magazine of Art (New York), July 1888, and reprinted in The Magazine
of Art, September 1888.

Dress'd in its russet suit of good Scotch cloth:
(Then what the told-out story of those twenty years? What of
  the future?)
1888   *1888–89*

Orange Buds by Mail from Florida[2]

[Voltaire closed a famous argument by claiming that a ship of war and the grand opera were
proofs enough of civilization's and France's progress, in his day.]

A lesser proof than old Voltaire's, yet greater,
Proof of this present time, and thee, thy broad expanse, America,
To my plain Northern hut, in outside clouds and snow,
Brought safely for a thousand miles o'er land and tide,
Some three days since on their own soil live-sprouting,   5
Now here their sweetness through my room unfolding,
A bunch of orange buds by mail from Florida.
1888   *1888–89*

Twilight[3]

The soft voluptuous opiate shades,
The sun just gone, the eager light dispell'd—(I too will soon be
  gone, dispell'd,)
A haze—nirwana—rest and night—oblivion.
1887   *1888–89*

You Lingering Sparse Leaves of Me[4]

You lingering sparse leaves of me on winter-nearing boughs,
And I some well-shorn tree of field or orchard-row;
You tokens diminute and lorn—(not now the flush of May, or
  July clover-bloom—no grain of August now;)
You pallid banner staves—you pennants valueless—you over-
  stay'd of time,
Yet my soul-dearest leaves confirming all the rest,   5
The faithfulest—hardiest—last.
1887   *1888–89*

2. First published in the *New York Herald*, March 19, 1888. MS in Barrett.
3. First published in *Century* 35 (December 1887): 264, the poet receiving $10. WW told
   Traubel he had had a number of letters objecting to the word "oblivion" as inconsistent with
   his philosophy. "But oblivion as I use it there is just the word, both as furnishing sense and
   rhythm to the idea I had in mind" (Traubel, I, 141). "Nirwana" (nirvana) in fact suggests in
   Indian Hinduism the emancipation from temporal life in a union with the eternal, and in
   Buddhism a spiritual beatification without transmigration.
4. First published in *Lippincott's Magazine*, November 1887. LC has a page of trial lines.

Not Meagre, Latent Boughs Alone[5]

Not meagre, latent boughs alone, O songs! (scaly and bare, like
    eagles' talons,)
But haply for some sunny day (who knows?) some future
    spring, some summer—bursting forth,
To verdant leaves, or sheltering shade—to nourishing fruit,
Apples and grapes—the stalwart limbs of trees emerging—the
    fresh, free, open air,
And love and faith, like scented roses blooming.   5
1887   *1888–89*

The Dead Emperor[6]

To-day, with bending head and eyes, thou, too, Columbia,
Less for the mighty crown laid low in sorrow—less for the
    Emperor,
Thy true condolence breathest, sendest out o'er many a salt
    sea mile,
Mourning a good old man—a faithful shepherd, patriot.
1888   *1888–89*

As the Greek's Signal Flame[7]

[For Whittier's eightieth birthday, December 17, 1887]

As the Greek's signal flame, by antique records told,
Rose from the hill-top, like applause and glory,
Welcoming in fame some special veteran, hero,
With rosy tinge reddening the land he'd served,
So I aloft from Mannahatta's ship-fringed shore,   5
Lift high a kindled brand for thee, Old Poet.
1887   *1888–89*

5. First published in *Lippincott's Magazine*, November 1887. The MS (Feinberg) is a fragment
   of the first two lines.
6. First published in the *New York Herald*, March 10, 1888. MSS are a rough draft (Barrett)
   and printer's draft (Berg). The emperor, Wilhelm I of Germany, died in Berlin, March 9,
   1888. To his friends, who protested this salute, WW replied, ". . . too many of the fellows
   forget that I include emperors, lords, kingdoms, as well as presidents, workmen, republics"
   (Traubel, I, 22).
7. First published in the *New York Herald*, December 15, 1887; reprinted in the *Boston Ad-
   vertizer*, December 17. A facsimile of the MS is reproduced in *CW*, X, 134–35. WW never
   met Whittier, but they corresponded. See Traubel, I, 127.

The Dismantled Ship[8]

In some unused lagoon, some nameless bay,
On sluggish, lonesome waters, anchor'd near the shore,
An old, dismasted, gray and batter'd ship, disabled, done,
After free voyages to all the seas of earth, haul'd up at last and
    hawser'd tight,
Lies rusting, mouldering.   5

1888   *1888–89*

Now Precedent Songs, Farewell[9]

Now precedent songs, farewell—by every name farewell,
(Trains of a staggering line in many a strange procession,
    waggons,
From ups and downs—with intervals—from elder years, mid-
    age, or youth,)
"In Cabin'd Ships," or "Thee Old Cause" or "Poets to Come"
Or "Paumanok," "Song of Myself," "Calamus," or "Adam,"   5
Or "Beat! Beat! Drums!" or "To the Leaven'd Soil they Trod,"
Or "Captain! My Captain!" "Kosmos," "Quicksand Years," or
    "Thoughts,"
"Thou Mother with thy Equal Brood," and many, many more
    unspecified,
From fibre heart of mine—from throat and tongue—(My life's
    hot pulsing blood,
The personal urge and form for me—not merely paper,
    automatic type and ink,)   10
Each song of mine—each utterance in the past—having its
    long, long history,
Of life or death, or soldier's wound, of country's loss or safety,
(O heaven! what flash and started endless train of all!
    compared indeed to that!
What wretched shred e'en at the best of all!)

1888   *1888–89*

8. First printed in the *New York Herald*, February 23, 1888. WW said the poem was suggested
   by a picture hanging in the parlor of his friend, Thomas B. Harned (Traubel, I, 390). Another
   source is suggested by the fact that a rough draft (Feinberg) of the poem was found in WW's
   copy of John G. C. Brainard's *Occasional Pieces of Poetry* (New York, 1825) at pages 47–48,
   where is printed Brainard's lyric, "The Captain—A Fragment," dealing with a legend of the
   sea. A facsimile of the MS is reproduced (page 103) in Donaldson. Another MS is owned by
   Dr. Max Thorek.
9. WW's own note at the foot of the page (see n. 2, below) is a clear record of the composition
   of this and the following poem. Traubel, I, 353–54, discusses the circumstances, which did
   not warrant more than a casual choice of the poems cited. See also Traubel, II, 10. First
   published in *November Boughs* (1888).

An Evening Lull[1]

After a week of physical anguish,
Unrest and pain, and feverish heat,
Toward the ending day a calm and lull comes on,
Three hours of peace and soothing rest of brain.[2]
1888   *1888–89*

Old Age's Lambent Peaks[3]

The touch of flame—the illuminating fire—the loftiest look at
    last,
O'er city, passion, sea—o'er prairie, mountain, wood—the
    earth itself;
The airy, different, changing hues of all, in falling twilight,
Objects and groups, bearings, faces, reminiscences;
The calmer sight—the golden setting, clear and broad: 5
So much i' the atmosphere, the points of view, the situations
    whence we scan,
Bro't out by them alone—so much (perhaps the best) unreck'd
    before;
The lights indeed from them—old age's lambent peaks.
1888   *1889*

After the Supper and Talk[4]

After the supper and talk—after the day is done,
As a friend from friends his final withdrawal prolonging,
Good-bye and Good-bye with emotional lips repeating,
(So hard for his hand to release those hands—no more will
    they meet,
No more for communion of sorrow and joy, of old and young,   5
A far-stretching journey awaits him, to return no more,)
Shunning, postponing severance—seeking to ward off the last
    word ever so little,

1. Traubel, II, 248–49, comments on the proofreading of this poem. First published in *November Boughs* (1888). Whitman's note to line 4 includes the poem preceding.
2. "The two songs on this page are eked out during an afternoon, June, 1888, in my seventieth year, at a critical spell of illness. Of course no reader and probably no human being at any time will ever have such phases of emotional and solemn action as these involve to me. I feel in them an end and close of all" [WW's note].
3. First printed in the *Century*, September 1888, this poem was not among the "Sands at Seventy" poems in *November Boughs* 1888, nor in *CPP* the same year. It was first collected in the Annex of 1884–88 *LG* reprints and the Birthday *LG* 1889. Upon hearing that his friend Harned liked the poem, WW said, "So do I . . . to me it is an essential poem—it needed to be made" (Traubel, II, 289). MS in Barrett.
4. First published in *Lippincott's Magazine*, November 1887, after having been rejected by H. M. Alden of *Harper's*, January 3, 1885 (Traubel, II, 211). Of the MSS, the Feinberg is entitled "So Loth to Depart" (reproduced in facsimile, *CW*, II, 322–23); the Barrett is an earlier draft.

E'en at the exit-door turning—charges superflous calling back
   —e'en as he descends the steps,
Something to eke out a minute additional—shadows of
   nightfall deepening,
Farewells, messages lessening—dimmer the forthgoer's visage
   and form,
Soon to be lost for aye in the darkness—loth, O so loth to depart!
Garrulous to the very last.
1887   *1888–89*

10

SECOND ANNEX
GOOD-BYE MY FANCY

Preface Note to 2d Annex[1]

CONCLUDING L. OF G.—1891

Had I not better withhold (in this old age and paralysis of me) such little tags and fringe-dots (maybe specks, stains,) as follow a long dusty journey, and witness it afterward? I have probably not been enough afraid of careless touches, from the first—and am not now—nor of parrot-like repetitions—nor platitudes and the commonplace. Perhaps I am too democratic for such avoidances. Besides, is not the verse-field, as originally plann'd by my theory, now sufficiently illustrated— and full time for me to silently retire?—(indeed amid no loud call or market for my sort of poetic utterance.)

In answer, or rather defiance, to that kind of well-put interrogation, here comes this little cluster, and conclusion of my preceding clusters. Though not at all clear that, as here collated, it is worth printing (certainly I have nothing fresh to write)—I while away the hours of my

Good-Bye My Fancy: The thirty-one poems of the "Second Annex—Good-Bye My Fancy," in *LG* 1891–92, had in some cases first been seen in periodical publication; they were then brought together in the first section of a miscellany of poetry and prose entitled *Good-Bye My Fancy* (1891). Like the poems of the "First Annex—Sands at Seventy," which were published in the miscellany *November Boughs* (1888), these were written, for the most part, after the poet had felt it necessary to complete the arrangement of his poetry as a whole in *LG* 1881, because of failing health and creativity as explained above (see note to "First Annex—Sands at Seventy"). Like the first annex, the second contains poems, if not so many, that have genuine merits and are related usefully to the themes of the 1881 volume. The text of *LG* 1891–92, including finally the present annex, was the last edition of *LG* to be published in the poet's lifetime. The complete MS of *Good-Bye My Fancy* is extant (Feinberg), fully assembled for the printer from proof sheets, clippings, and holograph leaves.
From the text of *LG* 1891–92, which is reproduced in the present edition, are excluded two pages (405–6) following the "First Annex—Sands at Seventy." These were printed on a single leaf, of which the recto read: "2D (ANNEX / GOOD-BYE MY FANCY. / Copyright, 1891, by WALT WHITMAN." / The verso (page 406) was the table of contents of this annex, now superseded by the contents page of the present edition.
1. This "Preface Note" was printed in *LG* 1891–92 without change from the plates of the separately published miscellany, *Good-Bye My Fancy* (1891). Its MS (Feinberg) is clearly written in black ink with comparatively little revision—an indication, as the text itself reveals—of the relaxation, even gaiety, that the poet confesses "I have in me perennially anyhow." The quatrain, "Last droplets . . ." is included in the "Excluded Poems and Passages" (*q.v.*).

72d year—hours of forced confinement in my den—by putting in shape this small old age collation:

Last droplets of and after spontaneous rain,
From many limpid distillations and past showers;
(Will they germinate anything? mere exhalations as they all are—
    the land's and sea's—America's;
Will they filter to any deep emotion? any heart and brain?)

However that may be, I feel like improving to-day's opportunity and wind up. During the last two years I have sent out, in the lulls of illness and exhaustion, certain chirps—lingering-dying ones probably (undoubtedly)—which now I may as well gather and put in fair type while able to see correctly—(for my eyes plainly warn me they are dimming, and my brain more and more palpably neglects or refuses, month after month, even slight tasks or revisions.)

In fact, here I am these current years 1890 and '91, (each successive fortnight getting stiffer and stuck deeper) much like some hard-cased dilapidated grim ancient shell-fish or time-bang'd conch (no legs, utterly non-locomotive) cast up high and dry on the shore-sands, helpless to move anywhere—nothing left but behave myself quiet, and while away the days yet assign'd, and discover if there is anything for the said grim and time-bang'd conch to be got at last out of inherited good spirits and primal buoyant centre-pulses down there deep somewhere within his gray-blurr'd old shell. . . . . (Reader, you must allow a little fun here—for one reason there are too many of the following poemets about death, &c., and for another the passing hours (July 5, 1890) are so sunny-fine. And old as I am I feel to-day almost a part of some frolicsome wave, or for sporting yet like a kid or kitten— probably a streak of physical adjustment and perfection here and now. I believe I have it in me perennially anyhow.)

Then behind all, the deep-down consolation (it is a glum one, but I dare not be sorry for the fact of it in the past, nor refrain from dwelling, even vaunting here at the end) that this late-years palsied old shorn and shell-fish condition of me is the indubitable outcome and growth, now near for 20 years along, of too over-zealous, over-continued bodily and emotional excitement and action through the times of 1862, '3, '4 and '5, visiting and waiting on wounded and sick army volunteers, both sides, in campaigns or contests, or after them, or in hospitals or fields south of Washington City, or in that place and elsewhere—those hot, sad, wrenching times—the army volunteers, all States,—or North or South—the wounded, suffering, dying—the exhausting, sweating summers, marches, battles, carnage—those trenches hurriedly heap'd by the corpse-thousands, mainly unknown —Will the America of the future—will this vast rich Union ever realize what itself cost, back there after all?—those hecatombs of battle-deaths—Those times of which, O far-off reader, this whole book is indeed finally but a reminiscent memorial from thence by me to you?

Sail Out for Good, Eidólon Yacht![2]

Heave the anchor short!
Raise main-sail and jib—steer forth,
O little white-hull'd sloop, now speed on really deep waters,
(I will not call it our concluding voyage,
But outset and sure entrance to the truest, best, maturest;)   5
Depart, depart from solid earth—no more returning to these
     shores,
Now on for aye our infinite free venture wending,
Spurning all yet tried ports, seas, hawsers, densities, gravitation,
Sail out for good, eidólon[3] yacht of me!
     1891   *1891–92*

Lingering Last Drops[4]

And whence and why come you?

We know not whence, (was the answer,)
We only know that we drift here with the rest,
That we linger'd and lagg'd—but were wafted at last, and are
     now here,
To make the passing shower's concluding drops.   5
     1891   *1891–92*

Good-Bye My Fancy[5]

Good-bye* my fancy—(I had a word to say,
But 'tis not quite the time—The best of any man's word or say,
Is when its proper place arrives—and for its meaning,
I keep mine till the last.)

*Behind a Good-bye there lurks much of the salutation of another beginning—to me, Development, Continuity, Immortality, Transformation, are the chiefest life-meanings of Nature and Humanity, and are the *sine qua non* of all facts, and each fact.

     Why do folks dwell so fondly on the last words, advice, appearance, of the departing? Those last words are not samples of the best, which involve vitality at its full, and balance, and perfect control and scope. But they are valuable beyond measure to confirm and endorse the varied train, facts, theories and faith of the whole preceding life.

     1891   *1891–92*

2. First published in *Lippincott's Magazine*, March 1891, together with three other poems, "Sound of the Winter," "The Unexpress'd," and "After the Argument"—all under the general title "Old-Age Echoes." Hanley has a page of rough draft, Barrett trial lines, and Feinberg the MS of the whole poem as well as a proof sheet with the deleted title "Old Age Recitatives."
3. See the poem "Eidólons," p. 6.
4. MS in Feinberg Collection. First published in *Good-Bye My Fancy* (1891).
5. WW's "word to say" on this theme is really uttered in the poem of the same title which closes the group. "Fancy" is here used in the sense of "creative imagination," now obsolescent but often so employed in the times of Coleridge and Poe. First published in *Good-Bye My Fancy* (1891).

On, on the Same, Ye Jocund Twain![6]

On, on the same, ye jocund twain!
My life and recitative, containing birth, youth, mid-age years,
Fitful as motley-tongues of flame, inseparably twined and
    merged in one—combining all,
My single soul—aims, confirmations, failures, joys—Nor single
    soul alone,
I chant my nation's crucial stage, (America's haply humanity's)
    —the trial great, the victory great,   5
A strange *eclaircissement* of all the masses past, the eastern
    world, the ancient, medieval,
Here, here from wanderings, strayings, lessons, wars, defeats—
    here at the west a voice triumphant—justifying all,
A gladsome pealing cry—a song for once of utmost pride and
    satisfaction;
I chant from it the common bulk, the general average horde,
    (the best no sooner than the worst)—And now I chant old
    age,
(My verses, written first for forenoon life, and for the
    summer's, autumn's spread,   10
I pass to snow-white hairs the same, and give to pulses winter-
    cool'd the same;)
As here in careless trill, I and my recitatives, with faith and love,
Wafting to other work, to unknown songs, conditions,
On, on, ye jocund twain! continue on the same!
1891   *1891–92*

My 71st Year[7]

After surmounting three-score and ten,
With all their chances, changes, losses, sorrows,
My parents' deaths, the vagaries of my life, the many tearing
    passions of me, the war of '63 and '4,
As some old broken soldier, after a long, hot, wearying march,
    or haply after battle,
To-day at twilight, hobbling, answering company roll-call, *Here*,
    with vital voice,   5
Reporting yet, saluting yet the Officer over all.
1889   *1891–92*

---

6. MSS include an early draft and proof sheet (Hanley) and four pages (Feinberg), including
    trial lines, rough draft, and final draft, dated May 10, 1890. First published in *Good-Bye My
    Fancy* (1891).
7. First published in *Century*, November 1889.

Apparitions[8]

A vague mist hanging 'round half the pages:
(Sometimes how strange and clear to the soul,
That all these solid things are indeed but apparitions,
    concepts, non-realities.)
1891   *1891–92*

The Pallid Wreath[9]

Somehow I cannot let it go yet, funereal though it is,
Let it remain back there on its nail suspended,
With pink, blue, yellow, all blanch'd, and the white now gray
    and ashy,
One wither'd rose put years ago for thee, dear friend;
But I do not forget thee. Hast thou then faded?   5
Is the odor exhaled? Are the colors, vitalities, dead?
No, while memories subtly play—the past vivid as ever;
For but last night I woke, and in that spectral ring saw thee,
Thy smile, eyes, face, calm, silent, loving as ever:
So let the wreath hang still awhile within my eye-reach,   10
It is not yet dead to me, nor even pallid.
1891   *1891–92*

An Ended Day[1]

The soothing sanity and blitheness of completion,
The pomp and hurried contest-glare and rush are done;
Now triumph! transformation! jubilate!*

*Note—*Summer country life.*—*Several years.*—In my rambles and explorations I found a woody place near the creek, where for some reason the birds in happy mood seem'd to resort in unusual numbers. Especially at the beginning of the day, and again at the ending, I was sure to get there the most copious bird-concerts. I repair'd there frequently at sunrise—and also at sunset, or just before . . . Once the question arose in me: Which is the best singing, the first or the latter-most? The first always exhilarated, and perhaps seem'd more joyous and stronger; but I always felt the sunset or late afternoon sounds more penetrating and sweeter—seem'd to touch the soul—often the evening thrushes, two or three of them, responding and perhaps blending. Though I miss'd some of the mornings, I found myself getting to be quite strictly punctual at the evening utterances.

    ANOTHER NOTE.—'He went out with the tide and the sunset,' was a phrase I heard from a surgeon describing an old sailor's death under peculiarly gentle conditions.

    During the Secession War, 1863 and '4, visiting the Army Hospitals around Washington, I form'd the habit, and continued it to the end, whenever the ebb or flood tide began the latter

---

8. The Feinberg MS of "Good-Bye My Fancy" shows these three lines as a holograph scrap pasted up for a third stanza of the poem "L. of G's Purport." First published in *Good-Bye My Fancy* (1891).
9. First published in the *Critic*, January 10, 1891. The MS (Berg) has the poet's notation, "My friends, Can you use this in the Critic? The price is $5 . . . ." In the first line, "funeral," the MS reading, was erroneously spelled "funeral" in the *Critic*. The error persisted in the collections *GBF* (1891) and *LG* 1891–92, both probably printed directly from a clipping of the *Critic* text, a procedure encouraged by WW's failing eyesight.
1. MS in Feinberg. First published in *Good-Bye My Fancy* (1891).

part of day, of punctually visiting those at that time populous wards of suffering men. Somehow (or I thought so) the effect of the hour was palpable. The badly wounded would get some ease, and would like to talk a little, or be talk'd to. Intellectual and emotional natures would be at their best: Deaths were always easier; medicines seem'd to have better effect when given then, and a lulling atmosphere would pervade the wards.

Similar influences, similar circumstances and hours, day-close, after great battles, even with all their horrors. I had more than once the same experience on the fields cover'd with fallen or dead.

1891   1891–92

Old Age's Ship & Crafty Death's[2]

From east and west across the horizon's edge,
Two mighty masterful vessels sailers steal upon us:
But we'll make race-a-time upon the seas—a battle-contest yet!
   bear lively there!
(Our joys of strife and derring-do to the last!)
Put on the old ship all her power to-day!   5
Crowd top-sail, top-gallant and royal studding-sails,
Out challenge and defiance—flags and flaunting pennants added,
As we take to the open—take to the deepest, freest waters.

1890   1891–92

To the Pending Year[3]

Have I no weapon-word for thee—some message brief and fierce?
(Have I fought out and done indeed the battle?) Is there no
   shot left,
For all thy affectations, lisps, scorns, manifold silliness?
Nor for myself—my own rebellious self in thee?

Down, down, proud gorge!—though choking thee;   5
Thy bearded throat and high-borne forehead to the gutter;
Crouch low thy neck to eleemosynary gifts.

1889   1891–92

Shakspere-Bacon's Cipher[4]

I doubt it not—then more, far more;
In each old song bequeath'd—in every noble page or text,

---

2. First published in *Century*, February 1890. MSS include a rough draft and proof sheet (Feinberg) and a printer's copy MS reproduced in facsimile in George M. Williamson's *Catalogue of a Collection of Books, Letters and Manuscripts, written by Walt Whitman* (1903).
3. First published in the *Critic*, January 5, 1889, under the title "To the Year 1889." Three MSS: an early draft varying widely from the printed version (Feinberg), a later draft (Lion), and a final draft (Yale).
4. MS, an early draft (Feinberg) with title "The Mystic Cipher" and subtitle "A hint for scientists." A proof sheet is reproduced in facsimile in Traubel, I, 180. First published in *The Cosmopolitan* (October 1887): 142.

(Different—something unreck'd before—some unsuspected
   author,)
In every object, mountain, tree, and star—in every birth and life,
As part of each—evolv'd from each—meaning, behind the
   ostent,   5
A mystic cipher waits infolded.
1891   *1891–92*

Long, Long Hence[5]

After a long, long course, hundreds of years, denials,
Accumulations, rous'd love and joy and thought,
Hopes, wishes, aspirations, ponderings, victories, myriads of
   readers,
Coating, compassing, covering—after ages' and ages'
   encrustations,
Then only may these songs reach fruition.   5
1891   *1891–92*

Bravo, Paris Exposition![6]

Add to your show, before you close it, France,
With all the rest, visible, concrete, temples, towers, goods,
   machines and ores,
Our sentiment wafted from many million heart-throbs, ethereal
   but solid,
(We grand-sons and great-grand-sons do not forget your
   grandsires,)
From fifty Nations and nebulous Nations, compacted, sent
   oversea to-day,   5
America's applause, love, memories and good-will.
1889   *1891–92*

Interpolation Sounds[7]

[General Philip Sheridan was buried at the Cathedral, Washington, D.C. August, 1888, with
all the pomp, music and ceremonies of the Roman Catholic service.]

Over and through the burial chant,
Organ and solemn service, sermon, bending priests,

5. MS in Feinberg. First published in *Good-Bye My Fancy* (1891).
6. First published in *Harper's Weekly,* September 28, 1889. MS and proof in Feinberg. The
   Paris Exposition, whose most famous exhibit was the Eiffel Tower, was open from May 6
   through November 6, 1889.
7. First published in the *New York Herald,* August 12, 1888, under the title "Over and Through
   the Burial Chant." LC has an earlier MS draft, and Yale the final MS of printer's copy, at the
   top of which WW has written the direction, "Put this in the day of Sheridan's burial
   ceremonies."

To me come interpolation sounds not in the show—plainly to
    me, crowding up the aisle and from the window,
Of sudden battle's hurry and harsh noises—war's grim game to
    sight and ear in earnest;
The scout call'd up and forward—the general mounted and his
    aids around him—the new-brought word—the
    instantaneous order issued;   5
The rifle crack—the cannon thud—the rushing forth of men
    from their tents;
The clank of cavalry—the strange celerity of forming ranks—
    the slender bugle note;
The sound of horses' hoofs departing—saddles, arms,
    accoutrements.*

---

*Note.—Camden. N. J., August 7, 1888.—Walt Whitman asks the *New York Herald* 'to add his tribute to Sheridan:'
  In the grand constellation of five or six names, under Lincoln's Presidency, that history will bear for ages in her firmament as marking the last life-throbs of secession, and beaming on its dying gasps, Sheridan's will be bright. One consideration rising out of the now dead soldier's example as it passes my mind, is worth taking notice of. If the war had continued any long time these States, in my opinion, would have shown and proved the most conclusive military talents ever evinced by any nation on earth. That they possess'd a rank and file ahead of all other known in points of quality and limitlessness of number are easily admitted. But we have, too, the eligibility of organizing, handling and officering equal to the other. These two, with modern arms, transportation, and inventive American genius, would make the United States, with earnestness, not only able to stand the whole world, but conquer that world united against us.'

1888   *1891–92*

To the Sun-Set Breeze[8]

Ah, whispering, something again, unseen,
Where late this heated day thou enterest at my window, door,
Thou, laving, tempering all, cool-freshing, gently vitalizing
Me, old, alone, sick, weak-down, melted-worn with sweat;
Thou, nestling, folding close and firm yet soft, companion
    better than talk, book, art,   5
(Thou hast, O Nature! elements! utterance to my heart beyond
    the rest—and this is of them,)
So sweet thy primitive taste to breathe within—thy soothing
    fingers on my face and hands,
Thou, messenger-magical strange bringer to body and spirit of me,
(Distances balk'd—occult medicines penetrating me from head
    to foot,)
I feel the sky, the prairies vast—I feel the mighty northern
    lakes,   10
I feel the ocean and the forest—somehow I feel the globe
    itself swift-swimming in space;

---

8. First published in *Lippincott's Magazine,* December 1890. Ezra Pound praised this poem in an unpublished essay (Yale) dated February 1, 1909: "And yet if a man has written lines like Whitman's to the 'sunset breeze' one has to love him. I think we have not yet paid enough attention to the deliberate artistry of the man, not in details but in the large" (Herbert Bergman, "Ezra Pound and Walt Whitman," *AL* 27 (March 1955): 60.

Thou blown from lips so loved, now gone—haply from endless
    store, God-sent,
(For thou art spiritual, Godly, most of all known to my sense,)
Minister to speak to me, here and now, what word has never
    told, and cannot tell,
Art thou not universal concrete's distillation? Law's, all
    Astronomy's last refinement?   15
Hast thou no soul? Can I not know, identify thee?
  1890   *1891–92*

Old Chants[9]

An ancient song, reciting, ending,
Once gazing toward thee, Mother of All,
Musing, seeking themes fitted for thee,
Accept for me, thou saidst, *the elder ballads,*
And name for me before thou goest each ancient poet.   5

(Of many debts incalculable,
Haply our New World's chieftest debt is to old poems.)

Ever so far back, preluding thee, America,
Old chants, Egyptian priests, and those of Ethiopia,
The Hindu epics, the Grecian, Chinese, Persian,   10
The Biblic books and prophets, and deep idyls of the Nazarene,
The Iliad, Odyssey, plots, doings, wanderings of Eneas,
Hesiod, Eschylus, Sophocles, Merlin, Arthur,
The Cid, Roland at Roncesvalles, the Nibelungen,
The troubadours, minstrels, minnesingers, skalds,   15
Chaucer, Dante, flocks of singing birds,
The Border Minstrelsy, the bye-gone ballads, feudal tales,
    essays, plays,
Shakspere, Schiller, Walter Scott, Tennyson,
As some vast wondrous weird dream-presences,
The great shadowy groups gathering around,   20
Darting their mighty masterful eyes forward at thee,
Thou! with as now thy bending neck and head, with courteous
    hand and word, ascending,
Thou! pausing a moment, drooping thine eyes upon them,
    blent with their music,
Well pleased, accepting all, curiously prepared for by them,
Thou enterest at thy entrance porch.   25
  1891   *1891–92*

---

9. First published in *New York Truth,* March 19, 1891. LG has a MS of the first five lines,
    Feinberg of the entire poem, with the alternative title "An ancient song reciting."

A Christmas Greeting[1]

From a Northern Star-Group to a Southern. 1889–90

Welcome, Brazilian brother—thy ample place is ready;
A loving hand—a smile from the north—a sunny instant hail!
(Let the future care for itself, where it reveals its troubles,
    impedimentas,
Ours, ours the present throe, the democratic aim, the
    acceptance and the faith;)
To thee to-day our reaching arm, our turning neck—to thee
    from us the expectant eye,   5
Thou cluster free! thou brilliant lustrous one! thou, learning well,
The true lesson of a nation's light in the sky,
(More shining than the Cross, more than the Crown,)[2]
The height to be superb humanity.
    1889   1891–92

Sounds of the Winter[3]

Sounds of the winter too,
Sunshine upon the mountains—many a distant strain
From cheery railroad train—from nearer field, barn, house,
The whispering air—even the mute crops, garner'd apples, corn,
Children's and women's tones—rhythm of many a farmer and
    of flail,   5
An old man's garrulous lips among the rest, *Think not we give
    out yet,*
Forth from these snowy hairs we keep up yet the lilt.
    1891   1891–92

A Twilight Song[4]

As I sit in twilight late alone by the flickering oak-flame,
Musing on long-pass'd war-scenes—of the countless buried
    unknown soldiers,

---

1. No record of publication. Both the MS in rough draft and the printer's copy in Feinberg Collection.
2. Two brilliant constellations in the Southern hemisphere; but WW's figure strongly recalls the historic failures of "cross and crown" in national destinies.
3. First published in *Lippincott's Magazine*, March 1891. Both Barrett and Lion have MSS, Feinberg the proof sheet.
4. First published in *Century* 40 (May 1890): 27, with the subtitle "For unknown buried soldiers, North and South." WW toiled much over this poem. No less than five drafts, three of which are mainly worksheets, are in the Brown Library; Huntington has a final draft, and Barrett three trial lines on the back of a letter dated August 14, 1889.

Of the vacant names, as unindented air's and sea's—the
    unreturn'd,
The brief truce after battle, with grim burial-squads, and the
    deep-fill'd trenches
Of gather'd dead from all America, North, South, East, West,
    whence they came up,   5
From wooded Maine, New-England's farms, from fertile
    Pennsylvania, Illinois, Ohio,
From the measureless West, Virginia, the South, the Carolinas,
    Texas, .
(Even here in my room-shadows and half-lights in the noiseless
    flickering flames,
Again I see the stalwart ranks on-filing, rising—I hear the
    rhythmic tramp of the armies;)
You million unwrit names all, all—you dark bequest from all
    the war,   10
A special verse for you—a flash of duty long neglected—your
    mystic roll strangely gather'd here,
Each name recall'd by me from out the darkness and death's
    ashes,
Henceforth to be, deep, deep within my heart recording, for
    many a future year,
Your mystic roll entire of unknown names, or North or South,
Embalm'd with love in this twilight song.   15
    1890   *1891–92*

When the Full-grown Poet Came[5]

When the full-grown poet came,
Out spake pleased Nature (the round impassive globe, with all
    its shows of day and night,) saying, *He is mine*;
But out spake too the Soul of man, proud, jealous and
    unreconciled, *Nay, he is mine alone*;
—Then the full-grown poet stood between the two, and took
    each by the hand;
And to-day and ever so stands, as blender, uniter, tightly
    holding hands,   5
Which he will never release until he reconciles the two,
And wholly and joyously blends them.
    1876   *1891–92*

---

5. One of four poems, cut from proofsheets and pasted on blank ends of pages in the "Cen-
tennial Edition" of *LG* 1876, the small edition bound in brown calf. It was printed in the
same position (p. 359) in the second issue of *LG* 1876 (bound in half cream-colored calf),
the final poem of the group, "Bathed in War's Perfume," not included in *LG* 1881. This
poem appeared in the volume *GBF* (1891), 14, and was retained in the same position in
GBF 1892, Second Annex—the only one of the 76 intercalations that was retained in 1892.
That the poet restored it to life in the present annex accords with his evident early approval
in selecting it to appear in the *New York Tribune* of February 19, 1876, with his preview of
his current *LG* edition. A ms fragment related to this poem is printed in *N and F*, I, 22,
item 185.

Osceola[6]

[When I was nearly grown to manhood in Brooklyn, New York, (middle of 1838,) I met one
of the return'd U. S. Marines from Fort Moultrie, S. C., and had long talks with him—learn'd
the occurrence below described—death of Osceola. The latter was a young, brave, leading
Seminole in the Florida war of the that time—was surrender'd to our troops, imprison'd and
literally died of "a broken heart," at Fort Moultrie. He sicken'd of his confinement—the doctor
and officers made every allowance and kindness possible for him; then the close:]

When his hour for death had come,
He slowly rais'd himself from the bed on the floor,
Drew on his war-dress, shirt, leggings, and girdled the belt
    around his waist,
Call'd for vermilion paint (his looking-glass was held before him,)
Painted half his face and neck, his wrists, and back-hands.   5

Put the scalp-knife carefully in his belt—then lying down,
    resting a moment,
Rose again, half sitting, smiled, gave in silence his extended
    hand to each and all,
Sank faintly low to the floor (tightly grasping the tomahawk
    handle,)
Fix'd his look on wife and little children—the last:

(And here a line in memory of his name and death.)[7]   10
1890   *1891–92*

A Voice from Death[8]

(The Johnstown, Penn., cataclysm, May 31, 1889.)

A voice from Death, solemn and strange, in all his sweep and
    power,
With sudden, indescribable blow—towns drown'd—humanity
    by thousands slain,
The vaunted work of thrift, goods, dwellings, forge, street, iron
    bridge,
Dash'd pell-mell by the blow—yet usher'd life continuing on,

6. First published in *Munson's Illustrated World,* April 1890. MSS include a rough draft MS
(Feinberg) and a later draft (Yale), probably printer's copy. The inspiration for the poem
derives in part from a large print of Osceola given to WW by the artist George Catlin. See
Edgeley W. Todd, "Indian Pictures and Two Whitman Poems," *HLQ* 19 (November 1955):
1–11.
7. The date of Osceola's death, January 30, 1838, verifies WW's date. A gallant young leader
of the second Seminole War (1835–37), he was treacherously seized and imprisoned while
conferring under an American truce agreement. He died within four months, substantiating
the widespread belief among whites of the time that his race could not survive either in
slavery or in captivity.
8. First published in the *New York World,* June 7, 1889, in front-page position only a week
after the flood. The printer's MS copy is in Yale. The Johnstown flood was caused by the
sudden collapse of a dam following unprecedented rains; some 2,200 lives were lost, and
property estimated at $12,000,000.

(Amid the rest, amid the rushing, whirling, wild debris,   5
A suffering woman saved—a baby safely born!)

Although I come and unannounc'd, in horror and in pang,
In pouring flood and fire, and wholesale elemental crash, (this
    voice so solemn, strange,)
I too a minister of Deity.

Yea, Death, we bow our faces, veil our eyes to thee,   10
We mourn the old, the young untimely drawn to thee,
The fair, the strong, the good, the capable,
The household wreck'd, the husband and the wife, the engulf'd
    forger in his forge,
The corpses in the whelming waters and the mud,
The gather'd thousands to their funeral mounds, and
    thousands never found or gather'd.   15

Then after burying, mourning the dead,
(Faithful to them found or unfound, forgetting not, bearing the
    past, here new musing,)
A day—a passing moment or an hour—America itself bends low,
Silent, resign'd, submissive.

War, death, cataclysm like this, America,   20
Take deep to thy proud prosperous heart.

E'en as I chant, lo! out of death, and out of ooze and slime,
The blossoms rapidly blooming, sympathy, help, love,
From West and East, from South and North and over sea,
Its hot-spurr'd hearts and hands humanity to human aid moves
    on;   25
And from within a thought and lesson yet.

Thou ever-darting Globe! through Space and Air!
Thou waters that encompass us!
Thou that in all the life and death of us, in action or in sleep!
Thou laws invisible that permeate them and all,   30
Thou that in all, and over all, and through and under all,
    incessant!
Thou! thou! the vital, universal, giant force resistless, sleepless,
    calm,
Holding Humanity as in thy open hand, as some ephemeral toy,
How ill to e'er forget thee!

For I too have forgotten,   35
(Wrapt in these little potencies of progress, politics, culture,
    wealth, inventions, civilization,)
Have lost my recognition of your silent ever-swaying power, ye
    mighty, elemental throes,

In which and upon which we float, and every one of us is
    buoy'd.
1889   *1891–92*

A Persian Lesson[9]

For his o'erarching and last lesson the greybeard sufi,[1]
In the fresh scent of the morning in the open air,
On the slope of a teeming Persian rose-garden,
Under an ancient chestnut-tree wide spreading its branches,
Spoke to the young priests and students.   5

"Finally my children, to envelop each word, each part of the
    rest,
Allah is all, all, all—is immanent in every life and object,
May-be at many and many-a-more removes—yet Allah, Allah,
    Allah is there.

"Has the estray wander'd far? Is the reason-why strangely hidden?
Would you sound below the restless ocean of the entire world?   10
Would you know the dissatisfaction? the urge and spur of
    every life;
The something never still'd—never entirely gone? the invisible
    need of every seed?

"It is the central urge in every atom,
(Often unconscious, often evil, downfallen,)
To return to its divine source and origin, however distant,   15
Latent the same in subject and in object, without one exception."
1891   *1891–92*

The Commonplace[2]

The commonplace I sing;
How cheap is health! how cheap nobility!
Abstinence, no falsehood, no gluttony, lust;
The open air I sing, freedom, toleration,
(Take here the mainest lesson—less from books—less from
    the schools,)   5
The common day and night—the common earth and waters,

---

9. MS printer's copy with cancelled title "A Sufi Lesson" in Feinberg. First published in *Good-
   Bye My Fancy* (1891).
1. A teacher of Sufism, an ecstatic spiritual tradition within Islam. Sufism has produced a rich
   poetic heritage much admired by WW and his contemporaries.
2. First published, in MS facsimile, in *Munson's Magazine*, March 1891. A rough draft (Fein-
   berg) shows minor variations.

Your farm—your work, trade, occupation,
The democratic wisdom underneath, like solid ground for all.
1891   *1891–92*

"The Rounded Catalogue Divine Complete"[3]

[Sunday, —— — ——.—Went this forenoon to church. A college professor, Rev. Dr.———, gave us a fine sermon, during which I caught the above words; but the minister included in his "rounded catalogue" letter and spirit, only the esthetic things, and entirely ignored what I name in the following:]

The devilish and the dark, the dying and diseas'd,
The countless (nineteen-twentieths) low and evil, crude and
    savage,
The crazed, prisoners in jail, the horrible, rank, malignant,
Venom and filth, serpents, the ravenous sharks, liars, the
    dissolute;
(What is the part the wicked and the loathesome[4] bear within
    earth's orbic scheme?)   5
Newts, crawling things in slime and mud, poisons,
The barren soil, the evil men, the slag and hideous rot.
1891   *1891–92*

Mirages[5]

(Noted verbatim after a supper-talk outdoors in Nevada with two old miners)

More experiences and sights, stranger, than you'd think for;
Times again, now mostly just after sunrise or before sunset,
Sometimes in spring, oftener in autumn, perfectly clear
    weather, in plain sight,
Camps far or near, the crowded streets of cities and the
    shopfronts,
(Account for it or not—credit or not—it is all true,   5
And my mate there could tell you the like—we have often
    confab'd about it,)
People and scenes, animals, trees, colors and lines, plain as
    could be,

---

3. First published in *Good-Bye My Fancy* (1891). Both an earlier draft and the final MS printer's copy are in Feinberg. The rough draft shows much revision and many lines not included in the final version. For example:

    > Buried and hid beneath the mountains of soil . . .
    > A lustrous sapphire blue, eternal, vital, slumbers
    >   ready (what is the part the wicked and the
    >   loathsome bear within the latent scheme?)

4. Correctly, "loathsome."
5. First published in *Good-Bye My Fancy* (1891). A MS printer's copy in Feinberg. The sub-heading has no biographical relevance. The western limit of WW's journeys was Denver, Colorado.

Farms and dooryards of home, paths border'd with box, lilacs
    in corners,
Weddings in churches, thanksgiving dinners, returns of long-
    absent sons,
Glum funerals, the crape-veil'd mother and the daughters,   10
Trials in courts, jury and judge, the accused in the box,
Contestants, battles, crowds, bridges, wharves,
Now and then mark'd faces of sorrow or joy,
(I could pick them out this moment if I saw them again,)
Show'd to me just aloft to the right in the sky-edge,   15
Or plainly there to the left on the hill-tops.
   1891   *1891–92*

L. of G.'s Purport[6]

Not to exclude or demarcate, or pick out evils from their
    formidable masses (even to expose them,)
But add, fuse, complete, extend—and celebrate the immortal
    and the good.

Haughty this song, its words and scope,
To span vast realms of space and time,
Evolution—the cumulative—growths and generations.   5

Begun in ripen'd youth and steadily pursued,
Wandering, peering, dallying with all—war, peace, day, and
    night absorbing,
Never even for one brief hour abandoning my task,
I end it here in sickness, poverty, and old age.

I sing of life, yet mind me well of death: 10
To-day shadowy Death dogs my steps, my seated shape, and
    has for years—
Draws sometimes close to me, as face to face.
   1891   *1891–92*

6. First published in *Good-Bye My Fancy* (1891). MS evidence exists in the LC and the Feinberg
collections that this poem, an old-age companion piece to earlier statements of intent such
as "One's-Self I Sing" and "Small the Theme of my Chant," was actually first projected, in
part, as three separate poems: the present lines 1 and 2 under the title "L. of G.'s Purport";
lines 6, 7, 8, and 9 under the title "My Task"; and lines 10, 11, and 12 under the title
"Death Dogs My Steps." To these three were added two lines under the title "For Us Two,
Reader Dear," which were finally published in another part of *Good-Bye My Fancy*, p. 44.
Another Feinberg MS gives lines, printed also on p. 44, under the title "L of G."

The Unexpress'd[7]

How dare one say it?
After the cycles, poems, singers, plays,
Vaunted Ionia's, India's—Homer, Shakspere—the long, long
    times' thick dotted roads, areas,
The shining clusters and the Milky Ways of stars—Nature's
    pulses reap'd,
All retrospective passions, heroes, war, love, adoration,   5
All ages' plummets dropt to their utmost depths,
All human lives, throats, wishes, brains—all experiences'
    utterance;
After the countless songs, or long or short, all tongues, all lands,
Still something not yet told in poesy's voice or print—
    something lacking,
(Who knows? the best yet unexpress'd and lacking.)   10
  1891   *1891–92*

Grand Is the Seen[8]

Grand is the seen, the light, to me—grand are the sky and stars,
Grand is the earth, and grand are lasting time and space,
And grand their laws, so multiform, puzzling, evolutionary;
But grander far the unseen soul of me, comprehending,
    endowing all those,
Lighting the light, the sky and stars, delving the earth, sailing
    the sea,   5
(What were all those, indeed, without thee, unseen soul? of
    what amount without thee?)
More evolutionary, vast, puzzling, O my soul!
More multiform far—more lasting thou than they.
  1891   *1891–92*

7. First published in *Lippincott's Magazine,* March 1891. The Yale MS bears WW's notation, "Sent to Alden Oct. 18 '90 100 asked rejected all returned." A later draft (Feinberg) is written on the back of a letter dated September 25, 1889; the MS printer's copy (Barrett) contains also the holograph of two other poems—"Sounds of the Winter" and "After the Argument." The three appeared together in *Lippincott's* under the general title "Old Age Echoes."
8. First published in *Good-Bye My Fancy.* In addition to the MS printer's copy (Feinberg), there are three MS versions of this poem, one at LG, a later one at Houghton, and a third—present whereabouts unknown—transcribed in *CW,* X, 130, None of the three contains the sixth line, which was inserted in the printer's copy.

Unseen Buds[9]

Unseen buds, infinite, hidden well,
Under the snow and ice, under the darkness, in every square
    or cubic inch,
Germinal, exquisite, in delicate lace, microscopic, unborn,
Like babes in wombs, latent, folded, compact, sleeping;
Billions of billions, and trillions of trillions of them waiting,   5
(On earth and in the sea—the universe—the stars there in the
    heavens,)
Urging slowly, surely forward, forming endless,
And waiting ever more, forever more behind.
1891   *1891–92*

Good-Bye My Fancy![1]

Good-bye my Fancy!
Farewell dear mate, dear love!
I'm going away, I know not where,
Or to what fortune, or whether I may ever see you again,
So Good-bye my Fancy.   5

Now for my last—let me look back a moment;
The slower fainter ticking of the clock is in me,
Exit, nightfall, and soon the heart-thud stopping.

Long have we lived, joy'd, caress'd together;
Delightful!—now separation—Good-bye my Fancy.   10

Yet let me not be too hasty,
Long indeed have we lived; slept, filter'd, become really
    blended into one;
Then if we die we die together, (yes, we'll remain one,)
If we go anywhere we'll go together to meet what happens,
May-be we'll be better off and blither, and learn something,   15
May-be it is yourself now really ushering me to the true songs,
    (who knows?)
May-be it is you the mortal knob really undoing, turning—so
    now finally,
Good-bye—and hail! my Fancy.
1891   *1891–92*

9. First published in *Good-Bye My Fancy.* In *The Evolution of Walt Whitman,* 14, Roger Asselineau suggests that in the development of *LG,* WW's poems themselves germinated in the fashion here described. The MS printer's copy is extant (Feinberg).
1. First published in *Good-Bye My Fancy.* In this farewell the poet rounds out the sense of self-communion, of colloquy with his *alter ego,* which may be thought of as his "demon," his poetic genius—a continuing dialogue with the self that began with "Song of Myself," notably the fifth canto. See note to the poem of the same title earlier in this annex (p. 453).

A BACKWARD GLANCE O'ER TRAVEL'D ROADS *AND* PREFATORY LETTER

Prefatory Letter to the Reader, *Leaves of Grass* 1889

May 31, 1889
CAMDEN, NEW JERSEY, U. S. AMERICA

To-day completes my three-score-and-ten years[1]—rounds and coheres the successive growths and stages of L. of G. with the following essay and (sort of) testament—my hurried epilogue of intentions-bequest—and gives me the crowning content, (for these lines are written at the last,) of feeling and definitely, per- 5 haps boastfully, reiterating, For good or bad, plain or not-plain, I have held out and now concluded my utterance, entirely its own way; the main wonder being to me, of the foregoing 404 pages entire, amid their many faults and omissions, that (after looking over them leisurely and critically, as the last week, night 10 and day,) they have adhered faithfully to, and carried out, for nearly 40 years, over many gaps, through thick and thin, peace and war, sickness and health, clouds and sunshine, my latent purposes, &c., even as measurably well and far as they do be- tween these covers. (Nature evidently achieves specimens only 15 —plants the seeds of suggestions—is not so intolerant of what is call'd evil—relies on *law* and *character* more than special cases or partialities; and in my little scope I have follow'd or tried to follow the lesson:[2] . . Probably that is about all.)

Yes, to-day finishes my 70th year; and even if but the merest 20 additional preface, (and not plain what tie-together it has with the following *Backward Glance*,) I suppose I must reel out some- thing to celebrate my old birthday anniversary and for this spe-

---

1. On his seventieth birthday, aged by illness and infirmity rather than by years, Whitman wrote this very characteristic letter to appear in the 1889 *Leaves of Grass*, which commemorated his last birthday, as he supposed. We have inserted it in its original position because it fixes historically the effective date of his determination to recommend that "A Backward Glance . . ." be included at the end of future editions of *LG* and that his final revised text be honored in any "future printing." This he did by means of the very specific footnote. Fortunately he was able to complete another miscellany, *Good-Bye My Fancy* (1891), and to add its poems as a "Second Annex" to the finally revised *LG* 1891–92, truly a "deathbed edition," which is reproduced in the present text. That edition, without this letter, repeated the footnote verbatim, except for the change from "422 pages" to 438, and gave it a more prominent position on the verse of the title page, where it also appears in the present edition.
2. That of nature, whose "successive growths and stages" from "seeds of suggestions" often remind Whitman how *LG* grew from his "latent purposes." These reiterations, and the la- borious revision in the MSS and successive editions, run counter to the theory that *LG* was originally planned as a whole. The present is one of the most concise and clear of WW's many pronouncements on this point.

cial edition of the latest completest L. of G. utterance.[3] Printers
send word, too, there is a blank here to be written up—and what   25
with?[4] . . . Probably I may as well transcribe and eke out this
note by the following lines of a letter last week to a valued friend
who demands to know my current personal condition: . . . "First
asking pardon for long neglect—The perfect physical health,
strength, buoyancy, (and inward impetus to back them,) which   30
were vouchsafed during my whole life, and especially throughout
the Secession War period, (1860 to '66,) seem'd to wane after
those years, and were closely track'd by a stunning paralytic sei-
zure, and following physical debility and inertia, (laggardness,
torpor, indifference, perhaps laziness,) which put me low in 1873   35
and '4 and '5—then lifted a little, but have essentially remain'd
ever since; several spirts or attacks—five or six of them, one time
or another from 1876 onward, but gradually mainly overcome—
till now, 1888 and '9, the worst and most obstinate seizure of
all. . . . Upon the whole, however, and even at this, and though   40
old and sick, I keep up, maintain fair spirits, partially read and
write—have publish'd last and full and revised editions of my
poems and prose (records and results of youth and early and mid
age—of absolute strength and health—o'erseen now during a
lingering ill spell)—But have had a bad year, this last one—have   45
run a varied gaunlet, chronic constipation, and then vertigo,
bladder and gastric troubles, and the foremention'd steady dis-
ability and inertia; bequests of the serious paralysis at Washing-
ton, D. C., closing the Secession War—that seizure indeed the
culmination of much that preceded, and real source of all my   50
woes since. During the past year, and now, with all these, (a
body and brain-action dull'd, while the spirit is perhaps willing
and live enough,) I get along more contentedly and comfortably
than you might suppose—sit here all day in my big, high, strong,
rattan-bottom'd chair (with great wolf-skin spread on the back   55
in cool weather)—as writing to you now on a tablet on my lap,
may-be my last missives of love, memories and cheer."

---

3. "As there are now several editions of L. of G., different texts and dates, I wish to say that I
   prefer and recommend the present one, complete, for future printing, if there should be any;
   a copy and fac-simile, indeed, of the text of these 422 pages. The subsequent interval which
   is so important to form'd and launch'd works, books especially, has pass'd; and waiting till
   fully after that, I give these concluding words" [WW's note].
4. The old printer and newsman whimsically remembered a constant affliction of his trade: "a
   blank here to be written up—and with what?" It may be part of the jest that he filled the
   blank with one of his countless letters dealing minutely and cheerfully with his appalling
   excretory and motor infirmities.

A Backward Glance O'er Travel'd Roads[5]

Perhaps the best of songs heard, or of any and all true love, or life's fairest episodes, or sailors', soldiers' trying scenes on land or sea, is the *résumé* of them, or any of them, long afterwards, looking at the actualities away back past, with all their practical excitations gone. How the soul loves to float amid such reminiscences!

So here I sit gossiping in the early candle-light of old age[6]—I and my book—casting backward glances over our travel'd road. After completing, as it were, the journey—(a varied jaunt of years, with many halts and gaps of intervals—or some lengthen'd ship-voyage, wherein more than once the last hour had apparently arrived, and we seem'd certainly going down—yet reaching port in a sufficient way through all discomfitures at last)—After completing my poems, I am curious to review them in the light of their own (at the time unconscious, or mostly unconscious) intentions, with certain unfoldings of the thirty years they seek to embody. These lines, therefore, will probably blend the weft of first purposes and speculations, with the warp of that experience afterwards, always bringing strange developments.

---

5. Appeared with the present title as the introduction to *November Boughs* (1888), a prose miscellany preceded by "Sands at Seventy," a cluster of new poems. The *November Boughs* volume was reissued in London (1889) and inserted in *Complete Poems and Prose* (1888) as a supplement without change of pagination. In *LG* 1889, a limited edition celebrating the poet's seventieth birthday, the new poems, "Sands at Seventy," appeared as an "Annex"; also "A Backward Glance . . ." was given its final position, following the completed poems as a retrospective essay.

Preceding "A Backward Glance . . . ," the poet included an untitled birthday letter to the reader, dated May 31, 1889 (see the text and footnote immediately above). Whitman's footnote to the letter was his first definition of the final text. Any "future printing, if there should be any; [should be] a copy and fac-simile" (as he had already told Horace Traubel: "leaving the book completely as I left it"). This footnote also appears with appropriate page references (as in *LG* 1891–92, the master text for this Norton Critical Edition). All editions of "A Backward Glance . . ." from 1888 to 1891–92 were printed from the same plates, without textual change except for the correction, in *LG* 1889, of two typographical errors (see footnotes below). Pages were not renumbered until the final *LG* 1891–92.

The essay was completed by May 28, 1888, and set in type three days later, on the poet's sixty-ninth birthday. It resulted from several previous ventures in literary autobiography, the first of which was "A Backward Glance on My Own Road" (*Critic*, January 5, 1884). This article, on two dominant themes, foreshadowed the two halves of the present essay. The second half of the *Critic* article was probably derived from the poet's article "How 'Leaves of Grass' Was Made," reported as having appeared "in 1885, in *The New York Star*," but this title is now known only by a posthumous article of the same name (allegedly reprinted from the *Star* as a memorial to Whitman) in *Frank Leslie's Popular Monthly* (June 1892). Every paragraph of the *Leslie's* text had also appeared before the final draft of 1888, with minor variants, in the poet's article "How I Made a Book," *Philadelphia Press*, July 11, 1886. Whitman then wrote the first half of his new essay, a revision of the first half of the 1884 ancestor, and this appeared as "My Book and I" in *Lippincott's Monthly Magazine* (January 1887). Every paragraph of "A Backward Glance O'er Travel'd Roads" appeared in some form in one of the preceding four articles. For a textual study of these essays see *Walt Whitman's Backward Glances*, ed. by Sculley Bradley and John A. Stevenson (Philadelphia, 1947), and see the edition of the essay in *Coll W, Prose*, II.

6. WW was only sixty-seven; this passage appeared in "My Book and I," *Lippincott's Monthly Magazine* (January 1887); see note 5 above.

Result of seven or eight stages and struggles[7] extending   20
through nearly thirty years, (as I nigh my three-score-and-ten I
live largely on memory,) I look upon "Leaves of Grass," now
finish'd to the end of its opportunities and powers, as my defin-
itive *carte visite* to the coming generations of the New World,[8]
if I may assume to say so. That I have not gain'd the acceptance   25
of my own time, but have fallen back on fond dreams of the
future—anticipations—("still lives the song, though Regnar
dies")[9]—That from a worldly and business point of view "Leaves
of Grass" has been worse than a failure—that public criticism
on the book and myself as author of it yet shows mark'd anger   30
and contempt more than anything else—("I find a solid line of
enemies to you everywhere,"—letter from W. S. K.,[1] Boston,
May 28, 1884)—And that solely for publishing it I have been
the object of two or three pretty serious special official
buffetings—is all probably no more than I ought to have ex-   35
pected. I had my choice when I commenc'd. I bid neither for
soft eulogies, big money returns, nor the approbation of existing
schools and conventions. As fulfill'd, or partially fulfill'd, the best
comfort of the whole business (after a small band of the dearest
friends and upholders ever vouchsafed to man or cause—doubt-   40
less all the more faithful and uncompromising—this little
phalanx!—for being so few) is that, unstopp'd and unwarp'd by
any influence outside the soul within me, I have had my say
entirely my own way, and put it unerringly on record—the value
thereof to be decided by time.   45
　　In calculating that decision, William O'Connor and Dr.
Bucke[2] are far more peremptory than I am. Behind all else that
can be said, I consider "Leaves of Grass" and its theory
experimental—as, in the deepest sense, I consider our American
republic itself to be, with its theory. (I think I have at least   50
enough philosophy not to be too absolutely certain of anything,
or any results.) In the second place, the volume is a *sortie*—
whether to prove triumphant, and conquer its field of aim and
escape and construction, nothing less than a hundred years from

7. WW authorized fifteen editions or reprints of *LG* poems. Those representing genuine "stages and struggles" were nine: 1855, 1856, 1860, 1867, 1871–72, 1876, 1881, 1888–89, and 1891–92. The Civil War poems, *Drum-Taps* (1865), might also be so regarded.
8. "When Champollion, on his death-bed, handed to the printer the revised proof of his 'Egyptian Grammar,' he said gayly, 'Be careful of this—it is my *carte de visite* to posterity' " [WW's note].
9. From "Alfred the Harper" (stanza 14, 1.3), a long ballad by John Sterling. King Alfred, disguised as a harper, appears at the feast of the Danes, who had ravaged the English coast and destroyed Regnar, the British defender; the Harper-King boldly praises him in the quoted line, then makes his escape to return victorious in Regnar's name. John Sterling (1806–1844) was a Scottish-born English poet, publisher, and curate, whose *Life* (1851) was written by Carlyle. WW copied the phrase about Regnar in his notes. *Cf. N and F*, IV, 167, item 52.
1. William Sloane Kennedy (1850–1929), critic and biographer, a late disciple of Whitman, of whom he wrote *Reminiscences* (1896) and—concerning *LG*—*The Fight of a Book for the World* (1926).
2. William Douglas O'Connor wrote *The Good Gray Poet* (1866), the earliest "vindication" of WW; Richard Maurice Bucke wrote an early biographical study, *Walt Whitman* (1883); both were the poet's devoted friends.

now can fully answer. I consider the point that I have positively 55
gain'd a hearing, to far more than make up for any and all other
lacks and withholdings. Essentially, *that* was from the first, and
has remain'd throughout, the main object. Now it seems to be
achiev'd, I am certainly contented to waive any otherwise mo-
mentous drawbacks, as of little account. Candidly and dispas- 60
sionately reviewing all my intentions, I feel that they were
creditable—and I accept the result, whatever it may be.

After continued personal ambition and effort, as a young fel-
low, to enter with the rest into competition for the usual rewards,
business, political, literary, &c.—to take part in the great *mèlée*,[3] 65
both for victory's prize itself and to do some good—After years
of those aims and pursuits, I found myself remaining possess'd,
at the age of thirty-one to thirty-three, with a special desire and
conviction. Or rather, to be quite exact, a desire that had been
flitting through my previous life, or hovering on the flanks, 70
mostly indefinite hitherto, had steadily advanced to the front,
defined itself, and finally dominated everything else. This was a
feeling or ambition to articulate and faithfully express in literary
or poetic form, and uncompromisingly, my own physical, emo-
tional, moral, intellectual, and aesthetic Personality, in the midst 75
of, and tallying, the momentous spirit and facts of its immediate
days, and of current America—and to exploit that Personality,
identified with place and date, in a far more candid and com-
prehensive sense than any hitherto poem or book.

Perhaps this is in brief, or suggests, all I have sought to do. 80
Given the Nineteenth Century, with the United States, and what
they furnish as area and points of view, "Leaves of Grass" is, or
seeks to be, simply a faithful and doubtless self-will'd record. In
the midst of all, it gives one man's—the author's—identity, ar-
dors, observations, faiths, and thoughts, color'd hardly at all with 85
any decided coloring from other faiths or other identities. Plenty
of songs had been sung—beautiful, matchless songs—adjusted
to other lands than these—another spirit and stage of evolution;
but I would sing, and leave out or put in, quite solely with ref-
erence to America and to-day.[4] Modern science and democracy 90
seem'd to be throwing out their challenge to poetry to put them
in its statements in contradistinction to the songs and myths of
the past. As I see it now (perhaps too late,) I have unwittingly
taken up that challenge and made an attempt at such
statements—which I certainly would not assume to do now, 95
knowing more clearly what it means.

For grounds for "Leaves of Grass," as a poem, I abandon'd the

3. The first "e" appears as a blank white space in the first edition, *November Boughs* (1888);
   so also in the two early reprints, *CPP* 1888–89 and the London edition, *NB* 1889. In *LG*
   1889 the word appeared as "mèleé." Posthumously corrected, "mêlée," in the Small, Maynard
   edition (1897), as Whitman had spelled it in his *Lippincott's* article, 1887 (see above).
4. That *LG* represents "one man's" identification with the "moral America" of his own experi-
   ence is repeated in the context of the entire article (*cf.* paragraph fourth from the last).

conventional themes, which do not appear in it: none of the stock ornamentation, or choice plots of love or war, or high, exceptional personages of Old-World song; nothing, as I may say, for beauty's sake—no legend, or myth,[5] or romance, nor euphemism, nor rhyme. But the broadest average of humanity and its identities in the now ripening Nineteenth Century, and specially in each of their countless examples and practical occupations in the United States to-day.

One main contrast of the ideas behind every page of my verses,[6] compared with establish'd poems, is their different relative attitude towards God, towards the objective universe, and still more (by reflection, confession, assumption, &c.) the quite changed attitude of the ego, the one chanting or talking, towards himself and towards his fellow-humanity. It is certainly time for America, above all, to begin this readjustment in the scope and basic point of view of verse; for everything else has changed. As I write, I see in an article on Wordsworth, in one of the current English magazines, the lines, "A few weeks ago an eminent French critic said that, owing to the special tendency to science and to its all-devouring force, poetry would cease to be read in fifty years." But I anticipate the very contrary. Only a firmer, vastly broader, new area begins to exist—nay, is already form'd —to which the poetic genius must emigrate. Whatever may have been the case in years gone by, the true use for the imaginative faculty of modern times is to give ultimate vivification to facts, to science, and to common lives, endowing them with the glows and glories and final illustriousness which belong to every real thing, and to real things only. Without that ultimate vivification—which the poet or other artist alone can give—reality would seem incomplete, and science, democracy, and life itself, finally in vain.

Few appreciate the moral revolutions, our age, which have been profounder far than the material or inventive or war-produced ones. The Nineteenth Century, now well towards its close (and ripening into fruit the seeds of the two preceding centuries[7])—the uprisings of national masses and shiftings of boundary-lines—the historical and other prominent facts of the United States—the war of attempted Secession—the stormy rush and haste of nebulous forces—never can future years wit-

5. "Great Are the Myths," which WW excluded from *LG*. More often than he remembered, he had referred in *LG* to the ancient heroic myths, and unconsciously he contributed to a new American myth rooted in the folklore of an expanding frontier, in the American earth, and in the democracy of the common man and natural faith.
6. This entire paragraph foreshadows those changes in poetry that, by 1925, fulfilled Whitman's prophecy that "the poetic genius must emigrate" into "a new area" of reality, of "ultimate vivification" of the new knowledge of man, society, and the "objective universe."
7. "The ferment and germination even of the United States to-day, dating back to, and in my opinion mainly founded on, the Elizabeth age in English history, the age of Francis Bacon and Shakspere. Indeed, when we pursue it, what growth or advent is there that does not date back, back, until lost—perhaps its most tantalizing clues lost—in the receded horizons of the past?" [WW's note].

ness more excitement and din of action—never completer change of army front along the whole line, the whole civilized world. For all these new and evolutionary facts, meanings, purposes, new poetic messages, new forms and expressions, are inevitable.

My Book and I—what a period we have presumed to span! those thirty years from 1850 to '80—and America in them! Proud, proud indeed may we be, if we have cull'd enough of that period in its own spirit to worthily waft a few live breaths of it to the future!

Let me not dare, here or anywhere, for my own purposes, or any purposes, to attempt the definition of Poetry, nor answer the question what it is. Like Religion, Love, Nature, while those terms are indispensable, and we all give a sufficiently accurate meaning to them, in my opinion no definition that has ever been made sufficiently encloses the name Poetry; nor can any rule or convention ever so absolutely obtain but some great exception may arise and disregard and overturn it.

Also it must be carefully remember'd that first-class literature does not shine by any luminosity of its own; nor do its poems. They grow of circumstances, and are evolutionary. The actual living light is always curiously from elsewhere—follows unaccountable sources, and is lunar and relative at the best. There are, I know, certain controlling themes that seem endlessly appropriated to the poets—as war, in the past—in the Bible, religious rapture and adoration—always love, beauty, some fine plot, or pensive or other emotion. But, strange as it may sound at first, I will say there is something striking far deeper and towering far higher than those themes for the best elements of modern song.

Just as all the old imaginative works rest, after their kind, on long trains of presuppositions, often entirely unmention'd by themselves, yet supplying the most important bases of them, and without which they could have had no reason for being, so "Leaves of Grass," before a line was written, presupposed something different from any other, and, as it stands, is the result of such presupposition. I should say, indeed, it were useless to attempt reading the book without first carefully tallying that preparatory background and quality in the mind. Think of the United States to-day—the facts of these thirty-eight or forty empires solder'd in one—sixty or seventy millions of equals, with their lives, their passions, their future—these incalculable, modern, American, seething multitudes around us, of which we are inseparable parts! Think, in comparison, of the petty environage and limited area of the poets of past or present Europe, no matter how great their genius. Think of the absence and ignorance, in all cases hitherto, of the multitudinousness, vitality, and the unprecedented stimulants of to-day and here. It almost seems as if a poetry with cosmic and dynamic features of magnitude and

limitlessness suitable to the human soul, were never possible
before. It is certain that a poetry of absolute faith and equality
for the use of the democratic masses never was.

In estimating first-class song, a sufficient Nationality, or, on
the other hand, what may be call'd the negative and lack of it,   190
(as in Goethe's case, it sometimes seems to me,) is often, if not
always, the first element. One needs only a little penetration to
see, at more or less removes, the material facts of their country
and radius, with the coloring of the moods of humanity at the
time, and its gloomy or hopeful prospects, behind all poets and   195
each poet, and forming their birth-marks. I know very well that
my "Leaves" could not possibly have emerged or been fashion'd
or completed, from any other era than the latter half of the Nine-
teenth Century, nor any other land than democratic America,
and from the absolute triumph of the National Union arms.   200

And whether my friend claim it for me or not, I know well
enough, too, that in respect to pictorial talent, dramatic situa-
tions, and especially in verbal melody and all the conventional
technique of poetry, not only the divine works that to-day stand
ahead in the world's reading, but dozens more, transcend (some   205
of them immeasurably transcend) all I have done, or could do.
But it seem'd to me, as the objects in Nature, the themes of
æstheticism, and all special exploitations of the mind and soul,
involve not only their own inherent quality, but the quality, just
as inherent and important, of *their point of view,*[8] the time had   210
come to reflect all themes and things, old and new, in the lights
thrown on them by the advent of America and democracy—to
chant those themes through the utterance of one, not only the
grateful and reverent legatee of the past, but the born child of
the New World—to illustrate all through the genesis and ensem-   215
ble of to-day; and that such illustration and ensemble are the
chief demands of America's prospective imaginative literature.
Not to carry out, in the approved style, some choice plot of for-
tune or misfortune, or fancy, or fine thoughts, or incidents, or
courtesies—all of which has been done overwhelmingly and   220
well, probably never to be excell'd—but that while in such
æsthetic presentation of objects, passions, plots, thoughts, &c.,
our lands and days do not want, and probably will never have,
anything better than they already possess from the bequests of
the past, it still remains to be said that there is even towards all   225
those a subjective and contemporary point of view appropriate
to ourselves alone, and to our new genius and environments,
different from anything hitherto; and that such conception of
current or gone-by life and art is for us the only means of their
assimilation consistent with the Western world.   230

Indeed, and anyhow, to put it specifically, has not the time

---

8. "According to Immanuel Kant, the last essential reality, giving shape and significance to all
the rest" [WW's note].

arrived when, (if it must be plainly said, for democratic America's
sake, if for no other) there must imperatively come a readjust-
ment of the whole theory and nature of Poetry? The question is
important, and I may turn the argument over and repeat it: Does   235
not the best thought of our day and Republic conceive of a birth
and spirit of song superior to anything past or present? To the
effectual and moral consolidation of our lands (already, as ma-
terially establish'd, the greatest factors in known history, and far,
far greater through what they prelude and necessitate, and are   240
to be in future)—to conform with and build on the concrete
realities and theories of the universe furnish'd by science, and
henceforth the only irrefragable basis for anything, verse
included—to root both influences in the emotional and imagi-
native action of the modern time, and dominate all that precedes   245
or opposes them—is not either a radical advance and step for-
ward, or a new verteber of the best song indispensable?

The New World receives with joy the poems of the antique,
with European feudalism's rich fund of epics, plays, ballads—
seeks not in the least[9] to deaden or displace those voices from   250
our ear and area—holds them indeed as indispensable studies,
influences, records, comparisons. But though the dawn-dazzle of
the sun of literature is in those poems for us to-day—though
perhaps the best parts of current character in nations, social
groups, or any man's or woman's individuality, Old World or   255
New, are from them—and though if I were ask'd to name the
most precious bequest to current American civilization from all
the hitherto ages, I am not sure but I would name those old and
less old songs ferried hither from east and west—some serious
words and debits remain; some acrid considerations demand a   260
hearing. Of the great poems receiv'd from abroad and from the
ages, and to-day enveloping and penetrating America, is there
one that is consistent with these United States, or essentially
applicable to them as they are and are to be? Is there one whose
underlying basis is not a denial and insult to democracy? What   265
a comment it forms, anyhow, on this era of literary fulfilment,
with the splendid day-rise of science and resuscitation of history,
that our chief religious and poetical works are not our own, nor
adapted to our light, but have been furnish'd by far-back ages
out of their arriere and darkness, or, at most, twilight dimness!   270
What is there in those works that so imperiously and scornfully
dominates all our advanced civilization, and culture?

Even Shakespere, who so suffuses current letters and art
(which indeed have in most degrees grown out of him,) belongs
essentially to the buried past. Only he holds the proud distinc-   275
tion for certain important phases of that past, of being the lof-

9. Read erroneously "in the last," in the first edition, *November Boughs* (1888), in the reprint
of that volume (1889), and in *CPP* 1888–89. Corrected in 1889, in the first edition of *Leaves
of Grass* that contained this essay.

tiest of the singers life has yet given voice to. All, however, relate
to and rest upon conditions, standards, politics, sociologies,
ranges of belief, that have been quite eliminated from the East-
ern hemisphere, and never existed at all in the Western. As au-
thoritative types of song they belong in America just about as
much as the persons and institutes they depict. True, it may be
said, the emotional, moral, and æsthetic natures of humanity
have not radically changed—that in these the old poems apply
to our times and all times, irrespective of date; and that they are
of incalculable value as pictures of the past. I willingly make
those admissions, and to their fullest extent; then advance the
points herewith as of serious, even paramount importance.

I have indeed put on record elsewhere my reverence and eu-
logy for those never-to-be-excell'd poetic bequests, and their in-
describable preciousness as heirlooms for America. Another and
separate point must now be candidly stated. If I had not stood
before those poems with uncover'd head, fully aware of their
colossal grandeur and beauty of form and spirit, I could not have
written "Leaves of Grass." My verdict and conclusions as illus-
trated in its pages are arrived at through the temper and incul-
cation of the old works as much as through anything else—
perhaps more than through anything else. As America fully and
fairly construed is the legitimate result and evolutionary outcome
of the past, so I would dare to claim for my verse. Without stop-
ping to qualify the averment, the Old World has had the poems
of myths, fictions, feudalism, conquest, caste, dynastic wars, and
splendid exceptional characters and affairs, which have been
great; but the New World needs the poems of realities and sci-
ence and of the democratic average and basic equality, which
shall be greater. In the centre of all, and object of all, stands the
Human Being, towards whose heroic and spiritual evolution po-
ems and everything directly or indirectly tend, Old World or
New.[1]

Continuing the subject, my friends have more than once
suggested—or may be the garrulity of advancing age is possess-
ing me—some further embryonic facts of "Leaves of Grass," and
especially how I enter'd upon them. Dr. Bucke has, in his vol-
ume, already fully and fairly described the preparation of my
poetic field, with the particular and general plowing, planting,
seeding, and occupation of the ground, till everything was fer-
tilized, rooted, and ready to start its own way for good or bad.
Not till after all this, did I attempt any serious acquaintance with

1. Conclusion of the first of the two divisions of this essay, dealing in general with WW's
preparation, motivation, and inspiration for *Leaves of Grass*. The following section emphasizes
certain themes, especially the theory of man, nature, and society, that this poetry embodies.
For the development of each section from earlier essays, see the footnote under the title "A
Backward Glance . . ."

poetic literature. Along in my sixteenth year I had become pos-
sessor of a stout, well-cramm'd one thousand page octavo volume   320
(I have it yet,) containing Walter Scott's poetry entire—an in-
exhaustible mine and treasury of poetic forage (especially the
endless forests and jungles of notes)—has been so to me for fifty
years, and remains so to this day.[2]

Later, at intervals, summers and falls, I used to go off, some-   325
times for a week at a stretch, down in the country, or to Long
Island's seashores—there, in the presence of outdoor influences,
I went over thoroughly the Old and New Testaments, and ab-
sorb'd (probably to better advantage for me than in any library
or indoor room—it makes such difference *where* you read,)   330
Shakespere, Ossian, the best translated versions I could get of
Homer, Eschylus, Sophocles, the old German Nibelungen, the
ancient Hindoo poems, and one or two other masterpieces,
Dante's among them. As it happen'd, I read the latter mostly in
an old wood. The Iliad (Buckley's prose version,) I read first thor- 335
oughly on the peninsula of Orient,[3] northeast end of Long Is-
land, in a shelter'd hollow of rocks and sand, with the sea on
each side. (I have wonder'd since why I was not overwhelm'd by
those mighty masters. Likely because I read them, as described,
in the full presence of Nature, under the sun, with the far-   340
spreading landscape and vistas, or the sea rolling in.)

Toward the last I had among much else look'd over Edgar
Poe's poems—of which I was not an admirer, tho' I always saw
that beyond their limited range of melody (like perpetual chimes
of music bells, ringing from lower *b* flat up to *g*) they were me- 345
lodious expressions, and perhaps never excell'd ones, of certain
pronounc'd phases of human morbidity. (The Poetic area is very
spacious—has room for all—has so many mansions!) But I was
repaid in Poe's prose by the idea that (at any rate for our occa-
sions, our day) there can be no such thing as a long poem. The   350
same thought had been haunting my mind before, but Poe's ar-
gument, though short, work'd the sum out and proved it to me.

Another point had an early settlement, clearing the ground
greatly. I saw, from the time my enterprise and questionings pos-
itively shaped themselves (how best can I express my own dis-   355
tinctive era and surroundings, America, Democracy?) that the
trunk and centre whence the answer was to radiate, and to which
all should return from straying however far a distance, must be
an identical body and soul, a personality—which personality, af-

---

2. "Sir Walter Scott's COMPLETE POEMS; especially including BORDER MINSTRELSY; then Sir
   Tristrem; Lay of the Last Minstrel; Ballads from the German; Marmion; Lady of the Lake;
   Vision of Don Roderick; Lord of the Isles; Rokeby; Bridal of Triermain; Field of Waterloo;
   Harold the Dauntless; all the Dramas; various Introductions, endless interesting Notes, and
   Essays on Poetry, Romance, &c.
   "Lockhart's 1833 (or '34) edition with Scott's latest and copious revisions and annotations.
   (All the poems were thoroughly read by me, but the ballads of the Border Minstrelsy over
   and over again)" [WW's note].
3. The northernmost of the two peninsulas into which Long Island divides at its eastern end.

ter many considerations and ponderings I deliberately settled   360
should be myself—indeed could not be any other. I also felt
strongly (whether I have shown it or not) that to the true and
full estimate of the Present both the Past and the Future are
main considerations.

These, however, and much more might have gone on and   365
come to naught (almost positively would have come to naught,)
if a sudden, vast, terrible, direct and indirect stimulus for new
and national declamatory[4] expression had not been given to me.
It is certain, I say, that, although I had made a start before, only
from the occurrence of the Secession War, and what it show'd   370
me as by flashes of lightning, with the emotional depths it
sounded and arous'd (of course, I don't mean in my own heart
only, I saw it just as plainly in others, in millions)—that only
from the strong flare and provocation of that war's sights and
scenes the final reasons-for-being of an autochthonic and pas-   375
sionate song definitely came forth.[5]

I went down to the war fields in Virginia (end of 1862), lived
thenceforward in camp—saw great battles and the days and
nights afterward—partook of all the fluctuations, gloom, despair,
hopes again arous'd, courage evoked—death readily risk'd—*the*   380
cause, too—along and filling those agonistic and lurid following
years, 1863–'64–'65—the real parturition years (more than
1776–'83) of this henceforth homogeneous Union. Without
those three or four years and the experiences they gave, "Leaves
of Grass" would not now be existing.[6]   385

But I set out with the intention also of indicating or hinting
some point-characteristics which I since see (though I did not
then, at least not definitely) were bases and object-urgings to-
ward those "Leaves" from the first. The word I myself put pri-
marily for the description of them as they stand at last, is the   390
word Suggestiveness. I round and finish little, if anything; and
could not, consistently with my scheme. The reader will always
have his or her part to do, just as much as I have had mine. I
seek less to state or display any theme or thought, and more to
bring you, reader, into the atmosphere of the theme or thought   395
—there to pursue your own flight. Another impetus-word is

4. In the earlier contributory essays, read "poetic"; the term "declamatory" was not then
disparaging.
5. This assertion may seem ambiguous; Whitman's poetry and ideas were well defined in the
three *LG* editions before "the direct stimulus" of the Civil War. But the war had long been
imminent: when the young journalist, during the Mexican War, supported "free soil"; when
he opposed Northern Democratic "hunker" politics, thus losing the editorship of the *Brooklyn
Eagle* in 1848; when he realized the flimsiness of the 1850 compromises. His first *LG* edition
(1855) strongly depicted the outrages of slavery, and he predicted a terrible vengeance in
his "Now Lucifer Was Not Dead" (see the "Passages Excluded from *LG* Poems" section).
He had, indeed, "made a start before."
6. A following sentence, which concludes this paragraph in the ancestor essay "How 'Leaves
of Grass' Was Made," supports the footnote immediately above with these words: "think of
the book as a whirling wheel, with the War of 1861–5 as the hub on which it all concentrates
and revolves."

Comradeship as for all lands, and in a more commanding and acknowledg'd sense than hitherto. Other word-signs would be Good Cheer, Content, and Hope.

The chief trait of any given poet is always the spirit he brings to the observation of Humanity and Nature—the mood out of which he contemplates his subjects. What kind of temper and what amount of faith report these things? Up to how recent a date is the song carried? What the equipment, and special raciness of the singer—what his tinge of coloring? The last value of artistic expressers, past and present—Greek æsthetes, Shakspere—or in our own day Tennyson, Victor Hugo, Carlyle, Emerson—is certainly involv'd in such questions. I say the profoundest service that poems or any other writings can do for their reader is not merely to satisfy the intellect, or supply something polish'd and interesting, nor even to depict great passions, or persons or events, but to fill him with vigorous and clean manliness, religiousness, and give him *good heart* as a radical possession and habit. The educated world seems to have been growing more and more ennuyed for ages, leaving to our time the inheritance of it all. Fortunately there is the original inexhaustible fund of buoyancy, normally resident in the race, forever eligible to be appeal'd to and relied on.

As for native American individuality, though certain to come, and on a large scale, the distinctive and ideal type of Western character (as consistent with the operative political and even money-making features of United States' humanity in the Nineteenth Century as chosen knights, gentlemen and warriors were the ideals of the centuries of European feudalism) it has not yet appear'd. I have allow'd the stress of my poems from beginning to end to bear upon American individuality and assist it—not only because that is a great lesson in Nature, amid all her generalizing laws, but as counterpoise to the leveling tendencies of Democracy—and for other reasons. Defiant of ostensible literary and other conventions, I avowedly chant "the great pride of man in himself," and permit it to be more or less a *motif* of nearly all my verse. I think this pride indispensable to an American. I think it not inconsistent with obedience, humility, deference, and self-questioning.

Democracy has been so retarded and jeopardized by powerful personalities, that its first instincts are fain to clip, conform, bring in stragglers, and reduce everything to a dead level. While the ambitious thought of my song is to help the forming of a great aggregate Nation, it is, perhaps, altogether through the forming of myriads of fully develop'd and enclosing individuals. Welcome as are equality's and fraternity's doctrines and popular education, a certain liability accompanies them all, as we see. That primal and interior something in man, in his soul's abysms, coloring all, and, by exceptional fruitions, giving the last majesty to him—something continually touch'd upon and attain'd by the

old poems and ballads of feudalism, and often the principal foun-
dation of them—modern science and democracy appear to be
endangering, perhaps eliminating. But that forms an appearance
only; the reality is quite different.[7] The new influences, upon the
whole, are surely preparing the way for grander individualities   450
than ever. To-day and here personal force is behind everything,
just the same. The times and depictions from the Iliad to Shak-
spere inclusive can happily never again be realized—but the el-
ements of courageous and lofty manhood are unchanged.

Without yielding an inch the working-man and working-   455
woman were to be in my pages from first to last. The ranges of
heroism and loftiness with which Greek and feudal poets en-
dow'd their god-like or lordly born characters—indeed prouder
and better based and with fuller ranges than those—I was to
endow the democratic averages of America. I was to show that   460
we, here and to-day, are eligible to the grandest and the best—
more eligible now than any times of old were. I will also want
my utterances (I said to myself before beginning) to be in spirit
the poems of the morning. (They have been founded and mainly
written in the sunny forenoon and early midday of my life.) I   465
will want them to be the poems of women entirely as much as
men. I have wish'd to put the complete Union of the States in
my songs without any preference or partiality whatever. Hence-
forth, if they live and are read, it must be just as much South
as North—just as much along the Pacific as Atlantic—in the   470
valley of the Mississippi, in Canada, up in Maine, down in Texas,
and on the shores of Puget Sound.

From another point of view "Leaves of Grass" is avowedly the
song of Sex and Amativeness, and even Animality—though
meanings that do not usually go along with those words are be-   475
hind all, and will duly emerge; and all are sought to be lifted
into a different light and atmosphere. Of this feature, intention-
ally palpable in a few lines, I shall only say the espousing prin-
ciple of those lines so gives breath of life to my whole scheme
that the bulk of the pieces might as well have been left unwritten   480
were those lines omitted. Difficult as it will be, it has become,
in my opinion, imperative to achieve a shifted attitude from su-
perior men and women towards the thought and fact of sexual-
ity, as an element in character, personality, the emotions, and a
theme in literature. I am not going to argue the question by   485
itself; it does not stand by itself. The vitality of it is altogether
in its relations, bearings, significance—like the clef of a sym-
phony. At last analogy the lines I allude to, and the spirit in
which they are spoken, permeate all "Leaves of Grass," and the
work must stand or fall with them, as the human body and soul   490
must remain as an entirety.

Universal as are certain facts and symptoms of communities

7. The earlier essay "How 'Leaves of Grass' Was Made" continues, more cautiously: "or involves,
at most, only a passing stage."

or individuals all times, there is nothing so rare in modern con-
ventions and poetry as their normal recognizance. Literature is
always calling in the doctor for consultation and confession, and   500
always giving evasions and swathing suppressions in place of that
"heroic nudity"[8] on which only a genuine diagnosis of serious
cases can be built. And in respect to editions of "Leaves of Grass"
in time to come (if there should be such) I take occasion now
to confirm those lines with the settled convictions and deliberate   505
renewals of thirty years,[9] and to hereby prohibit, as far as word
of mine can do so, any elision of them.

Then still a purpose enclosing all, and over and beneath all.
Ever since what might be call'd thought, or the budding of
thought, fairly began in my youthful mind, I had had a desire to   510
attempt some worthy record of that entire faith and acceptance
("to justify the ways of God to man" is Milton's well-known and
ambitious phrase) which is the foundation of moral America. I
felt it all as positively then in my young days as I do now in my
old ones; to formulate a poem whose every thought or fact   515
should directly or indirectly be or connive at an implicit belief
in the wisdom, health, mystery, beauty of every process, every
concrete object, every human or other existence, not only con-
sider'd from the point of view of all, but of each.

While I can not understand it or argue it out, I fully believe   520
in a clue and purpose in Nature, entire and several; and that
invisible spiritual results, just as real and definite as the visible,
eventuate all concrete life and all materialism, through Time.
My book ought to emanate buoyancy and gladness legitimately
enough, for it was grown out of those elements, and has been   525
the comfort of my life since it was originally commenced.

One main genesis-motive of the "Leaves" was my conviction
(just as strong to-day as ever) that the crowning growth of the
United States is to be spiritual and heroic. To help start and
favor that growth—or even to call attention to it, or the need of   530
it—is the beginning, middle and final purpose of the poems. (In
fact, when really cipher'd out and summ'd to the last, plowing
up in earnest the interminable average fallows of humanity—not
"good government" merely, in the common sense—is the justi-
fication and main purpose of these United States.)   535

Isolated advantages in any rank or grace or fortune—the direct
or indirect threads of all the poetry of the past—are in my opin-
ion distasteful to the republican genius, and offer no foundation
for its fitting verse. Establish'd poems, I know, have the very
great advantage of chanting the already perform'd, so full of glo-   540
ries, reminiscences dear to the minds of men. But my volume is

8. " 'Nineteenth Century,' July, 1883" [WW's note].
9. That is, since 1858, when "Sex and Amativeness" became dominant in the "Children of
   Adam" and "Calamus" clusters. Even to his benefactor, Emerson, who argued against in-
   cluding the outspoken "Children" in LG 1860, and to later critics, including those who
   "banned" the 1881 Boston edition, WW gave substantially the same defense of these poems
   as he gives above.

a candidate for the future. "All original art," says Taine, anyhow, "is self-regulated, and no original art can be regulated from without; it carries its own counterpoise, and does not receive it from elsewhere—lives on its own blood"—a solace to my frequent bruises and sulky vanity. ₅₄₅

As the present is perhaps mainly an attempt at personal statement or illustration, I will allow myself as further help to extract the following anecdote from a book, "Annals of Old Painters," conn'd by me in youth. Rubens, the Flemish painter, in one of his ₅₅₀ wanderings through the galleries of old convents, came across a singular work. After looking at it thoughtfully for a good while, and listening to the criticisms of his suite of students, he said to the latter, in answer to their questions (as to what school the work implied or belong'd,) "I do not believe the artist, unknown and ₅₅₅ perhaps no longer living, who has given the world this legacy, ever belong'd to any school, or ever painted anything but this one picture, which is a personal affair—a piece out of a man's life."

"Leaves of Grass" indeed (I cannot too often reiterate) has mainly been the outcropping of my own emotional and other ₅₆₀ personal nature—an attempt, from first to last, to put *a Person,* a human being (myself, in the latter half of the Nineteenth Century, in America,) freely, fully and truly on record. I could not find any similar personal record in current literature that satisfied me. But it is not on "Leaves of Grass" distinctively as *liter-* ₅₆₅ *ature,* or a specimen thereof, that I feel to dwell, or advance claims. No one will get at my verses who insists upon viewing them as a literary performance, or attempt at such performance, or as aiming mainly toward art or æstheticism.

I say no land or people or circumstances ever existed so needing ₅₇₀ a race of singers and poems differing from all others, and rigidly their own, as the land and people and circumstances of our United States need such singers and poems to-day, and for the future. Still further, as long as the States continue to absorb and be dominated by the poetry of the Old World, and remain un- ₅₇₅ supplied with autochthonous song, to express, vitalize and give color to and define their material and political success, and minister to them distinctively, so long will they stop short of first-class Nationality and remain defective.

In the free evening of my day I give to you, reader, the fore- ₅₈₀ going garrulous talk, thoughts, reminiscences,

> As idly drifting down the ebb,
> Such ripples, half-caught voices, echo from the shore.

Concluding with two items for the imaginative genius of the West, when it worthily rises—First, what Herder taught to the ₅₈₅ young Goethe, that really great poetry is always (like the Homeric or Biblical canticles) the result of a national spirit, and not the privilege of a polish'd and select few; Second, that the strongest and sweetest songs yet remain to be sung.

OLD AGE ECHOES

An Executor's Diary Note, 1891[1]

I said to W. W. today: "Though you have put the finishing touches on the *Leaves*, closed them with your good-by, you will go on living a year or two longer and writing more poems. The question is, what will you do with these poems when the time comes to fix their place in the volume?" "Do with them? I am not unprepared—I have even contemplated that emergency—I have a title in reserve: Old Age Echoes—applying not so much to things as to echoes of things, reverberant, an aftermath." "You have dropt enough by the roadside, as you went along, from different editions, to make a volume. Some day the world will demand to have that put together somewhere." "Do you think it?" "Certainly. Should you put it under ban?" "Why should I— how could I? So far as you may have anything to do with it I place upon you the injunction that whatever may be added to the *Leaves* shall be supplementary, avowed as such, leaving the book complete as I left it, consecutive to the point I left off, marking always an unmistakable, deep down, unobliteratable division line. In the long run the world will do as it pleases with the book. I am determined to have the world know what I was pleased to do."

Here is a late personal note from W. W.: "My tho't is to collect a lot of prose and poetry pieces—small or smallish mostly, but a few larger—appealing to the good will, the heart—sorrowful ones not rejected—but no morbid ones given."

There is no reason for doubt that "A Thought of Columbus," closing "Old Age Echoes," was W. W.'s last deliberate composition, dating December, 1891.

Old Age Echoes: This group of thirteen poems was first added to *LG* in its tenth (1897) edition, pp. 423–30: LEAVES OF GRASS / Including / Sands at Seventy, Good-Bye My Fancy / Old Age Echoes, and a Backward Glance / O'er Travel'd Roads / By / WALT WHIT-MAN / Boston / Small, Maynard & Company / 1897. The English imprint was issued in London the same year by G. P. Putnam's Sons.
1. Horace Traubel does not specify the date of this conversation with the poet, but obviously it resembles the almost daily notations of *With Walt Whitman in Camden* from 1888 to the end. The dating of the printed memorandum "1891" suggests relationship with the publication that year of the poet's last volume of poems.

To Soar in Freedom and in Fullness of Power[2]

I have not so much emulated the birds that musically sing,
I have abandon'd myself to flights, broad circles.
The hawk, the seagull, have far more possess'd me than the
     canary or mocking-bird,
I have not felt to warble and trill, however sweetly,
I have felt to soar in freedom and in the fullness of power, joy,
     volition.   5
1897   *1897*

Then Shall Perceive[3]

In softness, languor, bloom, and growth,
Thine eyes, ears, all thy sense—thy loftiest attribute—all that
     takes cognizance of beauty,
Shall rouse and fill—then shall perceive!
1897   *1897*

The Few Drops Known[4]

Of heroes, history, grand events, premises, myths, poems,
The few drops known must stand for oceans of the unknown,
On this beautiful and thick peopl'd earth, here and there a
     little specimen put on record,
A little of Greeks and Romans, a few Hebrew canticles, a few
     death odors as from graves, from Egypt—
What are they to the long and copious retrospect of antiquity?   5
1897   *1897*

One Thought Ever at the Fore[5]

One thought ever at the fore—
That in the Divine Ship, the World, breasting Time and Space,

2. In the Feinberg Collection, listed under the heading "My Poetry is more the Poetry of Sight than Sound," is a two-page MS prose fragment in black ink that WW had apparently intended as the beginning of a preface. From it the above five lines, arranged as verse, were directly transcribed, no doubt by Traubel.
3. The MS of this poem was sent by Traubel, in a letter of April 16, 1908, to an autograph collector named Sternberg (?). It contains a few more phrases, as follows, indicating that the poet had meant to compose further lines:

> April
> April and May, the sunrise fresh
> the balmy airs, the

4. Present location of MS unknown.
5. With its image of the voyage on which all peoples are bound together, this poem echoes a dominant idea in "Passage to India."

All Peoples of the globe together sail, sail the same voyage, are
    bound to the same destination.
1897   *1897*

While Behind All Firm and Erect[6]

While behind all, firm and erect as ever,
Undismay'd amid the rapids—amid the irresistible and deadly
    urge,
Stands a helmsman, with brow elate and strong hand.
1897   *1897*

A Kiss to the Bride[7]

Marriage of Nelly Grant, May 21, 1874

Sacred, blithesome, undenied,
With benisons from East and West,
And salutations North and South,
Through me indeed to-day a million hearts and hands,
Wafting a million loves, a million soul felt prayers;   5
—Tender and true remain the arm that shields thee!
Fair winds always fill the ship's sails that sail thee!
Clear sun by day, and light stars at night, beam on thee!
Dear girl—through me the ancient privilege too,
For the New World, through me, the old, old wedding
    greeting: 10
O youth and health! O sweet Missouri rose! O bonny bride!
Yield thy red cheeks, thy lips, to-day,
Unto a Nation's loving kiss.
1874   *1897*

Nay, Tell Me Not To-day the Publish'd Shame[8]

Winter of 1873, Congress in Session

Nay, tell me not to-day the publish'd shame,
Read not to-day the journal's crowded page,

---

6. Compare this poem with "The Pilot in the Mist"; both employ the image of the helmsman
   amid the rapids, and almost identical phrasing in the final lines. Compare also with line 55
   of "Thou Mother with Thy Equal Brood."
7. First published in the *New York Daily Graphic*, May 21, 1874, and again in the same news-
   paper two days later. Nelly Grant, President Grant's daughter, married a Mr. Sartoris.
8. First published in the *New York Daily Graphic*, March 5, 1873, this poem was reprinted by
   Traubel in *The Conservator*, October 1896. *LC* has five MS pages, two of which are trial
   lines, three the rough draft. The Feinberg Collection has a clipping of the *Graphic* text with
   corrections honored in the 1897 text. The "publish'd shame" refers to the scandals of the
   Crédit Mobilier and the "Salary Grab," an act doubling the president's salary and increasing
   that of other government officials. Public indignation later forced its modification.

The merciless reports still branding forehead after forehead,
The guilty column following guilty column.

To-day to me the tale refusing,   5
Turning from it—from the white capitol turning,
Far from these swelling domes, topt with statues,
More endless, jubilant, vital visions rise
Unpublish'd, unreported.

Through all your quiet ways, or North or South, you Equal
    States, you honest farms,   10
Your million untold manly healthy lives, or East or West, city
    or country,
Your noiseless mothers, sisters, wives, unconscious of their good,
Your mass of homes nor poor nor rich, in visions rise—
    (even your excellent poverties,)
Your self-distilling, never-ceasing virtues, self-denials, graces,
Your endless base of deep integrities within, timid but certain,   15
Your blessings steadily bestow'd, sure as the light, and still,
(Plunging to these as a determin'd diver down the deep hidden
    waters,)
These, these to-day I brood upon—all else refusing, these will
    I con,
To-day to these give audience.
1873   *1897*

Supplement Hours[9]

Sane, random, negligent hours,
Sane, easy, culminating hours,
After the flush, the Indian summer, of my life,
Away from Books—away from Art—the lesson learn'd, pass'd o'er,
Soothing, bathing, merging all—the sane, magnetic,   5
Now for the day and night themselves—the open air,
Now for the fields, the seasons, insects, trees—the rain and snow,
Where wild bees flitting hum,
Or August mulleins grow, or winter's snowflakes fall,
Or stars in the skies roll round—   10
The silent sun and stars.
1897   *1897*

9. Many MS pages of varying sizes (LC has fifteen, Feinberg seven, and Lion three) show that
WW worked extensively upon this poem, trying and rejecting many phrases and lines—
among them such title suggestions as "Notes as the wild Bee hums," "A September Supple-
ment," and "Latter-time Hours of a half-paralytic." Also there is a prose MS note (Lion),
apparently to be considered as a kind of gloss upon the poem. The sentiment of the poem
recalls the mood of WW's nature pieces in *Specimen Days*, e.g., "New Themes Entered
Upon" or "An Early Summer Reveille." *Cf.* also the poem "A Clear Midnight," whose second
line is echoed by the fourth line of this one.

Of Many a Smutch'd Deed Reminiscent[1]

Full of wickedness, I—of many a smutch'd deed reminiscent—
    of worse deeds capable,
Yet I look composedly upon nature, drink day and night the
    joys of life, and await death with perfect equanimity,
Because of my tender and boundless love for him I love and
    because of his boundless love for me.
1897   *1897*

To Be at All[2]

Cf. Stanza 27, "Song of Myself"

To be at all—what is better than that?
I think if there were nothing more developed, the clam in its
    callous shell in the sand were august enough.
I am not in any callous shell;
I am cased with supple conductors, all over,
They take every object by the hand, and lead it within me;   5
They are thousands, each one with his entry to himself;
They are always watching with their little eyes, from my head
    to my feet;
One no more than a point lets in and out of me such bliss and
    magnitude,
I think I could lift the girder of the house away if it lay
    between me and whatever I wanted.
1855   *1897*

Death's Valley[3]

*To accompany a picture; by request. "The Valley of the Shadow of
Death," from the painting by George Inness.*

Nay, do not dream, designer dark,
Thou hast portray'd or hit thy theme entire;

---

1. Although this poem first appeared in the "Old Age Echoes" of *LG* 1897, Dr. Bucke reprinted it two years later in his 1899 *N and F* as item 126, p. 39. MS in Barrett.
2. This poem also, first printed in the 1897 "Old Age Echoes," is reprinted in Dr. Bucke's *N and F* as item 134, p. 40. Trent has the MS. A related fragment, printed in *N and F* as item 102, p. 34, is in the Barrett Collection. Both fragments are obviously related to—indeed are rough drafts of—section 27 of "Song of Myself," as the subhead indicates.
3. This poem was first printed in *Harper's New Monthly Magazine*, April 1892, with the subtitle "To accompany a picture; by request," and the picture itself was reproduced on the page opposite. WW was paid $25 for the poem, and in fact, in a letter to WW of August 28, 1889, H. M. Alden, *Harper's* editor, had suggested its composition to accompany the picture. However, it was actually printed only in the wake of the poet's death, although WW had originally included its MS in his copy for *Good-Bye My Fancy* (Feinberg). Both Feinberg and Barrett have MSS. George Inness (1824–1894) was an American landscape painter famous for his romantic interpretations.

I, hoverer of late by this dark valley, by its confines, having
    glimpses of it,
Here enter lists with thee, claiming my right to make a symbol too.
For I have seen many wounded soldiers die,   5
After dread suffering—have seen their lives pass off with smiles;
And I have watch'd the death-hours of the old; and seen the
    infant die;
The rich, with all his nurses and his doctors;
And then the poor, in meagerness and poverty;
And I myself for long, O Death, have breath'd my every breath   10
Amid the nearness and the silent thought of thee.

And out of these and thee,
I make a scene, a song (not fear of thee,
Nor gloom's ravines, nor bleak, nor dark—for I do not fear thee,
Nor celebrate the struggle, or contortion, or hard-tied knot),   15
Of the broad blessed light and perfect air, with meadows,
    rippling tides, and trees and flowers and grass,
And the low hum of living breeze—and in the midst God's
    beautiful eternal right hand,
Thee, holiest minister of Heaven—thee, envoy, usherer, guide
    at last of all,
Rich, florid, loosener of the stricture-knot call'd life,
Sweet, peaceful, welcome Death.   20
1893   *1897*

On the Same Picture[4]

Intended for first stanza of "Death's Valley"

Aye, well I know 'tis ghastly to descend that valley:
Preachers, musicians, poets, painters, always render it,
Philosophs exploit—the battlefield, the ship at sea, the myriad
    beds, all lands,
All, all the past have enter'd, the ancientest humanity we know,
Syria's, India's, Egypt's, Greece's, Rome's;   5
Till now for us under our very eyes spreading the same to-day,
Grim, ready, the same to-day, for entrance, yours and mine,
Here, here 'tis limn'd.
1892   *1897*

---

4. The MS (Feinberg) of this eight-line passage indicates by its title—"Death's Valley"—that it
was indeed probably intended for one of the stanzas, if not the first, of the preceding poem.
The present title was evidently supplied by Traubel.

A Thought of Columbus[5]

The mystery of mysteries, the crude and hurried ceaseless
    flame, spontaneous, bearing on itself.

The bubble and the huge, round, concrete orb!
A breath of Deity, as thence the bulging universe unfolding!
The many issuing cycles from their precedent minute!
The eras of the soul incepting in an hour,   5
Haply the widest, farthest evolutions of the world and man.

Thousands and thousands of miles hence, and now four
    centuries back,
A mortal impulse thrilling its brain cell,
Reck'd or unreck'd, the birth can no longer be postpon'd:
A phantom of the moment, mystic, stalking, sudden,   10
Only a silent thought, yet toppling down of more than walls of
    brass or stone.
(A flutter at the darkness' edge as if old Time's and Space's
    secret near revealing.)
A thought! a definite thought works out in shape.
Four hundred years roll on.
The rapid cumulus—trade, navigation, war, peace, democracy,
    roll on;   15
The restless armies and the fleets of time following their leader
    —the old camps of ages pitch'd in newer, larger areas,
The tangl'd, long-deferr'd eclaircissement of human life and
    hopes boldly begins untying,
As here to-day up-grows the Western World.

(An added word yet to my song, far Discoverer, as ne'er before
    sent back to son of earth—
If still thou hearest, hear me,   20
Voicing as now—lands, races, arts, bravas to thee,
O'er the long backward path to thee—one vast consensus,
    north, south, east, west,
Soul plaudits! acclamation! reverent echoes!
One manifold, huge memory to thee! oceans and lands!
The modern world to thee and thought of thee!)   25
1891   *1897*

---

5. The MS of this poem was printed in facsimile in *Once a Week,* July 9, 1892; the next issue,
July 16, 1892, carried Traubel's account of its composition, "Walt Whitman's Last Poem,"
in which he tells how the poem, written on fragments pasted on two long strips of paper,
was handed to him by WW on the preceding March 16, ten days before his death. Some of
the fragments were old envelopes whose postmarks indicate that the composition began as
early as November 1891. Complete MS in Feinberg, both rough and final drafts. The Barrett
Collection has also a draft of the first six lines.

AN ALBUM OF
WHITMAN PORTRAITS

1. Whitman aged 30. The poet dates the photograph 1849, Bucke 1856. The signed copy in the Feinberg Collection is here reproduced by permission.

2. Whitman aged 35 (1854); engraved frontispiece, first edition, *Leaves of Grass*, 1855. The engraver, S. Hollyer, signed the Pierpont Morgan Library copy here reproduced by permission.

3. Whitman, about 40 (1859); engraved frontispiece, third edition, *Leaves of Grass*, 1860. Charles Hine, the painter of the portrait, signed the copy in the Feinberg Collection, here reproduced by permission.

4. Whitman aged 43 (1862)? This photograph was sent by the poet to William Rossetti for Mrs. Gilchrist with the comment: "I confess to myself a perhaps capricious fondness for it." The Saunders catalog dates it 1862, but the signed copy in the Feinberg Collection, here reproduced by permission, is inscribed 1863.

5. Whitman aged 44 (1863). Engraving by T. Johnson from photograph by Gardner. The copy in the Feinberg Collection is here reproduced by permission.

6. Whitman aged 50 (1869). Photograph by Frank Pearsall. The signed copy in the Feinberg Collection is here reproduced by permission.

7. Whitman aged 53 (1872). Photograph by Frank Pearsall. The signed copy in the Feinberg Collection is here reproduced by permission.

8. Whitman aged 61 (1880). Photograph by F. Gutekunst of Philadelphia. The signed copy in the Feinberg Collection is here reproduced by permission.

COPYRIGHT 1887
BY GEORGE C.COX

Walt Whitman 1887

9. Whitman aged 68 (1887). Photograph by George C. Cox. One of the poet's favorites. He called it "The Laughing Philosopher" and sent a copy to Tennyson. The signed copy in the Feinberg Collection is here reproduced by permission.

10. Whitman aged 69 (1888). Portrait in oils by Thomas Eakins. Reproduced by courtesy of the Pennsylvania Academy of the Fine Arts.

Walt Whitman
(Sculptor's profile)
May 1891

11. Whitman aged 72 (1891). Sculptor's profile photograph by the painter Thomas Eakins, and so inscribed by Whitman on the Feinberg copy here reproduced by permission. One of the last photographs, May 1891; frontispiece to *Good-Bye My Fancy* (1891).

OTHER POETRY AND PROSE

Note on the Texts

The following section includes two important categories of poetry associated with *Leaves of Grass*: (A) poems excluded from *Leaves of Grass*; (B) passages excluded from *Leaves of Grass* poems (for a list of titles, see the Table of Contents of this volume). The "excluded" poem is one that was canceled from a *Leaves of Grass* edition and not restored, or not present in the same form, in the canon of *LG* 1881 or *LG* 1891–92; and also those poems not transferred to *LG* from the poet's "Supplements" or supplementary volumes: *Drum-Taps*, "Songs Before Parting," *Passage to India, As a Strong Bird on Pinions Free, Two Rivulets, November Boughs, Good-Bye My Fancy,* and *Complete Prose Works*. This Norton Critical Edition includes all such poems, although they represent varying degrees of accomplishment or of substantive interest. By contrast, the second category—the "excluded passages"— represents a selection of those passages excluded from *LG* poems that have distinct merit and a certain independence of form and meaning. Where WW divided a poem, excluding part and preserving part in canon poems, or where parts of an excluded passage were independently dispersed for a time, this edition restores the original text.

The dating of each poem and passage, together with the first note, will show its first and last appearance in an *LG* edition and identify the source of the text reproduced. This was usually the text of its last appearance, or its last appearance as a whole in the case of those that Whitman abbreviated, of which some survived into the canon of 1881. The date at the left, below the poem, is that of the first appearance in *LG* or a supplement. The date at the right is that of last appearance. A date in parenthesis at the left indicates some form of earlier publication; a parenthesis at the right indicates date of survival of some fragment of the text. The range of these dates is generally from 1855 to 1876 (several were from *NB* 1888 or *GBF* 1891). Since the poet's style, including elisions and punctuation, varied considerably during this period, this edition follows in each case the form of the text in the edition from which it was extracted. An exception to this rule was the decision to ignore, with few exceptions, Whitman's numbering of lines or stanzas, which was whimsical until *LG* 1881, when he numbered only the large units, or cantos. It was necessary to supply some titles, particularly for the excluded passages and for certain poems drawn from *LG* editions before 1867. Such titles are shown between square brackets to distinguish them from Whitman's titles.

Poems Excluded from
Leaves of Grass

Great Are the Myths[1]

Great are the myths—I too delight in them,[2]
Great are Adam and Eve—I too look back and accept them,
Great the risen and fallen nations, and their poets,
    women, sages, inventors, rulers, warriors, and priests.

Great is Liberty! great is Equality! I am their follower,
Helmsmen of nations, choose your craft! where you sail, I sail,   5
Yours is the muscle of life or death—yours is the
    perfect science—in you I have absolute faith.

Great is To-day, and beautiful,
It is good to live in this age—there never was any better.

Great are the plunges, throes, triumphs, downfalls of
    Democracy,
Great the reformers, with their lapses and screams,   10
Great the daring and venture of sailors, on new explorations.

Great are Yourself and Myself,
We are just as good and bad as the oldest and youngest or any,
What the best and worst did, we could do,
What they felt, do not we feel it in ourselves?   15

---

1. Appeared in the first *Leaves of Grass* (1855), untitled, as the concluding poem, and in *LG* 1856 as "Poem of a Few Greatnesses." In *LG* 1860 (No. 2 in a "Leaves of Grass" cluster), it was increased from sixty-seven to seventy-one lines, the present text representing the fullest development of the poem. In 1867, with the present title, the poem was cut to forty-nine lines, perhaps in an effort to make it more objectives; see the interrelated stanzas that were then discarded: lines 7–16, 60–65, and 68–71. For the last group (lines 68–71) WW substituted one line: "Has Life much purport?—Ah, Death has the greatest purport." Line 6 was altered to read: "I weather it out with you, or sink with you." Lines 28, 29, and 50 were canceled in 1867. In later editions there were minor changes in punctuation and the poem was divided into five cantos, then permanently dropped in 1881, excepting the two couplets, lines 19–22, that became the poem "Youth, Day, Old Age, and Night."
2. A MS (Trent) earlier than the first *LG* (1855) is a draft of three stanzas (*N and F*, item 56), of which stanzas 1 and 3 compare closely with the present stanzas "1" and "5." The second MS stanza reads:

> And that's so, easy enough:
> And I am no shallowpate to go about singing them above
>   the rest and deferring to them;
> And they did not become great by singing and deferring.

What they wished, do we not wish the same?
Great is Youth—equally great is Old Age—great are the Day
    and Night,
Great is Wealth—great is Poverty—great is Expression—great
    is Silence.

Youth, large, lusty, loving—Youth, full of grace, force, fascination,
Do you know that Old Age may come after you,
    with equal grace, force, fascination?   20

Day, full-blown and splendid—Day of the immense sun,
    action, ambition, laughter,
The Night follows close, with millions of suns, and
    sleep, and restoring darkness.

Wealth with the flush hand, fine clothes, hospitality,
But then the Soul's wealth, which is candor, knowledge,
    pride, enfolding love;
(Who goes for men and women showing Poverty richer than
    wealth?)   25

Expression of speech! in what is written or said, forget
    not that Silence is also expressive,
That anguish as hot as the hottest, and contempt as
    cold as the coldest, may be without words,
That the true adoration is likewise without words, and without
    kneeling.

Great is the greatest Nation—the nation of clusters of equal
    nations.

Great is the Earth, and the way it became what it is;   30
Do you imagine it is stopped at this? the increase abandoned?
Understand then that it goes as far onward from this, as this is
    from the times when it lay in covering waters and gases,
    before man had appeared.

Great is the quality of Truth in man,
The quality of truth in man supports itself through all changes,
It is inevitably in the man—he and it are in love, and never
    leave each other.   35

The truth in man is no dictum, it is vital as eyesight,
If there be any Soul, there is truth—if there be man or
    woman, there is truth—if there be physical or moral,
    there is truth,
If there be equilibrium or volition, there is truth—if there be
    things at all upon the earth, there is truth.

O truth of the earth! O truth of things! I am determined
    to press my way toward you,
Sound your voice! I scale mountains, or dive in the sea after
    you.   40

Great is Language—it is the mightiest of the sciences,
It is the fulness, color, form, diversity of the earth, and of men
    and women, and of all qualities and processes,
It is greater than wealth—it is greater than buildings,
    ships, religions, paintings, music.

Great is the English speech—what speech is so great as the
    English?
Great is the English brood—what brood has so vast
    a destiny as the English?   45
It is the mother of the brood that must rule the earth with the
    new rule,
The new rule shall rule as the Soul rules, and as the
    love, justice, equality in the Soul, rule.

Great is Law—great are the old few landmarks of the law,
They are the same in all times, and shall not be disturbed.

Great are commerce, newspapers, books, free-trade, railroads,
    steamers, international mails, telegraphs, exchanges.   50

Great is Justice!
Justice is not settled by legislators and laws—it is in the Soul,
It cannot be varied by statutes, any more than love,
    pride, the attraction of gravity, can,
It is immutable—it does not depend on majorities—majorities
    or what not come at last before the same passionless and
    exact tribunal.

For justice are the grand natural lawyers and perfect
    judges—it is in their Souls,   55
It is well assorted—they have not studied for nothing—
    the great includes the less,
They rule on the highest grounds—they oversee all
    eras, states, administrations.

The perfect judge fears nothing—he could go front to front
    before God,
Before the perfect judge all shall stand back—life and death
    shall stand back—heaven and hell shall stand back.

Great is Goodness!   60
I do not know what it is, any more than I know what
    health is—but I know it is great.

Great is Wickedness—I find I often admire it, just as
    much as I admire goodness,
Do you call that a paradox? It certainly is a paradox.

The eternal equilibrium of things is great, and the
    eternal overthrow of things is great,
And there is another paradox.   65

Great is Life, real and mystical, wherever and whoever,
Great is Death—sure as Life holds all parts together,
    Death holds all parts together,
Death has just as much purport as Life has,
Do you enjoy what Life confers? you shall enjoy what Death
    confers,
I do not understand the realities of Death, but I know they are
    great,   70
I do not understand the least reality of Life—how then
    can I understand the realities of Death?
(*1855*) *1860*   *1860* (*1876*)

Poem of Remembrances
for a Girl or a Boy of These States[3]

You just maturing youth! You male or female!
Remember the organic compact of These States,
Remember the pledge of the Old Thirteen thenceforward to
    the rights, life, liberty, equality of man,
Remember what was promulged by the founders, ratified by
    The States, signed in black and white by the
    Commissioners, and read by Washington at the head of
    the army,
Remember the purposes of the founders,—Remember
    Washington;   5
Remember the copious humanity streaming from every
    direction toward America;
Remember the hospitality that belongs to nations
    and men; (Cursed be nation, woman, man, without
    hospitality!)
Remember, government is to subserve individuals,
Not any, not the President, is to have one jot more than you
    or me,

3. Originally a poem of forty-three lines in *LG* 1856, with the present title; reappeared in *LG*
1860 as "Chants Democratic—6," increased by the addition of the present first line. In *LG*
1867 WW excluded the present passage of twenty-one lines and retained the second section
(twenty-three lines) under the new title "Think of the Soul" (1867–76), which is reproduced
immediately below. The excluded passage, as shown above, has a certain unity and meaning
worthy of attention. The consecutive reading of this and the following "Think of the Soul"
reproduces the entire 1860 text, except that the serial numbers preceding stanzas have been
canceled.

Not any habitan of America is to have one jot less than you or
    me.   10

Anticipate when the thirty or fifty millions, are to become the
    hundred, or two hundred millions, of equal freemen and
    freewomen, amicably joined.

Recall ages—One age is but a part—ages are but a part;
Recall the angers, bickerings, delusions, superstitions,
    of the idea of caste,
Recall the bloody cruelties and crimes.

Anticipate the best women;   15
I say an unnumbered new race of hardy and well-defined
    women are to spread through all These States,
I say a girl fit for These States must be free, capable,
    dauntless, just the same as a boy.

Anticipate your own life—retract with merciless power,
Shirk nothing—retract in time—Do you see those
    errors, diseases, weaknesses, lies, thefts?
Do you see that lost character?—Do you see decay,
    consumption, rum-drinking, dropsy, fever, mortal cancer
    or inflammation?   20
Do you see death, and the approach of death?
    (1856) 1860   *1860*

Think of the Soul[4]

Think of the Soul;
I swear to you that body of yours gives proportions to
    your Soul somehow to live in other spheres;
I do not know how, but I know it is so.

Think of loving and being loved;
I swear to you, whoever you are, you can interfuse yourself
    with such things that everybody that sees you shall look
    longingly upon you.   5

Think of the past;
I warn you that in a little while others will find their
    past in you and your times.

4. Originally the last nine stanzas of "Poem of Remembrances . . . ," 1856 (*q.v.*, immediately
preceding), these twenty-three lines were preserved in the 1867 edition, from which the
earlier portion of the original poem was excluded. In the 1867 edition this poem, without
title, became No. 1 of the poem cluster entitled "Leaves of Grass." In 1868 it was included
as "Links" in Rossetti's English edition. With the present title and only a few changes,
principally in punctuation, the poem was retained in the editions of 1871–72 and 1876,
before being excluded from the 1881 edition. The text is that of the last edition, 1876.

The race is never separated—nor man nor woman escapes;
All is inextricable—things, spirits, Nature, nations, you
    too—from precedents you come.

Recall the ever-welcome defiers, (The mothers precede them;)   10
Recall the sages, poets, saviors, inventors, lawgivers, of the earth;
Recall Christ, brother of rejected persons—brother of slaves,
    felons, idiots, and of insane and diseas'd[5] persons.

Think of the time when you were not[6] yet born;
Think of times you stood at the side of the dying;
Think of the time when your own body will be dying.   15

Think of spiritual results,
Sure as the earth swims through the heavens, does every
    one of its objects pass into spiritual results.

Think of manhood, and you to be a man;
Do you count manhood, and the sweet of manhood, nothing?

Think of womanhood, and you to be a woman;   20
The creation is womanhood;
Have I not said that womanhood involves all?
Have I not told how the universe has nothing better
    than the best womanhood?
    (1856) 1867   *1876*

Respondez![7]

RESPONDEZ! Respondez!
(The war is completed—the price is paid—the title is
    settled beyond recall;)
Let every one answer! let those who sleep be waked! let none
    evade!
Must we still go on with our affectations and sneaking?
Let me bring this to a close—I pronounce openly for
    a new distribution of roles;   5
Let that which stood in front go behind! and let that which
    was behind advance to the front and speak;

5. Originally, "diseased"; the elision appeared from 1867 to 1876.
6. Originally, "you was not"; corrected in fourth edition, 1872.
7. Appeared initially as "Poem of the Propositions of Nakedness" in *LG* 1856 and appeared in
the 1860 edition without title, as number five of the "Chants Democratic and Native Amer-
ican." Entitled "Respondez," it appeared in all later editions until 1876, the source of this
text. Of the eleven lines gained by revision, the most striking were lines 2 and 17–19, which
reflected the Civil War and the postwar corruptions that WW excoriated the same year in
the prose of *Democratic Vistas* (1871). Excluding the poem as a whole in 1881, the poet
transposed several lines to other poems. Compare "Respondez," lines 6–8, 65, and 66 with
"Reversals"; and compare lines 22, 44, and 46 with "Transpositions."

Let murderers, bigots, fools, unclean persons, offer new
    propositions!
Let the old propositions be postponed!
Let faces and theories be turn'd inside out! let meanings
    be freely criminal, as well as results!
Let there be no suggestion above the suggestion of drudgery!   10
Let none be pointed toward his destination! (Say! do
    you know your destination?)
Let men and women be mock'd with bodies and mock'd with Souls!
Let the love that waits in them, wait! let it die, or pass
    still-born to other spheres!
Let the sympathy that waits in every man, wait! or let
    it also pass, a dwarf, to other spheres!
Let contradictions prevail! let one thing contradict another!
    and let one line of my poems contradict another!   15
Let the people sprawl with yearning, aimless hands! let their
    tongues be broken! let their eyes be discouraged! let none
    descend into their hearts with the fresh lusciousness of
    love!
(Stifled, O days! O lands! in every public and private
    corruption!
Smother'd in thievery, impotence, shamelessness, mountain-high;
Brazen effrontery, scheming, rolling like ocean's waves
    around and upon you, O my days! my lands!
For not even those thunderstorms, nor fiercest lightnings
    of the war, have purified the atmosphere;)   20
—Let the theory of America still be management, caste,
    comparison! (Say! what other theory would you?)
Let them that distrust birth and death still lead the rest! (Say!
    why shall they not lead you?)
Let the crust of hell be neared and trod on! let the days be
    darker than the nights! let slumber bring less slumber
    than waking time brings!
Let the world never appear to him or her for whom it was all made!
Let the heart of the young man still exile itself from the heart
    of the old man! and let the heart of the old man be exiled
    from that of the young man!   25
Let the sun and moon go! let scenery take the applause of the
    audience! let there be apathy under the stars!
Let freedom prove no man's inalienable right! every one who
    can tyrannize, let him tyrannize to his satisfaction!
Let none but infidels be countenanced!
Let the eminence of meanness, treachery, sarcasm, hate,
    greed, indecency, impotence, lust, be taken for granted
    above all! let writers, judges, governments, households,
    religions, philosophies, take such for granted above all!
Let the worst men beget children out of the worst women!   30
Let the priest still play at immortality!
Let death be inaugurated!
Let nothing remain but the ashes of teachers, artists,
    moralists, lawyers, and learn'd and polite persons!

Let him who is without my poems be assassinated!
Let the cow, the horse, the camel, the garden-bee—let the
    mud-fish, the lobster, the mussel, eel, the sting-ray, and
    the grunting pig-fish—let these, and the like of these, be
    put on a perfect equality with man and woman! 35
Let churches accommodate serpents, vermin, and the corpses
    of those who have died of the most filthy of diseases!
Let marriage slip down among fools, and be for none but fools!
Let men among themselves talk and think forever obscenely of
    women! and let women among themselves talk and think
    obscenely of men!
Let us all, without missing one, be exposed in public, naked,
    monthly, at the peril of our lives! let our bodies be freely
    handled and examined by whoever chooses!
Let nothing but copies at second hand be permitted to exist
    upon the earth! 40
Let the earth desert God, nor let there ever henceforth
    be mention'd the name of God!
Let there be no God!
Let there be money, business, imports, exports, custom,
    authority, precedents, pallor, dyspepsia, smut, ignorance,
    unbelief!
Let judges and criminals be transposed! let the prison-keepers
    be put in prison! let those that were prisoners take the
    keys! (Say! why might they not just as well be transposed?)
Let the slaves be masters! let the masters become slaves! 45
Let the reformers descend from the stands where they are
    forever bawling! let an idiot or insane person appear on
    each of the stands!
Let the Asiatic, the African, the European, the American, and
    the Australian, go armed against the murderous
    stealthiness of each other! let them sleep armed! let none
    believe in good will!
Let there be no unfashionable wisdom! let such be
    scorn'd and derided off from the earth!
Let a floating cloud in the sky—let a wave of the sea—let
    growing mint, spinach, onions, tomatoes—let these be
    exhibited as shows, at a great price for admission!
Let all the men of These States stand aside for a few
    smouchers![8] let the few seize on what they choose! let the
    rest gawk, giggle, starve, obey! 50
Let shadows be furnish'd with genitals! let substances
    be deprived of their genitals!
Let there be wealthy and immense cities—but still through
    any of them, not a single poet, savior, knower, lover!
Let the infidels of These States laugh all faith away!
If one man be found who has faith, let the rest set upon him!

8. *Cf.* "to smouch"—to gouge, to take unfair advantage. Colloquial in New York. *New English Dictionary,* IX, part 1.

Let them affright faith! let them destroy the power of breeding
    faith! 55
Let the she-harlots and the he-harlots be prudent!
    let them dance on, while seeming lasts!
    (O seeming! seeming! seeming!)
Let the preachers recite creeds! let them still teach
    only what they have been taught!
Let insanity still have charge of sanity!
Let books take the place of trees, animals, rivers, clouds!
Let the daub'd portraits of heroes supersede heroes! 60
Let the manhood of man never take steps after itself!
Let it take steps after eunuchs, and after consumptive and
    genteel persons!
Let the white person again tread the black person under his
    heel! (Say! which is trodden under heel, after all?)
Let the reflections of the things of the world be studied in
    mirrors! let the things themselves still continue unstudied!
Let a man seek pleasure everywhere except in himself! 65
Let a woman seek happiness everywhere except in herself!
(What real happiness have you had one single hour
    through your whole life?)
Let the limited years of life do nothing for the limitless years
    of death! (What do you suppose death will do, then?)
1856 *1876*

[In the New Garden][9]

In the new garden, in all the parts,
In cities now, modern, I wander,
Through the second or third result, or still further, primitive yet,
Days, places, indifferent—though various, the same,
Time, Paradise, the Mannahatta, the prairies, finding me
    unchanged, 5
Death indifferent—Is it that I lived long since?
    Was I buried very long ago?
For all that, I may now be watching you here, this moment;
For the future, with determined will, I seek—the woman of
    the future,
You, born years, centuries after me, I seek.
1860 *1860*

9. This poem appeared only in the third edition, *LG* 1860, identified as number "11" of the fifteen untitled poems comprising the section then called "Enfans d'Adam." All the others survived in the "Children of Adam" cluster, or elsewhere. "In the New Garden," however, in part resembles the first poem of the final "Children of Adam." That fine poem, called "To the Garden of the World" (*q.v.*) represents the "first man, Adam" with his Eve at the beginning; the present poem sees an Adam ever new but "primitive yet," in the "new garden," in "modern" cities, seeking the Eve "of the future."

[Who Is Now Reading This?][1]

Who is now reading this?

May-be one is now reading this who knows some
    wrong-doing of my past life,
Or may-be a stranger is reading this who has secretly loved me,
Or may-be one who meets all my grand assumptions
    and egotisms with derision,
Or may-be one who is puzzled at me.   5

As if I were not puzzled at myself!
Or as if I never deride myself! (O conscience-struck! O self-
    convicted!)
Or as if I do not secretly love strangers! (O tenderly,
    a long time, and never avow it;)
Or as if I did not see, perfectly well, interior in
    myself, the stuff of wrong-doing,
Or as if it could cease transpiring from me until it must cease.   10
1860   *1860*

[Long I Thought That Knowledge Alone Would Suffice][2]

Long I thought that knowledge alone would suffice
    me—O if I could but obtain knowledge!
Then my lands engrossed me—Lands of the prairies, Ohio's
    land, the southern savannas, engrossed me—For them I
    would live—I would be their orator;
Then I met the examples of old and new heroes—I heard of
    warriors, sailors, and all dauntless persons—And it
    seemed to me that I too had it in me to be as dauntless as
    any—and would be so;
And then, to enclose all, it came to me to strike up the songs
    of the New World—And then I believed my life must be
    spent in singing;
But now take notice, land of the prairies, land of
    the south savannas, Ohio's land,   5
Take notice, you Kanuck woods—and you Lake Huron—and

1. The first and only publication of this interesting poem occurred in *LG* 1860, where it was
without title, numbered "16" in the "Calamus" cluster. The present copy omits the stanza
numbering.
2. Appeared only in *LG* 1860, untitled, but numbered "8" in the cluster entitled "Calamus." It
is associated with another new poem of 1860, "Once I passed Through a Populous City"
(*q.v.*), which is more intense and stylistically impressive. In the MS version (ca. 1859) both
poems refer to the lover as a man. Before publication, Whitman changed the lover to a
woman in the other poem, which held its place into the final *LG* 1891–92. The present
poem WW canceled in his "Blue Copy" *LG* 1860. (See Bowers, 64 and 80.)

all that with you roll toward Niagara—and you Niagara
also,
And you, Californian mountains—That you each and all find
somebody else to be your singer of songs,
For I can be your singer of songs no longer—One who loves
me is jealous of me, and withdraws me from all but love,
With the rest I dispense—I sever from what I thought would
suffice me, for it does not—it is now empty and tasteless
to me,
I heed knowledge, and the grandeur of The States,
and the example of heroes, no more,   10
I am indifferent to my own songs—I will go with him I love,
It is to be enough for us that we are together—We never
separate again.
1860   1860

[Hours Continuing Long]³

Hours continuing long, sore and heavy-hearted,
Hours of the dusk, when I withdraw to a lonesome and
unfrequented spot, seating myself, leaning my face in my
hands;
Hours sleepless, deep in the night, when I go forth, speeding
swiftly the country roads, or through the city streets, or
pacing miles and miles, stifling plaintive cries;
Hours discouraged, distracted—for the one I cannot content
myself without, soon I saw him content himself without
me;
Hours when I am forgotten, (O weeks and months are
passing, but I believe I am never to forget!)   5
Sullen and suffering hours! (I am ashamed—but it
is useless—I am what I am;)
Hours of my torment—I wonder if other men ever
have the like, out of the like feelings?
Is there even one other like me—distracted—his
friend, his lover, lost to him?
Is he too as I am now? Does he still rise in the morning,
dejected, thinking who is lost to him? and at night,
awaking, think who is lost?
Does he too harbor his friendship silent and endless?
harbor his anguish and passion?   10
Does some stray reminder, or the casual mention of a name,
bring the fit back upon him, taciturn and deprest?
Does he see himself reflected in me? In these hours,
does he see the face of his hours reflected?
1860   1860

---

3. This was published, without title, as number "9" in the "Calamus" cluster of LG 1860. It
was not reprinted in subsequent editions, but among the "Calamus" poems it is a striking
expression of Whitman's theme of "comradeship."

[So Far, and So Far, and On Toward the End][4]

So far, and so far, and on toward the end,
Singing what is sung in this book, from the irresistible
    impulses of me;
But whether I continue beyond this book, to maturity,
Whether I shall dart forth the true rays, the ones that wait unfired,
(Did you think the sun was shining its brightest?   5
No—it has not yet fully risen;)
Whether I shall complete what is here started,
Whether I shall attain my own height, to justify these, yet
    unfinished,
Whether I shall make THE POEM OF THE NEW WORLD,
    transcending all others—depends, rich persons, upon you,
Depends, whoever you are now filling the current Presidentiad,
    upon you,   10
Upon you, Governor, Mayor, Congressman,
And you, contemporary America.
1860   *1860*

Thoughts—1: Visages[5]

Of the visages of things—And of piercing through
    to the accepted hells beneath;
Of ugliness—To me there is just as much in it as there is in
    beauty—And now the ugliness of human beings is
    acceptable to me;
Of detected persons—To me, detected persons are not, in any
    respect, worse than undetected persons—and are not in
    any respect worse than I am myself;
Of criminals—To me, any judge, or any juror, is equally
    criminal—and any reputable person is also—and the
    President is also.
1860   *1867*

---

4. Appeared only in *LG* 1860, as number "20" of twenty-four untitled poems of the cluster
entitled "Leaves of Grass."
5. First appeared in *LG* 1860; reprinted in *LG* 1867 without change, untitled, as number "1"
in the cluster of seven poems entitled "Thoughts." In the London selected edition by W. M.
Rossetti (*Poems by Walt Whitman,* 1868) it was entitled "Visages" and printed without verbal
change. It was excluded from the later editions. The MS (Huntington) lacks the last line.

Leaflets[6]

What General has a good army in himself, has a good army;
He happy in himself, or she happy in herself, is happy.
  (1860) 1867   *1867*

Thoughts—6: "Of What I Write"[7]

Of what I write from myself—As if that were not the resumé;[8]
Of Histories—As if such, however complete, were
    not less complete than the preceding poems;
As if those shreds, the records of nations, could possibly
    be as lasting as the preceding poems;
As if here were not the amount of all nations, and of all the
    lives of heroes.
  1860   *1876*

Says[9]

1

I say whatever tastes sweet to the most perfect person, that is
    finally right.

2

I say nourish a great intellect, a great brain;
If I have said anything to the contrary, I hereby retract it.

3

I say man shall not hold property in man;
I say the least developed person on earth is just as important
    and sacred to himself or herself, as the most developed
    person is to himself or herself.   5

6. Appeared independently only once, in *LG* 1867, with the present title, filling out the blank end of page 284. Earlier, in *LG* 1860, it was lines 4–5 of "Debris" (*q.v.*), a poem that appeared as a whole only in that edition.
7. Appeared in *LG* 1860 and, without alteration, in *LG* 1867 without title as number "6" among the seven poems of a cluster entitled "Thoughts." It was separately entitled "Thought" and slightly revised in editions from 1871 to 1876, the source of the present text. MS in Huntington.
8. So in WW's text.
9. Appeared in *LG* 1860 with the present text and title. Again entitled "Says" in 1867, it was cut from twenty-six to fifteen lines, retaining stanzas 1, 5, 7, and 8. If these stanzas alone are compared with the complete text, one sees that Whitman, after the Civil War and the publication of his *Drum-Taps*, rejected the passages dealing with slavery and reform, thus heightening in the remaining stanzas the theme of the dignity and potentialities of the democratic individual, already emphasized in stanza 5 by direct quotation from the last fifteen lines of paragraph 20 of his preface to *LG* 1855, his first manifesto on this subject. In the intensified version, the poem, now entitled "Suggestions," appeared in *LG* 1871, 1872, and for the last time in 1876, with the alteration of the epanaphora of initial phrases from "I say" (as above) to "That" or (in lines 13, 23, and 26) "And that."

4

I say where liberty draws not the blood out of
    slavery, there slavery draws the blood out of liberty,
I say the word of the good old cause in These States,
    and resound it hence over the world.

5

I say the human shape or face is so great, it must never be
    made ridiculous;
I say for ornaments nothing outre[1] can be allowed,
And that anything is most beautiful without ornament,   10
And that exaggerations will be sternly revenged in your own
    physiology, and in other persons' physiology also;
And I say that clean-shaped children can be jetted and
    conceived only where natural forms prevail in public, and
    the human face and form are never caricatured;
And I say that genius need never more be turned to romances,
(For facts properly told, how mean appear all romances.)

6

I say the word of lands fearing nothing—I will have no other
    land;   15
I say discuss all and expose all—I am for every topic openly;
I say there can be no salvation for These States without
    innovators—without free tongues, and ears willing to hear
    the tongues;
And I announce as a glory of These States, that they
    respectfully listen to propositions, reforms, fresh views and
    doctrines, from successions of men and women,
Each age with its own growth.

7

I have said many times that materials and the Soul
    are great, and that all depends on physique;   20
Now I reverse what I said, and affirm that all depends
    on the æsthetic or intellectual,
And that criticism is great—and that refinement is greatest of all;
And I affirm now that the mind governs—and that
    all depends on the mind.

8

With one man or woman—(no matter which one—
    I even pick out the lowest,)
With him or her I now illustrate the whole law;   25

---

1. *Sic*. Appears without accent also in Preface 1855; corrected in 1867.

I say that every right, in politics or what-not, shall be eligible
  to that one man or woman, on the same terms as any.
  1860   *1867 (1876)*

Apostroph[2]

O mater! O fils!
O brood continental!
O flowers of the prairies!
O space boundless! O hum of mighty products!
O you teeming cities! O so invincible, turbulent, proud!   5
O race of the future! O women!
O fathers! O you men of passion and the storm!
O native power only! O beauty!
O yourself! O God! O divine average!
O you bearded roughs! O bards! O all those slumberers!   10
O arouse! the dawn-bird's throat sounds shrill! Do
    you not hear the cock crowing?
O, as I walk'd the beach, I heard the mournful notes
    foreboding a tempest—the low, oft-repeated shriek of the
    diver, the long-lived loon;
O I heard, and yet hear, angry thunder;—O you
    sailors! O ships! make quick preparation!
O from his masterful sweep, the warning cry of the eagle!
(Give way there, all! It is useless! Give up your spoils;)   15
O sarcasms! Propositions! (O if the whole world
    should prove indeed a sham, a sell!)
O I believe there is nothing real but America and freedom!
O to sternly reject all except Democracy!
O imperator![3] O who dare confront you and me?
O to promulgate our own! O to build for that which builds for
    ˙ mankind!   20
O feuillage! O North! O the slope drained by the Mexican sea!
O all, all inseparable—ages, ages, ages!
O a curse on him that would dissever this Union for any
    reason whatever!
O climates, labors! O good and evil! O death!
O you strong with iron and wood! O Personality!   25
O the village or place which has the greatest man or
    woman! even if it be only a few ragged huts;
O the city where women walk in public processions in
    the streets, the same as the men;
O a wan and terrible emblem, by me adopted!

---

2. First appeared in the third edition, *LG* 1860, as the introductory poem of the section entitled
   "Chants Democratic and Native American," of which the remaining twenty-one poems were
   identified only by numerals. In the succeeding issue, 1867, the poem as a whole was replaced
   by a condensed and improved version of the concluding nineteen lines, which appeared in
   a new position as "Leaves of Grass: 1" (*cf.* "O Sun of Real Peace," below). Another derivative,
   not previously published, "O Brood Continental," appears among uncollected poems in this
   edition.
3. The Latin word for "emperor" also meant "commander" or "conqueror."

O shapes arising! shapes of the future centuries!
O muscle and pluck forever for me!   30
O workmen and workwomen forever for me!
O farmers and sailors! O drivers of horses forever for me!
O I will make the new bardic list of trades and tools!
O you coarse and wilful! I love you!
O South! O longings for my dear home! O soft and sunny airs!   35
O pensive! O I must return where the palm grows
    and the mocking-bird sings, or else I die!
O equality! O organic compacts! I am come to be your born poet!
O whirl, contest, sounding and resounding! I am
    your poet, because I am part of you;
O days by-gone! Enthusiasts! Antecedents!
O vast preparations for These States! O years!   40
O what is now being sent forward thousands of years to come!
O mediums! O to teach! to convey the invisible faith!
To promulge real things! to journey through all The States!
O creation! O to-day! O laws! O unmitigated adoration!
O for mightier broods of orators, artists, and singers!   45
O for native songs! carpenter's, boatman's, ploughman's
    songs! shoemaker's songs!
O haughtiest growth of time! O free and extatic!⁴
O what I, here, preparing, warble for!
O you hastening light! O the sun of the world will ascend,
    dazzling, and take his height—and you too will ascend;
O so amazing and so broad! up there resplendent, darting and
    burning;   50
O prophetic! O vision staggered with weight of light!
    with pouring glories!
O copious! O hitherto unequalled!
O Libertad! O compact! O union impossible to dissever!
O my Soul! O lips becoming tremulous, powerless!
O centuries, centuries yet ahead!   55
O voices of greater orators! I pause—I listen for you!
O you States! Cities! defiant of all outside authority! I spring at
    once into your arms! you I most love!
O you grand Presidentiads! I wait for you!
New history! New heroes! I project you!
Visions of poets! only you really last! O sweep on! sweep on!   60
O Death! O you striding there! O I cannot yet!
O heights! O infinitely too swift and dizzy yet!
O purged lumine! you threaten me more than I can stand!
O present! I return while yet I may to you!
O poets to come, I depend upon you!   65
1860   *1860 (1876)*

---

4. So spelled in both versions.

O Sun of Real Peace[5]

O sun of real peace! O hastening light!
O free and extatic![6] O what I here, preparing, warble for!
O the sun of the world will ascend, dazzling, and take his
    height—and you too, O my Ideal, will surely ascend!
O so amazing and broad—up there resplendent, darting and
    burning!
O vision prophetic, stagger'd with weight of light! with pouring
    glories!   5
O lips of my soul, already becoming powerless!
O ample and grand Presidentiads! Now the war, the war is over!
New history! new heroes! I project you!
Visions of poets! only you really last! sweep on! sweep on!
O heights too swift and dizzy yet!   10
O purged and luminous! you threaten me more than I can stand!
(I must not venture—the ground under my feet menaces
    me—it will not support me:
O future too immense,)—O present, I return, while yet I may,
    to you.
    (1860) 1867   *1876*

To You[7]

Let us twain walk aside from the rest;
Now we are together privately, do you discard ceremony;
Come! vouchsafe to me what has yet been vouchsafed to none
    —Tell me the whole story,
Let us talk of death—unbosom all freely,
Tell me what you would not tell your brother, wife, husband,
    or physician.   5
    (1860) 1872   *1876*

---

5. Whitman revised and reorganized the last nineteen lines of "Apostroph" (see above) to form
the thirteen lines of this poem, titled "O hastening light," in *LG* 1867. In *LG* 1871 it ap-
peared in a new cluster, "Marches now the War Is Over," whose motivation—the end of
the war—WW emphasized by adding the last half of line 7, by giving the poem its present
title, and by using the same phrase in the opening line. The present text is that of 1876, the
poem's last appearance.
6. So spelled in "Apostroph." See above.
7. Twelve years after this poem's first appearance, WW transformed it emotionally by the in-
sertion in *PI* 1871 and *TR* 1876 of the present fourth line, in which the "talk of death"
concentrates and defines a spiritual value. Without this line, in the 1860 version, the pro-
posed sharing of confidences suggests a somewhat gross familiarity. The ms (Barrett) has
the four-line version shown as the second of the two stanzas of a poem entitled "To You."
Each appeared separately with this title in *LG* 1860, printed in reverse order on p. 403
concluding the cluster "Messenger Leaves." The other poem, now the familiar couplet en-
titled "To You" among the *LG* "Inscriptions," simply declared that passing strangers should
talk freely together. The present poem did not appear in *PI* 1876. It reappeared only in the
revised edition of *Passage to India*, a supplement in *LG* 1872 and *TR* 1876. The contents
list in some copies ignored this poem ending page 114. WW did not include it in the final
selection of 1881, and it has not been revived.

Now Lift Me Close[8]

Now lift me close to your face till I whisper,
What you are holding is in reality no book, nor part of a book;
It is a man, flush'd and full-blooded—it is I—*So long!*
—We must separate awhile—Here! take from my lips this kiss;
Whoever you are, I give it especially to you;   5
So long!—And I hope we shall meet again.
1860   *1867 (1876)*

To the Reader at Parting[9]

Now, dearest comrade, lift me to your face,
We must separate awhile—Here! take from my lips this kiss;
Whoever you are, I give it especially to you;
So long!—And I hope we shall meet again.
(1860) 1871   *1876*

Debris[1]

*

He is wisest who has the most caution,
He only wins who goes far enough.

8. This poem, not previously collected, first appeared as a poem of six lines in *LG* 1860, iden-
tified only as "24," the last in the cluster "Leaves of Grass." In the same edition appeared
the extensive "So Long," which broadly echoes the six-line poem. In the 1867 edition, "Now
Lift Me Close" was the terminal poem of the "Leaves of Grass" cluster, while "So Long"
terminated the entire volume, at the end of "Songs before Parting," the last of three sup-
plements of recent poems. Although in lines 53–69 "So Long" expresses something of the
same idea as "Now Lift Me Close," the latter, in its six-line concentration, gives the effect
of an independent identity. In *LG* 1871, it was dropped in favor of "So Long"; but see a
four-line derivative, "To the Reader at Parting," immediately below.
9. This previously uncollected poem was a refinement of "Now Lift Me Close" (*q.v.*, above),
which was excluded from *LG* 1871. The revised text significantly canceled the previous lines
2 and 3, which had identified the "book" with the "man" (poet). Now the relationship with
the reader recalls the subtlety of meeting and parting expressed earlier in "Out of the Rolling
Ocean, the Crowd" (1865). "To the Reader at Parting" appeared as the penultimate poem
in the new volume, *Passage to India,* in 1871. *LG* 1871 ended with "So Long!" In *LG* 1872,
both poems appeared, each in the same relative place, since the volume included the "Pas-
sage to India" supplement. In 1881 the supplements were consolidated with *LG,* and "To
the Reader at Parting" was excluded in favor of "So Long!" as the terminating poem.
1. As a single poem of sixty lines "Debris" appeared only in *LG* 1860. In 1867 and later issues,
the poet excluded the poem as a whole but extracted certain passages and stanzas as separate
poems or parts of new poems. In the present text we see again the entire collage of associated
ideas, epigrams, characters, and events—with the poet present as commentator, producing
the tonal and emotional unity of a single composition. The thirty totally discarded lines
included, among other good things, the elusive and genuine lyric (lines 39–43) "I will take
an egg out of the robin's nest." Whitman thought so well of this poem that his memorandum
on the margin of the revised "Blue Book" copy of 1860, p. 424, read "with Religious Leaves
of Grass," referring to his dream of a second volume of *Leaves.* An epigram (lines 4 and 5)
appeared separately as "Leaflets" (*q.v.*) in *LG* 1867 and was then excluded. Seven of the
passages extracted from "Debris" survived in the final poems of *LG,* as follows:
    Lines 7–8: *cf.* "Stronger Lessons" in *Sands at Seventy.*

＊

Any thing is as good as established, when that is
    established that will produce it and continue it.

＊

What General has a good army in himself, has a good army;
He happy in himself, or she happy in herself, is happy,
But I tell you you cannot be happy by others, any more than   5
    you can beget or conceive a child by others.

＊

Have you learned lessons only of those who admired you, and
    were tender with you, and stood aside for you?
Have you not learned the great lessons of those who rejected
    you, and braced themselves against you? or who treated
    you with contempt, or disputed the passage with you?
Have you had no practice to receive opponents when they come?

＊

Despairing cries float ceaselessly toward me, day and night,   10
The sad voice of Death—the call of my nearest
    lover, putting forth, alarmed, uncertain,
This sea I am quickly to sail, come tell me,
Come tell me where I am speeding—tell me my destination.

＊

I understand your anguish, but I cannot help you,
I approach, hear, behold—the sad mouth, the look
    out of the eyes, your mute inquiry,   15
Whither I go from the bed I now recline on, come tell me;
Old age, alarmed, uncertain—A young woman's
    voice appealing to me, for comfort,
A young man's voice, *Shall I not escape?*

Lines 10–18 *cf.* "Yet, Yet, Ye Downcast Hours" (lines 5–13).
Lines 19–20: *cf.* "Offerings."
Lines 21–24: *cf.* "Visor'd."
Lines 34–35: *cf.* "Beautiful Women."
Lines 52–56: *cf.* "Not the Pilot."
Lines 57–60: *cf.* "As if a Phantom Caress'd Me" (lines 2–5).

*

A thousand perfect men and women appear,
Around each gathers a cluster of friends, and gay
    children and youths, with offerings.   20

*

A mask—a perpetual natural disguiser of herself,
Concealing her face, concealing her form,
Changes and transformations every hour, every moment,
Falling upon her even when she sleeps.

*

One sweeps by, attended by an immense train,   25
All emblematic of peace—not a soldier or menial among them.

*

One sweeps by, old, with black eyes, and profuse white hair,
He has the simple magnificence of health and strength,
His face strikes as with flashes of lightning whoever it turns
    toward.

*

Three old men slowly pass, followed by three others, and they
    by three others,   30
They are beautiful—the one in the middle of each
    group holds his companions by the hand,
As they walk, they give out perfume wherever they walk.

*

Women sit, or move to and fro—some old, some young,
The young are beautiful—but the old are more beautiful than
    the young.

*

What weeping face is that looking from the window?   35
Why does it stream those sorrowful tears?
Is it for some burial place, vast and dry?
Is it to wet the soil of graves?

*

I will take an egg out of the robin's nest in the orchard,
I will take a branch of gooseberries from the old bush in the
    garden, and go and preach to the world;
You shall see I will not meet a single heretic or scorner,
You shall see how I stump clergymen, and confound them,
You shall see me showing a scarlet tomato, and a
    white pebble from the beach.   40

*

Behavior—fresh, native, copious, each one for himself or herself,
Nature and the Soul expressed—America and freedom
    expressed—In it the finest art,   45
In it pride, cleanliness, sympathy, to have their chance,
In it physique, intellect, faith—in it just as much as to manage
    an army or a city, or to write a book—perhaps more,
The youth, the laboring person, the poor person, rivalling all
    the rest—perhaps outdoing the rest,
The effects of the universe no greater than its;
For there is nothing in the whole universe that can be more
    effective than a man's or woman's daily behavior can be,   50
In any position, in any one of These States.

*

Not the pilot has charged himself to bring his ship into port,
    though beaten back, and many times baffled,
Not the path-finder, penetrating inland, weary and long,
By deserts parched, snows chilled, rivers wet, perseveres till he
    reaches his destination,
More than I have charged myself, heeded or unheeded, to
    compose a free march for These States,   55
To be exhilarating music to them, years, centuries hence.

*

I thought I was not alone, walking here by the shore,
But the one I thought was with me, as now I walk by the shore,
As I lean and look through the glimmering light—
    that one has utterly disappeared,
And those appear that perplex me.   60
1860   *1860 (1881)*

[States!]²

States!
Were you looking to be held together by the lawyers?
By an agreement on a paper? Or by arms?
Away!
I arrive, bringing these, beyond all the forces of courts and
    arms,   5
These! to hold you together as firmly as the earth itself is held
    together.

The old breath of life, ever new,
Here! I pass it by contact to you, America.

O mother! have you done much for me?
Behold, there shall from me be much done for you.   10

There shall from me be a new friendship—It shall be called
    after my name,
It shall circulate through The States, indifferent of place,
It shall twist and intertwist them through and around each
    other—Compact shall they be, showing new signs,
Affection shall solve every one of the problems of freedom,
Those who love each other shall be invincible,   15
They shall finally make America completely victorious, in my name.

One from Massachusetts shall be a comrade to a Missourian,
One from Maine or Vermont, and a Carolinian and an
    Oregonese, shall be friends triune, more precious to each
    other than all the riches of the earth.
To Michigan shall be wafted perfume from Florida,
To the Mannahatta from Cuba or Mexico,   20
Not the perfume of flowers, but sweeter, and wafted beyond death.

No danger shall balk Columbia's lovers,
If need be, a thousand shall sternly immolate themselves for one,
The Kanuck shall be willing to lay down his life for the
    Kansian, and the Kansian for the Kanuck, on due need.

---

2. This poem as a whole (fifteen stanzas, forty-two lines) appeared only once, in *LG* 1860,
   "Calamus—5," the text shown here without the initial stanza numerals. However, WW ex-
   tracted from it materials for two poems of the final *LG*: in *Drum-Taps* (1865), "Over the
   Carnage Rose Prophetic a Voice" (*cf.* "States," lines 1–2, 14–25, and 31–35), and in *LG*
   1867, "A Song," later, the stirring "For You O Democracy" (*cf.* "States," last three stanzas,
   lines 36–42). Both new poems reflected the poet's Civil War experience. Before the war, the
   parent poem generalized the democratic idealism; both postwar revisions emphasized the
   comradeship engendered by the war.

It shall be customary in all directions, in the houses and
    streets, to see manly affection,   25
The departing brother or friend shall salute the remaining
    brother or friend with a kiss.

There shall be innovations,
There shall be countless linked hands—namely, the
    Northeasterner's and the Northwesterner's, and the
    Southwesterner's, and those of the interior, and all their
    brood,
These shall be masters of the world under a new power,
They shall laugh to scorn the attacks of all the remainder of
    the world.   30

The most dauntless and rude shall touch face to face lightly,
The dependence of Liberty shall be lovers,
The continuance of Equality shall be comrades.

These shall tie and band stronger than hoops of iron,
I, extatic,[3] O partners! O lands! henceforth with the love of
    lovers tie you.   35

I will make the continent indissoluble,
I will make the most splendid race the sun ever yet shone upon,
I will make divine magnetic lands.

I will plant companionship[4] thick as trees along all the rivers
    of America, and along the shores of the great lakes, and
    all over the prairies,
I will make inseparable cities, with their arms about each
    other's necks.   40

For you these, from me, O Democracy, to serve you, ma femme!
For you! for you, I am trilling these songs.
    1860   *1860 (1881)*

---

3. Misspelled throughout *LG* 1860.
4. In a footnote to "Democratic Vistas" (*CPW*, 247) WW wrote that "fervid comradeship [will]
    counterbalance and offset . . . our materialistic and vulgar American democracy. . . . I say
    democracy infers such loving comradeship as its most inevitable twin or counterpart."

Thoughts—2: "Of Waters, Forests, Hills"[5]

Of waters, forests, hills,
Of the earth at large, whispering through medium of me;
Of vista—Suppose some sight in arriere,[6] through the
    formative chaos, presuming the growth, fulness, life, now
    attained on the journey;
(But I see the road continued, and the journey ever continued;)
Of what was once lacking on the earth, and in due time has
    become supplied—And of what will yet be supplied,   5
Because all I see and know, I believe to have purport
    in what will yet be supplied.
1860   *1867 (1881)*

Thoughts—4: "Of Ownership . . ."[7]

Of ownership—As if one fit to own things could not at
    pleasure enter upon all, and incorporate them into himself
    or herself;
Of Equality—As if it harmed me, giving others the same
    chances and rights as myself—As if it were not
    indispensable to my own rights that others possess the
    same;
Of Justice—As if Justice could be any thing but the same
    ample law, expounded by natural judges and saviours,
As if it might be this thing or that thing, according to
    decisions.
1860   *1867 (1881)*

---

5. "Thoughts—2" and "Thoughts—4" (which follows) each lost its separate identity after *LG* 1867. They are here reproduced in the original text of *LG* 1860, where they appeared among the seven untitled poems of the cluster called "Thoughts." Of these, "3," "5," and "7," survived in the final edition without substantial change. "Thoughts—1" and "Thoughts—6," excluded from *LG*, are both included above. But in *LG* 1871 appeared a seven-line poem entitled "Thoughts," of which the first stanza was the first line of "Thoughts—4" (*q.v.* below) and the second stanza was the entire original text of "2" as given above. In 1881 Whitman revised this as a five-line stanza by discarding the first two lines of "Thoughts—2." See "Thoughts" in the cluster "By the Roadside." MS in Huntington.
6. Given without accent in all editions.
7. See footnote for "Thoughts—2" just preceding. When Whitman in 1871 transferred to that poem the first line of "Thoughts—4," he temporarily set aside the remnant of this poem. In 1881 he recovered two small epigrams, each entitled "Thought" in the new cluster of *LG* called "By the Roadside." Lines 3 and 4 became the second poem of that cluster entitled "Thought"; line 2 became the third so named (see *LG* text above).

Bathed in War's Perfume[8]

Bathed in war's perfume—delicate flag!
(Should the days needing armies, needing fleets, come again,)
O to hear you call the sailors and the soldiers! flag like a
    beautiful woman!
O to hear the tramp, tramp, of a million answering
    men! O the ships they arm with joy!
O to see you leap and beckon from the tall masts of ships!   5
O to see you peering down on the sailors on the decks!
Flag like the eyes of women.
1865   *1876*

Solid, Ironical, Rolling Orb[9]

Solid, ironical, rolling orb!
Master of all, and matter of fact!—at last I accept your terms;
Bringing to practical, vulgar tests, of all my ideal dreams,
And of me, as lover and hero.
1865   *1876*

Up, Lurid Stars![1]

Up, lurid stars! martial constellation!
Change, tattered cloth—your silver group withdrawing;
Bring we threads of scarlet, in vacant spots resetting,
    Thirty-four stars, red as blood.

World, take good notice! the silver group has vanished;   5
Notice clustering now, as coals of molten iron,
Time, warning baleful, off these western shores,
    Thirty-four stars, red as blood.
(1865)   *1865 (1881)*

8. First appeared in 1865, in *Drum-Taps*, where it was identical with the present text except
for the absence of the second line. It reappeared in the "Drum-Taps" section of *LG* 1867;
in Rossetti's English edition of 1868 it was entitled "The Flag." In *LG* 1871 Whitman added
the second line and made this the title poem of a cluster of seven poems saluting the flag,
which appeared with several other retrospective clusters of poems following the "Drum-Taps"
cluster. As a seven-line poem, without further change, it persisted in *LG* 1872 and 1876,
but not in later editions.

9. First appeared in *Drum-Taps* (1865); reappeared without change of text or title in all suc-
cessive editions of *LG* before the 1881 edition, from which it was excluded. After the 1867
edition, it was removed from the "Drum-Taps" cluster and appeared in the fifth cluster of
"Leaves of Grass" poems, which emphasized the nature of experience.

1. The present text, not before published, is related to the five-line poem "World Take Good
Notice" in *Drum-Taps* (1865), which is an intensified version of the same idea and symbol.
The version shown here is transcribed from an unpublished MS (Feinberg). An earlier or
more primitive MS (Yale) was reproduced in facsimile by J. H. Johnston in *Century Magazine*,
2nd ser., 49 (1911): 532; reprinted in Emory Holloway's Inclusive *LG*, notes, p. 652. The
Johnston text is also in two stanzas, but the refrains are comparatively more crude, the
phrasing less finished, and the wording more remote from the final choice. Comparison with
"World Take Good Notice" (*LG* text) may be rewarding.

Not My Enemies Ever Invade Me[2]

Not my enemies ever invade me—no harm to my pride from
    them I fear;
But the lovers I recklessly love—lo! how they master me!
Lo! me, ever open and helpless, bereft of my strength!
Utterly abject, grovelling on the ground before them.
    1865–66   *1867*

This Day, O Soul[3]

This day, O Soul, I give you a wondrous mirror;
Long in the dark, in tarnish and cloud it lay—But the
    cloud has pass'd and the tarnish gone;
. . . Behold, O Soul! it is now a clean and bright mirror,
Faithfully showing you all the things of the world.
    1865–66   *1876*

When I Read the Book[4]

When I read the book, the biography famous;
And is this, then, (said I,) what the author calls a man's life?
And so will some one, when I am dead and gone, write my life?
(As if any man really knew aught of my life;
As if you, O cunning Soul, did not keep your secret well!)   5
    1867   *1867 (1881)*

2. Appeared in *Sequel to Drum-Taps* (1865–66), p. 17; reprinted in the same position in *LG* 1867; excluded from later editions.
3. First published in *Sequel to Drum-Taps* (1865–66), p. 19, this poem appeared in the same position, unaltered, among the poems of the "Drum-Taps" group in *LG* 1867. It was not included in *LG* 1871 but was incorporated in the new volume of that year, *Passage to India* (p. 119). It survived in the *Passage to India* supplements—in *LG* 1872 and in *Two Rivulets* (1876), the companion volume to *LG* 1876. The poem was excluded from *LG* 1881 but it is related in idea with "My Picture-Gallery," which then appeared. Both resemble in phraseology a passage in ms (ca. 1855); see below in "Uncollected Poems"—"Pictures," lines 10–11.
4. In 1871 the poet took the poem above from the "Leaves of Grass" section of the 1867 edition, in which it first appeared (p. 268), and included it among a new group of "Inscriptions," then numbering nine small poems, which he placed at the front of the 1871 volume. Dropping line 5, the last line of the original poem above, he replaced it with three lines (see the ninth Inscription). If the new poem was a better inscription, the earlier was a poem in which genuine power and insight were concentrated in the last line.

Lessons[5]

There are who teach only the sweet lessons of peace and safety;
But I teach lessons of war and death to those I love,
That they readily meet invasions, when they come.

1871   *1871*

Ashes of Soldiers: Epigraph[6]

Again a verse for sake of you,
You soldiers in the ranks—you Volunteers,
Who bravely fighting, silent fell,
To fill unmention'd graves.

1871   *1876*

One Song, America, Before I Go[7]

One song, America, before I go,
I'd sing, o'er all the rest, with trumpet sound,
For thee—the Future.

I'd sow a seed for thee of endless Nationality;
I'd fashion thy Ensemble, including Body and Soul;   5
I'd show, away ahead, thy real Union, and how it may be
    accomplish'd.

(The paths to the House I seek to make,
But leave to those to come, the House itself.)
Belief I sing—and Preparation;
As Life and Nature are not great with reference to the Present
    only,
                                                                              10
But greater still from what is yet to come,
Out of that formula for Thee I sing.

1872   *1876*

---

5. Appeared in the volume *Passage to India* (1871), p. 116. It was absent from issues of that volume bound in as supplements to *LG* 1872 and *Two Rivulets* (1876); it was not included in the final collection of *LG* 1881.
6. No epigraph originally preceded "Ashes of Soldiers," then entitled "Hymn of Dead Soldiers," in *Drum-Taps* (1865) and in the "Drum-Taps" supplement, *LG* 1867. In the new volume *Passage to India* (1871), this epigraph appeared in italics above the poem, now revised, entitled "Ashes of Soldiers" and employed as title poem for a cluster of memorial poems. The epigraph remained in the "Passage to India" supplements of 1872 and 1876 but was canceled when "Ashes of Soldiers" was included with the poems finally selected for *LG* 1881.
7. One of two prefatory poems in *As a Strong Bird on Pinions Free* (1872), WW's poem for the Dartmouth College Commencement, June 26, 1872. The volume became a Supplement in *Two Rivulets* (1876). The commencement poem was revised under the title "Thou Mother with Thy Equal Brood" (*q.v.* above) in *LG* 1881, including a fundamental revision (in stanza 1) of the present poem, given here in its original form and separate identity. *Cf.* "Souvenirs of Democracy."

Souvenirs of Democracy[8]

The business man, the acquirer vast,
After assiduous years, surveying results, preparing for departure,
Devises houses and lands to his children—bequeaths
    stocks, goods—funds for a school or hospital,
Leaves money to certain companions to buy tokens,
    souvenirs of gems and gold;
Parceling out with care—And then, to prevent all cavil,   5
His name to his testament formally signs.

But I, my life surveying,
With nothing to show, to devise, from its idle years,
Nor houses, nor lands—nor tokens of gems or gold for my friends,
Only these Souvenirs of Democracy—In them—in
    all my songs—behind me leaving,   10
To You, whoever you are, (bathing, leavening this leaf
    especially with my breath—pressing on it a moment with
    my own hands;
—Here! feel how the pulse beats in my wrists!—
    how my heart's-blood is swelling, contracting!)
I will You, in all, Myself, with promise to never desert you,
To which I sign my name,

1872   *Walt Whitman*   *1876 (1881)*

From My Last Years[9]

From my last years, last thoughts I here bequeath,
Scatter'd and dropt, in seeds, and wafted to the West,
Through moisture of Ohio, prairie soil of Illinois—through
    Colorado, California air,
For Time to germinate fully.
    1876   *1876*

8. *Cf.* footnote to "One Song, America, Before I Go," immediately above. This was the second of the two inscription poems to *As a Strong Bird on Pinions Free,* the volume of 1872 and the supplement of 1876. In *LG* 1881, "My Legacy" appeared as an avatar of this poem, in a revision essentially changing the motivation (*q.v.*). Reducing the poem by four lines, the poet canceled out the bequest of himself—with the theatrical signature in facsimile—and made his legacy only "a bundle of songs . . . of camps and soldiers."
9. Appeared only once, in *Two Rivulets* (1876), p. 30. MS in Feinberg. Quoted in *N and F,* II, 67, item 43.

In Former Songs[1]

In former songs Pride have I sung, and Love, and passionate,
    joyful Life,
But here I twine the strands of Patriotism and Death.

And now, Life, Pride, Love, Patriotism and Death,
To you, O FREEDOM, purport of all!
(You that elude me most—refusing to be caught in songs of
    mine,)   5
I offer all to you.

2

'Tis not for nothing, Death,
I sound out you, and words of you, with daring tone—
    embodying you,
In my new Democratic chants—keeping you for a close,
For last impregnable retreat—a citadel and tower,   10
For my last stand—my pealing, final cry.
    1876   *1876*

The Beauty of the Ship[2]

When, staunchly entering port,
After long ventures, hauling up, worn and old,
Batter'd by sea and wind, torn by many a fight,
With the original sails all gone, replaced, or mended,
I only saw, at last, the beauty of the Ship.   5
    1876   *1876*

---

1. Appeared only once, in *Two Rivulets* (1876), p. 31.
2. In *LG* 1876, four "intercalations," as WW called them, were clippings from galley sheets pasted on blank end pages of some early issues and printed in the same position in later impressions of this edition. Only one survived in *LG* 1891–92 ("When the Full-Grown Poet Came," *q.v.* above). "The Beauty of the Ship" (*LG* 1876, p. 247) appeared before publication in a preview of the forthcoming volumes (*LG* and *TR*); this resembles WW's style and was published in the *New York Daily Tribune,* February 19, 1876. However, this poem and "After an Interval"—another "intercalation" that follows below—were excluded in later editions. The fourth "intercalation," "As In a Swoon" (*q.v.*, below) appeared again in *GBF* (1891), not in *LG*. But it was among poems WW included in *CPW* (1892).

After an Interval[3]

(Nov. 22, 1875, midnight—Saturn and Mars in conjunction.)

After an interval, reading, here in the midnight,
With the great stars looking on—all the stars of Orion looking,
And the silent Pleiades—and the duo looking of Saturn and
    ruddy Mars;[4]
Pondering, reading my own songs, after a long interval,
    (sorrow and death familiar now,)
Ere closing the book, what pride! what joy! to find them,   5
Standing so well the test of death and night!
And the duo of Saturn and Mars!
   1876   *1876*

Two Rivulets[5]

Two Rivulets side by side,
Two blended, parallel, strolling tides,
Companions, travelers, gossiping as they journey.

For the Eternal Ocean bound,
These ripples, passing surges, streams of Death and Life,   5
Object and Subject hurrying, whirling by,
The Real and Ideal,

Alternate ebb and flow the Days and Nights,
(Strands of a Trio twining, Present, Future, Past.)

---

3. See note to "The Beauty of the Ship," immediately above. "After an Interval" was another of the "intercalations" in *LG* 1876, pasted on the blank end of page 369 in early issues and printed in the same position in later impressions. It also appeared earlier in a preview of the forthcoming editions (presumably written by WW) in the *New York Daily Tribune*, February 19, 1876, but it was not included in *LG* editions after 1876.
4. On Whitman's strict observation of this conjunction, Joseph Beaver says (*Walt Whitman—Poet of Science*, 1951, p. 30): "Whitman had been watching the two bodies draw nearer together . . . *The Nautical Almanac* lists the phenomenon at 10:45 P.M. on November 21 . . . November 22 was the day that began" as the poet watched. Praised as a naturalist by his friend the naturalist Burroughs, Whitman knew that the ancients regarded Saturn as the grave patron of the sowing, Mars as god of war, Orion as the man-shaped constellation who slew Artemis for violating the chaste Aurora, and the Pleiades as seven sisters of whom one was hidden in shame for having loved a mortal.
5. Appeared only once, in the miscellany *Two Rivulets* (1876), twin-born with a new edition of *LG*, in uniform binding. In *Two Rivulets*, selected prose essays alternated with clusters of poems not yet incorporated in *LG*. Lines 4 and 5 of the poem served as epigraph on the title page, and the whole poem captioned the first cluster of fourteen new or recent poems. "Two Rivulets" suggested Whitman's commingled prose and verse themes, in unity with all things "for the eternal ocean bound." A version of the tercet of the present poem, lines 10–12, and also passages from another "excluded" poem, "Or From That Sea of Time," appear in "As Consequent," a later poem of genuine power, to which Whitman gave the first place in the new cluster of "Autumn Rivulets" in *LG* 1881. Quoted before publication in a preview of the new volumes (probably by WW) in *New York Daily Tribune*, February 19, 1876.

In You, whoe'er you are, my book perusing,   10
In I myself—in all the World—these ripples flow,
All, all, toward the mystic Ocean tending.

(O yearnful waves! the kisses of your lips!
Your breast so broad, with open arms, O firm, expanded shore!)
    1876   *1876 (1881)*

Or from That Sea of Time[6]

1

Or, from that Sea of Time,
Spray, blown by the wind—a double winrow-drift[7] of weeds
    and shells;
(O little shells, so curious-convolute! so limpid-cold and
    voiceless!
Yet will you not, to the tympans of temples held,
Murmurs and echoes still bring up—Eternity's music, faint
    and far,   5
Wafted inland, sent from Atlantica's rim—strains for the
    Soul of the Prairies,

Whisper'd reverberations—chords for the ear of the West,
    joyously sounding
Your tidings old, yet ever new and untranslatable;)
Infinitesimals out of my life, and many a life,
(For not my life and years alone I give—all, all I give;)   10
These thoughts and Songs—waifs from the deep—here, cast
    high and dry,
Wash'd on America's shores.

2

Currents of starting a Continent new,
Overtures sent to the solid out of the liquid,
Fusion of ocean and land—tender and pensive waves,   15
(Not safe and peaceful only—waves rous'd and ominous too,
Out of the depths, the storm's abysms—Who knows whence?
    Death's waves,
Raging over the vast, with many a broken spar and tatter'd sail.)
    1876   *1876 (1881)*

---

6. Appeared in the volume *Two Rivulets* (1876), p. 16. See note above to the poem "Two
   Rivulets," from which, as from the present poem, the poet incorporated lines in the new
   poem "As Consequent," which appeared in *LG* 1881 and survived into the final edition. That
   poem comprised twelve lines of new composition, followed by the motivating tercet from
   "Two Rivulets" and the entire eighteen lines of the present poem, with slight verbal altera-
   tions. However, Whitman reversed the order of stanzas, making the first stanza of the present
   poem the last stanza of the new poem (*q.v.*).
7. Corrected in 1881, "windrow-drift."

As in a Swoon[8]

As in a swoon, one instant,
Another sun, ineffable, full-dazzles me,
And all the orbs I knew—and brighter, unknown orbs;
One instant of the future land, Heaven's land.
1876   *1891 (1892)*

[Last Droplets][9]

Last droplets of and after spontaneous rain,
From many limpid distillations and past showers;
(Will they germinate anything? mere exhalations as they all are
        —the land's and sea's—America's;
Will they filter to any deep emotion? any heart and brain?)
1891   *1891*

Ship Ahoy![1]

In dreams I was a ship, and sail'd the boundless seas,
Sailing and ever sailing—all seas and into every port, or out
        upon the offing,
Saluting, cheerily hailing each mate, met or pass'd, little or big,
"Ship ahoy!" thro' trumpet or by voice—if nothing more, some
        friendly merry word at least,
For companionship and good will for ever to all and each.   5
1891   *1891 (1892)*

8. Appeared first in *LG* 1876, pasted on the blank end of page 207 in some early copies; printed
   in the same location in the later issue. It did not reappear in *LG* 1881. It was included in
   Good-Bye My Fancy (1891), but not when that supplement was added to *LG* 1891–92. In
   the same year WW included it among the few poems that he preserved in *CPW* 1892. See
   note to "The Beauty of the Ship," above.
9. This quatrain concluded the second paragraph of the poet's light-hearted "Preface Note" to
   Good-Bye My Fancy (1891)—a "little cluster," he wrote, of what "during the last two years
   I have sent out . . . , certain chirps . . . which now I may as well gather and put in fair type
   while able to see . . . , for here I am (each successive fortnight getting stiffer and stuck
   deeper) much like some hard-cased dilapidated grim ancient shell-fish or time-banged
   conch . . . ." The poem did not appear in the annex "Good-Bye My Fancy," in *LG*
   1891–92.
1. First appeared in *Good-Bye My Fancy* (1891), p. 28, the poet's last volume of miscellaneous
   prose and poetry. It was not among the poems that also appeared in the "Good-Bye My
   Fancy," annex to *LG* 1891–92. However, it was one of a few poems reprinted in *CPW* (1892).

For Queen Victoria's Birthday[2]

An American arbutus bunch to be put in a little vase on the royal breakfast table, May 24th, 1890

Lady, accept a birth-day thought—haply an idle gift and token,
Right from the scented soil's May-utterance here,
(Smelling of countless blessings, prayers, and old-time thanks,)[3]
A bunch of white and pink arbutus, silent, spicy, shy,
From Hudson's, Delaware's, or Potomac's woody banks.

1891 (1892)

L of G[4]

Thoughts, suggestions, aspirations, pictures,
Cities and farms—by day and night—book of peace and war,
Of platitudes and the commonplace.

For out-door health, the land and sea—for good will,
For America—for all the earth, all nations, the common
      people,   5
(Not of one nation only—not America only.)

In it each claim, ideal, line, by all lines, claims, ideals temper'd;
Each right and wish by other wishes, rights.
1891   *1891 (1892)*

---

2. Although Whitman's footnote to this poem (*q.v.*) reveals his appreciation of Queen Victoria's presumed foresight, he did not include this tribute among the poems from the 1891 *Good-Bye My Fancy* that made up the final "Annex" to LG the same year. It was reproduced, however, in *CPW* (1892). It appeared first in the *Philadelphia Public Ledger*, May 22, 1890.
3. "Note.—Very little, as we Americans stand this day, with our sixty-five or seventy millions of population, an immense surplus in the treasury, and all that actual power or reserve power (land and sea) so dear to nations—very little I say do we realize that curious crawling national shudder when the "Trent affair" promis'd to bring upon us a war with Great Britain—follow'd unquestionably, as that war would have, by recognition of the Southern Confederacy from all the leading European nations. It is now certain that all this then inevitable train of calamity hung on arrogant and peremptory phrases in the prepared and written missive of the British Minister, to America, which the Queen (and Prince Albert latent) positively and promptly cancell'd; and which her firm attitude did alone actually erase and leave out, against all the other official prestige and Court of St. James's. On such minor and personal incidents (so to call them,) often depend the great growths and turns of civilization. This moment of a woman and a queen surely swung the grandest oscillation of modern history's pendulum. Many sayings and doings of that period, from foreign potentates and powers, might well be dropt in oblivion by America—but never *this*, if I could have my way" [WW's note].
4. The poet's apostrophe to his book appeared in his last collection of new work, *Good-Bye My Fancy* (1891), and was collected, along with the prose of this volume, in *CPW* (1892). It was not among the poems of this volume that appeared in the concluding annex of *LG* 1891–92. MS in the Feinberg Collection.

After the Argument[5]

A group of little children with their ways and chatter flow in,
Like welcome, rippling water o'er my heated nerves and flesh.
1891   *1891 (1892)*

For Us Two, Reader Dear[6]

Simple, spontaneous, curious, two souls interchanging,
With the original testimony for us continued to the last.
1891   *1891 (1892)*

5. Appeared with other poems at the blank end of a prose piece on page 44 of *Good-Bye My Fancy* (1891), and again on the corresponding page of *CPW* (1892); not included in *LG* 1891–92. MS in the Feinberg Collection. First appeared in *Lippincott's Magazine*, March 1891, with three poems retained in *GBF* annex of *LG*—"Sounds of the Winter," "Sail out for Good, Eidólon Yacht," and "The Unexpressed."
6. Appeared with other poems at the blank end of a prose piece on page 44 of *Good-Bye My Fancy* (1891) and on the corresponding page of *CPW* (1892); not included in *LG* 1891–92. MS in the Feinberg Collection.

Passages Excluded from
Leaves of Grass Poems

[The Writer of Melodious Verses][1]

Do you think it would be good to be the writer of melodious
    verses?
Well, it would be good to be the writer of melodious verses;
But what are verses beyond the flowing character you could
    have? or beyond beautiful manners and behavior?
Or beyond one manly or affectionate deed of an apprentice-
    boy? or old woman? or man that has been in prison, or is
    likely to be in prison?
1855   *1860*

[This Is the Breath for America][2]

This is the breath for America, because it is my breath,
This is for laws, songs, behavior,
This is the tasteless water of Souls—this is the true sustenance.

This is for the illiterate, and for the judges of the Supreme
    Court, and for the Federal capitol and the State capitols,
And for the admirable communes of literats, com-
    posers, singers, lecturers, engineers, and savans,   5
And for the endless races of work-people, farmers, and seamen.
1855   *1860*

1. Originally the concluding stanza of "Song of the Answerer," which appeared without title in
    LG 1855, as "Poem of the Poet" in *LG* 1856, and "Leaves of Grass—3" in *LG* 1860, the
    source of the present text. These lines, discarded in *LG* 1867, epitomize one of Whitman's
    fundamental ideas. In *LG* 1881, "Song of the Answerer" was completed by the addition of
    canto 2, formerly an *LG* poem, "The Indications" (see note to "Song of the Answerer").
2. First appeared in *LG* 1855, p. 24, as a five-line stanza following that text now represented
    in canto 17, line 360, of "Song of Myself" (then untitled). It reappeared in the same relative
    position in *LG* 1856 ("Poem of Walt Whitman, An American") and finally in *LG* 1860 ("Walt
    Whitman," stanzas 83 and 84), the source of the present six-line text—in which the first
    line was reconstructed as two.

[Élèves I Salute You!][3]

I see the approach of your numberless gangs—I see
    you understand yourselves and me,
And know that they who have eyes and can walk are
    divine, and the blind and lame are equally divine,
And that my steps drag behind yours, yet go before them,
And are aware how I am with you no more than I am with
    everybody.
1855   *1860*

[Old Forever New Things][4]

Flour-works, grinding of wheat, rye, maize, rice—the barrels
    and the half and quarter barrels, the loaded barges, the
    high piles on wharves and levees,
Bread and cakes in the bakery, the milliner's ribbons, the
    dress-maker's patterns, the tea-table, the home-made
    sweetmeats;
Cheap literature, maps, charts, lithographs, daily and weekly
    newspapers,
The column of wants in the one-cent paper, the news
    by telegraph, amusements, operas, shows,
The business parts of a city, the trottoirs of a city when
    thousands of well-dressed people walk up and down,   5
The cotton, woolen, linen you wear, the money you make and
    spend,
Your room and bed-room, your piano-forte, the stove and cook-pans;
The house you live in, the rent, the other tenants, the deposit
    in the savings-bank, the trade at the grocery,
The pay on Seventh Day night, the going home, and the
    purchases; . . .
1855   *1860*

3. This title was the initial line of the passage in *LG* 1860, the source of this text. It was permanently retained, but in *LG* 1867 the other four lines were replaced by a single new line that foreshadowed and linked with the substance of the following passage, now canto 39 of "Song of Myself." The original passage, here restored, compactly suggested Whitman's persistent belief in the breeding of human values in humble origins, and it illustrated a familiar role in which the poet-prophet addressed "students" (here "élèves"—the French word appeared without accents in some *LG* texts).
4. In the first *LG* 1855 edition the untitled "A Song for Occupations" immediately followed the incomparable initial poem, "Song of Myself," which it resembled in its familiar spirit and its emphasis on the bountiful common life, found especially in its first title (*LG* 1856), "Poem of the Daily Work of the Workmen and Workwomen of these States." After 1860 the revisions introduced a more formal spirit reflected in new titles emphasizing the class, "Workingmen," and their "Occupations." Among exclusions in *LG* 1867 was a section of eighty consecutive lines that, in the last edition, would have stood between lines 3 and 5 of canto 5 (*q.v.*). The unit of nine lines here extracted, with their effective free association of what WW, in the beginning of the entire passage, had called the "old forever new things," conveyed the living sense of a way of life now lost.

[The Teeming Mother of Mothers][5]

Her daughters, or their daughters' daughters—who
    knows who shall mate with them?
Who knows through the centuries what heroes may come from
    them?

In them, and of them, natal love—in them that
    divine mystery, the same old beautiful mystery.
Have you ever loved the body of a woman?
Have you ever loved the body of a man?   5

Your father—where is your father?
Your mother—is she living? have you been much with her?
    and has she been much with you?
    1855   *1860*

[This Is Mastering Me][6]

O Christ! This is mastering me!
Through the conquered doors they crowd. I am possessed.

What the rebel said, gayly adjusting his throat to the rope-noose,
What the savage at the stump, his eye-sockets empty, his
    mouth spirting whoops and defiance,
What stills the traveller come to the vault at Mount Vernon,   5
What sobers the Brooklyn boy as he looks down the shores of
    the Wallabout and remembers the Prison Ships,[7]
What burnt the gums of the red-coat at Saratoga[8]
    when he surrendered his brigades,
These become mine and me every one—and they are but little,
I become as much more as I like.
    1855   *1860 [1867]*

---

5. In *LG* 1855 to 1860, this passage appeared after what is now line 3, canto 8 of "I Sing the Body Electric." The theme of inherited maternal responsibility for the race had been stated above; the present lyrical recapitulation was eroded by revisions in 1867 and 1881 to a remnant of lines 4 and 5. The text is "Enfans d'Adam—3," stanzas 28–30 (*LG* 1860), with the omission of the irrelevant last line.
6. These lines from page 80–81, *LG* 1860, followed the present canto 36, line 944 of "Song of Myself" (then "Walt Whitman"). They served to epitomize the poet's compassionate involvement in the episodes of human fortitude and faith portrayed in the previous three cantos. In *LG* 1867 WW excluded all except the first two lines, which now became the opening of canto 37. In *LG* 1881 he replaced the rhetorical first line with one more appropriate and retained the significant second line, which was added in *LG* 1860, the source of the present text.
7. See "The Wallabout Martyrs," WW's poem dealing with these victims of the American Revolution (*LG*, "Sands at Seventy").
8. British General John Burgoyne (1722–1792), having gallantly fought his way down the Hudson Valley, was not supported midway, as promised, by Howe's army from New York; the surrender terms (October 17, 1777) at Saratoga provided that he and his army be withdrawn from the war.

[O Hot-Cheek'd and Blushing][9]

O hot-cheek'd and blushing! O foolish hectic!
O for pity's sake, no one must see me now! my clothes
    were stolen while I was abed,[1]
Now I am thrust forth, where shall I run?

Pier that I saw dimly last night,[2] when I look'd from the windows!
Pier out from the main, let me catch myself with you,
    and stay—I will not chafe you,   5
I feel ashamed to go naked about the world.

I am curious to know where my feet stand and what this is
    flooding me, childhood or manhood—and the hunger that
    crosses the bridge between.

The cloth laps[3] a first sweet eating and drinking,
Laps life-swelling yolks—laps ear of rose-corn,[4] milky and just
    ripen'd;
The white teeth stay, and the boss-tooth advances in darkness,[5]   10
And liquor is spill'd on lips and bosoms by touching
    glasses, and the best liquor afterward.
1855   *1876*

9. This poem and the next, "Now Lucifer Was Not Dead," appeared in the first edition of *LG*
as cantos in "The Sleepers." They remained in the same positions, with slight alterations, in
all *LG* editions before 1881. In *LG* 1876, the source of the present text, the cantos of the
present poem were numbered "7" and "8" (stanzas 21–24). They gave the homogeneous
impression of an independent poem following the present first canto of "The Sleepers" (*q.v.*).
From the beginning "The Sleepers" was one of WW's greatest reflective poems, imbued with
a mystic vision of man and nature, in language and idea uniquely his own. By contrast, both
the "Lucifer" poem (see below) and the present one are violent although powerful lyrics.
Whitman must have felt strongly their impropriety in the context to exclude them after
twenty years, but why he did not then retain these little masterpieces as independent poems
remains a puzzle. "O Hot-Cheek'd and Blushing" represents a high order of symbolism, with
a compelling psychological movement, from the dream fantasy of being denuded in public
to the symbolic suggestion of a sexual act. This poem deserves close study.
1. In the preceding passage of "The Sleepers" the bardic narrator is a participant; beginning
his journey into night, he says, "I dream . . . all the dreams of the other dreamers."
2. At night the deserted wooden piers of the harbor of Brooklyn and New York—and often the
waters beneath them—became hiding places.
3. In its primitive use, the "lap" of a garment was the skirt or coattail that covered the sitting
person from belly to knee; hence, "to lap" meant to conceal or even (of a child) to cuddle.
4. The erotic symbols in the closing lines are among Whitman's most striking. *Cf.* the small,
rosy ear of the popcorn, then familiar.
5. *Stay*: in the context of the passage—to support or to remain steadfast, or to wait; *boss-tooth*:
as compared with the factually descriptive term "white teeth," note that "boss" originally
designated a swelling or extension of an internal organ; later, any protuberance of "embossed"
book covers, metal ornaments, armor, etc. Whitman also used the vernacular sense: the
"boss" workman, who commands. *Cf.* "ear of rose-corn," line 9.

[Now Lucifer Was Not Dead][6]

Now Lucifer[7] was not dead—or if he was, I am his sorrowful
    terrible heir;
I have been wrong'd—I am oppress'd—I hate him that
    oppresses me,[8]
I will either destroy him, or he shall release me.

Damn him! how he does defile me!
How he informs against my brother and sister, and
    takes pay for their blood!   5
How he laughs when I look down the bend, after the
    steamboat that carries away my woman!

Now the vast dusk bulk that is the whale's bulk,[9] it seems mine;
Warily, sportsman! though I lie so sleepy and slug-
    gish, the tap of my flukes is death.
1855   1876

6. This poem, like "O Hot-Cheek'd and Blushing" (*q.v.* above), was retained in "The Sleepers" without significant verbal change from the first *LG* edition until 1876, the source of the present text, which was then the whole of canto 14, following what is now canto 6 of "The Sleepers" (see *LG* above). "Lucifer" represents the height of Whitman's lyric invective. The poet speaking is not "simple separate" Whitman, but the voice of a bard, hurling maledictions against the oppressors of a people. Lucifer is traditionally the personification of evil and the symbol of "fallen" man; specifically, as Venus the morning star before sunrise, this "light-bringer" fell from heaven. The prophet Isaiah authorized the western literary tradition of the fallen archangel banished by God; he further identified a Babylonian ruler destroyed by the wrath of God for persecuting His people: "How art thou fallen from Heaven, O Lucifer, son of the morning! how art thou cut down to the ground, which didst weaken the nations" (Isaiah 14.12). Evidently Whitman's balladlike initial phrase, "Now Lucifer was not dead," recalls Isaiah's double meaning, which he specifically directed against the supporters of slavery, for whom the lurking power of avenging justice was biding its time to strike (lines 7–8).
7. The Latin name ("Light-bearer") defined his earliest mythical function as the morning star; but see the note above for the function of the myths of the fallen one.
8. Four pieces of MS (Virginia) showing revisions of this passage before *LG* 1855 strengthen its interpretation as an invective against slavery. Fragment 146 shows almost the final development of the first two stanzas. It begins significantly, "Black Lucifer," comparing the outcast angel with the enslaved people. Fragment 144 identifies the poem with the voice of the slave: "I am a curse: a negro thinks me / You cannot speak for yourself, negro / I dart like a snake from your mouth." The "negro" cries: "Iron necklace and red sores of the shoulders I do not mind / Hopple at the ankle will not detain me." He calls vengeance down from heaven—"Topple upon him, Light! for you seem to me all one lurid curse!" However the MS does not show the terrifying malediction of the last stanza of this poem, representing one of Whitman's most powerful expressions (*cf.* note below to line 7, "the whale's bulk"). In his transcription of Fragment 147 (*N and F*, I, 42, line 2), Bucke erroneously reports "defile" as "defy."
9. The Old Testament suggests an inherent natural avenger, a principle of retributive justice, or the "wrath of God"; these are represented as mammoths resembling the hippopotamus (behemoth, Job 40.15–24), or dragons, or whales, among them leviathan, of whom Job said, "When he raiseth himself . . . he maketh the sea to boil like a pot." *Cf.* Melville's *Moby Dick* (1851), four years earlier than *LG*: and see Job 3.8, Psalm 74.14, and Isaiah 27.1.

[Invocation: To Workmen and Workwomen][1]

Come closer to me;
Push close, my lovers, and take the best I possess;
Yield closer and closer, and give me the best you possess.

This is unfinish'd business with me—How is It with you?
(I was chill'd with the cold types, cylinder, wet paper between
   us.)   5

Male and Female!
I pass so poorly with paper and types, I must pass with
   the contact of bodies and souls.

American masses!
I do not thank you for liking me as I am, and liking the touch
   of me—I know that it is good for you to do so.
1855   1876

[Facts Showered Over with Light][2]

An American literat[3] fills his own place,
He justifies science—did you think the demonstrable
   less divine than the mythical?
He stands by liberty according to the compact of
   the first day of the first year of These States,
He concentrates in the real body and soul, and in the pleasure
   of things,
He possesses the superiority of genuineness over fiction and
   romance,   5
As he emits himself, facts are showered over with light,
The day-light is lit with more volatile light—the
   deep between the setting and rising sun goes deeper many
   fold,

1. This passage served to introduce "A Song for Occupations" under various titles in every *LG* edition through *LG* 1876. In the first (1855) edition the poem appeared (pp. 56–64) untitled, as the second in the volume. In *LG* 1881 WW gave the poem its final title and replaced this initial salutation by three lines emphasizing the "eternal meanings of the trades and tools." By contrast these canceled lines expressed the poet's comradely identification with working-men, although in *LG* 1860 he inserted two exclamations, "Male and Female!" and "American masses!" emphasizing the broad and impersonal intention of his fervent words.
2. This passage appeared once only, in the first edition of "By Blue Ontario's Shore" (*LG* 1856) in canto 10 following line 17. Like other parts of the poem, this resembles, in its last eight lines, the phraseology of the preface of *LG* 1855 (*cf.* the ninth paragraph before the end). It is a unified expression of a fundamental idea in *LG*, but it enlarges the central theme, the poet, to the man of letters in general (see following note). The parent poem, entitled "Poem of the Many in One" in *LG* 1856, appeared in all later *LG* editions, with concurrent alter-ations and two changes of title before 1881.
3. A learned person, a man of letters, presumably a writer of prose. *Cf.* Latin, *litteratus*, angli-cized as "literatus"—and note Poe's popularization of the plural form in *The Literati of New York City* (1846). An acceptable English substitute was the noun "literate"; hence Whitman's "literat" was not entirely new coinage. He used as plural both "literats" and "literati."

Each precise object, condition, combination, process, exhibits a
    beauty—the multiplication-table its, old age its, the
    carpenter's trade its, the grand-opera its,
The huge-hulled clean-shaped Manhattan clipper
    at sea, under steam or full sail, gleams with unmatched
    beauty,
The national circles and large harmonies of government
    gleam with theirs,   10
The commonest definite intentions and actions with theirs.
   1856   *1856*

[Language for America]⁴

Language-using controls the rest;
Wonderful is language!
Wondrous the English language, language of live men,
Language of ensemble, powerful language of resistance,
Language of a proud and melancholy stock, and of all who
    aspire,   5
Language of growth, faith, self-esteem, rudeness, justice,
    friendliness, amplitude, prudence, decision, exactitude,
    courage,
Language to well-nigh express the inexpressible,
Language for the modern, language for America.
   1856   *1856*

[His Shape Arises]⁵

His shape arises,
Arrogant, masculine, näive, rowdyish,
Laugher, weeper, worker, idler, citizen, countryman,
Saunterer of woods, stander upon hills, summer
    swimmer in rivers or by the sea,
Of pure American breed, of reckless health, his body perfect,
    free from taint from top to toe, free forever from
    headache and dyspepsia, clean-breathed,   5
Ample-limbed, a good feeder, weight a hundred and eighty
    pounds, full-blooded, six feet high, forty inches round the
    breast and back,

---

4. This passage, like "Facts Showered Over with Light" (*q.v.* above, and see note) appeared
only once, in the first version of "By Blue Ontario's Shores," in *LG* 1856. This also was a
separate and homogenous section, and it followed the passage just mentioned after an in-
terval of five lines, at a point that would occur between canto 10 and canto 11 in the final
LG text. The passage gains interest from Whitman's persistent concern with the power of
language and the development of an American speech. The gist of it was expressed in prose
in the preface to *LG* 1855, the third paragraph from the conclusion.
5. The *LG* 1856 "Broad-Axe Poem" and *LG* 1860 "Chants Democratic—2" concluded with
stanzas 33 and 34—these eighteen lines and a following group of eleven. In *LG* 1867, in
"Song of the Broad-Axe," stanza 33, the present text was excluded (between the concluding
cantos, 11 and 12). The passage gains in interest as an unmistakable self-portrait.

Countenance sun-burnt, bearded, calm, unrefined,
Reminder of animals, meeter of savage and gentleman on
    equal terms,
Attitudes lithe and erect, costume free, neck gray
    and open, of slow movement on foot,
Passer of his right arm round the shoulders of his
    friends, companion of the street,   10
Persuader always of people to give him their sweetest
    touches, and never their meanest,
A Manhattanese bred, fond of Brooklyn, fond of Broadway,
    fond of the life of the wharves and the great ferries,
Enterer everywhere, welcomed everywhere, easily understood
    after all,
Never offering others, always offering himself, corroborating
    his phrenology,
Voluptuous, inhabitive, combative, conscientious, alimentive,
    intuitive, of copious friendship, sublimity, firmness, self-
    esteem, comparison, individuality, form, locality,
    eventuality,   15
Avowing by life, manners, works, to contribute illustrations
    of results of The States,
Teacher of the unquenchable creed, namely, egotism,
Inviter of others continually henceforth to try their strength
    against his.
1856   *1860*

[A Thought of the Clef of Eternity][6]

What can the future bring me more than I have?
Do you suppose I wish to enjoy life in other spheres?

I say distinctly I comprehend no better sphere than this earth,
I comprehend no better life than the life of my body.

I do not know what follows the death of my body,   5
But I know well that whatever it is, it is best for me,
And I know well that whatever is really Me shall live
    just as much as before.

I am not uneasy but I shall have good housing to myself,
But this is my first—how can I like the rest any better?

6. This passage gives the impression of being an independent poem, but in *LG* 1856 the present nineteen-line text was the first "movement" (lines 4–22) of a thirty-four-line poem (finally titled "On the Beach at Night Alone," 1871). The exclusion of this passage reduced the parent poem in *LG* 1867 to fifteen lines (finally fourteen in *LG* 1881)—an objective treatment of the "similitude" that "interlocks" all existence, past, present, and eternal. By comparison the present poem is subjective, representing the poet's faith in individual survival coexistent in an eternity of other experience. The poem is here preserved with the strangeness and strength that characterized its last appearance as part of "Leaves of Grass—12" in *LG* 1860.

Here I grew up—the studs and rafters[7] are grown parts of me.   10
I am not uneasy but I am to be beloved by young and
     old men, and to love them the same,
I suppose the pink nipples of the breasts of women with whom
     I shall sleep will touch the side of my face the same,[8]
But this is the nipple of a breast of my mother, always near
     and always divine to me, her true child and son, whatever
     comes.

I suppose I am to be eligible to visit the stars, in my time,
I suppose I shall have myriads of new experiences—and that
     the experience of this earth will prove only one out of
     myriads;   15
But I believe my body and my Soul already indicate those
     experiences,
And I believe I shall find nothing in the stars more majestic
     and beautiful than I have already found on the earth,
And I believe I have this night a clew through the universes,
And I believe I have this night thought a thought of the clef[9]
     of eternity.
1856   *1860 (1881)*

[What Do You Hear, Walt Whitman?][1]

I hear the inimitable music of the voices of mothers,
I hear the persuasions of lovers,
I hear quick rifle-cracks from the riflemen of East
     Tennessee and Kentucky, hunting on hills, . . .
I hear the Virginia plantation chorus of negroes,
     of a harvest night, in the glare of pineknots,
I hear the strong baritone of the 'long-shore-men of
     Manahatta,—I hear the stevedores unlading the cargoes,
     and singing,   5
I hear the screams of the water-fowl of solitary northwest lakes,
I hear the rustling pattering of locusts, as they strike the grain

7. This homely phrase for the framework of a human body reminds us that the poet in his youth worked with his father as a house-builder.
8. In 1856 read: "taste the same to my lips." Nursing mothers learn that the suckling babe will first seek the nipple with its cheek. This was then nursery folklore; now it is established in pediatrics as the "rooting complex," described by C. A. and M. M. Aldrich (ca. 1938).
9. As a music lover Whitman uses the word strictly, as an indication or sign of the precise "tonality" (here, "meaning") of eternity. *Cf.* the phrase "a clew through the universe," just above.
1. These lines on things heard were among those of the present canto 3 of "Salut Au Monde" in its first edition, *LG* 1856 ("Poem of Salutation"). In that and other early editions the poem was not strictly a global courtesy or salutation from the "new" continent to older and disparate cultures—as it was in the final revision, *LG* 1881, of which the penultimate lines read: "Toward you all, in America's name, / I raise high the perpendicular hand." The majority of the excluded lines expressed the poet's appreciation of things American. The present passage, a group of associated aural images, constituted eight of the original sixteen lines between the present lines 3 and 11 of canto 3. Line 7 still remains in *LG*, but its locusts were expatriated to Syria. This was the most impressive of the excluded passages, excepting the almost unsurpassed transposition from canto 7, in *LG* 1881, "A Paumanok Picture."

and grass with the showers of their terrible clouds, . . .
I hear the bugles of raft-tenders on the streams of Canada . . .
1856   *1876*

[You Dumb Beautiful Ministers][2]

We descend upon you and all things—we arrest you all;
We realize the soul only by you, you faithful solids and fluids;
Through you color, form, location, sublimity, ideality;
Through you every proof, comparison, and all the suggestions
    and determinations of ourselves.
1856   *1876*

[Which Are My Miracles?][3]

What shall I give? and which are my miracles?

Realism is mine—my miracles—Take freely,
Take without end—I offer them to you wherever your
    feet can carry you, or your eyes reach. . . .

Or whether I go among those I like best, and that
    like me best—mechanics, boatmen, farmers,
Or among the savans—or to the soiree—or to the opera,[4]   5
Or stand a long while looking at the movements of machinery,
Or behold children at their sports,
Or the admirable sight of the perfect old man, or the perfect
    old woman,
Or the sick in hospitals, or the dead carried to burial,
Or my own eyes and figure in the glass; . . .   10

Every spear of grass—the frames, limbs, organs, of
    men and women, and all that concerns them,
All these to me are unspeakably perfect miracles.
1856   *1876*

2. This quatrain appeared in the first edition of "Crossing Brooklyn Ferry," *LG* 1856, then entitled "Sun-Down Poem." The passage introduced the section of eleven lines concluding the poem, later treated as a separate canto that in *LG* 1876 was numbered 12. The cantos were then consolidated, this passage was dropped, and the remaining seven lines concluded canto 9, still the last. The passage here reproduced appeared with only minor punctuation changes, from the beginning until 1876, the source of this text. The point of these lines is associated with "the impalpable sustenance of me from all things" (line 6 of the poem). *Cf.* Emerson's "Each and All."
3. Twelve lines pruned from the original thirty-five of "Miracles" (*q.v.*), then entitled "Poem of Perfect Miracles" in *LG* 1856. The resulting concentration of the remaining twenty-three lines intensified the effect of "Miracles." The first three lines, which introduced the original poem, were verbally improved, then dropped after *LG* 1867—the textual source for the present reading. Lines 4 to 10 followed the present line 14 of "Miracles" and the concluding couplet followed line 20; they remained without essential change until canceled in *LG* 1881.
4. *Savans*: WW seemingly preferred this vernacular form of "savants"; *soiree: cf.* "soirée," French term for an evening reception or party.

[You Who Celebrate Bygones!]⁵

But now I also, arriving, contribute something: . . .
Advancing, to give the spirit and the traits of new
    Democratic ages, myself, personally,
(Let the future behold them all in me—Me, so puzzling and
    contradictory—Me, a Manhattanese, the most loving and
    arrogant of men;)
I do not tell the usual facts, proved by records and documents,
What I tell, (talking to every born American,) requires no
    further proof than he or she who will hear me, will
    furnish, by silently meditating alone; . . .   5

I illuminate feelings, faults, yearnings, hopes—I have come at
    last, no more ashamed nor afraid . . .
1860   *1860*

[Creations for Strong Artists]⁶

There they stand—I see them already, each poised and in its
    place,
Statements, models, censuses, poems, dictionaries, biographies,
    essays, theories—How complete! How relative and
    interfused! No one supersedes another;
They do not seem to me like the old specimens,
They seem to me like Nature at last, (America has
    given birth to them, and I have also;)
They seem to me at last as perfect as the animals,
    and as the rocks and weeds—fitted to them,   5
Fitted to the sky, to float with floating clouds—to
    rustle among the trees with rustling leaves,
To stretch with stretched and level waters, where ships silently
    sail in the distance.
1860   *1860*

---

5. First a thirteen-line poem in *LG* 1860, No. 10 in the cluster "Chants Democratic"; in *LG* 1867 given its final title, "To a Historian," in the supplement "Songs Before Parting," where it was shortened by the exclusion of the present six lines (originally 4, 6 to 9, and 11). As the fifth of the "Inscriptions," the parent poem appeared in all later editions. The original distribution of the excluded lines was such that they represent a generalization of the whole poem, but the intimacy of their tone did not accord with Whitman's effort during this period to assume the communal objectivity of the national bard.
6. "Laws for Creations" (*q.v.*) emphasizes Whitman's organic theory of the creative artist and his artifact. In the original eighteen-line version (*LG* 1860, "Chants Democratic—13"), lines 6 to 12 shown above perhaps overemphasized the created work instead of the creative act, which was the central idea. They were excluded in *LG* 1867. Considered independently, they seem a unified statement of the concept that the artifact is to be organically related to the form of nature originally observed by the artist, and in the transcendental sense, that all natural facts are "interfused."

[Readers to Come][7]

Indeed, if it were not for you, what would I be?
What is the little I have done, except to arouse you?
I depend on being realized, long hence, where the broad fat
    prairies spread, and thence to Oregon and California
    inclusive,
I expect that the Texan and the Arizonian, ages hence, will
    understand me,
I expect that the future Carolinian and Georgian will
    understand me and love me,   5
I expect that Kanadians, a hundred, and perhaps many
    hundred years from now, in winter, in the splendor of the
    snow and woods, or on the icy lakes, will take me with
    them, and permanently enjoy themselves with me.

Of to-day I know I am momentary, untouched—I
    am the bard of the future. . . .
1860   *1860*

[O Bitter Sprig!][8]

O bitter sprig! Confession sprig!
In the bouquet I give you place also—I bind you in,
Proceeding no further till, humbled publicly,
I give fair warning, once for all.

I own that I have been sly, thievish, mean, a prevaricator,
    greedy, derelict,   5
And I own that I remain so yet.

What foul thought but I think it—or have in me the
    stuff out of which it is thought?
What in darkness in bed at night, alone or with a companion?
1860   *1860*

---

7. Seven lines, of the sixteen in "Poets to Come," when it first appeared in *LG* 1860 as "Chants Democratic—14," p. 186. In *LG* 1867, where the parent poem was given its present title, these lines were omitted (following the present line 4), evidently to clarify or intensify the meaning. The parent poem, which became one of the "Inscriptions" in 1881, now gives the impression of a salute to "poets to come," for whom this author left "a few indicative words." The two excluded stanzas, however, emphasize the emotional condition of WW poignantly destined to speak on winds of time to ears unborn.
8. These eight lines were the first three stanzas of "You Felons on Trial in Courts" in its first appearance as No. 13 in the cluster "Leaves of Grass" in *LG* 1860. In *LG* 1867 this passage was excluded and the remaining sixteen lines (reorganized as fifteen) were retained without significant change. The version of the poem retained is somewhat less specifically confessional, but each conveys a psychological compulsion having some religious interest, adroitly expressed.

[Nearing Departure][9]

O Soul!
Then all may arrive but to this;
The glances of my eyes, that swept the daylight,
The unspeakable love I interchanged with women,
My joys in the open air—my walks through the Mannahatta, 5
The continual good will I have met—the curious
  attachment of young men to me,
My reflections alone—the absorption into me from the
  landscape, stars, animals, thunder, rain, and snow, in my
  wanderings alone,
The words of my mouth, rude, ignorant, arrogant—my many
  faults and derelictions,
The light touches, on my lips, of the lips of my comrades, at
  parting,
The tracks which I leave, upon the side—walks and fields, 10
May but arrive at this beginning of me,
This beginning of me—and yet it is enough, O Soul,
O Soul, we have positively appeared—that is enough.
1860   *1860 (1881)*

[Let None Be Content with Me][1]

Yet not me, after all—let none be content with me,
I myself seek a man better than I am, or a woman better than
  I am,
I invite defiance, and to make myself superseded,
All I have done, I would cheerfully give to be trod under foot,
  if it might only be the soil of superior poems.

I have established nothing for good,[2]   5
I have but established those things, till things farther onward
  shall be prepared to be established,
And I am myself the preparer of things farther onward. . . .

Once more I enforce you to give play to yourself—and not to
  depend on me, or on any one but yourself,

9. "As the Time Draws Nigh," called "To My Soul" when it first appeared in *LG* 1860, con-
cluded with this stanza of thirteen lines, of which only four lines, the second and the last
three, fundamentally revised, were reflected in the final text. In *LG* 1867 it was entitled "As
Nearing Departure" (now a nine-line poem) in the supplement "Songs Before Parting." In
1871 it appeared with its present title and eight-line text, and with new punctuation in 1881.
The complete last stanza in the 1860 version, given above, has independent vitality and
interest.
1. These stanzas first appeared in "So Long!"—a new poem concluding *LG* 1860 and all later
LG editions. In the poem's second edition, *LG* 1867, Whitman divided the text by cantos,
excluding from the first canto stanzas 4 and 5 and 7 to 9 as given here, exuberantly intro-
ducing two themes—progress and individualism—expressed with more emotional propriety
in later passages.
2. Then quite prevalently used in the vernacular sense, meaning "finally" or "completely"; e.g.,
"he quit school for good."

Once more I proclaim the whole of America for each
    individual, without exception.

As I have announced the true theory of the youth,
    manhood, womanhood, of The States, I adhere to it;   10
As I have announced myself on immortality, the body,
    procreation, hauteur, prudence,
As I joined the stern crowd that still confronts the President
    with menacing weapons—I adhere to all,
As I have announced each age for itself, this moment I set the
    example.

I demand the choicest edifices to destroy them;
Room! room! for new far-planning draughtsmen and engineers!   15
Clear that rubbish from the building-spots and the paths!
    1860   *1860*

[Realities, the Visions of Poets][3]

For we support all, fuse all,
After the rest is done and gone, we remain;
There is no final reliance but upon us;
Democracy rests finally upon us, (I, my brethren, begin it,)
And our visions sweep through eternity.   5
    1860   *1876*

[Give Me the Clue . . . the Word Final][4]

O give me the clue! (it lurks in the night here somewhere;)
O if I am to have so much, let me have more!
O a word! O what is my destination? (I fear it is henceforth
    chaos;)
O how joys, dreads, convolutions, human shapes, and all
    shapes, spring as from graves around me!
O phantoms! you cover all the land and all the sea!   5
O I cannot see in the dimness whether you smile or frown
    upon me;

3. In *LG*1881, the final text of the reflective "As I Walked These Broad Majestic Days," WW excluded the last stanza. This passage, in all editions since the poem first appeared (*LG* 1860, "Chants Democratic—21") had functioned to elaborate the preceding idea that, among the modern realities, "the visions of poets" were still "the most solid." The text is that of 1876.
4. Originally stanza 31 in "A Word Out of the Sea" (*LG* 1860; in 1871 entitled "Out of the Cradle, Endlessly Rocking"), this passage, excepting the first two lines, was discarded in *LG* 1881. Critics wonder why Whitman canceled these impressive lines and they speculate on the actuality of the "well-beloved." (See *Handbook*, 142–43.) Comparing the excluded passage with the remaining twenty-two lines that conclude the poem, one remembers the poet's two companions "under the dusky cedars" ("When Lilacs Last in the Dooryard Bloom'd," canto 14): one, the "thought of death"—the immediate shock—as in the present lines the dread of "destination" and "chaos"; and the other, "the sacred knowledge," able to "fuse the song" of "two together" and "death." The poem was included in the 1871 *Passage to India* volume and supplements to *LG* 1872 and *TR* 1876, source of the present text.

O vapor, a look, a word! O well-beloved!
O you dear women's and men's phantoms!
1860   *1876*

[Orators Fit for America][5]

.... O I see arise orators fit for inland America;
And I see it is as slow to become an orator as to become a man;
And I see that all power is folded in a great vocalism.

Of a great vocalism, the merciless light thereof shall
    pour, and the storm rage,
Every flash shall be a revelation, an insult,   5
The glaring flame on depths, on heights, on suns, on stars,
On the interior and exterior of man or woman,
On the laws of Nature—on passive materials,
On what you called death—(and what to you therefore was
    death,
As far as there can be death.)   10
1860   *1876*

[Epigraph: A Carol of Harvest][6]

A song of the good green grass!
A song no more of the city streets;
A song of farms—a song of the soil of fields.

A song with the smell of sun-dried hay, where the
    nimble pitchers handle the pitch-fork;
A song tasting of new wheat, and of fresh-husk'd maize.   5
1871   *1876*

5. These stanzas in the 1876 text were the peroration concluding "Chants Democratic—12"
   in *LG* 1860. They were not retained by WW when, in 1881, he used the four preceding
   stanzas of the poem as canto 1 of "Vocalism," whose second canto was also an 1860 poem,
   numbered "21" in a "Leaves of Grass" cluster. "To Oratists" in *LG* 1876 is the source of the
   present text.
6. "A Carol of Harvest for 1867" appeared in *Passage to India* (1871) and remained in that
   collection when it was bound in as a supplement to *LG* 1872 and *TR* 1876. In these editions
   the two stanzas above introduced the poem in the manner of an epigraph (though not so
   designated). The poems of this supplement were redistributed in various parts of *LG* 1881,
   and the "Carol" appeared as "The Return of the Heroes," without this preliminary song.

[With Additional Songs Every Spring][7]

(With additional songs—every spring will I now strike
    up additional songs,
Nor ever again forget, these tender days, the chants of
    Death as well as Life;) . . .

To tally, drenched with them, tested by them,
Cities and artificial life, and all their sights and scenes,
My mind henceforth, and all its meditations—my recitatives,   5
My land, my age, my race, for once to serve in songs,
(Sprouts, tokens ever of death indeed the same as life,) . . .
  1871   *1876*

[Aroused and Angry][8]

Aroused and angry,
I thought to beat the alarum, and urge relentless war:
But soon my fingers fail'd me, my face droop'd, and I resign'd
    myself,
To sit by the wounded and soothe them, or silently watch the
    dead.
  1871   *1876 (1881)*

7. "Warble for Lilac Time" appeared in the first edition of *Passage to India* (1871) and in the later *PI* supplements of *LG* and *TR*. In *LG* 1881 the final text (*q.v.*) omitted the present stanzas after lines 21 and 24, respectively. The charming parent poem dealt entirely with the memorial significance of the lilac (Lincoln) and the shy preparations made by the gradual spring to celebrate love by this crowning luxuriance. However, the rejected lines reproduced above deserve attention as an expression of Whitman's compulsion to compare nature's life and death with mankind's artifices.
8. The 1865 *Drum-Taps*, which had been a supplement in some issues of *LG* 1867, was incorporated as a cluster in the *Leaves* of 1871. Whitman then inserted this epigraph in italics beneath the boldface heading, "Drum-Taps." Without change it reappeared in *LG* 1872 and 1876, the present text. In 1881 the poet interpolated this passage into "The Wound-Dresser," another poem in the "Drum-Taps" cluster, combining the four lines into three (lines 4–6), printed in roman between parentheses without verbal changes. The original epigraph is worth recovering as a lyrical epitomy of a major phase of WW's experience of the war.

Uncollected Poems

Pictures[1]

In a little house pictures I keep, ¶ many pictures[2]
  hanging suspended—It is not a fixed house,
It is round—it is but a few inches from one side of it to the
  other side,
But behold! it has room enough—in it, hundreds and
  thousands,—all the varieties;
—Here! do you know this? This is cicerone[3] himself;
And here, see you, my own States—and here the world itself,
  bowling
  rolling through the air;   5
And there, on the walls hanging, portraits of women and men,
  carefully kept,
This is the portrait of my dear mother—and this of my father
  —and these of my brothers and sisters;
This, (I name every thing as it comes,) This is a beautiful
  statue, long lost, dark buried, but never destroyed—now
  found by me, and restored to the light;
There five men, a group of sworn friends, stalwart, bearded,
  determined, work their way together through all the
  troubles and impediments of the world;
And that is a magical wondrous mirror—long it lay clouded,
  but the cloud has passed away,   10
It is now a clean and bright mirror—it will show you all you
  can conceive of, all you wish to behold;

1. Text first published in Emory Holloway's "Whitman's Embryonic Verse," *SWR* 10 (July 1925): 28–40. Reprinted, with introduction and notes by Holloway, as *Pictures: An Unpublished Poem* (New York, The June House; London, Faber & Gwyer, 1927). MS: Yale.
  The faded and battered twenty-nine-page notebook in which these lines were entered in ink, with penciled emendations, is an important preliminary, a kind of auspice of *LG* 1855, some of whose lines are here in rough draft. In its leaves the poet recorded the experience of his days and especially of his reading in phrases that had not achieved the rhythmic power to come, but that nevertheless reveal the poetic process, its pictures (images) being stored in the gallery of his mind.
  Underneath the title, centered on the first page of the notebook, the poet added in pencil: "Break all this into several 'pictures.' Walt Whitman." He persisted in such exercises after the appearance of *LG* 1855, as a number of fragments indicate (see below). In 1861 "Pictures" was to be a poem in the projected but never published *Banner of Daybreak* (Allen, 267); many years later in *The American* for October 30, 1880, WW published "My Picture-Gallery" (reprinted in *LG* 1881), whose six lines are a redaction of the first lines of the notebook, constituting an eloquently simple statement about his poetic storehouse that had served him so well. See also "Pictures" (Hanley MS) among the "Unpublished Poems."
2. The paragraph symbol is WW's own, later inserted in the MS, perhaps to indicate a new line at this point.
3. A guide for sightseers.

And that is a picture intended for Death—it is very beautiful
   —(what else is so beautiful as Death?)
There is represented the Day, full of effulgence—full of
   seminal lust and love—full of action, life, strength,
   aspiration,
And there the Night, with mystic beauty, full of love also, and
   full of greater life—the Night, showing where the stars are;
There is a picture of Adam in Paradise—side by side with him
   Eve, (the Earth's bride and the Earth's bridegroom;)   15
There is an old Egyptian temple—and again, a Greek temple,
   of white marble;
There are Hebrew prophets chanting, rapt, extatic—and here
   is Homer[4]
Here is one singing canticles in an unknown tongue, before
   the Sanskrit was,
And here a Hindu sage, with his recitative in Sanskrit;
And here the divine Christ expounds eternal truth—expounds
   the Soul,   20
And here he appears en-route to Calvary, bearing the cross—
   See you, the blood and sweat streaming down his face, his
   neck;
And here, behold, a picture of once imperial Rome, full of
   palaces—full of masterful warriors;
And here, the questioner, the Athenian of the classical time—
   Socrates, in the market place,
(O divine tongue! I too grow silent under your elenchus,[5]
(O you with bare feet, and bulging belly! I saunter along,
   following you, and obediently listen;)   25
And here Athens itself,—it is a clear forenoon,
Young men, pupils, collect in the gardens of a favorite master,
   waiting for him.
Some, crowded in groups, listen to the harangues or
   arguments of the elder ones,
Elsewhere, single figures, undisturbed by the buzz around
   them, lean against pillars, or within recesses, meditating,
   or studying from manuscripts,
Here and there, couples or trios, young and old, clear-faced,
   and of perfect physique, walk with twined arms, in divine
   friendship, happy,   30
Till, beyond, the master appears advancing—his form shows
   above the crowd, a head taller than they,
His gait is erect, calm and dignified—his features are colossal
   —he is old, yet his forehead has no wrinkles,
Wisdom undisturbed, self-respect, fortitude unshaken, are in
   his expression, his personality;
Wait till he speaks—what God's voice is that, sounding from
   his mouth?

---

4. Compare this and the following four lines with "Salut au Monde," lines 37–40.
5. A syllogism that refutes a proposition by proving the opposite. Note a close variant of lines
   23–25 in the fragments following the poem.

He places virtue and self-denial above all the rest,   35
He shows to what a glorious height the man may ascend,
He shows how independent one may be of fortune—how
     triumphant over fate;
—And here again, this picture tells a story of the Olympic games,
See you, the chariot races? See you, the boxers boxing, and the
     runners running?
See you, the poets off there reciting their poems and tragedies,
     to crowds of listeners?   40
—And here, (for I have all kinds,) here is Columbus setting
     sail from Spain on his voyage of discovery;
This again is a series after the great French revolution,
This is the taking of the Bastile, the prison—this is the
     execution of the king.
This is the queen on her way to the scaffold—those are
     guillotines;
But this opposite, (abruptly changing,) is a picture from the
     prison-ships of my own old city—Brooklyn city;[6]   45
And now a merry recruiter passes, with fife and drum, seeking
     who will join his troop;
And there is an old European martyrdom—See you, the
     cracking fire—See the agonized contortions of the limbs,
     and the writhing of the lips! See the head thrown back;
And here is a picture of triumph—a General has returned,
     after a victory—the city turns out to meet him,
And here is a portrait of the English king, Charles the First,
     (are you a judge of physiognomy?)
And here is a funeral procession in the country,   50
A beloved daughter is carried in her coffin—there follow the
     parents and neighbors;
And here, see you—here walks the Boston truckman, by the
     side of his string-team—see the three horses, pacing
     stately, sagacious, one ahead of another;
—And this—whose picture is this?
Who is this, with rapid feet, curious, gay—going up and down
     Mannahatta, through the streets, along the shores,
     working his way through the crowds, observant and
     singing?[7]
And this head of melancholy Dante, poet of penalties—poet of
     hell;   55
But this is a portrait of Shakespear, limner of feudal European
     lords (here are my hands, my brothers—one for each of you;)
—And there are wood-cutters, cutting down trees in my north
     east woods—see you, the axe uplifted;
And that is a picture of a fish-market—see there the shad, flat-

6. WW referred to these prison ships in the 1855 version of section 37, "Song of Myself." See
also "The Wallabout Martyrs" in the group "Sands at Seventy."
7. Clearly, a picture of the poet himself.

fish, the large halibut,—there a pile of lobsters, and there
    another of oysters;
Opposite, a drudge in the kitchen, working, tired—and there
    again the laborer, in stained clothes, sour-smelling, sweaty
    —and again black persons and criminals;[8]
And there the frivolous person—and there a crazy enthusiast—
    and there a young man lies sick of a fever, and is soon to
    die;   60
This, again, is a Spanish bull-fight—see, the animal with bent
    head, fiercely advancing;
And here, see you, a picture of a dream of despair, (—is it
    unsatisfied love?)
Phantoms, countless, men and women, after death, wandering;
And there are flowers and fruits—see the grapes, decked off
    with vine-leaves;
But see this!—see where graceful and stately the young queen-
    cow walks at the head of a large drove, leading the rest;   65
And there are building materials—brick, lime, timber, paint,
    glass, and iron, (so now you can build what you like;
And this black portrait—this head, huge, frowning, sorrowful
    —is Lucifer's portrait—the denied God's portrait,[9]
(But I do not deny him—though cast out and rebellious, he is
    my God as much as any;)
And again the heads of three other Gods—the God Beauty,
    the God Beneficence, and the God Universality, (they are
    mine, also;)
And there an Arab caravan, halting—See you, the palm trees,
    the camels, and the stretch of hot sand far away;   70
And there are my woods of Kanada, in winter, with ice and snow,
And here my Oregon hunting-hut, See me emerging from the
    door, bearing my rifle in my hand;
But there, see you, a reminiscence from over sea—a very old
    Druid, walking the woods of Albion;[1]
And there, singular, on ocean waves, downward, buoyant,
    swift, over the waters, an occupied coffin floating;
And there, rude grave-mounds in California—and there a path
    worn in the grass,   75
And there hang painted scenes from my Kansas life—and
    there from what I saw in the Lake Superior region;
And here mechanics work in their shops, in towns—There the
    carpenter shoves his jack-plane—there the blacksmith
    stands by his anvil, leaning on his upright hammer;[2]
This is Chicago with railroad depots, with trains arriving and

---

8. Compare this and the following line with *N and F*, I, item 16.
9. This and the following three lines are early workings of the ideas that went into the making of "Chanting the Square Deific"; and, among "Passages Excluded" above, see "Now Lucifer Was Not Dead."
1. Compare line 95, "Salut au Monde."
2. The phrases describing manual labor become much more vivid in "Song of Myself," as Holloway has noted.

departing—and, in their places, immense stores of grain, meat,
　　and lumber;[3]
And here are my slave-gangs, South, at work upon the roads,
　　the women indifferently with the men—see, how clumsy,
　　hideous, black, pouting, grinning, sly, besotted, sensual,
　　shameless;
And this of a scene afar in the North, the arctic—those are
　　the corpses of lost explorers, (no chaplets of roses will
　　ever cap their icy graves—but I put a chaplet in this
　　poem, for you, you sturdy English heros;)　　　　　　　　　80
But here, now copious—see you, here, the Wonders of eld, the
　　famed Seven,
The Olympian statue this, and this the Artemesian tomb,
Pyramid this, Pharos this, and this the shrine of Diana,
These Babylon's gardens, and this Rhodes' high-lifted marvel,
(But for all that, night at hand, see a wonder beyond any of
　　them,　　　　　　　　　　　　　　　　　　　　　　　　　85
Namely yourself—the form and thoughts of a man,
A man! because all the world, and all the inventions of the
　　world are but the food of the body and the soul of one man;)
And here, while ages have grown upon ages,
Pictures of youths and greybeards, Pagan, and Jew, and Christian,
Some retiring to caves—some in schools and piled libraries,　　90
To pore with ceaseless fervor over the myth of the Infinite,
But ever recoiling, Pagan and Jew and Christian,
As from a haze, more dumb and thick than vapor above the
　　hot sea;
—And here now, (for all varieties, I say, hang in this little house,)
A string of my Iroquois, aborigines—see you, where they
　　march in single file, without noise, very cautious, through
　　passages in the old woods;[4]　　　　　　　　　　　　　　95

Picture

O a husking-frolic in the West—see you, the large rude barn
　　—see you, young and old, laughing and joking, as they
　　husk the ears of corn;[5]
And there in a city, a stormy political meeting—a torch-light
　　procession—candidates avowing themselves to the people;
And here is the Lascar I noticed once in Asia—here he
　　remains still, pouring money into the sea, as an offering to
　　demons, for favor;
And there, in the midst of a group, a quell'd revolted slave,
　　cowering,

3. Compare this line with line 6, "Mediums."
4. Compare line 48, "Our Old Feuillage."
5. Compare line 755, "Song of Myself."

See you, the hand-cuffs, the hopple, and the blood-stain'd
    cowhide;   100
And there hang, side by side, certain close comrades of mine—
    a Broadway stage-driver, a lumberman of Maine, and a
    deck-hand of a Mississippi steamboat;
And again the young man of Mannahatta, the celebrated rough,[6]
(The one I love well—let others sing whom they may—him I
    sing for a thousand years!)
And there a historic piece—see you, where Thomas Jefferson
    of Virginia sits reading Rousseau, the Swiss, and
    compiling the Declaration of Independence, the American
    compact;
And there, tall and slender, stands Ralph Waldo Emerson, of
    New England, at the lecturer's desk lecturing,[7]   105
And there is my Congress in session in the Capitol—there are
    my two Houses in session;
And here, behold two war-ships, saluting each other—behold
    the smoke, bulging, spreading in round clouds from the
    guns and sometimes hiding the ships;
And there, on the level banks of the James river in Virginia
    stand the mansions of the planters;
And here an old black man, stone-blind, with a placard on his
    hat, sits low at the corner of a street, begging, humming
    hymn-tunes nasally all day to himself and receiving small
    gifts;
And this, out at sea, is a signal-bell—see you, where it is built
    on a reef, and ever dolefully keeps tolling, to warn
    mariners;   110
And this picture shows what once happened in one of
    Napoleon's greatest battles,
(The tale was conveyed to me by an old French soldier,)
In the height of the roar and carnage of the battle, all of a
    sudden, from some unaccountable cause, the whole fury
    of the opposing armies subsided—there was a perfect
    calm,
It lasted almost a minute—not a gun was fired—all was petrified,
It was more solemn and awful than all the roar and slaughter;   115
—And here, (for still I name them as they come,) here are my
    timber-towers, guiding logs down a stream in the North;
And here a glimpse of my treeless lianos, where they skirt the
    Colorado, and sweep for a thousand miles on either side
    of the Rocky Mountains;
And there, on the whaling ground, in the Pacific, is a sailor,
    perched at the top-mast head, on the look out,

---

6. In the 1855 version of line 497, "Song of Myself," the poet was to refer to himself as "Walt Whitman, an American, one of the roughs, a kosmos."
7. This line was added in pencil on the opposite blank page of the notebook. WW had heard Emerson lecture, as he noted in "Old Actors, Singers, Shows, etc. in New York," *Coll W, Prose*, II, 697.

(You can almost hear him crying out, *There-e-'s white water,* or
    The-e-re's black skin;)
But here, (look you well,) see here the phallic choice of
    America, a full-sized man or woman—a natural, well-
    trained man or woman   120
(The phallic choice of America leaves the finesse of cities, and
    all the returns of commerce or agriculture, and the
    magnitude of geography, and achievements of literature
    and art, and all the shows of exterior victory, to enjoy the
    breeding of full-sized men, or one full-sized man or
    woman, unconquerable and simple;)[8]
—For all those have I in a round house hanging—such
    pictures have I—and they are but little.
For wherever I have been, has afforded me superb pictures,
And whatever I have heard has given me perfect pictures,
And every hour of the day and night has given me copious
    pictures,   125
And every rod of land or sea affords me, as long as I live,
    inimitable pictures.[9]
    1924   *1927*

[Miscellaneous Fragments for "Pictures"]

And there a ship, long in a foreign port—but now, see you?
She is now ready to leave for home—
Short stay a-peak is her anchor,
See the pleased looks of the sailor men;
                —ms: Feinberg.

And here a tent and domestic utensils of the primitive
    Chippewa, the red-faced aborigines,
See you, the tann'd buffalo hides, the wooden dish, the
    drinking vessels of horn;
                —ms: Feinberg.

In the gymnasium leaping and lifting from
And here arguing the questioner in the classical time—
    Socrates in the market place
(O divine tongue! I too grow silent under your elenchus![1]

8. This line sums up the theme of the "Children of Adam" group of *LG*, and in the notebook WW—as if anticipating its potentiality—had penciled the direction: "take this out a ¶ by itself."
9. In *N and F*, I, item 26, WW has the line, "And to me each acre of the land and sea exhibits marvellous pictures."
1. *Elenchus*, from the ancient Greek word for "cross-examination," denotes Socrates' celebrated method of arriving at truth by rigorously (and often ironically) challenging the premises of his interlocutor's thinking. The word also occurs in the uncollected poem "Pictures," line 24.

O bare feet! O bulging belly! I saunter along by you and listen
  only.
                                          —MS: Yale.

See—there is Epicurus—see the old philosoph in a porch
  teaching
His physique is full—his voice clear and sonorous—his
  phrenology perfect,
He calls around him his school of young men—he gathers
  them in the street, or saunters with them along the banks
  of the river, arguing.
                          —N and F, I, item 139; MS: U of P.

[All That We Are]²

All that we are—the solid and liquid we are, we have advanced
  to,
We have advanced from what was our own cohesion and our
  own formation
We advance to just as much more, and just as much more.
Times suffices, and the laws suffice.—

Send any or all,—no matter what,   5
We have places for any and all—good places
We receive them, we have made preparation,
We have not only made preparation for a few developed persons
We have made preparation for undeveloped persons also

We effuse spirituality and immortality   10
We put a second brain to the brain,
We put second eyes to the eyes and second ears to the ears,
Then the drudge in the kitchen—then the laborer in his
  stained clothes—then the black person, criminals,
  barbarians—are no more inferior to the rest,
The frivolous and the blunderer are not to be laughed at as
  before,
The cheat, the crazy enthusiast, the unsuccessful man, come
  under the same laws as any.—   15
  1899   *1899*

2. Published, N and F, I, 12, items 14, 15, and 16. MS: Trent. These fifteen lines are written on a single sheet of yellow paper, showing many corrections in pencil and ink, and although Dr. Bucke printed them as three separate pieces, they possess an unmistakable unity of theme—both the eligibility and the promise of every soul. This is the poet's most persistent note. The last three lines are variants of lines 59 and 60 of the pre-1855 notebook, "Pictures" (see above), thus attesting early composition.

[I Am the Poet]³

I am the poet of reality
I say the earth is not an echo
Nor man an apparition;
But that all the things seen are real,
The witness and albic dawn of things equally real   5
I have split the earth and the hard coal and rocks and the
    solid bed of the sea
And went down to reconnoitre there a long time,
And bring back a report,
And I understand that those are positive and dense every one
And that what they seem to the child they are   10
[And the world is no joke,
Nor any part of it a sham]
1921   *1921*

[O I Must Not Forget!]⁴

O I must not forget!
To you I reach friendlily—

O I must not forget
To you I adhere!—

I do not flatter—I am not polite—but I adhere to you   5
Baffled, exiled, ragged, gaunt.
1899   *1899*

[Love Is the Cause of Causes]⁵

Love is the cause of causes,
Out of the vast, first Nothing
The ebbless and floodless vapor from the nostrils of Death,
It asked of God with undeniable will,

---

3. Published, *UPP*, II, 69–70. MS: LC *Whitman*, No. 80. These lines are written in pencil on two pages of WW's earliest extant notebook, dated 1847. The bracketed last two lines are lightly canceled in the MS. The first line is affirmed by line 483, "Song of Myself": "I accept Reality and dare not question it." Although they are but part of a remarkable outpouring that is a main source of the first edition of *LG*, these lines have an effect of unity, of a finished poem.
4. Published, *N and F*, I, 39, item 124. MS: Barrett. Six untitled penciled lines on a scrap of blue paper, probably composed before 1860, for in both diction and concept they are remindful of the phrasing of such early poems as "Starting from Paumanok" and "Song of the Open Road," and indeed they could serve as a motto or epigraph for the latter.
5. Published in "A Whitman Manuscript" by Emory Holloway, *The American Mercury* 3 (December 1924): 475–80. MS: Lion. These eight lines were inscribed in pencil on one page of a twenty-four page notebook with brown paper covers, which may be dated 1853–55. On an earlier page the poet had put the same reflection in a prose paragraph with much the same phraseology, whose stately rhetoric is still far from the rhythms of "Song of Myself."

Something to satisfy itself—   5
By then Chaos was staid with
And duly came from them a brood of beautiful children
Whom we call the laws of nature
1924   *1924*

[I Last Winter][6]

I last winter observed the Snow on a spree with the north west
    wind;
And it put me out of conceit of fences and imaginary lines.—
1899   *1899*

[I Cannot Be Awake][7]

I cannot be awake, for nothing looks to me as it did before,
Or else I am awake for the first time, and all before has been a
    mean sleep.
1899   *1899*

Light and Air![8]

Nothing ugly can be disgorged—
Nothing corrupt or dead set before them,
But it becomes translated or enclothed
Into supple youth or a dress of living richness
spring gushing out from under the roots of an old tree   5
barn-yard, pond, yellow-jagged bank with white pebblestones
timothy, sassafras, grasshopper, pismire, rail-fence
rye, oats, cucumbers, musk-melons, pumpkin-vine, long string
    of running blackberry—
regular sound of the cow crunching the grass—
the path worn in the grass—katy-did, locust, tree-toad, robin—
    wren—   10
1899   *1945*

6. Published, *N and F*, I, 35, item 105. MS: Berg. Two untitled lines in ink with penciled corrections on a small scrap of paper. In the MS "north west wind" is substituted for "Wild Drake," which is the "wood-drake" observed by the poet in line 237 of "Song of Myself." Probably composed about 1855.
7. Published, *N and F*, I, 49, item 170. MS: unavailable. This exceptionally sharp epigram is a poem in itself.
8. Published, *N and F*, I, 16, item 32; also in facsimile, p. 45, *Catalogue of the Whitman Collection*, Duke University Library, 1945. MS: Trent. Given its own title by the poet, this composition is in effect a complete poem, and although the last six lines do not begin with capitals, their line structure is unmistakable. The references to pismire, wren, running blackberry, and cow crunching the grass relate the piece to lines 664–68, sec. 31 of "Song of Myself," but its theme is closer to the poem "This Compost," a resemblance accented by the fact that in Bucke's transcript, it is preceded by a line not now in the MS:

   Under this rank coverlid stretch the corpses of young men.

[Of Your Soul]⁹

Of your soul I say truths to harmonize, if any thing can
    harmonize you,
Your body to me is sweet, clean, loving, strong, I am
    indifferent how it appears to others or to yourself,
Your eyes are more to me than poems, your lips do better than
    play music,
The lines of your cheeks, the lashes of your eyes, are eloquent to me,
The hold / gripe of your hand of your hand is richer than riches.—   5
    1899   *1899*

[What the Sun]¹

What the sun and sky do to the senses
What the landscape and waters, hills free vistas to the eye
He has done to the soul
Though / While ever the best remains untold
Though / While the secret and the solving still are hidden   5
    1948   *1948*

[Have You Supplied]²

Have you supplied the door of the house where the old one
    decayed away, and do not see that you also want your
    foundation and the roof?
Have you put only doors and windows to the house where they
    were crumbled?
Do you not see that the roof is also crumbled and this day,
    this night, may fall in ruins about your heads?
Do you not see that the old foundation beams of the floor
    have rotted under your feet, and who knows when they
    may break?
    1899   *1899*

9. Published, *N and F*, I, 26, item 58. MS: Barrett. These five fine lines are written in ink on
a small yellow scrap of paper. Complete in effect, they have the directness and simplicity of
the poet's most vigorous period—the middle or late 1850s.
1. Published, *Wake* 7 (Autumn 1948): 18. MS: Barrett. This composition, scribbled in pencil
on a single leaf, is—despite its lack of punctuation and alternative readings—a complete
and striking reflection upon one of the attributes of the poet—such as WW catalogued in
his 1855 Preface.
2. Published, *N and F*, I, 49, item 171. MS: Berg. These four lines in ink are so crowded and
intricately revised on a small scrap of paper that Bucke's transcription mistakes the first line
for two. Composition is probably early. For another line possibly intended for this compo-
sition, see "The power by which . . ." among the "Fragments" of this edition.

[I Do Not Expect]³

I do not expect to see myself in present magazines, reviews,
    schools, pulpits and legislatures—but presently I expect to
    see myself in magazines, schools and legislatures—or that
    my friends after me will see me there.
1899   *1899*

Scantlings⁴

White, shaved, foreign, soft-fleshed, shrinking,
Scant of muscle, scant of love-power,
Sant [*sic*] of gnarl and knot, modest, sleek in costumes,
Averse from the wet of rain, from the fall of snow, from the
    grit of the stones and soil,
A pretty race, each one just like hundreds of the rest,   5
A Race of scantlings from the strong growth of America.
1899   *1899*

Poem of Existence⁵

We call one the past, and we call another the future
But both are alike the present
It is not the past, though we call it so,—nor the future,
    though we call it so,
All the while it is the present only—both future and past are
    the present only.—

The curious realities now everywhere—on the surface of the
    earth,—in the interior of the earth   5
What is it? Is it liquid fire? Are there living creatures in that?
    Is it fire? solid? Is there not toward the core, some vast
    strange stifling vacuum?—Is there anything in that
    vacuum? any kind of curious flying or floating life with its
    nature fitted?

3. Published, *N and F*, I, 32, item 93. MS unavailable.
4. Published, *N and F*, I, 13, item 20. MS: Trent. These six lines, written in pencil on a small piece of paper, are headed by WW's own title, and there seems no question that they were intended as a complete poem, investing with vivid phrasing the scorn that the poet also expressed in line 1079 of "Song of Myself" about the "little plentiful manikins." This composition, no doubt, belongs to the same period. "Scantlings," familiar to WW's experience in carpentry, are small uprights used in house framing.
5. Published, *N and F*, I, 21, item 46; also in facsimile, p. 53, *Catalogue of the Whitman Collection*, Duke University Library, 1945. MS: Trent. This composition was written in ink on a single sheet in such a way as to suggest four distinct paragraph or stanzaic structures rather than conventional line arrangement. Yet it is indeed a poem, as the title—WW's own—declares, each part setting forth its own theme—the "present only" of time, the reality of the earth's interior, the existences on the stars, and the intercommunion of life. The date of writing is probably in the early 1850s.

The existence on the innumerable stars, with their varied
   degrees of perfection, climate, swiftness
—Some probably are but forming, not so advanced as the
   earth—(Some are no doubt more advanced—

There is intercommunion
One sphere cannot know another sphere,   10
(Communion of life is with life only, and of what is after life
(Each sphere knows itself only, and cannot commune beyond
   itself,
Life communes only with life,
Whatever it is that follows death.
1899   *1945*

[Until You Can Explain][6]

Priests!
Until you can explain a paving stone, do not try to explain God:
Until your creeds can do as much as apples and hen's eggs, let
   down your eyebrows a little,
Until your Bibles and prayer-books are able to walk like me,
And until your brick and mortar can procreate as I can,   5
I beg you, Sirs, do not presume to put them above me.
1899   *1899*

[Remembrances][7]

Remembrances I plant American ground with,
Lessons to think, I scatter as they come
I perceive that myriads of men and women never think
I perceive that ere visible effects can come, thought must come
I perceive that sages, poets, inventors, benefactors, lawgivers
   are only those who have thought,   5
That maugre all differences of ages and lands they differ not,
That what they leave is the common stock of the race.
1899   *1899*

---

6. Published, N *and* F, I, 32, item 89. MS: Feinberg. The reader will note a similarity of theme
   between these lines and the concluding lines (144–51) of "A Song for Occupations." Both
   passages make a contrast between life and nonlife, between the inanimate and the organic.
   Yet the above lines seem complete in themselves, a full poem, and may have been so in-
   tended. Their composition probably belongs to the period of the first edition—the middle
   1850s.
7. Published, N *and* F, I, 9, item 3. MS: Trent. These seven lines, written in pencil on a small
   sheet of ruled paper, are probably of early composition because on the verso is a list of rivers
   and cities of Europe (N *and* F, IV, item 11), one of the many notes the poet jotted down as
   preparation for his enterprise. The fourth line is lightly canceled in the MS, but still legible.

Thought[8]

Of that to come—Of experiences—Of vast unknown matter
   and qualities lying inert—much doubtless more than
   known matter & qualities,
Of many a covered embryo, owner and foetus—of the long
   patience through millions of years—of the slow formation,
Of countless germs waiting the due conjunction, the arousing
   touch,
Of all these tending fluidly and duly to myself, and duly and
   fluidly to reappear again out of myself.—

1899   *1899*

To the Future[9]

I see in you, as in the air, a divine volume, a thousand
   unformed poems, just indicated, waiting for me and The
   States,—no one preferred to ano[ther]
For I am the equal friend of each of The States, and I am the
   Poet of all,
Shall I wrest from you the thousand poems?
Shall I make the idiomatic book of my land?
Shall I yet finish the divine volume   5
I know not whether I am to finish the divine volume,
I shall go forth through the world. I shall traverse The States
   —But I cannot tell whither, or how long,—
Therefore I put upon record that I am well aware what floats
   suspended in you, you future, as qualities float suspended
   in the air.

1959   *1959*

---

8. Published, *N and F,* I, 45, item 150. MS: Trent. Although the essential theme of these four lines—the miracle of evolution—relates them closely to section 44 of "Song of Myself," particularly lines 1154–69, they are of later origin. They are written in pencil on the back of a partially clipped proof sheet of *LG* 1856, containing the beginning of "Sun-Down Poem" ("Crossing Brooklyn Ferry"). In effect the lines compose an entity, and WW supplies the title.
9. Published and edited in Roger Asselineau's "Three Uncollected 'Leaves of Grass,'" *HLQ* 22 (May 1959): 255–56. MS: Huntington. This poem is written in ink, with ink corrections, on the back of a single sheet of pink paper that contains a rough draft of the 1860 "To a Common Prostitute." The composition of both poems, then, may be assigned to the period between *LG* 1856 and *LG* 1860. Another link is that the seventh line of "To the Future" is a version of the present fourth line of the 1860 "As the Time Draws Nigh." Both poems express poignantly great ambition and momentary, but profound, uncertainty. The same note is also most movingly struck in the great terminal poem of 1860, "So Long!"

To an Exclusive.—[1]

Your tongue here? Your feet haunting The States?
But I also haunt The States, their born defender—I,
    determined brother of low persons and rejected and
    wronged persons—espouser of unhelped women,
From this hour sleeping and eating mainly that I wake and be
    muscular for their sakes,
Training myself in the gymnasium for their sakes, and
    acquiring a terrible voice for their sakes.—
Rapacious! I take up your challenge!   5
I fight, whether I win or lose, and hereby pass the feud to
    them that succeed me;
And I charge the young men that succeed me to train
    themselves and acquire terrible voices for disputes of life
    and death—and be ready to respond to whatever needs
    response,
For I prophecy that there will never come a time, North or
    South, when the rapacious tongue will not be heard, each
    age in its own dialect.
1899   *1955*

As of Forms.—[2]

Their genesis, all genesis,
They lost, all lost—for they include all.—

The earth and every thing in it,
The wave, the snake, the babe, the landscape, the human head,
Things, faces, reminiscences, presences, conditions, thoughts
    —tally and make definite a divine indistinct, spiritual
    delight in the Soul.—   5

Of the arts, as music, poems, architecture, outlines, and the
    rest, they are in their way to provoke this delight out of
    the soul,

1. Published, N and F, I, 26, item 60; also, Bowers, 259. MS: Barrett. These lines were written in ink on two leaves of pink paper, the title being centered and underlined at the top of the first. The poet is challenging the rapacious and the exclusive by championing the wronged and the rejected—a role vehemently, even exultantly undertaken in the poems of the 1850s. The probable period of composition is between 1856 and 1860.
2. Published, N and F, I, 26, item 59; also Bowers, 258. MS: Barrett. This poem was evidently composed by WW as one of the group of sixty-eight to seventy poems he worked upon in the summer of 1857 to realize his plan of having at least one hundred poems for his third edition. The surviving MS shows that it may have been rejected, for unlike the other poems in its group, it was left unnumbered; later Dr. Bucke, finding it among WW's papers, printed it in his collection of fragments. The MS evidence does not support the once-held theory that this poem is an early draft of the poem "Germs" (1860), to whose thought it bears only a general similarity in that both remark upon the spiritual significance of creation.

They are to seek it where it waits—for I see that it always
    patiently waits.—

Have you sought the inkling?
Have you wandered after the meanings of the earth? You need
    not wander:
Behold those forms.—   10
    1899   *1955*

[To This Continent]³

To this continent comes the offspring of the other continents,
And these poems are both offspring and fathers of superior
    offspring
And from these poems launches the same spirit that launched
    those ships, cities congress and the menaces that confront
    the President,
And these are for the lands.—

To the new continent come the offspring of the rest of the
    continents to bear offspring,   5
And these poems are both offspring and parents of superior
    offspring.
    1899   *1899*

[The Divinest Blessings]⁴

The divinest blessings are the commonest—bestowed everywhere,
And the most superb beauties are the cheapest the world over.
    1899   *1899*

Thought⁵

Of recognition—Come, I will no more trouble myself about
    recognition—
I will no longer look what things are rated to be, but what they
    really are to me.
    1899   *1899*

3. Published, N *and* F, I, 32, items 94 and 95. MS: Barrett. Written in black ink on two scraps
   of paper—one carrying the first four lines, and the other the last two, which are evidently
   a redaction of the first two lines. Bucke prints them as separate fragments in reverse order,
   but evidently they constitute a single pronouncement. Composition is probably between 1856
   and 1860.
4. Published, N *and* F, I, 49, item 172. MS unavailable. The phrase "blessings steadily bestow'd"
   is in WW's 1873 poem "Nay, Tell Me Not Today the Publish'd Shame," but these two lines
   are probably much earlier, remindful of the epigrams of the 1860 "Debris" or "Says."
5. Published, N *and* F, I, 30, item 80. MS: Trent. The title is WW's own, and under it the two
   lines are written in ink, with much revision, on a small scrap of paper. The composition
   probably belongs to the period when the poet was writing "Thoughts" for LG 1860.

[What Would It Bring You][6]

What would it bring you to be elected and take your place in
    the capitol?
I elect you to understand yourself: that is what all the offices
    in the republic could not do.
1899   *1899*

The Two Vaults[7]

Subject—Poem

—The vault at Pfaffs where the drinkers and laughers meet to
    eat and drink and carouse
While on the walk immediately overhead pass the myriad feet
    of Broadway
As the dead in their graves are underfoot hidden
And the living pass over them, recking not of them,
Laugh on laughers!   5
Drink on drinkers!
Bandy the jest!
Toss the theme from one to another!
Beam up—Brighten up, bright eyes of beautiful young men!
Eat what you, having ordered, are pleased to see placed before
    you—after the work of the day, now, with appetite eat,   10
Drink wine—drink beer—raise your voice,
Behold! your friend, as he arrives—Welcome him, where, from
    the upper step, he looks down upon you with a cheerful
    look
Overhead rolls Broadway—the myriad rushing Broadway
The lamps are lit—the shops blaze—the fabrics vividly are
    seen through the plate glass windows
The strong lights from above pour down upon them and are
    shed outside,   15
The thick crowds, well-dressed—the continual crowds as if
    they would never end
The curious appearance of the faces—the glimpse just caught
    of the eyes and expressions, as they flit along,
(You phantoms! oft I pause, yearning, to arrest some one of you!

---

6. Published, *N and F*, I, 30, item 82. MS: Berg. These two lines, inaccurately transcribed by Dr. Bucke, are on a small scrap of paper. Obviously, they are a complete "Thought," such as those of *LG* 1860, and were probably composed at the same time. The sentiment is illustrative of WW's untiring interest in private as well as public character.
7. Published, *UPP*, II, 92–93. MS: LC *Whitman*, No. 93. These lines were written, partly in pencil, partly in ink, on five pages of a green paper notebook of 1861–62. Lines 13–16 are badly smudged but readable. No doubt they were written on the spot—in Pfaff's, a basement restaurant at 653 Broadway, much frequented in mid-century by writers, especially the group associated with the *Saturday Press*. See Allen, 228–31. The poem, breaking off with an unfinished line, is more than descriptive; it broods on appearance and reality and confronts careless life with waiting death. Note the symbolism of the "two vaults."

Oft I doubt your reality—whether you are real—I suspect all
    is but a pageant.)
The lights beam in the first vault—but the other is entirely
    dark   20
In the first
1921   *1921*

Two Antique Records[8]

Two antique records there are—two religious platforms—
On the first one, stands the Greek sage, the classic
    masterpiece of virtue—
Eternal conscience is there—doubt is there—philosophy,
    questioning, reasoning is there.
On the second stands the jew the Christ, the Consolator . . .
There is love, there is drenched purity . . . there, subtle, is the
    unseen Soul, before which all the goods and greatnesses
    of the world become insignificant: 5
But now a third religion I give . . . I include the antique two
    . . . I include the divine Jew, and the Greek sage—
More still—that which is not conscience, but against it—that
    which is not the Soul I include
These and whatever exists, I include—I surround all, and dare
    not exclude one.
1921   *1921*

O Brood Continental[9]

O brood continental!
O you teeming cities! invincible, turbulent, proud!
O men of passion & the storm! O all you slumberers!
Arouse! arouse! the dawn-bird's throat sounds shrill!
Arouse! as I walk'd the beach, I heard the mournful notes
    foreboding a tempest!   5
The low, oft-repeated shriek of the diver, the long-lived loon, I
    heard;
I heard, & yet hear, angry thunder:—O sailors! O ships! make
    quick preparation![1]

8. Published, *UPP*, II, 91–92. MS: LC *Whitman*, No. 91. These lines are written in pencil on
    two pages of a black leather-covered notebook of sixty-nine pages, of whose contents only
    this poem is printed in Holloway's *UPP*. Internal evidence dates the poem as 1860–61. It
    bears obvious relation to "Chanting the Square Deific," which WW was to publish in "Sequel
    to Drum-Taps" five years later.
9. Published, Furness, 84. MS: LC *Whitman*, No. 1. Furness surmised that this poem was later
    incorporated in the 1860 "Apostroph," but the truth is, interestingly, the reverse. (See Arthur
    Golden, "A Note on a Whitman Holograph Poem," *PBSA* 55 (3rd quarter, 1961): 233–36.
    Golden's examination of WW's revisions in the "Blue Copy" *LG* 1860 demonstrates that "O
    Brood Continental" is actually a fair copy of the revisions the poet had made for the first
    fifteen lines of "Apostroph," the prior composition. The MS, neatly drafted and titled by WW,
    was evidently prepared for separate publication.
1. Inaccurately transcribed by Furness as "a quick preparation."

O from his masterful sweep, the warning cry of the eagle!
—Give way there all! it is useless—give up your spoils!
1928   *1928*

Kentucky[2]

Kentucky—young son of Virginia
Son of the noblest parent,—more faithful
—Virginia gave us Washington, and gave us, you

Land of the pleasant valleys! son of Virginia O could you know
With what anxious eyes from Manhattan we watch'd you,   5
How we said, questioning, Lo, the mother forgets herself—but
    would you forget her?
How, when the stars in our heaven—when the silver brothers
    on the blue
How the hearts throb
These hearts that throb in the North—how
Land of the centre—blind where the heart of the continent
    beats—O could you really know   10
These hearts that throb in Manhattan,
Son of Virgin[ia]

A young son of Virginia,
Your mother forgets herself a while—but you do not forget her;
Where you come, true to your own bright star, in the equal
    brothers, the silver brother of the blue,   15
Where you come, advancing with sinewy tendons, drest in your
    hunting shirt, with your rifle on your shoulder

Son of Virginia, in the land of hunters,
Land of sweet waters and offspring
Land of the sons of the mother Virginia
Land of the pleasant valleys and sweet-tasting rivers   20
Land of hunters—O could you know
How with anxious eyes from Manhattan we watch'd you

2. Published both in an arranged text by James E. Miller Jr., and in literal transcription from
the ms by William White, *Prairie Schooner* 32 (Fall 1958): 172–78. ms: Feinberg. Although
in essence complete, this poem was composed in rough draft on seven separate worksheets,
which show three different starts. How WW would have finally ordered the parts cannot be
known; hence the present order is necessarily provisional. The composition may be dated as
1861 because on the back of one of the worksheets is a first draft by WW of a letter of that
year concerning his brother, Jesse. This is, of course, the year when Kentucky wavered
between secession and loyalty to the Union, an issue to be fully decided for the North only
after a brief invasion late in the year by the Confederacy. With its occasionally powerful
phrasing and characteristic idiom, the poem seems to have been destined for *Drum-Taps*,
but WW could go no further. The only omission in this transcription is the repetition, set
down three times, of the title, "Kentucky." Other repetitions, obvious as the poem stands,
would undoubtedly have disappeared in a final draft.

O Land of the pleasant valleys and sweet-tasting rivers—O
    that you saw
These eyes that from island Manhattan so anxiously watch'd you.
O that you knew what ears waited to hear you, sons of
    hunters!   25

When the North felt the artery uncut
Then we knew the stars
Then we,—then America looking again at the sons of Virginia,
    and fields of the same,
Saw it was idle
Then she saw, without frowns, certain offspring of Virginia   30
And now she gazed content, on a battle-field in Virginia
And she frown'd no more on certain offspring

—And then, as to you Virginia, why will you strive against me,
    (we seem'd to hear America say.)
For more than I can conquer you you have provided me to
    conquer yourself,
For you provided me Washington, and have provided me these
    also.   35
O that you knew the angry and bitter tears shed at the North,
And the heart full of love and noble pride—full of
    brotherhood.
O that you knew the real heart of the North.

Son of hunters! Son of the pleasant valleys and sweet-tasting
    rivers!
Son of Virginia! would that you knew our joy in you today
    reflecting America's joy! anxiously waited,   40
O that you saw these million eyes of Manhattan!
Would that you knew how we felt, when the answer came to
    America's listening ears—
When she heard the sound of your sonorous cry as it rose
    clear and shrill, wafted across the Ohio;—
When she saw you, advancing, with sinewy tendons, drest in
    your hunting shirt, with your rifle on your shoulder

For do you, our American Mississippi carry the muttering news
    down swiftly with your running waters:—do not fail,   45
And do you whisper them low, O river—whisper them at night
    without fail wherever, in passing, you touch the shores on
    the east and on the west
Carry them on and on, you flowing daughter—carry them to
    the sea—pour them with your stream into the sea
And do you carry them swiftly to the whole world, you sea.
  1958   *1958*

To the Prevailing Bards[3]

Comrades! I am the bard of Democracy
Others are more correct and elegant than I, and more at home
    in the parlors and schools than I,
But I alone advance among the people en-masse, coarse and
    strong
I am he standing first there, solitary chanting the true
    America,
I alone of all bards, am suffused as with the common people.   5
I alone receive them with a perfect reception and love—and
    they shall receive me.
It is I who live in these, and in my poems,—O they are truly me!
But that shadow, my likeness, that goes to and fro seeking a
    livelihood, chattering, chaffering,
I often find myself standing and looking at it where it flits—
That likeness of me, but never substantially me.   10
1922   *1921*

[The Long, Long Solemn Trenches][4]

The long, long solemn trenches,
Has anyone thought who has stood in one of those trenches,
    what a measureless history it held?
What a stately poem and mighty and awful hymn it held?
What a history there holds in the crumbling contents of trenches?
What a poem beyond all ever written or chanted?   5
1960   *1960*

[There Rises in My Brain][5]

There rises in my brain the thought of graves—to my lips a
    word for dead soldiers
The Dead we left behind—there they lie, embedded low,
    already fused by Nature
Through broad Virginia's soil, through Tennessee—

---

3. Published, *UPP*, II, 91. MS: LC *Whitman*, No. 89, described by Holloway as an "old leather-bound notebook" containing the date June 26, 1859, and a pasted in photograph of an unidentified young woman.
4. Published, Walter Lowenfels, *Walt Whitman's Civil War* (1960), 13. MS: Feinberg. These five lines, complete in themselves, may be part of a projected longer poem on trenches, for accompanying the MS fragment is another, on which is a list of cities to be cited in such a poem: "Fredricksburg, Vicksburgh, trenches of Petersburgh & Richmond, Gettysburgh."
5. Published, Lowenfels, *Walt Whitman's Civil War*, 322. MS: Feinberg. In sentiment and theme, these seven lines are so closely related to the *Drum-Taps* "Ashes of Soldiers" that they may constitute a trial passage for this poem. However, they are in themselves an effective entity. Composed 1861–65.

The Southern states cluttered with cemeteries
the borders dotted with their graves—the Nation's dead.   5
Silent they lie—the passionate hot tears have ceased to flow—
time has assuaged the anguish of the living.
  1960   *1960*

Ship of Libertad[6]

Blow mad winds!
Rage, boil, vex, yawn wide, yeasty waves
Crash away—
Tug at the planks—make them groan—fall around, black
   clouds—clouds of death

Welcome the storm—welcome the trial—let the waves   5
Why now I shall see what the old ship is made of
Any body can sail with a fair wind, or a smooth sea

Why now I shall know whether there is anything in you, Libertad,
I shall see how much you can stand
Perhaps I shall see the crash—is all then lost?   10

Come now we will see what stuff you are made of Ship of
   Libertad
Let others tremble and turn pale—let them   ?
I want to see what   ?   before I die,
I welcome the menace—I welcome thee with joy

What then? Have those thrones there stood so long?   15
Does the Queen of England represent a thousand years?
And the Queen of Spain a thousand years?
And you

Ship of the World—Ship of Humanity
—Ship of the ages   20
Ship that circlest the world
Ship of the hope of the world—Ship of Promise
  1928   *1928*

6. Published, Furness, 84. MS: LC *Whitman*, No. 91. Obviously in rough draft, this poem was
   composed in pencil on six pages of a black leather notebook of 114 pages, belonging to the
   period 1860–61. The intended order of the six stanzas, a page to each, is difficult to deter-
   mine, but their structure is unmistakable although the Furness transcript, which is incom-
   plete, fails to indicate the stanzaic division. The question marks in the lines are the poet's
   own. The composition is an early attempt at the "Ship of State" theme in the months when
   the nation was deeply imperiled. The Spanish word "Libertad" (Liberty or Freedom) is, of
   course, a favorite borrowing, occurring many times in *LG*.

After Certain Disastrous Campaigns[7]

Answer me, year of repulses!
How will the poets, of ages hence, look back to you & to me
    also?
What themes will they make out of you, O year? (themes for
    ironical
    sarcastic laughter?)
What are the proofs to be finally shown out of you?
Are they not to be shown with pride as by bards descended
    from me? my children?   5
Are they really failures? are they sterile incompetent yieldings
    after all?
Are they not indeed to be victorious shouts from my children?
1921   *1921*

Sights—The Army Corps, Encamped on the War Field[8]

The cluster of tents—the brigades and divisions
The shelter tents—the peep through the open entrance flap—
    the debris around
The balloon up for reconnoisances
The sights of the hospital tent—the pale-faced wounded—the
    men lying flat on the ground, on the pine boughs,
The shebangs[9] of branches,—the fires built   5
The men emerging from their tents in the gray of the morning
The great camp of army corps, the divisions, the brigades and
    camps of the regiments
The sound of the drums—the different calls, the assembly, the
    early reveille, the tattoo at night, & the dinner call, etc.
The rows of tents, the streets through them
The squads out on the open ground going through their
    evolutions   10

7. Published, *UPP*, II, 101. ms: Morgan. These lines, on a single sheet, were originally titled
   by the first line, which the poet canceled for the present title. The year of repulses may well
   have been 1862, the disastrous campaigns being those of McClellan, who was halted by Lee
   until the battle of Antietam, September 17, 1862. Or possibly the year may have been 1863,
   when Lee and Jackson pushed northward until Lee was halted at Gettysburg, July 1–3. In
   any event the poem obviously belongs to the period when WW was writing the compositions
   that were to make *Drum-Taps* (1865). The ms contains a number of revisions, its final,
   amended version being honored here.
8. Published, Glicksberg, 124–25. ms: LC *Whitman*, No. 94. These lines were scribbled in an
   important notebook of 1862–63 in which WW kept record of many military actions to be
   reported both in his newspaper dispatches (see "Fifty-First New York City Veterans," *UPP*,
   II, 37–41, and Glicksberg, 63–83) and in his *Drum-Taps* poems (note particularly "The
   Artilleryman's Vision" and "A March in the Roads Hard-Prest, and the Road Unknown").
   The notebook is missing from the LC collection, but the ms of this poem is given in facsimile
   by Glicksberg, opposite page 125. It is "skeletal," as Glicksberg notes, but sufficiently de-
   veloped to give a unified impression.
9. It is characteristic of WW to use this now-familiar slang term, meaning "affair" or "con-
   trivance." The word is a variant of "shebeen," an Anglo-Irish term for a house where liquor
   is sold without license.

The long trains of baggage wagons—the huge clouds of smoke
    rising over the tents
The ambulances—
1933   *1933*

Sonnet[1]

Inscription, to precede Leaves of Grass, *when finished.*

I for the old round earth,
The World, ever varied and new, and the father of the new,
The Kronos,[2] huge, harsh, and brown-skinn'd—thence from
    eternal roots,
These Leaves utter—these, full of life, infolding all life.
By the heat of the sun—by ice and rain and air, through
    general nature ripen'd,   5
Electric, repellent enough—But be not you too soon repell'd.
—Does the sane and rocky Earth, the foot cutting Kronos,
    repel you?
Is not the Earth free, wicked, terrible, full of deserts?
Think you the fertile oases only are beautiful and mean
    something?
Do you suppose wickedness also does not mean something?   10
—Of those, with the rest, having come, I do not reject them—
    these I infold:
The same Old Man, composite am I—the same old body and
    soul,
The divine average—the great pride of man in himself, bad
    and good.
The combined purports of both are infolded in my following
    songs.
1959   *1959*

1. Published and edited, in Roger Asselineau's "Three Uncollected 'Leaves of Grass,' " *HLQ* 22 (May 1959): 257–58. MS: Huntington. "Sonnet" is a generic term with WW, meaning a lyric of indeterminate length, even though this piece happens to be fourteen lines. The subtitle, "Inscription, to precede Leaves of Grass, when finished," reminds us that the poet's introductory poem to *LG* 1867 is an "Inscription," and that, beginning with *LG* 1867, his opening cluster of poems is called "Inscriptions" in all succeeding editions. This "sonnet" is, like the other inscriptions, an announcement: the poet's acceptance of the "World, ever varied and new," from the beginnings as symbolized by Kronos (in Greek mythology the Titan who overthrew his father Uranus and was in turn dethroned by his son Zeus) to the present utterance of his "Leaves" infolding all life. This acceptance embraces, as central to the poet's philosophy, both the wicked and the good—both making up the "divine average," a key phrase in *LG*. The MS is in ink on two leaves of lined paper, with numerous penciled revisions; its composition was probably in the mid-1860s.
2. This symbol of primal creation appears both in the 1855 "Song of Myself," now at line 1029, and the 1865–66 "Chanting the Square Deific," line 7.

While the Schools and the Teachers Are Teaching[3]

While the schools and the teachers are teaching after their kind,
Some, obedience to look to the protection of the laws,
Some, to assert a sovereign and God, over all, to rely on,
Some, enjoining to build outside forts and embankments;
Solitary, I here, I to enjoin for you whoever you are you to
    build inside, invisible forts,   5
Counseling every man and woman to become the fortress, the
    lord and sovereign, of himself or herself,
To grow through infinite time finally to be a supreme God
    himself or herself,
Acknowledging none greater, now or after death, than himself
    or herself.
1959   *1959*

[Two Elegies on Lincoln][4]

UNVEIL THY BOSOM, FAITHFUL TOMB. [APRIL 1865]

Unveil thy bosom, faithful tomb,
Keep on—the precious gifts grow plentiful,
Thy soil, O land, indeed grows rich.

[THOU WEST THAT GAVE'ST HIM TO US]

Thou West that gave'st him to us,
That rear'dst him on thy ample prairie, and on the breasts of
    thy fresh rivers:
This day we return to thee bearing his body.
1959   *1962*

---

3. Published and edited by Roger Asselineau, in "Three Uncollected 'Leaves of Grass,' " *HLQ* 22 (May 1959): 259. MS: Huntington. Written on the same size of ruled paper and with the same sort of emendation in pencil and ink as its accompanying MS "sonnet," "Inscription, to precede Leaves of Grass . . . ," this piece is obviously an independent composition belonging to the same period. Its forthright counsel is Emersonian self-reliance carried to its further-most reach. In "lord . . . of himself" WW, interestingly enough, is borrowing a phrase already made illustrious by English poets—among them, Sir Henry Wotton, Dryden, and Byron. The final line is an echo of line 1271 of "Song of Myself."
4. Published in facsimile, opposite pages xxv and xliii in *Drum-Taps*, Facsimile Edition, ed. F. DeWolfe Miller (Gainesville, Fla., 1959). Printed in Harold W. Blodgett's "A Poet's Hero," *Symposium* 1 (Spring 1962): 29. MS: Feinberg. The first of these poems, whose title and bracketed date are WW's own, is written in ink on a small scrap of paper. It is not "Early lines for 'Lilacs . . . ,' " as suggested in its facsimile publication, but a rejected attempt to compose a burial lyric immediately upon the news of Lincoln's assassination—an attempt in which the poet succeeded with his "Hush'd be the Camps To-day," hastily inserted into *Drum-Taps* while it was still in press. The second poem, untitled, is still another attempt, composed on the verso of a scrap of paper bearing the MS lines of the first stanza of the *Drum-Taps* poem "Beat! Beat! Drums!" The second elegy is happier in its imagery than the first, but both are moving in their directness and simplicity, though unfulfilled.

April 1865[5]

I heard
      The blue birds singing
I saw the yellowish green where it covered the willows
I saw the eternal grass springing up
The light of the sun on the bay—the ships, dressed with
I saw in the distant city the gala flags flying   5
I saw on the ships the profusion of colors
I knew of the fete, the feasting
—Then I turned aside & mused on the unknown dead
I thought of the unrecorded, the heroes so sweet & tender
The young men   10
The returned—but where the unreturned
I thought of the unreturned, the sons of the mothers.
  1933   *1933*

beauty[6]

series of comparisons.

not the beautiful youth with features of bloom & brightness

but the bronzed old farmer & father

not the soldiers trim in handsome uniforms marching off to
    sprightly music with measured step

but the remnant returning thinned out,

not the beautiful flag with stainless white, spangled with silver
    & gold   5

But the old rag just adhering to the staff, in tatters—the
    remnant of many battle-fields

not the beautiful girl or the elegant lady with   ?   complexion,

But the mechanic's wife at work or the mother of many
    children, middle-aged or old

---

5. Published, Glicksberg, 128. MS: LC *Whitman*, No. 105. Although WW may have intended
to extend the poem beyond these twelve or so lines, some of which are incomplete, they do
suggest a certain completeness in themselves. Compare with "The Return of the Heroes" in
LG.

6. Published, Furness, 51–52. MS: Feinberg. These lines are written in ink on the last three
pages of an eighteen-page notebook with the name "Penitenzia" on the cover—a name
repeated on an accompanying notebook of six pages. Both notebooks carry rough-draft lines
and jottings for what may have been intended as a single poem under the title "Penitenzia."
However, these ten "series of comparisons" constitute an entity in themselves. At the top of
the first page WW had written, "good to bring in *lecture* or *reading*." Internal evidence
suggests that the notebooks belong to the period between *LG* 1867 and *LG* 1871.

Not the vaunted scenery of the tourist, picturesque,

But the plain landscape, the bleak sea shore, or the barren
    plain, with the common sky & sun,—or at night the moon
      & stars.   10
1925   *1928*

[Mask with Their Lids][7]

Mask with their lids thine eyes, O Soul!
The standards of the light & sense shut off
To darkness now retiring, inward from abysms,
The objective world behind thee left,
How curious, looking thence, appears the world, appear thy
    comrades,   5
Appears aloof thy life, each passion, each event.
And this thy visage [of thyself]?
1928   *1928*

Starry Union[8]

See! see! see! $\substack{\text{where} \\ \text{how}}$ the sun is beaming!
See! see! see! all the bright stars gleaming!
North or South in order moving,
All including, folding, loving
Union all! O its Union all!   5
O its all for $\substack{\text{each} \\ \text{one}}$ & $\substack{\text{each} \\ \text{one}}$ for all!
1921   *1921*

---

7. Published, Furness, 191. MS: Feinberg. These lines are written in the second of the two
"Penitenzia" notebooks (see preceding note); and they constitute, as here printed, the first
finally amended version, for the Furness transcript includes some canceled lines and erro-
neous readings. The draft is preceded by several pages of trial phrases, and one prose note
of particular interest: "Let the piece 'Droop-droop thine eyes, O Soul'—convey the idea of
a trance, yet with all the senses alert—only a state of high exalted musing—the tangible &
material with all its shows—the objective world suspended or surmounted for a while & the
powers in exaltation freedom, vision—yet the *senses* not lost or contemn'd—Then chant,
celebrate the unknown, the future hidden spiritual world—the real reality." Date of com-
position, about 1870.

8. Published, *UPP*, II, 101. MS: Morgan. Five lines in ink on a single sheet, with penciled
revisions, plus a sixth line in pencil, this passage may have been intended as a stanza for the
longer poem "Hands Round," below. Holloway surmises that it may have been designed as
a song for the cluster "Marches Now the War Is Over," which first appeared in *LG* 1871.
Note the employment of rhyme and meter as if the piece were to be a marching song of
comparatively conventional pattern, perhaps prepared for the Centennial Celebration of
1876. Actually, at least six MSS are extant in five different collections. Two—this one (Mor-
gan) and "Hands Round" (Trent)—are here printed as "Uncollected Poems": two—one with
the same title (Hanley) and "What the Word of Power" (Yale)—are in the "Unpublished
Poems" section; two outlines for poems of kindred intent in LC *Whitman*—one (No. 111)
printed by Furness, 206, the other (No. 230), unpublished—are not in the "Fragments"
section.

Hands Round[9]

[See!] see! where the sun is beaming!
See! see! see! all the bright stars, gleaming!
See by day how the sun is beaming
See by night all the far stars gleaming
What the charm of Power unbroken?   5
What the spell of ceaseless token?
? O its hand in hand, & a Union of all
What Columbia's? friendliest token?
'Tis the hands we take for the Union of all
Here's mine—give me thine—for the Union of all   10
What Columbia's friendliest token?
All hands round for the Union all!
Here's mine—give me thine—for the Union all

Stars up above in eternal lustre
Stars of the States in a compact clustre   15
Clasping, holding, earthward, heavenward
Circling, moving, roundward & onward
All hands round for the Union all
Here's mine—give me thine—for the Union all
Red, white, blue, to the westward   20
Red, white, blue, with the breezes waving
All combining, folding, loving,

Northward, Southward, Westward moving
O its all hands round for the Union all
Here's mine—give me thine—for the Union all   25
Clasping, circling earthward, heavenward!
Onward! onward! onward! onward!
Stars for the sky in an eternal lustre
Stars for the earth in a compact clustre
Then our hands here we give for the Union all!   30
O its all hand round—and each for all!
1949   *1949*

---

9. Published, *FCI*, 14–16. MS: Trent. These thirty-one lines, roughly arranged with considerable revision in four stanzas, are composed in ink on two sheets of green paper. Editors Gohdes and Silver note their obvious relation to the Morgan MS "Starry Union," and also to the "Comrades All (Hand-in-hand for once)," fragment printed by Furness, 206, from WW's lost Reading Book (LC *Whitman*, No. 111). For further relationships, see note on "Starry Union," the preceding poem. Its composition probably belongs to the year 1876, and the poem is no doubt designed as a rally poem for the centennial. Its employment of regular rhyme and meter is, of course, exceptional.

Wood Odors[1]

Morning after a night-rain
The fresh-cool summer-scent
Odors of pine and oak
The shade.

Wandering the negligent paths—the soothing silence,   5
The stillness and the veiled
The myriad living columns of the temple
The holy Sabbath morning

Incense and songs of birds in deep recesses
But most the delicate smells fitting the soul   10
The sky aloft, seen through the tree-tops

All the young growth & green maturity of May
White laurel-blossoms within reach, wood-pinks, below-
    overhead, stately tulip-trees with yellow cup-shaped
    flowers,
The meow meo-o-w of the cat-bird, cluck of robin, gurgle of
    thrush delicious

Over and under these, in the silence, delicate wood-odors   15
Birds flitting through the trees
Tangles of old grape-vines.
1960   *1960*

1. Published, *Harper's Magazine* 221 (December 1960): 43. MS: Livezey Collection, University of California. These lines, neatly transcribed in pencil, with few emendations, on two lined notebook pages, were composed at the time the poet was jotting down observations for the "Nature" notes of *Specimen Days and Collect* (1882–83)—a record, among much else, of the summer days he spent on Timber Creek at the Stafford farm in New Jersey in the mid-1870s. It may be argued that the lines are not a poem at all, but rather a listing of descriptive phrases such as WW wrote in his *Days* (see David Goodale, "Wood Odors," *WWR*, no. 8 (March 1962): 17. But it is also true that the form of the MS itself suggests planned poetic pattern with its differentiated lines and stanzas. As Rena V. Grant remarks in her footnote to the *Harper's Magazine* publication, its composition is remindful of "a skillful vers libre excursion into the realm of organic form."

Unpublished Poems

A Soul Duet.
A Dialogue between Pleasure and the Soul[1]

Come O my soul and let us take
   An evening walk becoming thee
But whither dost thou choose we shall bend our course
   Or to pleasant paths or to Calvary

O Calvary is a mountain high   5
   Tis a dreadful road for a youth like me
To eat or to drink would more suit my taste
   Far better than Mount Calvary

There is no time so good as [?]
   To ascend this mountain you can see   10
When old age comes on with its great load of [?]
   How then can you climb Mount Cal [vary?]

For I'd rather have peace and enjoy life's ease
   Than to be persuaded thus by thee
And I have heard them say there are lions in the way   15
   And they lurk in the passage to Calvary

Yes tis a straight and narrow road
   And lions lurk there for their [?]
But you shall have a guard, the angel [?]
   Shall conduct you over Cal [vary]   20

No, No I abide in the pleasant plain
   With my gay companions here to be,
I must tarry awhile in the joys of the world
   Before I climb Mount Calvary

1. MS: Hanley. Unmistakably in WW's hand, this composition harks back, both in theme and in treatment, to the journalist of the 1840s who wrote such effusions as "Fame's Vanity" or "The Playground"—see *The Early Poems and the Fiction* (Brasher, 1963)—and it must be assigned to the same period. It is written on five tattered strips pasted on dark-brown wrapping paper, and composed and amended in brown ink, black ink, purple crayon, and pencil. The many variants indicate much uncertainty in composition, an alternative title being "Climbing Mount Calvary." The hackneyed subject, the conventional structure, the expected phrasing are all related to a popular tradition: the contest between body and soul, which in American literature goes back to Anne Bradstreet's "The Flesh and the Spirit" (1678), and before that to many homilies of medieval Christianity.

Your gay companions ere long will be gone   25
   Short sighted ones, could they but see
But if ever you're to stand on Canaan's happy land
   You must travel up the mountain Calvary

Alas! I know what to do
   You greatly have alarmed me   30
I'm sure I'm going on till I fear I am undone
   Lord help me to climb Mount Calvary
   (ca. *1840*)

To the Poor—[2]

I have my place among you
Is it nothing that I have preferred to be poor—rather than to
   be rich?
The road to riches is easily open to me,
But I do not choose it
I choose to stay with you.—   5
   (ca. *1847–55*)

Pictures[3]

Lo! on a flat road runs a train'd runner, with muscular legs
   and thighs.—
He is thinly clothed,—he leans forward as he runs, with closed
   fists, and arms partially raised.
Lo! over the breast of the sea speeds a ship, under full sail—
   whitish gray, with her black hull underneath, she bends
   slightly sideways—a pennant is flying aloft—the waves
   seem to press forward—they topple and frolic with falling
   foam.
Lo! the woodcutter cutting down trees in the north-east woods
   in Wisconsin.
See you the attitude—see you the muscular limbs and the axe
   uplifted.   5
   (ca. *1855*)

2. MS: Feinberg. These lines, with title, are scribbled in pencil at the foot of one of two large sheets covered on both sides with prose notes on the Greek dramatists, the old Jersey prison ship, descriptions of birds, moral observations, and other miscellany, probably set down between 1847 and 1855. In none of his *LG* poems does WW so specifically vow himself to poverty, although he often expresses his sympathy for the poor; in line 15 of the 1855 "Great Are the Myths," later rejected, he asks:

     Who goes for men and women showing Poverty richer than wealth?

3. MS: Hanley. This MS, whose five lines are written in ink with penciled revisions on a small single sheet, may well be a trial exercise for the composition, "Pictures," to which the poet devoted an entire pre-1855 notebook. (See "Uncollected Poems.") The fourth line—about the woodcutter—is very close to line 57 of the notebook; the "ed" verbal ending in both this MS and the notebook is not yet contracted to " 'd": the script in both has the same characteristics generally—all of which leads to the supposition that the two have approximately the same date, some time between 1847 and 1855.

Broadway, 1861[4]

The sights now there
The splendid flags flying over all the stores
(The wind sets from the west—the flags are out stiff and broad
   —you can count every star of the thirty-four—you can
   count the thirteen stripes.)
The regiments arriving and departing,
The Barracks—the soldiers lounging around,   5
The recruiting band, preceded by the fifer—
The ceaseless din
  (1861)

[I Too Am Drawn][5]

I too am drawn:
Come, since it must be so—away from all parlors and offices!
Form the camp—plant the flag-staff in the middle—run up
   the flag on the halyards!
Unlimber the cannon—but not for mere salutes, for courtesy,
We will want something, henceforth, besides powder and
   wadding.   5
  (1861)

[I Have Lived][6]

I have lived forty years and seen only the soldiers the amateurs
I have heard from the cannon only courteous salutes
Now when I see the soldiers parading, I look on no longer in
   apathy
  (1861)

4. MS: Berg. These lines were written in ink on a single sheet under WW's own title, which sets the place and time. Like the two poems following, "[I Too Am Drawn]" and "[I Have Lived]," which were composed on the verso of the same sheet, this poem is closely related to the opening poem of *Drum-Taps*, "First O Songs for a Prelude," in its theme of the arousing of the energies of the great city—and of the nation–to the war.
5. MS: Berg. Written in ink on the verso of the "Broadway, 1861" MS, these lines, without title, give a unified impression by themselves, although it is possible that they may have been intended as a further stanza for the first poem. Both poems are related in spirit and occasion to "Beat! Beat! Drums!" as is also "[I Have Lived]," the poem following.
6. MS: Berg. These lines are scribbled in penciled rough draft, without title, just below the draft of "[I Too Am Drawn]" on the verso of the "Broadway, 1861" MS. They may have been intended simply as additional lines for a single composition. An alternative reading of the first line is:

     We have seen only the soldiers the amateurs.

[I Stand and Look][7]

I stand and look in the dark under a cloud,
But I see in the distance where the sun shines,
I see the thin haze on the tall white steeples of the city,—
I see the glistening of the waters in the distance.
 (ca. *1861–65*)

Of My Poems[8]

All the others were singing the distinctions, and what was to
 be preferred.
Therefore I thought I would sing a song of inherent qualities
 in a man, indifferent whether they are right or wrong.
 (ca. *1860–61*)

My Own Poems[9]

Aye, merchant, thou hast drawn a haughty draft
Upon the centuries yet to come
Yet hitherto unborn—the Americas of the future:
The trick is . . . *Will they pay?*
 (ca. *1860?*)

Of the Democratic Party 58–59–60[1]

They think they are providing planks of platforms on which
 they shall stand—
Of those planks it would be but retributive justice to make
 them coffins—
 (ca. *1860*)

---

7. MS: LC *Whitman*, No. 91. These lines are entered in pencil on one page of a sixty-nine-page black leather notebook of 1860–61. As an exercise in objective description, they are re- mindful of such *Drum-Taps* vignettes as "The Torch," "The Ship," and "A Farm Picture." The poem is remarkable for economy of expression, the scene itself complex but the im- pression fully rendered.
8. MS: LC *Whitman*, No. 91. This two-line jotting was entered in pencil on one page of the sixty-nine-page black leather notebook of 1860–61. One of WW's many announcements of intent, it could have fitted easily among the "Says" of *LG* 1860.
9. MS: LC *Whitman*, No. 228. This rough draft, in pencil with ink revisions, is on a single small scrap. It is impossible to date it, but WW began to make such epigrammatic pronouncements or "inscriptions" about his poetic role with his third edition—*LG* 1860.
1. MS: Trent. These two lines, under WW's title, are written in pencil on the verso of a scrap of prose jottings on the geography and populations of Europe. Compare with "To a President" and "To the States: To Identify the 16th, 17th, or 18th Presidentiad," which are also scornful pronouncements on the maneuverings of a Democratic Party organization that WW had rejected. See also the prose jeremiad "The Eighteenth Presidency!"

[To What You Said]²

To
   What you said, passionately clasping my hand, this is my
      answer:
   Though you have strayed hither, for my sake, you can never
      belong to me, nor I to you,
   Behold the customary loves and friendships—the cold
      guards,
   I am that rough and $\frac{\text{simple}}{\text{scornful}}$ person
   I am he who kisses his comrade lightly on the lips at
      parting, and I am one who is kissed in return,   5
   I introduce that new American salute
   Behold love choked, correct, polite, always suspicious
   Behold the received models of the parlors—What are they to
      me?
   What to these young men that travel with me?
   (ca. *1860*)

[While Some I So Deeply Loved]³

While some I so deeply loved (dear child, who stopt so often
   by you?, remember you me?
Remember you who kissed you while you lay so pale &
   lonesome in your cots?)
While those I knew, now dead, lie buried in their graves,
   unrecognized,
While the world of appearance & mirth goes on & goes on,
While so soon what is past forgotten, & the waves wash the
   imprints off the sand,   5
In nature's reverie sad, returning
   (*1864*)

2. MS: Feinberg. This poem is written in pencil on the verso of page 30 (WW's numbering) of
   the sixty-three-page rough draft of *Democratic Vistas*. (See item 37 of the Feinberg Exhibition
   Catalog, Detroit, 1955.) Considerably amended, the reading is nevertheless clear in its final
   form. Unmistakably a "Calamus" poem in sentiment, it was probably composed at about the
   same time as the others, 1857–60. When the poet came to compose his 1871 *Democratic
   Vistas*, he followed his customary frugal practice of using whatever bits of paper were at
   hand, this MS page being among them.
3. MS: Yale. These lines are written in ink with penciled corrections on the verso of a MS Civil
   War note, dated December 23, 1864, about a recruit, Frank Lester, whose mother had called
   on the poet. The fifth and sixth lines are variants of lines 21 and 22 of the *Drum-Taps* poem
   "The Wound-Dresser." Although this MS is, in effect, complete, it may well be a passage of
   an intended longer poem for *Drum-Taps*, perhaps another version of "The Wound-Dresser."

Reminiscences 64[4]

—I saw the bloody holocaust of the Wilderness & Manassas
I saw the wounded & the dead, & never forget them
(Ever since have they been with me—they have fused ever
    since in my poems:—)
They are here forever in my poems
How quick forgotten   5
   (ca. 1864)

[Disease and Death][5]

Not mere results of sin and law alone,
Sometimes I see in ye, Disease and Death!
The fear of evolution, knowledge, growth,
Reaching beyond the bounds—and so cut short.
   (ca. 1872)

Starry Union[6]

See by day
See! see! see! how the sun is blazing
See! see! see! all the bright stars shining

See by day the ^{great}/_{bright} sun blazing

4. MS: Huntington. This poem is a scrawl on one of ten pages of hospital notes, otherwise prose, which the poet jotted down in 1862–64. The title and the line structure are WW's own; for similar poetical jottings on battle scenes (the material to be perfected for *Drum-Taps*), see Glicksberg, 121–28. The figure 64, which is without apostrophe, may refer to the year 1864, since the bloody Battle of the Wilderness took place in early May of that year, when Grant crossed the Rapidan and engaged Lee's forces—the beginning of his campaign against Richmond. "Manassas" (or Second Bull Run) refers to the battle of August 29–30, 1862, when Lee and Jackson badly defeated the army of General Pope along Warrenton Pike, Virginia.
5. MS: Huntington. Originally, this reflection was three penciled lines—the second, third, and fourth—then another line was added in ink, tentatively canceled, and finally transposed to the top to become the poem's opening line. The composition is without title and undated. It may belong to the early 1870s, for line 113 of the 1872 Dartmouth Commencement poem "Thou Mother with Thy Equal Brood" may reflect its purport if "thee" and "ye" are both the poet's land:
    "In many a smiling mask death shall approach, beguiling thee, thou in disease shalt swelter,"
6. MS: Hanley. With the same title as the Morgan MS, printed in *UPP*, II, 101, and now in the present section of "Uncollected Poems," this composition is obviously part of the general effort most fully represented in the "Hands Round" MS of the Trent Collection, also in the "Uncollected Poems." Written in black ink on a tattered white sheet, and with penciled additions, it is probably an earlier draft of the Morgan MS, which in turn may be a revised stanza of the longer Trent MS. Compare with "What the Word of Power," below. Two MSS poem outlines of kindred theme are in the LC holdings. One is transcribed by Furness, 206 (LC *Whitman*, No. 111); the other (LC *Whitman*, No. 230) is unpublished. The probable date is 1876 since all these "Union" paeans are evidently inspired by the centennial.

See by night all the stars a-shining,   5
Shining, shining, ever shining.
The sun holding the stars
God holding the suns
As the Union holds the States
As the suns hold the stars   10
As the Power holds the Suns
All free yet all held inseparably
O by day comes the sun all blaz[ing]
O by night come the stars all shin[ing]
    (ca. *1876*)

[What the Word of Power][7]

What the word of power unbroken?
What the charm of heaven's own token
On & ever on from the Eastward
On & ever on to the westward
Union all! O its [*sic*] Union all!   5
O its [*sic*] all for each, & each for all!
    (ca. *1876*)

Last Words[8]

As to yet one more seance[9] (doubtless the last)
Recapitulating the same old themes—the emotional, the
    moral, the heroic,
By head and heart of me—by voice and pen—addressing old,
    old words,
To you here reading—Union, Equality, Love,
To you America, beginning, middle, end.   5
    (*1889*)

7. MS: Yale. These six lines, in ink with penciled corrections, bear obvious relation to other MSS
   that are parts of an attempted poem celebrating the Union, probably designed for the cen-
   tennial of 1876. See "Starry Union" and "Hands Round" among the "Uncollected Poems,"
   also a second "Starry Union" in the "Unpublished Poems," the fragment printed by Furness,
   206, and the unpublished fragment, LC *Whitman*, No. 230. The title is supplied.
8. MS: Feinberg. The MS materials for this poem are composed on five different pages made
   from the backs of letter sheets and split envelopes, bearing various dates in the year 1889.
   Two pages contain working notes and phrases only, the other three rough drafts, of which
   the one here printed is in the last, amended form. Since the poem remained unpublished,
   we may infer that the poet did not achieve the form he wanted. He did publish certain other
   late attempts to review his basic themes: *cf.* "A Carol Closing Sixty-Nine," "L. of G.'s Pur-
   port," and "Now Precedent Songs, Farewell."
9. By this word WW probably meant "mystical illumination."

[Glad the Jaunts for the Known][1]

Glad the jaunts for the known,
Trusting the unknown future,
With good heart, love, remembrance,
I finishing my three score and ten,
Giving this book to you   5
Sign with love my name
   (1888–89)

Champagne in Ice[2]

No use to argue temperance, abstinence only,
I've had a bad spell 40 hours, continuous
'Till now a heavy bottle of good champagne wine in my thirst,
Cold and tart-sweet drink'd from a big white mug half fill'd
   with ice,
It is started me in stomach and in head,   5
As I slowly drink, thanking my friend,
Feeling the day, and in myself, freedom and joy.
   (ca. 1891–92)

To the Soul[3]

All is for thee
Life and Death are for thee
The Body too is for thee
   (n.d.)

1. MS: LC *Whitman*, No. 32. Written and revised in pencil on the back of a letter to WW from James Gordon Bennett, editor of the *New York Herald*, dated January 23, 1888. Much revised, even in its rough draft, this piece is nevertheless complete as a sentiment to accompany an autographed book. Since the poet is finishing his "three score and ten," the book may well be the 1888 *Complete Poems and Prose* in one volume, or possibly the 1889 *LG*. The intended recipient is unidentified.
2. MS: Lion. Although these lines may be called a "poem" only by courtesy, they are both in form and intent an affecting and poetic note of thanks. In pencil with inked revisions on a single small sheet, they must have been composed in the poet's final days of invalidism. The MS, was sent to Oscar Lion with the following letter:

   > Dear Mr. Lion—Here's a bit of autobiography been havened on the floor of three twenty eight for a while and then drifted into sight again at my home today. Like it?
   >
   > Sept. 14—1942   Anne Traubel

   Anne Traubel was Horace Traubel's widow; "three twenty eight" was then the number of the poet's house on Mickle Street, Camden.
3. MS: LC *Whitman*, No. 229. Three lines in pencil under WW's title on a single sheet. Perhaps the poet had intended to go further. At the upper right corner of the MS he has penciled the one word: "crude."

[Two Little Buds]⁴

Two little ? human Buds.
One less, one larger, here we humbly place:
Quickly decayed on earth:
But now they bloom in God's immortal garden.
  (ca. *1870*)

[Sunrise]⁵

Darkies looking at the sun as it rose, a round red glistening
      ball through the vapory morning
"Don't it look pretty?" said one.
"Yes, said the other, but it looks mighty *ambitious*
  (*n.d.*)

---

4. MS: Berg. These four lines are written in ink on a small scrap of paper, which is accompanied
   by another scrap, the top of a piece of letterhead stationery of the Attorney General's Office,
   on which is scribbled, in the same ink and script, the tag:

    A youth beloved by all
    And in whom there was no guile.

   Since this is obviously quoted, the question arises: may not the "Buds" verses also be quoted,
   rather than composed? The question mark before "human" is WW's own.
5. MS: Feinberg. Written on a small scrap of paper with black ink, untitled, and in rough draft,
   this composition is just an anecdote—a "memo." But it has point, and WW gave it his
   customary form. The MS cannot be dated.

Uncollected Manuscript Fragments

[Sesostris][1]

Advance shapes like his shape—the king of Egypt's shape,
Shapes that tally Sesostris—gigantic in stature, wholesome,
  clean-eyed,
Six feet ten inches tall—every limb, every part and organ in
  proportion—strong, bearded, supple,
Conqueror of two continents in nine years,
Lover most of those that repelled him sternest—builder to
  them of phallic memorials,   5
Ruler wisely and friendly for sixty-two years—accepter of all
  religions—preferer of none,
Freer of slaves—divider among them of homesteads—maker of
  farmers.

After Death[2]

Now when I am looked back upon, I will hold levee,
I lean on my left elbow—I take ten thousand lovers, one after
  another, by my right hand.—

[America][3]

No Homer, Shakspere, Voltaire
No palaces, King's palaces nor courts,
Nor armies on the land, nor navies on the sea,

1. Published, N and F, I, 15–16, item 31. MS unavailable. Sesostris: legendary king of Egypt, considered to belong to the nineteenth dynasty and sometimes identified with Rameses II. According to Herodotus and Strabo, Sesostris conquered the whole known world. WW's description may be derived from his reading of Sir John Gardiner Wilkinson's Manners and Customs of the Ancient Egyptians (1836–40). See Stovall, "Notes on Whitman's Reading," AL 26 (November 1954): 347. Also it is to be remembered that in the 1850s WW frequented Dr. Henry Abbott's Egyptian Museum at 659 Broadway, New York. Cf. the "shapes" image in "Song of the Broad-Axe." See John Irwin's article in the criticism section of this Norton Critical Edition.
2. Published, N and F, I, 32, item 91. MS: Barrett. In the MS fragment the phrase "After death" is centered as a title. The Bucke transcription is slightly inaccurate.
3. Unpublished. MS: Feinberg. These phrases are written in pencil in this order under WW's own title on a sheet torn from the top of a larger sheet. Evidently they are rough drafts toward the beginning lines of a poem.

But countless living equal men:
Average   free

America to the Old World Bards[4]

Be thy task for once to thank in my name, the old world Bards
And be thy task to speak in my name to preserve the antique
    poems
Let them pass through
Let the phantoms walk the roads of thy soul
Call up the pale great   5
Let the procession pass—let the shadow walk through the very
    soul

[American Air][5]

American air I have breathed, breathe henceforth also of me,
American ground that supports me, I will support you also.

[War][6]

Armies & navies pass on the surface baleful
War & the passions of war pass on
War & the angry fight pass
War & the frantic tempers of men rage out their time & depart—
But we never depart   5

[As Nature][7]

As nature, inexorable, onward, resistless, impassive, amid the
    screams and din of disputants, so America.

---

4. Unpublished. ms: LC *Whitman*, No. 117. These six lines are penciled on two pages of a five-page notebook. In two further pages of jottings and phrases, the poet advises himself that they are to be a first stanza or canto, to be followed by a "strong Invocation." The sense of the opening lines seems to be that America is herself addressing the poet concerning the Old World bards. The title is the poet's own.
5. Published, *N and F*, I, 13, item 21. ms: Barrett. Conceivably, this is a complete poem, but the ms shows two more phrases below the line, indicating that it was probably intended for further development.
6. Unpublished. ms: Hanley. Written in pencil, these phrases on war are a poem outline, rather than a rough draft of the poem itself.
7. Published, *N and F*, I, 34, item 101. ms unavailable.

We Are[8]

As the turbulence of the expressions of the earth—as the great
   heat and the great cold—as the soiledness of animals and
   the bareness of vegetables and minerals
No more than these were the roughs among men shocking to me

[As to You][9]

As to you, if you have not yet learned to think, enter upon it now,
Think at once with directness, breadth, aim,
      conscientiousness—
You will feel a strange pleasure from the start, and grow
   rapidly each successive week.

[As We Are][1]

As we are content and dumb the amount of us in men and
   women is content and dumb,
As we cannot be mistaken at last, they cannot be mistaken.

? Ashes of Roses[2]

        Dust of the dead—
        Ashes of blue & grey,
        Ashes of battle-pits
        Solemn & strange cement—
        Not a crop grows hence in the fields of north or south   5
        Nor moisture of the river, nor falling rain

        Decoration day May 30. The *dust & debris* below in all the
cemeteries not only in Virginia & Tennessee but *all through
the land*   The names of the flowers   lilacs roses early
lilies   the colors, purple & white & yellow & red   the
graves   *Ashes of Armies*   The Unknown   Army-Ashes

8. Published, *N and F*, I, 13, item 18. MS: Berg. The Bucke transcript does not reproduce the
   "We are" that the poet had added above the first line, greatly improving its sense.
9. Published, *N and F*, I, 29, item 73. MS: Barrett. The last line of this trenchant counsel is
   canceled in the MS, but rightly preserved by Bucke, who transcribes it as part of a larger
   fragment, which begins with two lines now existing as a separate MS. See "Who wills . . . ,"
   below, p. 613.
1. Published, *N and F*, I, 11, item 12. MS: Barrett. This gnomic saying is the poet's expression
   of faith in the intuitional, of which the "we" of the poem are the agents.
2. Unpublished. MS: Feinberg. On each of two leaves the poet inscribed lines under the title
   (the question mark is his own), followed by a note in prose. The whole is an undated poem
   outline, bearing a close relationship to the *LG* poem "Ashes of Soldiers."

The dust of each fused in the dust of each—(i.e. the rebel &
the Union)

The Body—[3]

Why what do you suppose is the Body?
Do you suppose this that has always existed—this meat, bread,
    fruit, that is eaten, is the body?
No, those are visible parts of the body, materials that have
    existed in some way for billions of years—now entering
    into the form of the body
? But there is the real body too, not visible.

[Can ?][4]

Can ? make me so exuberant, yet so faintish?
The rage of an unconquerable fierceness is conquered by the
    touch [of the] tenderest hand
I cannot be awake, for nothing looks to me as it did before,
Or else I am awake for the first time, and all before has been a
    mean sleep.

[Decoration Day][5]

Lay on the graves of all dead soldiers
Wreaths of roses and branches of palms,

Not for the dead alone—for meanings, indications
All wars, contentions past, tokens reciprocal, over the north,
    and over the South
One day, at least, hot passions laid—peace—brotherhood
    uprisen,
We joining proud, remembering thankful, sorrowing

                                                     5

3. Published, N and F, I, 37–38, item 118; and item 169, p. 49. MS: Trent. Inadvertently the
  MS was twice transcribed, and with slight inaccuracy, by Bucke. In a marginal note on the
  MS leaf, the poet instructed himself, "make this more rhythmic." The question mark before
  the last line is WW's own. The fragment is perhaps related to the LG poem "I Sing the Body
  Electric."
4. Published, N and F, I, 37, item 116. MS: Barrett. The question mark after "Can" in the first
  line of this interesting fragment is the poet's own–proposing, in effect, a riddle for the reader.
  The two words supplied in the second line are in the Bucke transcript.
5. Unpublished. MS: Feinberg. The penciled MS shows these to be trial lines in very rough draft,
  with the title "Decoration Day" halfway down the leaf rather than in position. Cf. the last
  four stanzas of "Ashes of Soldiers."

[Divine Is the Person][6]

Devine is the person/body —it is all—it is the soul also
How can there be immortality, except through mortality?
How can the ultimate realities of visible things be visible?
How can the real body ever die and [?]

Ebb and Flood Tides[7]

Advancing, retreating, and hand in hand
Duly with rhythmic steps turning and mouths to the right or
the left reverting
You chorus of brothers, and sisters
Moving forever round the circles of the earth

[The Epos of a Life][8]

The Epos of a life I sing—varied the road, the way by farm &
hum of city, & frequent trackless wild—by river, lake, &
ocean—by shows of peace & war;
Him of The Lands, identical, I sing, along the single thread, so
interspersed,

[The Grappler][9]

the grappler with his
grappling irons—I
see him ahold of
the long handles—
working them deep in   5
the water, carefully
feeling

---

6. Unpublished. MS: Barrett. A small scrap, with lines much worked over, this MS is related to
the fragment "The Body," as both are to "I Sing the Body Electric" and to "Song of Myself,"
especially sections 24–25.
7. Unpublished. MS: Feinberg. Although these are trial lines, much revised and amended, a
distinguished image emerges, and the lyric achieves a kind of completion.
8. Unpublished. MS: Feinberg. Written in pencil with many corrections and cancellations. Un-
doubtedly in trial form, still the lines convey vitality and a sense of completion.
9. Unpublished. MS: LC Whitman, No. 91. This is a jotting in a leather-bound notebook of
1860–61 that contains a miscellany of drawings, prose, and verse. Although WW did not
use this particular line in LG, it could well have been a part of canto 5 of "A Song for
Occupations," in which the grappler is listed (line 114).

[Have I Refreshed][1]

Have I refreshed and elevated you?
Though I have uttered no word about your particular
    employment, have you received from me new and valuable
    hints about your employment?
Have you gone aside after listening to me, and created for
    yourself?
Have I proved myself strong by provoking strength out of you?

[Hear My Fife!][2]

Hear my life!—I am a recruiter
Come, who will join my troop?

[I Have Appeared][3]

I have appeared among you to say that what you do is right,
    and what you affirm is right;
But that they are only the alphabet of right.—
And that you shall use them as beginnings and first attempts—
I have not appeared with violent hands to pull up by the roots
    any thing that has grown,
Whatever has grown, has grown well—   5
Do you fancy there is some water in the semen of the
    perpetual copulation
Do you suppose the laws might be reformed and rectified?

[Immortality][4]

How can there be immortality except through mortality?
How can the ultimate reality of visible things be visible?
How can the real body ever die?

---

1. Published, N and F, I, 30, item 78. MS: Barrett. Although the poet did not see fit to print these lines, their sentiment is basic in LG.
2. Published, N and F, I, 15, item 29. MS: Barrett. Cf. line 46 of the uncollected poem "Pictures," in which the poet does not identify himself as the recruiter.
3. Unpublished. MS: Feinberg. These lines, preceded by prose jottings, apparently unrelated, are penciled on a fragment that definitely seems to be pre-1855. Interestingly, they constitute a primitive, early form of the passage in canto 22 of "Song of Myself," lines 464–69.
4. Published, N and F, I, 48, item 168. MS unavailable.

[I Admire]⁵

I admire a beautiful woman . . . I am easy about who paints
    her portrait.
Poet go!
I am ready to swear never to write another word.

[I Am a Look]⁶

I am a look—mystic—in a trance—exaltation.
Something wild and untamed—half savage.
Common things—the trickling sap that flows from the end of
    the manly maple.

[I Am a Student]⁷

I am a student, free of a Library,—it is limitless and eternally
    open to me;
The books are written in numberless tongues, always perfect
    and alive,—
They do not own the library who buy the books and sell them
    again,
I am the owner of the library, for I read every page, and enjoy
    the meaning of the same

[I Am Become]⁸

I am become the poet of babes and little things.
I descend many steps—I go backward primeval
I retrace steps oceanic—I pass around not "merely my own
    kind," but all the objects I see.—

[I Am Not Content]⁹

I am not content now with a mere majority . . . . I must have
    the love of all men and all women,

5. Published, N and F, I, 81, item 182. MS unavailable.
6. Published, N and F, I, 40, item 135. MS unavailable. WW uses the "trickling sap" metaphor
    in line 537, "Song of Myself."
7. Published, N and F, I, 36, item 110. MS: Barrett. In several LG poems, e.g., lines 14–20,
    "Song of Myself," and line 20, "Thou Mother with Thy Equal Brood," the indoor library is
    a symbol of book experience in contrast with nature's experience.
8. Published, N and F, I, 35, item 103. MS: Barrett. The Bucke transcript does not indicate
    the "quote" in the third line. Cf. canto 44, "Song of Myself," lines 1148 ff.
9. Published, N and F, I, 45, item 151. MS: Trent. In transcribing, Bucke included at the end
    of the second line the words—"and stand upright before him"—that are canceled in the MS,
    with the period after "one."

If there be one left in any country who has no faith in me, I
will travel to that country, and go to that one.

[I Am That Halfgrown Angry Boy][1]

I am that halfgrown angry boy, fallen asleep,
The tears of foolish passion yet undried upon my cheeks.

Years with all their events pass for me,
Some are spent in travel—some in the usual hunt after
fortune.

I pass through the travels and fortunes of thirty years, and
become old,   5
Each in its due order comes and goes,
And then a message for me comes.
The

[I Know Many Beautiful Things][2]

I know many beautiful things about men and women,
But do not know anything more beautiful than to be
freehanded and always go on the square.

I see an aristocrat;
I see a smoucher grabbing the good dishes exclusively to
himself and grinning at the starvation of others as if it
were funny,
I gaze on the greedy hog; he snorts as he roots in the delicate
greenhouse.   5
How those niggers smell!
Must that hod-boy occupy the same stage with me?
Doth the dirt doze and forget itself?
And let tomatoes ripen for busters and night walkers,
And do no better for me—   10
Who am a regular gentleman or lady,
With a stoop and a silver door-plate and a pew in church?
And is the day here when I vote at the polls,
One with the immigrant that last August strewed lime in my
gutter?
One with the thick-lipped black?   15

1. Published, N and F, I, 41, item 137. MS: Trent. Possibly pre-1855 verse, for on the verso of
   the MS is a holograph of unpublished journalistic prose. Furthermore, the sentimental phras-
   ing of the first two lines is almost exactly duplicated in a story fragment (CW, IX, 146)
   belonging in mood to the fiction of the 1840s.
2. Published, N and F, I, 17–18, item 36. MS unavailable. A rough draft—perhaps only a poem
   outline, certainly not a complete poem. The highly idiomatic and concrete diction and the
   satiric vehemence suggest composition in the early or middle 1850s.

And can dew wet the air after such may be elected to Congress,
And make laws over me?
Have you heard the gurgle of gluttons perfectly willing to stuff
themselves
While they laugh at the good fun of the starvation of others,
But when the gaunt and the starved awkwardly come for their
slices   20
The quiet changes to angry hysterics.

It is for babies to lift themselves out of the . . .
I go not with the babies who . . .

I am none of the large baby sort;
I have no wish to lift myself above breathing air, and be
specially eminent or attractive;   25
I am not quite such a fool as that,
I remain with people on average terms—
I am too great to be a mere leader.

[I Know That Amativeness][3]

I know that amativeness is just as divine as spirituality—and
this which I know I put freely in my poems.
I know that procreation is just as divine as spirituality—and
this which I know I put freely in my poems.

[I Shall Venerate][4]

I shall venerate hours and days and think them immeasurable
hereafter;
I am finding how much I can pass through in a few minutes.
I was a good friend to all things before,
But now what I was seems to me limpsey and little.

[I Subject All the Teachings][5]

I subject all the teachings of the schools, and all dicta and
authority to the tests of myself

3. These two lines, separately transcribed in *N and F*, I, as item 132, p. 40, and item 175, p. 49, respectively, have obvious association as one composition. No doubt the two MSS, now untraced, were somehow disjoined.
4. Published, *N and F*, I, 35, item 107. MS unavailable. WW was fond of the dialectal word "limpsey" (weak), sometimes using the alternative spelling, "limpsy."
5. Published, *N and F*, I, 30, item 79. MS: Barrett. This dictum could stand as a small poem by itself, but it was probably intended, judging from the MS leaf, as part of a larger composition.

And I encourage you to subject the same to the tests of
yourself—and to subject me and my words to the
strongest tests of any

[In American Schools][6]

In American schools sit men and women—
Schools for men and women are more necessary than for
children.

[I'll Trace This Garden][7]

1

I'll trace this garden oer & oer
Meditate on each sweet flower
Thinking of each happy hour

2

Some say my love is gone to France

3

I'll sell my frock—I'll sell my where   5

4

I wish I was on yonder hill
It's there I'd sit & cry my fill
So every tear should turn a mill

5

I'll dye my dress—I'll dye it red
Over the world I'll beg my bread   10
My parents dear shall think me dead

---

6. Published, N and F, I, 23, item 49. MS unavailable. As one-time schoolmaster, as journalist,
and as poet, WW's interest in education was unremitting. See Florence Bernstein Freedman's
Walt Whitman Looks at the Schools (1950).
7. Unpublished. MS: Feinberg. Since WW wrote these experimental ballad lines on letterhead
of the Attorney General's Office, Washington, D.C., where be was first employed July 1,
1865, the MS can be roughly dated. But this verse is most atypical of WW's poems of the
period. One can only surmise that either the poet was recalling a ballad he had heard, or
that he was trying his own hand. He never lost—even after 1855—a fondness for occasional
practice of conventional patterns.

[It Were Easy to Be Rich][8]

It were easy to be rich owning a dozen banks
But to be rich

It was easy to grant offices and favor being President
But to grant largess and favor

It were easy to be beautiful with a fine complexion and regular
    features
But to be beautiful

It were easy to shine and attract attention in grand clothes
But to outshine?   in sixpenny muslin

[Life, Light][9]

Life light and the in-bound tides
? only only through ye,
Through death and waning day and the ebb's depletion
Life, light, and the inbound tides

[Living Bulbs][1]

Living bulbs, melons with polished rinds smooth to the
    reached hand
Bulbs of life, lilies, polished melons, flavored for the mildest
    hand that shall reach.

[Nor Humility's Book][2]

Nor humility's book nor the book of despair nor of old
    restrictions;
Book of a new soldier, bound for new campaigns;
Book of the sailor that sails the sea stormier, vaster than any.

8. Published, *UPP*, II, 72. MS: LC *Whitman*, No. 80. Like the uncollected poem "I am the poet of reality," this is winnowed from the important 1847 notebook, the lines penciled on a single leaf. Still a fragment, still in outline, the piece has begun to achieve concise form.
9. Unpublished. MS: LC *Whitman*, No. 119. These trial phrases are written in purple pencil on two lined notebook pages. It is impossible to date them, although in mood they belong to the poems of the "Sea-Drift" cluster.
1. Published, *N and F*, I, 41, item 136. MS: Trent. These two lines in pencil on a small piece of paper remind us that in his 1855 Preface the poet spoke of the compact shape of melons, and that in "Song of Myself," line 1296 he wrote of "the polish'd breast of melons." In a prose fragment (*N and F*, IV, item 41) is a sentence closely echoing the first line of this fragment: "Sweet-gum, bulb, and melons with bulbs grateful to the hand."
2. Published, *N and F*, I, 23, item 51. MS unavailable. This fragment could stand by itself as a poem and may have been intended as such, but it seems more likely that the three lines are part of an unfinished composition.

[O I See Now][3]

(O I see now that I have the make of materialism and things,
And that intellect is to me but as hands, or eyesight, or as a
   vessel,

[Osirus][4]

Osirus—to give forms.
I am he who finds nothing more divine than simple and
   natural things are divine.

[The Poet Is a Recruiter][5]

The poet is a recruiter
He goes forth beating
the drum,—O, who
will not join his troop?

[The Power by Which][6]

The power by which the carpenter plumbs his house is the
   same power that dashes his brains out if he fall from the
   roof.—

[Prince of Wales][7]

Prince of Wales in New York 1860
The Good Queen's Eldest Son
One rapid look I gave and saw
The Queen's Son
A fair youth   5

3. Published, N and F, I, 14, item 24. MS: Trent. These verses are written in pencil at the foot
   of a prose passage on the same theme. See N and F, III, item 26. The MS is a single sheet
   —a single composition, both prose and verse.
4. Published, N and F, I, 9, item 2. MS unavailable. Properly, "Osiris," Egyptian god of the
   lower world, mentioned by WW in line 1030, "Song of Myself."
5. Unpublished. MS: LC Whitman, No. 83. This little fragment is penciled in this form at the
   foot of a page of a small notebook belonging to the period 1854–55. Cf. the fragment "Hear
   my fife," above, p. 609.
6. Published, N and F, I, 31, item 84. MS: Berg. It is possible that the poet intended to add
   this single-line fragment to the composition "Have you supplied . . . ." See the "Uncollected
   Poems" section. Both deal with carpentry or home-building as symbolic of life-building.
7. Unpublished. MS: LC Whitman, No. 92. This impression is entered on a page of a Brooklyn-
   Washington notebook of 1860–64. The Prince of Wales, who visited New York City on
   October 11, 1860, was saluted by WW in the poem "Year of Meteors," line 11, with words
   probably suggested by this notebook entry.

In the barouche drawn by the champing horses
Pass'd a fair youth with downcast eyes

[A Procession Without Halt][8]

A procession without halt,
Apparent at times and hid at times
Rising the rising grounds in relief against the clear sky lost in
    the hollows, stretched interminably over the plains,
No eye that ever saw the starting—no eyes that ever need wait
    for the ending
Where any one goes, however ahead, the rest duly coming,
    however far behind,   5
Marches a marching procession

[Remember If You Are Dying][9]

Remember if you are dying, that you are dying, . . . is it so,
    then?
If it be so, I bring no shuffling consolation of doctors and
    priests,
I tell the truth . . . I tell with unvarying voice.—

[Sanity and Ensemble][1]

Sanity and ensemble characterize the great masters,
Innocence and nakedness are resumed,
Theories of the special depart as dreams,
Nothing happens, or ever has happened, or ever can happen,
    but the vital laws are enough,
None were or will be hunted, none were or will be retarded.   5
A vast, clear scheme, each learner learning it for himself,
Taking men, women, laws, the earth, and the things of the
    earth as they are,
Starting from one's-self and coming back to one's-self,
Looking always toward the poet,
Seeing all tend eternally toward happiness,   10
What is narrower than gravitation, light, life, of no account,
What is less than the sure formation of density, or the patient
    upheaving of strata, of no account,

8. Published, N and F, I, 13, item 22. ms: Bayley. "All is a procession," said WW (line 89, "I
    Sing the Body Electric"), and the image, a great favorite, occurs many times in LG. These
    lines, however, are a poem outline rather than a fragment that has actually kindled into
    poetry.
9. Published, N and F, I, 13, item 19. ms: Barrett. The sentiment of this verse fragment is basic
    in LG, and in effect it is a complete poem in itself.
1. Published, N and F, I, 15, item 28. ms: U of Penn. Probably not a poem, but an outline of
    ideas to be expanded into a poem that never got written, although the mood faintly suggests
    "A Song of the Rolling Earth."

What is less than that which follows the thief, the liar, the
    glutton, the drunkard, through this experience, and
    doubtless afterwards, that too of no account.
What does not satisfy each one and convince each one—that
    too is of no account.

[Shall We Sky-lark][2]

Shall we sky-lark with God
The poet seems to say to the rest of the world
Come, God and I are now here
What will you have of us

[Ships Sail upon the Waters][3]

Ships sail upon the waters,—some arriving others departing
Ten thousand cities rich, learned, populous cities—they have
    grown or certainly to grow
The States spread amply—old states and new states—they
    front on the two seas—they are edged or cleft by the
    Mississippi,
Congress is in session in the Capitol, or will be in session the
    appointed time,
See the President is menaced face to face by the common
    people, for his derelictions.   5

The Soul's Procession[4]

The idea—after carrying the Soul   through all
    experiences   tableaux situations   sufferings   heroism
    especially at Sea wrecks   storms picture of a ship in a
    storm at sea
The Soul then stalks on by itself
Swims on—sails on like a sufficient splendid solitary ship by
    itself—There is space enough—
There are the orbs of the worlds in space with ample room
    enough
& there are the orbs of souls also swimming in space   5

2. Published, *UPP*, II, 83. MS: LC *Whitman*, No. 85. These four lines are penciled on one page
   of a twenty-three-page notebook belonging to the late 1840s or early 1850s when *LG* 1855
   was in gestation.
3. Published, *N and F*, I, 30, item 77. MS: Barrett. In effect a complete poem, but the MS,
   without title on a single sheet, and much worked over, gives the impression of being a
   fragment of a larger whole.
4. Unpublished. MS: Barrett. A thirteen-page notebook whose cover is inscribed by the poet
   with the above title, underlined. Within are a number of prose jottings such as the first
   sentence of this composition. Then some of the jottings break into rhythmic trial lines, as
   above. The whole constitutes an interesting early working upon a theme that is central in
   the poet's vision, and to which he gave expression many times—most notably in "Passage to
   India."

612   ♦   Uncollected Manuscript Fragments

Each one composite in itself
And the spirit of God holding them together
The orbs as the suns & worlds swim in space,
But the Souls swim in the Spirit of God in greater space

[Spirituality, the Unknown][5]

Spirituality, the unknown, the great aspirations of the soul, the
idea of justice, divinity, immortality.

[That Is Profitable][6]

great to you
That is profitable which you carry with you after death
I will carefully earn riches to be carried with me after the
death of my body
I will . . . . .

[These Are the Caravan][7]

These are the caravan of the desert—the close of the day—the
encampment and the camels.

Proem[8]

These are the sights that I have absorbed in Manhattan Island,
and in all These States,
These are the thoughts that have come to me—some have
come by night, and some by day, as I walked,

I know that Personality is divine, and gives life and identity to
a man or woman—And I know that egotism is divine,
I know that the woman is to be equal to the man. And I know
that there is to be nothing excepted,

5. Published, N and F, I, 39, item 127. MS unavailable. A line summing up meaning and
intention.
6. Unpublished. MS: Feinberg. This interesting reflection is penciled in regular line formation
on a page of a substantial 212-page notebook that, by internal evidence, can be dated as
belonging to the period 1856–57.
7. Published, N and F, I, 32, item 92. MS unavailable.
8. Published, N and F, I, 16, item 33. MS: Trent. A fragment penciled on a piece of ruled paper
with the poet's own title at the top, suggesting that these four lines are the beginning passage
of a prefatory poem.

[Undulating, Swiftly Merging][9]

Undulating, swiftly merging from womb to birth, from birth to
   fullness and transmission, quickly transpiring—
Conveying the sentiment of the mad, whirling, *fullout* speed of
   the stars, in their circular orbits.

[What, Think You][1]

What, think you, does our Continent mean in reference to our
   race? I say it means with radical and resistless power to
   assert the *Individual*—raise a refuge strong and free for
   practical average use, for man and woman:
That will America build and curiously looking around writes
   thereof a poem thereof.

[Who Wills with His Own Brain][2]

Who wills with his own brain, the sweet of the float of the
   earth descends and surrounds him,
If you be a laborer or apprentice or solitary farmer, it is the
   same

Have you known that your limbs must not dangle?
Have you known that your hands are to grasp vigorously?
You are also to grasp with your mind vigorously   5

Remember how many pass their whole lives and hardly once
   think and never learned themselves to think,
Remember before all realities must exist their thoughts.

As to you, if you have not yet learned to think, enter upon it
   now,
Think at once with directness, breadth, aim, conscientiousness,
You will find a strange pleasure from the start and grow rapidly
   each successive week.   10

9. Published, *N and F,* I, 48, item 164. MS unavailable.
1. Published, *N and F,* I, 48, item 163. MS unavailable. This sentiment would have interested
   Alexis de Tocqueville who, in his *Democracy in America* (1835, 1840), remarked: "I readily
   admit that the Americans have no poets; I cannot allow that they have no poetic ideas."
2. Published, *N and F,* I, 28–29, item 73. MS: Barrett (lines 1–2 and 8–10); MS of lines 3–7
   unavailable. The first two lines are now a separate fragment, as are also lines 8–10. See "As
   to You," above, p. 600. The entire composition, as transcribed here and in *N and F,* consti-
   tutes an incomplete poem, of which other parts may have been lost or never written.

[Why Should I Subscribe][3]

Why should I subscribe money to build some hero's statue?
That butcher boy is just as great a hero
He does not know what fear is.

[Will You Have the Walls][4]

Will you have the walls of the world with the air and the
    fringed clouds?
The Poet says God and me, What do you want from us? Ask
    and maybe we will give it you.
The Soul addresses God as his equal—as one who knows his
    greatness—as a younger brother.

[The Woman That Sells][5]

The woman that sells candies and apples, at the street-stand,
The boy crying his newspapers in the morning.

[Poetic Lines in 1855–56 Notebook][6]

Cursed is that age or nation that does not realize itself, and
    esteem itself
Wretched is that man who does not esteem himself
                                                        —page 9

Of me the good comes by wrestling for it,
I am not he bringing ointments and soft wool for you,
I am he with whom you must wrestle. . . . I am
The good of you is not in me. . . . the good of you is
    altogether in yourself.

3. Published, *N and F*, I, 35, item 108. MS unavailable.
4. Published, *N and F*, I, 29, item 76. MS unavailable. Probably composed in the early 1850s,
   for the sentiment is like that of "Song of Myself"—such lines as:
       And I know that the hand of God is the promise of my own,
       And I know that the spirit of God is the brother of my own,
5. Published, *N and F*, I, 28, item 67. MS unavailable. These lines could have been intended
   for canto 15, "Song of Myself," which so brilliantly details the sight and show of daily actions
   in America.
6. Published, *An 1855–56 Notebook Toward the Second Edition of Leaves of Grass*, ed. by
   Harold W. Blodgett (1959). MS: Feinberg. Although most of the poetry entries in this im-
   portant ninety-eight-page notebook are trial lines and phrases toward the second edition (*LG*
   1856), those here printed were never used in any *LG* poem. A few of them are so
   distinguished—for example those on page 33 of the notebook—that it is hard to understand
   why the poet never published them. He could be prodigal.

I am the one who indicates, and the one who provokes and
    tantalizes   5
                                 —page 28

I believe whatever happens I shall not forget this earth,
I believe I shall walk and walk among men and women.—
Wherever I go I believe I shall often return
There are many words and deeds that will happen that will
    allure me,
Where any one thinks of me or wishes me that will allure me,   5
Where the happy young husband and wife are, and the happy
    old husband and wife are, will allure me
                                   —page 33

Where the great renunciation is made in secret, that will allure
    me,
Where personal love reaches toward me, that will allure me.
    . . . to the prisoner in his cell, or the slave, or the solitary
    sick person, it will certainly allure me,
I do not know what is waiting for me to be—
But I know that I shall be in great form and nature
I cannot prove it to you or any one. . . . but I know it is so.   5
                                   —page 35

What the earth is and where the earth is [?]
Not more spiritual, not more divine and beautiful than this
    earth
                                   —page 45

I have all lives, all effects, all hidden invisibly in myself. . . .
    they proceed from me
                                   —page 94

Prefaces

Preface 1855—*Leaves of Grass*, First Edition[1]

America[2] does not repel the past or what it has[3] produced
under its forms or amid other politics or the idea of castes or
the old religions. . . . accepts the lesson with calmness . . . is
not so impatient as has been supposed that the slough[4] still sticks
to opinions and manners and literature while the life which   5
served its requirements has passed into the new life of the new
forms . . . perceives that the corpse is slowly borne from the
eating and sleeping rooms of the house . . . perceives that it
waits a little while in the door . . . that it was fittest for its days
. . . that its action has descended to the stalwart and wellshaped[5]   10
heir who approaches . . . and that he shall be fittest for his days.
    The Americans of all nations at any time upon the earth have
probably the fullest poetical nature. The United States them-
selves are essentially the greatest poem. In the history of the
earth hitherto the largest and most stirring appear tame and or-   15
derly to their ampler largeness and stir. Here at last is something
in the doings of man that corresponds with the broadcast doings
of the day and night. Here is not merely a nation but a teeming
nation of nations.[6] Here is action untied from strings necessarily
blind to particulars and details magnificently moving in vast   20

---

1. Whitman has not generally been credited with having written prose of a power commensurate
with his poetry. However, the preface to the first edition of *Leaves of Grass* is prose of
noteworthy power and intellectual persuasiveness, with a corresponding stylistic authority.
It is in fact one of the important landmarks of American literary criticism and it has contin-
ued to exert an influence on modern literature. Further comment on this preface will be
found in the introduction to this Norton Critical Edition. "Preface 1855" was collected with
other prose works in *SDC* 1882, *CCP* 1888, and *CPW* 1892. The two London reprints of
this preface (1868 and 1881) do not concern us here. The revisions, of which the bulk were
made in *Specimen Days and Collect*, represented changes in Whitman's practices with re-
spect to punctuation and other conventions, but a more important alteration was the can-
cellation of a number of passages that decreased the essay in bulk by about one-third. The
shorter version of "Preface 1855" appears in *CPW*, and in *Coll W, Prose Works 1892*, II.
The footnotes here, for the first edition, indicate passages canceled in later editions of the
preface, including lines that were translated into certain new poems, principally in *LG* 1856
and *LG* 1860. Poems significantly affected by such transfers are "By Blue Ontario's Shore,"
the most noteworthy, and also "Song of Prudence," "Song of the Answerer," "To You, (who-
ever you are)," "Tests," "Perfections," "Says," and "A Child's Amaze." See also the footnotes
for the texts of these poems. Phrases or ideas from twenty-two of the twenty-four original
paragraphs of the "Preface 1855" appear in the poems.
2. Lines 1–11, *cf.* "By Blue Ontario's Shore," 51–57.
3. Later editions read: "what the past has."
4. Later editions read: "not impatient because the slough."
5. Later editions read: "well-shaped."
6. The sentence ending here was omitted in later editions.

616

masses.[7] Here is the hospitality which forever[8] indicates heroes. . . . Here are the roughs and beards and space and ruggedness and nonchalance that the soul loves.[9] Here the performance disdaining the trivial unapproached in the tremendous audacity of its crowds and groupings and the push of its perspective spreads with crampless and flowing breadth and showers its prolific and splendid extravagance.[1] One sees it must indeed own the riches of the summer and winter, and need never be bankrupt while corn grows from the ground or the orchards drop apples or the bays contain fish or men beget children upon women. 25 30

Other states indicate themselves in their deputies. . . . but the genius of the United States is not best or most in its executives or legislatures, nor in its ambassadors or authors or colleges or churches or parlors, nor even in its newspapers or inventors . . . but always most in the common people.[2] Their manners speech dress friendships—the freshness and candor of their physiognomy—the picturesque looseness of their carriage . . . their deathless attachment to freedom—their aversion to anything indecorous or soft or mean—the practical acknowledgment of the citizens of one state by the citizens of all other states—the fierceness of their roused resentment—their curiosity and welcome of novelty—their self-esteem and wonderful sympathy—their susceptibility to a slight—the air they have of persons who never knew how it felt to stand in the presence of superiors—the fluency of their speech—their delight in music, and sure symptom of manly tenderness and native elegance of soul[3] . . . their good temper and openhandedness—the terrible significance of their elections—the President's taking off his hat to them not they to him—these too are unrhymed poetry. It awaits the gigantic and generous treatment worthy of it. 35 40 45 50

The largeness[4] of nature or the nation were monstrous without a corresponding largeness and generosity of the spirit of the citizen. Not nature nor swarming states[5] nor streets and steamships nor prosperous business nor farms nor capital nor learning may suffice for the ideal of man . . . nor suffice the poet. No reminiscences may suffice either. A live nation can always cut a deep mark and can have the best authority the cheapest . . . namely from its own soul. This is the sum of the profitable uses of individuals or states and of present action and grandeur and of the 55

---

7. Later editions omit "vast."
8. Later editions read "for ever."
9. This sentence was omitted in later editions.
1. Lines 12–27, *cf.* "By Blue Ontario's Shore," 58–65.
2. In the later editions the remainder of this paragraph is omitted, but the 1855 phrase "common people," was extended by the words: "south, north, west, east, in all its States, through all its mighty amplitude."
3. Lines 35–47, *cf.* "By Blue Ontario's Shore," 95–98.
4. Does not begin a paragraph in the later editions, but runs on without interruption after line 35, "common people," where the previous paragraph was cut; "of nature or" omitted in the later texts.
5. Later editions read: "Not swarming states."

subjects of poets.[6]—As if it were necessary to trot back genera-   60
tion after generation to the eastern records! As if the beauty and
sacredness of the demonstrable must fall behind that of the
mythical! As if men do not make their mark out of any times!
As if the opening of the western continent by discovery and what
has transpired since[7] in North and South America were less than   65
the small theatre of the antique or the aimless sleep-walking of
the middle ages! The pride of the United States leaves the wealth
and finesse of the cities and all returns of commerce and agri-
culture and all the magnitude of geography or shows of exterior
victory to enjoy the breed of fullsized men[8] or one fullsized man   70
unconquerable and simple.

The American poets[9] are to enclose old and new for America
is the race of races.[1] Of them a bard is to be commensurate with
a people. To him the other continents arrive as contributions
. . . he gives them reception for their sake and his own sake. His   75
spirit responds to his country's spirit. . . . he incarnates its ge-
ography and natural life and rivers and lakes. Mississippi with
annual freshets and changing chutes, Missouri and Columbia
and Ohio and Saint Lawrence with the falls and beautiful mas-
culine Hudson, do not embouchure where they spend them-   80
selves more than they embouchure into him. The blue breadth
over the inland sea of Virginia and Maryland and the sea off
Massachusetts and Maine and over Manhattan bay and over
Champlain and Erie and over Ontario and Huron and Michigan
and Superior, and over the Texan and Mexican and Floridian   85
and Cuban seas and over the seas off California and Oregon, is
not tallied by the blue breadth of the waters below more than
the breadth of above and below is tallied by him. When the long
Atlantic coast[2] stretches longer and the Pacific coast stretches
longer he easily stretches with them north or south. He spans   90
between them also from east to west and reflects what is between
them. On him rise solid growths that offset the growths of pine
and cedar and hemlock and liveoak and locust and chestnut and
cypress and hickory and limetree and cottonwood and tuliptree
and cactus and wildvine and tamarind and persimmon. . . . and   95
tangles as tangled as any canebrake or swamp. . . . and forests
coated with transparent ice and icicles hanging from the boughs
and crackling in the wind. . . . and sides and peaks of mountains.
. . . and pasturage sweet and free as savannah or upland or
prairie. . . . with flights and songs and screams that answer those   100
of the wildpigeon and highhold and orchard oriole and coot and

---

6. In the later editions the four following sentences ending "the middle ages!" (line 67) are
   between parentheses.
7. In later texts, "since" is cancelled.
8. Later texts read: "the sight and realization of full-sized men," etc.
9. Lines 72–81 and 105–6, 705–10, cf. "By Blue Ontario's Shore," 66–76.
1. In later texts the following forty-eight lines are omitted, ending at line 131, "lips cease."
2. Lines 89–131, cf. "By Blue Ontario's Shore," 77–94 and 99–106.

surf-duck and redshouldered-hawk and fish-hawk and white-ibis
and indian-hen and cat-owl and water-pheasant and qua-bird
and pied-sheldrake and blackbird and mockingbird and buz-
zard and condor and night-heron and eagle. To him the heredi-   105
tary countenance descends both mother's and father's. To him
enter the essences of the real things and past and present events
—of the enormous diversity of temperature and agriculture and
mines—the tribes of red aborigines—the weatherbeaten vessels
entering new ports or making landings on rocky coasts—the first   110
settlements north or south—the rapid stature and muscle—the
haughty defiance of '76, and the war and peace and formation
of the constitution. . . . the union always surrounded by blath-
erers and always calm and impregnable—the perpetual coming
of immigrants—the wharf hem'd cities and superior marine—   115
the unsurveyed interior—the loghouses and clearings and wild
animals and hunters and trappers. . . . the free commerce—the
fisheries and whaling and golddigging—the endless gestation of
new states—the convening of Congress every December, the
members duly coming up from all climates and the uttermost   120
parts. . . . the noble character of the young mechanics and of
all free American workmen and workwomen. . . . the general
ardor and friendliness and enterprise—the perfect equality of
the female with the male. . . . the large amativeness—the fluid
movement of the population—the factories and mercantile life   125
and laborsaving machinery—the Yankee swap—the New-York
firemen and the target excursion—the southern plantation life
—the character of the northeast and of the northwest and
southwest—slavery and the tremulous spreading of hands to pro-
tect it, and the stern opposition to it which shall never cease till   130
it ceases or the speaking of tongues and the moving of lips cease.
For such the expression of[3] the American poet is to be transcen-
dant and new.[4] It is to be indirect and not direct or descriptive
or epic. Its quality goes through these to much more. Let the
age and wars of other nations be chanted and their eras and   135
characters be illustrated and that finish the verse. Not so the
great psalm of the republic. Here the theme is creative and has
vista.[5] Here comes one among the wellbeloved stonecutters and
plans with decision and science and sees the solid and beautiful
forms of the future where there are now no solid forms.   140

Of all nations the United States with veins full of poetical stuff
most need poets and will doubtless have the greatest and use
them the greatest.[6] Their Presidents shall not be their common
referee so much as their poets shall.[7] Of all mankind the great

---

3. In later texts, read: "The expression of."
4. Lines 133–40, *cf.* "By Blue Ontario's Shore," 119–26.
5. The passage that follows, originally 33 lines in length, ending "draw blood" (line 162), is
   omitted in later editions.
6. Lines 141–43, *cf.* "By Blue Ontario's Shore," 132–33.
7. Lines 141–62, and 139–48, *cf.* "By Blue Ontario's Shore," 137–53.

poet is the equable man. Not in him but off from him things are grotesque or eccentric or fail of their sanity. Nothing out of its place is good and nothing in its place is bad. He bestows on every object or quality its fit proportions neither more nor less. He is the arbiter of the diverse and he is the key. He is the equalizer of his age and land. . . . he supplies what wants supplying and checks what wants checking. If peace is the routine out of him speaks the spirit of peace, large, rich, thrifty, building vast and populous cities, encouraging agriculture and the arts and commerce—lighting the study of man, the soul, immortality—federal, state or municipal government, marriage, health, freetrade, intertravel by land and sea. . . . nothing too close, nothing too far off . . . the stars not too far off. In war he is the most deadly force of the war. Who recruits him recruits horse and foot . . . he fetches parks of artillery the best that engineer ever knew. If the time becomes slothful and heavy he knows how to arouse it . . . he can make every word he speaks draw blood. Whatever stagnates in the flat of custom or obedience or legislation he never stagnates.[8] Obedience does not master him, he masters it. High up out of reach he stands turning a concentrated light . . . he turns the pivot with his finger . . . he baffles the swiftest runners as he stands and easily overtakes and envelops them. The time straying toward infidelity and confections and persiflage he withholds by his steady faith[9] . . . he spreads out his dishes . . . he offers the sweet firmfibred meat that grows men and women. His brain is the ultimate brain. He is no arguer . . . he is judgment. He judges not as the judge judges but as the sun falling around a helpless thing. As he sees the farthest he has the most faith. His thoughts are the hymns of the praise of things. In the talk on the soul and eternity and God off of his equal plane he is silent. He sees eternity less like a play with a prologue and denouement. . . . he sees eternity in men and women . . . he does not see men and women as dreams or dots. Faith is the antiseptic of the soul . . . it pervades the common people and preserves them . . . they never give up believing and expecting and trusting. There is that indescribable freshness and unconsciousness about an illiterate person that humbles and mocks the power of the noblest expressive genius. The poet sees for a certainty how one not a great artist may be just as sacred and perfect as the greatest artist. . . . . .[1] The power to destroy or remould is freely used by him[2] but never the power[3] of attack. What is past is past. If he does not expose superior models and prove himself by every step he takes he is

---

8. Later texts read: "the great poet never."
9. Later texts omit "his." The passage following, ending "dreams or dots" (line 178), is omitted in the later editions.
1. In later texts a new paragraph begins here.
2. In later texts, read: "by the greatest poet."
3. In later texts, read: "seldom the power."

not what is wanted. The presence of the greatest poet conquers
. . . not parleying or struggling or any prepared attempts. Now
he has passed that way see after him! there is not left any vestige   190
of despair or misanthropy or cunning or exclusiveness or the
ignominy of a nativity or color or delusion of hell or the necessity
of hell. . . . . and no man thenceforward shall be degraded for
ignorance or weakness or sin.[4]

    The greatest poet hardly knows pettiness or triviality. If he   195
breathes into any thing[5] that was before thought small it dilates
with the grandeur and life of the universe. He is a seer. . . . he
is individual . . . he is complete in himself. . . . the others are
as good as he, only he sees it and they do not. He is not one of
the chorus. . . . he does not stop for any regulation . . . he is the   200
president of regulation. What the eyesight does to the rest he
does to the rest. Who knows the curious mystery of the eyesight?
The other senses corroborate themselves,[6] but this is removed
from any proof but its own and foreruns the identities of the
spiritual world. A single glance of it mocks all the investigations   205
of man and all the instruments and books of the earth and all
reasoning. What is marvellous? what is unlikely? what is impos-
sible or baseless or vague? after you have once just opened the
space of a peachpit and given audience to far and near and to
the sunset and had all things enter with electric swiftness softly   210
and duly without confusion or jostling or jam.

    The land and sea, the animals fishes and birds, the sky of
heaven and the orbs, the forests mountains and rivers, are not
small themes . . . but folks expect of the poet to indicate more
than the beauty and dignity which always attach to dumb real   215
objects . . . . they expect him to indicate the path between reality
and their souls.[7] Men and women perceive the beauty well
enough . . probably as well as he. The passionate tenacity of
hunters, woodmen, early risers, cultivators of gardens and or-
chards and fields, the love of healthy women for the manly form,   220
seafaring persons, drivers of horses, the passion for light and the
open air, all is an old varied sign of the unfailing perception of
beauty and of a residence of the poetic in outdoor people. They
can never be assisted by poets to perceive . . . some may but
they never can. The poetic quality is not marshalled in rhyme or   225
uniformity or abstract addresses to things nor in melancholy
complaints or good precepts, but is the life of these and much
else and is in the soul. The profit of rhyme is that it drops seeds
of a sweeter and more luxuriant rhyme, and of uniformity that
it conveys itself into its own roots in the ground out of sight.   230

---

4. No paragraph break occurs here in later texts (*cf*. line 184, note).
5. In later texts, read: "anything."
6. Lines 203–11, *cf*. "Tests," 4–5.
7. Lines 212–41, *cf*. "Song of the Answerer" (the poet) who serves others by indicating "the
path between reality and their souls." Lines transferred from the present essay are found in
the second canto of the poem: see notes below to lines 397, 406, 737. Further detail on
"the Answerer" appears in the note to that poem.

The rhyme and uniformity of perfect poems show the free growth
of metrical laws and bud from them as unerringly and loosely as
lilacs or roses[8] on a bush, and take shapes as compact as the
shapes of chestnuts and oranges and melons and pears, and shed
the perfume impalpable to form. The fluency and ornaments of
the finest poems or music or orations or recitations are not in-
dependent but dependent. All beauty comes from beautiful blood
and a beautiful brain. If the greatnesses are in conjunction in a
man or woman it is enough . . . . the fact will prevail through
the universe . . . . but the gaggery and gilt of a million years will
not prevail. Who troubles himself about his ornaments or fluency
is lost. This is what you shall do:[9] Love the earth and sun and
the animals, despise riches, give alms to every one that asks,
stand up for the stupid and crazy, devote your income and labor
to others, hate tyrants, argue not concerning God, have patience
and indulgence toward the people, take off your hat to nothing
known or unknown or to any man or number of men, go freely
with powerful uneducated persons and with the young and with
the mothers of families, read these leaves in the open air every
season of every year of your life,[1] re-examine all you have been
told at school or church or in any book, dismiss whatever insults
your own soul, and your very flesh shall be a great poem and
have the richest fluency not only in its words but in the silent
lines of its lips and face and between the lashes of your eyes and
in every motion and joint of your body. . . . . . . The poet shall
not spend his time in unneeded work. He shall know that the
ground is always ready ploughed[2] and manured . . . . others may
not know it but he shall. He shall go directly to the creation. His
trust shall master the trust of everything he touches . . . . and
shall master all attachment.

The known universe has one complete lover and that is the
greatest poet. He consumes an eternal passion and is indifferent
which chance happens and which possible contingency of for-
tune or misfortune and persuades daily and hourly his delicious
pay. What balks[3] or breaks others is fuel for his burning progress
to contact and amorous joy. Other proportions of the reception
of pleasure dwindle to nothing to his proportions. All expected
from heaven or from the highest he is rapport with in the sight
of the daybreak or a scene[4] of the winter woods or the presence
of children playing or with his arm round the neck of a man or
woman. His love above all love has leisure and expanse . . . . he
leaves room ahead of himself. He is no irresolute or suspicious
lover . . . he is sure . . . he scorns intervals. His experience and

8. In later texts, read: "and roses."
9. Lines 242–60, cf. "By Blue Ontario's Shore," 235–47.
1. The preceding clause is omitted from the later editions.
2. In later editions, read: "already plough'd."
3. In later editions, read "baulks"; both spellings are correct.
4. In later editions, read: "the scenes."

the showers and thrills are not for nothing. Nothing can jar him
. . . . suffering and darkness cannot—death and fear cannot. To   275
him complaint and jealousy and envy are corpses buried and
rotten in the earth . . . . he saw them buried. The sea is not
surer of the shore or the shore of the sea than he is of the
fruition[5] of his love and of all perfection and beauty.

The fruition of beauty is no chance of hit or miss[6] . . . it is   280
inevitable[7] as life . . . . it is exact and plumb as gravitation. From
the eyesight[8] proceeds another eyesight and from the hearing
proceeds another hearing and from the voice proceeds another
voice eternally curious of the harmony of things with man. To
these respond perfections[9] not only in the committees that were   285
supposed to stand for the rest but in the rest themselves just the
same. These understand the law of perfection in masses and
floods . . . that its finish is to each for itself and onward from
itself[1] . . . that it is profuse and impartial . . . that there is not
a minute of the light or dark nor an acre of the earth or sea[2]   290
without it—nor any direction of the sky nor any trade or em-
ployment nor any turn of events. This is the reason that about
the proper expression of beauty there is precision and balance
. . . one part does not need to be thrust above another. The best
singer is not the one who has the most lithe and powerful organ   295
. . . the pleasure of poems is not in them that take the handsom-
est measure and similes and sound.[3]

Without effort and without exposing in the least how it is done
the greatest poet brings the spirit of any or all events and pas-
sions and scenes and persons some more and some less to bear   300
on your individual character as you hear or read. To do this well
is to complete with the laws that pursue and follow time. What
is the purpose must surely be there and the clue of it must be
there . . . . and the faintest indication is the indication of the
best and then becomes the clearest indication. Past and present   305
and future are not disjoined but joined. The greatest poet forms
the consistence of what is to be from what has been and is. He
drags the dead out of their coffins and stands them again on
their feet . . . . he says to the past, Rise and walk before me that
I may realize you. He learns the lesson . . . . he places himself   310
where the future becomes present. The greatest poet does not
only dazzle his rays over character and scenes and passions . . .
he finally ascends and finishes all . . . he exhibits the pinnacles
that no man can tell what they are for or what is beyond . . . .

5. Erroneously printed "he is the fruition," in *SDC* 1882 and later editions.
6. In later texts read: "miss or hit."
7. Later editions read: "is as inevitable."
8. Lines 281–84, *cf.* "Assurances," 7.
9. The poem "Perfections," an epigram, reflects the idea at large in lines 285–97 and 318–24.
   This sentence was omitted in later texts.
1. The preceding clause was omitted in later texts.
2. Later texts read "earth and sea," (note added comma).
3. Later texts omit "and similes."

he glows a moment on the extremest verge. He is most wonderful 315
in his last half-hidden smile or frown . . . by that flash of the
moment of parting the one that sees it shall be encouraged or
terrified afterward for many years. The greatest poet does not
moralize or make applications of morals . . . he knows the soul.
The soul has that measureless pride which consists in never ac- 320
knowledging any lessons but its own.[4] But it has sympathy as
measureless as its pride and the one balances the other and nei-
ther can stretch too far while it stretches in company with the
other. The inmost secrets of art sleep with the twain. The
greatest poet has lain close betwixt both and they are vital in his 325
style and thoughts.

The art of art, the glory of expression and the sunshine of the
light of letters is simplicity. Nothing is better than simplicity
. . . . nothing can make up for excess or for the lack of definite-
ness. To carry on the heave of impulse and pierce intellectual 330
depths and give all subjects their articulations are powers neither
common nor very uncommon. But to speak in literature with the
perfect rectitude and insousiance[5] of the movements of animals
and the unimpeachableness of the sentiment of trees in the
woods and grass by the roadside is the flawless triumph of art. 335
If you have looked on him who has achieved it you have looked
on one of the masters of the artists of all nations and times. You
shall not contemplate the flight of the graygull over the bay or
the mettlesome action of the blood horse or the tall leaning of
sunflowers on their stalk or the appearance of the sun journeying 340
through heaven or the appearance of the moon afterward with
any more satisfaction than you shall contemplate him. The
greatest[6] poet has less a marked style and is more the channel
of thoughts and things without increase or diminution, and is
the free channel of himself. He swears to his art, I will not be 345
meddlesome, I will not have in my writing any elegance or effect
or originality to hang in the way between me and the rest like
curtains. I will have nothing hang in the way, not the richest
curtains. What I tell I tell for precisely what it is. Let who may
exalt or startle or fascinate or sooth[7] I will have purposes as 350
health or heat or snow has and be as regardless of observation.
What I experience or portray shall go from my composition with-
out a shred of my composition. You shall stand by my side and
look in the mirror with me.

The old red blood and stainless gentility of great poets will be 355
proved by their unconstraint.[8] A heroic person walks at his ease

4. In later texts, "lessons or deductions but." Lines 320–24, cf. "Song of Prudence," 43–45, a
direct borrowing; cf. note on "perfections," line 285. See line 615 note for all borrowings in
"Prudence."
5. In later texts, correctly spelled, "insouciance."
6. In later texts, "great."
7. Spelled correctly, "soothe," in the later editions. Lines 349–56 parallel the idea of "Song of
Myself." Section 19, lines 382–88.
8. Lines 355–56 and 360–64, cf. "By Blue Ontario's Shore," 221–23.

through and out of that custom or precedent or authority that
suits him not. Of the traits of the brotherhood of writers[9] savans
musicians inventors and artists nothing is finer than silent defi-
ance advancing from new free forms. In the need of poems phi-   360
losophy politics mechanism science behaviour,[1] the craft of art,
an appropriate native grand-opera, shipcraft, or any craft, he is
greatest forever and forever[2] who contributes the greatest origi-
nal practical example. The cleanest expression is that which finds
no sphere worthy of itself and makes one.   365

The messages of great poets[3] to each man and woman are,
Come to us on equal terms, Only then[4] can you understand us,
We are no better than you, What we enclose you enclose,[5] What
we enjoy you may enjoy. Did you suppose there could be only
one Supreme?[6] We affirm there can be unnumbered Supremes,   370
and that one does not countervail another any more than one
eyesight countervails another . . and that men can be good or
grand only of the consciousness of their supremacy within them.
What do you think is the grandeur of storms[7] and dismember-
ments and the deadliest battles and wrecks and the wildest fury   375
of the elements and the power of the sea and the motion of
nature and of the throes of human desires and dignity and hate
and love? It is that something in the soul which says, Rage on,
Whirl[8] on, I tread master here and everywhere, Master of the
spasms of the sky and of the shatter of the sea, Master of nature   380
and passion and death, And of[9] all terror and all pain.

The American bards shall be marked for generosity and affec-
tion and for encouraging competitors . . They shall be kosmos[1]
. . without monopoly or secresy[2] . . glad to pass any thing[3] to any
one . . hungry for equals night and day. They shall not be careful   385
of riches and privilege . . . . they shall be riches and privilege
. . . . they shall perceive who the most affluent man is. The most
affluent man is he that confronts all the shows he sees by equiv-
alents out of the stronger wealth of himself. The American bard
shall delineate no class of persons nor one or two out of the   390
strata of interests nor love most nor truth most nor the soul most
nor the body most . . . . and not be for the eastern states more

---

9. In later texts, "of first class writers," (note comma). In his revisions, WW restored some of
   the commas experimentally excluded in his earlier prose.
1. Spelled "behavior" in later editions; both are correct.
2. In later editions, "for ever and ever."
3. In later texts, "great poems."
4. In 1882, read "only." The capital letter beginning each of a succession of clauses was an
   early experiment. In 1881 Whitman restored the small initial letter in most cases.
5. In later texts, spelled "inclose."
6. Lines 368–73, cf. "By Blue Ontario's Shore," 25–26.
7. Lines 373–81, cf. "To You, (whoever you are)," 42–43. The entire poem is motivated by this
   paragraph—see lines 6–17 and 33–38.
8. In later texts, "whirl."
9. In later texts, "death, and."
1. In later texts, "Kosmos," but WW was not consistent in capitalizing this word.
2. Correctly spelled as "secrecy" in later texts.
3. In later texts, read: "anything."

than the western or the northern states more than the southern.[4]

Exact science and its practical movements are no checks on the greatest poet but always his encouragement and support. The outset and remembrance are there . . there the arms that lifted him first and brace him[5] best . . . . there he returns after all his goings and comings. The sailor and traveler[6] . . the anatomist, chemist, astronomer, geologist, phrenologist, spiritualist, mathematician, historian and lexicographer are not poets, but they are the lawgivers of poets and their construction underlies the structure of every perfect poem. No matter what rises or is uttered they sent the seed of the conception of it . . . of them and by them stand the visible proofs of souls . . . . . always of their fatherstuff[7] must be begotten the sinewy races of bards. If there shall be love and content between the father and the son[8] and if the greatness of the son is the exuding of the greatness of the father there shall be love between the poet and the man of demonstrable science. In the beauty of poems are the tuft[9] and final applause of science.

Great is the faith of the flush of knowledge and of the investigation of the depths of qualities and things. Cleaving and circling here swells the soul of the poet yet it president[1] of itself always. The depths are fathomless and therefore calm. The innocence and nakedness are resumed . . . they are neither modest nor immodest. The whole theory of the special and supernatural[2] and all that was twined with it or educed out of it departs as a dream. What has ever happened . . . . what happens and whatever may or shall happen, the vital laws enclose all . . . . they[3] are sufficent[4] for any case and for all cases . . . none to be hurried or retarded . . . . any miracle[5] of affairs or persons inadmissible in the vast clear scheme where every motion and every spear of grass and the frames and spirits of men and women and all that concerns them are unspeakably perfect miracles[6] all referring to all and each distinct and in its place. It is also not consistent with the reality of the soul to admit that there is anything in the known universe more divine than men and women.

Men and women and the earth and all upon it are simply[7] to

395

400

405

410

415

420

425

---

4. In later texts, "Eastern," "Western," "Northern," and "Southern," and in general when signifying a region.
5. In later texts, "braced him."
6. Lines 398–402, cf. "Song of the Answerer," 73–74.
7. The preceding phrase and the remainder of the sentence canceled in later texts.
8. Lines 405–9, cf. "Song of the Answerer," 69–70.
9. In later texts, "are henceforth the tuft."
1. Correctly, in later texts, "is president."
2. Later texts read: "The whole theory of the supernatural."
3. Later texts read: "inclose all. They."
4. Corrected in later texts: "sufficient."
5. Later texts read: "any special miracle."
6. Lines 418–25 (see also lines 288–91), cf. "Miracles," 15–20. The poem originally contained other lines from the same locations but these were excluded in 1881.
7. Later texts cancel "simply."

be taken as they are, and the investigation of their past and 430
present and future shall be unintermitted and shall be done with
perfect candor. Upon this basis philosophy speculates ever look-
ing toward the poet,[8] ever regarding the eternal tendencies of all
toward happiness never inconsistent with what is clear to the
senses and to the soul. For the eternal tendencies of all toward 435
happiness make the only point of sane philosophy. Whatever
comprehends less than that . . . whatever is less than the laws
of light and of astronomical motion . . . or less than the laws
that follow the thief the liar the glutton and the drunkard
through this life and doubtless afterward . . . . . . or less than 440
vast stretches of time or the slow formation of density or the
patient upheaving of strata—is of no account. Whatever would
put God in a poem or system of philosophy as contending against
some being or influence is also of no account.[9] Sanity and en-
semble characterise the great master . . . spoilt in one principle 445
all is spoilt. The great master has nothing to do with miracles.
He sees health for himself in being one of the mass . . . . he
sees the hiatus in singular eminence. To the perfect shape comes
common ground. To be under the general law is great for that
is to correspond with it. The master knows that he is unspeakably 450
great and that all are unspeakably great . . . . that nothing for
instance is greater than to conceive children and bring them up
well . . . that to be[1] is just as great as to perceive or tell.

In the make of the great masters the idea of political liberty
is indispensible.[2] Liberty takes the adherence of heroes wherever 455
men and women[3] exist . . . . but never takes any adherence or
welcome from the rest more than from poets. They are the voice
and exposition of liberty. They out of ages are worthy the grand
idea . . . . to them it is confided and they must sustain it. Nothing
has precedence of it and nothing can warp or degrade it.[4] The 460
attitude of great poets is to cheer up slaves and horrify despots.
The turn of their necks, the sound of their feet, the motions of
their wrists, are full of hazard to the one and hope to the other.
Come nigh them awhile and though they neither speak or advise
you shall learn the faithful American lesson.[5] Liberty is poorly 465
served by men whose good intent is quelled from one failure or
two failures or any number of failures, or from the casual indif-
ference or ingratitude of the people, or from the sharp show of
the tushes of power, or the bringing to bear soldiers and cannon
or any penal statutes. Liberty relies upon itself, invites no one, 470

8. Later texts read "towards."
9. Lines 442–44, *cf.* "A Child's Amaze," 2–3.
1. In later texts, "*be*" (in italics).
2. Lines 454–61, *cf.* "By Blue Ontario's Shore," 154–56.
3. Later texts read: "man and woman."
4. The passage following, ending "part of the earth" (line 511), is omitted from the later texts, but thirty of the originally sixty-four lines were transposed; see following note 5.
5. Lines 461–82, revised and condensed, appear in the same order in "To A Foil'd European Revolutionaire," lines 1–8, 14–16, and 19–24. Lines 508–11 compare with the poem, lines 25–26. Fifteen lines of the poem, most important the last eight, were new composition.

promises nothing, sits in calmness and light, is positive and com-
posed, and knows no discouragement. The battle rages with
many a loud alarm and frequent advance and retreat . . . . the
enemy triumphs . . . . the prison, the handcuffs, the iron neck-
lace and anklet, the scaffold, garrote and leadballs do their work   475
. . . . the cause is asleep . . . . the strong throats are choked with
their own blood . . . . the young men drop their eyelashes toward
the ground when they pass each other . . . . and is liberty gone
out of that place? No never. When liberty goes it is not the first
to go nor the second or third to go . . it waits for all the rest to   480
go . . it is the last . . . When the memories of the old martyrs
are faded utterly away . . . . when the large names of patriots
are laughed at in the public halls from the lips of the orators
. . . . when the boys are no more christened after the same but
christened after tyrants and traitors instead . . . . when the laws   485
of the free are grudgingly permitted and laws for informers and
bloodmoney are sweet to the taste of the people . . . . when I
and you walk abroad upon the earth stung with compassion at
the sight of numberless brothers answering our equal friendship
and calling no man master—and when we are elated with noble   490
joy at the sight of slaves . . . . when the soul retires in the cool
communion of the night and surveys its experience and has
much extasy over the word and deed that put back a helpless
innocent person into the gripe of the gripers or into any cruel
inferiority . . . . when those in all parts of these states who could   495
easier realize the true American character but do not yet—when
the swarms of cringers, suckers, doughfaces, lice of politics,
planners of sly involutions for their own preferment to city of-
fices or state legislatures or the judiciary or congress or the pres-
idency, obtain a response of love and natural deference from the   500
people whether they get the offices or no . . . . when it is better
to be a bound booby and rogue in office at a high salary than
the poorest free mechanic or farmer with his hat unmoved from
his head and firm eyes and a candid and generous heart . . . .
and when servility by town or state or the federal government or   505
any oppression on a large scale or small scale can be tried on
without its own punishment following duly after in exact pro-
portion against the smallest chance of escape . . . . or rather
when all life and all the souls of men and women are discharged
from any part of the earth—then only shall the instinct of liberty   510
be discharged from that part of the earth.
  As the attributes of the poets of the kosmos concentrate in
the real body and soul[6] and in the pleasure of things they possess
the superiority of genuineness over all fiction and romance. As
they emit themselves facts are showered over with light . . . . the   515
daylight is lit with more volatile light . . . . also the deep[7] between

6. The later texts omit "and soul."
7. The later texts omit "also."

the setting and rising sun goes deeper many fold. Each precise object or condition or combination or process exhibits a beauty . . . . the multiplication table its—old age its—the carpenter's trade its—the grand-opera its . . . . the hugehulled cleanshaped[8] New-York clipper at sea under steam or full sail gleams with unmatched beauty . . . . the American circles and large harmonies of government gleam with theirs . . . . and the commonest definite intentions and actions with theirs. The poets of the kosmos advance through all interpositions and coverings and turmoils and stratagems to first principles. They are of use . . . . they dissolve poverty from its need and riches from its conceit. You large proprietor they say shall not realize or perceive more than any one else. The owner of the library is not he who holds a legal title to it having bought and paid for it. Any one and every one is owner of the library[9] who can read the same through all the varieties of tongues and subjects and styles, and in whom they enter with ease[1] and take residence and force toward paternity and maternity, and make supple and powerful and rich and large . . . .[2] These American states strong and healthy and accomplished shall receive no pleasure from violations of natural models and must not permit them. In paintings or mouldings or carvings in mineral or wood, or in the illustrations of books or newspapers,[3] or in any comic or tragic prints, or in the patterns of woven stuffs or any thing[4] to beautify rooms or furniture or costumes, or to put upon cornices or monuments or on the prows or sterns of ships, or to put anywhere before the human eye indoors or out, that which distorts honest shapes or which creates unearthly beings or places or contingencies in a nuisance and revolt. Of the human form especially it is so great it must never be made ridiculous.[5] Of ornaments to a work nothing outre can be allowed . . but those ornaments can be allowed that conform to the perfect facts of the open air and that flow out of the nature of the work and come irrepressibly from it and are necessary to the completion of the work. Most works are most beautiful without ornament . . . Exaggerations will be revenged in human physiology. Clean and vigorous children are jetted and conceived only in those communities where the models of natural forms are public every day . . . . . Great genius and the people of these states[6] must never be demeaned to romances.

520
525
530
535
540
545
550
555

---

8. The later texts read "huge-hull'd clean-shap'd."
9. After "library" the later texts read: "(indeed he or she alone is owner,) who."
1. Later texts omit the next clause "and take . . . maternity."
2. Later texts begin a new paragraph here.
3. Later texts omit the next phrase: "or in . . . prints."
4. In later texts: "anything."
5. Lines 545–57, *cf.* "Says" ("Excluded Poems"), 8–14. Stanza 6 ("Says," line 15), based on the idea of the next paragraph (following line 557) praises social candor and truth as the necessary conditions for freedom; stanza 7 reflects a theme in the following text (after line 623): the social need for the prudent governance of the mind over human choice.
6. Later editions capitalize "States" whenever the word substitutes for "United States."

As soon as histories are properly told there is no more need of romances.[7]

The great poets are also to be known[8] by the absence in them of tricks and by the justification of perfect personal candor. Then folks echo a new cheap joy[9] and a divine voice leaping from their brains: How beautiful is candor! All faults may be forgiven of him who has perfect candor. Henceforth let no man of us lie, for we have seen that openness wins the inner and outer world and that there is no single exception, and that never since our earth gathered itself in a mass have deceit or subterfuge or prevarication attracted its smallest particle or the faintest tinge of a shade—and that through the enveloping wealth and rank of a state or the whole republic of states a sneak or sly person shall be discovered and despised . . . . and that the soul has never been once fooled[1] and never can be fooled . . . . and thrift without the loving nod of the soul is only a fœtid puff . . . . and there never grew up in any of the continents of the globe nor upon any planet or satellite[2] or star, nor upon the asteroids, nor in any part of ethereal space, nor in the midst of density, nor under the fluid wet of the sea, nor in that condition which precedes the birth of babes, nor at any time during the changes of life,[3] nor in that condition that follows what we term death, nor in any stretch of abeyance or action afterward of vitality,[4] nor in any process of formation or reformation anywhere, a being whose instinct hated the truth.

Extreme caution or prudence, the soundest organic health, large hope and comparison and fondness for women and children, large alimentiveness and destructiveness and causality, with a perfect sense of the oneness of nature and the propriety of the same spirit applied to human affairs . . these are called up of the float of the brain of the world to be parts of the greatest poet from his birth out of his mother's womb and from her birth out of her mother's. Caution seldom goes far enough. It has been thought that the prudent citizen was the citizen who applied himself to solid gains and did well for himself and his family[5] and completed a lawful life without debt or crime. The greatest poet sees and admits these economies as he sees the economies of food and sleep, but has higher notions of prudence than to think he gives much when he gives a few slight attentions at the latch of the gate. The premises of the prudence of life are not the hospitality of it or the ripeness and harvest of it. Beyond the independence of a little sum laid aside for burial-money, and

560

565

570

575

580

585

590

595

7. Later editions read: "told, no more need."
8. Later texts omit "also."
9. The later editions omit the two clauses beginning here and ending "beautiful is candor."
1. In later editions, "once been."
2. Later editions omit five phrases, beginning with "or star" and ending with "wet of the sea."
3. Later editions omit the clause which follows: "nor in . . . death."
4. Later texts omit "afterward."
5. Later texts read, "and for his family," (note comma).

of a few clapboards around and shingles overhead on a lot[6] of
American soil owned, and the easy dollars that supply the year's
plain clothing and meals, the melancholy prudence of the aban-   600
donment of such a great being as a man is to the toss and pallor
of years of moneymaking with all their scorching days and icy
nights and all their stifling deceits and underhanded dodgings,
or infinitessimals of parlors, or shameless stuffing while others
starve . . and all the loss of the bloom and odor of the earth and   605
of the flowers and atmosphere and of the sea and of the true
taste of the women and men you pass or have to do with in youth
or middle age, and the issuing sickness and desperate revolt at
the close of a life without elevation or naivete,[7] and the ghastly
chatter of a death without serenity or majesty, is the great fraud   610
upon modern civilization and forethought, blotching the surface
and system which civilization undeniably drafts, and moistening
with tears the immense features it spreads with such velocity
before the reached kisses of the soul. . .[8] Still the right expla-
nation remains to be made about prudence.[9] The prudence of   615
the mere wealth and respectability of the most esteemed life
appears too faint for the eye to observe at all when little and
large alike drop quietly aside at the thought of the prudence
suitable for immortality.[1] What is wisdom[2] that fills the thinness
of a year or seventy or eighty years to wisdom spaced out by ages   620
and coming back at a certain time with strong reinforcements
and rich presents and the clear faces of wedding-guests as far as
you can look in every direction running gaily toward you? Only
the soul is of itself[3] . . . . all else has reference to what ensues.
All that a person does or thinks is of consequence.[4] Not a move   625
can a man or woman make that affects him or her in a day or a
month or any part of the direct lifetime or the hour of death but
the same affects him or her onward afterward through the in-
direct lifetime. The indirect is always as great and real as the
direct. The spirit receives from the body just as much as it gives   630
to the body. Not one name of word or deed . . not of venereal
sores or discolorations . . not the privacy of the onanist . . not
of the putrid veins of gluttons or rumdrinkers . . . not peculation

6. A small parcel or allotment of land; not as in the vernacular sense, "a great deal."
7. Correctly in later texts, "naïveté"; immediately following, WW inserted new copy in paren-
   theses: "(even if you have achiev'd a secure 10,000 a year, or election to Congress or the
   Governorship,)."
8. In the later texts a new paragraph begins here, with change of the opening phrase to "Ever
   the right."
9. Lines 614–704, *cf.* "Song of Prudence," 3–56. Of the fifty-six lines of this poem, all but the
   first two are borrowed, with appropriate intensification, from the lines of the preface, in
   approximately the same order except that lines 43–45 of the poem reflect an earlier preface
   passage, lines 320–24 (see note, line 321). The other notes citing parallel passages occur
   below at lines 619, 624, 642, and 691.
1. Lines 615–19, *cf.* "Song of Prudence," 3–4. See also line 615, note.
2. In later editions, "the wisdom"; so also, "to wisdom" becomes "to the wisdom," later in this
   sentence (*cf.* line 620).
3. Lines 623–32, *cf.* "Song of Prudence," 5–13. See also line 615, note 9.
4. The four sentences following, originally twenty-five lines, ending "returned again" (line 644),
   are omitted in later editions.

or cunning or betrayal or murder . . no serpentine poison of
those that seduce women . . not the foolish yielding of women   635
. . not prostitution . . not of any depravity of young men . . not
of the attainment of gain by discreditable means . . not any nas-
tiness of appetite . . not any harshness of officers to men or
judges to prisoners or fathers to sons or sons to fathers or of
husbands to wives or bosses to their boys . . not of greedy looks   640
or malignant wishes . . . nor any of the wiles practised by people
upon themselves . . . ever is or ever can be stamped on the
programme but it is duly realized and returned,[5] and that re-
turned in further performances . . . and they returned again. Nor
can the push of charity or personal force ever be any thing[6] else   645
than the profoundest reason, whether it bring arguments to hand
or no. No specification is necessary . . to add or subtract or divide
is in vain. Little or big, learned or unlearned, white or black,
legal or illegal, sick or well, from the first inspiration down the
windpipe to the last expiration out of it, all that a male or female   650
does that is vigorous and benevolent and clean is so much sure
profit to him or her in the unshakable order of the universe and
through the whole scope of it forever.[7] If the savage or felon
is wise it is well . . . . if the greatest poet or savan is wise it is
simply the same . . if the President or chief justice is wise it is   655
the same . . . if the young mechanic or farmer is wise it is no
more or less . . if the prostitute is wise it is no more nor less.
The interest will come round . . all will come round. All the best
actions of war and peace . . . all help given to relatives and
strangers and the poor and old and sorrowful and young children   660
and widows and the sick, and to all shunned persons . . all fur-
therance of fugitives and of the escape of slaves . . all the self-
denial that stood steady and aloof on wrecks and saw others take
the seats of the boats . . . all offering of substance or life for the
good old cause, or for a friend's sake or opinion's sake . . . all   665
pains of enthusiasts scoffed at by their neighbors . . all the vast
sweet love and precious suffering of mothers . . . all honest men
baffled in strifes recorded or unrecorded . . . . all the grandeur
and good of the few ancient nations whose fragments of annals
we inherit . . and all the good of the hundreds of far mightier   670
and more ancient nations unknown to us by name or date or
location . . . . all that was ever manfully begun, whether it suc-
ceeded or no . . . . all that has at any time been well suggested
out of the divine heart of man or by the divinity of his mouth or
by the shaping of his great hands . . and all that is well thought   675
or done this day on any part of the surface of the globe . . or on
any of the wandering stars or fixed stars by those there as we are
here . . or that is henceforth to be well thought or done by you

5. Lines 642–88, cf. "Song of Prudence," 14–42. See also line 615, note 9.
6. In later editions, "anything."
7. The six sentences following, originally forty-three lines, ending "soul is truth" (line 686),
   omitted in later editions, were merged in "Song of Prudence" (see note 5 above).

whoever you are, or by any one—these singly and wholly inured
at their time and inure now and will always to the identities from
which they sprung or shall spring . . . Did you guess any of them
lived only its moment? The world does not so exist . . no parts
palpable or impalpable so exist . . . no result exists now without
being from its long antecedent result, and that from its antece-
dent, and so backward without the farthest mentionable spot
coming a bit nearer the beginning than any other spot . . . .
Whatever satisfies the soul is truth. The prudence of the greatest
poet answers at last the craving and glut of the soul,[8] is not
contemptuous of less ways of prudence if they conform to its
ways, puts off nothing, permits no let-up for its own case or any
case, has no particular sabbath or judgment-day, divides not the
living from the dead or the righteous from the unrighteous,[9] is
satisfied with the present, matches every thought or act by its
correlative, knows[1] no possible forgiveness or deputed atone-
ment[2] . . . knows that the young man who composedly periled
his life and lost it has done exceeding well for himself, while the
man who has not periled his life and retains it to old age in riches
and ease has perhaps achieved nothing for himself worth men-
tioning . . and that only that person has no great prudence to
learn who has learnt to prefer real longlived things, and favors
body and soul the same, and perceives the indirect assuredly
following the direct, and what evil or good he does leaping on-
ward and waiting to meet him again—and who in his spirit in
any emergency whatever neither hurries or avoids death.

The direct trial of him who would be the greatest poet is to-
day.If he does not flood himself with the immediate age as with
vast oceanic tides . . . . .[3] and if he does not attract his own land
body and soul to himself and hang on its neck with incomparable
love and plunge his semitic muscle into its merits and demerits
. . . and if he be not himself the age transfigured . . . . and if to
him is not opened the eternity which gives similitude to all per-
iods and locations and processes and animate and inanimate
forms, and which is the bond of time, and rises up from its
inconceivable vagueness and infiniteness in the swimming shape
of today,[4] and is held by the ductile anchors of life,[5] and makes
the present spot the passage from what was to what shall be,
and commits itself to the representation of this wave of an hour
and this one of the sixty beautiful children of the wave—let him

---

8. The following clause, "is not . . . to its ways," is omitted in the later editions.
9. Lines 691–703, *cf.* "Song of Prudence," 46–56. See also line 615, note 9 above.
1. In later texts, "and knows."
2. This ends the paragraph in later editions, when the passage following, originally thirteen
   lines ending "hurries or avoids death" (line 703), had been merged in "Song of Prudence."
3. In later editions the three following clauses are omitted, the present sentence continuing,
   "if he be not himself" (line 710). For "semitic muscle" (line 709) read "seminal muscle" as
   in "By Blue Ontario's Shore," line 8 of canto 6, which as a whole reflects the ideas of the
   present paragraph.
4. In later texts, "shapes."
5. *Cf.* "A Noiseless Patient Spider," line 9.

merge in the general run and wait his development. . . . .
Still the final test[6] of poems or any character or work remains.   720
The prescient poet projects himself centuries ahead and judges
performer or performance after the changes of time. Does it live
through them? Does it still hold on untired? Will the same style
and the direction of genius to similar points be satisfactory now?
Has no new discovery in science or arrival at superior planes of   725
thought and judgment and behaviour fixed him or his so that
either can be looked down upon?[7] Have the marches of tens and
hundreds and thousands of years made willing detours to the
right hand and the left hand for his sake? Is he beloved long and
long after he is buried? Does the young man think often of him?   730
and the young woman think often of him? and do the middle-
aged[8] and the old think of him?

A great poem is for ages and ages in common and for all de-
grees and complexions and all departments and sects and for a
woman as much as a man and a man as much as a woman. A   735
great poem is no finish to a man or woman but rather a begin-
ning.[9] Has any one fancied he could sit at last under some due
authority and rest satisfied with explanations and realize and be
content and full? To no such terminus does the greatest poet
bring . . . he brings neither cessation or sheltered fatness and   740
ease. The touch of him tells[1] in action. Whom he takes he takes
with firm sure grasp into live regions previously unattained . . . .
thenceforward is no rest . . . . they see the space and ineffable
sheen that turn the old spots and lights into dead vacuums.[2] The
companion of him beholds the birth and progress of stars and   745
learns one of the meanings. Now there shall be a man cohered
out of tumult and chaos . . . . the elder encourages the younger
and shows him how . . . they two shall launch off fearlessly
together till the new world fits an orbit for itself and looks un-
abashed on the lesser orbits of the stars and sweeps through the   750
ceaseless rings and shall never be quiet again.

There will soon be no more priests.[3] Their work is done.[4] They
may wait awhile . . . perhaps a generation or two . . dropping off
by degrees. A superior breed shall take their place . . . . the gangs
of kosmos and prophets en masse shall take their place. A new   755
order shall arise and they shall be the priests of man, and every
man shall be his own priest.[5] The churches built under their
umbrage shall be the churches of men and women. Through the

6. In later editions this phrase begins a new paragraph.
7. The preceding sentence was omitted in later editions.
8. In later texts, read "middle-aged."
9. Lines 735–51, cf. "Song of the Answerer," 80–83.
1. In later editions, read: "of him, like Nature, tells."
2. Later editions omit the following sentence: "The companion . . . meanings."
3. Lines 752–61, cf. "By Blue Ontario's Shore," 226, and cursim, 224–30.
4. The two sentences following, "They may wait" through "take their place," are omitted in
   later editions.
5. The two sentences following, originally five lines ending "all events and things" (line 761),
   are omitted in the later editions.

divinity of themselves shall the kosmos and the new breed of
poets be interpreters of men and women and of all events and   760
things. They shall find their inspiration in real objects today,
symptoms of the past and future. . . . They shall not deign to
defend immortality or God or the perfection of things or liberty
or the exquisite beauty and reality of the soul. They shall arise
in America and be responded to from the remainder of the earth.   765
   The English language befriends the grand American expres-
sion . . . . it is brawny enough and limber and full enough. On
the tough stock of a race who through all change of circum-
stance was never without the idea of political liberty, which is
the animus of all liberty, it has attracted the terms of daintier   770
and gayer and subtler and more elegant tongues. It is the pow-
erful language of resistance . . . it is the dialect of common sense.
It is the speech of the proud and melancholy races and of all
who aspire. It is the chosen tongue to express growth faith self-
esteem freedom justice equality friendliness amplitude prudence   775
decision and courage. It is the medium that shall well nigh ex-
press the inexpressible.
   No great literature nor any like style of behaviour or oratory
or social intercourse or household arrangements or public insti-
tutions or the treatment by bosses of employed people, nor ex-   780
ecutive detail or detail of the army or navy, nor spirit of legis-
lation or courts or police or tuition or architecture or songs or
amusements[6] or the costumes of young men, can long elude the
jealous and passionate instinct of American standards. Whether
or no the sign appears from the mouths of the people,   785
it throbs a live interrogation in every freeman's and freewoman's
heart after that which passes by, or this built to remain. Is it
uniform with my country? Are its disposals without ignominious
distinctions? Is it for the evergrowing communes of brothers and
lovers, large, well-united, proud beyond the old models,[7] gener-   790
ous beyond all models? Is it something grown fresh out of the
fields or drawn from the sea for use to me today here? I know
that what answers for me an American must[8] answer for any
individual or nation that serves for a part of my materials. Does
this answer?[9] or is it without reference to universal needs? or   795
sprung of the needs of the less developed society of special
ranks? or old needs of pleasure overlaid by modern science and
forms? Does this acknowledge liberty with audible and absolute
acknowledgment, and set slavery at nought for life and death?
Will it help breed one goodshaped and wellhung man, and a   800
woman to be his perfect and independent mate? Does it improve

6. The words that follow, "or the costumes of young men," are omitted from the later texts.
7. In later editions an added comma modifies the meaning: "well united, proud, beyond the old models," (cf. "well-united").
8. In later editions, read: "an American, in Texas, Ohio, Canada, must."
9. The eight clauses following, originally nine lines, ending "improve manners?" (line 802), are omitted in the later editions.

manners? Is it for the nursing of the young of the republic? Does it solve[1] readily with the sweet milk of the nipples of the breasts of the mother of many children?[2] Has it too the old ever-fresh forbearance and impartiality? Does it look with the same love on the last born and on those hardening toward stature, and on the errant, and on those who disdain all strength of assault outside of their own? 805

The poems distilled from other poems will probably pass away.[3] The coward will surely pass away. The expectation of the vital and great can only be satisfied by the demeanor of the vital and great. The swarms of the polished deprecating and reflectors and the polite float off and leave no remembrance.[4] America prepares with composure and goodwill for the visitors that have sent word. It is not intellect that is to be their warrant and welcome. The talented, the artist, the ingenious, the editor, the statesman, the erudite . . they are not[5] unappreciated . . they fall in their place and do their work. The soul of the nation also does its work.[6] No disguise can pass on it . . no disguise can conceal from it. It rejects none, it permits all. Only toward as good as itself and toward the like of itself[7] will it advance half-way. An individual is as superb as a nation when he has the qualities which make a superb nation. The soul of the largest and wealthiest and proudest nation may well go half-way to meet that of its poets.[8] The signs are effectual. There is no fear of mistake. If the one is true the other is true. The proof of a poet is that his country absorbs him as affectionately as he has absorbed it. 810 815 820 825

Prefatory Letter to Ralph Waldo Emerson—
Leaves of Grass 1856

To Emerson's letter in praise of *Leaves of Grass,* Whitman replied a year later, in an "open letter" (published but not sent) that was virtually a preface to his *Leaves of Grass* of 1856, in which it appeared in the appendix following Emerson's letter, below:

1. *Cf.* "dissolve," not present but inevitably suggested. In the context of the entire paragraph the solution in "the sweet milk . . . of the mother of many children" is the ideas of nature and liberty.
2. The six sentences following were omitted from the later texts—originally thirteen lines, including the first six lines of the new paragraph, ending "leave no remembrance" (line 813). But see following note 3.
3. Lines 809–27, *cf.* "By Blue Ontario's Shore," 213–19.
4. In the later texts, the last paragraph of the preface begins here, the earlier lines having been transferred (see preceding notes 2 and 3).
5. In later editions, "erudite, are not."
6. The sentence following is omitted from the later texts.
7. The preceding phrase in later editions reads: "Only toward the like of itself."
8. In the later editions, the preface ends here; the following four sentences were excluded.

Emerson to Whitman, 1855[1]

Concord, Massachusetts, *21 July, 1855.*

Dear Sir—I am not blind to the worth of the wonderful gift of "Leaves of Grass." I find it the most extraordinary piece of wit and wisdom that America has yet contributed. I am very happy in reading it, as great power makes us happy. It meets the demand I am always making of what seemed the sterile and stingy nature, as if too much handiwork, or too much lymph in the temperament, were making our western wits fat and mean.

I give you joy of your free and brave thought. I have great joy in it. I find incomparable things said incomparably well, as they must be. I find the courage of treatment which so delights us, and which large perception only can inspire.

I greet you at the beginning of a great career, which yet must have had a long foreground somewhere, for such a start. I rubbed my eyes a little, to see if this sunbeam were no illusion; but the solid sense of the book is a sober certainty. It has the best merits, namely, of fortifying and encouraging.

I did not know until I last night saw the book advertised in a newspaper that I could trust the name as real and available for a post-office. I wish to see my benefactor, and have felt much like striking my tasks, and visiting New York to pay you my respects.

R. W. Emerson.

1. Whitman's text of this letter shows two negligible departures in punctuation from the MS (Feinberg). These accidentals stand as in Whitman's text. It is not entirely clear that the MS intends a third paragraph beginning at "I greet," but logic is on the side of retaining it. In all cases, Emerson writes the ampersand instead of spelling "and," but this Norton Critical Edition follows Whitman's text in this respect, and also in showing the place and date on one line, without abbreviation and with standard punctuation.

The open letter to Emerson, which Whitman included in his second *LG* edition (1856), may be regarded as a preface to that edition. It is astonishing that it has not before been presented in this capacity. Excepting the brief, epistolary address to Emerson at the beginning and end, in its magnitude and style this is evidently intended for an essay; its substance is purposefully related to the poems of the volume. Whitman included this letter, which Emerson had not seen, in the appendix, where also, and without Emerson's authorization, he associated it with the now-famous letter that Emerson had sent him a year before on reading Whitman's gift copy of the first *LG* volume. In fact, Whitman had already made public Emerson's letter of praise by joyfully showing it to friends, by allowing Dana, the editor, to publish it without consulting Emerson in the *New York Tribune*, and by pasting clippings of the letter in presentation copies of *LG* to Longfellow and others. Finally, on the spine of the 1856 volume, he displayed Emerson's golden words, "I greet you at the beginning of a great career." Despite its familiarity, the present edition lets Emerson's letter stand as it was in the 1856 edition, preceding Whitman's "Letter to Ralph Waldo Emerson." This preface-letter is a penetrating and vivacious statement of Whitman's objectives as poet in his first phase of creativity, and of his theories of man, nature, and democratic society. It is also his best statement of his demand for "an avowed, empowered, unabashed development of sex. The only salvation" against the threatening deterioration of democratic individualism and society was for the creative artist and thinker to combat the prevailing "infidelism" by asserting "the eternal decency of the amativeness of Nature, the motherhood of all."

Whitman to Emerson, 1856

Brooklyn, *August, 1856.*

Here are thirty-two Poems,[2] which I send you, dear Friend and Master, not having found how I could satisfy myself with sending any usual acknowledgment of your letter. The first edition, on which you mailed me that till now unanswered letter, was twelve poems—I printed a thousand copies, and they readily sold;[3] these thirty-two Poems I stereotype, to print several thousand copies of. I much enjoy making poems. Other work I have set for myself to do, to meet people and The States face to face, to confront them with an American rude tongue;[4] but the work of my life is making poems. I keep on till I make a hundred, and then several hundred—perhaps a thousand. The way is clear to me. A few years, and the average annual call for my Poems is ten or twenty thousand copies[5]—more, quite likely. Why should I hurry or compromise? In poems or in speeches I say the word or two that has got to be said, adhere to the body, step with the countless common footsteps, and remind every man and woman of something.

Master, I am a man who has perfect faith. Master,[6] we have not come through centuries, caste, heroisms, fables, to halt in this land today. Or I think it is to collect a ten-fold impetus that any halt is made. As nature, inexorable, onward, resistless, impassive amid the threats and screams of disputants, so America. Let all defer. Let all attend respectfully the leisure of These States, their politics, poems, literature, manners, and their free-handed modes of training their own offspring. Their own comes, just matured, certain, numerous and capable enough, with egotistical tongues, with sinewed wrists, seizing openly what belongs to them. They resume Personality, too long left out of mind. Their shadows are projected in employments, in books, in the cities, in trade; their feet are on the flights of the steps of the Capitol; they dilate, a larger, brawnier, more candid, more democratic, lawless, positive native to The States, sweet-bodied, completer, dauntless, flowing, masterful, beard-faced, new race of men.

2. I.e., twelve from the 1855 first edition and twenty new poems in *LG* 1856.
3. The facts are not entirely ascertainable, and variously reported (See C. J. Furness, *Introduction, Leaves of Grass, 1855,* New York, 1939; and Allen, 150–54). Whitman plausibly told Traubel in 1888 that when he wrote to Emerson many copies had been consigned to dealers but sales reports had not been made. It is likely that from 800 to 1000 copies were printed, of which about 300 were clothbound; that very few were sold; that copies were given to influential writers and reviewers, and the rest "remaindered" unbound or in paper covers. The rarity of the 1856 edition does not suggest that "several thousand" copies were run off, even from stereotype plates.
4. Whitman's mission called him to the public forum but his efforts, early and late, were not successful. Some critics find the effects of oratory in his written style.
5. He should have known that only Longfellow among American poets then approached these sales figures.
6. *Cf.* first paragraph. The term, as applied to the teacher, writer, or artist, did not suggest servility. Emerson was indeed the "Master" of the school of literary idealism; perhaps WW is too lavish, but see the last two paragraphs of the letter.

Swiftly, on limitless foundations, the United States too are 35
founding a literature. It is all as well done, in my opinion, as
could be practicable. Each element here is in condition. Every
day I go among the people of Manhattan Island, Brooklyn, and
other cities, and among the young men, to discover the spirit of
them, and to refresh myself. These are to be attended to; I am 40
myself more drawn here than to those authors, publishers, im-
portations, reprints, and so forth. I pass coolly through those,
understanding them perfectly well, and that they do the indis-
pensable service, outside of men like me, which nothing else
could do. In poems, the young men of The States shall be rep- 45
resented, for they out-rival the best of the rest of the earth.

The lists of ready-made literature which America inherits by the
mighty inheritance of the English language—all the rich reper-
toire of traditions, poems, histories, metaphysics, plays, classics,
translations, have made, and still continue, magnificent prepara- 50
tions for that other plainly signified literature, to be our own, to
be electric, fresh, lusty, to express the full-sized body, male and
female—to give the modern meanings of things, to grow up
beautiful, lasting, commensurate with America, with all the pas-
sions of home, with the inimitable sympathies of having been boys 55
and girls together, and of parents who were with our parents.

What else can happen The States,[7] even in their own despite?
That huge English flow, so sweet, so undeniable, has done in-
calculable good here, and is to be spoken of for its own sake
with generous praise and with gratitude. Yet the price The States 60
have had to lie under for the same has not been a small price.
Payment prevails; a nation can never take the issues of the needs
of other nations for nothing. America, grandest of lands in the
theory of its politics, in popular reading, in hospitality, breadth,
animal beauty, cities, ships, machines, money, credit, collapses 65
quick as lightning at the repeated, admonishing, stern words,
Where are any mental expressions from you, beyond what you
have copied or stolen? Where the born throngs of poets, literats,
orators, you promised? Will you but tag after other nations? They
struggled long for their literature, painfully working their way, 70
some with deficient languages, some with priest-craft, some in
the endeavor just to live—yet achieved for their times, works,
poems, perhaps the only solid consolation left to them through
ages afterward of shame and decay. You are young, have the
perfectest of dialects, a free press, a free government, the world 75
forwarding its best to be with you. As justice has been strictly
done to you, from this hour do strict justice to yourself. Strangle
the singers who will not sing you loud and strong. Open the
doors of The West. Call for new great masters to comprehend
new arts, new perfections, new wants. Submit to the most robust 80
bard till he remedy your barrenness. Then you will not need to

7. Presumably, "to The States."

adopt the heirs of others; you will have true heirs, begotten of yourself, blooded with your own blood.

With composure I see such propositions, seeing more and more every day of the answers that serve. Expressions do not yet serve, for sufficient reasons; but that is getting ready, beyond what the earth has hitherto known, to take home the expressions when they come, and to identify them with the populace of The States, which is the schooling cheaply procured by any outlay any number of years. Such schooling The States extract from the swarms of reprints, and from the current authors and editors. Such service and extract are done after enormous, reckless, free modes, characteristic of The States. Here are to be attained results never elsewhere thought possible; the modes are very grand too. The instincts of the American people are all perfect, and tend to make heroes. It is a rare thing in a man here to understand The States.

All current nourishments to literature serve. Of authors and editors I do not know how many there are in The States, but there are thousands, each one building his or her step to the stairs by which giants shall mount. Of the twenty-four modern mammoth two-double, three-double, and four-double cylinder presses now in the world, printing by steam, twenty-one of them are in These States. The twelve thousand large and small shops for dispensing books and newspapers—the same number of public libraries, any one of which has all the reading wanted to equip a man or woman for American reading—the three thousand different newspapers, the nutriment of the imperfect ones coming in just as usefully as any—the story papers, various, full of strong-flavored romances, widely circulated—the one-cent and two-cent journals—the political ones, no matter what side—the weeklies in the country—the sporting and pictorial papers—the monthly magazines, with plentiful imported feed—the sentimental novels, numberless copies of them—the low-priced flaring tales, adventures, biographies—all are prophetic; all waft rapidly on. I see that they swell wide, for reasons. I am not troubled at the movement of them, but greatly pleased. I see plying shuttles, the active ephemeral myriads of books also, faithfully weaving the garments of a generation of men, and a generation of women, they do not perceive or know. What a progress popular reading and writing has made in fifty years! What a progress fifty years hence! The time is at hand when inherent literature will be a main part of These States, as general and real as steampower, iron, corn, beef, fish. First-rate American persons are to be supplied. Our perennial materials for fresh thoughts, histories, poems, music, orations, religions, recitations, amusements, will then not be disregarded, any more than our perennial fields, mines, rivers, seas. Certain things are established, and are immovable; in those things millions of years stand justified. The mothers and fathers of whom modern centuries have come, have not existed for nothing; they too had brains and hearts. Of course all literature, in all nations and years, will share marked attributes in common, as we all, of all ages, share the common human attributes. America is to be kept coarse and broad. What is to be done is to withdraw from precedents, and be directed to men and women—also to The States in their federalness; for the union of the parts of the body is not more necessary to their life than the union of These States is to their life.

A profound person can easily know more of the people than they know of themselves. Always waiting untold in the souls of the armies of common people, is stuff better than anything that can possibly appear in the leadership of the same. That gives final verdicts. In every department of These States, he who travels with a coterie, or with selected persons, or with imitators, or with infidels, or with the owners of slaves, or with that which is ashamed of the body of a man, or with that which is ashamed of the body of a woman, or with any thing less than the bravest and the openest, travels straight for the slopes of dissolution. The genius of all foreign literature is clipped and cut small, compared to our genius, and is essentially insulting to our usages, and to the organic compacts of These States. Old forms, old poems, majestic and proper in their own lands here in this land are exiles; the air here is very strong. Much that stands well and has a little enough place provided for it in the small scales of European kingdoms, empires, and the like, here stands haggard, dwarfed, ludicrous, or has no place little enough provided for it. Authorities, poems, models, laws, names, imported into America, are useful to America today to destroy them, and so move disencumbered to great works, great days.

Just so long, in our country or any country, as no revolutionists advance, and are backed by the people, sweeping off the swarms of routine representatives, officers in power, book-makers, teachers, ecclesiastics, politicians, just so long, I perceive, do they who are in power fairly represent that country, and remain of use, probably of very great use. To supersede them, when it is the pleasure of These States, full provision is made; and I say the time has arrived[8] to use it with a strong hand. Here also the souls of the armies have not only overtaken the souls of the officers, but passed on, and left the souls of the officers behind out of sight many weeks' journey; and the souls of the armies now go en-masse without officers. Here also formulas, glosses, blanks, minutiæ, are choking the throats of the spokesmen to death. Those things most listened for, certainly those are the things

8. The period since 1847 had been increasingly characterized by the futile effort to balance slavery and free-soil forces; by the disruption of the Democratic Party, which lost WW his editorship of the *Brooklyn Eagle*; by the Mexican War, desperate compromises, the fateful treachery of the Kansas-Nebraska legislation, the resulting "bloody Kansas" strife, and the generally weak, vacillating leaders in Washington. See David S. Reynolds's article in the Criticism section of this Norton Critical Edition.

least said. There is not a single History of the World. There
is not one of America, or of the organic compacts of These   175
States, or of Washington, or of Jefferson, nor of Language, nor
any Dictionary of the English Language. There is no great au-
thor; every one has demeaned himself to some etiquette or some
impotence. There is no manhood or life-power in poems; there
are shoats and geldings more like. Or literature will be dressed 180
up, a fine gentleman, distasteful to our instincts, foreign to our
soil. Its neck bends right and left wherever it goes. Its costumes
and jewelry prove how little it knows Nature. Its flesh is soft; it
shows less and less of the indefinable hard something that is
Nature. Where is any thing but the shaved Nature of synods and 185
schools? Where is a savage and luxuriant man? Where is an over-
seer? In lives, in poems, in codes of law, in Congress, in tuitions,
theatres, conversations, argumentations, not a single head lifts
itself clean out, with proof that it is their master, and has sub-
ordinated them to itself, and is ready to try their superiors. None 190
believes in These States, boldly illustrating them in himself. Not
a man faces round at the rest with terrible negative voice, refus-
ing all terms to be bought off from his own eye-sight, or from
the soul that he is, or from friendship, or from the body that he
is, or from the soil and sea. To creeds, literature, art, the army, 195
the navy, the executive, life is hardly proposed, but the sick and
dying are proposed to cure the sick and dying. The churches are
one vast lie; the people do not believe them, and they do not
believe themselves; the priests are continually telling what they
know well enough is not so, and keeping back what they know 200
is so. The spectacle is a pitiful one. I think there can never be
again upon the festive earth more bad-disordered persons delib-
erately taking seats, as of late in These States, at the heads of
the public tables—such corpses' eyes for judges—such a rascal
and thief in the Presidency.[9]   205

Up to the present, as helps best, the people, like a lot of large
boys, have no determined tastes, are quite unaware of the gran-
deur of themselves, and of their destiny, and of their immense
strides—accept with voracity whatever is presented them in nov-
els, histories, newspapers, poems, schools, lectures, every thing. 210
Pretty soon, through these and other means, their development
makes the fibre that is capable of itself, and will assume deter-
mined tastes. The young men will be clear what they want, and
will have it. They will follow none except him whose spirit leads

---

9. "Rascal and thief" could have been Whitman's terms for several recent presidents. However
Franklin Pierce, president since 1853, the instrument of the proslavery party's treacherous
compromises (see preceding note 8), was supplanted in June 1856 as the Democratic can-
didate by James Buchanan, whose platform promised even stronger support of the proslavery
policies. In this letter of August 1856, WW could have been referring to either or both. In
The Eighteenth Presidency, Whitman's unpublished campaign pamphlet, he excoriated the
current and gigantic corruptions but did not openly support any candidate. Those "corpse's
eyes," the "judges," he had just accused of conniving to subvert the penalties for the slave-
traders of New York City in an article (*Life Illustrated*, August 2). See Allen, 191–99.

them in the like spirit with themselves. Any such man will be   215
welcome as the flowers of May. Others will be put out without
ceremony. How much is there anyhow, to the young men of
These States, in a parcel of helpless dandies, who can neither
fight, work, shoot, ride, run, command—some of them devout,
some quite insane, some castrated—all second-hand, or third,   220
fourth, or fifth hand—waited upon by waiters, putting not this
land first, but always other lands first, talking of art, doing the
most ridiculous things for fear of being called ridiculous, smirk-
ing and skipping along, continually taking off their hats—no one
behaving, dressing, writing, talking, loving, out of any natural   225
and manly tastes of his own, but each one looking cautiously to
see how the rest behave, dress, write, talk, love—pressing the
noses of dead books upon themselves and upon their country—
favoring no poets, philosophs, literats here, but dog-like danglers
at the heels of the poets, philosophs, literats, of enemies' lands   230
—favoring mental expressions, models of gentlemen and ladies,
social habitudes in These States, to grow up in sneaking defiance
of the popular substratums of The States? Of course they and
the likes of them can never justify the strong poems of America.
Of course no feed of theirs is to stop and be made welcome to   235
muscle the bodies, male and female, for Manhattan Island,
Brooklyn, Boston, Worcester, Hartford, Portland, Montreal, De-
troit, Buffalo, Cleaveland, Milwaukee, St. Louis, Indianapolis,
Chicago, Cincinnati, Iowa City, Philadelphia, Baltimore, Ra-
leigh, Savannah, Charleston, Mobile, New Orleans, Galveston,   240
Brownsville, San Francisco, Havana, and a thousand equal cities,
present and to come. Of course what they and the likes of them
have been used for, draws toward its close, after which they will
all be discharged, and not one of them will ever be heard of any
more.   245
    America, having duly conceived, bears out of herself offspring
of her own to do the workmanship wanted. To freedom, to
strength, to poems, to personal greatness, it is never permitted
to rest, not a generation or part of a generation. To be ripe be-
yond further increase is to prepare to die. The architects of   250
These States laid their foundations, and passed to further
spheres. What they laid is a work done; as much more remains.
Now are needed other architects, whose duty is not less difficult,
but perhaps more difficult. Each age forever needs architects.
America is not finished,[1] perhaps never will be; now America is   255
a divine true sketch. There are Thirty-Two States sketched—the
population thirty millions. In a few years there will be Fifty
States. Again in a few years there will be A Hundred States, the
population hundreds of millions, the freshest and freest of men.

1. It is often overlooked that Whitman's poetic vision of America was prophetic and that (see
   lines 160–333) he was at the same time deeply disturbed by the immediate corruption and
   violent actualities of public life and by the psychic immaturity in private life that seemed to
   determine the course of this disastrous mid-century in America.

Of course such men stand to nothing less than the freshest and freest expression. ₂₆₀

Poets here, literats here, are to rest on organic different bases from other countries; not a class set apart, circling only in the circle of themselves, modest and pretty, desperately scratching for rhymes, pallid with white paper, shut off, aware of the old pictures and traditions of the race, but unaware of the actual race around them—not breeding in and in among each other till they all have the scrofula. Lands of ensemble, bards of ensemble! Walking freely out from the old traditions, as our politics has walked out, American poets and literats recognize nothing behind them superior to what is present with them—recognize with joy the sturdy living forms of the men and women of These States, the divinity of sex, the perfect eligibility of the female with the male, all The States, liberty and equality, real articles, the different trades, mechanics, the young fellows of Manhattan Island, customs, instincts, slang, Wisconsin, Georgia, the noble Southern heart, the hot blood, the spirit that will be nothing less than master, the filibuster spirit, the Western man, native-born perceptions, the eye for forms, the perfect models of made things, the wild smack of freedom, California, money, electric-telegraphs, free-trade, iron and the iron mines—recognize without demur those splendid resistless black poems, the steam-ships of the sea-board states, and those other resistless splendid poems, the locomotives, followed through the interior states by trains of rail-road cars.

A word remains to be said, as of one ever present, not yet permitted to be acknowledged, discarded or made dumb by literature, and the results apparent.[2] To the lack of an avowed, empowered, unabashed development of sex, (the only salvation for the same,) and to the fact of speakers and writers fraudulently assuming as always dead what every one knows to be always alive, is attributable the remarkable non-personality and indistinctness of modern productions in books, art, talk; also that in the scanned lives of men and women most of them appear to have been for some time past of the neuter gender; and also the stinging fact that in orthodox society today, if the dresses were changed, the men might easily pass for women and the women for men.

Infidelism usurps most with fœtid polite face; among the rest infidelism about sex. By silence or obedience the pens of savans, poets, historians, biographers, and the rest, have long connived at the filthy law, and books enslaved to it,[3] that what makes the manhood of a man, that sex, womanhood, maternity, desires,

---

2. For comment on the importance of the following discourse, see the first note to this letter, above, and see the introduction to this volume.
3. I.e., by laws censoring literature; in 1881 Whitman's final revision of the canon *LG* was to be withdrawn in Boston as the result of Comstockery (i.e., prudish censorship, thus named after Anthony Comstock, first enforcer of heavy censorship in the U.S.).

lusty animations, organs, acts, are unmentionable and to be
ashamed of, to be driven to skulk out of literature with whatever   305
belongs to them. This filthy law has to be repealed—it stands in
the way of great reforms. Of women just as much as men, it is
the interest that there should not be infidelism about sex, but
perfect faith. Women in These States approach the day of that
organic equality with men, without which, I see, men cannot   310
have organic equality among themselves. This empty dish, gal-
lantry, will then be filled with something. This tepid wash, this
diluted deferential love, as in songs, fictions, and so forth, is
enough to make a man vomit; as to manly friendship, everywhere
observed in The States, there is not the first breath of it to be   315
observed in print. I say that the body of a man or woman, the
main matter, is so far quite unexpressed in poems; but that the
body is to be expressed, and sex is. Of bards for These States, if
it come to a question, it is whether they shall celebrate in poems
the eternal decency of the amativeness of Nature, the mother-   320
hood of all, or whether they shall be the bards of the fashionable
delusion of the inherent nastiness of sex, and of the feeble and
querulous modesty of deprivation. This is important in poems,
because the whole of the other expressions of a nation are but
flanges out of its great poems. To me, henceforth, that theory of   325
any thing, no matter what, stagnates in its vitals, cowardly and
rotten, while it cannot publicly accept, and publicly name, with
specific words, the things on which all existence, all souls, all
realization, all decency, all health, all that is worth being here
for, all of woman and of man, all beauty, all purity, all sweetness,   330
all friendship, all strength, all life, all immortality depend. The
courageous soul, for a year or two to come, may be proved by
faith in sex, and by disdaining concessions.

　　To poets and literats—to every woman and man, today or any
day, the conditions of the present, needs, dangers, prejudices,   335
and the like, are the perfect conditions on which we are here,
and the conditions for wording the future with undissuadable
words. These States, receivers of the stamina of past ages and
lands, initiate the outlines of repayment a thousand fold. They
fetch the American great masters, waited for by old worlds and   340
new, who accept evil as well as good, ignorance as well as eru-
dition, black as soon as white, foreign-born materials as well as
home-born, reject none, force discrepancies into range, surround
the whole, concentrate them on present periods and places,
show the application to each and any one's body and soul, and   345
show the true use of precedents. Always America will be agitated
and turbulent. This day it is taking shape, not to be less so, but
to be more so, stormily, capriciously, on native principles, with
such vast proportions of parts! As for me, I love screaming, wres-
tling, boiling-hot days.   350

　　Of course, we shall have a national character, an identity. As
it ought to be, and as soon as it ought to be, it will be. That,

with much else, takes care of itself, is a result, and the cause of greater results. With Ohio, Illinois, Missouri, Oregon—with the states around the Mexican sea—with cheerfully welcomed im- 355 migrants from Europe, Asia, Africa—with Connecticut, Vermont, New Hampshire, Rhode Island—with all varied interests, facts, beliefs, parties, genesis—there is being fused a determined character, fit for the broadest use for the freewomen and freemen of The States, accomplished and to be accomplished, with- 360 out any exception whatever—each indeed free, each idiomatic, as becomes live states and men, but each adhering to one enclosing general form of politics, manners, talk, personal style, as the plenteous varieties of the race adhere to one physical form. Such character is the brain and spine to all, including literature, 365 including poems. Such character, strong, limber, just, openmouthed, American-blooded, full of pride, full of ease, of passionate friendliness, is to stand compact upon that vast basis of the supremacy of Individuality—that new moral American continent without which, I see, the physical continent remained in- 370 complete, may-be a carcass, a bloat—that newer America, answering face to face with The States, with ever-satisfying and ever-unsurveyable seas and shores.

Those shores you found. I say you have led The States there —have led Me there. I say that none has ever done, or ever can 375 do, a greater deed for The States, than your deed. Others may line out the lines, build cities, work mines, break up farms; it is yours to have been the original true Captain who put to sea, intuitive, positive, rendering the first report, to be told less by any report, and more by the mariners of a thousand bays, in each 380 tack of their arriving and departing, many years after you.

Receive, dear Master, these statements and assurances through me, for all the young men, and for an earnest that we know none before you, but the best following you; and that we demand to take your name into our keeping, and that we un- 385 derstand what you have indicated, and find the same indicated in ourselves, and that we will stick to it and enlarge upon it through These States.

Walt Whitman.

Preface 1872—As a Strong Bird on Pinions Free

The impetus and ideas urging me, for some years past, to an
utterance, or attempt at utterance, of New World songs, and an
epic of Democracy, having already had their published[1] expres-
sion, as well as I can expect to give it, in LEAVES OF GRASS, the
present and any future pieces from me are really but the sur-   5
plusage forming after that Volume, or the wake eddying behind
it. I fulfilled in that an imperious conviction, and the commands
of my nature as total and irresistible as those which make the
sea flow, or the globe revolve. But of this Supplementary Vol-
ume, I confess I am not so certain.[2] Having from early manhood   10
abandoned the business pursuits and applications usual in my
time and country, and obediently yielded myself up ever since to
the impetus mentioned, and to the work of expressing those
ideas, it may be that mere habit has got dominion of me, when
there is no real need of saying any thing further.[3] . . . But what 15
is life but an experiment? and mortality but an exercise? with
reference to results beyond. And so shall my poems be. If in-
complete here, and superfluous there, n'importe—the earnest
trial and persistent exploration shall at least be mine, and other
success failing, shall be success enough. I have been more anx-   20
ious, anyhow, to suggest the songs of vital endeavor, and manly
evolution, and furnish something for races of outdoor athletes,
than to make perfect rhymes, or reign in the parlors. I ventured

---

Preface 1872: Appeared in *Specimen Days and Collect,* as "PREFACE, 1872 / *to 'As a Strong
Bird on Pinions Free,'* / (now *'Thou Mother with thy Equal Brood' in permanent ed'n)*"; so
also in later collections, *CPP,* and *CPW.* The volume of 1872 contained six smaller poems
besides the title poem, which WW read, on the invitation of the students, at the Dartmouth
Commencement, June 26, 1872. This preface is especially interesting because it discloses
that WW then felt that he had perhaps accomplished what he intended in *Leaves of Grass*
and that he proposed a second, companion volume, to deal poetically with "democratic
nationality"—to which this title poem, at least, might ultimately belong (see further footnotes
below). He included the entire volume as one of the supplements bound up in his miscellany
Two Rivulets (1876). The present text is that of 1872. Many revisions appear in the *SDC*
text, which was newly stereotyped, nearly all of them in punctuation and typography, in-
cluding the reduction of capital letters, and the normalizing of the ampersand and points of
suspension. The present footnotes show only the verbal or other alterations affecting mean-
ing or emphasis. A collation of all texts, in *Prose Works 1892,* vol. II of *Collected Writings,*
shows that later editions of this preface were printed from the *SDC* plates, without change,
in *SDC* Glasgow (1883), *CPP,* and *CPW.*

1. In *SDC* and later collections, read "publish'd." During the later period, Whitman's revisions
   and new composition showed a characteristic elision of the unvoiced "e" in the terminal "ed"
   of past-tense verbs and verbals (*cf.* preceding note above).
2. I.e., whether this 1872 volume was "surplusage" of *LG* (considered as completed) or whether
   it foreshadowed a new companion volume on "democratic nationalism" (*cf.* the last two
   paragraphs of this preface). Actually, *Passage to India* (1871) was WW's last distinguished
   addition to the *Leaves,* of which the poems then in print included almost all his destined
   major work. His physical decline and diminution of creative power began with his stroke of
   paralysis and his mother's death (1873). See following note on "any thing further."
3. He added a few major poems—e.g., "Song of the Redwood Tree," "Prayer of Columbus,"
   and numerous small but genuine lyrics; also, in 1881, his final revision and reorganization
   of the *LG* poems added much to the meaning of the work as a whole. Thereafter he revised
   and collected his prose works and added one master work, "A Backward Glance . . ." (*q.v.,*
   above).

from the beginning, my own way, taking chances—and would
keep on venturing.   25

   I will therefore not conceal from any persons, known or un-
known to me, who take interest in the matter, that I have the
ambition of devoting yet a few years to poetic composition. . . .
The mighty present age! To absorb, and express in poetry, any
thing of it—of its world—America—cities and States—the   30
years, the events of our Nineteenth Century—the rapidity of
movement—the violent contrasts, fluctuations of light and
shade, of hope and fear—the entire revolution made by science
in the poetic method—these great new underlying facts and new
ideas rushing and spreading everywhere;—Truly a mighty age!   35
As if in some colossal drama, acted again like those of old, under
the open sun, the Nations of our time, and all the characteristics
of Civilization, seem hurrying, stalking across, flitting from wing
to wing, gathering, closing up, toward some long-prepared, most
tremendous denouement. Not to conclude the infinite scenas[4]   40
of the race's life and toil and happiness and sorrow, but haply
that the boards be cleared from oldest, worst incumbrances,[5]
accumulations, and Man resume the eternal play anew, and un-
der happier, freer auspices. . . . To me, the United States are
important because, in this colossal drama, they are unquestion- 45
ably designated for the leading parts, for many a century to
come. In them History and Humanity seem to seek to culmi-
nate.[6] Our broad areas are even now the busy theatre of plots,
passions, interests, and suspended problems, compared to which
the intrigues of the past of Europe, the wars of dynasties, the   50
scope of kings and kingdoms, and even the development of peo-
ples, as hitherto, exhibit scales of measurement comparatively
narrow and trivial. And on these areas of ours, as on a stage,
sooner or later, something like an *eclaircissement* of all the past
civilization of Europe and Asia is probably to be evolved.   55

   The leading parts. . . . Not to be acted, emulated here, by us
again, that role till now foremost in History—Not to become a
conqueror Nation, or to achieve the glory of mere military, or
diplomatic, or commercial superiority—but to become the grand
Producing Land[7] of nobler Men and Women—of copious races,   60
cheerful, healthy, tolerant, free—To become the most friendly
Nation, (the United States indeed,)—the modern composite
Nation, formed from all, with room for all, welcoming all
immigrants—accepting the work of our own interior develop-

4. Latin: "scenes." *Cf.* line 36, "colossal drama . . . like those of old."
5. Then an allowable spelling.
6. WW's faith in the "manifest destiny" of the United States was fortified by his acceptance of
   the ancient and persistent dogma that in the perpetual changes there is a selection of the
   good, which perhaps spirals toward an ultimate perfection. See, especially, the "crowning
   stage" (two paragraphs below) and WW's note thereon.
7. The initial capital for emphasis was generally absent in later editions.

ment, as the work fitly filling ages and ages to come;—the lead-   65
ing Nation of peace, but neither ignorant nor incapable of being
the leading Nation of war;—not the Man's Nation only, but the
Woman's Nation—a land of splendid mothers, daughters, sis-
ters, wives.

Our America to-day I consider in many respects as but indeed   70
a vast seething mass of *materials*, ampler, better, (worse also,)
than previously known—eligible to be used to carry toward[8] its
crowning stage, and build for good the great Ideal Nationality of
the future, the Nation of the Body and the Soul,[9]—no limit here
to land, help, opportunities, mines, products, demands, supplies,   75
&c.;—with (I think) our political organization, National, State,
and Municipal, permanently established, as far ahead as we can
calculate—but, so far, no social, literary, religious, or esthetic
organizations, consistent with our politics, or becoming to us—
which organizations can only come, in time, through native   80
schools or teachers of great Democratic Ideas,[1] Religion—
through Science, which now, like a new sunrise, ascending, be-
gins to illuminate all—and through our own begotten Poets and
Literatuses. . . . (The moral of a late well-written book on Civi-
lization seems to be that the only real foundation-walls and   85
basis[2]—and also *sine qua non* afterward—of true and full Civi-
lization, is the eligibility and certainty of boundless products for
feeding, clothing, sheltering every body[3]—perennial fountains of
physical and domestic comfort, with inter-communication, and
with civil and ecclesiastical freedom;—and that then the esthetic   90
and mental business will take care of itself. . . . Well, the United
States have established this basis, and upon scales of extent,
variety, vitality, and continuity, rivaling those of Nature; and
have now to proceed to build an Edifice upon it. I say this Edifice
is only to be fitly built by new Literatures, especially the Poetic.   95
I say a modern Image-Making creation is indispensable to fuse
and express the modern Political and Scientific creation[4]—and
then the Trinity[5] will be complete.)

---

8. Later texts read "towards."
9. "The problems of the achievement of this crowning stage through future first-class National
   Singers, Orators, Artists, and others—of creating in literature an *imaginative* New World,
   the correspondent and counterpart of the current Scientific and Political New Worlds—and
   the perhaps distant, but still delightful prospect, (for our children, if not in our own day,)
   of delivering America, and, indeed, all Christian lands everywhere, from the thin, moribund,
   and watery, but appallingly extensive nuisance of conventional poetry—by putting something
   really alive and substantial in its place—I have undertaken to grapple with, and argue, in
   DEMOCRATIC VISTAS" [WW's note].
1. Later texts omit "native schools or teachers of."
2. Later texts read "bases."
3. Corrected in *SDC* to "everybody."
4. In view of the twentieth-century changes in the understanding and use of image, myth, and
   symbol "to fuse and express" society and science, WW's statement is farsighted.
5. Later texts read "trinity."

When I commenced, years ago, elaborating the plan of my
poems, and continued turning over that plan, and shifting it in   100
my mind through many years, (from the age of twenty-eight to
thirty-five,) experimenting much, and writing and abandoning
much, one deep purpose underlay the others, and has underlain
it and its execution ever since—and that has been the Religious
purpose. Amid many changes, and a formulation taking far dif-   105
ferent shape from what I at first supposed,[6] this basic purpose
has never been departed from in the composition of my verses.
Not of course to exhibit itself in the old ways, as in writing hymns
or psalms with an eye to the church-pew, or to express conven-
tional pietism, or the sickly yearnings of devotees, but in new   110
ways, and aiming at the widest sub-bases and inclusions of Hu-
manity, and tallying the fresh air of sea and land. I will see, (said
I to myself,) whether there is not, for my purposes as poet, a
Religion, and a sound Religious germenancy in the average Hu-
man Race, at least in their modern development in the United   115
States, and in the hardy common fibre and native yearnings and
elements, deeper and larger, and affording more profitable re-
turns, than all mere sects or churches—as boundless, joyous,
and vital as Nature itself—A germenancy that has too long been
unencouraged, unsung, almost unknown. . . . With Science, the   120
Old Theology of the East, long in its dotage, begins evidently to
die and disappear. But (to my mind) Science—and may be such
will prove its principal service—as evidently prepares the way for
One indescribably grander—Time's young but perfect offspring
—the New Theology—heir of the West—lusty and loving, and   125
wondrous beautiful. For America, and for to-day, just the same
as any day, the supreme and final Science is the Science of
God—what we call science being only its minister[7]—as Democ-
racy is or shall be also. And a poet of America (I said) must fill
himself with such thoughts, and chant his best out of them. . .   130
. . . And as those were the convictions and aims, for good or
bad, or LEAVES OF GRASS, they are no less the intention of this
Volume. As there can be, in my opinion, no sane and complete
Personality—nor any grand and electric Nationality, without the
stock element of Religion imbuing all the other elements, (like   135
heat in chemistry, invisible itself, but the life of all visible life,)
so there can be no Poetry worthy the name without the element
behind all. . . . . . The time has certainly come to begin to dis-
charge the idea of Religion, in the United States, from mere   140

6. The persistent supposition that WW consciously foreshadowed the ultimate *Leaves of Grass*
in *LG* 1855 he several times denied, as here.
7. It was also an idea of contemporary European and New England transcendentalism that
science (or "knowing") in its general sense was only a minister to "the supreme . . . Science
of God," since the "All"—the macrocosm—contains every microcosm (*cf.* Emerson's poem
"Each and All"). It is in this sense that WW's "underlying" purpose was religious, and that
he distrusted the specialized clerical authority of ecclesiastical creeds (see below, same
paragraph).

ecclesiasticism, and from Sundays and churches and church-
going, and assign it to that general position, chiefest, most in-
dispensable, most exhilarating, to which the others are to be
adjusted, inside of all human character, and education, and af-
fairs. The people, especially the young men and women of Amer-   145
ica, must begin to learn that Religion, (like Poetry,) is something
far, far different from what they supposed. It is, indeed, too im-
portant to the power and perpetuity of the New World to be
consigned any longer to the churches, old or new, Catholic or
Protestant—Saint this, or Saint that. . . . It must be consigned   150
henceforth to Democracy *en masse,* and to Literature. It must
enter into the Poems of the Nation. It must make the Nation.

The Four Years' War is over—and in the peaceful, strong,
exciting, fresh occasions of To-day, and of the Future, that
strange, sad war is hurrying even now to be forgotten. The camp,   155
the drill, the lines of sentries, the prisons, the hospitals,—(ah!
the hospitals!)—all have passed away—all seem now like a
dream. A new race, a young and lusty generation,[8] already
sweeps in with oceanic currents, obliterating that war, and all
its scars, its mounded graves, and all its reminiscences of hatred,   160
conflict, death. So let it be obliterated. I say the life of the pres-
ent and the future makes undeniable demands upon us each and
all, South, North, East, West. . . . To help put the United States
(even if only in imagination) hand in hand, in one unbroken
circle in a chant—To rouse them to the unprecedented grandeur   165
of the part they are to play, and are even now playing—to the
thought of their great Future, and the attitude conformed to it
—especially their great Esthetic, Moral, Scientific Future, (of
which their vulgar material and political present is but as the
preparatory tuning of instruments by an orchestra,)—these, as   170
hitherto, are still, for me, among my hopes, ambitions.

Leaves of Grass, already published, is, in its intentions, the
song of a great composite *Democratic Individual,* male or female.
And following on and amplifying the same purpose, I suppose I
have in my mind to run through the chants of this Volume, (if   175
ever completed,) the thread-voice, more or less audible, of an
aggregated, inseparable, unprecedented, vast, composite, electric
Democratic Nationality.

Purposing, then, to still fill out, from time to time through
years to come, the following Volume,[9] (unless prevented,) I con-   180

---

8. The standard "Author's Edition" of *Two Rivulets,* 1876, reads "living generation." The limited
   "Centennial Edition" of that issue reads "lusty," as in the present first edition text. So also
   do all later collections—*SDC, CPP,* and *CPW.*
9. I.e., a suggested companion work to *LG* (see note 2, p. 647).

clude this Preface to the first installment[1] of it, pencilled in the open air, on my fifty-third birth-day, by wafting to you, dear Reader, whoever you are, (from amid the fresh scent of the grass, the pleasant coolness of the forenoon breeze, the lights and shades of tree-boughs silently dappling and playing around me,   185 and the notes of the cat-bird for undertone and accompaniment,) my true good-will and love.

Washington, D. C., May 31, 1872.   W. W.

Preface 1876—*Leaves of Grass* and *Two Rivulets*

At the eleventh hour, under grave illness, I gather up the pieces of Prose and Poetry left over since publishing, a while since, my first and main Volume, LEAVES OF GRASS—pieces, here, some new, some old—nearly all of them (sombre as many are, making this almost Death's book)[1] composed in by-gone at-   5 mospheres of perfect health—and, preceded by the freshest collection, the little Two RIVULETS,[2] and by this rambling Prefatory gossip,[3] now send them out, embodied in the present Melange, partly as my contribution and outpouring to celebrate, in some sort, the feature of the time, the first Centennial of our New   10

---

1. Read "instalment" in *SDC, CPP,* and *CPW.*

Preface 1876: Simply "Preface" when the essay first appeared in *Two Rivulets* (1876), this title was enlarged in later collections (*SDC, CPP,* and *CPW*) to read, "PREFACE, 1876 / *to the two-volume Centennial Edition / of L. of G. and Two Rivulets.*' " Note WW's 1876 assignment of the preface to both volumes in his first footnote (*q.v.*). Both *LG* and *TR* in 1876 were designated, on the title page, as "Author's Edition." "About two hundred copies" of each volume (Wells) were differently bound and further identified as the "Centennial Ed'n 1876" by the gold-stamped label on the spine. Numerous alterations in the preface appear in the *SDC* (1882) text, which was then reproduced in the later collections. The alterations in *SDC* were largely the reduction of capitals and other mechanical changes. Only verbal changes and such others as may affect the interpretation are shown in the present footnotes. A collation based on the final edition appears in *Prose Works 1892,* vol. II of *Collected Writings.*

1. In the 1872 Preface (*q.v.*) WW proposed writing a book on the democratic society as a companion poem to *LG.* In the present essay (paragraph 8) he writes, "I only wish I were a younger and fresher man, to attempt the enduring Book . . . about it." After years of mounting infirmities, he now observes that the unwritten book was foreshadowed in *LG* and is represented by such prose works as *Democratic Vistas* (1871) in the present collection of *TR.* The "dual forms" of prose and poetry in the collection correspond with certain subjects— "Politics for one, and for the other, the pensive thought of Immortality"—the latter to be found in the "Passage to India" poems, a section of *TR.* Gay W. Allen observes (*The Solitary Singer,* 462–66) that the dualism of this book appears in the "two rivulets" of alternating prose and verse; in the conceptual duality of life—death, mortality—immortality, time— eternity, the present—the historical past. However, this polarity is resolved in the "Calamus" motivation, which unites poet and reader and the common people of disparate countries. The dualism extends formally to this preface, of which the text emphasizes the nature of the life and social changes of WW's times, while the footnotes, almost the same in bulk, provide a corresponding running commentary on the purports of *Leaves of Grass.*

2. The following phrase and its corresponding footnote were excluded from later editions, in which there appeared the enlarged title shown in the note on title, above.

3. "This Preface is not only for the present collection, but, in a sort, for all my writings, both Volumes" [WW's note. In later editions this information appears beneath the title].

World Nationality—and then as chyle and nutriment to that moral, Indissoluble Union, equally representing All, and the mother of many coming Centennials.

And e'en for flush and proof of our America—for reminder, just as much, or more, in moods of towering pride and joy, I keep my special chants of Death and Immortality[4] to stamp the

15

4. "PASSAGE TO INDIA.—As in some ancient legend-play, to close the plot and the hero's career, there is a farewell gathering on ship's deck and on shore, a loosing of hawsers and ties, a spreading of sails to the wind—a starting out on unknown seas, to fetch up no one knows whither—to return no more—And the curtain falls, and there is the end of it—So I have reserv'd that Poem, with its cluster, to finish and explain much that, without them, would not be explain'd, and to take leave, and escape for good, from all that has preceded them. (Then probably *Passage to India,* and its cluster, are but freer vent and fuller expression to what, from the first, and so on throughout, more or less lurks in my writings, underneath every page, every line, every where.)

"I am not sure but the last enclosing sublimation of Race or Poem is, What it thinks of Death. . . . . . After the rest has been comprehended and said, even the grandest—After those contributions to mightiest Nationality, or to sweetest Song, or to the best Personalism, male or female, have been glean'd from the rich and varied themes of tangible life, and have been fully accepted and sung, and the pervading fact of visible existence, with the duty it devolves, is rounded and apparently completed, it still remains to be really completed by suffusing through the whole and several, that other pervading invisible fact, so large a part, (is it not the largest part?) of life here, combining the rest, and furnishing, for Person or State, the only permanent and unitary meaning to all, even the meanest life, consistently with the dignity of the Universe, in Time. . . . . . As, from the eligibility to this thought, and the cheerful conquest of this fact, flash forth the first distinctive proofs of the Soul, so to me, (extending it only a little further,) the ultimate Democratic purports, the ethereal and spiritual ones, are to concentrate here, and as fixed stars, radiate hence. For, in my opinion, it is no less than this idea of Immortality, above all other ideas, that is to enter into, and vivify, and give crowning religious stamp, to Democracy in the New World.

"It was originally my intention, after chanting in LEAVES OF GRASS the songs of the Body and Existence, to then compose a further, equally needed Volume, based on those convictions of perpetuity and conservation which, enveloping all precedents, make the unseen Soul govern absolutely at last. I meant, while in a sort continuing the theme of my first chants, to shift the slides, and exhibit the problem and paradox of the same ardent and fully appointed Personality entering the sphere of the resistless gravitation of Spiritual Law, and with cheerful face estimating Death, not at all as the cessation, but as somehow what I feel it must be, the entrance upon by far the greatest part of existence, and something that Life is at least as much for, as it is for itself. [The paragraph break does not occur in later editions. *Ed.*]

"But the full construction of such a work (even if I lay the foundation, or give impetus to it) is beyond my powers, and must remain for some bard in the future. The physical and the sensuous, in themselves or in their immediate continuations, retain holds upon me which I think are never entirely relea's'd; and those holds I have not only not denied, but hardly wish'd to weaken.

"Meanwhile, not entirely to give the go-by to my original plan, and far more to avoid a mark'd hiatus in it, than to entirely fulfil it, I end my books with thoughts, or radiations from thoughts, on Death, Immortality, and a free entrance into the Spiritual world. In those thoughts, in a sort, I make the first steps or studies toward the mighty theme, from the point of view necessitated by my foregoing poems, and by Modern Science. In them I also seek to set the key-stone to my Democracy's enduring arch. I re-collate them now, for the press, (much the same, I transcribe my *Memoranda* following, of gloomy times out of the War, and Hospitals,) [This parenthetical clause does not appear in later editions. *Ed.*] in order to partially occupy and offset days of strange sickness, and the heaviest affliction and bereavement of my life; and I fondly please myself with the notion of leaving that cluster to you, O unknown Reader of the future, as 'something to remember me by,' more especially than all else. Written in former days of perfect health, little did I think the pieces had the purport that now, under present circumstances, opens to me.

"[As I write these lines, May 31, 1875, it is again early summer—again my birth-day—now my fifty-sixth. Amid the outside beauty and freshness, the sunlight and verdure of the delightful season, O how different the moral atmosphere amid which I now revise this Volume, from the jocund influences surrounding the growth and advent of LEAVES OF GRASS. I occupy

coloring-finish of all, present and past. For terminus and tem-
perer to all, they were originally written; and that shall be their
office at the last.

For some reason—not explainable or definite to my own mind,   20
yet secretly pleasing and satisfactory to it—I have not hesitated
to embody in, and run through the Volume, two altogether dis-
tinct veins, or strata—Politics for one, and for the other, the
pensive thought of Immortality. Thus, too, the prose and poetic,
the dual[5] forms of the present book. . . . . . [6] The pictures from   25
the Hospitals during the War, in *Memoranda*, I have also decided
to include. Though they differ in character and composition
from the rest of my pieces, yet I feel that that they ought to go
with them, and must do so. . . . . The present Volume,[7] therefore,
after its minor episodes, probably divides into these Two, at first   30
sight far diverse, veins of topic and treatment. One will be found
in the prose part of Two Rivulets, in *Democratic Vistas*, in the
Preface to *As a Strong Bird*, and in the concluding Notes to
Memoranda of the Hospitals. The other, wherein the all-engross-
ing thought and fact of Death is admitted, (not for itself so much   35
as a powerful factor in the adjustments of Life,) in the realistic
pictures of *Memoranda*, and the free speculations and ideal es-
capades of *Passage to India*.

Has not the time come, indeed, in the development of the New
World, when its Politics should ascend into atmospheres and   40
regions hitherto unknown—(far, far different from the miserable
business that of late and current years passes under that
name)—and take rank with Science, Philosophy and Art?[8] . . . .
. . . Three points, in especial, have become very dear to me, and

myself, arranging these pages for publication, still envelopt in thoughts of the death two
years since of my dear Mother, the most perfect and magnetic character, the rarest combi-
nation of practical, moral and spiritual, and the least selfish, of all and any I have ever
known—and by me O so much the most deeply loved . . . . . . and also under the physical
affliction of a tedious attack of paralysis, obstinately lingering and keeping its hold upon me,
and quite suspending all bodily activity and comfort . . . . {The following sentence,
concluding the paragraph, does not appear in later editions. Ed.} I see now, much clearer
than ever—perhaps these experiences were needed to show—how much my former poems,
the bulk of them, are indeed the expression of health and strength, and sanest, joyfulest
life.]

"Under these influences, therefore, I still feel to keep *Passage to India* for last words even
to this Centennial dithyramb. Not as, in antiquity, at highest festival of Egypt, the noisome
skeleton of Death was also sent on exhibition to the revellers, for zest and shadow to the
occasion's joy and light—but as the perfect marble statue of the normal Greeks at Elis,
suggesting death in the form of a beautiful and perfect young man, with closed eyes, leaning
on an inverted torch—emblem of rest and aspiration after action—of crown and point which
all lives and poems should steadily have reference to, namely, the justified and noble ter-
mination of our identity, this grade of it, and outlet-preparation to another grade" [WW's
note].

5. See "dualism," note 1 above on "Death's book."
6. The following sentence and the next were excluded in WW's later collections.
7. In WW's later collections, "present," was dropped before "Volume," because obviously
irrelevant.
8. The previous passage, thirteen lines in the first edition from "One will be found," line 31,
to "Philosophy and Art," were omitted in the later texts. The canceled proposal that democ-
racy must ultimately sublimate "politics" at the level of "science, philosophy, and art," em-
phasized in other passages of the essay, may be thought to reflect his motivation for the
second, unwritten book.

all through I seek to make them again and again, in many forms   45
and repetitions, as will be seen: 1. That the true growth-
characteristics of the Democracy of the New World are hence-
forth to radiate in superior Literary, Artistic and Religious
Expressions, far more than in its Republican forms, universal
suffrage, and frequent elections, (though these are unspeakably   50
important) . . . . . . 2. That the vital political mission of The
United States is, to practically solve and settle the problem of
two sets of rights—the fusion, thorough compatibility and junc-
tion of individual State prerogatives, with the indispensable ne-
cessity of centrality and Oneness—the National Identity power   55
—the sovereign Union, relentless, permanently comprising all,
and over all, and in that never yielding an inch . . . . then
3d. Do we not, amid a general malaria of Fogs and Vapors, our
day, unmistakably see two Pillars of Promise, with grandest, in-
destructible indications—One, that the morbid facts of Ameri-   60
can politics and society everywhere are but passing incidents and
flanges of our unbounded impetus of growth—weeds, annuals,
of the rank, rich soil—not central, enduring, perennial things?
—The Other, that all the hitherto experience of The States,[9]
their first Century, has been but preparation, adolescence—and   65
that This Union is only now and henceforth (*i. e.*, since the
Secession war) to enter on its full Democratic career?

Of the whole, Poems and Prose, (not attending at all to chron-
ological order, and with original dates and passing allusions in
the heat and impression of the hour, left shuffled in, and undis-   70
turb'd,) the chants of LEAVES OF GRASS, my former Volume, yet
serve as the indispensable deep soil, or basis, out of which, and
out of which only, could come the roots and stems more defi-
nitely indicated by these later pages. (While that Volume radiates
Physiology alone, the present One, though of the like origin in   75
the main, more palpably doubtless shows the Pathology which
was pretty sure to come in time from the other.)[1]

In that former and main Volume, composed in the flush of my
health and strength, from the age of 30 to 50 years, I dwelt on
Birth and Life, clothing my ideas in pictures, days, transactions   80
of my time, to give them positive place, identity—saturating
them with that vehemence of pride and audacity of freedom nec-
essary to loosen the mind of still-to be-form'd America from the
accumulated folds, the superstitions, and all the long, tenacious
and stifling anti-democratic authorities of the Asiatic and Eu-   85
ropean past—my enclosing purport being to express, above all

9. Misspelled as "Sates" in all later collections.
1. One might find the pathological in several of these works: "Democratic Vistas" (1871), con-
taining a blistering attack on the postwar corruption of personality and politics in the "gilded
age"; "Preface 1872," containing comments on the unrealized cultural potentialities of the
United States; and "Memoranda During the War" (1875–76), notes on battlefront scenes,
hospital service, and the dead.

artificial regulation and aid, the eternal Bodily Character of
One's-Self.[2]

2. [In the later texts the clause reads: "the eternal bodily composite, cumulative natural char-
acter of one's self." *Ed.*]
"Leaves of Grass.—Namely, a Character, making most of common and normal elements,
to the superstructure of which not only the precious accumulations of the learning and
experiences of the Old World, and the settled social and municipal necessities and current
requirements, so long a-building, shall still faithfully contribute, but which, at its foundations
and carried up thence, and receiving its impetus from the Democratic spirit, and accepting
its gauge, in all departments, from the Democratic formulas, shall again directly be vitalized
by the perennial influences of Nature at first hand, and the old heroic stamina of Nature,
the strong air of prairie and mountain, the dash of the briny sea, the primary antiseptics—
of the passions, in all their fullest heat and potency, of courage, rankness, amativeness, and
of immense pride. . . . . . Not to lose at all, therefore, the benefits of artificial progress and
civilization, but to re-occupy for Western tenancy the oldest though ever-fresh fields, and
reap from them the savage and sane nourishment indispensable to a hardy nation, and the
absence of which, threatening to become worse and worse, is the most serious lack and
defect to-day of our New World literature.
"Not but what the brawn of Leaves of Grass is, I think, thoroughly spiritualized every-
where, for final estimate, but, from the very subjects, the direct effect is a sense of the Life,
as it should be, of flesh and blood, and physical urge, and animalism. . . . . . While there
are other themes, and plenty of abstract thoughts and poems in the Volume—While I have
put in it (supplemented in the present Work by my prose *Memoranda*,) [This parenthetical
clause does not appear in later editions. *Ed.*] passing and rapid but actual glimpses of the
great struggle between the Nation and the Slave-power, (1861–'65,) as the fierce and bloody
panorama of that contest unroll'd itself—While the whole Book, indeed, revolves around
that Four Years' War, which, as I was in the midst of it, becomes, in *Drum-Taps*, pivotal to
the rest entire—follow'd by *Marches now the War is Over*—[This phrase between dashes is
not present in later editions. *Ed.*] and here and there, before and afterward, not a few
episodes and speculations—*that*—namely, to make a type-portrait for living, active, worldly,
healthy Personality, objective as well as subjective, joyful and potent, and modern and free,
distinctively for the use of the United States, male and female, through the long future—
has been, I say, my general object. (Probably, indeed, the whole of these varied songs, and
all my writings, both Volumes, only ring changes in some sort, on the ejaculation, How vast,
how eligible, how joyful, how real, is a Human Being, himself or herself.)
"Though from no definite plan at the time, I see now that I have unconsciously sought, by
indirections at least as much as directions, to express the whirls and rapid growth and in-
tensity of the United States, the prevailing tendency and events of the Nineteenth Century,
and largely the spirit of the whole current World, my time; for I feel that I have partaken of
that spirit, as I have been deeply interested in all those events, the closing of long-stretch'd
eras and ages, and, illustrated in the history of the United States, the opening of larger ones.
(The death of President Lincoln, for instance, fitly, historically closes, in the Civilization of
Feudalism, many old influences—drops on them, suddenly, a vast, gloomy, as it were, sep-
arating curtain. [The parenthetical matter ends here in later editions. *Ed.*] The world's entire
dramas afford none more indicative—none with folds more tragic, or more sombre or far
spreading.)
"Since I have been ill, (1873–74–75,) mostly without serious pain, and with plenty of time
and frequent inclination to judge my poems, (never composed with eye on the book-market,
nor for fame, nor for any pecuniary profit,) I have felt temporary depression more than once,
for fear that in Leaves of Grass the *moral* parts were not sufficiently pronounc'd. But in
my clearest and calmest moods I have realized that as those Leaves, all and several, surely
prepare the way for, and necessitate Morals, and are adjusted to them, just the same as
Nature does and is, they are what, consistently with my plan, they must and probably should
be. . . . . . (In a certain sense, while the Moral is the purport and last intelligence of all
Nature, there is absolutely nothing of the moral in the works, or laws, or shows of Nature.
Those only lead inevitably to it—begin and necessitate it.)
"Then I meant Leaves of Grass, as published, to be the Poem of Identity, (of *Yours*,
whoever you are, now reading these lines). . . . . . [The sentence beginning here does not
appear in later editions. *Ed.*] For genius must realize that, precious as it may be, there is
something far more precious, namely, simple Identity, One's-self. A man is not greatest as
victor in war, nor inventor or explorer, nor even in science, or in his intellectual or artistic
capacity, or exemplar in some vast benevolence. To the highest Democratic view, man is
most acceptable in living well the average, practical life and lot which happens to him as
ordinary farmer, sea-farer, mechanic, clerk, laborer, or driver—upon and from which position
as a central basis or pedestal, while performing its labors, and his duties as citizen, son,
husband, father and employed person, he preserves his physique, ascends, developing, ra-
diating himself in other regions—and especially where and when, (greatest of all, and nobler

The varieties and phases,[3] (doubtless often paradoxical, con-
tradictory,) of the two Volumes, of LEAVES, and of these RIVU-   90
LETS, are ultimately to be considered as One in structure, and
as mutually explanatory of each other—as the multiplex results,
like a tree, of series of successive growths, (yet from one central
or seed-purport)—there having been five or six such cumulative
issues, editions, commencing back in 1855 and thence progress-   95
ing through twenty years down to date, (1875–76)—some things
added or re-shaped from time to time, as they were found
wanted, and other things represt. Of the former Book, more ve-
hement, and perhaps pursuing a central idea with greater
closeness—join'd with the present One, extremely varied in   100
theme—I can only briefly reiterate here, that all my pieces, al-
ternated through Both, are only of use and value, if any, as such
an interpenetrating, composite, inseparable Unity.

---

than the proudest mere genius or magnate in any field,) he fully realizes the Conscience,
the Spiritual, the divine faculty, cultivated well, exemplified in all his deeds and words,
through life, uncompromising to the end—a flight loftier than any of Homer's or
Shakspere's—broader than all poems and bibles—namely, Nature's own, and in the midst
of it, Yourself, your own Identity, body and soul. (All serves, helps—but in the centre of all,
absorbing all, giving, for your purpose, the only meaning and vitality to all, master or mistress
of all, under the law, stands Yourself.) . . . . . To sing the Song of that divine law of Identity,
and of Yourself, consistently with the Divine Law of the Universal, is a main intention of
those LEAVES.
    "Something more may be added—for, while I am about it, I would make a full confession.
I also sent out LEAVES OF GRASS to arouse and set flowing in men's and women's hearts,
young and old, (my present and future readers,) [This parenthetical phrase is not present in
later editions. *Ed.*] endless streams of living, pulsating love and friendship, directly from
them to myself, now and ever. To this terrible, irrepressible yearning, (surely more or less
down underneath in most human souls,)—this never-satisfied appetite for sympathy, and
this boundless offering of sympathy—this universal democratic comradeship—this old, eter-
nal, yet ever-new interchange of adhesiveness, so fitly emblematic of America—I have given
in that book, undisguisedly, declaredly, the openest expression. [The present paragraph ends
here in later editions, thus excluding the more personal interpretation of the "Calamus" motif
in favor of the social role emphasized in the following paragraph. *Ed.*] . . . . . . Poetic literature
has long been the formal and conventional tender of art and beauty merely, and of a narrow,
constipated, special amativeness. I say, the subtlest, sweetest, surest tie between me and
Him or Her, who, in the pages of *Calamus* and other pieces realizes me—though we never
see each other, or though ages and ages hence—must, in this way, be personal affection.
And those—be they few, or be they many—are at any rate *my readers*, in a sense that belongs
not, and can never belong, to better, prouder poems.
    "Besides, important as they are in my purpose as emotional expressions for humanity, the
special meaning of the *Calamus* cluster of LEAVES OF GRASS, (and more or less running
through that book, and cropping out in *Drum-Taps*,) mainly resides in its Political signifi-
cance. In my opinion it is by a fervent, accepted development of Comradeship, the beautiful
and sane affection of man for man, latent in all the young fellows, North and South, East
and West—it is by this, I say, and by what goes directly and indirectly along with it, that
the United States of the future, (I cannot too often repeat,) are to be most effectually welded
together, intercalated, anneal'd into a Living Union.
    "Then, for enclosing clue of all, it is imperatively and ever to be borne in mind that LEAVES
OF GRASS entire is not to be construed as an intellectual or scholastic effort or Poem mainly,
but more as a radical utterance out of the abysms of the Soul ["abysms of the Soul" omitted
in later editions. *Ed.*], the Emotions and the Physique—an utterance adjusted to, perhaps
born of, Democracy and Modern Science [later editions read "the Modern." *Ed.*], and in its
very nature regardless of the old conventions, and, under the great Laws, following only its
own impulses" [WW's note].
3. Beginning with this phrase, three successive paragraphs, ending with the words, "allows
    them," were excluded in the later editions. Evidently, much of this had relevance primarily
    in context with the *TR* volume. However, three ideas have general interest: that WW's poetry
    and prose works correspond in a "composite, inseparable Unity"; that the ordinary people of
    all lands have a common interest; and that his poetry was experimental, under the "irresistible
    urge" of spiritual dictation.

Two of the pieces in this Volume were originally Public Recitations—the College Commencement Poem, *As a Strong Bird*—and then the *Song of the Exposition,* to identify these great Industrial gatherings, the majestic outgrowths of the Modern Spirit and Practice—and now fix'd upon, the grandest of them, for the Material event around which shall be concentrated and celebrated, (as far as any one event can combine them,) the associations and practical proofs of the Hundred Years' life of the Republic. The glory of Labor, and the bringing together not only representatives of all the trades and products, but, fraternally, of all the Workmen of all the Nations of the World, (for this is the Idea behind the Centennial at Philadelphia,) is, to me, so welcome and inspiring a theme, that I only wish I were a younger and a fresher man, to attempt the enduring Book, of poetic character, that ought to be written about it.

The arrangement in print of Two Rivelets—the indirectness of the name itself, (suggesting meanings, the start of other meanings, for the whole Volume)—are but parts of the Venture which my Poems entirely are. For really they have all been Experiments, under the urge of powerful, quite irresistible, perhaps wilful influences, (even escapades,) to see how such things will eventually turn out—and have been recited, as it were, by my Soul, to the special audience of Myself, far more than to the world's audience. [See, further on, Preface of *As a Strong Bird,* &c., 1872.] Till now, by far the best part of the whole business is, that, these days, in leisure, in sickness and old age, my Spirit, by which they were written or permitted erewhile, does not go back on them, but still and in calmest hours, fully, deliberately allows them.

Estimating the American Union as so far and for some time to come, in its yet formative condition, I therefore now bequeath Poems and Essays[4] as nutriment and influences to help truly assimilate and harden, and especially to furnish something toward what The States most need of all, and which seems to me yet quite unsupplied in literature, namely, to show them, or begin to show them, Themselves distinctively, and what They are for. For though perhaps the main points of all ages and nations are points of resemblance, and, even while granting evolution, are substantially the same, there are some vital things in which this Republic, as to its Individualities, and as a compacted Nation, is to specially stand forth, and culminate modern humanity. And these are the very things it least morally and mentally knows—(though, curiously enough, it is at the same time faithfully acting upon them.)

I count with such absolute certainty on the Great Future of The United States—different from, though founded on, the

---

4. Later texts omit "therefore now" after "I" and read simply: "I bequeath poems . . ."

past—that I have always invoked that Future, and surrounded
myself with it, before or while singing my Songs. . . . (As ever,   150
all tends to followings—America, too, is a prophecy. What, even
of the best and most successful, would be justified by itself
alone? by the present, or the material ostent alone? Of men or
States, few realize how much they live in the future. That, rising
like pinnacles, gives its main significance to all You and I are   155
doing to-day. Without it, there were little meaning in lands or
poems—little purport in human lives. . . . . . . All ages, all
Nations and States, have been such prophecies. But where any
former ones with prophecy so broad, so clear, as our times, our
lands—as those of the West?)[5]   160

    Without being a Scientist, I have thoroughly adopted the con-
clusions of the great Savans and Experimentalists of our time,
and of the last hundred years, and they have interiorly tinged
the chyle of all my verse, for purposes beyond. Following the
Modern Spirit, the real Poems of the Present, ever solidifying   165
and expanding into the Future, must vocalize the vastness and
splendor and reality with which Scientism has invested Man and
the Universe (all that is called Creation,) and must henceforth
launch Humanity into new orbits, consonant with that vastness,
splendor, and reality, (unknown to the old poems,) like new sys-   170
tems of orbs, balanced upon themselves, revolving in limitless
space, more subtle than the stars. Poetry, so largely hitherto and
even at present wedded to children's tales, and to mere amor-
ousness, upholstery and superficial rhyme, will have to accept,
and, while not denying the Past, nor the Themes of the past,   175
will be revivified by, this tremendous innovation, the Kosmic
Spirit, which must henceforth, in my opinion, be the background
and underlying impetus, more or less visible, of all first-class
Songs.

    Only, (for me, at any rate, in all my Prose and Poetry,) joyfully   180
accepting Modern Science, and loyally following it without the
slightest hesitation, there remains ever recognized still a higher
flight, a higher fact, the Eternal Soul of Man, (of all Else too,)
the Spiritual, the Religious—which it is to be the greatest office
of Scientism, in my opinion, and of future Poetry also, to free   185
from fables, crudities and superstitions, and launch forth in re-
newed Faith and Scope a hundred fold. To me, the worlds of
Religiousness, of the conception of the Divine, and of the Ideal,
though mainly latent, are just as absolute in Humanity and the

---

5. WW perhaps reflects the current philosophical adherence to the theory of human progress
and the belief in the "Manifest Destiny" of the United States; so also in "Preface 1872"
(*q.v.*, text and editorial comment).

Universe as the world of Chemistry,[6] or any thing in the objective   190
worlds. To me,

> The Prophet and the Bard,
> Shall yet maintain themselves—in higher circles yet,
> Shall mediate to the Modern, to Democracy—interpret yet
>   to them,
> God and Eidólons.   195

To me, the crown of Savantism is to be, that is surely opens
the way for a more splendid Theology, and for ampler and diviner
Songs. No year, nor even century, will settle this. There is a
phase of the Real, lurking behind the Real, which it is all for.
There is also in the Intellect of man, in time, far in prospective   200
recesses, a judgment, a last appellate court, which will settle it.

In certain parts, in these flights, or attempting to depict or
suggest them, I have not been afraid of the charge of obscurity,[7]
in either of my Two Volumes—because human thought, poetry
or melody, must leave dim escapes and outlets—must possess a   205
certain fluid, aerial character, akin to space itself, obscure to
those of little or no imagination, but indispensable to the highest
purposes. Poetic style, when address'd to the Soul, is less definite
form, outline, sculpture, and becomes vista, music, half-tints,
and even less than half-tints. True, it may be architecture; but   210
again it may be the forest wild-wood, or the best effects[8] thereof,
at twilight, the waving oaks and cedars in the wind, and the
impalpable odor.

Finally, as I have lived in fresh lands, inchoate, and in a rev-
olutionary age, future-founding, I have felt to identify the points   215
of that age, these lands, in my recitatives, altogether in my own
way. Thus my form has strictly grown from my purports and
facts, and is the analogy of them. . . . . . . Within my time the
United States have emerg'd from nebulous vagueness and sus-
pense, to full orbic, (though varied) decision—have done the   220
deeds and achiev'd the triumphs of half a score of centuries—
and are henceforth to enter upon their real history—the way
being now, (i. e. since the result of the Secession War,) clear'd
of death-threatening impedimenta, and the free areas around
and ahead of us assured and certain, which were not so before   225

---

6. Cf. the previous paragraph. WW's interest in the developing concepts of science is reflected
   in LG (See Joseph Beaver, Walt Whitman, Poet of Science, 1951). In the present paragraph
   and the following, his belief that science must seek the humanistic sanction may have rel-
   evance to the condition of the twentieth century.
7. Many of the powerful images of LG have a meaningful obscurity: the rediscovery of his
   poetry by American poets early in the present century probably encouraged their inclination
   toward a heightened intensity and subtely of imagery.
8. Properly, "effect"; corrected in later texts.

—(the past century being but preparations, trial-voyages and experiments of the Ship, before her starting out upon deep water.)

In estimating my Volumes, the world's current times and deeds, and their spirit, must be first profoundly estimated. Out of the Hundred Years just ending, (1776–1876), with their genesis of inevitable wilful events, and new introductions,[9] and many unprecedented things of war and peace, (to be realized better, perhaps only realized, at the remove of another Century hence)—Out of that stretch of time, and especially out of the immediately preceding Twenty-Five Years, (1850–75,) with all their rapid changes, innovations, and audacious movements— and bearing their own inevitable wilful birth-marks—my Poems[1] too have found genesis.

W. W.

230

235

---

9. SDC and later texts read: "wilful events, and new experiments and introductions, . . ."
1. SDC and later texts read: "the experiments of my poems . . ." *Cf.* previous note; in 1882 these alterations suggest WW's continuing sense of the "experimental" nature of his poetry.

Text of 1855 *Leaves of Grass*

I Celebrate myself,
And what I assume you shall assume,
For every atom belonging to me as good belongs to you.

I loafe and invite my soul,
I lean and loafe at my ease . . . . observing a spear of summer
    grass.   5

Houses and rooms are full of perfumes . . . . the shelves are
    crowded with perfumes,
I breathe the fragrance myself, and know it and like it,
The distillation would intoxicate me also, but I shall not let it.

The atmosphere is not a perfume . . . . it has no taste of the
    distillation . . . . it is odorless,
It is for my mouth forever . . . . I am in love with it,   10
I will go to the bank by the wood and become undisguised and
    naked,
I am mad for it to be in contact with me.

The smoke of my own breath,
Echos, ripples, and buzzed whispers . . . . loveroot, silkthread,
    crotch and vine,
My respiration and inspiration . . . . the beating of my heart
    . . . . the passing of blood and air through my lungs,   15
The sniff of green leaves and dry leaves, and of the shore and
    darkcolored sea-rocks, and of hay in the barn,
The sound of the belched words of my voice . . . . words
    loosed to the eddies of the wind,
A few light kisses . . . . a few embraces . . . . a reaching
    around of arms,
The play of shine and shade on the trees as the supple boughs wag,
The delight alone or in the rush of the streets, or along the
    fields and hillsides,   20

This, the poetic text of the first (1855) *LG*, contains twelve poems, printed without section
numbers or individual titles. In order to read the entire text of the first *LG*, the reader should
also refer to the "Preface 1855" in the "Prefaces" section of this volume. The first poem,
occupying more than half of the first edition, was entitled "Poem of Walt Whitman, an
American" in the 1856 edition, "Walt Whitman" in the 1860 edition, and "Song of My-
self" in 1881.

The feeling of health . . . . the full-moon trill . . . . the song of
    me rising from bed and meeting the sun.

Have you reckoned a thousand acres much? Have you
    reckoned the earth much?
Have you practiced so long to learn to read?
Have you felt so proud to get at the meaning of poems?

Stop this day and night with me and you shall possess the
    origin of all poems,   25
You shall possess the good of the earth and sun . . . . there are
    millions of suns left,
You shall no longer take things at second or third hand . . . .
    nor look through the eyes of the dead . . . . nor feed on
    the spectres in books,
You shall not look through my eyes either, nor take things
    from me,
You shall listen to all sides and filter them from yourself.

I have heard what the talkers were talking . . . . the talk of the
    beginning and the end,   30
But I do not talk of the beginning or the end.

There was never any more inception than there is now,
Nor any more youth or age than there is now;
And will never be any more perfection than there is now,
Nor any more heaven or hell than there is now.   35

Urge and urge and urge,
Always the procreant urge of the world.

Out of the dimness opposite equals advance . . . . Always
    substance and increase,
Always a knit of identity . . . . always distinction . . . . always a
    breed of life.

To elaborate is no avail . . . . Learned and unlearned feel that
    it is so.   40

Sure as the most certain sure . . . . plumb in the uprights, well
    entretied, braced in the beams,
Stout as a horse, affectionate, haughty, electrical,
I and this mystery here we stand.

Clear and sweet is my soul . . . . and clear and sweet is all that
    is not my soul.

Lack one lacks both . . . . and the unseen is proved by the
    seen,   45
Till that becomes unseen and receives proof in its turn.

Showing the best and dividing it from the worst, age vexes age,
Knowing the perfect fitness and equanimity of things, while
    they discuss I am silent, and go bathe and admire myself.

Welcome is every organ and attribute of me, and of any man
    hearty and clean,
Not an inch nor a particle of an inch is vile, and none shall be
    less familiar than the rest.   50

I am satisfied . . . . I see, dance, laugh, sing;
As God comes a loving bedfellow and sleeps at my side all
    night and close on the peep of the day,
And leaves for me baskets covered with white towels bulging
    the house with their plenty,
Shall I postpone my acceptation and realization and scream at
    my eyes,
That they turn from gazing after and down the road,   55
And forthwith cipher and show me to a cent,
Exactly the contents of one, and exactly the contents of two,
    and which is ahead?

Trippers and askers surround me,
People I meet . . . . . the effect upon me of my early life . . . .
    of the ward and city I live in . . . . of the nation,
The latest news . . . . discoveries, inventions, societies . . . .
    authors old and new,   60
My dinner, dress, associates, looks, business, compliments,
    dues,
The real or fancied indifference of some man or woman I love,
The sickness of one of my folks—or of myself . . . . or ill-doing
    . . . . or loss or lack of money . . . . or depressions or
    exaltations,
They come to me days and nights and go from me again,
But they are not the Me myself.   65

Apart from the pulling and hauling stands what I am,
Stands amused, complacent, compassionating, idle, unitary,
Looks down, is erect, bends an arm on an impalpable certain rest,
Looks with its sidecurved head curious what will come next,
Both in and out of the game, and watching and wondering at it.   70

Backward I see in my own days where I sweated through fog
    with linguists and contenders,
I have no mockings or arguments . . . . I witness and wait.

I believe in you my soul . . . . the other I am must not abase
    itself to you,
And you must not be abased to the other.

Loafe with me on the grass . . . . loose the stop from your
    throat,   75
Not words, not music or rhyme I want . . . . not custom or
    lecture, not even the best,
Only the lull I like, the hum of your valved voice.

I mind how we lay in June, such a transparent summer morning;
You settled your head athwart my hips and gently turned over
    upon me,
And parted the shirt from my bosom-bone, and plunged your
    tongue to my barestript heart,   80
And reached till you felt my beard, and reached till you held
    my feet.

Swiftly arose and spread around me the peace and joy and
    knowledge that pass all the art and argument of the earth;
And I know that the hand of God is the elderhand of my own,
And I know that the spirit of God is the eldest brother of my own,
And that all the men ever born are also my brothers . . . . and
    the women my sisters and lovers,   85
And that a kelson of the creation is love;
And limitless are leaves stiff or drooping in the fields,
And brown ants in the little wells beneath them,
And mossy scabs of the wormfence, and heaped stones, and
    elder and mullen and pokeweed.

A child said, What is the grass? fetching it to me with full
    hands;   90
How could I answer the child? . . . . I do not know what it is
    any more than he.

Or I guess it must be the flag of my disposition, out of hopeful
    green stuff woven.

Or I guess it is the handkerchief of the Lord,
A scented gift and remembrancer designedly dropped,
Bearing the owner's name someway in the corners, that we
    may see and remark, and say Whose?   95

Or I guess the grass is itself a child . . . . the produced babe of
    the vegetation.

Or I guess it is a uniform hieroglyphic,
And it means, Sprouting alike in broad zones and narrow zones,
Growing among black folks as among white,
Kanuck, Tuckahoe, Congressman, Cuff, I give them the same,
    I receive them the same.   100

And now it seems to me the beautiful uncut hair of graves.

Tenderly will I use you curling grass,
It may be you transpire from the breasts of young men,
It may be if I had known them I would have loved them;
It may be you are from old people and from women, and from
    offspring taken soon out of their mothers' laps,   105
And here you are the mothers' laps.

This grass is very dark to be from the white heads of old mothers,
Darker than the colorless beards of old men,
Dark to come from under the faint red roofs of mouths.

O I perceive after all so many uttering tongues!   110
And I perceive they do not come from the roofs of mouths for
    nothing.

I wish I could translate the hints about the dead young men
    and women,
And the hints about old men and mothers, and the offspring
    taken soon out of their laps.

What do you think has become of the young and old men?
And what do you think has become of the women and
    children?   115

They are alive and well somewhere;
The smallest sprout shows there is really no death,
And if ever there was it led forward life, and does not wait at
    the end to arrest it,
And ceased the moment life appeared.

All goes onward and outward . . . . and nothing collapses,   120
And to die is different from what any one supposed, and luckier.

Has any one supposed it lucky to be born?
I hasten to inform him or her it is just as lucky to die, and I
    know it.

I pass death with the dying, and birth with the new-washed
    babe . . . . and am not contained between my hat and
    boots,
And peruse manifold objects, no two alike, and every one good,   125
The earth good, and the stars good, and their adjuncts all
    good.

I am not an earth nor an adjunct of an earth,
I am the mate and companion of people, all just as immortal
    and fathomless as myself;
They do not know how immortal, but I know.

Every kind for itself and its own . . . . for me mine male and
    female,   130
For me all that have been boys and that love women,
For me the man that is proud and feels how it stings to be slighted,
For me the sweetheart and the old maid . . . . for me mothers
    and the mothers of mothers,
For me lips that have smiled, eyes that have shed tears,
For me children and the begetters of children.   135

Who need be afraid of the merge?
Undrape . . . . you are not guilty to me, nor stale nor discarded,
I see through the broadcloth and gingham whether or no,
And am around, tenacious, acquisitive, tireless . . . . and can
    never be shaken away.

The little one sleeps in its cradle,   140
I lift gauze and look a long time, and silently brush away flies
    with my hand.

The youngster and the redfaced girl turn aside up the bushy hill,
I peeringly view them from the top.

The suicide sprawls on the bloody floor of the bedroom.
It is so . . . . I witnessed the corpse . . . . there the pistol had
    fallen.   145

The blab of the pave . . . . the tires of carts and sluff of
    bootsoles and talk of the promenaders,
The heavy omnibus, the driver with his interrogating thumb,
    the clank of the shod horses on the granite floor,
The carnival of sleighs, the clinking and shouted jokes and
    pelts of snowballs;
The hurrahs for popular favorites . . . . the fury of roused mobs,
The flap of the curtained litter—the sick man inside, borne to
    the hospital,   150
The meeting of enemies, the sudden oath, the blows and fall,
The excited crowd—the policeman with his star quickly
    working his passage to the centre of the crowd;
The impassive stones that receive and return so many echoes,
The souls moving along . . . . are they invisible while the least
    atom of the stones is visible?

What groans of overfed or half-starved who fall on the flags
    sunstruck or in fits,
What exclamations of women taken suddenly, who hurry home
    and give birth to babes,
What living and buried speech is always vibrating here . . . .
    what howls restrained by decorum,
Arrests of criminals, slights, adulterous offers made,
    acceptances, rejections with convex lips,
I mind them or the resonance of them . . . . I come again and
    again.

The big doors of the country-barn stand open and ready,
The dried grass of the harvest-time loads the slow-drawn wagon,
The clear light plays on the brown gray and green intertinged,
The armfuls are packed to the sagging mow:
I am there . . . . I help . . . . I came stretched atop of the load,
I felt its soft jolts . . . . one leg reclined on the other,
I jump from the crossbeams, and seize the clover and timothy,
And roll head over heels, and tangle my hair full of wisps.

Alone far in the wilds and mountains I hunt,
Wandering amazed at my own lightness and glee,
In the late afternoon choosing a safe spot to pass the night,
Kindling a fire and broiling the freshkilled game,
Soundly falling asleep on the gathered leaves, my dog and gun
    by my side.

The Yankee clipper is under her three skysails . . . . she cuts
    the sparkle and scud,
My eyes settle the land . . . . I bend at her prow or shout
    joyously from the deck.

The boatmen and clamdiggers arose early and stopped for me,
I tucked my trowser-ends in my boots and went and had a
    good time,
You should have been with us that day round the chowder-kettle.

I saw the marriage of the trapper in the open air in the far-
    west . . . . the bride was a red girl,
Her father and his friends sat near by crosslegged and dumbly
    smoking . . . . they had moccasins to their feet and large
    thick blankets hanging from their shoulders;
On a bank lounged the trapper . . . . he was dressed mostly in
    skins . . . . his luxuriant beard and curls protected his
    neck,
One hand rested on his rifle . . . . the other hand held firmly
    the wrist of the red girl,
She had long eyelashes . . . . her head was bare . . . . her

coarse straight locks descended upon her voluptuous limbs
   and reached to her feet.

The runaway slave came to my house and stopped outside,
I heard his motions crackling the twigs of the woodpile,
Through the swung half-door of the kitchen I saw him limpsey
   and weak,   185
And went where he sat on a log, and led him in and assured him,
And brought water and filled a tub for his sweated body and
   bruised feet,
And gave him a room that entered from my own, and gave him
   some coarse clean clothes,
And remember perfectly well his revolving eyes and his
   awkwardness,
And remember putting plasters on the galls of his neck and
   ankles;   190
He staid with me a week before he was recuperated and
   passed north,
I had him sit next me at table . . . . my firelock leaned in the
   corner.

Twenty-eight young men bathe by the shore,
Twenty-eight young men, and all so friendly,
Twenty-eight years of womanly life, and all so lonesome.   195

She owns the fine house by the rise of the bank,
She hides handsome and richly drest aft the blinds of the window.

Which of the young men does she like the best?
Ah the homeliest of them is beautiful to her.

Where are you off to, lady? for I see you,   200
You splash in the water there, yet stay stock still in your room.

Dancing and laughing along the beach came the twenty-ninth
   bather,
The rest did not see her, but she saw them and loved them.

The beards of the young men glistened with wet, it ran from
   their long hair,
Little streams passed all over their bodies.   205

An unseen hand also passed over their bodies,
It descended tremblingly from their temples and ribs.

The young men float on their backs, their white bellies swell to
   the sun . . . . they do not ask who seizes fast to them,
They do not know who puffs and declines with pendant and
   bending arch,
They do not think whom they souse with spray.   210

The butcher-boy puts off his killing-clothes, or sharpens his
    knife at the stall in the market,
I loiter enjoying his repartee and his shuffle and breakdown.

Blacksmiths with grimed and hairy chests environ the anvil,
Each has his main-sledge . . . . they are all out . . . . there is a
    great heat in the fire.

From the cinder-strewed threshold I follow their movements,   215
The lithe sheer of their waists plays even with their massive arms,
Overhand the hammers roll—overhand so slow—overhand so sure,
They do not hasten, each man hits in his place.

The negro holds firmly the reins of his four horses . . . . the
    block swags underneath on its tied-over chain,
The negro that drives the huge dray of the stoneyard . . . .
    steady and tall he stands poised on one leg on the
    stringpiece,   220
His blue shirt exposes his ample neck and breast and loosens
    over his hipband,
His glance is calm and commanding . . . . he tosses the slouch
    of his hat away from his forehead,
The sun falls on his crispy hair and moustache . . . . falls on
    the black of his polish'd and perfect limbs.

I behold the picturesque giant and love him . . . . and I do not
    stop there,
I go with the team also.   225

In me the caresser of life wherever moving . . . . backward as
    well as forward slueing,
To niches aside and junior bending.

Oxen that rattle the yoke or halt in the shade, what is that you
    express in your eyes?
It seems to me more than all the print I have read in my life.

My tread scares the wood-drake and wood-duck on my distant
    and daylong ramble,
They rise together, they slowly circle around.   230
. . . . I believe in those winged purposes,
And acknowledge the red yellow and white playing within me,
And consider the green and violet and the tufted crown
    intentional;
And do not call the tortoise unworthy because she is not
    something else,   235

And the mockingbird in the swamp never studied the gamut,
    yet trills pretty well to me,
And the look of the bay mare shames silliness out of me.

The wild gander leads his flock through the cool night,
Ya-honk! he says, and sounds it down to me like an invitation;
The pert may suppose it meaningless, but I listen closer,   240
I find its purpose and place up there toward the November sky.

The sharphoofed moose of the north, the cat on the housesill,
    the chickadee, the prairie-dog,
The litter of the grunting sow as they tug at her teats,
The brood of the turkeyhen, and she with her halfspread wings,
I see in them and myself the same old law.   245

The press of my foot to the earth springs a hundred affections,
They scorn the best I can do to relate them.

I am enamoured of growing outdoors,
Of men that live among cattle or taste of the ocean or woods,
Of the builders and steerers of ships, of the wielders of axes
    and mauls, of the drivers of horses,   250
I can eat and sleep with them week in and week out.

What is commonest and cheapest and nearest and easiest is Me,
Me going in for my chances, spending for vast returns,
Adorning myself to bestow myself on the first that will take me,
Not asking the sky to come down to my goodwill,   255
Scattering it freely forever.

The pure contralto sings in the organloft,
The carpenter dresses his plank . . . . the tongue of his
    foreplane whistles its wild ascending lisp,
The married and unmarried children ride home to their
    thanksgiving dinner,
The pilot seizes the king-pin, he heaves down with a strong
    arm,   260
The mate stands braced in the whaleboat, lance and harpoon
    are ready,
The duck-shooter walks by silent and cautious stretches,
The deacons are ordained with crossed hands at the altar,
The spinning-girl retreats and advances to the hum of the big
    wheel,
The farmer stops by the bars of a Sunday and looks at the oats
    and rye,   265
The lunatic is carried at last to the asylum a confirmed case,

He will never sleep any more as he did in the cot in his
    mother's bedroom;
The jour printer with gray head and gaunt jaws works at his case,
He turns his quid of tobacco, his eyes get blurred with the
    manuscript;
The malformed limbs are tied to the anatomist's table,   270
What is removed drops horribly in a pail;
The quadroon girl is sold at the stand . . . . the drunkard nods
    by the barroom stove,
The machinist rolls up his sleeves . . . . the policeman travels
    his beat . . . . the gate-keeper marks who pass,
The young fellow drives the express-wagon . . . . I love him
    though I do not know him;
The half-breed straps on his light boots to compete in the
    race,   275
The western turkey-shooting draws old and young . . . . some
    lean on their rifles, some sit on logs,
Out from the crowd steps the marksman and takes his position
    and levels his piece;
The groups of newly-come immigrants cover the wharf or levee,
The woollypates hoe in the sugarfield, the overseer views them
    from his saddle;
The bugle calls in the ballroom, the gentlemen run for their
    partners, the dancers bow to each other;   280
The youth lies awake in the cedar-roofed garret and harks to
    the musical rain,
The Wolverine sets traps on the creek that helps fill the Huron,
The reformer ascends the platform, he spouts with his mouth
    and nose,
The company returns from its excursion, the darkey brings up
    the rear and bears the well-riddled target,
The squaw wrapt in her yellow-hemmed cloth is offering
    moccasins and beadbags for sale,   285
The connoisseur peers along the exhibition-gallery with
    halfshut eyes bent sideways,
The deckhands make fast the steamboat, the plank is thrown
    for the shoregoing passengers,
The young sister holds out the skein, the elder sister winds it
    off in a ball and stops now and then for the knots,
The one-year wife is recovering and happy, a week ago she
    bore her first child,
The cleanhaired Yankee girl works with her sewing-machine or
    in the factory or mill,   290
The nine months' gone is in the parturition chamber, her
    faintness and pains are advancing;
The pavingman leans on his twohanded rammer—the
    reporter's lead flies swiftly over the notebook—the
    signpainter is lettering with red and gold,
The canal-boy trots on the towpath—the bookkeeper counts at
    his desk—the shoemaker waxes his thread,

The conductor beats time for the band and all the performers
    follow him,
The child is baptised—the convert is making the first
    professions,   295
The regatta is spread on the bay . . . . how the white sails sparkle!
The drover watches his drove, he sings out to them that would
    stray,
The pedlar sweats with his pack on his back—the purchaser
    higgles about the odd cent,
The camera and plate are prepared, the lady must sit for her
    daguerreotype,
The bride unrumples her white dress, the minutehand of the
    clock moves slowly,   300
The opium eater reclines with rigid head and just-opened lips,
The prostitute draggles her shawl, her bonnet bobs on her
    tipsy and pimpled neck,
The crowd laugh at her blackguard oaths, the men jeer and
    wink to each other,
(Miserable! I do not laugh at your oaths nor jeer you,)
The President holds a cabinet council, he is surrounded by the
    great secretaries,   305
On the piazza walk five friendly matrons with twined arms;
The crew of the fish-smack pack repeated layers of halibut in
    the hold,
The Missourian crosses the plains toting his wares and his cattle,
The fare-collector goes through the train—he gives notice by
    the jingling of loose change,
The floormen are laying the floor—the tinners are tinning the
    roof—the masons are calling for mortar,   310
In single file each shouldering his hod pass onward the laborers;
Seasons pursuing each other the indescribable crowd is
    gathered . . . . it is the Fourth of July . . . . what salutes
    of cannon and small arms!
Seasons pursuing each other the plougher ploughs and the
    mower mows and the wintergrain falls in the ground;
Off on the lakes the pikefisher watches and waits by the hole
    in the frozen surface,
The stumps stand thick round the clearing, the squatter strikes
    deep with his axe,   315
The flatboatmen make fast toward dusk near the cottonwood
    or pekantrees,
The coon-seekers go now through the regions of the Red river,
    or through those drained by the Tennessee, or through
    those of the Arkansas,
The torches shine in the dark that hangs on the
    Chattahoochee or Altamahaw;
Patriarchs sit at supper with sons and grandsons and great
    grandsons around them,

In walls of abode, in canvass tents, rest hunters and trappers
    after their day's sport.   320
The city sleeps and the country sleeps,
The living sleep for their time . . . . the dead sleep for their time,
The old husband sleeps by his wife and the young husband
    sleeps by his wife;
And these one and all tend inward to me, and I tend outward
    to them,
And such as it is to be of these more or less I am.   325

I am of old and young, of the foolish as much as the wise,
Regardless of others, ever regardful of others,
Maternal as well as paternal, a child as well as a man,
Stuffed with the stuff that is coarse, and stuffed with the stuff
    that is fine,
One of the great nation, the nation of many nations—the
    smallest the same and the largest the same,   330
A southerner soon as a northener, a planter nonchalant and
    hospitable,
A Yankee bound my own way . . . . ready for trade . . . . my
    joints the limberest joints on earth and the sternest joints
    on earth,
A Kentuckian walking the vale of the Elkhorn in my deerskin
    leggings,
A boatman over the lakes or bays or along coasts . . . . a
    Hoosier, a Badger, a Buckeye,
A Louisianian or Georgian, a poke-easy from sandhills and
    pines,   335
At home on Canadian snowshoes or up in the bush, or with
    fishermen off New foundland,
At home in the fleet of iceboats, sailing with the rest and tacking,
At home on the hills of Vermont or in the woods of Maine or
    the Texan ranch,
Comrade of Californians . . . . comrade of free
    northwesterners, loving their big proportions,
Comrade of raftsmen and coalmen—comrade of all who shake
    hands and welcome to drink and meat;   340
A learner with the simplest, a teacher of the thoughtfulest,
A novice beginning experient of myriads of seasons,
Of every hue and trade and rank, of every caste and religion,
Not merely of the New World but of Africa Europe or Asia . . . .
    a wandering savage,
A farmer, mechanic, or artist . . . . a gentleman, sailor, lover or
    quaker,   345
A prisoner, fancy-man, rowdy, lawyer, physician or priest.

I resist anything better than my own diversity,
And breathe the air and leave plenty after me,
And am not stuck up, and am in my place.

The moth and the fisheggs are in their place,   350
The suns I see and the suns I cannot see are in their place,
The palpable is in its place and the impalpable is in its place.

These are the thoughts of all men in all ages and lands, they
    are not original with me,
If they are not yours as much as mine they are nothing or next
    to nothing,
If they do not enclose everything they are next to nothing,   355
If they are not the riddle and the untying of the riddle they are
    nothing,
If they are not just as close as they are distant they are nothing.

This is the grass that grows wherever the land is and the water is,
This is the common air that bathes the globe.

This is the breath of laws and songs and behaviour,   360
This is the tasteless water of souls . . . . this is the true
    sustenance,
It is for the illiterate . . . . it is for the judges of the supreme
    court . . . . it is for the federal capitol and the state
    capitols,
It is for the admirable communes of literary men and
    composers and singers and lecturers and engineers and
    savans,
It is for the endless races of working people and farmers and
    seamen.

This is the trill of a thousand clear cornets and scream of the
    octave flute and strike of triangles.   365

I play not a march for victors only . . . . I play great marches
    for conquered and slain persons.

Have you heard that it was good to gain the day?
I also say it is good to fall . . . . battles are lost in the same
    spirit in which they are won.

I sound triumphal drums for the dead . . . . I fling through my
    embouchures the loudest and gayest music to them,
Vivas to those who have failed, and to those whose war-vessels
    sank in the sea, and those themselves who sank in the
    sea,   370
And to all generals that lost engagements, and all overcome

heroes, and the numberless unknown heroes equal to the
    greatest heroes known.

This is the meal pleasantly set . . . . this is the meat and drink
    for natural hunger,
It is for the wicked just the same as the righteous . . . . I make
    appointments with all,
I will not have a single person slighted or left away,
The keptwoman and sponger and thief are hereby invited . . . .
    the heavy-lipped slave is invited . . . . the venerealee is
    invited,
There shall be no difference between them and the rest. 375

This is the press of a bashful hand . . . . this is the float and
    odor of hair,
This is the touch of my lips to yours . . . . this is the murmur
    of yearning,
This is the far-off depth and height reflecting my own face,
This is the thoughtful merge of myself and the outlet again. 380

Do you guess I have some intricate purpose?
Well I have . . . . for the April rain has, and the mica on the
    side of a rock has.

Do you take it I would astonish?
Does the daylight astonish? or the early redstart twittering
    through the woods?
Do I astonish more than they? 385

This hour I tell things in confidence,
I might not tell everybody but I will tell you.

Who goes there! hankering, gross, mystical, nude?
How is it I extract strength from the beef I eat?

What is a man anyhow? What am I? and what are you? 390
All I mark as my own you shall offset it with your own,
Else it were time lost listening to me.

I do not snivel that snivel the world over,
That months are vacuums and the ground but wallow and filth,
That life is a suck and a sell, and nothing remains at the end
    but threadbare crape and tears. 395

Whimpering and truckling fold with powders for invalids . . . .
    conformity goes to the fourth-removed,
I cock my hat as I please indoors or out.

Shall I pray? Shall I venerate and be ceremonious?

I have pried through the strata and analyzed to a hair,
And counselled with doctors and calculated close and found
    no sweeter fat than sticks to my own bones.   400

In all people I see myself, none more and not one a barleycorn
    less,
And the good or bad I say of myself I say of them.

And I know I am solid and sound,
To me the converging objects of the universe perpetually flow,
All are written to me, and I must get what the writing means.   405

And I know I am deathless,
I know this orbit of mine cannot be swept by a carpenter's
    compass,
I know I shall not pass like a child's carlacue cut with a burnt
    stick at night,

I know I am august,
I do not trouble my spirit to vindicate itself or be understood,   410
I see that the elementary laws never apologize,
I reckon I behave no prouder than the level I plant my house
    by after all.

I exist as I am, that is enough,
If no other in the world be aware I sit content,
And if each and all be aware I sit content.   415

One world is aware, and by far the largest to me, and that is
    myself,
And whether I come to my own today or in ten thousand or
    ten million years,
I can cheerfully take it now, or with equal cheerfulness I can wait.

My foothold is tenoned and mortised in granite,
I laugh at what you call dissolution,   420
And I know the amplitude of time.

I am the poet of the body,
And I am the poet of the soul.

The pleasures of heaven are with me, and the pains of hell are
    with me,
The first I graft and increase upon myself . . . . the latter I
    translate into a new tongue.   425

I am the poet of the woman the same as the man,
And I say it is as great to be a woman as to be a man,
And I say there is nothing greater than the mother of men.

I chant a new chant of dilation or pride,
We have had ducking and deprecating about enough,   430
I show that size is only development.

Have you outstript the rest? Are you the President?
It is a trifle . . . . they will more than arrive there every one,
    and still pass on.

I am he that walks with the tender and growing night;
I call to the earth and sea half-held by the night.   435

Press close barebosomed night! Press close magnetic
    nourishing night!
Night of south winds! Night of the large few stars!
Still nodding night! Mad naked summer night!

Smile O voluptuous coolbreathed earth!
Earth of the slumbering and liquid trees!   440
Earth of departed sunset! Earth of the mountains misty-topt!
Earth of the vitreous pour of the full moon just tinged with blue!
Earth of shine and dark mottling the tide of the river!
Earth of the limpid gray of clouds brighter and clearer for my sake!
Far-swooping elbowed earth! Rich apple-blossomed earth!   445
Smile, for your lover comes!

Prodigal! you have given me love! . . . . therefore I to you give love!
O unspeakable passionate love!

Thruster holding me tight and that I hold tight!
We hurt each other as the bridegroom and the bride hurt each
    other.   450

You sea! I resign myself to you also . . . . I guess what you mean,
I behold from the beach your crooked inviting fingers,
I believe you refuse to go back without feeling of me;
We must have a turn together . . . . I undress . . . . hurry me
    out of sight of the land,
Cushion me soft . . . . rock me in billowy drowse,   455
Dash me with amorous wet . . . . I can repay you.

Sea of stretched ground-swells!
Sea breathing broad and convulsive breaths!
Sea of the brine of life! Sea of unshovelled and always-ready graves!
Howler and scooper of storms! Capricious and dainty sea!   460
I am integral with you . . . . I too am of one phase and of all
    phases.

Partaker of influx and efflux . . . . extoler of hate and
    conciliation,
Extoler of amies and those that sleep in each others' arms.

I am he attesting sympathy;
Shall I make my list of things in the house and skip the house
    that supports them?   465

I am the poet of commonsense and of the demonstrable and of
    immortality;
And am not the poet of goodness only . . . . I do not decline to
    be the poet of wickedness also.

Washes and razors for foofoos . . . . for me freckles and a
    bristling beard.

What blurt is it about virtue and about vice?
Evil propels me, and reform of evil propels me . . . . I stand
    indifferent,   470
My gait is no faultfinder's or rejecter's gait,
I moisten the roots of all that has grown.

Did you fear some scrofula out of the unflagging pregnancy?
Did you guess the celestial laws are yet to be worked over and
    rectified?

I step up to say that what we do is right and what we affirm is
    right . . . . and some is only the ore of right,   475
Witnesses of us . . . . one side a balance and the antipodal
    side a balance,
Soft doctrine as steady help as stable doctrine,
Thoughts and deeds of the present our rouse and early start.

This minute that comes to me over the past decillions,
There is no better than it and now.   480

What behaved well in the past or behaves well today is not
    such a wonder,
The wonder is always and always how there can be a mean
    man or an infidel.

Endless unfolding of words of ages!
And mine a word of the modern . . . . a word en masse.

A word of the faith that never balks,   485
One time as good as another time . . . . here or henceforward
    it is all the same to me.

A word of reality . . . . materialism first and last imbueing.

Hurrah for positive science! Long live exact demonstration!
Fetch stonecrop and mix it with cedar and branches of lilac;
This is the lexicographer or chemist . . . . this made a grammar
    of the old cartouches,   490
These mariners put the ship through dangerous unknown seas,
This is the geologist, and this works with the scalpel, and this
    is a mathematician.

Gentlemen I receive you, and attach and clasp hands with you,
The facts are useful and real . . . . they are not my dwelling
    . . . . I enter by them to an area of the dwelling.

I am less the reminder of property or qualities, and more the
    reminder of life,   495
And go on the square for my own sake and for others' sakes,
And make short account of neuters and geldings, and favor
    men and women fully equipped,
And beat the gong of revolt, and stop with fugitives and them
    that plot and conspire.

Walt Whitman, an American, one of the roughs, a kosmos,
Disorderly fleshy and sensual . . . . eating drinking and
    breeding,   500
No sentimentalist . . . . no stander above men and women or
    apart from them . . . . no more modest than immodest.

Unscrew the locks from the doors!
Unscrew the doors themselves from their jambs!

Whoever degrades another degrades me . . . . and whatever is
    done or said returns at last to me,
And whatever I do or say I also return.   505

Through me the afflatus surging and surging . . . . through me
    the current and index.

I speak the password primeval . . . . I give the sign of democracy;
By God! I will accept nothing which all cannot have their
    counterpart of on the same terms.

Through me many long dumb voices,
Voices of the interminable generations of slaves,   510
Voices of prostitutes and of deformed persons,
Voices of the diseased and despairing, and of thieves and dwarfs,
Voices of cycles of preparation and accretion,
And of the threads that connect the stars—and of wombs, and
    of the fatherstuff,
And of the rights of them the others are down upon,   515

Of the trivial and flat and foolish and despised,
Of fog in the air and beetles rolling balls of dung.

Through me forbidden voices,
Voices of sexes and lusts . . . . voices veiled, and I remove the veil,
Voices indecent by me clarified and transfigured.   520

I do not press my finger across my mouth,
I keep as delicate around the bowels as around the head and heart,
Copulation is no more rank to me than death is.

I believe in the flesh and the appetites,
Seeing hearing and feeling are miracles, and each part and tag
    of me is a miracle.   525

Divine am I inside and out, and I make holy whatever I touch
    or am touched from;
The scent of these arm-pits is aroma finer than prayer,
This head is more than churches or bibles or creeds.

If I worship any particular thing it shall be some of the spread
    of my body;
Translucent mould of me it shall be you,   530
Shaded ledges and rests, firm masculine coulter, it shall be you,
Whatever goes to the tilth of me it shall be you,
You my rich blood, your milky stream pale strippings of my life;
Breast that presses against other breasts it shall be you,
My brain it shall be your occult convolutions,   535
Root of washed sweet-flag, timorous pond-snipe, nest of
    guarded duplicate eggs, it shall be you,
Mixed tussled hay of head and beard and brawn it shall be you,
Trickling sap of maple, fibre of manly wheat, it shall be you;
Sun so generous it shall be you,
Vapors lighting and shading my face it shall be you,   540
You sweaty brooks and dews it shall be you,
Winds whose soft-tickling genitals rub against me it shall be you,
Broad muscular fields, branches of liveoak, loving lounger in
    my winding paths, it shall be you,
Hands I have taken, face I have kissed, mortal I have ever
    touched, it shall be you.

I dote on myself . . . . there is that lot of me, and all so
    luscious,   545
Each moment and whatever happens thrills me with joy.

I cannot tell how my ankles bend . . . . nor whence the cause
    of my faintest wish,
Nor the cause of the friendship I emit . . . . nor the cause of
    the friendship I take again.

To walk up my stoop is unaccountable . . . . I pause to
    consider if it really be,
That I eat and drink is spectacle enough for the great authors
    and schools,   550
A morning-glory at my window satisfies me more than the
    metaphysics of books.

To behold the daybreak!
The little light fades the immense and diaphanous shadows,
The air tastes good to my palate.

Hefts of the moving world at innocent gambols, silently rising,
    freshly exuding,   555
Scooting obliquely high and low.

Something I cannot see puts upward libidinous prongs,
Seas of bright juice suffuse heaven.

The earth by the sky staid with . . . . the daily close of their
    junction,
The heaved challenge from the east that moment over my
    head,   560
The mocking taunt, See then whether you shall be master!

Dazzling and tremendous how quick the sunrise would kill me,
If I could not now and always send sunrise out of me.

We also ascend dazzling and tremendous as the sun,
We found our own my soul in the calm and cool of the
    daybreak.   565

My voice goes after what my eyes cannot reach,
With the twirl of my tongue I encompass worlds and volumes
    of worlds.

Speech is the twin of my vision . . . . it is unequal to measure
    itself.

It provokes me forever,
It says sarcastically, Walt, you understand enough . . . . why
    don't you let it out then?   570

Come now I will not be tantalized . . . . you conceive too
    much of articulation.

Do you not know how the buds beneath are folded?
Waiting in gloom protected by frost,
The dirt receding before my prophetical screams,
I underlying causes to balance them at last,   575
My knowledge my live parts . . . . it keeping tally with the
      meaning of things,
Happiness . . . . which whoever hears me let him or her set
      out in search of this day.

My final merit I refuse you . . . . I refuse putting from me the
      best I am.

Encompass worlds but never try to encompass me,
I crowd your noisiest talk by looking toward you.   580

Writing and talk do not prove me,
I carry the plenum of proof and every thing else in my face,
With the hush of my lips I confound the topmost skeptic.

I think I will do nothing for a long time but listen,
And accrue what I hear into myself . . . . and let sounds
      contribute toward me.   585

I hear the bravuras of birds . . . . the bustle of growing wheat
      . . . . gossip of flames . . . . clack of sticks cooking my
      meals.

I hear the sound of the human voice . . . . a sound I love,
I hear all sounds as they are tuned to their uses . . . . sounds
      of the city and sounds out of the city . . . . sounds of the
      day and night;
Talkative young ones to those that like them . . . . the
      recitative of fish-pedlars and fruit-pedlars . . . . the loud
      laugh of workpeople at their meals,
The angry base of disjointed friendship . . . . the faint tones of
      the sick,   590
The judge with hands tight to the desk, his shaky lips
      pronouncing a death-sentence,
The heave'e'yo of stevedores unlading ships by the wharves . . . .
      the refrain of the anchor-lifters;
The ring of alarm-bells . . . . the cry of fire . . . . the whirr of
      swift-streaking engines and hose-carts with premonitory
      tinkles and colored lights,
The steam-whistle . . . . the solid roll of the train of
      approaching cars;
The slow-march played at night at the head of the association,   595
They go to guard some corpse . . . . the flag-tops are draped
      with black muslin.

I hear the violincello or man's heart's complaint,
And hear the keyed cornet or else the echo of sunset.

I hear the chorus . . . . it is a grand-opera . . . . this indeed is
    music!

A tenor large and fresh as the creation fills me,   600
The orbic flex of his mouth is pouring and filling me full.

I hear the trained soprano . . . . she convulses me like the
    climax of my love-grip;
The orchestra whirls me wider than Uranus flies,
It wrenches unnamable ardors from my breast,
It throbs me to gulps of the farthest down horror,   605
It sails me . . . . I dab with bare feet . . . . they are licked by
    the indolent waves,
I am exposed . . . . cut by bitter and poisoned hail,
Steeped amid honeyed morphine . . . . my windpipe squeezed
    in the fakes of death,
Let up again to feel the puzzle of puzzles,
And that we call Being.   610

To be in any form, what is that?
If nothing lay more developed the quahaug and its callous
    shell were enough.

Mine is no callous shell,
I have instant conductors all over me whether I pass or stop,
They seize every object and lead it harmlessly through me.   615

I merely stir, press, feel with my fingers, and am happy,
To touch my person to some one else's is about as much as I
    can stand.

Is this then a touch? . . . . quivering me to a new identity,
Flames and ether making a rush for my veins,
Treacherous tip of me reaching and crowding to help them,   620
My flesh and blood playing out lightning, to strike what is
    hardly different from myself,
On all sides prurient provokers stiffening my limbs,
Straining the udder of my heart for its withheld drip,
Behaving licentious toward me, taking no denial,
Depriving me of my best as for a purpose,   625
Unbuttoning my clothes and holding me by the bare waist,
Deluding my confusion with the calm of the sunlight and
    pasture fields,
Immodestly sliding the fellow-senses away,
They bribed to swap off with touch, and go and graze at the
    edges of me,
No consideration, no regard for my draining strength or my
    anger,   630
Fetching the rest of the herd around to enjoy them awhile,
Then all uniting to stand on a headland and worry me.

The sentries desert every other part of me,
They have left me helpless to a red marauder,
They all come to the headland to witness and assist against
    me.   635

I am given up by traitors;
I talk wildly . . . . I have lost my wits . . . . I and nobody else
    am the greatest traitor,
I went myself first to the headland . . . . my own hands carried
    me there.

You villain touch! what are you doing? . . . . my breath is tight
    in its throat;
Unclench your floodgates! you are too much for me.   640

Blind loving wrestling touch! Sheathed hooded sharptoothed
    touch!
Did it make you ache so leaving me?

Parting tracked by arriving . . . . perpetual payment of the
    perpetual loan,
Rich showering rain, and recompense richer afterward.

Sprouts take and accumulate . . . . stand by the curb prolific
    and vital,   645
Landscapes projected masculine full-sized and golden.

All truths wait in all things,
They neither hasten their own delivery nor resist it,
They do not need the obstetric forceps of the surgeon,
The insignificant is as big to me as any,   650
What is less or more than a touch?

Logic and sermons never convince,
The damp of the night drives deeper into my soul.

Only what proves itself to every man and woman is so,
Only what nobody denies is so.   655

A minute and a drop of me settle my brain;
I believe the soggy clods shall become lovers and lamps,
And a compend of compends is the meat of a man or woman,
And a summit and flower there is the feeling they have for
    each other,
And they are to branch boundlessly out of that lesson until it
    becomes omnific,   660
And until every one shall delight us, and we them.

I believe a leaf of grass is no less than the journeywork of the stars,
And the pismire is equally perfect, and a grain of sand, and
    the egg of the wren,
And the tree-toad is a chef-d'ouvre for the highest,
And the running blackberry would adorn the parlors of heaven,   665
And the narrowest hinge in my hand puts to scorn all machinery,
And the cow crunching with depressed head surpasses any statue,
And a mouse is miracle enough to stagger sextillions of infidels,
And I could come every afternoon of my life to look at the
    farmer's girl boiling her iron tea-kettle and baking
    shortcake.

I find I incorporate gneiss and coal and long-threaded moss
    and fruits and grains and esculent roots,   670
And am stucco'd with quadrupeds and birds all over,
And have distanced what is behind me for good reasons,
And call any thing close again when I desire it.

In vain the speeding or shyness,
In vain the plutonic rocks send their old heat against my
    approach,   675
In vain the mastadon retreats beneath its own powdered bones,
In vain objects stand leagues off and assume manifold shapes,
In vain the ocean settling in hollows and the great monsters
    lying low,
In vain the buzzard houses herself with the sky,
In vain the snake slides through the creepers and logs,   680
In vain the elk takes to the inner passes of the woods,
In vain the razorbilled auk sails far north to Labrador,
I follow quickly . . . . I ascend to the nest in the fissure of the
    cliff.

I think I could turn and live awhile with the animals . . . . they
    are so placid and self-contained,
I stand and look at them sometimes half the day long.   685

They do not sweat and whine about their condition,
They do not lie awake in the dark and weep for their sins,
They do not make me sick discussing their duty to God,
Not one is dissatisfied . . . . not one is demented with the
    mania of owning things,
Not one kneels to another nor to his kind that lived thousands
    of years ago,   690
Not one is respectable or industrious over the whole earth.

So they show their relations to me and I accept them;
They bring me tokens of myself . . . . they evince them plainly
    in their possession.

I do not know where they got those tokens,
I must have passed that way untold times ago and negligently
    dropt them,   695
Myself moving forward then and now and forever,
Gathering and showing more always and with velocity,
Infinite and omnigenous and the like of these among them;
Not too exclusive toward the reachers of my remembrancers,
Picking out here one that shall be my amie,   700
Choosing to go with him on brotherly terms.

A gigantic beauty of a stallion, fresh and responsive to my
    caresses,
Head high in the forehead and wide between the ears,
Limbs glossy and supple, tail dusting the ground,
Eyes well apart and full of sparkling wickedness . . . . ears
    finely cut and flexibly moving.   705

His nostrils dilate . . . . my heels embrace him . . . . his well
    built limbs tremble with pleasure . . . . we speed around
    and return.

I but use you a moment and then I resign you stallion . . . .
    and do not need your paces, and outgallop them,
And myself as I stand or sit pass faster than you.

Swift wind! Space! My Soul! Now I know it is true what I
    guessed at;
What I guessed when I loafed on the grass,   710
What I guessed while I lay alone in my bed . . . . and again as
    I walked the beach under the paling stars of the morning.

My ties and ballasts leave me . . . . I travel . . . . I sail . . . .
    my elbows rest in the sea-gaps,
I skirt the sierras . . . . my palms cover continents,
I am afoot with my vision.

By the city's quadrangular houses . . . . in log-huts, or camping
    with lumbermen,   715
Along the ruts of the turnpike . . . . along the dry gulch and
    rivulet bed,
Hoeing my onion-patch, and rows of carrots and parsnips . . . .
    crossing savannas . . . trailing in forests,
Prospecting . . . . gold-digging . . . . girdling the trees of a new
    purchase,
Scorched ankle-deep by the hot sand . . . . hauling my boat
    down the shallow river;
Where the panther walks to and fro on a limb overhead . . . .
    where the buck turns furiously at the hunter,   720
Where the rattlesnake suns his flabby length on a rock . . . .
    where the otter is feeding on fish,

Where the alligator in his tough pimples sleeps by the bayou,
Where the black bear is searching for roots or honey . . . .
   where the beaver pats the mud with his paddle-tail;
Over the growing sugar . . . . over the cottonplant . . . . over
   the rice in its low moist field;
Over the sharp-peaked farmhouse with its scalloped scum and
   slender shoots from the gutters; 725
Over the western persimmon . . . . over the longleaved corn
   and the delicate blue-flowered flax;
Over the white and brown buckwheat, a hummer and a buzzer
   there with the rest,
Over the dusky green of the rye as it ripples and shades in the
   breeze;
Scaling mountains . . . . pulling myself cautiously up . . . .
   holding on by low scragged limbs,
Walking the path worn in the grass and beat through the
   leaves of the brush; 730
Where the quail is whistling betwixt the woods and the wheatlot,
Where the bat flies in the July eve . . . . where the great
   goldbug drops through the dark;
Where the flails keep time on the barn floor,
Where the brook puts out of the roots of the old tree and
   flows to the meadow,
Where cattle stand and shake away flies with the tremulous
   shuddering of their hides, 735
Where the cheese-cloth hangs in the kitchen, and andirons
   straddle the hearth-slab, and cobwebs fall in festoons from
   the rafters;
Where triphammers crash . . . . where the press is whirling its
   cylinders;
Wherever the human heart beats with terrible throes out of its
   ribs;
Where the pear-shaped balloon is floating aloft . . . . floating
   in it myself and looking composedly down;
Where the life-ear is drawn on the slipnoose . . . . where the
   heat hatches pale-green eggs in the dented sand, 740
Where the she-whale swims with her calves and never forsakes
   them,
Where the steamship trails hindways its long pennant of smoke,
Where the ground-shark's fin cuts like a black chip out of the
   water,
Where the half-burned brig is riding on unknown currents,
Where shells grow to her slimy deck, and the dead are
   corrupting below; 745
Where the striped and starred flag is borne at the head of the
   regiments;
Approaching Manhattan, up by the long-stretching island,
Under Niagara, the cataract falling like a veil over my
   countenance;
Upon a door-step . . . . upon the horse-block of hard wood
   outside,

Upon the race-course, or enjoying pic-nics or jigs or a good
    game of base-ball,   750
At he-festivals with blackguard jibes and ironical license and
    bull-dances and drinking and laughter,
At the cider-mill, tasting the sweet of the brown sqush . . . .
    sucking the juice through a straw,
At apple-pealings, wanting kisses for all the red fruit I find,
At musters and beach-parties and friendly bees and huskings
    and house-raisings;
Where the mockingbird sounds his delicious gurgles, and
    cackles and screams and weeps,   755
Where the hay-rick stands in the barnyard, and the dry-stalks
    are scattered, and the brood cow waits in the hovel,
Where the bull advances to do his masculine work, and the
    stud to the mare, and the cock is treading the hen,
Where the heifers browse, and the geese nip their food with
    short jerks;
Where the sundown shadows lengthen over the limitless and
    lonesome prairie,
Where the herds of buffalo make a crawling spread of the
    square miles far and near;   760
Where the hummingbird shimmers . . . . where the neck of
    the longlived swan is curving and winding;
Where the laughing-gull scoots by the slappy shore and laughs
    her near-human laugh;
Where beehives range on a gray bench in the garden half-hid
    by the high weeds;
Where the band-necked partridges roost in a ring on the
    ground with their heads out;
Where burial coaches enter the arched gates of a cemetery;   765
Where winter wolves bark amid wastes of snow and icicled
    trees;
Where the yellow-crowned heron comes to the edge of the
    marsh at night and feeds upon small crabs;
Where the splash of swimmers and divers cools the warm
    noon;
Where the katydid works her chromatic reed on the walnut-
    tree over the well;
Through patches of citrons and cucumbers with silver-wired
    leaves,   770
Through the salt-lick or orange glade . . . . or under conical
    furs;
Through the gymnasium . . . . through the curtained saloon
    . . . . through the office or public hall;
Pleased with the native and pleased with the foreign . . . .
    pleased with the new and old,
Pleased with women, the homely as well as the handsome,
Pleased with the quakeress as she puts off her bonnet and
    talks melodiously,   775
Pleased with the primitive tunes of the choir of the
    whitewashed church,

Pleased with the earnest words of the sweating Methodist
    preacher, or any preacher . . . . looking seriously at the
    camp-meeting;
Looking in at the shop-windows in Broadway the whole
    forenoon . . . . pressing the flesh of my nose to the thick
    plate-glass,
Wandering the same afternoon with my face turned up to the
    clouds;
My right and left arms round the sides of two friends and I in
    the middle;   780
Coming home with the bearded and dark-cheeked bush-boy
    . . . . riding behind him at the drape of the day;
Far from the settlements studying the print of animals' feet, or
    the moccasin print;
By the cot in the hospital reaching lemonade to a feverish
    patient,
By the coffined corpse when all is still, examining with a candle;
Voyaging to every port to dicker and adventure;   785
Hurrying with the modern crowd, as eager and fickle as any,
Hot toward one I hate, ready in my madness to knife him;
Solitary at midnight in my back yard, my thoughts gone from
    me a long while,
Walking the old hills of Judea with the beautiful gentle god by
    my side;
Speeding through space . . . . speeding through heaven and
    the stars,   790
Speeding amid the seven satellites and the broad ring and the
    diameter of eighty thousand miles,
Speeding with tailed meteors . . . . throwing fire-balls like the
    rest,
Carrying the crescent child that carries its own full mother in
    its belly:
Storming enjoying planning loving cautioning,
Backing and filling, appearing and disappearing,   795
I tread day and night such roads.

I visit the orchards of God and look at the spheric product,
And look at quintillions ripened, and look at quintillions green.

I fly the flight of the fluid and swallowing soul,
My course runs below the soundings of plummets.   800

I help myself to material and immaterial,
No guard can shut me off, no law can prevent me.

I anchor my ship for a little while only,
My messengers continually cruise away or bring their returns
    to me.

I go hunting polar furs and the seal . . . . leaping chasms with
    a pike-pointed staff . . . . clinging to topples of brittle and
    blue.   805

I ascend to the foretruck . . . . I take my place late at night in
    the crow's nest . . . . we sail through the arctic sea . . . . it
    is plenty light enough,
Through the clear atmosphere I stretch around on the
    wonderful beauty,
The enormous masses of ice pass me and I pass them . . . .
    the scenery is plain in all directions,
The white-topped mountains point up in the distance I
    fling out my fancies toward them;
We are about approaching some great battlefield in which we
    are soon to be engaged,   810
We pass the colossal outposts of the encampments . . . . we
    pass with still feet and caution;
Or we are entering by the suburbs some vast and ruined city
    . . . . the blocks and fallen architecture more than all the
    living cities of the globe.

I am a free companion . . . . I bivouac by invading watchfires.

I turn the bridegroom out of bed and stay with the bride myself,
And tighten her all night to my thighs and lips.   815

My voice is the wife's voice, the screech by the rail of the stairs,
They fetch my man's body up dripping and drowned.

I understand the large hearts of heroes,
The courage of present times and all times;
How the skipper saw the crowded and rudderless wreck of the
    steamship, and death chasing it up and down the storm,   820
How he knuckled tight and gave not back one inch, and was
    faithful of days and faithful of nights,
And chalked in large letters on a board, Be of good cheer, We
    will not desert you;
How he saved the drifting company at last,
How the lank loose-gowned women looked when boated from
    the side of their prepared graves,
How the silent old-faced infants, and the lifted sick, and the
    sharp-lipped unshaved men;   825
All this I swallow and it tastes good . . . . I like it well, and it
    becomes mine,
I am the man . . . . I suffered . . . . I was there.

The disdain and calmness of martyrs,
The mother condemned for a witch and burnt with dry wood,
    and her children gazing on;

The hounded slave that flags in the race and leans by the
    fence, blowing and covered with sweat,   830
The twinges that sting like needles his legs and neck,
The murderous buckshot and the bullets,
All these I feel or am.

I am the hounded slave . . . . I wince at the bite of the dogs,
Hell and despair are upon me . . . . crack and again crack the
    marksmen,   835
I clutch the rails of the fence . . . . my gore dribs thinned with
    the ooze of my skin,
I fall on the weeds and stones,
The riders spur their unwilling horses and haul close,
They taunt my dizzy ears . . . . they beat me violently over the
    head with their whip-stocks.

Agonies are one of my changes of garments;   840
I do not ask the wounded person how he feels . . . . I myself
    become the wounded person,
My hurt turns livid upon me as I lean on a cane and observe.

I am the mashed fireman with breastbone broken . . . .
    tumbling walls buried me in their debris,
Heat and smoke I inspired . . . . I heard the yelling shouts of
    my comrades,
I heard the distant click of their picks and shovels;   845
They have cleared the beams away . . . . they tenderly lift me forth.

I lie in the night air in my red shirt . . . . the pervading hush
    is for my sake,
Painless after all I lie, exhausted but not so unhappy,
White and beautiful are the faces around me . . . . the heads
    are bared of their firecaps,
The kneeling crowd fades with the light of the torches.   850

Distant and dead resuscitate,
They show as the dial or move as the hands of me . . . . and I
    am the clock myself.

I am an old artillerist, and tell of some fort's bombardment
    . . . . and am there again.

Again the reveille of drummers . . . . again the attacking
    cannon and mortars and howitzers,
Again the attacked send their cannon responsive.   855

I take part . . . . I see and hear the whole,
The cries and curses and roar . . . . the plaudits for well aimed
    shots,
The ambulanza slowly passing and trailing its red drip,

Workmen searching after damages and to make indispensible
    repairs,
The fall of grenades through the rent roof . . . . the fan-shaped
    explosion,   860
The whizz of limbs heads stone wood and iron high in the air.

Again gurgles the mouth of my dying general . . . . he furiously
    waves with his hand,
He gasps through the clot . . . . Mind not me . . . . mind . . . .
    the entrenchments.

I tell not the fall of Alamo . . . . not one escaped to tell the
    fall of Alamo,
The hundred and fifty are dumb yet at Alamo.   865

Hear now the the tale of a jetblack sunrise,
Hear of the murder in cold blood of four hundred and twelve
    young men.

Retreating they had formed in a hollow square with their
    baggage for breastworks,
Nine hundred lives out of the surrounding enemy's nine times
    their number was the price they took in advance,
Their colonel was wounded and their ammunition gone,   870
They treated for an honorable capitulation, received writing
    and seal, gave up their arms, and marched back prisoners
    of war.

They were the glory of the race of rangers,
Matchless with a horse, a rifle, a song, a supper or a courtship,
Large, turbulent, brave, handsome, generous, proud and
    affectionate,
Bearded, sunburnt, dressed in the free costume of hunters,   875
Not a single one over thirty years of age.

The second Sunday morning they were brought out in squads
    and massacred . . . . it was beautiful early summer,
The work commenced about five o'clock and was over by eight.

None obeyed the command to kneel,
Some made a mad and helpless rush . . . . some stood stark
    and straight,   880
A few fell at once, shot in the temple or heart . . . . the living
    and dead lay together,
The maimed and mangled dug in the dirt . . . . the new-
    comers saw them there;
Some half-killed attempted to crawl away,
These were dispatched with bayonets or battered with the
    blunts of muskets;

A youth not seventeen years old seized his assassin till two
    more came to release him,   885
The three were all torn, and covered with the boy's blood.

At eleven o'clock began the burning of the bodies;
And that is the tale of the murder of the four hundred and
    twelve young men,
And that was a jetblack sunrise.

Did you read in the seabooks of the oldfashioned frigate-fight?   890
Did you learn who won by the light of the moon and stars?

Our foe was no skulk in his ship, I tell you,
His was the English pluck, and there is no tougher or truer,
    and never was, and never will be;
Along the lowered eve he came, horribly raking us.

We closed with him . . . . the yards entangled . . . . the
    cannon touched,   895
My captain lashed fast with his own hands.

We had received some eighteen-pound shots under the water,
On our lower-gun-deck two large pieces had burst at the first
    fire, killing all around and blowing up overhead.

Ten o'clock at night, and the full moon shining and the leaks
    on the gain, and five feet of water reported,
The master-at-arms loosing the prisoners confined in the after-
    hold to give them a chance for themselves.   900

The transit to and from the magazine was now stopped by the
    sentinels,
They saw so many strange faces they did not know whom to trust.

Our frigate was afire . . . . the other asked if we demanded
    quarters? if our colors were struck and the fighting done?

I laughed content when I heard the voice of my little captain,
We have not struck, he composedly cried, We have just begun
    our part of the fighting.   905

Only three guns were in use,
One was directed by the captain himself against the enemy's
    mainmast,
Two well-served with grape and canister silenced his musketry
    and cleared his decks.

The tops alone seconded the fire of this little battery,
    especially the maintop,
They all held out bravely during the whole of the action.   910

Not a moment's cease,
The leaks gained fast on the pumps . . . . the fire eat toward
the powder-magazine,
One of the pumps was shot away . . . . it was generally
thought we were sinking.

Serene stood the little captain,
He was not hurried . . . . his voice was neither high nor low,   915
His eyes gave more light to us than our battle-lanterns.

Toward twelve at night, there in the beams of the moon they
surrendered to us.

Stretched and still lay the midnight,
Two great hulls motionless on the breast of the darkness,
Our vessel riddled and slowly sinking . . . . preparations to pass
to the one we had conquered,   920
The captain on the quarter deck coldly giving his orders
through a countenance white as a sheet,
Near by the corpse of the child that served in the cabin,
The dead face of an old salt with long white hair and carefully
curled whiskers,
The flames spite of all that could be done flickering aloft and
below,
The husky voices of the two or three officers yet fit for duty,   925
Formless stacks of bodies and bodies by themselves . . . . dabs
of flesh upon the masts and spars,
The cut of cordage and dangle of rigging . . . . the slight shock
of the soothe of waves,
Black and impassive guns, and litter of powder-parcels, and the
strong scent,
Delicate sniffs of the seabreeze . . . . smells of sedgy grass and
fields by the shore . . . death-messages given in charge to
survivors,
The hiss of the surgeon's knife and the gnawing teeth of his saw, 930
The wheeze, the cluck, the swash of falling blood . . . . the
short wild scream, the long dull tapering groan,
These so . . . . these irretrievable.

O Christ! My fit is mastering me!
What the rebel said gaily adjusting his throat to the rope-noose,
What the savage at the stump, his eye-sockets empty, his
mouth spirting whoops and defiance,   935
What stills the traveler come to the vault at Mount Vernon,
What sobers the Brooklyn boy as he looks down the shores of
the Wallabout and remembers the prison ships,
What burnt the gums of the redcoat at Saratoga when he
surrendered his brigades,

These become mine and me every one, and they are but little,
I become as much more as I like.   940

I become any presence or truth of humanity here,
And see myself in prison shaped like another man,
And feel the dull unintermitted pain.

For me the keepers of convicts shoulder their carbines and
    keep watch,
It is I let out in the morning and barred at night.   945

Not a mutineer walks handcuffed to the jail, but I am
    handcuffed to him and walk by his side,
I am less the jolly one there, and more the silent one with
    sweat on my twitching lips.

Not a youngster is taken for larceny, but I go up too and am
    tried and sentenced.

Not a cholera patient lies at the last gasp, but I also lie at the
    last gasp,
My face is ash-colored, my sinews gnarl . . . . away from me
    people retreat.   950

Askers embody themselves in me, and I am embodied in them,
I project my hat and sit shamefaced and beg.

I rise extatic through all, and sweep with the true gravitation,
The whirling and whirling is elemental within me.

Somehow I have been stunned. Stand back!   955
Give me a little time beyond my cuffed head and slumbers and
    dreams and gaping,
I discover myself on a verge of the usual mistake.

That I could forget the mockers and insults!
That I could forget the trickling tears and the blows of the
    bludgeons and hammers!
That I could look with a separate look on my own crucifixion
    and bloody crowning!   960

I remember . . . . I resume the overstaid fraction,
The grave of rock multiplies what has been confided to it . . . .
    or to any graves,
The corpses rise . . . . the gashes heal . . . . the fastenings roll
    away.

I troop forth replenished with supreme power, one of an
    average unending procession,
We walk the roads of Ohio and Massachusetts and Virginia
    and Wisconsin and New York and New Orleans and Texas

and Montreal and San Francisco and Charleston and
    Savannah and Mexico, 965
Inland and by the seacoast and boundary lines . . . . and we
    pass the boundary lines.

Our swift ordinances are on their way over the whole earth,
The blossoms we wear in our hats are the growth of two
    thousand years.

Eleves I salute you,
I see the approach of your numberless gangs . . . . I see you
    understand yourselves and me, 970
And know that they who have eyes are divine, and the blind
    and lame are equally divine,
And that my steps drag behind yours yet go before them,
And are aware how I am with you no more than I am with
    everybody.

The friendly and flowing savage . . . . Who is he?
Is he waiting for civilization or past it and mastering it? 975

Is he some southwesterner raised outdoors? Is he Canadian?
Is he from the Mississippi country? or from Iowa, Oregon or
    California? or from the mountains? or prairie life or bush-
    life? or from the sea?

Wherever he goes men and women accept and desire him,
They desire he should like them and touch them and speak to
    them and stay with them.

Behaviour lawless as snow-flakes . . . . words simple as grass
    . . . . uncombed head and laughter and naivete; 980
Slowstepping feet and the common features, and the common
    modes and emanations,
They descend in new forms from the tips of his fingers,
They are wafted with the odor of his body or breath . . . . they
    fly out of the glance of his eyes.

Flaunt of the sunshine I need not your bask . . . . lie over,
You light surfaces only . . . . I force the surfaces and the
    depths also. 985

Earth! you seem to look for something at my hands,
Say old topknot! what do you want?

Man or woman! I might tell how I like you, but cannot,
And might tell what it is in me and what it is in you, but
    cannot,
And might tell the pinings I have . . . . the pulse of my nights
    and days. 990

Behold I do not give lectures or a little charity,
What I give I give out of myself.

You there, impotent, loose in the knees, open your scarfed
    chops till I blow grit within you,
Spread your palms and lift the flaps of your pockets,
I am not to be denied . . . . I compel . . . . I have stores plenty
    and to spare,   995
And any thing I have I bestow.

I do not ask who you are . . . . that is not important to me,
You can do nothing and be nothing but what I will infold you.

To a drudge of the cottonfields or emptier of privies I lean
    . . . . on his right cheek I put the family kiss,
And in my soul I swear I never will deny him.   1000

On women fit for conception I start bigger and nimbler babes,
This day I am jetting the stuff of far more arrogant republics.

To any one dying . . . . thither I speed and twist the knob of
    the door,
Turn the bedclothes toward the foot of the bed,
Let the physician and the priest go home.   1005

I seize the descending man . . . . I raise him with resistless will.

O despairer, here is my neck,
By God! you shall not go down! Hang your whole weight upon me.

I dilate you with tremendous breath . . . . I buoy you up;
Every room of the house do I fill with am armed force . . . .
    lovers of me, bafflers of graves: 1010
Sleep! I and they keep guard all night;
Not doubt, not decease shall dare to lay finger upon you,
I have embraced you, and henceforth possess you to myself,
And when you rise in the morning you will find what I tell you
    is so.

I am he bringing help for the sick as they pant on their backs, 1015
And for strong upright men I bring yet more needed help.

I heard what was said of the universe,
Heard it and heard of several thousand years;
It is middling well as far as it goes . . . . but is that all?

Magnifying and applying come I,   1020
Outbidding at the start the old cautious hucksters,

The most they offer for mankind and eternity less than a spirt
    of my own seminal wet,
Taking myself the exact dimensions of Jehovah and laying
    them away,
Lithographing Kronos and Zeus his son, and Hercules his
    grandson,
Buying drafts of Osiris and Isis and Belus and Brahma and
    Adonai,   1025
In my portfolio placing Manito loose, and Allah on a leaf, and
    the crucifix engraved,
With Odin, and the hideous-faced Mexitli, and all idols and
    images,
Honestly taking them all for what they are worth, and not a
    cent more,
Admitting they were alive and did the work of their day,
Admitting they bore mites as for unfledged birds who have
    now to rise and fly and sing for themselves,   1030
Accepting the rough deific sketches to fill out better in myself
    . . . . bestowing them freely on each man and woman I
    see,
Discovering as much or more in a framer framing a house,
Putting higher claims for him there with his rolled-up sleeves,
    driving the mallet and chisel;
Not objecting to special revelations . . . . considering a curl of
    smoke or a hair on the back of my hand as curious as any
    revelation;
Those ahold of fire-engines and hook-and-ladder ropes more to
    me than the gods of the antique wars,   1035
Minding their voices peal through the crash of destruction,
Their brawny limbs passing safe over charred laths . . . .
    their white foreheads whole and unhurt out of the
    flames;
By the mechanic's wife with her babe at her nipple interceding
    for every person born;
Three scythes at harvest whizzing in a row from three lusty
    angels with shirts bagged out at their waists;
The snag-toothed hostler with red hair redeeming sins past and
    to come,   1040
Selling all he possesses and traveling on foot to fee lawyers for
    his brother and sit by him while he is tried for forgery:
What was strewn in the amplest strewing the square rod about
    me, and not filling the square rod then;
The bull and the bug never worshipped half enough,
Dung and dirt more admirable than was dreamed,
The supernatural of no account . . . . myself waiting my time
    to be one of the supremes,   1045
The day getting ready for me when I shall do as much good as
    the best, and be as prodigious,
Guessing when I am it will not tickle me much to receive
    puffs out of pulpit or print;
By my life-lumps! becoming already a creator!

Putting myself here and now to the ambushed womb of the
    shadows!

. . . . A call in the midst of the crowd,   1050
My own voice, orotund sweeping and final.

Come my children,
Come my boys and girls, and my women and household and
    intimates,
Now the performer launches his nerve . . . . he has passed his
    prelude on the reeds within.

Easily written loosefingered chords! I feel the thrum of their
    climax and close.   1055

My head evolves on my neck,
Music rolls, but not from the organ . . . . folks are around me,
    but they are no household of mine.

Ever the hard and unsunk ground,
Ever the eaters and drinkers . . . . ever the upward and
    downward sun . . . . ever the air and the ceaseless tides,
Ever myself and my neighbors, refreshing and wicked and real,   1060
Ever the old inexplicable query . . . . ever that thorned thumb
    —that breath of itches and thirsts,
Ever the vexer's hoot! hoot! till we find where the sly one hides
    and bring him forth;
Ever love . . . . ever the sobbing liquid of life,
Ever the bandage under the chin . . . . ever the tressels of death.

Here and there with dimes on the eyes walking,   1065
To feed the greed of the belly the brains liberally spooning,
Tickets buying or taking or selling, but in to the feast never
    once going;
Many sweating and ploughing and thrashing, and then the
    chaff for payment receiving,
A few idly owning, and they the wheat continually claiming.

This is the city . . . . and I am one of the citizens;   1070
Whatever interests the rest interests me . . . . politics,
    churches, newspapers, schools,
Benevolent societies, improvements, banks, tariffs, steamships,
    factories, markets,
Stocks and stores and real estate and personal estate.

They who piddle and patter here in collars and tailed coats
    . . . . I am aware who they are . . . . and that they are not
    worms or fleas,
I acknowledge the duplicates of myself under all the scrape-
    lipped and pipe-legged concealments.   1075

The weakest and shallowest is deathless with me,
What I do and say the same waits for them,
Every thought that flounders in me the same flounders in them.

I know perfectly well my own egotism,
And know my omniverous words, and cannot say any less,   1080
And would fetch you whoever you are flush with myself.

My words are words of a questioning, and to indicate reality;
This printed and bound book . . . . but the printer and the
    printing-office boy?
The marriage estate and settlement . . . . but the body and
    mind of the bridegroom? also those of the bride?
The panorama of the sea . . . . but the sea itself?   1085
The well-taken photographs . . . . but your wife or friend close
    and solid in your arms?
The fleet of ships of the line and all the modern improvements
    . . . . but the craft and pluck of the admiral?
The dishes and fare and furniture . . . . but the host and
    hostess, and the look out of their eyes?
The sky up there . . . . yet here or next door or across the way?
The saints and sages in history . . . . but you yourself?   1090
Sermons and creeds and theology . . . . but the human brain,
    and what is called reason, and what is called love, and
    what is called life?

I do not despise you priests;
My faith is the greatest of faiths and the least of faiths,
Enclosing all worship ancient and modern, and all between
    ancient and modern,
Believing I shall come again upon the earth after five thousand
    years,   1095
Waiting responses from oracles . . . . honoring the gods . . . .
    saluting the sun,
Making a fetish of the first rock or stump . . . . powowing with
    sticks in the circle of obis,
Helping the lama or brahmin as he trims the lamps of the idols,
Dancing yet through the streets in a phallic procession . . . .
    rapt and austere in the woods, a gymnosophist,
Drinking mead from the skull-cup . . . . to shasta and vedas
    admirant . . . . minding the koran,   1100
Walking the teokallis, spotted with gore from the stone and
    knife—beating the serpent-skin drum;
Accepting the gospels, accepting him that was crucified,
    knowing assuredly that he is divine,
To the mass kneeling—to the puritan's prayer rising—sitting
    patiently in a pew,
Ranting and frothing in my insane crisis—waiting dead-like till
    my spirit arouses me;

Looking forth on pavement and land, and outside of pavement
and land,   1105
Belonging to the winders of the circuit of circuits.

One of that centripetal and centrifugal gang,
I turn and talk like a man leaving charges before a journey.

Down-hearted doubters, dull and excluded,
Frivolous sullen moping angry affected disheartened
atheistical,   1110
I know every one of you, and know the unspoken
interrogatories,
By experience I know them.

How the flukes splash!
How they contort rapid as lightning, with spasms and spouts of
blood!

Be at peace bloody flukes of doubters and sullen mopers,   1115
I take my place among you as much as among any;
The past is the push of you and me and all precisely the same,
And the night is for you and me and all,[1]
And what is yet untried and afterward is for you and me and all.

I do not know what is untried and afterward,   1120
But I know it is sure and alive and sufficient.

Each who passes is considered, and each who stops is
considered, and not a single one can it fail.

It cannot fail the young man who died and was buried,
Nor the young woman who died and was put by his side,
Nor the little child that peeped in at the door and then drew
back and was never seen again,   1125
Nor the old man who has lived without purpose, and feels it
with bitterness worse than gall,
Nor him in the poorhouse tubercled by rum and the bad disorder,
Nor the numberless slaughtered and wrecked . . . . nor the
brutish koboo, called the ordure of humanity,
Nor the sacs merely floating with open mouths for food to slip in,
Nor any thing in the earth, or down in the oldest graves of the
earth,   1130
Nor any thing in the myriads of spheres, nor one of the
myriads of myriads that inhabit them,
Nor the present, nor the least wisp that is known.

---

1. This line reads "And the day and night are for you and me and all" in many copies of
the 1855 *LG*. See Gary Schmidgall, "1855: A Stop-Press Revision," *WWQR* 18, nos. 1–2
(Summer/Fall 2000): 73–75.

It is time to explain myself . . . . let us stand up.

What is known I strip away . . . . I launch all men and women
    forward with me into the unknown.

The clock indicates the moment . . . . but what does eternity
    indicate? 1135

Eternity lies in bottomless reservoirs . . . . its buckets are rising
    forever and ever,
They pour and they pour and they exhale away.

We have thus far exhausted trillions of winters and summers;
There are trillions ahead, and trillions ahead of them.

Births have brought us richness and variety, 1140
And other births will bring us richness and variety.

I do not call one greater and one smaller,
That which fills its period and place is equal to any.

Were mankind murderous or jealous upon you my brother or
    my sister?
I am sorry for you . . . . they are not murderous or jealous
    upon me; 1145
All has been gentle with me . . . . . . I keep no account with
    lamentation;
What have I to do with lamentation?

I am an acme of things accomplished, and I an encloser of
    things to be.

My feet strike an apex of the apices of the stairs,
On every step bunches of ages, and larger bunches between
    the steps, 1150
All below duly traveled—and still I mount and mount.

Rise after rise bow the phantoms behind me,
Afar down I see the huge first Nothing, the vapor from the
    nostrils of death,
I know I was even there . . . . I waited unseen and always,
And slept while God carried me through the lethargic mist, 1155
And took my time . . . . and took no hurt from the fœtid carbon.

Long I was hugged close . . . . long and long.

Immense have been the preparations for me,
Faithful and friendly the arms that have helped me.

Cycles ferried my cradle, rowing and rowing like cheerful
boatmen;   1160
For room to me stars kept aside in their own rings,
They sent influences to look after what was to hold me.

Before I was born out of my mother generations guided me,
My embryo has never been torpid . . . . nothing could overlay it;
For it the nebula cohered to an orb . . . . the long slow strata
piled to rest it on . . . . vast vegetables gave it sustenance,   1165
Monstrous sauroids transported it in their mouths and
deposited it with care.

All forces have been steadily employed to complete and delight me,
Now I stand on this spot with my soul.

Span of youth! Ever-pushed elasticity! Manhood balanced and
florid and full!

My lovers suffocate me!   1170
Crowding my lips, and thick in the pores of my skin,
Jostling me through streets and public halls . . . . coming
naked to me at night,
Crying by day Ahoy from the rocks of the river . . . . swinging
and chirping over my head,
Calling my name from flowerbeds or vines or tangled underbrush,
Or while I swim in the bath . . . . or drink from the pump at
the corner . . . . or the curtain is down at the opera . . . .
or I glimpse at a woman's face in the railroad car;   1175
Lighting on every moment of my life,
Bussing my body with soft and balsamic busses,
Noiselessly passing handfuls out of their hearts and giving
them to be mine.

Old age superbly rising! Ineffable grace of dying days!

Every condition promulges not only itself . . . . it promulges
what grows after and out of itself,   1180
And the dark hush promulges as much as any.

I open my scuttle at night and see the far-sprinkled systems,
And all I see, multiplied as high as I can cipher, edge but the
rim of the farther systems.

Wider and wider they spread, expanding and always expanding,
Outward and outward and forever outward.   1185

My sun has his sun, and round him obediently wheels,
He joins with his partners a group of superior circuit,
And greater sets follow, making specks of the greatest inside them.

There is no stoppage, and never can be stoppage;
If I and you and the worlds and all beneath or upon their
    surfaces, and all the palpable life, were this moment
    reduced back to a pallid float, it would not avail in the
    long run,   1190
We should surely bring up again where we now stand,
And as surely go as much farther, and then farther and farther.

A few quadrillions of eras, a few octillions of cubic leagues, do
    not hazard the span, or make it impatient,
They are but parts . . . . any thing is but a part.

See ever so far . . . . there is limitless space outside of that,   1195
Count ever so much . . . . there is limitless time around that.

Our rendezvous is fitly appointed . . . . God will be there and
    wait till we come.

I know I have the best of time and space—and that I was
    never measured, and never will be measured.

I tramp a perpetual journey,
My signs are a rain-proof coat and good shoes and a staff cut
    from the woods;   1200
No friend of mine takes his ease in my chair,
I have no chair, nor church nor philosophy;
I lead no man to a dinner-table or library or exchange,
But each man and each woman of you I lead upon a knoll,
My left hand hooks you round the waist,   1205
My right hand points to landscapes of continents, and a plain
    public road.

Not I, not any one else can travel that road for you,
You must travel it for yourself.

It is not far . . . . it is within reach,
Perhaps you have been on it since you were born, and did not
    know,   1210
Perhaps it is every where on water and on land.

Shoulder your duds, and I will mine, and let us hasten forth;
Wonderful cities and free nations we shall fetch as we go.

If you tire, give me both burdens, and rest the chuff of your
    hand on my hip,
And in due time you shall repay the same service to me;   1215
For after we start we never lie by again.

This day before dawn I ascended a hill and looked at the
    crowded heaven,
And I said to my spirit, When we become the enfolders of
    those orbs and the pleasure and knowledge of every thing
    in them, shall we be filled and satisfied then?
And my spirit said No, we level that lift to pass and continue
    beyond.

You are also asking me questions, and I hear you;   1220
I answer that I cannot answer . . . . you must find out for
    yourself.

Sit awhile wayfarer,
Here are biscuits to eat and here is milk to drink,
But as soon as you sleep and renew yourself in sweet clothes I
    will certainly kiss you with my goodbye kiss and open the
    gate for your egress hence.

Long enough have you dreamed contemptible dreams,   1225
Now I wash the gum from your eyes,
You must habit yourself to the dazzle of the light and of every
    moment of your life

Long have you timidly waded, holding a plank by the shore,
Now I will you to be a bold swimmer,
To jump off in the midst of the sea, and rise again and nod to
    me and shout, and laughingly dash with your hair.   1230

I am the teacher of athletes,
He that by me spreads a wider breast than my own proves the
    width of my own,
He most honors my style who learns under it to destroy the
    teacher.

The boy I love, the same becomes a man not through derived
    power but in his own right,
Wicked, rather than virtuous out of conformity or fear,   1235
Fond of his sweetheart, relishing well his steak,
Unrequited love or a slight cutting him worse than a wound cuts,
First rate to ride, to fight, to hit the bull's eye, to sail a skiff, to
    sing a song or play on the banjo,
Preferring scars and faces pitted with smallpox over all
    latherers and those that keep out of the sun.

I teach straying from me, yet who can stray from me?   1240
I follow you whoever you are from the present hour;
My words itch at your ears till you understand them.

I do not say these things for a dollar, or to fill up the time
    while I wait for a boat;

It is you talking just as much as myself . . . . I act as the
    tongue of you,
It was tied in your mouth . . . . in mine it begins to be
    loosened.   1245

I swear I will never mention love or death inside a house,
And I swear I never will translate myself at all, only to him or
    her who privately stays with me in the open air.

If you would understand me go to the heights or water-shore,
The nearest gnat is an explanation and a drop or the motion of
    waves a key,
The maul the oar and the handsaw second my words.   1250

No shuttered room or school can commune with me,
But roughs and little children better than they.

The young mechanic is closest to me . . . . he knows me pretty
    well,
The woodman that takes his axe and jug with him shall take
    me with him all day,
The farmboy ploughing in the field feels good at the sound of
    my voice,   1255
In vessels that sail my words must sail . . . . I go with
    fishermen and seamen, and love them,
My face rubs to the hunter's face when he lies down alone in
    his blanket,
The driver thinking of me does not mind the jolt of his wagon,
The young mother and old mother shall comprehend me,
The girl and the wife rest the needle a moment and forget
    where they are,   1260
They and all would resume what I have told them.

I have said that the soul is not more than the body,
And I have said that the body is not more than the soul,
And nothing, not God, is greater to one than one's-self is,
And whoever walks a furlong without sympathy walks to his
    own funeral, dressed in his shroud,   1265
And I or you pocketless of a dime may purchase the pick of
    the earth,
And to glance with an eye or show a bean in its pod
    confounds the learning of all times,
And there is no trade or employment but the young man
    following it may become a hero,
And there is no object so soft but it makes a hub for the
    wheeled universe,
And any man or woman shall stand cool and supercilious
    before a million universes.   1270

And I call to mankind, Be not curious about God,
For I who am curious about each am not curious about God,

No array of terms can say how much I am at peace about God
 and about death.

I hear and behold God in every object, yet I understand God
 not in the least,
Nor do I understand who there can be more wonderful than
 myself.   1275

Why should I wish to see God better than this day?
I see something of God each hour of the twenty-four, and
 each moment then,
In the faces of men and women I see God, and in my own
 face in the glass;
I find letters from God dropped in the street, and every one is
 signed by God's name,
And I leave them where they are, for I know that others will
 punctually come forever and ever.   1280

And as to you death, and you bitter hug of mortality . . . . it is
 idle to try to alarm me.

To his work without flinching the accoucheur comes,
I see the elderhand pressing receiving supporting,
I recline by the sills of the exquisite flexible doors . . . . and
 mark the outlet, and mark the relief and escape.

And as to you corpse I think you are good manure, but that
 does not offend me,   1285
I smell the white roses sweetscented and growing,
I reach to the leafy lips . . . . I reach to the polished breasts of
 melons.

And as to you life, I reckon you are the leavings of many deaths,
No doubt I have died myself ten thousand times before.

I hear you whispering there O stars of heaven,   1290
O suns . . . . O grass of graves . . . . O perpetual transfers and
 promotions . . . . if you do not say anything how can I say
 anything?

Of the turbid pool that lies in the autumn forest,
Of the moon that descends the steeps of the soughing twilight,
Toss, sparkles of day and dusk . . . . toss on the black stems
 that decay in the muck,
Toss to the moaning gibberish of the dry limbs.   1295

I ascend from the moon . . . . I ascend from the night,
And perceive of the ghastly glitter the sunbeams reflected,
And debouch to the steady and central from the offspring great
 or small.

There is that in me . . . . I do not know what it is . . . . but I
  know it is in me.

Wrenched and sweaty . . . . calm and cool then my body
  becomes;   1300
I sleep . . . . I sleep long.

I do not know it . . . . it is without name . . . . it is a word unsaid,
It is not in any dictionary or utterance or symbol.

Something it swings on more than the earth I swing on,
To it the creation is the friend whose embracing awakes me.   1305

Perhaps I might tell more . . . . Outlines! I plead for my
  brothers and sisters.

Do you see O my brothers and sisters?
It is not chaos or death . . . . it is form and union and plan
  . . . . it is eternal life . . . . it is happiness.

The past and present wilt . . . . I have filled them and emptied
  them,
And proceed to fill my next fold of the future.   1310

Listener up there! Here you . . . . what have you to confide to me?
Look in my face while I snuff the sidle of evening,
Talk honestly, for no one else hears you, and I stay only a
  minute longer.

Do I contradict myself?
Very well then . . . . I contradict myself;   1315
I am large . . . . I contain multitudes.

I concentrate toward them that are nigh . . . . I wait on the
  door-slab.

Who has done his day's work and will soonest be through with
  his supper?
Who wishes to walk with me?

Will you speak before I am gone? Will you prove already too
  late?   1320

The spotted hawk swoops by and accuses me . . . . he
  complains of my gab and my loitering.

I too am not a bit tamed . . . . I too am untranslatable,
I sound my barbaric yawp over the roofs of the world.

The last scud of day holds back for me,
It flings my likeness after the rest and true as any on the
    shadowed wilds,   1325
It coaxes me to the vapor and the dusk.

I depart as air . . . . I shake my white locks at the runaway sun,
I effuse my flesh in eddies and drift it in lacy jags.

I bequeath myself to the dirt to grow from the grass I love,
If you want me again look for me under your bootsoles.   1330

You will hardly know who I am or what I mean,
But I shall be good health to you nevertheless,
And filter and fibre your blood.

Failing to fetch me me[2] at first keep encouraged,
Missing me one place search another,   1335
I stop some where waiting for you

Leaves of Grass[3]

Come closer to me,
Push close my lovers and take the best I possess,
Yield closer and closer and give me the best you possess.

This is unfinished business with me . . . . how is it with you?
I was chilled with the cold types and cylinder and wet paper
    between us.   5

I pass so poorly with paper and types . . . . I must pass with
    the contact of bodies and souls.

I do not thank you for liking me as I am, and liking the touch
    of me . . . . I know that it is good for you to do so.

Were all educations practical and ornamental well displayed
    out of me, what would it amount to?
Were I as the head teacher or charitable proprietor or wise
    statesman, what would it amount to?
Were I to you as the boss employing and paying you, would
    that satisfy you?   10

The learned and virtuous and benevolent, and the usual terms;
A man like me, and never the usual terms.

2. The second "me," probably an accidental repetition, is omitted in subsequent editions of *LG*.
   In the 1855 edition, the poem ends, as here, without a period.
3. Entitled "A Song for Occupations" in 1881.

Neither a servant nor a master am I,
I take no sooner a large price than a small price . . . . I will
    have my own whoever enjoys me,
I will be even with you, and you shall be even with me.   15

If you are a workman or workwoman I stand as nigh as the
    nighest that works in the same shop,
If you bestow gifts on your brother or dearest friend, I demand
    as good as your brother or dearest friend,
If your lover or husband or wife is welcome by day or night, I
    must be personally as welcome;
If you have become degraded or ill, then I will become so for
    your sake;
If you remember your foolish and outlawed deeds, do you
    think I cannot remember my foolish and outlawed deeds?   20
If you carouse at the table I say I will carouse at the opposite
    side of the table;
If you meet some stranger in the street and love him or her,
    do I not often meet strangers in the street and love them?
If you see a good deal remarkable in me I see just as much
    remarkable in you.

Why what have you thought of yourself?
Is it you then that thought yourself less?
Is it you that thought the President greater than you? or the   25
    rich better off than you? or the educated wiser than you?

Because you are greasy or pimpled—or that you was once
    drunk, or a thief, or diseased, or rheumatic, or a prostitute
    —or are so now—or from frivolity or impotence—or that
    you are no scholar, and never saw your name in print
    . . . . do you give in that you are any less immortal?

Souls of men and women! it is not you I call unseen, unheard,
    untouchable and untouching;
It is not you I go argue pro and con about, and to settle
    whether you are alive or no;
I own publicly who you are, if nobody else owns . . . . and see
    and hear you, and what you give and take;   30
What is there you cannot give and take?

I see not merely that you are polite or whitefaced . . . .
    married or single . . . . citizens of old states or citizens of
    new states . . . . eminent in some profession . . . . a lady
    or gentleman in a parlor . . . . or dressed in the jail
    uniform . . . . or pulpit uniform,
Not only the free Utahan, Kansian, or Arkansian . . . . not only
    the free Cuban . . . not merely the slave . . . . not
    Mexican native, or Flatfoot, or negro from Africa,
Iroquois eating the warflesh—fishtearer in his lair of rocks and
    sand . . . . Esquimaux in the dark cold snowhouse . . . .

Chinese with his transverse eyes . . . . Bedowee—or
wandering nomad—or tabounschik at the head of his
droves,
Grown, half-grown, and babe—of this country and every
country, indoors and outdoors I see . . . . and all else is
behind or through them.   35

The wife—and she is not one jot less than the husband,
The daughter—and she is just as good as the son,
The mother—and she is every bit as much as the father.

Offspring of those not rich—boys apprenticed to trades,
Young fellows working on farms and old fellows working on
farms;   40
The naive . . . . the simple and hardy . . . . he going to the
polls to vote . . . . he who has a good time, and he who
has a bad time;
Mechanics, southerners, new arrivals, sailors, mano'warsmen,
merchantmen, coasters,
All these I see . . . . but nigher and farther the same I see;
None shall escape me, and none shall wish to escape me.

I bring what you much need, yet always have,   45
I bring not money or amours or dress or eating . . . . but I
bring as good;
And send no agent or medium . . . . and offer no
representative of value—but offer the value itself.

There is something that comes home to one now and
perpetually,
It is not what is printed or preached or discussed . . . . it
eludes discussion and print,
It is not to be put in a book . . . . it is not in this book,   50
It is for you whoever you are . . . . it is no farther from you
than your hearing and sight are from you,
It is hinted by nearest and commonest and readiest . . . . it is
not them, though it is endlessly provoked by them . . . .
What is there ready and near you now?

You may read in many languages and read nothing about it;
You may read the President's message and read nothing about
it there,
Nothing in the reports from the state department or treasury
department . . . . or in the daily papers, or the weekly
papers,   55
Or in the census returns or assessors' returns or prices current
or any accounts of stock.

The sun and stars that float in the open air . . . . the
appleshaped earth and we upon it . . . . surely the drift of
them is something grand;

I do not know what it is except that it is grand, and that it is
  happiness,
And that the enclosing purport of us here is not a speculation,
  or bon-mot or reconnoissance,
And that it is not something which by luck may turn out well
  for us, and without luck must be a failure for us,   60
And not something which may yet be retracted in a certain
  contingency.

The light and shade—the curious sense of body and identity—
  the greed that with perfect complaisance devours all
  things—the endless pride and outstretching of man—
  unspeakable joys and sorrows,
The wonder every one sees in every one else he sees . . . . and
  the wonders that fill each minute of time forever and each
  acre of surface and space forever,
Have you reckoned them as mainly for a trade or farmwork? or
  for the profits of a store? or to achieve yourself a position?
  or to fill a gentleman's leisure or a lady's leisure?

Have you reckoned the landscape took substance and form
  that it might be painted in a picture?   65
Or men and women that they might be written of, and songs
  sung?
Or the attraction of gravity and the great laws and harmonious
  combinations and the fluids of the air as subjects for the
  savans?
Or the brown land and the blue sea for maps and charts?
Or the stars to be put in constellations and named fancy names?
Or that the growth of seeds is for agricultural tables or
  agricultural itself?   70

Old institutions . . . . these arts libraries legends collections—
  and the practice handed along in manufactures . . . . will
  we rate them so high?
Will we rate our prudence and business so high? . . . . I have
  no objection,
I rate them as high as the highest . . . . but a child born of a
  woman and man I rate beyond all rate.

We thought our Union grand and our Constitution grand;
I do not say they are not grand and good—for they are,   75
I am this day just as much in love with them as you,
But I am eternally in love with you and with all my fellows
  upon the earth.

We consider the bibles and religions divine . . . . I do not say
  they are not divine,
I say they have all grown out of you and may grow out of you still,

It is not they who give the life . . . . it is you who give the life;   80
Leaves are not more shed from the trees or trees from the
    earth than they are shed out of you.

The sum of all known value and respect I add up in you
    whoever you are;
The President is up there in the White House for you . . . . it
    is not you who are here for him,
The Secretaries act in their bureaus for you . . . . not you here
    for them,
The Congress convenes every December for you,   85
Laws, courts, the forming of states, the charters of cities, the
    going and coming of commerce and mails are all for you.

All doctrines, all politics and civilization exurge from you,
All sculpture and monuments and anything inscribed anywhere
    are tallied in you,
The gist of histories and statistics as far back as the records
    reach is in you this hour—and myths and tales the same;
If you were not breathing and walking here where would they
    all be?   90
The most renowned poems would be ashes . . . . orations and
    plays would be vacuums.

All architecture is what you do to it when you look upon it;
Did you think it was in the white or gray stone? or the lines of
    the arches and cornices?

All music is what awakens from you when you are reminded by
    the instruments,
It is not the violins and the cornets . . . . it is not the oboe nor
    the beating drums—nor the notes of the baritone singer
    singing his sweet romanza . . . . nor those of the men's
    chorus, nor those of the women's chorus,   95
It is nearer and farther than they.

Will the whole come back then?
Can each see the signs of the best by a look in the
    lookingglass? Is there nothing greater or more?
Does all sit there with you and here with me?

The old forever new things . . . . you foolish child! . . . . the
    closest simplest things—this moment with you,   100
Your person and every particle that relates to your person,
The pulses of your brain waiting their chance and
    encouragement at every deed or sight;
Anything you do in public by day, and anything you do in
    secret betweendays,
What is called right and what is called wrong . . . . what you
    behold or touch . . . . what causes your anger or wonder,

The anklechain of the slave, the bed of the bedhouse, the
    cards of the gambler, the plates of the forger;   105
What is seen or learned in the street, or intuitively learned,
What is learned in the public school—spelling, reading,
    writing and ciphering . . . . the blackboard and the
    teacher's diagrams:
The panes of the windows and all that appears through them
    . . . . the going forth in the morning and the aimless
    spending of the day;
(What is it that you made money? what is it that you got what
    you wanted?)
The usual routine . . . . the workshop, factory, yard, office,
    store, or desk;   110
The jaunt of hunting or fishing, or the life of hunting or fishing,
Pasturelife, foddering, milking and herding, and all the
    personnel and usages;
The plum-orchard and apple-orchard . . . . gardening . .
    seedlings, cuttings, flowers and vines,
Grains and manures . . marl, clay, loam . . the subsoil plough
    . . the shovel and pick and rake and hoe . . irrigation and
    draining;
The currycomb . . the horse-cloth . . the halter and bridle and
    bits . . the very wisps of straw,   115
The barn and barn-yard . . the bins and mangers . . the mows
    and racks:
Manufactures . . commerce . . engineering . . the building of
    cities, and every trade carried on there . . and the
    implements of every trade,
The anvil and tongs and hammer . . the axe and wedge . . the
    square and mitre and jointer and smoothingplane;
The plumbob and trowel and level . . the wall-scaffold, and the
    work of walls and ceilings . . or any mason-work:
The ship's compass . . the sailor's tarpaulin . . the stays and
    lanyards, and the ground-tackle for anchoring or mooring,   120
The sloop's tiller . . the pilot's wheel and bell . . the yacht or
    fish-smack . . the great gay-pennanted three-hundred-foot
    steamboat under full headway, with her proud fat breasts
    and her delicate swift-flashing paddles;
The trail and line and hooks and sinkers . . the seine, and
    hauling the seine;
Smallarms and rifles . . . . the powder and shot and caps and
    wadding . . . . the ordnance for war . . . . the carriages;
Everyday objects . . . . the housechairs, the carpet, the bed
    and the counterpane of the bed, and him or her sleeping
    at night, and the wind blowing, and the indefinite noises:
The snowstorm or rainstorm . . . . the tow-trowsers . . . . the
    lodge-hut in the woods, and the still-hunt: 125
City and country . . fireplace and candle . . gaslight and heater
    and aqueduct;

The message of the governor, mayor, or chief of police . . . .
    the dishes of breakfast or dinner or supper;
The bunkroom, the fire-engine, the string-team, and the car or
    truck behind;
The paper I write on or you write on . . and every word we
    write . . and every cross and twirl of the pen . . and the
    curious way we write what we think . . . . yet very faintly;
The directory, the detector, the ledger . . . . the books in ranks
    or the bookshelves . . . . the clock attached to the wall,   130
The ring on your finger . . the lady's wristlet . . the hammers
    of stonebreakers or coppersmiths . . the druggist's vials
    and jars;
The etui of surgical instruments, and the etui of oculist's or
    aurist's instruments, or dentist's instruments;
Glassblowing, grinding of wheat and corn . . casting, and what
    is cast . . tinroofing, shingledressing,
Shipcarpentering, flagging of sidewalks by flaggers . .
    dockbuilding, fishcuring, ferrying;
The pump, the piledriver, the great derrick . . the coalkiln and
    brickkiln,   135
Ironworks or whiteleadworks . . the sugarhouse . . steam-saws,
    and the great mills and factories;
The cottonbale . . the stevedore's hook . . the saw and buck of
    the sawyer . . the screen of the coalscreener . . the mould
    of the moulder . . the workingknife of the butcher;
The cylinder press . . the handpress . . the frisket and tympan
    . . the compositor's stick and rule,
The implements for daguerreotyping . . . . the tools of the
    rigger or grappler or sail-maker or blockmaker,
Goods of guttapercha or papiermache . . . . colors and brushes
    . . . . glaziers' implements,   140
The veneer and gluepot . . the confectioner's ornaments . . the
    decanter and glasses . . the shears and flatiron;
The awl and kneestrap . . the pint measure and quart measure
    . . the counter and stool . . the writingpen of quill or metal;
Billiards and tenpins . . . . the ladders and hanging ropes of
    the gymnasium, and the manly exercises;
The designs for wallpapers or oilcloths or carpets . . . . the
    fancies for goods for women . . . . the bookbinder's stamps;
Leatherdressing, coachmaking, boilermaking, ropetwisting,
    distilling, signpainting, limeburning, coopering,
    cottonpicking,   145
The walkingbeam of the steam-engine . . the throttle and
    governors, and the up and down rods,
Stavemachines and plainingmachines . . . . the cart of the
    carman . . the omnibus . . the ponderous dray;
The snowplough and two engines pushing it . . . . the ride in
    the express train of only one car . . . . the swift go
    through a howling storm:
The bearhunt or coonhunt . . . . the bonfire of shavings in the
    open lot in the city . . the crowd of children watching;

The blows of the fighting-man . . the upper cut and one-two-
    three;   150
The shopwindows . . . . the coffins in the sexton's wareroom
    . . . . the fruit on the fruitstand . . . . the beef on the
    butcher's stall,
The bread and cakes in the bakery . . . . the white and red
    pork in the pork-store;
The milliner's ribbons . . the dressmaker's patterns . . . . the
    tea-table . . the homemade sweetmeats:
The column of wants in the one-cent paper . . the news by
    telegraph . . . . the amusements and operas and shows:
The cotton and woolen and linen you wear . . . . the money
    you make and spend;   155
Your room and bedroom . . . . your piano-forte . . . . the stove
    and cookpans,
The house you live in . . . . the rent . . . . the other tenants
    . . . . the deposite in the savings-bank . . . . the trade at
    the grocery,
The pay on Saturday night . . . . the going home, and the
    purchases;
In them the heft of the heaviest . . . . in them far more than
    you estimated, and far less also,
In them, not yourself . . . . you and your soul enclose all
    things, regardless of estimation,   160
In them your themes and hints and provokers . . if not, the
    whole earth has no themes or hints or provokers, and
    never had.

I do not affirm what you see beyond is futile . . . . I do not
    advise you to stop,
I do not say leadings you thought great are not great,
But I say that none lead to greater or sadder or happier than
    those lead to.

Will you seek afar off? You surely come back at last.   165
In things best known to you finding the best or as good as the
    best,
In folks nearest to you finding also the sweetest and strongest
    and lovingest,
Happiness not in another place, but this place . . not for
    another hour, but this hour,
Man in the first you see or touch . . . . always in your friend
    or brother or nighest neighbor . . . . Woman in your
    mother or lover or wife,
And all else thus far known giving place to men and women.   170

When the psalm sings instead of the singer,
When the script preaches instead of the preacher,
When the pulpit descends and goes instead of the carver that
    carved the supporting desk,
When the sacred vessels or the bits of the eucharist, or the

lath and plast, procreate as effectually as the young
    silversmiths or bakers, or the masons in their overalls,
When a university course convinces like a slumbering woman
    and child convince,   175
When the minted gold in the vault smiles like the
    nightwatchman's daughter,
When warrantee deeds loafe in chairs opposite and are my
    friendly companions,
I intend to reach them my hand and make as much of them as
    I do of men and women.

Leaves of Grass[4]

To think of time . . . . to think through the retrospection,
To think of today . . and the ages continued henceforward.

Have you guessed you yourself would not continue? Have you
    dreaded those earth-beetles?
Have you feared the future would be nothing to you?

Is today nothing? Is the beginningless past nothing?   5
If the future is nothing they are just as surely nothing.

To think that the sun rose in the east . . . . that men and
    women were flexible and real and alive . . . . that every
    thing was real and alive;
To think that you and I did not see feel think nor bear our part,
To think that we are now here and bear our part.

Not a day passes . . not a minute or second without an
    accouchement;   10
Not a day passes . . not a minute or second without a corpse.

When the dull nights are over, and the dull days also,
When the soreness of lying so much in bed is over,
When the physician, after long putting off, gives the silent and
    terrible look for an answer,
When the children come hurried and weeping, and the
    brothers and sisters have been sent for,   15
When medicines stand unused on the shelf, and the camphor-
    smell has pervaded the rooms,
When the faithful hand of the living does not desert the hand
    of the dying,

---

4. Entitled "To Think of Time" in 1871.

When the twitching lips press lightly on the forehead of the dying,
When the breath ceases and the pulse of the heart ceases,
Then the corpse-limbs stretch on the bed, and the living look
    upon them,   20
They are palpable as the living are palpable.

The living look upon the corpse with their eyesight,
But without eyesight lingers a different living and looks
    curiously on the corpse.

To think that the rivers will come to flow, and the snow fall,
    and fruits ripen . . and act upon others as upon us now
    . . . . yet not act upon us;
To think of all these wonders of city and country . . and others
    taking great interest in them . . and we taking small
    interest in them.   25

To think how eager we are in building our houses,
To think others shall be just as eager . . and we quite indifferent.

I see one building the house that serves him a few years . . . .
    or seventy or eighty years at most;
I see one building the house that serves him longer than that.

Slowmoving and black lines creep over the whole earth . . . .
    they never cease . . . . they are the burial lines,   30
He that was President was buried, and he that is now
    President shall surely be buried.

Cold dash of waves at the ferrywharf,
Posh and ice in the river . . . . half-frozen mud in the streets,
A gray discouraged sky overhead . . . . the short last daylight of
    December,
A hearse and stages . . . . other vehicles give place,   35
The funeral of an old stagedriver . . . . the cortege mostly drivers.

Rapid the trot to the cemetery,
Duly rattles the deathbell . . . . the gate is passed . . . . the
    grave is halted at . . . . the living alight . . . . the hearse
    uncloses,
The coffin is lowered and settled . . . . the whip is laid on the
    coffin,
The earth is swiftly shovelled in . . . . a minute . . no one
    moves or speaks . . . . it is done,   40
He is decently put away . . . . is there anything more?

He was a goodfellow,
Freemouthed, quicktempered, not badlooking, able to take his
    own part,

Witty, sensitive to a slight, ready with life or death for a friend,
Fond of women, . . played some . . eat hearty and drank
    hearty,   45
Had known what it was to be flush . . grew lowspirited toward
    the last . . sickened . . was helped by a contribution,
Died aged forty-one years . . and that was his funeral.

Thumb extended or finger uplifted,
Apron, cape, gloves, strap . . . . wetweather clothes . . . . whip
    carefully chosen . . . . boss, spotter, starter, and hostler,
Somebody loafing on you, or you loafing on somebody . . . .
    headway . . . . man before and man behind,   50
Good day's work or bad day's work . . . . pet stock or mean
    stock . . . . first out or last out . . . . turning in at night,
To think that these are so much and so nigh to other drivers
    . . and he there takes no interest in them.

The markets, the government, the workingman's wages . . . . to
    think what account they are through our nights and days;
To think that other workingmen will make just as great
    account of them . . yet we make little or no account.

The vulgar and the refined . . . . what you call sin and what
    you call goodness . . to think how wide a difference;   55
To think the difference will still continue to others, yet we lie
    beyond the difference.

To think how much pleasure there is!
Have you pleasure from looking at the sky? Have you pleasure
    from poems?
Do you enjoy yourself in the city? or engaged in business? or
    planning a nomination and election? or with your wife and
    family?
Or with your mother and sisters? or in womanly housework? or
    the beautiful maternal cares?   60

These also flow onward to others . . . . you and I flow onward;
But in due time you and I shall take less interest in them.

Your farm and profits and crops . . . . to think how engrossed
    you are;
To think there will still be farms and profits and crops . . yet
    for you of what avail?

What will be will be well—for what is is well,   65
To take interest is well, and not to take interest shall be well.

The sky continues beautiful . . . . the pleasure of men with
    women shall never be sated . . nor the pleasure of women
    with men . . nor the pleasure from poems;
The domestic joys, the daily housework or business, the
    building of houses—they are not phantasms . . they have
    weight and form and location;
The farms and profits and crops . . the markets and wages and
    government . . they also are not phantasms;
The difference between sin and goodness is no apparition;   70
The earth is not an echo . . . . man and his life and all the
    things of his life are well-considered.

You are not thrown to the winds . . you gather certainly and
    safely around yourself,
Yourself! Yourself! Yourself forever and ever!

It is not to diffuse you that you were born of your mother and
    father—it is to identify you,
It is not that you should be undecided, but that you should be
    decided;   75
Something long preparing and formless is arrived and formed
    in you,
You are thenceforth secure, whatever comes or goes.

The threads that were spun are gathered . . . . the weft crosses
    the warp . . . . the pattern is systematic.

The preparations have every one been justified;
The orchestra have tuned their instruments sufficiently . . . .
    the baton has given the signal.   80

The guest that was coming . . . . he waited long for reasons
    . . . . he is now housed,
He is one of those who are beautiful and happy . . . . he is one
    of those that to look upon and be with is enough.

The law of the past cannot be eluded,
The law of the present and future cannot be eluded,
The law of the living cannot be eluded . . . . it is eternal,   85
The law of promotion and transformation cannot be eluded,
The law of heroes and good-doers cannot be eluded,
The law of drunkards and informers and mean persons cannot
    be eluded.

Slowmoving and black lines go ceaselessly over the earth,
Northerner goes carried and southerner goes carried . . . . and
    they on the Atlantic side and they on the Pacific, and they
    between, and all through the Mississippi country . . . .
    and all over the earth.   90

The great masters and kosmos are well as they go . . . . the
    heroes and good-doers are well,
The known leaders and inventors and the rich owners and
    pious and distinguished may be well,
But there is more account than that . . . . there is strict
    account of all.

The interminable hordes of the ignorant and wicked are not
    nothing,
The barbarians of Africa and Asia are not nothing,   95
The common people of Europe are not nothing . . . . the
    American aborigines are not nothing,
A zambo or a foreheadless Crowfoot or a Camanche is not
    nothing,
The infected in the immigrant hospital are not nothing . . . .
    the murderer or mean person is not nothing,
The perpetual succession of shallow people are not nothing as
    they go,
The prostitute is not nothing . . . . the mocker of religion is
    not nothing as he goes.   100

I shall go with the rest . . . . we have satisfaction:
I have dreamed that we are not to be changed so much . . . .
    nor the law of us changed;
I have dreamed that heroes and good-doers shall be under the
    present and past law,
And that murderers and drunkards and liars shall be under the
    present and past law;
For I have dreamed that the law they are under now is
    enough.   105

And I have dreamed that the satisfaction is not so much
    changed . . . . and that there is no life without
    satisfaction;
What is the earth? what are body and soul without
    satisfaction?

I shall go with the rest,
We cannot be stopped at a given point . . . . that is no
    satisfaction;
To show us a good thing or a few good things for a space of
    time—that is no satisfaction;   110
We must have the indestructible breed of the best, regardless
    of time.

If otherwise, all these things came but to ashes of dung;
If maggots and rats ended us, then suspicion and treachery
    and death.

Do you suspect death? If I were to suspect death I should die
    now,

Do you think I could walk pleasantly and well-suited toward
    annihilation?   115

Pleasantly and well-suited I walk,
Whither I walk I cannot define, but I know it is good,
The whole universe indicates that it is good,
The past and the present indicate that it is good.

How beautiful and perfect are the animals! How perfect is my
    soul!   120
How perfect the earth, and the minutest thing upon it!
What is called good is perfect, and what is called sin is just as
    perfect;
The vegetables and minerals are all perfect . . and the
    imponderable fluids are perfect;
Slowly and surely they have passed on to this, and slowly and
    surely they will yet pass on.

O my soul! if I realize you I have satisfaction,   125
Animals and vegetables! if I realize you I have satisfaction,
Laws of the earth and air! if I realize you I have satisfaction.

I cannot define my satisfaction . . yet it is so,
I cannot define my life . . yet it is so.

I swear I see now that every thing has an eternal soul!   130
The trees have, rooted in the ground . . . . the weeds of the
    sea have . . . . the animals.

I swear I think there is nothing but immortality!
That the exquisite scheme is for it, and the nebulous float is
    for it, and the cohering is for it,
And all preparation is for it . . and identity is for it . . and life
    and death are for it.

Leaves of Grass[5]

I wander all night in my vision,
Stepping with light feet . . . . swiftly and noiselessly stepping
    and stopping,
Bending with open eyes over the shut eyes of sleepers;
Wandering and confused . . . . lost to myself . . . . ill-assorted
    . . . . contradictory,
Pausing and gazing and bending and stopping.   5

How solemn they look there, stretched and still;
How quiet they breathe, the little children in their cradles.

5. Entitled "The Sleepers" in 1871.

The wretched features of ennuyees, the white features of
    corpses, the livid faces of drunkards, the sick-gray faces of
    onanists,
The gashed bodies on battlefields, the insane in their strong-
    doored rooms, the sacred idiots,
The newborn emerging from gates and the dying emerging
    from gates,   10
The night pervades them and enfolds them.

The married couple sleep calmly in their bed, he with his palm
    on the hip of the wife, and she with her palm on the hip
    of the husband,
The sisters sleep lovingly side by side in their bed,
The men sleep lovingly side by side in theirs,
And the mother sleeps with her little child carefully wrapped.   15

The blind sleep, and the deaf and dumb sleep,
The prisoner sleeps well in the prison . . . . the runaway son
    sleeps,
The murderer that is to be hung next day . . . . how does he
    sleep?
And the murdered person . . . . how does he sleep?

The female that loves unrequited sleeps,   20
And the male that loves unrequited sleeps;
The head of the moneymaker that plotted all day sleeps,
And the enraged and treacherous dispositions sleep.

I stand with drooping eyes by the worstsuffering and restless,
I pass my hands soothingly to and fro a few inches from them;   25
The restless sink in their beds . . . . they fitfully sleep.

The earth recedes from me into the night,
I saw that it was beautiful . . . . and I see that what is not the
    earth is beautiful.

I go from bedside to bedside . . . . I sleep close with the other
    sleepers, each in turn;
I dream in my dream all the dreams of the other dreamers,   30
And I become the other dreamers.

I am a dance . . . . Play up there! the fit is whirling me fast.

I am the everlaughing . . . . it is new moon and twilight,
I see the hiding of douceurs . . . . I see nimble ghosts
    whichever way I look,
Cache and cache again deep in the ground and sea, and where
    it is neither ground or sea.   35

Well do they do their jobs, those journeymen divine,
Only from me can they hide nothing and would not if they could;

I reckon I am their boss, and they make a pet besides,
And surround me, and lead me and run ahead when I walk,
And lift their cunning covers and signify me with stretched
    arms, and resume the way;   40
Onward we move, a gay gang of blackguards with
    mirthshouting music and wild-flapping pennants of joy.

I am the actor and the actress . . . . the voter . . the politician,
The emigrant and the exile . . the criminal that stood in the
    box,
He who has been famous, and he who shall be famous after
    today,
The stammerer . . . . the wellformed person . . the wasted or
    feeble person.   45

I am she who adorned herself and folded her hair expectantly,
My truant lover has come and it is dark.

Double yourself and receive me darkness,
Receive me and my lover too . . . . he will not let me go
    without him.

I roll myself upon you as upon a bed . . . . I resign myself to
    the dusk.   50

He whom I call answers me and takes the place of my lover,
He rises with me silently from the bed.

Darkness you are gentler than my lover . . . . his flesh was
    sweaty and panting,
I feel the hot moisture yet that he left me.

My hands are spread forth . . I pass them in all directions,   55
I would sound up the shadowy shore to which you are
    journeying.

Be careful, darkness . . . . already, what was it touched me?
I thought my lover had gone . . . . else darkness and he are
    one,
I hear the heart-beat . . . . I follow . . I fade away.

O hotcheeked and blushing! O foolish hectic!   60
O for pity's sake, no one must see me now! . . . . my clothes
    were stolen while I was abed,
Now I am thrust forth, where shall I run?

Pier that I saw dimly last night when I looked from the windows,
Pier out from the main, let me catch myself with you and stay
        . . . . I will not chafe you;
I feel ashamed to go naked about the world,   65
And am curious to know where my feet stand . . . . and what
        is this flooding me, childhood or manhood . . . . and the
        hunger that crosses the bridge between.

The cloth laps a first sweet eating and drinking,
Laps life-swelling yolks . . . . laps ear of rose-corn, milky and
        just ripened:
The white teeth stay, and the boss-tooth advances in darkness,
And liquor is spilled on lips and bosoms by touching glasses,
        and the best liquor afterward.   70

I descend my western course . . . . my sinews are flaccid,
Perfume and youth course through me, and I am their wake.

It is my face yellow and wrinkled instead of the old woman's,
I sit low in a strawbottom chair and carefully darn my
        grandson's stockings.

It is I too . . . . the sleepless widow looking out on the winter
        midnight,   75
I see the sparkles of starshine on the icy and pallid earth.

A shroud I see—and I am the shroud . . . . I wrap a body and
        lie in the coffin;
It is dark here underground . . . . it is not evil or pain here
        . . . . it is blank here, for reasons.

It seems to me that everything in the light and air ought to be
        happy;
Whoever is not in his coffin and the dark grave, let him know
        he has enough.   80

I see a beautiful gigantic swimmer swimming naked through
        the eddies of the sea,
His brown hair lies close and even to his head . . . . he strikes
        out with courageous arms . . . . he urges himself with his
        legs.

I see his white body . . . . I see his undaunted eyes;
I hate the swift-running eddies that would dash him
        headforemost on the rocks.

What are you doing you ruffianly red-trickled waves?   85
Will you kill the courageous giant? Will you kill him in the
        prime of his middle age?

Steady and long he struggles;
He is baffled and banged and bruised . . . . he holds out while
    his strength holds out,
The slapping eddies are spotted with his blood . . . . they bear
    him away . . . . they roll him and swing him and turn him:
His beautiful body is borne in the circling eddies . . . . it is
    continually bruised on rocks,   90
Swiftly and out of sight is borne the brave corpse.

I turn but do not extricate myself;
Confused . . . . a pastreading . . . . another, but with darkness
    yet.

The beach is cut by the razory ice-wind . . . . the wreck-guns
    sound,
The tempest lulls and the moon comes floundering through
    the drifts.   95

I look where the ship helplessly heads end on . . . . I hear the
    burst as she strikes . . . . I hear the howls of dismay . . . .
    they grow fainter and fainter.

I cannot aid with my wringing fingers;
I can but rush to the surf and let it drench me and freeze
    upon me.

I search with the crowd . . . . not one of the company is
    washed to us alive;
In the morning I help pick up the dead and lay them in rows
    in a barn.   100

Now of the old war-days . . the defeat at Brooklyn;
Washington stands inside the lines . . he stands on the
    entrenched hills amid a crowd of officers,
His face is cold and damp . . . . he cannot repress the weeping
    drops . . . . he lifts the glass perpetually to his eyes . . . .
    the color is blanched from his cheeks,
He sees the slaughter of the southern braves confided to him
    by their parents.

The same at last and at last when peace is declared,   105
He stands in the room of the old tavern . . . . the wellbeloved
    soldiers all pass through.

The officers speechless and slow draw near in their turns,
The chief encircles their necks with his arm and kisses them
    on the cheek,
He kisses lightly the wet cheeks one after another . . . . he
    shakes hands and bids goodbye to the army.

728 ◆ 1855 LEAVES OF GRASS

Now I tell what my mother told me today as we sat at dinner
    together,   110
Of when she was a nearly grown girl living home with her
    parents on the old homestead.

A red squaw came one breakfasttime to the old homestead,
On her back she carried a bundle of rushes for rushbottoming
    chairs;
Her hair straight shiny coarse black and profuse halfenveloped
    her face,
Her step was free and elastic . . . . her voice sounded
    exquisitely as she spoke.   115

My mother looked in delight and amazement at the stranger,
She looked at the beauty of her tallborne face and full and
    pliant limbs,
The more she looked upon her she loved her,
Never before had she seen such wonderful beauty and purity;
She made her sit on a bench by the jamb of the fireplace . . . .
    she cooked food for her,   120
She had no work to give her but she gave her remembrance
    and fondness.

The red squaw staid all the forenoon, and toward the middle
    of the afternoon she went away;
O my mother was loth to have her go away,
All the week she thought of her . . . . she watched for her
    many a month,
She remembered her many a winter and many a summer,   125
But the red squaw never came nor was heard of there again.

Now Lucifer was not dead . . . . or if he was I am his
    sorrowful terrible heir;
I have been wronged . . . . I am oppressed . . . . I hate him
    that oppresses me,
I will either destroy him, or he shall release me.

Damn him! how he does defile me,   130
How he informs against my brother and sister and takes pay
    for their blood,
How he laughs when I look down the bend after the steamboat
    that carries away my woman.

Now the vast dusk bulk that is the whale's bulk . . . . it seems
    mine,
Warily, sportsman! though I lie so sleepy and sluggish, my tap
    is death.

A show of the summer softness . . . . a contact of something
    unseen . . . . an amour of the light and air;   135
I am jealous and overwhelmed with friendliness,

And will go gallivant with the light and the air myself,
And have an unseen something to be in contact with them also.

O love and summer! you are in the dreams and in me,
Autumn and winter are in the dreams . . . . the farmer goes
    with his thrift,   140
The droves and crops increase . . . . the barns are wellfilled.

Elements merge in the night . . . . ships make tacks in the
    dreams . . . . the sailor sails . . . . the exile returns home,
The fugitive returns unharmed . . . . the immigrant is back
    beyond months and years;
The poor Irishman lives in the simple house of his childhood,
    with the wellknown neighbors and faces,
They warmly welcome him . . . . he is barefoot again . . . . he
    forgets he is welloff;   145
The Dutchman voyages home, and the Scotchman and
    Welchman voyage home . . and the native of the
    Mediterranean voyages home;
To every port of England and France and Spain enter wellfilled
    ships;
The Swiss foots it toward his hills . . . . the Prussian goes his
    way, and the Hungarian his way, and the Pole goes his
    way,
The Swede returns, and the Dane and Norwegian return.

The homeward bound and the outward bound,   150
The beautiful lost swimmer, the ennuyee, the onanist, the
    female that loves unrequited, the moneymaker,
The actor and actress . . those through with their parts and
    those waiting to commence,
The affectionate boy, the husband and wife, the voter, the
    nominee that is chosen and the nominee that has failed,
The great already known, and the great anytime after to day,
The stammerer, the sick, the perfectformed, the homely,   155
The criminal that stood in the box, the judge that sat and
    sentenced him, the fluent lawyers, the jury, the audience,
The laugher and weeper, the dancer, the midnight widow, the
    red squaw,
The consumptive, the erysipalite, the idiot, he that is wronged,
The antipodes, and every one between this and them in the
    dark,
I swear they are averaged now . . . . one is no better than the
    other,   160
The night and sleep have likened them and restored them.

I swear they are all beautiful,
Every one that sleeps is beautiful . . . . every thing in the dim
    night is beautiful,
The wildest and bloodiest is over and all is peace.

Peace is always beautiful,   165
The myth of heaven indicates peace and night.

The myth of heaven indicates the soul;
The soul is always beautiful . . . . it appears more or it appears
    less . . . . it comes or lags behind,
It comes from its embowered garden and looks pleasantly on
    itself and encloses the world;
Perfect and clean the genitals previously jetting, and perfect
    and clean the womb cohering,   170
The head wellgrown and proportioned and plumb, and the
    bowels and joints proportioned and plumb.

The soul is always beautiful,
The universe is duly in order . . . . every thing is in its place,
What is arrived is in its place, and what waits is in its place;
The twisted skull waits . . . . the watery or rotten blood waits,   175
The child of the glutton or venerealee waits long, and the child
    of the drunkard waits long, and the drunkard himself
    waits long,
The sleepers that lived and died wait . . . . the far advanced
    are to go on in their turns, and the far behind are to go
    on in their turns,
The diverse shall be no less diverse, but they shall flow and
    unite . . . . they unite now.

The sleepers are very beautiful as they lie unclothed,
They flow hand in hand over the whole earth from east to west
    as they lie unclothed;   180
The Asiatic and African are hand in hand . . . . the European
    and American are hand in hand,
Learned and unlearned are hand in hand . . and male and
    female are hand in hand;
The bare arm of the girl crosses the bare breast of her lover
    . . . . they press close without lust . . . . his lips press her
    neck,
The father holds his grown or ungrown son in his arms with
    measureless love . . . . and the son holds the father in his
    arms with measureless love,
The white hair of the mother shines on the white wrist of the
    daughter,   185
The breath of the boy goes with the breath of the man . . . .
    friend is inarmed by friend,
The scholar kisses the teacher and the teacher kisses the
    scholar . . . . the wronged is made right,
The call of the slave is one with the master's call . . and the
    master salutes the slave,
The felon steps forth from the prison . . . . the insane becomes
    sane . . . . the suffering of sick persons is relieved,
The sweatings and fevers stop . . the throat that was unsound

is sound . . the lungs of the consumptive are resumed . .
  the poor distressed head is free, 190
The joints of the rheumatic move as smoothly as ever, and
  smoother than ever,
Stiflings and passages open . . . . the paralysed become supple,
The swelled and convulsed and congested awake to themselves
  in condition,
They pass the invigoration of the night and the chemistry of
  the night and awake.

I too pass from the night; 195
I stay awhile away O night, but I return to you again and love
  you;
Why should I be afraid to trust myself to you?
I am not afraid . . . . I have been well brought forward by you;
I love the rich running day, but I do not desert her in whom I
  lay so long:
I know not how I came of you, and I know not where I go
  with you . . . . but I know I came well and shall go
  well. 200

I will stop only a time with the night . . . . and rise betimes.

I will duly pass the day O my mother and duly return to you;
Not you will yield forth the dawn again more surely than you
  will yield forth me again,
Not the womb yields the babe in its time more surely than I
  shall be yielded from you in my time.

Leaves of Grass[6]

The bodies of men and women engirth me, and I engirth them,
They will not let me off nor I them till I go with them and
  respond to them and love them.

Was it dreamed whether those who corrupted their own live
  bodies could conceal themselves?
And whether those who defiled the living were as bad as they
  who defiled the dead?

The expression of the body of man or woman balks account, 5
The male is perfect and that of the female is perfect.

6. Entitled "I Sing the Body Electric" in 1867.

The expression of a wellmade man appears not only in his face,
It is in his limbs and joints also . . . . it is curiously in the
    joints of his hips and wrists,
It is in his walk . . the carriage of his neck . . the flex of his
    waist and knees . . . . dress does not hide him,
The strong sweet supple quality he has strikes through the
    cotton and flannel;   10
To see him pass conveys as much as the best poem . . perhaps
    more,
You linger to see his back and the back of his neck and
    shoulderside.

The sprawl and fulness of babes . . . . the bosoms and heads
    of women . . . . the folds of their dress . . . . their style as
    we pass in the street . . . . the contour of their shape
    downwards;
The swimmer naked in the swimmingbath . . seen as he swims
    through the salt transparent greenshine, or lies on his
    back and rolls silently with the heave of the water;
Framers bare-armed framing a house . . hoisting the beams in
    their places . . or using the mallet and mortising-chisel,   15
The bending forward and backward of rowers in rowboats . . . .
    the horseman in his saddle;
Girls and mothers and housekeepers in all their exquisite offices,
The group of laborers seated at noontime with their open
    dinnerkettles, and their wives waiting,
The female soothing a child . . . . the farmer's daughter in the
    garden or cowyard,
The woodman rapidly swinging his axe in the woods . . . . the
    young fellow hoeing corn . . . . the sleighdriver guiding his
    six horses through the crowd,   20
The wrestle of wrestlers . . two apprentice-boys, quite grown,
    lusty, goodnatured, nativeborn, out on the vacant lot at
    sundown after work,
The coats vests and caps thrown down . . the embrace of love
    and resistance,
The upperhold and underhold—the hair rumpled over and
    blinding the eyes;
The march of firemen in their own costumes—the play of the
    masculine muscle through cleansetting trowsers and
    waistbands,
The slow return from the fire . . . . the pause when the bell
    strikes suddenly again—the listening on the alert,   25
The natural perfect and varied attitudes . . . . the bent head,
    the curved neck, the counting:
Suchlike I love . . . . I loosen myself and pass freely . . . . and
    am at the mother's breast with the little child,
And swim with the swimmer, and wrestle with wrestlers, and
    march in line with the firemen, and pause and listen and
    count.

I knew a man . . . . he was a common farmer . . . . he was the
   father of five sons . . . and in them were the fathers of
   sons . . . and in them were the fathers of sons.

This man was of wonderful vigor and calmness and beauty of
   person; 30
The shape of his head, the richness and breadth of his
   manners, the pale yellow and white of his hair and beard,
   the immeasurable meaning of his black eyes,
These I used to go and visit him to see . . . . He was wise also,
He was six feet tall . . . . he was over eighty years old . . . . his
   sons were massive clean bearded tanfaced and handsome,
They and his daughters loved him . . . all who saw him loved
   him . . . they did not love him by allowance . . . they
   loved him with personal love;
He drank water only . . . . the blood showed like scarlet
   through the clear brown skin of his face; 35
He was a frequent gunner and fisher . . . he sailed his boat
   himself . . . he had a fine one presented to him by a
   shipjoiner . . . . he had fowling-pieces, presented to him
   by men that loved him;
When he went with his five sons and many grandsons to hunt
   or fish you would pick him out as the most beautiful and
   vigorous of the gang,
You would wish long and long to be with him . . . . you would
   wish to sit by him in the boat that you and he might
   touch each other.

I have perceived that to be with those I like is enough,
To stop in company with the rest at evening is enough, 40
To be surrounded by beautiful curious breathing laughing flesh
   is enough,
To pass among them . . to touch any one . . . . to rest my arm
   ever so lightly round his or her neck for a moment . . . .
   what is this then?
I do not ask any more delight . . . . I swim in it as in a sea.

There is something in staying close to men and women and
   looking on them and in the contact and odor of them that
   pleases the soul well,
All things please the soul, but these please the soul well. 45

This is the female form,
A divine nimbus exhales from it from head to foot,
It attracts with fierce undeniable attraction,
I am drawn by its breath as if I were no more than a helpless
   vapor . . . . all falls aside but myself and it,
Books, art, religion, time . . the visible and solid earth . . the
   atmosphere and the fringed clouds . . what was expected
   of heaven or feared of hell are now consumed, 50

Mad filaments, ungovernable shoots play out of it . . the
    response likewise ungovernable,
Hair, bosom, hips, bend of legs, negligent falling hands—all
    diffused . . . . mine too diffused,
Ebb stung by the flow, and flow stung by the ebb . . . .
    loveflesh swelling and deliciously aching,
Limitless limpid jets of love hot and enormous . . . . quivering
    jelly of love . . . white-blow and delirious juice,
Bridegroom-night of love working surely and softly into the
    prostrate dawn,   55
Undulating into the willing and yielding day,
Lost in the cleave of the clasping and sweetfleshed day.

This is the nucleus . . . after the child is born of woman the
    man is born of woman,
This is the bath of birth . . . this is the merge of small and
    large and the outlet again.
Be not ashamed women . . your privilege encloses the rest . . it
    is the exit of the rest,   60
You are the gates of the body and you are the gates of the soul.

The female contains all qualities and tempers them . . . . she
    is in her place . . . . she moves with perfect balance,
She is all things duly veiled . . . . she is both passive and active
    . . . . she is to conceive daughters as well as sons and sons
    as well as daughters.

As I see my soul reflected in nature . . . . as I see through a
    mist one with inexpressible completeness and beauty . . . .
    see the bent head and arms folded over the breast . . . .
    the female I see,
I see the bearer of the great fruit which is immortality . . . .
    the good thereof is not tasted by roues, and never can be.   65

The male is not less the soul, nor more . . . . he too is in his
    place,
He too is all qualities . . . . he is action and power . . . . the
    flush of the known universe is in him,
Scorn becomes him well and appetite and defiance become
    him well,
The fiercest largest passions . . bliss that is utmost and sorrow
    that is utmost become him well . . . . pride is for him,
The fullspread pride of man is calming and excellent to the
    soul;   70
Knowledge becomes him . . . . he likes it always . . . . he
    brings everything to the test of himself,
Whatever the survey . . whatever the sea and the sail, he
    strikes soundings at last only here,
Where else does he strike soundings except here?

The man's body is sacred and the woman's body is sacred . . . .
    it is no matter who,
Is it a slave? Is it one of the dullfaced immigrants just landed
    on the wharf?   75

Each belongs here or anywhere just as much as the welloff
    . . . . just as much as you,
Each has his or her place in the procession.

All is a procession,
The universe is a procession with measured and beautiful
    motion.

Do you know so much that you call the slave or the dullface
    ignorant?   80
Do you suppose you have a right to a good sight . . . and he or
    she has no right to a sight?
Do you think matter has cohered together from its diffused
    float, and the soil is on the surface and water runs and
    vegetation sprouts for you . . and not for him and her?

A slave at auction!
I help the auctioneer . . . . the sloven does not half know his
    business.

Gentlemen look on this curious creature,   85
Whatever the bids of the bidders they cannot be high enough
    for him,
For him the globe lay preparing quintillions of years without
    one animal or plant,
For him the revolving cycles truly and steadily rolled.

In that head the allbaffling brain,
In it and below it the making of the attributes of heroes.   90

Examine these limbs, red black or white . . . . they are very
    cunning in tendon and nerve;
They shall be stript that you may see them.

Exquisite senses, lifelit eyes, pluck, volition,
Flakes of breastmuscle, pliant backbone and neck, flesh not
    flabby, goodsized arms and legs,
And wonders within there yet.   95

Within there runs his blood . . . . the same old blood . . the
    same red running blood;
There swells and jets his heart . . . . There all passions and
    desires . . all reachings and aspirations:
Do you think they are not there because they are not
    expressed in parlors and lecture-rooms?

This is not only one man . . . . he is the father of those who
    shall be fathers in their turns,
In him the start of populous states and rich republics,   100
Of him countless immortal lives with countless embodiments
    and enjoyments.

How do you know who shall come from the offspring of his
    offspring through the centuries?
Who might you find you have come from yourself if you could
    trace back through the centuries?

A woman at auction,
She too is not only herself . . . . she is the teeming mother of
    mothers,   105
She is the bearer of them that shall grow and be mates to the
    mothers.

Her daughters or their daughters' daughters . . who knows who
    shall mate with them?
Who knows through the centuries what heroes may come from
    them?

In them and of them natal love . . . . in them the divine
    mystery . . . . the same old beautiful mystery.

Have you ever loved a woman?   110
Your mother . . . . is she living? . . . . Have you been much
    with her? and has she been much with you?
Do you not see that these are exactly the same to all in all
    nations and times all over the earth?

If life and the soul are sacred the human body is sacred;
And the glory and sweet of a man is the token of manhood
    untainted,
And in man or woman a clean strong firmfibred body is
    beautiful as the most beautiful face.   115

Have you seen the fool that corrupted his own live body? or
    the fool that corrupted her own live body?
For they do not conceal themselves, and cannot conceal
    themselves.

Who degrades or defiles the living human body is cursed,
Who degrades or defiles the body of the dead is not more cursed.

Leaves of Grass[7]

Sauntering the pavement or riding the country byroad here
    then are faces,
Faces of friendship, precision, caution, suavity, ideality,
The spiritual prescient face, the always welcome common
    benevolent face,
The face of the singing of music, the grand faces of natural
    lawyers and judges broad at the backtop,
The faces of hunters and fishers, bulged at the brows . . . . the
    shaved blanched faces of orthodox citizens,   5
The pure extravagant yearning questioning artist's face,
The welcome ugly face of some beautiful soul . . . . the
    handsome detested or despised face,
The sacred faces of infants . . . . the illuminated face of the
    mother of many children,
The face of an amour . . . . the face of veneration,
The face as of a dream . . . . the face of an immobile rock,   10
The face withdrawn of its good and bad . . a castrated face,
A wild hawk . . his wings clipped by the clipper,
A stallion that yielded at last to the thongs and knife of the
    gelder.

Sauntering the pavement or crossing the ceaseless ferry, here
    then are faces;
I see them and complain not and am content with all.   15

Do you suppose I could be content with all if I thought them
    their own finale?

This now is too lamentable a face for a man;
Some abject louse asking leave to be . . cringing for it,
Some milknosed maggot blessing what lets it wrig to its hole.

This face is a dog's snout sniffing for garbage;   20
Snakes nest in that mouth . . I hear the sibilant threat.

This face is a haze more chill than the arctic sea,
Its sleepy and wobbling icebergs crunch as they go.

This is a face of bitter herbs . . . . this an emetic . . . . they
    need no label,
And more of the drugshelf . . laudanum, caoutchouc, or hog's
    lard.   25

This face is an epilepsy advertising and doing business . . . . its
    wordless tongue gives out the unearthly cry,

7. Entitled "Faces" in 1871.

Its veins down the neck distend . . . . its eyes roll till they
    show nothing but their whites,
Its teeth grit . . the palms of the hands are cut by the turned-
    in nails,
The man falls struggling and foaming to the ground while he
    speculates well.

This face is bitten by vermin and worms,   30
And this is some murderer's knife with a halfpulled scabbard.

This face owes to the sexton his dismalest fee,
An unceasing deathbell tolls there.

Those are really men! . . . . the bosses and tufts of the great
    round globe.

Features of my equals, would you trick me with your creased
    and cadaverous march?   35
Well then you cannot trick me.

I see your rounded never-erased flow,
I see neath the rims of your haggard and mean disguises.

Splay and twist as you like . . . . poke with the tangling fores
    of fishes or rats,
You'll be unmuzzled . . . . you certainly will.   40

I saw the face of the most smeared and slobbering idiot they
    had at the asylum,
And I knew for my consolation what they knew not;
I knew of the agents that emptied and broke my brother,
The same wait to clear the rubbish from the fallen tenement;
And I shall look again in a score or two of ages,   45
And I shall meet the real landlord perfect and unharmed, every
    inch as good as myself.

The Lord advances and yet advances:
Always the shadow in front . . . . always the reached hand
    bringing up the laggards.

Out of this face emerge banners and horses . . . . O superb!
    . . . . I see what is coming,
I see the high pioneercaps . . . . I see the staves of runners
    clearing the way,   50
I hear victorious drums.

This face is a lifeboat;
This is the face commanding and bearded . . . . it asks no odds
    of the rest;
This face is flavored fruit ready for eating;
This face of a healthy honest boy is the programme of all good.   55

These faces bear testimony slumbering or awake,
They show their descent from the Master himself.

Off the word I have spoken I except not one . . . . red white or
    black, all are deific,
In each house is the ovum . . . . it comes forth after a
    thousand years.

Spots or cracks at the windows do not disturb me,   60
Tall and sufficient stand behind and make signs to me;
I read the promise and patiently wait.

This is a fullgrown lily's face,
She speaks to the limber-hip'd man near the garden pickets,
Come here, she blushingly cries . . . . Come nigh to me
    limber-hip'd man and give me your finger and thumb,   65
Stand at my side till I lean as high as I can upon you,
Fill me with albescent honey . . . . bend down to me,
Rub to me with your chafing beard . . rub to my breast and
    shoulders.

The old face of the mother of many children:
Whist! I am fully content.   70

Lulled and late is the smoke of the Sabbath morning,
It hangs low over the rows of trees by the fences,
It hangs thin by the sassafras, the wildcherry and the catbrier
    under them,

I saw the rich ladies in full dress at the soiree,
I heard what the run of poets were saying so long,   75
Heard who sprang in crimson youth from the white froth and
    the water-blue,

Behold a woman!
She looks out from her quaker cap . . . . her face is clearer
    and more beautiful than the sky.

She sits in an armchair under the shaded porch of the
    farmhouse,
The sun just shines on her old white head.   80

Her ample gown is of creamhued linen,
Her grandsons raised the flax, and her granddaughters spun it
    with the distaff and the wheel.

The melodious character of the earth!
The finish beyond which philosophy cannot go and does not
    wish to go!
The justified mother of men!   85

A young man came to me with a message from his brother,[8]
How should the young man know the whether and when of his
    brother?
Tell him to send me the signs.

And I stood before the young man face to face, and took his
    right hand in my left hand and his left hand in my right
    hand,
And I answered for his brother and for men . . . . and I
    answered for the poet, and sent these signs.   5

Him all wait for . . . . him all yield up to . . . . his word is
    decisive and final,
Him they accept . . . . in him lave . . . . in him perceive
    themselves as amid light,
Him they immerse, and he immerses them.

Beautiful women, the haughtiest nations, laws, the landscape,
    people and animals,
The profound earth and its attributes, and the unquiet ocean,   10
All enjoyments and properties, and money, and whatever
    money will buy,
The best farms . . . . . others toiling and planting, and he
    unavoidably reaps,
The noblest and costliest cities . . . . others grading and
    building, and he domiciles there;
Nothing for any one but what is for him . . . . near and far are
    for him,
The ships in the offing . . . . the perpetual shows and marches
    on land are for him if they are for any body.   15

He puts things in their attitudes,
He puts today out of himself with plasticity and love.
He places his own city, times, reminiscences, parents, brothers
    and sisters, associations employment and politics, so that
    the rest never shame them afterward, nor assume to
    command them.

He is the answerer,
What can be answered he answers, and what cannot be
    answered he shows how it cannot be answered.   20

A man is a summons and challenge,
It is vain to skulk . . . . Do you hear that mocking and
    laughter? Do you hear the ironical echoes?

8. This poem became the first half of "Song of the Answerer" in 1881.

Books friendships philosophers priests action pleasure pride
    beat up and down seeking to give satisfaction;
He indicates the satisfaction, and indicates them that beat up
    and down also.

Whichever the sex . . . whatever the season or place he may go
    freshly and gently and safely by day or by night,   25
He has the passkey of hearts . . . . to him the response of the
    prying of hands on the knobs.

His welcome is universal . . . . the flow of beauty is not more
    welcome or universal than he is,
The person he favors by day or sleeps with at night is blessed.

Every existence has its idiom . . . . every thing has an idiom
    and tongue;
He resolves all tongues into his own, and bestows it upon men
    . . and any man translates . . and any man translates
    himself also: 30
One part does not counteract another part . . . . He is the
    joiner . . he sees how they join.

He says indifferently and alike, How are you friend? to the
    President at his levee,
And he says Good day my brother, to Cudge that hoes in the
    sugarfield;
And both understand him and know that his speech is right.

He walks with perfect ease in the capitol,   35
He walks among the Congress . . . . and one representative
    says to another, Here is our equal appearing and new.

Then the mechanics take him for a mechanic,
And the soldiers suppose him to be a captain . . . . and the
    sailors that he has followed the sea,
And the authors take him for an author . . . . and the artists
    for an artist,
And the laborers perceive he could labor with them and love
    them;   40
No matter what the work is, that he is one to follow it or has
    followed it,
No matter what the nation, that he might find his brothers
    and sisters there.

The English believe he comes of their English stock,
A Jew to the Jew he seems . . . . a Russ to the Russ . . . .
    usual and near . . removed from none.

Whoever he looks at in the traveler's coffeehouse claims him,   45
The Italian or Frenchman is sure, and the German is sure, and
    the Spaniard is sure . . . . and the island Cuban is sure.

The engineer, the deckhand on the great lakes or on the
     Mississippi or St Lawrence or Sacramento or Hudson or
     Delaware claims him.

The gentleman of perfect blood acknowledges his perfect blood,
The insulter, the prostitute, the angry person, the beggar, see
     themselves in the ways of him . . . . he strangely
     transmutes them,
They are not vile any more . . . . they hardly know themselves,
     they are so grown: 50

You think it would be good to be the writer of melodious
     verses,
Well it would be good to be the writer of melodious verses;
But what are verses beyond the flowing character you could
     have? . . . . or beyond beautiful manners and behaviour?
Or beyond one manly or affectionate deed of an
     apprenticeboy? . . or old woman? . . or man that has been
     in prison or is likely to be in prison?

———————

Suddenly out of its stale and drowsy lair, the lair of slaves,[9]
Like lightning Europe le'pt forth . . . . half startled at itself,
Its feet upon the ashes and the rags . . . . Its hands tight to
     the throats of kings.

O hope and faith! O aching close of lives! O many a sickened
     heart!
Turn back unto this day, and make yourselves afresh.   5

And you, paid to defile the People . . . . you liars mark:
Not for numberless agonies, murders, lusts,
For court thieving in its manifold mean forms,
Worming from his simplicity the poor man's wages;
For many a promise sworn by royal lips, And broken, and
     laughed at in the breaking,   10
Then in their power not for all these did the blows strike of
     personal revenge . . or the heads of the nobles fall;
The People scorned the ferocity of kings.

But the sweetness of mercy brewed bitter destruction, and the
     frightened rulers come back:
Each comes in state with his train . . . . hangman, priest and
     tax-gatherer . . . . soldier, lawyer, jailer and sycophant.

Yet behind all, lo, a Shape,   15

9. This poem, the earliest of the twelve of 1855, first appeared in the *New York Daily Tribune*
   of June 21, 1850, under the title "Resurgemus." WW gave it the title "Europe, The 72d and
   73d Years of These States" in 1860.

Vague as the night, draped interminably, head front and form
    in scarlet folds,
Whose face and eyes none may see,
Out of its robes only this . . . . the red robes, lifted by the arm,
One finger pointed high over the top, like the head of a snake
    appears.

Meanwhile corpses lie in new-made graves . . . . bloody
    corpses of young men: 20
The rope of the gibbet hangs heavily . . . . the bullets of
    princes are flying . . . . the creatures of power laugh
    aloud,
And all these things bear fruits . . . . and they are good.

Those corpses of young men,
Those martyrs that hang from the gibbets . . . those hearts
    pierced by the gray lead,
Cold and motionless as they seem . . live elsewhere with
    unslaughter'd vitality.   25

They live in other young men, O kings,
They live in brothers, again ready to defy you:
They were purified by death . . . . They were taught and exalted.

Not a grave of the murdered for freedom but grows seed for
    freedom . . . . in its turn to bear seed,
Which the winds carry afar and re-sow, and the rains and the
    snows nourish.   30

Not a disembodied spirit can the weapons of tyrants let loose,
But it stalks invisibly over the earth . . whispering counseling
    cautioning.

Liberty let others despair of you . . . . I never despair of you.

Is the house shut? Is the master away?
Nevertheless be ready . . . . be not weary of watching,   35
He will soon return . . . . his messengers come anon.

Clear the way there Jonathan![1]
Way for the President's marshal! Way for the government
    cannon!
Way for the federal foot and dragoons . . . . and the phantoms
    afterward.

1. WW entitled this poem "A Boston Ballad" in 1871.

I rose this morning early to get betimes in Boston town;
Here's a good place at the corner . . . . I must stand and see
    the show.

I love to look on the stars and stripes . . . . I hope the fifes will
    play Yankee Doodle.

How bright shine the foremost with cutlasses,
Every man holds his revolver . . . . marching stiff through
    Boston town.

A fog follows . . . . antiques of the same come limping,
Some appear wooden-legged and some appear bandaged and
    bloodless.

Why this is a show! It has called the dead out of the earth,
The old graveyards of the hills have hurried to see;
Uncountable phantoms gather by flank and rear of it,
Cocked hats of mothy mould and crutches made of mist,
Arms in slings and old men leaning on young men's shoulders.

What troubles you, Yankee phantoms? What is all this
    chattering of bare gums?
Does the ague convulse your limbs? Do you mistake your
    crutches for firelocks, and level them?

If you blind your eyes with tears you will not see the
    President's marshal,
If you groan such groans you might balk the government
    cannon.

For shame old maniacs! . . . . Bring down those tossed arms,
    and let your white hair be;
Here gape your smart grandsons . . . . their wives gaze at them
    from the windows,
See how well-dressed . . . . see how orderly they conduct
    themselves.

Worse and worse . . . . Can't you stand it? Are you retreating?
Is this hour with the living too dead for you?

Retreat then! Pell-mell! . . . . Back to the hills, old limpers!
I do not think you belong here anyhow.

But there is one thing that belongs here. . . . Shall I tell you
    what it is, gentlemen of Boston?

I will whisper it to the Mayor . . . . he shall send a committee
    to England,
They shall get a grant from the Parliament, and go with a cart
    to the royal vault.

Dig out King George's coffin . . . . unwrap him quick from the
   graveclothes . . . . box up his bones for a journey: 30
Find a swift Yankee clipper . . . . here is freight for you
   blackbellied clipper,
Up with your anchor! shake out your sails! . . . . steer straight
   toward Boston bay.

Now call the President's marshal again, and bring out the
   government cannon,
And fetch home the roarers from Congress, and make another
   procession and guard it with foot and dragoons.

Here is a centrepiece for them: 35
Look! all orderly citizens . . . . look from the windows women.

The committee open the box and set up the regal ribs and glue
   those that will not stay,
And clap the skull on the top of the ribs, and clap a crown on
   the top of the skull.

You have got your revenge old buster! . . . . The crown is come
   to its own and more than its own.

Stick your hands in your pockets Jonathan . . . . you are a
   made man from this day,   40
You are mighty cute . . . . and here is one of your bargains.

———————————

There was a child went forth every day,[2]
And the first object he looked upon and received with wonder
   or pity or love or dread, that object he became,
And that object became part of him for the day or a certain
   part of the day . . . . or for many years or stretching cycles
   of years.

The early lilacs became part of this child,
And grass, and white and red morningglories, and white and
   red clover, and the song of the phœbe-bird,   5
And the March-born lambs, and the sow's pink-faint litter, and
   the mare's foal, and the cow's calf, and the noisy brood of
   the barnyard or by the mire of the pond-side . . and the
   fish suspending themselves so curiously below there . .
   and the beautiful curious liquid . . and the water-plants
   with their graceful flat heads . . all became part of him.

And the field-sprouts of April and May became part of him . . . .
   wintergrain sprouts, and those of the light-yellow corn,
   and of the esculent roots of the garden,
And the appletrees covered with blossoms, and the fruit

2. WW entitled this poem "There Was a Child Went Forth" in 1871.

afterward . . . . and woodberries . . and the commonest
    weeds by the road;
And the old drunkard staggering home from the outhouse of
    the tavern whence he had lately risen,
And the schoolmistress that passed on her way to the school
    . . and the friendly boys that passed . . and the
    quarrelsome boys . . and the tidy and freshcheeked girls . .
    and the barefoot negro boy and girl,
And all the changes of city and country wherever he went.

His own parents . . he that had propelled the fatherstuff at
    night, and fathered him . . and she that conceived him in
    her womb and birthed him . . . . they gave this child more
    of themselves than that,
They gave him afterward every day . . . . they and of them
    became part of him.

The mother at home quietly placing the dishes on the suppertable,
The mother with mild words . . . . clean her cap and gown
    . . . . a wholesome odor falling off her person and clothes
    as she walks by:
The father, strong, selfsufficient, manly, mean, angered, unjust,
The blow, the quick loud word, the tight bargain, the crafty lure,
The family usages, the language, the company, the furniture
    . . . . the yearning and swelling heart,
Affection that will not be gainsayed . . . . The sense of what is
    real . . . . the thought if after all it should prove unreal,
The doubts of daytime and the doubts of nighttime . . . the
    curious whether and how,
Whether that which appears so is so . . . . Or is it all flashes
    and specks?
Men and women crowding fast in the streets . . if they are not
    flashes and specks what are they?
The streets themselves, and the facades of houses . . . . the
    goods in the windows,
Vehicles . . teams . . the tiered wharves, and the huge crossing
    at the ferries;
The village on the highland seen from afar at sunset . . . . the
    river between,
Shadows . . aureola and mist . . light falling on roofs and
    gables of white or brown, three miles off,
The schooner near by sleepily dropping down the tide . . the
    little boat slacktowed astern,
The hurrying tumbling waves and quickbroken crests and slapping;
The strata of colored clouds . . . . the long bar of maroontint
    away solitary by itself . . . . the spread of purity it lies
    motionless in,
The horizon's edge, the flying seacrow, the fragrance of
    saltmarsh and shoremud;

These became part of that child who went forth every day, and
    who now goes and will always go forth every day,
And these become of him or her that peruses them now.

Who learns my lesson complete?[3]
Boss and journeyman and apprentice? . . . . churchman and
    atheist?
The stupid and the wise thinker . . . . parents and offspring
    . . . . merchant and clerk and porter and customer . . . .
    editor, author, artist and schoolboy?

Draw nigh and commence,
It is no lesson . . . . it lets down the bars to a good lesson,   5
And that to another . . . . and every one to another still.

The great laws take and effuse without argument,
I am of the same style, for I am their friend,
I love them quits and quits . . . . I do not halt and make salaams.

I lie abstracted and hear beautiful tales of things and the
    reasons of things,   10
They are so beautiful I nudge myself to listen.

I cannot say to any person what I hear . . . . I cannot say it to
    myself . . . . it is very wonderful.

It is no little matter, this round and delicious globe, moving so
    exactly in its orbit forever and ever, without one jolt or the
    untruth of a single second;
I do not think it was made in six days, nor in ten thousand
    years, nor ten decillions of years,
Nor planned and built one thing after another, as an architect
    plans and builds a house.   15

I do not think seventy years is the time of a man or woman,
Nor that seventy millions of years is the time of a man or
    woman,
Nor that years will ever stop the existence of me or any one
    else.

Is it wonderful that I should be immortal? as every one is
    immortal,
I know it is wonderful . . . . but my eyesight is equally
    wonderful . . . . and how I was conceived in my mother's
    womb is equally wonderful,   20
And how I was not palpable once but am now . . . . and was
    born on the last day of May 1819 . . . . and passed from a

3. WW entitled this poem "Who Learns My Lesson Complete?" in 1871.

babe in the creeping trance of three summers and three
winters to articulate and walk . . . . are all equally
wonderful.

And that I grew six feet high . . . . and that I have become a
man thirty-six years old in 1855 . . . . and that I am here
anyhow—are all equally wonderful;
And that my soul embraces you this hour, and we affect each
other without ever seeing each other, and never perhaps
to see each other, is every bit as wonderful:
And that I can think such thoughts as these is just as
wonderful,
And that I can remind you, and you think them and know
them to be true is just as wonderful,   25
And that the moon spins round the earth and on with the
earth is equally wonderful,
And that they balance themselves with the sun and stars is
equally wonderful.

Come I should like to hear you tell me what there is in
yourself that is not just as wonderful,
And I should like to hear the name of anything between
Sunday morning and Saturday night that is not just as
wonderful.

Great are the myths . . . . I too delight in them,[4]
Great are Adam and Eve . . . . I too look back and accept
them;
Great the risen and fallen nations, and their poets, women,
sages, inventors, rulers, warriors and priests.

Great is liberty! Great is equality! I am their follower,
Helmsmen of nations, choose your craft . . . . where you sail I
sail,   5
Yours is the muscle of life or death . . . . yours is the perfect
science . . . . in you I have absolute faith.

Great is today, and beautiful,
It is good to live in this age . . . . there never was any better.

Great are the plunges and throes and triumphs and falls of
democracy,
Great the reformers with their lapses and screams,   10
Great the daring and venture of sailors on new explorations.

Great are yourself and myself,
We are just as good and bad as the oldest and youngest or any,
What the best and worst did we could do,

4. WW entitled this poem "Great Are the Myths" in 1867.

What they felt . . do not we feel it in ourselves?   15
What they wished . . do we not wish the same?

Great is youth, and equally great is old age . . . . great are the
     day and night;
Great is wealth and great is poverty . . . . great is expression
     and great is silence.

Youth large lusty and loving . . . . youth full of grace and force
     and fascination,
Do you know that old age may come after you with equal
     grace and force and fascination?   20

Day fullblown and splendid . . . . day of the immense sun, and
     action and ambition and laughter,
The night follows close, with millions of suns, and sleep and
     restoring darkness.

Wealth with the flush hand and fine clothes and hospitality:
But then the soul's wealth—which is candor and knowledge
     and pride and enfolding love:
Who goes for men and women showing poverty richer than
     wealth?   25

Expression of speech . . in what is written or said forget not
     that silence is also expressive,
That anguish as hot as the hottest and contempt as cold as the
     coldest may be without words,
That the true adoration is likewise without words and without
     kneeling.

Great is the greatest nation . . the nation of clusters of equal
     nations.

Great is the earth, and the way it became what it is,   30
Do you imagine it is stopped at this? . . . . and the increase
     abandoned?
Understand then that it goes as far onward from this as this is
     from the times when it lay in covering waters and gases.

Great is the quality of truth in man,
The quality of truth in man supports itself through all changes,
It is inevitably in the man . . . . He and it are in love, and
     never leave each other.   35

The truth in man is no dictum . . . . it is vital as eyesight,
If there be any soul there is truth . . . . if there be man or
     woman there is truth . . . . If there be physical or moral
     there is truth,
If there be equilibrium or volition there is truth . . . . if there
     be things at all upon the earth there is truth.

O truth of the earth! O truth of things! I am determined to
    press the whole way toward you,
Sound your voice! I scale mountains or dive in the sea after
    you.   40

Great is language . . . . it is the mightiest of the sciences,
It is the fulness and color and form and diversity of the earth
    . . . . and of men and women . . . . and of all qualities and
    processes;
It is greater than wealth . . . . it is greater than buildings or
    ships or religions or paintings or music.

Great is the English speech . . . . What speech is so great as
    the English?
Great is the English brood . . . . What brood has so vast a
    destiny as the English?   45
It is the mother of the brood that must rule the earth with the
    new rule,
The new rule shall rule as the soul rules, and as the love and
    justice and equality that are in the soul rule.

Great is the law . . . . Great are the old few landmarks of the
    law . . . . they are the same in all times and shall not be
    disturbed.

Great are marriage, commerce, newspapers, books, freetrade,
    railroads, steamers, international mails and telegraphs and
    exchanges.

Great is Justice;   50
Justice is not settled by legislators and laws . . . . it is in the
    soul,
It cannot be varied by statutes any more than love or pride or
    the attraction of gravity can,
It is immutable . . it does not depend on majorities . . . .
    majorities or what not come at last before the same
    passionless and exact tribunal.

For justice are the grand natural lawyers and perfect judges
    . . . . it is in their souls,
It is well assorted . . . . they have not studied for nothing . . . .
    the great includes the less,   55
They rule on the highest grounds . . . . they oversee all eras
    and states and administrations,

The perfect judge fears nothing . . . . he could go front to
    front before God,
Before the perfect judge all shall stand back . . . . life and
    death shall stand back . . . . heaven and hell shall stand
    back.

Great is goodness;
I do not know what it is any more than I know what health is
    . . . . but I know it is great.   60

Great is wickedness . . . . I find I often admire it just as much
    as I admire goodness:
Do you call that a paradox? It certainly is a paradox.

The eternal equilibrium of things is great, and the eternal
    overthrow of things is great,
And there is another paradox.

Great is life . . and real and mystical . . wherever and whoever,   65
Great is death . . . . Sure as life holds all parts together, death
    holds all parts together;
Sure as the stars return again after they merge in the light,
    death is great as life.

Live Oak, with Moss[1]

I.

Not the heat flames up and consumes,
Not the sea-waves hurry in and out,
Not the air, delicious and dry, the air of the ripe summer,
    bears lightly along white down-balls of myriads of seeds,
    wafted, sailing gracefully, to drop where they may,
Not these—O none of these, more than the flames of me,
    consuming, burning for his love whom I love—O none,
    more than I, hurrying in and out;
Does the tide hurry, seeking something, and never give up?—
    O I, the same, to seek my life-long lover;   5
O nor down-balls, nor perfumes, nor the high rain-emitting
    clouds, are borne through the open air, more than my
    copious soul is borne through the open air, wafted in all
    directions, for friendship, for love.—

II.

I saw in Louisiana a live-oak growing,
All alone stood it, and the moss hung down from the branches,
Without any companion it grew there, glistening out joyous
    leaves of dark green,
And its look, rude, unbending, lusty, made me think of myself;
But I wondered how it could utter joyous leaves, standing
    alone there without its friend, its lover—For I knew I
    could not;   5
And I plucked a twig with a certain number of leaves upon it,
    and twined around it a little moss, and brought it away—
And I have placed it in sight in my room,
It is not needed to remind me as of my friends, (for I believe
    lately I think of little else than of them,)
Yet it remains to me a curious token—I write these pieces,
    and name them after it;[2]

1. These twelve verse manuscripts served WW as the nucleus for the "Calamus" section of *LG*. In 1953 Fredson Bowers first printed the sequence in *Studies in Bibliography*, from the manuscripts in the Clifton Waller Barrett Library, Special Collections, University of Virginia. The texts here are based on Hershel Parker's editing of a fresh collation from those manuscripts, prepared by Mark Niemeyer.
2. This line has previously been edited to read, "Yet it remains to me a curious token—it makes me think of manly love." For the rationale for the present emendation, see Steven Olsen-Smith's forthcoming article, "The Growth and Dispersion of Walt Whitman's 'Live Oak, with Moss' Sequence."

For all that, and though the live oak glistens there in
    Louisiana, solitary in a wide flat space, uttering joyous
    leaves all its life, without a friend, a lover, near—I know
    very well I could not.   10

III.

When I heard at the close of the day how I had been praised
    in the Capitol, still it was not a happy night for me that
    followed;
Nor when I caroused—Nor when my favorite plans were
    accomplished—was I really happy,
But that day I rose at dawn from the bed of perfect health,
    electric, inhaling sweet breath,
When I saw the full moon in the west grow pale and disappear
    in the morning light,
When I wandered alone over the beach, and undressing,
    bathed, laughing with the waters, and saw the sun rise,   5
And when I thought how my friend, my lover, was coming,
    then O I was happy;
Each breath tasted sweeter—and all that day my food
    nourished me more—And the beautiful day passed well,
And the next came with equal joy—And with the next, at
    evening, came my friend,
And that night, while all was still, I heard the waters roll
    slowly continually up the shores
I heard the hissing rustle of the liquid and sands, as directed
    to me, whispering to congratulate me,—For the friend I
    love lay sleeping by my side,   10
In the stillness his face was inclined towards me, while the
    moon's clear beams shone,
And his arm lay lightly over my breast—And that night I was
    happy.

IV.

This moment as I sit alone, yearning and pensive, it seems to
    me there are other men, in other lands, yearning and
    pensive.
It seems to me I can look over and behold them, in Germany,
    France, Spain—Or far away in China, India, or Russia—
    talking other dialects,
And it seems to me if I could know those men I should love
    them as I love men in my own lands,
It seems to me they are as wise, beautiful, benevolent, as any
    in my own lands;
O I think we should be brethren—I think I should be happy
    with them.   5

V.

Long I thought that knowledge alone would suffice me—O if I
    could but obtain knowledge!
Then the Land of the Prairies engrossed me—the south
    savannas engrossed me—For them I would live—I would
    be their orator;
Then I met the examples of old and new heroes—I heard of
    warriors, sailors, and all dauntless persons—And it
    seemed to me I too had it in me to be as dauntless as any,
    and would be so;
And then to finish all, it came to me to strike up the songs of
    the New World—And then I believed my life must be
    spent in singing;
But now take notice, Land of the prairies, Land of the south
    savannas, Ohio's land,   5
Take notice, you Kanuck woods—and you, Lake Huron—and
    all that with you roll toward Niagara—and you Niagara
    also,
And you, Californian mountains—that you all find some one
    else that he be your singer of songs,
For I can be your singer of songs no longer—I have ceased to
    enjoy them.
I have found him who loves me, as I him, in perfect love,
With the rest I dispense—I sever from all that I thought would
    suffice me, for it does not—it is now empty and tasteless
    to me,   10
I heed knowledge, and the grandeur of The States, and the
    examples of heroes, no more,
I am indifferent to my own songs—I am to go with him I love,
    and he is to go with me,
It is to be enough for each of us that we are together—We
    never separate again.—

VI.

What think you I have taken my pen to record?
Not the battle-ship, perfect-model'd, majestic, that I saw to day
    arrive in the offing, under full sail,
Nor the splendors of the past day—nor the splendors of the
    night that envelopes me—Nor the glory and growth of the
    great city spread around me,
But the two men I saw to-day on the pier, parting the parting
    of dear friends.
The one to remain hung on the other's neck and passionately
    kissed him—while the one to depart tightly prest the one
    to remain in his arms.   5

VII.

You bards of ages hence! when you refer to me, mind not so
    much my poems,
Nor speak of me that I prophesied of The States and led them
    the way of their glories,
But come, I will inform you who I was underneath that
    impassive exterior—I will tell you what to say of me,
Publish my name and hang up my picture as that of the
    tenderest lover,
The friend, the lover's portrait, of whom his friend, his lover,
    was fondest,   5
Who was not proud of his songs, but of the measureless ocean
    of love within him—and freely poured it forth,
Who often walked lonesome walks thinking of his dearest
    friends, his lovers,
Who pensive, away from one he loved, often lay sleepless and
    dissatisfied at night,
Who, dreading lest the one he loved might after all be
    indifferent to him, felt the sick feeling—O sick! sick!
Whose happiest days were those, far away through fields, in
    woods, on hills, he and another, wandering hand in hand,
    they twain, apart from other men.   10
Who ever, as he sauntered the streets, curved with his arm the
    manly shoulder of his friend—while the curving arm of
    his friend rested upon him also.

VIII.

Hours continuing long, sore and heavy-hearted,
Hours of the dusk, when I withdraw to a lonesome and
    unfrequented spot, seating myself, leaning my face in my
    hands,
Hours sleepless, deep in the night, when I go forth, speeding
    swiftly the countryroads, or through the city streets, or
    pacing miles and miles, stifling plaintive cries,
Hours discouraged, distracted,—For he, the one I cannot
    content myself without—soon I saw him content himself
    without me,
Hours when I am forgotten—(O weeks and months are
    passing, but I believe I am never to forget!)   5
Sullen and suffering hours—(I am ashamed—but it is useless
    —I am what I am;)
Hours of torment—I wonder if other men ever have the like,
    out of the like feelings?
Is there even one other like me—distracted—his friend, his
    lover, lost to him?
Is he too as I am now? Does he still rise in the morning,
    dejected, thinking who is lost to him?
And at night, awaking, think who is lost?   10
Does he too harbor his friendship silent and endless? Harbor
    his anguish and passion?

Does some stray reminder, or the casual mention of a name,
    bring the fit back upon him, taciturn and deprest?
Does he see himself reflected in me? In these hours does he
    see the face of his hours reflected?

IX.

I dreamed in a dream of a city where all the men were like
    brothers,
O I saw them tenderly love each other—I often saw them, in
    numbers, walking hand in hand;
I dreamed that was the city of robust friends—Nothing was
    greater there than manly love—it led the rest,
It was seen every hour in the actions of the men of that city,
    and in all their looks and words.—

X.

O you whom I often and silently come where you are, that I
    may be with you,
As I walk by your side, or sit near, or remain in the same room
    with you,
Little you know the subtle electric fire that for your sake is
    playing within me.—

XI.

Earth! Though you look so impassive, ample and spheric there
    —I now suspect that is not all,
I now suspect there is something terrible in you, ready to
    break forth,
For an athlete loves me,—and I him—But toward him there is
    something fierce and terrible in me,
I dare not tell it in words—not even in these songs.

XII.

To the young man, many things to absorb, to engraft, to
    develop, I teach, that he be my eleve,
But if through him speed not the blood of friendship, hot and
    red—if he be not silently selected by lovers, and do not
    silently select lovers—of what use were it for him to seek
    to become eleve of mine?

From Democratic Vistas[1]

As the greatest lessons of Nature through the universe are
perhaps the lessons of variety and freedom, the same present the
greatest lessons also in New World politics and progress. If a
man were ask'd, for instance, the distinctive points contrasting
modern European and American political and other life with the [5]
old Asiatic cultus, as lingering-bequeath'd yet in China and
Turkey, he might find the amount of them in John Stuart Mill's
profound essay on Liberty[2] in the future, where he demands two
main constituents, or sub-strata, for a truly grand nationality—
1st, a large variety of character—and 2d, full play for human [10]
nature to expand itself in numberless and even conflicting
directions—(seems to be for general humanity much like the
influences that make up, in their limitless field, that perennial
health-action of the air we call the weather—an infinite number
of currents and forces, and contributions, and temperatures, and [15]
cross purposes, whose ceaseless play of counterpart upon
counterpart brings constant restoration and vitality.) With this
thought—and not for itself alone, but all it necessitates, and
draws after it—let me begin my speculations.

America, filling the present with greatest deeds and problems, [20]
cheerfully accepting the past, including feudalism, (as, indeed,
the present is but the legitimate birth of the past, including
feudalism,) counts, as I reckon, for her justification and success,
(for who, as yet, dare claim success?) almost entirely on the
future. Nor is that hope unwarranted. To-day, ahead, though [25]
dimly yet, we see, in vistas, a copious, sane, gigantic offspring.
For our New World I consider far less important for what it has
done, or what it is, than for results to come. Sole among
nationalities, these States have assumed the task to put in forms
of lasting power and practicality, on areas of amplitude rivaling [30]
the operations of the physical kosmos, the moral political
speculations of ages, long, long deferr'd, the democratic repub-
lican principle, and the theory of development and perfection
by voluntary standards, and self-reliance. Who else, indeed,

---

1. *Democratic Vistas* (1871) brings together, along with additional material, substantial amounts
of two essays, "Democracy" and "Personalism," that WW had published in 1867 and 1868,
respectively.
2. John Stuart Mill (1806–1873), English philosopher whose essay *On Liberty* appeared in
1859.

except the United States, in history, so far, have accepted in   35
unwitting faith, and, as we now see, stand, act upon, and go
security for, these things?

But preluding no longer, let me strike the key-note of the
following strain. First premising that, though the passages of
it have been written at widely different times, (it is, in fact,   40
a collection of memoranda, perhaps for future designers,
comprehenders,) and though it may be open to the charge of
one part contradicting another—for there are opposite sides to
the great question of democracy, as to every great question—I
feel the parts harmoniously blended in my own realization and   45
convictions, and present them to be read only in such oneness,
each page and each claim and assertion modified and temper'd
by the others. Bear in mind, too, that they are not the result of
studying up in political economy, but of the ordinary sense,
observing, wandering among men, these States, these stirring   50
years of war and peace. I will not gloss over the appaling dangers
of universal suffrage in the United States. In fact, it is to admit
and face these dangers I am writing. To him or her within whose
thought rages the battle, advancing, retreating, between
democracy's convictions, aspirations, and the people's crudeness,   55
vice, caprices, I mainly write this essay. I shall use the words
America and democracy as convertible terms. Not an ordinary
one is the issue. The United States are destined either to
surmount the gorgeous history of feudalism, or else prove the
most tremendous failure of time. Not the least doubtful am I   60
on any prospects of their business, material success. The tri-
umphant future of their business, geographic and productive
departments, on larger scales and in more varieties than ever, is
certain. In those respects the republic must soon (if she does
not already) outstrip all examples hitherto afforded, and   65
dominate the world.[3]

---

3. " 'From a territorial area of less than nine hundred thousand square miles, the Union has
expanded into over four millions and a half—fifteen times larger than that of Great Britain
and France combined—with a shore-line, including Alaska, equal to the entire circumfer-
ence of the earth, and with a domain within these lines far wider than that of the Romans
in their proudest days of conquest and renown. With a river, lake, and coastwise commerce
estimated at over two thousand millions of dollars per year; with a railway traffic of four to
six thousand millions per year, and the annual domestic exchanges of the country running
up to nearly ten thousand millions per year; with over two thousand millions of dollars
invested in manufacturing, mechanical, and mining industry; with over five hundred millions
of acres of land in actual occupancy, valued, with their appurtenances, at over seven thou-
sand millions of dollars, and producing annually crops valued at over three thousand millions
of dollars; with a realm which, if the density of Belgium's population were possible, would
be vast enough to include all the present inhabitants of the world; and with equal rights
guaranteed to even the poorest and humblest of our forty millions of people—we can, with
a manly pride akin to that which distinguish'd the palmiest days of Rome, claim,' &c., &c.,
&c.,—*Vice-President Colfax's Speech, July 4, 1870.*
              LATER—*London "Times," (Weekly,) June 23, '82.*
  " 'The wonderful wealth-producing power of the United States defies and sets at naught
the grave drawbacks of a mischievous protective tariff, and has already obliterated, almost
wholly, the traces of the greatest of modern civil wars. What is especially remarkable in the
present development of American energy and success is its wide and equable distribution.
North and south, east and west, on the shores of the Atlantic and the Pacific, along the

Admitting all this, with the priceless value of our political
institutions, general suffrage, (and fully acknowledging the
latest, widest opening of the doors,) I say that, far deeper than
these, what finally and only is to make of our western world a   70
nationality superior to any hither known, and out-topping the
past, must be vigorous, yet unsuspected Literatures, perfect
personalities and sociologies, original, transcendental, and
expressing (what, in highest sense, are not yet express'd at all,)
democracy and the modern. With these, and out of these, I   75
promulge new races of Teachers, and of perfect Women,
indispensable to endow the birth-stock of a New World. For
feudalism, caste, the ecclesiastic traditions, though palpably
retreating from political institutions, still hold essentially, by
their spirit, even in this country, entire possession of the more   80
important fields, indeed the very subsoil, of education, and of
social standards and literature.

I say that democracy can never prove itself beyond cavil, until
it founds and luxuriantly grows its own forms of art, poems,
schools, theology, displacing all that exists, or that has been   85
produced anywhere in the past, under opposite influences. It
is curious to me that while so many voices, pens, minds, in
the press, lecture-rooms, in our Congress, &c., are discussing
intellectual topics, pecuniary dangers, legislative problems, the
suffrage, tariff and labor questions, and the various business and   90
benevolent needs of America, with propositions, remedies, often
worth deep attention, there is one need, a hiatus the
profoundest, that no eye seems to perceive, no voice to state.
Our fundamental want to-day in the United States, with closest,
amplest reference to present conditions, and to the future, is   95
of a class, and the clear idea of a class, of native authors,
literatures, far different, far higher in grade than any yet known,
sacerdotal, modern, fit to cope with our occasions, lands,
permeating the whole mass of American mentality, taste, belief,
breathing into it a new breath of life, giving it decision, affecting 100
politics far more than the popular superficial suffrage, with
results inside and underneath the elections of Presidents or
Congresses—radiating, begetting appropriate teachers, schools,
manners, and, as its grandest result, accomplishing, (what
neither the schools nor the churches and their clergy have   105
hitherto accomplish'd, and without which this nation will no

chain of the great lakes, in the valley of the Mississippi, and on the coasts of the gulf of
Mexico, the creation of wealth and the increase of population are signally exhibited. It is
quite true, as has been shown by the recent apportionment of population in the House of
Representatives, that some sections of the Union have advanced, relatively to the rest, in an
extraordinary and unexpected degree. But this does not imply that the States which have
gain'd no additional representatives or have actually lost some have been stationary or have
receded. The fact is that the present tide of prosperity has risen so high that it has overflow'd
all barriers, and has fill'd up the back-waters, and establish'd something like an approach to
uniform success' " [WW's note].

more stand, permanently, soundly, than a house will stand without a substratum,) a religious and moral character beneath the political and productive and intellectual bases of the States. For know you not, dear, earnest reader, that the people of our land may all read and write, and may all possess the right to vote—and yet the main things may be entirely lacking?—(and this to suggest them.)

View'd, to-day, from a point of view sufficiently over-arching, the problem of humanity all over the civilized world is social and religious, and is to be finally met and treated by literature. The priest departs, the divine literatus comes. Never was anything more wanted than, to-day, and here in the States, the poet of the modern is wanted, or the great literatus of the modern. At all times, perhaps, the central point in any nation, and that whence it is itself really sway'd the most, and whence it sways others, is its national literature, especially its archetypal poems. Above all previous lands, a great original literature is surely to become the justification and reliance, (in some respects the sole reliance,) of American democracy.

Few are aware how the great literature penetrates all, gives hue to all, shapes aggregates and individuals, and, after subtle ways, with irresistible power, constructs, sustains, demolishes at will. Why tower, in reminiscence, above all the nations of the earth, two special lands, petty in themselves, yet inexpressibly gigantic, beautiful, columnar? Immortal Judah lives, and Greece immortal lives, in a couple of poems.

Nearer than this. It is not generally realized, but it is true, as the genius of Greece, and all the sociology, personality, politics and religion of those wonderful states, resided in their literature or esthetics, that what was afterwards the main support of European chivalry, the feudal, ecclesiastical, dynastic world over there—forming its osseous structure, holding it together for hundreds, thousands of years, preserving its flesh and bloom, giving it form, decision, rounding it out, and so saturating it in the conscious and unconscious blood, breed, belief, and intuitions of men, that it still prevails powerful to this day, in defiance of the mighty changes of time—was its literature, permeating to the very marrow, especially that major part, its enchanting songs, ballads, and poems.[4]

To the ostent of the senses and eyes, I know, the influences

4. "See, for hereditaments, specimens, Walter Scott's Border Minstrelsy, Percy's collection, Ellis's early English Metrical Romances, the European continental poems of Walter of Aquitania, and the Nibelungen, of pagan stock, but monkish-feudal redaction; the history of the Troubadours, by Fauriel; even the far-back cumbrous old Hindu epics, as indicating the Asian eggs out of which European chivalry was hatch'd; Ticknor's chapters on the Cid, and on the Spanish poems and poets of Calderon's time. Then always, and, of course, as the superbest poetic culmination-expression of feudalism, the Shaksperean dramas, in the attitudes, dialogue, characters, &c., of the princes, lords and gentlemen, the pervading atmosphere, the implied and express'd standard of manners, the high port and proud stomach, the regal embroidery of style, &c." [WW's note].

which stamp the world's history are wars, uprisings or downfalls of dynasties, changeful movements of trade, important inventions, navigation, military or civil governments, advent of powerful personalities, conquerors, &c. These of course play 150 their part; yet, it may be, a single new thought, imagination, abstract principle, even literary style, fit for the time, put in shape by some great literatus, and projected among mankind, may duly cause changes, growths, removals, greater than the longest and bloodiest war, or the most stupendous merely 155 political, dynastic, or commercial overturn.

In short, as, though it may not be realized, it is strictly true, that a few first-class poets, philosophs, and authors, have substantially settled and given status to the entire religion, education, law, sociology, &c., of the hitherto civilized world, by 160 tinging and often creating the atmospheres out of which they have arisen, such also must stamp, and more than ever stamp, the interior and real democratic construction of this American continent, to-day, and days to come. Remember also this fact of difference, that, while through the antique and through the 165 mediæval ages, highest thoughts and ideals realized themselves, and their expression made its way by other arts, as much as, or even more than by, technical literature, (not open to the mass of persons, or even to the majority of eminent persons,) such literature in our day and for current purposes, is not only more 170 eligible than all the other arts put together, but has become the only general means of morally influencing the world. Painting, sculpture, and the dramatic theatre, it would seem, no longer play an indispensable or even important part in the workings and mediumship of intellect, utility, or even high esthetics. 175 Architecture remains, doubtless with capacities, and a real future. Then music, the combiner, nothing more spiritual, nothing more sensuous, a god, yet completely human, advances, prevails, holds highest place; supplying in certain wants and quarters what nothing else could supply. Yet in the civilization 180 of to-day it is undeniable that, over all the arts, literature dominates, serves beyond all—shapes the character of church and school—or, at any rate, is capable of doing so. Including the literature of science, its scope is indeed unparallel'd.

Before proceeding further, it were perhaps well to discriminate 185 on certain points. Literature tills its crops in many fields, and some may flourish, while others lag. What I say in these Vistas has its main bearing on imaginative literature, especially poetry, the stock of all. In the department of science, and the specialty of journalism, there appear, in these States, promises, perhaps 190 fulfilments, of highest earnestness, reality, and life. These, of course, are modern. But in the region of imaginative, spinal and essential attributes, something equivalent to creation is, for our age and lands, imperatively demanded. For not only is it not enough that the new blood, new frame of democracy shall be 195 vivified and held together merely by political means, superficial suffrage, legislation, &c., but it is clear to me that, unless it goes deeper, gets at least as firm and as warm a hold in men's hearts, emotions and belief, as, in their days, feudalism or ecclesiasticism, and inaugurates its own perennial sources, welling from the centre forever, its strength will be defective, its growth doubtful, and its main charm wanting. I suggest, therefore, the possibility, should some two or three really original American poets, (perhaps artists or lecturers,) arise, mounting the horizon like planets, stars of the first magnitude, that, from their eminence, fusing contributions, races, far localities, &c., together they would give more compaction and more moral identity, (the quality to-day most needed,) to these States, than all its Constitutions, legislative and judicial ties, and all its hitherto political, warlike, or materialistic experiences. As, for instance, there could hardly happen anything that would more serve the States, with all their variety of origins, their diverse climes, cities, standards, &c., than possessing an aggregate of heroes, characters, exploits, sufferings, prosperity or misfortune, glory or disgrace, common to all, typical of all—no less, but even greater would it be to possess the aggregation of a cluster of mighty poets, artists, teachers, fit for us, national expressers, comprehending and effusing for the men and women of the States, what is universal, native, common to all, inland and seaboard, northern and southern. The historians say of ancient Greece, with her ever-jealous autonomies, cities, and states, that the only positive unity she ever own'd or receiv'd, was the sad unity of a common subjection, at the last, to foreign conquerors. Subjection, aggregation of that sort, is impossible to America; but the fear of conflicting and irreconcilable interiors, and the lack of a common skeleton, knitting all close, continually haunts me. Or, if it does not, nothing is plainer than the need, a long period to come, of a fusion of the States into the only reliable identity, the moral and artistic one. For, I say, the true nationality of the States, the genuine union, when we come to a mortal crisis, is, and is to be, after all, neither the written law, nor, (as is generally supposed,) either self-interest, or common pecuniary or material objects—but the fervid and tremendous Idea, melting everything else with resistless heat, and solving all lesser and definite distinctions in vast, indefinite, spiritual, emotional power.

It may be claim'd, (and I admit the weight of the claim,) that common and general worldly prosperity, and a populace well-to-do, and with all life's material comforts, is the main thing, and is enough. It may be argued that our republic is, in performance, really enacting to-day the grandest arts, poems, &c., by beating up the wilderness into fertile farms, and in her railroads, ships, machinery, &c. And it may be ask'd, Are these not better, indeed,

for America, than any utterances even of greatest rhapsode, artist, or literatus? 245
I too hail those achievements with pride and joy: then answer that the soul of man will not with such only—nay, not with such at all—be finally satisfied; but needs what, (standing on these and on all things, as the feet stand on the ground,) is address'd to the loftiest, to itself alone. 250

* * *

As to the political section of Democracy, which introduces and breaks ground for further and vaster sections, few probably are the minds, even in these republican States, that fully comprehend the aptness of that phrase, "THE GOVERNMENT OF THE PEOPLE, BY THE PEOPLE, FOR THE PEOPLE," which we inherit from 255 the lips of Abraham Lincoln; a formula whose verbal shape is homely wit, but whose scope includes both the totality and all minutiæ of the lesson.
The People! Like our huge earth itself, which, to ordinary scansion, is full of vulgar contradictions and offence, man, 260 viewed in the lump, displeases, and is a constant puzzle and affront to the merely educated classes. The rare, cosmical, artistmind, lit with the Infinite, alone confronts his manifold and oceanic qualities—but taste, intelligence and culture, (so-called,) have been against the masses, and remain so. There is plenty of 265 glamour about the most damnable crimes and hoggish meannesses, special and general, of the feudal and dynastic world over there, with its *personnel* of lords and queens and courts, so welldress'd and so handsome. But the People are ungrammatical, untidy, and their sins gaunt and ill-bred. 270
Literature, strictly consider'd, has never recognized the People, and, whatever may be said, does not to-day. Speaking generally, the tendencies of literature, as hitherto pursued, have been to make mostly critical and querulous men. It seems as if, so far, there were some natural repugnance between a literary 275 and professional life, and the rude rank spirit of the democracies. There is, in later literature, a treatment of benevolence, a charity business, rife enough it is true; but I know nothing more rare, even in this country, than a fit scientific estimate and reverent appreciation of the People—of their measureless wealth of latent 280 power and capacity, their vast, artistic contrasts of lights and shades—with, in America, their entire reliability in emergencies, and a certain breadth of historic grandeur, of peace or war, far surpassing all the vaunted samples of book-heroes, or any *haut-ton*[5] coteries, in all the records of the world. 285

The movements of the late secession war, and their results, to any sense that studies well and comprehends them, show that

5. French: "High-toned," pretentious.

popular democracy, whatever its faults and dangers, practically justifies itself beyond the proudest claims and wildest hopes of its enthusiasts. Probably no future age can know, but I well know, how the gist of this fiercest and most resolute of the world's war-like contentions resided exclusively in the unnamed, unknown rank and file; and how the brunt of its labor of death was, to all essential purposes, volunteer'd. The People, of their own choice, fighting, dying for their own idea, insolently attack'd by the secession-slave-power, and its very existence imperil'd. Descending to detail, entering any of the armies, and mixing with the private soldiers, we see and have seen august spectacles. We have seen the alacrity with which the American born populace, the peaceablest and most good-natured race in the world, and the most personally independent and intelligent, and the least fitted to submit to the irksomeness and exasperation of regimental discipline, sprang, at the first tap of the drum, to arms—not for gain, nor even glory, nor to repel invasion—but for an emblem, a mere abstraction—for the life, *the safety of the flag*. We have seen the unequal'd docility and obedience of these soldiers. We have seen them tried long and long by hopelessness, mismanagement, and by defeat; have seen the incredible slaughter toward or through which the armies, (as at first Fredericksburg, and afterward at the Wilderness,) still unhesitatingly obey'd orders to advance. We have seen them in trench, or crouching behind breastwork, or tramping in deep mud, or amid pouring rain or thick-falling snow, or under forced marches in hottest summer (as on the road to get to Gettysburg)—vast suffocating swarms, divisions, corps, with every single man so grimed and black with sweat and dust, his own mother would not have known him—his clothes all dirty, stain'd and torn, with sour, accumulated sweat for perfume—many a comrade, perhaps a brother, sun-struck, staggering out, dying, by the roadside, of exhaustion—yet the great bulk bearing steadily on, cheery enough, hollow-bellied from hunger, but sinewy with unconquerable resolution.

We have seen this race proved by wholesale by drearier, yet more fearful tests—the wound, the amputation, the shatter'd face or limb, the slow hot fever, long impatient anchorage in bed, and all the forms of maiming, operation and disease. Alas! America have we seen, though only in her early youth, already to hospital brought. There have we watch'd these soldiers, many of them only boys in years—mark'd their decorum, their religious nature and fortitude, and their sweet affection. Wholesale, truly. For at the front, and through the camps, in countless tents, stood the regimental, brigade and division hospitals; while everywhere amid the land, in or near cities, rose clusters of huge, white-wash'd, crowded, one-story wooden barracks; and there ruled agony with bitter scourge, yet seldom brought a cry; and there stalk'd death by day and night along the narrow aisles between the rows of cots, or by the blankets on the ground, and touch'd lightly many a poor sufferer, often with blessed, welcome touch.

I know not whether I shall be understood, but I realize that it is finally from what I learn'd personally mixing in such scenes that I am now penning these pages. One night in the gloomiest period of the war, in the Patent office hospital in Washington city, as I stood by the bedside of a Pennsylvania soldier, who lay, conscious of quick approaching death, yet perfectly calm, and with noble, spiritual manner, the veteran surgeon, turning aside, said to me, that though he had witness'd many, many deaths of soldiers, and had been a worker at Bull Run, Antietam, Fredericksburg, &c., he had not seen yet the first case of man or boy that met the approach of dissolution with cowardly qualms or terror. My own observation fully bears out the remark.

What have we here, if not, towering above all talk and argument, the plentifully-supplied, last-needed proof of democracy, in its personalities? Curiously enough, too, the proof on this point comes, I should say, every bit as much from the south, as from the north. Although I have spoken only of the latter, yet I deliberately include all. Grand, common stock! to me the accomplish'd and convincing growth, prophetic of the future; proof undeniable to sharpest sense, of perfect beauty, tenderness and pluck, that never feudal lord, nor Greek, nor Roman breed, yet rival'd. Let no tongue ever speak in disparagement of the American races, north or south, to one who has been through the war in the great army hospitals.

* * *

Assuming Democracy to be at present in its embryo condition, and that the only large and satisfactory justification of it resides in the future, mainly through the copious production of perfect characters among the people, and through the advent of a sane and pervading religiousness, it is with regard to the atmosphere and spaciousness fit for such characters, and of certain nutriment and cartoon-draftings proper for them, and indicating them for New World purposes, that I continue the present statement —an exploration, as of new ground, wherein, like other primitive surveyors, I must do the best I can, leaving it to those who come after me to do much better. (The service, in fact, if any, must be to break a sort of first path or track, no matter how rude and ungeometrical.)

We have frequently printed the word Democracy. Yet I cannot too often repeat that it is a word the real gist of which still sleeps, quite unawaken'd, notwithstanding the resonance and the many angry tempests out of which its syllables have come, from pen or tongue. It is a great word, whose history, I suppose, remains unwritten, because that history has yet to be enacted. It is, in some sort, younger brother of another great and often-used word, Nature, whose history also waits unwritten. As I perceive,

the tendencies of our day, in the States, (and I entirely respect
them,) are toward those vast and sweeping movements, influ-   385
ences, moral and physical, of humanity, now and always current
over the planet, on the scale of the impulses of the elements.
Then it is also good to reduce the whole matter to the consid-
eration of a single self, a man, a woman, on permanent grounds.
Even for the treatment of the universal, in politics, metaphysics,   390
or anything, sooner or later we come down to one single, solitary
soul.

* * *

Of course, in these States, for both man and woman, we must
entirely recast the types of highest personality from what the
oriental, feudal, ecclesiastical worlds bequeath us, and which yet   395
possess the imaginative and esthetic fields of the United States,
pictorial and melodramatic, not without use as studies, but
making sad work, and forming a strange anachronism upon the
scenes and exigencies around us. Of course, the old undying
elements remain. The task is, to successfully adjust them to new   400
combinations, our own days. Nor is this so incredible. I can con-
ceive a community, to-day and here, in which, on a sufficient
scale, the perfect personalities, without noise meet; say in some
pleasant western settlement or town, where a couple of hundred
best men and women, of ordinary worldly status, have by luck   405
been drawn together, with nothing extra of genius or wealth, but
virtuous, chaste, industrious, cheerful, resolute, friendly and de-
vout. I can conceive such a community organized in running
order, powers judiciously delegated—farming, building, trade,
courts, mails, schools, elections, all attended to; and then the   410
rest of life, the main thing, freely branching and blossoming in
each individual, and bearing golden fruit. I can see there, in
every young and old man, after his kind, and in every woman
after hers, a true personality, develop'd, exercised proportionately
in body, mind, and spirit. I can imagine this case as one not   415
necessarily rare or difficult, but in buoyant accordance with the
municipal and general requirements of our times. And I can re-
alize in it the culmination of something better than any stereo-
typed *eclat* of history or poems. Perhaps, unsung, undramatized,
unput in essays or biographies—perhaps even some such com-   420
munity already exists, in Ohio, Illinois, Missouri, or somewhere,
practically fulfilling itself, and thus outvying, in cheapest vulgar
life, all that has been hitherto shown in best ideal pictures.

In short, and to sum up, America, betaking herself to forma-
tive action, (as it is about time for more solid achievement, and   425
less windy promise,) must, for her purposes, cease to recognize
a theory of character grown of feudal aristocracies, or form'd by
merely literary standards, or from any ultramarine, full-dress for-
mulas of culture, polish, caste, &c., and must sternly promulgate

her own new standard, yet old enough, and accepting the old, 430
the perennial elements, and combining them into groups, uni-
ties, appropriate to the modern, the democratic, the west, and
to the practical occasions and needs of our own cities, and of
the agricultural regions. Ever the most precious in the common.
Ever the fresh breeze of field, or hill, or lake, is more than any 435
palpitation of fans, though of ivory, and redolent with perfume;
and the air is more than the costliest perfumes.

And now, for fear of mistake, we may not intermit to beg our
absolution from all that genuinely is, or goes along with, even
Culture. Pardon us, venerable shade! if we have seem'd to speak 440
lightly of your office. The whole civilization of the earth, we
know, is yours, with all the glory and the light thereof. It is,
indeed, in your own spirit, and seeking to tally the loftiest teach-
ings of it, that we aim these poor utterances. For you, too, mighty
minister! know that there is something greater than you, namely, 445
the fresh, eternal qualities of Being. From them, and by them,
as you, at your best, we too evoke the last, the needed help, to
vitalize our country and our days. Thus we pronounce not so
much against the principle of culture; we only supervise it, and
promulge along with it, as deep, perhaps a deeper, principle. As 450
we have shown the New World including in itself the all-leveling
aggregate of democracy, we show it also including the all-varied,
all-permitting, all-free theorem of individuality, and erecting
therefor a lofty and hitherto unoccupied framework or platform,
broad enough for all, eligible to every farmer and mechanic—to 455
the female equally with the male—a towering self-hood, not
physically perfect only—not satisfied with the mere mind's and
learning's stores, but religious, possessing the idea of the infinite,
(rudder and compass sure amid this troublous voyage, o'er
darkest, wildest wave, through stormiest wind, of man's or na- 460
tion's progress)—realizing, above the rest, that known humanity,
in deepest sense, is fair adhesion to itself, for purposes beyond
—and that, finally, the personality of mortal life is most impor-
tant with reference to the immortal, the unknown, the spiritual,
the only permanently real, which as the ocean waits for and 465
receives the rivers, waits for us each and all.

Much is there, yet, demanding line and outline in our Vistas,
not only on these topics, but others quite unwritten. Indeed, we
could talk the matter, and expand it, through lifetime. But it is
necessary to return to our original premises. In view of them, we 470
have again pointedly to confess that all the objective grandeurs
of the world, for highest purposes, yield themselves up, and de-
pend on mentality alone. Here, and here only, all balances, all
rests. For the mind, which alone builds the permanent edifice,
haughtily builds it to itself. By it, with what follows it, are con- 475
vey'd to mortal sense the culminations of the materialistic, the

known, and a prophecy of the unknown. To take expression, to incarnate, to endow a literature with grand and archetypal models—to fill with pride and love the utmost capacity, and to achieve spiritual meanings, and suggest the future—these, and these only, satisfy the soul. We must not say one word against real materials; but the wise know that they do not become real till touched by emotions, the mind. Did we call the latter imponderable? Ah, let us rather proclaim that the slightest songtune, the countless ephemera of passions arous'd by orators and tale-tellers, are more dense, more weighty than the engines there in the great factories, or the granite blocks in their foundations.

Approaching thus the momentous spaces, and considering with reference to a new and greater personalism, the needs and possibilities of American imaginative literature, through the medium-light of what we have already broach'd, it will at once be appreciated that a vast gulf of difference separates the present accepted condition of these spaces, inclusive of what is floating in them, from any condition adjusted to, or fit for, the world, the America, there sought to be indicated, and the copious races of complete men and women, along these Vistas crudely outlined. It is, in some sort, no less a difference than lies between that long-continued nebular state and vagueness of the astronomical worlds, compared with the subsequent state, the definitely-form'd worlds themselves, duly compacted, clustering in systems, hung up there, chandeliers of the universe, beholding and mutually lit by each other's lights, serving for ground of all substantial foothold, all vulgar uses—yet serving still more as an undying chain and echelon of spiritual proofs and shows. A boundless field to fill! A new creation, with needed orbic works launch'd forth, to revolve in free and lawful circuits—to move, self-poised, through the ether, and shine like heaven's own suns! With such, and nothing less, we suggest that New World literature, fit to rise upon, cohere, and signalize in time, these States.

* * *

Their politics the United States have, in my opinion, with all their faults, already substantially establish'd, for good, on their own native, sound, long-vista'd principles, never to be overturn'd, offering a sure basis for all the rest. With that, their future religious forms, sociology, literature, teachers, schools, costumes, &c., are of course to make a compact whole, uniform, on tallying principles. For how can we remain, divided, contradicting ourselves, this way?[6] I say we can only attain harmony and stability

6. "Note, to-day, an instructive, curious spectacle and conflict. Science, (twin, in its fields, of Democracy in its)—Science, testing absolutely all thoughts, all works, has already burst well upon the world—a sun, mounting, most illuminating, most glorious—surely never again to set. But against it, deeply entrench'd, holding possession, yet remains, (not only through the churches and schools, but by imaginative literature, and unregenerate poetry,) the fossil theology of the mythic-materialistic, superstitious, untaught and credulous, fable-loving, primitive ages of humanity" [WW's note].

by consulting ensemble and the ethic purports, and faithfully building upon them. For the New World, indeed, after two grand stages of preparation-strata, I perceive that now a third stage, being ready for, (and without which the other two were useless,) with unmistakable signs appears. The First stage was the planning and putting on record the political foundation rights of immense masses of people—indeed all people—in the organization of republican National, State, and municipal governments, all constructed with reference to each, and each to all. This is the American programme, not for classes, but for universal man, and is embodied in the compacts of the Declaration of Independence, and, as it began and has now grown, with its amendments, the Federal Constitution—and in the State governments, with all their interiors, and with general suffrage; those having the sense not only of what is in themselves, but that their certain several things started, planted, hundreds of others in the same direction duly arise and follow. The Second stage relates to material prosperity, wealth, produce, labor-saving machines, iron, cotton, local, State and continental railways, intercommunication and trade with all lands, steamships, mining, general employment, organization of great cities, cheap appliances for comfort, numberless technical schools, books, newspapers, a currency for money circulation, &c. The Third stage, rising out of the previous ones, to make them and all illustrious, I, now, for one, promulge, announcing a native expression-spirit, getting into form, adult, and through mentality, for these States, self-contain'd, different from others, more expansive, more rich and free, to be evidenced by original authors and poets to come, by American personalities, plenty of them, male and female, traversing the States, none excepted—and by native superber tableaux and growths of language, songs, operas, orations, lectures, architecture—and by a sublime and serious Religious Democracy sternly taking command, dissolving the old, sloughing off surfaces, and from its own interior and vital principles, reconstructing, democratizing society.

For America, type of progress, and of essential faith in man, above all his errors and wickedness—few suspect how deep, how deep it really strikes. The world evidently supposes, and we have evidently supposed so too, that the States are merely to achieve the equal franchise, an elective government—to inaugurate the respectability of labor, and become a nation of practical operatives, law-abiding, orderly and well off. Yes, those are indeed parts of the task of America; but they not only do not exhaust the progressive conception, but rather arise, teeming with it, as the mediums of deeper, higher progress. Daughter of a physical revolution—mother of the true revolutions, which are of the interior life, and of the arts. For so long as the spirit is not changed, any change of appearance is of no avail.

The old men, I remember as a boy, were always talking of

American independence. What is independence? Freedom from all laws or bonds except those of one's own being, control'd by the universal ones. To lands, to man, to woman, what is there at last to each, but the inherent soul, nativity, idiocrasy, free, highest-poised, soaring its own flight, following out itself?   570

At present, these States, in their theology and social standards, (of greater importance than their political institutions,) are entirely held possession of by foreign lands. We see the sons and daughters of the New World, ignorant of its genius, not yet in-   575
augurating the native, the universal, and the near, still importing the distant, the partial, and the dead. We see London, Paris, Italy—not original, superb, as where they belong—but second-hand here, where they do not belong. We see the shreds of He-brews, Romans, Greeks; but where, on her own soil, do we see,   580
in any faithful, highest, proud expression, America herself? I sometimes question whether she has a corner in her own house.

*   *   *

Long ere the second centennial arrives, there will be some forty to fifty great States, among them Canada and Cuba. When the present century closes, our population will be sixty or seventy   585
millions. The Pacific will be ours, and the Atlantic mainly ours. There will be daily electric communication with every part of the globe. What an age! What a land! Where, elsewhere, one so great? The individuality of one nation must then, as always, lead the world. Can there be any doubt who the leader ought to be?   590
Bear in mind, though, that nothing less than the mightiest original non-subordinated SOUL has ever really, gloriously led, or ever can lead. (This Soul—its other name, in these Vistas, is LITERATURE.)

In fond fancy leaping those hundred years ahead, let us survey   595
America's works, poems, philosophies, fulfilling prophecies, and giving form and decision to best ideals. Much that is now un-dream'd of, we might then perhaps see establish'd, luxuriantly cropping forth, richness, vigor of letters and of artistic expres-sion, in whose products character will be a main requirement,   600
and not merely erudition or elegance.

Intense and loving comradeship, the personal and passionate attachment of man to man—which, hard to define, underlies the lessons and ideals of the profound saviours of every land and age, and which seems to promise, when thoroughly develop'd,   605
cultivated and recognized in manners and literature, the most substantial hope and safety of the future of these States, will then be fully express'd.[7]

---

7. It is to the development, identification, and general prevalence of that fervid comradeship, (the adhesive love, at least rivaling the amative love hitherto possessing imaginative literature, if not going beyond it,) that I look for the counterbalance and offset of our materialistic and vulgar American democracy, and for the spiritualization thereof. Many will say it is a dream, and will not follow my inferences: but I confidently expect a time when there will be seen,

A strong-fibred joyousness and faith, and the sense of health *al fresco,* may well enter into the preparation of future noble American authorship. Part of the test of a great literatus shall be the absence in him of the idea of the covert, the lurid, the maleficent, the devil, the grim estimates inherited from the Puritans, hell, natural depravity, and the like. The great literatus will be known, among the rest, by his cheerful simplicity, his adherence to natural standards, his limitless faith in God, his reverence, and by the absence in him of doubt, ennui, burlesque, persiflage, or any strain'd and temporary fashion. 610

615

* * *

I hail with joy the oceanic, variegated, intense practical energy, the demand for facts, even the business materialism of the current age, our States. But wo to the age or land in which these things, movements, stopping at themselves, do not tend to ideas. As fuel to flame, and flame to the heavens, so must wealth, science, materialism—even this democracy of which we make so much—unerringly feed the highest mind, the soul. Infinitude the flight: fathomless the mystery. Man, so diminutive, dilates beyond the sensible universe, competes with, outcopes space and time, meditating even one great idea. Thus, and thus only, does a human being, his spirit, ascend above, and justify, objective Nature, which, probably nothing in itself, is incredibly and divinely serviceable, indispensable, real, here. And as the purport of objective Nature is doubtless folded, hidden, somewhere here—as somewhere here is what this globe and its manifold forms, and the light of day, and night's darkness, and life itself, with all its experiences, are for—it is here the great literature, especially verse, must get its inspiration and throbbing blood. Then may we attain to a poetry worthy the immortal soul of man, and which, while absorbing materials, and, in their own sense, the shows of Nature, will, above all, have, both directly and indirectly, a freeing, fluidizing, expanding, religious character, exulting with science, fructifying the moral elements, and stimulating aspirations, and meditations on the unknown. 620

625

630

635

640

The process, so far, is indirect and peculiar, and though it may be suggested, cannot be defined. Observing, rapport, and with intuition, the shows and forms presented by Nature, the sensuous luxuriance, the beautiful in living men and women, the actual play of passions, in history and life—and, above all, from 645

---

running like a half-hid warp through all the myriad audible and visible worldly interests of America, threads of manly friendship, fond and loving, pure and sweet, strong and life-long, carried to degrees hitherto unknown—not only giving tone to individual character, and making it unprecedently emotional, muscular, heroic, and refined, but having the deepest relations to general politics. I say democracy infers such loving comradeship, as its most inevitable twin or counterpart, without which it will be incomplete, in vain, and incapable of perpetuating itself" [WW's note].

those developments either in Nature or human personality in
which power, (dearest of all to the sense of the artist,) transacts
itself—out of these, and seizing what is in them, the poet, the   650
esthetic worker in any field, by the divine magic of his genius,
projects them, their analogies, by curious removes, indirections,
in literature and art. (No useless attempt to repeat the material
creation, by daguerreotyping the exact likeness by mortal mental
means.) This is the image-making faculty, coping with material   655
creation, and rivaling, almost triumphing over it. This alone,
when all the other parts of a specimen of literature or art are
ready and waiting, can breath into it the breath of life, and en-
dow it with identity.

"The true question to ask," says the librarian of Congress in a   660
paper read before the Social Science Convention at New York,
October, 1869, "The true question to ask respecting a book, is,
has it help'd any human soul?" This is the hint, statement, not
only of the great literatus, his book, but of every great artist. It
may be that all works of art are to be first tried by their art   665
qualities, their image-forming talent, and their dramatic, picto-
rial, plot-constructing, euphonious and other talents. Then,
whenever claiming to be first-class works, they are to be strictly
and sternly tried by their foundation in, and radiation, in the
highest sense, and always indirectly, of the ethic principles, and   670
eligibility to free, arouse, dilate.

As, within the purposes of the Kosmos, and vivifying all me-
teorology, and all the congeries of the mineral, vegetable and
animal worlds—all the physical growth and development of man,
and all the history of the race in politics, religions, wars, &c.,   675
there is a moral purpose, a visible or invisible intention, certainly
underlying all—its results and proof needing to be patiently
waited for—needing intuition, faith, idiosyncrasy, to its realiza-
tion, which many, and especially the intellectual, do not have—
so in the product, or congeries of the product, of the greatest   680
literatus. This is the last, profoundest measure and test of a first-
class literary or esthetic achievement, and when understood and
put in force must fain, I say, lead to works, books, nobler than
any hitherto known. Lo! Nature, (the only complete, actual
poem,) existing calmly in the divine scheme, containing all, con-   685
tent, careless of the criticisms of a day, or these endless and
wordy chatterers. And lo! to the consciousness of the soul, the
permanent identity, the thought, the something, before which
the magnitude even of democracy, art, literature, &c., dwindles,
becomes partial, measurable—something that fully satisfies,   690
(which those do not.) That something is the All, and the idea of
All, with the accompanying idea of eternity, and of itself, the
soul, buoyant, indestructible, sailing space forever, visiting every
region, as a ship the sea. And again lo! the pulsations in all

matter, all spirit, throbbing forever—the eternal beats, eternal   695
systole and diastole of life in things—where-from I feel and
know that death is not the ending, as was thought, but rather
the real beginning—and that nothing ever is or can be lost, nor
ever die, nor soul, nor matter.

* * *

From Specimen Days[1]

Down at the Front.

FALMOUTH, Va., *opposite Fredericksburgh, December 21, 1862.*—Begin my visits among the camp hospitals in the army of the Potomac. Spend a good part of the day in a large brick mansion on the banks of the Rappahannock, used as a hospital since the battle—seems to have receiv'd only the worst cases. Out doors, at the foot of a tree, within ten yards of the front of the house, I notice a heap of amputated feet, legs, arms, hands, &c., a full load for a one-horse cart. Several dead bodies lie near, each cover'd with its brown woolen blanket. In the door-yard, towards the river, are fresh graves, mostly of officers, their names on pieces of barrel-staves or broken boards, stuck in the dirt. (Most of these bodies were subsequently taken up and transported north to their friends.) The large mansion is quite crowded upstairs and down, everything impromptu, no system, all bad enough, but I have no doubt the best that can be done; all the wounds pretty bad, some frightful, the men in their old clothes, unclean and bloody. Some of the wounded are rebel soldiers and officers, prisoners. One, a Mississippian, a captain, hit badly in leg, I talk'd with some time; he ask'd me for papers, which I gave him. (I saw him three months afterward in Washington, with his leg amputated, doing well.) I went through the rooms, downstairs and up. Some of the men were dying. I had nothing to give at that visit, but wrote a few letters to folks home, mothers, &c. Also talk'd to three or four, who seem'd most susceptible to it, and needing it.

After First Fredericksburg.

December 23 to 31.—The results of the late battle are exhibited everywhere about here in thousands of cases, (hundreds die every day,) in the camp, brigade, and division hospitals. These are merely tents, and sometimes very poor ones, the wounded lying on the ground, lucky if their blankets are spread on layers of pine or hemlock twigs, or small leaves. No cots; seldom even

---

1. *Specimen Days* (1882) is composed of about 250 prose "memoranda," many of them evoking WW's experiences of either the heroic suffering of Civil War soldiers or the restorative powers of a life in nature.

a mattress. It is pretty cold. The ground is frozen hard, and there
is occasional snow. I go around from one case to another. I do
not see that I do much good to these wounded and dying; but I
cannot leave them. Once in a while some youngster holds on   10
to me convulsively, and I do what I can for him; at any rate, stop
with him and sit near him for hours, if he wishes it.

Besides the hospitals, I also go occasionally on long tours
through the camps, talking with the men, &c. Sometimes at
night among the groups around the fires, in their shebang en-   15
closures of bushes. These are curious shows, full of characters
and groups. I soon get acquainted anywhere in camp, with of-
ficers or men, and am always well used. Sometimes I go down
on picket with the regiments I know best. As to rations, the army
here at present seems to be tolerably well supplied, and the men   20
have enough, such as it is, mainly salt pork and hard tack. Most
of the regiments lodge in the flimsy little shelter-tents. A few
have built themselves huts of logs and mud, with fire-places.

Hospital Scenes and Persons.

Letter Writing.—When eligible, I encourage the men to write,
and myself, when called upon, write all sorts of letters for
them, (including love letters, very tender ones.) Almost as I reel
off these memoranda, I write for a new patient to his wife.
M. de F., of the 17th Connecticut, company H, has just come   5
up (February 17th) from Windmill point, and is received in ward
H, Armory-square. He is an intelligent looking man, has a foreign
accent, black-eyed and hair'd, a Hebraic appearance. Wants a
telegraphic message sent to his wife, New Canaan, Conn. I agree
to send the message—but to make things sure I also sit down   10
and write the wife a letter, and despatch it to the post-office
immediately, as he fears she will come on, and he does not wish
her to, as he will surely get well.

Saturday, January 30th.—Afternoon, visited Campbell hospi-
tal. Scene of cleaning up the ward, and giving the men all clean   15
clothes—through the ward (6) the patients dressing or being
dress'd—the naked upper half of the bodies—the good-humor
and fun—the shirts, drawers, sheets of beds, &c., and the gen-
eral fixing up for Sunday. Gave J. L. 50 cents.

Wednesday, February 4th.—Visited Armory-square hospital,   20
went pretty thoroughly through wards E and D. Supplied paper
and envelopes to all who wish'd—as usual, found plenty of men
who needed those articles. Wrote letters. Saw and talk'd with
two or three members of the Brooklyn 14th regt. A poor fellow
in ward D, with a fearful wound in a fearful condition, was hav-   25
ing some loose splinters of bone taken from the neighborhood
of the wound. The operation was long, and one of great pain—
yet, after it was well commenced, the soldier bore it in silence.

He sat up, propp'd—was much wasted—had lain a long time
quiet in one position (not for days only but weeks,) a bloodless,
brown-skinn'd face, with eyes full of determination—belong'd to
a New York regiment. There was an unusual cluster of surgeons,
medical cadets, nurses, &c., around his bed—I thought the
whole thing was done with tenderness, and done well. In one
case, the wife sat by the side of her husband, his sickness typhoid
fever, pretty bad. In another, by the side of her son, a mother—
she told me she had seven children, and this was the youngest.
(A fine, kind, healthy, gentle mother, good-looking, not very old,
with a cap on her head, and dress'd like home—what a charm
it gave to the whole ward.) I liked the woman nurse in Ward E
—I noticed how she sat a long time by a poor fellow who just
had, that morning, in addition to his other sickness, bad
hemorrhage—she gently assisted him, reliev'd him of the blood,
holding a cloth to his mouth, as he coughed it up—he was so
weak he could only just turn his head over on the pillow.

One young New York man, with a bright, handsome face, had
been lying several months from a most disagreeable wound, re-
ceiv'd at Bull Run. A bullet had shot him right through the blad-
der, hitting him front, low in the belly, and coming out back. He
had suffer'd much—the water came out of the wound, by slow
but steady quantities, for many weeks—so that he lay almost
constantly in a sort of puddle—and there were other disagree-
able circumstances. He was of good heart, however. At present
comparatively comfortable, had a bad throat, was delighted with
a stick of horehound candy I gave him, with one or two other
trifles.

Some Specimen Cases.

June 18th.—In one of the hospitals I find Thomas Haley, com-
pany M, 4th New York cavalry—a regular Irish boy, a fine spec-
imen of youthful physical manliness—shot through the lungs—
inevitably dying—came over to this country from Ireland to
enlist—has not a single friend or acquaintance here—is sleeping
soundly at this moment, (but it is the sleep of death)—has a
bullet-hole straight through the lung. I saw Tom when first
brought here, three days since, and didn't suppose he could live
twelve hours—(yet he looks well enough in the face to a casual
observer.) He lies there with his frame exposed above the waist,
all naked, for coolness, a fine built man, the tan not yet bleach'd
from his cheeks and neck. It is useless to talk to him, as with
his sad hurt, and the stimulants they give him, and the utter
strangeness of every object, face, furniture, &c., the poor fellow,
even when awake, is like some frighten'd, shy animal. Much of
the time he sleeps, or half sleeps. (Sometimes I thought he knew

more than he show'd.) I often come and sit by him in perfect
silence; he will breathe for ten minutes as softly and evenly as
a young babe asleep. Poor youth, so handsome, athletic, with
profuse beautiful shining hair. One time as I sat looking at
him while he lay asleep, he suddenly, without the least start,
awaken'd, open'd his eyes, gave me a long steady look, turning
his face very slightly to gaze easier—one long, clear, silent look—
a slight sigh—then turn'd back and went into his doze again.
Little he knew, poor death-stricken boy, the heart of the stranger
that hover'd near.

    W. H. E., Co. F., 2d N. J.—His disease is pneumonia. He lay
sick at the wretched hospital below Aquia creek, for seven or
eight days before brought here. He was detail'd from his regi-
ment to go there and help as nurse, but was soon taken down
himself. Is an elderly, sallow-faced, rather gaunt, gray-hair'd
man, a widower, with children. He express'd a great desire for
good, strong green tea. An excellent lady, Mrs. W., of Washing-
ton, soon sent him a package; also a small sum of money. The
doctor said give him the tea at pleasure; it lay on the table by
his side, and he used it every day. He slept a great deal; could
not talk much, as he grew deaf. Occupied bed 15, ward I, Ar-
mory. (The same lady above, Mrs. W., sent the men a large pack-
age of tobacco.)

    J. G. lies in bed 52, ward I; is of company B, 7th Pennsylvania.
I gave him a small sum of money, some tobacco, and envelopes.
To a man adjoining also gave twenty-five cents; he flush'd in the
face when I offer'd it—refused at first, but as I found he had
not a cent, and was very fond of having the daily papers to read,
I prest it on him. He was evidently very grateful, but said little.

    J. T. L., of company F., 9th New Hampshire, lies in bed 37,
ward I. Is very fond of tobacco. I furnish him some; also with a
little money. Has gangrene of the feet; a pretty bad case; will
surely have to lose three toes. Is a regular specimen of an old-
fashion'd, rude, hearty, New England countryman, impressing
me with his likeness to that celebrated singed cat, who was better
than she look'd.

    Bed 3, ward E, Armory, has a great hankering for pickles,
something pungent. After consulting the doctor, I gave him a
small bottle of horse-radish; also some apples; also a book. Some
of the nurses are excellent. The woman-nurse in this ward I like
very much. (Mrs. Wright—a year afterwards I found her in Man-
sion house hospital, Alexandria—she is a perfect nurse.)

    In one bed a young man, Marcus Small, company K, 7th
Maine—sick with dysentery and typhoid fever—pretty critical
case—I talk with him often—he thinks he will die—looks like
it indeed. I write a letter for him home to East Livermore,
Maine—I let him talk to me a little, but not much, advise him
to keep very quiet—do most of the talking myself—stay quite a

while with him, as he holds on to my hand—talk to him in a   65
cheering, but slow, low and measured manner—talk about his
furlough, and going home as soon as he is able to travel.

Thomas Lindly, 1st Pennsylvania cavalry, shot very badly
through the foot—poor young man, he suffers horribly, has to
be constantly dosed with morphine, his face ashy and glazed,   70
bright young eyes—I give him a large handsome apple, lay it in
sight, tell him to have it roasted in the morning, as he generally
feels easier then, and can eat a little breakfast. I write two letters
for him.

Opposite, an old Quaker lady is sitting by the side of her son,   75
Amer Moore, 2d U. S. artillery—shot in the head two weeks
since, very low, quite rational—from hips down paralyzed—he
will surely die. I speak a very few words to him every day and
evening—he answers pleasantly—wants nothing—(he told me
soon after he came about his home affairs, his mother had been   80
an invalid, and he fear'd to let her know his condition.) He died
soon after she came.

The Real War Will Never Get in the Books.

And so good-bye to the war. I know not how it may have been,
or may be, to others—to me the main interest I found, (and still,
on recollection, find,) in the rank and file of the armies, both
sides, and in those specimens amid the hospitals, and even the
dead on the field. To me the points illustrating the latent per-   5
sonal character and eligibilities of these States, in the two or
three millions of American young and middle-aged men, North
and South, embodied in those armies—and especially the one-
third or one-fourth of their number, stricken by wounds or dis-
ease at some time in the course of the contest—were of more   10
significance even than the political interests involved. (As so
much of a race depends on how it faces death, and how it stands
personal anguish and sickness. As, in the glints of emotions un-
der emergencies, and the indirect traits and asides in Plutarch,
we get far profounder clues to the antique world than all its more   15
formal history.)

Future years will never know the seething hell and the black
infernal background of countless minor scenes and interiors,
(not the official surface-courteousness of the Generals, not the
few great battles) of the Secession war; and it is best they should   20
not—the real war will never get in the books. In the mushy
influences of current times, too, the fervid atmosphere and typ-
ical events of those years are in danger of being totally forgotten.
I have at night watch'd by the side of a sick man in the hospital,
one who could not live many hours. I have seen his eyes flash   25
and burn as he raised himself and recurr'd to the cruelties on
his surrender'd brother, and mutilations of the corpse afterward.

(See, in the preceding pages, the incident at Upperville—the seventeen kill'd as in the description, were left there on the ground. After they dropt dead, no one touch'd them—all were made sure of, however. The carcasses were left for the citizens to bury or not, as they chose.)

Such was the war. It was not a quadrille in a ball-room. Its interior history will not only never be written—its practicality, minutiæ of deeds and passions, will never be even suggested. The actual soldier of 1862–'65, North and South, with all his ways, his incredible dauntlessness, habits, practices, tastes, language, his fierce friendship, his appetite, rankness, his superb strength and animality, lawless gait, and a hundred unnamed lights and shades of camp, I say, will never be written—perhaps must not and should not be.

The preceding notes may furnish a few stray glimpses into that life, and into those lurid interiors, never to be fully convey'd to the future. The hospital part of the drama from '61 to '65, deserves indeed to be recorded. Of that many-threaded drama, with its sudden and strange surprises, its confounding of prophecies, its moments of despair, the dread of foreign interference, the interminable campaigns, the bloody battles, the mighty and cumbrous and green armies, the drafts and bounties—the immense money expenditure, like a heavy-pouring constant rain—with, over the whole land, the last three years of the struggle, an unending, universal mourning-wail of women, parents, orphans—the marrow of the tragedy concentrated in those Army Hospitals—(it seem'd sometimes as if the whole interest of the land, North and South, was one vast central hospital, and all the rest of the affair but flanges)—those forming the untold and unwritten history of the war—infinitely greater (like life's) than the few scraps and distortions that are ever told or written. Think how much, and of importance, will be—how much, civic and military, has already been—buried in the grave, in eternal darkness.

A Winter Day on the Sea-Beach.

One bright December mid-day lately I spent down on the New Jersey sea-shore, reaching it by a little more than an hour's railroad trip over the old Camden and Atlantic. I had started betimes, fortified by nice strong coffee and a good breakfast (cook'd by the hands I love, my dear sister Lou's—how much better it makes the victuals taste, and then assimilate, strengthen you, perhaps make the whole day comfortable afterwards.) Five or six miles at the last, our track enter'd a broad region of salt grass meadows, intersected by lagoons, and cut up everywhere by watery runs. The sedgy perfume, delightful to my nostrils, reminded me of "the mash" and south bay of my native island. I could have journey'd contentedly till night through these flat and odorous sea-prairies. From half-past 11 till 2 I was nearly all the time along the beach, or in sight of the ocean, listening to its hoarse murmur, and inhaling the bracing and welcome breezes. First, a 15 rapid five-mile drive over the hard sand—our carriage wheels hardly made dents in it. Then after dinner (as there were nearly two hours to spare) I walk'd off in another direction, (hardly met or saw a person,) and taking possession of what appear'd to have been the reception-room of an old bath-house range, had a broad 20 expanse of view all to myself—quaint, refreshing, unimpeded— a dry area of sedge and Indian grass immediately before and around me—space, simple, unornamented space. Distant vessels, and the far-off, just visible trailing smoke of an inward bound steamer; more plainly, ships, brigs, schooners, in sight, 25 most of them with every sail set to the firm and steady wind.

The attractions, fascinations there are in sea and shore! How one dwells on their simplicity, even vacuity! What is it in us, arous'd by those indirections and directions? That spread of waves and gray-white beach, salt, monotonous, senseless—such 30 an entire absence of art, books, talk, elegance—so indescribably comforting, even this winter day—grim, yet so delicate-looking, so spiritual—striking emotional, impalpable depths, subtler than all the poems, paintings, music, I have ever read, seen, heard. (Yet let me be fair, perhaps it is because I have read those poems 35 and heard that music.)

A Sun-Bath—Nakedness.

Sunday, Aug. 27.—Another day quite free from mark'd prostration and pain. It seems indeed as if peace and nutriment from heaven subtly filter into me as I slowly hobble down these country lanes and across fields, in the good air—as I sit here in solitude with Nature—open, voiceless, mystic, far removed, yet 5 palpable, eloquent Nature. I merge myself in the scene, in the perfect day. Hovering over the clear brook-water, I am sooth'd by its soft gurgle in one place, and the hoarser murmurs of its three-foot fall in another. Come, ye disconsolate, in whom any latent eligibility is left—come get the sure virtues of creek-shore, 10 and wood and field. Two months (July and August, '77,) have I absorb'd them, and they begin to make a new man of me. Every day, seclusion—every day at least two or three hours of freedom, bathing, no talk, no bonds, no dress, no books, no *manners.*

Shall I tell you, reader, to what I attribute my already much- 15 restored health? That I have been almost two years, off and on, without drugs and medicines, and daily in the open air. Last summer I found a particularly secluded little dell off one side by my creek, originally a large dugout marl-pit, now abandon'd, fill'd with bushes, trees, grass, a group of willows, a straggling bank, 20

and a spring of delicious water running right through the middle
of it, with two or three little cascades. Here I retreated every hot
day, and follow it up this summer. Here I realize the meaning
of that old fellow who said he was seldom less alone than when
alone. Never before did I get so close to Nature; never before   25
did she come so close to me. By old habit, I pencill'd down from
time to time, almost automatically, moods, sights, hours, tints
and outlines, on the spot. Let me specially record the satisfaction
of this current forenoon, so serene and primitive, so convention-
ally exceptional, natural.   30

An hour or so after breakfast I wended my way down to the
recesses of the aforesaid dell, which I and certain thrushes, cat-
birds, &c., had all to ourselves. A light south-west wind was
blowing through the tree-tops. It was just the place and time for
my Adamic air-bath and flesh-brushing from head to foot. So   35
hanging clothes on a rail near by, keeping old broadbrim straw
on head and easy shoes on feet, havn't I had a good time the
last two hours! First with the stiff-elastic bristles rasping arms,
breast, sides, till they turn'd scarlet—then partially bathing in
the clear waters of the running brook—taking everything very   40
leisurely, with many rests and pauses—stepping about bare-
footed every few minutes now and then in some neighboring
black ooze, for unctuous mud-bath to my feet—a brief second
and third rinsing in the crystal running waters—rubbing with
the fragrant towel—slow negligent promenades on the turf up   45
and down in the sun, varied with occasional rests, and further
frictions of the bristle-brush—sometimes carrying my portable
chair with me from place to place, as my range is quite extensive
here, nearly a hundred rods, feeling quite secure from intrusion,
(and that indeed I am not at all nervous about, if it accidentally   50
happens.)

As I walk'd slowly over the grass, the sun shone out enough
to show the shadow moving with me. Somehow I seem'd to get
identity with each and every thing around me, in its condition.
Nature was naked, and I was also. It was too lazy, soothing, and   55
joyous-equable to speculate about. Yet I might have thought
somehow in this vein: Perhaps the inner never lost rapport we
hold with earth, light, air, trees, &c., is not to be realized through
eyes and mind only, but through the whole corporeal body,
which I will not have blinded or bandaged any more than the   60
eyes. Sweet, sane, still Nakedness in Nature!—ah if poor, sick,
prurient humanity in cities might really know you once more! Is
not nakedness then indecent? No, not inherently. It is your
thought, your sophistication, your fear, your respectability, that
is indecent. There come moods when these clothes of ours are   65
not only too irksome to wear, but are themselves indecent. Per-
haps indeed he or she to whom the free exhilarating extasy of
nakedness in Nature has never been eligible (and how many
thousands there are!) has not really known what purity is—nor

what faith or art or health really is. (Probably the whole curriculum of first-class philosophy, beauty, heroism, form, illustrated by the old Hellenic race—the highest height and deepest depth known to civilization in those departments—came from their natural and religious idea of Nakedness.) 70

Many such hours, from time to time, the last two summers— I attribute my partial rehabilitation largely to them. Some good people may think it a feeble or half-crack'd way of spending one's time and thinking. May-be it is. 75

Whitman on His Art

Comments, 1855–1892

In his published prefaces to *Leaves of Grass,* in a number of unpublished introductions, in *Democratic Vistas,* in various pieces collected in the *Complete Prose Works* (1892), and above all in "A Backward Glance O'er Travel'd Roads," Whitman set forth his convictions about the nature and purpose of his poetry.

The most important of these pronouncements are a basic part of this edition. Less formal—but no less revealing—are the notes and observations with which the poet constantly reviewed his poetic strategy, sometimes addressing himself in private diary entries, sometimes confiding opinions on his work to his trusted friends. A selection follows.

My poems when complete should be a *unity,* in the same sense that the earth is, or that the human body, (senses, soul, head, trunk, feet, blood, viscera, man-root, eyes, hair) or that a perfect musical composition is.

Great constituent elements of my poetry—Two, viz: Materialism—Spirituality—The Intellect is what is to be the medium of these and to beautify and make serviceable there.[1]

To change the book—go over the whole with great care—to make it more intensely the poem of *Individuality*—addressed more *distinctly to the single personality listening to it*—ruling out, perhaps, some parts that stand in the way of this—cull out the egot[istic] somewhat.[2]

In future *Leaves of Grass. Be more severe* with the final revision of the poem, nothing will do, not one word or sentence that is not *perfectly clear*—with positive purpose—harmony with the name, nature, drift of the poem. Also *no ornaments,* especially *no ornamental adjectives,* unless they have come molten hot, and imperiously prove themselves. *No ornamental similes at all—not one: perfect transparent clearness* sanity, and health are wanted—*that* is the *divine style*—O if it can be attained—[3]

---

1. *N and F,* II, 55, item 1. Undated; probably written in 1855–56.
2. Quoted in Emory Holloway, "Notes from a Whitman Student's Scrapbook," *American Scholar* 2 (1933), 274. Quoted from an undated MS scrap; probably written in 1856.
3. *N and F,* II, 69, item 55. Undated.

Make *the Works*—Do not go into criticisms or arguments at all. Make full-blooded, rich, natural *works*. Insert natural things, indestructibles, idioms, characteristics, rivers, states, persons, etc. Be full of *strong, sensual germs*.[4]

Sat. June 21 [1856]
It seems to me quite clear and determined that I should concentrate my powers [on] *Leaves of Grass*—not diverting any of my means, strength, interest to the construction of anything else—of any other book.[5]

Feb. 25, '57. Dined with Hector Tyndale. Asked H. T. where he thought I needed particular attention to be directed for my improvement—where I could especially be bettered in my poems. He said: "In massiveness, breadth, large sweeping effects, without regard to details.—As in the Cathedral at York (he said) I came away with great impressions of its largeness, solidity, and spaciousness, without troubling myself with its parts."

Asked F. Le B. same question, viz: What I most lacked. He said: "In *euphony*—your poems seem to me to be full of the raw material of poems, but crude, and wanting finish and rhythm."

Put in my poems: *American things, idioms, materials, persons, groups, minerals, vegetables, animals, etc.*[6]

The Great Construction of the New Bible. Not to be diverted from the principle object—the main life work—the three hundred and sixty-five.—It ought to be ready in 1859 (June '57).[7]

It may be Drum-Taps may come out this winter, yet, (in the way I have mentioned in times past.) It is in a state to put right through, a perfect copy being ready for the printers—I feel at last, & for the first time without any demur, that I am satisfied with it—content to have it go to the world verbatim & punctuation. It is in my opinion superior to Leaves of Grass—certainly more perfect as a work of art, being adjusted in all its proportions, & its passion having the indispensable merit that though to the ordinary reader let loose with wildest abandon, the true artist can see it is yet under control. But I am perhaps mainly satisfied with Drum-Taps because it delivers my ambition of the task that has haunted me, namely to express in a poem (& in the way I like, which is not at all by directly stating it) the pending action of this *Time & Land we swim in,* with all their large conflicting fluctuations of despair & hope, the shiftings, masses, & the whirl & deafening din, (yet over all, as by invisible hand, a definite purport & idea)—with the unprecedented anguish of wounded & suffering, the beautiful young men, in wholesale death & agony, everything some-

4. *N and F*, II, 57, item 16. In footnote Bucke says, "Written about 1856."
5. *N and F*, III, 84, item 22.
6. *N and F*, III, 126, item 151.
7. *N and F*, I, 57, item 14.

times as if in blood color, & dripping blood. The book is therefore unprecedently sad, (as these days are, are they not?)—but it also has the blast of the trumpet, & the drum pounds & whirrs in it, & then an undertone of sweetest comradeship & human love, threading its steady thread inside the chaos, & heard at every lull & interstice thereof—truly also it has clear notes of faith & triumph.[8]

No one of the Themes generally considered as the stock fit for or motif for poetry is taken by W. W. for his foundation. No romantic occurrence, nor legend, nor plot of mystery, nor sentimentalizing, nor historic personage or event, nor any woven tale of love, ambition or jealousy is in his work. The usual dominant requirements—beauty, art, hero and heroine, form, meter, rhyme, regularity, have not only not been the laws of its creation but might almost seem at first glance to have never been suspected by the author. Thus compared with the rich ornamentation of the plots and passions of the best other poems, the palace hall, the velvet, the banquet, the master-pieces of paintings and statues, the costly vessels and furnishings, the melody, the multitudinous wealth of conceit, trope, incident, florid and dulcet versification and the much elaborated beauty of the accepted poets, there is something in Leaves of Grass that seems singularly simple and bare . . .

Indeed, the qualities which characterize "Leaves of Grass" are not the qualities of a fine book or poem or any work of art but the qualities of a living and full-blooded man, amativeness, pride, adhesiveness, curiosity, yearning for immortality, joyousness and sometimes uncertainty. You do not read, it is someone that you see in action, in war, or on a ship, or climbing the mountains, or racing along and shouting aloud in pure exultation.

A certain vagueness almost passing into chaos (it remains to be acknowledged) is in a few pieces or passages; but this is apparently by the deliberate intention of the author.[9]

. . . I have just concluded a contract with J. R. Osgood and Co of Boston for the publishing of my poems complete in one volume, under the title of "Walt Whitman's Poems" (the old name of "Leaves of Grass" running through the same as ever)—to be either a $2. book or a $2.50 one—if the former, I to have 25 cts royalty, if the latter, 30 cts)—The proposition for publication came from them. The bulk of the pieces will be the same as hitherto—only I shall secure now the consecutiveness and *ensemble* I am always thinking of—Book will probably be out before winter.[1]

Even as a boy, I had the fancy, the wish, to write a piece, perhaps a poem, about the seashore—that suggesting, dividing line, contact, junction, the solid marrying the liquid—that curious, lurking some-

---

8. Letter to William Douglas O'Connor, January 6, 1865. In *Corr.*, I, 246–47.
9. *N and F*, II, 63–64, item 38. An omitted sentence—"W. W. is now fifty-two years old"— dates this passage as written in 1871.
1. Letter to John Burroughs, June 17, 1881. In *Corr.*, III, 230–31.

thing (as doubtless every objective form finally becomes to the subjective spirit) which means far more than its mere first sight, grand as that is—blending the real and ideal, and each made portion of the other. Hours, days, in my Long Island youth and early manhood, I haunted the shores of Rockaway or Coney Island, or away east to the Hamptons or Montauk. Once, at the latter place (by the old lighthouse, nothing but sea-tossings in sight in every direction as far as the eye could reach), I remember well, I felt that I must one day write a book expressing this liquid, mystic theme. Afterward, I recollect, how it came to me that instead of any special lyrical or epical or literary attempt, the seashore should be an invisible *influence*, a pervading gauge and tally for me, in my composition. (Let me give a hint here to young writers. I am not sure but I have unwittingly followed out the same rule with other powers besides sea and shores—avoiding them, in the way of any dead set at poetizing them, as too big for formal handling—quite satisfied if I could indirectly show that we have met and fused, even if only once, but enough—that we have really absorbed each other and understand each other.)

There is a dream, a picture, that for years at intervals (sometimes quite long ones, but surely again, in time) has come noiselessly up before me, and I really believe, fiction as it is, has entered largely into my practical life—certainly into my writings, and shaped and colored them. It is nothing more or less than a stretch of interminable white-brown sand, hard and smooth and broad, with the ocean perpetually, grandly, rolling in upon it, with slow-measured sweep, with rustle and hiss and foam, and many a thump as of low bass drums. This scene, this picture, I say, has risen before me at times for years. Sometimes I wake at night and can hear and see it plainly.[2]

"I have found the law of my own poems," was the unspoken but more and more decided feeling that came to me as I pass'd, hour after hour, amid all this grim yet joyous elemental abandon—this plentitude of material, entire absence of art, untrammel'd play of primitive Nature—the chasm, the gorge, the crystal mountain stream, repeated scores, hundreds of miles—the broad handling and absolute un-crampedness—the fantastic forms, bathed in transparent browns, faint reds and grays, towering sometimes a thousand, sometimes two or three thousand feet high—at their tops now and then huge masses pois'd and mixing with the clouds, with only their outlines, hazed in misty lilac, visible. ("In Nature's grandest shows," says an old Dutch writer, an ecclesiastic, "amid the ocean's depth, if so might be, or countless worlds rolling above at night, a man thinks of them, weighs all, not for themselves or the abstract, but with reference to his own personality, and how they may affect him or color his destinies.")[3]

2. "Sea-shore Fancies," in *Prose Works 1892, Vol. I, Specimen Days,* ed. Floyd Stovall (New York: New York University Press, 1963–64), 138–39.
3. "An Egotistical 'Find,' " in *Specimen Days,* 210–11.

The *worry* of Ruskin—he has at various times sent to me for six sets of my ($10, two Vol.) centennial Edition—& sent the money for them—with *Leaves of Grass* is that they are too *personal*, too emotional, launched from the fires of *myself*, my spinal passions, joys, yearnings, doubts, appetites etc etc.—which is really what the book is mainly for, (as a type however for those passions, joys, workings etc *in all the race*, at least as shown under modern & especially American auspices)—Then I think he winces at what seems to him the *Democratic* brag of L. of G.—I have heard from R several times through English visitor friends of his—It is quite certain that he has intended writing to me at length—& has doubtless made draughts of such writing—but defers & *fears*—& has not yet written—R like a true Englishman evidently believes in the high poetic art of (only) making abstract works, poems, of some fine plot or subject, stirring, beautiful, very noble, completed within their own centre & radius, & nothing to do with the poet's special personality, nor exhibiting the least trace of it—like Shakespere's great unsurpassable dramas. But I have dashed at *the greater drama going on within myself & every human being—that is what I have been after*—[4]

Well—the lilt is all right: yes, right enough: but there's something anterior—more imperative. The first thing necessary is the thought— the rest may follow if it chooses—may play its part—but must not be too much sought after. The two things being equal I should prefer to have the lilt present with the idea, but if I got down my thought and the rhythm was not there I should not work to secure it. I am very deliberate—I take a good deal of trouble with words: yes, a good deal: but what I am after is the content not the music of words. Perhaps the music happens—it does no harm: I do not go in search of it.[5]

My last, my final, my conclusive, message (conclusive for me) is in A Backward Glance: the steel of its strength is there—the screwpoint—the heart-spot of it, too—is there, in that, where I say, 'But it is not in Leaves of Grass distinctly as *literature* or a specimen'— and so on (you remember the passage): that's me—the last of me if not the first—doctrine or no doctrine, Bucke or no Bucke. Taking it in that spirit—freely, bravely, according to its design—with that paragraph and others closely connected—you will see that all my parts cohere—that there are no loose joints: one reason explains all: Leaves of Grass—(intact, unbroken, not a comma removed) from first to last—from the very earliest poems to the very latest—from Starting from Paumanok to Sands at Seventy.[6]

There is a tally-stamp and stage-result of periods and nations, elusive, at second or third hand, often escaping the historian of matter-

4. Letter to William Douglas O'Connor, October 7, 1882. In *Corr.*, III, 307.
5. Conversation with Horace Traubel, Wednesday, May 16, 1888. Quoted in Traubel, I, 163.
6. Conversation with Horace Traubel, Monday, September 10, 1888. Quoted in Traubel, II, 297.

of-fact—in some sort the nation's spiritual formative ferment or chaos—the getting in of its essence, formulating identity—a law of it, and significant part of its progress. (Of the best of events and facts, even the most important, there are finally not the events and facts only, but something flashing out and fluctuating like tuft-flames or eidólons, from all.) My going up and down amidst these years, and the impromptu jottings of their sights and thoughts, of war and peace, have been in accordance with that law, and probably a result of it. . . . In certain respects, (emotionality, passions, spirituality, the invisible trend,) I therefore launch forth the divisions of the following book as not only a consequent of that period and its influences, but in one sort a History of America, the past 35 years, after the rest, after the adjuncts of that history have been studied and attended to.[7]

As I conclude . . . the interrogative wonder-fancy rises in me whether (if it be not too arrogant to even state it,) the 33 years of my current time, 1855–1888, with their aggregate of our New World doings and people, have not, indeed, created and formulated the foregoing leaves—forcing their utterance as the pages stand—coming actually from the direct urge and developments of those years, and not from any individual epic or lyrical attempts whatever, or from my pen or voice, or any body's special voice. Out of that supposition, the book might assume to be consider'd an autochthonic record and expression, freely render'd, of and out of these 30 to 35 years—of the soul and evolution of America—and of course, by reflection, not ours only, but more or less of the common people of the world. . . . In another sense (the warp crossing the woof, and knitted in,) the book is probably a sort of autobiography; an element I have not attempted to specially restrain or erase. . . .[8]

I will not reject any theme or subject because the treatment is too personal. As my stuff settles into shape, I am told (and sometimes myself discover, uneasily, but feel all right about it in calmer moments) it is mainly autobiographic, and even egotistic after all—which I finally accept, and am contented so.[9]

7. "Note at Beginning," in CPP.
8. From "Note at End," in CPP, 141–42.
9. From "Memoranda," in GBF, 45.

A Whitman Manuscript

Whitman's poetry began to take its radically original shape in the pages of pocket notebooks he carried with him. Here is one such page, this one bearing the beginnings of a key passage from "Song of Myself."

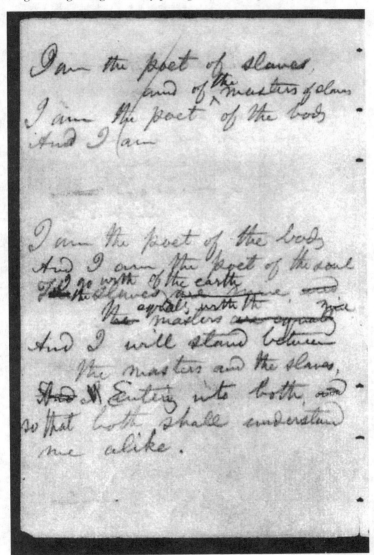

Page 68 of an early notebook of WW's now in the Library of Congress (which may be viewed in digitized form through the Library of Congress Web site).

CRITICISM

Criticism 1855–1955

[WALT WHITMAN]

Leaves of Grass: A Volume of Poems Just Published†

To give judgment on real poems, one needs an account of the poet himself. Very devilish to some, and very divine to some, will appear the poet of these new poems, the "Leaves of Grass;" an attempt, as they are, of a naive, masculine, affectionate, contemplative, sensual, imperious person, to cast into literature not only his own grit and arrogance, but his own flesh and form, undraped, regardless of models, regardless of modesty or law, and ignorant or silently scornful, as at first appears, of all except his own presence and experience, and all outside the fiercely loved land of his birth, and the birth of his parents, and their parents for several generations before him. Politeness this man has none, and regulation he has none. A rude child of the people!—No imitation—No foreigner—but a growth and idiom of America. No discontented—a careless slouch, enjoying today. No dilettante democrat—a man who is art-and-part with the commonalty, and with immediate life—loves the streets—loves the docks—loves the free rasping talk of men—likes to be called by his given name, and nobody at all need Mr. him—can laugh with laughers—likes the ungenteel ways of laborers—is not prejudiced one mite against the Irish—talks readily with them—talks readily with niggers—does not make a stand on being a gentleman, nor on learning or manners—eats cheap fare, likes the strong flavored coffee of the coffee-stands in the market, at sunrise—likes a supper of oysters fresh from the oyster-smack—likes to make one at the crowded table among sailors and work-people—would leave a select soiree of elegant people any time to go with tumultuous men, roughs, receive their caresses and welcome, listen to their noise, oaths, smut, fluency, laughter, repartee—and can preserve his presence perfectly among these, and the like of these. The effects he produces in his poems are no effects of artists or the arts, but effects of the original eye or arm, or the actual atmosphere, or tree, or bird. You may feel the unconscious teaching of a fine brute, but will never feel the artificial teaching of a fine writer or speaker.

† Unsigned review by Whitman, "*Leaves of Grass*: A Volume of Poems Just Published," in the *Brooklyn Daily Times*, September 29, 1855. This text was first collected by Whitman's literary executors in the miscellany *In Re Walt Whitman* (1893).

793

Other poets celebrate great events, personages, romances, wars, loves, passions, the victories and power of their country, or some real or imagined incident—and polish their work and come to conclusions, and satisfy the reader. This poet celebrates natural propensities in himself; and that is the way he celebrates all. He comes to no conclusions, and does not satisfy the reader. He certainly leaves him what the serpent left the woman and the man, the taste of the Paradisaic tree of the knowledge of good and evil, never to be erased again.

What good is it to argue about egotism? There can be no two thoughts on Walt Whitman's egotism. That is avowedly what he steps out of the crowd and turns and faces them for. Mark, critics! Otherwise is not used for you the key that leads to the use of the other keys to this well-enveloped man. His whole work, his life, manners, friendships, writings, all have among their leading purposes an evident purpose to stamp a new type of character, namely his own, and indelibly fix it and publish it, not for a model but an illustration, for the present and future of American letters and American young men, for the south the same as the north, and for the Pacific and Mississippi country, and Wisconsin and Texas and Kansas and Canada and Havana and Nicaragua, just as much as New York and Boston. Whatever is needed toward this achievement he puts his hand to, and lets imputations take their time to die.

First be yourself what you would show in your poem—such seems to be this man's example and inferred rebuke to the schools of poets. He makes no allusions to books or writers; their spirits do not seem to have touched him; he has not a word to say for or against them, or their theories or ways. He never offers others; what he continually offers is the man whom our Brooklynites know so well. Of pure American breed, large and lusty—age thirty-six years, (1855,)—never once using medicine—never dressed in black, always dressed freely and clean in strong clothes—neck open, shirt collar flat and broad, countenance tawny transparent red, beard well-mottled with white, hair like hay after it has been mowed in the field and lies tossed and streaked —his physiology corroborating a rugged phrenology—a person singularly beloved and looked toward, especially by young men and the illiterate—one who has firm attachments there, and associates there —one who does not associate with literary people—a man never called upon to make speeches at public dinners—never on platforms amid the crowds of clergymen, or professors, or aldermen, or congressmen —rather down in the bay with pilots in their pilot-boat—or off on a cruise with fishers in a fishing-smack—or riding on a Broadway omnibus, side by side with the driver—or with a band of loungers over the open grounds of the country—fond of New York and Brooklyn— fond of the life of the great ferries—one whom, if you should meet, you need not expect to meet an extraordinary person—one in whom you will see the singularity which consists in no singularity—whose contact is no dazzle or fascination, nor requires any deference, but has the easy fascination of what is homely and accustomed—as of something you knew before, and was waiting for—there you have Walt Whitman, the begetter of a new offspring out of literature, taking with easy nonchalance the chances of its present reception, and, through all misunderstandings and distrusts, the chances of its future reception—preferring always to speak for himself rather than have others speak for him.

EDWARD EVERETT HALE

Leaves of Grass: Brooklyn, 1855[†]

Everything about the external arrangement of this book was odd and out of the way. The author printed it himself, and it seems to have been left to the winds of heaven to publish it. So it happened that we had not discovered it before our last number, although we believe the sheets had then passed the press. It bears no publisher's name, and, if the reader goes to a bookstore for it, he may expect to be told at first, as we were, that there is no such book, and has not been. Nevertheless, there is such a book, and it is well worth going twice to the bookstore to buy it. Walter Whitman, an American,—one of the roughs,—no sentimentalist,—no stander above men and women, or apart from them,—no more modest than immodest,—has tried to write down here, in a sort of prose poetry, a good deal of what he has seen, felt, and guessed at in a pilgrimage of some thirty-five years. He has a horror of conventional language of any kind. His theory of expression is, that, "to speak in literature with the perfect rectitude and *insouciance* of the movements of animals, is the flawless triumph of art." Now a great many men have said this before. But generally it is the introduction to something more artistic than ever,—more conventional and strained. Antony began by saying he was no orator, but none the less did an oration follow. In this book, however, the prophecy is fairly fulfilled in the accomplishment. "What I experience or portray shall go from my composition without a shred of my composition. You shall stand by my side and look in the mirror with me."

So truly accomplished is this promise,—which anywhere else would be a flourish of trumpets,—that this thin quarto deserves its name. That is to say, one reads and enjoys the freshness, simplicity, and reality of what he reads, just as the tired man, lying on the hillside in summer, enjoys the leaves of grass around him,—enjoys the shadow, —enjoys the flecks of sunshine—not for what they "suggest to him," but for what they are.

So completely does the author's remarkable power rest in his simplicity, that the preface to the book—which does not even have large letters at the beginning of the lines, as the rest has—is perhaps the

† From the *North American Review* 82 (January 1856): 275–77.

very best thing in it. We find more to the point in the following analysis of the "genius of the United States," than we have found in many more pretentious studies of it.

"Other states indicate themselves in their deputies, but the genius of the United States is not best or most in its executives or legislatures, nor in its ambassadors or authors or colleges or churches or parlors, nor even in its newspapers or inventors;—but always most in the common people. Their manners, speech, dress, friendships;—the freshness and candor of their physiognomy, the picturesque looseness of their carriage, their deathless attachment to freedom, their aversion to everything indecorous or soft or mean, the practical acknowledgement of the citizens of one State by the citizens of all other States, the fierceness of their roused resentment, their curiosity and welcome of novelty, their self-esteem and wonderful sympathy, their susceptibility to a slight, the air they have of persons who never knew how it felt to stand in the presence of superiors, the fluency of their speech, their delight in music (the sure symptom of manly tenderness and native elegance of soul), their good temper and open-handedness, the terrible significance of their elections, the President's taking off his hat to them, not they to him,—these too are unrhymed poetry. It awaits the gigantic and generous treatment worthy of it."

The book is divided into a dozen or more sections, and in each one of these some thread of connection may be traced, now with ease, now with difficulty,—each being a string of verses, which claim to be written without effort and with entire *abandon*. So the book is a collection of observations, speculations, memories, and prophecies, clad in the simplest, truest, and often the most nervous English,—in the midst of which the reader comes upon something as much out of place as a piece of rotten wood would be among leaves of grass in the meadow, if the meadow had no object but to furnish a child's couch. So slender is the connection, that we hardly injure the following scraps by extracting them.

> I am the teacher of Athletes;
> He that by me spreads a wider breast than my own, proves the
>   width of my own;
> He most honors my style who learns under it to destroy the
>   teacher;
> The boy I love, the same becomes a man, not through derived
>   power, but in his own right,
> Wicked rather than virtuous out of conformity or fear,
> Fond of his sweetheart, relishing well his steak,
> Unrequited love, or a slight, cutting him worse than a wound
>   cuts,
> First-rate to ride, to fight, to hit the bull's-eye, to sail a skiff, to
>   sing a song, or to play on the banjo,
> Preferring scars, and faces pitted with small-pox, over all
>   latherers and those that keep out of the sun.

Here is the story of the gallant seaman who rescued the passengers on the San Francisco:—

I understand the largest heart of heroes,
The courage of present times and all times;
How the skipper saw the crowded and rudderless wreck of the
    steamship, and death chasing it up and down the storm,
How he knuckled tight, and gave not back one inch, and was
    faithful of days and faithful of nights,
And chalked in large letters on a board, 'Be of good cheer, we
    will not desert you';
How he saved the drifting company at last,
How the lank, loose-gowned women looked when boated from
    the side of their prepared graves,
How the silent old-faced infants, and the lifted sick, and the
    sharp-lipped, unshaved men;
All this I swallowed, and it tastes good; I like it well, and it
    becomes mine:
I am the man, I suffered, I was there.

Claiming in this way a personal interest in every thing that has ever happened in the world, and, by the wonderful sharpness and distinctness of his imagination, making the claim effective and reasonable, Mr. "Walt. Whitman" leaves it a matter of doubt where he has been in this world, and where not. It is very clear, that with him, as with most other effective writers, a keen, absolute memory, which takes in and holds every detail of the past,—as they say the exaggerated power of the memory does when a man is drowning,—is a gift of his organization as remarkable as his vivid imagination. What he has seen once, he has seen for ever. And thus there are in this curious book little thumb-nail sketches of life in the prairie, life in California, life at school, life in the nursery,—life, indeed, we know not where not,— which, as they are unfolded one after another, strike us as real,—so real that we wonder how they came on paper.

For the purpose of showing that he is above every conventionalism, Mr. Whitman puts into the book one or two lines which he would not address to a woman nor to a company of men. There is not anything, perhaps, which modern usage would stamp as more indelicate than are some passages in Homer. There is not a word in it meant to attract readers by its grossness, as there is in half the literature of the last century, which holds its place unchallenged on the tables of our drawing-rooms. For all that, it is a pity that a book where everything else is natural should go out of the way to avoid the suspicion of being prudish.

FANNY FERN

Fresh Fern Leaves: *Leaves of Grass*†

Well baptized: fresh, hardy, and grown for the masses. Not more welcome is their natural type to the winter-bound, bedridden, and spring-emancipated invalid. *Leaves of Grass* thou art unspeakably delicious, after the forced, stiff, Parnassian exotics for which our admiration has been vainly challenged.

Walt Whitman, the effeminate world needed thee. The timidest soul whose wings ever drooped with discouragement, could not choose but rise on thy strong pinions.

> Undrape—you are not guilty to me, nor stale nor discarded;
> I see through the broadcloth and gingham whether or no.

> O despairer, here is my neck,
> You shall *not* go down! Hang your whole weight upon me.

Walt Whitman, the world needed a "Native American" of thorough, out and out breed—enamored of *women* not *ladies*, men not *gentlemen*; something beside a mere Catholic-hating Know-Nothing; it needed a man who dared speak out his strong, honest thoughts, in the face of pusillanimous, toadeying, republican aristocracy; dictionary-men, hypocrites, cliques and creeds; it needed a large-hearted, un-tainted, self-reliant, fearless son of the Stars and Stripes, who disdains to sell his birthright for a mess of pottage; who does

> Not call one greater or one smaller, That which fills its period
> and place being equal to any;

who will

> Accept nothing which all cannot have their counterpart of on the
> same terms.

Fresh *Leaves of Grass*! not submitted by the self-reliant author to the fingering of any publisher's critic, to be arranged, rearranged and disarranged to his circumscribed liking, till they hung limp, tame, spiritless, and scentless. No. It were a spectacle worth seeing, this glorious Native American, who, when the daily labor of chisel and plane was over, himself, with toil-hardened fingers, handled the types to print the pages which wise and good men have since delighted to endorse and to honor. Small critics, whose contracted vision could see no beauty, strength, or grace, in these *Leaves*, have long ago repented that they so hastily wrote themselves down shallow by such a premature confession. Where an Emerson, and a Howitt have commended, my woman's voice of praise may not avail; but happiness was born a twin,

---

† From *New York Ledger*, May 10, 1856, 4.

and so I would fain share with others the unmingled delight which these "Leaves" have given me.

I say unmingled; I am not unaware that the charge of coarseness and sensuality has been affixed to them. My moral constitution may be hopelessly tainted or—too sound to be tainted, as the critic wills, but I confess that I extract no poison from these *Leaves*—to me they have brought only healing. Let him who can do so, shroud the eyes of the nursing babe lest it should see its mother's breast. Let him look carefully between the gilded covers of books, backed by high-sounding names, and endorsed by parson and priest, lying unrebuked upon his own family table; where the asp of sensuality lies coiled amid rhetorical flowers. Let him examine well the paper dropped weekly at his door, in which virtue and religion are rendered disgusting, save when they walk in satin slippers, or, clothed in purple and fine linen, kneel on a damask "*prie-dieu.*"

Sensual!—No—the moral assassin looks you not boldly in the eye by broad daylight; but Borgia-like takes you treacherously by the hand, while from the glittering ring on his finger he distils through your veins the subtle and deadly poison.

Sensual? The artist who would inflame, paints you not nude Nature, but stealing Virtue's veil, with artful artlessness now conceals, now exposes, the ripe and swelling proportions.

Sensual? Let him who would affix this stigma upon *Leaves of Grass,* write upon his heart, in letters of fire, these noble words of its author:

> In woman I see the bearer of the great fruit, which is immortality.
> . . . the good thereof is not tasted by *roues*, and never can be.
> . . . .
> Who degrades or defiles the living human body is cursed,
> Who degrades or defiles the body of the dead is not more cursed.

Were I an artist I would like no more suggestive subjects for my easel than Walt Whitman's pen has furnished.

> The little one sleeps in its cradle,
> I lift the gauze and look a long time, and silently brush away
>   flies with my hand.
> The farmer stops by the bars of a Sunday and looks at the
>   oats and rye.
> . . . .
> Earth of the slumbering and liquid trees!
> Earth of departed Sunset,
> Earth of the mountain's misty topt!
> Earth of the vitreous pour of the full moon just tinged with
>   blue!
> Earth of shine and dark mottling the tide of the river!
> Earth of the limpid grey of clouds brighter and clearer for
>   my sake!
> Far swooping elbowed earth! Rich apple-blossomed earth!
> Smile, for your lover comes!"

I quote at random, the following passages which appeal to me:

A morning glory at my window, satisfies me more than the
    metaphysics of books.
. . . .

Logic and sermons never convince.
The damp of the night drives deeper into my soul.

Speaking of animals, he says:

I stand and look at them sometimes, half the day long.
They do not make me sick, discussing their duty to God.
. . . .

—Whoever walks a furlong without sympathy, walks to his
    own funeral dressed in his shroud.
. . . .

I hate him that oppresses me,
I will either destroy him, or he shall release me.
. . . .

I find letters from God dropped in the street, and every one
    is signed by God's name,
And I leave them where they are, for I know that others will
    punctually come forever and ever.
. . . .

———Under Niagara, *the cataract falling like a veil over
my countenance.*

Of the grass he says:

It seems to me *the beautiful uncut hair of graves.*

I close the extracts from these *Leaves*, which it were easy to multiply,
for one is more puzzled what to leave unculled, than what to gather,
with the following sentiments; for which, and for all the good things
included between the covers of his book Mr. Whitman will please
accept the cordial grasp of a woman's hand:

"The wife—and she is not one jot less than the husband,
The daughter—and she is just as good as the son,
The mother—and she is every bit as much as the father."

HENRY DAVID THOREAU

[Excerpts from two letters to H. G. O. Blake]†

[19 Nov. 1856]
Alcott has been here three times, and, Saturday before last, I went
with him and Greeley, by invitation of the last, to G.'s farm, thirty-six
miles north of New York. The next day A. and I heard Beecher preach;

---

† From *The Correspondence of Henry David Thoreau*, ed. W. Harding and C. Bode (New York,
1958), 441–42 and 444–45.

and what was more, we visited Whitman the next morning (A. had already seen him), and were much interested and provoked. He is apparently the greatest democrat the world has seen. Kings and aristocracy go by the board at once, as they have long deserved to. A remarkably strong though coarse nature, of a sweet disposition, and much prized by his friends. Though peculiar and rough in his exterior, his skin (all over (?)) red, he is essentially a gentleman. I am still somewhat in a quandary about him,—feel that he is essentially strange to me, at any rate; but I am surprised by the sight of him. He is very broad, but, as I have said, not fine. He said that I misapprehended him. I am not quite sure that I do. He told us that he loved to ride up and down Broadway all day on an omnibus, sitting beside the driver, listening to the roar of the carts, and sometimes gesticulating and declaiming Homer at the top of his voice. He has long been an editor and writer for the newspapers,—was editor of the 'New Orleans Crescent' once; but now has no employment but to read and write in the forenoon, and walk in the afternoon, like all the rest of the scribbling gentry . . .

[7 Dec. 1856]

That Walt Whitman, of whom I wrote to you, is the most interesting fact to me at present. I have just read his 2nd edition (which he gave me) and it has done me more good than any reading for a long time. Perhaps I remember best the poem of Walt Whitman an American & the Sun Down Poem.[1] There are 2 or 3 pieces in the book which are disagreeable to say the least, simply sensual. He does not celebrate love at all. It is as if the beasts spoke. I think that men have not been ashamed of themselves without reason. No doubt, there have always been dens where such deeds were unblushingly recited, and it is no merit to compete with their inhabitants. But even on this side, he has spoken more truth than any American or modern that I know. I have found his poem exhilirating encouraging. As for its sensuality,—& it may turn out to be less sensual than it appeared—I do not so much wish that those parts were not written, as that men & women were so pure that they could read them without harm, that is, without understanding them. One woman told me that no woman could read it as if a man could read what a woman could not. Of course Walt Whitman can communicate to us no experience, and if we are shocked, whose experience is it that we are reminded of?

On the whole it sounds to me very brave & American after whatever deductions. I do not believe that all the sermons so called that have been preached in this land put together are equal to it for preaching—

We ought to rejoice greatly in him. He occasionally suggests something a little more than human. You can't confound him with the other

---

1. Of the two poems Thoreau mentions here, "Poem of Walt Whitman an American" was subsequently retitled "Song of Myself," and "Sun Down Poem" became "Crossing Brooklyn Ferry."

inhabitants of Brooklyn or New York. How they must shudder when they read him! He is awfully good.

To be sure I sometimes feel a little imposed on. By his heartiness & broad generalities he puts me into a liberal frame of mind prepared to see wonders—as it were sets me upon a hill or in the midst of a plain—stirs me well up, and then—throws in a thousand of brick. Though rude & sometimes ineffectual, it is a great primitive poem,— an alarum or trumpet-note ringing through the American camp. Wonderfully like the Orientals, too, considering that when I asked him if he had read them, he answered, "No: tell me about them."

I did not get far in conversation with him,—two more being present,—and among the few things which I chanced to say, I remember that one was, in answer to him as representing America, that I did not think much of America or of politics, and so on, which may have been somewhat of a damper to him.

Since I have seen him, I find that I am not disturbed by any brag or egoism in his book. He may turn out the least of a braggart of all, having a better right to be confident.

He is a great fellow.

ANNE GILCHRIST

An Englishwoman's Estimate of Walt Whitman†

I think it was very manly and kind of you to put the whole of Walt Whitman's poems into my hands; and that I have no other friend who would have judged them and me so wisely and generously.

I had not dreamed that words could cease to be words, and become electric streams like these. I do assure you that, strong as I am, I feel sometimes as if I had not bodily strength to read many of these poems. In the series headed "Calamus," for instance, in some of the "Songs of Parting," the "Voice out of the Sea,"[1] the poem beginning "Tears, tears,"[2] &c., there is such a weight of emotion, such a tension of the heart, that mine refuses to beat under it—stands quite still—and I am obliged to lay the book down for a while. Or again, in the piece called "Walt Whitman," and one or two others of that type, I am as one hurried through stormy seas, over high mountains, dazed with sunlight, stunned with a crowd and tumult of faces and voices, till I am breathless, bewildered, half-dead. Then come parts and whole poems in which there is such calm wisdom and strength of thought, such a cheerful breadth of sunshine, that the soul bathes in them renewed and strengthened. Living impulses flow out of these that make me

---

† Gilchrist's "Estimate" first appeared in *The Radical* (Boston) 7 (May 1870): 345–59; the abridged text here is from Herbert H. Gilchrist, *Anne Gilchrist—Her Life and Writings* (New York, 1887), 287–307.
1. Gilchrist means "A Word Out of the Sea," the title of "Out of the Cradle Endlessly Rocking" in the 1860 and 1867 editions of *LG*.
2. The poem "Tears" was first added to *LG* in 1867.

exult in life, yet look longingly towards "the superb vistas of Death."[3] Those who admire this poem, and do not care for that, and talk of formlessness, absence of metre, and so forth, are quite as far from any genuine recognition of Walt Whitman as his bitter detractors. Not, of course, that all the pieces are equal in power and beauty, but that all are vital; they grew—they were not made. We criticise a palace or a cathedral; but what is the good of criticising a forest? Are not the hitherto-accepted masterpieces of literature akin rather to noble architecture; built up of material rendered precious by elaboration; planned with subtile art that makes beauty go hand in hand with rule and measure, and knows where the last stone will come, before the first is laid; the result stately, fixed, yet such as might, in every particular, have been different from what it is (therefore inviting criticism), contrasting proudly with the careless freedom of nature, opposing its own rigid adherence to symmetry to her wilful dallying with it? But not such is this book. Seeds brought by the winds from north, south, east, and west, lying long in the earth, not resting on it like the stately building, but hid in and assimilating it, shooting upwards to be nourished by the air and the sunshine and the rain which beat idly against that,—each bough and twig and leaf growing in strength and beauty its own way, a law to itself, yet, with all this freedom of spontaneous growth, the result inevitable, unalterable (therefore setting criticism at naught), above all things vital,—that is, a source of ever-generating vitality: such are these poems. . . .[4]

I see that no counting of syllables will reveal the mechanism of the music; and that this rushing spontaneity could not stay to bind itself with the fetters of metre. But I know that the music is there, and that I would not for something change ears with those who cannot hear it. And I know that poetry must be one of two things,—either own this man as equal with her highest, completest manifestors, or stand aside, and admit that there is something come into the world nobler, diviner than herself, one that is free of the universe, and can tell its secrets as none before. . . .

I am persuaded that one great source of this kindling, vitalizing power—I suppose *the* great source—is the grasp laid upon the present, the fearless and comprehensive dealing with reality. Hitherto the leaders of thought have (except in science) been men with their faces resolutely turned backwards; men who have made of the past a tyrant that beggars and scorns the present, hardly seeing any greatness but what is shrouded away in the twilight, underground past; naming the present only for disparaging comparisons, humiliating distrust that tends to create the very barrenness it complains of; bidding me warm myself at fires that went out to mortal eyes centuries ago; insisting, in religion above all, that I must either "look through dead men's eyes," or shut my own in helpless darkness. Poets fancying themselves so happy over the chill and faded beauty of the past, but not making me

---

3. "Song at Sunset," line 21.
4. Here Gilchrist quotes "Roots and Leaves Themselves Alone," one of the "Calamus" poems.

happy at all,—rebellious always at being dragged down out of the free air and sunshine of to-day.

But this poet, this "athlete, full of rich words, full of joys,"[5] takes you by the hand, and turns you with your face straight forwards. The present is great enough for him, because he is great enough for it. It flows through him as a "vast oceanic tide," lifting up a mighty voice. Earth, "the eloquent, dumb, great mother,"[6] is not old, has lost none of her fresh charms, none of her divine meanings; still bears great sons and daughters, if only they would possess themselves and accept their birth-right,—a richer, not a poorer, heritage than was ever provided before,—richer by all the toil and suffering of the generations that have preceded, and by the further unfolding of the eternal purposes. Here is one come at last who can show them how; whose songs are the breath of a glad, strong, beautiful life, nourished sufficingly, kindled to unsurpassed intensity and greatness by the gifts of the present. . . .

See, again, in the pieces gathered together under the title "Calamus," and elsewhere, what it means for a man to love his fellow-man. Did you dream it before? These "evangel-poems of comrades and of love"[7] speak, with the abiding, penetrating power of prophecy, of a "new and superb friendship;" speak not as beautiful dreams, unrealizable aspirations to be laid aside in sober moods, because they breathe out what now glows within the poet's own breast, and flows out in action toward the men around him. Had ever any land before her poet, not only to concentrate within himself her life, and, when she kindled with anger against her children who were treacherous to the cause her life is bound up with, to announce and justify her terrible purpose in words of unsurpassable grandeur (as in the poem beginning, "Rise, O days, from your fathomless deeps"), but also to go and with his own hands dress the wounds, with his powerful presence soothe and sustain and nourish her suffering soldiers,—hundreds of them, thousands, tens of thousands,—by day and by night, for weeks, months, years?

> I sit by the restless all the dark night; some are so young,
> Some suffer so much: I recall the experience sweet and sad.
> Many a soldier's loving arms about this neck have crossed and
>   rested,
> Many a soldier's kiss dwells on these bearded lips:—[8]

Kisses, that touched with the fire of a strange, new, undying eloquence the lips that received them! The most transcendent genius could not, untaught by that "experience sweet and sad," have breathed out hymns for her dead soldiers of such ineffably tender, sorrowful, yet triumphant beauty. . . .

Nor do I sympathize with those who grumble at the unexpected

5. The last line of "A Song of Joys," as it read in the 1860 and 1867 editions of *LG*.
6. "A Song of the Rolling Earth," line 41.
7. "Starting from Paumanok," line 92.
8. "The Wound-Dresser," lines 62–65.

words that turn up now and then. A quarrel with words is always, more or less, a quarrel with meanings; and here we are to be as genial and as wide as nature, and quarrel with nothing. If the thing a word stands for exists by divine appointment (and what does not so exist?), the word need never be ashamed of itself; the shorter and more direct, the better. It is a gain to make friends with it, and see it in good company. Here, at all events, "poetic diction" would not serve,—not pretty, soft, colourless words, laid by in lavender for the special uses of poetry, that have had none of the wear and tear of daily life; but such as have stood most, as tell of human heart-beats, as fit closest to the sense, and have taken deep hues of association from the varied experiences of life—those are the words wanted here. We only ask to seize and be seized swiftly, overmasteringly, by the great meanings. We see with the eyes of the soul, listen with the ears of the soul; the poor old words that have served so many generations for purposes, good, bad, and indifferent, and become warped and blurred in the process, grow young again, regenerate, translucent . . .

You [W. M. Rossetti] argued rightly that my confidence would not be betrayed by any of the poems in this book. None of them troubled me even for a moment; because I saw at a glance that it was not, as men had supposed, the heights brought down to the depths, but the depths lifted up level with the sunlit heights, that they might become clear and sunlit too. Always, for a woman, a veil woven out of her own soul—never touched upon even, with a rough hand, by this poet. But, for a man, a daring, fearless pride in himself, not a mock-modesty woven out of delusions—a very poor imitation of a woman's. Do they not see that this fearless pride, this complete acceptance of them-selves, is needful for her pride, her justification? What! is it all so ignoble, so base, that it will not bear the honest light of speech from lips so gifted with "the divine power to use words?"[9] Then what hateful, bitter humiliation for her, to have to give herself up to the reality! Do you think there is ever a bride who does not taste more or less this bitterness in her cup? But who put it there? It must surely be man's fault, not God's, that she has to say to herself, "Soul, look another way—you have no part in this. Motherhood is beautiful, fatherhood is beautiful; but the dawn of fatherhood and motherhood is not beau-tiful." Do they really think that God is ashamed of what He has made and appointed? And, if not, surely it is somewhat superfluous that they should undertake to be so for Him.

The full-spread pride of man is calming and excellent to the soul,[1]

Of a woman above all. It is true that instinct of silence I spoke of is a beautiful, imperishable part of nature too. But it is not beautiful when it means an ignominious shame brooding darkly. Shame is like a very flexible veil, that follows faithfully the shape of what it covers, —beautiful when it hides a beautiful thing, ugly when it hides an ugly

9. "Vocalism," line 1.
1. "I Sing the Body Electric," line 80.

one. It has not covered what was beautiful here; it has covered a mean distrust of a man's self and of his Creator. It was needed that this silence, this evil spell, should for once be broken, and the daylight let in, that the dark cloud lying under might be scattered to the winds. It was needed that one who could here indicate for us "the path between reality and the soul" should speak. That is what these beautiful, despised poems, the "Children of Adam," do, read by the light that glows out of the rest of the volume: light of a clear, strong faith in God, of an unfathomably deep and tender love for humanity,—light shed out of a soul that is "possessed of itself."

. . . Yet I feel deeply persuaded that a perfectly fearless, candid, ennobling treatment of the life of the body (so inextricably intertwined with, so potent in its influence on the life of the soul) will prove of inestimable value to all earnest and aspiring natures, impatient of the folly of the long prevalent belief that it is because of the greatness of the spirit that it has learned to despise the body, and to ignore its influences; knowing well that it is, on the contrary, just because the spirit is not great enough, not healthy and vigorous enough, to transfuse itself into the life of the body, elevating that and making it holy by its own triumphant intensity; knowing, too, how the body avenges this by dragging the soul down to the level assigned itself. Whereas the spirit must lovingly embrace the body, as the roots of a tree embrace the ground, drawing thence rich nourishment, warmth, impulse. Or, rather, the body is itself the root of the soul,—that whereby it grows and feeds. The great tide of healthful life that carries all before it must surge through the whole man, not beat to and fro in one corner of his brain.

> O the life of my senses and flesh, transcending my senses and flesh![2]

. . . He [Whitman], the beloved friend of all, initiated for them a "new and superb friendship;" whispered that secret of a god-like pride in a man's self, and a perfect trust in woman, whereby their love for each other, no longer poisoned and stifled, but basking in the light of God's smile, and sending up to Him a perfume of gratitude, attains at last a divine and tender completeness. He gave a faith-compelling utterance to that "wisdom which is the certainty of the reality and immortality of things, and of the excellence of things." Happy America, that he should be her son! One sees, indeed, that only a young giant of a nation could produce this kind of greatness, so full of the ardour, the elasticity, the inexhaustible vigour and freshness, the joyousness, the audacity of youth. But I, for one, cannot grudge anything to America. For, after all, the young giant is the old English giant,—the great English race renewing its youth in that magnificent land, "Mexican-breathed, Arctic-braced,"[3] and girding up its loins to start on a new career that shall match with the greatness of the new home.

2. "A Song of Joys," line 100; the line should begin, "The real life . . ."
3. "Starting from Paumanok," line 208, "Far breath'd land! Arctic braced! Mexican breez'd!"

OSCAR WILDE

The Gospel According to Walt Whitman†

"No one will get at my verses who insists upon viewing them as a literary performance, or as aiming mainly towards art and æstheticism. *Leaves of Grass* has been chiefly the outcropping of my own emotional and other personal nature—an attempt from first to last to put a *Person*, a human being (myself, in the latter half of the nineteenth century, in America) freely, fully and truly on record. I could not find any similar personal record in current literature that satisfied me." In these words Walt Whitman gives us the true attitude we should adopt towards his work, having indeed a much saner view of the value and meaning of that work than either his eloquent admirers or noisy detractors can boast of possessing. His last book, *November Boughs* as he calls it, published in the winter of the old man's life, reveals to us, not indeed a soul's tragedy, for its last note is one of joy and hope and noble and unshaken faith in all that is fine and worthy of such faith, but certainly the drama of a human soul, and puts on record with a simplicity that has in it both sweetness and strength the record of his spiritual development and of the aim and motive both of the manner and the matter of his work. His strange mode of expression is shown in these pages to have been the result of deliberate and self-conscious choice. The "barbaric yawp," which he sent over "the roofs of the world" so many years ago, and which wrung from Mr. Swinburne's lips such lofty panegyric in song and such loud clamorous censure in prose, appears here in what will be to many an entirely new light. For in his very rejection of art Walt Whitman is an artist. He tried to produce a certain effect by certain means and he succeeded. There is much method in what many have termed his madness, too much method indeed some may be tempted to fancy.

In the story of his life, as he tells it to us, we find him at the age of sixteen beginning a definite and philosophical study of literature:—

> Summers and falls, I used to go off, sometimes for a week at a stretch, down in the country, or to Long Island's seashores—there in the presence of outdoor influences, I went over thoroughly the Old and New Testaments, and absorb'd (probably to better advantage for me than in any library or indoor room—it makes such difference *where* you read) Shakspere, Ossian, the best translated versions I could get of Homer, Æschylus, Sophokles, the old German Nibelungen, the ancient Hindoo poems, and one or two other masterpieces, Dante's among them. As it happen'd I read the latter mostly in an old wood. The Iliad I read first thoroughly on the peninsula of Orient, north-east end of Long Island, in a sheltered hollow of rocks and sand, with the sea on each side. (I have wondered since why I was not overwhelmed by those mighty

† From *Pall Mall Gazette*, January 25, 1889.

masters. Likely because I read them, as described, in the full presence of Nature, under the sun, with the far-spreading landscapes and vistas, or the sea rolling in.)

Edgar Allan Poe's amusing bit of dogmatism that, for our occasions and for our day, there can be no such thing as a long poem, fascinated him: "The same thought had been haunting my mind before," he says, "but Poe's argument, though short, work'd the sum out and proved it to me:" and the English translation of the Bible seems to have suggested to him the possibility of a poetic form which while retaining the spirit of poetry would still be free from the trammels of rhyme and of a definite metrical system. Having thus to a certain degree settled upon what one might call the *technique* of Whitmanism, he began to brood upon the nature of that spirit that was to give life to the strange form. The central point of the poetry of the future seemed to him to be necessarily "an identical body and soul," a personality in fact, which personality he tells us frankly, "after many considerations and ponderings I deliberately settled should be myself." However for the true creation and revealing of this personality, at first only dimly felt, a new stimulus was needed. This came from the Civil War. After describing the many dreams and passions of his boyhood and early manhood he goes on to say:—

> These, however, and much more might have gone on and come to naught (almost positively would have come to naught) if a sudden, vast, terrible, direct and indirect stimulus for new and national declamatory expression had not been given to me. It is certain, I say, that, although I had made a start before, only from the occurrence of the Secession War, and what it showed me as by flashes of lightning, with the emotional depths it sounded and arous'd (of course, I don't mean in my own heart only, I saw it just as plainly in others, in millions) that only from the strong flare and provocation of that war's sights and scenes the final reasons-for-being of an autochthonic and passionate song definitely came forth. I went down to the war-fields of Virginia, lived thenceforward in camp, saw great battles and the days and nights afterwards—partook of all the fluctuations, gloom, despair, hopes again aroused, courage evoked—death readily risked—the *cause* too—along and filling those agonistic and lurid following years, the real parturition years of the henceforth homogeneous Union. Without those three or four years and the experiences they gave, "Leaves of Grass" would not now be existing.

Having thus obtained the necessary stimulus for the quickening and awakening of the personal self, some day to be endowed with universality, he sought to find new notes of song, and passing beyond the mere passion for expression—he aimed at "Suggestiveness" first. "I round and finish little, if anything; and could not, consistently with my scheme. The reader will have his or her part to do, just as much as I have had mine. I seek less to state or display any theme of thought, and more to bring you, reader, into the atmosphere of the theme or thought—there to pursue your own flight." Another "impetus word" is Comradeship, and other "word-signs" are Good Cheer, Content, and Hope. Individuality, especially, he sought for:—

> I have allowed the stress of my poems from beginning to end to bear upon American individuality and assist it—not only because that is a great lesson in Nature, amid all her generalizing laws, but as a counterpoise to the levelling tendencies of Democracy— and for other reasons. Defiant of ostensible literary and other conventions, I avowedly chant "the great pride of a man in him-self," and permit it to be more or less a *motif* of nearly all my verse. I think this pride indispensable to an American. I think it not inconsistent with obedience, humility, deference, and self-questioning.

A new theme also was to be found in the relation of the sexes, con-ceived in a natural, simple, and healthy form, and he protests against poor Mr. William Rossetti's attempt to Bowdlerize and expurgate his song.

> From another point of view "Leaves of Grass" is avowedly the song of Sex, and Amativeness, and even Animality—though meanings that do not usually go with these words are behind all, and will duly emerge; and all are sought to be lifted into a different light and atmosphere. Of this feature intentionally palpable in a few lines, I shall only say the espousing principle of those lines so gives breath to my whole scheme that the bulk of the pieces might as well have been left unwritten were those lines omitted. . . . Universal as are certain facts and symptoms of communities there is nothing so rare in modern conventions and poetry as their nor-mal recognizance. Literature is always calling in the doctor for consultation and confession, and always giving evasions and swathing suppressions in place of that "heroic nudity" on which only a genuine diagnosis can be built. And in respect to editions of "Leaves of Grass" in time to come (if there should be such) I take occasion now to confirm those lines with the settled convic-tions and deliberate renewals of thirty years, and to hereby pro-hibit, as far as mine can do so, any elision of them.

But beyond all these notes and moods and motives is the lofty spirit of a grand and free acceptance of all things that are worthy of exis-tence. "I desired," he says, "to formulate a poem whose every thought or fact should indirectly or directly be or connive at an implicit belief in the wisdom, health, mystery, or beauty of every process, every con-crete object, every human or other existence, not only consider'd from the point of view of all, but of each." His two final utterances are that really great poetry is always the result of a national spirit, and not the privilege of a polished and select few; and that the sweetest and strong-est songs yet remain to be sung.

Such are the views contained in the opening essay, "A Backward Glance o'er Travel'd Roads," as he calls it; but there are many other essays in this fascinating volume, some on poets such as Burns and

Lord Tennyson, for whom Walt Whitman has a profound admiration: some on old actors and singers, the elder Booth, Forrest, Alboni, and Mario being his special favourites: others on the native Indians, on the Spanish element in American nationality, on Western slang, on the poetry of the Bible, and on Abraham Lincoln. But Walt Whitman is at his best when he is analyzing his own work, and making schemes for the poetry of the future. Literature to him has a distinctly social aim. He seeks to build up the masses by "building up grand individuals." And yet literature itself must be preceded by noble forms of life. "The best literature is always the result of something far greater than itself—not the hero but the portrait of the hero. Before there can be recorded history or poem there must be the transaction." Certainly in Walt Whitman's views there is a largeness of vision, a healthy sanity, and a fine ethical purpose. He is not to be placed with the professional *littérateurs* of his country, Boston novelists, New York poets, and the like. He stands apart, and the chief value of his work is in its prophecy not in its performance. He has begun a prelude to larger themes. He is the herald to a new era. As a man he is the precursor of a fresh type. He is a factor in the heroic and spiritual evolution of the human being. If Poetry has passed him by, Philosophy will take note of him.

WILLIAM DEAN HOWELLS

[Whitman in Retrospect]†

Mr. Walt Whitman calls his latest book *November Boughs*, and in more ways than one it testifies and it appeals beyond the letter to the reader's interest. For the poet the long fight is over; he rests his cause with what he has done; and we think no one now would like to consider the result without respect, without deference, even if one cannot approach it with entire submission. It is time, certainly, while such a poet is still with us, to own that his literary intention was as generous as his spirit was bold, and that if he has not accomplished all he intended, he has been a force that is by no means spent. Apart from the social import of his first book ("without yielding an inch, the working-man and working-woman were to be in my pages from first to last"), he aimed in it at the emancipation of poetry from what he felt to be the trammels of rhyme and metre. He did not achieve this; but he produced a new kind in literature, which we may or may not allow to be poetry, but which we cannot deny is something eloquent, suggestive, moving, with a lawless, formless beauty of its own. He dealt literary conventionality one of those blows which eventually show as internal injuries, whatever the immediate effect seems to be. He made

† From William Dean Howells, "Editor's Study," *Harper's Monthly* 78 (February 1889): 488–92. Howells, in his ninth year as editor of *Harper's*, was the foremost critical voice in the American literary world. Although he could not honestly recognize Whitman as a major poet, he had liked him for many years (see *Literary Friends and Acquaintances* [1900], 73–76).

it possible for poetry hereafter to be more direct and natural than hitherto; the hearing which he has braved nearly half a century of contumely and mockery to win would now be granted on very different terms to a man of his greatness. This is always the way; and it is always the way that the reformer (perhaps in helpless confession of the weakness he shares with all humankind) champions some error which seems as dear to him as the truth he was born to proclaim. Walt Whitman was not the first to observe that we are all naked under our clothes, but he was one of the greatest, if not the first, to preach a gospel of nudity; not as one of his Quaker ancestry might have done for a witness against the spiritual nakedness of his hearers, but in celebration of the five senses and their equal origin with the three virtues of which the greatest is charity. His offence, if rank, is quantitatively small; a few lines at most; and it is one which the judicious pencil of the editor will some day remove for him, though for the present he "takes occasion to confirm those lines with the settled convictions and deliberate renewals of thirty years." We hope for that day, not only because it will give to all a kind in poetry which none can afford to ignore, and which his cherished lines bar to most of those who read most in our time and country, but because we think the five senses do not need any celebration. In that duality which every thoughtful person must have noticed composes him, we believe the universal experience is that the beast half from first to last is fully able to take care of itself. But it is a vast subject, and, as the poet says, "it does not stand by itself; the vitality of it is altogether in its relations, bearings, significance." In the mean while we can assure the reader that these *November Boughs* are as innocent as so many sprays of apple blossom, and that he may take the book home without misgiving.

We think he will find in reading it that the prose passages are, some of them, more poetic than the most poetic of the rhythmical passages. "Some War Memoranda," and "The Last of the War Cases"—notes made twenty-five years ago—are alive with a simple pathos and instinct with a love of truth which recall the best new Russian work, and which make the poet's psalms seem vague and thin as wandering smoke in comparison. Yet these have the beauty of undulant, sinuous, desultory smoke forms, and they sometimes take the light with a response of such color as dwells in autumn sunsets. The book is well named *November Boughs*: it is meditative and reminiscent, with a sober fragrance in it like the scent of fallen leaves in woods where the leaves that still linger overhead,

> Or few, or none, do shake against the cold—
> Bare ruined choice where late the sweet birds sang.[1]

It is the hymn of the runner resting after the race, and much the same as he chants always, whether the race has been lost or won.

1. Howells misquotes the passage from Shakespeare's Sonnet 73, which reads:

> . . . or none, or few, do hang
> Upon those boughs which shake against the cold,
> Bare ruin'd choirs where late the sweet birds sang.

II.

To get the final lilt of songs;
To penetrate the inmost lore of poets; to know the mighty
    ones—
Job, Homer, Æschylus, Dante, Shakespeare, Tennyson,
    Emerson;
To diagnose the shifting, delicate tints of love and pride and
    doubt; to truly understand,
To encompass these, the last keen faculty and entrance price,
Old age, and what it brings from all its past experiences—

this is now the "good gray poet's" aspiration, and he throws it "out at
the object," as Matthew Arnold says, with the syntactical incomplete-
ness of a sigh. It is the mood and the manner of several other lyrical
passages in the book, and is more important only because it bears
incidentally upon the question lately asked by Mr. Edmund Gosse,
"Has America produced a poet?" Mr. Gosse says he asks it rather in
compliance with an editorial wish than from his own impulse, and
certainly he asks it with all the grace and gentleness inseparable from
his literature. In answering it negatively he confines himself to poets
no longer alive, and so no longer susceptible to hurts of pride or vanity.
At the same time he intimates that if it were a question of living poets
it could not be a question at all; or, if he does not intimate this, he
leaves the living poets to infer it from the kindness of the terms he
uses toward them. He names Chaucer, Spenser, Shakespeare, Milton,
Dryden, Pope, Gray, Burns, Wordsworth, Coleridge, Byron, Shelley,
and Keats as the British worthiest; and he asks, "What dead American
is worthy to join the twelve, and make an Anglo-Saxon's baker's
dozen?" He thinks none, and he gives his reasons: perfectly good rea-
sons for those who are already of his opinion; charming reasons for
all; courteous reasons, respectful, even reverential reasons, but carry-
ing conviction to no contrary mind. This is in the nature of things; for
as no one can say what poetry is, so no one can say who is a poet.
One may quite easily defy Mr. Gosse to say what touch in all Dryden
thrills and lifts like many touches in Emerson. One may challenge him
to prove the art of Pope finer than the art of Longfellow, or bid him
show where and how Burns is better than Bryant. But at the end of
the ends the case is what it was: he remains as unpersuaded as you
do. Still, as true Americans, and as the most provincial people on the
planet in certain respects, we could not leave the case as it was. One
of the literary newspapers invited a symposium of American authors
to sit upon Mr. Gosse and his reasons, and they all, or nearly all,
declared that Emerson was worthy to be the baker's dozenth: there
might be doubts about Longfellow, or there might be doubts about
Bryant, but there could not be any doubt about Emerson. The verdict
was interesting as a proof that Emerson holds the first place in the
critical esteem of those among us best fitted to judge him; but it seems
odd that at a feast where there were so many living poets (whose

worthiness Mr. Gosse refused to question) none was found ready to sacrifice either his brother or himself, and so provide an immortal thirteenth on the spot.

HAVELOCK ELLIS

Whitman†

"Whatever tastes sweet to the most perfect person, that is finally right"—this, it has been said, is the maxim on which Whitman's morality is founded, and it is the morality of Aristotle. But no Greek ever asserted and illustrated it with such emphatic iteration.

From the days when the Greek spirit found its last embodiment in the brief songs, keen or sweet, of the "Anthology,"[1] the attitude which Whitman represents in the "Song of Myself" has never lacked representatives. Throughout the Middle Ages those strange haunting echoes to the perpetual chant of litany and psalm, the Latin student-songs, float across all Europe with their profane and gay paganism, their fresh erotic grace, their "In taberna quando sumus," their "Ludo cum Cæcilia," their "Gaudeamus igitur."[2] In the sane and lofty sensuality of Boccaccio, as it found expression in the history of Alaciel and many another wonderful story, and in Gottfried of Strasburg's[3] assertion of human pride and passion in "Tristan and Isolde," the same strain changed to a stronger and nobler key. Then came the great wave of the Renaissance through Italy and France and England, filling art and philosophy with an exaltation of physical life, and again later, in the movements that center around the French Revolution, an exaltation of arrogant and independent intellectual life. But all these manifestations were sometimes partial, sometimes extravagant; they were impulses of the natural man surging up in rebellion against the dominant Christian temper; they were, for the most part consciously, of the nature of reactions. We feel that there is a fatal lack about them which Christianity would have filled; only in Goethe is the antagonism to some extent reconciled. Beneath the vast growth of Christianity, for ever exalting the unseen by the easy method of pouring contempt on the seen, and still ever producing some strange and exquisite flower of ascêsis—some Francis or Theresa or Fénelon[4]—a slow force was working underground. A tendency was making itself felt to find in the

---

† From *The New Spirit* (1890), 107–25. This excerpt comprises most of the third and the entire fourth section of a five-part essay on Whitman. All notes are by the editor of this Norton Critical Edition.
1. The Greek Anthology is a collection of thousands of epigrammatic poems in Greek literature, ranging from the seventh century to the tenth century B.C.E.
2. Respectively, "When we are in the tavern," "I sport with Cecilia," "Let us therefore rejoice."
3. A thirteenth-century poet now remembered for his version in Middle High German, ca. 1210, of the familiar Tristram and Isolde legend.
4. St. Francis of Assisi (1182–1226); St. Theresa (1515–1582), Spanish Carmelite nun; Fénelon (1651–1715), a French prelate and writer.

theoretically despised physical—in those every-day stones which the builders of the Church had rejected—the very foundation of the mysteries of life; if not the basis for a new vision of the unseen, yet for a more assured vision of the seen.

No one in the last century expressed this tendency more impressively and thoroughly, with a certain insane energy, than William Blake— the great chained spirit whom we see looking out between the bars of his prisonhouse with those wonderful eyes. Especially in "The Marriage of Heaven and Hell," in which he seems to gaze most clearly "through narrow chinks of his cavern," he has set forth his conviction that "first the notion that man has a body distinct from his soul is to be expunged," and that "if the doors of perception were cleansed, everything would appear to man, as it is, infinite." This most extraordinary book is, in his own phraseology, the Bible of Hell.

Whitman appeared at a time when this stream of influence, grown mighty, had boldly emerged. At the time that "Leaves of Grass" sought the light Turgenev was embodying in the typical figure of Bassaroff[5] the modern militant spirit of science, positive and audacious—a spirit marked also, as Hinton[6] pointed out, by a new form of asceticism, which lay in the denial of emotion. Whitman, one of the very greatest emotional forces of modern times, who had grown up apart from the rigid and technical methods of science, face to face with a new world and a new civilization, which he had eagerly absorbed so far as it lay open to him, had the good inspiration to fling himself into the scientific current, and so to justify the demands of his emotional nature; to represent himself as the inhabitant of a vast and coordinated cosmos, tenoned and mortised in granite:

> All forces have been steadily employed to complete and
>   delight me,
> Now on this spot I stand with my robust soul.

That Whitman possessed no trained scientific instinct is unquestionably true, but it is impossible to estimate his significance without understanding what he owes to science. Something, indeed, he had gained from the philosophy of Hegel—with its conception of the universe as a single process of evolution, in which vice and disease are but transient perturbations—with which he had a second-hand acquaintance that has left distinct, but not always well assimilated, marks on his work; but, above all, he was indebted to those scientific conceptions which, like Emerson, he had absorbed or divined. It is these that lie behind "Children of Adam."

This mood of sane and cheerful sensuality, rejoicing with a joy as massive and calm-eyed as Boccaccio's, a moral-fibered joy that Boccaccio never knew, in all the manifestations of the flesh and blood of the world—saying, not: "Let us eat and drink, for to-morrow we die," but, with Clifford: "Let us take hands and help, for this day we are

---

5. The youthful revolutionary hero of Turgenev's novel *Fathers and Sons* (1862).
6. James Hinton (1822–1875), English sociologist, author of *Philosophy and Religion* (1881) and other books.

alive together"[7]—is certainly Whitman's most significant and impressive mood. Nothing so much reveals its depth and sincerity as his never-changing attitude towards death. We know the "fearful thing" that Claudio, in Shakespeare's play, knew as death:

> to die and go we know not where;
> To lie in cold obstruction and to rot;
> . . . . to be worse than worst
> Of those that lawless and uncertain thoughts
> Imagine howling!

And all the Elizabethans in that age of splendid and daring life—even Raleigh and Bacon—felt that same shudder at the horror and mystery of death. Always they felt behind them some vast medieval charnel-house, gloomy and awful, and the sunniest spirits of the English Renaissance quail when they think of it. There was in this horror something of the child's vast and unreasoned dread of darkness and mystery, and it scarcely survived the scientific and philosophic developments of the seventeenth century. Whitman's attitude is not the less deep-rooted and original. For he is not content to argue, haughtily indifferent, with Epicurus and Epictetus, that death can be nothing to us, because it is no evil to lose what we shall never miss. Whitman will reveal the loveliness of death. We feel constantly in "Leaves of Grass" as to some extent we feel before the "Love and Death" and some other pictures of one of the greatest of English artists. "I will show," he announces, "that nothing can happen more beautiful than death." It must not be forgotten that Whitman speaks not merely from the standpoint of the most intense and vivid delight in the actual world, but that he possessed a practical familiarity with disease and death which has perhaps never before fallen to the lot of a great writer. At the end of the "Song of Myself" he bequeaths himself to the dust, to grow from the grass he loves:

> If you want me again, look for me under your bootsoles,
> You will hardly know who I am or what I mean,
> But I shall be good health to you nevertheless,
> And filter and fiber your blood.

And to any who find that dust but a poor immortality, he would say with Schopenhauer, "Oho! do you know, then, what dust is?" The vast chemistry of the earth, the sweetness that is rooted in what we call corruption, the life that is but the leavings of many deaths, is nobly uttered in "This Compost," in which he reaches beyond the corpse that is good manure to sweet-scented roses, to the polished breasts of melons; or again, in the noble elegy, "Pensive on her dead gazing," on those who died during the war. In his most perfectly lyrical poem, "Out of the Cradle endlessly rocking," Whitman has celebrated death—"that strong and delicious word"—with strange tenderness; and never has the loveliness of death been sung in a more sane and

7. William Kingdon Clifford (1845–1879), English mathematician, author of *Elements of Dynamics* (1879–87).

virile song than the solemn death-carol in "When Lilacs last in the Dooryard bloomed":

> Dark mother, always gliding near with soft feet,
> Have none chanted for thee a chant of fullest welcome?
> Then I chant it for thee, I glorify thee above all,
> I bring thee a song, that when thou must indeed come, come
>   unfalteringly.

*   *   *   *   *

> Over the tree-tops I float thee a song,
> Over the rising and sinking waves, over the myriad fields and the
>   prairies wide,
> Over the dense-packed cities all and the teeming wharves and
>   ways,
> I float this carol with joy, with joy to thee, O Death.

Whitman's second great thought on life lies in his egoism. His intense sense of individuality was marked from the first; it is emphatically asserted in the "Song of Myself"—

> And nothing, not God, is greater to one than one's self is—

where it lies side by side with his first great thought. But even in the "Song of Myself" it asserts a separate existence:

> This day before dawn I ascended a hill and looked at the crowded
>   heaven,
> And I said to my spirit, *When we become the enfolders of those
>   orbs and the pleasure and knowledge of everything in them,
>   shall we be filled and satisfied then?*
> And my spirit said, *No, we but level that lift to pass and continue
>   beyond.*

In the end he once, at least, altogether denies his first thought; he alludes to that body which he had called the equal of the soul, or even the soul itself, as excrement:

> Myself discharging my excrementitious body to be burned, or re-
>   duced to powder, or buried,
> My real body doubtless left to me for other spheres.

The first great utterance was naturalistic; this egoism is spiritualistic. It is the sublime apotheosis of Yankee self-reliance. "I only am he who places over you no master, owner, better, God, beyond what waits intrinsically in yourself." This became the dominant conception in Whitman's later work, and fills his universe at length. Of a God, although he sometimes uses the word to obtain emphasis, he at no time had any definite idea. Nature, also, was never a living vascular personality for him; when it is not a mere aggregate of things, it is an order, sometimes a moral order. Also he wisely refuses with unswerving consistency to admit an abstract Humanity; of "man" he has nothing to say; there is nothing anywhere in the universe for him but individuals, undying, everlastingly aggrandizing individuals. This egoism is practical, strenuous, moral; it cannot be described as religious. Whitman is lacking—and in this respect he comes nearer to Goethe than to any other great modern man—in what may be possibly the disease of "soul," the disease that was so bitterly bewailed by Heine. Whitman was congenitally deficient in "soul"; he is a kind of Titanic Undine.[8] "I never had any particular religious experiences," he told Bucke, "never felt the need of spiritual regeneration"; and although he describes himself as "pleased with the earnest words of the sweating Methodist preacher, impressed seriously at the camp-meeting," we know what weight to give to this utterance when we read elsewhere, of animals:

> They do not sweat and whine about their condition,
> They do not lie awake in the dark and weep for their sins,
> They do not make me sick discussing their duty to God,
> Not one is dissastisfied, not one is demented with the mania of
>   owning things,
> Not one kneels to another, nor to his kind that lived thousands
>   of years ago,
> Not one is respectable or unhappy over the whole earth.

We may detect this lack of "soul" in his attitude towards music; for, in its highest development, music is the special exponent of the modern soul in its complexity, its passive resignation, its restless mystical ardors. That Whitman delighted in music is clear; it is equally clear, from the testimony of his writings and of witnesses, that the music he delighted in was simple and joyous melody as in Rossini's operas; he alludes vaguely to symphonies, but

>   when it is a grand opera,
>   Ah, this indeed is music—this suits me.

That Whitman could have truly appreciated Beethoven, or understood Wagner's "Tannhäuser," is not conceivable.

With Whitman's egoism is connected his strenuousness. There is a stirring sound of trumpets always among these "Leaves of Grass." This man may have come, as he tells us, to inaugurate a new religion, but he has few or no marks upon him of that mysticism—that Eastern spirit of glad renunciation of the self in a larger self—which is of the essence of religion. He is at the head of a band of sinewy and tan-faced pioneers, with pistols in their belts and sharp-edged axes in their hands:

> And he going with me leaves peace and routine behind him,
> And stakes his life to be lost at any moment.

This strenuousness finds expression in the hurried jolt and bustle of the lines, always alert, unresting, ever starting afresh. Passages of sweet and peaceful flow are hard to find in "Leaves of Grass," and the more precious when found. Whitman hardly succeeds in the expression of joy; to feel exquisitely the pulse of gladness a more passive and

---

8. Female water sprite familiar in European folklore.

feminine sensibility is needed, like that we meet with in "Towards Democracy";[9] we must not come to this focus of radiant energy for repose or consolation.

This egoism, this strenuousness, reaches at the end to heights of sublime audacity. When we read certain portions of "Leaves of Grass" we seem to see a vast phalanx of Great Companions passing for ever along the cosmic roads, stalwart Pioneers of the Universe. There are superb young men, athletic girls, splendid and savage old men—for the weak seem to have perished by the roadside—and they radiate an infinite energy, an infinite joy. It is truly a tremendous diastole of life to which the crude and colossal extravagance of this vision bears witness; we weary soon of its strenuous vitality, and crave for the systole of life, for peace and repose. It is not strange that the immense faith of the prophet himself grows hesitant and silent at times before "all the meanness and agony without end," and doubts that it is an illusion and "that may-be identity beyond the grave a beautiful fable only." Here and again we meet this access of doubt, and even amid the faith of the "Prayer of Columbus" there is a tremulous, pathetic note of sadness.

Yet there is one keen sword with which Whitman is always able to cut the knot of this doubt—the sword of love. He has but to grasp love and comradeship, and he grows indifferent to the problem of identity beyond the grave. "He a-hold of my hand has completely satisfied me." He discovers at last that love and comradeship—adhesiveness—is, after all, the main thing, "base and finale, too, for all metaphysics"; deeper than religion, underneath Socrates and underneath Christ. With a sound insight he finds the roots of the most universal love in the intimate and physical love of comrades and lovers:

> I mind how once we lay, such a transparent summer morning,
> How you settled your head athwart my hips and gently turned
> over upon me,
> And parted the shirt from my bosom-bone, and plunged your
> tongue to my bare-stript heart,
> And reached till you felt my beard, and reached till you held my
> feet.
> "Swiftly arose and spread around me the peace and knowledge
> that pass all the argument of the earth,
> And I know that the hand of God is the promise of my own,
> And I know that the spirit of God is the brother of my own,
> And that all the men ever born are also my brothers, and the
> women my sisters and lovers,
> And that a kelson of the creation is love.

---

9. A book of poems (1883) by Edward Carpenter (1844–1929), an English author much influenced by Whitman.

IV

This "love" of Whitman's is a very personal matter; of an abstract Man, a *solidaire* Humanity, he never speaks; it does not appear ever to have occurred to him that so extraordinary a conception can be formulated; his relations to men generally spring out of his relations to particular men. He has touched and embraced his fellows' flesh; he has felt throughout his being the mysterious reverberations of the contact:

> There is something in staying close to men and women and
>   looking on them, and in the contact and odor of them,
>   that pleases the soul well,
> All things please the soul, but these please the soul well.

This personal and intimate fact is the center from which the whole of Whitman's morality radiates. Of an abstract Humanity, it is true, he has never thought; he has no vision of Nature as a spiritual Presence; God is to him a word only, without vitality; to Art he is mostly indifferent; yet there remains this great moral kernel, springing from the sexual impulse, taking practical root in a singularly rich and vivid emotional nature, and bearing within it the promise of a city of lovers and friends.

This moral element is one of the central features in Whitman's attitude towards sex and the body generally. For the lover there is nothing in the loved one's body impure or unclean; a breath of passion has passed over it, and all things are sweet. For most of us this influence spreads no farther; for the man of strong moral instinct it covers all human things in infinitely widening circles; his heart goes out to every creature that shares the loved one's delicious humanity; henceforth there is nothing human that he cannot touch with reverence and love. "Leaves of Grass" is penetrated by this moral element. How curiously far this attitude is from the old Christian way we realize when we turn to those days in which Christianity was at its height, and see how Saint Bernard with his mild and ardent gaze looked out into the world of Nature and saw men as "stinking spawn, sacks of dung, the food of worms."

But there is another element in Whitman's attitude—the artistic. It shows itself in a two-fold manner. Whitman came of a vigorous Dutch stock; these Van Velsors from Holland have fully as large a part in him as anything his English ancestry gave him, and his Dutch race shows itself chiefly in his artistic manner. The supreme achievement in art of the Dutch is their seventeenth century painting. What marked those Dutch artists was the ineradicable conviction that every action, social or physiological, of the average man, woman, child, around them might be, with love and absolute faithfulness, phlegmatically set forth. In their heroic earthliness they could at no point be repulsed; color and light may aureole their work, but the most commonplace things of Nature shall have the largest nimbus. That is the temper of Dutch art throughout; no other art in the world has the same characteristics. In the art of Whitman alone do we meet with it again, impatient indeed and broken up into fragments, pierced through with shafts of light from other sources, but still constant and unmistakable. The other artistic element in Whitman's attitude is modern; it is almost the only artistic element by which, unconsciously perhaps, he allies himself to modern tradition in art instead of breaking through them by his own volcanic energy—a curious research for sexual imagery in Nature, imagery often tinged by bizarre and mystical color. Rossetti occasionally uses sexual imagery with rare felicity, as in "Nuptial Sleep":

> And as the last slow sudden drops are shed
> From sparkling eaves when all the storm has fled,
> So singly flagged the pulses of each heart.

With still greater beauty and audacity Whitman, in "I sing the body electric," celebrates the last abandonment of love:

> Bridegroom night of love working surely and softly into the
>   prostrate dawn,
> Undulating into the willing and yielding day,
> Lost in the cleave of the clasping and sweet-fleshed day.

Or, again, in the marvelously keen "Faces"—so realistic and so imaginative—when the "lily's face" speaks out her longing to be filled with albescent honey. This man has certainly felt the truth of that deep saying of Thoreau's, that for him to whom sex is impure there are no flowers in Nature. He cannot help speaking of man's or woman's life in terms of Nature's life, of Nature's life in terms of man's; he mingles them together with an admirably balanced rhythm, as in "Spontaneous Me." All the functions of man's or woman's life are sweet to him because they bear about them a savor of the things that are sweet to him anywhere in the world,

> Of the smell of apples and lemons, of the pairing of birds,
> Of the wet of woods, of the lapping of waves.

Sometimes when he is on this track he seems to lose himself in mystic obscurity; and the words in which he records his impressions are mere patches of morbid color.

There is a third element in Whitman's attitude. It is clear that he had from the outset what may be vaguely called a scientific purpose in that frank grasp of the body, which has a significance to be measured by the fierce opposition it aroused, and by the tenacity with which, in the latest volume of his old age, "November Boughs," he still insists that the principle of those lines so gives breath to the whole scheme that the bulk of the pieces might as well have been left unwritten were those lines omitted. He has himself admirably set this forth in "A Memorandum at a Venture" in "Specimen Days and Collect." In religion and politics we have after a great struggle, gained the priceless possibility of liberty and sincerity. But the region of sex is still, like our moral and social life generally, to a large extent unreclaimed; there still exist barbarous traditions which medieval Christianity has helped to perpetuate, so that the words of Pliny regarding the contaminating touch of a woman, who has always been regarded as in a peculiar manner the symbol of sex—"Nihil facile reperiabatur mulierum profluvio magis monstrificum"[1]—are not even yet meaningless. Why should the sweetening breath of science be guarded from this spot? Why should not "freedom and faith and earnestness" be introduced here? Our attitude towards this part of life affects profoundly our attitude towards life altogether. To realize this, read Swift's "Strephon and Chloe," which enshrines, vividly and unshrinkingly, in a classic form, a certain emotional way of approaching the body. It narrates the very trivial experiences of a man and woman on their bridal night. The incidents are nothing; they are perfectly innocent; the interesting fact about them is the general attitude which they enfold. The unquestioning faith of the man is that in setting down the simple daily facts of human life he has drowned the possibilities of love in filth. And Swift here represents, in an unflinchingly logical fashion, the opinions, more or less realized, more or less disguised, of most people even to-day. Cannot these facts of our physical nature be otherwise set down? Why may we not "keep as delicate around the bowels as around the head and heart?" That is, in effect, the question which, in "A Memorandum at a Venture," Whitman tells us that he undertook to answer. This statement of it was probably an afterthought; else he would have carried out his attempt more thoroughly and more uncompromisingly.

For I doubt if even Whitman has fully realized the beauty and purity of organic life; the scientific element in him was less strong than the moral, or even the artistic. While his genial poetic manner of grasping things is of prime importance, the new conceptions of purity are founded on a scientific basis which must be deeply understood. Swift's morbid and exaggerated spiritualism, a legacy of medievalism—and the ordinary "common-sense" view is but the unconscious shadow of medieval spiritualism—is really founded on ignorance, in other words, on the traditional religious conceptions of an antique but still surviving barbarism.

From our modern standpoint of science, opening his eyes anew, the wonderful cycles of normal life are for ever clean and pure, the loathsomeness, if indeed anywhere, lies in the conceptions of hypertrophied and hyperæsthetic brains. Some who have striven to find a vital natural meaning in the central sacrament of Christianity have thought that the Last Supper was an attempt to reveal the divine mystery of food, to consecrate the loveliness of the mere daily bread and wine which becomes the life of man. Such sacraments of Nature are everywhere subtly woven into the texture of men's bodies. All loveliness of the body is the outward sign of some vital use.

Doubtless these relationships have been sometimes perceived and

---

1. The quotation, from Pliny the Elder's *Natural History*, Book 7, chapter 15, is slightly garbled. It means, "Nothing could easily be found that is more remarkable than the monthly flux of women."

their meaning realized by a sort of mystical intuition, but it is only of recent years that science has furnished them with a rational basis. The chief and central function of life—the omnipresent process of sex, ever wonderful, ever lovely, as it is woven into the whole texture of our man's or woman's body—is the pattern of all the process of our life. At whatever point touched, the reverberation, multiplexly charged with uses, meanings, and emotional associations of infinite charm, to the sensitive individual more or less conscious, spreads throughout the entire organism. We can no longer intrude our crude distinctions of high and low. We cannot now step in and say that this link in the chain is eternally ugly and that is eternally beautiful. For irrational disgust, the varying outcome of individual idiosyncrasy, there is doubtless still room; it is incalculable, and cannot be reached. But that rational disgust which was once held to be common property has received from science its death-blow. In the growth of the sense of purity, which Whitman, not alone, has annunciated, lies one of our chief hopes for morals, as well as for art.

HENRY JAMES

[Review of *Calamus*]†

* * *

What sense shall I speak of as affected by the series of letters published, under the title of "Calamus," by Dr. R. M. Bucke, one of the literary executors of Walt Whitman? The democratic would be doubtless a prompt and simple answer, and as an illustration of democratic social conditions their interest is lively. The person to whom, from 1868 to 1880, they were addressed was a young labouring man,[1] employed in rough railway work, whom Whitman met by accident—the account of the meeting, in his correspondent's own words, is the most charming passage in the volume—and constituted for the rest of life a subject of a friendship of the regular "eternal," the legendary sort. The little book appeals, I daresay, mainly to the Whitmanite already made, but I should be surprised if it has actually failed of power to make a few more. I mean by the Whitmanite those for whom the author of "Leaves of Grass" is, with all his rags and tatters, an upright figure, a *successful* original. It has in a singular way something of the same relation to poetry that may be made out in the luckiest—few, but fine—of the writer's other pages; I call the way singular because it squeezes through the narrowest, humblest gate of prose.

There is not even by accident a line with a hint of style—it is all flat, familiar, affectionate, illiterate colloquy. If the absolute natural

---

† From a review originally published in *Literature*, April 16, 1898. James as a young man had published a highly critical review of WW's Civil War poetry, but subsequently he came to admire the poet.
1. Peter Doyle.

be, when the writer is interesting, the supreme merit of letters, these, accordingly, should stand high on the list. (I am taking for granted, of course, the interest of Whitman.) The beauty of the natural is, here, the beauty of the particular nature, the man's own overflow in the deadly dry setting, the personal passion, the love of life plucked like a flower in a desert of innocent, unconscious ugliness. To call the whole thing vividly American is to challenge, doubtless, plenty of dissent— on the ground, persumably, that the figure in evidence was no less queer a feature of Camden, New Jersey, than it would have been of South Kensington. That may perfectly be; but a thousand images of patient, homely, American life, else undistinguishable, are what its queerness—however startling—happened to express. In this little book is an audible New Jersey voice, charged thick with such impressions, and the reader will miss a chance who does not find in it many odd and pleasant human harmonies. Whitman wrote to his friend of what they both saw and touched, enormities of the common, sordid occupations, dreary amusements, undesirable food; and the record remains, by a mysterious marvel, a thing positively delightful. If we ever find out why, it must be another time. The riddle meanwhile is a neat one for the sphinx of democracy to offer.

* * *

D. H. LAWRENCE

Whitman†

Whitman is the greatest of the Americans. One of the greatest poets of the world, in him an element of falsity troubles us still. Something is wrong; we cannot be quite at ease in his greatness.

This may be our own fault. But we sincerely feel that something is overdone in Whitman; there is something that is too much. Let us get over our quarrel with him first.

All the Americans, when they have trodden new ground, seem to have been conscious of making a breach in the established order. They have been self-conscious about it. They have felt that they were trespassing, transgressing, or going very far, and this has given a certain stridency, or portentousness, or luridness to their manner. Perhaps that is because the steps were taken so rapidly. From Franklin to Whitman is a hundred years. It might be a thousand.

The Americans have finished in haste, with a certain violence and violation, that which Europe began two thousand years ago or more. Rapidly they have returned to lay open the secrets which the Christian epoch has taken two thousand years to close up.

With the Greeks started the great passion for the ideal, the passion

† From *Nation & Athenaeum* 29 (July 23, 1921): 616–18. This essay is the forerunner of Lawrence's chaper on Whitman in *Studies in Classic American Literature* (1923).

for translating all consciousness into terms of spirit and ideal or idea. They did this in reaction from the vast old world which was dying in Egypt. But the Greek, though they set out to conquer the animal or sensual being in man, did not set out to annihilate it. This was left for the Christians.

The Christians, phase by phase, set out actually to *annihilate* the sensual being in man. They insisted that man was in his reality *pure spirit*, and that he was perfectible as such. And this was their business, to achieve such a perfection.

They worked from a profound inward impulse, the Christian religious impulse. But their proceeding was the same, in living extension, as that of the Greek esoterics, such as John the Evangel or Socrates. They proceeded, by will and by exaltation, to overcome *all* the passions and all the appetites and prides.

Now, so far, in Europe, the conquest of the lower self has been objective. That is, man has moved from a great impulse within himself, unconscious. But once the conquest has been effected, there is a temptation for the conscious mind to return and finger and explore, just as tourists now explore battlefields. This self-conscious *mental* provoking of sensation and reaction in the great affective centres is what we call sentimentalism or sensationalism. The mind returns upon the affective centres, and sets up in them a deliberate reaction.

And this is what all the Americans do, beginning with Crêvecœur, Hawthorne, Poe, all the transcendentalists, Melville, Prescott, Wendell Holmes, Whitman, they are all guilty of this provoking of mental reactions in the physical self, passions exploited by the mind. In Europe, men like Balzac and Dickens, Tolstoi and Hardy, still act direct from the passional motive, and not inversely, from mental provocation. But the æsthetes and symbolists, from Baudelaire and Maeterlinck and Oscar Wilde onwards, and nearly all later Russian, French, and English novelists set up their reactions in the mind and reflect them by a secondary process down into the body. This makes a vicious living and a spurious art. It is one of the last and most fatal effects of idealism. Everything becomes self-conscious and spurious, to the pitch of madness. It is the madness of the world of to-day. Europe and America are all alike; all the nations self-consciously provoking their own passional reactions from the mind, and *nothing* spontaneous.

And this is our accusation against Whitman, as against the others. Too often he deliberately, self-consciously *affects* himself. It puts us off, it makes us dislike him. But since such self-conscious secondariness is a concomitant of all American art, and yet not sufficiently so to prevent that art from being of rare quality, we must get over it. The excuse is that the Americans have had to perform in a century a curve which it will take Europe much longer to finish, if ever she finishes it.

Whitman has gone further, in actual living expression, than any man, it seems to me. Dostoevsky has burrowed underground into the decomposing psyche. But Whitman has gone forward in life-knowledge. It is he who surmounts the grand climacteric of our civilization.

Whitman enters on the last phase of spiritual triumph. He really arrives at that stage of infinity which the seers sought. By subjecting the *deepest centres* of the lower self, he attains the maximum consciousness in the higher self: a degree of extensive consciousness greater, perhaps, than any man in the modern world.

We have seen Dana and Melville, the two adventurers, setting out to conquer the last vast *element*, with the spirit. We have seen Melville touching at last the far end of the immemorial, prehistoric Pacific civilization, in "Typee." We have seen his terrific cruise into universality.

Now we must remember that the way, even towards a state of infinite comprehension, is through the externals towards the quick. And the vast elements, the cosmos, the big things, the universals, these are always the externals. These are met first and conquered first. That is why science is so much easier than art. The quick is the living being, the quick of quicks is the individual soul. And it is here, at the quick, that Whitman proceeds to find the experience of infinitude, his vast extension, or concentrated intensification into Allness. He carries the conquest to its end.

If we read his pæans, his chants of praise and deliverance and accession, what do we find? All-embracing, indiscriminate, passional acceptance; surges of chaotic vehemence of invitation and embrace, catalogues, lists, enumerations. "Whoever you are, to you endless announcements. . . ." "And of these one and all I weave the song of myself." "Lovers, endless lovers."

Continually the one cry: I am everything and everything is me. I accept everything in my consciousness; nothing is rejected:—

I am he that aches with amorous love:
  Does the earth gravitate? does not all matter, aching, attract all
    matter?
So the body of me to all I meet or know.

At last everything is conquered. At last the lower centres are conquered. At last the lowest plane is submitted to the highest. At last there is nothing more to conquer. At last all is one, all is love, even hate is love, even flesh is spirit. The great oneness, the experience of infinity, the triumph of the living spirit, which at last includes everything, is here accomplished.

It is man's accession into wholeness, his knowledge in full. Now he is united with everything. Now he embraces everything into himself in a oneness. Whitman is drunk with the new wine of this new great experience, really drunk with the strange wine of infinitude. So he pours forth his words, his chants of praise and acclamation. It is man's maximum state of consciousness, his highest state of spiritual being. Supreme spiritual consciousness, and the divine drunkenness of supreme consciousness. It is reached through embracing love. "And whoever walks a furlong without sympathy walks to his own funeral dressed in his own shroud." And this supreme state, once reached, shows us the One Identity in everything, Whitman's cryptic *One Identity*.

Thus Whitman becomes in his own person the whole world, the whole universe, the whole eternity of time. Nothing is rejected. Because nothing opposes him. All adds up to one in him. Item by item he identifies himself with the universe, and this accumulative identity he calls Democracy, En Masse, One Identity, and so on.

But this is the last and final truth, the last truth is at the quick. And the quick is the single individual soul, which is never more than itself, though it embrace eternity and infinity, and never *other* than itself, though it include all men. Each vivid soul is unique, and though one soul embrace another, and include it, still it cannot *become* that other soul, or livingly dispossess that other soul. In extending himself, Whitman still remains himself, he does not become the other man, or the other woman, or the tree, or the universe: in spite of Plato.

Which is the maximum truth, though it appears so small in contrast to all these infinites, and En Masses, and Democracies, and Almightynesses. The essential truth is that a man is himself, and only himself, throughout all his greatnesses and extensions and intensifications.

The second truth which we must bring as a charge against Whitman is the one we brought before, namely, that his Allness, his One Identity, his En Masse, his Democracy, is only a half-truth—an enormous half-truth. The other half is Jehovah, and Egypt, and Sennacherib: the other form of Allness, terrible and grand, even as in the Psalms.

Now Whitman's way to Allness, he tells us, is through endless sympathy, merging. But in merging you must merge away from something, as well as towards something, and in sympathy you must depart from one point to arrive at another. Whitman lays down this law of sympathy as the one law, the direction of merging as the one direction. Which is obviously wrong. Why not a right-about-turn? Why not turn slap back to the point from which you started to merge? Why not *that* direction, the reverse of merging, back to the single and overweening self? Why not, instead of endless dilation of sympathy, the retraction into isolation and pride?

Why not? The heart has its systole diastole, the shuttle comes and goes, even the sun rises and sets. We know, as a matter of fact, that all life lies between two poles. The direction is twofold. Whitman's *one direction* becomes a hideous tyranny once he has attained his goal of Allness. His One Identity is a prison of horror, once realized. For identities are manifold and each jewel-like, different as a sapphire from an opal. And the motion of merging becomes at last a vice, a nasty degeneration, as when tissue breaks down into a mucous slime. There must be the sharp retraction from isolation, following the expansion into unification, otherwise the integral being is overstrained and will break, break down like disintegrating tissue into slime, imbecility, epilepsy, vice, like Dostoevsky.

And one word more. Even if you reach the state of infinity, you can't sit down there. You just physically can't. You either have to strain still further into universality and become vaporish, or slimy: or you have to hold your toes and sit tight and practise Nirvana; or you have to come back to common dimensions, eat your pudding and blow your nose and be just yourself; or die and have done with it. A grand experience is a grand experience. It brings a man to his maximum. But even at his maximum a man is not more than himself. When he is infinite he is still himself. He still has a nose to wipe. The state of infinity is *only* a state, even if it be the supreme one.

But in achieving this state Whitman opened a new field of living. He drives on to the very centre of life and sublimates even this into consciousness. Melville hunts the remote white whale of the deepest passional body, tracks it down. But it is Whitman who captures the whale. The pure sensual body of man, at its deepest remoteness and intensity, this is the White Whale. And this is what Whitman captures.

He seeks his consummation through one continual ecstacy: the ecstacy of *giving himself*, and of being taken. The ecstacy of his own reaping and merging with another, with others; the sword-cut of sensual death. Whitman's motion is always the motion of *giving himself*: This is my body—take, and eat. It is the great sacrament. He knows nothing of the other sacrament, the sacrament in pride, where the communicant envelops the victim and host in a flame of ecstatic consuming, sensual gratification, and triumph.

But he is concerned with others beside himself: with woman, for example. But what is woman to Whitman? Not much? She is a great function—no more. Whitman's "athletic mothers of these States" are depressing. Muscles and wombs: functional creatures—no more.

As I see myself reflected in Nature,
As I see through a mist, One with inexpressible completeness,
    sanity, beauty,
See the bent head, and arms folded over the breast, the Female
    I see.

That is all. The woman is reduced, really, to a submissive function. She is no longer an individual being with a living soul. She must fold her arms and bend her head and submit to her functioning capacity. Function of sex, function of birth.

This, the nucleus—after the child is born of woman, man is born
    of woman,
This is the bath of birth, the merge of small and large, and the
    outlet again—

Acting from the last and profoundest centres, man acts womanless. It is no longer a question of race continuance. It is a question of sheer, ultimate being, the perfection of life, nearest to death. Acting from these centres, man is an extreme being, the unthinkable warrior, creator, mover, and maker.

And the polarity is between man and man. Whitman alone of all moderns has known this positively. Others have known it negatively, *pour épater les bourgeois.*[1] But Whitman knew it positively, in its tremendous knowledge, knew the extremity, the perfectness, and the fatality.

Even Whitman becomes grave, tremulous, before the last dynamic truth of life. In *Calamus* he does not shout. He hesitates: he is reluctant, wistful. But none the less he goes on. And he tells the mystery of manly love, the love of comrades. Continually he tells us the same truth: the new world will be built upon the love of comrades, the new great dynamic of life will be manly love. Out of this inspiration the creation of the future.

The strange Calamus has its pink-tinged root by the pond, and it sends up its leaves of comradeship, comrades at one root, without the intervention of woman, the female. This comradeship is to be the final cohering principle of the new world, the new Democracy. It is the cohering principle of perfect soldiery, as he tells in "Drum Taps." It is the cohering principle of final *unison* in creative activity. And it is extreme and alone, touching the confines of death. It is something terrible to bear, terrible to be responsible for. It is the soul's last and most vivid responsibility, the responsibility for the circuit of final friendship, comradeship, manly love.

> Yet, you are beautiful to me, you faint-tinged roots, you make me
>   think of death;
> Death is beautiful from you (what, indeed, is finally beautiful
>   except death and love?).
> I think it is not for life I am chanting here my chant of lovers, I
>   think it must be for death.
> For how calm, how solemn it grows to ascend to the atmosphere
>   of lovers;
> Death or life, I am then indifferent, my soul declines to prefer (I
>   am not sure but the high soul of lovers welcomes death most),
> Indeed, O death, I think now these leaves mean precisely the
>   same as you mean—

Here we have the deepest, finest Whitman, the Whitman who knows the extremity of life, and of the soul's responsibility. He has come near now to death, in his creative life. But creative life must come near to death, to link up the mystic circuit. The pure warriors must stand on the brink of death. So must the men of a pure creative nation. We shall have no beauty, no dignity, no essential freedom otherwise. And so it is from Sea-Drift, where the male bird sings the lost female: not that she is lost, but lost to him who has had to go beyond her, to sing on the edge of the great sea, in the night. It is the last voice on the shore.

> Whereto answering, the sea
> Delaying not, hurrying not,
> Whispered me through the night, very plainly before daybreak,
> Lisp'd to me the low and delicious word death,

---

1. "To shock [or annoy] the middle class."

And again death, death, death, death,
Hissing melodious, neither like the bird nor like my aroused
    child's heart,
But edging near as privately for me rustling at my feet,
Creeping thence steadily up to my ears and laving me softly all
    over,
Death, death, death, death, death—

What a great poet Whitman is: great like a great Greek. For him
the last enclosures have fallen, he finds himself on the shore of the
last sea. The extreme of life: so near to death. It is a hushed, deep
responsibility. And what is the responsibility? It is for the new great
era of mankind. And upon what is this new era established? On the
perfect circuits of vital flow between human beings. First, the great
sexless normal relation between individuals, simple sexless friendships,
unison of family, and clan, and nation, and group. Next, the powerful
sex relation between man and woman, culminating in the eternal orbit
of marriage. And, finally, the sheer friendship, the love between com-
rades, the manly love which alone can create a new era of life.

The one state, however, does not annul the other: it fulfils the other.
Marriage is the great step beyond friendship, and family, and nation-
ality, but it does not supersede these. Marriage should only give repose
and perfection to the great previous bonds and relationships. A wife
or husband who sets about to annul the old, pre-marriage affections
and connections ruins the foundations of marriage. And so with the
last, extremest love, the love of comrades. The ultimate comradeship
which sets about to destroy marriage destroys its own *raison d'être*.
The ultimate comradeship is the final progression from marriage; it is
the last seedless flower of pure beauty, beyond purpose. But if it de-
stroys marriage it makes itself purely deathly. In its beauty, the ulti-
mate comradeship flowers on the brink of death. But it flowers from
the root of all life upon the blossoming tree of life.

The life-circuit now depends entirely upon the sex-unison of mar-
riage. This circuit must never be broken. But it must be still surpassed.
We cannot help the laws of life.

If marriage is sacred, the ultimate comradeship is utterly sacred,
since it has no ulterior motive whatever, like procreation. If marriage
is eternal, the great bond of life, how much more is this bond eternal,
being the great life-circuit which borders on death in all its round. The
new, extreme, the sacred relationship of comrades awaits us, and the
future of mankind depends on the way in which this relation is en-
tered upon by us. It is a relation between fearless, honorable, self-
responsible men, a balance in perfect polarity.

The last phase is entered upon, shakily, by Whitman. It will take us
an epoch to establish the new, perfect circuit of our being. It will take
an epoch to establish the love of comrades, as marriage is really es-
tablished now. For fear of going on, forwards, we forwards, we turn
round and destroy, or try to destroy, what lies behind. We are trying
to destroy marriage, because we have not the courage to go forward

from marriage to the new issue. Marriage must never be wantonly attacked. *True* marriage is eternal; in it we have our consummation and being. But the final consummation lies in that which is beyond marriage.

And when the bond, or circuit of perfect comrades is established, what then, when we are on the brink of death, fulfilled in the vastness of life? Then, at last, we shall know a starry maturity.

Whitman put us on the track years ago. Why has no one gone on from him? The great poet, why does no one accept his greatest word? The Americans are not worthy of their Whitman. They take him like a cocktail, for fun. Miracle that they have not annihilated every word of him. But these miracles happen.

The greatest modern poet! Whitman, at his best, is purely himself. His verse springs sheer from the spontaneous sources of his being. Hence its lovely, lovely form and rhythm: at the best. It is sheer, perfect, *human* spontaneity, spontaneous as a nightingale throbbing, but still controlled, the highest loveliness of human spontaneity, undecorated, unclothed. The whole being is there, sensually throbbing, spiritually quivering, mentally, ideally speaking. It is not, like Swinburne, an exaggeration of the one part of being. It is perfect and whole. The whole soul speaks at once, and is too pure for mechanical assistance of rhyme and measure. The perfect utterance of a concentrated, spontaneous soul. The unforgettable loveliness of Whitman's lines!

> Out of the cradle endlessly rocking.

Ave America!

RANDALL JARRELL

Some Lines from Whitman[†]

Whitman, Dickinson, and Melville seem to me the best poets of the 19th Century here in America. Melville's poetry has been grotesquely underestimated, but of course it is only in the last four or five years that it has been much read; in the long run, in spite of the awkwardness and amateurishness of so much of it, it will surely be thought well of. (In the short run it will probably be thought entirely too well of. Melville is a great poet only in the prose of *Moby Dick.*) Dickinson's poetry has been thoroughly read, and well though undifferentiatingly loved—after a few decades or centuries almost everybody will be able to see through Dickinson to her poems. But something odd has happened to the living changing part of Whitman's reputation: nowadays it is people who are not particularly interested in poetry, people who say that they read a poem for what it says, not for how it says it, who admire Whitman most. Whitman is often written about, either ap-

---

† From *Poetry and the Age* (New York: Alfred A. Knopf, 1953), 112–20, 131–32. Copyright © 1952, 1953 by Randall Jarrell. Reprinted by permission of Alfred A. Knopf, Inc.

provingly or disapprovingly, as if he were the Thomas Wolfe of 19th Century democracy, the hero of a de Mille movie about Walt Whitman. (People even talk about a war in which Walt Whitman and Henry James chose up sides, to begin with, and in which you and I will go on fighting till the day we die.) All this sort of thing, and all the bad poetry that there of course is in Whitman—for any poet has written enough bad poetry to scare away anybody—has helped to scare away from Whitman most "serious readers of modern poetry." They do not talk of his poems, as a rule, with any real liking or knowledge. Serious readers, people who are ashamed of not knowing all Hopkins by heart, are not at all ashamed to say, "I don't really know Whitman very well." This may harm Whitman in your eyes, they know, but that is a chance that poets have to take. Yet "their" Hopkins, that good critic and great poet, wrote about Whitman, after seeing five or six of his poems in a newspaper review: "I may as well say what I should not otherwise have said, that I always knew in my heart Walt Whitman's mind to be more like my own than any other man's living. As he is a very great scoundrel this is not a very pleasant confession." And Henry James, the leader of "their" side in that awful imaginary war of which I spoke, once read Whitman to Edith Wharton (much as Mozart used to imitate, on the piano, the organ) with such power and solemnity that both sat shaken and silent; it was after this reading that James expressed his regret at Whitman's "too extensive acquaintance with the foreign languages." Almost all the most "original and advanced" poets and critics and readers of the last part of the 19th Century thought Whitman as original and advanced as themselves, in manner as well as in matter. Can Whitman really be a sort of Thomas Wolfe or Carl Sandburg or Robinson Jeffers or Henry Miller—or a sort of Balzac of poetry, whose every part is crude but whose whole is somehow great? He is not, nor could he be; a poem, like Pope's spider, "lives along the line," and all the dead lines in the world will not make one live poem. As Blake says, "all sublimity is founded on minute discrimination," and it is in these "minute particulars" of Blake's that any poem has its primary existence.

To show Whitman for what he is one does not need to praise or explain or argue, one needs simply to quote. He himself said, "I and mine do not convince by arguments, similes, rhymes,/ We convince by our presence." Even a few of his phrases are enough to show us that Whitman was no sweeping rhetorician, but a poet of the greatest and oddest delicacy and originality and sensitivity, so far as words are concerned. This is, after all, the poet who said, "Blind loving wrestling touch, sheath'd hooded sharp-tooth'd touch"; who said, "Smartly attired, countenance smiling, form upright, death under the breastbones, hell under the skull-bones"; who said, "Agonies are one of my changes of garments"; who saw grass as the "flag of my disposition," saw "the sharp-peak'd farmhouse, with its scallop'd scum and slender shoots from the gutters," heard a plane's "wild ascending lisp," and saw and heard how at the amputation "what is removed drops horribly in a pail." This is the poet for whom the sea was "howler and scooper of storms," reaching out to us with "crooked inviting fingers"; who went "leaping chasms with a pike-pointed staff, clinging to topples of brittle and blue"; who, a runaway slave, saw how "my gore dribs, thinn'd with the ooze of my skin"; who went "lithographing Kronos . . . buying drafts of Osiris"; who stared out at the "little plentiful manni-kins skipping around in collars and tail'd coat,/ I am aware who they are, (they are positively not worms or fleas)." For he is, at his best, beautifully witty: he says gravely, "I find I incorporate gneiss, coals, long-threaded moss, fruits, grain, esculent roots,/ And am stucco'd with quadrupeds and birds all over"; and of these quadrupeds and birds "not one is respectable or unhappy over the whole earth." He calls advice: "Unscrew the locks from the doors! Unscrew the doors from their jambs!" He publishes the results of research: "Having pried through the strata, analyz'd to a hair, counsel'd with doctors and cal-culated close,/ I find no sweeter fat than sticks to my own bones." Everybody remembers how he told the Muse to "cross out please those immensely overpaid accounts,/ That matter of Troy and Achilles' wrath, and Aeneas', Odysseus' wanderings," but his account of the arrival of the "illustrious emigré" here in the New World is even better: "Bluff'd not a bit by drainpipe, gasometer, artificial fertilizers,/ Smiling and pleas'd with palpable intent to stay,/ She's here, install'd amid the kitchenware." Or he sees, like another Breughel, "the mechanic's wife with the babe at her nipple interceding for every person born,/ Three scythes at harvest whizzing in a row from three lusty angels with shirts bagg'd out at their waists,/ The snag-toothed hostler with red hair re-deeming sins past and to come"—the passage has enough with not only (in Johnson's phrase) to keep it sweet, but enough to make it believable. He says:

> I project my hat, sit shame-faced, and beg.
>
> Enough! Enough! Enough!
> Somehow I have been stunn'd. Stand back!
> Give me a little time beyond my cuff'd head, slumbers, dreams, gaping,
> I discover myself on the verge of a usual mistake.

There is in such changes of tone as these the essence of wit. And Whitman is even more far-fetched than he is witty; he can say about Doubters, in the most improbable and explosive of juxtapositions: "I know every one of you, I know the sea of torment, doubt, despair and unbelief./ How the flukes splash! How they contort rapid as lightning, with splashes and spouts of blood!" Who else would have said about God: "As the hugging and loving bed-fellow sleeps at my side through the night, and withdraws at the break of day with stealthy tread,/ Leav-ing me baskets cover'd with white towels, swelling the house with their plenty"?—the Psalmist himself, his cup running over, would have looked at Whitman with dazzled eyes. (Whitman was persuaded by friends to hide the fact that it was God he was talking about.) He says, "Flaunt of the sunshine I need not your bask—lie over!" This unusual employment of verbs is usual enough in participle-loving Whitman, who also asks you to "look in my face while I snuff the sidle of evening," or tells you, "I effuse my flesh in eddies, and drift it in lacy jags." Here are some typical beginnings of poems: "City of orgies, walks, and joys. . . . Not heaving from my ribb'd breast only. . . . O take my hand Walt Whitman! Such gliding wonders! Such sights and sounds! Such join'd unended links. . . ." He says to the objects of the world, "You have waited, you always wait, you dumb, beautiful ministers"; sees "the sun and stars that float in the open air,/ The apple-shaped earth"; says, "O suns— O grass of graves— O perpetual transfers and promotions,/ If you do not say anything how can I say anything?" Not many poets have written better, in queerer and more convincing and more individual language, about the world's *gliding wonders*: the phrase seems particularly right for Whitman. He speaks of those "circling rivers the breath," of the "savage old mother incessantly crying,/ To the boy's soul's questions sullenly timing, some drown'd secret hissing"—ends a poem, once, "We have voided all but freedom and our own joy." How can one quote enough? If the reader thinks that all this is like Thomas Wolfe he *is* Thomas Wolfe; nothing else could explain it. Poetry like this is as far as possible from the work of any ordinary rhetorician, whose phrases cascade over us like suds of the oldest and most-advertised detergent.

The interesting thing about Whitman's worst language (for, just as few poets have ever written better, few poets have ever written worse) is how unusually absurd, how really ingeniously bad, such language is. I will quote none of the most famous examples; but even a line like *O culpable! I acknowledge. I exposé!* is not anything that you and I could do—only a man with the most extraordinary feel for language, or none whatsoever, could have cooked up Whitman's worst messes. For instance: what other man in all the history of this planet would have said, "I am a habitan of Vienna"? (One has an immediate vision of him as a sort of French-Canadian halfbreed to whom the Viennese are offering, with trepidation, through the bars of a zoological garden, little mounds of whipped cream.) And *enclaircise*—why, it's as bad as *explicate*! We are right to resent his having made up his own horrors, instead of sticking to the ones that we ourselves employ. But when Whitman says, "I dote on myself, there is that lot of me and all so luscious," we should realize that we are not the only ones who are amused. And the queerly bad and merely queer and queerly good will often change into one another without warning: "Hefts of the moving world, at innocent gambols silently rising, freshly exuding,/ Scooting obliquely high and low"—not good, but *queer*!—suddenly becomes, "Something I cannot see puts up libidinous prongs,/ Seas of bright juice suffuse heaven," and it is sunrise.

But it is not in individual lines and phrases, but in passages of some lengths, that Whitman is at his best. In the following quotation Whitman has something difficult to express, something that there are many formulas, all bad, for expressing; he expresses it with complete success, in language of the most dazzling originality:

The orchestra whirls me wider than Uranus flies,
It wrenches such ardors from me I did not know I possess'd them,
It sails me, I dab with bare feet, they are lick'd by the indolent
    waves,
I am cut by bitter and angry hail, I lose my breath,
Steep'd amid honey'd morphine, my windpipe throttled in fakes
    of death,
At length let up again to feel the puzzle of puzzles,
And that we call Being.

One hardly knows what to point at—everything works. But *wrenches*
and *did not know I possess'd them*; the incredible *it sails me, I dab with
bare feet; lick'd by the indolent; steep'd amid honey'd morphine; my
windpipe throttled in fakes of death*—no wonder Crane admired Whit-
man! This originality, as absolute in its way as that of Berlioz' orches-
tration, is often at Whitman's command:

I am a dance—play up there! the fit is whirling me fast!
I am the ever-laughing—it is new moon and twilight,
I see the hiding of douceurs, I see nimble ghosts whichever way
    I look,
Cache and cache again deep in the ground and sea, and where it
    is neither ground nor sea.
Well do they do their jobs those journeymen divine,
Only from me can they hide nothing, and would not if they could,
I reckon I am their boss and they make me a pet besides,
And surround me and lead me and run ahead when I walk,
To lift their cunning covers to signify me with stretch'd arms and
    resume the way;
Onward we move, a gay gang of blackguards! with mirth-shouting
    music and wild-flapping pennants of joy!

If you did not believe Hopkins' remark about Whitman, that *gay gang
of blackguards* ought to shake you. Whitman shares Hopkins' passion
for "dappled" effects, but he slides in and out of them with ambiguous
swiftness. And he has at his command a language of the calmest and
most prosaic reality, one that seems to do no more than present:

The little one sleeps in its cradle.
I lift the gauze and look a long time, and silently brush away flies
    with my hand.
The youngster and the red-faced girl turn aside up the bushy hill,
I peeringly view them from the top.
The suicide sprawls on the bloody floor of the bedroom.
I witness the corpse with its dabbled hair, I note where the pistol
    has fallen.

It is like magic: that is, something has been done to us without our
knowing how it was done; but if we look at the lines again we see the
gauze, silently, youngster, red-faced, bushy, peeringly, dabbled—not that
this is all we see. "Present! present!" said James; these are presented,
put down side by side to form a little "view of life," from the cradle to

the last bloody floor of the bedroom. Very often the things presented form nothing but a list:

The pure contralto sings in the organ loft,
The carpenter dresses his plank, the tongue of his foreplane whis-
tles its wild ascending lisp,
The married and unmarried children ride home to their
Thanksgiving dinner,
The pilot seizes the king-pin, he heaves down with a strong arm,
The mate stands braced in the whale-boat, lance and harpoon are
ready,
The duck-shooter walks by silent and cautious stretches,
The deacons are ordain'd with cross'd hands at the altar,
The spinning-girl retreats and advances to the hum of the big wheel,
The farmer stops by the bars as he walks on a First-day loafe and
looks at the oats and rye,
The lunatic is carried at last to the asylum a confirm'd case,
(He will never sleep any more as he did in the cot in his mother's
bed-room;)
The jour printer with gray head and gaunt jaws works at his case,
He turns his quid of tobacco while his eyes blur with the
manuscript,
The malform'd limbs are tied to the surgeon's table,
What is removed drops horribly in a pail; . . .

It is only a list—but what a list! * * *
They might have put on his tombstone WALT WHITMAN: HE HAD HIS
NERVE. He is the rashest, the most inexplicable and unlikely—the most
impossible, one wants to say—of poets. He somehow *is* in a class by
himself, so that one compares him with other poets about as readily
as one compares *Alice* with other books. (Even his free verse has a
completely different effect from anybody else's.) Who would think of
comparing him with Tennyson or Browning or Arnold or Baudelaire?
—it is Homer, or the sagas, or something far away and long ago, that
comes to one's mind only to be dismissed; for sometimes Whitman *is*
epic, just as *Moby Dick* is, and it surprises us to be able to use truth-
fully this word that we have misused so many times. Whitman *is* grand,
and elevated, and comprehensive, and real with an astonishing reality,
and many other things—the critic points at his qualities in despair and
wonder, all method failing, and simply calls them by their names. And
the range of these qualities is the most extraordinary thing of all. We
can surely say about him, "He was a man, take him for all in all. I
shall not look upon his like again"—and wish that people had seen
this and not tried to be his like: one Whitman is miracle enough, and
when he comes again it will be the end of the world.

I have said so little about Whitman's faults because they are so plain:
baby critics who have barely learned to complain of the lack of ambigu-
ity in *Peter Rabbit* can tell you all that is wrong with *Leaves of Grass*. But
a good many of my readers must have felt that it is ridiculous to write
an essay about the obvious fact that Whitman is a great poet. It is

ridiculous—just as, in 1851, it would have been ridiculous for anyone to write an essay about the obvious fact that Pope was no "classic of our prose" but a great poet. Critics have to spend half their time reiterating whatever ridiculously obvious things their age or the critics of their age have found it necessary to forget: they say despairingly, at parties, that Wordsworth is a great poet, and *won't* bore you, and tell Mr. Leavis that Milton is a great poet whose deposition *hasn't* been accomplished with astonishing ease by a few words from Eliot. . . . There is something essentially ridiculous about critics, anyway: what is good is good without our saying so, and beneath all our majesty we know this.

Let me finish by mentioning another quality of Whitman's—a quality, delightful to me, that I have said nothing of. If some day a tourist notices, among the ruins of New York City, a copy of *Leaves of Grass*, and stops and picks it up and reads some lines in it, she will be able to say to herself: "How very American! If he and his country had not existed, it would have been impossible to imagine them."

WILLIAM CARLOS WILLIAMS

An Essay on *Leaves of Grass*†

Leaves of Grass! It was a good title for a book of poems, especially for a new book of American poems. It was a challenge to the entire concept of the poetic idea, and from a new viewpoint, a rebel viewpoint, an American viewpoint. In a word and at the beginning it enunciated a shocking truth, that the common ground is of itself a poetic source. There has been inklings before this that such was the case in the works of Robert Burns and the poet Wordsworth, but in this instance the very forms of the writing had been altered: it had gone over to the style of the words as they appeared on the page. Whitman's socalled "free verse" was an assault on the very citadel of the poem itself; it constituted a direct challenge to all living poets to show cause why they should not do likewise. It is a challenge that still holds good after a century of vigorous life during which it has been practically continuously under fire but never defeated.

From the beginning Whitman realized that the matter was largely technical. It had to be free verse or nothing with him and he seldom varied from that practice—and never for more than the writing of an occasional poem. It was a sharp break, and if he was to go astray he had no one but himself to blame for it. It was a technical matter, true enough, and he would stick it out to the end, but to do any more with it than simply to write the poems was beyond him.

He had seen a great light but forgot almost at once after the first revelation everything but his "message," the idea which originally set

† First published in *Leaves of Grass: One Hundred Years After*, ed. Milton Hindus (Stanford University Press, 1955). Copyright © 1955 by Florence H. Williams. Reprinted by permission of New Directions Publishing Corp., agents for Mrs. William Carlos Williams.

him in motion, the idea on which he had been nurtured, the idea of democracy—and took his eye off the words themselves which should have held him.

The point is purely academic—the man had his hands full with the conduct of his life and couldn't, if they had come up, be bothered with other matters. As a result, he made no further progress as an artist but, in spite of various topical achievements, continued to write with diminishing effectiveness for the remainder of his life.

He didn't know any better. He didn't have the training to construct his verses after a conscious mold which would have given him power over them to turn them this way, then that, at will. He only knew how to give them birth and to release them to go their own way. He was preoccupied with the great ideas of the time, to which he was devoted, but, after all, poems are made out of words not ideas. He never showed any evidence of knowing this and the unresolved forms consequent upon his beginnings remained in the end just as he left them.

Verses, in English, are frequently spoken of as measures. It is a fortunate designation as it gives us, in looking at them, the idea of elapsed time. We are reminded that the origin of our verse was the dance—and even if it had not been the dance, the heart when it is stirred has its multiple beats, and verse at its most impassioned sets the heart violently beating. But as the heart picks up we also begin to count. Finally, the measure for each language and environment is accepted. In English it is predominantly the iambic pentameter, but whether that is so for the language Whitman spoke is something else again. It is a point worth considering, but apart from the briefest of notices a point not to be considered here. It may be that the essential pace of the English and the American languages is diametrically opposed each to the other and that that is an important factor in the writing of their poetry, but that is for the coming generations to discover. Certainly not only the words but the meter, the measure that governed Whitman's verses, was not English. But there were more pressing things than abstract discussions of meter to be dealt with at that time and the poet soon found himself involved in them.

Very likely the talk and the passionate talk about freedom had affected him as it had infected the French and many others earlier. It is said that, when as a young man he lived in New Orleans, he had fallen in love with a beautiful octoroon but had allowed his friends and relatives to break up the match. It is possible that the disappointment determined the pattern of his later rebellion in verse. Free verse was his great idea! *Versos sueltos* the Spanish call them. It is not an entirely new idea, but it was entirely new to the New York Yankee who was, so to speak, waiting for it with open arms and an overcharged soul and the example of Thomas Jefferson to drive him on.

But verse had always been, for Englishmen and the colonials that imitated them, a disciplined maneuver of the intelligence, as it is today, in which measure was predominant. They resented this American with his new idea, and attacked him in a characteristic way—*on moral grounds*. And he fell for it. He had no recourse but to defend himself and the fat was in the fire. How could verse be free without being immoral? There is something to it. It is the same attack, with a more modern tilt to it, that undoubtedly bothers T. S. Eliot. He is one of the best informed of our writers and would do us a great service, if free verse—mold it as he will—is not his choice, to find us an alternative. From the evidence, he has tried to come up with just that, but up to the present writing he has not brought the thing off.

The case of Mr. Eliot is in this respect interesting. He began writing at Harvard from a thoroughly well-schooled background and produced a body of verse that was immediately so successful that when his poem *The Waste Land* was published, it drove practically everyone else from the field. Ezra Pound, who had helped him arrange the poem on the page, was confessedly jealous. Other American poets had to take second place. A new era, under domination of a return to a study of the classics, was gratefully acknowledged by the universities, and Mr. Eliot, not Mr. Pound, was ultimately given the Nobel Prize. The drift was plainly away from all that was native to America, Whitman among the rest, and toward the study of the past and England.

Though no one realized it, a violent revolution had taken place in American scholarship and the interests from which it stemmed. Eliot had completely lost interest in all things American, in the very ideology of all that America stood for, including the idea of freedom itself in any of its phases. Whitman as a symbol of indiscriminate freedom was completely antipathetic to Mr. Eliot, who now won the country away from him again. The tendency toward freedom in the verse forms, which seemed to be thriving among American poets, was definitely checked and the stage was taken over for other things. I shall never forget the impression created by *The Waste Land*. It was as if the bottom had dropped out of everything. I had not known how much the spirit of Whitman animated us until it was withdrawn from us. Free verse became overnight a thing of the past. Men went about congratulating themselves as upon the disappearance of something that had disturbed their dreams; and indeed it was so—the dreams of right-thinking students of English verse had long been disturbed by the appearance among them of the horrid specter of Whitman's free verse. Now it was as if a liberator, a Saint George, had come just in the nick of time to save them. The instructors in all the secondary schools were grateful.

Meanwhile, Mr. Eliot had become a British subject and removed himself to England where he took up residence. He became a member of the Church of England. He was determined to make the break with America complete, as his fellow artist Henry James had done before him, and began to publish such poems as *Ash Wednesday* and the play *Murder in the Cathedral*, and the *Four Quartets*. Something had happened to him, something drastic, something to do, doubtless, with man's duty and his freedom in the world. It is a far cry from this to Whitman's thought of man as a free agent. The pendulum had gone the full swing.

It is inevitable for us to connect the happenings in the world generally with what takes place in the poem. When Mr. Eliot quit writing, when he quit writing poems, it looked as if he had got to a point where he had nowhere else to turn, and as if in his despair he had given up not only the poem but the world. A man as clever and well informed as he was had the whole world at his feet, but the only conclusion that he reached was that he wanted none of it. Especially did he want none of the newer freedom.

Not that he didn't in his verse try it on, for size, let us say, in his later experiments, particularly in *Four Quartets*, but even there he soon came to the end of his rope. The accented strophe he had definitely given up, as Wagner in the prelude to *Parsifal* had done the same, but to infer from that fact that he had discovered the freedom of a new measure was not true. It looked to me, at least, as if there were some profound depth to his probing beyond which he dared not go without compromising his religious faith. He did not attempt it. It is useful to record the limits of his penetration and the point at which he gave up his attempts to penetrate further. Just how far shall we go in our search for freedom and, more importantly, how shall our efforts toward a greater freedom be conditioned in our verses? All these decisions, which must be reached in deciding what to do, have implications of general value in our lives.

The young men who are students of literature today in our universities do not believe in seeking within the literary forms, the lines, the foot, the way in which to expand their efforts to know the universe, as Whitman did, but are content to follow the theologians and Mr. Eliot. In that, they are children of the times; they risk nothing, for by risking an expanded freedom you are very likely to come a cropper. What, in the words of Hjalmar Ekdal in *The Wild Duck*, are you going to invent?

Men, offering their heads, have always come up with new proposals, and the world of events waits upon them, and who shall say whether it were better to close one's eyes or go forward like Galileo to the light or wait content in the darkness like the man in the next county? Whitman went forward to what to him seemed desirable, and so if we are to reject him entirely we must at least follow him at the start to find out what his discoveries were intended to signify and what not to signify.

Certainly, we are in our day through with such loose freedom as he employed in his verses in the blind belief that it was all going to come out right in the end. We know now that it is not. But are we, because of that, to give up freedom entirely? Merely to put down the lines as they happen to come into your head will not make a poem, and if, as happened more than once in Whitman's case, a poem result, who is going to tell what he has made? The man knew what he was doing, but he did not know all he was doing. Much still remains to discover, but that freedom in the conduct of the verses is desirable cannot be questioned.

There is a very moving picture of Whitman facing the breakers coming in on the New Jersey shore, when he heard the onomatopoeic waves talk to him direct in a Shakespearean language which might have been Lear himself talking to the storm. But it was not what it seemed; it was a new language, an unnamed language which Whitman could not identify or control.

For as the English had foreseen, this freedom of which there had been so much talk had to have limits somewhere. If not, it would lead you astray. That was the problem. And there was at about that time a whole generation of Englishmen, prominent among whom was Frank Harris, whom it did lead astray in moral grounds, just as there were Frenchmen at the time of the French Revolution who were led astray and are still being led astray under the difficult conditions that exist today. It is the reaction against such patterns of thought that moved Eliot and that part of the present generation which is not swallowed up by its fascination with the scene which draws them to Paris whenever they get the opportunity to go there. For in your search for freedom—which is desirable—you must stop somewhere, but where exactly shall you stop? Whitman could not say.

To propose that the answer to the problem should lie in the verse itself would have been to those times an impertinence—and the same would be the case even now. The Greeks had their Dionysia in the spring of the year, when morals could be forgotten, and then the control of life resumed its normal course. In other words, they departmentalized their lives, being of an orderly cast of mind, but we do not lend ourselves easily to such a solution. With us it is all or nothing, provided we are not caught at it. Either we give ourselves to a course of action or we do not give ourselves. Either we are to be free men or not free men—at least in theory. Whitman, like Tom Paine, recognized no limits and that got him into trouble.

But the waves on the Jersey shore still came tumbling in, quieting him as their secret escaped him, isolating him and leaving him lonesome—but possessed by the great mystery which won the world to his side. For he was unquestionably the child of the years. What was the wave that moved the dawning century also moved him and demanded his recognition, and it was not to be denied. All the discoveries and inventions which were to make the twentieth century exceed all others, for better or worse, were implicit in his work. He surpassed the ritualistic centuries which preceded him, just as Ehrlich and Koch and finally Einstein were to exceed Goethe. It was destined to be so, and the New World of which he was a part gave him birth. He had invented a new way of assaulting fate. "Make new!" was to him as it was to Pound much later an imperious command which completely controlled him.

If he was to enlarge his opportunity he needed room, in verse as in everything else. But there were to be no fundamental changes in the concepts that keep our lives going at an accepted pace and within normal limits. The line was still to be the line, quite in accord with the normal contours of our accepted verse forms. It is not so much that which brought Whitman's verse into question but the freedom with which he laid it on the page. There he had abandoned all sequence and all order. It was as if a tornado had struck.

A new order had hit the world, a relative order, a new measure with which no one was familiar. The thing that no one realized, and this includes Whitman himself, is that the native which they were dealing with was no longer English but a new language akin to the New World to which its nature accorded in subtle ways that they did not recognize. That made all the difference. And not only was it new to America— it was new to the world. There was to be a new measure applied to all things, for there was to be a new order operative in the world. But it has to be insisted on that it was not disorder. Whitman's verses seemed disorderly, but ran according to an unfamiliar and a difficult measure. It was an order which was essential to the new world, not only of the poem, but to the world of chemistry and physics. In this way, the man was more of a prophet than he knew. The full significance of his innovations in the verse patterns has not yet been fully disclosed.

The change in the entire aesthetic of American art as it began to differ not only from British but from all the art of the world up to this time was due to this tremendous change in measure, a relative measure, which he was the first to feel and to embody in his works. What he was leaving behind did not seem to oppress him, but it oppressed the others and rightly so.

It is time now to look at English and American verse at the time Whitman began to write, for only by so doing can we be led to discover what he did and the course that lay before him. He had many formidable rivals to face on his way to success. But his chief opponent was, as he well knew, the great and medieval Shakespeare. And if any confirmation of Shakespeare's sacrosanct position in the language is still sought it is easily to be obtained when anything is breathed mentioning some alteration in the verse forms which he distinguished by using them. He may be imitated as Christopher Fry imitates him, but to vary or depart from him is heresy. Taken from this viewpoint, the clinical sheets of Shakespeare as a writer are never much studied. That he was the greatest word-man that ever existed in the language or out of it is taken for granted but there the inquiry ends.

Shakespeare presented Whitman with a nut hard to crack. What to do with the English language? It was all the more of a problem since the elements of it could not be presented at all or even recognized to exist. As far as the English language was concerned, there was only to use it and to use it well according to the great tradition of the masters.

And indeed it was a magnificent tradition. At the beginning of the seventeenth century it had reached an apogee which it had, to a great extent, maintained to the present day and of which it was proud and jealous. But when Shakespeare wrote, the laurels were new and had so recently been attained and had come from such distinguished achievements that the world seemed to pause for breath. It was a sort of noon and called for a halt. The man himself seemed to feel it and during an entire lifetime did no more than develop to the full his talents. It was noon sure enough for him, and he had only to stretch out in the sun and expand his mood.

Unlike Whitman, he was or represented the culmination of a historic as well as literary past whose forms were just coming to a head after the great trials which were to leave their marks on the centuries. There had been Chaucer, but the language had come of age since then as had the country. Now America had been discovered and the world could not grow much larger. Further expansion, except in a limited degree, was unlikely, so that the poet was left free to develop his world of detail but was not called upon to extend it. More was not necessary than to find something to do and develop it for the entire span of a long life. But as always with the artist, selection was an important point in the development.

For instance, as his sonnets show, Shakespeare was an accomplished rhymer, but he gave it up early. The patches of heroic couplet which he wrote for the Players in *Hamlet* are among the best examples of that form. Yet his main reliance was on blank verse—though he did, on occasion, try his hand at a triple accent which he rejected without more than a thought. The demands of the age called for other things and he was, above everything else, a practical man.

Practicing for so long a time upon the iambic pentameter, he had the opportunity to develop himself prodigiously in it. Over the years he shows a technical advance, a certain impatience with restraint in his work which makes it loose and verges more toward the conformation of prose. There is a great difference between Shakespeare's earlier and later work, the latter being freer and more natural in tone.

A feeling for prose began to be felt all through his verse. But at his death the form began to lapse rapidly into the old restrictions. It got worse and worse with the years until all the Elizabethan tenor had been stripped away, or as Milton phrased it speaking of his illustrious predecessor:

> Sweetest Shakespeare, Nature's child,
> Warbled his native woodnotes wild.

With Milton came Cromwell and the English Revolution, and Shakespeare was forgotten, together with the secrets of his versification, just as Whitman today is likely to be forgotten and the example of his verses and all that refers to him.

The interest that drove Whitman on is the same one that drove Shakespeare at the end of his life in an attempt to enlarge the scope of written verse, to find more of expression in the forms of the language employed. But the consequences of such experimentation are always drastic and amount in the end to its suppression, which in the person of a supreme genius is not easy.

From what has been said thus far, you can see why it is impossible to imitate Shakespeare; he was part of a historic process which cannot repeat itself. All imitations of the forms of the past are meaningless, empty shells, which have merely the value of decorations. So that, if anything is now to be created, it must be in a new form. Whitman, if he was to do anything of moment, could not, no matter how much he may have bowed down to the master, imitate him. It would not have had any meaning at all. And his responsibility to the new language was such that he had no alternative but to do as it bade him.

Though he may not have known it, with Whitman the whole spirit of the age itself had been brought under attack. It was a blind stab which he could not identify any more than a child. How could he, no matter how acute his instincts were, have foreseen the discoveries in chemistry, in physics, in abnormal psychology, or even the invention of the telephone or the disclosure of our subterranean wealth in petroleum? He knew only, as did those who were disturbed by his free verse, that something had occurred to the normal structure of conventional aesthetic and that he could not accept it any longer. Therefore, he acted.

We have to acknowledge at once in seeking a meaning involving the complex concerns of the world that the philosophic, the aesthetic, and the mechanical are likely to stem in their development from the same root. One may be much in advance of the other in its discoveries, but in the end a great equalizing process is involved so that the discovery of the advance in the structure of the poetic line is equated by an advance in the conception of physical facts all along the line. Man has no choice in these matters; the only question is, will he recognize the changes that are taking place in time to make the proper use of them? And when time itself is conceived of as relative, no matter how abstruse that may sound, the constructions, the right constructions, cannot be accepted with a similar interpretation. It may take time to bring this about, but when a basic change has occurred in our underlying concern it brooks no interference in the way it will work itself out.

Whitman didn't know anything about this, nor does Mr. Eliot take it into his considerations nor Father Merton either, but if they had to construct a satisfactory poetic line it had and still has to be done according to this precept. For we have learned, if we have learned anything from the past, that the principles of physics are immutable. Best, if you do not approve of what writing has become, to follow in Mr. Eliot's footsteps.

For it is important to man's fate that these matters be—if anything is important to man's fate in this modern world. At least, you cannot retrace steps that have been taken in the past. And you don't know, you simply do not know, what may come of it. No more than Whitman knew what his struggle to free verse may have implied and may still imply for us no matter how, at the moment, the world may have forsaken him. The books are not closed even though the drift in the tide of our interest may at the moment be all the other way. It cannot so soon have reversed itself. Something is still pending, though the final shape of the thing has not yet crystallized. Perhaps that is the reason for the regression. There are too many profitable leads in other associated fields of the intelligence for us to draw back now.

Where have the leads which are *not* aesthetic tended to take us in the present country? By paying attention to detail and our telescopes and microscopes and the reinterpretations of their findings, we realize that man has long since broken from the confinement of the more rigid of his taboos. It is reasonable to suppose that he will in the future, in spite of certain setbacks, continue to follow the same course.

Man finds himself on the earth whether he likes it or not, with nowhere else to go. What then is to become of him? Obviously we can't stand still or we shall be destroyed. Then if there is no room for us on the outside we shall, in spite of ourselves, have to go *in*: into the cell, the atom, the poetic line, for our discoveries. We have to break the old apart to make room for ourselves, whatever may be our tragedy and however we may fear it. By making room within the line itself for his inventions, Whitman revealed himself to be a worthy and courageous man of his age and, to boot, a farseeing one.

Recent Criticism

DAVID S. REYNOLDS

To Heal a Nation†

In several senses, the first two editions of *Leaves of Grass*, published in 1855 and 1856, were poetic versions of the leading ideas of the two parties that dominated the North's political scene in these years, the Know-Nothings and the Republicans. Several of Whitman's central themes—extreme valuation of the common person, intense Americanism, a cleansing impulse—tie him to these parties.

Both the Know-Nothings and Republicans, besides being opposed to slavery, presented themselves as fresh, populist alternatives to previous parties, which were viewed as rotten to the core. They grew with amazing rapidity between 1854 and '56 partly because, with the disappearance of the Whig Party and the proslavery apostasy of the Democrats, they advertised a fresh beginning, a new world of political purity in a time of overriding ugliness and corruption. As Alexander H. Stephens, who moved, like Whitman, out of the Democratic Party into the Republican, wrote at the end of 1854: "Old parties, old names, old issues, and old organizations are passing away. A day of new things, new issues, new leaders, and new organizations is at hand."[1] Whitman caught the spirit of the time when he wrote in the first paragraph of the 1855 preface that America "has passed into the new life of the new forms."

The old party leaders, insisted the Know-Nothings and Republicans, were grotesque representatives of a party system that had grown corrupt and detached from the people. Below the corruption of America's rulers lay the genuineness of average Americans whose values should be the basis of political action. One Know-Nothing typically called for a leader who was "fresh from the loins of the people." The two Republican presidential nominees of the fifties—the hardy explorer John Frémont and the Illinois rail-splitter Abraham Lincoln—epitomized this populist, antiparty impulse. In the 1856 race Frémont was pushed as "a new man, fresh from the people and one of themselves." Among

---

† From *Walt Whitman's America* (New York: Alfred A. Knopf, 1995), 148–53. Copyright © 1995 by David S. Reynolds. Reprinted by permission of Alfred A. Knopf, a Division of Random House, Inc.
1. William E. Gienapp, *Origins of the Republican Party* (New York: Oxford University Press, 1986), p. 167.

his supporters was Whitman, whose whole family abandoned the Democrats and turned Republican.

Whitman shared the new populist impulse. He had once been snobbish, as witnessed by his snide aspersions of the simple Woodbury villagers in his 1840 letters to Abraham Leech. His sympathy for the masses had increased between 1846 and '48 with the rise of the Free-Soil movement, when the territorial dispute led him to praise publicly American working people whose values he suddenly championed. But he had then still been very much within the framework of the party hierarchy, and he retained an almost sheepish veneration of the presidency and the party leadership. With the corruption and political collapse of the fifties, however, his veneration for entrenched rulers disappeared and his respect for common people increased exponentially.

He espoused a dialectical mode of thinking that was new to him, one that lay behind the parties of the midfifties, involving fierce rejection of entrenched authority coupled with equally intense praise of simple artisan values. In his notebook he wrote: "I know that underneath all this putridity of Presidents and Congressmen that has risen to the top, lie pure waters a thousand fathoms deep." Eric Foner has shown that the Republican Party rose to prominence in large part because of its appeal to the ideology of free labor, epitomized in average workers such as independent shopkeepers, farmers, and artisans of all kinds, whose values were posed as preferable to those of exploitative moguls and politicians. Whitman shared this outlook.[2] His tract "The Eighteenth Presidency!" follows the Republican dialectic. In it he unsparingly attacks the powers that be and sings praise to "the true people, . . . mechanics, farmers, boatmen, manufacturers, and the like." He hopes some "healthy-bodied, middle-aged, beard-faced American blacksmith or boatman" will "come down from the West across the Alleghanies, and walk into the Presidency."

A similar dialectic runs through the early editions of *Leaves of Grass*. In 1847 he had written in the *Eagle* that the presidency was the most sublime office on earth. Now his attitude was exactly reversed. The people, he stressed in the 1855 preface, should not take off their hats to presidents: it should be the other way around. The president would no longer be the people's referee: now the poet would be. The genius of the United States, he wrote, was not in presidents or legislatures but "always most in their common people," as it was better to be a poor free mechanic or farmer than "a bound booby and rogue in office." His early poems are full of long catalogs of average people at work. The party collapse and the devaluation of authority figures, in other words, had fueled his ardent populism, just as it had helped give rise to the new party organizations.

He also shared with the new parties an intense Americanism that tended toward jingoism. It has often been thought that his nationalistic

2. See Eric Foner, *Free Soil, Free Labor, Free Men: The Ideology of the Republican Party before the Civil War* (New York: Oxford University Press, 1970).

instinct derived from the Young America movement or from Emerson. But by the early fifties the Young America movement had turned sour. Its intense Americanism, which had in the early forties engendered literary nationalism, had been swept up in the politics of expansionism, which by the fifties was allied with the proslavery forces. Two great champions of Young America, John L. O'Sullivan and Stephen Douglas, had by the fifties become defenders of the South. The organ of Young America, the *Democratic Review*, which had published several of Whitman's early stories, ceased publication in 1852. As for Emerson, it is likely that he directly influenced the nationalistic stance of Whitman's poetry, despite Whitman's later denials. It is important to note, however, that at the only two *documented* moments of Whitman's awareness of Emerson—in 1842 and 1847—the Concord sage had no fertilizing effect on his imagination. It was only after Whitman had escaped the shackles of party and had experienced the political crisis of the fifties that he gave literary form to the Americanism Emerson represented. The timing of Whitman's intense nationalism coincided exactly with the dominance of that most nationalistic of all political movements, the Know-Nothings.

After the collapse of the Whig Party in early 1854, the strongly pro-American Know-Nothings suddenly became the most powerful new party in the nation. The Know-Nothings (probably so named because they started as a secret order whose members professed ignorance of it) tapped into long-smoldering nativist sentiment in the North. As a result of developments abroad, especially the Irish potato famine, immigrants were arriving in America at a pace never known before or since. Between 1845 and 1855, 3 million foreigners swarmed to America's shores, peaking in 1854, when 427,833 arrived. This was the largest proportionate increase in immigrants at any time in American history. The large majority were Roman Catholic. The Know-Nothings responded to a deep-seated fear that Catholic foreigners would infiltrate American institutions and possibly even take over the government. Since many foreigners, particularly the Irish, supported slavery, the Know-Nothings appealed to antislavery activists. They also incorporated defenders of the working class.

Above all, they were the party of intense, unabashed Americanism. "America for Americans" was their motto, the Star-Spangled Banner was their emblem, and in 1855 "American Party" became their public name. Their success in the Northern elections of 1854 and '55 was stunning. They elected eight governors, more than a hundred congressmen, mayors in three major cities, and thousands of other local officials. Their height of popularity was reached in June 1855, the month before *Leaves of Grass* appeared, with their number at about 1.5 million members.

Whitman later recalled that the Know-Nothings were "the great party of those days." Although he said he did not join the organization (but then, what Know-Nothing would say?), he had a history of flirtation with nativism. In 1842 he had come out strongly against Bishop John Hughes on the issue of public funding for Catholic schools, an issue that came back with redoubled fury in the fifties and fueled the Know-Nothing debate. The politician in the 1850s he most admired, John P. Hale, was an ardent nativist. Since the Know-Nothings in 1854 and early '55 were championing his favorite causes—antislavery, temperance, and rights for working people—he may have found the American Party appealing.

At any rate, the jingoistic moments in his early poetry smacked of nativism. In one poem he wrote, "America isolated I sing; / I say that works here made in the spirit of other lands, are so much poison to these States," adding, "Bards for my own land only I invoke." In the first two editions, at the peak of the nativist frenzy, he identified himself in his signature poem as "Walt Whitman, an American"—changed later, in less nativist times, to "Walt Whitman, of Manhattan the son." Trying to appeal to the nativist readership, he began a self-review of his poetry by boasting, "An American bard at last!" redoubling the boast in another self-review: "No imitation—No foreigner—but a growth and idiom of America."

If he was a nativist, though, he was one with a difference. His first woman reviewer, Fanny Fern, saw this when she called him "this glorious Native American" but specified that he was "no Catholic-baiting Know Nothing." On the one hand, he did adopt some of the attitudes of the Know-Nothings, to the extent that he would once say that America's digestion was strained by the "millions of ignorant foreigners" coming to its shores. Sketching plans for a lecture to be given to a Protestant group, he sounded like a Know-Nothing when he wrote that Catholics were sufficiently numerous to put all American enterprises in their grasp. He warned, "Beware of churches! beware of priests!" and wondered what America had to do with "all this mummery of prayer and rituals."

On the other hand, as was true with his attitude toward antislavery groups, he wanted to avoid extremes and in fact extended a friendly hand to foreigners in his poetry. In "Song of Myself" he announced himself "Pleas'd with the native and pleas'd with the foreign." In another poem he wrote, "See, in my poems immigrants continually coming and landing." His claim elsewhere that his poetry does not separate "the white from the black, or the native from the immigrant just landed at the wharf" in fact has validity, as is evidenced particularly by his poetic paean to international friendship, "Salut au Monde!" The American Party, while it stimulated his nationalism, became one more narrow political group he rejected. It made him wish to wrest the word "American" from partial definitions and seek the largest possible applications for the term.

Time would tell he had good reason to do so. The American Party rapidly fell prey to the same kind of sectional divisions that had killed off the Whigs. The ascendant Republicans, meanwhile, spent more energy attacking the Southern slavocracy than on representing the interests of Northern workers. Both the problems and the proposed solutions of the parties were addressed to specific, practical needs of the moment.

For Whitman, American's problem was far deeper than the immigrant explosion or the Southern slave power. Corruption in America was not superficial or easily removed. It was, he wrote, "in the blood." His disgust with the political process was more profound than that of any other commentator of the fifties. He wrote that the parties had become "empty flesh, putrid mouths, mumbling and squeaking the tones of these conventions, the politicians standing back in the shadow, telling lies." Those responsible for selecting America's leaders came "from political hearses, and from the coffins inside, and from the shrouds inside the coffins; from the tumors and abscesses of the land; from the skeletons and skulls in the vaults of the federal almshouses; from the running sores of the great cities."

The final effect of the dramatic political changes of the fifties was to drive him beyond parties altogether. In his 1856 notebook the former party loyalist could proclaim himself "no[t] the particular representative of any one party—no tied and ticketed democrat, whig, abolitionist, republican,—no bawling spokesman of natives against foreigners."

The history of parties and reforms had shown him that the former led to institutionalized corruption, the latter to narrow views and sometimes wild fanaticism. He now reminded himself, "We want no *reforms*, no *institutions*, no *parties*—We want a *living principle* as nature has, under which nothing can go wrong—This must be vital through the United States." He had once believed the American system would perpetually purify itself through party debates and periodic elections. But with the party system having collapsed in a morass of bad principle and outright knavery, he had to look elsewhere for purification and ennoblement.

If the political and social crises represented the grim aspects of American life, there were other cultural arenas that offered hope and restoration. Even as he had lost confidence in politics as usual, he had been surveying more positive, fruitful areas of cultural life. His omnivorous imagination profited from recent developments in popular performance, science, literature, sexual discourse, and the visual arts —all of which, along with freshly fashioned nature imagery, could remind Americans of the extraordinary potential of their nation.

In 1855 Whitman believed that the United States, cut adrift from its original ideals, desperately needed poets. He was confident too that America's veins were full of poetical stuff.

KAREN SANCHEZ-EPPLER

To Stand Between: Walt Whitman's Poetics of Merger and Embodiment†

* * *

At that moment in his early notebook jottings when Whitman first assumes his new voice and verse form, he defines what it means to be a poet, and specifically to be the poet of the body, in terms provided by American slavery. Claiming to reconcile racially distinct bodies, Whitman locates the poet in the sexually charged middle space between masters and slaves:

> I am the poet of slaves and of the masters of slaves
> I am the poet of the body
> And I am
>
> I am the poet of the body
> And I am the poet of the soul
> I go with the slaves of the earth equally with the masters
> And I will stand between the masters and the slaves
> Entering into both so that both shall understand me alike.[1]

Only two of these lines are actually preserved in *Leaves of Grass*: "I am the poet of the body, / And I am the poet of the soul" introduces the twenty-first section of the poem Whitman ultimately called "Song of Myself," offering a self-defining summation that has informed most subsequent readings of Whitman's poetics.[2] Slavery is not mentioned in any published version of section 21; it has disappeared, leaving the pairing of body and soul as its only trace. A sense of the political import of Whitman's poetics of embodiment is similarly absent from most critical assessments of his work. Yet in these notebook lines Whitman depicts his strategy of singing the body as a practice derived from the dynamics of American slavery. My discussion of Whitman's poetics reassesses the political sources and implications of his corporeal poetry, demonstrating that his celebration of the body not only reinterprets the body but also uses that reinterpretation to redefine the political. Even Whitman's effacement of the political origins of his poetics, as in his deletion of master and slave from these lines, ultimately serves not to dismiss the political in favor of the personal and bodily, but rather to absorb each into the other, to demonstrate that the same issues that inform political practice also designate individual identity.

In locating the poet between master and slave, and between body

---

† From *Touching Liberty: Abolition, Feminism, and the Politics of the Body* (Berkeley: University of California Press, 1993), 50–57. Copyright © 1993 by Karen Sanchez-Eppler. Reprinted by permission of the University of California Press. The author's notes have been edited.

1. *Collected Writings of Walt Whitman: Notebooks and Unpublished Prose Manuscripts*, ed. Edward F. Grier (New York: New York University Press, 1984), vol. I, p. 67.
2. *Walt Whitman's Leaves of Grass: The First (1855) Edition*, ed. Malcolm Cowley (New York: Penguin, 1986), lines 422–23.

and soul, Whitman attempts to claim for his poetry the power to mediate oppositions. Able to speak for both sides, the poet alone seems capable of overcoming both the difference between slave and master that divides American society and the division between body and soul that makes the identity of each individual problematic. Moreover, in locating the poet between these two concerns, Whitman proposes to equate political questions with the question of the body, and hence to relate the structure of social practices to the structure of personal identity. What I call Whitman's poetics of merger and embodiment refers, then, both to his poetic goal of healing radical divisions, social and personal, and to the poetic strategies by which he attempts to effect that goal.

Merger and embodiment are linked strategies in this poetics: merger, the perfect melding of opposites into a complete undifferentiated oneness, is best exemplified for Whitman in the physical imagery of the sexual embrace. What Whitman seeks in his poetry is simultaneously to express the particularity of bodily experience—he frequently compares his poetry to the human body—and to promote the healing sameness of merger. The practice of miscegenation or racial amalgamation associated with plantation slavery thus provides within Whitman's writings an historically resonant vocabulary with which to examine his poetics: in the scene of miscegenation racially distinct bodies merge. Presenting the poet as standing between master and slave, body and soul, the political and the personal, the ideals of merger and of bodily specificity, Whitman asserts the power of poetry, but such a presentation also inadvertently reveals the limitations of that power, the ways in which such poetry must remain contingent upon the very divisions it claims to heal.

Whitman's first notebook poetry records his developing sense of what it means to call himself "poet." The lines begin with a feat of autogenesis: "I am the poet," he writes, in a triumph of essentialism, a gesture of autonomous identity and agency. No sooner is this self-assured assertion of being made, however, than it is undermined. The "of" that relates the poet to his topic also appears as the tie between master and slave. Here Whitman recognizes that to assume the name of poet is to assume mastery and possession, but, as he further demonstrates, the line also weakens all claims to autonomy, for the slave comes first, identifying and so delimiting what it means to be master: after all, to be the "master of slaves" is a lesser, more circumscribed claim than that of being "master." The relation signaled by "of" remains simultaneously possessive and partitive: does the topic belong to the poet or is the poet part of his topic?

In identifying himself as the poet of the body in the subsequent line, Whitman might appear to evade these problems, since the topic of the body seems to replace the dynamics of possession and mastery with one of identity. I would argue, however, that these lines ought to be read as apposites, and that in defining himself as both the poet of slavery and the poet of the body Whitman points to the interdependence of these two concerns. The question of mastery and the question of identity are ultimately the same question. * * *[T]he practices of American slavery call attention to the ways in which the condition and status of one's body designate identity. Whitman shared this insight, asserting in "Crossing Brooklyn Ferry" that "I too have received identity by my body" (l. 63); thus Whitman's focus on the body repeats rather than escapes the failure of autonomy and the strictures of mastery with which these lines began. Whitman gives up here, breaking off the next line, inscribing only a beginning that trails away into blankness; in its incompleteness, "And I am" pathetically echoes Jehovah's own self-identifying tautology: I am what I am.

Whitman drew a slash across this verse, left a few lines of blank space on the page, and began again. The second version reverses the sequence so that now the pairing of body and soul introduces that of slave and master: the very ease of the reversal emphasizes Whitman's sense of these pairs as fundamentally the same. The third line originally read "Thus the slaves are mine and the masters are equally mine," making explicit the identification of poetry with mastery and the reliance of both on a notion of ownership. In the canceled line the poet stands as ultimate master, claiming ownership of all that the masters have, and beyond that, of the masters themselves. Here the equality of master and slave lies in their being "equally" possessed. Whitman's revision displaces the identification of poet with master, providing in its stead a concept of the poet as companion "go[ing] . . . equally with" slave and master. In making this change Whitman redefines the role of the poet: he replaces an essentialist conception of the self-created poet with the anti-essentialist insight that poetic power results from occupying a specific relational position. The "I" who "will stand between" gains the ability to be "understood," and so takes the name of poet, by occupying the place of linkage between the opposing but interdependent roles of master and slave. That the desire to be under*stood* punningly recapitulates the hierarchic standing of master and slave suggests the precariousness, if not the impossibility, of Whitman's poetic goal.

Whitman's first notebook poetry thus charts the development of his conception of the poet from an autonomous, self-made being to a site of mediation. In this latter view the poet is simply what stands between. If the poet articulates body and soul, master and slave, these terms and relations similarly constitute the place and role of the poet. In these early lines Whitman does more than merely stake out a topic. Rather, by identifying the poet as mediator, he traces the ways in which the oppositional nature of his subject matter defines his poetic voice.[3] So later, in *Leaves of Grass*, Whitman identifies miscegenation

3. Allen Grossman says of these lines (and of Whitman's early formal experiments in "Resurgemus," "Blood-Money," and "Wounded in the House of Friends") that "the 'open' line as formal principle appears simultaneously with the subject of liberation and is the enabling condition of the appearance of that subject" ("The Poetics of Union in Whitman and Lincoln," in *The American Renaissance Reconsidered*, ed. Walter Benn Michaels and Donald E. Pease [Baltimore, MD: Johns Hopkins University Press, 1985], 192). [See pp. 872–89 in this volume.] Although my analysis is deeply indebted to Grossman's insights, I wish to stress the difference between our readings: my focus on Whitman's identification of the role of the poet with that of the mediator lays the basis for a quite different conception of Whitman's poetics and produces a more reciprocal understanding of the relation between the form and subject of these lines than that Grossman describes.

—the erotic merger of racially distinct bodies—as a model for poetic power, even as this new voice makes the uttering of such topics possible.

"I Sing the Body Electric" comprises Whitman's most insistent demonstration of his ideal of poetic embodiment, that the supple, flexing body of the "wellmade man," "conveys as much as the best poem . . . perhaps more" (l. 11). His claim that the wellmade body and the best poem are equally expressive suggests that flesh and words can serve as substitutes for each other. The programmatic aim of this poem is to collapse the two meanings of *convey*: to present what is carried by the body and what can be communicated by words as the same. Significantly, Whitman fashions this "Poem of the Body," as it was perhaps more appropriately entitled in 1856, out of the least celebratory, most exploitative of discourses on the body: the chant of the auctioneer hawking slaves.

> A slave at auction!
> I help the auctioneer, . . . the sloven does not half know his
>   business.
>
> Gentlemen look on this curious creature,
> Whatever the bids of the bidders they cannot be high enough
>   for him,
> For him the globe lay preparing quintillions of years without one
>   animal or plant,
> For him the revolving cycles truly and steadily rolled.
>   (ll. 83–87)

Like the poet, the auctioneer stands between slave and master, product and buyer; the business of both is to sing the value of the thing at hand and to extract the assent of purchase from their audience. In usurping the place of the auctioneer, Whitman is, of course, criticizing his office, demonstrating that even the hyperbole of the auctioneer's pitch grossly understates the value of the item on the block: the human body, he opines, is hardly paid for by all time and the entire world. But he is also inadvertently demonstrating the uneasy parallels between his poetics and the practices of American slavery, the ways in which the act of celebrating a body resembles the act of selling one so that his task as poet corresponds to that of the auctioneer. The parallels prove even closer, for Whitman's concept of embodiment is delimited by the body of the slave.

On the auction block, regardless of any other claims to identity a slave might express, he or she is nothing but body, flesh for sale. The slave at auction provides the quintessential instance of what it means for one's identity to be entirely dependent upon one's body. Though many other human bodies are celebrated in this poem, and throughout Whitman's poetry, to a significant degree Whitman's fundamental image of the body remains that of the slave: one central example of the completely corporeal person. The description of the negro driver in "Song of Myself" suggestively matches in the details of dress and posture the drawing of Whitman that replaces his name on the title page of the 1855 *Leaves of Grass*.

> The negro that drives the huge dray of the stoneyard. . . . steady
>   and tall he stands poised on one leg on the stringpiece,
> His blue shirt exposes his ample neck and breast and loosens over
>   his hipband,
> His glance is calm and commanding. . . . he tosses the slouch of
>   his hat away from his forehead,
> The sun falls on his crispy hair and moustache. . . . falls on the
>   black of his polish'd and perfect limbs.
>
> (ll. 220–23)

Whitman's placement of the drawing, as has often been argued, privileges flesh, or at least the image of flesh, over name or word as a pointer to identity. It is the first instance of the book's complex and self-conscious strategies of self-incarnation: "Whoever touches this book touches a man." The substitution of a portrait for his name, and the similarities between that portrait and his description of a black man indicate comparable efforts on Whitman's part to assert the corporeality of his own identity.

To argue that in Whitman's poems the challenge of bodiliness gains its absoluteness and urgency from even an indirect comparison of the black salable body of the slave and his own is, however, to tell only half the story. Whitman proposes to unify a discordant America by creating a poetry that would reconcile bodily differences. The intense bodiliness of the slave at auction thus simultaneously initiates Whitman's poetic project and poses the major obstacle to its achievement. The auction block initiates Whitman's poetic project by staging his attempt to negotiate the space between master and slave. It poses the major obstacle to the achievement of this project of poetic reconciliation because, though Whitman insists on the materiality of all being, and particularly of our sense of otherness, he can find no way to heal these divisions that does not dissolve the bodies out of which his poetry is made. Despite his exuberant rhetoric of celebration, despite his insistence that in singing the body this poem overcomes all bodily differences, the costs and contradictions inherent in his double goals of merger and embodiment remain visible. So, as auctioneer in "I Sing the Body Electric," Whitman gradually strips away the slave's skin, dismembering the body in the act of celebrating it, until all that is left is eternal and ubiquitous blood.

> Examine these limbs, red black or white. . . . they are very cunning
>   in tendon and nerve;
> They shall be stript that you may see them.
>
> Exquisite senses, lifelit eyes, pluck, volition,
> Flakes of breastmuscle, pliant backbone and neck, flesh not
>   flabby, goodsized arms and legs,
> And wonders within there yet.

Within there runs his blood. . . . the same old blood. . the same
   red running blood;

(ll. 91–96)

Here Whitman evokes blood as a physical equalizer: something of
the body that is, nevertheless, not implicated in the bodily differences
of skin "red, black or white." In asking us to imagine this blood as
distinct from the bodies that contained it, Whitman nevertheless in-
sists that it serve as a metonym for those bodies, recalling them even
as it would replace them. The refrain of blood promises to function as
refrains usually do, to promote the comfort of repetitive, nostalgic
sameness. Yet Whitman's reliance on blood in his effort to merge the
body of the slave into a generalized humanity is, to say the least, dis-
turbing. From the auction block an appeal to blood too easily recalls
the bloody backs of whipped slaves. In the lore of plantation slavery,
as in all racist discourses, blood is precisely where race dwells, and
the genealogy and value of light-skinned slaves is traditionally mea-
sured in drops of black and white blood.[4] Whitman's poetics of merger
and his poetics of embodiment both initiate and contradict each other.
For just as Whitman's celebration of the body results in pulling apart
the slave's flesh to facilitate the merger of the slave's notoriously dif-
ferent body into a vision of human sameness, Whitman's chorus of
merger and inclusion repeats the bloody, physical differentiations of
plantation life.

MICHAEL MOON

The Twenty-Ninth Bather: Identity, Fluidity, Gender, and Sexuality in Section 11 of "Song of Myself"[†]

Few readers would deny that Leaves of Grass in general, and "Song of
Myself" in particular, are, in some ways, difficult texts. Some of the
most celebrated passages in the latter text—e.g., section 5, in which
"the soul" and "the body" are said to enter into some kind of ecstatic
union with each other; or section 11, in which a young woman peeks
out of the window of her house at a party of male bathers, and also,
somehow, seems to join them at play in the water—have elicited nu-
merous, and often conflicting, critical responses. I want to examine
section 11 of "Song of Myself" closely, and to explore its representa-
tions of gender and sexuality, and of touching and writing, on the one

---

4. See Whitman's own description of the creole Margaret in his early novel Franklin Evans
(1842), in Collected Writings of Walt Whitman: The Early Poems and the Fiction (New York:
New York University Press, 1963).
† A version of this essay appeared in Disseminating Whitman: Revision and Corporeality in
"Leaves of Grass" (Cambridge, Mass: Harvard University Press, 1991), 36–47. Copyright ©
1991 by the President and Fellows of Harvard College. Reprinted by permission of Harvard
University Press.

hand, and what one might call the complex fluidity of identity, on the other. In doing so, I shall be especially interested in the question of how Whitman extends the means of representing the "flow" of identification and contact (such as that between a woman and a group of men, between clothed bodies and naked ones, or between visible actants and invisible agents, and so on) that energize and compel much of his most powerful poetry.

The first (1855) edition of *Leaves of Grass* seems in some ways even more difficult than the subsequent editions of the book because in the first version the author provides so few of the conventional demarcations on which readers depend in order to construe the relative status of the parts of a text, such as titles, stanza breaks, and rhyme schemes. The so-called 1855 "Preface" actually appears without a title, as do the poems that follow, the first six of which are headed "Leaves of Grass." Of the latter six, the four which do not commence at the top of a page are headed only with double rules. (Whitman thus enacts in literature Paine's pronouncement on the repudiation of aristocratic labels in the new republics of his time: "The . . . Constitution says *there shall be no titles.*") The long lines of the 1855 text run on down its long pages almost unbroken, and the pages in turn proliferate almost without any suggestion as to how the reader is supposed to organize them. The *mise en page* of the 1855 *Leaves* is the volume's most striking manifestation of its program of aggressively drawing the reader into "contact" with the author (by forcing the reader to "cut into" the text without many directives as to where it may lead).

In these "complications" of the text, I believe, one can readily detect the kind of difficulty Annabel Patterson has identified as an unmistakable "sign of the hermeneutics of censorship" at work in a text. Patterson points out "the social uses of indeterminacy": it allows writers to develop practices which exploit the ungroundable quality of language in order to allow them to treat proscribed subjects with relative impunity. Such a practice is readily apparent in those passages in Whitman in which the ungrounded condition of the text's language permits him to treat censorable material in "permissible," because indeterminable, language.[1] * * *

The indeterminacies of the 1855 *Leaves of Grass* also serve the purpose of rendering the text and the dispositions of the body which it represents fluid. Rather than presenting a single liminal decor or "atmosphere" in which the culture's oppressive codes of embodiment may be liquidated, the first several editions of *Leaves of Grass*, while continuing to extend the project of evoking the (male) body "literally," also produce a whole repertory of the kinds of liminal "flows" I have described.

Section 11 is perhaps most obviously consonant with the terms that I have argued are paradigmatic ones for the first edition of *Leaves of Grass*: the "fluidity," substitutability, and indeterminacy of masculine

---

1. *Censorship and Interpretation: The Conditions of Writing and Reading in Early Modern England* (Madison: University of Wisconsin Press, 1984), p. 243.

identity and sexuality. This passage is the eighteen-line one from the 1855 *Leaves of Grass* which later became section 11 of "Song of Myself":

Twenty-eight young men bathe by the shore,
Twenty-eight young men, and all so friendly,
Twenty-eight years of womanly life, and all so lonesome.

She owns the fine house by the rise of the bank,
She hides handsome and richly drest aft the blinds of the
window.

Which of the young men does she like the best?
Ah the homeliest of them is beautiful to her.

Where are you off to, lady? for I see you,
You splash in the water there, yet stay stock still in your room.

Dancing and laughing along the beach came the twenty-ninth
bather,
The rest did not see her, but she saw them and loved them.

The beards of the young men glistened with wet, it ran from
their long hair,
Little streams passed all over their bodies.

An unseen hand also passed over their bodies,
It descended tremblingly from their temples and ribs.

The young men float on their backs, their white bellies swell to
the sun. . . . they do not ask who seizes fast to them,
They do not know who puffs and declines with pendant and
bending arch,
They do not think whom they souse with spray.

The action of the passage serves to bring the excluded figure through the window and incorporate her into the "fluid" circle. Male and female are placed in strong and direct appositional relationship from its opening lines: "Twenty-eight young men . . . / . . . and all so friendly, / Twenty-eight years of womanly life, and all so lonesome." Here, at least to begin with, masculinity bears a positive affective charge ("so friendly") and femininity a negative one ("so lonesome"). Moreover, insofar as they are both "twenty-eight," the large group of young men is made not only numerically parallel but also in some sense equivalent with the solitary woman and her life.

In the poetic passage, economic and class difference are aligned with gender difference. The young men are said to "bathe," but the woman to "own[ ]" and "hide[ ]," a contrast which suggests that while male homosociality can be untrammeled by economic constraints, bourgeois female domesticity ("She owns the fine house by the rise of the bank, / She hides handsome and richly drest . . .") is at least as much a privation as it is a privilege. Another way of putting this would be to say that while what the young men are represented as having they hold in common (each other, "twenty-eight young men . . . all so friendly"), what the woman is represented as having is private property, "fine" and "rich[ ]," but in some fundamental sense disjunct from herself ("Twenty-eight years of womanly life, and all so lonesome").

The passage makes two things clear about the "lonesome" woman's "fine house" and "rich[ ]" clothes: they are compensatory substitutes for her for what the twenty-eight young men possess in one another, and they are inadequate ones. What she proves to "have going for her," so to speak, is not her wealth or even her good looks (she is not said simply to be "handsome," after all, but to "hide[ ] handsome . . . aft the blinds of the window"), but the restless and frustrated desire she shares with Whitman's ideal readers as he describes them in the note to the 1876 Preface. Like them, she is subject to a "terrible, irrepressible yearning, (surely more or less down underneath in most human souls)," and it is this lack, rather than her wealth, that Whitman conceives of as impelling and empowering her to desire to plunge into the "endless streams of living, pulsating love and friendship" which *Leaves of Grass* was designed "to arouse and set flowing in men's and women's hearts."

In representing her wish to do so, the text releases this rich "lady" ("Where are you off to, lady?") from the constraints of gender and class which have hitherto relegated her to "[t]wenty-eight years of womanly [which in this text, at least to begin with, is to say "lonesome"] life." In the poem's liminal space, she can have her "fine house" to "hide" in, but also fly out of it, "Dancing and laughing," at the same time: "You splash in the water there, yet stay stock still in your room."

The speaker of the passage could be said to emerge from his strictly narrative role at this point, as he claims to see the "lady" not only maintaining her hidden position as she stands "handsome and richly drest aft the blinds of the window," but also (invisibly) passing out onto the beach and into the water to join the twenty-eight young men already disporting themselves there. However, it is also the case that the speaker's emergence into a more active role in the passage is set up perhaps as early as its opening lines, where the repetition of the words "Twenty-eight . . . / . . . and all so" to describe two very different entities and situations, the young men bathing and the woman watching them, may make the reader want to inquire of the speaker how these two entities can be said to be parallel.

The speaker in the passage assumes powers, derived from the watching-and-desiring position of the young woman, which include not only his phantasmatic powers of passing unseen among the twenty-eight bathers and touching their bodies at will but also the power to write about these pleasures. In a reading which *only* sees the male speaker appropriating the position of the female voyeur, Robert K. Martin reads the last three lines of this passage, where "[t]he young men float on their backs, their white bellies swell[ing] to the sun," as representing actual "*physical* intimacies," between them and the speaker, who "puffs and declines" over their bodies with "pendant and bending arch" until "they souse [him] with spray" (that is, they are fellated by him).[2] Whitman might have opposed such a literally "sex-ual" reading of these lines, not so much because such a reading would be inaccurate or irrelevant as because limiting the determinate grounds for the exchanges which are represented in a passage like this one to specifically sexual ones is inevitably to produce a hermeneutic dead-end in a text which was designed to retain its fluidity and mobility of meaning(s). Various kinds of male-homosexual desires and inter-actions *are* being represented here, as they are elsewhere in Whitman's writing, and it is important to recognize them as such. But there are also other kinds of highly significant factors represented as being at work in this passage, such as economies of gender (male versus fe-male), age (young versus mature), general sexual epistemology (ac-knowledgment and acceptance of oneself as sexual subject and/or object versus refusal or rejection of such knowledge and acceptance), and socioeconomic class (a "life-style" of private bourgeois acquisitive-ness versus one grounded in more egalitarian and communitarian kinds of pleasure-taking).

Rather than attempting to ground the exchanges transacted in the course of the passage unequivocally in a single sub-vocabulary, such as that of the repertory of male-homosexual acts, one might do better to attend to the often peculiar terms in which these exchanges are conducted in Whitman's writing. Male-homosexual acts are, after all, a set of behaviors which is itself not stable or closed, since most of these acts (for example, fellatio, anal intercourse) are practiced by het-erosexuals as well—although I would not overlook the difference that homosexuals acts are symmetrically reversible in ways that correspond-ing heterosexual acts are not. In the passage in question, for example, the crucial exchange effected may well be not the final one (whatever it is) between the speaker and the young men, but that between the speaker and the young woman. The nature of the exchange that takes place midway in the passage might be interpreted as the speaker's appropriation of the woman's position for his own. Leaving her stand-ing at her window, he passes from one of its sides to the other on the energy of her desire, as it were. To pursue this interpretive line, one might argue that the feminine position invoked and described in the first half of the passage disappears halfway through it, or, rather, that the woman is dislocated from her position and replaced by the (male) speaker. It would then be the (male) speaker who assumes the privilege of becoming the "twenty-ninth bather"; in a grammatically transvestite moment halfway through the passage ("Dancing and laughing along the beach came the twenty-ninth bather, / The rest did not see her, but she saw them and loved them"), he would briefly but consequen-tially pass through feminine identity. Then, according to this reading, as feminine identity and feminine pronouns disappear altogether from the passage, the figure of the rich and lonely woman would vanish

2. Robert K. Martin, *The Homosexual Tradition in American Poetry* (Austin: University of Texas Press, 1979), p. 21.

after having served as springboard for the speaker's remarkable flight.

Rather than interpreting the passage as necessarily involving the exclusion of the young woman and the femininity she represents at its midway point, I want to argue that it would be more appropriate, in view of the significant role the female figure occupies in the first half of this section, to interpret her as being incorporated into the passage at its crucial midpoint and for the rest of the section *as* a feminine figure (and as a figure of femininity), and not merely as a transvestite "cover" or mask for the (male) speaker's prohibited and/or unspeakable desire for the male bathers he "spies" through the window. The speaker (in the interpretation I am arguing for) passes through the window and across the space between into the water with the twenty-eight bathers *along with* the young woman (both of them alike empowered by her desire), without necessarily ceasing to identify himself with her. Having merged with the young woman (but without necessarily having merged *her* into himself), the speaker (now in his merged state with the young woman neither determinately male nor female) extends his/her identification farther, partly with the young men and partly with the fluid medium in which they are immersed and enjoying themselves: the "wet" which "[runs] from their long hair" and "over their bodies" is represented as being homologous with the "unseen hand [which] also passe[s] over their bodies."

* * * Whitman in the twenty-eight-bathers episode of the 1855 text definitively inverts the two canonical bathing scenes in the Bible—David watching Bathsheba (2 Samuel II) and Susannah and the Elders (Apochrypha). These narratives were doubtless burdened for readers in his culture with several kinds of oppressive patriarchal significances, such as (from the point of view of the figures of Bathsheba and Susannah) women's being made the unwitting and/or unwilling objects of male voyeurism as well as other forms of male power, and (from the point of view of David and the Elders) scopic pleasure's (that is, pleasure in eroticized watching) necessarily taking the form of a stealthy and guilty voyeurism that inevitably carries the exposure and punishment of the watcher(s) in its wake. By contrast, the figure of "the twenty-ninth bather"—a composite of the young woman and the (male) bather—escapes traditional circuits of authority and desire which render the biblical bathers victimized women and their observers guilty evildoers, in order to enter and occupy a utopian space in which a figure representative of feminine desire and identity can effectively be incorporated into a scene of masculine *jouissance*.

Granted, the section may not represent female orgasm at all, and certainly does not represent it with anything like the directness and specificity with which it represents something like male orgasm ("They ["The young men"] do not think whom they souse with spray"). Still, there is a significant difference between not representing female orgasm in a given section of the text and excluding femininity from its representational program altogether. If this passage falls short of representing a woman (women's) attaining full physical sexual satisfaction, it does incorporate feminine sexuality to a considerable degree, and to a higher degree than most English-language texts contemporaneous with it that one might adduce; the female figure is, after all, represented with notable (and exceptional) straighforwardness desiring to join and at least in some way(s) to possess the young male bathers, and then passing out in tandem with the speaker into the water to do so.

The "unseen hand [which] . . . passe[s] over [the bathers'] bodies" is at least in part hers, a sign of the metonymic feminine agency she bears into what would otherwise be an uninflected scene of orgiastic male-homoerotic utopianism. That this key scene of male "fluidity," one of the most determinately and specifically erotic of all such scenes in *Leaves of Grass, is* inflected as it is with feminine erotic desire argues against the assumption that Whitman's privileging of male-homoeroticism in itself precludes his also representing feminine sexuality and feminine agency in his text. Literally almost from the beginning of the 1855 text, as this episode allows one to see, the figure of a woman's (women's) hand(s) is disseminated with other figures for physical presence and absence as well as masculine ones.

It is not to diminish but to confirm the real role of feminine agency in this representative section of the poetry of the first edition of *Leaves of Grass* that I also point out the female figure's role in the complex act of self-censorship the passage performs. It would be too direct a challenge to state censorship and criminal prosecution for Whitman simply to stage a scene (so to speak) in which a rich and handsome but repressed and lonely "mature" or "older" *man* gazes desirously out at a group of younger men bathing; the obvious tactical advantage of placing a woman in the voyeur's position is that in doing so the author does not outwardly violate powerful cultural proscriptions against (and against representing) erotic desire between men. Here, as at many other points in his writing, Whitman uses self-censorship strategically, making it a means of extending rather than contracting the range of his writing's meanings. Rather than engaging in a simple, straightforward act of self-censorship and de-eroticizing the desirous gaze which the passage launches, he insists not only on its erotic quality but on the *commonness* (in both senses of the word, ordinariness and sharedness) of intense sexual desire ("surely more or less down underneath in most human souls"), "in men's and women's hearts, young and old." In merging without excluding either the (male) speaker and the woman into a composite "twenty-ninth bather," Whitman effectively destabilizes the genders of both the source and object(s) of the erotic gaze, projecting a space in which both women and men are free not only to direct such a gaze at (other) men, but also to fulfill the desires that impel the gaze.

What I am arguing here is that had he chosen to pursue a more common kind of self-censorship, Whitman might have represented sexual desire in de-eroticized and idealized forms, as his culture generally preferred to do—as a desire for "love and friendship" that excluded the corporeal to the degree that the erotic was conceived of as being antagonistic to, even actively disruptive of, "orderly" familial and domestic relations among people. Alongside the officially prohibited representation of a man feeling, enacting, and fulfilling his desire for other men, Whitman posits the hardly less transgressive representation of a woman doing the same thing.

* * *

The significance of this figure is one of intense indeterminacy, like others in the 1855 text, such as the "grass" that is turned into metonyms for numerous classes of persons and various parts of their bodies in what became section 6 of "Song of Myself," beginning "A child said, What is the grass? . . ." Supplementarity is a pronounced feature of the significance of such figures, signaled in the "twenty-eight bathers" section by the recurrence of the words "all so" ("also") in its opening lines. No unconsidered metonym, the "unseen hand" of the closing lines of this passage is also a sign of the poet's projected physical presence among the twenty-eight bathers as well as among his readers in general. It is a sign of the hand of the writer unseen by the reader, who has only the print on the page to signify the desire to provide affectionate physical presence which impels Whitman's writing—or, one might say, only the print on the page *and* the elaborate eroticized image of writing contained in the closing lines of the passage, where it is not (or not only) fellatio that is being figured but (or but also) the writer's "unseen hand[s]" in motion, "seiz[ing] fast" with one hand to the pages—the young men's "white bellies swell[ing]" in the light— and with the other covering them with the "pendant and bending arch" of his "flowing" script. Here is a point (by no means the only one in *Leaves of Grass*) at which the fluidity of writing (that is, *écriture*) and the fluidity of handwriting—and of Whitman's handwriting—intersect. Whitman has told us a few pages earlier in "I celebrate myself" that one of the meanings that his "leaves" (pages) includes is "the breasts of young men" ("It may be you [curling leaves of grass] transpire from the breasts of young men"); in the closing lines of the "twenty-eight-bathers" passages we learn that the pages of his book are intended to represent their bellies, too—and to serve as yet another metonymic substitute for the never more than liminal presence to the reader of these (male) bodies and their constituent parts.

Here, in the figure of the "unseen hand" and its activities, is also a point in Whitman's text where genders meet—both in the "unseen[ness]" of the hand and also in the invisibility of its agency, a quality which does not necessarily lessen the reality of its agency ("Little streams passed over their bodies," then, "An unseen hand also passed over their bodies"). Woman and (male) speaker meet in the "unseen hand," which is also a sign of the substitutive relationship in which the poem *makes* seen what is unseen (hidden or proscribed desire) through the substitution for it of language and writing. Of this the hand is a doubly gendered metonym. In one sense a hand without a body, in another sense the hand is derived from both a woman's *and* a man's bodies. It is finally a figure for the metonymic text itself, and the kinds of exchanges it effects, which involve the mobilization ("pass[ing] over") of body parts and actions which are rendered as pairs of verbs which tend to denote discontinuous motions (for example, in the last lines, "float" and "swell," and "puffs and declines").

JOHN IRWIN

Whitman: Hieroglyphic Bibles and Phallic Songs†

* * * In "Song of Myself" Whitman says that the grass

> . . . is a uniform hieroglyphic
> And it means, Sprouting alike in broad zones and narrow zones,
> Growing among black folks as among white,
> Kanuck, Tuckahoe, Congressman, Cuff, I give them the same, I
> receive them the same.
>
> (ll. 106–09)

Later in the poem, Whitman cites Champollion's[1] decipherment as an example of the progress of science:

> Hurrah for positive science! long live exact demonstration!
> Fetch stonecrop mixt with cedar and branches of lilac,
> This is the lexicographer, this the chemist, this made a grammar
> of the old cartouches. . . .
>
> (ll. 485–87)

A cartouche is an oval ring used in hieroglyphic writing to set off the characters of a royal or divine name. The earliest examiners of the Rosetta stone had noticed that a group of characters enclosed in an oval appeared at a point in the hieroglyphic inscription corresponding to the place where the name of the pharaoh Ptolemy Epiphanes occurred in the Greek inscription. The general surmise had been that these characters comprised the pharaoh's name and that the oval ring was an unvarying marker of royal names. Since the name Ptolemy was Greek in origin, the investigators reasoned that it must have been written phonetically in Egyptian, and they proceeded to isolate the name's phonetic elements in the demotic text of the Rosetta stone. Champollion, following the lead of earlier researchers like de Sacy, Akerblad, and Young, concentrated his efforts at decipherment on proper names and on establishing the relationship between demotic writing and the hieroglyphics. Having at first rejected Young's contention that demotic writing was a cursive script ultimately derived from the hieroglyphics, Champollion finally accepted it; and in September 1822, working with copies of inscriptions from the temple at Abu Simbel, he deciphered the names of the pharaohs Rameses and Thothmes. Champollion sud-

---

† From *American Hieroglyphics: The Symbol of the Egyptian Hieroglyphics in the American Renaissance* (New Haven, Conn.: Yale University Press, 1980), 20–40. Copyright © 1980 by John Irwin. Reprinted by permission of Yale University Press. Line and page references have been changed to correspond to this Norton Critical Edition.
1. Jean-François Champollion (1790–1832) first deciphered Egyptian hieroglyphic writing in the 1820s, using the bilingual text of the Rosetta stone as an aid.

denly realized that phonetic signs were used for writing not only for-
eign names but Egyptian names as well, indeed that they were "original
and integral elements of the hieroglyphical system as such." It was this
discovery that he announced in the letter to Monsieur Dacier, though
"the actual demonstration and proof of this revolutionary assertion was
reserved for a subsequent publication."[2]

Whitman's interest in Egyptian antiquities seems to date from the
years 1853 or 1854. At about that time he began to visit the Egyptian
museum of Dr. Henry Abbott in New York. In *Good-Bye My Fancy* he
says, "The great 'Egyptian Collection' was well up in Broadway, and I
got quite acquainted with Dr. Abbott, the proprietor—paid many visits
there, and had long talks with him, in connection with my readings of
many books and reports on Egypt—its antiquities, history, and how
things and the scenes really look, and what the old relics stand for, as
near as we can now get."[3] Whitman's visionary description of Egypt in
"Salut au Monde!" may well be based on some of the things that he
had seen and discussed at Dr. Abbott's museum:

> I see Egypt and the Egyptians, I see the pyramids and obelisks,
> I look on chisell'd histories, records of conquering kings,
>   dynasties, cut in slabs of sand-stone, or on granite-blocks,
> I see at Memphis mummy-pits containing mummies embalm'd,
>   swathed in linen cloth, lying there many centuries,
> I look on the fall'n Theban, the large-ball'd eyes, the side-drooping
>   neck, the hands folded across the breast.
>
>   (ll. 145–50)

Floyd Stovall notes that an article "on 'The Egyptian Museum' pub-
lished in *Life Illustrated* for December 8, 1855, was almost certainly
written by Whitman. This article shows that Whitman had absorbed a
good deal of information about ancient Egypt, some of it from Abbott,
no doubt, some of it from lectures by Gliddon and others, but probably
a good deal more from his reading of the many books, reviews, and
magazine and newspaper articles on Egypt published during the 1840's
and 1850's."[4] In the article Whitman discusses the "satisfactory con-
clusion" to the "perplexing subject" of decipherment and remarks that
Champollion "probably contributed more to that conclusion than any
other man. When he returned from Egypt he knew his death was
rapidly approaching. With feverish haste he completed his great work,
a 'grammar of Egyptian Hieroglyphics'—he corrected the proofs on his
death-bed. 'Preserve these,' said he, handing them to his friends, 'they
are my visiting-cards to posterity.'" Three decades later, in *A Backward
Glance O'er Travel'd Roads* (1888), Whitman used this story again, as
an image of his own achievement: "Result of seven or eight stages and
struggles extending through nearly thirty years, (as I nigh my three-

2. Erik Iversen, *The Myth of Egypt and Its Hieroglyphics in European Tradition* (Copenhagen,
   1961), p. 142.
3. *The Collected Writings of Walt Whitman*, eds. Gay Wilson Allen, Sculley Bradley *et al.* (New
   York: New York University Press), vol. 9, p. 696.
4. Floyd Stovall, *The Foreground of Leaves of Grass* (Charlottesville: University of Virginia Press,
   1974), p. 163.

score-and-ten I live largely on memory,) I look upon 'Leaves of Grass,' now finish'd to the end of its opportunities and powers, as my definitive *carte visite* to the coming generations of the New World, if I may assume to say so" [p. 478]. And in a footnote he repeats the story of Champollion's death-bed reference to his "Egyptian Grammar" as his "*carte de visite* to posterity' " [p. 478]. * * *

Like Emerson's admiring references to Champollion, Whitman's praise of positive science and the man who "made a grammar of the old cartouches" carries a qualification. In "Song of Myself," he says:

> Gentlemen, to you the first honors always!
> Your facts are useful, and yet they are not my dwelling.
> I but enter by them to an area of my dwelling.
>
> (ll. 490–92)

The physical fact is not the dwelling place because for Whitman the physical is the path to the metaphysical ("path" not in the sense that the metaphysical is located elsewhere, but in the sense that the metaphysical is a radically different way of experiencing the physical). In the preface to the 1855 edition of *Leaves of Grass*, Whitman says: "Exact science and its practical movements are no checks on the greatest poet but always his encouragement and support. . . . The anatomist, chemist, astronomer, geologist, phrenologist, spiritualist, mathematician, historian, and lexicographer are not poets, but they are the lawgivers of poets and their construction underlies the structure of every perfect poem. . . . In the beauty of poems are the tuft and final applause of science" [p. 633]. And in "A Passage to India" (1871), he expresses once more the notion that the poet completes the work of the scientist:

> After the seas are all cross'd, (as they seem already cross'd,)
> After the great captains and engineers have accomplish'd their
>   work,
> After the noble inventors, after the scientists, the chemist, the
>   geologist, ethnologist,
> Finally shall come the poet worthy that name
> The true son of God shall come singing his songs.
>
> Then not your deeds only O voyagers, O scientists and inventors,
>   shall be justified, . . .
> All affection shall be fully responded to, the secret shall be told,
> All these separations and gaps shall be taken up and hook'd and
>   link'd together,
> The whole earth, this cold, impassive, voiceless earth, shall be
>   completely justified,
> Trinitas divine shall be gloriously accomplish'd and compacted by
>   the true son of God, the poet. . . .
>
> (ll. 101–11)

When Whitman says that with the coming of the true poet "the secret shall be told," he echoes Emerson's belief that the significance of nature is concealed beneath the surface complexity of the physical objects examined by empirical science. In *Democratic Vistas* Whitman says, "As the purport of objective Nature is doubtless folded, hidden, somewhere here—as somewhere here is what this globe and its manifold forms, and the light of day, and night's darkness, and life itself, with all its experiences, are for—it is here the great literature, especially verse, must get its inspiration and throbbing blood" [pp. 778–79]. Whitman maintains that the test of the "great literatus" who shall pierce that complexity and tell the secret of nature will be "his cheerful simplicity, his adherence to natural standards" [p. 778]. One is reminded of Emerson's remark that Goethe had penetrated the multiplicity of physical nature "through the rare turn for unity and simplicity of his mind." The doctrine of correspondence is clear: one penetrates the obscure hieroglyphic "characters" of the language of nature to reach the inner simplicity of their meaning by means of the inner simplicity of the human "character." Like reveals like.

One of the major image patterns associated with the hieroglyph of nature in the works of the American Renaissance is that of the cipher and the key. As Emerson speaks of "the cipher of the world," so Whitman in a poem from *Good-Bye My Fancy* called "Shakspere-Bacon's Cipher" says:

> In each old song bequeath'd—in every noble page or text,
> (Different—something unreck'd before—some unsuspected
>   author,)
> In every object, mountain, tree, and star—in every birth and life,
> As part of each—evolv'd from each—meaning, behind the ostent,
> A mystic cipher waits infolded.

And as Emerson says that the poet-scientist Goethe "contributed a key to many parts of nature," so Whitman in the preface to the 1855 *Leaves of Grass* says that the poet who draws "his encouragement and support" from science is "the arbiter of the diverse and he is the key" [p. 620].

Closely related to the figure of the cipher and key is the image of natural signatures. Commenting on the Renaissance belief that "buried similitudes must be indicated on the surface of things," Michel Foucault notes that in this tradition

> there are no resemblances without signatures. The world of similarity can only be a world of signs. Paracelsus says:
>
> > It is not God's will that what he creates for man's benefit and what he has given us should remain hidden. . . . And even though he has hidden certain things, he has allowed nothing to remain without exterior and visible signs in the form of special marks—just as a man who has buried a hoard of treasure marks the spot that he may find it again.
>
> A knowledge of similitudes is founded upon the unearthing and deciphering of these signatures. . . . the face of the world is covered with blazons, with characters, with ciphers and obscure words—with "hieroglyphics," as Turner called them. And the

space inhabited by immediate resemblances becomes like a vast open book; it bristles with written signs; every page is seen to be filled with strange figures that intertwine and in some places repeat themselves. All that remains is to decipher them.[5]

In this same vein Emerson, in his essay on Goethe, depicts the operations of nature as a continuous act of writing:

> Nature will be reported. All things are engaged in writing their history. The planet, the pebble, goes attended by its shadow. The rolling rock leaves its scratches on the mountain; the river its channel in the soil; the animal its bones in the stratum; the fern and leaf their modest epitaph in the coal. The falling drop makes its sculpture in the sand or the stone. Not a foot steps into the snow or along the ground, but prints, in characters more or less lasting, a map of its march. Every act of the man inscribes itself in the memories of his fellows and in his own manners and face. The air is full of sounds; the sky, of tokens; the ground is all memoranda and signatures, and every object covered over with hints which speak to the intelligent.[6]

According to the tradition that Foucault cites, God has written two books—the book of nature and the Bible. Both are written in hieroglyphics that require interpretation, yet this continuity in the form of their writing means that they can be used to interpret one another, each book somehow being the hidden key to the other's meaning. Oegger's *The True Messiah*, which employs this mode of reciprocal interpretation, is dominated by the image of the hieroglyph. Oegger says:

> Man is the true hieroglyphic of the Divinity; a hieroglyphic, infinite in its details, even when man is considered only as a material form, since his material form itself, is but the emblem of his moral being. . . . All animals, by their corporeal forms, as well as by their instincts, are hieroglyphics of the different degradations of human nature, or of detached parts of the collection of organs of life, called man.[7]

Since there are "millions of hieroglyphics which any one may easily find," Oegger proposes to provide "simple keys, by means of which the reader can, by himself, penetrate farther into the immense domains of nature." In general, Oegger follows the method employed by Swedenborg[8] in *Arcana Coelestia* (1749–56), though with greater flexibility. (The *Arcana Coelestia* is a decipherment of Genesis and Exodus by means of the hieroglyphical key to the language of nature.) Of Swedenborg's method, Emerson remarks: "He fastens each natural object to a theologic notion;—a horse signifies carnal understanding; a tree, perception; the moon, faith; a cat means this; an ostrich that; an artichoke this other;—and poorly tethers every symbol to a several ec-

5. Michel Foucault, *The Order of Things* (New York: Random House, 1973), pp. 26–27.
6. Ralph Waldo Emerson, *The Complete Works of Ralph Waldo Emerson*, ed. E. W. Emerson (Boston, 1903), vol. 4, p. 261.
7. Kenneth W. Cameron, *Emerson the Essayist* (Raleigh, N.C., 1945), vol. 2, pp. 95–96.
8. Emanuel Swedenborg (1688–1772), Swedish philosopher and religious writer [Ed.].

clesiastic sense. . . . His theological bias thus fatally narrowed his interpretation of nature, and the dictionary of symbols is yet to be written. But the interpreter whom mankind must still expect, will find no predecessor who has approached so near to the true problem" (4:121).

Swedenborg's and Oegger's readings of the hieroglyphs of Scripture are closely related to the tradition of hieroglyphic Bibles, which began in the seventeenth century and continued well into the nineteenth. According to W. A. Clouston, the first hieroglyphic Bible was published in Augsburg in 1687 by Melchior Mattsperger.[9] Its title was *The Spiritual Heart-Fancies, in Two Hundred and Fifty Biblical Picture-Texts*. The book contains eighty-four copperplate engravings in which the 250 Biblical quotations are reproduced. In each quotation, key words are replaced by pictures of the objects that the words signify. In his preface Mattsperger says that he has provided these "Biblical Figure-Sayings" so that "simple people may learn . . . many a text which all their life long they might never have considered." And he adds, "I have had printed the accompanying table of all the texts comprised in it, word by word in themselves, in which the figure is always indicated by larger type, which those who are unable to name the right word may use instead of a key."

* * *

The first English version to derive from Mattsperger's work was published in London by T. Hodgson in 1780. Entitled *A Curious Hieroglyphick Bible*, it was meant "for the Amusement of Youth: designed chiefly to familiarize tender Age, in a pleasing and diverting Manner, with early Ideas of the Holy Scriptures" through "Select Passages in the Old and New Testaments, represented with Emblematical Figures" (p. 9). Some, if not all, of the woodcuts were done by the well-known English engraver Thomas Bewick. The work was so well received that it "went through no fewer than twenty large editions—besides four reprints published at Dublin—down to the year 1812," and it was reprinted in America by Isaiah Thomas. In 1794 a rival work to Hodgson's entitled *A New Hieroglyphical Bible* was published in London by G. Thompson. Thompson's work was the progenitor of numerous English hieroglyphic Bibles and at least three Continental versions, one of which (a German edition printed in Leipzig in 1842) contains a preface with an explicit statement of the relationship between the hieroglyphic book of nature and Sacred Scripture:

> 1. The book of Nature, which God wrote himself, of old alone announced to man the truths needed by the heart to enable it to face every fortune.
> 2. But, alas, finite natures did not comprehend the glorious book. The divine word, in which it was written, remained unintelligible for many a century in every land.
> 3. The book was too great for finite spirits, the characters

9. W. A. Clouston, *Hieroglyphic Bibles* (Glasgow, 1948), p. 124.

themselves prevented the characters from being read, and when they were seen, men, though endowed with the keenest intelligence, failed to interpret them for want of the necessary light.

4. The wisest men looked on the sun and moon, the glittering stars in the bright night, as only floating spheres in boundless space, not as revealers of the divine power. . . .

7. They read and read, but for all they read, they read not aright, but only confused themselves, and all their wisdom and prudence was a prolific field for all kinds of error:

8. Then God, by men, taught from within by the illuminating power of His spirit, caused the Book to arise, which destroys the darkness in the minds of men in human fashion. . . .

10. Since he gave this Book to men, creation is intelligible and clear to them, and what they now read from earth and heaven is no longer error, but perfectly clear. . . .

In both Hodgson's edition and Thompson's, a key to the cipher accompanies each hieroglyphic passage: "The whole Sentences, which give an Explanation of the Figures, are placed at the Bottom of each Page; and the Words, which are represented by Figures, are particularly distinguished in *Italic*," says the author of the preface to Hodgson's second edition. In other editions the key is often placed at the back of the book and is preceded by a picture of a key. The image of the cipher and key is basic to the format of the hieroglyphic Bible, and that image is invariably connected with the motif of learning to call things by their right names. In Mattsperger's original work a table gave the names of all the flowers, trees, fruits, and so forth, whose pictures decorated the borders of each page. According to the title page of the Hamburg version, one of the purposes of the book is to teach children "how to draw everything very neatly, and to name it with its proper name." * * *

To call objects by their right names means to call them by their original names. It is an Adamic task that reminds us of Whitman's effort to recapture the language of physical objects in his role as poet of the Edenic New World:

A song of the rolling earth, and of words according,
Were you thinking that those were the words, those upright lines? those curves, angles, dots?
No, those are not the words, the substantial words are in the ground and sea,
They are in the air, they are in you. . . .

Human bodies are words, myriads of words. . . .

Air, soil, water, fire—those are words. . . .

The masters know the earth's words and use them more than audible words. . . .

I swear I begin to see little or nothing in audible words,
All merges toward the presentation of the unspoken meanings of the earth,

Toward him who sings the songs of the body and of the truths of
    the earth,
Toward him who makes the dictionaries of words that print
    cannot touch.[1]

* * *

I have discussed at some length hieroglyphic Bibles and the tradition
of the hieroglyphical interpretation of the Bible represented by Swe-
denborg and Oegger because there is reason to believe that at one
point Whitman conceived of *Leaves of Grass* as a kind of hieroglyphic
Bible. The evidence is circumstantial but ample. To begin with, there
is Whitman's interest in the hieroglyphics and Egyptology, the fact that
he called his major symbol "a uniform hieroglyphic," and that in *A
Backward Glance* he implicitly compared *Leaves of Grass*, "his *carte
visite* to the coming generations," to Champollion's hieroglyphic gram-
mar. Indeed, Whitman may have had in mind Emerson's remark that
for Swedenborg the world was a "grammar of hieroglyphs." Next, we
know that as late as June 1857 Whitman considered his ongoing work
on *Leaves of Grass* as "the Great Construction of the New Bible."[2] The
Bible was, of course, the major influence on Whitman's prosody, shap-
ing his cadenced verse with its repetitions and parallelisms. Further,
many of the elements found in the format of the hieroglyphic Bible
are to be found in *Leaves of Grass* as well. * * *

* * *

In characterizing *Leaves of Grass* as a kind of hieroglyphic Bible, we
should keep in mind that its model is not the Bible of orthodox Chris-
tianity. Whitman's is not a religion of the triune God but rather a
religion of the human body and the body of nature conjoined in
a cosmic unity. In Whitman's poetry, the physical is the pathway to
the metaphysical precisely because in his poetic vision the physi-
cal is transformed into the metaphysical—man's body becomes his
soul. * * *
The poetic transformation of the physical into the metaphysical is
synonymous with the attempt to recapture the original language of
objects, for in that language physical objects were, to use Emerson's
term, "transparent," their significances shone through their material
shapes. Physical objects were transparently metaphysical objects, signs
in which no separation or discontinuity between form and content
existed because as pictographic ideograms their form was their con-
tent. Whitman's attempt to regain the original language of natural
signs, his effort to replace "audible words" with "the presentation of
the unspoken meanings of the earth," involves the paradoxical use of
phonetic signs to restore the unspoken (nonphonetic) language of pic-
tographic ideograms, the paradox involved in *singing* "the songs of the
body." And it is in light of the Romantic concept of song as the tran-

1. "A Song of the Rolling Earth," ll. 1–4, 7, 10, 16, 98–101 [*Ed.*].
2. Walt Whitman, *Notes and Fragments*, ed. Richard Maurice Bucke (Folcroft, Pa: Folcroft
    Library Editions, 1972), p. 57.

scending of the mediation of spoken language *through* the mediation of spoken language that Whitman's effort to transform the physical into the metaphysical must be understood.

For Whitman, "song" is a rhetorical figure, a trope that depicts the discontinuity between self and world, between spoken word and physical object, as a form/content dichotomy capable of being overcome by music. * * * "Song" is Whitman's name for that Paterian "condition of music" where "in its consummate moments, the end is not distinct from the means, the form from the matter, the subject from the expression; they inhere in and completely saturate each other."[3] In the Whitmanian trope, "song" signifies an ideal interpenetration in which form fuses with content, the spoken word with the object, the poet's self (the poem's subject) with the song, and the song with the world. And it signifies all of this precisely because, in Whitman's aesthetic, song is understood to be at once a literal and figurative *expiration*, the singer's breathing out of the self (pneuma) into the world and a filling of the self by the world, a prefigurative *Liebestod*[4] in which the self expires into, and becomes one with, the world, so that self-consciousness becomes "cosmic consciousness." In "Out of the Cradle Endlessly Rocking," the poet travels by means of his song back to his own childhood (and thus toward man's ultimate origin, "the cosmic float," symbolized by the sea) in order to hear once again the song of the bird calling to its lost mate. And he realizes that the singing of the bird has a double meaning: it is at once an image of the world calling to the separated self of the poet and an image of the poet singing in order to "expire," to breath himself into the world:

> Demon or bird! (said the boy's soul,)
> Is it indeed toward your mate you sing? or is it really to me?
> For I, that was a child, my tongue's use sleeping, now I have heard
>   you,
> Now in a moment I know what I am for, I awake
> And already a thousand singers, a thousand songs, clearer, louder
>   and more sorrowful than yours,
> A thousand warbling echoes have started to life within me, never
>   to die.
>
> O you singer solitary, singing by yourself, projecting me,
> O solitary me listening, never more shall I cease perpetuating
>   you. . . .
>
> (ll. 144–51)

In Whitman's idealized conception of song, the musical component of poetry, by raising spoken language to that condition in which its sonic form is its content (in which vocal expiration is a return to origin, to that original interpenetration of sign and meaning), transforms spoken language into the audible equivalent of that original language of natural signs in which the form of the pictographic physical object was

---

3. Walter Pater, *The Renaissance* (London: Macmillan, 1910), p. 139.
4. German term meaning "love-death," from the ecstatic closing section of Richard Wagner's opera *Tristan and Isolde* [Ed.].

transparently its meaning. Thus in Whitman's poetry, song is presented as the mode of the poet's return to a childlike simplicity of character, to those radically simple, written characters of the original language of natural signs through which the poet's character is expressed. Whitman aims, through the fusing power of song, to turn the phallic tree of spoken language back into the cosmic tree of the language of natural signs within his own cosmic written self, the Walt Whitman whose song (*Leaves of Grass*) is his poetic self. In one of the poems in *Children of Adam* he says,

> Ages and ages returning at intervals,
> Undestroy'd, wandering immortal,
> Lusty, phallic, with the potent original loins, perfectly sweet,
> I, chanter of Adamic songs,
> Through the new garden the West, the great cities calling,
> Deliriate, thus prelude what is generated, offering these, offering
>   myself. . . .
>
> ("Ages and Ages . . . ," ll. 1–6)

In the ideal transparency of embodiment, the singer becomes his song, the object its meaning. For Whitman song is an audible hieroglyph, a musical emblem.

ALLEN GROSSMAN

The Poetics of Union in Whitman and Lincoln: An Inquiry toward the Relationship of Art and Policy[†]

I

To begin with, I shall suppose that both policy and art are addressed to the solution of problems vital to the continuity of the social order, and, therefore, to the human world. In the period of America's Civil War (the "renaissance" moment both of America's literary and its constitutional authenticity) there arose two great and anomalous masters, the one of policy and the other of poetry: Abraham Lincoln and Walt Whitman. Both men addressed the problem of the reconstruction of their common human world—the Union as a just and stable polity—at a time when the elements necessary to the intelligibility of that world seemed fallen, in Seward's words, into "irrepressible conflict."[1]

The political and constitutional situation, as both men understood it, was clear. The Missouri Compromise of 1820, which had reconciled the equality requirement of the Declaration of Independence with the continuity requirements of the Constitution (among them slavery), was

† From Walter Benn Michaels and Donald E. Pease, eds., *The American Renaissance Reconsidered* (Baltimore: Johns Hopkins University Press, 1985), 183–204. Copyright © 1985 by Allen Grossman. Reprinted by permission of the Johns Hopkins University Press. The author's notes have been edited.
1. The argument of this paper is extensively indebted to James Buechler, "Abraham Lincoln, American Literature, and the Affirmation of Union" (1955), a Harvard Honors essay.

undone between 1846 and 1857 by the outcome of the Mexican War, the Fugitive Slave Law, Kansas-Nebraska, and Dred Scott. In effect, competition between the claims of two incompatible systems of labor with their attendant social structures, precipitated by the acquisition of new territory in the Mexican War and the opening of the Northwest, required deliberated choices, as if in an "original position," among contradictory descriptions of the human world. By the accident of history, these choices involved the staggeringly primitive question as to which human beings were persons.[2] That deliberation was, in the end, condensed upon the figure and discourse of Lincoln, whose "mould-smashing mask" (as Henry James put it) was a bizarre picture of *concordia discors*, the imagination's conquest of irreconcilables; it was interrupted and restated by the cruel, integrative, and perhaps artificial catastrophe of the Civil War; and at last ironically inscribed in the Thirteenth, Fourteenth, and Fifteenth amendments.[3]

On the literary side, Emerson, Thoreau, Melville, and Whitman addressed the same problem of the union or connectedness of the human world, which they also saw by deliberated fictions as if for the first time in a new territory where the worth of persons was subject to the risk of finding a form. The long aftermath of the Revolution had destroyed the old America, a confederation of separately constituted religious communities, in which personhood was validated or canceled by reference to the eucharistic mystery of the hypostatic union. Whitman and others worked toward a reconstructive poetics appropriate to a modern political society, in which this same validating function was equivocally provided in the centerless rationality of the Constitution legislated by the secular decree of the people. Authentic American art, as well as true American constitutionality, awaited a solution to the crisis of the establishment of the person.[4]

In America at midcentury, both art and policy confronted a culture that lacked an effective structure (a meter, a genre, an epistemology,

2. See Arthur Bestor, "The American Civil War as a Constitutional Crisis," in Lawrence M. Friedman and Harry N. Scheiber, *American Law and the Constitutional Order* (Cambridge: Harvard University Press, 1978), p. 234:

> But the abstractness of Constitutional issues has nothing to do, one way or the other, with the role they may happen to play at a moment of crisis. Thanks to the structure of the American Constitutional system itself, the abstruse issue of slavery in the territories was required to carry the burden of well-nigh all the emotional drives, well-nigh all the political and economic tensions, and well-nigh all the moral perplexities that resulted from the existence in the United States of an archaic system of labor and an intolerable policy of racial subjection.

3. The analysis of Lincoln's meanings that follows is not psychological in method. I have, however, greatly benefited from the findings of Dwight G. Anderson, *Abraham Lincoln, The Quest for Immortality* (New York: Alfred A. Knopf, 1982); also, George B. Forgie, *Patricide in the House Divided* (New York: W. W. Norton, 1979), and Charles B. Strozier, *Lincoln's Quest for Union* (New York: Basic Books, 1982).

4. The destruction by the Revolution of the older "prestige order," based on inherited class or status, was accompanied by the development of an "indigenous class structure . . . based upon property." See Jackson Turner Main, *The Social Structure of Revolutionary America* (Princeton: Princeton University Press, 1965), pp. 282, 283. The loss of feudal status-criteria, and the loss also of the model of the hypostatic union (the union of persons in the Trinity), were correlative shocks contributing to the crisis. Emerson and Whitman attempted to recuperate the former development by reconstructing on a secular basis the empowerments lost as a consequence of the latter.

a law) between the pragmatic ideal of political unity—the unwritten poem of these states—and the mutually excluding legitimacies for which right and place were claimed in consciousness and the nation —Declaration and Constitution, equality and order, body and soul. Lincoln supplied that structure in the form of a conservative ideology of union based in ethical constitutionalism, promulgated by a rational style of discourse of unfailing adequacy and persuasiveness. He was a *novus homo*, a man impersonated by his language, the structure of whose song of self-invention (a recapitulation of the significant past of America, as he understood it) came in the event to be repeated as America's present, the Civil War. The literary master of union was Whitman for whom also the one justifiable order of the world was the order of the discourse by which he invented himself, his song. ("The United States themselves," he said, "are essentially the greatest poem.") Neither of these men could appear, except as a function of their language which bore upon them, and subsequently upon their world, as Emerson remarked of perception in general, not as a whim but as a fate.

The only social role that could make actual the enigmatic particularity of Lincoln's self-invention, speaking the pure language of individual personhood by which he discovered the tragic laws of its social peace, was the citizen presidency. The only social role that could express the function of the person for Whitman—immanent, comedic, doxological, choral—was the poet-nurse, commissioned healer of the violence of language of another sort. At the end of the war, Whitman signified the inclusion of the tragedy of policy within the comedy of his art by receiving Lincoln into the night—"hiding, receiving"—of his elegy, as he had received in his arms so many of the dead of Lincoln's war.

Insofar as the actuality of both policy and poetry require sentences a man can speak, the material upon which poetry works and the material upon which policy works are identical because of the ubiquity of language, and present the same resistances. The reasons that one cannot make just any poem, or just any policy, good are the same. An entailment of any style a person speaks is the structure of a social world that can receive it—a political formation and its kind of conscious life. Consequently, Whitman and Lincoln were autodidact masters. As such, they received the implications of acculturation without interposition of mediating social forms, and restated its structure directly as the structure of the worlds they intended.

Whereas Lincoln was born in the wilderness Thoreau deliberately chose to live there. Lincoln's literacy derived from personal labor. For Lincoln the crisis of union repeated the enigma of his own socialization. His legendary honesty specifies him as a man of his word, as Whitman's theatrical "nakedness" makes him a man whose self is his song. For Whitman as for Lincoln, the legitimation of his personhood (the crisis of union) involves the justification of a mode of discourse, not merely a particular case of practice. But the autodidact self-invention of Whitman—his self-commissioning praxis—identified him with the ethos of poetry. In his understanding poetry is the leisure of receptivity, not the rational labor of the will—"I loafe and invite my soul." A poetry that authorizes a personhood reflexively validated by its own discourse can have no category of fictionality. (He who touches this book touches all the man there is.) A poetry that has no category of fictionality is a policy.[5] Correlatively, a policy that intends, as did Lincoln's, the same structure as its discourse is a poetry. In this sense, both Whitman and Lincoln are profoundly conservative figures. Both bind the world, with totalitarian immediacy, to the configurative implication of the central sentences of a cultural instrument.

Therefore, one may ask the question whether, as between Lincoln's politics and Whitman's poetry, there are two policies of union, or only one insofar as they are representative of two distinct cultural modes? Does poetry know anything that policy does not? One may also ask, given the singular nature of these two figures, both of whom practice language that intends as a function of its structure a just order of the human world, whether there really is a nontragic, open-form, egalitarian version of the reconciliation of justice and order, or only the brilliant, closed, individualist, logic-based Lincolnian version so profoundly implicated with our world as it has come to pass.

II

The supposition, with which I began, that art and policy are addressed to the same problems, assumes that prior to both art and policy is the common intention of an order of the human world, and that the world has a stake in knowing (and criticism a means of inquiring) what art and policy cannot do.

Lincoln's strategy of order was an amplification of a legal grammar (Blackstonian) adapted to political use, the structure of which was based in the Aristotelian laws of thought—identity, non-contradiction, the excluded middle. He judged the world that he constructed by a hermeneutic criterion of intelligibility, modeled on Euclid. A house divided against itself, like a sentence that asserts contradictories, cannot stand because it makes no sense and accords with no possible state of affairs.[6] He judged the substantial moral world similarly, ac-

---

5. See John T. Irwin, "Self-Evidence and Self-Reference: Nietzsche and Tragedy, Whitman and Opera" in *New Literary History* 9, no. 1 (Autumn 1979): 177–92. I fully agree with his notion of the "endlessly oscillating grounding" of self and text in Whitman, but not with his assimilation of Whitman's song to Schopenhauer's music.
6. In a conversation with the Reverend J. P. Gulliver in 1860, Lincoln specified two biographical moments in which his style was formed. As a child, he says:

> I used to get irritated when anybody talked to me in a way I could not understand. I don't think I ever got angry at anything else in my life. I was not satisfied until I had repeated it over and over, until I had put it in language plain enough, as I thought, for any boy I knew to comprehend. This was a kind of passion with me. . . . I am never easy now, when I am handling a thought, till I have bounded it North, and bounded it South, and bounded it East, and bounded it West.

The other moment he describes as the discovery of a means to make *demonstration* result, as Webster's dictionary promised, in "certain proof." He supplied the means by secluding himself in his father's house "til I could give any proposition in the six books of Euclid at sight." Gulliver's report was published in the New York *Independent*, 1 September 1864, rpt. in James Mellon, *The Face of Lincoln* (New York: Viking Press, 1979). Lincoln's source for the "house divided" image as a logical contradiction is Tom Paine's *Common Sense*, 1:8 of *The Complete Writings*, ed. Philip Foner (New York: Citadel Press, 1945).

cording to the criterion of simplicity. Lincoln accepted as self-evident
the distinction between good and evil, implied as a restriction on
choice by the Declaration of Independence (all men are created equal),
and assumed that there was a state of fact in accord with the criterion
that the two authoritative documents of his reality (Declaration and
Constitution) meant the same thing. Correspondingly, the meaning of
the law, for Lincoln, was "the intention of the law-giver," and all the
givers of authentic law, including God, intended the same thing.[7] "The
will of God," he notes in 1862, "prevails. In great contests each party
claims to act in accordance with the will of God. Both may be, and
one must be, wrong. God cannot be for and against the same thing at
the same time." Hence, Lincoln's speaking induced a sentiment of
what Marianne Moore called his "intensified particularity," deriving
first from a willed overcoming of complexity and consequent clarifi-
cation of the world, and second from the indissociability of that clar-
ification from his own person.[8] Thus, Lincoln's policy subordinated
and conserved an ineradicable autochthony against a reality of im-
mense complexity. In its severest form, the form given it in history by
the hands of Grant and Sherman, his rhetoric was obliterative. "Both
may be, and one must be, wrong."[9]

In the crossing of kinds of discourse in history, poetry situates itself
where other instruments of mind find impossibility. Thus, Walt Whit-
man found his truth, and the unity of his world, precisely at the crisis
of contradiction where Lincoln found disintegrative instability. Unlike
Lincoln's God, who cannot be for and against the same thing at the
same time, Whitman's "greatest poet" inferred from the traditional
fame-powers of his art a fundamental principle of undifferentiated rep-
resentation, which constituted a massive trope of inclusion. Represen-
tation (the class of all classes) was itself an implicit unification, the
fame of the world; and the great bard, "by whom only can series of
peoples and states be fused into the compact organism of a Nation,"
promulgated the goodness of simple presence as human state of af-
fairs. Of *his* legislator Whitman says in the "Poem of Many in One":
"He judges not as the judge judges but as light falling round a helpless
thing." Whitman's originality consisted in the discovery of a regulative
principle that permitted an art based in the representative function

7. The centrality in Lincoln's mind, and the minds of his audiences, of the hermeneutic
proposition—"the intention of the law-giver is the law"—is attested by its place in "The First
Inaugural." Roy P. Basler et al., *The Collected Works of Abraham Lincoln* (New Brunswick,
N.J.: Rutgers University Press, 1954), 4:263; hereafter cited as Basler.
8. Marianne Moore's "Lincoln and the Art of the Word" in *A Marianne Moore Reader* (New
York: Viking Press, 1965) characterizes him as a "Euclid of the heart." The standard essay
on Lincoln as a writer is Roy P. Basler, "Lincoln's Development as a Writer" in *A Touchstone
for Greatness* (Westport, Conn.: Greenwood Press, 1973). See also, Edmund Wilson, *Patri-
otic Gore* (New York: Oxford University Press, 1962), pp. 119ff.
9. Lincoln's identification of the deontological distinction between right and wrong with the
rhetorical authority of "logic" can be seen in the following reply to Douglas at Alton (Basler
3:315): "He says he 'don't care whether it [slavery] is voted up or voted down' in the terri-
tories. . . . Any man can say that who does not see anything wrong with slavery, but no man
can logically say he don't care whether a wrong is voted up or voted down. He may say he
don't care whether an indifferent thing is voted up or down, but he must logically have a
choice between a right thing and a wrong thing."

itself, and organized in its ideal-typical moments (for example, the world-inventories in #15 and #33 of "Song of Myself") as a taxonomy of which the sorting index is mere being-at-all. The argument that made the meter of Whitman was the unification of the world in the one power of language, the secret authority of the poet (his "Santa Spirita"), the bestowal of presence across time. The theater of that presence is the poetic line; and the poetics of the line is the multiplicative logic of presence by which Whitman replaces, and contradicts, the world-dividing logic of argument of Lincoln's rational sentence.

The English poetic line, as Whitman found it, was the synergetic outcome of two orders of form: an abstract and irrational pattern of counted positions, on the one hand, and the natural stress characteristics of language heightened and articulated by the semantic concerns of the reader, on the other. But the repertory of abstract patterns that the reader received was, in his view, indelibly stained by the feudal contexts of its most prestigious instances, and in addition required the subordination of the natural stress characteristics of language, and therefore an abridgment of the freedom of the speaker. But Whitman was an end-stopped line-writer. And for him the abstract patterns (the "mechanical" aspects of structure) served, at the least, two indispensable functions: the provision, first of all, of an external and (by convention) timeless *locus communis* where the "I" and the "you" could meet, a principle of access; and, second, the establishment of a finite term which sealed utterance against silence and granted form. Whitman compensated his deletion of the metrical aspect of the line by revising the mechanism of access on the basis of the "transparence," or reciprocal internality, of persons one to the other ("What I shall assume you shall assume"), and by the hypothesis of a world composed of a "limitless" series of brilliant finite events each of which imposed closure at the grammatical end of its account. But it is opposition to the meaning-intending will by the resistance of abstract form that produces, in the English poetic line, the sentiment of the presence of the person as a singular individual; and this Whitman could not restore.

We see, therefore, the paradox: the logic of poetic construction posed to Whitman, the ideologist of union as happiness, is analogous to the logic of clarification posed to Lincoln, the ideologist of union as "fairness." In Lincoln's case the unification of the world required the dissolution of one term of any set of contradictories in order to obtain the thereby inherent simplification required by truth—a totalitarianism of hypotaxis. In the poet's case, the abandonment of abstract pattern put in question the validity of the instrument of fame itself by dissolving its subject—a totalitarianism of parataxis. The problem for both Whitman and Lincoln was how to preserve the ends of the enterprise from the predation of the means.

III

When Matthiessen named Whitman "the central figure of our literature affirming the democratic faith," he did so because he saw Whitman as the champion, not only of liberty and equality, but also (unlike Emerson, Thoreau, and even Melville) of fraternity—the master of union as social love.[1] But Lincoln was the great speaker of the American Renaissance whose imagination empowered the democratic faith. Its way, he said, is "plain, peaceful, generous, just." In the 1850s, both Whitman and Lincoln held more or less the same politics, including the view that slavery *and also abolition* were barbarisms: abolition because it interrupted contract and exchange without which there was no social world in which anyone *could* be free; slavery because, as an impermissible variation of the practice of liberty (you cannot choose to enslave), it destroyed the value both of labor and leisure without which freedom was empty of praxis.[2] Lincoln's characteristic strategy for freeing slaves was *compensated* emancipation, the completion of the Revolution by the co-optation in its service of the constitutional principle of contract—the justification, in effect, of logical discourse. Whitman supposed that the same result could only be obtained by a more fundamental revision of the central nature of relationship—the establishment of a new basis of speaking in the counterlogic, and infinite distributability, of affectionate presence. Both Lincoln and Whitman intended the same thing. The two systems (the closed and the open) that they sponsored aspire each to specify the inclusion of the other as the best outcome of its own nature. The limits of each of these two systems in view of their common goal becomes plain in the two related issues of *hierarchy*, the constraints upon variation consistent with union as structure, and equality, the management of access of persons one to the other consistent with union as *value*.

In Lincoln's "First Inaugural," a performative utterance at the moment of oath-taking, which he described as an account of his own worthiness of credence, Lincoln identified secession as a transgressive practice of freedom—a disordering variation—inconsistent with the intactness of the organic law of the nation; and he defined by contrast the true democratic sovereign:

> Plainly, the central idea of secession is the essence of anarchy. A majority, held in restraint by constitutional checks, and limitations, and always changing easily, with deliberate changes of popular opinions and sentiments is the only true sovereign. Whoever rejects it does of necessity fly to anarchy or to despotism. Unanimity is impossible; the rule of the minority, as a permanent arrangement is wholly inadmissible; so that, rejecting the majority principle, anarchy or despotism is all that is left.[3]

1. F. O. Matthiessen, *From the Heart of Europe* (New York: Oxford University Press, 1948), p. 90.
2. For Whitman on abolition, see Whitman's essays in *The Brooklyn Daily Eagle* in 1846 and 1847, reprinted in Cleveland Rodgers and John Black, *The Gathering of Forces* (New York: G. P. Putnam's Sons, 1920), 1:179–238. Note also Whitman's essays in the same volume on union. Whitman and Lincoln held the same political views, except that Whitman's attitude toward government and political parties displayed his aversion to units of social organization other than the individual and the whole. For the development of the Transcendental writers of the period toward the acceptance of abolition, see Daniel Aaron, *The Unwritten War* (New York: Alred A. Knopf, 1973).
3. Basler, 4:264.

Oath-taking is Lincoln's peculiar form of honesty. At the moment of the "First Inaugural" he identifies himself with the union, grown suddenly abstract with the secession of seven states, and establishes himself as its regulative presence by articulating the grammar of the one authentic sentence that expresses both equality and intelligible structure.[4] But the world the Constitution describes is organized around the conservation of the singular person by the concession of totalistic right—excluding despotism, anarchy, *and also unanimity*. By the principle of majority rule, equality is delegated and unanimity eternally postponed. This delegation takes the form of an exchange whereby autonomy is given up, and social life, the human scale of the person, received in return. Lincoln's true sovereign is a collectivity less than the whole, a "majority held in restraint" by a regulative principle external to itself which by its measure produces freedom in the form of resistances to the will structured to conserve its own nature. At the heart of Lincoln's conception of constitution is a commutative process: life is given up for meaning, the significance of the whole sentence; and the interest of all persons (and, therefore, potentially the whole interest of each) is exchanged for a rational sociability based in a hierarchy of ends of which the highest term is external to the person, and not within his power of choice. Paramount among these exchanges, and implied in all, is the exchange of life for meaning, an idea that Lincoln repeated as a hermeneutic principle in his explanation of the war (e.g., "From these honored dead we take increased devotion to that cause for which they gave the last full measure of devotion"). Since secession was a transgressive exercise of choice (the repudiation of the social bond) on behalf of slavery, and slavery a perversion of contract to repudiate rather than affirm personhood, the urgency of restoring Union was doubly driven by the ethical motive, not only (and perhaps not primarily) to establish all human beings as persons, but also to revalidate the principle of the whole social world. Secession made inescapably apparent the inherently conflictual character of the legal understanding of the Constitution by making unmistakable the incompatibility of the freedom of the individual (the freedom, for instance, to enslave) with the order of the state—the inherently imperfect inclusion under rational auspices of the many in the one.

Whitman's motive, by contrast, was to get death out of sociability, to devise "death's outlet song." The bard is the better president because he is the "perfect" agent of human presence—the voice's announcement, prior to all other messages, of the presence of the person prior to all other characteristics. As such, the bard distributes the value of personhood which is the value commuted in all other economic transactions. The poem is of the same nature as central value, because the whole function of its discourse is acknowledgment. Consequently,

---

4. "I therefore declare that, in view of the Constitution and the laws, the Union is unbroken; and, to the extent of my ability, I shall take care, as the Constitution itself expressly enjoins me, that the laws of the Union be faithfully executed in all the States" (Basler, 4:265).

universal access to the poem is a policy to overcome scarcity. To effect this, Whitman devised a "song" that would reconcile variety and order, equality and constitution, one and many without compromising either term. Once again Whitman situates his new American organic law and true sovereign precisely where Lincoln finds impossibility, at the zero point of unanimity.

The destruction of the constitutional settlement of the 1820s precipitated the crisis of the Union in the form of the scarcity of personhood. A characteristic recuperative episode of the 1850s is the Dred Scott decision which solved the problem of such scarcity by ruling the African slave out of the human community by a distinction as severe and of the same effect as that between the redeemed and the unregenerate.[5] In the slave codes of the South the chattel slave must call every man "master." By his uncanny difference—a human being who is not a person—the slave precisely specifies and thereby generates and maintains (this is his work) the boundary between the nonperson and the person upon which the distinction of the person is established.[6] The refounding of personhood, the historical function of the poet, was the deferred business both of the American Revolution and of American literature. But the perfect equality of all human beings requires, as Whitman understood, an infinite resource of fame.

Whitman's policy was to establish a new principle of access that would effect multiplication, or pluralization (the getting many into one), without the loss entailed by exchange—the glory of the perfect messenger. In the chronology of Whitman's work, the "open" line as formal principle appears simultaneously with the subject of liberation, and is the enabling condition of the appearance of that subject. That is to say, his first poems in the new style are also his first poems on the subject of slavery and freedom (specifically, "Resurgemus," "Blood-Money," "Wounded in the House of Friends"). His first lines in the new style altogether (so far as I can tell) are recorded in a notebook as follows:

> I am the poet of the slave, and of the masters of the slave
> . . . .
> I am the poet of the body
> And I am the poet of the soul
> I go with the slaves of the earth equally with the masters

5. Taney in Dred Scott makes plain the primary function of the Constitution as a regulative document which creates by secular means rights-bearing human beings, according to the principle of difference: "The words 'people of the United States' and 'citizens' are synonomous terms, and mean the same thing. . . . It is true, every person, and every class of persons, who were at the time of the adoption of the Constitution recognized as citizens in the several States, became also citizens of this new political body; but none other; it was formed by them, and for them and their posterity, but for no one else" in Henry Steele Commager, *Documents of American History* (New York: Appleton-Century-Crofts, 1949), pp. 339–45.

6. This was a conscious and practical matter. E. Merton Coulter (*The Confederate States of America, 1861–1865* [Baton Rouge: Louisiana State University Press, 1950], p. 10) cites a Georgia editor (*Atlanta Southern Confederacy*, 25 October 1862) who says of slavery that it made "the poor man respectable." It gave the poor "an elevated position in society that they would not otherwise have." * * *

And I will stand between the masters and the slaves,
Entering into both, so that both shall understand me alike[7]

In another early notebook Whitman gives an account of what he calls "translation," the power he uses in place of the Coleridgean poetic "imagination." (He sometimes, as in the Lincoln elegy, calls it "tally-ing.")

> Every soul has its own individual language, often unspoken, or feebly spoken; but a true fit for that man and perfectly adapted for his use—The truths I tell to you or to any other may not be plain to you, because I do not translate them fully from my idiom into yours.—If I could do so, and do it well, they would be as apparent to you as they are to me; for they are truths. No two have exactly the same language, and the great translator and joiner of the whole is the poet.[8]

Instead of a "poetic language" (always a mimetic version of the language of one class) Whitman has devised a universal "conjunctive principle" whose manifest structure is the sequence of end-stopped, nonequivalent, but equipollent lines. By it he intends the power of the God to whom (as in the "Collect for Purity" which opens the Mass) "all hearts are open . . . desires known . . . from whom no secrets are hid." His poetic authority is J. S. Mill's "overheard" soliloquy of feeling, and his physicalist basis is the phrenological continuity between inner and outer mind. The drama of translation is enacted at the beginning of an early poem, "The Answerer":

> Now list to my morning's romanza, I tell the signs of the Answerer,
> To the cities and farms I sing as they spread in the sunshine
>   before me.
>
> A young man comes to me bearing a message from his brother,
> How shall the young man know the whether and when of his
>   brother?
> Tell him to send me the signs.
>
> And I stand before the young man face to face, and take his right
>   hand in my left hand and his left hand in my right hand
> And I answer for his brother and for men. . . .

By curing the human colloquy, the poet (the translator, answerer, perfect messenger, better president) intends to establish a boundless resource of the central acknowledgment-value, and to rid sociability of death by overcoming the scarcity of fame, a process that requires the mechanical checks and balances (reifications of the competing will of the inaccessible other) that characterize the poetics of Lincoln's constitutionalism. But Whitman's new principle of access—his line—is

---

7. Emory Holloway, *The Uncollected Poetry and Prose of Walt Whitman* (Garden City, N.Y.: Doubleday, Page & Co., 1921), 2:69; hereafter cited as Holloway. For the functional analogy between body/matter/slave, and soul/spirit/master, see Davis, p. 304.
8. Holloway, 2:65.

not "organic" in Matthiessen's Coleridgean sense. It has the virtuality of a paradigm; and the negotiation of its actualization against the resistances of history and mind is Whitman's major subject.

The primal scene of that negotiation is the "transparent morning" of part 5 of "Song of Myself." It is the inaugural moment of Whitman's candor, and as such it recapitulates the first subject matter liberated by his line. The form is the confession of a creed:

> I believe in you my soul, the other I am must not abase itself
>   to you
> And you must not be abased to the other.

The rewriting of hierarchies—soul/body, collective/individual, nation/state—as equalities, and the rewriting as identities of conventional dualities, above all the self and the other, is the task of the "translator," whose goal is union as the fraternalization of the community. In the Nicene Creed what follows is, of course, the hypostatic union. What follows in Whitman's creed is the greater mystery of the mortal union of two, the competent number of acknowledgment, and the archetype of all political relationship. For Lincoln, labor is prior to capital and is the praxis of the individual will by which all selfhood, and therefore all value, is produced.[9] It is indistinguishable from the act of clarification (the intention of the lawgiver) by which univocal meaning is derived, many made one. To loaf ("Loafe with me on the grass . . . ") is to exchange the posture of hermeneutic attention for the posture of receptivity, the unity of all things in the last sorting category of mere consciousness prior to interpretation ("the origin of all poems") of which the voice is the "hum," the sound of the blood doing the cultural work of God (a further secularization of the "sound of many waters" of Revelation, repeated by Wordsworth as the mystically integrative speaking of the Leech Gatherer), the doggerel of life. What follows, then, is the sexual union reconstructed as a moment of primal communication, the tongue to the heart. The principle of the language of the soul is the deletion, as in Whitman's metricality as a whole, of centralizing hypotactic grammar, and the difference-making prosodies both of individual meaning-intention and abstractly patterned (stress/no stress) metricality. What is obtained is an unprecedented trope of inclusion—the sign, embodied in that revision of primary human relationship ("gently turned over upon me"), of which the greater inclusions of emancipation and union are the things signified:

> And limitless are the leaves stiff and drooping in the fields
> And brown ants in the little wells beneath them
> And mossy scabs of the worm fence, heap'd stones, elder, mullein
>   and poke-weed.

But what is created, paradoxically, is a new slave culture. The Whitmanian voice, like the slave, is uncanny—a servant of persons, but not

9. See "Fragment on Free Labor" (Basler, 3:462), and "Address before the Wisconsin State Agricultural Society, Milwaukee, Wisconsin," 30 September 1859 (*ibid.*, pp. 471ff.).

itself personal—a case of delegated social death: "A generalized art language, a literary algebra" (Sapir). "Comradeship—part of the death process. The new Democracy—the brink of death. One identity— death itself" (Lawrence). "To put the paradox in a nutshell, he wrote poetry out of poetry writing" (Pavese).[1] There is truth in these judgments. The logic of presence, Whitman's "profound lesson of reception," has its own violence. The Whitmanian convulsion ("And parted the shirt from my bosom-bone, and plunged your tongue to my bare-stripped heart"), attendant upon the reduction of all things to appearance, is the counter-violence to that which flows from the logic of clarification, the reduction of all things to univocal meaning. The tongue of the soul is the principle of continuity figured as the "hum" of subvocal, absorbed, multitudinous, continuously regulated "valved voice," or "this soul," as Whitman elsewhere says, ". . . its other name is Literature."[2] The tongue sacrifices the subject of justice in the interest of personal immediacy that overcomes the difference of the social body, but at the same time destroys (tongue to bare-stripped heart) the destiny of the secular person that the social body is.

In a tract Whitman wrote in 1856 on behalf of Fremont (whom Lincoln also supported), Whitman produces his model of "The Redeemer President" whose way will be "not exclusive, but inclusive."[3] Lincoln was not Whitman's redeemer president. Lincoln was the type of the "unknown original" (Sapir's expression) from which, as from the utterance of the hermit thrush of the elegy, Whitman translated his song. Whitman's taxonomic line runs "askant" history (the abstract pattern he deletes is precisely the element of the line that has a history).[4] That variation produces the infinite access he required for his "peace that passes the art and argument of earth." In Lincoln's terms such a variation is as transgressive (and of the same nature) as Douglas's "squatter sovereignty," or slavery itself.

Lincoln's sentence, by contrast, prolongs the history of each soul beyond mortality in a never-darkened theater of judgment. In the midst of an argument in his "Second Annual Address" (1862) in support of compensated emancipation, Lincoln inserts the following sentence: "In times like these men should utter nothing for which they would not be responsible through time and in eternity."[5] In the straitening of choice, Lincoln in his language grows thick with character, the pure case of tragic personhood enacting the indissolubility of a moral identity that persists across eschatological boundaries in continuous space

1. Edward Sapir, *Language: An Introduction to the Study of Speech* (New York: Harcourt Brace, 1949), p. 224; D. H. Lawrence, *Studies in Classical American Literature* (New York: Viking Press, 1964), p. 170. For Cesare Pavese, see Gay Wilson Allen, *The New Walt Whitman Handbook* (New York: New York University Press, 1975), p. 317.
2. In "Democratic Vistas" at p. 981, *Walt Whitman: Complete Poetry and Collected Prose* (New York: Library of America, 1982).
3. "The Eighteenth Presidency!" in Clifton Joseph Furness, *Walt Whitman's Workshop* (Cambridge: Harvard University Press, 1928), p. 109.
4. *Cf.* 15.171 of "When Lilacs Last . . .": "And I saw askant the armies." The "crossing" moment, as in "Calvary Crossing a Ford," or the crossing of bodies in #5 of "Song of Myself," signifies for Whitman immediacy of access, unqualified by space or time. So, also, in "Crossing Brooklyn Ferry": "I see you face to face."
5. Basler, 5:535.

and time (the cosmological expression of ethical contract)—unmistakable, eternally situated, judged. The peroration of the same speech begins: "Fellow citizens, *we* cannot escape history. We of this Congress and this administration, will be remembered in spite of ourselves. No personal significance, or insignificance, can spare one or another of us. The fiery trial through which we pass, will light us down, in honor or dishonor, the lastest generation."[6] By deleting the abstract pattern of internal marks that closes the traditional line and carries it across time, Whitman deleted history, founded an infinite resource of acknowledgment, dissolved the moral praxis of the singular individual, and "launched forth" (as he says at the end of the "Song of the Answerer") into the desituate universe of transparent minds, generated by an open metrical contract, "to sweep through the ceaseless rings and never be quiet again." Lincoln's language, unlike Whitman's, is empowered because it is of the same nature as the institutions that invented him, and his space and time are institutional space and time. In such a world, judgment and acknowledgment are inseparable; and the economy of scarcity is reconstituted in the oldest economic terms of our civilization—honor or dishonor.

Both Whitman and Lincoln are captives of a system of representation, which they are commissioned to justify and put in place as an order of the human world—a policy for union. Are there two policies, or only one? On the one hand, a Whitmanian policy—open, egalitarian, in a sense socialist (as Matthiessen thought it to be), generalized from the fame-power of art, and darkly qualified by that abjection of the subject of value which is the other side of receptivity; and, on the other hand, a Lincolnian system—closed, republican, capitalist, a regulative policy driven by the logic of clarification, and darkly qualified in its turn by the obliterative implications both of moral exclusiveness and the delegatory economies of labor? We have seen that the centered, hierarchical, Lincolnian ethical rationality is precisely the enemy element from which Whitman is bent upon exempting his human world. We see also that the resonant, scale-finding, integrative vocality of Lincoln is the most severe criticism our literature affords of Whitman's indeterminate realization of the person—"You whoever you are." Whitman's "Word over all, beautiful as the sky" reconciles what Lincoln's ethical dualism drives into division, yet only at that distance; Lincoln's sentiment of ethical difference cruelly specifies the limit of variation in which regulative rationality can produce the actual life of all men. But despite the reciprocally canceling nature of Whitman and Lincoln as liberators, the gravity of representation itself unites them in a common conservatism.

In the "Preface of 1855" Whitman lays down his own regulative sentence: "Nothing out of its place is good and nothing in its place is bad."[7] For Whitman the final sorting category of presence, the place

6. *Ibid.*, p. 537.
7. On honor and dishonor as a zero-sum transaction see the "Epilogue" to Gregory Nagy, *Comparative Studies in Greek and Indic Meter* (Cambridge: Harvard University Press, 1974), p. 261.

of good life, is (as I have said) mere existence, of which the dwelling is the open air, and the poetic structure the internally unmarked line manifesting "as amid light" the natural stress characteristics of language in the natural order, determined at the end by the objectively finite plenitude of each of an infinite number of facts of being *caught in a brilliant virtuality from which it cannot depart*: "Passing the yellow-speared wheat, every grain from its shroud in / the dark-brown fields uprisen."[8] For Lincoln that same place of good life is "the national homestead"—a boundless, mastered autochthony specified, rendered continuously intelligible and therefore free, by the internal markings of superordinate measure. It is Lincoln who says: "There is no line, straight or crooked, on which to divide."

IV

One reason we turn to criticism of poetry is to bring to pass projects that become possible only when we make statements about poetic texts. We do criticism because we are busy about something else. In this sense, we do not intend the poem; we intend the intention that brought the poet to poetry, which is not the poem but the reason for taking poetry in hand. Our judgment upon the poem is an assessment of the likelihood of the coming to pass of what is intended. And our judgment, or the poet's, upon poetry itself is an assessment of its usefulness as an instrument of our urgent, common work.

In "a society waiting," as Whitman says of his America, "unformed . . . between things ended and things begun," Whitman intended a revision of all "conjunctive relations."[9] Of this revision the "great poet" was the sign, and also the incarnation of the regulative principle of his own signifier, the poem—man of his word. As the world over which Lincoln presided darkened through the Civil War, Whitman saw the defeat of fraternity which was the substance of his policy. The seal of that defeat, the murder of the president, he inscribed with his great reconstructive "Burial Hymn," "When Lilacs Last in the Dooryard Bloom'd." During that period, Lincoln in his speeches drew the world with justificatory intensity and comprehensiveness ever deeper into the system of representation whose structure was expressed in his political and strategic judgments, as in the "Second Inaugural": "Until every drop of blood drawn by the lash shall be paid by another drawn by

8. Bradley, p. 714, 11.123–24.
9. The expression is William James's. James's "radical empiricism" is fundamentally explanatory of Whitman's epistemology.

> To be radical, an empiricism must neither admit into its constructions any element that is not directly experienced, nor exclude from them any element that is not directly experienced. For such a philosophy, *the relations that connect experiences must themselves be experienced relations, and any kind of relation experienced must be accounted as "real" as anything else in the system.* . . . . *Radical empicirism*, as I understand it, *does full justice to conjunctive relations*, without however treating them as rationalism always tends to treat them as being true in some supernal way, as if the unity of things and their variety belonged to different orders of truth and vitality altogether.

> William James, *Essays in Radical Empiricism and a Pluralistic Universe* (New York: E. P. Dutton, 1971) pp. 25, 26.

the Sword." Whitman, on the other hand, tended more and more to modify his regulative principles to release the world from the over-determination of all systems of representation, as in the consummatory cry of perfect translation: "I spring out of these pages into your arms —decease calls me forth."[1]

As is the case with pastoral elegy in general, "When Lilacs Last" is, first of all, a gesture of riddance of a prior representational dispensa-tion unable to "keep" its children. (Whitmanian celebration by plural-ization extinguishes all personhood which has *only* singular form— ["Nor for you, for one alone / Blossoms and branches green to coffins all I bring."])[2] Second, the elegy effects the reconstitution of the world on the basis of the new supersessory system (in "Lycidas" the "unex-pressive nuptial song," in Whitman's poem "yet varying ever-altering song"). Finally, it investigates the implications of a "passing," or para-tactic transcendence, of that new system of representation toward a right state of the world undeformed by any mediation of discourse. One reason for the fullness of articulation of Whitman's poem lies in the complexity of its judgment, not only on the failed predecessor sys-tem of which all that survives is love without an object, but also on itself as a policy toward the consummation of that love—a union not broken by the means of its accomplishment. In this judgment of the judge whose justice does not divide consists the final profundity of Whitman, his "delicacy" as the late James Wright called it.

"When Lilacs Last" repeats the millennial archetype of the death of the Beloved Companion whose *nostos* it completes ("Nothing out of its place is good; and nothing in its place is bad"). The elegy returns to the West; Lincoln had departed four years earlier on his journey from West to East (displacing an autochthonous power in the service of an alien rationality) with the great sentences of farewell at Spring-field, Illinois (11 February 1861), which begin with double negatives that seal, at the moment of deracination, untranslatable individuality into irreducible space and time: "Friends: no one not in my situation, can appreciate my sadness at this parting. . . . Here I have lived . . . , and have passed from a young to an old man. Here my children have been born, and one is buried."[3] By contrast, Whitman's correlative rehearsal of departure in the opposite direction, from East to West (his revision in 1862 of the opening stanza to "Starting from Pauma-nok") sets the self at large in the field of consciousness—at the other end from Lincoln of the truth table for the particle /or/:

> Aware of the fresh free giver the flowing Missouri, aware of the
>   mighty Niagara,

1. Whitman's equivocation of the difference of sign and signified, word and thing, body and soul, "I" and "you" expresses an intention to rid conjunctive transactions (whether seeing, loving, speaking, or political bonding) of all representational mediations. This is the reason of his use of Lucretian optics (as in "Crossing Brooklyn Ferry"), his interest in phrenology, his dislike of political parties, poetic diction, mythology, and so on.
2. "Celebration" in Whitman (as in "I celebrate myself") invokes the meaning of pluralization which inheres in all cognates of Latin *celebrare*. * * *
3. Basler, 4:90.

Aware of the buffalo herds grazing the plains, the hirsute and
    strong-breasted bull,
Of earth, rocks, Fifth-month flowers experienced, stars, rain,
    snow, my amaze . . . ,

released from the rational justice of situation, inclusive of many places
at once (here and also there) not as seeing is but as light is. And yet
"Solitary, singing in the West." The old situated world of unexchange-
able Euclidean marks provided the object of love—the Beloved
Companion—to Whitman as elegist; but the new world of the open
principle provides the elegy. It springs forth at the death of the loved
person, released from the hermeneutic bondage ("O the black murk
that hides the star!") which invented that person and destroyed him
—a supersessive culture of keeping as union one and many ("each to
keep and all"), by its nature requiring his loss. The loss of the com-
panion precipitates the speaker in the poem upon a new autonomy—
a searching of the boundaries of representation ("dusk and dim") for
an instrument of sociability that does not produce the disappearance
of its object.

At the heart of Whitman's elegy is the scene of the reading of the
song of the hermit thrush named "Solitary," the "loud human song"
of the unknown original, the singular person. This scene is a repetition
of the inaugural action of translation (as pluralization) by which in
"Out of the Cradle Endlessly Rocking" the poet received his commis-
sioning ("Now in a moment I know what I am for . . . / And already
a thousand singers . . . have started to life within me, never to die").
To accomplish this katabasis requires a re-fraternalization by which
the poet becomes the conjunctive term between the "thought" of death
and its "knowledge," general and particular, many and one—the hand
in hand of union mediated only by the consciousness of continuous
vitality. In this relationship, the poet becomes the "Answerer," who
addresses the central question of freedom which is suffering, as rec-
ognition itself, the signifier of nothing. From the renewal of his central
originality Whitman receives the vision of things as they are with the
living and the dead. He translates Lincoln's death without exchanging
it for any term whatsoever, and the "slain soldiers of the war" without
the commutation of any rational value:

I saw battle-corpses, myriads of them,
And the white skeletons of young men, I saw them,
I saw debris and debris of all the slain soldiers of the war,
But I saw they were not as was thought,
They themselves were fully at rest, they suffer'd not,
The living remain'd and suffer'd, the mother suffer'd,
And the wife and the child and the musing comrade suffer'd,
And the armies that remain'd suffer'd.

Through the establishment of difference between the living and the
dead—a laying of ghosts, including Lincoln and his meanings—the
elegist recovers the perceptibility of his world, as Lincoln had estab-
lished the difference between persons and things by the emancipation

of the slaves, and thus restored the rationality of the polity. But the act of perceptual autonomy ("free sense") finds Whitman, at the moment of his greatest originality, at the greatest distance also from the social world in which alone his intention can have meaning, that world over which Lincoln presided as emancipator, accounting for the same facts of suffering (at Gettysburg, for example, or in the "Second Inaugural") according to compensatory economies of theodicy, those of dedication, sacrifice, and the vengeance of God.

Both Whitman (poet citizen) and Lincoln (citizen president) intended a "just and lasting peace" in a polity that had lost regulative stability and consequently postponed the antinomy of those two terms. Each took in hand a millenial instrument of representation the nature of which he articulated as policy with singular fidelity: in Lincoln's case, the political principle of sociability based in commutative justice, the logic of noncontradiction, singular identity, and the hierarchy of rational order—the language of tragic personhood; in Whitman's case, the poetic principle of sociability, based in an abstraction from the representational function of art, and organized in accord with a redistributive counterlogic of presence as pluralization and the transparence of affection—a comedy of justice without exchange. But the Whitmanian distributive politics of "transparence" fails to obtain unanimity because it has no natural standpoint (there is no transparence consistent with the social life of the person), and thus obtains only justice without constitution. Likewise the Lincolnian poetics of fairness does not obtain fairness because the nature of the person on whose behalf it acts limits the systemic change possible to the institutions that represent the person—constitution without justice. Both men succeeded in mastering their instrument, but not (as each so profoundly intended) in overcoming its nature. Both men succeeded in mastering their instrument, *but not (as each so profoundly intended) in overcoming its nature.* The contradiction between equality and perpetuation—Declaration as justice, and Constitution as structure— was more powerful than the systems of representation that invented these men (and which they sponsored) could conciliate, because the contradiction is of the same nature as the system.

Thus, having made one out of many, the common work of policy and poetry, Lincoln and Whitman left behind the inherently unfinished, reconstructive task of making many, once again of one—the creation of a real world consistent with its principles both of value and of order. Near the close of his "Second Annual Message" in which he promulgated the Emancipation, Lincoln distinguished between imagining and doing, and between the present and the past:

> It is not "Can any of us *imagine* better?" but "can we all *do* better?" . . . The dogmas of the quiet past, are inadequate to the stormy present. The occasion is piled high with difficulty, and we must rise with the occasion. As our case is new, so we must think

anew and act anew. We must disenthrall ourselves, and then we shall save our country.[4]

Both men, together with most of their literary contemporaries, saw the historical moment as one requiring new structures of response; both deprecated the category of the imaginary, and both intended to "disenthrall" the self in the interest of national authenticity. In the end, however, the freedom conferred by Whitman and Lincoln remained, as I have suggested, virtual and paradoxical. The empowered master, Lincoln, was unable, by the very nature of his power, to legislate a social world in which his intention could become actual. Whitman, the master of social love (the better president as he understood it), was unable, by the nature of his fundamental revision of personhood, to enter the world by any act, except the deathwatch of the wounded in Lincoln's war.

The fate of Whitmanian policy brings to mind the observation that words in poetry are only as effective as the institutions in which they have meaning. More particularly, "bad faith" attaches to open form in that it anticipates, by the radical nature of its truth, no institution in which its words can have effect, no world in which its text is transmitted, and yet no presence of the self-authorized person it liberates except the image or eidolon of the poem. Correlatively, we note from the fate of Lincolnian policy, which is our history: that the language of closed form is empowered because it is of the same structure as human institutions; but that such institutions, or for that matter such poems (Yeats's for example), are only as moral as the grammar of their construction, and powerless to mediate by secular means the irrepressible conflict of legitimacies which is the principle of their life.

Are there then, as between Whitman and Lincoln, two policies of union or only one? There is, on the showing of this argument, only one—with this qualification: A faithful response to Whitman's originality will be a continual critique, in view of a policy toward institutions, of the structures of representation, in the light of the revelation of personhood unmistakably presented in Lincoln's language and countenance—the archetype of the doomed companion laboring in history, whom we now know and hope to love. The open road is the one line that is not imaginary.

4. Basler, 5:537.

BETSY ERKKILA

The Poetics of Reconstruction: Whitman the Political Poet after the Civil War†

Whitman was never able to carry out his plan to write a new volume of poems centered on the theme of democratic nationality. On January 23, 1873, he suffered a paralytic stroke that left him virtually immobilized for a few weeks and crippled for the rest of his life. In May he made a trip to Camden, New Jersey, to see his mother a few days before her death on May 23, 1873. "I feel that the blank in life & heart left by the death of my mother is what will never to me be fill'd," he wrote to his friends John and Ursula Burroughs (*Corr.*, II, 225). Physically handicapped, as well as emotionally depressed by his mother's death, Whitman was unable to return to his job in Washington. Although he hired a substitute for a time, on July 1, 1874, his services as a clerk in the attorney general's office were officially terminated. He spent the remainder of his life in Camden, first at his brother George's house and finally, beginning in 1884, in his own home at 328 Mickle Street.

Referring to his physical disability as the "war-paralysis," Whitman attributed his stroke to his service in the hospitals during the war years. Although he may not literally have inhaled poisons in the war hospitals, as he sometimes claimed, his stroke was at least partly a result of the psychic demons that came to haunt him during and after the war years. According to Whitman, his Washington physician Dr. Drinkard told him that "it was the result of too extreme bodily and emotional strain continued at Washington and 'down in front,' in 1863, '4 and '5."[1] Immediately after the war, Whitman appears to have suffered from a kind of shell shock that manifested itself in physical symptoms and psychic stress.

This stress intensified in 1870 when he suffered another emotional crisis, probably related to his love relationship with a horse-car conductor named Peter Doyle. In a notebook entry dated July 15, 1870, Whitman's public image as the good gray poet struggles with his personal desire as a closeted gay poet, leading him to resolve "TO GIVE UP ABSOLUTELY & *for good, from this present hour,* this FEVERISH, FLUCTUATING, *useless undignified pursuit of 164—too long, (much too long)* persevered in, —so humiliating—*It must come at last* & had better come now—(*It cannot possibly be a success*)." He comments on the need to suppress his love for men: "Depress the adhesive nature[.] It is in excess—making life a torment All this diseased, feverish disproportionate *adhesiveness*" (*UPP*, II, 96). During this same period

† From *Whitman the Political Poet* (New York: Oxford University Press, 1989), 279–92. Copyright © 1989 by Betsy Erkkila. Reprinted by permission of Oxford University Press. Line numbers have been changed to correspond to this Norton Critical Edition.
1. Floyd Stovall, ed., *Walt Whitman: Prose Works 1892*, vol. II (New York: New York University Press, 1964), pp. 704–5. Further citations to this volume are given in the text of *PW*.

Whitman carried on an extensive and loving correspondence with Doyle.[2] Although he does not mention Doyle by name in his notebooks, it is commonly assumed that 164 is a code for the initials PD, corresponding to letters 16 and 4 in the alphabet. Whereas during the war years, Whitman's homosexual desire became a source of sustenance and utopian vision, in the postwar period, as the more conservative sexual ideology of the new bourgeois order took hold, his love relationships with men became a heightened source of self-torment and self-doubt.

There is a rather tragic irony in the fact that the democratic poet of bodily health and free-wheeling mobility should become in his later years a "half-paralytic." And yet there had always been a curious correspondence between Whitman's body and the body politic of America: His body seemed at times a kind of national seismograph, registering disturbances in the political sphere. In the postwar period in particular, his physical paralysis and the corresponding lack of vitality in his work seemed to reflect the diseased condition of the political republic. Whitman frequently described his physical state in a way that suggested its connection with the state of the Union in the postwar years. "It is singular how much nervous disease there is—and many cases of paralysis & apoplexy," he wrote his mother after his own stroke. "I think there is something in the air" (Corr., II, 220). He referred to the physical problems of his later years as "bequests of the serious paralysis at Washington, D.C., closing the Secession war—that seizure indeed the culmination of much that preceded, and real source of all my woes since" (PW, II, 736). Later on his first trip west in 1879, Whitman, perhaps confronted with the conflict between his dream vision of the West and the reality of rough conditions and "plenty of hard-up fellows," became physically ill and had to return to the East (Corr., III, 168).

In a prefatory note to Leaves of Grass (1889), Whitman traced the course of his bodily ills in such a way as to connect them with the socioeconomic ills of America in the latter half of the nineteenth century: "The perfect physical health, strength, buoyancy . . . which were vouchsafed during my whole life, and especially throughout the Secession War period, (1860 to '66,) seem'd to wane after those years, and were closely track'd by a stunning paralytic seizure, and following physical debility and inertia, (laggardness, torpor, indifference, perhaps laziness,) which put me low in 1873 and '4 and '5—then lifted a little, but have essentially remain'd ever since" (PW, II, 736). The physical and emotional debility that put Whitman "low" between 1873 and 1875 coincided with the worst economic depression in American history. "There is an awful amount of want & suffering, from no work, hereabout," Whitman wrote to Pete Doyle of conditions in New Jersey

2. In "What's in a Title? Whitman's 'Calamus' and Bucke's Calamus," Studies in the American Renaissance, ed. Joel Myerson (Boston: Twayne, 1979), Artem Lozynsky contends that Richard Maurice Bucke's publication of Whitman's letters to Peter Doyle in 1897 was intended to deal with the problem of Whitman's homosexuality by demonstrating that his relationship to Doyle was spiritual and chaste (pp. 475–88).

in 1874 (*Corr.*, II, 275). By 1875, 500,000 workers were unemployed nationwide. During the same period, the worst scandals of the Grant administration were also exposed. The Credit Mobilier scandal, implicating several congressmen in a railroad fraud, broke in the fall of 1872; in February and March the "salary grab" act caused public outrage; in the summer, the secretary of the treasury exposed several treasury officials who had taken bribes from the whiskey-ring conspiracy of distillers; and five of Grant's cabinet members were implicated in illegal financial dealings.

Whitman's low mood in the period initially following his stroke is evident in "Prayer of Columbus," which appeared in *Harper's Magazine* in March 1874. In his notes for the poem Whitman wrote under the heading "Portraiture of Columbus": "pourtray [*sic*] him as a mystic he *was a mystic.*"[3] He had already included a "portraiture" of Columbus as a figure of himself in "Passage to India," but in "Prayer of Columbus" he makes that identification complete. "As I see it now," he wrote Ellen O'Connor, "I shouldn't wonder if I have unconsciously put a sort of autobiographical dash in it" (*Corr.*, II, 272). In the voice of Columbus ailing and ship-wrecked on the island of Jamaica, Whitman utters his own woe and the woefulness of his times:

> A batter'd, wreck'd old man,
> Thrown on this savage shore, far, far from home,
> Pent by the sea, and dark rebellious brows, twelve dreary months,
> Sore, stiff with many toils, sicken'd, and nigh to death,
> I take my way along the island's edge,
> Venting a heavy heart.
>
> (ll. 1–6)

Physically paralysed and politically disillusioned, Whitman moves in "Prayer of Columbus," as in "Passage to India," toward a more traditional religious faith. Whereas the early Whitman had consistently railed against those religion systems that postulated a divine authority outside the self, in "Prayer of Columbus," he utters his own prayer, yielding the authority of self and the command of the democratic ship to the divine "Steersman" in the sky. The gesture measures the distance between the early and late Whitman and the extent of his disillusionment with America's experiment in democracy.

Wavering, like Columbus, between the hope that his work was part of a divine plan for "newer, better worlds" and his "mocking" suspicion that he was the "raving" victim of some cosmic joker, Whitman struggled to accommodate the scandals of the Grant administration and the rankness of the Gilded Age in a saving national vision. Grant was, in Whitman's view, "nothing heroic, as the authorities put it—and yet the greatest hero." His rise from the son of a tanner to general and

---

3. Library of Congress (Feinberg), Item no. 39. The idea for the poem came from his reading an article on "The Last Days of Columbus," published in *The Irish Republic* (May 1869). Across the margin of the article, he wrote: "Poems—Columbus—(? that name for piece)— make the poem an utterance of Columbus—there on Jamaica Island (read first *Ulysses* by Tennyson)." The article was abstracted from Sir Arthur Phelps's *The Spanish Conquest in America.*

president was the essence of the American success myth, illustrating "the capacities of that American individuality common to us all."[4] To Whitman, Grant's acts as both general and president were instrumental in preserving and solidifying the Union; and his reelection in 1872, despite the challenge to his Southern policy and his corrupt administration by the liberal Republicans, confirmed both the Union victory and the policies of radical reconstruction.

In a diary entry for March 4, 1874, Whitman noted that Grant's election "confirmed for the second time, the Principle of Nationality, as the principle dominating all others in American politics." His overwhelming victory established "the Reconstruction measures and the 13th, 14th, and 15th Amendments to the Constitutions [sic] as organic and immutable elements of the Constitution through the time to come."[5] Although Whitman had disagreed with his friend William Douglas O'Connor over the wisdom of immediately enfranchising black men, he did support the Reconstruction policies and constitutional amendments that would give to black persons, if not the reality then at least the promise of, equal civil and political rights.[6]

To give Grant a "moment's diversion from the weighty stream of official and political cares," in February 1874 Whitman sent him a copy of his war memoranda, " 'Tis But Ten Years Since," which had appeared in the New York Daily Graphic. "You of all men can best return to them, in the vein in which they are composed," the poet wrote. "I am not sure whether you will remember me—or my occasional salute to you in Washington" (Corr., II, 280). Whitman regarded the corruption of the Grant administration and the failure of moral energy in the nation as passing symptoms rather than as signs of terminal illness in the democratic body of America. The loss of idealism in the nation was symbolized for some by the death in 1874 of Charles Sumner, who had led the move in Congress for a civil rights bill to ensure the full equality of black freemen. Responding to Ellen O'Connor's anxiety about "political & public degradation—Sumner's death & inferior men &c. being rampant &c.," Whitman assured her: "I look on all such states of things exactly as I look on a cloudy & evil state of weather, or a fog, or long sulk meteorological—it is a natural result of things, a growth of something deeper, has its uses, & will hasten to exhaust itself, & yield to something better—" (Corr., II, 289).

The scandals of the Grant administration are the subject of "Nay, Tell Me Not To-day the Publish'd Shame," which was published in the Daily Graphic during the winter session of Congress in 1873:

Nay, tell me not to-day the publish'd shame,
Read not to-day the journal's crowded page,

4. "The Silent General," PW, I, 226–27; and "Rulers Strictly Out of the Masses," PW, II, 534–35.
5. Library of Congress (Feinberg), Item no. 32.
6. For a discussion of Whitman's dispute with O'Connor, see Jerome Loving, Walt Whitman's Champion: William Douglas O'Connor (College Station: Texas A&M Press, 1978), pp. 94–102.

The merciless reports still branding forehead after forehead,
The guilty column following guilty column.

To-day to me the tale refusing,
Turning from it—from the white capitol turning,
Far from the swelling domes, topt with statues,
More endless, jubilant, vital visions rise
Unpublish'd, unreported.

(ll. 1–9)

Whitman's initial *Nay* is significant, for the poem marks his refusal to read or hear the "publish'd shame" of the time, which included the recent exposure of the Credit Mobilier scandal and the "salary grab" act. He turns away from the "swelling domes" of the Capitol to an "unpublish'd, unreported" vision of the country, but the vision he evokes is at once "unpublished" and unreal:

> Through all your quiet ways, or North or South, you Equal States,
>   you honest farms,
> Your million untold manly healthy lives, or East or West, city or
>   country,
> Your noiseless mothers, sisters, wives, unconscious of their good,
> Your mass of homes nor poor nor rich, in visions rise—(even your
>   excellent poverties,)
> Your self-distilling, never-ceasing virtues, self-denials, graces,
> Your endless base of deep integrities within, timid but certain.

(ll. 10–15)

Refusing the journalistic accounts of his time, Whitman "unimagines" the "publish'd shame" of America in a willfully idealized vision of "honest farms" and virtuous, self-denying citizens inhabiting a land-based Jeffersonian republic in which even poverty is excellent.

Whitman's desire to unmake the present in dreams of the democratic future is evident in the two-volume edition of his works that he published in conjunction with the Centennial Exhibition in Philadelphia in 1876. "O how different the moral atmosphere amid which I now revise this Volume, from the jocund influences surrounding the growth and advent of LEAVES OF GRASS,"[7] Whitman wrote in a note on his birthday in 1875. In a later note on his personal state when he prepared the centennial edition of his works, he wrote: "I was seriously paralyzed from the Secession war, poor, in debt, was expecting death . . . and I had the books printed during the lingering interim to occupy the tediousness of glum days and nights" (*PW*, II, 699). The moral atmosphere and gloom to which he refers allude specifically to his paralysis and his continued sadness over his mother's death, but the atmosphere also includes the dark days of the nation to which Whitman repeatedly refers in his new volume: "Thee, seated coil'd in evil

---

7. The full text from which this sentence is quoted appears as note 4 to "Preface 1876" in this Norton Critical Edition (p. 653). The sentence quoted here appears in the sixth paragraph of the note [*Ed.*].

times, my Country, with craft and black dismay—with every meanness, treason thrust upon thee."[8] He feared that the "Pathology" of the present would enter into his new work, and indeed it did, both in the recurrent image of the "time's thick murk" and in the failure of inspiration evident in the centennial edition.

The first volume of the centennial edition was a reprint of the 1871–72 *Leaves of Grass*, with a few minor "Intercalations" added at the end of some editions. His second volume, entitled *Two Rivulets*, consisted primarily of previously published poetry and prose: *Democratic Vistas, As a Strong Bird on Pinions Free, Memoranda During the War,* and *Passage to India* all are reprinted from original plates with separate pagination.

In his preface to *Two Rivulets,* Whitman avows his earlier intent to turn the *Passage to India* cluster into a new volume of poems: "It was originally my intention, after chanting in LEAVES OF GRASS the songs of the Body and Existence, to then compose a further, equally needed Volume, [exhibiting] the problem and the paradox of the same ardent and fully appointed Personality entering the sphere of the resistless gravitation of Spiritual Law, and with cheerful face estimating Death." Unable to carry out his original plan, he decided to conclude his work with the *Passage to India* cluster and "thoughts, or radiations from thoughts, on Death, Immortality, and a free entrance into the Spiritual world."[9]

Two Rivulets is, as its title suggests, double—split between politics and death. "I have not hesitated to embody in, and run through the Volume," Whitman says, "two altogether distinct veins, or strata— Politics for one, and for the other, the pensive thought of Immortality. Thus, too, the prose and poetic, the dual forms of the present book" (*LGC,* p. 748). This duality of perspective—between life and death, real and ideal, body and soul, present and future—structures the volume. The preface is itself divided between reflections on democratic nationality in the body of the essay and reflections on the purport of *Leaves of Grass* in a sequence of discursive footnotes. The contents of the volume is divided thematically between pieces on democracy, such as *Democratic Vistas* and the preface to *As a Strong Bird,* and pieces on death, such as *Memoranda During the War* and *Passage to India.* Just as this dualism of perspective is bound in a single volume, so in his epigraph Whitman establishes the idea of a union of opposites as the controlling metaphor of *Two Rivulets:* "For the Eternal Ocean bound,/These ripples, passing surges, streams of Death and Life" (*LG: Variorum,* III, 655). The differences between *Leaves of Grass* and *Two Rivulets,* the first representing his earlier emphasis on the "Body and Existence" and the second representing his later emphasis on "Death and the Spiritual World," are also, the poet says, "One in structure," part of "an interpenetrating, composite, inseparable Unity" (*LGC,* p. 751).

8. Sculley Bradley et al., eds., *Leaves of Grass: A Textual Variorum of the Printed Poems,* 3 vols. (New York: New York University Press, 1980), III, 669.
9. *Leaves of Grass: Comprehensive Reader's Edition,* ed. Harold W. Blodgett and Sculley Bradley (New York: Norton, 1965), p. 748. Further citations to this volume are given in the text as *LGC.*

In the poems of *Two Rivulets* Whitman accommodates "the bad majority—the varied, countless frauds of men and States" in an Hegelian scheme in which "Only the Good is universal" ("Song of the Universal," ll. 26, 28). But by locating the drama of democracy in the "Spiritual World" outside the "Body and Existence" of his haughty, electric, contradictory, and frequently vulnerable persona, Whitman loses the vitality and specificity of his early verse. His poetry begins to limp with the hollow abstractions of democracy. Although Whitman continued to grope toward a more communal form, he lacked the stamina to complete such a work. Reflecting on the products of labor on display at the Centennial Exhibition in Philadelphia, he wrote: "The glory of Labor, and the bringing together not only representatives of all the trades and products, but, fraternally, of all the Workmen of all the Nations of the World, (for this is the Idea behind the Centennial at Philadelphia,) is, to me, so welcome and inspiring a theme, that I only wish I were a younger and a fresher man, to attempt the enduring Book, of poetic character, that ought to be written about it" (*LGC*, p. 751).

If in his early poetry Whitman struggled with and against the paradoxes and contradictions of democratic self and nation, in his centennial poems he seems content to be the poet of public policy. Rather than engage the political contradiction between clearing the West for settlement and developing a race "proportionate to Nature," in "Song of the Redwood-Tree" he celebrates the felling of trees as part of an "unseen moral essence" or "hidden national will" that molds the New World, "unswerv'd by all the passing errors, perturbations of the surface" (ll. 58, 60, 62). Rather than explore the contradiction between the advance of "broad humanity" and the extermination of native Americans carried out by government agency, he sounds a "trumpet-note" for General George A. Custer, representing his last stand as a "lightning flash" of heroism amid the "dark days" of the present ("From far Dakota's Cañons," ll. 3, 18, 13).

Stiffened into his public pose as the good gray poet of democracy, Whitman seems no longer willing to give voice to his questions and fears about the future of America. But these questions and fears nevertheless come out, if only as in "Passage to India," indirectly and subterraneously. In "To a Locomotive in Winter" he celebrates the locomotive as a "Type of the modern! emblem of motion and power! pulse of the continent!" The poem registers the public fascination with the railroad which, as the key to western settlement, mass production and consumption, and the binding of the nation, dominated the economics, politics, and imagination of late-nineteenth-century America. Despite the poem's upbeat tone, however, the poet's language of celebration is fraught with alarm. The "black cylindric body" of the locomotive, with its "great protruding headlight, fix'd in front" and its smoke stacks out-belching "dense and murky clouds" as it pants and roars and "shrieks" through the countryside, bears traces of an anxiety about machine technology that anticipates Frank Norris's train as Iron Monster, grasping the land and the people in the stranglehold of "The Octopus" (*LG: Variorum*, III, 666–67).

Like the republic itself in 1876, Whitman's centennial volume is full of centrifugal impulses, held together not organically from within but by binding from without. The volume is a patchwork, with each of the different sections paginated separately. For a volume intended to honor the centennial of the republic, there is also something foreboding about the pairing of politics and death, or as Whitman says of his songs, "Strands of Patriotism and Death." Death in these songs is no longer balanced with life as part of an ongoing process; rather, as in "Lilacs," death becomes a deliverance from life, a "last impregnable retreat—a citadel and tower" ("In Former Songs," l. 10). Politically, Whitman celebrates the future, but his mind, like *Two Rivulets* itself, is turned toward thoughts "on Death, Immortality, and a free entrance into the Spiritual world" (*LGC*, p. 748). Concluding with the "Passage to India" cluster, Whitman's centennial volume marks the course of the American republic itself, leaping not toward the democratic future but toward death.

For all Whitman's effort to celebrate the national birthday, his centennial volume *had* absorbed the "pathology" of a country "coil'd in evil times." While America displayed its material wealth and industrial prowess at the Centennial Exposition in Philadelphia, thousands of workers remained unemployed. On July 4, 1876, a skirmish between black militiamen and white civilians led to an armed confrontation that was settled by the intervention of federal troops. Occurring on the very day of the republic's centennial birthday, the conflict was a reminder of unresolved political tensions within the union. Whatever reconstruction had taken place in the South was largely the result of the threat or actual exercise of federal military power.

The presidential election of 1876 revealed the growing power and resistance of the Democratic party in the South. Samuel Tilden, the Democratic candidate, won a majority of the popular vote against the Republican candidate Rutherford B. Hayes. But Tilden lacked one electoral vote to win the election. The political stalemate, which lasted several months, resulted in the Compromise of 1877: in exchange for the votes of southern Democrats, Hayes agreed as president to withdraw the last remaining troops from Louisiana and South Carolina, to include Democrats in his government, and to support policies favorable to southern whites. Returning the nation to sectional compromise and the South to home rule, the Compromise of 1877 marked the official end of Reconstruction. For almost a century, racism and segregation were upheld by the courts and institutionalized as the official policy of the nation, North as well as South.[1]

---

1. For a discussion of the Compromise of 1877, see Kenneth M. Stampp, *The Era of Reconstruction* (New York: Knopf, 1966); Rembert W. Patrick, *The Reconstruction of the Nation* (New York: Oxford University Press, 1967); and Keith J. Polakoff, *The Politics of Inertia: The Election of 1876 and the End of Reconstruction* (Baton Rouge: Louisiana State University Press, 1973). For studies of racial attitudes during and after Reconstruction, see especially C. Vann Woodward, *American Counterpoint: Slavery and Racism in the North-South Dialogue* (Boston: Little, Brown, 1971); George M. Fredrickson, *The Black Image in the White Mind* (New York: Harper and Row, 1972); and Eric Foner, *Nothing But Freedom: Emancipation and Its Legacy* (Baton Rouge: Louisiana State University Press, 1983).

As the nation began to move toward economic recovery and a new political regime under the presidency of Rutherford B. Hayes (1877–81), Whitman, too, began to move toward a renewed sense of bodily health. He was aided in his recovery by articulating his war experiences in *Memoranda During the War,* which was published in 1875. He was also invigorated by the visits to the New Jersey farm of Susan and George Stafford that he began making in 1876. Among the Staffords, whom he met through his affectionate relationship with their son Harry, he retrieved some of his own familial past in rural Long Island; and on the banks of Timber Creek, he practiced a rigorous regime of mud baths, scrubbing, and nude sunbathing that shocked the neighbors but restored his physical strength and vigor.

After 1876, there was also a turn in Whitman's literary fortunes. It is perhaps one of the ironies of poetic history that his centennial *Leaves,* which in some ways marked a low point in the life of both poet and nation, also marked an upward swing in his reputation as a poet. Under the impetus of a subscription campaign on his behalf carried out by his admirers in England and America, the centennial *Leaves* became his first book to sell well nationally and internationally. Several prominent British writers, including William Michael and Dante Gabriel Rossetti, Edward Dowden, Alfred Tennyson, John Ruskin, George Saintsbury, and Ford Madox Brown, bought copies of Whitman's books, sometimes paying double and triple the price. "Severely scann'd, it was perhaps no very great or vehement success," Whitman wrote, "but the tide had palpably shifted at any rate, and the sluices were turn'd in my own veins and pockets. That emotional, audacious, open-handed, friendly-mouth'd just-opportune English action, I say, pluck'd me like a brand from the burning, and gave me life again, to finish my book, since ab't completed" (PW, II, 699–700).

The restoration of balance is reflected in Whitman's final ordering of his poems in the 1881 edition of *Leaves of Grass.* In this edition, he integrated all of his annexes, thus signifying his abandonment of the plan to write a new volume of poems centered on the theme of democratic nationality and spiritual union. Unlike Whitman's postwar volume of *Leaves of Grass,* the 1881 volume once again includes a picture of the poet, but it is not, as in earlier volumes, a current picture of himself. Rather, he returns to the 1855 daguerreotype engraving of himself, which appears opposite his longest poem, now retitled "Song of Myself." The new title confirms the move toward the recreation of himself in the image of his book that had intensified during and after the war years. But the 1855 daguerreotype is also a sign of difference. Like James Fenimore Cooper returning to the youth of both hero and country in *The Deerslayer* (1841), Whitman's return to his 1855 portrait is another leap away from the present, signifying his desire to identify himself, his book, and the nation not with the "half-paralytic" of the postwar period but with the healthy and robust democrat of the prewar years.

And yet, while this idealized Jacksonian common man stands at the head of the 1881 *Leaves,* there are signs that Whitman has lost the revolutionary fire that marked his early period. Although he does not renounce the political radicalism of his early years, his deletions, additions, and changes reveal a quest for stability and balance and a corresponding falling off of the moral passion, political commitment, and struggle to resolve contradiction that characterized his earlier verse. At the very time that the Knights of Labor and the Farmer's Alliance were beginning to gain adherents, Whitman weakened his assault on the "grip of capital" by dropping the *Songs of Insurrection* cluster and distributing the poems in this grouping through *Leaves of Grass*. He also deleted "Respondez," the poem that had over the years registered the ironic gap between ideal and reality in the American republic. He deleted his comradely invocation to workmen and workwomen at the outset of "A Song for Occupations." And in "The Sleepers," he suppressed two of his most radical utterances: his erotically charged "O hot-cheek'd and blushing" sequence and his powerful attack on slavery in the black "Lucifer" passage. He also suppressed several passages and a few poems that revealed his doubts about the future of self and nation: He deleted "Solid, Ironical, Rolling Orb" and the "chaos" passage in "Out of the Cradle" that begins "O a word! O what is my destination? (I fear it is henceforth chaos;)" (*LGC*, p. 639). These changes had the effect of removing sites of historical struggle from the poems and reinforcing the image of national growth as natural growth.

Whitman added only twenty new poems to the 1881 *Leaves*, the best of which is "The Dalliance of the Eagles," a poem depicting in violent and graphic language the copulation of two eagles in flight. The other 1881 poems are minor, occasional poems, including poems on Whitman's trip west in 1879 ("Italian Music in Dakota," "The Prairie States," and "Spirit That Form'd This Scene"), a poem on Grant's triumphant return from his world tour in 1879 ("What Best I See in Thee"), a poem on the death of his mother ("As at Thy Portals Also Death"), and a poem on the death of President James Garfield, who was shot on July 2, 1881, in the dispute over spoils and patronage that followed the election of 1880.

Whitman was depressed by the shooting of Garfield, whom he had known when the latter was a congressman in Washington. Coming only a few days before the Fourth of July, the shooting revived his Carlylean doubts about the prospects of democracy in the New World: "We had the most horrible *celebration* here I ever knew," he wrote of the national birthday; "ruffians yelling, crackers, and all the old guns & pistols of all Jersey, with all the bad elements of humanity completely let loose & making the most infernal din possible to conceive for over thirty hours" (*Corr.*, III, 232–33).

Garfield's death on September 19, 1881, made him the second president to be assassinated in less than twenty years. And yet "The Sobbing of the Bells," like Whitman's Lincoln elegy, effaces the violent circumstances of Garfield's death. In six short lines that approximate the conventional language and sentiment of Longfellow and Whittier, Whitman evokes the "heart-beats of a Nation" sobbing in unison with the bells that toll on the occasion of Garfield's death. Ironically, the shooting of presidents has become, along with war, the most effective means of bringing the country together in a truly national union.

The most significant change in the 1881 *Leaves* is not the addition of new poems but Whitman's restructuring of the entire volume into a final coherent form. Introduced by a series of inscriptions that reach from the "One's Self" of the poet to the "Thou" of the reader, the poems repeat this outward motion, developing not chronologically but thematically from a focus on self in "Starting from Paumanok" and "Song of Myself," to a focus on the relation of self to other in the amative theme of *Children of Adam* and the adhesive theme of *Calamus*, and then toward the national and international focus of poems such as "Salut au Monde!," "Crossing Brooklyn Ferry," "Song of the Exposition," and "A Song for Occupations." These songs are followed by three new clusters: *Birds of Passage,* which focuses on the evolutionary advance of democracy; *Sea-Drift,* which collects several of the seashore poems, including "Out of the Cradle" and "As I Ebb'd"; and *By the Roadside,* a miscellany of vignettes of the poet's life and times, including "A Boston Ballad," "Europe," and "To the States, to Identify the 16th, 17th, or 18th Presidentiad."

The poems of the war and its aftermath are now included in a single *Drum-Taps* grouping. The change signifies the move of both poet and nation away from a central preoccupation with the war in the post-Reconstruction period. The war is still the axis of *Leaves of Grass,* but the poems are not distributed over three separate groupings, as in 1871 and 1876. No longer collected in a separate volume, Whitman's Lincoln poems logically follow the *Drum-Taps* poems in a grouping entitled *Memories of President Lincoln* (still the only place in which Lincoln is specifically named as the subject of the poems). The poems on the death of Lincoln are followed by the clusters *Autumn Rivulets, Whispers of Heavenly Death,* and *From Noon to Starry Night.* Like the poems collected in the *Passage to India* annex, these clusters concentrate on the themes of death, immortality, and the spiritual world. The *Songs of Parting* cluster still closes the volume with a leap toward the sea in "Now Finale to the Shore" and a parting kiss to the reader in "So Long!"

These clusters radiate in ever-widening concentric circles from a focus on self, life, body, light, day, and the social world toward a focus on the cosmos, death, soul, darkness, night, and the spiritual world. At the same time, the clusters and the poems they include continually fold back on one another chronologically and thematically, temporally and spatially, in a manner that suggests the image of ensemble—of "form and union and plan"—that is the final design and desire of *Leaves of Grass.*

Walt Whitman: A Chronology

1819	Born May 31 at West Hills, near Huntington, Long Island.
1823	May 27, Whitman family moves to Brooklyn.
1825–30	Attends public school in Brooklyn.
1830	Office boy for doctor, lawyer.
1830–34	Learns printing trade.
1835	Printer in New York City until great fire August 12.
1836–38	Summer of 1836, begins teaching at East Norwich, Long Island; by winter 1837–38 has taught at Hempstead, Babylon, Long Swamp, and Smithtown.
1838–39	Edits weekly newspaper, the *Long Islander*, at Huntington.
1840–41	Autumn 1840, campaigns for Van Buren; then teaches school at Trimming Square, Woodbury, Dix Hills, and Whitestone.
1841	May, goes to New York City to work as printer in *New World* office; begins writing for the *Democratic Review*.
1842	Spring, edits a daily newspaper in New York City, the *Aurora*; edits *Evening Tattler* for short time.
1845–46	August, returns to Brooklyn, writes for *Long Island Star* from September until March.
1846–48	From March 1846, until January 1848, edits *Brooklyn Daily Eagle*; February 1848, goes to New Orleans to work on the *Crescent*; leaves May 27 and returns via Mississippi and Great Lakes.
1848–49	September 9, 1848, to September 11, 1849, edits a "free soil" newspaper, the *Brooklyn Freeman*.
1850–54	Operates printing office and stationery store; does freelance journalism; builds and speculates in houses.
1855	Early July, *Leaves of Grass* is printed by Rome Brothers in Brooklyn; father dies July 11; Emerson writes to poet on July 21.
1856	Writes for *Life Illustrated*; publishes second edition of *Leaves of Grass* in summer and writes "The Eighteenth Presidency!"
1857–59	From spring of 1857 until about summer of 1859 edits the *Brooklyn Times*; unemployed winter of 1859–60; frequents Pfaff's bohemian restaurant.
1860	March, goes to Boston to see third edition of *Leaves of Grass* through the press.
1861	April 12, Civil War begins; brother George Whitman enlists.

901

1862	December, goes to Fredericksburg, Virginia, scene of recent battle in which George was wounded; stays in camp two weeks.
1863	Remains in Washington, D. C., working part time in Army Paymaster's office; visits soldiers in hospitals.
1864	June 22, returns to Brooklyn because of illness.
1865	January 24, appointed clerk in Department of Interior, returns to Washington; meets Peter Doyle; witnesses Lincoln's second inauguration; Lincoln assassinated, April 14; May, *Drum-Taps* is printed; June 30, is discharged from position by Secretary James Harlan but re-employed next day in Attorney General's office; autumn, prints *Drum-Taps and Sequel,* containing "When Lilacs Last in the Dooryard Bloom'd."
1866	William D. O'Connor publishes *The Good Gray Poet.*
1867	John Burroughs publishes *Notes on Walt Whitman as Poet and Person;* July 6, William Michael Rossetti publishes article on Whitman's poetry in *London Chronicle;* "Democracy" (part of *Democratic Vistas*) published in December *Galaxy.*
1868	Rossetti's *Poems of Walt Whitman* (selected and expurgated) published in England; "Personalism" (second part of *Democratic Vistas*), in May *Galaxy;* second issue of fourth edition of *Leaves of Grass,* with *Drum-Taps and Sequel* added.
1869	Mrs. Anne Gilchrist reads Rossetti edition and falls in love with the poet.
1870	July, is very depressed for unknown reasons; prints fifth edition of *Leaves of Grass,* and *Democratic Vistas* and *Passage to India,* all dated 1871.
1871	September 3, receives Mrs. Gilchrist's first love letter; September 7, reads "After All Not to Create Only" at opening of American Institute Exhibition in New York.
1872	June 26, reads "As a Strong Bird on Pinions Free" at Dartmouth College commencement.
1873	January 23, suffers paralytic stroke; mother dies May 23; unable to work, stays with brother George in Camden, New Jersey.
1874	"Song of the Redwood-Tree" and "Prayer of Columbus."
1875	Prepares Centennial Edition of *Leaves of Grass* and *Two Rivulets* (dated 1876).
1876	Controversy in British and American press over America's neglect of Whitman; spring, meets Harry Stafford and begins recuperation at Stafford farm, at Timber Creek; September, Mrs. Gilchrist arrives and rents house in Philadelphia.
1877	January 28, gives lecture on Tom Paine in Philadelphia; goes to New York in March and is painted by George W. Waters; during summer gains strength by sunbathing at Timber Creek.

1878	Spring, too weak to give projected Lincoln lecture, but in June visits J. H. Johnston and John Burroughs in New York.
1879	April to June, in New York, where he gives first Lincoln lecture and says farewell to Mrs. Gilchrist, who returns to England; September, goes to the West for the first time and visits Colorado; because of illness remains in St. Louis with brother Jeff from October to January.
1880	Gives Lincoln lecture in Philadelphia; summer, visits Dr. R. M. Bucke in London, Ontario.
1881	April 15, gives Lincoln lecture in Boston; returns to Boston in August to read proof of *Leaves of Grass*, being published by James R. Osgood; poems receive final arrangement in this edition.
1882	Meets Oscar Wilde; Osgood ceases to distribute *Leaves of Grass* because District Attorney threatens prosecution unless the book is expurgated; publication is resumed in June by Rees Welsh in Philadelphia, who also publishes *Specimen Days and Collect*; both books transferred to David McKay, Philadelphia.
1883	Dr. Bucke publishes *Walt Whitman*, a critical study closely "edited" by the poet.
1884	Buys house on Mickle Street, Camden, New Jersey.
1885	In poor health; friends buy a horse and phaeton so that the poet will not be "house-tied"; November 29, Mrs. Gilchrist dies.
1886	Gives Lincoln lecture four times in Elkton, Maryland, Camden, Philadelphia, and Haddonfield, New Jersey; is painted by John White Alexander.
1887	Gives Lincoln lecture in New York; is painted by Thomas Eakins.
1888	Horace Traubel raises funds for doctors and nurses; *November Boughs* printed; money sent from England.
1889	Seventieth birthday, proceedings published in *Camden's Compliments*.
1890	Writes angry letter to J. A. Symonds, dated August 19, denouncing Symonds's interpretation of "Calamus" poems, claims six illegitimate children.
1891	*Good-Bye My Fancy* is printed, and the "death-bed edition" of *Leaves of Grass* (dated 1891–92).
1892	Dies March 26, buried in Harleigh Cemetery, Camden, New Jersey.

Selected Bibliography

EDITIONS AND TEXTUAL BIBLIOGRAPHIES

Bradley, Sculley, Harold W. Blodgett, Arthur Golden, and William White, eds. *Leaves of Grass: A Textual Variorum of the Printed Poems*. 3 vols. New York: New York University Press, 1980.

BIOGRAPHIES

Allen, Gay Wilson. *Solitary Singer: A Critical Biography of Walt Whitman*. New York: Macmillan, 1955.
Kaplan, Justin. *Walt Whitman: A Life*. New York: Simon and Schuster, 1980.
Loving, Jerome. *Walt Whitman: The Song of Himself*. Berkeley, CA: University of California Press, 2000.
Schmidgall, Gary. *Walt Whitman: A Gay Life*. New York: Dutton, 1997.
Zweig, Paul. *Walt Whitman: The Making of the Poet*. New York: Basic Books, 1984.

GENERAL INTRODUCTIONS

Allen, Gay Wilson. *The New Walt Whitman Handbook*. New York: New York University Press, 1975.
Miller, Edwin Haviland. *Walt Whitman's "Song of Myself": A Mosaic of Interpretations*. Iowa City: University of Iowa Press, 1989.

REFERENCE WORKS AND CRITICAL BIOGRAPHIES

Giantvalley, Scott, ed. *Walt Whitman, 1838–1939: A Reference Guide*. Boston: G. K. Hall, 1981.
Kummings, Donald D., ed. *Walt Whitman 1940–1975: A Reference Guide*. Boston: G. K. Hall, 1982.
LeMaster, J. R., and Donald D. Kummings, eds. *Walt Whitman: An Encyclopedia*. New York: Garland, 1998.
Myerson, Joel. *Walt Whitman: A Descriptive Biography*. Pittsburgh: University of Pittsburgh Press, 1993.

CRITICAL STUDIES

• indicates works excerpted in this Norton Critical Edition.

Allen, Gay Wilson, and Ed Folsom, eds. *Walt Whitman and the World*. Iowa City: University of Iowa Press, 1995.
Bauerlein, Mark. *Walt Whitman and the American Idiom*. Baton Rouge: Louisiana State University Press, 1991.
Ceniza, Sherry. *Walt Whitman and Nineteenth-Century Women Reformers*. Tuscaloosa: University of Alabama Press, 1998.
Dougherty, James. *Walt Whitman and the Citizen's Eye*. Baton Rouge: Louisiana State University Press, 1993.
• Erkkila, Betsy. *Whitman the Political Poet*. New York: Oxford University Press, 1989.
———, and Jay Grossman, eds. *Breaking Bounds: Whitman and American Cultural Studies*. New York: Oxford University Press, 1996.
Folsom, Ed. *Walt Whitman's Native Representations*. New York: Cambridge University Press, 1994.
———, ed. *Walt Whitman: The Centennial Essays*. Iowa City: University of Iowa Press, 1994.
Greenspan, Ezra. *The Cambridge Companion to Walt Whitman*. New York: Cambridge University Press, 1995.
• Grossman, Allen. "The Poetics of Union in Whitman and Lincoln: An Inquiry toward the Relationship of Art and Policy." In Walter Benn Michaels and Donald E. Pease, eds.,

The American Renaissance Reconsidered. Baltimore: The Johns Hopkins University Press, 1985. 183–204.

Hollis, C. Carroll. *Language and Style in "Leaves of Grass."* Baton Rouge: Louisiana State University Press, 1983.

Hutchinson, George B. *The Ecstatic Whitman: Literary Shamanism and the Crisis of the Union.* Columbus: Ohio State University Press, 1986.

• Irwin, John. *American Hieroglyphics: The Symbol of the Egyptian Hieroglyphics in the American Renaissance.* New Haven, Conn.: Yale University Press, 1980.

Killingsworth, M. Jimmie. *Whitman's Poetry of the Body: Sexuality, Politics, and the Text.* Chapel Hill: University of North Carolina Press, 1989.

Klammer, Martin. *Whitman, Slavery, and the Emergence of "Leaves of Grass."* University Park: University of Pennsylvania Press, 1995.

Larson, Kerry C. *Whitman's Drama of Consensus.* Chicago: University of Chicago Press, 1988.

Mancuso, Luke. *The Strange Sad War Revolving: Walt Whitman, Reconstruction, and the Emergence of Black Citizenship, 1865–76.* Columbia, S.C.: Camden House, 1997.

Martin, Robert K. *The Homosexual Tradition in American Poetry.* Austin: University of Texas Press, 1979.

• Moon, Michael. *Disseminating Whitman: Revision and Corporeality in "Leaves of Grass."* Cambridge, Mass.: Harvard University Press, 1991.

Nathanson, Tenny. *Whitman's Presence: Body, Voice, and Writing in "Leaves of Grass."* New York: New York University Press, 1992.

Perlman, Jim, Ed Folsom, and Dan Campion, eds. *Walt Whitman: The Measure of His Song.* 2nd rev. ed. Duluth, Minn.: Holy Cow! Press, 1998.

Price, Kenneth M. *Whitman and Tradition: The Poet in His Century.* New Haven, Conn.: Yale University Press, 1990.

• Reynolds, David S. *Walt Whitman's America: A Cultural Biography.* New York: Alfred A. Knopf, 1995.

• Sanchez-Eppler, Karen. *Touching Liberty: Abolition, Feminism, and the Politics of the Body.* Berkeley: University of California Press, 1993.

Shively, Charley, ed. *Drum Beats: Walt Whitman's Civil War Boy Lovers.* San Francisco: Gay Sunshine Press, 1989.

Thomas, M. Wynn. *The Lunar Light of Whitman's Poetry.* Cambridge, Mass.: Harvard University Press, 1987.

INTERNET SITES

Library of Congress Walt Whitman Home Page
The Walt Whitman Hypertext Archive

Index of Titles and
First Lines

907

Thither as I look I see each result and glory retracing itself, 12
Thou Mother with Thy Equal Brood, 381
Thou Orb Aloft Full-Dazzling, 387
Thou Reader, 14
Thou who hast slept all night upon the storm, 215
Thought (As I sit with others at a great feast), 380
Thought (Of equality—), 232
Thought (Of justice—), 232
Thought (Of obedience, faith, adhesiveness), 231
Thought (Of persons arrived at high positions), 326
Thought (Of recognition), 575
Thought (Of that to come), 573
Thought No. 5 (1860); see Thought (As I sit . . .)
Thought of Columbus, A, 491
Thoughts (Of ownership—), 227
Thoughts (Of public opinion), 401
Thoughts (Of these years I sing), 413
Thoughts No. 2 (1860); see Thoughts— 4 (Of ownership)
Thoughts No. 3 (1860); see Thought (Of persons)
Thoughts No. 4 (1860); see Thoughts— 4 (Of ownership); Thought (Of Justice); Thought (Of Equality)
Thoughts No. 7 (1860); see Thought (Of obedience)
Thoughts, suggestions, aspirations, pictures, 542
Thoughts—1: Visages, 521
Thoughts—2: "Of Waters, Forests, Hills," 533
Thoughts—4: "Of Ownership . . .," 533
Thoughts—6: "Of What I Write," 522
Through the ample open door of the peaceful country barn, 230
Through the soft evening air enwinding all, 337
To a Cantatrice; see To a Certain Cantatrice
To a Certain Cantatrice, 11
To a Certain Civilian, 272
To a Common Prostitute, 325
To a Foil'd European Revolutionaire, 311
To a Foiled Revolter or Revoltress; see To a Foil'd European Revolutionaire
To a Historian, 5
To a Locomotive in Winter, 395
To a President, 228

To a Pupil, 328
To a Stranger, 109
To a Western Boy, 115
To an Exclusive, 574
To Be at All, 489
To conclude, I announce what comes after me, 422
To Foreign Lands, 5
To get betimes in Boston town I rose this morning early, 221
To Get Betimes in Boston Town; see A Boston Ballad
To Get the Final Lilt of Songs, 438
To Him That Was Crucified, 323
To My Soul; see As the Time Draws Nigh
To Old Age, 233
To One Shortly to Die, 378
To Oratists; see Vocalism
To Other Lands; see To Foreign Lands
To Rich Givers, 229
To Soar in Freedom and in Fullness of Power, 486
To the East and to the West, 114
To the Future, 573
To the Garden the World, 78
To the Leaven'd Soil They Trod, 275
To the Man-of-War-Bird, 215
To the Pending Year, 456
To the Poor, 590
To the Prevailing Bards, 580
To the Reader at Parting, 527
To the Sayers of Words; see A Song of the Rolling Earth
To the Soul, 596
To the States, 10
To the States: To Identify the 16th, 17th, or 18th Presidentiad, 233
To the Sun-Set Breeze, 458
To Thee Old Cause, 6
To Think of Time, 364
[To This Continent], 575
To Those Who've Fail'd, 426
[To What You Said], 593
To Workingmen; see Song for Occupations
To You (Stranger, if you . . .), 14
To You (whoever you are), 195
To You (Let us twain . . .), 526
To-day a rude brief recitative, 219
To-day and Thee, 429
To-day, from each and all, a breath of prayer, 430
To-day, with bending head and eyes, 448
Torch, The, 333
Transpositions, 364
Trickle Drops, 107
True Conquerors, 442